# SELECTED LETTERS OF
# LUCRETIA COFFIN MOTT

WOMEN IN AMERICAN HISTORY

*Series Editors*
Anne Firor Scott
Nancy A. Hewitt
Stephanie Shaw

*A list of books in the series appears
at the end of this book.*

# Selected Letters of
# Lucretia Coffin Mott

EDITED BY
BEVERLY WILSON PALMER

*Holly Byers Ochoa, Associate Editor*
*Carol Faulkner, Editing Fellow*

UNIVERSITY OF ILLINOIS PRESS
URBANA AND CHICAGO

FRONTISPIECE
Portrait by William H. Furness, 1858
(Courtesy of the Friends Historical Library
of Swarthmore College)

Publication of this book was supported by a grant (#2001-004)
from the National Historical Publications and Records Commission.

The paper in this book meets the guidelines for permanence and dura-
bility of the Committee on Production Guidelines for Book Longevity
of the Council on Library Resources. ∞

Library of Congress Cataloging-in-Publication Data
Mott, Lucretia, 1793–1880.
Selected letters of Lucretia Coffin Mott / edited by Beverly Wilson
Palmer ; with the assistance of Holly Byers Ochoa, associate editor,
and Carol Faulkner, editing fellow.
p.   cm. — (Women in American history)
Includes bibliographical references (p. ) and index.
ISBN 0-252-02674-8 (cloth : acid-free paper)
1. Mott, Lucretia, 1793–1880—Correspondence. 2. Feminists—United
States—Correspondence. 3. Women abolitionists—United States—
Correspondence. 4. Quakers—United States—Correspondence.
I. Palmer, Beverly Wilson, 1936– . II. Ochoa, Holly Byers, 1951– .
III. Faulkner, Carol. IV. Title. V. Series.
HQ1413.M68S45      2002
303.484'092      2001000377

TO

HARRIET SKINNER WILSON (1908–99)

BETTY STEIN BYERS (1923–98)

# Contents

# Acknowledgments

Several institutions and many individuals have made possible the publication of this volume. Swarthmore College, most specifically the staff at Friends Historical Library, has not only contributed photocopies of the extensive Lucretia Coffin Mott manuscript collection but has also shared expertise on Quaker records there. My thanks to Mary Ellen Chijioke, former curator of the Friends Historical Library (now library director at Guilford College), and J. William Frost, professor of religion and director of the library. Also of great assistance during my several trips to the library were archivists Susanna K. Morikawa and Patricia C. O'Donnell and administrative assistant Charlotte Blandford.

Grants from the National Historical Publications and Records Commission in 1997–2001 have constituted major funding for this publication. My colleagues and I could not have completed our work on schedule without the NHPRC Editing Fellowship in 1998–99. The contributions of the editing fellow, Carol Faulkner, are recognized on the title page. At the NHPRC I wish to thank particularly Laurie Baty, Roger Bruns, Richard Cameron, Timothy Connelly, Dane Hartgrove, and Michael Meier for their advice and encouragement. The American Philosophical Society formally initiated this project by funding archival work at Smith College. Finally, a grant from the Anna H. and Elizabeth Chace Foundation has supplemented the NHPRC's funding. I am grateful for all the financial support.

At Pomona College Associate Editor Holly Byers Ochoa has brought her excellent editing and analytical talents to this publication. Pomona College has provided office space, computer expertise, and research support; my thanks to Pomona's History Department, especially Evelyn Khalili and Jan Ginther, administrative aides; Fred Grieman and Patricia Smiley, associate deans; and the staff at the Office for Information Technology, especially Denis Recendez. Undergraduates Hetal Sheth and Jennifer Jones have rendered dedicated, intelligent help.

The History Department at the Claremont Graduate University generously furnished the funds for graduate student help. Special thanks go to Petula Iu and Jennifer Hillman Helgren, graduate students whose capable assistance with research and proofreading has been a great asset.

At the University of Illinois Press, Karen Hewitt, former executive editor, Michele A. May, acquisitions associate, and Theresa Sears, managing editor, have thoughtfully guided the production of this volume.

The list of other individuals supplying advice and information is headed by Margaret Hope Bacon, author of *Valiant Friend: The Life of Lucretia Mott* (1980, 1999). Together we have worked to publicize the accomplishments of this remarkable woman, and I value our friendship and Margaret's expert help. Members of the Editorial Advisory Board, listed on the title page, have offered advice and information on women's history and the Society of Friends, as well as welcome encouragement. I especially thank Nancy Hewitt, Thomas Hamm, and the two anonymous readers chosen by the University of Illinois Press for their insightful comments on drafts of the introductory essay. Thomas Hamm shared his extensive knowledge of nineteenth-century Quaker practices. Christopher Densmore, archivist at SUNY-Buffalo, has unfailingly offered information on the New York Quakers. James Gould of Cotuit, Massachusetts, compiled a list of the Mott descendants, which has been invaluable to us in tracing the numerous in-laws and grandchildren of Lucretia Coffin Mott. Mary Gilmore of the Seymour Library and Stephanie Przybylek at the Cayuga Museum have enabled us to flesh out some of the Auburn, New York, personalities to whom Mott referred in her letters to her sister. Although the list of short titles reflects the work of scholars whose work has made our research easier, I wish to acknowledge especially Ann D. Gordon, editor of the *Selected Papers of Elizabeth Cady Stanton and Susan B. Anthony,* Louis Ruchames and Walter Merrill, editors of *The Letters of William Lloyd Garrison,* and John B. Pickard, editor of *The Letters of John Greenleaf Whittier.*

Margery Post Abbott, Elizabeth Post Falconi, and Hester Davis generously sent us photocopies of Lucretia Coffin Mott letters in their families' possession. The repositories contributing documents to this project for publication are listed under "Key to Editorial Notations."

Finally, the support of my husband, Hans C. Palmer, and my children, Margaret Palmer Woodruff and David E. Palmer, has been unfailing and essential.

Although these advisors and assistants have been crucial to the completion of this edition, whatever faults remain are entirely my own.

# Introduction: Lucretia Coffin Mott—
# Wife, Mother, Quaker, Activist

In her efforts to eradicate as many evils from the earth as she humanly could, Lucretia Coffin Mott stands out among her peers. Indeed, given her prolonged speaking tours, attendance at dozens of conventions and Quaker meetings, and efforts on behalf of slaves, Native Americans, women, and peace, we imagine her life as almost wholly devoted to public service. Yet her domestic life was equally rich and varied. Its intersection with her public life carries important implications for the study of women and women's activism in the nineteenth century. In her constant concern for the welfare and activities of both her extended family and the larger society, Mott wrote letters that reveal the struggles women faced as both public figures and private arbiters. These letters express the anxieties and joys of a nineteenth-century woman with political ideals and domestic commitments. Although she is known today primarily as a woman's rights leader, Mott viewed those rights as only one part of a broad-based reform agenda for American society and as intimately linked to women's and men's most personal relations.

Born in 1793 to Quaker parents, Lucretia Coffin learned as a child to lead an independent life. Her description of family dynamics in Nantucket, the seaport town of her birth, indicates the unusual place some women occupied in the early republic: "During the absence of their husbands, Nantucket women have been compelled to transact business, often going to Boston to procure supplies of goods— . . . They have kept their own accounts, & indeed acted the part of men—" (letter to Elizabeth Cady Stanton, 16 March 1855).

When Lucretia was thirteen, the Coffins, then living in Boston, decided to send their daughter to a coeducational Quaker school, Nine Partners, in Dutchess County, New York. It was here that the young student met James Mott. From 1808 to 1810 she served as an assistant teacher of "Reading, Grammar and Arithmetick" at Nine Partners,[1] and during that time the Coffin family moved to Philadelphia. In 1811 James and Lucretia married and established their home in Philadelphia; that city and its environs would be their residence for the rest of their lives. There James engaged in the cotton and wool trade but later focused only on wool trading as a protest against the slave-driven cotton industry in the South. Between 1812 and 1828 Lucretia bore six children, of whom five, four daughters and a son, lived to adulthood. In addition to meeting the domestic demands of bearing and raising her children, Lucretia briefly taught at a Friends select school for girls in 1817. She began to speak at Quaker meetings a year later, and in 1821 she was recognized as a minister in the Society of Friends in Philadelphia.

The Quaker tradition enabled women to take public positions on a variety of social problems. Recognized as a minister when she was only twenty-eight and later as the clerk of the Philadelphia Women's Yearly Meeting, Lucretia enjoyed the privilege of speaking in her own meeting as well as traveling widely to minister to other meetings. During the 1820s a conflict between the stricter, more conservative Quakers and the tolerant, less orthodox followers of Elias Hicks (known as the Hicksites) caused the Motts to break with their original meeting. In 1827 first James and then Lucretia followed the Hicksite branch (Hicksites insisted it was the Orthodox Quakers who left the fold), which espoused free interpretation of the Bible and reliance on inward authority, as opposed to the guidance of historic Christian authority. Moreover, Hicks's strong condemnation of slavery resonated with the Motts' antislavery beliefs. Nevertheless, the split deeply disturbed the devout Lucretia. The separation affected her personally because her sister Eliza Coffin Yarnall and her family, as well as James's parents, sided with the Orthodox.[2] This division did not end her differences with her fellow Quakers in years to come. Although remaining a Hicksite Quaker throughout her life and appearing only in simple, plain clothing, Mott often spoke outside Quaker meetings, and her sermons show her full commitment to liberal religious issues such as the inherent goodness of all humans, the importance of good works, and resistance to clerical authority.

Although Lucretia's Quaker background led to her activism, her friendship with William Lloyd Garrison, whom she met in 1830, strengthened her embrace of abolitionism and nonresistance. She was present as an observer (women were not permitted as delegates) when Garrison and others founded the American Anti-Slavery Society (AASS). Until their striking differences in 1865 as to whether the AASS had accomplished its goals, these two radical abolitionists put forth similar agendas. Mott and Garrison sought the immediate emancipation of the slaves and believed this freedom could be obtained solely through moral suasion. Moreover, Mott's Quaker beliefs were in keeping with Garrison's no-government stance; like many Quakers, she tended to eschew involvement in electoral politics. As active members of the Non-Resistance Society, Mott and Garrison preached resistance to violence and to participation in politics. The society discouraged members from resorting to violence to bring about change and from supporting public officials who possessed the power to use force.[3]

Lucretia Mott's letters reflect these and other causes she espoused and provide a guide to her activist itinerary. She traveled throughout the East and Midwest addressing reform organizations, such as the Non-Resistance Society, and at the antislavery conventions of American women, while locally she spoke to medical students and quarterly and yearly Quaker meetings. In June 1846 when war between the United States and Great Britain over the Oregon territory seemed imminent, Mott drafted a petition from the women of Philadelphia to the women of Exeter, England, urging them to join in preventing any hostilities. She obtained over five thousand signatures. Complementing the idealism expressed in her sermons and speeches, her letters demonstrate her commitment to practical action. She organized middle-class women in Philadelphia to offer employment and nursery care for poor women, regardless of race, through the Northern Association for the Relief of Poor Women. Typical is an 1850 letter to her sister Martha Coffin Wright: "I have been visiting 3 or 4 colored schools this morng & distributg 50 garments among them" (c. 6 February).

Mott traveled abroad only once, in 1840. Chosen as one of six women delegates from the several American antislavery societies to the World's Anti-Slavery Convention, she sailed with James for England on 7 May. On 12 June the convention refused to seat the women delegates, despite the protest of other American participants such as Garrison and Wendell Phillips, a Boston lawyer. Kathryn Kish Sklar has described Mott's sensible reaction to this rejection: since Mott was an "experienced organizer," she realized that the women's defeat was a "hopeless cause," and instead used her time in England to strengthen ties with other women at the convention.[4] It was in London that Mott formed a friendship with Elizabeth Cady Stanton, who attended the convention as the bride of delegate Henry B. Stanton.

The year 1848, which saw revolutionary movements in Europe and the expansion of the antislavery cause in the United States, also saw Mott and Stanton joined in the cause of woman's rights. Meeting with her sister Martha Coffin Wright, two other Quakers, Jane Master Hunt and Mary Ann McClintock, and Stanton in Waterloo, New York, Mott helped organize the Seneca Falls Woman's Rights Convention, scheduled for 19–20 July. This convention is considered the birthplace of the woman's rights movement. On 16 July this group had drawn up the Declaration of Sentiments, which served as the basis for the two-day convention. In it they called for equal treatment of women in the family, the workplace, the professions, the church, and the political arena.

Although much has been made of Stanton's brilliant suggestion that the convention pattern its declaration on the Declaration of Independence, the resolutions the women presented closely resemble sentiments expressed earlier by female abolitionists. For example, Mott, as one of the founders of the Philadelphia Female Anti-Slavery Society (PFASS), an interracial organization established in 1833, repeated ideas expressed initially at the first Anti-Slavery Convention of American Women in 1837 (see her 16 March 1855 letter to Stanton). These ideas often combined concerns about limits on women's spiritual and social authority. The eighth resolution offered in Seneca Falls contains similar language to one offered in 1837: "Resolved, That woman has too long rested satisfied in the circumscribed limits which corrupt customs and a perverted application of the Scriptures have marked out for her, and that it is time she should move in the enlarged sphere which her greater Creator has assigned her."[5]

Throughout the turbulent 1850s, Mott moved in that "enlarged sphere" as she engaged in further antislavery and nonresistant activities. For example, in 1851 she helped raise funds for the defense of Caster Hanway when he and thirty-eight other free blacks were tried for helping slaves escape. Later she assisted another fugitive slave, Jane Johnson, and still later she extended hospitality to Mary Ann Brown, the wife of John Brown, during his December 1859 trial for murder and conspiracy. As a Quaker preaching nonviolence, Mott denounced both Brown's attack on Harpers Ferry and the Civil War. Still, like other abolitionists, she hoped the war would end slavery. And she rejoiced when the slaves were finally freed in 1865.

Until the end of her life Mott continued to speak regularly at a variety of meetings advocating woman's rights, peace, temperance, and rights for freedpeople. In recognition of her long service to both the antislavery and the woman's rights causes she was chosen the first president of the American Equal Rights Association (AERA) in May 1866. This association split in 1868 over support for what would become the Fifteenth Amendment, which granted suffrage to freedmen but not to any women. The advocates of woman's rights were at the heart of the division, with Stanton and Susan B. Anthony demanding suffrage for freedmen and all women while Lucy Stone, Henry Blackwell, and their supporters advocated suffrage for freedmen first. Ever the peacemaker, Mott tried to heal the breach. Her blessing was sought by both sides (see her 17 April 1866 letter to Wendell Phillips), and she remained friendly with both. She begged them to "merge their interests in one common cause" (see her 18 March 1870 letter to Theodore Tilton), but to no avail. The two new organizations, Stanton and Anthony's National Woman Suffrage Association (NWSA) and Stone and Blackwell's American Woman Suffrage Association (AWSA), both formed in 1869, did not unite until 1890.

In her eighty-fifth year Mott delivered her last public address when woman's rights advocates celebrated the thirtieth anniversary of the Seneca Falls convention in Rochester, New York. Coping with frequent bouts of ill health and the deaths of her husband, her beloved sister Martha, and two of her daughters in the 1860s and 1870s, Mott still continued to travel and to speak. As a lifelong critic of sects and creeds, she became active in the Free Religious Association, an organization composed of both Christians and Jews seeking religious reform. Throughout her life, an incisive, challenging mind, a clear sense of her mission, and a level-headed personality made her a natural leader and a major force in nineteenth-century American life.

Despite her public persona, Mott's letters vividly illustrate her efforts to balance the roles of wife, mother, aunt, cousin, cook, seamstress, and household manager with those of Quaker preacher, speaker, committee member, and organizer. In her 1849 "Discourse on Woman," delivered on 17 December in Philadelphia, Mott asserted women's capacity for combining "domestic relations" with public "responsibilities," a combination borne out in her life. A wife and mother's "self-respect will be increased; preserving the dignity of her being, she will not suffer herself to be degraded into a mere dependent. Nor will her feminine character be impaired."[6] The home life of James and Lucretia demonstrated the conventional division of labor and, as Blanche Hersh points out, the Motts' understanding of their family responsibilities was no different from that of other middle-class reform couples. Along with their public obligations, James ran his wool business and later farmed, while Lucretia mended his shirts and baked the pies. Indicating her priorities, in a short, unfinished memoir written sometime before 1853, she spoke of her goal "to make *home* attractive and comfortable, appropriating a portion of time & means to minister to the wants of those in straitened circumstances."[7] Yet in their public activities, Lucretia led the way, while James played the role of supporter.

Throughout their long marriage, James encouraged his wife in her many activities outside the home. Their marriage exemplified a true partnership. Since the two regularly traveled together, few letters to him exist, and during the infrequent times when they were apart, she often addressed the whole family in her letters home (for a rare expression of her love for James, see her letter to James and their children begun c. 19 June 1849). The devotion between the outgoing Lucretia and the quiet, stalwart James was well known in their time ("never a cloud overshadowed us in the conjugal relation" she wrote William Lloyd Garrison Jr. on 4 March 1864) and has been cited as evidence of a highly compatible marriage. Such happy partnerships were rare among unions with one prominent activist.[8] Deliberately or not, the eighteen-year-old Lucretia gained a life partner who would steadily endorse her every endeavor, travel with her, and readily accept a supporting public role while she spoke throughout the eastern and midwestern United States. Her letters show, too, that James was equally involved in the causes so dear to Lucretia; in fact the two often composed joint letters (see, e.g., their letter to Adam Mott and Anne Mott of 7–9 November 1813 and their letter to Lucy Stone of 9 December 1856). He chaired many an abolitionist meeting, as well as the second day of the 1848 Seneca Falls convention, and the two frequently took turns serving as officers in the Pennsylvania Anti-Slavery Society and the AASS.

The marriage promises these two exchanged on 10 April 1811 were certainly in keeping with Lucretia's later views.[9] In a letter to fellow Quaker and cousin Nathaniel Barney discussing his daughter's marriage, she affirmed that she could reluctantly accept an officiant at the wedding "provided that part of the *church* marriage, promise, of *obedience on the part of the wife*, were omitted. I could never submit to that" (19 March 1852). Years later, describing the Quaker doctrine on marriage to the British reformer Josephine Butler, Mott testified eloquently to her own: "There is no assumed authority or admitted inferiority; no *promise* of *obedience*. Their independence is equal, their dependence mutual, and their obligations reciprocal" (20 April 1869). Considering this "mutual dependence," one wonders if Lucretia realized how crucial James's support was to her efforts. A letter to her sister Martha (from 21 January 1868) conveys little sense of alarm at the pneumonia that caused her husband's death a few days later. She seems just as concerned about her own fever and "night sweats" as James's condition, breaking a long letter to Martha filled with family gossip, relatives' business, and problems with the AERA to write casually, "Now I ought to go up to my husband." Ironically the frail Lucretia, who suffered from chronic dyspepsia for over thirty years, outlived her beloved husband by almost thirteen years.

Because there are few references to the raising of her offspring in the early letters (1812–30), we do not know how Mott treated her five young children. In her unfinished memoir she generalized about her relationship with her married children: "Always having a large family, the reasonable duty of division of labor has been urged and practiced by us." But while Mott's childhood on Nantucket may have seemed "reasonable," her parents' marriage did not illustrate the traditional separation between domestic female and commercial male roles (a separation Mott followed to some degree in her own marriage). While Thomas Coffin was absent on whaling missions Anna Folger Coffin ran a dry goods store on School Street. Later comments to young woman's rights activists such as Elizabeth Neall Gay and Elizabeth Cady Stanton suggest that early on Lucretia indeed saw her duty as more than guarding the homeplace. In 1856 she wrote Gay, "Come out of thy privacy let the babies take care of themselves, just watched by their nurse to keep them out of mischief— I sought thee in vain at the Anniversy. in New Y— Didn't thy *aged* frd. leave babies too, to go there?" (27 May 1856; see also her letter to Elizabeth McClintock and Elizabeth Cady Stanton of 27 November 1849 and her letter to Martha Coffin Wright and Eliza Wright Osborne of 19 March 1861). Furthermore, two of Mott's four daughters adopted to some degree her complex balancing of public and private responsibilities: Maria Mott Davis was active in the antislavery movement while Anna Mott Hopper, also active in the PFASS, was elected one of the first managers, or trustees, of Swarthmore College. Yet Mott criticized women who employed nurses for their children ("blessed were we to be without them," she wrote Martha on 23 May 1873). And she relished her daughters' proximity to Philadelphia, regarding Pattie's move to New York City in 1863 as an affront. As Margaret Hope Bacon points out, Lucretia never believed that Pattie could fend for herself.[10] Like many women, she vacillated between protecting her children and making them independent.

Lucretia Mott's home was populated mostly by women, as letters to her sister Martha, her niece Anna Temple Brown, and her daughter Pattie Mott Lord testify. Lucretia revered her mother, but thought somewhat less of her father's business acumen (see her letter to Martha of 4 February 1871). Moreover, until she was eleven and the family moved from Nantucket to Boston, Thomas Coffin regularly left his family for long whaling voyages. Her only brother, Thomas Mayhew Coffin, appeared to be quietly competent, but not a major influence in her life. Her letters rarely criticize her four daughters, but occasionally disparage her only son's extravagant tastes. Carroll Smith-Rosenberg has described the nineteenth-century world of the middle class as one in which women "helped one another with the burdens of housewifery and motherhood, nursed one another's sick, and mourned for one another's dead," and where "men made only a shadowy appearance."[11] The former observation, but not the latter, certainly holds true for Mott.

Indeed, Mott's world encompassed women and men, blacks and whites, family and political allies. She especially valued her intellectual exchanges with men, illustrated by her correspondence with Nathaniel Barney, the Scottish phrenologist George Combe, and the Irish Quaker Richard D. Webb. Although only a few perfunctory letters to William Lloyd Garrison survive, the editor of the *Liberator* also loomed large in her life. And Mott's letters to her sister Martha describe animated conversations with family and friends like the abolitionists Robert Purvis and James Miller McKim as well as the Unitarian minister Robert Collyer about topics such as antislavery violence in Kansas, suicide, and divorce laws. Her home, first the houses in Philadelphia and then Roadside (the farm north of Philadelphia to which she and James retired in 1857), was a focus for discussing public affairs as well as nurturing her family.

Lucretia's class status provided her with some advantages in juggling social activism and family care. Even during economic downturns in James's business (see, e.g., her letter to Martha Coffin Wright of 8 November 1857), the Motts usually employed several servants to assist in maintaining their home and grounds. But the circles in which the Motts moved also increased Lucretia's workload. A large house and the customary Quaker hospitality assured a steady supply of company. And her far-flung connections to Quaker meetings, relatives, and co-workers in a variety of causes put constant demands on her time.

Moreover, Mott's extensive correspondence was a burden itself, both physically and emotionally. The spoken word, not the written one, was her forte. She did not consider herself adept with the pen, as she wrote her old Nantucket friend Nathaniel Barney in 1852: "Pretty note-paper 'lines' are less in *my line*, than hurried scraps, such as cousin Phebe G—can testify to. . . . Thou can hardly conceive the dread I have of answerg. the letters of invitation recd. from Ohio, Western N.Y., Mass., & other places, to attend A. S. & Wom. Conventions; knowing the custom of publishing such answers" (19 March 1852; see also her letter to Elizabeth Cady Stanton of 3 October 1848).

Thus readers of Mott's letters to other reformers will find a matter-of-fact correspondent employing simple, direct prose to describe a convention, get the meeting organized, raise the funds. In letters to her fellow Quakers, however, she engaged in thoughtful discussions of her differences with the religious establishment. Letters to her family (those "hurried scraps") present still quite another kind of letter-writer. We catch glimpses of friendly arguments, of reading tastes, and of caustic opinions about contemporary newspaper articles, all sprinkled amid news of the family's health, its comings and goings, births, deaths, pregnancies, and servants' behavior. Rarely in these family letters did Mott pause to elaborate on any subject, personal or public, but instead offered only a few brief tantalizing sentences on Aunt Lydia's financial straits or Abraham Lincoln's inaugural address. Her granddaughter Anna Davis Hallowell aptly described these letters as "kaleidoscopic."[12] Lucretia once wrote her sister Martha, "You may not 'make head or tail' of this sheet—and tis of no consequence that you should— I have just written on as if I had been talkg. to my dear Sister here in this Library" (3 September 1867). The family letters, especially those to Martha and to Lucretia's daughter Pattie, contain the abrupt shifts of topic, rhetorical questions, and code words so common to conversation. The Motts enthusiastically enjoyed the nineteenth-century customs of gathering to hear letters read aloud and circulating them to sisters, daughters, sons-in-law, cousins, nieces, and nephews. She begged for more news ("we want a letter"; letter to Maria Mott and Edward M. Davis, 7 August 1855) from her widespread family and enthusiastically followed their varied lives.

Those more matter-of-fact letters to her fellow reformers illustrate, in contrast, Mott's forcefulness and organizing skill, but shed little light on the quality and tone of her public speaking, the gift for which she was renowned. Fortunately Dana Greene's edition of Mott's speeches and sermons preserves the text of many of these works. But it is still difficult to envision the magical transformation she effected when she won skeptical audiences over to the causes for which she fought so courageously. This account of her speaking in Maysville, Kentucky, on 16 October 1853 is only one of the many testimonies to her eloquence:

> She spoke for about an hour and a half, holding an immense audience enchained. She presented views bold, startling, and at least, to this community, original. No crying evil of the day escaped exposure and condemnation. . . . Her manner of speech was mild, winning and attractive. Her discourse gave strong evidence of the fact, that a woman, when she is qualified properly, has a right to be heard in public assemblages. From the misrepresentations of the press, our people had expected to see a sour, disappointed-looking woman, who, if the truth was fully known, was unhappy in her domestic relations. Her own appearance and that of her husband at once gave strong presumptive evidence of a quiet, happy life. Every auditor—even the strongest pro-slavery man—listened with attention, if not conviction.[13]

Such public recognition of her power did not affect this modest woman who came forward only when duty and the spirit called; for example, in the British Isles she termed the cheers that followed her speeches in Birmingham and Dublin "not merited" (letter to Maria Weston Chapman, 29 July 1840).

The power of the spirit governed all Mott's actions; her Quaker heritage gave meaning and context to every aspect of her life. Her demand for equality for African Americans and women was based on her belief that every human being must be open to be led by the promptings of the spirit. An 1867 sermon at the Brooklyn Unitarian Church epitomizes her convictions: "I believe that such proving all things, such trying all things, and holding fast only to that which is good, is the great religious duty of our age. The superstitions of the past must give way to this incorruptible spirit which searcheth all things. Our own conscience and the Divine Spirit's teaching are always harmonious and this Divine illumination is as freely given to man as his reason, or as are many of his natural powers."[14] Impelled by "this incorruptible spirit which searcheth all things," Lucretia expressed her distrust of authority in meeting when she was a young housewife. She asked James's grandfather why a Quaker should be disowned (i.e., removed from membership) for marrying outside the faith (29 June 1822). She wondered how "those of unblemished lives" could be taken to task by the meeting's elders (letter to Anne Mott, 26 February 1827). Elias Hicks's preaching in the 1820s, challenging scriptural and hierarchical authority, thus struck a responsive chord in Lucretia, and after the 1827 Hicksite separation she never hesitated to articulate her beliefs, even when they appeared shocking to other Hicksites. "Oh how our Discipline needs revising—& stripping of its objectionable features," she wrote Richard D. Webb and Hannah Webb. "I know not how far yours may differ from ours, but I know we have far too many disownable offences. Still with all our faults, I know of no religious association I would prefer to it" (25 February 1842).

Mott's distress over sectarian religion, expressed more formally in her frequent sermons, appears in numerous letters, especially to the Webbs and Nathaniel Barney. She asked Barney, "When will men learn that there are other & more indissoluble bonds of union than agreement in opinion in Creed or form?—" (14 March 1848). To Stanton, Mott wrote of her concern: "It is lamentable, that the simple & benign religion of Jesus should be so encumbered with the creeds & dogmas of sects— Its primitive beauty obscured by these gloomy appendages of man" (23 March 1841).

In her letters Mott frequently complained about the Hicksites' reluctance to take on the abolitionist, woman's rights, and other causes she considered important. Quakers were often "so filled with fears and cautions, that they would have been glad to forbid the subject of slavery," she remarked to Nathaniel Barney (14 February 1843). Mott wrote Barney and his wife in 1839 that the New York Meeting "took umbrage at my going to a Non-Resistance Meeting & talked themselves into an idea that it was almost a wicked step" (8 November 1839).

Conservative criticism, however, did not deter Lucretia or James. In 1848 the Motts had signed a call to an anti-sabbath convention in Boston, she insisted, "with our eyes wide open. We knew it wd subject us to added censure & reproach. But it has been a 'testimony' with me for years—not to measure devotion by Sabbath observances—& as zeal has increased in this direction, to try to counteract it—" (letter to Nathaniel Barney, 14 March 1848). The historian Nancy Hewitt speculates that the Hicksite split produced a "disruption and decline of male authority [which] was accompanied by the nurturance and expansion of women's power" in both the Orthodox and Hicksite organizations.[15] At least among the Hicksites, the independent Lucretia Mott served as a living example for her sisters of women's political power.

The historian Susan Mosher Stuard cogently expresses the religious legacy Mott and other Quaker women inherited: "Women among the Friends may be credited with helping to arouse righteous indignation against the whole corpus of received scholarly thought and the mental constructs by which thinkers arrived at their conclusions. By rejecting the very endeavor of formulating orthodox doctrines and rules, Quakerism as a movement found a way to discard the gender ideology that lay embedded within Western thought."[16] Mott understood and was empowered by this inheritance. She wrote Josephine Butler, "In the executive department of the Society, the right conceded to woman to act conjointly with man has had its influence, not only in making her familiar with the routine of business relating to our 'Discipline,' but in giving her self-reliance in mingling with the various reformatory societies in the great movements of the age" (20 April 1869). It is no coincidence that the majority of women signing the Declaration of Sentiments at Seneca Falls were Quakers or former Quakers.[17]

In a speech to the Pennsylvania Anti-Slavery Society in November 1869, Mott recalled how her Quaker faith had led to her participation in antislavery activities in the 1820s. She explained that she had felt herself obliged "to abstain from the products of the slave's labor [e.g., cotton, sugar, and other plantation products], knowing that Elias Hicks long, long before, had done this." Earlier at Nine Partners School, she related, students had learned about cruelties of the slave trade and had become familiar with Thomas Clarkson's appeals to abolish it. Although she was "somewhat prepared" to speak out against the slave trade in meeting, she described the "unexpected" call in moving and personal language: "It was a trial to be obliged to appear needlessly peculiar. It was like parting with the right hand or the right eye, but when I left the meeting I yielded to the obligation, and then, for forty years from that time, whatever I did I did under the conviction that it was wrong to partake of the products of the labor of slavery."[18]

The preceding statement underlines Mott's conviction that faith was fruitless unless connected to action. In her study of Mott and four other antislavery women Anna Speicher maintains, "For these women, the most egregious injustice in their world, and therefore the one most in need of Christian action, was slavery, the bondage of millions of God's children in involuntary servitude."[19]

As a believer in the influence that organizations could bring to bear on social problems, Mott founded and remained a leader of many antislavery organizations, beginning with the racially integrated AASS and the PFASS. She organized many a petition to Congress protesting her country's recognition of slavery. She and James housed fugitive slaves and befriended many free blacks. Her letters are sprinkled with references to visits from the Fortens and the Purvises, prominent Philadelphia black families and fellow activists on behalf of abolition. For more than twenty years she delivered numerous talks, sermons, and testimonies before state legislatures on the subject of antislavery, although only a few of these have survived.

When the U.S. government was finally roused to confront slavery as a real threat to a civil society in 1861, the ensuing war compelled Mott, who espoused nonviolence and had spoken at nonresistance meetings since 1839, to make hard choices. The forcible settlement of disputes should be one of the "relics of the dark ages," Mott had proclaimed in 1858.[20] This peace-loving woman protested the Civil War but not without some anguish. When her son-in-law Edward Davis returned from the front, Lucretia expressed surprise to Martha that his earlier pacifist efforts had become eclipsed by a resort to military force: "who wd. have thot. . . . that he wd. now be among the active officers in this war? He flatter[s?] himself that the abolitn. of slavery—end, justifies the means."[21] For Mott such means were problematic. In July 1861 she wrote a letter to the editor of the *National Anti-Slavery Standard* disputing the newspaper's coverage of a recent speech she had given in Boston because it imputed that she supported the war. She protested that "instead of the whole armor of God, we have the battle of the warrior, which is ever with confused noise and garments rolled in blood." Still, she continued, "terrible as war ever must be, let us hope that it may not be *stayed* by any compromise which shall continue the unequal, cruel war on the rights and liberties of millions of our unoffending fellow-beings" (6 July 1861). Not only did the Civil War impose this inner conflict but it forced Mott to endure the injuries and deaths of relatives and close friends (her nephew Willie Wright fought in the Battle of Gettysburg and several cousins were killed in 1863–64).

Yet whatever doubts she entertained, Mott saw that with the war came "an increase of hope for the Slave" (letter to Anna Temple Brown and Martha Coffin Wright, 27 December 1862). She wrote two sisters teaching freed slaves at Port Royal, South Carolina: "Is not the change in feeling, & conduct toward this oppressed class, beyond all that we could have anticipated—& marvellous in our eyes?" (letter to Anne Heacock and possibly Jennie Heacock, 23 July 1863). She also helped James Miller McKim send supplies to newly liberated freedpeople in Port Royal. In 1864, quoting Corinthians, the ever hopeful pacifist wrote Martha, Anna Temple Brown, and Martha Mott Lord: "The AntiS. sentiment is spreadg—not by battles with carnal weapons but the mighty 'armor of righteousness on the right hand & on the left'— It is no evidence of inconsistency, to be glad when the right is uppermost in the army—even if yr. depende. is *not* on the arm of flesh" (letter begun 21 January 1864). She echoed this belief more formally and realistically at the Pennsylvania Peace Society meeting in November 1868: "I regard the abolition of slavery as being much more the result of this moral warfare which was waged against the great crime of our nation: than as coming from the battle field, and I always look upon it as the result of the great moral warfare. It is true that Government had not risen to the high moral point which was required to accomplish this great object, and it must use the weapons it was accustomed to employ, and in its extremity it was compelled to do this great work. So in regard to war, it must be held in its true light and the enormity of the crime be laid where it belongs."[22]

Despite her prominence in these antislavery and nonresistance efforts, Mott's leadership in the antebellum woman's rights movement is the role for which she is chiefly remembered. Mott's abolitionist stance and her advocacy of woman's rights coincided frequently in these years, in particular when women delegates were denied representation at the 1840 World's Anti-Slavery Convention in London. Scholars agree about the significance of this convention, at which Mott first met Stanton, for the formation of the 1848 woman's rights conventions in Seneca Falls and Rochester and for Mott's germinal influence on Stanton's determination to seek equality for all women.[23]

As many historians have pointed out, the Seneca Falls convention was largely a congruence of the right women at the right time and place.[24] In July 1848 while Mott and her sister Martha were in Waterloo, New York, visiting Jane Hunt, a Quaker friend, Stanton, residing in nearby Seneca Falls, came to tea. They were joined by Mary Ann McClintock, a Philadelphia Friend and an antislavery activist then living in Waterloo. Little did these five women realize that July what they had initiated. In fact, when Mott described her summer to Edmund Quincy (24 August 1848), only at her letter's close did she mention the two conventions at Seneca Falls and Rochester, which had been called "to consider the relative position of woman in society." Instead, the bulk of her letter described her travels with James to the residences of fugitive slaves in Ontario and a stay with the Seneca at the Cattaraugus Reservation. Indeed, as Nancy Hewitt and others have argued, 1848 was filled with so many promising changes that this little meeting at an obscure New York town was only part of a wider pattern of revolution.[25]

Still, only a year later, Mott claimed that the agitation for women's equal treatment "has claimed my earnest interest for many years." During her youthful teaching days at Nine Partners School, she learned that, although the school charged the same tuition for boys and girls, women teachers were paid only half the salary of the men teachers.[26] In 1830, as the clerk of the women's meeting, she altered a letter John Comly, clerk of the men's meeting, had composed for the London Yearly Meeting, inserting "and sisters" after his term "brethren" (see the letter of 14 April 1830). Already by the mid-1830s she was well known as a founder of the PFASS. Moreover, her travels in the 1830s and 1840s took her to Quaker meetings and state legislatures throughout the mid-Atlantic states, where she determinedly introduced discussions of a woman's right to speak publicly and to hold property.

By 1848, Mott had already served as the president and manager of the PFASS, as the vice president of the American Free Produce Association, and on the executive committee of the AASS for eastern Pennsylvania. Through her efforts in those years to get Friends' meetings to take a stand against slavery, she had frequently encountered responses ranging from apathy to outright opposition. In all her work, she had become acutely attuned to the ways in which skillful opponents, through parliamentary maneuvering, might thwart causes dear to her. And she did not hesitate to refute the opinions of male speakers, even one as esteemed as the Unitarian clergyman Theodore Parker, when she thought he tended to compromise on observance of the sabbath.[27] Her reputation as a fighter for her beliefs was well-established when she came to Seneca Falls.

Thus it is no surprise that Mott's name heads the list of the one hundred delegates who signed the convention's Declaration of Sentiments. But, except for a few impromptu letters, we do not have her assessment of this significant event. In contrast, Stanton, Anthony, and Matilda Gage recorded the genesis of the Seneca Falls convention as that first meeting around the tea table at Jane Hunt's. In the summer of 1848 Stanton described herself as engulfed in "tempest-tossed" domesticity, with three sons under the age of six. Stanton's account accentuates the helplessness of the group, for she says they "were quite innocent of the herculean labors they proposed."[28] To be sure, this version may illustrate Stanton's feelings, but those feelings contrast markedly with the public courage and experience of Mott.

Mott's initial reluctance to include suffrage in the 1848 Declaration of Sentiments has placed her in the shadow of those woman's rights leaders who concentrated almost solely on voting rights. Mott, however, endorsed a broad woman's rights agenda; suffrage was not the only, nor was it the most important, goal for this reformer who shunned participation in electoral politics. In her "Discourse on Woman," she argued that a woman should be granted the right to vote, whether or not she chose to exercise it. Answering the question, "'What does woman want?'" she declared, "She wants to be acknowledged a moral, responsible being. She is seeking not to be governed by laws, in the making of which she has no voice. She is deprived of almost every right in civil society, and is a cypher in the nation, except in the right of presenting a petition. . . . In marriage, there is assumed superiority, on the part of the husband, and admitted inferiority, with a promise of obedience on the part of the wife. This subject calls loudly for examination, in order that the wrong may be redressed." Woman was physically different from man, she believed, but, echoing Mary Wollstonecraft's words from over half a century earlier, Mott stressed that woman should not "degenerate into a kind of effeminacy, in which she is satisfied to be the mere plaything or toy of society, content with her outward adorning, and with the tone of flattery and fulsome adulation too often addressed to her."

When Mott asked her audience, "Why should not woman seek to be a reformer?" she directly linked woman's rights with her other concerns. In the present age, "notable for its works of mercy and benevolence," women could contribute equally with men to the improvement of their fellow beings: "They are efficient co-workers, their talents are called into profile exercise, their labors are effective in each department of reform."[29]

After the Civil War, suffrage became an even more dominant part of the woman's rights agenda as the debates about rights and suffrage for freedmen took center stage. Mott tried to please advocates for the Fourteenth and Fifteenth Amendments as well as opponents who denounced the amendments because women were excluded. She initially believed that pursuing woman suffrage at this time was inadvisable in view of the "all-absorbg. negro questn." (letter to Martha Coffin Wright and Martha Mott Lord, 2 November 1865). Yet a year later she sent a letter to the Equal Rights Convention in Albany stating that the freedman had "Advocates not a few for his right to the ballot— Intelligent as these advocates are, they must see that this right cannot be consistently withheld from woman" (18 November 1866). Moreover, as president of the AERA she signed a letter protesting any changes in the Constitution that would withhold rights from women (10 May 1867) and suggested in the spring of 1868 that AERA efforts for freedmen's suffrage should be "discontinued," since they had adequate support elsewhere, and asked that woman's rights conventions be resumed (before 14 May 1868). Still, she subsequently signed public letters seeking passage of the Fifteenth Amendment granting universal male suffrage (see her letter to the Senate, c. 3 February 1869, and her letter to fellow abolitionists, December 1869), perhaps in hopes it would lead to the passage of a proposed sixteenth amendment giving the vote to women. Because of her stature and her good relations with woman's rights activists on both sides of the issue, her support was sought by all parties seeking constitutional recognition of African Americans and women.

In this edition of her letters, Mott's private views on the breach between the two woman's rights organizations over the Fifteenth Amendment are readily available for the first time. She rendered candid opinions of the conflict between the Stone and Blackwell faction (founders of the AWSA) and her old friends Stanton and Anthony (organizers of the NWSA). (Mott had probably met Anthony, whom she described as an "efficient, practical woman" [letter to Elizabeth Cady Stanton, 16 March 1855], at the 1852 Syracuse convention, at which the former presided and the latter was a secretary.) Logically, Mott's long devotion to the abolitionist cause should make her a partisan of Stone's organization. However, although Mott criticized Stanton and Anthony's tactics ("they may make some mistakes—and perhaps mis statements"; letter to Martha Coffin Wright, 6 June 1869) and refused to subscribe to their publication, the *Revolution,* she found it impossible to desert them. Regarding an invitation to a recent woman's rights convention organized by Stone and others in Boston, Mott wrote

Martha, "Thou'lt see, my dear Sister how respectfully I am bidden, or *was* rather, to the late convention. But, as going where Susan B. A. & E. C. Stanton were denied wd. be partisan-like, *that* wd. have prevented if age wd.n't.—" (3 December 1868). Mott's primary ties to Stanton and Anthony might have been personal and emotional; after all, her friendship with Stanton dated back to 1840. Mott may have simply loved "dear Elizabeth" so much that she could overlook the latter's racist remarks (see her letter to Martha Coffin Wright of 21 January 1868, n. 9). And the peripatetic Anthony was always warmly received at the Motts' home. Perhaps Mott found Lucy Stone too quarrelsome (see letter to Martha Coffin Wright, 3 December 1868). Moreover, as her letters in this period indicate, she was tired. Mott wished the antagonists "wd. simply say, 'I dont agree with her'—instd. of makg it a *principle*," she wrote Martha (16 July 1870). A younger, more energetic Mott might have tried more assiduously to resolve this conflict and bring the two sides together. Instead, the usually optimistic peacemaker was resigned to a separation (see her letter to Martha Coffin Wright of 7 April 1870) and she permitted her name to be added to the roster of Stanton and Anthony's organization. Despite her repeated professions of "I don't care," her letters suggest a vital interest in the women's efforts. She spoke at the NWSA annual meetings in 1871 and 1873, but thereafter confined her appearances, largely symbolic, to the centennial celebration in Philadelphia and the thirtieth anniversary celebration of the Seneca Falls convention. Mott devoted much of her remaining strength and years instead to the Free Religious Association and the cause of peace (e.g., see her letter to Richard D. Webb of 22 January 1871 and her letter to Ulysses S. Grant of 12 November 1873).

Scholars analyzing the history of the woman's rights movement have concentrated on a causal linkage: women's activism in the antislavery and temperance movements led to the pursuit of their own rights. In these earlier movements, they argue, women gained confidence, organizing skills, and a sense of their deprivations that fueled their quest for the privileges men enjoyed.[30] Thus woman's rights are seen as the goal, and the other endeavors as the means. Such a development may apply to some nineteenth-century feminists, but not to Lucretia Mott. When scholars include her in their discussion of antebellum woman's rights leaders, but overlook her other reform impulses, they confuse her ends and means.

For Mott, the cause of women was *both* an end and a means. She wanted women to have more power, not only to secure personal rights such as the vote, but also so they could work more effectively to eliminate the problems of the day: war, slavery, poverty, drunkenness, illiteracy. Denial of the franchise to women was just one of many wrongs to be righted. In Mott's view women should be able to agitate in legislatures for nondiscriminatory property rights, integrate schools and streetcars, enter any profession. Women's power and voice were also needed to establish a serene and comfortable life for husbands, children, and grandchildren.

The historian Nancy Isenberg writes that the "legacy of the antebellum women's rights campaign extended beyond the vote or even the terms of what was to be the Fifteenth Amendment. The larger contribution came from the varied and ingenious arguments for women's full entitlement as citizens." The 1848 Seneca Falls convention approved a resolution stating that, since woman possessed the same "capabilities" and "consciousness of responsibility" as man, woman should "promote every righteous cause, by every righteous means; and especially in regard to the great subjects of morals and religion, it is self-evidently her right to participate with her brother in teaching them, both *in private* and in public."[31] Isenberg believes that Mott most likely wrote this resolution and it certainly illustrates her thinking, as succinctly expressed in an 1853 sermon: "all these great reformatory movements are in accordance with each other."[32]

Mott was not alone in either her belief in these crucial connections or in her insistence on the private as well as the public dimensions of reform. She provided a model for a life of social activism larger than just the demand for suffrage—or even for woman's rights in general—that numerous other antebellum women activists embraced. Many Quakers, free black women, and radicals from other backgrounds shared Mott's vision for social change. Moreover, by maintaining friendships throughout her life with such African American colleagues as Robert Purvis, Harriet Tubman, and Sojourner Truth, Mott refused to participate in any division between women's interests and those of blacks, a division that plagued the suffrage movement and the broader women's movement beginning in the late nineteenth century.

Lucretia Mott's letters demonstrate how dramatically her life embodied this interweaving of politics and daily life so central to most nineteenth-century women activists. A letter to George Combe and his wife, Cecilia, several weeks after the 1848 Seneca Falls and Rochester conventions is illustrative. Besides the two conventions, Mott commented on the uprisings in Rome and France, an anti-sabbath meeting, a Theodore Parker sermon, Elihu Burritt's peace mission, Philadelphia friends who had recently visited the Combes, and her nine grandchildren. She concluded, "reform is 'certainly the order of the day'" (10 September 1848). Reform of almost every kind—temperance, peace, equal rights, woman suffrage, school, prisons, abolition of slavery—was clearly the order of Lucretia Coffin Mott's busy days.

## Notes

1. Otelia Cromwell, *Lucretia Mott* (Cambridge, Mass.: Harvard University Press, 1958), 18.

2. *James and Lucretia Mott: Their Life and Letters,* ed. Anna Davis Hallowell (Boston: Houghton Mifflin, 1884), 100.

3. See Margaret Hope Bacon, "Antislavery Women and Nonresistance," in *The Abolitionist Sisterhood: Women's Political Culture in Antebellum America,* ed. Jean Fagan Yellin and John C. Van Horne (Ithaca, N.Y.: Cornell University Press, 1994), 275–97.

4. Kathryn Kish Sklar, "The World Anti-Slavery Convention," in ibid., 315.

5. "Woman's Rights Convention, Held at Seneca Falls," in *Selected Papers of Elizabeth Cady Stanton and Susan B. Anthony,* ed. Ann D. Gordon, 2 vols. (New Brunswick, N.J.: Rutgers University Press, 1997, 2000), 1:77; compare with earlier resolution in *Liberator,* 16 June 1837, 98.

6. Lucretia Coffin Mott, "Discourse on Woman," *Lucretia Mott: Her Complete Speeches and Sermons,* ed. Dana Greene (New York: Edwin Mellen Press, 1980), 151.

7. Blanche G. Hersh, *The Slavery of Sex* (Urbana: University of Illinois Press, 1978), 209; Lucretia Coffin Mott, memoir, Mott Manuscripts, Friends Historical Library, Swarthmore College, Swarthmore, Pa.

8. Margaret Hope Bacon, *Valiant Friend: The Life of Lucretia Mott* (New York: Walker, 1980), 31; Hersh, *The Slavery of Sex,* 225–27; see also Chris Dixon, *Perfecting the Family: Antislavery Marriages in Nineteenth-Century America* (Amherst: University of Massachusetts Press, 1997), chap. 3.

9. See Bacon, *Valiant Friend,* 30.

10. Ibid., 186.

11. Carroll Smith-Rosenberg, "Hearing Women's Words," *Disorderly Conduct: Visions of Gender in Victorian America* (New York: Oxford University Press, 1986), 28.

12. *James and Lucretia Mott,* 379. Moreover, references in Mott's letters to her family are even more "kaleidoscopic" to outsiders because most incoming letters have not been recovered.

13. "Maysville," *Liberator,* 4 November 1853, 174.

14. Lucretia Coffin Mott, "When the Heart Is Attuned to Prayer," *Complete Speeches and Sermons,* 302.

15. Nancy Hewitt, "The Fragmentation of Friends," in *Witnesses for Change: Quaker Women over Three Centuries,* ed. Elizabeth Brown and Susan Mosher Stuard (New Brunswick, N.J.: Rutgers University Press, 1989), 94, see also 100, 104; see also Hewitt's study of upstate New York Quakers, "Feminist Friends: Agrarian Quakers and the Emergence of Woman's Rights in America," *Feminist Studies* 12 (Spring 1986): 27–49, and Margaret Hope Bacon, *Mothers of Feminism* (Philadelphia: Friends General Conference, 1986), 93.

16. Susan Mosher Stuard, "Women's Witnessing," in *Witnesses for Change,* 14.

17. See Judith Wellman's study on the convention participants, "The Seneca Falls Women's Rights Convention: A Study of Social Networks," *Journal of Women's History* 3 (Spring 1991): 27; *Selected Papers of Stanton and Anthony,* 1:87; Hewitt, "Feminist Friends," 29.

18. "Proceedings of the Annual Meeting of the Pennsylvania Anti-Slavery Society," 17 November 1869, *National Anti-Slavery Standard,* 27 November 1869, 1.

19. Anna Speicher, *The Religious World of Antislavery Women: Spirituality in the Lives of Five Abolitionist Lecturers* (Syracuse: Syracuse University Press, 2000), 89.

20. Lucretia Coffin Mott, "Religious Instinct in the Constitution of Man," *Complete Speeches and Sermons,* 246.

21. Lucretia Coffin Mott to Martha Coffin Wright, 15 October 1861, Mott Manuscripts, Swarthmore; see also Mott's letter to Martha of 6 November 1861, below.

22. Lucretia Coffin Mott, "Going to the Root of the Matter," *Complete Speeches and Sermons,* 311–12.

23. On the London convention, see Mott's letter to Maria Weston Chapman, 29 July 1840, below; see also Bonnie Anderson, *Joyous Greetings: The First International Women's Movement, 1830–60* (New York: Oxford University Press, 2000), 126–28; Bacon, "Antislavery Women and Nonresistance," 293; *Elizabeth Cady Stanton, Susan B. Anthony: Correspondence, Writings, Speeches,* ed. Ellen Carol DuBois (New York: Shocken Books,

1981), 11–12; and Elisabeth Griffith, *In Her Own Right: The Life of Elizabeth Cady Stanton* (New York: Oxford University Press, 1984), 10, 76, 175.

24. See, e.g., Wellman, "The Seneca Falls Women's Rights Convention," 9–13, 25–29.

25. Nancy Hewitt, "Re-Rooting American Women's Activism: Global Perspectives on 1848," *Österreichische Zeitschrift für Geschichtswissenschaften* 4 (1998): 457–70; Anderson, *Joyous Greetings,* 128.

26. Mott, "Discourse on Woman," 143; Mott, memoir.

27. See Lucretia Coffin Mott, "Remarks, Delivered to the Anti-Sabbath Convention," 23–24 Mar. 1848, *Complete Speeches and Sermons,* 59–60.

28. Elizabeth Cady Stanton, Susan B. Anthony, and Matilda Joslyn Gage, *History of Woman Suffrage* (New York: Fowler and Wells, 1881), 1:68; on the *History of Woman Suffrage*'s special slant, see Hersh, *The Slavery of Sex,* 72; on Mott's antebellum "experience and expertise," see Anderson, *Joyous Greetings,* 123–24.

29. Mott, "Discourse on Woman," 147–48, 154; Mary Wollstonecraft, *A Vindication of the Rights of Woman* (London: Penguin Classics, 1985), 100, 254–55.

30. See, e.g., DuBois, *Stanton, Anthony,* 22, 32; Keith Melder, *The Beginnings of Sisterhood* (New York: Schocken Books, 1977), 16; Suzanne Marilley, *Woman Suffrage and the Origins of Liberal Feminism in the United States* (Cambridge, Mass.: Harvard University Press, 1996), 20–21.

31. Nancy Isenberg, *Sex and Citizenship in Antebellum America* (Chapel Hill: University of North Carolina Press, 1998), 20, 190; "Woman's Rights Convention," 1:77–78, emphasis added.

32. Isenberg, *Sex and Citizenship,* 31; Lucretia Coffin Mott, "To the Hearts of Temperance Reformers," *Complete Speeches and Sermons,* 199.

# Editorial Principles

## Search, Selection, and Organization

The largest collection of Mott correspondence is located at Swarthmore College, with approximately 485 holograph letters and 60 letter fragments, mostly written by Lucretia Coffin Mott (LCM). The second largest collection is at Smith College, with a total of 340 letters to and from LCM, including fragments. Many other letters are held in smaller numbers in libraries or by individuals. Selections from this large body of writings formed the 1884 collection published by LCM's granddaughter Anna Davis Hallowell, *Lucretia and James Mott: Their Life and Letters.* Typical of nineteenth-century conventions in editing, Hallowell abridged, combined, and expurgated the original manuscript letters to create the appearance of a less spontaneous, more logical, and primmer correspondent. Hallowell changed phrases and words so that, for example, "not by a jug full" became "by any means," "writing" replaced "scribbling," and "gossiping" emerged as "trifling." Published here for the first time are the authentic texts of LCM's letters as closely and clearly as my colleagues and I can reproduce them.

Unfortunately, numerous letters, both to and from LCM, were destroyed, sometimes at her insistence. In other correspondence we have found references to letters LCM wrote to Frederick Douglass, Lucy Stone, and Henry B. Blackwell, among others, which have not been recovered. Although LCM herself mentioned writing to fellow reformers such as Amy Post and Abby Kelley Foster (and it can be safely assumed that she continued her correspondence after 1850 with liberal Quakers like Richard D. Webb and Hannah Webb), none of those letters has apparently survived. A complete list of all known extant letters to and from LCM can be found in the appendix.

We have selected about one-quarter of the approximately 950 surviving letters written by LCM for inclusion in this volume. The letters fall into two broad categories, family and nonfamily, with family letters being the larger category, mainly because these have survived. Our goal has been to choose letters covering the length and breadth of LCM's public life as a leading reformer while retaining a sense of her central role in her family. Indeed, it would be impossible to separate the personal and public dimensions of her life since the subjects are interwoven in the letters and since many family members participated with LCM in woman's rights, antislavery, and other progressive causes. Notable in this respect were LCM's husband, James, her sister Martha Coffin Wright, and her daughter and son-in-law Maria Mott Davis and Edward Davis.

Letters that were only accepting, declining, or issuing invitations were eliminated from our consideration for inclusion at the outset. Letters that dealt only with family matters were also generally excluded. While the majority of letters are presented in their entirety, on occasion we have taken the liberty of selecting one or two interesting daily entries from long letters written over a period of several days. We chose these daily entries to avoid either rejecting a significant letter because of its length or taxing the reader with an excess of domestic details or information about now-obscure individuals. In general, the selections demonstrate the key involvement of LCM in the political, social, and religious movements of nineteenth-century America. They also reveal the thinking behind the actions of this family-oriented woman who managed to satisfy home and community obligations while working to secure justice for women and persons of color.

This volume is organized into four sections, each of which corresponds to a significant phase in LCM's personal life: 1813–40, her early years, culminating in her trip to the British Isles; 1840–56, her years in Philadelphia as a radical preacher and an activist grandmother; 1857–68, her years at the family's farm, Roadside, ending with James Mott's death; and 1868–80, her years as the family matriarch until her death.

## Transcription and Annotation

This collection contains transcriptions of holograph letters, printed letters, circulars, and petitions. Each item has been given a standardized heading indicating the name of the recipient. In cases where my colleagues and I have had to infer the name, we have enclosed it in brackets. Guesses are indicated by question marks. Many of the letters LCM wrote to her sister Martha were intended, as her text indicates, to be sent on to other family members. Unless that member is clearly addressed as a recipient, we have omitted the name in the heading.

If LCM's letter is an addition to one written by another person, we have placed the date and location in brackets before the text of the letter unless LCM included her own information. We have then inserted an identifying phrase in brackets and have italicized this material, for example, "[*Added to JM's of the same date*]." Similarly, when we have omitted an entry from a multiple-date letter, we have indicated that, such as "[*Continuation of a letter begun 4 Septem-*

*ber from New York City*]." In these cases a location is included only if it differs from the original.

The date of the letter and LCM's location when writing it have standardized positions. Our additions of this information are italicized and appear in brackets. The name of the state is supplied for cities and towns outside Pennsylvania that are not well known. We have retained LCM's Quaker references to days of the week, in which "First Day," for example, stands for Sunday and "Fourth Day" stands for Wednesday. We have also retained her nineteenth-century date style in which "6 mo. 18th. 1838" means 18 June 1838. The locations of the greeting, complimentary closing, and signature have also been regularized. Since LCM often reused incoming letters as her own stationery, we have not noted the nature of the stationery unless it bears some significance to her letter.

Spacing within the text of the letter and paragraph indentions have been regularized. Material on a new page that seems to indicate a new thought is treated as a new paragraph. LCM's underlining has been rendered as italic.

All material, whether handwritten or reproduced from a printed source, whether original letter, copy, circular, or petition, is transcribed as written, with misspellings and erratic punctuation retained. Misspellings of names are corrected in notes identifying individuals or events. Especially in her informal letters, LCM spelled words inconsistently. She also capitalized unevenly, sometimes even beginning a new sentence with a lowercase letter. We have retained this inconsistent practice, but have inserted extra space to indicate each probable sentence break. Her end-of-line word divisions have not been reproduced. Words crossed out have been omitted unless the cancellation shows a significant change in meaning.

Interlineations that merely correct an omission or detail (e.g., "32 no I mean 33") are not noted with a caret unless the sentence would be difficult to follow. All other material inserted by LCM is between carets. LCM's square brackets have been converted to braces to avoid confusion with our additions.

LCM frequently used superscripts for her numerous abbreviations, as in "morn$^g$" and "yest$^y$," for "morning" and "yesterday." We have lowered all superscripts, converting the small dash mark sometimes found under the superscript to a period. (If there was no mark under the superscript, we have not added a period.) However, if an abbreviated word with an underscored superscript appears with a period indicating the end of a sentence, we have not included the second period. An exception to this lowered superscript policy has been made for the name of her daughter-in-law, Marianna Pelham Wright, whom she usually refers to as "Mari$^a$." We have retained this superscripted form to avoid confusion with LCM's daughter Maria. We have also retained the superscripted abbreviation of the Hallowell family's name, usually written as "Hall$^l$.," for easier reading of the triple letter.

LCM observed an almost entirely consistent abbreviation pattern in her letters, adding after one or more syllables the last letter of the word, as in "famy."

and "Caroe.," for "family" and "Caroline." When these abbreviations seem likely to pose an obstacle for the reader, we have added the missing letters in brackets; for example, LCM's "dicy." becomes "dic[tionar]y." To avoid cluttering the text, each word expansion generally appears only once per letter. When an abbreviated word contains sufficient letters to be comprehensible, however, we have not expanded it; for example, "corresponde." is not expanded but "correspe." is. If a word or part of a word group can be deciphered or easily inferred, though not clearly read on the manuscript, we have added the missing letters in brackets, as in "[trou]ble" or "try[ing to]." Tentative readings also appear in brackets but include a question mark.

To reduce the number of annotations, we have added identifying words, such as a missing first or last name, in italics and brackets, for example, "Pattie [*Lord*]" or "[*Wendell*] Phillips." Family members and other frequently mentioned individuals are identified in the "Biographical Directory." Others are usually identified on their first mention in the volume. Birth and death dates, marriages, and occupational data are supplied when known. Individuals mentioned only in the notes are not fully identified. We do not explain when people, events, and allusions cannot be identified. We have assumed that readers have a general knowledge of well-known figures and events—Job, Abraham Lincoln, the Civil War—and have not supplied citations for major reference works, such as the *Dictionary of American Biography,* William W. Hinshaw's *Encyclopedia of American Quaker Genealogy, Notable American Women,* and the RLIN (English short title catalog). The annotations identify obscure individuals, indicate sources of quotations, clarify LCM's meaning, provide background for her comments, and refer readers to other relevant letters. Our additions to quotations in the notes are signaled by italics and brackets.

Any postscript, whether designated "P.S." by LCM or by us, is placed at the end of the letter or, in a multiple-date letter, the section of the letter to which it pertains. Material marked with an asterisk or other symbol to be added somewhere in a letter is also placed at the end of the letter. Each document ends with information about its format and an indication of its source. The few letter fragments are indicated as such in the sourcelines. LCM's habit of using every inch of the paper when writing—sometimes failing to include a signature or even ending punctuation—makes her letters look incomplete at times, but all letters, except where noted, have been reproduced in their entirety.

# Key to Editorial Notations

## Abbreviations

| | |
|---|---|
| AASS | American Anti-Slavery Society |
| AERA | American Equal Rights Association |
| AL | autograph letter |
| ALS | autograph letter with signature |
| AWSA | American Woman Suffrage Association |
| c. | circa |
| C | contemporary copy |
| Env | envelope |
| Extr | extract |
| Frag | fragment |
| JM | James Mott |
| LCM | Lucretia Coffin Mott |
| LS | letter written in another's hand except signature |
| MCW | Martha Coffin Wright |
| MML | Martha ("Pattie") Mott Lord |
| ms. | manuscript |
| NWSA | National Woman Suffrage Association |
| PASS | Pennsylvania Anti-Slavery Society |
| PFASS | Philadelphia Female Anti-Slavery Society |
| PL | printed letter |
| PLS | printed letter with holograph signature |
| TTR | transcription from another source |
| XC | photocopy of original |

## Short Citations

| | |
|---|---|
| Bacon | Margaret Hope Bacon, *Valiant Friend: The Life of Lucretia Mott* (New York: Walker, 1980) |
| Diary | *Slavery and "The Woman Question": Lucretia Mott's Diary of Her Visit to Great Britain to Attend the World's Anti-Slavery Convention of 1840,* ed. Frederick B. Tolles (Haverford, Pa.: Friends Historical Association, 1952) |
| Gordon | *Selected Papers of Elizabeth Cady Stanton and Susan B. Anthony,* ed. Ann D. Gordon, 2 vols. (New Brunswick, N.J.: Rutgers University Press, 1997, 2000) |
| Hallowell | *James and Lucretia Mott: Their Life and Letters,* ed. Anna Davis Hallowell (Boston: Houghton Mifflin, 1884) |
| HWS | Elizabeth Cady Stanton, Susan B. Anthony, and Matilda Joslyn Gage, *History of Woman Suffrage,* vols. 1 and 2 (New York: Fowler and Wells, 1881) |
| Ingle | Larry Ingle, *Quakers in Conflict: The Hicksite Reformation* (Wallingford, Pa.: Pendle Hill Publications, 1998) |
| JGW | *The Letters of John Greenleaf Whittier,* ed. John B. Pickard, 3 vols. (Cambridge, Mass.: Belknap Press, 1971–75) |
| NASS | *National Anti-Slavery Standard* (New York newspaper) |
| Sermons | *Lucretia Mott: Her Complete Speeches and Sermons,* ed. Dana Greene (New York: Edwin Mellen Press, 1980) |
| Stanton-Anthony Papers | *Papers of Elizabeth Cady Stanton and Susan B. Anthony,* ed. Patricia G. Holland and Anne D. Gordon, microfilm ed. (Wilmington, Del.: Scholarly Resources, 1992) |
| Sterling | Dorothy Sterling, *Ahead of Her Time: Abby Kelley and the Politics of Anti-Slavery* (New York: W. W. Norton, 1991) |
| Taylor | Clare Taylor, *Women of the Antislavery Movement: The Weston Sisters* (New York: St. Martin's Press, 1995) |
| WLG | *Letters of William Lloyd Garrison,* ed. Louis Ruchames and Walter Merrill, 5 vols. (Cambridge, Mass.: Harvard University Press, 1971–81) |

## Letter Sources

The following individuals and repositories (listed according to their Library of Congress *National Union Catalog* designations), to the extent that they possess rights to the manuscript letters in their possession, have kindly granted permission for these materials to be included in this edition.

| | |
|---|---|
| CSmH | Huntington Library, San Marino, Calif. |
| CULA | Box 121, Collection 100, Miscellaneous Manuscripts Collection, Department of Special Collections, Charles E. Young Research Library, University of California, Los Angeles |
| Davis | Private collection of Hester Davis, Fayetteville, Ark. |

| | |
|---|---|
| DLC | Blackwell Family Papers, National American Woman Suffrage Association Papers, and Elizabeth Cady Stanton Papers, Manuscript Division, Library of Congress, Washington, D.C. |
| DNA | Records of the U.S. Senate, 40th Cong., 3d sess., RG 46, National Archives, Washington, D.C. |
| Falconi | Private collection of Elizabeth Post Falconi, Newtown, Pa. |
| GBNLS | Combe Papers, National Library of Scotland, Edinburgh (letters published courtesy of the Trustees of the National Library of Scotland) |
| IaDPm | Putnam Museum of History and Natural Science, Davenport, Ia. |
| InFwL | Lincoln Museum, Fort Wayne, Ind. |
| MB | Rare Books and Manuscripts, Boston Public Library (letters published courtesy of the Trustees of the Boston Public Library) |
| MCR | A/M921, Schlesinger Library, Radcliffe Institute, Harvard University, Cambridge, Mass. |
| MH-H | Houghton Library, Harvard University, Cambridge, Mass. |
| MHi | Caroline Wells Healey Dall Papers, Massachusetts Historical Society, Boston |
| MiUc | Diedrich Collection, Manuscripts Division, William L. Clements Library, University of Michigan, Ann Arbor |
| MNHi | Nantucket Historical Association, Nantucket, Mass. |
| MNS | Garrison Family Papers, Sophia Smith Collection, Smith College, Northampton, Mass. |
| MSaE | Salem Female Anti-Slavery Society Papers, Phillips Library, Peabody Essex Museum, Salem, Mass. |
| MWA | American Antiquarian Society, Worcester, Mass. |
| NBu | James Fraser Gluck Collection, Grosvenor Rare Book Room, Buffalo and Erie County Public Library, Buffalo, N.Y. |
| NHP | Women's Rights National Historical Park, Seneca Falls, N.Y. |
| NICO | May Anti-Slavery Collection (#4601), Division of Rare and Manuscript Collections, Cornell University Library, Ithaca, N.Y. |
| NjP | General Manuscripts, Bound, CO199, Department of Rare Books and Special Collections, Princeton University Library, Princeton, N.J. |
| NjRD | Elizabeth Cady Stanton Memorial Collection, Mabel Smith Douglass Library, Rutgers, the State University of New Jersey, New Brunswick |
| NN | Maloney Collection of McKim-Garrison Family Papers, Manuscripts and Archives Division, New York Public Library, Astor, Lenox, and Tilden Foundations |
| NNCB | Sydney Howard Gay Papers, Josephine S. Griffing Papers, and Caroline Bonsall Kelley Papers, Rare Book and Manuscript Library, Columbia University, New York |

NPV　　　　Special Collections, Vassar College Libraries, Poughkeepsie, N.Y.

NRU　　　　Department of Rare Books and Special Collections, Rush Rhees Library, University of Rochester, Rochester, N.Y.

NSyU　　　　Gerritt Smith Papers, Department of Special Collections, Syracuse University Library, Syracuse, N.Y.

OHi　　　　Charles E. Rice Papers, Archives/Library Division, Ohio Historical Society, Columbus

PHi　　　　Society Collection, Historical Society of Pennsylvania (HSP), Philadelphia

PSCHi　　　Mott Manuscripts, Heacock Manuscripts, and Ross Manuscripts, Friends Historical Library, Swarthmore College, Swarthmore, Pa.

# Chronology

Most sermons published in *Lucretia Mott: Her Complete Sermons and Speeches,* edited by Dana Greene, are not listed here. Speeches and remarks that have hitherto been unrecorded are included instead.

| | |
|---|---|
| 20 June 1788 | JM born |
| 3 January 1793 | born in Nantucket, Mass., to Thomas and Anna Folger Coffin |
| July 1804 | Coffin family moves to Boston |
| July 1806 | attends Nine Partners School in Dutchess County, near Poughkeepsie, New York |
| 1808–10 | assists girls' teacher at Nine Partners School |
| c. January 1809 | Coffin family moves to Philadelphia |
| 10 April 1811 | marries JM |
| 6 August 1812 | daughter Anna born |
| 23 August 1814 | son Thomas born |
| 26 January 1815 | Thomas Coffin dies; JM moves to New York City briefly |
| 16 April 1817 | son Thomas dies |
| April 1817 | teaches at Select School for Girls, Philadelphia |
| 30 March 1818 | daughter Maria born |
| 1818 | gives first speech at Twelfth Street (Orthodox) Meeting, Philadelphia |
| 1821 | recognized as minister in Society of Friends |
| 8 August 1823 | second son Thomas born |
| 14 December 1825 | daughter Elizabeth born |
| 1826 | JM helps organize Philadelphia Free Produce Society to protest slave products |
| 1827 | with JM joins followers of Elias Hicks in split of Quaker church; both join Cherry Street Meeting; disowned by Twelfth Street Meeting |

| | |
|---|---|
| 30 October 1828 | daughter Martha ("Pattie") born |
| August 1830 | meets William Lloyd Garrison in Philadelphia |
| 1830 | JM's firm sells wool instead of cotton |
| 1830–35 | serves as clerk of Philadelphia Women's Yearly Meeting |
| 24 April 1833 | daughter Anna marries Edward Hopper |
| 4–6 December 1833 | attends founding meeting of AASS in Philadelphia; meets James Miller McKim |
| 9 December 1833 | helps organize PFASS; serves first as corresponding clerk, later as president |
| 26 October 1836 | daughter Maria marries Edward M. Davis |
| 9–12 May 1837 | speaks at Anti-Slavery Convention of American Women in New York City |
| 17 May 1838 | mob attacks and burns Pennsylvania Hall during second Anti-Slavery Convention of American Women in Philadelphia |
| 20 May 1839 | speaks at AASS of Eastern Pennsylvania |
| 25 September 1839 | speaks to Non-Resistance Society, Boston |
| February 1840 | attacked by anti-Hicksite mob on return trip from Southern Quarterly Meeting in Delaware |
| 7–27 May 1840 | with JM sails to England as prospective delegate to World's Anti-Slavery Convention, representing AASS |
| 12 June 1840 | refused a seat in convention, which ends June 23 |
| 24 June 1840 | speaks before a group of British abolitionists in London |
| 22 July 1840 | delivers a temperance lecture in Dublin |
| 9 August 1840 | speaks to Glasgow Emancipation Society |
| 26 August 1840 | with JM leaves Great Britain; they arrive in New York City 24 September |
| c. January 1841 | testifies against slavery before state legislatures in Delaware, Pennsylvania, New Jersey |
| 6 October 1841 | protests disownment of Isaac T. Hopper and others in sermon at Rose Street Meeting, New York City |
| October–November 1842 | speaks in Maryland, Virginia, and Washington, D.C., on abolition and woman's rights |
| 26 March 1844 | has serious illness; Anna Coffin dies |
| 21 July 1845 | daughter Elizabeth marries Thomas Cavender |
| 28 July 1845 | son Thomas marries Marianna Pelham |
| August 1845 | travels to Ohio Yearly Meeting in Salem |
| 6 February 1847 | addresses Women of Philadelphia meeting on slavery |
| mid-August 1847 | gives sermons at Unitarian Church, Nantucket; Second Congregational (Unitarian) Society, Worcester; Syracuse Unitarian Church |
| late August 1847 | attends Ohio and Indiana Yearly Meetings and antislavery conventions |
| 9–11 May 1848 | in "The Law of Progress," first major speech at AASS in New York City, advocates immediate abolition of slavery |

| | |
|---|---|
| 11 June 1848 | speaks at Genesee Yearly Meeting, Waterloo, New York |
| pre–13 July 1848 | with JM tours Cattaraugus Indian reservation and set-tlements of "self-emancipated slaves" in Canada |
| 13–16 July 1848 | meets with Elizabeth Cady Stanton, Jane Hunt, Mary Ann McClintock, and MCW in Waterloo, New York, to organize Seneca Falls Woman's Rights Convention and write Declaration of Sentiments |
| 19–20 July 1848 | Seneca Falls Woman's Rights Convention held |
| 2 August 1848 | speaks at Rochester Woman's Rights Convention |
| 8 May 1849 | speaks at AASS annual meeting |
| 4–6 June 1849 | attends Yearly Meeting of Congregational Friends, Wa-terloo, New York; speaks in Seneca Falls on 6 June on woman's rights |
| 12 July 1849 | brother Thomas dies |
| 15–17 October 1849 | speaks at PASS meeting, Norristown |
| 17 December 1849 | delivers "Discourse on Woman" in Philadelphia as an-swer to Richard Henry Dana Sr.'s lecture criticizing the woman's rights movement |
| 4 July 1850 | speaks at commencement at New York Central College in upstate New York |
| 23–24 October 1850 | attends first National Woman's Rights Convention in Worcester, Mass. |
| January 1851 | JM retires to farming; with JM buys farm outside Phil-adelphia |
| 15–16 October 1851 | attends Worcester Woman's Rights Convention |
| November–December 1851 | assists black prisoners in Christiana fugitive slave case and attends their trial in Philadelphia; raises funds for Quaker defendant Caster Hanway |
| 8–10 September 1852 | elected president of Syracuse Woman's Rights Conven-tion; delivers remarks at meeting |
| 25–27 October 1852 | denounces Fugitive Slave Law at PASS meeting in West Chester |
| 15–17 December 1852 | speaks at PASS meeting in Philadelphia |
| mid-May 1853 | speaks at meeting of PFASS; Sojourner Truth also speaks |
| 8 June 1853 | daughter Pattie marries George Lord |
| 1–2 September 1853 | addresses World Temperance Conference, New York City |
| 5–7 October 1853 | delivers "The Laws in Relation to Women" at National Woman's Rights Convention, Cleveland |
| 14 October 1853 | speaks at woman's rights meeting in Cincinnati; Lucy Stone also speaks |
| 16 October 1853 | speaks at Maysville, Ky., courthouse |
| 24–26 October 1853 | addresses PASS meeting in Norristown |
| 4–5 December 1853 | delivers remarks at Second Decade celebration of AASS in Philadelphia |

| | |
|---|---|
| 10–11 May 1854 | delivers remarks at AASS meeting in New York City |
| 18–20 October 1854 | speaks at fifth National Woman's Rights Convention in Philadelphia |
| August 1855 | assists fugitive slave Jane Johnson; protests Passmore Williamson's imprisonment |
| October 1855 | speaks at Cincinnati Woman's Rights Convention; travels to Cleveland, Syracuse, Albany, New York City |
| 7–8 May 1856 | delivers remarks at AASS meeting in New York City |
| 25–26 November 1856 | delivers remarks at New York Woman's Rights Convention |
| c. 1 March 1857 | with JM moves to Roadside farm, on York Rd., outside Philadelphia |
| 5 December 1857 | speaks at Odd Fellows Hall, Columbia, Pa. |
| 11 May 1859 | speaks at AASS annual meeting in New York City |
| 12 May 1859 | speaks at National Woman's Rights Convention in New York City |
| December 1859 | hosts Mary Ann Brown, John Brown's wife, during his trial |
| 7–8 February 1861 | travels to New York State Woman's Rights Convention in Albany; testifies on divorce to New York legislature |
| 10 April 1861 | with JM celebrates golden wedding anniversary |
| 16 June 1861 | preaches at Congregational Society, Boston |
| October 1862 | with JM serves on committee to discuss formation of Swarthmore College |
| 1862 | helps organize Women's Association for Aid of Freedmen |
| 10 January 1863 | speaks at Philadelphia meeting celebrating Emancipation Proclamation chaired by JM |
| 12 July 1863 | speaks to black soldiers at Camp William Penn, established near Roadside |
| 3–4 December 1863 | speaks at Third Decade celebration of AASS in Philadelphia |
| January 1864 | with JM helps organize Friends' Association for Aid and Elevation of the Freedman |
| 4 May 1864 | acts of incorporation for Swarthmore College are drawn up |
| 9 May 1865 | William Lloyd Garrison retires from AASS |
| 4 September 1865 | daughter Elizabeth dies at Roadside |
| January 1866 | helps found Pennsylvania Peace Society |
| 10 May 1866 | speaks at Woman's Rights Convention in New York City; elected first president of newly formed AERA |
| 13 June 1866 | Congress approves Fourteenth Amendment, introducing for the first time the word *male* into the Constitution |
| 22 November 1866 | in speech at PASS supports continuation of its work |
| 17 January 1867 | speaks at Equal Rights Convention in Philadelphia |

| | |
|---|---|
| 9–10 May 1867 | speaks at AERA convention in New York City |
| 30 May 1867 | addresses first meeting of the Free Religious Association in Boston |
| 25 August 1867 | speaks at meeting of Pennsylvania Peace Society in Abington |
| 26 January 1868 | JM dies at Lords' home in Brooklyn |
| 28 July 1868 | Fourteenth Amendment ratified |
| 21 January 1869 | speaks at Universal Peace Union meeting, Washington, D.C. |
| 11 February 1869 | speaks at PFASS celebration of its thirty-fifth anniversary |
| 26 February 1869 | Congress approves Fifteenth Amendment, granting universal male suffrage |
| March 1869 | George W. Julian proposes Sixteenth Amendment to grant woman suffrage |
| 12–13 May 1869 | chairs and speaks at AERA meeting in New York City, where resolution to oppose Fifteenth Amendment is defeated |
| 14 May 1869 | speaks at meeting in Brooklyn for purpose of forming a woman suffrage organization |
| 15 May 1869 | Stanton and Anthony form NWSA |
| June 1869 | Anna Hopper appointed to Swarthmore College Board of Managers |
| 20 October 1869 | speaks at Friends' Meeting House and Unitarian Church in Wilmington, Del. |
| c. 1 November 1869 | speaks at twenty-eighth Congregational Society, Boston |
| 10 November 1869 | speaks at official opening of Swarthmore College |
| 17 November 1869 | speaks at PASS annual meeting |
| 24–25 November 1869 | AWSA founded in Cleveland |
| 24 March 1870 | makes remarks at final meeting of the PFASS |
| 30 March 1870 | Fifteenth Amendment ratified |
| 6 April 1870 | with Theodore Tilton tries to reconcile AWSA and NWSA |
| 24 May 1870 | speaks at New England Woman Suffrage Association, Boston |
| 19–21 October 1870 | speaks at Second Decade Convention of national woman's rights movement in New York City |
| November 1870 | AWSA meets in Cleveland and votes against merger with NWSA |
| 1870–80 | serves as president of Pennsylvania Peace Society |
| 3 May 1871 | speaks at Essex County Woman Suffrage Society, East Orange, New Jersey |
| 9 May 1871 | speaks at first Reform League Meeting, New York City |
| 11–12 May 1871 | speaks at NWSA meeting in New York City |
| 26 May 1872 | delivers sermon, "Peace of Nations," at Quaker meeting, Rutherford, New Jersey |

| | |
|---|---|
| 3 July 1872 | Marianna Mott dies in Switzerland |
| Fall 1872 | meets Ulysses S. Grant and urges him to pardon Modoc Indians condemned to death |
| 6 May 1873 | speaks at NWSA meeting, New York City |
| 13 June 1874 | James Miller McKim dies |
| 3 August 1874 | daughter Anna Hopper dies |
| 4 January 1875 | sister MCW dies |
| 14 April 1875 | speaks at centennial celebration of Pennsylvania Abolition Society |
| 4 July 1876 | suffrage activists excluded from U.S. Centennial Celebration in Philadelphia; presides and speaks at woman suffrage meeting at First Unitarian Church, Philadelphia |
| 20 July 1876 | honored at NWSA reception in Philadelphia |
| 19 July 1878 | delivers last public address in Rochester, New York, on thirtieth anniversary of Seneca Falls Woman's Rights Convention |
| 11 November 1880 | dies at Roadside |

# Biographical Directory

This directory has been prepared with the assistance of James Gould of Cotuit, Massachusetts, and these reference works: Thomas C. Cornell, *Adam and Anne Mott: Their Ancestors and Their Descendants* (Poughkeepsie, N.Y.: A. V. Haight, 1890); William Wade Hinshaw, *Encyclopedia of American Quaker Genealogy,* 7 vols. (Ann Arbor, Mich.: Edwards Bros., 1936–50); and Helen S. Weary, comp., "Descendants of Adam Mott," copy in Pamphlet Group 7, Mott Family Papers, PSCHi.

*Abbott, Sarah Yarnall* (b. 1826): daughter of Benjamin Horner (1790–1867) Yarnall and Elizabeth ("Eliza") Coffin Yarnall (1794–1870); married William H. Abbott on 28 November 1866; had one child, Charles Abbott (b. 1870).

*Anthony, Susan Brownell* (1820–1906): Rochester, New York, abolitionist, temperance, and woman suffrage activist; a founder of the National Woman Suffrage Association.

*Barney, Nathaniel* (1792–1869): Nantucket cousin of LCM; son of Abial Coffin Barney and Jonathan Barney; oil and candle manufacturer; married Elisa Starbuck (1802–89) in 1820; had two children who survived infancy: Joseph Barney (1827–1905) and Sarah Barney Swain (1829–1905).

*Barney, Elisa Starbuck* (1802–89): woman's rights and antislavery activist; married Nathaniel Barney (1792–1869) in 1820; had two children who survived infancy: Joseph Barney (1827–1905) and Sarah Barney Swain (1829–1905).

*Birney, Laura Stratton* (d. 1868): daughter of Caroline Chase Stratton (d. c. January 1879); married Fitzhugh Birney (d. 1864), son of James Birney, on 25 December 1863; had a daughter, Bettie Birney (b. 1864).

*Brown, Anna Temple* (c. 1820–1900): daughter of Solomon Temple and Mary Coffin Temple (d. 1824), LCM's sister; married wool merchant Walter Brown (d. May 1879); had three children: Harry Brown, Walter Brown (d. 1863), and Marion ("Minnie") Brown (b. 1855).

*Brown, Mary Yarnall* (b. 1821): daughter of Benjamin Horner Yarnall (1790–1867) and Elizabeth ("Eliza") Coffin Yarnall (1794–1870); married George T. Brown, brother of

Walter Brown (d. May 1879), on 29 May 1844; their son Ellis Brown married Sarah Willet in January 1878.

*Cavender, Elizabeth ("Lib") Mott* (1825–65): daughter of LCM and JM; married Thomas S. Cavender (1821–96) on 21 July 1845; four children survived infancy: Frances ("Fanny") Cavender Parrish (1846–83), Henry ("Harry") Cavender (1849–63), Mary Cavender (b. 1851), and Charles Cavender (b. c. 1855); lived on farm called Eddington, 1860–65.

*Cavender, Frances ("Fanny").* See Parrish, Frances ("Fanny") Cavender

*Cavender, Thomas S.* (1821–96): son of John H. Cavender and Hannah Shoemaker Cavender; farmer; married Elizabeth ("Lib") Mott (1825–65), LCM and JM's daughter, on 21 July 1845; four children survived infancy: Frances ("Fanny") Cavender Parrish (1846–83), Henry ("Harry") Cavender (1849–63), Mary Cavender (b. 1851), and Charles Cavender (b. c. 1855); lived on farm called Eddington, 1860–65.

*Chase, Mary Ann Wistar:* married William B. Chase (b. 1814), son of Borden Chase (d. 1829) and Ruth Bunker Chase (c. 1778–1860), in 1839.

*Chase, Ruth Bunker* (c. 1778–1860): daughter of LCM's aunt Judith Folger Bunker (b. 1750), and widow of Borden Chase (d. 1829); mother of Caroline Chase Stratton (d. c. January 1879) and mother-in-law of Mary Ann Wistar Chase; lived in Mt. Holly, New Jersey

*Coffin, Anna Folger* (1771–1844): mother of LCM; wife of Capt. Thomas Coffin Jr. (1766–1815); had five other children: Sarah Coffin (d. 1824), Elizabeth ("Eliza") Coffin Yarnall (1794–1870), Thomas Mayhew Coffin (1798–1849), Mary Coffin Temple (d. 1824), and MCW.

*Coffin, Elizabeth ("Eliza").* See Yarnall, Elizabeth ("Eliza") Coffin

*Coffin, Thomas Mayhew* (1798–1849): unmarried brother of LCM; Philadelphia merchant.

*Davis, Anna Coffin.* See Hallowell, Anna Coffin Davis

*Davis, Edward Morris* (1811–87): abolitionist, nonresistant, woman's rights leader, and merchant; son of Evan Davis and Elizabeth Davis; married Maria Mott (1818–97), LCM and JM's daughter, on 26 October 1836; had four children who survived infancy: Charles James Davis (1845–50), Anna Coffin Davis Hallowell (1838–1913), Henry Corbit Davis (1839–1901), and William ("Will") Morris Davis (1850–1934).

*Davis, Henry Corbit* (1839–1901): son of Edward Morris Davis (1811–87) and Maria Mott Davis (1818–97); merchant; married Martha ("Pattie") Mellor (1842–74) on 7 May 1862; had two children with her: Lucy Davis (b. 1863) and Charley Davis (b. 1865); married Naomi Lawton (b. 1842) on 14 June 1876.

*Davis, Maria Mott* (1818–97): daughter of LCM and JM; married Edward Morris Davis (1811–87) on 26 October 1836; had four children who survived infancy: Charles James Davis (1845–50), Anna Coffin Davis Hallowell (1838–1913), Henry Corbit Davis (1839–1901), and William ("Will") Morris Davis (1850–1934).

*Davis, William ("Will") Morris* (1850–1934): son of Edward Morris Davis (1811–87) and Maria Mott Davis (1818–97), LCM and JM's daughter; geologist; married Ellen Bliss Warner (1854–1913) in 1879.

*Dennis, Anne McKim* (1841–93): adopted daughter of James Miller McKim (1810–74); married Frederick Dennis (d. 1886) in the fall of 1863; married Wendell Phillips Garrison (1840–1907), son of William Lloyd Garrison (1805–79), in 1891.

*Earle, Mary Hussey* (1798–1886): first cousin of LCM; daughter of Uriel Hussey (1766–1802) and Phebe Folger Hussey (1768–1864) of Nantucket; married Thomas Earle (1796–1849), a Germantown banker and broker; had four children: Phebe Earle Gibbons (1821–93), Henry Earle (1829–74), Caroline Earle White (1833–1916), and George H. Earle.

*Earle, Phebe.* See Gibbons, Phebe Earle

*Gardner, Edward W.* (1804–63): son of Tristam Gardner and Kezia Gardner; Nantucket seaman; married Phebe Hussey (1800–63), cousin of LCM, in 1840; had son William Gardner (b. 1829) by a previous marriage.

*Gardner, Phebe Hussey* (1800–63): Nantucket cousin of LCM; daughter of Uriel Hussey (1766–1802) and Phebe Folger Hussey (1768–1864); married Edward W. Gardner (1804–63) in 1840.

*Garrison, Ellen Wright* (1840–1931): daughter of David Wright (1806–97) and MCW; married William Lloyd Garrison Jr. (1838–1909) on 14 September 1864; had four children: Agnes Garrison (1866–1950), Charles Garrison (1868–1951), Frank Wright Garrison (1871–1961), and William Lloyd Garrison III (1874–1906).

*Garrison, Lucy McKim* (1842–77): daughter of James Miller McKim (1810–74) and Sarah Allibone Speakman McKim (1813–91); musician; married Wendell Phillips Garrison (1840–1907), son of William Lloyd Garrison (1805–79), on 6 December 1865; had three children: Lloyd McKim Garrison (1867–1900), Philip Garrison (1869–1936), and Katherine Garrison (1873–1948).

*Garrison, William Lloyd* (1805–79): abolitionist and editor of the antislavery newspaper the *Liberator;* founded the New England Anti-Slavery Society in 1831; organized the AASS in 1833; married Helen Benson (1811–76) on 4 September 1834; children include Wendell Phillips Garrison (1840–1907) and William Lloyd Garrison Jr. (1838–1909).

*Garrison, William Lloyd, Jr.* (1838–1909): son of William Lloyd Garrison (1805–79) and Helen Benson Garrison (1811–76); married Ellen Wright (1840–1931) on 14 September 1864; had four children: Agnes Garrison (1866–1950), Charles Garrison (1868–1951), Frank Wright Garrison (1871–1961), and William Lloyd Garrison III (1874–1906).

*Gibbons, Phebe Earle* (1821–93): daughter of Mary Hussey Earle (1798–1886) and Thomas Earle (1796–1849); married Dr. Joseph Gibbons (1818–83), antislavery activist from Lancaster; had three children: Fanny Gibbons, Caroline Gibbons (d. 1900), and Mary Anna Gibbons.

*Hallowell, Anna Coffin Davis* (1838–1913): daughter of Edward Morris Davis (1811–87) and Maria Mott Davis (1818–97), LCM and JM's daughter; married Richard Price Hallowell (1835–1904) on 25 October 1859; editor of *James and Lucretia Mott: Their Life and Letters;* had four children: Maria ("May") Hallowell (1860–1916), Penrose Hallowell (1862–72), James Hallowell (1865–1928), and Lucretia Hallowell (1867–1958).

*Harrison, Margaret.* See Yarnall, Margaret Harrison

*Hopper, Anna Mott* (1812–74): daughter of LCM and JM; married Edward Hopper (1812–93) on 24 April 1833; had four children who survived infancy: Lucretia ("Lue") Hopper (1838–61), Maria Hopper (1845–99), George Hopper (1847–56), and Isaac Hopper (1855–74).

*Hopper, Edward* (1812–93): son of Isaac T. Hopper and Sarah Tatum Hopper; Philadelphia lawyer; married Anna Mott (1812–74), LCM and JM's daughter, on 24 April 1833; had four children who survived infancy: Lucretia ("Lue") Hopper (1838–61), Maria Hopper (1845–99), George Hopper (1847–56), and Isaac Hopper (1855–74).

*Hussey, Mary.* See Earle, Mary Hussey

*Hussey, Phebe* (Nantucket cousin of LCM). See Gardner, Phebe Hussey

*Hussey, Phebe Folger* (1768–1864): aunt of LCM; married Uriel Hussey (1766–1802) of Nantucket; had four children: Phebe Hussey Gardner (1800–63), Mary Hussey Earle (1798–1886), Edward Hussey, and George Hussey (d. 1815).

*Lord, Ellen ("Nelly")* (1855–97): daughter of George Waite Lord (1830–80) and MML.

*Lord, George Waite* (1830–80): son of George Lord and Ellen Waite Lord; wool merchant in business with Walter Brown (d. May 1879) in New York City; married MML on 8 June 1853; had four children who survived infancy: Ellen ("Nelly") Lord De Schweinitz (1855–97), Mary ("Molly") Mott Lord (1861–1931?), Anna Lord (1865–1949), and Lucretia ("Lulu") Lord (1867–1935); lived in New York City, Brooklyn, and Orange, New Jersey.

*Lord, Martha ("Pattie") Mott* (1828–1916): daughter of LCM and JM; married George Waite Lord (1830–80) on 8 June 1853; had four children who survived infancy: Ellen ("Nelly") Lord De Schweinitz (1855–97), Mary ("Molly") Mott Lord (1861–1931?), Anna Lord (1865–1949), and Lucretia ("Lulu") Lord (1867–1935); lived in New York City, Brooklyn, and Orange, New Jersey.

*McKim, Anne.* See Dennis, Anne McKim

*McKim, Charles Follen* (1847–1909): architect; son of Sarah Allibone Speakman McKim (1813–91) and James Miller McKim (1810–74); married Annie Bigelow in 1874.

*McKim, James Miller* (1810–74): a Presbyterian convert to the Society of Friends; active in the abolitionist and freedpeople's aid movement; married Quaker Sarah Allibone Speakman (1813–91) on 1 October 1840; had two children: Charles Follen McKim (1847–1909) and Lucy McKim Garrison (1842–77); adopted his niece Anne McKim Dennis (1841–93).

*McKim, Lucy.* See Garrison, Lucy McKim

*McKim, Sarah Allibone Speakman* (1813–91): Quaker, abolitionist; married James Miller McKim (1810–74) on 1 October 1840; had two children: Charles Follen McKim (1847–1909) and Lucy McKim Garrison (1842–77); adopted her husband's niece Anne McKim Dennis (1841–93).

*Mott, Anna.* See Hopper, Anna Mott

*Mott, Elizabeth ("Lib").* See Cavender, Elizabeth ("Lib") Mott

*Mott, Emily.* See Shaw, Emily Mott

*Mott, Isabella ("Bel").* See Parrish, Isabella ("Bel") Mott

*Mott, James* (1788–1868): husband of LCM; Philadelphia merchant; son of Adam Mott and Anne Mott; siblings: Sarah Mott Cornell, Mary Mott Hicks, Abigail Mott Moore, and Richard Mott (1804–88); married LCM on 10 April 1811; children: Anna Mott Hopper (1812–74), Thomas Mott (1823–99), Maria Mott Davis (1818–97), Elizabeth ("Lib") Mott Cavender (1825–65), and MML.

*Mott, Lucretia Coffin* (1793–1880): daughter of Capt. Thomas Coffin Jr. (1766–1815) and Anna Folger Coffin (1771–1844); siblings: Sarah Coffin (d. 1824), Elizabeth ("Eliza") Coffin Yarnall (1794–1870), Thomas Mayhew Coffin (1798–1849), Mary Coffin Temple (d. 1824), and MCW; married JM on 10 April 1811; children: Anna Mott Hopper (1812–74), Thomas Mott (1823–99), Maria Mott Davis (1818–97), Elizabeth ("Lib") Mott Cavender (1825–65), and MML.

*Mott, Maria* (LCM and JM's daughter). See Davis, Maria Mott

*Mott, Marianna* (*"Mariᵃ."*) *Pelham* (1825–72): daughter of MCW and Capt. Peter Pelham (1785–1826); married Thomas Mott (1823–99) on 28 July 1845; had three children: Isabella ("Bel") Mott Parrish (1846–1929), Emily Mott Shaw (1848–1927), and Maria ("May") Mott (1858–1938).

*Mott, Martha.* See Lord, Martha ("Pattie") Mott

*Mott, Richard* (1804–88): brother of JM; realtor in Toledo, Ohio; U.S. congressman, 1855–59; married Elizabeth Mitchell Smith (1804–55) on 12 November 1828; had two daughters, Mary S. Mott (1831–60) and Anna Caroline ("Cannie") Mott (b. 1835).

*Mott, Thomas* (1823–99): fourth child of LCM and JM; wool merchant; married first cousin Marianna ("Mariᵃ.") Pelham (1825–72) on 28 July 1845; had three children: Isabella ("Bel") Mott Parrish (1846–1929), Emily Mott Shaw (1848–1927), and Maria ("May") Mott (1858–1938).

*Neall, Daniel, Sr.* (1783?-1846): Philadelphia Quaker, dentist, and abolitionist; married Rebecca Bunker (c. 1787–1880) in 1840.

*Neall, Rebecca Bunker* (c. 1787–1880): daughter of LCM's aunt Judith Folger Bunker (b. 1750); married Daniel Neall Sr. (1783?-1846) in 1840; lived in Mt. Holly, New Jersey.

*Needles, Augusta Stratton:* daughter of Caroline Chase Stratton (d. c. January 1879); married John Amos Needles (b. 1828) in December 1857.

*Osborne, David Munson* (1822–86): New York farm machinery manufacturer; son of John Hall and Caroline Bulkley Osborne; married Eliza Wright (1830–1911) on 3 September 1851; had four children: Emily ("Milly") Osborne Harris (1853–1940), Florence ("Floy") Osborne (1856–77), Helen ("Nell") Osborne (1864–1944), and Thomas ("Tom") Mott Osborne (1859–1926).

*Osborne, Eliza Wright* (1830–1911): daughter of David Wright (1806–97) and MCW; married David Munson Osborne (1822–86) on 3 September 1851; had four children: Emily ("Milly") Osborne Harris (1853–1940), Florence ("Floy") Osborne (1856–77), Helen ("Nell") Osborne (1864–1944), and Thomas ("Tom") Mott Osborne (1859–1926).

*Osborne, Emily ("Milly")* (1853–1940): daughter of David Munson Osborne (1822–86) and Eliza Wright Osborne (1830–1911).

*Parrish, Frances ("Fanny") Cavender* (1846–83): daughter of Thomas S. Cavender (1821–96) and Elizabeth ("Lib") Mott Cavender (1825–65), LCM and JM's daughter; married Thomas Clarkson Parrish (1847–99) on 10 April 1868.

*Parrish, Isabella ("Bel") Mott* (1846–1929): daughter of Thomas Mott (1823–99) and Marianna ("Mariᵃ.") Pelham Mott (1825–72); married Joseph Parrish (1843–93) on 3 September 1868; had three daughters, Ethel Parrish (1869–1959), Grace Parrish (1871–1960), and Mariana Parrish (1874–1965).

*Pelham, Marianna.* See Mott, Marianna ("Mariᵃ.") Pelham

*Pugh, Sarah* (1800–1884): teacher, abolitionist, and woman's rights leader.

*Shaw, Emily Mott* (1848–1927): daughter of Thomas Mott (1823–99) and Marianna ("Mariᵃ.") Pelham Mott (1825–72); married George Russell Shaw (1848–1937) on 31 August 1874.

*Stanton, Elizabeth Cady* (1815–1902): suffrage activist and a founder of the NWSA; married Henry B. Stanton (1805–87) in 1840.

*Stanton, Henry B.* (1805–87): New York lawyer and abolitionist; active in the political wing of the antislavery movement; married Elizabeth Cady (1815–1902) in 1840.

*Stratton, Augusta.* See Needles, Augusta Stratton

*Stratton, Caroline Chase* (d. c. January 1879): daughter of LCM's first cousin Ruth Bunker Chase (c. 1778–1860); married Jacob Stratton; had two daughters: Augusta Stratton Needles and Laura Stratton Birney (d. 1868); married Charles P. Wood (1818–78) of Auburn, New York, in April 1855 in Philadelphia; divorced c. 1860; reassumed her first husband's last name.

*Stratton, Laura.* See Birney, Laura Stratton

*White, Caroline Earle* (1833–1916): daughter of Mary Hussey Earle (1798–1886) and Thomas Earle (1796–1849); married Philadelphia attorney Richard White on 28 September 1854.

*Wood, Caroline Chase Stratton.* See Stratton, Caroline Chase

*Wood, Charles P.* (1818–78): Auburn, New York, businessman and banker; second husband of Caroline Chase Stratton (d. c. January 1879); had children from a previous marriage: Hetty Wood, Bel Wood, Frank Wood (c. 1840–64), Linn Wood (d. 1858), Louis Wood (c. 1853–1862), Julia Wood, and Mary Wood; divorced c. 1860; married Emma Parker (1817–98) in 1864.

*Wright, David* (1806–97): Auburn, New York, lawyer; married MCW on 18 November 1829; had six children, including Matthew Tallman Wright (1832–54) and William ("Willie") Pelham Wright (1842–1902); one child died in infancy.

*Wright, Eliza.* See Osborne, Eliza Wright

*Wright, Ellen.* See Garrison, Ellen Wright

*Wright, Francis ("Frank")* (1844–1903): son of David Wright (1806–97) and MCW; merchant; married Fanny B. Pell (1848–92) on 23 April 1867; had one daughter, Mabel Wright (1869–1963).

*Wright, Martha Coffin Pelham* (1806–75): sister of LCM; married Capt. Peter Pelham (1785–1826); had one daughter, Marianna ("Mariᵃ.") Pelham Mott (1825–72); married David Wright (1806–97) on 18 November 1829; had six more children, including

Matthew Tallman Wright (1832–54) and William ("Willie") Pelham Wright (1842–1902); one child died in infancy; lived in Auburn, New York.

*Wright, Matthew Tallman* (1832–54): son of David Wright (1806–97) and MCW; drowned in California.

*Wright, William ("Willie") Pelham* (1842–1902): son of David Wright (1806–97) and MCW; Florida citrus grower; married Flora McMartin (1843–98) on 28 October 1869; had two daughters, Anne Wright (1872–1951) and Edith Wright (1874–1960).

*Yarnall, Benjamin Horner* (1790–1867): son of Mary Horner Yarnall and Ellis Yarnall; Philadelphia merchant; married Elizabeth ("Eliza") Coffin (1794–1870), LCM's sister, on 23 November 1814; had six children who lived to adulthood: Thomas Coffin Yarnall (1815–1911), Ellis Yarnall (1817–1905), William Yarnall (1819–1903), Mary Yarnall Brown (b. 1821), Rebecca Yarnall (b. 1830), and Sarah Yarnall Abbott (b. 1826).

*Yarnall, Elizabeth ("Eliza") Coffin* (1794–1870): sister of LCM; married Benjamin Horner Yarnall (1790–1867) on 23 November 1814; had six children who lived to adulthood: Thomas Coffin Yarnall (1815–1911), Ellis Yarnall (1817–1905), William Yarnall (1819–1903), Mary Yarnall Brown (b. 1821), Rebecca Yarnall (b. 1830), and Sarah Yarnall Abbott (b. 1826).

*Yarnall, Ellis* (1817–1905): son of Elizabeth ("Eliza") Coffin Yarnall (1794–1870) and Benjamin Horner Yarnall (1790–1867); merchant and shipper; married Helen Cox (d. before 1855); married Margaret Harrison (1827–1899) on 10 June 1858; with Harrison had four children who lived to adulthood: Agnes Yarnall (1859–1910), Mildred Yarnall (b. 1862), Charlton Yarnall (b. 1864), and Harold Yarnall (1867–1917); lived at Ellerslie in Germantown in 1860s.

*Yarnall, Margaret Harrison* (1827–1899): British; niece of writer Mary Howitt (1799–1888); second wife of Ellis Yarnall (1817–1905); had four children who lived to adulthood: Agnes Yarnall (1859–1910), Mildred Yarnall (b. 1862), Charlton Yarnall (b. 1864), and Harold Yarnall (1867–1917); lived at Ellerslie in Germantown in 1860s.

*Yarnall, Mary.* See Brown, Mary Yarnall

*Yarnall, Sarah.* See Abbott, Sarah Yarnall

*Yarnall, Thomas Coffin* (1815–1911): son of Elizabeth ("Eliza") Coffin Yarnall (1794–1870) and Benjamin Horner Yarnall (1790–1867); Episcopal minister; married Sarah Price Rose (d. 1909) on 9 July 1846; had nine children: Helen Yarnall, William Yarnall (1819–1903), Charles Herbert Yarnall, Sarah Rose Yarnall, Elizabeth Yarnall, George Hunter Yarnall, Henry Yarnall, Thomas Coffin Yarnall Jr., and Francis Yarnall.

*Yarnall, William* (1819–1903): son of Elizabeth ("Eliza") Coffin Yarnall (1794–1870) and Benjamin Horner Yarnall (1790–1867); Philadelphia furniture dealer; married Elizabeth Moore Massey on 20 October 1844; had two children: Emily Yarnall (b. 1855) and Benjamin Horner Yarnall (1852–82).

# Quaker Terminology

*Clerk:* The presiding officer at a meeting, the clerk was chosen annually by that meeting and was authorized to sign communications to other meetings.

*Disownment:* A Friend could be refused membership, or disowned, for marrying a non-Quaker, owning a slave, or other conduct considered unsuitable by the monthly meeting. The former Friend could still attend meetings for worship, but not business meetings.

*Meeting for Sufferings:* This meeting was the equivalent of an executive committee, authorized to act on behalf of the yearly meetings in cases that could not be delayed until the yearly meeting. After the 1827 separation, the Hicksites called this meeting the Representative Committee.

*Minute:* A minute was the conclusion of a business meeting, whether preparative, monthly, quarterly, or yearly, and the record could be made up of a number of minutes. Ministers could also receive a traveling minute from their monthly meetings, stating that they were in unity with the Society of Friends and had that meeting's approval to travel to other Friends' meetings.

*Monthly Meeting:* This meeting was authorized to receive and disown members, to marry couples, and to own property.

*Preparative Meeting:* A reference both to an organization of individuals and an event, this meeting was sometimes called "preparatory." Events included congregational meetings for worship, which usually took place on both First Day (Sunday) and at midweek on either Fourth Day (Wednesday) or Fifth Day (Thursday). They also included business meetings, theoretically open to all members, which occurred once a month to prepare business for the monthly meeting.

*Quarterly Meeting:* Comprised of two or more monthly meetings, it attended to doctrinal and organizational issues.

*Select Meeting:* This term usually referred to meetings of ministers and elders at any one of the levels: preparative, monthly, quarterly, or yearly. "Select" could also mean meetings restricted to Quakers, such as business meetings.

*Yearly Meeting:* This meeting heard and acted on cases of disownment, if appealed, and decided other issues referred to it. Each yearly meeting was independent of other yearly meetings and could not make decisions for another. Along with its capacity as the final authority in all cases, the yearly meeting was a major social event, bringing thousands of Friends together.

# SELECTED LETTERS OF
# LUCRETIA COFFIN MOTT

# PART 1

# November 1813–July 1840

Besides demonstrating her family preoccupations, LCM's early letters reveal her growing sense of a destiny beyond that of wife and mother. LCM began to speak at Quaker meetings in 1818, and in 1821 she was recognized as a minister in the Society of Friends in Philadelphia. In these early letters we see Elias Hicks's appeal for her, but since no letters of the period survive, only in retrospect do we learn how painful did she find the Hicksite/Orthodox separation of 1827 (see letter to the London Yearly Meeting of Friends, c. 14 April 1830). Even after this split, the feuds and differences among the Hicksite Quakers, along with those in abolitionist organizations, troubled LCM in the 1820s and 1830s and continued to plague her throughout her life. Her sensitivities, however, did not prevent her from criticizing both publicly and privately her "timid" and apathetic colleagues (see letter to James Miller McKim, 8 May 1834, and to Phebe Post Willis, 13 September 1834). She hoped that "Friends will only keep pace with the advance of public sentiment on the subject" and join with her in "uniting their efforts in Society capacity with those they are pleased to call 'the world'" (letter to Phebe Post Willis, 2 September 1835).

LCM never shut out "the world." On an 1819 ministry to Virginia, she had her first "affecting" encounter with slavery (letter to unidentified recipient, 15 December 1819). In 1833 as a founder of the PFASS, she officially commenced her long career to seek freedom and justice for African Americans. Letters to Phebe Post Willis (e.g., 1 March 1834), as well as her new friends James Miller McKim and George Combe (8 May 1834, 13 June 1839), signal the activism that characterized her long life. She shared the organizational efforts and problems of their respective female antislavery societies with her New England cohort Maria Weston Chapman (29 May 1839, 20 February 1840). Ever optimistic and determined, she made light of the mob's destruction of the Philadelphia hall where the second Anti-Slavery Convention of American Women met. The gathering she recalled primarily as a "rich feast," one "not seriously interrupted even by the burning of the Hall" (letter to Edward M. Davis, 18 June 1838).

To Abby Kelley and to Nathaniel Barney and Elisa Barney, LCM indicated her concern, one she had voiced since a student at Nine Partners, about the unequal treatment of women. In these letters she articulated a woman's right to speak and participate in "promiscuous" (mixed-sex) meetings, whether Quaker or secular. She thrust herself into other causes, such as nonresistance and equitable treatment of Native Americans. And these involvements occurred against a background of child-rearing, sharing households with two married daughters and their husbands, as well as continuous visiting by Quakers, abolitionists, and relatives.

During her three months' tour of the British Isles in 1840 LCM kept a diary for the first and last time in her life (to our knowledge). It is an invaluable chronicle of the places she and JM visited, the people they met, and the speeches she gave. But, not surprisingly, given their busy schedule and LCM's aversion to extended writing, her diary provides little elaboration on the trip. While she presented the convention delegates' arguments for and against seating the women in her diary, she expressed no reaction to these speeches. This section of her correspondence includes, however, both her public and her private responses to the refusal by the World's Anti-Slavery Convention to seat the eight women delegates from the United States in June 1840 (see letter to Daniel O'Connell, 17 June 1840). In her letter to Chapman of 29 July she defended her decision not to protest the convention's exclusion and described her efforts to educate the British on the equality of the sexes: "I never failed in our several tea-parties,— soirees, &c to avail myself of every offer made for utterance for our cause—& then I shrunk not from the whole truth as those who heard can testify Egotism must be excused for Woman's sake."

LCM and JM received a thorough education during the summer they toured England, Scotland, and Ireland. Their encounters and the new friendships formed during this trip would reverberate in LCM's letters throughout the next decades.

## To Adam Mott and Anne Mott[1]

[*Philadelphia 8 November 1813*]
2nd day

*[Added to JM's letter to "My dear Parents" of 7 November]*

I dont like to contradict people but I believe I only went so far as to tell my JM.—that I feared he was not qualified to take Gould's place judging from what I had heard of his (G's) acquirements— I hope some one will appear to supply his place—we can't spare James—& he never was in his element in that business— —[2] I hope the School will prosper I wish it every good & trust suitable teachers will be found without sending so far as Philada.— You have not mentioned Aunt Lydia in your last letters we should be very glad to hear how she gets along & how poor Edward is—does Grand Father intend spending the winter with her?—[3] We have very satisfactory letters from Uncle Mayhew[4] he says he never was more easy on acct of the safety of himself & family & never felt more at home—that several houses have been raised in the town within a few weeks, house lots in demand & that T. Rotch had sold a small tract of his land for *$200 per Acre*— — —

Our Aunt E. B. & companions returned this morning from Baltimore— they will probably spend a few days in the city I suppose Anna Thorne[5] has reached her home ere this we were not half satisfied that we had so little of their company please remember us to her— — — Peter & Abbey Barker have lately spent a week in the city attending the marriage of their neice Betsey Barker to Dr Saml. Jackson a brother of E. Kimber's wife— — Emmor & wife are absent on a visit to her sister Enoch Lewis' wife who is thought to be fast going in a consumption—[6] its said Emmor has improved very much while in your parts— — — — We have not recd. a letter from uncle Richard[7] lately—it would indeed be dreary to be settled there so far from the factory where James will have to spend most of his time. I am not out of hopes but that by continuing here till Spring we shall be able to get that house near the factory.— then if you return & settle in the neighborhood I have not a doubt but that I shall be entirely contented there Mary must make an agreement with Robert to settle at Mamaroneck, are they to be married in the spring?— —[8]

Rachel Offley is making preparation for her change—her Mother left the city today to accompany Hannah Evans on a religious visit in Jersey to be absent several weeks.—

Anna is very well & is learning to talk but its now near her bed time & she is crying for me to take her I must there[fore?], bid you affectionately farewell with much love to [*ms. damaged*]

*Lucretia C. Mott*

[*JM continues his letter on 9 November; there is a one-line postscript by LCM; ms. damaged*]

ALS PSCHi-Mott
Env: "Adam Mott, Washington, Dutchess County, State of New York"

1. Adam Mott (1762–1839) and Anne Mott (1768–1852), whose maiden name was also Mott, were married in 1785. They had five children who lived to adulthood: JM, Sarah, Mary, Abigail, and Richard (Thomas C. Cornell, *Adam and Anne Mott: Their Ancestors and Their Descendants* [Poughkeepsie, N.Y.: A. V. Haight, 1890], chap. 24).

2. In his portion of the letter, JM told his parents that he might consider teaching at "the school" (presumably Nine Partners) for the winter term, but Thomas Coffin needed his help in their financially precarious nail manufacturing business. The two were listed as "Coffin & Mott, Merchants" in the 1813 Philadelphia City Directory. "Gould" is probably Goold Brown (1791–1875), a Rhode Island Quaker and educator (Bacon, 31–33; *JGW*, 2:278).

3. Lydia P. Mott (1775–1862) was Anne Mott's sister-in-law and the widow of Robert Mott (1771–1805). A son, Edward Mott, would die on 1 January 1814 (Cornell, *Adam and Anne Mott*, 213). James Mott Sr. (1743–1823), Anne Mott's father and a former New York City merchant who briefly headed Nine Partners School, had retired to Mamaroneck, New York.

4. Uncle Mayhew Folger (1774–1828), Anna Coffin's brother, was a former ship captain. In a letter of 27 April 1813, JM had said that Folger was moving to Ohio (Hallowell, 47).

5. Elizabeth Folger Barker (b. 1766) was the sister of Anna Coffin. Anna Thorne (1766–1838) was a member of Nine Partners Monthly Meeting (*Memorial concerning Anna M. Thorne [et al.] Deceased of the Religious Society of Friends, within the Limits of the Yearly Meeting of New York* [New York: M. Day, 1841], 3, 36).

6. "Abbey Barker" is possibly Abigail Barker (d. 1840; *Calumny Refuted; or, A Glance at John Wilbur's Book* [London: John Hasler, 1845]). Emmor Kimber (1773–1850), a Quaker minister and schoolmaster in Chester County, had married Susanna Jackson (1773–1854) in 1796 (*Friends' Intelligencer*, 7 September 1850, 189). Samuel Jackson (1787–1872), a brother of Susanna Kimber, was a professor at the University of Pennsylvania Medical School. Her sister had married Enoch Lewis (1776–1856), a Quaker and a mathematics teacher at Westtown School in Chester County.

7. Richard Mott (1767–1856), a brother of Anne Mott, was a cotton manufacturer in Mamaroneck. LCM and JM would join him for about six months in 1814 when JM's nail business with Thomas Coffin failed. In October 1814 JM would obtain a position in a wholesale plow store in Philadelphia (Hallowell, 48; Bacon, 32–33).

8. JM's sister Mary Underhill Mott (1793–1862) would marry Robert Hicks (1793–1849) on 19 May 1814.

## To James Mott Sr.

PHILA., 1st mo. 24th, 1819

I have been so negligent of late with my pen, that I feel almost unable to express an idea in this way; but the many kind acts of remembrance and interest in our welfare, manifested towards us in an epistolary way, by our dear grandfather, having been, I trust, gratefully received by us, I have thought some acknowledgment of the same due from us; and not having succeeded in my endeavors to convince my J. M. that this was exclusively his province, I have made an attempt myself . . . .[1] Although in re-perusing some of thy former letters, the excellent advice therein contained may be compared (as respects myself) to "bread cast upon the waters,"[2] yet I tremblingly hope the time is approaching when it may be found. Still my want of faith is such, that in looking at the high profession we are making, and the terms of admission into the Kingdom, I am ready at times to shrink, and to cry out with the disciples formerly, "Who then can be saved;" and the many instances of late, of departure from the simplicity of Quakerism as respects trade, with the consequent embarrassment attendant thereon, and that too in some from whom we have looked for better things, add not a little to the discouraging side of the prospect. I know the "difficulty of the times" stands chargeable with it all, and we must charitably conclude that it has a share in it, still we cannot believe the requisition, "do justly," to have been made, and the power of compliance withheld. What then must be the conclusion? I am sensible, however, I have sufficient within to correct, without "fretting myself because of evil-doers;" and I hope by "studying to be quiet and doing my own business,"[3] to be enabled to leave the pronouncing of judgment to Him who will do it righteously, and not according to the appearance of man.

A few tracts accompany this, forwarded by Wm. Merritt, who has spent a few days with us, and is, we think, a very fine young man, and a warm advocate for Elias Hicks; many Friends this way not being prepared to unite with him altogether, in his views on some subjects. Dost thou agree in sentiment with him, respecting spreading the Scriptures and the First-day of the week.[4]

Elizabeth Walker has had much to say to-day at Arch St. mg,—we were not there. Her daughter's appearance is very much altered since she was at Nine-Partners School. She looks rather smart for a companion to a travelling Friend; but is there not danger of our placing too much stress on externals, and of becoming justly chargeable with the faults of the Scribes and Pharisees?

With much affection, in which my James cordially unites, I conclude.

LUCRETIA.

PL Hallowell, 64–65

1. Ellipses are in Hallowell's edition.
2. Eccles. 11:1.
3. Ps. 37:1; 1 Thess. 4:11.
4. William Merritt (1796–1882) was a member of the New York Monthly Meeting (*Friends' Intelligencer*, 7 October 1882, 536). According to Bacon, LCM had first met Elias Hicks (1748–1830), the Quaker preacher from Long Island, in 1809 when she taught at Nine Partners School; Hicks had spent a week in Philadelphia in December 1817. Hicks's sermons criticized the Bible, missionary societies, and the sabbatarian movements that many Friends with Orthodox sympathies were joining. In a 19 May 1818 letter to Phebe Willis, Hicks had stated that parts of the Bible, especially the Old Testament with its emphasis on war and violence, need not necessarily be considered an authority; the "Inward Light of Christ," not the Bible, was the highest authority and best guide. Copies of Hicks's letter circulated among the Philadelphia Friends (Bacon, 23–24; *Journal of the Life and Religious Labors of Elias Hicks* [New York: I. T. Hopper, 1832], 318–20; Ingle, 82–83, 95).

## To Unidentified Recipient

[*Philadelphia*] 12 mo. 15th, 1819.

I have not many fine traveller's stories to relate. We took the direct road to Winchester, and after a pleasant journey of six days, arrived safely, having met with one accident, the breaking of our axle-tree, which detained us a few hours. The country through which we passed was most of it under fine cultivation, and in some places, particularly near Harper's Ferry, the scenery was romantic. We met with many clever Friends in and near Winchester. Sarah Zane's principal object in going was to attend their meeting in a new house that was built upon a lot she had purchased for them. She has interested herself for Friends there. It was the time for their Quarterly Mg at Hopewell, six miles from Winchester, which we attended, and there met with Edward Stabler and wife, and many others.[1] He is one of the very interesting men. We lodged at the same house, and sat up very late to hear him talk. The sight of the poor slaves was indeed affecting; though in that neighborhood, we were told their situation was rendered less deplorable, by kind treatment from their masters.

We returned by the same route through Fredericktown, York, Lancaster, etc., and reach home after a little less than three weeks' absence.

PL Hallowell, 68–69

1. Sarah Zane was a Quaker minister, probably from Philadelphia (Hallowell, 68). Edward Stabler (1769–1831) was an elder, and his second wife, Mary Hartshorne Stabler (c. 1783–1853), was an overseer of the Alexandria, Virginia, Monthly Meeting.

## To James Mott Sr.

Philada. 3d. mo. 15th. 1822—

I hope that no remissness on our part will be the means of our losing the correspondence of our beloved Grand-Parent, tho' we have now to acknowledge the receipt of two communications which have remained too long unanswered the former giving us some particulars of dear Mary J. Alsop's resigned situation which were interesting; together with the account of the manner in which aunt Lydia [*Mott*] & thy-self had spent the summer.— We shall rejoice to hear of her restoration to health— Thy request respecting the letter to the young women from England was attended to—but there has not been any sent from them directed to J. M's care—they have had some discouragements in their business here and one I believe is now teaching school, the other learning cloakmaking.— — We felt obliged by thy introduction of Jethro Wood,[1] he was with us about ten days and we were much pleased with his company—he amused us with some of his anecdotes— —his health improved while here,—we are now daily expecting his wife and son, to whom he wrote before he left us wishing them to meet him here on his return from Washington—perhaps they will stay to attend our Yearly Meeting— —and how gratifying would it be to us to have the company of our dear Grandfather at that time—for altho' we are not likely to be settled at house keeping agreeably to our wish and expectation—still our Mother's family is not large and we shall reserve a room for thy accommodation if thou wilt indulge us with a hope of seeing thee— Dr. Moore and wife[2] wish it much and were inquiring the last time we were there if we were expecting thee—

We hear Anna Almy of Providence has a certificate to attend this Yearly Meeting— — we know of no others from that way—but what an affecting state of things among them![3] the account of it is widely circulating in the newspapers—it has always been a painful subject—to me—accusation having been brought against some of those whom we had always estimated as among the "very elect"—that I have been willing to disbelieve most of the reports concerning them—but they have now gone to such lengths that we can no longer remain incredulous—but dost thou think it quite right for a society professing as we do—to suffer any of its poor deluded members to lie in prison? and to take them from meeting by force? no doubt they have borne long with some of them— a friend of this City lately expressed a fear that a disposition had been too much indulged that would be ready to "call down fire from Heaven"—and it has appeared as if some here were ready to conclude that these poor things were "sinners above all men"—without sufficiently bearing in mind that "except we repent we shall likewise perish"[4]— — We had not heard of the book on the observance of the Sabbath till thou mentioned it— we have since read it with some interest, & unite with thee that the reasoning of Leland is mild yet forcible, the author of the last piece we are told is no other than (to use our Mother Mott's expression a *few years ago*) "the great and good *Elias*" [*Hicks*]— didst thou not place it upon him. I suspected that both Mother & thyself thought of him—we are wisely forbidden to judge of the motives of one of another, that being the case, I thought his language too severe— — Thos. McClintock[5] who signs Leland is a young man who joined our society by request when about nineteen years old—his talents are considered good—he has occasionally written for the newspapers and I understand corresponds with Elias Hicks— he is an Apothecary and having been obliged to keep his shop open on first days as well as others has perhaps *enlarged* his views on that subject— — — We last evening met with Emmor Kimber's oldest daughter who married George Massey's son she is nicely settled about 8 miles from her Father. her sister takes her place in the school which has been larger this winter than at any preceding time—[6] Emmor still intends appealing to our Yearly Mg— John Comly lately paid him a satisfactory visit had much to say to him which was well received— he reminded him that as long as Job justified himself his afflictions were continued, but when he acknowledged himself "vile" there was a change— I have never known a fall in our society that seemed so affecting[7]—in looking at his situation I have remembered that under the Law those of the seed of Aaron who had a blemish were not suffered to offer upon the Altar yet they were permitted to partake of the Holy and of the most Holy—and that this at times may be Emmor's experience is the fervent wish of my heart for him—

Tomorrow we expect to attend the funeral of Benjamin Johnson[8] an estimable friend and overseer of our meeting— I believe we mentioned last fall his going with his wife to spend the winter in Richmond on account of his health— they offered us their house free of rent in their absence—but we did not think best to accept it— he has been gradually declining all winter & was so desirous to return to his family once more, that they attempted it, and came by steam-boats as far as French-town, where he was met by his oldest son and after an interview of a few hours, he yielded his life apparently in much resignation, his remains were yesterday brought to the City that his little family of 7 children might have the melancholy satisfaction of looking upon him once more— his wife mentions, in a letter soon after their arrival in Richmond, having attended the preparative meeting there where were only five females & remarks that "nothing short of the same Power that preserved a Lot in Sodom, could have kept alive a remnant of His Israel in that land of Slavery"— — We understand George Withy[9] is on his return from that land—& expected to be at Columbia, about 70 miles from here, by the 15th of this month—he will likely be at our yearly Mg—

Last accounts from William Foster state that he expects to go to New England & will probably be at their next yearly Mg—an excellent messenger!— — We just parted with John Cox & wife  they have been here several days—they enquired after you & thought Uncle Richd. could not be very fond of his pen— please inform him & Aunt A. that their friends generally look for a visit from them next mo.[10]—Jane Shoemakers health is much improved— — — We are shortly to lose our very good monthly & quarterly meeting's clerk—Anne Biddle, but our loss will be John Tatum's great gain[11]—

I had no idea of filling the sheet when I commenced but such as it is please accept it with much affection from—

Lucretia Mott

James will likely write by this oppy. to our Parents

ALS Davis Env: "James Mott Snr., New York"

1. Jethro Wood (1774–1834), a New York City inventor and Quaker, was married to Sarah Howland Wood.

2. This is probably Dr. John Wilson Moore (c. 1791–1865) and his wife, Rachel Wilson Moore (c. 1791–1877). Rachel, a Quaker minister, would later marry Samuel Townsend (*Friends' Intelligencer*, 23 July 1865, 312, 15 December 1877, 682).

3. Anna Almy, later Jenkins (1790–1849), would found the Providence Shelter for Colored Children. LCM is referring to the imprisonment and trial in March 1822 of John Alley Jr., Preserved Sprague (1777–1848), and two others for having "committed riots in the Quaker Meeting House at Lynn," Massachusetts, in February. The four were part of

the New Light movement, which in 1822–24 protested the elders' rule and had Unitarian leanings (*A Review of the Trial of John Alley, Jr., and Others on the Charges of Riot, etc.* [n.p., 1823]; Frederick B. Tolles, "The New-Light Quakers of Lynn and New Bedford," *New England Quarterly* [September 1959]: 298–303).

4. 2 Kings 1:12; LCM is adapting Luke 13:3: "except ye repent, ye shall all likewise perish."

5. Thomas McClintock (c. 1792–1876), an abolitionist and a Quaker minister, lived in Philadelphia until 1836, when he moved to Waterloo, New York.

6. Anna Kimber (1798–1876) married Robert Valentine Massey, the son of George Massey (c. 1767–1848). Abby Kimber (1804–71), a sister of Anna Kimber, taught at the Kimberton School, which Emmor Kimber founded in 1817 and which advocated the absence of authority (J. Smith Futhey and Gilbert Cope, *History of Chester County, Pennsylvania* [Philadelphia: Louis H. Everts, 1881], 305).

7. In May 1820 the overseers of the Uwchlan Monthly Meeting had begun an investigation into the indebtedness of Emmor Kimber. Despite Kimber's appeals to the quarterly and yearly meetings, he was disowned. Kimber subsequently published a pamphlet charging the monthly meeting with exceeding its authority and concluded, "I advise no one to follow my example in opposing arbitrary power in individual members who are out of the order of the gospel." Many Friends withdrew their children from Kimberton School (Emmor Kimber, *Facts Stated, That the Truth May Not Be Blamed* [Philadelphia: William Brown, 1823], 9–15; Ingle, 50). John Comly (1773–1850), a former schoolmaster, had become a full-time Quaker minister and farmer in 1815.

8. Benjamin Johnson (d. 1822) was a Philadelphia printer and the author of the *Philadelphia School Dictionary* (1812, 3d ed.) and other titles.

9. The British Quaker George Withy (1763?-1837) would visit the United States in 1822–23 (Ingle, 32, 123). In a sermon in Burlington, New Jersey, on 10 May 1822, Withy would stress the divinity of Christ and the necessity of salvation only through his intercessions (*A Sermon, Preached at Friends' Meeting House* [Philadelphia: n.p., 1822], 19–21).

10. LCM is probably referring to William Forster (1784–1854), a British Quaker who visited the United States in 1820–25. John Cox (1754–1847) and his wife, Ann Dillwyn Cox (1746–1838), lived in Burlington, New Jersey (Susanna Parrish Wharton, *The Parrish Family* [Philadelphia: n.p., 1925], 245–88). Richard Mott had married Abigail Field (1766–1851) in 1787.

11. Anne Biddle (1780–1870) of Philadelphia would marry John Tatum of Gloucester County, New Jersey, on 26 June 1822 (*Friends' Review*, 8 October 1870, 107).

## To James Mott Sr.

PHIL., 6th mo. 29th, 1822.

I believe our beloved grandparent promised to write to us, if we would let him know whether we reached home in safety; and that information having been conveyed by letter to our parents, we may now, I think, reasonably expect a fulfilment of his promise.

I have hardly sufficient by me at this time to warrant my taking the pen. I have re-perused thy book on Education since our return, and hope its instructive contents will be usefully remembered by me.[1]

We are now engaged in reading "Southey's Life of Wesley, with the Rise and

Progress of Methodism."[2] An interesting work, though some parts we thought might have been omitted, such as the supernatural appearances. The author appears as much attached to the doctrines of the Episcopal Church, as some of us Quakers are to ours. I was pleased with the rule laid down for Wesley, by his mother, to enable him to judge of the lawfulness or unlawfulness of pleasure, which is as follows: "Whatever weakens your reason, impairs the tenderness of your conscience, obscures your sense of God, or takes off the relish of spiritual things; in short, whatever increases the strength and authority of your body over your mind, that thing is sin to you, however innocent it may be in itself."

Cannot you enlightened ones set us a good example by making some improvement in the Discipline relative to out-goings in marriage? Our meeting has lately disowned two daughters of Rebecca Paul, a minister, on that account, and last month a complaint was entered against their mother for "conniving" at it. Her son was present at the marriage, so that probably four of the family will lose their right of membership.[3] One of the young men requested to be received as a member, after he was engaged to be married. This was not granted. Rebecca is a poor widow who has had to make exertion for the support of her family. She told the overseers that clever young men appearing for her daughters, and considering that she had nothing to offer them if they stayed with her, she could not hold them, and should feel too much like an Ananias[4] to sit under a complaint against them, stating "without the consent of their mother." It has been what Friends call "a trying case." Last week a young couple were disowned who married, being first cousins. What is to be done in such cases?

The opportunity we have had of being again with our revered grandfather, and many others very dear to us, is a subject of grateful recollection. We still indulge the hope of seeing thee in this city.

Affectionately,    LUCRETIA.

PL Hallowell, 77–79

1. James Mott Sr., *"Observations on the Education of Children" and "Hints to Young People on the Duties of Civil Life"* (New York: Samuel Wood, 1816).

2. Robert Southey (1774–1843) wrote *The Life of Wesley and the Rise and Progress of Methodism* (London: Longman, Hurst, Rees, Orme, and Brown, 1820). John Wesley (1703–91), English theologian, founded the Methodist church.

3. Rebecca Paul, the second wife of Jeremiah Paul, would be disowned by the Philadelphia Monthly Meeting in 1823 for supporting her daughters' marriages to non-Friends. Her daughters, Elizabeth Donaldson (b. 1799) and Lydia Austin (b. 1802), had been disowned the previous year for their marriages "contrary to the order established among Friends." The committee in the case of Rebecca's son Nathan Paul (b. 1797) later wrote to him "on the subject of the charge against him, who it seems at present resides remote from any Monthly Meeting of Friends" (Philadelphia Monthly Meeting minutes, 30 May 1822, 27 June 1822, 30 January 1823, PSCHi).

4. Ananias lied to Peter the apostle about money he had made through the sale of his possessions and kept to himself (Acts 5:1–5).

# To Adam Mott and Anne Mott

*[Philadelphia 29 December 1822]*

*[Added to JM's letter of the same date]*

James's last letter was finished & sent when I was from home but from what he has told me he then wrote, added to the above— I judge you have a pretty full account of the transactions of *some* friends in this City in regard to Elias [*Hicks*][1]—& it may not be necessary for me to add much— I have been pleased to observe a disposition to prevail among a large majority to hear & judge for themselves— We have been much in his company & find him the same consistant exemplary man that he was many years ago—& I believe the criterion still remains—that the tree is known by its fruit— We had a very pleasant visit from him & dined in company with him at Dr. Moore's, who has had independence enough to remain his fast friend. John Comly also came into the City to be with him in his time of trial— an elder of Green st. meeting accompanied him in his family visits & expressed much or entire satisfaction—as did many, many others & when he was about leaving the city Hannah L. Smith[2] expressed a belief that He who had delivered him in six troubles would not forsake him in the seventh, but that the language of his heart would be, "return unto thy rest oh my soul for the Lord hath dealt bountifully with thee"[3] after which in a very broken manner he desired to commemorate the loving kindness of our gracious Creator, in that he had been with him & followed him from meeting to meeting &c— I never saw such crowded meetings as those on 1st. days were & very quiet solemn sittings

I dont know whether James acknowledged the receipt of a very acceptable letter from our dear Father & sister Mary [*Hicks*] with an addition from Mother after her return from Rahway—we were glad to hear the family visits were satisfactory— Well I suppose the time is drawing near when we must part with Silas & Sarah[4] & I should rejoice to see them once more before they go, for our little visit last spring seems but a peep at them & I see no prospect of going again very soon, tho' my J.M. may— but cannot they wind up their concerns at Flushing in time to pay us a little visit previously to going so far— We were quite surprised to hear of the birth of Abbey's boy—not knowing of any expectation of such an event—have not yet learned its name, we were glad to hear they were so comfortable & that the school continues to prosper— — We learned through Sarah Collins[5] that br. Robert [*Hicks*] was poorly—but did not know he had been so seriously affectd as to occasion the anxious nursing that sister Mary mentions— — do they feel settled in N York or does Robert still talk of a farm—& what does Richard intend doing. I am pleased to hear his health is restored & think he might employ an evening occasionally in writing to his brother & sister It would be an advantage to himself as well as give us pleasure the bearer of your last letter, Anna Powell has visited us—she appears to be a clever young woman—she talks of spending the winter with her sister—they feel alone in this large city & such are to be felt for— Elizh. B. Robinson intends to find them out

We have made some inquiry but have not yet ascertained whether John Billings is writing for the Reformer—[6] I frequently see him passing in the street— — have you seen T. Eddy's letter & accompanying remarks[7]—we have a copy—if you wish it we will forward it to you—we heard the overseers had taken it up—is it so?— — Elias's book on the subject of Slavery is in the hands of J. Rakestraw[8] to be printed— — We frequently call to see Andrew Under-hill[9] who is rapidly declining—he appears at times sensible of his situation, & at others when he feels a little better he mentions what he intends to do when he recovers—his Mother appears much affected with it— She lately showed me an interesting letter she had recd. from Aunt Lydia— I suppose our vener-able GrandParent is again with you, if so please remind him a letter would be very acceptable to us—

Our family are in usual health, except colds— Our Mother has many cares having a family of 18 to provide for—but she has good spirits & we get along very comfortably—having a convenient house & good help—& she observed a few days ago that she should be very glad to have a visit from you this winter & I can assure you that you could be made very comfortable  we have a fire to ourselves in which room you should lodge—& I have no doubt we should find much to talk about—do come—

in love—    L. Mott

ALS Davis

1. In the fall of 1822, Hicks had been preaching outside the bounds of the Philadel-phia Yearly Meeting, upsetting some Quakers in Maryland and Delaware. Two Quak-ers, Ezra Comfort and Isaiah Bell, reported back to Jonathan Evans (c. 1765–1839), the clerk of the Philadelphia Meeting for Sufferings, and other Philadelphia Quakers that Hicks was referring to Christ as having "no more power given him than man" (Ingle, 17–18, 108).

2. Hannah Logan Smith (1777–1846), a Philadelphia Quaker, became a minister at age seventeen and married James Smith at age thirty (Mary R. Darby Smith, *Brief Memori-als of Departed Worth: Being Sketches of the Character, Life, and Death of Hannah Logan Smith* [London: A. Napier, 1882]).

3. Ps. 116:7.

4. Silas Cornell (1789–1864) had married JM's sister Sarah (1791–1872) in 1815.

5. Sarah Collins was a Quaker minister from Westchester, New York (*Journal of the Life and Religious Labours of John Comly* [Philadelphia: T. E. Chapman, 1853], 166).

6. The Philadelphia newspaper *Reformer* ran from 1820 to 1835 and was published by Joseph Rakestraw.

7. Thomas Eddy (1758–1827), a founder of the American Bible Society, was involved in prison reform, antislavery, Native American welfare, and the colonization of African Americans. In a letter to John Warder of 18 October 1822, Eddy had urged Warder to copy and circulate, with or without his attribution, Eddy's "Facts and Observations Illustra-tive of the Present State of Society in New York," which criticized Hicks's Unitarian lean-ings. Hicks had "asserted that he was not obliged to believe what our reason could not

comprehend," and Eddy cautioned: "If Friends in Philadelphia should allow this man to visit families, and in this way spread his poisonous principles, divisions among them will assuredly be the consequence" (Thomas Eddy, *The Cabinet; or, Works of Darkness Brought to Light* [Philadelpia: T. Eddy, 1824], 6–7, 12–13, 17, 19).

8. Elias Hicks's *Observations on the Slavery of the Africans and Their Descendants: Recommended to the Serious Perusal, and Impartial Consideration of the Citizens of the United States of America, and Others Concerned* was originally published in New York City by S. Wood in 1811.

9. Andrew Underhill (1797–1823) was a Philadelphia Quaker (*A Short Memoir of Andrew Underhill: Who Departed This Life, at Philadelphia, on the Eighteenth of the First Month, 1823, in the Twenty-Sixth Year of His Life* [Philadelphia: Benj. and Thos. Kite, 1826]).

## To Adam Mott and Anne Mott

Phila., 4th mo. 23rd, 1826.

Our Yearly Meeting does not furnish much to pen, although it was acknowledged by all whom I heard speak of it, to be very satisfactory. Anna Braithwaite, E. Robeson, Rebecca Updegraff, attended with certificates, all of whom had full opportunities to relieve their minds, and we had much preaching.[1] I was obliged to leave the Meeting on Seventh-day morning, and did not get out again till Second-day, after which I felt better every day. The children did pretty well, though were more exposed to the air, by running out while we were at Meeting, than I liked. Thomas is still poorly, very fretful, and requires patient attention. I wrote the foregoing with my babe [*Elizabeth*] in my arms. I wish you could see what a lovely, fat, little pet she is; and her father already flatters himself she looks pleased when he takes her. If she has had the measles, it was very light; there was a slight eruption which Dr. Moore thought looked like it, but no fever. The crape gown will be useful to make over for Anna, unless I conclude to keep it for Maria, as I have just prepared Anna to go to Westtown boarding-school.[2] They have both had their bombazines made up this winter.

James' present partner is a young man, and appears in good spirits. They have already some goods consigned to them, and their friends think their prospects good. I confess I should be much better satisfied, if they could do business that was in no wise dependent on slavery, and perhaps some will appear after a while.[3]

PL Hallowell, 95–96

1. In her trips to the United States (1823, 1825, 1827), Anna Braithwaite (1788–1859), a British evangelical Quaker, opposed the doctrines of Elias Hicks. Elizabeth Robson (1771–1843), a Yorkshire Quaker, traveled in the United States from 1824 to 1828 and from 1838 to 1842. Robson was recorded as a minister in 1810 and, like Braithwaite, was opposed to Hicks (Ingle, 63, 126, 161; *Friends Historical Society Journal*, 14 [1917]: 75–78). Rebecca T. Updegraff (b. 1790) was a Quaker minister from Ohio and the mother of David Upde-

graff, also a minister (J. Brent Bill, *David B. Updegraff: Quaker Holiness Preacher* [Richmond, Ind.: Friends United Press, 1983], 13–14).

2. The Westtown Boarding School was a Quaker school founded in 1799 in Chester County. In 1827 the Motts would remove Anna from Westtown because of its Orthodox affiliation (Bacon, 46; Otelia Cromwell, *Lucretia Mott* [Cambridge, Mass.: Harvard University Press, 1958], 27, 35).

3. JM was then engaged in the cotton and wool wholesale business (Bacon, 39, 42).

## To Anne Mott

Phil., 2nd mo. 26th, 1827.

It is with heartfelt regret that we learn the state of things at Jericho Mg., as well as in many others.[1] If we cd. only do as our beloved grandfr. advised, "leave the present unprofitable discussion, and endeavor to go on unto perfection," how much better wd. it be for us all. The apostle has truly forewarned us, "But if ye bite and devour one another, take heed that ye be not consumed one of another:"[2] for have we not found this to be the case, that the stronger are consuming the weaker, in the several Mgs. where these party feelings exist. I know it is a serious thing to set up individual judgement against that of a Mo. Mg.; but when we see those of unblemished lives repeatedly arraigned before their tribunal, and remember the test which the Blessed Master laid down, "By their fruits shall ye know them,"[3] it is difficult always to refrain, though we still endeavor to do so.

PL Hallowell, 97–98

1. Evidently the break in the Quaker community over the preachings of Elias Hicks was beginning in Jericho Monthly Meeting on Long Island, where Hicks was a minister. The meeting sided with Hicks and registered dissatisfaction with Thomas Willis, a Quaker minister of Jericho, who opposed Hicks "on acct. of the disunity" (Jericho Men's Monthly Meeting minutes, 18 January 1827, 15 February 1827, 17 May 1827, PSCHi). After Hicks's death, Willis published *The Answers by Elias Hicks to the Six Queries Addressed to Him* (New York: Mahlon Day, 1831), which demonstrated "wherein his opinions were at variance with the Christian doctrines they [*Orthodox Quakers*] held." Willis included excerpts from Hicks's sermons to demonstrate Hicks's renunciation of scriptural authority (4, 16–17; see also Bliss Forbush, *Elias Hicks: Quaker Liberal* [New York: Columbia University Press, 1956], 151, 192–93, 239, 244–47).

2. Gal. 5:15.

3. LCM is adapting Matt. 7:16: "Ye shall know them by their fruits. Do we gather grapes of thorns, or figs of thistles?"

## To the London Yearly Meeting of Friends

*[Philadelphia c. 14 April 1830]*

Dear Friends:—

Your communication, under cover of a letter from Josiah Forster to the clerk of this meeting, was duly received; and, notwithstanding the obstacles you have placed in the way of our communion, we have thought it right, on mature deliberation, again to address you in the language of brotherly love, with desires that, on further reflection, you may be induced to open the channel of Christian intercourse between us.[1]

On looking over the annals of our religious society, it is pleasing to perceive that for more than one hundred and forty years the Yearly Meeting of London and that of Pennsylvania preserved the most cordial relations. During this time an affectionate interchange of their views and sentiments was maintained, to their mutual edification and comfort, binding them more firmly together in the bonds of gospel fellowship. Greatly desiring to preserve such an intercourse uninterrupted, this meeting, in the fourth month, 1828, addressed to you an affectionate epistle, in which we adverted to the division which had taken place in the Yearly Meeting of Philadelphia, and stated our views of the causes which had led to that event. We did this in the hope that by making you acquainted with our case as we understood it ourselves, you might be preserved from any improper bias, and be induced to suspend your decision on the subject, until time and a further investigation of circumstances might enable you to form an impartial judgment. By your answer to this ~~brotherly~~ {friendly}[2] effort for the preservation of harmony between us, we perceive, that on the *ex parte* evidence of a committee, acting as the representatives of a small minority of Friends in this section of our country, you have pronounced us "separatists," and have declared it the judgment of your meeting, "neither to read, nor accept the communication" we sent you!

We would affectionately request you to review the course you have adopted on this occasion; to consider whether it comports with the precepts of the Christian religion—{the practice of early Friends}—or even with common justice—to condemn your brethren {and sisters} *unheard*. "Whatsoever ye would that men should do to you, do ye even so to them." (Matt. vii. 12.) This is the positive precept of Christ, whose friends we are only so far as we do whatsoever he commands us. By this act, if you persevere in the course you have prescribed, you will cut yourselves off from religious communion with {upwards of} eighteen thousand of your fellow-professors of the gospel of Christ within this one Yearly Meeting! You will separate yourselves from a religious community whose aim is to exalt the standard of Truth and righteousness; whose ardent desire is to promote peace on earth and good-will to men.

We are aware, dear friends, that our ~~adversaries~~ {opponents} have pronounced us infidels and deists! They have said we have departed from the Christian faith, and renounced the religion of our worthy predecessors in the Truth. Nothing is easier than to make such charges as these; but, in the present case, we are happily assured that nothing is harder than to prove them. We are not sensible of any dereliction on our part from the principles laid down by our blessed Lord. The history of the birth, life, acts, death, and resurrection of the holy Jesus, as in the volume of the book it is written of him, we reverently believe. "We are not ashamed of the gospel of Christ, because it is the power of God until salvation to all them that believe."[3] Neither do we hesitate to acknowledge the divinity ~~ascribed to~~ {of} its author; because we know from living experience that he is the *power* of God and the *wisdom* of God; that, under the present glorious dispensation, he is the *one* holy principle of Divine *life* and *light*—the unlimited *word* of grace and truth, which only can build us up in the true faith, and give us an inheritance among all those who are sanctified.

Neither are we sensible of any departure from the faith or principles of our primitive Friends. We are not ignorant that on some points of a speculative nature, they had different views, and expressed themselves diversely; but notwithstanding this was the case, such were the aboundings of the love of God and of one another, that these differences did not interrupt the excellent harmony {that existed among them}. In the fundamental principle of the Christian faith, "*the light of Christ within, as God's gift for man's salvation,*" and which, as William Penn[4] declares, "is {as} the root of the goodly tree of doctrines, which grew and branched out from it," they were all united. And in that which united them we are united with them; believing in the same *fundamental principle,* and in all *the blessed doctrines* which grow from it as their root, both as they are laid down in the Scriptures of Truth, and in their writings; desiring above all things the growth and advancement of this principle in ourselves, and in the world at large.

The peculiar testimonies which the Society of Friends have borne from the beginning, are near and dear to us; not only because of the blessed Root from which they spring, but because we believe, that as they are faithfully supported, they will be a means of advancing that glorious day, spoken of by the Lord's prophets, when the people "shall beat their swords into ploughshares, and their spears into pruning-hooks; when nation shall not lift up sword against nation, neither shall they learn war any more; but they shall sit, every man under his vine and under his fig-tree, and none shall make them afraid." (Mic. iv. 4.)

The charges brought against *us* by our opposers, to injure and invalidate our character as a Christian people, are the same that were preferred against our primitive Friends; and, we ~~believe~~ {apprehend,} upon the same grounds. In that day, those who, like Diotrephes, loved to have the preeminence,[5] could not bear to see a people rising up and bearing testimony to the truth and practical importance of that humbling doctrine, {"Be not ye called Rabbi; for} one is your master, even Christ, and all ye are brethren." (Matt. xxiii. 8.) We do not believe that the dissensions which have appeared among us, had their origin {so much} in differences of opinion {on doctrinal points}, as in a disposition, apparent in some ~~of their society~~, to exercise an oppressive authority in the church. These, in our meetings for discipline, although a small minority of the whole, assumed the power to direct a course of measures, painful to the feelings and contrary to the deliberate judgment of their brethren. Thus the few usurped a power over the many, subversive of our established order, and destructive to the peace and harmony of society. After long and patient forbearance, in the hope that our opposing brethren might see the impropriety of such a course, the great body of the Yearly Meeting saw no way to regain ~~peace~~ {a state of tranquility,} but by a *disconnection* with those who had produced, and were promoting such disorders among us.

After much painful exercise on our part, through all which we had abundant evidence of the extension of Divine regard, affording strength proportioned to the labour of the day—such a *disconnection* was effected. And, with gratitude to our heavenly Father, we are now enabled to say, that harmony and brotherly love abound among us; under the feeling of which, we have often experienced the Divine presence to be the crown and diadem of our solemn assemblies.

By official accounts (which we believe to be nearly correct) from all parts of this Yearly Meeting, it appears that out of about *twenty-five* thousand adults and children, which composed it {at the time of the division}, about *eighteen thousand* remain in connection with this body.[6]

Finally, brethren {and sisters,} we are concerned to express, in the language of the apostle, the desire for ourselves and for you, that we may "give all diligence to add to our faith virtue; and to virtue, *knowledge;* and to knowledge, temperance; and to temperance, patience; and to patience, godliness; and to godliness, brotherly kindness; and to brotherly kindness, *charity.*"[7] For if these things be in us, and abound, they will make us that we shall neither be barren nor unfruitful in the knowledge of our Lord Jesus Christ.

With the salutation of love, we remain your friends.

Signed by direction, and on behalf of said meeting, by

JOHN COMLY,
*Clerk to the Men's Meeting.*
LUCRETIA MOTT,
*Clerk to the Women's Meeting.*[8]

PL *Journal of the Life and Religious Labours of John Comly, Late of Byberry, Pennsylvania* (Philadelphia: T. Ellwood Chapman, 1853), 638–41.

1. Josiah Forster (1782–1870), a British abolitionist, was the clerk of the London Yearly Meeting for twelve years (*Diary,* 25). In 1828, the Philadelphia Yearly Meeting had split into two groups: the Hicksites, followers of Elias Hicks, and the Orthodox, who were influenced by evangelical Protestantism. The Hicksites advocated a close adherence to the doctrine of inner light, or individual conscience, in religious belief and practice, while the Orthodox opposed Hicks's questioning of the divinity of Christ, original sin, and

the authority of the Scriptures (Thomas Hamm, *The Transformation of American Quakerism: Orthodox Friends, 1800–1907* [Bloomington: Indiana University Press, 1988], 15–20). Since 1828, the London Yearly Meeting had supported the Orthodox Philadelphia Yearly Meeting. Samuel Bettle, clerk of the Orthodox Yearly Meeting, had sent an epistle to the London Yearly Meeting in 1828 declaring that the Hicksites' beliefs were "not the principles of the Christian religion, and cannot therefore be received by our religious Society" (London Yearly Meeting, Epistles Received, 1828, 426, Library of the Religious Society of Friends, London). In its 31 May 1828 minutes, the London Yearly Meeting had referred to an address from the Philadelphia Hicksites and concluded that since "the said Address was from the body in Philadelphia who have separated themselves from Friends," it would not "read or accept the same" (London Yearly Meeting minutes, 1828, 282–83, Library of the Religious Society of Friends, London). In contrast, an expression of sympathy and support had been sent to the Orthodox members in May 1829 (London Yearly Meeting, Epistles Sent, 1829, 206–8, Library of the Religious Society of Friends, London).

2. Strikethroughs and words in braces indicate changes LCM made to Comly's original letter (notes taken by Margaret Hope Bacon from the original draft of the 1830 epistle, PSCHi; see also Bacon, 47–49).

3. Rom. 1:16.

4. William Penn (1644–1718), a Quaker leader, founded the commonwealth of Pennsylvania.

5. Diotrephes, the leader of a congregation of early Christians, opposed the work of John and the other apostles (3 John 9–10).

6. Of the 26,800 members of the Philadelphia Yearly Meeting in 1827, approximately 17,380 became Hicksites and 9,000 became Orthodox (Ingle, 218).

7. 2 Pet. 1:5–7.

8. On the same day as this epistle is dated, the Philadelphia Yearly Meeting instructed its clerk to sign the epistle and send it to the London Yearly Meeting (minutes, 1830, 67–68, PSCHi). According to Bacon (47–48), LCM protested Comly's original letter during the women's meeting as too conciliatory and made the changes noted above. Records of the London Yearly Meeting contain no recognition of epistles received by the Philadelphia Hicksites. In an epistle to the Philadelphia Orthodox dated 18–27 May 1831, Josiah Forster as clerk stated that the London meeting "hereby further declares that it does not recognize as in connexion with itself as a Christian community under the Religious denomination of Friends or Quakers any Meeting, Association, institution, Community of body of persons within the district of the Yearly Meeting . . . other than sd. Yearly Meeting" (London Yearly Meeting minutes, 1831, 79–81).


# To Phebe Post Willis[1]

Philada. 3 mo. 1st. 1834—

My dear P. P. W.

I did not intend spring should appear ere I acknowledged thy acceptable letter recd. some weeks if not months since— The account of the decease of dear Rachel Hicks's son[2] had reached us—but none of the particulars of the funeral &c—had we heard before—all of which were interesting & altogether unexpected that her Father should get out to Mg. again—that he attended with her on so solemn & affecting an occasion must have been particularly grateful

& consolatory to her—she has had a large share of affliction— Thy accot. of her thro' all was encouraging— she & thou too would have been cheered I think, could you have witnessed the deep & lively interest evinced here 3 months since at the Anti-Slavery Convention— if Elias [*Hicks*] could have lived to see this cause spread as we now behold it—how would he have rejoiced—not among friends tho'—the delegation was composed of Unitarians, Baptists Presbyterians—a few Orthodox Friends & still fewer of our side—a few females were there by sufferance—& a more interesting session we never witnessed—for all seem'd absorbed in the object for which they met—engaging in the righteous cause of exertion for suffering humanity— have you had their "Declaration" I cant fill my sheet in telling thee about it for it would fill the whole of it— Some of the proceedings are published in the "Friend"—also in the "Genius"—& a full accot. in the "Liberator"— do take that paper among you The Emancipator too published in New York is well worth circulating—in these you will see how Anti Slavery Societies are increasing & on what correct principles they are established— We have formed a female Anti Slavery society to aid the cause the *little all* in our power[3] and we have before us the subject of reprinting what Elias Hicks has written on the subject, can you tell us what his last work was?—& indeed—all that he wrote on the subject we should like to have— Do read "Mrs Childs Appeal in favor of that class of Americans called Africans"—tis a noble work—& by a woman too[4]—if I had only known of it when we were in Boston I would have tried to see her— Our house was open to the strangers who were here at that time & it was as interesting as any yearly Mg week I have known— We had 3 presbyterians to lodge with us— One of whom [*James Miller McKim*] became so much interested in inquiries concerng friends & in attending our Mgs. that he remained here 2 weeks—& altho' he was qualifying himself for the Ministry with the expectation of devoting himself to the missionary cause in Asia—yet before he left here he said all his props were knocked away—& he could not pursue his studies with the same object in view as when he came— he now feels as if his exertions must be directed to the Abolition cause in some way whether to visit the Southern States or in what way he cannot yet tell— he took home many books & writes to us that he has been readg some of these & finds the arguments against the supreme Divinity of Christ, the Trinity & the atonement, irresistible to his mind—that he held on as long as he could to these doctrines but had been obliged at last to let go— still he would like to see how we get over some passages that are adduced by our opponents in support of these views— he then adds (a sentiment that I hope he may cherish) that "it is true no text of scripture however plain can shake my belief in a truth which I perceive by intuition, nor make me believe a thing which is contrary to my innate sense of right & wrong"— on the subject of slavery he says "since my mind is enlightened on this subject I can hardly think, speak, read or dream of any thing else— I am convinced there is much of a slave holdg spirit in the north as in the south— we are more indebted to circumstances than to our virtue for our freedom from this crime— I can only find relief in consecrating my self & my all to God to be employed as long as I live in his behalf—& I thank him that he has opened my eyes & touched my heart so that I can feel in any measure aright on this momentous subject"— —he is not yet 23—an orphan—& has the charge of 5 younger brothers & sisters— we feel deeply interested in his progress for he resides entirely away from Friends in Carlisle in this state— thou must excuse me if I have made too long a story of it— several more about his age attended the convention—& some of them are writing on the subject of abstinence from slave labor— one a young man from Portland, Me. writes in the Liberator & signs "Mott"—[5] you would be interested in reading them—they commence in the numbers of this year— —

John G. Whittier too of Haverhill Mass. a young man orthodox friend writes beautifully— his letter addressed to the New England AntiSlavery Society published in No. 3 of the present volume of the Liberator is very interesting[6]—& several other articles in that number do read them— I doubt his being very orthodox—for he told me that some in his neighborhood would have been glad to see us there last summer— Some friends think it *wicked* to mingle with other societies in these exertions for good—but I feel differently & can rejoice that subjects in which we ought, with the light—we have had, to be pioneers, are now taken hold of spiritedly by sincere professors of other folds— Now I will return to thy letter— I have a not a copy of Moses Browns birth day as noticed in the paper or I would send it thee— We hear very little of our frds. in New England— Edwd. Hicks[7] has given up his minute & says he was all wrong when he got it—so he will not be likely to go nor do I hear of John Comly or any one else going— a letter from Ruthy Buffum to George Truman dated 30th. of 10th. Mo. says they continued to be so disturbed with Swedenborgians reading &c that she and her husband— Preserved Sprague & Wm. Luscomb have left the Mg.—[8] they went to the extent of their feelings— John Alley thot. them hasty—but he has since given them ^the Swedenborgians^ his views so clearly of the new church doctrine that its advocates have abandoned the prospect of establishing their meeting in his Hall— Ruthy says they found themselves too much attached to their former mode of worship to relinquish it— Lois Purinton says she now finds something that satisfies her respecting futurity—& some others are much taken with his speculations & they did not think best to keep the appearance of unity when they were twain—for she & others could not feed on such husks as Sweden[borgian] imaginations—neither did they think any good would be gained [by?] controversy—- many are quite gratified in knowing they did not [*ms. damaged*]

N. Spencer & Ruth and Asa & Mary Hoag paid them a visit—when they had visited their Mg. & were clear of them— Ruthy opened their situation to them— Ruth said it confirmed her former feelings for she felt burdened in their Mg.—they expressed much feeling for them— Asa reminded them that Christ trod the wine press alone Ruth added that in these seasons of desertion he was tempted to command the stones to be made bread—& admonished them not to try too long to assimilate in their Mgs.— —she mentions havg. lately had something like an apoplectic fit—that she fell lifeless & continued to all appearance dead for some time—

I have just filled a sheet to her, the first I have written except a short one to E. Fry soon after our return— I have also written to Wm. Rotch—apologizing for his letter being published as it was with inaccuracies— we hear nothing lately from them or their Mg.—except that their Mg has been regularly attended by about 40 members— Elizh. Rodman has seldom been at it this winter.— Benj. Rodman has failed in business & many others in New Bedford—[9] Some of their large houses have been sold at a great sacrifice— — Nor do we hear much more from our Nant. Frds.— Sylvanus Macy & his wife Anna are both deceased—

9th—

I met with the enclosed last evening & the description answered so well to that interesting young man we met with on board the boat last summer, that I thot. I would send it to thee—perhaps thou learned his name— I did not— he came on in the same boat with Jas. & self from New York—& we heard nothing from him afterwards—& think this must be the same dear fellow— I have no recollection at all of the person thou alludes to, who travelled several days in compy. with us— many circumstances however I do remember & love to dwell upon—particularly our private opportunities in our rooms & our wakeful & talkative night hours— — I dont know what Henry [*Willis*] & thyself can have to prevent your coming this spring to yearly Mg.—when we could revive each others remembrance of those times— You may not always be able to leave home so easily—& your havg. been here last year need make no difference—for ours is an affection that deserves such an interchange— do think of it & let us know your conclusion— you can introduce br. John and Mary—[10] we should be pleased to have them accompany you & make their long talked of visit— — —

Does not sister Lydia too think a journey would be of use to her this spring— her company with her husbands would be pleasant to us and if you will inform us that you will come—we will reserve places for you— Uncle Saml.[11] has not written us— I suppose we ought to have remembered him in that way & I hope James will write to him by this opportunity—his & thy kind attentions will not soon be forgotten by me—& if you also can look back with satisfaction—it adds to mine— — My arm "is restored whole as the other"— I was confined 4 weeks with it, owing to imprudence in going out & makg. pies &c—when I arose & departed on that little journey which occupied us two weeks & 2 days—& ended well—since which—Slavery has been my *hobby*— I have had 6 appointed Mgs. for the people of colour in their several places of worship & expect to have 3 more which will embrace all—

We were glad to hear that your br. & sister from Scipio made you a visit— Mother enjoyed it for them— she is always glad to hear from her Scipio frds—she desires love to you all— sister Eliza too wishes to be affecty remembered— her youngest child has been ill with catarrh fever— P. Hussey
is still at Nant.— Benjn. Ferris[12] was in the City not long since [& took?] tea
with us—he is cheerful Ann Chapman has [*ms. damaged*] moved into 6th
st.—her son has commenced business on his own accot. [*ms. damaged*] in
appears in our Mg.

AL NRU Env: "Phebe P. Willis, care of Henry Willis, Jericho, Long Island"

1. Phebe Post Willis (1790–1846), a Hicksite Quaker and cousin of JM, had married
Henry Willis (1786–1865) in 1813.

2. Rachel Hicks (1789–1878) was a minister in the Hicksite New York City meeting.

3. William Lloyd Garrison, Lewis Tappan, Samuel J. May and others had formed the
AASS in Philadelphia on 4–6 December 1833. Its Declaration of Sentiments, signed by
Garrison, JM, James Miller McKim, Robert Purvis, and others, called on citizens "to
remove slavery by moral and political action." The declaration resolved to establish
antislavery societies, hire antislavery agents, and "enlist the PULPIT and the PRESS" on
behalf of slaves. LCM and others had founded the PFASS on 9 December (*Liberator,* 14
December 1833, 198, 21 December 1833, 102; Bacon, 59).

4. *The Appeal in Favor of That Class of Americans Called African* by the writer and
abolitionist Lydia Maria Child (1802–80) was published in Boston by Allen and Ticknor
in 1833.

5. The four letters by "Mott" had appeared in the *Liberator* on 18 January 1834, 11, 25
January 1834, 13–14, 1 February 1834, 19, and 22 February 1834, 30.

6. The Quaker John Greenleaf Whittier (1807–92) was a poet, journalist, and abolitionist. His letter of 10 January 1834 (*JGW,* 1:136–40) had appeared in the *Liberator* (18
January 1834, 10). In it he criticized the timidity and hypocrisy of Northerners in dealing with slavery and called for open, civil discussion with Southerners on that institution.

7. Moses Brown (1738–1836), a Quaker merchant and abolitionist from Rhode Island,
had been born on 12 September. Edward Hicks (1780–1849), a cousin of Elias Hicks, was
a Pennsylvania farmer and itinerant painter.

8. George Truman (c. 1798–1877) was a dentist and Hicksite minister from Philadelphia. Ruthy Buffum (d. 1866), her husband, Israel Buffum (1787–1874), and Preserved
Sprague had all been members of the Lynn Preparative Meeting, part of Salem Monthly Meeting. Israel Buffum and Sprague had been disowned in 1822, William Luscomb
in 1828, and Ruthy Buffum in 1833, after having been absent from the meeting for several years. The meeting from which they had recently left, then, was probably some other
group they had joined or formed (Salem Monthly Meeting, men's minutes, 1811–23, and
Salem Monthly Meeting, women's minutes, 1815–46, New England Yearly Meeting Archives, Rhode Island Historical Society Library; see also LCM to James Mott Sr., 15 March
1822, above). The Swedenborgians followed the teachings of Emanuel Swedenborg (1688–
1772), a Swedish mystic and philosopher. Swedenborg had written that all physical phe-
nomena have a spiritual correspondence and that both reside in human beings. He considered Christ not divine but rather an exemplary human being.

9. William Rotch Jr. (1759–1850), the son of a Nantucket and New Bedford Quaker
whaling merchant by the same name, was a merchant and the clerk of the New England Yearly Meeting, 1788–1818. Rotch's sister, Elizabeth Rotch Rodman (1757–1856), along
with her son Benjamin Rodman (1794–1876) had, as New Light Quakers, challenged the

"Old Light" Quakers in 1823 (Frederick B. Tolles, "The New-Light Quakers of Lynn and New Bedford," *New England Quarterly* 32 [September 1959]: 306–14; John M. Bullard, *The Rotches* [Milford, N.H.: Cabinet Press, 1947], 71–72, 451–52).

 10. Henry Willis's brother, John Willis (1790–1864), and his wife, Mary Kirby Willis (c. 1787–1873), lived in Jericho.

 11. Samuel Mott (1773–1864) married Catharine Appleby (1775–1862).

 12. A brother of Phebe Post Willis, the abolitionist Isaac Post (1798–1872) and his second wife, Amy Kirby Post (1802–89), lived in Scipio, New York. Benjamin Ferris (1780–1867) was the clerk of the Philadelphia Hicksite meeting and a leader in the separation of 1827 (Ingle, 58–59).

## To James Miller McKim

Philada. 5 Mo. 8th.—1834

My dear friend J. M. M'Kim

 Thine by H. Duffield was received yesterday.— I did not learn who he was before he left the door— —hope however we shall yet see him, as he told Maria [*Mott*] he would call today— — He didn't mention where he put up, or we would send for the package of books, and not trouble him to bring them.—

 By him I send a specimen of our 'Anti Slavery Sweets'— Our girls desire me to clear them of the suspicion of composing the rhymes, as they are not ambitious of the talent display'd, they were mostly written by the pupils of S. Pugh's school— Chandler, the editor of the 'United States Gazette' furnished a few,[1]—also a friend of abolition in Bucks Co.—Saml Johnson, 70 years of age.—

 I cannot doubt that the good feeling subsisting between us hitherto in our discussions, will continue, in any future examination of subjects, even should we find ourselves not so nearly united in sentiment as we anticipated last winter.—

 When my husband called on Wm. Furness[2] to enquire where he should find the controversy, thou wished to see, he read parts of thy letter to him, which induced a desire for a correspondence with thee— —he wished the same suggested to thee when if it was agreeable to thee—he expected thee to signify it by writing to him first. He has called here several times since & enquired after thee.— — He is becoming increasingly interested in the Abolition cause & we hope it will ere long be with him a pulpit theme—

 Last week we had the renewed pleasure of a visit from Wm. L. Garrison—he passed several days in the City—addressed the coloured people at the Wesleyan & Bethel churches.—would have delivered a public address—had he met with more encouragement from our timid Philada. Abolitionists— he was even discouraged in the desire he felt to say a few words to our young men on the evening of their forming themselves into a Society.—[3] he was present but at the request of one or two took no part—they thinking the feeling here of opposition, to his zeal & ardent measures in the cause, was such, that it would be rather a disadvantage.— How much more congenial with my feelings, was the noble appeal on his behalf made by Lewis Tappan & others at the Convention!— —[4] This is not known out of his particular circle & I have some doubts since I began of the propriety of mentioning it— So please say nothing about it— It appears to me Important that he should have the countenance & support of his friends, he expects to come again in a month or 6 weeks & deliver public addresses here— — Two young Theological students from the Lane Seminary—Thome & Stanton—also passed thro' the city—delegates to the great Antislavery Mg. in New York—[5] We passed an evening with them & Wm. L. Garrison & Phelps, of Boston at our friend Jas. Forten's & were highly interested in their relation of circumstances.—[6] The cause is certainly making rapid progress—we may yet live to see the desire of our Souls, with regard to this oppressed people.—

A letter was received from Benj Lundy[7] a week since, dated at Cincinnatti— he has strong hopes of ultimate success in his project—but had to come back thus far for a supply of funds— A number of his friends will be likely to unite & furnish him with the sum required— —

Thomas Chandler deceased lately a few miles below Wilmington—he has left from 15 to $20,000 to be applied to the education of colored children on the Manual labor plan— Benj. Ferris is one of the executors, he will however be likely to have some [trou]ble [*ms. damaged*] from the nephews of the deceased, who are try[ing to] [*ms. damaged*] set aside the will on the plea of insanity— which he [thi]nks [*ms. damaged*] they will find a difficulty in proving— —

If thy expectation of coming to the City next week should be realised—I can assure thee it will give us great pleasure to see thee—& again have a free interchange of sentiments—such as we cannot so fully enjoy on paper—

Our family are in usual health except the two youngest Elizh. & Martha who are recovering from a light attack of scarlet fever— Elizh. has also had the mumps— —

All unite in affecte. remembrance

Thy frd—     L. Mott—

ALS PSCHi-Mott
Env, written in another hand: "J. Miller Mc.Kim, Carlisle, Penn. pr H. Duffield"

1. "Anti Slavery Sweets" probably refers to mottos or short poems that accompanied candies from free produce stores (Bacon, 41). Joseph R. Chandler (1792–1880) published the *United States Gazette* from 1826 to 1847.

2. William Henry Furness (1802–96) was a Philadelphia Unitarian clergyman and theologian.

3. The Philadelphia Anti-Slavery Society was formed on 30 April (Dwight L. Dumond, *A Bibliography of Antislavery in America* [Ann Arbor, Michigan: University of Michigan Press, 1967], 92).

4. Lewis Tappan (1788–1873), a New York City merchant, was a founder of the New York Anti-Slavery Society and the AASS. At the December meeting of the latter society, defending Garrison against charges that his goal of immediate emancipation was imprudent, Tappan had said: "What is prudence? Is it succumbing to a majority of our frail

fellow mortals? . . . That man is imprudent who is afraid to speak as God commands him to speak, when the hour of danger is near" (*Liberator,* 21 December 1833, 102).

5. The AASS was to meet on 6 May. Addressing the adjourned meeting of the society on 8 May, both Henry B. Stanton and James A. Thome (1809–73) would denounce the colonization of African Americans (*Liberator,* 17 May 1834, 79).

6. Amos A. Phelps (1804–47) was a New England minister and abolitionist. James Forten (1766–1842) was a prosperous sailmaker in Philadelphia.

7. Benjamin Lundy (1789–1839), an old friend of LCM and JM and an abolitionist, was no doubt soliciting funds for his Baltimore-based *Genius of Universal Education.* It ceased publication in 1835.

## To Phebe Post Willis

Philada. 9 Mo. 13th. 1834—

I hope my dear P. P. W. is not in her heart accusing me of designed neglect in so long delaying to acknowledge the receipt of hers—so acceptable—last Spring— I will not use the time & paper now to apologise or offer excuses will only try to do better in future— Rachel Brown will leave the City in a day or two—after letting us have a little peep at her— she shortens her stay owing to anxiety about her husband & frds. in New York—while the Cholera is producing so much mortality there— how affecting was the sudden removal of Jacob—Corlies!—his wife on a visit to her Father—[1] Our City is very healthy thus far— My Jas. had an attack of fever a week since & his head affected as it was when he had that long illness but with prompt remedies—cupping &c—health was restored without the Drs. aid— Dr. Moore has been confined to the house & much of the time to his bed these three weeks past—with rheumatism or gout affecting his shoulder & back—he has been much reduced & is now slowly recovering  Others of our friends well—how is it with you?, for the time is long that we hear nothing from you, only by inquiry of our N. York frds. Cousin Josiah Macy[2] made us a short visit & from him we learned all we could of your welfare— The pamphlet of Elias's [*Hicks*] I received, and felt with thee, as if there must be something more— I have since looked over the volume of his letters hoping to collect something then tho' I dont know that we need be anxious about it, when we see the same principle at work with his successors under other names & producing consistent fruits too— I cant restrain the wish at times, that he could have lived to see this cause spread as it has. There are able defenders springing up in many parts of the country & going to the root of the evil too by writing & practicing too on the consistency of abstinence from Slave labor— We hope Josh. Beale will do well by his business notwithstandg all his discouragements— Is it your opinion that the late outrages & all the opposition we meet with will temporarily hinder the progress of the work?—or will it tend rather to the furtherance thereof—[3] I want to see us in no wise—terrified of our adversaries which is to them an evident token of perdition &c—& have we to experience that some of our veriest adversaries—are those of our own household.— I fear 'twill prove too true, that the opposition to a unity of labor in this holy cause will be as fully manifested by the members of our society from whom we should look for better things—as from those professedly hostile to abolition— I hope I err in this view of the subject—but it is not without cause I judge attempts are already made to proscribe the subject altogether from our galleries— I think I am aware of the need of caution in introducing it without a clear evidence of a requiring so to do—for to those deeply interested therein, it is an exciting subject—hence—I willingly receive cautionary hints but proscription I cannot bear—we have suffered enough from such attempts in years past— I can never willingly submit— Wm. Penn said he hated "obedience upon authority without conviction"—dont conclude from the above that there is any serious want of unity among us—it is only from the desire with some to pass smoothly along in this time of 'party spirit,' as they consider it—& thus they would have us "cry peace, peace, where there is no peace"—[4] Cousin Josiah when here appeared very confident that *Friends* had nothing to do in these Anti Slavery movements in conjunction with Reverends &c of other Societies & if we could see frds. marching onward, in the cause—as formerly many did— I might unite with him—but taking us as we are—I never more cordially nor more peacefully gave the right hand of fellowship to any congregated body than to that Noble Convention of pleaders in the cause of suffering humanity last winter— We have since had repeated opportunities of intercourse with the members of Antislavery Societies from different parts— & the evidence given of "truth speaking the same language in all however scattered"—(a favorite epistolary expression with us) has rejoiced my heart—[5]

That fine young man Thome from Lane Seminary—whose speech in New York was so thrilling—made his home with us & delivered addresses here in the City—which several of our orthodox frds. attended and were much pleased— Abm. L. Pennock[6] came to me after one of them & asked how much he should give—he afterward called on Thome here & spent the eve after 5 years absence from our house—said he had not had his Abolition feelings so aroused for 9 years—presented 100 New testaments to the schools for cold childn. in Cincinnatti—& the next day sent a note to Amos A. Phelps the author of those admirable "Lectures on slavery & its remedy"—who also was stayg. with us—directg. him to draw on him for fifty dollars—believg. it right to give that sum to the Anti S. society

Saml. Emlen of Burlington also called & handed $15— Thos. Kite introduced the subject of the late sufferings of our poor colored brethren into Arch St. Mo. Mg.—seconded by Saml. Bettle & Thos. Stewardson[7]—all of whom made some pertinent remarks on the subject— Thos. has since taken pains to recommend the perusal of "Mrs. Childs Appeal" to his young frds.—now such things I like to hear let them come from which side the house they will but to our shame be it spoken that while some of us are drawing back unto perdition—

many others are pressing onward & will be mainly instruments in breakg. the chains of the oppressed—by their faithfulness in honestly attacking the prejudices of the oppressed— If you know Gerritt Smith an influential man in your State a great advocate in the temperance cause—and a reputed Colonizationist—let me whisper in your ears as it has been in mine that he has come over to the Abolition ranks and is preparing to come out— I felt sure last winter when I read his speeches at Washington at the Colonization Mg.—that he was not far from the kingdom of Abolition—have you read J. G. Birneys letter—[8] I dont want to fill my paper with this subject tho I confess it is an engrossing one— We have had another visit from our young Carlisle friend J. M. M'Kim—& we have also kept up a regular correspondence since— he finds he cant give up all his outward props as easily as he thought he could tho he acknowledges his views have undergone a change since his conferences with us— he has produced considerable sentiment in his neighbord. by lecturing on the subject of Sl[aver]y & Dr. Parrish too has been drawn in rather unintentionally at Columbia A young Colonizationist in a lecture there had represented the 'blacks' here as a nuisance—the Dr. going there soon afterwards & knowg. so well the contrary thot. he would deliver an address in defence of the character of our colored citizens—& was urged so to do— he procured the necessary documents from here & notified the people of his intentions—or rather a col[ore]d. man residg. there gave public notice of it—when a few who were hostile to the people of color—thratened a mob—which when Dr. P. was informed of— he promptly refused to have any thing to say to them— the excitement however was kept up 2 or 3 nights & some damage done to the property of the said colored man— these things have rather alarmed Dr. P. & a few weeks since Prudence Crandall (Phillio)—came here with the intention of giving up her school at Canterbury & opening a day school for col[ore]d childn. in this City—[9] we went round among them & soon had 50 scholars engaged @ $4 per quarter—but the Dr. & some others were apprehensive of the consequences & discouraged her comg for the present  she will wait till after our Elections are past—when if nothing unfavorable occurs she contemplates movg. here— Our female Society had appointed a committee to look out for a suitable teacher & try to get up such a school before we had heard of her intention of coming— We have devoted several days to visiting all the schools in the city & found such a one was much needed

J & self have been down among our poor sufferers by the late riots & found much injury done to their property—say to the amot. of 5 or $6000—[10] Jas. is one of a committee of a town Mg. called to investigate the subject & report the amot. of damages— they are to meet tomorrow eveg. when it is to be hoped something will be raised for their reliefs— I recd. some weeks since a long letter 3 sheets from our friend Elisha Fry at Lynn—setting forth his trials & discouragements— it seems he has left John Alley & has but a poor opinion of him & some others there—& feeling so much alone he would like to come this

way & settle if there was any opening for business for him—[11] I wish there was—
he says he feels entirely alone on the earth—& wants to open his mind to some
one— his wife & childn. have had repeated attacks of illness—& his own life
despaired of— they feel as strangers in a strange land— he reminds me that
he could not unite in the desire expressed when we were there that they should
have a Mg.—& tho some may blame him for not helping to keep it up, he must
bear it patiently as he endeavored to his other trials—but he knew how things
stood with those poor bewildered scattered wandering creatures &c—& thot.
he could be of no use to them in a Mg. capacity— If I have an opportunity
after I have answered the letter I will send it to thee as he writes freely of the
situation of many we met there— he acknowledges the reception of the books
which were just what he wanted— he desires his love to thee & to Uncle Samuel

Ruthy Buffum has also written lately—says she is "twice dead plucked up
by the roots"—their Mg. is dropped but was kept up long enough to get her
disowned—her daughr. is soon to be married— Amos Peasley has a prospect
of going there—[12] Lois Purinton's satisfaction I understood to be in Sweden-
borgian views—

From all we can learn from N Bedford we conclude that Mg is satisfactorily
kept up & rather increases— We expect our Mother & Aunt P. Hussey will be
there this fall on their return from N—t where they have spent 2 months—when
we shall hear particularly from our friends there— We had a visit of a day from
Thos. & Eunice Macy after they had attended your quarty. Mg. in the Spring—
Phebe Hussey often speaks of her visit to you with pleasure & desired me to give
her love affectionately to you  she occasionally attends our Mg but not regularly— John Comly has gone to Ohio and Indiana to be absent 5 months—if he
has not read Job Scott's writings[13] so much as to get in a low spot & turn back—
he wrote quite discouragingly to Wm. Wharton lately  Benjn. Price is with him—
since he left home Charles Comly has lost their youngest child about a year old—
Anna & Emmor Comly have marriage in prospect—the former to John Bowman—the latter to Johns sister Hannah Bowman—both very suitable—[14] Thou
asks what we think of the appearances of Ann Chapmans son— he appears
wholly dedicated to his Master & improves in his manner of speaking— he is
at times rather *lengthy* for a new beginner but I believe his frds. think he will
get along he & his br. are very industrious & seem desirous of supportg. their
Mother more comfortably than she has been  they have moved near us & are
better fixed than ever before here  Lydia White[15] is going to board there— Our
childn. go to school in the same house to Martha Jones who boards with Ann—
They are expectg. a visit from Jemima Reese this fall— We shall be glad to see
her here— We heard an interestg. accot. of your new yearly Mg— Dr. Parrish's 2 sons were there  George Truman has just gone to attend the opening of
Fishing Creek half year's Mg.

[*P.S.*] Anna [*Hopper*] has been laughing at my uninteresting sheet  she says
there is only one subject in it— I have not answered all thy inquiries but con-

clude thou hast had other opportunities of hearg. from Philada since the date of thine

Priscilla Townsends daughr.[16] has been confined to her bed the last 6 weeks—her spine so much affected that they wish to try that means of restoration— Debh. Whartons child has recovered from those attacks— Edwd. & Anna are still with us—they are in haste now to get to housekeeping—but have to wait till the tenants year is up at the house where Edwds. store is— Anna with our Elizh. & Martha boarded several weeks at Charles Comly's thro' the warm weather our Thos. has been 8 weeks near West Chester at Benjn. Price's learng. to work

Sister Eliza desires her love she & her family are well—our daughrs. too join J. & self in affectionate remembrances to our Long Island cousins— The information thou gave of the several families whom we so pleasantly visited when there was acceptable do write soon again— how is thy dear sister Lydia—

If I had known I had so much to say I would have written closer for I dont like cross lining— H. Williams[17] & self attended all the Mgs. of the Southern Quarter—& witnessed the blight of Slavery over the land— Jas & self have since been to Caln Qr. & attended the mg of the Anti-Slavery Society composed of men & women in that neighborhood—except those visits I have been at home

Thine in much affection    LM
J & L Motts love specially to
uncle S. Mott & Aunt Caty

ALS NRU

Env: "Henry Willis, For P. P. W.—, Jericho, Long Island, attention of R. N. Brown"

1. Rachel Hopper Brown (c. 1798–1887) was a daughter of Isaac T. Hopper. Jacob Corlies and Hannah Corlies (c. 1780–1866) were members of the Hicksite New York Monthly Meeting. Jacob had died on 4 September 1834 at age fifty-six.

2. Josiah Macy (1785–1872) was a member of the Hicksite New York Monthly Meeting.

3. Joseph Beale was also a member of the Hicksite New York Monthly Meeting. By "late outrages" LCM may be referring to the suit that Orthodox Quakers in New York had brought in October 1833 against the Hicksites to reclaim all property belonging to the Society of Friends at the time of the 1828 separation. The Orthodox Monthly Meeting claimed it was the true Quaker organization, while the Hicksites argued that they had been seeking a compromise since the separation (*Statement of the Efforts Made by Friends, to Effect an Amicable Settlement with the Orthodox* [New York: n.p., c. 1833], 1–8; *Summary Statement Facts, on Affirmation, Submitted to the Vice Chancellor* [New York, c. 1834], 5, 15, 21, 24).

4. Jer. 6:14.

5. "Noble Convention of pleaders" is a reference to the founding meeting of the AASS on 4–6 December 1833. LCM's reference to "truth speaking the same language in all however scattered" is possibly an adaptation of Gen. 11:1: "And the whole earth was of one language, and of one speech."

6. Abraham L. Pennock (1786–1868) was a Quaker merchant and antislavery leader.

7. Thomas Kite (1785–1845) was an Orthodox Quaker printer (*Memoir of Thomas Kite*

[Philadelphia: Friends Book Store, 1883]). Samuel Bettle (c. 1774–1861) was a tailor, an Orthodox Quaker, and the clerk of the Philadelphia Yearly Meeting, 1817–31. Thomas Stewardson (c. 1762–1841) was a wealthy Orthodox Quaker (Ingle, 22, 24).

8. At the American Colonization Society Meeting in Washington in January 1834, the New York philanthropist Gerrit Smith (1797–1874) had expressed concern about a perception that the society "obstructs the progress of emancipation." Smith had admitted that criticism of the society as *"deficient in pity for the free people of color"* had some merit. He had argued that African Americans should not be forced to immigrate to Liberia (*Liberator,* 8 February 1834, 22). In his lengthy letter to Rev. Thornton J. Mills of the Kentucky Colonization Society, the lawyer James G. Birney (1792–1857) had stated that since his views on colonization had changed, he could not accept the position of vice president in that organization. Among Birney's objections to colonization was its premise that immigration was the only solution to the problem of slavery. Colonization also, wrote Birney, "has *taken up and sustained* the vital principle of slavery, when it declares that *slavery now is right.* . . . It gives favor to an unscriptural, therefore unreasonable, prejudice against the colored man" (*Liberator,* 16 August 1834, 129–31).

9. Dr. Joseph Parrish (1779–1840) was the president of the Pennsylvania Society for Promoting the Abolition of Slavery and the Mott family's physician. Prudence Crandall Phillio (1803–89) had tried to establish a school for black girls in Canterbury, Connecticut, but was discouraged by townspeople and the state legislature.

10. The *Liberator* (23 August 1834, 136) had reported that forty-four buildings, including two churches, in the region of Seventh, Baker, and Small Streets had been destroyed by rioters apparently targeting the residences of Philadelphia African Americans.

11. Elisha Fry (1789–1849), a carriage maker, had moved to Lynn in 1833 (Ellen Frye Barker, *Frye Genealogy* [New York: Tobias Wright, 1929], 19, 25).

12. In 1828 Amos Peaslee had supported Elias Hicks when the Ohio Yearly Meeting divided (Bliss Forbush, *Elias Hicks: Quaker Liberal* [New York: Columbia University Press, 1956], 270–72).

13. Thomas Macy (c. 1787–1864) and Eunice Coffin Macy (b. 1788) were Nantucket Quakers (MNHi records). With his emphasis on the spiritual resources within individuals, Job Scott (1751–93) of Providence, Rhode Island, had precipitated the Quaker reform movement of the 1820s (Ingle, 7–9).

14. William Wharton (1790–1856), a Hicksite Quaker, married Deborah Fisher Wharton (1795–1888), a Hicksite Quaker minister of Ninth and Spruce Street Meeting. Benjamin Price (1793–1872) was a Chester County Quaker (*Golden Wedding of Benjamin and Jane Price* [Philadelphia: J. B. Lippincott, 1870]). The children of John Comly were Charles (1808–94), Ann (1806–72), and Emmor (1811–89); the latter's wife was Hannah Bowman Comly (1815–50) (Comly Genealogy, PSCHi).

15. Lydia White (1788–1871), a Hicksite Quaker and the librarian of the PFASS, was active in the free produce movement.

16. The Hicksite Quakers Priscilla Kirk and Charles Townsend had four daughters.

17. Hannah Williams (1784–1848), an elder and overseer at Plymouth Meeting (Hicksite), ran a boarding school in Plymouth (*Memoir of Jesse and Hannah Williams* [Philadelphia: Wm. H. Pile, 1875], 59–62, 202).

## To Phebe Post Willis

Philada 9 Mo. 2nd. 1835

My dear Phebe

I have not even so good an excuse as thou in thy kindness admitted for me, that I have not written before— the day after we parted I told Jas. I should begin a sheet immediately to tell thee how we fared after you parted from us—but I let one time after another pass until now—so I must try to be as agreeable as I can to make up for it— In the first place I will acknowledge the reception of thy acceptable letter by Willet Robbins, who we were in hopes would have come to see us—but were disappointed[1] We were interested with all the particulars thou gave us of our friends on Long Island— We didn't doubt you would find all things had gone on well in your absence and I suppose you might have made a longer visit— As it proved we were glad we had not succeeded in inducing you to go to Peterborro'—for we did not find Gerritt Smith at home— the school too was smaller than we expected to see—only about 13—several more expected in a few days— we were however much interested in witnessing the exercises of the pupils who were mostly young Men— We arrived there over a rough & uninteresting road—in time to go into the school while our supper was preparing— they work on the farm & in the garden the middle of the day & have school early in the Morng & late in the afternoon— the teacher, an intelligent Scotchman & an Abolitionist— G. Smith attends the Meetings of the Anti Slavery Society in that place—but as yet takes no active part— After tea we walked up to his house, a large beautiful place, with pleasure grounds handsomely laid out—fine garden &c— they were all absent except a housekeeper—havg left that morng to visit their relatives at the West & perhaps attend the Temperance Convention at Buffalo—[2] some of their neighbrs. & an intimate friend came in & made us welcome—had some strawberries prepared with *free* sugar & cream— they told us the family had pretty much come to the conclusion to use no more Slave produce— he is much respected in the place & has a large property there—the proceeds of which enables him to aid greatly in benevolent objects— James left a note for him—expressive of the object of our visit & invitg him to come & see us when he passed again thro' our City— we returned to the Tavern to lodge—rose early the next morng & rode back to Chittenanga to breakfast— a Stage soon came along nearly filled with delegates to the Temperance Convention—just room for us & we had a pleasant day's journey back to Auburn— — Joshua Leavitt an Abolition Editor—was one of the number—[3] We concluded the pleasant compy of that day made up for our disappointment— we reached Auburn in time to hire a conveyance to Aurora that night—arrived before dark— Jeffries had called & let them know Jas.'s intention of returng— Anna & Hannah[4] were very glad to see him because they were not quite satisfied to be left to stay so long—and I was much better pleased for Jas. to lengthen his visit a little than for him to hurry home with scarcely seeing br. David [*Wright*]'s family— We improved the time well till the follow 2nd. day when as Isaac [*Post*] wrote thee they left us there to stay three weeks longer—but in consequence of a letter Eliza recd from Benjn. [*Yarnall*] we shortened our visit a week— Our time was very pleasantly passed—but it will be twice told I presume to state particulars as from what our Mother writes we suppose you have Isaac and Amy [*Post*] with you— They will tell you how nicely we succeeded in getting to the Ridge Anti S. Mg notwithstandg our kind John Merritt held us by the wheel so long— it always calls forth a smile when I recur to that evenings ride—for till we turned the corner from the village—I was in fear that we should be called back—& very gratifying it was to attend that Meetg— We hope you are planning a visit to this City with Isaac and Amy— we should be exceedingly pleased to see you here—and would do all in our power to make it pleasant— — We shall not soon forget their many kindnesses to us— Altho' we have so lately met & paid many pleasant visits together— I some times feel as if we had few good opportunities to talk over former days &.c. and as J. & self have no prospect of seeing Long Island soon—I think you can do no less than persuade Isaac & Amy to accompany you here— We can then recur together to the events of this summer, which afford a pleasant & peaceful retrospect— — We were quite disposed to visit you on our way home & I proposed it to Eliza & Maria [*Mott*]— E said she had hoped that we should have a day to spare that we might pass it with you—but all the arrangements were made to receive us at home at that time & it seemed best to make no stop— We found our house cleaned & ready for our reception— Anna & Hannah Wharton here to meet us—& every thing connected with home looked pleasant— After a week's rest & enjoyment of our friends we again shut up house— Maria went out & passed a few days at Wm. Wharton's & we went to West Chester to see our Thos. at Benjn Price's—then to Concord Qy Mg were absent 4 or 5 days— on our return Maria went to Mount Holly with E. Hopper & brot. our childn. home—so that our family began to look of some consequence Our cousin Saml. Mott[5] came & passed a few days with us—also a cousin arrived from Liverpool—and the last week we have had cousin Rebecca [*Bunker*] from Mount Holly— she will leave us tomorrow for New York & by her I shall send this— We have had several Abolition friends from Boston to visit us—but not many public meetgs— the evg we arrived home we went to hear the Anniversary Address of the British Emancipation—delivered by 2 young men—one from Boston—but the late excitement has induced our Men's society to suspend their Meetgs a few weeks—[6] We doubt not that good will eventually come of all this present evil—and we already see some symptoms of a reaction in the public mind—and I hope we shall pursue "the even tenor of our way"—"not soon shaken in mind" or moved with fear[7] We hear of new Societies forming in various parts of the country—so that there is no cause of discouragement & if Friends will only keep pace with the advance of public sentiment on the subject—I will have no controversy with them relative to their uniting their efforts in Society capacity with those they are pleased to call "the world"— More than this I want they should read C. Marriott's arguments on our inconsistency in the use of Slave produce—so that we may cleanse ourselves from this unrighteousness— — — I was right glad to hear of S. Archer's[8] scruples and hope he will attend to them  there is no other way of advancement than by individual faithfulness— Aunt L[ydia]. is able to endure hardness as a good Soldier— it is by misunderstandg & mispresentg her that she has so many opposers—

5th. day Morn 3rd.

I have to hasten this to a clo[se] [*ms. damaged*] we have the company of our frds. David L. Child[9] & his wife Maria—the Authors of the Anti-Slavery works which you have seen— they arrived last evening & will pass a few days with us—

I can only add much love to all our frds. Eliza desires hers affecy tendered— & our girls too as well as their Father send kind remembrances— — Write soon & tell us whether you will come— I have no City news worth penning—

AL NRU Env: "Henry Willis, Jericho, For P. P. W., Long Island"

1. Willet Robbins (1781–1861) was a member of the Jericho Monthly Meeting and a New York City merchant.

2. Smith had opened the Peterboro Manual Labor School for African Americans in 1834 with Colquhoun Grant as instructor (Milton C. Sernett, *Abolition's Axe* [Syracuse: Syracuse University Press, 1986], 42). The semiannual meeting of the New York State Temperance Society had been held in Buffalo on 9–10 July 1835 (*Buffalo Commercial Advertiser*, 6–16 July 1835).

3. Joshua Leavitt (1794–1873) was a Congregational minister and newspaper editor.

4. Anna Hopper had been visiting in Aurora with Hannah Wharton (1818–93), daughter of Deborah Fisher Wharton and William Wharton, who would marry Robert Haydock in 1843 (LCM to Anna Coffin, August 6, 1835, MNS).

5. This Samuel Mott is either JM's cousin (1775–1845) or a cousin by the same name from New York City (d. 1859; LCM to MCW, 3 August 1859, Mott Manuscripts, PSCHi).

6. The Young Men's Anti-Slavery Society of Philadelphia had announced a "public" antislavery meeting for 1 August at which Samuel L. Gould of Boston was scheduled to speak (*United States Gazette*, 1 August 1835, 2). After two black men had tried to kill two whites, rioting erupted in the vicinity of Catherine and Eighth Streets in Philadelphia in late July (*Liberator*, 25 July 1835, 120).

7. The first quotation is possibly an adaptation of Thomas Gray's "Elegy in a Country Churchyard" (l. 76): "The noiseless tenor of their way." "Not soon shaken in mind" is from 2 Thess. 2:2.

8. Charles Marriott (d. 1843) wrote *An Address to the Members of the Religious Society of Friends, on the Duty of Declining the Use of the Products of Slave Labour* (New York: I. T. Hopper, 1835). Stephen Archer was a member of the Hicksite New York Monthly Meeting.

9. David L. Child (1794–1874), a lawyer and journalist, was the husband of Lydia Maria Child.

## To the Anti-Slavery Societies and Friends of the
## Oppressed Generally

*Philadelphia, Nov.* 10, 1836.

Respected and Beloved Friends:

Believing that you are always ready for every good word and work in the cause of emancipation, we hail with grateful joy this opportunity of commending to your attention and kind offices, our beloved sister, Angelina E. Grimké.[1] As she comes among you the authorized Agent of the American Anti-Slavery Society, and as in many places her works have preceded her, it is necessary for us only to express our approval of her course, and our earnest prayers for her prosperity.

Where our friend is known, no "letters of commendation" from us will be necessary to insure her a welcome reception. To those who do not know her, we would say, that as a friend of the slave, and a fearless champion of human rights, she is worthy to be received and esteemed very highly in love for her works' sake. She is entering a new field of labor, and will meet with peculiar difficulties. She must encounter not only the sneers of the heartless multitude, which are the portion of every faithful abolitionist, but grave charges of infractions of the laws of female delicacy and propriety, will doubtless be preferred against her by a more serious class of the community. This will be hard to bear! How hard, they know who have endured it. While, then, our sister is willing to dedicate herself to this arduous part of the work, and for Christ's sake and the gospel's, welcomes the keen reproach and bitter contempt incident to it, we entreat you to give her your support, your sympathy, and your prayers.

From this dear member of our Society we part with mingled feelings of joy and sorrow, commending her to God and the word of his grace—trusting that amid the perils of her way, she will find relief and encouragement in your friendship and confidence, and earnestly praying that He who "makes the wrath of man to praise him,"[2] and restrains the remainder thereof, will cause all things to work for her good, and for the prosperity of the blessed cause in which our hearts are so firmly united.

Signed on behalf of
the Philadelphia Anti-Slavery Society,
Esther Moore, *President.*
Lucretia Mott, *V. President.*
Sarah Pugh, *Rec. Secretary.*
Sidney Ann Lewis, *Librar'n.*
Mary Grew, *Cor. Secretary.*
Lydia B. Pierce.                      Mary C. Pennock,
Sarah L. Forten,                     Sarah Lewis,

Lydia White,                          Grace Douglass,
Susan Grew,                           Charlotte Forten,
Mary Needles.                         Hetty Reckless,
Olive W. Bacon,                       Hetty Burr.[3]

PL *National Enquirer,* 19 November 1836, 42

1. Angelina Grimké (1805–79) was the Quaker daughter of South Carolina slaveholders and an intermittent member of the PFASS. At a meeting on 11 November 1836, Grimké would inform the PFASS that she had decided to become an agent of the AASS, "for the purpose of advancing the object of our Societies by traveling throughout the land and by conversation or otherwise giving expositions of the views held by Abolitionists" (PFASS minutes, Pennsylvania Abolition Society Papers, reel 30, PHi).

2. LCM is adapting Ps. 76:10: "Surely the wrath of man shall praise thee."

3. White members of the PFASS not previously identified are Esther Moore (1774–1854), a Hicksite Quaker and the wife of Dr. Robert Moore; Orthodox Quaker Sidney Anne Lewis (c. 1795–1882), the owner of a free produce store that opened in 1836; Mary Grew (1813–96), a graduate of Hartford Female Seminary, a journalist, and a woman's rights activist; Susan Grew (1804–81), the half-sister of Mary Grew; Mary Needles (1787?–1873), a wealthy Quaker and the wife of the abolitionist Edward Needles; Olive Bacon (d. 1874), the wife of B. C. Bacon; and Mary C. Pennock, possibly a Quaker of West Chester (c. 1807–86) or a Quaker of Coatesville (c. 1801–91). The black members are Sarah L. Forten (1814–?), a poet who in 1838 married Joseph Purvis, the brother of the prominent abolitionist Robert Purvis; her mother, Charlotte Forten (1784–1884), wife of James Forten; Sarah Lewis, who taught school with Sarah Pugh; Grace Bustill Douglass (d. 1842), a Quaker and the wife of the prosperous barber Robert Douglass; Hetty Reckless (1776–1881), active in the Underground Railroad and temperance and anti-prostitution movements and a promoter of black sabbath schools; and Hetty Burr, a founder of the PFASS and the wife of John P. Burr (1792–?), a barber and a leader in Philadelphia's black community. (Biographical sources include Jean Fagan Yellin and John C. Van Horne, eds., *The Abolitionist Sisterhood: Women's Political Culture in Antebellum America* [Ithaca, N.Y.: Cornell University Press, 1994], 71, 80, 161, 164, 278; Peter C. Ripley, ed., *Black Abolitionist Papers* [Chapel Hill: University of North Carolina Press, 1991], 3:91, 145; *WLG*, 3:60, 4:33, 529; Ira Brown, *Mary Grew: Abolitionist and Feminist* [Selinsgrove, Pa.: Susquehanna University Press, 1991], 13; Ruth Nuremberger, *The Free Produce Movement* [New York: AMS Press, 1942], 119; Shirley J. Yee, *Black Female Abolitionists: A Study in Activism, 1828–1860* [Knoxville: University of Tennessee Press, 1992], 82, 95, 98; Charles Blockson, *The Underground Railroad in Pennsylvania* [Jacksonville, N.C.: Flame International, 1981], 25; LCM to MML, 9 January 1874, Mott Manuscripts, PSCHi; *Friends' Review,* 15 April 1882, 570; and *Friends' Intelligencer,* 22 May 1886, 329, 25 July 1891, 473.)

## To James Miller McKim

[*Philadelphia 15 March 1838*]

[*Added to Anna M. Hopper's letter of the same date*]

Anna brought over her sheet so far filled, feeling as if it was too "forlorn" to send— She has left it however and I will devote an hour or so to pleasing communion with thee— Not that I have much to communicate from 'Highland farm'—else would a letter have been speedily forwarded immediately on our return.

The visit to us was particularly pleasant, much was done to render it so, by each member of the family. They had a house full of 'Friends' on our arrival there, including 5 of Emmor Kimber's family. I soon found that Sarah would have preferred our being there the next day, when they rarely had lodgers as all went towards their home after the Meetg. was over.[1] We had planned too to come as far as Downingtown & lodge at G. Massey's the next night, but Sarah at length resorted to an expedient which would oblige us to go back that we should leave our horse & carriage there & go to Meetg with them in their sleigh—this we readily acceded to & instead of 14 lodgers had only one a cousin of theirs who I thought had perhaps gone under the guise of relationship with other motives— he appeared to be a nice young man— Penquite Linton from Bucks Co. we found there—a widower thou knows— Gertrude K[imber]. was amused with the pains he took to let Sarah's Father know that he united with him in an argument between Emmor & him— Much was said against the influence of the 'Priests' in the Anti-Slavery cause— Micah. wondered that Jas. Mott could sign a pledge[2] as contained in the Declaration,' *to enlist the pulpit* in behalf of the oppressed  He had also noticed that 18 out of 24 whose names were advertised as agents were Reverends— We found his prejudices strong against that Class— tho he acknowledged Miller M'Kim was better than some of them— William [*Speakman*] took some pains to draw forth our opinion of "the young man"— I afterward learned from Sarah that he (Wm.) was made acquainted with circumstances. When we meet, which event is pleasantly anticipated, I will tell thee more of our conversation the next eveg when alone with him on the limits of Parental influence over children, on his unwillingness to part with Sarah &.c— and all this without a suspicion being excited that we had any cause for the remarks made— More than once I thought Sarah's characteristic openness & candor would have betray'd her— I was surprised to see him so unsuspecting  She improved every oppor[tunit]y. for a lone chat with me—and her freedom as before was truly grateful. She told me she had written once since her return home—in her sister's letter, but thought she should not again, as you were situated in relation to her Father. She shew'd me a letter to Rebecca[3] found on her arrival home containg. "pencillings by the way"— I thought the likeness good but told her when she came to the city again I would shew her one which tho' more flattered I thot. did the Artist more credit. We regretted not seeing Rebecca—she had been quite sick & was not able to be at her Father's—proposed our stayg another day & visitg her, but our arrangets. were such we cou [*ms. damaged*] The affection between Wm. & Sarah was as thou had described them & was '*very* [*ms. damaged*] their Mother too was kind & very clever—took Sarah's part in the conversa[tio]n. allud [*ms. damaged*] I admired Sarah's innocent willingness to run down towards the barn & sing, cold as it was, for our gratification in hearg. the echo—in the presence too of this said cousin of theirs— If thou had heard her there on your first acquaintance I should have almost concluded that it was thy organ of ideality, romance, tune or some other that was sweetly playd upon and inspired the immediate attachment—but stop— I dont mean to fill my paper with this subject pleasing tho' it may be— for I want room to acknowledge the reception of thy letter of last Mo. from Pittsburg & which I hoped to receive before we went to Caln. We were sorry to hear of thy havg a cold— Shall I copy for thee what Gertrude [*Kimber?*] says in a letter to Maria [*Davis*]—"How very interestg Miller M'Kim's letters were, in the last Emancipator. It as just like him to use no deception to obtain his purpose of seeing the prisons, and the keeper himself, if he should see the account cannot help but feel that there is one honorable Abolitionist at least."[4] She further says—"*All of us* think you shamefully neglected C. C. Burleigh & L. Gunn by allowg. the Cyrus to go to St. Domingo,[5] without either letter or paper, and we dont wonder they felt hurt— We hold you inexcusable— And they write to you so frequently— Does thee remember the letter where Lewis spoke of the women there being so fascinating?— One of the girls after readg. it exclaimed 'Well if I ever want to fascinate Lewis C. Gunn I'll look *black* at him'! Tell thy Mother that we have had a visit from Penquite & that he was not more captivating than he proved at frd. Speakmans, but was equally amusing." Dost thou know that Thos. Janney of Bucks Co. has proved so captivating to Mary Kimber as to induce her to yield her interest in that school & become his companion[6]—or did I mention this in my other letter? for I find I'm growing old— We have had a pleasant visit from Emmor lately—I'm just informed he is in town again today & Abby with him— J. G. Whittier we have here too—tho *we* are not much benefitted by his coming I mean personally— he was here the night he arrived & we expected he would abide with us awhile at least—but his friend Thayer[7] seemed to have a claim on him—he cal [*ms. damaged*] once since & assured us we should see enough of him & that is the last of him— The paper will speak for him in other respects— I never saw him more aggreeable than the last evening he passed here— Wm. Burleigh[8] is with us now takg a rest— he has had a bad cold for a few weeks past & has not been able to pursue his vocation— The eveg of his arrival they had a discussion with some Colonizationists in the session room of the new Hall in which he took part—it will be resumed next 4th. day eveg— They are workg with all speed to finish the Hall by the time *We* shall want it in the 5th. Month. We were pleading with the com. to let us have it at a lower rate than $25 a day— P. Wright[9] remarked that they might as well for he supposed it would have to come out of their pockets— I told him not before we had done our part by our own industry to place it there as the mutual or common depository.— How hard it is to correct the low estimate set on Woman's labors!— The Grimkes are doing a noble part in this great work—think of A.E.G. addressing the Mass. Legislar. for hours repeatedly!— Wm. H. Johnson[10] says "The unfetterg the Female intellect from the thraldom of prejudice I consider of even more value than the original object of A. S.

movements."— Apropos—hast thou seen the caricature at the print shops—
A post office the *Mistress* busily engaged with her female clerks assorting letters—one or more of them employed in peeping in at the ends—&c

Thank thee for the extracts from thy Diary—I believe thou wilt yet have
to let all thou hast learned "*at the feet of Gamaliel*"[11] go for what it is worth without going "from one form into another." The "Christians" may be a pious and
Christ-like sect, but I dont admire their numbering the Commandments.—
Whatsoever he—the Spirit of Truth biddeth us do, that we are to do, without
vainly seekg to ascertain the exact number of the Jewish or other written
commands. It is quite time we read & examined the Bible more rationally in
order that truth may shine in its native brightness. I dont wonder at thy doubts
of the propriety of occupying thy "station as Minister" in preaching any system of Faith and care not how soon thy Orthodox brethren detect thy heresies—tho' I shall be careful how I expose thee— I did tell Father Speakman
that thy religious or theological opinions had been for some years past undergoing a change—perhaps I said *a great* change— I want thee to have done
with calling Unitarian rationalities—"icy philosophizing"— Thou dont know
what thou may be thyself yet— I do consider the subject a serious one & thy
conclusions of great importance & pray that thou may be rightly directed in
thy decision.

Great excitement prevails among our Quaker Orthodox relative to J. J. Gurney.[12]—he has met with some opposition from an influential quarter—but a
large majority are in his favor— Edwd. H. is writg out some ½ doz. sermons—
taking advantage of this time to add a few dollars to his purse. Anna has no
suspicion of the reality of the case with S & thyself—nor has any member of
her family—

affecy &c    L. Mott

1st. day 19th—

This sheet has really seemed too frivolous to send & I have kept it a day or
two hesitatg but a short letter from thee to E M. D. recd. yesterday, expressive
of thy "*impatience*" induces me to forward it—let us hear from thee soon—when
shall we see thee? H[annah]. Wharton's aged Grandfather died last week—
Wm.'s wealth will be increased.[13] I suppose thou wilt hear thro' R. Potts whether
Sarah is coming to our Yearly Mg which commences the 8th. of next month—
She had not determined when we were there—her Mother is coming & thot.
she should need Sarah to wait on her about the City. E. M. Davis wished me to
inform thee that he had furnished Andrew[14] money to the amount of $59—
Andrew called here a few weeks since & seemed to feel neglected by his friends
in the way of writing— Edwd has been so much engaged in Henry's absence
that he says he has not had the time to extend the Fatherly care over Andrew
that thou desired  he has generally let him know what he has wanted money for
when he has called for it.

ALS PSCHi-Mott
Env: "James H. M'Kim, care of Dr. Joseph Gazzam, Pittsburg, Penna."

1. In her part of the letter Anna M. Hopper had described the visit of LCM and JM to the Speakman farm after attending Western and Caln Quarterly Meetings. James Miller McKim would propose to Sarah Speakman, a Lancaster County Quaker, in May 1838 and they would marry on 1 October 1840 (Bacon, 70; LCM to Richard D. Webb and Hannah Webb, 12 October 1840, MB; William Cohen, "James Miller McKim: Pennsylvania Abolitionist," Ph.D. diss., New York University, 1968, 164–65, 211).

2. Gertrude Kimber (d. 1869) would marry Charles C. Burleigh (1810–78) in 1842 (*NASS*, 4 December 1869, 3; Kimber Genealogy, PSCHi). Micajah Speakman (1781–1852) was Sarah's father (Dena Epstein, "Lucy McKim Garrison: American Musician," *Bulletin of the New York Public Library* 67 [October 1963]: 530). The "pledge as contained in the Declaration" possibly refers to the "Address of the Pennsylvania Anti-Slavery Society to the Ministers of the Gospel in the State of Pennsylvania." One minister's reply objecting to the address's criticism of clergy's timid response to slavery is contained in the *Liberator* (20 April 1838, 61).

3. Sarah's brother was possibly William Speakman (c. 1805–92) of Chester County, and Sarah's sister was Rebecca Potts (1803–82) of Pottstown (*Friend,* 20 May 1882, 328).

4. McKim's letters to Joshua Leavitt from a slave prison at Pittsburgh were also published in the *Pennsylvania Freeman.* In the second letter (published 15 March 1838, 1) McKim recounted his conversation with the keeper of the slave prison.

5. Lewis C. Gunn (1813–92) and Burleigh had left the United States on 28 November 1837 on a fact-finding trip, arriving in Haiti on 18 December 1837. Their reports on the condition of the Haitian people appeared in the *Pennsylvania Freeman.* In a letter published in the *Freeman* (1 March 1838, 97), Gunn had asked how his friends in Philadelphia would have let the *Cyrus* sail to St. Domingo without sending them any letters (*Pennsylvania Freeman,* 30 November 1837, 47, 8 February 1838, 86; Lewis C. Gunn, *Records of a California Family* [San Diego: n.p., 1928], 4–5).

6. Mary Kimber (1807–59), daughter of Emmor Kimber, would marry Thomas Janney (c. 1794–1879) of Bucks County (Kimber Genealogy, PSCHi; *Friends' Intelligencer,* 19 March 1859, 12, 22 February 1879, 26).

7. Abijah Wyman Thayer (1796–1864), a newspaper editor and a friend and benefactor of Whittier, had moved to Philadelphia in 1835 and convinced Whittier to follow him in 1838 (*JGW,* 1:8).

8. William H. Burleigh (1812–71), the brother of C. C. Burleigh, was an abolitionist lecturer and newspaper editor.

9. Peter Wright was a Philadelphia abolitionist and one of the builders of Pennsylvania Hall.

10. In addresses to the Massachusetts legislature on 21 and 23 February 1838, Angelina Grimké had spoken against slavery and for women's rights as citizens (Gerda Lerner, *The Grimké Sisters from South Carolina* [New York: Schocken Books, 1967], 1–12). William H. Johnson was a founder and the corresponding secretary of the Bucks County Anti-Slavery Society (*Pennsylvania Freeman,* 6 December 1838, 3; *Liberator,* 20 August 1836, 135).

11. Acts 22:3.

12. Joseph John Gurney (1787–1847), a British evangelical Quaker, had begun a three-year tour of the United States in 1837, during which his preaching, especially his emphasis of the authority of the Bible over the doctrine of inner light, had a profound impact on Orthodox Quakers (Bacon, 175; Thomas Hamm, *The Transformation of American Quakerism: Orthodox Friends, 1800–1907* [Bloomington: Indiana University Press, 1988], 20–23).

13. William Wharton's father, Charles Wharton (1743–1838), was a successful Philadelphia merchant.

14. This is a reference to McKim's brother, Andrew McKim (c. 1820–45) (*Pennsylvania Freeman*, 1 January 1846, 3).

## To Anne Warren Weston[1]

[*Philadelphia 7 June 1838*]

[*Added to JM's letter of the same date*]

Yes, My dear Anne—we were in a painful state of suspense for a few days & our anticipations were fearful—[2] It would be but a repetition of the foregoing to dwell on the events or to express my gratitude that all is now well with you & us, and as only 15 minutes are allowed me to add my mite I will use part of that time to remove the impression which I fear will be made that any of our thorough Anti-Slavery friends are turning back & discouraging the colored people from co-operating with our movements it is only our half-way Abolitionists & some timid ones like Dr. Parrish who have never joined our societies & who are now quaking with fear— These it is to be regretted are not well understood by the colored people whom they attempt to influence—they think them wholly identified with us & confiding in them as their best advisers they are in danger of being led astray— I told Dr. P. that the course he was pursuing would make it necessary for counter influence to be exerted by some of us—he assured me he should do all he could to get the colored people to protest against such intercourse as that resolution contemplated[3] & he has already called some of them together for that purpose— Tell Chs. Burleigh this if he is with you—he will understand it—tell him too that I had attended to his coat long before I recd. his letter— I shall write to him—

My letter is called for & I have only time in the warmest affection to subscribe myself

thy affect. friend    L. Mott.—

I found the enclosed pen under the bureau & presumed it was left by one of your compy

I hope C. Sampson's health did not suffer from the excitement— Love to her & all

I sent Maria's towel by Charles—

ALS MB Env: "Anne Warren Weston, care of Henry G. Chapman, Boston"

1. Anne Warren Weston (1812–90) and her sister Maria Weston Chapman (1806–85) were Boston abolitionists and woman's rights advocates.

2. Maria Chapman had come down with brain fever during the excitement of the second Anti-Slavery Convention of American Women in Philadelphia in May 1838. On 17 May, as Abigail Kelley, LCM, and others were addressing the meeting, a mob had attacked Pennsylvania Hall. They then burned it after the convention delegates had left (Sterling, 66–67). For accounts of the convention and the burning of the hall see *Pennsylvania Freeman,* 24 May 1838, 2–3; and *Liberator,* 25 May 1838, 82.

3. Before being disrupted by the mob, convention delegates had contemplated a resolution against prejudice that called for white abolitionists to associate with blacks in their everyday lives (Sterling, 66).

## To Edward M. Davis

Philada. 6 mo. 18th. 1838—

My dear Edward

I have just returned from "over the way" where I have listened with a grateful heart to thy letters announcing thy safe arrival— We heard the pleasing news of the return of the 'Great Western' last eveg on coming home from a day's excursion in the country— Maria [*Davis*] met us at the door with the welcome intelligence & this morng Miller [*McKim*] was the first to espy H. C. Corbit[1] at Edward's door with the letters— We were quickly all assembled there waiting as patiently as we well could for Maria to give them the first glance—"poor fellow"! we said—"to be so sick"!— the hope however prevailed that it might eventually benefit thy general health—

The numerous & circumstantial letters thou wilt receive in the oft repeated intercourse by steam & otherwise between the two countries, will render my poor attempt of little worth to thee, but the promptings of Motherly affection, added to the request thou made that we should write, at least the Anti-Slavery news, forbid my thus reasoning, so I proceed.

The papers will inform thee of the Anniversary in N. York of our Womens Convention here, as well as the general one in New England[2]—but they cannot impart to thee, nor is it in my power, to portray the deep interest manifested by those in attendance on these occasions, suffice it to say that even Maria could leave her babe, scarce four weeks old [*Anna Davis*], & risk her own health, to participate in the rich feast we had here & which was not seriously interrupted even by the burning of the Hall— — Our proceedings tho' not yet published have greatly roused our pseudo-Abolitionists, as well as alarmed such timid ones as our good Dr. Parrish—who has left no means untried to induce us to expunge from our minutes a resolution relating to social intercourse with our colored brethren,—in vain we urged the great departure from order & propriety in such a procedure after the Convention had separated.— he and Charles Townsend[3] were willing to take the responsibility if the publishing Committee would consent to have it withdrawn—and when he failed in this effort, he called some of the respectable part of the colored people together at Robert Douglas's[4] & advised them not to accept such intercourse as was proffered them—& to issue a disclaimer of any such wish— This they have not yet done—but it has caused not a little excitement among us.— In Boston the bone of contention has been the admission of another proscribed class—women—to equal participation in the doings of the Convention— An interesting account of the discussion from C. C. Burleigh I would send thee but for its length—— Charles often expressed regret on his arrival from Hayti, that thy departure had not been delayed till his return or at least of great disappointment at not finding thee here— We were sorry to see him so little improved by his winter's residence— Lewis [*Gunn*] looks finely & is busily engaged writing a book—a narrative of the events of the past Month in connexion with the burning of the Hall.— Charles intends to spend some time with me on Long Island next month.— Wm. [*Burleigh*] is in the City takg charge of the "Freeman" in Whittier's absence—he desires remembrance to thee— Miller will add to this—he is much occupied now in addressing a letter to his Presbytery, resigning his office as minister among them & avowing a change in his Theological opinions with his reasons for the same—[5] It is to be published in pamphlet form— He has been in gradual preparation for this step these 2 or 3 years & it has little connexion with other important interests of which Maria has apprised thee—[6] How I longed to whisper the secret in thy ears before thy departure!—but I could not betray the generous confidence that had reposed the tender trust to us.— What dost thou think of it?— "Is it not nice"?— Sarah is every way lovely— Of his "worth & well tried virtues" I need not write to thee. We contemplate with peculiar satisfaction as a union calculated to promote their mutual happiness.— Theodore & Angelina too![7] what an eventful two months!— They are now on a visit to his friends, in the full enjoyment of connubial bliss after which they will settle down on a pretty little place on the banks of the Hudson 12 miles from N. York.

I was glad to hear thou hadst received letters from W. L. G[arrison]. introducing thee to AntiSlavery friends—whether or not there is one to H. Martineau[8] I hope thou wilt call on her if thou hast opportunity—as far as the tendering of our affectionate regards may serve as an introduction, avail thyself of it—assure her of the satisfaction we have had in the perusal of her late works & the desire we feel that her pen will not cease to be employed in aid of personal & political freedom until every vestige of slavery shall be effaced from our land.

Pleased we are with thy determination to return to us, as speedily as possible, I would nevertheless encourage thy remaining long enough in England to make inquiry whether something may not be done to promote the manufacture of free cotton———

I will leave the remainder of the room for Miller to fill, only adding how grateful to my feelings have been thy acknowledgement of Divine support in thy hour of trial bringing into resignation to thy lot & inspiring the hope that all would be well.

In warm affection<br>
thy Mother—    L. Mott.

ALS MH-H (shelf mark bMS Am 1054 [135])<br>
Env: "Edward M. Davis, care of Coates & Co., London"

1. Henry Cowgill Corbit (1800–1851) was a Philadelphia Quaker and a close friend of Edward M. Davis (*Diary*, 35).

2. LCM is referring to meetings of the AASS in New York City, 2–8 May 1838; the second Anti-Slavery Convention of American Women in Philadelphia; and the annual meeting of the New England Anti-Slavery Society in Boston, 30–31 May 1838. The New England Anti-Slavery Society had passed a controversial resolution stating that all present, men and women, were invited to take seats and participate in the convention. Mott had attended the women's convention but not the two other meetings (*Liberator*, 11 May 1838, 75, 18 May 1838, 78, 8 June 1838, 90).

3. Charles Townsend was a Philadelpia Hicksite Quaker and the husband of Priscilla Kirk Townsend.

4. Robert Douglass was a Philadelphia barber and an abolitionist leader. His wife, Grace Bustill Douglass, and his daughter, Sarah Douglass Mapps (1806–82), were members of the PFASS.

5. James Miller McKim, *Letter to the Wilmington Presbytery* (Philadelphia: Merrihew and Gunn, 1838).

6. LCM is referring to McKim's courtship of Sarah Speakman.

7. Angelina Grimké had married Theodore Dwight Weld (1803–95), a former student at Lane Seminary and an antislavery lecturer, on 14 May 1838 in Philadelphia.

8. Harriet Martineau (1802–76), a British author and an abolitionist, had met LCM in 1836 while touring the United States (Bacon, 67).

## To Thomas A. Greene and Lydia Greene

Philada. 11 mo. 22nd. 1838.

My dear friends Thos. & Lydia Greene[1]

By the return of our cousins Anna Robeson & daughr. I feel an inclination to write a few lines to you, if only to express my feelings of grateful remembrance of your kindness to us when in New Bedford last summer, which with that of our friends on Nantucket & Long Island contributed so much to the restoration of my health.

I have been gradually improving since our return home, and have now little to complain of on that score.—— The pamphlets Thos. furnished me with I have had satisfaction in looking over, and hope the enlightened example of Massachusetts will have its effect on other States.—— What do you think of the Peace Convention lately held in Boston & their ultra "Declaration" and Constitution?[2]— Will not Friends be left far in the rear, if these new converts carry out their principles—

With this I forward some of our late Anti-Slavery papers that you may see what progress we are making in the cause dear to my heart. Our principles and measures are beginning to be better understood & approved by the Members of our Yearly Meeting some of the younger part of whom are giving efficient aid to the Righteous work of emancipation by devotion of much of their time— talents & means.—

Our friends generally are well— You have not given us sufficient of your company to make acquaintance with many of them— You may make it up in time to come.— Our Yearly Meeting is at some distance—the time for hold- ing it being changed to the 5th. Month. Should you not visit us before, we should be gratified to have you as our guests at that time.— We had a pleasant tho' short visit from cousin Henry Willis a few weeks since—he brought his daugh- ter & two cousins & placed them in Kimberton School. By him we received a letter from our friend John Ketcham,[3] informing that they had made some movement towards forming an AntiSlavery Society at Jericho— So much for the efforts of C. C. Burleigh last summer.— — Danl. Neall Jr.[4] has been stir- ring up our Nant. friends we understand in the same cause while engaged there in his avocation as dentist—through him we were glad to hear mention made of you & some other of our friends in New Bedford— —to whom we desire kind remembrances— — I rejoiced with you in the safe return of your dear friends James Arnold[5] & family. The delightful walk we had over their beautiful plea- sure ground, is often recurred to among th[e] incidents of our visit to your place—not the least impressive of which was the interview with Dr. Channing.[6]

My husband may have some addition to make other than the expression of his love—so with mine to your sister, her interesting son—and to yourselves in large mea[s]ure I conclude.— —

Lucretia Mott

ALS MNS Env: "Thomas A. Greene, New Bedford, Mass."

1. Thomas A. Greene (1794–1867) and Lydia Greene of New Bedford, Massachusetts, were Hicksite Quakers.

2. The New England Non-Resistance Society had been established in Boston in Sep- tember 1838 by William Lloyd Garrison, Samuel J. May, Henry C. Wright, and others. Its constitution stated that no member should "engage in or countenance any plot or effort to revolutionize, or change, by physical violence, any government, however cor- rupt or oppressive" (Sterling, 72; *Liberator,* 28 September 1838, 154).

3. John Ketcham (c. 1780–1865) was a member of the Hicksite Jericho Meeting. His wife was Rebecca Sherman Ketcham (c. 1793–1881).

4. Daniel Neall Jr. (1817–94) was a Philadelphia abolitionist.

5. James Arnold (1781–1868), a New Bedford merchant and a Quaker, became a Con- gregationalist during the Hicksite split. He and Thomas Greene were members of a debate society known as the Old Dialectic Society (William J. Potter, *A Tribute to the Memory of James Arnold* [New Bedford, Mass.: Fessenden and Baker, 1868], i–iii).

6. William Ellery Channing (1780–1842) was a Unitarian minister and a peace advo- cate. In "Remarks on the Slavery Question" (1839), Channing described LCM after the burning of Pennsylvania Hall: "Who that has heard the tones of her voice, and looked on the mild radiance of her benign and intelligent countenance, can endure the thought that such a woman was driven by a mob from a spot to which she had gone . . . on a

mission of Christian sympathy" (*Works of William Ellery Channing, D.D.* [Boston: American Unitarian Association, 1891], 813).

## To Abigail Kelley[1]

Philada. 3 mo. 18th. 1839—

My dear friend Abby Kelly

Thy letter of 1st. Mo. last, tho apparently so neglected, has been read again and again with deep interest;—and has been lent to such as have the cause of human rights at heart, asking their aid in making a suitable reply.— They have failed to furnish such arguments as I wanted to meet thine;—and had I not been somewhat at a loss to find convincing reasons, even to satisfy my own mind, I should not have been thus remiss in replying to thee.— — —

I should be very glad if women generally and men too, could so lose sight of distinctions of sex as to act in public meetings, on the enlightened and true ground of Christian equality. But that they cannot yet do this is abundantly evinced, by the proceedings of your New England Convention last spring, as well as by the more recent movements in Massachusetts.[2]— — There is perhaps no better or speedier mode of preparing them for this equality, than for those women whose "eyes are blessed that they see",[3] to act in accordance with the light they have, and avail themselves of every opportunity offered them to mingle in discussions and take part with their brethren.

At the same time without compromise of the principle of equality—or sanction of any error as I conceive, *in their present circumstances,* they may meet by themselves for special purposes, in the same manner as the Society of Friends have ever done, and thus prepare themselves for more public and general exercise of their rights.

Will not the ground thou assumes, oblige thee to withdraw from the Society of Friends?—as all their meetings for discipline are with closed doors,—not only against the "worlds people", but men against women, and women against men.

And yet their meetings of women imperfect as they are, have had their use, in bringing our sex forward, exercising their talents, and preparing them for united action with men, as soon as we can convince them that this is both our right and our duty.

Again I think we may yield in some measure, to the conscientious objections of those whose education has kept them in the dark on this subject, but who are in other respects valuable co-adjutors;—at least until we have labored more to convince them that "in Christ Jesus there is neither male nor female".[4]—

— — It is already acknowledged that our Conventions have done something towards bringing woman to a higher estimate of her powers,—and it will be a subject of regret, if those who are qualified to enlighten ~~their sisters~~ others, and who may be instrumental in removing the prejudice by which so many are bound, should hastily withdraw and leave their sisters "to serve alone".

I would therefore use what little influence I may have in endeavoring to persuade thee and such as thyself, to suspend the conclusions to which your arguments are leading you, in order that you may give us your company this spring, when we may examine the whole ground more fully than I have yet been able to do,—and if it can clearly be shewn that the course we are pursuing is inconsistent with the principles we recognise, I shall then be willing to abandon it.

Thou wilt observe that we have changed the time first concluded upon for our Convention,[5] and have fixed on the 1st. of 5 Mo. to meet here at such place as we may succeed in obtaining for the purpose.— We have applied for several places of worship—those of Friends as well as others have so far been refused to us, with the exception of the Universalist's house in Callowhill street, which we shall probably have, if we can find persons willing to guarantee the Safety of the building.

We are making some progress in our City society—two of our youngest members delivered each an address before a large meeting of *women* invited for the occasion, and we have another appointment for next week, to hear Elizabeth Stickney. They have begun as S. & A. E. Grimke did, and in as short time they may be prepared for a mixed audience.[6]

affectionately

thy frd.—    L. Mott.

ALS MWA Env: "Abby Kelly Millbury Mass. attention Wm. Bassett."

1. Abigail Kelley, later Foster (1810–87), was an abolitionist and woman's rights lecturer. Although Kelley spoke at the second Anti-Slavery Convention of American Women, by 1839 she had come to believe that separate women's meetings were no longer wise (Sterling, 80–81).

2. At the New England Anti-Slavery Society Convention in Boston, 29–31 May 1838, the society had resolved that both men and women could participate. Amos Phelps, Henry B. Stanton, and others had protested this resolution as introducing another issue into the antislavery cause. They subsequently formed their own newspaper, the *Massachusetts Abolitionist,* which, unlike the *Liberator,* would focus solely on antislavery. At the quarterly meeting of the Massachusetts Anti-Slavery Society on 26 March 1839, Phelps would resign in protest against the society's position on woman's rights (Sterling, 68–71; *Liberator,* 18 May 1839, 59, 15 February 1839, 27, 22 February 1839, 31, 29 March 1839, 51).

3. Matt. 13:16.

4. Gal. 3:28.

5. Both the PFASS and the third Anti-Slavery Convention of American Women were meeting in Philadelphia in May 1839. The latter convention was held 1–3 May in the Pennsylvania Riding School on Filbert Street (*Pennsylvania Freeman,* 9 May 1839, 2).

6. Elizabeth Stickney (1811–1906), the stepdaughter of the Boston abolitionist Henry Clarke Wright (1797–1870), would marry Lewis Carstairs Gunn in 1839. Stickney would deliver an address on racial prejudice before the PFASS on 29 March (*Pennsylvania Free-*

man, 21 March 1839, 3; PFASS minutes, 29 March 1839, Pennsylvania Abolition Society Papers, reel 30, PHi; Lewis C. Gunn, *Records of a California Family* [San Diego: n.p., 1928], 4–5; Lewis Perry, *Childhood, Marriage, and Reform: Henry Clarke Wright, 1797–1870* [Chicago: University of Chicago Press, 1980], 173–79). Sarah Grimké (1792–1873), the sister of Angelina Grimké, was an abolitionist and an advocate of woman's rights.

## To Maria Weston Chapman

Philada. 5 Mo 29th. 1839.

My dear friend Maria W. Chapman

Thou must think I set a low value on thy long and painfully interesting letter received at the time of our Convention, else some acknowledgment of it would have been made before now. It was not the case however,—the letter has been read again and again—its details dwelt upon—and desirous as I was to hide myself "till these calamities be overpast,"[1] the claim upon our sympathy is such as to enlist my feelings in your behalf.

True I could hardly bear the harsh epithets applied to those whom we had almost venerated; & may we not still indulge the hope (even against hope) that they will see that the measures they are pursuing will scatter & divide—rather than further the great enterprise, to accomplish which so many, of diverse opinions on other subjects, harmoniously conjoined. I can't believe that Mary S. Parker will be satisfied to work with a sectarian *few*, against the united *many*—but that she and some others will retrace their steps—[2] You must keep as near to them as you can, so as to draw them back to the true fold. We could not possibly spare to you our Charles C. Burleigh, pressing as seemed your exigency. We feared for his health & for the excitement into which he would necessarily be drawn. Moreover he is needed here to *prevent* the 'flames extending to this part of the camp.' We shall look for his return to us next week. J. G. Whittier will soon withdraw from the Freeman. What his next course will be we are left to surmise—. He must not array himself against our dear Wm. L. Garrison.— I should regret to lose him more than any other who lists that way. I would far rather he should be neutral than write as he does. Moses Cartland is here & will probably succeed him as Editor of our paper.[3]

Hast thou any prospect of being at the great Anti-Slavery Convention in London next year?— How I shall long to go! Our next Womens Convention must not interfere with the time for leaving the country to attend that meeting. As 'Chairman' of the committee in Philada., to make the appointment of time; I would thus early consult thee, whether immediately following the New-England Convention will not be the best arrangement we can make, if it will allow time to cross the Atlantic. Dost thou know what month is concluded on for that glorious event?—[4] Please let me hear from thee on this subject, as well as all others in which we are mutually interested.

Our Female Society here are stirring themselves on behalf of the colored people—trying to improve their situation.[5] We have divided ourselves into committees & taken all the districts in the city where they reside—in order to carry out, as far as we can, that resolution of our Convention relative to them. Would it not be well for all our Female Societies to do likewise?

This will probably be handed thee by our son Thomas Mott who is going with his cousin Wm. Yarnall to take a little journey, as relaxation from his studies. He is quite a young & new traveller, but I hope will not be too bashful to call on thee.

Affectionate remembrances to thy sister Anne whose letter was truly acceptable, though I have not yet said so to her.— Also to sister Mary[6] and indeed to all our dear friends there—

very affectionately
thy L. Mott

ALS MB Env: "Maria W. Chapman, Boston, Mass."

1. The third Anti-Slavery Convention of American Women had met in Philadelphia on 1–3 May 1839. The quotation is from Ps. 57:1.

2. Mary S. Parker (1801–41), president of the Boston Female Anti-Slavery Society, had sided with those members who rejected issues like woman's rights and nonresistance— issues Chapman and others supported—as part of the society's agenda (Jean Fagan Yellin and John C. Van Horne, eds., *The Abolitionist Sisterhood: Women's Political Culture in Antebellum America* [Ithaca, N.Y.: Cornell University Press, 1994], 45, 60–62; *Liberator,* 19 April 1839, 63).

3. John Greenleaf Whittier would give up the editorship in February 1840 and Burleigh would assume it. Whittier's rift with Garrison stemmed from the latter's allegations that Whittier compromised on the slavery issue (see Whittier's letter to Garrison, 24 February 1839, *JGW,* 1:331–34). Moses Cartland (1805–63), Whittier's cousin, had edited the *Freeman* in Whittier's absence, but left it to start an academy in New Hampshire (ibid., 1:166, 1:351).

4. The British and Foreign Anti-Slavery Society would issue a call in the fall of 1839 for the World's Anti-Slavery Convention to be held in London in June 1840; a second call in February 1840 would ask explicitly for the names of "gentleman" delegates (*Diary,* 8–9).

5. The PFASS's annual report for 1838 noted among its accomplishments the society's operation of a school for African American girls, which had thirty students (*Pennsylvania Freeman,* 14 February 1839, 4).

6. Mary Gray Chapman (d. 1874) was Chapman's sister-in-law (Taylor, 122).

# To George Combe[1]

Philada 6 Mo. 13th. 1839—

My dear friend Geo. Combe

I was much gratified with the reception of thy letter of 20th. Ult. kindly congratulating us on the success of our Convention. Fully do I accord with thee in the sentiment, that the cause of Abolition be 'pleaded by the moral sentiments and addressed to the moral sentiments;'—and it is because this power has been mainly relied upon, from the commencement of the enterprise, that it has had my most hearty, tho' feeble co-operation.— — — That there may have been, in some instances, an intemperate zeal exhibited, we admit;—but when we consider how just is the indignation kindled in the breast of every friend of humanity, who contemplates American Slavery, with all its concomitant enormities, and atrocities, our surprise is, that Combativeness and Destructiveness should be so quiescent, with those who in all other grievances, claim the right of redress by calling into activity these organs.— — A reference to the documents of the American Anti-Slavery Society, I presume will show a greater amount of appeal to the intellect and conscience—more well-directed arguments against the known evils of slavery, and less harrowing invective on its supposed cruelties, than is to be found in treating of any other oppression under the sun. But we have been so long accustomed to look complacently on the condition of the slaveholder, and to make many apologies for the system in which he is involved, that now, the plain truth uttered in the language of righteous abhorrence is regarded as vituperative, and calculated solely to insult and exasperate.— — True, the plain dealing of Abolitionists has given offence to many,—but to more, it has served as the trumpet tone to rouse them from the deep sleep into which they had sunk. Now that they are waking up to an examination of the subject, they may require less urgency of appeal.

I wish, in this short space, I could make thee understand why Colonizationists and Abolitionists cannot harmonize. I would gladly furnish thee with some works on the subject, but travellers dont like to be burdened in this way. Permit me however to recommend to thy perusal "Jay's Inquiry"[2] in—J. G. Birney's "Letter on Colonization" (once a slaveholder & Colonizationist) & the "Elmore Correspondence,"[3] all found at the Anti-Slavery Office in New York, or at thy service when thou shall again gratify us with thy company in our city. These would not occupy much of thy valuable time, devoted as it is to the disenthralment of the mind from a captivity, scarcely less deplorable, to existing customs,—a false Philosophy,—and a *falser* Theology. In the meantime I will give thee a few extracts from some of the Reports, and standard works of the Colonization Society,—enough to convince thee, that theirs and ours are essentially antagonist principles. A Colonization Society 'in the abstract' we do not object to, but we regard the present one as based on selfishness and unchristian prejudice—consequently 'inadequate in its design, injurious in its tendency and contrary to sound principles;'[4]—creating an indifference to the advancement of the free people of color in this—their legitimate home. Many who planned the Society were undoubtedly actuated by Benevolence, but how much more effective would have been their efforts, so mis-directed, had they been exerted to remove the disabilities imposed by public opinion and by legislative power. It is objectionable because it satisfies the minds of those who wish to do something, as redress to injured Africa, and who vainly suppose their contributions to this cause will make amends for the deep injuries they have aided to inflict. It receives its most efficient support from the slave-holders. The Presidents and other officers of the Society have not liberated their own slaves, even on the conditions of their leaving the country. Henry Clay who presided at its 1st Meeting said, as found in their Annual Report, that he was "not prepared to emancipate his Slaves, if the means were provided of sending them from the country".[5] It is solemnly pledged not to interfere in the system of slavery, or in any manner to disturb the repose of the planters. In one of their Reports, Randolph says, "So far from being connected with the Abolition of Slavery, the measure proposed would prove one of the greatest securities, to enable the master to keep in possession his own property." In the 11th. Report, Harrison of Va. "It has declared itself in no wise allied to any abolition society, but is ready whenever there is need *to pass censure upon such Societies* in America".——— [6] "Into their accounts the subject of Emancipation does not enter at all. They consider any attempt to promote the increase of the free colored population by manumission, unnecessary, premature, & dangerous. Attempts for their instruction would be inconsistent with public safety. Emancipation, with the liberty to remain this side the Atlantic, is but an act of dreamy madness."[7] &c  Hence between Colonization & Abolition Societies there is no affinity of feeling or action; and this is the cause inexplicable to many, why they cannot pursue their objects amicably together. I presume thou art acquainted with the creed of the Abolitionists; the fundamental of which is, that 'man cannot rightfully hold property in man'. In this essential point then they & the Colonization Society antagonize each other. The latter say "the execution of their scheme would augment instead of diminishing the value of the property left behind. It would provide and keep open a drain for the excess beyond the occasions of profitable employment".[8]

One word more in reply to thy complaint of denunciatory language.— Wm. L. Garrison, upon whose writings I have drawn for a part of the foregoing, says "It is a self-evident proposition, that, so far as you alleviate the pressure of guilt upon the conscience of evil-doers, you weaken the power of motive to repent, and encourage them to sin with impunity.[9]— — —  The rebukes of Pitt, Fox, Wilberforce, & Clarkson were once deemed fanatical and outrageous by good men, but now that the concentrated execration of the civilized world is poured upon those engaged in the slave trade, how mild & inefficient comparatively, their rebukes! So the denunciations now hurled against slavery which seem to many so violent and unmerited, will be considered moderate, pertinent and just, when this murderous system shall have been overthrown".[10] Certain also of your own excellent speakers & writers used strong & bold epithets— Algernon Sidney & the celebrated & eloquent Dr. Thompson[11]—*to whose head thou introduced us in thy lectures* hesitated not to denounce such an usurpation as an evidence of "degeneracy into the worst of beasts" &c "a system inimical to all that is merciful in the heart & holy in the conduct; subject to the curse of Almighty God."

Thus I have endeavored to give thee some of my views—& hope by dwelling so long on the subject & taxing thy patience to such an extent, I have not
deprived myself the pleasure of another let[ter] from thee. I will promise that
my answers in future sh[all?] not be so long. We all felt very sorry for your loss
of Mo[ney?] & hope ere [this?] it is recovered— I was glad it was not a *bla[ck]*
man who disappeared with it.— So many weeks devotion to so small a class,
was matter of regret with us before we heard of the robbery, & increasingly so,
when informed that so much of the proceeds of it was borne off in that way.

We were pleased with the introduction to your cousin Fanny Butler—&
particularly so with the freedom of her call on us—while she seemed to think
it required an apology— I have since accepted a kind invitation from Anne
Morrison to ride out to their place, and passed an hour or two very pleasantly
with her.[12]— I shall endeavor to profit by thy warning with regard to her, altho' not in immediate danger of falling into the error of an over-estimate of
her powers. She has a mind of no common order—& moral sentiments rendered active by reason of use— Still I regard her so much a child of impulse,
that she rather calls forth my compassionate feelings, than any approach to
idolatry. I hear she is going to repeat—her visit to us & shall be glad of an opportunity for further acquaintance. The veneration to which I am more prone
is, for that moral sublimity which is found in connexion with an enlarged mind
& liberal principles, of this "noblest work of God" I indulge an admiration
almost amounting to idolatry & conclude *that* is the "?" organ, which thou hast
given me 'large.' We hear too little of Phrenology since thy departure— We
need an efficient Lecturer to secure an interest, that shall lead to further investigation of the Subject. I attended this afternoon a meeting of a Female Lyceum—composed of quite young women & was gratified to hear an essay by my
cousin Phebe Earle—on the question "Does the Science of Phrenology lead to
Fatalism[?"]

From what we can learn there has not yet been a sufficient sum subscribed
to call Wilderspin to this country.[13] B. Richards has taken some steps towards
it—of which he may have informed thee. The controllers of the Public Schools
do not encourage his coming. If we had not met with a heavy pecuniary loss by
fire within the last year, we would gladly contribute more than will now be in
our power toward his coming.

My dear love to thy Cecilia[14]— I felt increased attachment to her each time
we met—& hope to enjoy as much of your company a[s] possible when you
again come to our City. My Husband & children join in this desire & unite in
kind remembrances. Thy messages were delivered to our frd—Dr Parrish &
family and to A. D. Morrison—who were glad to be remembered.

Most Sincerely<br>
thy friend    Lucretia Mott

ALS GBNLS Env: "George Combe, Montreal, Canada"

1. George Combe (1788–1858), a Scot, advocated the study of the skull's shape as a diagnosis of personality and means of understanding social problems. He lectured on phrenology and education in the United States from 1838 to 1840. Combe's works include *Physiology Applied to Health and Education* (1834), *Physiology of Digestion* (1836), and *The Physiological and Moral Management of Infancy* (1840), as well as many articles in the *Phrenological Journal*. In his book about his American travels, Combe described meeting LCM: "To the soft delicacy of a refined and accomplished woman, Lucretia Mott adds the clear and forcible intellect of a philosopher" (*Notes on the United States of North America during a Phrenological Visit in 1838–9–40* [Edinburgh: Maclachlan, Stewart, 1841], 2:28).

2. William Jay (1789–1858), a member of the AASS, wrote *An Inquiry into the Character and Tendency of the American Colonization, and American Anti-Slavery Society,* published in 1835 by the AASS. Jay's *Inquiry* went through ten editions (*WLG,* 2:99–100).

3. In corresponding with Franklin Harper Elmore (1799–1850), a Democratic congressman from South Carolina, James G. Birney defended the work of the antislavery movement, declaring that it sought "the immediate abandonment, without expatriation," of slavery in the United States. This correspondence had been reprinted in the *Pennsylvania Freeman* earlier in the month (7 June 1838, 1) and continued into July.

4. William Lloyd Garrison, *Thoughts on African Colonization* (Boston: Garrison and Knapp, 1832), 2.

5. Garrison reprinted the words of Clay (1772–1852), a Whig senator from Kentucky, in *Thoughts on African Colonization,* 42.

6. Garrison quoted the remarks of John Randolph (1773–1833), a senator and representative from Virginia, which were included in the American Colonization Society's second report, 1818, and a speech by a "Mr. Harrison of Virginia" from the society's eleventh annual report (ibid., 43–44).

7. Ibid., 57.

8. Ibid., 75.

9. Ibid., 66.

10. Ibid., 9. Garrison named four prominent figures in British abolitionism: William Pitt, the younger (1759–1806); George Fox (1624–91), the founder of the Society of Friends; William Wilberforce (1759–1833); and Thomas Clarkson (1760–1846).

11. Algernon Sidney (1622–83) participated in the Whig plot against King Charles and was executed for treason. Garrison frequently cited Sidney's *Discourses concerning Government* and believed him to be an abolitionist. George Thompson (1804–78) was a leading British abolitionist (*WLG,* 1:99, 103, 2:217–22).

12. Fanny Kemble Butler (1809–93), an English actress and an author, had married Philadelphian Pierce Butler in 1834. Her father, Charles Kemble, was an uncle of Combe's wife, Cecilia. Anne Morrison (d. 1866) was the president of the Women's Hospital of Philadelphia in 1864 (*Friends' Review,* 31 January 1863, 349; LCM to MML, 5 April 1866, Mott Manuscripts, PSCHi).

13. Samuel Wilderspin (1792–1866) was a British schoolmaster.

14. Combe's wife, Cecilia Siddons Combe (1794–1868), was the daughter of Sara Kemble Siddons, the British actress.

# To James Miller McKim

Philada. 7 Mo. 19th. 1839

My dear Miller

I have thy two letters of 4th. & 13th Inst. before me—& sat down with the intention of telling thee how truly welcome they were, in a hurried page to send by Charles [*Burleigh*] and Aunt Lydia P. Mott, who are now on the eve of their departure, but on second thought it seems best to wait till they are off, then fill this sheet if I find material & forward it by Mail to anticipate their arrival among you & let you know that all thy kind wishes for a longer stay with you availed them nothing—the route having been previously so marked out and notice given, as to admit of no change.

23d.

I am glad for Aunt L. to have even the little opportunity of seeing one of whom she has heard me say *so much,* & doubt not she & Charles too will prize the few hours stay with you—as well as that which they allotted themselves at 'Highland Farm'. Our Aunt has been *in her day* a fine, accomplished woman, & it affected me to see that like the rest of us, she is growing old.

Thy acknowledgment of cherished kindness & friendship for Charles felt grateful to me, and I doubt not will be heartily reciprocated. I cant now recollect what passed between Sarah & myself relative to thy esteem for him;—but I had not regarded the freedom with which thou had sometimes spoken of his "foibles" to *us who knew* him, as of so censurable a character or the 'judgment so severe' as to call for so *much* condemnation as thy remarks evince. In one or two instances as I mentioned to thee at the time I fear'd there was unprofitable indulgence in talk on some subjects, with our household—but as though sayst "enough on this point". Thou hast had it seems a delightful time of retirement for a review of the past 2 years—and as far as circumstances & associations have had an effect to contaminate or sully the purity which becometh a follower of Christ. thou hast had access to the fountain whence healing virtue is drawn— & the renewal of "a clean heart" and "a right spirit" is now thy enjoyment. "Keep thy hearts (then) with all diligence".[1] Thou knows I feared for thee last summer, while we were all enjoying such happy hours of relaxation & entire unbending—that the *mirthfulness* of "uncle Tom"—to say nothing of the hilarity of others around thee, would endanger thy wonted circumspection— And then the jestings of dear J. G. W[hittier].—and *my own* freedom of chat with thee etc. etc. were enough to enfeeble thy Spiritual health.— As for myself—I have not even time for such an inspection into my own state as the deranged nature of it requires— We are in bustle continually—more company than common lately— — Chs. & aunt L. left Ann Moore our neice & Abby Gibbons with her two children here—[2] When Jas. came up to dinner he informed that our br. Robert Hicks was coming from New York that afternoon to attend a meeting

of the Indian Committee— he arrived & our Thomas with him tired of waiting for the "British Queen"— The Mg of the Com. was interesting rendered
so by a full report from those appointed to visit the tribes under our care.

A council is to be held with them & the Secretary of War relative to their
removal— The President has invited the attendance of our friends who are
interested for them—& we have accordingly agreed to send a delegation to join
one from New York & Gennesee Yy. Mgs. & also some from the Orthodox Mgs—
all to assemble on the 12th of next Month—[3] I write this in part for Aunt Ly-
dias information—as she has taken a deep interest in that injured class of our
fellow beings.— No women are sent—of course— The Com. reported a sad
state of things in their domestic arrangements. I held out to the Mg. a prospective view that the sorry picture presented in the female department, might lead
to a council of *Squaws,* when some women might be required. It provoked a
smile from some & called forth the reproof of Ruth Pyle & a demand for more
solemnity. I thot. she willingly found occasion for censure.— Benjn. Ferris is
one of the chosen—he accepted the appointt. "nothing loth". He with Samuel
Comfort came home with us & joined by br. Robert passed a social eveg.—
Edwd. Moore came in from the Asylum on 1st. day & finding no intelligence of
Edwd. & Maria—he & Ann left us yesterday morng. for Rochester, hoping to
meet them in New York, but by the arrival of the "Great Western" we learn that
the "British Queen" would not leave London before the 10th. & perhaps not
then—[4] A long & interesting letter from Maria is our only amend for the disappointment— They had performed the 2 weeks tour much to their satisfaction and were now very homesick. We shall not look eagerly for them till the 1st
of next week.— — We had a pleasant visit from J. G. Whittier & Moses A Cartland yesterday— The former spoke of his visit to Carlisle with evident satisfaction.— We are right glad to hear of thy restoration to health & of thy cheerfulness— — He thinks too that thou wilt accept the agency.— I wish thou
had never left it, but that is poor employt. so will only hope "all things will work
together for good".[5] Dont engage in a school unless it be a boarding school, so
that thou can employ suitable assistants. The confinement would not suit thee.

Please say to Aunt L. who will probably arrive among you on 6th. day—that
I recd. her short note this morng but not till after the box was packed & nailed
up— If it can be easily opened I will attend to her request— There was abundant room for more than was put in—Jas. not findg a box of just the suitable
size— We filled in with Abolition papers & pamphlets which she will please
not suffer to be destroy'd or used as waste paper for that is contrary to all Anti-
Slavery rules—but circulate them to the best advantage. Some Friends' tracts
too she will find among them & her bundles in the Centre—also a package of
our Convention Proceedings for Ohio & Indiana with a note from Anna concerning their distribution *which she must not forget to look for.* Joshua Coffin[6]
called here just after they left with a small package directed to Stephen Gloces-

ter—Cincinnatti.—wh. he desired might be put in the box but it was forgotten— If it is opened we will put it in— Tell Charles I received another letter
by Thos. from M. W. Chapman on the subject of their difficulties— Also one
by mail yesterday from Mary S. Parker—on the same subject He will recollect
that I suggested to M. W. Chapman an early consultation relative to next year's
Convention—because of the London Convention She accordingly requested
a meetg of the Com. sayg—"Philada. frds. are waitg to hear from us".— This
excited the jealousy of M. S. Parker & she immediately wrote to know *why* we
wished such early action—if we feared they would soon pass into oblivion &c—
I feel so sorry for them, that all confidence one in another is lost—& suspicion
& jealousy fill their minds. Thomas had a pleasant jaunt with his cousin Wm.
[*Yarnall*]—went to Salem, Lynn, Nahant, Mount Auburn, Cambridge College—
&c He reached Jericho on 5th day & stayed till 2nd. day.

In a letter from P. P. Willis by him she says "Tell aunt Lydia I recd. her accepte.
little note with the bundle that accompd. it—& remind C. C. B. that he promised to write again".

We are trying to have a Meeting appointed here for the 1st. Augt. have applied for the Wesley Church in Lombard St.—

4th day Morng.—

We recd. a letter from Charles last eveg. giving us the pleasant informn. of
their safe travel as far as Lampeter,—& the good meetings they had had—but
neither he nor Aunt Lydia told us whether *she* attended the Mgs—nor whether
she preached at Uwchlan Mg—nor anything of their call at Abm. L. Pennock's—
if they found him at home & if they recd. Aunt L. as Orthodox Frds. *ought* to—
these are items I wish to be remembered in Chs. letter from Carlisle or Pittsburg as he may find time to write— It "brought them near us" last eveg to get
a letter written in the morng—but acceptable as is his attention in writg—he
must not take the time that belongs to his frds. where he is stopping—but *must
render himself right agreeable*—& he must take all the rest that his much speakg,
added to his additional *new* care of driving & waitg on a *lady* require.

We shall open the box today & put in some books from Joseph Healy[7] sent
to Wm. Donaldson— He will write to Wm. explanatory of them— I shall send
a copy of John Woolman's Works—new edition with additional matter on Slavery which Aunt L. or Chs. will please present to our personally unknown friend
Augustus Wattles.—[8] I fear the books sent for the school will be found many
of them so old—& some obsolete—as scarcely to pay for sending so far Aunt
L. says *all* remembrances are pleasant to her of her acceptable visit to us tell her
so they are to us except that I feel disappointed in havg not enough quiet enjoyment of her compy— Excuse me for makg my letter to thee the medium of
so much of so little interest for others— We had Father & Mother Jones from
the Gulf yesterday hopg to find Edwd. & Maria—Henry & Sarah Corbit & Isaac
Davis joined them here to tea[9]—but no Edwd. & Maria yet— I shall write di-

rected to Pittsburg if they come in time— Love to Eliza—& to all—Let us hear from thee

L Mott

ALS NICO Env, written in JM's hand: "J. Miller McKim, Carlisle, Penna."

1. Ps. 51:10; Prov. 4:23.

2. Ann Mott Moore (b. 1818) was the daughter of JM's sister Abigail Moore (1795–1846) and her husband, Lindley Moore (1788–1871). Abigail Hopper Gibbons (1801–93), a philanthropist, an abolitionist, a prison reformer, and the sister of Edward Hopper, was married to the dry goods merchant James Sloan Gibbons (1810–92).

3. Joel Roberts Poinsett (1779–1851) had become President Martin Van Buren's secretary of war in 1837. In this position Poinsett was responsible for relocating forty thousand Native Americans west of the Mississippi. LCM is referring to Quaker concern for the government's treatment of the Seneca in New York State. On 1 November members of the Genesee, New York, Philadelphia, and Baltimore Yearly Meetings would petition the president urging that the United States abide by the treaty, pay sums due Seneca chiefs, and refrain from forcible removal of the Native Americans (*The Case of the Seneca Indians in the State of New York* [Philadelphia: Merrihew and Thompson, 1840], 20–32, 54–56).

4. Samuel Comfort was a Hicksite Quaker from Bucks County (Ingle, 198). Edward Mott Moore (b.1814) was the son of Abigail Moore and Lindley Moore. The Davises had been scheduled to sail from London on 1 July, after a tour of Britain and France (LCM to Wendell Phillips, 8 June 1839, MH-H; LCM to George Combe, 8 September 1839, GBNLS).

5. Rom. 8:28.

6. Joshua Coffin (1792–1864), a letter carrier from Newburyport, Massachusetts, and a founder of the New England Anti-Slavery Society, was removed from office for rescuing kidnapped African Americans.

7. Joseph Healy was a Philadelphia Orthodox Quaker.

8. John Woolman (1720–72) was a Quaker minister and abolitionist whose writings were published as *The Works of John Woolman* (Philadelphia: Benjamin and Jacob Johnson, 1800). In November 1838, the manual labor school founded by Augustus Wattles (1807–83) in Mercer County, Ohio, had enrolled thirty students and he was also assisting blacks to buy farms in the area of his school, making it "the largest colored settlement now in Ohio" (*Pennsylvania Freeman,* 14 March 1839, 2, 16 May 1839, 1).

9. Henry Corbit married Sarah Bolton (d. 1852). Isaac Roberts Davis (d. 1857), the brother of Edward M. Davis, married Lydia Cowgill Corbit (1810–73).

# To Nathaniel Barney and Elisa Barney

Philada. 11 Mo. 8th. 1839

My much-loved N. & E. Barney

I fondly hoped to meet you at the Anniversary in Boston, and with regret learned by Nathanl.'s acceptable letter, that sickness was one cause of his absence. Do be careful in the observance of the laws of health, for I cant learn resignation to the Good—& the Useful not living 'out half their days.'

I can assure you the word of encouragement never reached me when more needed, than at the time of the reception of that letter. Our New York friends took umbrage at my going to a Non-Resistance Meeting[1] & talked themselves into an idea that it was almost a wicked step. G. F. White[2] made the subject of War his theme the 1st. day following, and after admitting that no consistent Christian could take arms, he added, that still he could believe the warrior with his weapon in hand, ready to destroy his brother, might be nearer the kingdom of Heaven, than a member of a Non-Resistance Society. So he might have said of a member of a Quaker Socy.— We all know that simple membership does not confer a testimony. Else might *he* have a clearer one against Slavery.— Not satisfied with that opp[ortunit]y. he came here had the members of our 3 Mgs collected at Cherry St. house with many others not of our fold. His text was "He who will resist God will resist man". He went on to shew how the hirelings of the day were resisting God—as that class ever had done—how preposterous then for such to profess the principles of non-resistance. That these hirelings first approached Friends with the plausible offer of union in circulating the Scriptures—many were led away by them—then with Abolition knowg the testimony of the Socy against Slavery—again with Women's Rights & lastly with Non-Resistance  Warned the young people against being caught in their snares—their vine was as the vine of Sodom & their grapes bitter—that some were well nigh hugged to death by them. What did woman want in the name of rights, but liberty to roam over the country from Dan to Beersheba spurning the protection of man—to traverse the streets & lanes of the City—to travel in stages and steamboats by day Lines & night Lines without a male protector—for himself, before he would submit to the dictation of an imperious woman, he would traverse the earth while there was a foot of ground to tread upon & swim the rivers while there was water to swim in—that an elder in Socy said at his table that she did not intend to marry until she found a man to whose judgment she could surrender her own—these were the sentiments that would win the hearts of men—to such as these a man would bring his treasures & pour into her lap & kneel at her feet &.c"— All this in the name of the Gospel of Jesus Christ!— This is nearly verbatim—similar denunciations of Anti-Slavery & Non-R. Socs. were repeated at the Western & Caln Qrs. wh. he attended with a minute of unity from his Mo. Mg.— Benjn. Ferris accompanied him & in a letter to R. Price reported what he said, as setting in a true & clear light the delusion of modern Abolitionism—exposing those who had been led away by it—&c

I should not give you these particulars—but that these said meetings have produced some excitement among us & party spirit is in danger of having the ascendancy, and with the hope that you may exercise the holy office of Peace-Makers I want you to be apprised early of the state we are in. Some of our dear young people are much puzzled to understand how Stephen Treadwell and G. F. White can both be right & their messages diametrically opposite.

A young man from the Western Qr. writes thus to me— "It is not enough that we are opposed by all the profane & vulgar—as well as by many sober-minded men but we must also be opposed and most violently denounced by those minuted & accredited Gospel preachers!!— It never fails to strengthen the current of opposition to all practical righteousness—because he inculcates the doctrine that every evil should remain unmolested— His theology is dark & mysterious—contradictory & absurd— he said that Non-Resistance was another child of the devil—converts made, like mushrooms of a nights growth by a lecture from an hireling—that he could not conceive of greater blasphemy than to profess it—that Jesus was not a Non-Resistant until a short time before his death. &c I write to try to dispel the burden that is resting upon me— It is distressing to honest minds to see two or more public friends travellg around, both professing to be led by the unerring light & yet their doctrines diverging to the widest extremes— His attack upon Non-Resistants was most unexpect-ed— I almost shuddered as he heaped his denunciations upon them. [In?]stantly my mind glanced over the names of a Chapman, a Garrison, a May—[*ms. damaged*] a Capron—a Burleigh & a Quincy[3] and my spirit sank with despondency & a [*ms. damaged*] with something of indignation when I recollected that he was an accredited minister of the Socy of Friends!— Shame on such professors—a few of them will scatter our Socy. to the winds & Quak-erism will no longer have an organized form! Oh how diffe[rent] were his doc-trines from that which inculcates an every day religion that [*ms. damaged*] to live & work by as well as profess—a religion which a man can carry with [*ms. damaged*] on all occasions & practically apply in all cases." Now this is a young man w[ho a] few years ago when but a stripling—took a stand alone on the subject of Temperance when not a society was in existence in his neighd. but havg a br. who fell a victim to that dire sin—he was awakened to the subject & totally abstained— His faithfulness in this particular prepared his mind for the reception of other subjects of moral reform & he became an active aboli-tionist made sacrifices of gain & health by lecturing on the subject— He has also done much among his associates to improve their taste in literature, by establishg a library of useful works—& as a Friend tho' not yet in the *sectarian* exterior is without reproach. How desirable that such efforts should meet with every encouragement!— It may appear strange to you that I should thus write—& if I could detect in myself any germ of unkind feeling toward G. F. W. I should hesitate—indeed I do even now pause because of the wellknown axi-om that "two of trade dont agree".[4] But I have been so cast down in view of what awaits the Society—if this spirit of judging & condemning is not arrested, that I have sought relief by expression in this way— As to replying from the gal-lery—my fervent prayer is to be enabled to "answer not again"—but havg done well & sufferg for it to take it patiently.

On my return from Boston I found N. York Mo. Mg. at hand & after pass-ing a day or two delightfully with our Jericho frds. I attended that Mg accompd by cousins P. P. Willis—John & Mary W.—Lydia Rushmore & her son—br. Robert Hicks had told his Mary that he doubted my makg any stop in N.Y. presumg I suppose, that I should be ashamed of my course—he thinkg that I was travelling alone—and what if I was!—the fact however was—that my Jas. had introduced me to Wm. Hacker on board the boat here & asked his escort wh. he kindly rendered all the way to Boston— Joseph Post & Saml. Willis[5] were all attention in returng—as far as Jericho— on my arrival at N. York—I recd. a letter from James saying he should be at the depot on the arrival of the eveg line in waitg for me—wh. induced me to change my first plan of waitg till the next day—& come on in that line unattended— Jas. was afterword informed by Elias Hicks who came on the day before I did, that I should not come till the next day—so when I arrived after midnight he was not there & I walked home alone, but nothing befel me— I felt not that there was anything amiss in it— & should not have thot. it worth speakg of again—but that it was spoken of to my disadvantage in N. York—they hearg of my walkg home alone—& doubtless was the cause of a part of George's 'concern' here— I judge so from the manner in which br. Robert rallied me on the subject in a late visit here, on his way to Washington. Griffith M. Cooper too has been here & very acceptable was his visit—[6] He has accepted the Agency for the Indians. He tells me that they in their Yearly Mg have come to the conclusion to "judge not one another any more," as to their course on these points alluded to—& well may they—when such as Ths. M'Clintock finds their duty to lie in uniting with their brethren of other denominations in carrying on the work of righteousness[7]

Our frd. G. Truman seems rather favorable to George's views & I fear he may lose some of that charity wh. has hitherto marked his character— Now if you think I have written too freely—cast that goodly mantle over it & the writer & do not condemn, but deal plainly. I have left little room to speak of other matters— The Mg. in Boston was indeed deeply interestg & instructive— I was sorry to see Peter & Elizh. leavg & supposed I should see them there again— I regretted afterward that I had not followed them out—as I knew not where to find them—& feared that Elizh. was sick

How sorry I am to see so much in the Liberator that ought not to be told in Gath— I wish they would entirely separate if they can no longer work in harmony—the female Socy I mean—[8] There is encouragement from Ohio & other quarters that the cause is makg progress

A family of 7 fugitives passed thro' the City on their way to Canada this week—such travellers increase— Our Mg has been much disturbed with Mary & Susan Cox lately.— It continues large & frequently very satisfactory— I expect to have a Mg with the prisoners at Moyamen[sing] next [*ms. damaged*] day—[9] I have just recd. a letter [from?] Geo C [*ms. damaged*]—should like to shew you our correspondence—

affecy   L Mott

23rd—

After writg the foregoing & giving into Aunt Phebe's hands to send by Captn. Gardner I found he was not going so soon as I thought he was—& the feeling that prompted this being somewhat allayed I recalled it intending to destroy it & write a less complaing one—but not havg had time to do better—  I will send this & trust to your goodness—read & destroy it

ALS MNHi Env: "Nathaniel Barney, Nantucket"

1. LCM had spoken briefly at the meeting of the New England Non-Resistance Society in Boston on 25 September 1839 (*Liberator*, 11 October 1839, 164).

2. George F. White (1789–1847) was a New York City Hicksite Quaker.

3. Those Massachusetts abolitionists not previously identified are Samuel J. May (1797–1871), a Unitarian clergyman; Effingham Capron (1791–1859), a Quaker who helped found the Non-Resistance Society; and Edmund Quincy (1808–77), a newspaper editor.

4. John Gay, "The Rat Catcher and Cats," l. 44.

5. William Hacker was a Philadelphia merchant. Samuel Willis (1815–70) was Henry Willis's son.

6. Elias Hicks (1815–53) was the husband of JM's niece Sarah Hicks. Griffith M. Cooper (c. 1790–1864) of Williamson, New York, was a Quaker abolitionist (*Pennsylvania Freeman*, 11 April 1844, 4; *Liberator*, 7 July 1865, 106; Gordon, 1:272).

7. Rom. 14:13. Thomas McClintock had written a letter to the *Liberator* explaining his continued allegiance to Garrison in the face of the defection of many of Garrison's former friends (*Liberator*, 27 September 1839, 153).

8. Gath was a Philistine city during biblical times visited by plagues (1 Sam. 4–6). The dispute within the Boston Female Anti-Slavery Society revolved around nominations and votes received for society president at the meeting in October 1839, but reflected larger political splits over women's public activism and the influence of ministers within the movement. This internal dispute was covered extensively in the *Liberator* (1 November 1839, 174, 8 November 1839, 179, and 15 November 1839, 182, 183; Debra Gold Hansen, "The Boston Female Anti-Slavery Society and the Limits of Gender Politics," in *The Abolitionist Sisterhood: Women's Political Culture in Antebellum America*, ed. Jean Fagan Yellin and John C. Van Horne [Ithaca, N.Y.: Cornell University Press, 1994], 45–65).

9. Mary L. Cox (1791–1869) and Susan H. Cox Luther (1795–1876) were Philadelphia Quakers. Mary had been speaking at the Cherry Street Meeting about nonresistance and antislavery (*Journal*, 14 February 1877; *Non-Resistant*, 8 January 1840, 3; see also LCM to Maria Weston Chapman, 20 February 1840, below). Combe had visited the Moyamensing prison in Philadelphia on his tour of the United States and described it as a place with "no baths, cold or warm, for the prisoners, and no yard for exercise. I should imagine a warm bath once a-week would produce, both morally and physically, a beneficial influence on these convicts" (Combe, *Notes on the United States of North America during a Phrenological Visit in 1838–9–40* [Edinburgh: Maclachlan, Stewart, 1841], 2:229).

## To George Combe

Philada. 11 Mo. 25th. 1839

My dear friend Geo. Combe

When I received thy acceptable letter of 5th—Inst., I intended before many days to reply, if only to remove the impression, that the remarks of our friend

Fanny K. Butler had made on thy mind, relative to my shewing her thy comparison of our organs. That I did read to her a part of thy letter is true.—but not *the* part, where thou awarded any superiority to my developements. For however my Love of Approbation might be gratified with such an opinion of our respective minds, a sense of propriety would forbid my shewing it to her, as it has done indeed, to all out of our own family circle and immediate friends. I have taken pleasure in reading that letter to many, because of the expression it contained, of confidence in the success of our Anti-Slavery enterprise. Should thou publish my answers to it, the propriety of which I leave to thy decision, I hope thou wilt print also thy letter.[1] The copy thou asks for, of the part alluding to F. Butler, is as follows:

"We were glad to hear that you had met with Mrs. Butler. She was always a great favorite of mine, and she appeared to me to be more gentle, kind & affectionate when I saw her last here, than I had ever seen her before. She seems to improve as she grows older. I warn you however against committing an idolatry which is very commonly fallen into, by her friends in this country—namely—do not over-estimate her Causality". Here I stopped in reading the letter to her—omitting the following: You have much more of the organ yourself, and you are capable of taking deeper and wider views than she. You have less Self-Esteem, & if you were to reverse your relative positions, that is to say, you to look up to her as your superior in reasoning power, you would often be puzzled and she not benefitted by your wisdom." I acknowledge I feel some misgivings in copying what seems to me more than my due, for if she would yield herself wholly to her convictions of right & of duty, she would have few superiors *among women.*

Thou asks what we here would think of thy speaking plain truths of the American people. We should be far from "ashamed" of thy thus exposing us, and should hope that good would result from such plain dealing as we require, if done in a proper spirit, with a manifest desire for our improvement. I recollect, at the time thou spoke of our Acquisitiveness,[2] in one of thy lectures, I thought thou made more apologies for us, than we could make for ourselves; and feared it would give too much encouragement to those who are pursuing wealth, with an avidity, as if they counted "Gain to be Godliness." I should have been better pleased, if thou had then given us a merited reproof, for I thought there was too much of flattery in thy remarks. Shall I "forfeit" *thy* "good opinion" by speaking thus plainly? We shall look with interest for thy book, and hope thy friends at home will advise favorably to its publication.

I delivered thy messages to Geo. M. Justice[3] &c. The books alluded to have arrived, and he intended writing to thee very soon.

A. D. Morrison and self were wishing there was sufficient inducement for thee to deliver another course here similar to that nearly completed in Boston. She talked of an attempt to ascertain the public feeling on this subject. I dont know that she took any step however. If she did she probably informed thee.

We shall wish to hear your conclusions for next month, and hope the time may pass pleasantly to you both. The prospect of seeing you once more before your departure from this country is very pleasant. You must allow us as much time as you can. I regret to hear of the affection of "Cecy"'s eyes. She must be aware of the need of great care in using them, after even a light attack. My husband and children unite in love to you both. We hope you have met with our particular friends Wm. Lloyd Garrison, and Maria W. Chapman in Boston. I rejoiced to hear that thou had had conversation with John Pierpont on the subject of Colonization. What an admirable defence he has made against the charges of the Anti-Temperance & Anti-Abolition members of his congregation![4]

My Jas. Mott just bids me say, that he met G. M. Justice today—and he wished his respects to thee, with a tender of his thanks for the books, as he had not yet written.

very Sincerely
thy friend—    L. Mott

ALS GBNLS Env: "George Combe, Boston, Mass."

1. Combe did not reprint the letter regarding LCM and Fanny Kemble Butler. Regarding American slavery, he wrote: "If they nourish in the bosom of their country a system at open enmity with benevolence and justice, and if they harden their higher feelings in such a way as to become blind to its cruelty and injustice, it is morally impossible that minds thus perverted in their perceptions can esteem and practise justice in all other relations of life" (Combe, *Notes on the United States of North America during a Phrenological Visit in 1838–9–40* [Edinburgh: Maclachlan, Stewart, 1841], 1:256–57).

2. On American acquisitiveness, Combe wrote: "The Americans, although highly acquisitive, are not sordid as a nation. They expend their wealth freely, and where the object meets with their approbation, they are even munificent in their donations" (ibid., 2:198–99).

3. George Middleton Justice was a Philadelphia Hicksite Quaker.

4. John Pierpont (1785–1866) was a Boston Unitarian minister and a reformer. In 1838 his parishioners at Hollis Street Church had tried to remove him for his liberal reform interests. Pierpont had responded, "I protest . . . that there are some subjects which may be interdicted to the pulpit, on the grounds that they are 'exciting topics'" (*JGW*, 1:300; *Liberator*, 4 October 1839, 157, 25 October 1839, 171, 8 November 1839, 177).

## To Maria Weston Chapman

Philada. 12 mo. 16th. 1839

My dear Maria

Thy kind letter of "17th. Oct" and "5th. Nov." were duly received with their accompaniments—the "Liberty Bell"[1] and "North Star," with which we were much interested.

I sent the two copies as directed. Sarah M. Douglass desired me to make her acknowledgments to thee for thy kindness in remembering her, and to say that she should appreciate such a gift from thee, even though it had not contained

W. L. Garrison's and L. M. Child's essays. Margaretta Forten[2] too, asked me to thank thee on their behalf.

My copy has been kept in circulation. It contains some excellent pieces. W. L. G.'s I was particularly pleased with.

The "North Star" too shed its appropriate light for the occasion. How brilliant is its prototype just now, in its early rising!—[3] Do you see it sometimes?— The Managers of our Fair had fixed on that name for their book before they heard of your paper, and it was too late to alter it,—so we must bear the character of copyists. I hoped ours would be out in time to send thee one, before it is offered here. Thy repeated kindnesses to me in this way, call for more than the mere expression of thanks—they are highly valued, I assure thee—— Our Anna M. Hopper is hoping, the box of treasures so thoughtfully contributed by thee to their sale, will be forth-coming.

Now, my dear Maria, what shall I say as to the main subject of thy letter? I am so at a loss that I have delayed from day to day, to make the attempt. Not that I would conceal from any, my disapprobation of the proceedings of the new organization, from the beginning—the plans and manouevres of the Ex. Com. in New York, &c, &c—[4] But if I spoke out my whole heart, it would be, in pleading with my dear friends of the other side, not to be moved by these things, nor suffer themselves to be driven from the ground of Non-Resistance. I judge you not, as having acted improperly in your defense against the high-handed measures of your opponents.— indeed I rather regard you as laboring for the *whole;*—and that whatever security we may enjoy from similar encroachments, we are in great measure indebted to your quick-sighted discovery and prompt exposure of. Still, the local dissensions and the detail of divisions in your meetings and societies, I have not been willing should be told "in Gath;" and have therefore wished with L. M. Child, that "our dear and much-respected friend Garrison would record them more sparingly in his paper." The ~~painful~~ censurable occurrences in your Female Socy., altho painfully interesting, I would much have preferred, not to gratify the enemy with the recital of.

I have felt little inclination to read the "Mass Abolitionist," and have not seen any save the 1st. No.[5] C. C. Burleigh mentioned the perverted use made of my remarks, but I had not seen the article till thou sent it to me. It is so entirely out of my line to write for publication, that I must be excused from making the attempt;—but I should be glad for E. Wright[6] to know that the turn he gave to my "explanation" in the Non-Resistance meeting—viz. an admission of the right to be intolerant, was just the opposite of what was intended by me in the remarks made. It reminded me of the comment of the Edinburgh Reviewers, on Stuarts complaint of Channings want of Charity in their controversy.[7] After a full recognition of the right of opinion, they say, "but who ever heard of tolerating *intolerance?*"

When we declare the self-evident truth of man's inalienable right to the pursuit of happiness, we certainly do not confer or acknowledge the right to

injure hi[s] neighbor. Nor ought we to pre-suppose man's better nature so cor-
rupted, & his judgment and inclination so distorted, that his happiness shall
consist in so-doing. Should any prove themselves so regardless of the rights of
their neighbor, as to claim the authority of the text for the liberty of trampling
upon him, they must be met with a suitable remonstrance, and restored to a
sound mind and pure heart, by applying correct reasoning and all the remedies
which the Gospel furnishes. Now these you have abundantly within your reach
in Boston and need not my feeble aid— Thou art at perfect liberty however to
make such use of this attempt to explain myself, as in thy judgment may be best.

As to my closing remarks in the Non-Resistance Mg., I would willingly furnish them could I call them to mind.[8] I made the attempt soon after the meeting, but succeeded so poorly, that it was like "the manna of yesterday"—& I gave
it up. Adin Ballou's excellent speech is a treasure.[9] Have you the Non-Resistant
from the beginning? I requested B. A. S Jones to procure me all the numbers, as
I had disposed of mine, & he promised to write for them. I was much pleased
with the article on Phrenology in the Liberator.[10] I expressed to Geo Combe the
hope that he would meet with thee and our friend W. L. G. while in Boston. Will
you let him have the pleasure— He writes me that he has convened with J.
Pierpont on Colonisation & now understands our views better than he did.

The account of your Fair was indeed cheering.[11] Also the fact that the colored people are not entirely discouraged in view of the dissensions among us—
Let all the notice be taken of them in the Liberator that you can— I doubt there
being any effort made to apply the proceeds of our Fair to the use of the N. Y.
Ex. Com.—nor do I think J. G. W. would recommend it. I think they are learning by the things they have suffered. How heartily can I respond the wish that
we may oftener meet. My visit to you is a source of unmingled pleasure—the
acquaintance with dear Edmund Quincy & others, whom not having seen I
loved  The kind regard of thy Henry G. was more than I looked for[12]—as I knew
he did not fully unite in our Non Resistance views— I feared he would be
pained by my ultraism— I can fully sympathize in his annoyances in the shape
of C. [E.?] Gifford & his like. We have no lack of such here

I have not room to send all the love I feel for thy sisters and our frds. generally

very truly thine    L Mott

excuse my little sheets of *free* paper—made of linen

with this a friend of mine Sarah Jackson sends $5 for the Liberator she has
not paid for a year or two

I enclose $3 for the Non-Resistance cause—should like to have some tracts

ALS MB Env: "Maria W. Chapman, Boston Mass. per [S.?] C. Coleman"

1. In 1838 Chapman had begun the *Liberty Bell,* a collection of antislavery writings
by such authors as Garrison and Lydia Maria Child to be sold at the Boston Female
Anti-Slavery Society's annual bazaar, and she published it sporadically until 1858 (Taylor, 87–88).

2. Margaretta Forten (1808–75) was the sister of Sarah L. Forten and a member of the PFASS (C. Peter Ripley, ed., *Black Abolitionist Papers* [Chapel Hill: University of North Carolina Press, 1991], 3:91).

3. *The North Star: The Poetry of Freedom by Her Friends* (Philadelphia: Merrihew and Thompson, 1840) was compiled by J. G. Whittier for the Philadelphia Anti-Slavery Fair, 23 December 1839.

4. Nonresistance was one issue that split the AASS. The New York State Anti-Slavery Society disapproved of the Garrisonians' stance against any participation in politics (*Pennsylvania Freeman*, 10 October 1839, 2).

5. In 1839 some male members of the Massachusetts Anti-Slavery Society, objecting to the introduction of woman's rights issues into the society's agenda, formed the Massachusetts Abolition Society. The latter, which LCM and others often called the "new organization," was open only to men (Henry Mayer, *All on Fire: William Lloyd Garrison and the Abolition of Slavery* [New York: St. Martin's Press, 1998], 267). Its newspaper, the *Massachusetts Abolitionist*, stated that Garrison's *Liberator* had not accurately presented the Boston Female Anti-Slavery Society's alleged partiality to the new, anti-Garrisonian organization (7 November 1839, 150). The issue of the *Massachusetts Abolitionist* to which LCM refers has not been uncovered.

6. Elizur Wright (1804–85), the secretary of the New York Anti-Slavery Society and a founder of the AASS, resigned from the AASS in 1839 and became editor of the *Massachusetts Abolitionist* (*WLG*, 2:111).

7. Moses Stuart (1780–1852), a Calvinist at Andover Theological Seminary, had criticized a controversial sermon by William Ellery Channing preached at the ordination of Jared Sparks, in which Channing spelled out the beliefs of the Unitarians and their reasons for rejecting Trinitarian dogma and Calvinism (Stuart, *Letters to the Rev. Wm. Ellery Channing, Containing Remarks on His Sermon Recently Preached and Published in Baltimore* [Andover, Mass.: Flagg and Gould, 1819]; Jack Mendelsohn, *Channing: The Reluctant Radical* [Boston: Little, Brown, 1971], 158–67).

8. LCM's closing remarks at the nonresistance meeting on 27 September 1839 have not been recovered, probably because she could not recall them to her satisfaction. The *Non-Resistant* noted that it was waiting for LCM to send a copy: "Lucretia Mott addressed the meeting in an eloquent and impressive manner. The meeting requested a report from herself of her remarks, to be published with the proceedings, which it is hoped will soon be received" (7 December 1839, 3). LCM also spoke on two resolutions at this meeting. She admonished Henry Clarke Wright and other ministers to keep their speeches short, thereby "giving opportunity to the least" members of the society, and told a brief story from her family life to illustrate the ineffectuality of punishment: "One of our little girls when told to go to bed, felt disinclined to obey, and some time after, she was discovered hid under the table, thinking it a good piece of fun. No notice was taken of it, and she took her own time. We had forgotten the affair, when she came running down stairs with her little bare feet, saying, 'do mother forgive me!'" (*Non-Resistant*, 2 November 1839, 1, 16 November 1839, 3).

9. Adin Ballou (1803–90) was a Universalist minister, a reformer, and a nonresistant. Ballou had addressed the relationship of nonresistants to human and divine government (*Liberator*, 6 December 1839, 196; *Non-Resistant*, 16 November 1839, 1).

10. Benjamin Smith Jones (1812–62) was a Philadelphia abolitionist. With Whittier, he helped compile *The North Star* (see note 3). The editorial "Phrenology," which promoted Combe's lectures, had been published in the *Liberator* (29 November 1839, 191).

11. The Boston Female Anti-Slavery Society had held a fair on 29 and 30 October 1839 to sustain the work of the Massachusetts Anti-Slavery Society. Maria Weston Chapman's

account of the fair appeared in the *Liberator* (1 November 1839, 174; see also *Liberator,* 4 October 1839, 159).

12. Henry Grafton Chapman (1804–42), a Boston merchant, had married Maria Weston in 1830.

## To James Miller McKim

Philada—12 Mo. 29th. 1839—

My dear Miller

It is so long since I have written to thee that thou really begins to feel to me somewhat like a stranger; but this coming visit in the 2nd. month, will restore thee to us again, as one of our household—and a dear one too— We all look forward to it with delight— Be sure to come directly to "136"—we'll let thee visit John G. W., if he is here then, as often as thou wishes. I find by E. M. D[avis]. that they are planning somewhat for thee to take the charge of the Depository—whether anything will be fixed on that will offer an inducement to thee, I know not

I fear however that they cannot afford sufficient salary, to enable thee to prosecute all thy wishes.— I have two letters from thee unacknowledged,— one of "July 13th."—the other "Oct. 21[st"] both very acceptable—as thine ever have been— But I am not going to plead guilty to the charge thou hints at— either in thy case or Charles [*Burleigh*]'s;—nor yet in the 2 or 3 that have since been confided to me of a similar character. What can I do, if you young people will come to me, whispering in my ear, your hearts best affections. You cant expect one of my temperament, to hear with coldness & indifference. If then in the ardor of feeling, my sympathies are with you, & I express myself accordingly—you must not attribute it to an impatience of all necessary delay.— — — We are expecting a visit from Sarah next week, when we can talk over matters; for now my name is up, I may as well go on in characteristic style.— As to Charles's affairs, I'll refer thee to him for all information; as well as for a further clearance of myself from tha[t] meddling to which "Match-Makers" are prone. Enough of this, however.

We regretted that Sarah [*Speakman*] was not here last week during "the Sale". It was an animating time, and their success was encouraging. They took more than $800. and have many books left.— We feared the exertion would be too much for our Anna [*Hopper*] who is by no means strong; but the excitement was so pleasant that she has not suffered materially by the exposure. Maria [*Davis*] is so tied down to her babes, that they had not much of her help.— She seldom comes here to stay long— Little Henry C. is a fine growing boy—and Anna one of the sweetest of children. Not however so forward and smart as our dear little Lu [*Hopper*] whose Father continues his unwearied pains to "develope" and then exhibit her.— He is quite encouraged in his profession since his admission.— Thou dont know how disappointed my sister Martha [*Wright*] was, that thou didn't visit us during her stay here this fall— She mentioned it again & again. Now, she has taken Marianna [*Pelham*] home, we may not expect a visit from her soon again. They have removed from Aurora to Auburn, and David is doing well there.

Sarah Pugh called yesterday and read to us a letter she had received from Northumberland containing most gratifying information of thy visit there. It was just what I loved to hear said of thee—thy preaching—and all  Why dont thy letters appear oftener in the Freeman? We have H. B. Stanton pleasantly with us now—he dined here on 6th. day—& lectured that evening to a small audience—owing to the storm. He is to speak again tomorrow evening.[1] He bore very well an allusion to their wrong-doings in New York & Mass.— We hope they begin to see the error of their ways. What a pity to waste any of our precious time—& devote any of the valuable space in our Abolition Papers in childish quarrellings among ourselves!— If the Resolutions which our Female Society here, passed at its last Meeting—and the letter accompanying it, both written by Mary Grew to our Sisters in Boston should appear in any of their papers—I think thou wilt be pleased with a prerusal of them.[2] I am glad to hear thou read the proceedings of the Non-Resistant Meeting with interest. The words of truth & soberness were spoken forth there and the meeting altogether was of deep interest to me— On one account, more so than our first Anti-Slavery Convention— That *women* were there by right, and not by sufferance and stood on equal ground. Adin Ballou's speech was considered the best exposition of our principles that was offered— With this I forward thee a few, to hand to those, to whom "it is lawful to speak wisdom."— — I will also send a copy of the several addresses, issued by our Yearly Mgs. Com. on the subject of slavery—so that thou may see, how the cause is advancing among us— Our "Frds Association" too is increasing in numbers & interest  Charles can tell thee that he is regarded so much a "plain Friend" as to be invited to speak in two of our meetings.

Who dost thou think will go to the Grand Convention in London?— We are speculating largely here— What if Jas. & myself should crowd in among the number?— Edwd. & Maria are trying to make us think we can go.— J. G. W. must go— Gerritt Smith we hope will, tho' he says not— H. B. Stanton expects to go. Wm. L. G. certainly. S. Pugh holds herself ready—Elizabeth J Neall also[3]— I wish Marias Chapman & Child could go— Abm. L. Pennock says Charles must go— What an interesting event it will be!—

While on the subject of matrimony just now—I ought to have told thee of two engagements of that nature in our family connexion—likely soon to be consummated—and both not only without my help, but without my knowledge or slightest suspicion until all fixed betwn. the parties—and that is more than Edwd. & Anna can say for they were needful auxiliaries in our case—viz. that of Danl. Neall with our cousin Rebecca Bunker— Dost thou recollect

The Executive Committee of the PASS, 1839. *Back row, left to right:* Mary Grew, Edward M. Davis, Haworth Wetherald, Abby Kimber, James Miller McKim, Sarah Pugh; *front row, left to right:* Cyrus Burleigh, Margaret Jones Burleigh, Benjamin Bacon, Robert Purvis, LCM, JM. (Courtesy of the Friends Historical Library of Swarthmore College)

her?—of Mount Holly—a fine woman—tho' of hidden worth owing to her diffidence—of suitable age—and they appear as happy together as much younger people— She is now with us on a visit—& thou wilt believe me, when I tell thee that it is with pleasure I prepare a room for their select conferences. I pity Charles when he is watching my preparations for them & tell him, it may be his turn some day—when it will give me equal pleasure to accommodate them— Danl. has asked for a certif[icat]e. on accot. of marriage and the time fixed is early in the 2nd Month. The other case is our cousin Phebe Hussey with Captn. Edwd. J. Gardner of Nt.—a widower with 2 children—very suitable & pleasing every way. She has been there since the 9 Mo last— They are to be married on New Years day 1840— Neither her Mother nor sister Mary Earle can be present on the occasion. I shall have to draw my undignified sheet to a close— Thou'lt think I have not treated thee much like a stranger. Destroy it when read—and write me a better—

Affectionate remembrances to your household—Eliza must be very glad to have Mary with her again.

truly thine— L. Mott—

My Jas. Mott says Give my love to Miller—tell him we shall be glad to see him here as soon as can come".

ALS PSCHi-Mott Env: "James M. McKim, Carlisle, or wherever found, Pa., By Charles"

1. Henry Stanton had spoken before the Junior Anti-Slavery Society at Temperance Hall on 27 December and would speak again on 30 and 31 December 1839 (*Pennsylvania Freeman*, 2 January 1840, 3).

2. At a meeting of the PFASS on 12 December, the members had resolved "That we earnestly entreat the members of the Boston Female Anti-Slavery Society by all the love they bear the suffering slave by all the regard which they cherish for the honor of the Anti-Slavery enterprise in our Country, to eradicate at once & forever the 'root of bitterness' which has sprung up among them; and again to dwell together in unity" (Pennsylvania Abolition Society Papers, reel 30, PHi).

3. Elizabeth J. Neall, later Gay (1819–1907), the daughter of Daniel Neall Sr., went to the World's Anti-Slavery Convention in London as a representative of the PFASS.


## To Maria Weston Chapman

[*Philadelphia 20 February 1840*]

[*Added to Anna Hopper's letter of the same date*]

My dear Maria

I too felt sorry that the acknowledgment of your generous contribution to the Fair should be so long delayed. I was absent from the City nearly 2 weeks—and since my return I have waited for an opportunity to send our Annual Report &.c  If the package of "Wright & Wrong"[1] & "Liberator extra" had reached us two days earlier, we could have distributed nearly all of them at our Meetg of the Female AntiS. Society. With Sarah Pugh's assistance we have sent many of them as directed & shall soon forward all of them. Several of our friends expressed their thanks—& satisfaction with the opportunity to read & judge for themselves of your difficulties. The box I was glad to have—to shew, with your circular of the weekly contribution plan received some time since. We may have to adopt some similar plan for our treasury is nearly empty—& money very difficult to obtain.— At our last meeting we agreed to subscribe for the same number of copies of the Liberator as heretofore. It was a close vote however for many of our members thought we ought to give the preference to a German paper published in this State. That class of our community standing so in need of light. It was urged too that the Liberator contained more of local matter than was needed here. But on the other hand it was stated, that there was less of an objectionable character than was found in it last year & our taking fewer copies now might be construed by its enemies as passing a censure on it & its Editor. Its advocacy of Liberty on the broad ground, might also have been offered as another reason; but as that would have laid some of us open to the charge of "lugging in the woman question," &c we forebore to adduce it. The vote was 27 to 25.[2]

Thou asks, whose was the single vote in the negative—on the letter sent to your Society— It was Grace Douglass. Your answer will be read at our next meeting.[3] S. Pugh & myself have read it together with the account of your meeting. We deeply lament the existing state of things among you. But understand me not as entering into judgment of the propriety of the steps you have felt bound to take in this affair. We read the reasons offered by 'the Board' of the Mass. A. S. Socy. for decling aid to the Parent Society, with much interest—& thought them abundantly sufficient. I mean—my husband & self.— We dread the approach of this controversy—and hope it may not reach us— There will be some difficulty in procuring a satisfactory Editor for the "Freeman" in the place of J. G. Whittier who leaves us this week—regretted by all I presume. We shall not find his equal in many respects. Standing just as he does, between our Orthodox Friends & *our Side* which together compose a large proportion of Penna. Abolitionists he has pleased all.— The seeming countenance he gave to the new organization—we could make allowance for in his close intimacy with H. B. Stanton— And we have ever hoped he would be dealt very gently with for that error of judgment. He is most sensitive now on that subject & somewhat sore from wounds inflicted by sundry resolutions passed in Chester Co. some time since—as well as by the remarks of individuals (perhaps myself included.) There was rather a mis-representation to him of what I said at our board. Mg. when we were discussing the question of takg the Libr. & Freeman.—[4] On this account S. Pugh, A. M. Hopper & self were sorry there was any allusion to him & the Freeman, in your letter to our Society. We thought of suppressing it, but felt that we had no right to do that— Then we hoped he would not hear of it— But that was vain—for there were enough to report— So on the whole we concluded it will be better to let him see for himself before he leaves us, just what is said— so that an exaggerated picture need not be presented to him. I hope you will meet in Boston & discuss the matter face to face—[5] Specially do I wish dear Maria Child to see & talk with him. My best love to her—'thy sisters'—& all

We have a little stir here too in our Moral Reform Society The com: to procure a room for our Annual Mg accepted the session room of a Presbytn. Mg house with the understandg that women should not speak— I was informed of this the day before the Mg—of course did no go— At the next stated Mg of our Socy I offered a resolution something after this sort "That we can only effect the object of our association as our Sex seek an elevation from the low estate which existing customs, & the influence of the Priesthood have placed them," Remarkg upon it in reference to the proscription at our *own* meeting. Some excitement was manifest & several left the Mg. It was late however & they may have had other reasons for withdrawg— The subject will be taken up at our Mg 3 months hence— I expect to withdraw from the society I regretted to see in the Non-Resistant, that letter from M. L. Cox—[6] I was not at the Mg when the circumstances occurred of which she wrote—but she ought in justice to us, to have stated that the forcible seizure of her sister, was not only wholly unauthorized, but that the next "Preparative Mg" came out unanimously against such a procedure—& forbade its repetition. The man who was the prominent actor in the affair altho nominally a member has nev[er] taken an interest in the "concerns of our Society." He was not a constable but simply a clerk of the Market & claimed the right to act as police officer in virtue of his office—he judging her a disturber of the Peace. Our Friends think almost every statement in that letter would bear another face but eschewing controversy they forbear a defence of themselves  They deny that the cause of dissatisfaction is Susan Cox's advocacy of the cause of the oppressed &c. I felt a wish that we might clear ourselves from some of these charges—& asked Dr. Parrish to write an answer for the Non-Resistant but he declined.

I yesterday paid B. S. Jones my subscription to the Non-Resistant for this year. It was in my heart to give more liberally but present exgences forbid. My husband is likely to come out better than very many in these perilous times— being able to meet all his engagements in money matters without as much embarrassment as he feared—

I regret that even "such a worthy cause" is likely to prevent thy going to England. I see no way for us to leave home yet—

Kindest remembrances to thy husband—his parents & sister Mary

ever thine—     L. Mott

Thanks to A. W. Weston for the sonnet—  It was good

ALS MB Env: "Maria Weston Chapman, Boston, Mass. pr J. G. W."

1. *Right and Wrong in Boston: Annual Report of the Boston Female Anti-Slavery Society* was written by Chapman and published annually from 1836 to 1844 (Taylor, 27).

2. At a meeting the previous year LCM had requested an increase in the number of subscriptions to the *Liberator* as "evidence" of the PFASS's support of Garrison's activities, but some members objected that such a stand could be construed as taking sides "on a disputed point in the Mass. A. S. Society" (PFASS minutes, 14 February 1839, Pennsylvania Abolition Society Papers, reel 30, PHi; see also PFASS minutes, 13 February 1840, reel 30).

3. The minutes of the 12 March meeting simply state that the letter from "several members" of the Boston Female Anti-Slavery Society was read (reel 30).

4. An abolitionist from Chester County, James Fulton Jr. had declared in the fall of 1839 that Whittier sided with Garrison's antagonists in the Massachusetts Abolition Society, the "new organization" (*JGW*, 1:365, 367). The minutes of the PFASS board meeting state that the board had agreed to subscribe to forty copies of the *Pennsylvania Freeman*, but because of disagreement, the matter of *Liberator* subscriptions would be referred to the society as a whole (6 February 1840, Pennsylvania Abolition Society Papers, reel 30, PHi).

5. On 13 February the PFASS had passed a resolution applauding Whittier for his "invaluable offerings" to the *Freeman* and the antislavery cause and regretting that his health caused him to leave Philadelphia (PFASS minutes, 6 February 1840, Pennsylvania Abolition Society Papers, reel 30). On 29 February Whittier would write Elizabeth Neall from Amesbury, Massachusetts, that he had met with Chapman and left some letters from LCM: "Knowing that unless I began hostilities at once, she would, I gave her a regular lecture, and then listened to hers" (*JGW*, 1:385).

6. Mary L. Cox's letter of 13 November 1839 in the *Non-Resistant* (of which Chapman was an editor) described how her sister, Susan H. Cox Luther, and their mother, living at Race and Seventh Streets, had attended the Cherry Street Friends' meeting in Philadelphia on 10 November. When Joshua Mitchell, a clerk of the market and according to Cox "high-constable, and withal a member of the Society of Friends," asked Luther to leave, she refused. Mitchell and Thomas Ellwood Chapman, another "guard," then physically forced Luther to leave the meeting, which she did without resisting, saying, "Fear God and give glory to his name, for the hour of judgment is come." Cox went on to state that when she appeared on the scene, a "mob" followed them to their front door. Cox claimed that all three of the women were birth-right Quakers and that they had every right to attend the meeting (*Non-Resistant*, 8 January 1840, 3). Cox would be disowned for disunity in 1843; Luther had been previously disowned for marrying outside the Society of Friends (*Journal*, 14 February 1877).

## To Maria Weston Chapman

Philada. 5 mo. 13th. 1840.

My dear Maria

I have a hurried few minutes that I must devote to thee—and to the acknowledgment of thy dear Sister Anne's kindness in penning the several interesting items in thy last acceptable sheet recd. 2 or 3 weeks since. Dont apologise for writing often, for each double & single fold is read with much interest. Sometimes painful 'tis true, but the confidence & freedom which prompt the affecting details of your Society Mgs., is grateful to me— When the package arrived containg the "Libr extra" "Right & Wrong" &c, in our eagerness to open it & read the several sheets accompanying it—we missed one half sheet of a later date which was stitched to the envelope— It lay in a closet several weeks before I discovered it— It announced the new book—"Despotism in America"—wh. we have since read with deep interest. Who would have thought so many new views & arguments could be presented?— What a nice little history, in the Introduction, of the progress of Democracy in this country!—[1] When I finished it I felt as if I should like to begin & read it again. The accots. too of your doings in the Legislature, we have been glad to receive. G. Bradburn has truly done wonders.[2]

The information Anne gave of D. L. & Maria Child's having left Northampton, was new to us[3]— Maria has not written to me in a long time— I wish she would— How glad I should be if Philada. offered any inducement to them to settle here to advantage!— Anna M. Hopper was saying lately—she wished they would come & that Maria would open a school for young children—she and our Maria Davis would like to place theirs under such guardianship. But I should prefer her going to the World's Convention first. Are you not going to send her?— As she was disappointed accompanying her husband when he went—she ought to go now.— Had I the means, how gladly would I aid her in the undertaking. My husband & self really are making ready for the voyage— It is a late conclusion. Sarah Pugh and Elizabeth J. Neall will accompany us. We hear of very few going from Penna.— We should like to be informed who are actually going from Mass. We see a long list in the Libr.— Thy name among the rest. So we conclude *all* are not going. How sorry I am that circumstances will prevent thy being there.— Why cant Caroline[4] or Anne W. represent your Socy— Who of the New-Organization will be sent?— No women I conclude.

We should not be at the Anniversary Mg. in N. Y. if we were in the country—for it occurs during the week of our Yearly Mg. which would keep us at home. We now expect to leave N. York in one of the packet Ships—about the 7th or 9th. of next Mo.—[5] Let me hear from thee before we leave— Wm. L. Garrison, it seems, feels bound to stay till the battle is over in New York—at the risk of his not reaching London in time for the opening of the Convention.[6] I am more & more convinced that new and old organization can no more walk together Joshua Leavitt's editorials of late—& Gerrit Smith's letter with the charges against his brethren—surprised and grieved me much— I have ever hoped that J. G. W. would have his eyes opened—by such letters & denunciations—but he certainly seems to be blinded—& pours all his censures upon one party.—[7] We received the letter thou alluded to, from your self called "Board", stating their grievances & calling for our sympathy, putting several questions to us as to what they should do &.c—begging the favor of an answer— It was read at our last Meeting & a motion was made to answer or rather to acknowledge its reception & decline any further participation in your unhappy divisions— I opposed this on the ground of our having taken no notice of your letter, which also contained some inquiries as to how we would have proceeded under similar circumstances & asking too a repetition of *our favor*. Some members thot. the request not so direct for an answer, & that courtesy demanded that we should notice the last— I then moved as an amendment, that we should reply to both—which was accepted—but the motion was lost altogether—so you will not be likely to have further communication from us. I was not at the meeting—being absent from the City, when your letter was read— It called forth no remark I was told— —[8] Anne asked for further information of our Delaware treatment—but it is such an old story now that I dont feel like filling my page with it— The scene was truly awful at the time. D. Neall's new wife [*Rebecca*] was not inured to Mobs as some of us are—she shook, as with an ague fit from head to foot. I plead hard with them to take me as I was the offender— if offence had been committed, & give him up to his wife—but they declined saying "you are a woman & we have nothing to say to you."—to wh. I answered "I ask no courtesy at your hands on accot of my sex". but they had heard of him before as Prest. of Penna. Hall— Our presence & remonstrances no doubt moderated their purposes—for they treated us with respect—told me "all that was said in Mg was well liked, till that subject was touched upon. They only put tar enough on his coat not any on his person to [redeem?] their [pledge?] adding a few feathers—& obtaing a rail from a fence near made use of it but a few minutes commencg a song "ridg on a rail" when they released him sayg "Now old man, you are at liberty" He turned to them sayg. "Now my Smyrna friends—if any of you shd. be in Philada. & would come to my house I would give you as much to eat & drink as you want." they asked "Will you give us brandy" "No," he replied, "Nothing but water, I am a thorough cold water man" "thank you Sir" several said—& as we walked from them—not one followed, nor offered the least insult.— It was really a *respectful* mob—& I rejoiced to have no feeling in my heart toward them other than pity—& love for the lads standg around who listened to all I said— —

As respects M. L. Cox's letter— The charge may perhaps as well rest uncontradicted—altho' I have no objection to any publicity given to what I wrote— I mentioned it to Mary[9] & found her letter was written before our prepy Mg. occurred so if I called hers an *unfair* statement I would rather say *erroneous* statemt Moreover we cant say much for ourselves—for while we do not *forcibly carry* out her sister,—we employ a guard of young men at our gates to *keep her out* This is done to be sure without physical violence or rather without personal injury—but it is not so thoroughly non-resistant as some of us could desire.

I enclose $1 for the Non-Resistant—to be sent to Sarah Pearson[10] No 104 North 9th St Philada. And as we may not return before our next years subscription to the Liberator & Non Resistant will be due I enclose $5 to be credited to our account for the 2 papers

Love unfeigned to [*ms. damaged*] household, with wa[rm? at]tachment

thine,    L. Mott

By this opp[ortunit]y I shall write a few lines to Wm. L. Garrison enclosing $20 from the new subscriber to the Non Resistant Sarah Pearson—she has taken the Liberator for years & highly approves its course— When thou writes please say whether it is recd.— I dont wish to trouble him to acknowledge it— with his many engagements

ALS MB Env: "Maria W. Chapman, care of Henry G. Chapman, Boston, Mass."

1. The author (later revealed as Richard Hildreth) of *Despotism in America; or, An Inquiry into the Nature and Results of the Slaveholding System in the United States,* published anonymously in Boston in 1840, distinguished between the democratic Northern states and the slaveholding Southern states, calling the latter: "aristocracies of the sternest and most odious kind." He predicted a "desperate and dreadful struggle" between the two regions (Boston: J. P. Jewett, 1854, 8–9).

2. As a member of the Massachusetts legislature (1839–42), George Bradburn (1806–80), a Whig abolitionist and a Unitarian minister from Nantucket, had recently helped pass resolutions protesting the gag rule that forbade the introduction of antislavery petitions in the U.S. Congress (see Whittier to Daniel Neall Jr., 12 March 1840, *JGW,* 1:390).

3. The Childs were to stay on their rented beet farm outside Northampton until 1841 (*Lydia Maria Child: Selected Letters, 1817–80,* ed. Milton Meltzer and Patricia Holland [Amherst: University of Massachusetts Press, 1982], 130).

4. The *Liberator* listed thirty members of the Massachusetts Anti-Slavery Society, including Chapman, who had been appointed convention delegates (3 April 1840, 55). The

"circumstances" are probably the birth of a daughter, Gertrude Chapman, in 1840 (Taylor, 5). Caroline Weston (1808–82) was Chapman's sister.

5. On 1 May the Cherry Street Meeting had sent "To the Abolitionists of Great Britain" a certificate of membership "as a testimony of the respect and affection with which we regard" LCM and JM (Mott Manuscripts, PSCHi).

6. Tensions had been mounting all spring on several issues regarding the AASS's policies, particularly how deeply members should be involved in politics and elections and the position of women as officers and committee members in the organization. Garrison had written LCM on 28 April 1840 that "duty requires me to be at the anniversary of the Parent Society, which is pregnant with good or evil to our sacred cause" (*WLG*, 2:591).

7. In the *Emancipator*, editor Joshua Leavitt had criticized certain parties within the AASS for manipulating the actions of the executive committee. The *Non-Resistant* had criticized Leavitt for having "joined in the vulgar cry" against the Massachusetts Anti-Slavery Society because it had supported the Non-Resistance Society: "The abolitionists of the United States do not employ him for the purpose of doing battle with Non-Resistance" (*Emancipator*, 16 April 1840, 202; *Non-Resistant*, 8 April 1840, 27). Gerrit Smith's letter to Garrison of 6 April referred to an earlier exchange about the constitution of the AASS and its stand on participation in elections. Smith wrote that "the doctrine, that it is immoral to participate in politics, is of very recent origin." Garrison was wrong, declared Smith, in asserting that three of the framers of the society's constitution (Isaac Winslow, Samuel J. May, and George W. Benson) thought it "immoral to vote." Smith believed that if differences over this issue remained unresolved, a large group would withdraw from the AASS (*Liberator*, 24 April 1840, 65). Whittier blamed the Garrison faction for the divisiveness in the AASS and supported the formation of the Liberty party (see *JGW*, 1:400–401).

8. The minutes of the PFASS simply state that the Boston letter was read at its 9 April meeting (Pennsylvania Abolition Society Papers, reel 30, PHi).

9. This is probably Mary Grew, the corresponding secretary of the PFASS and a delegate to the World's Anti-Slavery Convention in London.

10. Sarah Pearson (d. 1865) was a Hicksite Quaker.


# To Daniel O'Connell[1]

London, 6th mo. 17, 1840

*To Daniel O'Connell, M. P.*

The rejected delegates from America to the "General Anti-Slavery Conference," are desirous to have the opinion of one of the most distinguished advocates of universal liberty, as to the reasons urged by the majority for their rejection, viz: that the admission of women, being contrary to English usage, would subject them to ridicule, and that such recognition of their acknowledged principles would prejudice the cause of human freedom.[2]

Permit me, then, on behalf of the delegation, to ask of Daniel O'Connell the favor of his sentiment, as incidentally expressed in the meeting on the morning of the 13th inst.,[3] and oblige his sincere friend,

LUCRETIA MOTT

PL *Pennsylvania Freeman,* 17 September 1840, 4

1. Daniel O'Connell (1775–1847), an Irish Whig in Parliament, advocated full rights for Roman Catholics.

2. The World's Anti-Slavery Convention had voted on 12 June 1840 to exclude all eight of the American woman delegates (see *Diary*, 30; LCM to Maria Weston Chapman, 29 July 1840, below; LCM to her children, 14 June 1840, NRU).

3. In her 15 June diary entry LCM had described O'Connell as "excellent—amusing" (*Diary*, 33). O'Connell's reply to LCM's letter of 20 June, which would be published in the *Freeman, Liberator,* and other papers, stated that the convention's fear of ridicule "was an unworthy, and indeed, a cowardly motive." Among O'Connell's reasons for opposing the exclusion was the prominent role that American women had played in the antislavery cause. He argued that the struggle to abolish slavery was not a military one, and its adherents depended "entirely on reason and persuasion common to both sexes, and on the emotions of benevolence and charity, which are more lovely and permanent amongst women, than amongst men." He apologized that his absence on the day of the vote had prevented him from "sooner urging these considerations on the Convention" (*Pennsylvania Freeman,* 17 September 1840, 4).

# To Maria Weston Chapman[1]

Dublin 7 Mo. 29th. 1840.—

My dear Maria

I remember how many—and kind and long have been thy messages of this sort to me, and now that our dear Wm. L. G. & N. P. Rogers are about to leave us setting their faces homeward,[2] I feel that somewhat is due from me to thee— But how to accomplish it 'I find not', for we are from day to day so in the midst of bustle & commotion & excitement—pleasurable & otherwise, that to write seems quite out of the question. Our friends too can tell you so much better than I can narrate here, the story of our coming across the Atlantic to attend a 'World's Convention'—simple souls! and on our arrival the grave information awaited us, that it was no more than a Conference of the British & Foreign A. S. Society, to be composed of such members as their 'Com. of Arrangement' should choose to select—that the name "The Worlds Convention" was merely a "poetical license"—(alias—a rhetorical flourish—)—and that the 'Com.' in their wisdom had seen meet to ordain and enact, that women should not compose part of their august body. That they further *as wise men should,* had a resolution prepared for this said 'Conference' as one of its first measures,— 'That all the arrangements of said committee be sanctioned & approved by the Conference.— Of course we would not "thrust ourselves forward" into *such* a meeting, but having come so far to see what could be done for the Slave, & being thus prevented doing anything ourselves, we were willing to be mere lookers on & listeners from without, as, by so doing we should be the means of many more women having an invitation to sit as spectators—which we found was accounted a very high privilege, in this land—by their women, who had hitherto, most submissively gone forth into all the streets, lanes, high-ways & bye paths to get Signers to petitions, & had been lauded—long & loud, for this drudgery, but who had not been *permitted*,—even to *sit* with their brethren, nor indeed much by themselves in public meetings—having transacted their business, as we were informed, by Committees.

In vain we endeavored to have a public meeting called for women—altho a few—Anne Knight, Elizh. Pease &.c—did all they could to promote it.[3] At length we gave up in despair & left London satisfied—that "when for the time they ought to be teachers, they have need that one teach them which be the first principles"[4] of Human Freedom. I might say more but time forbids—and much doubtless has already been written you in Boston, by those who keenly felt our grievances.— We had many opportunities with members of the 'New-Organization,' & with the com. & with individuals, to present to them their injustice to us—to the cause of the slave—as well as their own inconsistency. These we improved & had many a battle wherein we came off as we think victorious. But a 'World's Convention' has yet to be held— That the feelings of the British public would not have been so outraged as we were given to understand, by our admission, is abundantly evinced, in the readiness with which I have been heard in other places.— In Birmingham my appearance on the platform, in a large Meeting at the Town-Hall was as heartily cheered as if I had been worth hearing. And an invitation sent to the Chair to me to appoint a special meeting.— George Harris of Glasgow delivered an excellent lecture at the Meeting alluded to—on Capital punishment.[5] I intend to get a copy if possible of *three* which we are told he has delivered in Glasgow on the same subject[x].

Since we came to Dublin I have accepted an invitation to speak in a Temperance Mg.[6]—not the least manifestation of dissatisfaction—altho' unexpected to most present—but on the contrary "cheers long & loud"—& not merited neither—but such is the custom in this land—and I mention it as proof that the objections to our admission were all hollow—

Abby Kelly asks W. L. G. in a letter, if, as they fear, L. Mott has sacrificed *principle* at the altar of Peace— Now I dont know how far she will consider me as having done so— I have sometimes shrunk from a defence of our rights, when others have gone forward & stood in the breach—& I am very willing to crown such with laurels that I may not deserve—

We discovered before we left Philada. that the name of the convention was changed & saw the letter of Josh. Sturge[7]—hence we recd. our credentials conditionally—& after being refused by the Com. we felt satisfied not to present them to the Meeting. I was glad however that Wendell Phillips & Ann were not so easily put by & that he came forward & manfully plead for the right— I shall ever love Ann Phillips for her earnest appeals to her husband to stand firm in that hour of trial—and him for doing so—[8] Tell Abby Kelly if I am not much bold myself I respect those most who are so.— Tho' I fully believe if our English and Irish friends thought there were any in America whose foreheads were more as adamant than mine, they would be awe-struck—yea, horrified! I never failed in our several tea-parties,—soirees, &c to avail myself of every offer made for utterance for our cause—& then I shrunk not from the whole truth as those who heard can testify  Egotism must be excused for Woman's sake.

In addition to several letters written home giving an account of ourselves— I have filled one sheet to C. C. Burleigh—remarking on some of our speakers &c—which I have concluded to enclose unsealed—thinkg, thou might like to look over it—when thou wilt oblige me by sealg & forwg. it as directed—  If Wm. M. C. is with you ask him to let it serve instead of a letter to him, as I have sometimes thought of writing since I recd. a dear affect. message from him in a letter from Charles—  Our Irish friends tell me I take too sombre a view of the Meeting & Speakers—  I admit it may be so but I tell them to put their souls in our Souls stead & perhaps they too will be affected with a morbid sensitiveness.

Wm. L. G. will tell you—what glorious meetings they have had in Scotland.—  We rejoice that we have stayed here to see them once more.

We rejoice too to hear of thy well-doing in thy chamber—as well as of Helen Garrison's— — How affecting is the death of J. A. Collin's wife![9] We feel a deep interest in your doings across the wide water & hope truth & the right will yet be triumphant— — How I wish you could win back J. G. W. & Gerritt Smith![10] It is much best that a separation has taken place in the National Society—as we were—  We could not walk together unless more agreed—

Love to thy husband & every one of you—

ever thine    *L. Mott*

xFor the Non-Resistant.

ALS MB Env: "Maria W. Chapman, Boston, [yr.?] W. L. G. & N. P. R."

1. LCM wrote the letter on stationery of the British and Foreign Anti-Slavery Society.

2. Garrison and the New Hampshire newspaperman Nathaniel P. Rogers (1794–1846), delegates to the World's Anti-Slavery Convention in London, had, in protest against the women's delegates' exclusion, refused to participate. They left Ireland on 29 July and sailed from the British Isles for the United States on 4 August.

3. Anne Knight (1792–1862), a Chelmsford writer, socialized frequently with LCM and JM in London. LCM had met the Quaker reformer and antislavery leader Elizabeth Pease (1807–97) on 6 June, when Pease "talked orthodoxy" en route to a hat maker's shop (*Diary*, 23–25).

4. Heb. 5:12.

5. In her diary LCM briefly described a speech she had given before a group of British abolitionists in London on 24 June. Her letter to her children adds more detail to the event as she "addressed the brethren on the importance of effort to supply us with manufactured goods from free cotton and answered some objections urged during the sittings of the convention—  I was listened to patiently—  In the course of my remarks I most unwittingly came across Josiah Fosters prejudices by speaking of ourselves as Friends alluding to the sentiments of some in America & to those expressed by some here. . . . I did not remember while I was speaking that there had been a division, I had no sooner sat down than he was up desiring the audience to understand that I was not a member of the Society of Friends" (27 June 1840, NRU). The Unitarian minister George Harris (1794–1859) had preached before a crowd of twenty-five hundred (*Diary*, 46–47, 60).

6. On 22 July LCM had spoken at the temperance meeting and recorded in her diary that "people appeared satisfied" (*Diary,* 62).

7. Joseph Sturge (1793–1859), a member of the executive committee of the British and Foreign Anti-Slavery Society, had sent a letter discouraging the women delegates from attending: "Such a step would be any thing rather than a help to our cause" (letter of 3 March 1840, *Liberator,* 8 May 1840, 75). Despite Sturge's stand, LCM and JM had several social encounters with the Quaker corn merchant from Birmingham (*Diary,* 18).

8. Wendell Phillips (1811–84), a Boston lawyer and an antislavery leader, and his wife, Ann Terry Greene Phillips (1813–86), were both delegates to the convention. On 12 June, arguing for the acceptance of the women delegates, Phillips had said that in the United States, "we think it right for women to sit by our side there, and we think it right for them to do the same here" (*Proceedings of the General Anti-Slavery Convention* [London: British and Foreign Anti-Slavery Society, 1841], 36).

9. Helen Benson (1811–76) had married Garrison in 1834. Their third son, Wendell Phillips Garrison (d. 1907), had been born on 4 June 1840. John A. Collins (1810–79) was a supporter of Garrison and an agent for both the American and the Massachusetts Anti-Slavery societies.

10. After the AASS meeting in New York City in May 1840, Smith had joined the American and Foreign Anti-Slavery Society, which LCM and others also called the "new organization" (see LCM to Maria Weston Chapman, 13 May 1840, above; see also LCM to Elizabeth Cady Stanton, 16 March 1855, below).

# PART 2

# December 1840–December 1856

Returning to the United States in September 1840, LCM was immediately cast into myriad domestic and reform responsibilities. The friendships forged with Elizabeth Pease Nichol, Richard D. Webb, Hannah Webb, and Richard Allen during her trip abroad prompted extensive correspondence in which she showed her commitment to international agitation against slavery. Letters to these friends, as well as to Nathaniel Barney, Elisa Barney, and George W. Julian, describe her conflicts with her fellow Hicksites over her increasing activism and her radical theological beliefs. She criticized New York Hicksites' disownment of three antislavery activists and later splits in Midwestern yearly meetings over slavery. In doing so, LCM indicated her refusal to be guided, as she wrote Sarah Dugdale, by the "lovers of ease and quiet" (7 October 1845). Her declaration to Richard D. Webb and Hannah Webb, "I glory in radicalism or ultraism" (14 May 1849), epitomizes her life as a reformer.

LCM's friendship with Elizabeth Cady Stanton, which developed during her 1840 trip abroad, offered many opportunities for LCM to express affection for her young friend and to mentor Stanton in her work for woman's rights. Besides her regular exchanges with Stanton, LCM corresponded with a network of reformers, including William Lloyd Garrison, Lucy Stone, and Hannah Darlington, discussing women's employment and educational opportunities and planning woman's rights conventions. The historic Seneca Falls and Rochester conventions of 1848 constituted only a portion of LCM's efforts to establish public recognition of the rights women lacked.

During these years, as LCM traveled with JM throughout the Midwest and New England, she continued her passionate speaking not only for woman's rights but also for abolition and temperance. She confessed she sometimes "shocked" her audience with radical statements, such as her denial of human depravity (see her letter to Joseph Dugdale and Ruth Dugdale of 12 July 1850). Locally she was instrumental in assisting fugitive slaves and in sending books, clothes, and supplies to fugitives who had settled in Canada (see, e.g., her letter to Joseph Dugdale and Ruth Dugdale of 28 March 1849). In letters to other reformers she recounted the almost miraculous escape of Henry "Box" Brown and other fugitives. Later in the 1850s visitors from Kansas reminded the Philadelphians of the struggle for Free-Soilers' settlement in that territory and prompted lively discussions about the possibility of a peaceful resolution to the escalating crisis there (letter to MCW, 26 February 1856).

Letters to family back home composed as LCM traveled provide a distinct contrast in intimacy and informality with those to reformers. Besides the Philadelphia family, LCM wrote her sister MCW, living in Auburn, New York, sometimes as often as three times a week. Although MCW had left the Society of Friends when she married a non-Quaker, the two women continued to share tastes in liberal theology, reading, and politics. A co-worker in the woman's rights movement, MCW became increasingly a cherished confidante. Fourteen years older than her sister, LCM did not refrain from admonishing MCW in subjects ranging from the kind of stationery the latter used to raising a troublesome son. For example, the thirty-five-year-old MCW, wrote LCM, "must be careful not to fall from her step-ladder— They are dangerous for one who is increasg in flesh as she approaches middle age" (letter to MCW and David Wright, 28 August 1841).

In the family letters to her sister and her children, LCM discussed public events such as Theodore Parker's sermons, the Mexican War, fugitive slaves, and the popularity of *Uncle Tom's Cabin*, and commented on childbirth, servant problems, and picking blackberries. But no matter how urgently these public and domestic concerns pressed, she always welcomed her children, sisters, nieces, and nephews—in fact *insisted* that they visit JM and her in Philadelphia. Despite her attempts to keep her children as close to her side as possible, she had to endure frequent separations from them. As her married children raised their own children, strayed from the Quaker way of life, and traveled to Europe, LCM found her already broad horizons extended.

# To Aaron S. Lippincott[1]

Philada 12/8/40—

Respected friend A. S. Lippincott

I hope before this, thou hast received an acknowledgment from Jas. S. Gibbons of thy generous contribution in aid of the National Standard.[2] I have waited to hear from him before I thanked thee for the sum given, and the note accompanying it, which I sent to New York. A letter from James to C. C. Burleigh makes mention of it in grateful terms.

I entirely accord with thy remarks on the importance of that paper as well as other Abolition Periodicals not being turned aside from their direct object, to assail one another. There has been too much of it, and it has, doubtless, checked the onward course of the Anti-Slavery movement. But the attentive reader will discover that much in the "Old Organization" Papers has been on the defensive side—if that will excuse it.

A sectarian spirit found its way into our ranks and made similar ravages to those made in our Religious Society some ten or twelve years ago, when many thought it necessary to defend our simple faith by replies to Orthodox accusations. I never however, felt much interest in those controversies; neither now do I read with any satisfaction the criminations and re-criminations which sometimes mark our pages.

I hope therefore thy word of exhortation will be suffered among them, and that thou wilt retain an interest and guardian care over the advocates of the cause of the suffering and the dumb.

With thanks, In behalf of the Society for thy gift,

I am thine, for Truth and Liberty,
*Lucretia Mott*

ALS PSCHi-Mott Env: "Aaron S. Lippincott, 2nd. Street."

1. Aaron S. Lippincott (c. 1816–96) was a Philadelphia dry goods merchant and at his death a member of the Chester Monthly Meeting (Philadelphia City Directory, 1840; *Friends' Intelligencer,* 30 May 1896, 354).

2. The *NASS* had been established in June 1840 as the organ of the AASS after that society had fractured.

# To Elizabeth Pease

Philadelphia 2 Mo. 18th. 1841

My dear Elizabeth Pease

I have been writing a long letter to Fanny C. Wade[1] of Leicester Eng. acknowledging the reception of a valuable gift for our Anti-Slavery cause—a case filled with beautifully neat & tasteful articles, many of which have found a ready sale here.

I supposed Sarah Pugh was improving this opportunity to write to thee & perhaps to our dear brother George Thompson too, but she just called with letters to some other of our highly valued friends in your land, and says she has not had it in her power to do more at this time. She wrote you both I think some two months since. I wish thou could see a joint letter from Abby Kimber & herself to Louisa Bigg—Banbury Oxfordshire—sent by this conveyance—if we find that Joseph Adshead[2] is willing to be thus burdened. He kindly called on us 2 days since. I regretted much that we could not have more of his company. It does my heart good to meet any one from England, since our most delightful visit in that far-famed land, and specially so to greet any one so closely united with thy Father & thyself—George Thompson, Wm. Adam, & others in the British India enterprise.[3] We want to hear of your successful efforts. I liked to see Joseph evince some zeal in the cause. I wish he had made a longer stay in this city—or that we had known sooner of his being here.

I cant now say half that I want should be said to thee & which I hoped Sarah would find time to do.

How we rejoice at thy allegiance to Wm. L. Garrison and the right!— The exposure of such doings as have disgraced N. Colver, will open the eyes of some of our half-new-organized brethren.[4] How base to speak of J. A. Collins in the manner he did! Some of us feared he ∧Collins∧ was following too soon in the wake of so many *beggars*—Dawes & Keep, J. C. Fuller, *Chs. E. Lester,* &.c. &.c., but he & others thought the exigencies of our cause demanded it & I hope he may not be disappointed.[5] I was never quite satisfied with the Oberlin agents calling so much sympathy to their aid, while there are so many more direct ways of aiding the Anti-Slavery work. It is a Theological seminary & I fear will be new-organized. They already oppose Augustus Wattles in his manual labor school in Mercer County Ohio which is doing much more to elevate the colored man. These however are my private fears— I will hope better things as I told Wm. Dawes. We have had some most pleasant meetings lately of our English company—or rather our ship's company. Our beloved Isaac Winslow[6] is here & we have been from house to house in social parties, where we have talked over many of the scenes thro' which we passed so pleasantly together. The high-handed measures to which some of us were subjected were placed in the far-distant ground, as well as the petty indulgence of the spirit of Sectarism, while very near to our view as well as to our hearts best feelings, were the great kindness & attention of our many dear friends. It ever affords a delightful retrospect. That 3 months travel and sojourn, came up to my fondest anticipations, & I shall not cease to love you all dearly. But dont thou think our [*poetic brother, J. G. Whittier*] said more for his orthodox brother[*hood, than they could say*] for themselves? I hope thou reads his letter & C. C. Burleigh's reply to it, which we thot. good.[7]

With this I send our Annual Report written by Mary Grew—also Dr. Channings Emancipation which I know thou wilt like.[8] One also for George Thompson which please forward to him with my husbands & my kindest regards—no, with our dear love— How oft I dwell with pleasure on our "tour to the Lakes" & over the high-lands in his company! He made himself so agreeable. His comfortable dwelling too with his dignified Ann[9] & the dear little ones—the peerless five, including that "little fragment of humanity," I love to think of them all. Has Patrick Brewster, the friend of the struggling Chartist, succeeded in convincing George that a double honor awaits him if he will take up their cause?[10] Do write & tell us of all your doings. Excuse this so hasty & imperfect scratch of a letter  If I could do better I would not send it, but this is my only moment for writing—& thy goodness must excuse it.

My husband has been with me to the Legislatures of Delaware—New Jersey & our own State, where a patient & respectful audience was granted while I plead the cause of the oppressed. I have also attended 5 of our Quarterly Mgs since our return home, & have some more in prospect.

Angelina E. G. Weld has her second son[11]—of course she will be still longer immured in her nursery & her sister with her— With kind regards to thy Parents and the love of us all in large measure to thyself—I am thine with a sisters freedom

AL PSCHi-Mott Env: "Elizabeth Pease, Darlington, England"

1. LCM had met Fanny C. Wade in England on 10 July 1840 (*Diary*, 58). The minutes of the PFASS reflect that a letter to F. C. Wade was read (11 March 1841, Pennsylvania Abolition Society Papers, reel 30, PHi).

2. Joseph Adshead (1800–1861) was a British reformer known for his interest in prison improvement (*WLG*, 3:18).

3. Elizabeth's father, Joseph Pease (1772–1846), a wealthy British Quaker, was interested in the British East India Company, the abolition of slavery, and the condition of the English working class (*WLG*, 3:14; *Diary*, 23). William Adam, formerly in service of the British East India Company, was an officer of the British India Society in 1840 (*Diary*, 25, 27).

4. Nathaniel Colver (1794–1870), a Boston clergyman and a reformer, had gone to the "new organization" after the split of the AASS. In a speech before the Massachusetts Anti-Slavery Society he criticized Garrison and John Collins (*WLG*, 3:14).

5. John Keep (1781–1870) and William Dawes, trustees of Oberlin College, were visiting Great Britain to raise funds for the school. Charles E. Lester (1815–90), a Utica, New York, minister, had written a humorous account of the debate over the admission of women to the World's Anti-Slavery Convention in London entitled *The Glory and Shame of England* (New York: Harper and Brothers, 1841; *Diary*, 24, 35). James C. Fuller (1793?–1847), an Irish Quaker, had immigrated to New York State in the 1830s (*JGW*, 1:411).

6. Isaac Winslow (1787–1867), a Quaker merchant of Portland, Maine, had attended the London convention (*Diary*, 13).

7. The italicized words in brackets were written on the damaged manuscript in a hand other than LCM's. Whittier's letter that LCM mentions was probably one of 6 July 1840 to "Dear Charles" published in the *NASS* in which Whittier stated that, while not officially a member, he did "sympathize with the faithful abolitionists of the American and

Foreign Anti-Slavery Society" and noted that he did not believe that abolishing civil and church governments was the means to abolishing slavery. In response, C. C. Burleigh commented that no member of the AASS believed in the abolition of civil and church government "as the best means of abolishing slavery" (*NASS*, 13 August 1840, 37–38; *JGW*, 1:420–23).

8. In *Emancipation*, written 15 November 1840 (Boston: E. P. Peabody, 1840), William Ellery Channing had responded to Quaker minister Joseph John Gurney's report on the success of West Indian emancipation. Channing had denounced the American support of slavery and had ended by commenting on the duty of individuals, especially women, and free states to speak against slavery and help abolish it.

9. Anne Erksine Spry was the wife of George Thompson (*WLG*, 2:27).

10. Patrick Brewster (1788–1859) was a Scottish minister, a Chartist, an abolitionist, and a temperance and education advocate (*Diary*, 72).

11. Theodore "Sody" Weld was born on 3 January 1841 (Gerda Lerner, *The Grimké Sisters from South Carolina* [New York: Schocken Books, 1967], 288).

# To Nathaniel Barney

*[Philadelphia 6 March 1841]*

*[Added to JM's letter of the same date]*

My dear Nathaniel

Before the receipt of thine yesterday I had just closed a hurried few lines to our cousin Phebe Gardner, in which I requested her to tell thee we had recd. thy last, with its acceptable enclosure which was immediately appropriated toward the payment of the same number of the Liberator we have heretofore taken. We felt grateful for the donation.

I have been so much from home attendg 5 Qy Mgs, beside the places Jas. has mentioned, that I have not had time from other duties to write to my dear friends as I could wish. Many items in thine were particularly interesting, as was also the letter published in the Islander respectg the Atheneum, which we were glad to receive. We took it to Sadsbury for Lindley Coates to read—[1] It is indeed an encouraging fact that public sentiment is changing in reference to the colored people—and does not the late discussion in the Kentucky Legislature evince progress in the work of Emancipation?[2] What dost thou think of Oliver Johnson's correspondence with Geo. F. White?[3] I should have preferred a silent endurance of George's anathemas, not doubting it would be manifest whence his revilings came. Things begin to wear a threatening aspect. Much opposition has been acted out lately here towards Mary S. Gove who is delivering a course of lectures to an intelligent class of women on Anatomy & Physiology.[4] I am atteng. with our Anna—Maria & Elizh. Many Cherry—Green—& Spruce St. Friends go— She having been disowned by the Orthodox at the Eastward—& slandered by others—some of our good friends would have preferred that no countenance be given her by any of us;—but I had long wished that subject properly presented to Females & after examining her certificates & hearing her own story I was fully satisfied that she could suitably demonstrate to our children, and the more I heard her slandered the more it became a principle with me to countenance her efforts. We are all well satisfied so far—

How noble was your Womens contribution to the Boston Fair![5] I was so glad to hear of their good works. My views underwent precisely the change that thou mentions relative to Fairs. On being repeatedly called on to give my reasons against them—I was constrained to admit that it was the abuse of them that was objectionable. I hope Eliza did not get her sickness by going to Boston & attending the sale. I was sorry to hear she had suffered with rheumatism. Are you not comg to our Yearly Mg.? How rejoiced we should be to have you under our roof where we could say so much

Please thank G. Bradburn for the paper contg his letter

Love to all our dear [frds]

ever yours,    L. Mott

We were obliged by thy mention of our cousin Phebe Gardner

ALS MNHi

1. In a letter, a "member of the Atheneum" had protested an upcoming resolution from the Atheneum denying access to African Americans (*Nantucket Islander,* 16 January 1841, 2). Lindley Coates (1794–1856), a Chester County Hicksite, was a founder of the AASS (*WLG,* 3:158).

2. Earlier that year an act had been introduced into the Kentucky legislature that would have allowed slaves to be purchased and brought into Kentucky, thus repealing an 1833 law. When the act failed to pass, legislator Cassius M. Clay (1820–1903) gave a widely publicized speech denouncing slavery (*Pennsylvania Freeman,* 24 February 1841, 1; Robert McElroy, *Kentucky in the Nation's History* [New York: Moffat, Yard, 1909], 411).

3. Oliver Johnson (1809–89), an abolitionist and a newspaper editor, published *Correspondence between Oliver Johnson and George F. White: A Minister of the Society of Friends* (New York: privately published, 1841). Johnson had initiated the correspondence in November 1840 in response to some negative remarks White had made regarding the Non-Resistance Society and Quaker participation in nonresistance.

4. Mary Sargeant Gove, later Nichols (1810–84), was an author, an advocate of free love, and a water-cure physician originally from New Hampshire.

5. The Massachusetts Anti-Slavery Fair, held 22–26 December 1840, had raised over $2,000 (*Liberator,* 4 December 1840, 195; *NASS,* 7 January 1841, 122).

## To Elizabeth Cady Stanton[1]

Philada. 3 mo. 23rd. 1841

My dear Elizh.

With Sarah Pugh and 'Lizzy' Neall for thy correspondents, I cannot hope to convey much that will be new or interesting; but for the love I bear thee, my dear girl, thy cousins must not go without a line, expressive of my interest in

you both; for let me assure Henry, that from the hour he came here—an unso-
phisticated "Lane Seminary boy," he has had our best wishes; as well as of late
our fears, lest he would give too much aid to New-Organization; But we'll let
that pass— He and J. G. W. too must not forget their first love. If such a thing
is possible as an honest & *Christian* lawyer, in this day of over-reaching, I hope
he may be successful in his new pursuit.

And my dear, what is the result of all the enquiries of thy open, generous
confiding spirit? Art thou settled on the sure foundation, of the revealed will of
God to the inner sense? Or is thy mind still perplexed with the schemes of Salvation, and plans of redemption which are taught in the schools of Theology?
It is lamentable, that the simple & benign religion of Jesus should be so encumbered with the creeds & dogmas of sects— Its primitive beauty obscured by
these gloomy appendages of man— The investigations of the honest inquirer
checked by the cry of heresy—infidelity! Thou knows how it was in London—
thou knows too, that I have no wish to proselyte to any speculative opinions I
may hold; but all may know, for I proclaim it abroad, that I long to see obedience to manifested duty—leading to practical righteousness, as the christian's
standard—the test of discipleship—the fruit of faith. Then large liberty—un-
bounded toleration—yes "Religious right," as to forms of worship and abstract
theories.

This most excellent Charity will not forbid our calling the attention of those,
who are superstitiously dwelling in the shadows & figures of the *true,* to what
we may deem a more enlightened and better understanding of the law of
Christ.— But this is not what I took the pen for. It was to tell thee how well I
love you both, and how much we want to see you. When are we to have this said
visit? It must be soon or we fear not at all, this year. Dont let peculiar circumstances discourage. We are all "own folks" here. At least we feel so, & it will give
us the most sincere pleasure to welcome you at 136 North 9th. St. Thou must
not feel as thou did in England when travelling with Henry & stopping at Frds.
houses. But was'nt that, take it altogether—a pleasant visit & tour? I ever dwell
on it with delight. George Combe, in a letter to us, speaks of Henry's call as giving
him pleasure. He has presented me a copy of his "Notes," on this country. The
work will be out in a week or two. I have a nice letter from Dr. Channing acknowlg Lady Byron's present  Come and see it. We have also a lot of beautiful
gifts from our Anti-S. frds. in England—the Ashursts—Wade's &.c[2]

We regret much that we have had so little of the company of thy cousins.
We have been waiting for the returning health of Gerrit Smith, so as to enjoy
their society, and here now they are going away to leave us.

Elizh. [*Neall*] kindly called with thy letter this morng. And thou art a Ho-
meopathist—a believer in Animal Magnetism too!— Well there is no harm in
investigation—and surely the 'Faculty' have need to be distrustful of their
conflicting theories. Tell Henry to remember the Anniversary of our State Society is approaching. He must not let the Study of Law be all-absorbing—forget

not that he early dedicated himself to the slave's cause. How glad we were that you went to Dublin & saw our dear friends there![3] Come & talk about them. My Husband dont know that I am writing, but he loves thee dearly & often talks about thee.

Most fondly thine    L. Mott

ALS DLC-Stanton

1. LCM wrote this letter on the stationery of the British and Foreign Anti-Slavery Society.

2. When Lady Byron, Anna Isabella Milbanke (1792–1860), had met LCM at the London convention, Lady Byron had asked her to carry an engraving to Channing (*Diary*, 54). At the convention LCM had also met William H. Ashurst (1792–1855), a London solicitor interested in woman's rights and the abolition of capital punishment, and his daughter, Elizabeth A. Ashurst (c. 1820–50) (*Diary*, 29, 34; Gordon, 1:23).

3. The PASS had been founded in 1837. The Stantons visited the Quaker printer Richard D. Webb (1805–72) and his wife, Hannah Webb (1809–62), as well as James Haughton (1795–1873), president of the Hibernian Anti-Slavery Society (Gordon, 1:24).

## To Richard D. Webb and Hannah Webb

Philada. 4 Mo. 2nd. 1841—

My dear friends Richard & Hannah Webb

How little I can write that will be interesting, after the long letters of my husband, Abby Kimber and perhaps Sarah Pugh! As to Theology, I am sick of disputes on that subject; though I cannot say just as my husband has—that he "don't care a fig about it"—for I do want those I love, should see their way out of the darkness and error with which they are surrounded. Moreover, I think so much harm is done by teaching the doctrine of human depravity & a dependance on a vicarious atonement, that I feel constrained to call on all every where, to yield such a mistaken and paralyzing dogma. As to the mere opinion of 'Trinity'—or 'Unity' or any such purely speculative indulgence, affecting not the life or practice, "the long-headed, reasoning man," & "the warm, enthusiastic, poetic-minded man" may each follow his convictions harmlessly. But Richard is greatly mistaken in saying *our* Friends are "*declaredly* Unitarian." Why, they would be horror-struck at the idea of it—as the quotation from the letters of G. Truman & John Jackson[1] proves—as well as many other confessions of faith since our Separation,—equally ambiguous. George F White the notable "Hicksite Priest," who "in season & out of season"[2] assails Abolitionists, Non-Resistants & Temperance men, has lately been here, warning our Meeting against "modern Unitarianism." Now, what man of straw he has been building for himself with that cognomen I know not; but we perceive some are searching Elias Hicks's writings & remembering his sayings in proof that he was as much opposed to Unitarians as to any other sect. They are nevertheless, Unitarian in sentiment, whether they know it or not; and so was Wm. Penn & some other of our early Friends. But they as well as some of our modern Friends threw a veil of mysticism, and obscure expressions around them—reserving to themselves an understanding of "Christ the Light," which many of their readers fail to perceive. This practice strikes me, as not quite honest—and yet when questions are put, to see how we may be caught in our words, we have high authority for parrying a little, at least so far as to say, "I will also ask you," &.c. George Combe's "notes on the U. S. A. during a Phrenelogical visit" is just out, in which he represents our Friends as Unitarians  Many of our members are sorely aggrieved by this statement, as well as his saying that we left the Society, instead of the fact, that they left us, and the Original doctrines of Friends. It troubles me not at all, for our stability & usefulness as a society, depend, not on the opinions *of* us, so much as on our strict adherance to our cardinal doctrine of the sufficiency of the "Light within," & righteousness *without*. We hoped to send you some books by this opportunity, but the bearer of our letters declines taking parcels. Now I'll have done with Theology.

I felt just as Richard expressed about our letter to you on our arrival, it was not such a letter as I wanted to send you. I told James after it was gone that I was not satisfied with it. Yours in return with our dear Charles L. Corkran's addition was most acceptable,[3]—as well as the privilege we enjoyed of reading Sarah's & Abby's full sheet, which they were so happy to receive. I felt great affection for all the dear friends with whom we so delightfully mingled in Dublin & shall long have yearnings of heart towards them,—but specially for your nice C. C. were my interests enlisted. I cherish the hope of seeing him comfortably settled here at no distant day. His honesty in the avowal of sentiments, that however correct, have little countenance with your benighted sectarians,—his moral courage in acting in accordance with his convictions, when it might affect his living, & the devotion of his time to the moral improvement of his degraded & oppressed fellow beings—then, his kind attentions to us & his interest in the company & conversation of that noble man Wm. L. Garrison—as well as his ready perception of the rights & willing acknowledgment of a change of views, on Woman—Non-resistance, &c  all these traits of character render him an important personage in our estimation. I have read his addition to your letter many times & have only one amendment to propose viz. where he says, "I am now quite of opinion that any female, who possesses the talent for publicly helping to advance & improve the human race, should be allowed to exercise it." I move, that the words "be allowed to" be omitted. Our freedom has so long been "by suff'rance and at will of a Superior," that we cannot expect a ready recognition of independent judgment—then, the servitude of woman is by so many of her kind "kept and guarded as a sacred thing,"[4] that we need not look for her mental fetters to be soon broken. I wish we could send him some of our papers & periodicals without subjecting him to postage.

We felt obliged for Hannah's kindness in copying for us that part of Richard's letter which she feared would be illegible, even tho' she did add anything from her own original mind. We claim however part of the page she filled in that good long letter of yours to S. P. & A. K.— How near it makes you feel to us, to read your comments on such recent transactions as are recorded in the Liberator! I fear the Sabbath, Church, & Ministry Convention will not effect much, the time is so occupied by St. Clair—Phelps—Torrey—Colver & other bigots—[5] It may set the people of Priest-ridden New England to thinking for themselves, & ultimately do good. I wish we could send you O. A. Brownson's writings on the Laboring Classes—the Priesthood?—&.c.[6] He lectured in this City lately on the "Democracy of Christianity," to a delighted audience. C. C. Burleigh delivered an address on the same subject & won a heap of applause. What a partial committee is that British & Foreign Executive, to publish J. G. W.'s letter & take no notice of Charles's mild and able answer![7] If we could spare him for a while from our Anti-Slavery field, I should rejoice for you to have him to fill the vacancy that *your* Charles's absence has left, and encourage your poor teetotalers to persevere in every good word & work. I wonder if that young woman whose Mother called on me at your house, has ever come over to this Country.

I was right glad you had an opp[ortunit]y to see & admire that bright, open, lovely Elizh. Stanton. We had not seen her till we met in England & I love her now as one belonging to us— I never could regard her Henry quite as a New-Organizationist—altho' he has acted improperly in some instances. He & Whittier & Birney ought to leave that Clan and return to their first love. They all seem to be retiring from the Anti-Slavery field— Birney has married a rich wife & therefore cannot longer serve the slave I suppose—[8] Stanton is studying Law & prays us to have him excused—and Whittier has gone to his farm & wishes to prove it, perhaps— We hear he is on his way hither & how pleased Elizh. Neale is I cannot say—but they certainly like each other very well.

I have the "tremendous name" Richard asked for, across the title page of "Garrison Thoughts [*on African Colonization*]," &c— We shall send it the earliest oppy. to Wm. Rathbone's care.[9] It is a treasure— I want to send our Annual Report written by Mary Grew—& a heap more papers.

I must not fill up my paper without telling you how shamefully our Hicksite—Orthodox Frds. in N. Y. are treating I. T. Hopper & his son-in-law Jas. S. Gibbons. You will see Oliver Johnson's statement in the "Standard" of his & George White's doings—[10] Well, G. Whites pro-slavery frds. overseers of N. Y. Mo. Mg. have brot. Isaac & J. G. before the Mg. as offenders on the charge of aiding in circulating a paper wh. promotes discord among Friends. G. F. White has been preaching from the gallery for 2 years past that which has sowed more discord than we shall soon be able to root out and destroy— He has been encouraged in his denunciations by those who are now active in passing church censure on I. T. H. & J S Gibbons. Some of us look forward to troublous times in our Church on account of the opposing sentiment & action on the subject of Abolition. Our "Cherry St. Mg." has not yet anything unpleasant to disturb our harmony— They bear with me & my wanderings wonderfully well. But when our Yearly Mg. comes together, we may meet with some opposition. Our Yy. Mgs. committee on Slavery have published a nice tract on the subject since our return.

What a good letter Harriet Martineau has written to J. A. Collins on New & Old Organiztn. We are sorry Collins did not know better than to apply to so vain a source as the British & Foreign Com. for funds.[11] Indeed we regretted his going to England on a begging expedition at this time—after Dawes & Keep had dunned everybody—by the way— I fear Oberlin will be New-Organized—but we don't know yet We do not cease to regret that our E. M. Davis did not take the time to go over to Dublin & see you all—& let you see him. His countenance is as open & his heart as generous as is Elizabeth Stanton's. He came home late in the autumn. I have not room to send the love I feel for you all— I'll attempt no names.

truly yours—    L. Mott

ALS MB Env: "Richard D. Webb, Dublin, Ireland"

1. John Jackson (1809–55), the son of the prominent Hicksite minister Halliday Jackson, established the Sharon Female Boarding School in Darby around 1837 with his wife, Rachel Tyson Jackson (1807–83).

2. 2 Tim. 4:2.

3. LCM had met Charles L. Corkran, sometimes mistakenly written "Cockran," at the London convention. He was active in the Irish Temperance Union and edited the union's newspaper, the *Dublin Weekly Herald*. He later became a Unitarian minister (Richard S. Harrison, *Richard Davis Webb: Dublin Quaker Printer, 1805–1872* [Skeagh, Ireland: Red Barn Publishing, 1993], 20).

4. William Cowper, *The Task*, book 5, "The Winter Morning Walk," l. 304.

5. The Sabbath, Church, and Ministry Convention, convened 17–19 November 1840, had discussed the "nature and authority of the Church, the Ministry, and the Sabbath" (*Liberator*, 13 November 1840, 183, 27 November 1840, 190, 4 December 1840, 194). Alanson St. Clair (1804–77) had left the Massachusetts Anti-Slavery Society in 1839–40 to join the Massachusetts Abolition Society. Charles Torrey (1813–46) was a founding member of the Massachusetts Abolition Society (*WLG*, 3:12, 26).

6. Orestes Augustus Brownson (1803–76) was a reformer, a minister, and an author. LCM is referring to his *The Laboring Classes: An Article from the Boston Quarterly Review* (Boston: B. H. Green, 1840) and *New Views of Christianity, Society, and the Church* (Boston: J. Munroe, 1839) (*WLG*, 2:348).

7. See LCM to Elizabeth Pease, 18 February 1841, note 7, above.

8. Elizabeth P. Fitzhugh had married James Birney on 3 March 1841.

9. William Rathbone (1787–1868) was a reformer, a philanthropist, and a politician from Liverpool, England (*WLG*, 3:14).

10. According to Robert Hicks, Isaac T. Hopper (1771–1852), a New York City Hicksite Quaker abolitionist, and James S. Gibbons had "been laboring with great zeal to draw our society [*New York Monthly Meeting*] into modern abolitionism" and had participated in Oliver Johnson's attack on George F. White. Johnson introduced the letter from Robert Hicks by saying that his pamphlet proved that White had made untrue statements regarding abolitionists and that White's actions had been "very extraordinary." White

and his friends had not replied publicly to Johnson's charges but instead privately employed "the *tongue* and the *pen*" (Hicks to Samuel Griffith, 26 March 1841, *NASS*, 26 August 1841, 45).

11. Harriet Martineau's letter to "My Dear Friend" expressed her regret at the divisions in the American antislavery movement but offered her support for the Garrisonians: "All believe that truth will finally prevail; and you and I, dear friend, have a firm faith that therefore the old organization, with Garrison at its head, will prevail at length, over the base enmity of the seceders." (*NASS*, 1 April 1841, 171). The American and Foreign Anti-Slavery Society had foiled John Collins's fundraising trip to London. A representative of the British and Foreign Anti-Slavery Society wrote: "That cause [*antislavery*] in the United States the Committee now consider as more truly represented by the American and Foreign A. S. Society" (*NASS*, 11 March 1841, 158, 25 March 1841, 166; see also LCM to Maria Weston Chapman, 29 July 1840, above).

## To Martha Coffin Wright and David Wright

Philada. 8 Mo. 28th. 40 [*1841*]

Seventh day work done—The time I like to begin a letter & sum up the week's doings. I shall try with Anna [*Hopper*]'s help to send you a decent missive, not only to return all due acknowlmts. for your very acceptable sheet wh. came at last, on 4th day after Meetg. but also to 'make up' for that mere scratch of 8 or 9 pages written while Silas & Sarah [*Cornell*] were preparg to take their leave, after 4 or 5 days pleasantly passed with us. Silas said it would be a bright spot— They seemed to enjoy all they saw, and we didn't spare to make their visit agreeable. Alice was rather impatient to see her sister [*Anna*], whom she resembles—rather more sprightly & could run & play with Patty [*Mott*] & Rebecca Yarnall as smart as either of them. Neither of Sarah's childn. is like herself. James looks more like *our* Grandfather Mott than any of the descendants.[1] Gilbert is doing nothing in the money-making line—not so in the line of family inheritance—his wife has a babe her 3rd.—[2] One is not—"a favor"! Abby [*Mott Moore*] is in poor health—coughs & raises a good deal— The day before they left, some blood. Edwd. has a moderate share of practice—is making rather more than a living. Lindley out of business at present, talks of a school— Sarah wishes he would engage in one at once— They would like the Superintendence of Havreford. They talk of sending their Mary[3] this way, to finish her education next winter—either to Westown or to a day school in this City—and would like to know what she could be *boarded* for in Philada. I recommended a boardg. school as preferable, & said nothing about City prices. If Mother [*Ann*] Mott remains in New York, Ann Moore is coming down to pass the winter, but Sarah hoped she would conclude to go home with her. Richard's wife[4] is so weakly at Toledo, that she is going to remain next winter in Rochester where she now is with her childrn. And as soon as Richard can wind up his business, he will leave there altogether. Silas's sons are doing well for themselves as engineers.[5] This is the sum of family news from them. They took home a copy

of Three Months in G. B. & Edwd. presented a copy of the History of Penna.
Hall with engravgs wh. would suit Silas. Nothing else in the line of presents, save
Moll Pitcher,[6] Anna gave them. I wonder if Martha ever read that— I know
she would like it. I hope you will be able to get Parker's sermon.[7] It is a beautiful production & the sentiments so just & yet so horrifying to Orthodoxy. Ellis
[*Yarnall*] brot. a review of it wh. does him injustice as all such pious critics do,
by making him say what he has not said. How widely our tastes vary! Thos.
Yarnall had read that, & afterwd. one of Bishop Onderdonk's—"Episcopacy—
the Scriptural warrant for it in controversy with Barnes[8]—wh. he wrote Ellis had
strengthened his convictions "with reference to Apostolic usage as binding upon
the present age." He says "Bishop Ondks. tracts are models in controversy.
Strangely contrasted, both with the style & arguments of our good Bishop, is
an Ordin[atio]n. sermon preached in Boston, by Theodore Parker—a stranger
production professg to be a sermon from a Christian Pastor I never perused.
Denyg every possible groundwork of scripture & antiquity & yet full of rich
poetic thought & beautiful imagery, it is a lamentable exhibition of the absurdities wh. the human mind may believe, when it deserts Catholic principles."
But he is cheered with the hope that "the wild rationalism of the Transcendental School is producing a strong counter movement & doctrines wh. of old were
held, are beginning to re-assert their proper claims." Among the encouraging
signs, he says "Brownson has deserted the flag & commences an article "We
would speak respectfully of Unit[aria]nism., as we would always do of the dead"
&.c." I should be glad to send you his letter—a page or more in this strain, very
well written & yet betraying sentiments, in my opinion, so much darker than
those he is reviewing. For, Parker is full of faith in the true groundwork of religion in all ages on wh. all truths of scripture are based—not on miracles, nor
inexplicable creeds. But what lamentable absurdities those are involved in, who
bind themselves to Church Theologies! Lindley Coates says how easily we can
make ourselves believe that wh. we wish to take place. *We* hear nothing like reaction among Unitarians, tho' Ellis came home from Boston full of the idea. The
truth is that all orthodox sects have modified their faith or their creeds with the
advance of rational principles of religion, & now that a large class of Unitarians are moving forward and leaving the Fathers of that reformation behind,
these are, in their turn, raising the cry of 'heresy' wh dying othodoxy seizes as a
straw whereon it may rest its expiring hope. What think you of Robert Hicks's
letter in the last Standard?[9] What miserable employt. is furnished by sectarian
funds. I have a letter from Saml. Philbrick[10] by Isaac Winslow who returned from
Boston last evg. wh I should like to copy. But I must stop or I shall not have room
for other things. It may be an opp[ortunit]y will offer, when I will send a pack
of letters to you to read & return. On 4th. day we met Eliza [*Yarnall*] by appt.
after Mg. & came home to read your entertaing. letter. Martha may think just
as much of Mother's protest against her sendg her well filled sheets, as I do, when
I have been rather circumstantial in some narration, & read it to her, thinkg I

had done well, she will say "*that* is not what Martha wants to hear"! Again she will say "do tell me what there is to write"— I mention sundry vastly interestg items—she will explain "Oh bless me! I wouldn't write that for a dollar." We always rejoice when an Auburn fold is handed us. And if the hand is only heavy & no crosslining, it is numbered with our pleasantest reading. Mary Yarnall has begun a sheet to Anna so that I need not enlarge on her part. We can fancy Mother as plainly as need be, fast marching to the house & lending a helping hand wherever she can, in order that all may be speedily accomplished & the furniture placed & the occupants in possession.[11] I *would not* move in to gratify her impatience of delay, while those painted floors & stairs are too green to walk on. A week or so will make a great diff. in the hardeng of fresh paint—and not much in your rent. We were glad you had the carpenter to put the strips on right. As to Eliza [*Yarnall*]'s makg a late visit, this season, she has not said so, but I rather think she will prefer to wait till James has repaired his fallen fortunes so far as for me not to feel the expense too much to bear her compy. It is among our pleasant anticipations, tho' may not be realized till Martha has made us one or two visits. We shall look for another letter soon with a copy of Marianna [*Pelham'*]s, so as to know what are her prospects of returning. All about Aunt Lydia [*Mott*] & sister & J. [*C.*] I. was acceptable. It is not so pleasant for the latter to be unsettled in his place of residence. He may be a useful man wherever he is. I didn't know that he was "instant in season" at funerals. It is quite relieving when you find those you fear you have slighted, think *they* must apologize. Mother took after her Father or Grandfr. in findg. a knife. Was it stickg high?— Why didn't you mention whether the letter sent by Debh. Coates,[12] via Syracuse, was by private conveyance or by post from there— I told Debh. Coates if she met with anyone going to Auburn to hand it to him. You didn't say how you liked the extracts I favored you with & divers other parts of those three letters— Martha might have commented on. It is quite flattering for our letters to rivet David, more than your fascinatg society. It is always a pleasant part of yours to hear of his success in law cases. I suppose it is partly because he will only engage on the side of equity. Mind & tell how he liked that slip from the ledger on monopolies—sent by Silas & Sarah. I have another on capital punishment to send next oppy. I expected you would be more struck with Mary Parker's death. It caused such a sensation here.— Emma seems just as ever now, only that she speaks of her sister, more as if she was alive than gone forever![13] Sarah M'Kim has written a very pretty & suitable letter to them. I was glad Martha made thee go down & see her compy. How much I have wanted thee & Anna too sometimes when you have had so little notion of helpg. to entertain callers. You made out to have a pretty clever table full, at your party. When Martha has a housewarming she can invite the others again. When we read that Anna spent most of her time in paintg & readg, Eliza said, it would not be so well for her as using more exercise. Do you think it a good way to put clothes in soak? I have thot. that the dirt soakg into other parts made them harder to wash, & lying so long in dirty water gave them a grey look. I tried it but did not like it. Moreover it makes one more handling of them all & I always should dread to get them out over night. It used to seem dismal when cousin Ruth [*Chase*] was going about 1st. day eveg in Vandewater St. collectg the clothes to soak. I like to place them in the basket before I dress for Mg. 1st. day morng & have no more trouble with them. We feel quite provoked that the careless managers of the 'Freeman' should have sent a bill—for the one you have was paid for here—& the Liberator was paid for by our Socy.—one of the 30 copies for wh. we subscribe. I am only waitg for Miller to come home to go to the office & scold about it.[14] Much as poor Charles [*Burleigh*] has been 'berated' as an editor, we never had so poor a paper of his preparg. as last weeks was—no—this week's I mean. Martha had mentioned before her regret at not stoppg it before Miller's administration, & I had conveyed that balsam to him, "robbing Peter." She needn't have taken up 15 lines such "large print" in explanation. Now Ive done. I fully agree with Martha as to the "beautiful traits" in our Mothers character & have often compared or rather contrasted myself with her—especially when our childn. were going to France & breakg up housekeepg—  I have so many things to take my attention, that, I have been pained sometimes at the little help I could give my childn.  As to Anna it is the other way. If there are to be collars or capes or frocks made for Elizh. & Martha or yokes for anything, I depend on her. How I couldn't put in weights on windows, but when that part was read, Eliza said so could she. Has Mother told how nicely Anna & Elizh. put new ladders to our blinds. The front parlor will soon need a similar renewing. We felt sorry for Sarah to have such a fall & her friend to have his Buggy broken—you didn't say whether it was ruined. I feared her teeth would be loose after such a blow. What a wonder that she escaped with so slight a hurt. Should she go to Wilmington, be sure you encourage her to come here on the way & stay with us. We shall like to become acquainted with her. Martha must be careful not to fall from her step-ladder— They are dangerous for one who is increasg in flesh as she approaches middle age. I always dreaded high ceilings—& extra work about house—so much is necessary for our comfort, that superfluous labor should be avoided and yet Mary Earle said "do look how Aunt Coffin's countenance brightens since she understands its that house in the Main St. so it is "we love it and yet loath it." As to there being no sacrifice of pride if you have to part with it & go into an inferior one, it reminded me of Susan Kimber's reply to me once (100 years gone) when I made some such speech about dress: "I thought thou knew thyself better". Anna's explantn. of Mother's "tidyg up" was droll. I was much amused once when Benjn. [*Yarnall*] offered Mother an umbrella—she thanked him but she "had nothing on that rain wouldn't help." Hasn't David learned better yet than to be "disobliging" to Tallman because he had been so? How much more kindly impression he could have made on his mind during their ride to Sherwood's corner, by moralizing on the advantages of kindness. I never forgot how hard it seemed to me for my Grandmr. to tell me she had intend-

ed to let me ride up to the field with GrandFr. & home on the load of corn or
hay— If I had not been naughty— What I had done left no impression, but
her unkindness I couldn't forget—for it would have been the height of happiness to go with him in those rare days of a "drive". When shall we learn that
retaliation is never in imitation of Him who "causeth his sun to shine on the
evil & on the good".[15] What possessed you to Dutch part of the letter & try Elizh.s
eyes so to pick it out? It would seem that Sarah is not as happy as she ought to
be, if she would prefer death. Much as I dislike revenge—a little retort like Eliza's when all set up a laugh at you is admissible. Now havg made due replies to
every part of your letter & all the sage reflections growing out of it I will proceed with my diary—after sayg Barty's house is to be sold but we hear of no
purchaser. They are to remain in it till spring & Mary Ann [*Chase*] to make part
of the family. Anna wrote out to Maria [*Davis*] that Wm. had his hat in mourng.
Caroline [*Stratton*] saw the note & exclaimed "What mockery["] & burst into
tears. She is going to furnish her chambers with some of Wm.'s furniture—or
Mary Ann  She would prefer other—but told Maria she should be obliged to
take theirs. We suppose he is in debt to them. After readg your letter on 4th day
we had one from England with a box of fancy articles designed for last Fair—
It will be quite as acceptable next  It is small 8 or $10 worth perhaps.

[*P.S.*] probably knew each others feelings Anna then said he told her he a
year ago that he hoped he should find her as he left her when he returned this
summer  How such speeches get out by being told to a sister & from her to a
*few* confidential frds.  Robt. Biddle said he knew well enough that the thing was
fixed for Hannah [*Wharton?*] was up to see his sister Anna before Mg in private & seeing there were so many confidants he thot. he had a right to guess so
he went up to Danl. Miller's[16] & there met with Wm. & Rachel & they guessed
it among them & when Edwd & Maria were walkg down to Mg. they heard a
great laughg in at D. Millers & stopped at the window & were obliged to acknowledge the fact seeing Hannah had been so little private herself. I have not made
as short a story as Mother would but it is all the '*go*' here so we must give you
such as we have. We joked Fredk. about Mary Channing but it embarrassed him
so that it was no fun.[17] He was very lovely & free on other subject[s]

He loved dearly to tell what Dr. Chan[nin]g thought of this & that as is very
natural you know. Mary will send her letter by Mail in a few days. She is preparing for a party  I'll leave her to tell about it. Our childn. like John Simmon's
school very much[18] Martha said he couldn't get her name right  He called her
several names— Anna told her she should tell him it was Martha & then he
would have it *Pat*. I asked Maria why she didn't come in oftener  Edwd. said he
had very hard work to get her to visit *his* relations in 9th street. Anna Davis has
been round twice by herself [bringing?] a note to Anna & feeling as grand as
[Cuffee?]

AL MNS

1. James (1820–68), Sarah Alice (1830–74), and Anna (b. 1824) were the children of Silas Cornell and Sarah Mott Cornell, JM's sister (Thomas C. Cornell, *Adam and Anne Mott: Their Ancestors and Their Descendants* [Poughkeepsie, N.Y.: A. V. Haight, 1890], 367–70).

2. Gilbert Hicks Moore (1816–68) was the son of JM's sister Abigail Mott Moore and Lindley Moore. He had married Anna Maria Comstock in 1836.

3. Mary S. Mott (1831–60) was the daughter of Richard Mott and Elizabeth Mott.

4. Elizabeth M. Smith (1804–55), a New Bedford Quaker, had married JM's brother, Richard, in 1828.

5. Another son of Silas Cornell and Sarah Cornell was Thomas Clapp Cornell (b. 1819; Cornell, *Adam and Anne Mott*, 367).

6. JM's *Three Months in Great Britain* (Philadelphia: J. Miller McKim, 1841) described numerous incidents in which British Orthodox Quakers shunned the American Hicksites (see 16–17, 30, 65–69; Pennsylvania Hall Association, *History of Pennsylvania Hall* [Philadelphia: Merrihew and Gunn, 1838]; John Greenleaf Whittier, *Moll Pitcher, a Poem* [Boston: Carter and Hendee, 1832]).

7. Theodore Parker (1810–60), a Unitarian clergyman, had preached "The Transient and Permanent in Christianity" in Boston on 19 May 1841, in which he had challenged the authority of churches and Christianity: "But looking at the history of what men call Christianity, nothing seems more uncertain and perishable. While true religion is always the same thing, in each century and every land, in each man that feels it, the Christianity of the pulpit, which is the religion taught, the Christianity of the people, which is the religion that is accepted and lived out, has never been the same thing in two centuries or lands, except only in name" (Henry Steele Commager, *Theodore Parker: An Anthology* [Boston: Beacon Press, 1960], 40).

8. *Episcopacy Tested by Scripture* (New York: Protestant Episcopal Tract Society, 1831) and *Episcopacy Examined and Reexamined* (New York: Protestant Episcopal Tract Society, 1835) were both written by Henry Ustick Onderdonk (1789–1858), bishop of Pennsylvania.

9. See LCM to Richard D. Webb and Hannah Webb, 2 April 1841, above.

10. Samuel Philbrick (1789–1859) was a leather merchant, the treasurer of the Massachusetts Anti-Slavery Society, and a generous contributor to the *Liberator*.

11. Anna Coffin was helping the Wright family move into their new house (Hallowell, 259).

12. Deborah Coates was a Hicksite Quaker minister.

13. Mary Parker had died of consumption at age thirty-nine (*Liberator,* 23 July 1841, 119). Emma Parker, later Wood (1817–98), Mary's sister, was a member of the PFASS and a Philadelphia Hicksite Quaker until she was released from membership in 1851.

14. McKim had been the publishing agent for the PASS since January 1840. From February to April 1840, he had acted as the temporary editor of the *Pennsylvania Freeman* after Whittier's resignation (William Cohen, "James Miller McKim: Pennsylvania Abolitionist," Ph.D. diss., New York University, 1968, 171, 197, 211–12).

15. Matt. 5:45.

16. Robert Biddle (1823–91) was a Philadelphia Hicksite Quaker. "Danl. Miller" is either Daniel Leeds Miller Jr. (1820–71) or his father (1788–1866), also named Daniel, both Philadelphia Hicksites.

17. William Ellery Channing's daughter Mary Channing (b. 1818) would soon marry Frederick Augustus Eustis (d. 1871), who had graduated from Harvard Divinity School in 1830.

18. John Simmons (c. 1802–64) was a Philadelphia abolitionist (*NASS*, 29 October 1864, 2).

## To Phebe Post Willis

Philada 1 mo. 6th. 1842

My dear Phebe P.

Another year has commenced its rapid course, and with it I have entered my 49th year. May the few remaining years allotted me, be devoted to the cause of suffering humanity, and to my own improvement!

Thy acceptable sheet was handed me just after my return from an absence from home of 5 weeks. Thou may recollect a com. was appointed to unite with one from Baltimore on the application of Centre Qy & Fishing Creek half Yearly Mg. for a Yearly Meeting. Chalkley Gillingham & George Truman expected to go together, but George had so much business on hand, & being also engaged evenings, in visiting the families of our Mo. Mg. he thot. best to stay at home. Chalkley then offered me a seat in his carriage & proposed that Elizh. Paxson (Grace Knight's daughr) another member of the Com. should go. She declined. My Husband then applied to Cathe. Truman to bear me compy. as no member of the Com. appeared. George & their childn all encouraged her. Our elders also approvg she consented to go. An excellent companion & friend she proved herself to be. Mary L. Rowland came forward too late & offered to go, but as she is quite a preacher our friends thought she had better go at some future time on her own concern.[1] Mary Biddle giving her to understand that she might bear her company. We travelled thro' 19 counties of this State and had large public Mgs. at West Chester, York, Lewistown, Bellefonte Clearfield town, Williamsport, Danville, Catawissa, Shamokin, Pottsville &.c., besides attending the Qy, Half Yearly & some Monthly Mgs. We found great openness to receive us & our views. Repeated requests to have another Meeting—and in some places where Abolitionists had not been so well received. Wm. Stabler[2] and John Smith of Virginia were in attendance of most of the Mgs with us—members of the Com. from Balt[imor]e. It was evident that prejudice had closed my way with them at first—indeed J. Smith acknowledged as much to Cathe., but before we separated—all obstructions seemed removed & there was entire freedom & affection. I mention this to thee knowing thou wilt understand it, & excuse the egotism. Oh, if we could only mingle more as Christians should, in brotherly & sisterly affection, the impending evils in our borders might be averted! We have just had a pleasant mg. of the Indian Com. Philip Thomas has since sent me two of his books. James was urged to go New York tomorrow to attend the com. there on 7th day but he cant leave his business. Jas. Walton[3] tells us that John Comly's views have undergone some change on Abolition & other reforms. He is better satisfied that those who feel it right should labor in them, and feels much more comfortable since he has come to this conclusion— Now if this is true, it will go far towards redeeming us from threatening divisions. I cant bear to think, after all we suffered 12 or 14 years ago, that we are again forming two parties.[4]

As to G. F. White's vagaries, I have not wanted to put pen to paper touching him—I ever hoping—even against hope, that he would be restored to his right mind. That is one reason that I have so seldom communed with thee of late. I really dread to make our present difficulties a subject of comment. We are favored with a *good degree* of unity in our Mo. Mg. In our late travels we found a large body of friends of the right stamp. Wm. S. & J. Smith look very favorably to the formation of another Yearly Mg as requested. All this will help to liberalize Society at large. See how Genessee Yearly is advancing. So is Ohio. Thou knows my disposition is to look at the bright side.— I can but hope there is a favorable change taking place in the minds of many. We feel anxious for New York Mo. Mg.— John Jackson we hope was a saviour there yesterday. Stephen Treadwell is holding large & satisfactory meetings in the neighbd. of the City. He does not expect to come here till our Qy. Mg. time. Sarah Underwood was at our eveg Mg on 1st day. Her childn. are in J. Jackson's school & she is spending the winter there & thereaway. Elizah. Newport has lately returned from a long travel into the limits of Balte. Yearly, accompd. by Thos. Longstreth & wife.[5]

I have gone on, one subject after another occurring, without saying what I intended to when I began—that was to allude to that very wet day and eveg. that we passed in New York. I greatly feared thou would be sick after such a drenching—& for weeks after our return home I intended to write purposely to ask after thy health. Great as was the gratification of passing even those few hours with you, and having your compy to New York with that of our dear John Ketcham, I feared the effects of the rain in giving you colds & spoiling your clothes, would make you regret going, & that we shold wish we had pursued our way home. Moreover havg. compy with me, I had not the opporty I longed for in going, to hear thee unbosom thy grief for thy dear departed! I saw that in all the bustle of our abrupt entrance upon you and your building engagements, that no suitable time would occur to tread on such hallowed ground. I even reproached myself for the allusion I made. In recurrence to the day now, it seems a very dream. Yet it was a pleasant one— To Sarah Pugh particularly so. She has no other than agreeable impressions of that visit. I am sure thou need not have felt anything about your confusion—for we saw very little of it. Cousin Henry [*Willis*] & the childn. as well as thyself laid all aside so readily & cheerfully, as is your wont, to receive & entertain not only us, but the dear friends & cousins who joined us there & added to our pleasures, that I am filled with grateful recollections of that day-dream.

It would have given me no small pleasure to pass that night at Saml. Willets', in compy with you—but under our circumstances, it was best we did not. Thy cousin Saml. has ever felt almost "as bone of my bone" since he first so kindly tendered his services as fellow-traveller, & the many attentions in my frequent visits to New York—thro' good & evil report, have been at times as balm to me. He can tell thee of the correspondence between Nathanl. Merritt & Jas. Martin,[6] induced by my wish to have notice given of my prospect of being at that Meeting  Jas. Martin has generously permitted me to take copies of the letter & also to answer for myself. If Saml. has not seen it & thou would like to hear further concerng it I will send thee the correspondence to read

When thou hast opp[ortunit]y—please return the letters I left with thee also if thou hast recd. from thy brother [*Isaac Post*] those English scrawls. We were sorry to hear of their illness at Rochester— I presume C. C. Burleigh has been with them. We have heard less frequently from him, except thro' his published letters, than at any former time when he has been travelling. I have had but one letter & that was written months ago. We felt as if we could not hold a State [meetg?] without him & wrote pressing him to come, but his arrangements would not admit of it & they did very well without him. It was a grand meeting they say. I regretted much losing the treat, but perhaps it was all for the best. James kept me well supplied with letters & so did George his Cathe. The papers also he J. sent to me—but I must have missed that to which thou alludes about Knapp's censures of Garrison—neither has Jas. seen it. Garrison did much to keep the poor fellow from sinking.[7] He wrote to me more than a year ago on his behalf—altho' he ^K^ had become quite intemperate. I imagine where he is known he cannot hurt Garrison.

We had heard of the death of your uncle Saml. Pearsoll but not of your mothers illness. She will have to be more careful of herself than when she was younger. I remember how handsome she looked as she lay in bed the morng. I stepped in to see her. My love to her & to John & Mary—J. & R. Ketcham & all the childn. Joseph & Mary too— Thou did not mention them in thy letter— nor thy Mother— Is she still with you? affecte. remembr. to her. Dont Cathe[8] begin to talk of a visit to Kimberton & to us. I feel sorry that I. T. Hopper has lost so good a member of his Com. Thos. Greene had not been informed of the Mg of that com. He & Lydia were here a few evegs since, but I was not at home. He expects to meet the Com. the day before your Qy Mg. The sermon to wh. cousin John alluded, I suppose was some weeks ago when G. F. White in illustration of something he was saying—touched on slavery & said if there was one link blacker than another in the chain it was the consumer of the produce  This would appear so if he reasoned on the subject but he judged no man & called none sinners.

Thos. McClintock's meetgs were not so large as they would have been, if he had mentioned his wish to have them in time for notice to be given at the close of our 1st day Meetings. I heard no such comparison here between his & G. F. Whites  George's meetings are always large here—

Maurice [Plaser?] and wife made their home with us while in this City. We were pleased with them— Maurice was cautious as thou says but before they left us, we found how much they had been proscribed at home because of their Anti-Slavery sentiments  His wife told me that was the reason he was here without a minute  She also told me of some things in their Yearly Mg wh. look as if trouble awaited them  I wish Geo. Hatten & such as he would learn wisdom by the things we have suffered. James took them out to Darby to attend Concord Qy Mg I am pleased to hear of the change in Eliza Seaman's views. As to Rachel Hicks if she preaches as she did when last here, I cannot feel much interest in her meetings I mourn her change! I wish thou would tell her so— I rejoiced to hear that Saml. Willets told frds in New York Mo Mg. that he had tried to go with his frds but he could not He will be much happier I am persuaded to be honest to his conviction.

Mary Townsend is very poorly mostly confined to [the?] house & frequently to her bed her spine is affected. She has labored too hard in works of benevolence. Hannah is better tho not well—[9] My sister Eliza had a severe hurt some weeks ago occasioned by a fall downstairs—her knee was so much bruised & swelled, that we feared a serious injury. She was confined to the house 4 or 5 weeks but it appears nearly well now.

Thy love was acceptable & she returns good measure & so does my Mother We have sister Martha's daughr Marianna Pelham passing the winter with us & going to school— She & Elizh. [Mott] send love to Cathe. She ^C.^ was well beloved by all at Kimberton. Wm. Parrish's little son Joseph is lying very low with inflammation of the brain—4 years old—a great trial to his parents— not expected to live thro' the night[10] I have filled my paper & can only say

most affecy    L Mott

We had a nice letter from Nath.ls lately— How much he feels & Elisa [Barney] too.

ALS NRU Env: "Phebe P. Willis, Jericho, L. Island"

1. Chalkley Gillingham (1807–81) was a minister of the Alexandria, Virginia, Monthly Meeting. Catherine Master Truman (1797–1884) had married George Truman in 1821. Mary L. Rowland would preach at the Indiana Yearly Meeting in 1845 (JM to Nathaniel Barney and Elisa Barney, 26 October 1847, MNHi).

2. William Stabler was the clerk of the Baltimore Yearly Meeting, 1833–40, 1850–51 (Bliss Forbush, *Three Hundred Years of Quakerism in Maryland, Virginia, District of Columbia, and Central Pennsylvania* [Baltimore: Baltimore Yearly Meeting, 1972], 158).

3. Philip E. Thomas (1776–1861), the clerk of the Baltimore Yearly Meeting, 1821–32, was the president of the Baltimore and Ohio Railroad and chaired the Indian Affairs Committee, 1808–61 (ibid., 60). James Walton (d. 1856) was a Hicksite Quaker.

4. In August 1841, Isaac T. Hopper and James S. Gibbons had been disowned by the New York Monthly Meeting for publishing antislavery articles in the *NASS*; Charles Marriott had been disowned in November. On 7 September LCM had spoken at the Rose Street Meeting in New York City. Describing her address, Lydia Maria Child wrote that LCM was "liable to precisely the same censure . . . and would doubtless receive it, if she were amenable to the Monthly-Meetings of New York." In her sermon LCM had focused on "the sacredness of individual freedom," wrote Child, "the necessity of leaving others to judge for themselves concerning their line of duty; and here she alluded to existing divisions in the society. . . . She earnestly deprecated the tendency to disparage all good works, not done within the enclosure of our own particular sect." In February 1842, the Westbury, Long Island, Quarterly Meeting would confirm the monthly meeting's disownment of Hopper and Gibbons; Marriott's case was referred to another commit-

tee (*NASS,* 7 October 1841, 70, 11 November 1841, 91, 3 February 1842, 138; see also LCM to Richard D. Webb and Hannah Webb, 25 February 1842, below).

5. Thomas Longstreth (c. 1788–1867) was a member of the Hicksite Green Street Meeting (*Friends' Intelligencer,* 14 September 1867, 441).

6. Nathaniel S. Merritt (1802–90) was a member of the Hicksite New York Monthly Meeting. James Martin (c. 1808–86) was an elder of the Hicksite Philadelphia Monthly Meeting (*Friends' Intelligencer,* 10 March 1886, 9).

7. Isaac Knapp (1804–43), a former partner of Garrison and later a printer at the *Liberator,* had published in December 1841 a circular complaining of unfair treatment by Garrison and withdrew from the paper (*WLG,* 3:40–42).

8. Phebe Post Willis's mother-in-law was Rachel Pearsall Willis (1765–1855); her brother was Joseph Post (1803–88); his wife was Mary Robbins Post (1806–92); Phebe's daughter was Catherine Willis (1822–82) and Phebe's mother was Catherine Willets Post (1766–1844) (Post Family Genealogy, private collection of Margery Post Abbott).

9. Mary Townsend (b. 1814) and her sister, Hannah Townsend (b. 1812), were the daughters of Charles Townsend and Priscilla Townsend.

10. William Dillwyn Parrish (1815–63), son of the late Dr. Joseph Parrish and Susanna Cox Parrish, would lose his son on 13 January 1842.

## To Richard D. Webb and Hannah Webb

Philada. 2 Mo. 25th. 1842.

My dear Richard & Hannah Webb
And our other dear friends in Dublin,

For when writing to any one of our precious circle, I feel as if I were addressing all—C Corkran inclusive, in the yearnings of undiminished affection. As the result of our travel abroad, nothing affords more unmingled pleasure, than the reception of some 3 or 4 sheets of Richards "illegible scribblings." The very difficulty we have in deciphering seems to heighten the gratification for we know that when we have puzzled it out, we shall be paid for the effort. The last, to Sarah Pugh was the more interesting, from the fact of Sarah's hastening hither with it unopened, and letting us share the pleasure of the first reading with her. We often wish for Abby Kimber to enjoy with us the first impressions—but some of her notes to Sarah help to supply her absence. I wish Sarah would copy for you what she wrote at the close of the last year. It was so expressive of my feelings that the rapid flight of Time was placing our delightful visit in the more distant view; and so on, a heap of pretty sentiments, just what I felt, but had not the ability to write out.

It happened soon after the reception of Richds. letter, that J. M. & self were meeting with the Indian Committee of the several Yearly Mgs. *of our Frds.* (of course). Philip E. Thomas was present—the author of the Balte. reply to J. J. Gurney.[1] After our business was concluded—, I read to them the ^Richds.^ comments, on the language used—"itinerant foreigner". I did not know that P. E. Thomas had written the book, till I perceived all eyes directed to him, with a smile—& he commenced a defence of the expressions used. He said, he could

not call [him?] [*Gurney*]—a "travelling Friend", for he did not consider him
one—that there was nothing contemptuous in the term "itinerant" nor in that
of "foreigner". He considered the man very much out of *his place*, in attempting to address them, without having mingled with them at all, or knowing their
sentiments, save by ex-parte statements. His conduct he regarded as *impudent,*
& if that term would answer as a substitute, he would think it quite as expressive. He then offered to supply our Dublin friends, with some copies of the review of the work, with his additional remarks. We have since received a parcel
of that & another production of his pen; which at his request we herewith send.
I fear you will not get it without having to pay more postage on it, than it will
be worth to you. If Richard & Anne Allen[2] are not too orthodox to read what
may be said by our side, please hand them one. I always feel rather more as if
they belonged to English Friends, than I feel when writing to you. I cannot remember whether my husband wrote to Richard, after receiving his acceptable
letter in 9 Mo last—or of that date; with a small addition from Anne. I shall take
great pleasure in enclosing in this, for her, Whittier's autograph, at her request.
Since I find she could bear our Anna's playful lines for her friend Sarah M'Kim,
I should like to send her some others by the same author. We can hear with
evident satisfaction, a little raillery at the expense of other sects, but few can bear
to have their own, made the subject of satire, or even pleasantry. Our veneration is trained to pay homage to ancient usage, rather than to truth, which is
older than all. Else, why Church censure on marriages that are not of *us?*—on
Parents conniving? on our members being present at such &c? Oh how our
Discipline needs revising—& stripping of its objectionable features. I know not
how far yours may differ from ours, but I know we have far too many disownable
offences. Still with all our faults, I know of no religious association I would prefer
to it. And I would rather hear of R. D. Webb laboring very faithfully, & with all
Christian daring, *in* his society, than withdrawing from it. I felt so with regard
to Wm. Bassett[3] & hoped that his influence within the pale, might 'turn many
to *righteousness*' I have frequently noticed that persons who were once useful
in our society, withdrawg from it, became rather contracted & selfish—shut
themselves out from society at large, and grew censorious. Their children also
havg no rallying point, as they grew older, following their natural inclination
for Association, connected themselves with sects far behind the intelligence &
light of their parents. This has been remarkably the case with the families of
those who were cruelly severed from our society some 20 years ago in New
England—called New lights  A case has lately occurred in this region. A daughr.
of enlightened Parents, who withdrew from us 15 years ago, has lately joined the
Catholics, & has in view to become a 'sister of charity.' Job Scott's childn. are
Swedenborgians. These remarks may not apply to all. Wm. L. Garrison never
was attached to any sect. Sarah Pugh, from the time of the separation among
us, never felt her interests enlisted with either side; I have no fear of her talents
rusting for want of use. N. P. Rogers, bound as he was, with a set of bigots &

superstitious devotees, may increase his usefulness by his severance from such a denomination. J. A. Collins, ditto. What a Radical, and ultra reformer he is! I did not know him, nor much of his sentiments till since his return from England. I told him, consistency required of him to wear coarser clothing. He would not admit this, as his efforts were not so much to level the rich, as to raise the poor—& furnish them with all the comforts & enjoyments of their wealthy neighbors. What has become of those queer separatists,—Jacobites, to whom we essayed to speak, but they would not? When you write, we should be glad to be informed how our aged friends, Dr. Hutton & wife are. Do they yet live? If from them our dear James Haughton could learn anything of their son Dr. Hutton & family of London, and impart it to us, it would be very acceptable. Dr. Drummond too.[4] Is he yet alive? and have you prevailed with him, to unite his talents & labors with those, engaged in works of reform.

It has been gratifying to see Jas. Haughton's name so frequently in public Meetgs. for the good of the people, & the spread of sound principles. His letter recd. last summer is valued by us even tho' we have made no adequate return. I want to send him a heretical sermon, preached by Theodore Parker in Boston last year—The "Transient & Permanent in Christianity." It created a great stir in New-England & led some of the old Unitarians to tremble for their reputation as Christians. The Orthodox were out upon them in all quarters; which led some of them to issue their disclaimers; whereupon, the Evangelicals, catching at a straw, foresaw a strong counter-movement, and were cheered with the belief that "doctrines which of old were held, would begin to re-assert their former claims; and Truth, hallowed by time & reverend by Apostolic teaching, & holy, from its conformity to the blessed lessons of the Son of God would become & remain the only standard of the Christian Life". Thus wrote my nephew Thos. C. Yarnall, who is studying in College for the ministry in the Episcopal Church. But to my understanding & reading Parker is equally full of faith in the real ground-work of religion in all ages, on which the truths of Scripture are based: not on miracles, or inexplicable creeds. We shall not make much progress as Christians, until we dare to read & examine the Jewish Scriptures, as we would any other of the ancient records. By what authority do we set so high a value on every text that may be drawn from this volume? Certainly not by any command therein found. On the contrary, again & again is there an appeal to the inner sense,—"why even of yourselves, judge ye not what is right?["]⁵ Parker's remarks on the Bible, in the Discourse above mentioned, I like very much—that its real & proper estimate will not be lessened by breaking through the Idolatry which is now paid to it. I read its pages ^I mean the scriptures^ over & over again with a keen relish and encourage our childn. to do the same, but I cannot do, as we saw Friends in England & Ireland do—make the reading of that book a religious rite in the family—and adopt a peculiar tone & solemn style of pronunciation—all the e.d. terminations full &.c. Let us venerate the Good & the True, while we respect not prejudice & Superstition!

R. D. Webb thinks I am a Humanitarian. I have never given my faith a name. The distinctions among Christian professors are found on an analysis, to be but hair-breadth, and it is puzzling to bear in mind the distinctive points in their creeds. We give a more Orthodox hue to ours, by retaining some expressions which do not convey our real sentiments. I do not wonder that Richard asks, what we mean by our professions. If he should hear some of our preachers, he would understand us better. The hearers are often told that they are not called to rest their hopes of salvation on the "Sacrifice without the gates of Jerusalem". The Divinity of Christ is held—not by miraculous power—so much as his spiritual creation—"the son of God with power *according to the spirit of holiness.*" We never attempt to draw or define the precise relation to the Father—nor is a trinity acknowledged in our galleries. We rather, urge obedience to manifested duty, as the means of acceptance with the Searcher of hearts. This is the old-fashioned Quaker doctrine—"neither is there salvation as in any other".[6] I have no doubt of the kindness & sincerity of the friend who warned you of the danger of association with some of us. Should she hear Richard say, how loosely society attachments rest upon him, she would feel as if there was a cause for her concern. He must be careful how he gives utterance to such sentiments. I have often felt the restraints & seen the evils of which he speaks; but after much consideration, I have come to the conclusion that the advantages preponderate—I mean of religious Associations. It requires constant watching and care that we yield no principle; but only concede minor points, for the sake of unity. If the bearing of a faithful testimony to the world subjects us to excommunication, why then let us seek another rallying point for our childns. sake—as well as for the preservation of ourselves. You will see by the Standard how the New York pseudo-Quakers are conducting towards I. T. Hopper, J. S. Gibbons, & C. Marriott. I bear my testimony against their intolerance in every circle. In our Indian Committee of the Yearly Meetgs united—C Marriott has been a faithful & active member. In a meeting of that Com. last week, I expressed the regret I felt that he should be so unjustly deprived of his right to labor with us in that cause— Some present thot. we should be careful how we judged another Mo. Mg. I told them we did not hesitate 15 years ago, to judge of the persecuting spirit of our Orthodox opposers, and I viewed the treatment of these frds. in N. York in the same light. We were then struggling for freedom of opinion. We are now claimg the right of *practice* in accordance with our convictions. I wish you could see a correspondence growing out of my going to Boston last Autumn, to attend the Non-Resistance Anniversary and attendg New York Mg. on my way home.[7] The Elders & others there have been quite desirous to make me an offender for joining with those not in membership with us & accepting offices in these Societies. But our Friends here, know full well that such a position is neither contrary to our Discipline, to Scripture, to reason nor common sense. I was permitted to answer for myself & I found proof enough in the practice of Friends from the days of Wm. Penn to the present—of such "mixtures." They failed of bringing action against me. Richard says truly,—that "oil & water would unite as readily as G. F. White & L. M."[8] I can only account for some things in his course, on the ground of insanity. Some months ago he sent in a kind of resignation of his right of Membership. The Mo. Mg. had the paper examined, by a few frds., who reported unfavorably to its being read. It was all hushed & not more than a dozen individuals knew what the paper contained   The next month he obtained a minute to attend Indiana Yearly Mg. On his return, when appearances indicated the restoration of I. T. Hopper & J. S. Gibbons to their rights, G. F. White announced to his Mg. what he had done & that he then repeated it—calling at the same time on the young people present to be prepared to act in the approachg hour of trial in the Society. Since the Quary Mg. confirmed the judgment, they appear satisfied—but as the Yearly Meeting draws near, another threat will doubtless be held out—as is the practice with the politicians in our Southern States;—unless indeed we should do as the Mass. petitioners have done—ask, *ourselves,* for a dissolution of the Union. But I don't wish to fill my whole sheet with these matters. Have you taken an interest in our Congressional proceedings this winter? or rather will you—when you hear or read how bravely our veteran J. Q. Adams is acquitting himself in Washington.[9] Before quite leaving the former subject, which Richard says fills his head from morning till night, I meant to tell you how Anne Knight in a letter to Margaretta Forten, & to M. W. Chapman, that to me I find was wholly on Woman's Rights, deplores my heresy. She says "Her forbearance of the wrongs encountered in Father-land would merit the term *Christian,* had she not so utterly disowned & insulted her Lord *and Savior.* The dreadful mistakes of her Theology have, I am sorry to say, excluded her from the hearts of many of our A. S. women; & their hospitality on that account was less warm. For my own part dearly as I love my savior—as the Lamb slain from the foundation of the world" &. c —a half a page just as Orthodox writers express themselves,—she goes on to say "and knowing from Lucretia that she rejects her Lord, & turns with disgust from "his hanging on a tree" his being slain, his blood shed,—that she recoils from what she calls so gross an idea, and desires not, what the angels desire to look into—the scheme of Redemption".—   ["]Awfully as I regard this state of deep & hardened revolt, yet do I love L. M for her work's sake.—   It was a joy to have the opporty of offering those attentions which others neglected" &.c. &.c.—   She then goes on to speak of the narrow-minded bigotry of those at the Convention, who excluded women—not seeing herself on another subject, equally a bigot. "Oh, wad some Power"[10] &c. I can truly say "Father forgive her," &c I loved her for her courage in paying us so much attention & identifying herself with us. I shall write to her as soon as I finish this sheet, & try to convince her that altho' I do not interpret the "sacred text" precisely as she does, I am not on that count entitled to all the hard names, branded by a self-stiled orthodoxy. She expresses a wish to have some of J. M.'s Books, wh. I shall take great pleasure in sending her—   We have not sent one to England for we did not know but they would regard it an insult. I intend also to write & send one to Elizh. Pease. She wrote a kind letter to us last summer, which we have not yet acknowledged. I have little time to write—save a constant correspondence with my absent sister & a few friends in this land. I am travelling from home so much that, I have to be the more devoted to my family & domestic avocations when with them. And until I do as Richard approves in Sarah Pugh—break off my attachment to our religious Society, I shall have frequent demand on my time & services in its behalf. An application has been made to our & Balte. Yearly Mg. for the establishment of a new Yearly-Mg. west of the Alleghany Mountains in this State. I visited the meetings to compose this Mg. this winter in co. with several of the Com. furnished also with a minute to appoint Meetings. We were absent 5 weeks,—travelled near 700 miles, and averaged nearly a Meeting a day during our absence. In some places where Orthodoxy pro-slavery had hitherto closed the door against us, access was now readily found. Elizh. Robson & companions preceded us & were not slow to represent the "Hicksites" as denyers of all that was sacred. We met with a gentleman in Mifflin County an entire stranger to Friends of either division. He told us what 'Mrs.' Robson & Co. had said & remarked this difference, that while they had much to say against us, we seemed to have nothing to say against them. He exerted himself to procure a house for a Mg. for us, & induced several who were opposed to Womens preaching to go & hear for themselves. He has since been in this City & took pains to come & see us & assure us, we should ever have a ready hearing at Lewistown.

You wish to hear all we can tell you of J. G. Whittier. Truly he is almost lost to us. Months & months pass without our hearing from him. New-Organizn. claims him and not without far too much reason. Maria Chapman wrote me, that he was in, a few moments, at the Boston Fair; adding, "he sins against the clearest light, & I may say—when I recall what our love for him was, before he destroyed it— —the truest love. He was in the Office a few months since, bemoaning to Garrison, that there should have been any divisions. 'Why could we not all go on together?' 'Why not indeed' said Garrison, '*we* stand just where we did. I see no reason, why you cannot co-operate with the American Socy.' 'Oh,' replied Whittier, 'but the Am. Soc is not what it once was. It has the hat, & the coat & the waistcoat of the old Socy. but the life has passed out of it'. 'Are you not ashamed then,' said Garrison 'to come here, wondering why we cant go on together. No wonder you cant co-operate with a *suit of old clothes'*." Now I would far prefer to write something pleasant about him. He seemed to enjoy going from place to place with Joseph Sturge, and we were glad of their little calls on us.[11] I cant help loving Whittier & J. Sturge too, even tho' they have wronged us, in the course they have pursued. So long as they retain any sympathy for the suffering bondsman, I shall feel a tender regard for them, even tho' in other respects they go halting. This is especially my feeling toward each component part of that London Convention—with the very slight exception of N. Colver & one or two others. Even Jesus—"the son of the Blessed", treated hypocrites with severity. You will see in the *Liberator,* that Colver was ready to make excuse for the Mg. houses being refused. "A work of Grace was going on," &c[12]

What an interesting account of the Mass. Meetg. & of J. C. Fuller N. P. Rogers gives in the Herald of Freedom and how characteristic of the man, are his leading editorials! You will be pleased, as we have been, to hear how well Remond has been received since his return from your land; laden with the praises of Ireland—and with the Irish Address.[13] Miller M'Kim says, there has been quite a run on the A. S. Office here by the Repealers since that Address has been reprinted for gratuitous distribution. The seed sown seems to be taking root in Irish hearts. We are cheered on by some late manifestations in that quarter.

You will see H. B. Stanton's name among the 3rd. party speakers in Boston. How sorry I am that he has thus sold himself! They might have had Colver, if we could have kept him—and Whittier—& T. D. Weld. You will see in the Standard Feb. 3 or *Liberator,* the Washington correspondence of the N. York American, signed R. M. T. H.—giving an account of Adams's defence. It is supposed & with some reason, tho' yet a secret, that Theodore D. Weld is the writer of that & sundry other letters from Washn.[14] He has been there several months. Our New-Organ. Abolitionists are not idle. Let us give them credit for all the good they do. Elizabeth C. Stanton—noble soul! is at Johnstown N.Y. at her Father's; where they will remain while Henry is but a student at Law. The latest accot. of her is in a letter I lately recd. from C. C. Burleigh. I have half a mind to enclose it to Anne Allen, as another specimen of his familiar style;—only I fear it will give the impression, of a want of becoming reverence for institutions, regarded sacred. I will see what Jas. says to it. E. Stanton writes to her frd. E. J. Neall, that she has lately made her debut in public,—in a Temperance speech, & was so eloquent in her appeals, as to affect not only her audience, but herself to tears— About 100 women were present. She infused into her speech a homoepathic dose of Womans Rights, & does the same in many private conversations. She wishes as many copies of S. Grimkes Letter on the Equality of the Sexes, we can send her—for that little book does execution. In a letter to me some time ago she says—"The more I think on the present condition of woman, the more am I oppressed with the reality of her degradation. The laws of our Country, how unjust are they!—our customs how vicious! What God has made sinful, both in man & woman,—custom has made sinful in woman alone. In talking with many people I have been much struck with this fact." After saying much more wh. my limits forbid my copying—she adds, "I have commenced the study of medicine. Having a great horror of both medical & theological quacks, I have come to the conclusion to take care of my own soul & body. I am examining Homoepathy." &c— She will probably become a Mother in a few weeks.[15]

I can readily imagine your brother James a fond Father; from the little evidence I had of his affection in the conjugal relations. I was pleased with his nice wife—and the addition since made to their family, is all that seems necessary in their beautiful abode, to render their bliss complete. We are glad that he &

Thomas, do not leave their br. Richd. 'to serve alone'. We notice their honorable names occasionally, in the proceedings of your meetings. Oh; that delightful day at the sea-side with Thos. & Mary & the 3 little ones! how is the little lame daughter? The walk up Killiney hills—the prospect from the top—the addition to our company—all, all are remembered with dear delight. When, think you will come here? I cannot convey by expression how much I want to see you again. Why, we are far better acquainted now, than when we were with you. These dear, familiar letters to S. Pugh & A. Kimber & to ourselves—some of wh. are lying before me, bind you to our hearts, as bosom friends. Richd. takes pains to make us well acquainted with your valued friend R. R. R. Moore.[16] He forgets that we knew him so well in the 'Convention.' We were glad however of all he wrote about him. Among the scenes wh. made an indelible impression, was his very earnest speech & rapid utterance standing I think not far from the excluded women Deleg[at]es. then—when we made a visit to you, at your lodgings—he was quite as earnest in protesting against some measure under discussion. I often smile when recurring to that visit. For I had scarcely learned where we were going—or to distinguish you from the numerous English Frds. who had been introduced. Hannah walked with me—took me thro' part of Covent Garden Market, which I had so oft read of when a child. Reaching your house, there were so many couples of the same name; beside Richd. & Anne Allen, that it was long before I could learn "who was who". Then your venerable Father sat there looking so grave as if he had some misgivings as to the propriety of his juxtaposition with heretics of the Hicksites order—his prudential silence when I ventured a little ultraism.—and withal the "Irish hospitality" with which we were entertained—each one doing so much to minister to our hungry appetites—and then crowning the eveg by R. D. Webb & R. Allen taking that long walk home with us— If I forget these things my *memory* will forget its office. Again, when in your social circle in Dublin, I *presumed* to read what I had written home, of your non-committal course in matters of Theology—suggesting as one reason, the fear of your Orthodox leaders—the earnestness & openness of countenance with which your brother Thomas ejaculated, "*I'm not afraid,*" gave me a sensation of delight. It needs some to be "not afraid", in order to withstand the high-handed measures of the Quaker Hierarchy. I doubt whether the domination of any sect is more arbitrary. A handful of the distinct order in Rhode Island Yearly Mg placed their veto on the opening of Mg. houses for the lectures of the Abolitionists, and lo! they are nearly all closed. Hereaway the young people are kept from the benevolent efforts of the day—as if there would be defilement in the touch. I dont wonder that Richd. Webb feels the evils of these Sectarian organizations. Altho' I have written as I have on another page— I agree with him, (*in the abstract,*) that for those who are accustomed to reflect & come to conclusions for themselves, they are unnecessary.

When you have read the controversy between Paul & Amicus,[17] we should like to have your opinion of the work. It was first published in the 'Berean,'* a

periodical, edited, in Wilmington Del. by Dr. Gibbons, Benjn. Ferris & a number more Friends of talent & worth—as well as of liberal views. 'Amicus' was
Benjn. Ferris. He told us that every answer to Paul was written after his family
had retired for the night—that frequently when he went to put his effusions into
the Office, it was daylight. He never submitted one of them to the criticism of
his friends, & never had any objection made to them. After the controversy was
ended, the "Mg. for Sufferings" issued a kind of disclaimer of it—or protest
against it—at the suggestion of Jonan. Evans—the Pope of that day, because it
had not been submitted to their Orthodox tribunal, previously to its publication according to the 'good' order', prescribed in the Discipline. This occurred
about a year or two before the 'Separation'. ^say 1823 or 4^ Our friends did not
relish a reproof from that quarter— All the Editors of that paper, were on *our*
side when the division took place. Not long after this Fanny Wright—R. D. Owen
& some others of that school were at Wilmington, & some of these liberal writers & their childn. went to hear them lecture on 'knowledge'—'education' &.c.
This alarmed Dr. G., B. Ferris, &.c—& they came out with an "Expose of Modern Skepticism". Immediately another Paper was issued by B. Webb &.c—called
the "Delaware Free Press". Whereupon Dr. G. & co. entered a complaint to the
Mg. of their Ultraism, & about 5 or 6 were disowned.[18] They appealed in vain
to our Yearly Mg. many thinking it were better these should suffer, than that our
august body should be in any manner identified with the 'Infidel Owenites'. The
childn. of these persecuted brethren withdrew & Wilmington Mg. has had 'Ichabod' on its walls from that time to the present. These disowned members were
among their most active, benevolent citizens and have continued respected &
beloved. Now such arbitrary measures I detest. My husband & self came near
"losing our place", by uttering our indignant protest against their intolerance.
These are the evils of religious—or sectarian organizns. We cry out against assumption of power & oppression— But no sooner do we successfully resist
their influence, than the same weapons are wielded by us against those who take
one step in advance of ourselves. We can be mighty charitable to the poor weak-
lings we consider *behind* us—but let some go on *before,*—we are as ready to cry
stop & to condemn, as were those at whose hands we suffered such abuse. Where
is our confidence in the Truth, that we are so fearful to meet error without denunciation. I never felt any special interest in Owen or his followers, but desired
to meet them in a Christian spirit—knowing they would not ultimately prevail,
only as they were in the right. Our dear Elizh. Pease & some others quaked with
fear when Owen called on Wm. L. G. & the other American frds. at Mark
Moore's, lest it might give us a bad name, but I regarded not such fears. How
could a common observer of *heads* & countenance tremble for the influence of
such a man. The most successful refutation of his visionary scheme is to suffer
him to be his own expositor.[19]

I forgot to tell you when speaking of E. Robson, that she has lately met with
a little 'damper', by the Mo. Mg. of the Southern district of this City, refusing

to receive family visits from her. She had been thro' the two or (I believe) three other Meetgs.— What the obstruction was, we have not heard. Josh. J. Gurney knew better than to try to his strength at that Mg. They have the name of being opposed to him—but we had thot. E. Robson was Anti-Gurney too. Perhaps her frds. thot. she was staying here too long.

Your frd. Elizh. [Cosins?] I have not seen since I took her Richard's letter last summer. She was highly gratified to receive it—& may have acknowledged it before now. Neither have we seen for a year past, the Irish ~~Friend~~ or stranger against whom Richd. kindly warned us, with a graphic description of his appearance—"as if butter would not melt in his mouth" &c. We gave his partner a hint of his character—of wh. he appeared to be somewhat apprised; but hoped he would retrieve his good name

The few lines from Hannah in your last letter to S. Pugh were much to my liking. The liberal Spirit breathed thro' it—and her remarks on Elisha Bates just suited me. It is truly astonishing that one who once occupied the place he did in the Society of Friends, should be a ranting,—'Hellfire,' Methodist preacher—or indeed a preacher of any other Society—(unless it be Unitarian & not then for hire.)[20] Several *young* Frds. of the Orthodox order have joined the church. This is not surprising, educated as they have been, these 10 years past, seeking "to be made perfect by the flesh".[21] Not having the inspection of the Boston Bazaar boxes we had not the opp[ortunit]y. to see the Articles or Letters on Slavery—& find out which was written by Hannah. Wasn't that description of the Fair, by M[aria]. W. C[hapman]. good? When anything of interest appears in the Libr, Standard, or Herald of Freedom, I read it with the more zest, knowg. you will enjoy it too.

I have not told you what a nice visit we had from Lord Morpeth. It will do to place with yours from Father Mathew—the accot. of wh., & your remarks of him pleased us well. We felt some hesitancy about calling on "his Lordship," thinking he would not remember us—but in a letter from Dr. Channing to his son who is passing the winter here, he expressed a hope that we would see him.[22] So we went to his lodgings, card in hand reducing him to a common man, on our Republican principles. He was not at home. He soon returned the call, made himself very agreeable, accepted an invitn. the day following to breakfast with us & came each time unattended, *walking* as any of our Citizens would. We were pleased with the ease with which he accommodated himself to our American & Quaker simplicity. We invited an intelligent few Abolitionists to meet him here, and had a delightful time. He gives general satisfaction in passing thro' the country. His amiable disposition & manner are pleasing, 'tho' rather awkward at the graces. Elizh. J. Neall has since met him in Washington. I wish she had a correspondent in Dublin—so that she might give you a description of their meeting.

I began this letter as dated. It is now 3 Mo. 7th. I can only write a little each day—having many interruptions. Another Lion has just arrived in the City—

Charles Dickens. Our childn. have a strong desire to see him. I too have admired the benevolent character of his writings—tho' I have read very little in them. I did not expect to seek an interview, nor to invite him here, as he was not quite one of our sort—but just now there was left at the door, his & his wife's card, with a kind & sweet letter from our dear friend E. J. Reid—London—introducing them & expressing a strong desire that we would make their acquaintance.[23] There is not a woman in London whose draft I would more gladly honor. So now I have a grand excuse to call on them, and our girls are in high glee. I regret that in Boston & New York, they have been so extravagant in their reception of the man.

I wonder if I could not keep on to the end of the year & find something to write you from day to day. I must stop so as to leave somewhat for Sarah Pugh & Abby Kimber to tell you. There may be much in this that they have already written—for Sarah filled & sent Abby's last to you, without my seeing it. Abby has lately made a short, but pleasant visit to the City. Her enjoyment in retrospect is fresh as ever—& when she comes, Sarah accompanies her hither, so that we may all talk over past scenes. E. Neall too comes in for her share. Elizh. Reid asks me in her letter recd today, if the report is true that E. J. N[eall]. & J. G. Whittier are married. How wide of the truth it is! Mary Grew has lived too far from us quite in the lower part of the City, to meet with us often, when our Friends are with us—but there is a strong binding tie of affection with the band of rejected Delegates. Isaac Winslow is now in France, attendg to his br. Jereh's. business, while he is in this country. He was in the City last week with two of his sisters—but we had only a little share of their compy. E Neall was more favored, having been at his house at Havre. Emily will probably return with her Father. We yesterday attended the funeral of Jas. Forten. You will see an accot. of his death in the Standard—an obituary written probably by Mary Grew.[24*][*] It was a real amalgamation funeral—hundreds of white people & thousands of colored— Kindest remembrances to all thy loved circle. Will your Father come to America this season?— Remember us with much affection to C. Corkran when you write—

Yours truly    Lucretia Mott

*James tells me I am mistaken— It was not published in the Berean—but in another Wilmington Paper— Paul is a Presbyterian Minister by the name of Gilbert.

*[*]No—that written by Mary Grew did not reach New York in time—the notice published was quite inferior to that written by Mary.

12th [*March*].

I have opened my envelope to say how rejoiced we are at the news of the safety of the Caledonia. Great anxiety has been felt. We have recd. several Dublin papers and the Irish Friend—all of which interested us & we are obliged by these continued marks of your attention. The article on Free Produce I rejoiced to see, for consistency calls loudly on us for this stand to be made—ask R. Allen to write on. His sympathy & appeals for the poor murderer Delahunt were grateful to my feelings.[25] How I felt that they were in vain! But the appeal will not be lost. Neither will Jas. Haughton's to his poor brethren on Peace—Slavery—&c—I liked his proposal to tax waste land. We called on Dickens—but he was [*ms. damaged*] ired that we could have but a few minutes interview We tried to engage a visit from him, but his stay in this City was only 3 or 4 days & was engaged all the time. 5 or 600 gentlemen called on him the morng. we were there. Jas. Mott talked to him about his travels in the South and hoped he would not be deceived by the outside appearance—but try to get a peep behind the scenes— I too said a word or two on the same subject.—[26]

How gratifying is the decision of your Parliament on the Creole case—that & the Amistad are doing well for our cause—[27]

17th [*March*]

J. M. M'Kim's letter giving an account of Jas. Forten's funeral in todays Standard is good—& true—so was H. C. Wrights announcing his death[28]

I have written my letter to Anne Knight   M. W. Chapman says "Poor, dear Anne Knight! how sorry she will be to see my name to the call for the Bible Convention actually thinking me as good as Orthodox![29] I grieve to grieve her or any one else; but it would never do to be obliged to despise myself for a whole life-time, for neglecting an opport[unit]y. to do good, lest I should give offence". I was glad that C. Corkran withdrew from those Temperance bigots in London

I have filled my sheets with out a word on Non-Resistance, Capital punishment, & other subjects, wh., tho' they do not "fill my head from morng till night," yet occupy much of my thought. Thanks for the "Rhymes for the people"—, "[Hints?] about the Army" & c Such appeals cannot fail to do good. I saw a lecture on Education I think, by the same author when in Lond[on] & have it somewhere among my papers. A parcel was just left at the door, containg 50 copies of "Four Letters to the Rev Jas. Caughy"— I turned to that from R. Allen wh. is all I have had time to read.[30] I am glad he dealt so faithfully with the Priest. We shall circulate them   Jas. Motts love he cant add

Jas. thinks it not best to send more than one of each of P. E. Thomas's books— If you would like to have more you can send for them.

ALS MB Env: "Richard D. Webb, 160 Great Brunswick St., Dublin, Ireland"

1. In his pamphlet, *Review of Gurney's Attack on Friends of Baltimore, and of Their Defence* (Baltimore: Wm. Wooddy, 1841), Philip E. Thomas had criticized a lengthy letter Joseph J. Gurney had written to the Hicksite Friends in Baltimore declining to visit their Lombard Street Meeting. Thomas had quoted passages from the Hicksites' answer to Gurney (their "Defence") in which they professed their belief "in the Scriptures concerning Christ, both as to his outward manifestation in the flesh, and in relation to that Divine Principle of Light and Truth in man, which in Scripture is called 'the Christ.'" Thomas had concluded that a reading of Gurney's attack and the "Defence" showed "that the Spirit of Orthodoxy is every where the same, that of insolence, assumption, and denunciation, that it is impossible for the meekest to keep any terms with it, except those

of base, unmanly submission." He had criticized Gurney as possessing the "assumption and narrow-mindedness of a foreigner" (10–14, 17–19, 22).

2. Richard Allen (1803–86) was an abolitionist, an orthodox Quaker, and a cotton merchant; his wife, Anne Webb Allen, was a cousin of Richard D. Webb (LCM to Richard D. Webb and Hannah Webb, 28 May 1850, MB). LCM and JM had first met the Allens in London (*Diary*, 34).

3. William Bassett (1803–71), originally an orthodox Quaker from Lynn, Massachusetts, became a Unitarian and was ardently pro-Garrison.

4. The Jacobites were led in part by Joshua Jacob of Dublin, who publicly criticized those Quakers who did not adhere to the group's custom of extreme simplicity in dress and living habits; they wore nothing but white clothing and were often referred to as "White Quakers" (Isabel Grubb, *Quakers in Ireland, 1654–1900* [London: Swarthmore Press, 1927], 126–29). Dr. Joseph Hutton (1790–1860) was a Unitarian minister in London. LCM and JM had met his father and mother in Dublin on 23 July 1840. William Hamilton Drummond (1778–1865) was a Presbyterian preacher in Dublin (*Diary*, 27, 31, 62, 64).

5. Luke 12:57.

6. "The son of God with power according to the spirit of holiness" is from Rom. 1:4; "neither is there salvation as in any other" is from Acts 4:12.

7. At the New England Non-Resistance Meeting held in Boston on 21 and 22 September 1841, LCM had said that "the feeling among us seemed truer and deeper" than at the meeting she had attended in 1839, and "I would ever have it more felt than expressed. Whatever we do express, I hope will be in fewer words and to the point" (*Liberator*, 19 November 1841, 188). An editorial in the *Practical Christian* (reprinted in the *Liberator*, 12 November 1841, 184) had criticized the organization for not recognizing the prominence of the Christian religion in its proceedings.

8. In a letter to her husband, Maria Mott Davis would describe White's criticism of those persons "*disturbing religious Congregations*—that they had no more right to do so from a sense duty, than to go the wharf, load a dray with sugar & rice & send it to some benevolent society, under a sense of duty" (10 December 1843, Mott Manuscripts, PSCHi).

9. In the House of Representatives, John Quincy Adams (1767–1848) continued to protest Congress's refusal to allow him to submit antislavery petitions.

10. "Oh wad some Pow'r the giftie gie us / To see oursels as ithers see us!" (Robert Burns, "To a Louse," ll. 43–44).

11. Sturge had visited the United States in the spring of 1841 and traveled with Whittier, meeting abolitionists (see Whittier to Moses Cartland, 12 May 1841, *JGW*, 1:500).

12. In a letter signed "W.," the writer had described the Liberty Party convention taking place in Boston on 16 February, at which Rev. Nathaniel Colver declared that Boston churches were already occupied "in the work of grace going on in the city" and therefore unavailable for the next day's session (*Liberator*, 25 February 1842, 31).

13. Two articles reprinted from the *Herald of Freedom* had described an antislavery meeting at the Massachusetts State House at which Wendell Phillips, Abby Kelley, and Frederick Douglass spoke. About James C. Fuller, N. P. Rogers wrote, "We have never known him speak so well" (*Liberator*, 18 February 1842, 26). Charles Lenox Remond (1810–73), a black abolitionist from Salem, Massachusetts, and a founder of the AASS, had stayed with the Webbs when visiting Ireland in December 1841. He had returned to the United States with an address to the Irish Americans written by Richard D. Webb and James Haughton, urging them to work to abolish slavery (*Liberator*, 11 March 1842, 39; Richard S. Harrison, *Richard Davis Webb: Quaker Printer* [Dublin: Red Barn Publishing, 1993], 26).

14. In his letter of 25 January, R.M.T.H. had described in vivid language John Quincy Adams's confrontation with the congressional Southern caucus: "In a tone of insulted majesty and reinvigorated spirit, [*Adams*] said, in reply to the audacious and atrocious charge of '*high treason*,'—'I call for the reading of the first paragraph of the DECLARATION OF INDEPENDENCE! Read it! READ IT! And see what THAT says of the right of a people to reform, to change, to dissolve their government'" (*NASS*, 3 February 1842, 139). Theodore D. Weld had agreed to go to Washington to research colonization and the slave trade for a group of antislavery congressmen, including Adams (Weld to Lewis Tappan, 14 December 1841, *Weld-Grimké Letters,* ed. Gilbert H. Barnes and Dwight Dumond [New York: D. Appleton-Century, 1934], 2:879–80, 905).

15. No record of Stanton's speech has been recovered. LCM cites Stanton's letter to Neall of 26 November 1841. A son, Daniel Stanton, would be born on 2 March (Elisabeth Griffith, *In Her Own Right: The Life of Elizabeth Cady Stanton* [New York: Oxford University Press, 1984], 41; Gordon, 1:25, 34). Sarah Grimké published *Letters on the Equality of the Sexes and the Condition of Woman* in 1838 (Boston: Isaac Knapp).

16. In addition to Richard D. Webb and Hannah Webb, members of the Webb family were James Webb Sr. (1776–1854), his sons Thomas Webb (1806–84) and James H. Webb Jr. (1810–68), and James Jr.'s wife, Ann Webb, all of whom attended the 1840 London convention. LCM described her visits with the Webb family in Dublin on 24–25 July in her diary. Robert Ross Rowan Moore (1811–64) was active in antislavery and peace reform (*Diary,* 34, 63–64; Harrison, *Richard Davis Webb,* 23, 28).

17. In a long series of exchanges from May 1821 until November 1822 in the *Christian Repository,* the Presbyterian clergyman Eliphalet Gilbert (1793–1853), writing as "Paul," had attacked Friends for "the characteristic notions and conduct of your society," describing Quakers as "Deists" and "Infidels." Writing as "Amicus," liberal Quakers, including William Gibbons (1781–1845), a Wilmington, Delaware, doctor, had denounced "Paul" and repudiated the doctrine of the Trinity (Ingle, 98–102).

18. The Hicksite Wilmington meeting had disowned Benjamin Webb for supporting the views of the woman's rights advocate and liberal reformer Frances Wright (1795–1852) and the socialist and newspaper editor Robert Dale Owen (1801–77) (ibid., 61, 131).

19. When LCM had met the British utopian socialist and textile manufacturer Robert Owen (1771–1858), father of Robert Dale, in London on 30 June 1840, she had described him as "altogether visionary—great benevolence" (*Diary,* 51).

20. Elisha Bates (c. 1779–1861), a printer and an orthodox Ohio Quaker, had been disowned in 1837.

21. Gal. 3:3.

22. George William Frederick Howard (1802–64), then Lord Morpeth, later the seventh Earl of Carlisle, was on an extended tour of the United States. Father Theobold Mathew (1790–1856) was a Franciscan priest and an Irish temperance leader. William Francis Channing (1820–1901) was then a medical student at the University of Pennsylvania.

23. The visit of Charles Dickens (1812–70) to Philadelphia is briefly described in chapter 7 of his *American Notes.* Elizabeth Jesser Reid (1795?-1866) was a Unitarian and a close friend of Harriet Martineau (*WLG,* 2:663).

24. Both Isaac Winslow (1787–1867) and Jeremiah Winslow had lived in France for some years while engaged in whaling. Isaac Winslow's daughter, Emily Annette Winslow (later Taylor), had accompanied her father on his trip to the 1840 London convention (*WLG,* 2:209; *Diary,* 13). The obituary of James Forten, who had died on 4 March, was published in the *NASS* (10 March 1842, 159).

25. John Delahunt, who had pleaded not guilty, was being tried in Dublin for the murder of a child (*Times* [London], 17 January 1842, 6).

26. Theodore Cuyler reported that, on a visit to Dickens in London later in 1842, the latter told him, "If you see Mrs. Lucretia Mott tell her that I have not forgotten the slave" (*Letters of Charles Dickens,* ed. Madeline House, Graham Storey, and Kathleen Tillotson [Oxford: Clarendon Press, 1974], 3:357).

27. On a voyage from the United States in November 1841, slaves on the American ship the *Creole* had mutinied and forced the vessel to dock at the British port of Nassau. When British officials freed all the slaves except those in the mutineering crew, U.S. government officials demanded that all the crew be returned to the United States for criminal proceedings. The British, however, refused. In another slave mutiny off Long Island in June 1839 on the *Amistad,* the slaves were also freed, thanks to John Quincy Adams's defense before the U.S. Supreme Court in 1841.

28. McKim's obituary on Forten appeared in the *NASS* (17 March 1842, 162). H. C. Wright's tribute and description of the funeral on 6 March was published in the *Liberator* (11 March 1842, 89).

29. Chapman was one of four signers to a call for a Bible convention for a "public discussion of the credibility and authority of the Scriptures" to be held in Boston on 29 March 1842 (*Liberator,* 21 January 1842, 11).

30. *Rhymes for the People about Battle, Glory, and Murder* (Dublin: Webb and Chapman, n.d.). *Four Letters to the Reverend James Caughy, Methodist Episcopal Minister; on the Participation of the American Methodist Episcopal Church in the Sin of American Slavery/Three from Robert Johnston and One from Richard Allen* (Dublin: S. J. Machen, 1841).


## To Richard Allen

Philadelphia 6. Mo. 25th. 1842

Dear friend Richard Allen

Allow me to introduce to thy acquaintance our young friend Theodore Ledyard Cuyler,[1] who is about to travel in Europe & who I hope will visit Dublin.

When we were leaving your shores, R. D. Webb assured us that any Abolition friends of ours would be sure to meet a hearty welcome with you. Of this we had then & have had since full evidence. I hope our friend may prove himself of this number. His nearest relatives in N. York state are among our active laborers in the great Cause. On the subject of Temperance you will find him sound, and interested in the progress of this notable reform in your land, as well as our own.

I sent a long letter to R. D. Webb some 2 months since, & as writing to one of your band is addressing all, I have not much to say now. By that opportunity I forwarded to thy Anne at her request J. G. Whittiers autograph, which I hope she has received.

Thou hast probably become so inured to having thy letters made public, as readily to excuse me for taking that liberty with thy welcome sheet of 3rd Mo. last. Thy remarks on the several subjects were so good, that I could not forbear sharing the treat with the readers of the Standard.[2]

We have been much interested in the report of the Delegates to the Paris Convention. The Glasgow papers containing it were sent us. Did you observe the similarity in the reasons urged, with those by which we were excluded from the London Conference? And applied to the very men who were so zealous for our exclusion!—Josiah Forster, G. W. Alexander, &c— Truly, "What measure ye mete, shall be measured to you again."[3] And they consoled themselves too as we did that althogh denied the privilege of holding the Convention, their mission was not without its use &.c.

We recd. lately a paper—the Nenagh Guardian I think giving a report of Wm. Knibb's speech at your late Anniversary Meeting in London, setting forth the privations & sufferings of the poor Irish emigrants to Jamaica. It was truly heart-rending. I thought of you while reading it, and how earnestly you remonstrated with them against such removal. We have also George Thompson's speeches in Glasgow on the Affgananistan war—and on war in general. Excellent he was on that subject.[4] Surely, "the habitations of the earth are full of cruelty"! How much there is for Joseph Sturge to do, should he be elected to Parliament, and how much for us all to do![5] The evidences that James Haughton, R. D. Webb & brothers & thyself are still laboring for your poor in Ireland, are truly gratifying to

your sincere friend
Lucretia Mott

Sarah Pugh has just sent a well filled sheet to R. D. Webb so "what can I say more"?

ALS OHi

1. Theodore Ledyard Cuyler (1822–1909), a recent Princeton graduate, later became a Presbyterian minister.

2. Richard Allen's letter of 3 March 1842, supporting the Irish Temperance Union, responded to Maria Edgeworth's efforts in the temperance cause (*NASS*, 19 May 1842, 200).

3. George William Alexander (1802–90) was an English Quaker and an abolitionist (*WLG*, 3:25; *Diary*, 25, 46). The French Anti-Slavery Society had planned to hold a "great public meeting in Paris," but the government, fearing a riot, forbade it. Several delegates from Britain and Ireland went anyway in hopes of persuading the French to emancipate immediately slaves in their colonies (Charles L. Corkran to William Lloyd Garrison, 5 May 1842, *Liberator*, 24 June 1842, 99). The quotation is from Matt. 7:2.

4. In his address to the British and Foreign Anti-Slavery Society meeting in May, Rev. William Knibb, a delegate to the 1840 London convention from the Baptists Western Union of Jamaica, had addressed the poverty and economic exploitation that, despite emancipation in the West Indies, blacks still suffered. The British were also to blame for the poor treatment of Irish immigrants there, added Knibb: "There have been scenes in Jamaica, within the last two years, unequaled in atrocity by all those abominations connected with the foreign slave trade" (*NASS*, 23 June 1842, 10). In two lectures in early June, George Thompson had denounced the Anglo-Afghan War, in which the British sought to extend their influence westward from India: "This war taxes our poverty. . . . It will absorb the thoughts of others, though it should have none of our own" (*Liberator*, 8 July 1842, 106).

5. LCM is adapting Ps. 74:20: "For the dark places of the earth are full of the habitations of cruelty." Joseph Sturge lost the election to Parliament by eighty-four votes.

## To Nathaniel Barney

2nd mo., 14th, 1843.

Here this letter has lain, nearly three mos, waiting for me to fill and send it, while I have delayed from time to time. My health has not been very good since my return, and writing has been rather a dread to me. Some parts of the above will be old and stale, if indeed it was necessary to be so minute about my little fulfilments of duty. It needs care that we do not magnify our missions of love.

As so much is told, I may as well complete the narrative by informing you that I was not easy to return my minute, without going again to Washington, and seeking an interview with those in power, and the representatives of this boastful nation. We applied for the Hall of Congress, but that being granted on condition of silence on slavery, we of course could not accept it. The Unitarian house proved a far better place, and was crowded to excess,—many members of Congress present—all quiet and respectful. I have recd a letter from Dr. Macauly, who was present, requesting my views, as there expressed, on woman's duties and responsibilities.[1] I have written him at length. Some other notes and letters have been sent us, expressive of unity. We marveled that the people, both there and in Virginia, were so open to hear the truth on the subject of slavery. We called on Pres. Tyler. I told him "a part of my mission was to interest those in power on the subject of emancipation." He professed some interest in the subject, but thought the blacks should be colonized. James told him that the South could not do without them, and he thought they should be left free to choose their location, as other people were. He asked if we would be willing to have them at the North. I replied, "Yes—as many as incline to come, but most of them would prefer to remain on the plantations, and work for wages." He spoke of the discussions of the subject years ago in Virginia, "but the Missouri question and other agitations had put the cause back." I hoped it was not too late to resume it. He liked the way Friends treated the subject; he had lately read the address from Baltimore, and liked it. I did not,—it was calculated to set the slave-holder's conscience too much at ease,—it made more apology for him, than he could make for himself. He replied, "I should like to hand Mr. Calhoun over to you."[2] On our coming away, he wished me success in my benevolent enterprises.

We called on John Quincy Adams, who seemed much discouraged that anything would be effected this Congress, or the next, on the subject of slavery. The message of the new governor of N. Y.[3] had "made his blood boil with indignation." Our hopes of success must not rest on those in power, but on the common people, whose servants they are. These hear truth gladly, when free access is obtained to their unprejudiced hearts. I ever have hope of a meeting made up of such.

We seem in rather a tame state in our own Meeting. Nothing very exciting since Rachel Hicks' visit, save some remarks from Nicholas Brown, in the men's Mg, charging the abolitionists with having been the means of making the situation of the col[ore]d people worse in Richmond, where he and Margt. had been. He made some false statements, which were corrected by Danl. Neall, Geo. Truman, and others. He was afterwards reproved for his speech by one of our overseers.

I have lately read M. W. Chapman's "Ten Years of Experience," or Ninth Annual Report, with much interest, as I do everything from her pen. I like what she says on associations; for, if properly conducted, they need not destroy individuality. Are our sectarian associations thus conducted? I am more and more persuaded that they encroach far too much on individual rights, and infringe the freedom of the Gospel.[4]

George Truman has been called out lately to defend the abolitionists in public and private. He was a near sympathizer with me during Balt[imor]e Yearly Mg; when Friends there were so filled with fears and cautions, that they would have been glad to forbid the subject of slavery.

Have you seen the memorial to the Maryland legislature from the "Balte Mg for Sufferings"?[5] It seems very much as if it was to redeem their character after that slanderous "document" from their Yearly Mg. I doubt not it has been drawn from them by abolitionists. There is considerable good anti-slavery feeling in that Yearly Mg, if they only dare speak out. That "document" was "a lie." There was no exercise in that meeting corresponding with the expressions and assertions contained in it. All that had been expressed was of an anti-slavery character. Samuel Janney[6] had made a good speech, which James says would have graced any of our anti-slavery papers. A *sham* committee was appointed "to define the position of the Society on the subject." In the committee this "document" was immediately produced, having been prepared two or three weeks before, and, with one reading, passed; some objections were made, which were silenced. We have since heard that it was submitted to John Comly and others, two weeks before the meeting. These things are calculated to sever the bond of union in our Socy, and already this is the case to some extent in Indiana.[7]

I was pleased to find by thy letter some months back, that thy practice and thy preaching were such as to develop the real character of some of your "worshippers"; for, as thou says, "we have but to do right, and let consequences take care of themselves." If there were more of this confidence and less practical infidelity, we should see greater results from our labors than have yet marked them.

With continued affection, thy friend,

L. Mott.

PL Hallowell, 237–40

1. On 15 January 1843, at the Unitarian Church in Washington, D.C., LCM had preached a sermon on Prov. 14:34: "Righteousness exalteth a Nation, but sin is a reproach to any people." She had told the audience that she spoke with all "the disadvantages of a woman breaking through the proscribed customs of the times" and stated, "There has been a great advancement among the people with regard to woman. Her condition is destined

to become improved and elevated—she is already regarded in a very different light from that assigned to her from the dark ages; and she should come also to appreciate herself and be seeking to something higher than she has formerly done" (*Sermons,* 43).

2. President John Tyler (1790–1862), a Virginia Whig, as a U.S. congressman had voted against the Missouri Compromise of 1820. The "address from Baltimore" was the "Address to Members on Slavery" issued in 1842 from the Baltimore Yearly Meeting, which warned Friends not to advocate the abolition of slavery through "*political* or other means of a *coercive* nature," but instead "mind our own business" (*Niles' National Register,* 10 December 1842, 229–30; Thomas Drake, *Quakers and Slavery in America* [New Haven, Conn.: Yale University Press, 1950], 148–49; *NASS,* 1 December 1842, 2). John C. Calhoun (1782–1850) was a proslavery Democratic senator from South Carolina (1832–43, 1845–50).

3. Democrat William C. Bouck (1786–1859) served as governor of New York from 1843 to 1845. In a recent address, Bouck had stated that New York had no right to interfere in the laws of other states, nor did he think that the national government should extend greater power over the states, even in regards to slavery: "We have happily relieved ourselves from the evil of slavery. But we have no right to interfere with that institution as it exists in other States. We have virtually agreed that it shall not be done, and until we are prepared to break up the national compact, and take the hazard of a civil war, our obligations to other States should be faithfully discharged" (*NASS,* 12 January 1843, 125–26).

4. In her *Ninth Annual Report of the Boston Female Anti-Slavery Society: Presented October 12, 1842* (Boston: Oliver Johnson, 1842) Chapman had described the principles of the society's association: "Association was our first and most important means. *It* is the order of nature, that when any human beings earnestly wish the accomplishment of any particlar object, they look around them for help—they unite their forces—they become associated. Regularity, division of labor, mutual understanding, being always advantageous, they consequently become organized" (9–19).

5. In the memorial to the Maryland legislature, Baltimore Friends had expressed concern over "propositions for the enactment of laws, the effect of which, if passed, would be further to abridge the priveleges of the colored population of our State, and to multiply the difficulties of those who, under a sense of duty, are desirous of emancipating their slaves." According to the *NASS,* the "memorial was so unfavorably received by the body to whom it was addressed, that the memorialists were permitted to withdraw it" (*NASS,* 16 March 1843, 162).

6. Samuel McPherson Janney (1801–80) was a Virginia Quaker minister, a member of the Baltimore Yearly Meeting, and a Quaker historian.

7. The Indiana Yearly Meeting had also expressed disapproval of members participating in antislavery societies, and by February 1843, antislavery friends had separated to form their own meeting, the Indiana Yearly Meeting of Anti-Slavery Friends (Drake, *Quakers and Slavery in America,* 163–65).

## To Richard D. Webb and Hannah Webb

Philada. 3 Mo. 17th. 1843

My dear Richard & Hannah Webb

My particular object in writing at the time is to introduce to your notice our friend Henry Colman, who is about to visit your land, and to spend some time in your Country and in Great Britain. You may have seen some notice in the Standard of his valuable labors for agricultural improvement. and that he is to

act as the European correspondent of the 'Gennessee Farmer'.[1] I would further
commend him to you as a liberal minded Christian, whose writings are calculated to enlarge & improve the mind. He talks of attending the next London
Conference, but is not committed to New Organization I need not say more,
for R. D. Webb assured us that any of our abolition friends would be kindly
received; and your attention to all such as have visited you, fulfils that assurance.

H. C. Wright seemed to find it hard work to leave you. His letters home, as
well as those in the Liberator have been read by us with great interest. They took
us to your drawing-room & brought all your family including the visitors into
near communion with us. We were glad to hear he is likely to do so well with
his book. We perceive by the Papers kindly sent to us, that he has obtained the
public ear. We had not heard of his leaving Dublin, till a Manchester paper reported his speech at that Meeting The Anti-corn law agitators really are in earnest. If they can only effect their object, one great cause of the suffering & distress among you will be removed[2] But many will remain, that ought to claim
equal attention. How can any benevolent heart & enlightened mind rest easy
under your oppressive tythe exactions? Then your enormous expenditures for
the support of Royalty! Why does not your cry wax louder & louder? Even as it
has done against the Army & Navy. There is certainly much to encourage the
Reformer, in the growing public sentiment in favor of the right. Witness the
increasing dislike of Capital punishment. This subject is claiming attention in
many parts of this country. Literary & debating societies are taking it up for
discussion, and petitions are presented to our several Legislatures.

The probability of speedy success in our efforts for human freedom, may
be as apparent to you, in your abundant access to our Anti-Slavery Papers, as
my prophetic vision can delineate it. Before this will reach you, whatever of
interest is occurring with us, you will be made acquainted with. Sarah Pugh
intends to write by this opportunity and as your last delightful sheet was addressed to her or to A. Kimber, I have it not by me to reply to. I can only say it
gave us great pleasure to participate in the perusal of it. All the information given
of the several families in whom we feel such a near interest, as well as of the
vagaries of the Jacobites or White Quakers, is very acceptable. How is it that
neither yours nor Richard Allen's letters told us anything of Anna Jenkins' religious visit to your land and to England? We understood she attended both the
Yearly Meetings. Her return home was much sooner than was anticipated. In a
letter to Richard Allen some months ago, I asked the favor of an explanation,
how far your Yearly Meeting was subordinate to the London Yearly—whether
you were governed by the same discipline &.c—[3] Please remember when you
write to answer this, for I have an object in ascertaining the fact in the case.

I wish to indulge in no selfish feeling as regards our correspondence, particularly as Sarah Pugh is so kind as to bring her letters here to open them, so
that we may read them together; still, 'turn about is fair play', and I would just
hint that a certain long letter sent you some time last year, has not yet been

honored with a direct reply. I think Sarah Pugh has not written you since the reception of your last. I would not forestall her in any remark she may wish to make. Much of her time for months past has been occupied with the sick, in her uncle Enoch Lewis's family, and at home, where they have had the birth of a little babe, though not of her sister's; but of a near relative whom, in the goodness of their hearts, they invited to pass such an eventful period in their family. Thus some new features or points of our dear Sarah's character are developed;—and you would smile to see how confidently she can come into our kitchen & instruct me in the mystery of making rye mush & the like. Another trait—for I must say all I can for her in return for the abundant eulogy heaped on me,—to say nothing of the likeness she sent you, of which I was not apprised till your letter bespoke you enamored of the neat cap &.c— she has really come out a public speaker in our A. S. Meetings & astonished the natives.' in Chester Co. with her eloquence. Abby Kimber & herself keep up an active correspondence, and in that too I share. Abby is ever lively & witty—her letters contain much good sense too. Her remarks on passing events are always worth reading. I wish Sarah would copy parts for you. We are preparing our youngest daughter—Martha, to go to Kimberton next term for a year or more.

Now all the rest of the acts of your friends—how they have travelled to Washington, and the South, holding meetings with slaveholders & others, and how they have attended conventions at the North,—are they not written in words of flattery, in the chronicles of the Standard—& the Burleighs & the Garrisons?[4]

But oh, we are going to lose L. M. Child, as editor of the Standard; and have D. L. Child as principal editor. She is so beset on on all sides, and such demands on her talents for other purposes that she has resolved to retire,—and will only occasionally furnish a 'Letter' or an article. Her husband is most too much a whig politician to give satisfaction to all. Moreover he is rather a prosy writer, and after having such a delightful one, the contrast will be more striking.[5] What do you think of the separation among the Orthodox Friends in Indiana? There is trouble also among *our* Friends in that quarter. What the result will be remains to be seen. G. F. White is out in the West on business—so there is quiet in his home neighborhood. This is a long letter of introduction.

Greet all our loved ones in yours—Richard Allen's—James Haughton's—& your brothers' [*James and Thomas*] families. How are Dr. Drummond and the venerable Joseph Hutton & wife?

most affectionately yours    L. Mott

My J. M. is much engaged with his business. He has met with heavy losses the last year or two—but is not discouraged quite. He sends love.

We were much gratified to see Wm. Bell of Belfast a few weeks since.[6] He and his son dined with us & we talked over our visit to Ireland in fine style. He is likely to settle in New York I believe. He is very liberal considering how or-

thodox he is. I could say much more if I had time & room—such as it is—receive & answer direct—

ever yours    LM—

ALS MB Env: "Richard D. Webb, Dublin, Ireland, H. Colman"

1. Henry Colman (1785–1849) was a Massachusetts Unitarian minister, the former
editor of *New England Farmer,* and the agricultural commissioner of Massachusetts
(*NASS,* 16 February 1843, 147).

2. Henry C. Wright had been in the British Isles since October 1842 and his book, *A
Kiss for a Blow,* was published by Webb (Dublin, 1843). In letters printed in the *Liberator,* he reported that he was to attend a meeting of the Anti–Corn Law League, which
opposed the high protective tariffs placed on imported corn: "If the revenue is taken off
from corn, it must be put on something else—on houses and lands; and the burden must
finally come down, as now, on the poor laborer who rents lands and houses" (*Liberator,*
13 January 1843, 7, 3 March 1843, 33, 10 March 1843, 37).

3. In 1842–43 Anna Jenkins traveled as a minister to Great Britain, Ireland, and Eu-
rope ("Dictionary of Quaker Biography," Library of the Religious Society of Friends in
Britain, Friends' House, London). The Dublin Yearly Meeting was independent of the
London meeting (Olive C. Goodbody, *Guide to Irish Quaker Records* [Dublin: Irish
Manuscript Commission, 1967], 2–3).

4. LCM was apparently embarrassed by the published reports of her trip to Washington, D.C., and the South, which included an account of her meeting in Richmond, Virginia, in the *Liberator* (10 February 1843, 22). She had preached to three thousand persons who seemed "highly pleased" with her views on slavery. A poem about her written
by "Worcester" had been published in the *NASS* (2 March 1843, 156). One stanza of the
poem read thus:

> Thine is that glad and holy faith which tells
>     That man shall not forever be prey
> Unto his fellow man—whose splendor wells,
>     Fresh from the source of everlasting day;
> Thine is the hymn which loud and louder swells
>     And yet shall swell until have died away
> The mingling cries of war, oppression, hate,
> And wrong, which long have laid the earth desolate!

5. David Child would become editor of the *NASS* in May 1843, but he held the position for only one year, since other abolitionists shared LCM's suspicion of his political
views (*WLG,* 3:163).

6. LCM had met William Bell, editor of the *Irish Friend,* in Dublin in 1840 (*Diary,* 65).

## To George Combe and Cecilia Combe

Philada. 3 Mo. 24th 1843

My dear Friends Geo. & Cecilia Combe
     I was truly glad again to recognize your well-known hand. Do you know the
pleasurable sensation on receiving a letter from those we love—just from the
hand-writing, before we quite recollect the writer? Yours of 6th. Ult. reached us

a week since. It had a long passage in the Great Western. We had long been looking and wishing to hear from you. Reports had reached here of the ill health of
G. Combe, and that you talked of coming again to this Country. Your letter gave
us the first certain intelligence from you since you left Edinburgh for Germany.
We regretted much that your pleasure & usefulness were limited while there by
too close study & consequent indisposition. I should have supposed G. Combe
too nearly perfected in the observance of the physical laws, to have to "learn
obedience by the things which he suffered."[1] Increased care & attention will be
necessary after so much suffering.

Your anxiety on your brother Andrew's account must have been great.[2] I was
rejoiced that you arrived in time to see him before he sailed for Madeira—
Would not a voyage across the Atlantic be likely to be advantageous to him? How
gladly should we welcome him to this country. I was glad to hear that your niece
was able to accompany him.

The Pamphlet containing the correspondence on Prison discipline came to
hand a day or two after your letter. We have read it with interest & approval. The
sentiments correspond with those before expressed in the 'Moral Philosophy.'[3]
There always has seemed to me great cruelty in doing such violence to man's
social nature, to say nothing of the effect on the nervous system, as to place him
in solitary confinement. Years ago I felt that true benevolence would lead to more
discrimination in the treatment of offenders, so that our Prisons might be really Penitentiaries. As far as a plan or system is proposed in the 'Correspondence'
it seems to me founded on a due regard to the best interests of our erring fellow beings—and as such I fully unite with the views expressed. As regards the
comparative advantages of ours & the N. York plan, I have not been able to point
them out, and have found my self wavering as the advocates of each have presented their arguments.[4] The evils pointed out in the two, in the Correspondence
met my difficulties—and I hope by canvassing the subject thus publicly, that
generous minds will be awakened to its importance both in Europe and America. My husband took the Pamphlet to the Editor of the Pennsylvanian, with thy
request to publish it. That man, unwise as other knowing men acknowledge
themselves to be, is ruining his health by excessive mental exercise. I see within
a day or two a copy of the 'Correspondence', in the "Pathfinder" a new Literary
paper, edited in New York by Godwin—a son-in-law of Bryant.[5]

Speaking of abuse of ourselves, I may as well acknowledge my own errors
too—having been a sufferer the last winter, owing to undertaking more than
my strength was adequate to. After passing some weeks on my native Isle—
Nantucket, I returned home with improved health— Soon after, Jas. & self took
a tour of 4 or 5 weeks thro' Delaware, Maryland and part of Virginia—holding
meetings with Slaveholders & others—frequenty 2 in a day. They listened with
more patience than we expected and always treated us with respect. We repeated our visit to Washington during the session of Congress—and made application for the Hall of Representatives for a meeting—which was granted on

condition that the exciting subject of Slavery should not be mentioned. Of course we could not accept it on these terms. The Unitarian Mg. house was granted without restriction, and a large Mg. was held—many members of Congress—some from the far South present. Their courtesy led them to bear from a woman what they would probably have resisted in a man. A report of what was said on the subject of slavery went the rounds of the Papers. We held several Meetings also in the neighborhood of Washn. Since our return home I have suffered much with dyspepsia my old complaint & have lost 15 lbs flesh. I am now recovering however & though not perhaps quite so penitent as G. Combe, I hope to obtain pardon—and to do better in future.

'Our Cause' is prospering we hope. Public sentiment is certainly changing. Articles on the subject of slavery are admitted into several of our daily papers and public journals which formerly excluded them. The Legislative action of some of the States has been on the right side—and some of the Southern Presses begin to speak out. Still there is a strong political or partisan influence against the Cause—as well as all the imagined advantages that avarice &c covetousness can bring to sustain the iniquitous system. We read with interest all that transpires abroad on this subject. The London Com. of the British & Foreign Socy. seem to be actively engaged in collecting & disseminating information— They have issued their call for another Convention.[6] The bearer of this—Henry Colman expects to attend it. He goes to Europe, as the Correspondent of an Agricultural Paper in this country, and to make a tour of observation. If you should meet, you would find him a liberal minded Christian—late a Unitarian Minister.

You have doubtless mourned with us the death of our revered Dr. Channing! He was in this City last summer, and it was our high privilege to share in his society. He never seemed more lovely than in our free interchange of sentiments at that time. F. A. Eustis, who is engaged to be married to his daughter thus writes of him in a letter to his friend: "The death of Dr. C. which I was privileged to witness awakened all the natural longings of my spirit for perfection. It has not saddened me—death never does—especially such a death as his. But it has aroused me anew to my allegiance to Truth & to Duty. + + + + + The world has honored him & will honor him still more for his intellect consecrated to religion & to morals. But to me & mine his intellect was the least part of him. It was the spirit of the man, which controlled the expression of his thoughts, which beamed in the kindness of his eye, which spoke in the sweet affection of his voice,—his modesty—his sense of justice—his uniform gentleness, not the mere gifts of nature, but acquired by a long & patient struggle with himself— the work of a lifetime devoted to self culture, which we have lost in him—and yet not lost, for the memory of them is with us still. Dr. C. as he appeared to his own family never was & never can be known to the world. The blank which his removal has caused in his own family, the world can never estimate." & c My paper is filling up or I should like to extract more of his just tribute to this excellent man. You had some opportunity to become acquainted with him & his family. His last Public Address was at Lenox, on the subject of Slavery.[7]

Have you seen Lord Morpeth's letter to M. W. Chapman—for our "Liberty Bell"? It was published in several of the daily papers. He manifested considerable interest in the subject of Slavery when travelling thro this country. We hope he will write as plainly as Charles Dickens has.[8] We had a pleasant visit from him in company with a select number of our Anti-Slavery friends—among whom was a colored man.

I am glad to hear of the advance in Phrenology in your land. Altho' little appears to be done here just now in lectures or publications, yet the form of the head is evidently more observed & talked of—& beginning to be understood—and Moral philosophy & Theology are modified by this growing knowledge. But how much have we yet to learn! The more I read "Moral Philosophy" the better I like it. Your dissensions between church & state are rather encouraging. We may hope for melioration of the condition of your suffering poor, only as your Priestly & Kingly monopolies are trampled down  Our country it is true has suffered much from frauds & Bankruptcies—& is sinning much in oppressing nearly 3 millions of her inhabitants, but neither do I despair that the rightful remedy will yet be applied to yours & ours until "violence shall no more be heard in the land—wasting & destruction within her borders."[9]

It was grateful to be remembered by you both after your long absence. Cecy's addition & 'affectionate greeting' was most acceptable. I sent the letter to Anne Morrison & she I presume will write by this opportunity. She has had much to feel for a near cousin whose husband is among the defaulters in a large Insurance company. My Jas. has met with some heavy losses by failures & great depression in trade & business of all kinds. He is not wholly discouraged however, for which I feel thankful. Our son is engaged with him in the Wool business & they are now doing their share I suppose—  Our Edwd Hopper is succeeding well as a Lawyer. We still make our family as when you were here—  Our little "daughter with dark eyes" has grown a tall girl of 14 [*Martha "Patty"*]— We are preparg her to go to boarding school. The *blue* eyed one [*Elizabeth*] is hoping to spend next summer with her cousin at Auburn N.Y. Our friends generally in health. Dr. Hartshorne[10] & family have had a severe affliction in the loss of a promising son who sailed from the West Indies for this place last summer & the vessel has never been heard of  A violent storm occurred a day or two after

Geo M. Justice is also mourng the loss of a lovely son about 20 years old. Dr Parrish's family have moved to their country residence near Burlington. I think when I wrote you last—acknowledging the books kindly presented me I tried to write a decent letter & ended in just such a scrawl. I did not know that I should find it so hard to stop

ever yours   L. Mott<br>ALS GBNLS

**To the Senate and House of Representatives of the United States.**

The undersigned, women of Pennsylvania, respectfully request that you will immediately effect such alteration of the constitution and laws of the United States as will relieve the citizens of Pennsylvania from all participation in the support of American slavery.

Lucretia Mott
Esther Phillips
Mary Fisher
Dorcas Swift
Rebecca B. Neall
Sarah Clark
Phebe Hussey
E. C. Garrad
Anna C. Brown
Phebe W. Thomas
Martha Beans
Martha Hampton
Elizabeth Pickering
Mary H. Middleton
Lydia Gillingham
Hannah F. Clothier
Susan C. Hallowell
Priscilla M. Clothier
Rebecca S. Hart
Ellen Woolley
Anna M. Hopper
Elizabeth Perkins
Abigail M. Bacon
Martha Rhodes
Rachel Purvis
Jane Brooks
Margaret Wade
Hannah Hates
Mary P. Guzman
Elizabeth L. Paxton
Elizabeth Paxson

Charlotte S. Thorn
Huldah Justice
Catharine McNamee
Amy Clendenon
Mercy Clendenon
Elizabeth Clendenon
Margaret Hart
Lydia Hart
Elizabeth Justice
Lydia Ann Albinger
Harriet Ogden
Esther P. Justice
Mary P. Blackhouse
Sarah Parrish
Hannah J. Jenkins
Hannah McClure
Mary S. Brown
Sarah Yarnall
Sarah H. Palmer
Susan Hopper
Susanne H. Dorsey
Mira Townsend
Sarah H. Gillingham
Martha Gillingham
Sarah Dorsey
Mary H. Gillingham
Rebecca P. Hart
Mary W. Magill
Rebecca J. Magill
Maria M. Davis
Martha Mott
M. E. Hill

"To the Senate and House of Representatives of the United States," tabled slavery petitions, 16 February 1846–7 July 1846. (National Archives, RG 46, SEN 29A-H3)

1. Heb. 5:8.

2. Andrew Combe (1797–1847), a Scottish phrenologist like his brother, George, was also a physician.

3. Carl Mittermaier and George Combe, *On the Application of Phrenology to Criminal Legislation and Prison Discipline, from the Phrenological Journal for January, 1843* (London: n.p., 1843); Combe, *Lectures on Moral Philosophy, Delivered before the Philosophical Association at Edinburgh, in the Winter Session of 1835–36* (Boston: Marsh, Capen, Lyon, and Webb, 1840).

4. The New York plan of penitentiaries was known as the Auburn or congregate system, in which prisoners slept in separate cells but worked together during the day. The rival Pennsylvania plan, called the separate system, kept prisoners entirely isolated from each other. Combe believed the Auburn system was superior in some respects: "The Auburn system of social labour, is better, in my opinion, than that of Pennsylvania, in so far as it allows of a little more stimulus to the social faculties, and does not weaken the nervous system to so great an extent." But he believed that the Pennsylvania system "preserves the convict from contamination by evil communications with his fellow-prisoners" (David Rothman, *The Discovery of the Asylum: Social Order and Disorder in the New Republic* [Boston: Little, Brown, 1971], 79–88; Combe, *Notes on the United States of North America during a Phrenological Visit in 1838–9–40* [Edinburgh: Maclachlan, Stewart, 1841], 2:16).

5. The *Pennsylvanian,* a Democratic paper published by Benjamin Mifflin and Rowland Parry, apparently did not publish Combe's writings (see the March and April 1843 issues). Parke Godwin (1816–1904), an editor and an author, married Frances Bryant, the daughter of William Cullen Bryant (1794–1878), a poet and a newspaper editor. Godwin's paper, the *Pathfinder,* ran for a few months in 1843.

6. The British and Foreign Anti-Slavery Society would hold another world convention in London on 15 June 1843 (*Liberator,* 7 July 1843, 106).

7. Channing, who had died on 2 October 1842, had spoken in Lenox, Massachusetts, on 1 August 1842 on the anniversary of emancipation in the West Indies (*The Works of William Ellery Channing, D.D.* [Boston: American Unitarian Association, 1891], 907–24).

8. In his letter dated 26 October 1842 to Maria Weston Chapman, Lord Morpeth had written that he did not wish to be a contributor to the *Liberty Bell* because, although he sympathized with the antislavery movement, he did not believe his "foreign interference" would benefit the cause (*Liberty Bell* [Boston: Massachusetts Anti-Slavery Fair, 1843], 38–47). In *American Notes,* Dickens appealed to "common sense" and "common humanity" when he asked: "With these revolting evidences of the state of society which exists in and about the slave districts of America before them, can they have a doubt of the real condition of the slave, or can they for a moment make a compromise between the institution or any of its flagrant fearful features, and their own just consciences?" (Harmondsworth, England: Penguin Books, 1972, 283).

9. Isa. 60:18.

10. Joseph Hartshorne (1779–1850) was a Pennsylvania physician.

## To C. W. Pennock[1]

Philada. 10 Mo. 26th. 43.

Respected frd C. W. Pennock

Since the reception of thy note, relative to the emancipated slaves, I have mentioned the circumstance to a number of our friends, and have spoken of it in our Anti-Slavery Meetings; with the hope that suitable places would be found for the family on their arrival here; but as yet we have had no application for their services.

If situations can be found for them in the country, it would be preferable, to adding more to the number already too crowded in our City.

While the iniquitous system of Slavery continues in our land, there will remain an unchristian prejudice against the race, which will stand in the way of their advancement or success in trades and the more profitable employments. They will have to be "hewers of wood and drawers of water" in our midst.[2]

We will however make further exertions, and if successful, will give thee the earliest information.

very respectfully    Lucretia Mott

ALS PSCHi-Mott

1. This is possibly Caspar Wistar Pennock (1799–1867), a Philadelphia physician and Quaker.
2. Josh. 9:21.

## To Martha Coffin Wright

[*Philadelphia 12 January 1844*][1]

Rod will com[e] home tonight & from all appearances will be as welcome as other lovers. No sooner had they returned than Mother began begging to see the letter—but in vain. I reckon it will be hermetically sealed from public view— & I am much of the mind of the Author of the "World without souls" that "such sayings like the wines of the south are delicious in their proper soil, but they will not bear transporting."[2] (except to be poured into a *Mothers* heart.) Elizh. [*Mott*] appears to have had a pleasant eveg. at the Hutchinson last Concert,[3] yesternight—with T[homas]. S. C[avender]. I endeavor as much as possible to be resigned to any turn wh. that intimacy may take—for at one time they appear to be 'very friends—' when something will occur to make them comparative strangers. I cannot of course conceal—any more than can James nor *would* I, the high regard I entertain for the youth—but knowg that tastes differ—& that *our* liking would not secure mutual happiness, unless there was 'love unfeigned' *betwn. themselves* I would be the *farthest,* from endeavg to promote an alliance that was not so based. As to little Landis, Elizh. assured me, & I was disposed to

believe her, that the countenance she gave him, was with no other than feelgs
of friendship & a desire to encourage him in his resolve, to break off from his
bad habits—smokg—wine-drinkg—fire companies. &.c— This was a benevolent motive on her part—& had a good effect—he signed the pledge and
seemed bent on changg his course of life—but it was very evident that he regarded her in another light than a *mere* friend—his visits became very frequent
& repeated attention betrayed an increasg attachmt— Elizh. discovg this thot.
proper to give him a check not wishg it to produce an estrangement—but the
youth took it so to heart, that he ceased his visits & they seem to be becomg
strangers. Now I suppose Elizh. will take offen[ce] at all the above & I should
be sorry that it shd be proclaimed—but I know M Anna [*Pelham*] w[ill?] tell
thee on her return—& that I should speak of it, shd. we meet face to face,—to
say nothg [of?] Mothers entertaing powers. And I shall keep this from public
gaze; till it is sent & thou w[ill?] of course destroy it— I would hide it from
Lib & M.Anna only they would think it was some [*ms. damaged*]

AL Frag MNS

1. This letter is so dated because the reverse of the fragment from Anna Folger Coffin
describes the sixth birthday "yesterday" of Lucretia Hopper, born 11 January 1838.
    2. John William Cunningham (1780–1861), the author of *A World without Souls* (Bos-
ton: Manning and Loring, 1808), was also the coauthor of *The Life and Works of William Cowper.*
    3. Organized in 1841, the Hutchinson family singers toured the United States and
Europe until they disbanded in 1849 (*WLG*, 3:158).

## To E.H.R.

Philadelphia, Pennsylvania.<br>[*c. 14 March 1844*][1]

MY DEAR FRIEND, E. H. R.

I HAVE not been unmindful of the contents of thy letter.[2] Could an answer
have been given in accordance with thy wish for the poor objects of thy sympathy, it should sooner have been done.

After a free and full discussion of the question of purchase, at a meeting of
our Female Anti-Slavery Society, the following resolution was passed by a large
majority:—

"Resolved, That while we deeply sympathise with those who are making
efforts for their own emancipation, or that of their relatives and friends, by soliciting funds to purchase their freedom from those who unjustly hold them in
bondage, we nevertheless must decline all pecuniary aid in such purchase, regarding contributions for this object as a worse than useless appropriation of
money, and as an indirect support of slavery.

"Resolved, That we will discourage such contributions, because those who give aid in this way, erroneously imagine they are promoting the cause of human freedom, when they may, in fact, be only transferring the bonds to others, equally entitled to their liberty."

The case of the poor victim of the oppressor's power, so feelingly depicted, is a peculiarly hard one. But, were the circumstances attending the imprisonment and sale of other inmates of that horrible prison, made known, we might find most of them claiming the especial sympathy of hearts interested in their behalf. Should all the victims of this monstrous oppression be purchased from the inhuman trader in men, he would doubtless advertise for more. And while the disposition of the slave-holder is unchanged, and the trade is legalized, the supply would be furnished.

It is worthy of consideration, whether such purchase be not indeed an acknowledgment of the right of property in man, and therefore inconsistent for abolitionists to encourage.

For years, my sympathy was so wrought upon by the many cases of peculiar hardship, which an intimate acquaintance with the atrocious system of American slavery discloses, that, without much reflection, I contributed my mite toward the purchase of slaves. But further reflection and observation convinced me that it was misdirected benevolence—not in accordance with the dictates of true humanity. The sum obtained in this way is often used for the purchase of other slaves,—thus keeping up the inducement, either to kidnap the poor creatures on the coast of Africa, or to "breed" and raise them for sale in the northern slave States. Here, an indirect support is given to the system, even while we would fain persuade ourselves that we are aiding in its abolition. If the sums, raised for this object, were appropriated to the enlightening of the public mind on the enormity of the whole system, how much more effective would it be!

Many young people, in this city, are disposed to curtail their expenses in dress, and other indulgences, in order to aid in the circulation of the anti-slavery truth, through the length and breadth of the land. We have evidence that the appeals to the conscience and best interests of the slave-holder, are not made in vain. The occasional response from the South, as well as the reiterated cry for liberty from our Northern land, cheers us onward in our holy enterprise.

Let us then extend our benevolence to the whole class of "the suffering and the dumb," rather than expend our means in acts of sympathy towards a few isolated cases.

Thine for the oppressed
L. MOTT.

PL *Liberty Bell*, 1846, 253–57

1. The minutes of the PFASS for 14 March 1844 record that LCM "read a letter in answer to one, lately read before the Society. In this answer, she expressed her views, and those of the society, concerning the purchase of slaves" (Pennsylvania Abolition Society Papers, reel 30, PHi).

2. An introduction to this letter explained that the slave had been imprisoned in the state prison in Baltimore because the family who owned her had become bankrupt. She was at risk of being sold away from "all her relatives and friends." A request for funds to purchase her freedom had been made more than a year earlier to "the friends of Freedom in Philadelphia" (*Liberty Bell* [Boston: Massachusetts Anti-Slavery Fair, 1846], 253).

## To Sarah Dugdale[1]

Philada. 10 Mo. 7th. 1845

My dear Friend Sarah Dugdale

For many weeks I have had it on my mind to write to thee—believing some little account of thy dear *Joseph's* visit this way, beside that which he and his sympathizing Ruth may have to relate, will not be unacceptable to thee and thy husband, as well as to some others, who are similarly tried with yourselves.[2] We thought the course he pursued judicious, in presenting his minute—asserting his right of membership & unity as a minister. He varied a little in his practice, at our Yearly Meeting, more in submission to the advice of some timid Anti-Slavery Friends here, lest the opposition should overpower him & them, than in accordance with his own judgment. The course he pursued however, may have had an effect to soften the hearts of some of the opposers—who manifested more friendly feelings than was anticipated. Indeed his ministry seem'd to carry an evidence to many, beyond *Church* authority—and all opposition—with a slight exception, was silenced. Their stay with us during that week was pleasant to us. We regretted that our Aunt L. P. M[ott]. and companion who were with us at the same time, pursued a non-committal course toward them—owing as we supposed, to a kind of pledge given to their friends at home. When once compromise of principles is made, for peace-sake and to please men, we may expect darkness and opposition to follow. Joseph will tell you how keenly he felt the treatment he afterward received from our dear Aunt, at Rochester. We felt it too. But to shew you that others equally estimable, judged very differently of what they heard, I enclose a letter recd. from a dear cousin of ours [*Phebe Post Willis?*], residing on Long Island, who was on a visit to her brother Isaac Post. She has long had much to feel, on account of the proscriptive intolerant course pursued by Westbury Qr. towards I. T. Hopper, C. Marriott and others. I have not her liberty to send it—so you will see the propriety of not making any public use of it. What will be the ultimate result of all these high-handed measures, we cannot foresee. If all can preserve the temper & spirit toward our persecutors, that Joseph & Ruth manifest, there will be little to fear. It is hard, to have two such ordeals to pass through in our short generation. But such things must needs be, while an Ecclesiastical establishment finds place among us. Our duty therefore is, to submit with Christian grace—for surely "they know not what they do." How little have those, who cried out against "a ministry shackled by human authority," been able to bear *Church* promotion, themselves. When once we depart from the ground,—that "God is the Sovereign Lord of Conscience,"[3] despotism & cruelty are the unfailing result. Well for us that the age does not now license the stake and the halter.

We have lately received a letter from our friend Griffith M. Cooper of Farmington, informing that the meeting of Ministers and Elders had reported him to the Monthly Meeting as no longer worthy to be regarded a minister among them. He says he was a doomed man from the time that he bore his testimony against the proceedings of New York Meeting in the case of I. T. Hopper and Charles Marriott. Thus we have mournful evidence that an Orthodox Spirit still bears sway in various parts of our Society. Knowing full well what this spirit is, by what we formerly suffered at its hands, we may pray to be fortified with Christian patience to the end. Still there may be something for us to do, in bearing a faithful protest against intolerance as well as sympathizing with those, who have become discouraged & disaffected so far as to meditate a withdrawal from the Society. Some resignations are already offered in this & Gennessee Yearly Meetings.

I have not been able to see that another division & re-organization will afford more than a temporary remedy for the evils under which we are laboring. While our present Discipline remains as it is, giving power to a few over the ministry, we may expect such results to follow. A radical change is called for. Many among us would feel little inclined to associate under restrictions, which they have felt all too binding. Entire come-outerism is to be feared in its [sca?]ttering tendency with our young people. What then is the right step to pursue? It may be well for Friends to confer together and report the results of such conferences. Whatever is done should be done "openly, uncondemned". "In secret" let us "do nothing."[4]

My husband & self propose to attend a conference of Friends in Chester Co. next week. Our present feeling is to urge that no movement may be made through impatience. If we are thr[own?] out of the synagogue as some of you have been, it may then be tim[e] to consider what course is most for the promotion of truth and righteousness. At present our duty leads to a faithful advocacy of what we believe right, whether the lovers of ease and quiet will hear or forbear.

You have had your keen & bitter trials. We have oft felt sympathy with you, and have rejoiced to hear how you have been supported through all. It is certainly "a small thing to be judged of man's judgment.["]⁵

Very affectionately<br>
thy friend    Lucretia Mott

ALS PSCHi-Mott Env: "John Dugdale, Selma, Clark Co., Ohio"

1. Sarah B. Dugdale (1787–1880) was an Ohio Quaker minister and an abolitionist (*Pennsylvania Freeman,* 9 March 1854, 39).

2. Joseph Dugdale (1810–96), the son of Sarah Dugdale, was a Quaker farmer, a teacher, and a minister. He and his wife, Ruth Dugdale (1801–98), were active in the antislavery and temperance movements. The Dugdales and their allies, members of Green Plain Meeting (Clark County, Ohio), had split with the Indiana Yearly Meeting in 1842–43, after calling on George F. White to repent, and had formed the Anti-Slavery Friends. They also had accused the Indiana Quakers of being too worldly and concerned with wealth. The Indiana split was part of a wider split among American Quakers between evangelical Gurneyites and Orthodox Wilburites. With other Hicksite Quakers and Garrisonian abolitionists, Joseph Dugdale had helped found the Society for Universal Inquiry and Reform in 1842, which was based on principles of nonresistance and the government of God on earth (*Friends' Intelligencer,* 21 March 1896; *NASS,* 6 July 1843, 18; Thomas Hamm, *The Transformation of American Quakerism: Orthodox Friends, 1800–1907* [Bloomington: Indiana University Press, 1988], 32–33; Thomas Hamm, *God's Government Begun: The Society for Universal Inquiry and Reform, 1842–46* [Bloomington: Indiana University Press, 1995], 63–87). JM had visited Green Plain Friends in 1844 and feared then that the Dugdales would be disowned (LCM to Nathaniel Barney and Elizabeth Barney, 17 September 1844, MNHi).

3. "They know not what they do" is from Luke 23:34; LCM is adapting from the Westminster Confession of Faith: "God alone is the Sovereign Lord of the conscience; and hath left it free from the doctrines and commandments of men" (XX, 1643).

4. LCM is adapting John 18:20: "In secret have I said nothing."

5. 1 Cor. 4:3.

## To George Combe and Cecelia Combe

Philada. 3 Mo. 2nd. 1846.

My dear Geo. & Ceca. Combe

I am a debtor to you, and acknowledge my bankruptcy. You must not measure my affection for you, by the expression given to it with my pen. Your kind remembrance of us, again & again, without return, is appreciated more fully than you may have been led to conclude. For more than a year after the fit of illness which prostrated me so much, I could not give my mind to reading or writing much— The advice of our Physician was, not to attempt either for a time—so that the brain might have a perfect rest. That sickness furnished confirmation strong of the truth of Phrenology. I had travelled over several of the neighboring counties, the previous autumn & Winter, appointing meetings for successive days, some 2 or 3 weeks at a time.— My husband & self in returning from these excursions in New Jersey, crossed the Delaware eleven times in as many weeks, through the winter, after 10 oclock in the evening. Added to this, the care & oversight of a family of twelve, and sometimes fourteen, proved too much for me, and the penalty for these repeated violations, although just, was severe. My nervous system was greatly affected—inflammation of the lungs followed. My dear Mother was seized at the same time with bilious pleurisy, which terminated her life in a few days. This stroke was too much for my already excited brain— and dreadful spasms with loss of reason followed for several days. At intervals however I was sensible of the progress of the irritation—first of the organs of the affections—then the moral portion—& lastly the intellectual—so as to require the ice & cold water removed to each part of the head—and the manifestations were in accordance with the advance of the disease. The physicians were told they must treat me on Phrenological principles. They had attended Geo. Combe's Lectures & were familiar with the subject. Drs. Noble & Parrish.[1] They asked me, if I should not wish to write to George Combe on my recovery— I told them I was constantly thinking of it & composing letters as I was lying in bed—for sleep departed from me for several days & nights. The activity of my Causality was distressing to me at times, as well as to my attendants. My husband & children were devoted to me for weeks—until at length James was taken with the disease, as it first made its appearance in my Mother & self and which was an epidemic in the City at the time. He was ill about a week. I was confined to my room for more than a month.

The loss of our dear Mother was keenly felt by her children & grandchildren. She was 73 years old. We thought ten years might have been added to her life, before we could regard her, as having attained to the "good old age", where we might resign her with fewer pangs. Her constitution was vigorous—more so than that of either of her children— —her spirits uniformly good—she was often the life of the family circle. She had given no evidence of her mental powers declining— —we were therefore unprepared for her sudden removal from us. Her memory is precious to us—more so probably, than if she had manifested a decay of her organs, or had outlived her faculties. When this is the case, as Geo. C. has said, "death is not an evil to be deprecated". Other changes have taken place in our family since that event—reducing our numbers, and leaving quite a void in our circle.

Our Edward Hopper and Anna, with their little daughter left us more than a year ago—and took a house and office together, where Edward is receiving a fair share of business as a Lawyer. They have another daughter added to their family [*Maria*]. Our third daughter, Elizh., was married about 7 months since to Thos. S. Cavender—a Conveyancer—settled in business in the northern part of this City. They are at housekeeping several squares from us. Our son, Thomas, married about the same time a cousin, residing in N. York State. He & his Marianna are now making part of our family—but preparing to keep house in a few months. Your having been in this country & knowing so well our custom of early marriages, will not be surprised, that those little children, when you saw them, are now man—and wife, at 22—and 20 yrs. old. It is far from right, that the cares & duties of married life should be entered into, at so early an age. But how are we to prevent it? Theorizing & moralizing have not yet done it. I remember when you were here, you thought your youthful Queen would take the advice of her enlightened physician, not to form such an alliance before she was 20 or upwards— But facts have abundantly proved that her propensities are not under the best control.[2]

We have made a little change too in our residence— Our son-in-law E. M Davis and my husband purchased the 2 houses next above where we have lived these 12 years past, had the fence removed—opening the yards together—the lot extending 200 ft. back—wh. makes a handsome garden & playground for their 3 children [*Anna, Henry, and Charles*]. We also made improvements in the houses—a balcony & conveniences of baths &.c—which have added to our comfort. We met with some serious losses in the fluctuation of mercantile business a few years ago—but better success since that time has nearly restored us to a moderate competency. We have only one daughter remaining with us—and we mean to try to keep her longer than we have her sisters. E. M. Davis will leave us again the Spring for a few months in Paris on business.

I have been thus egotistical, not as writing to mere transient acquaintances, formed as a bare privilege, among many others equally well entitled to your remembrance & regard—but in the freedom & confidence of a friendship fondly cherished since our introduction in 1838. The refined pleasures of that winter are a frequent theme of delightful recurrence. I was saying to James lately, that I never passed the Museum or entered the Musical Fund Hall, without being reminded of the benefit & enjoyment derived there, by those Lectures on Phrenology. Then the gratification of visiting you at your own home, and being so cordially received there—not only by yourselves, but by your brother [*Andrew*] also, whose writings we had so highly valued—served to form a cement to our friendship & affection, which I trust will be lasting as our lives. The mention of the several particulars of your family & friends—in your letters—your change of home—even to the painting and papering of your house—was truly acceptable to us. We were very glad to hear of dear 'Cecy's health being restored—(I can't say Cecelia—it is too stiff for very friends) The invitation to your "spare bed room" is most grateful to us—altho' not likely soon if ever, to be accepted. We did talk of accompanying E. M. Davis across the Atlantic, tak[ing] with us our daughr. Martha, and should probably have done so, had not the addition of a little son to their family, prevented his Maria's going, as was their first plan. James Mott would like nothing better than to visit your land again—so it is among the possibles that we may meet once more, even if America do not attract you hither again. I have always had a hope that your brother would come here. We, as well as many others, would welcome him most cordially. We were gratified to hear of his improved health.

The note of introduction of Thomas Spencer of Bath was handed to us by himself.[3] We felt obliged for that, as well as other testimonials of your regard. He passed part of an evening with us, but he was so occupied during his short stay in our City, that we did not succeed in having his company again. We attended one of his Temperance lectures, & were pleased with his gentlemanly bearing, as well as his moral appeals to the Audience. It is a rare occurrence for a Church Minister to be interested in *Moral* reform. We hear less of Father Mathew of late. What is the reason? Have his pecuniary difficulties clouded his

fair fame or has his interest waxed less for the inebriate sons of Ireland & Scotland & England?

The numbers of the Scotsman you sent us were read with interest. James had
the articles on the reform in Germany, printed in our Friends' Intelligencer. The
daily Papers here also copied these accounts. We may hope for some relief to a
priest-ridden people, when a Ronge comes out with the boldness of a Reformer.[4] But after all, such a little step is taken at each revolution, and such a tendency to retrograde among all sectarians, that I confess some discouragement
as to permanent advance in liberal Christianity. The Unitarians are carrying
themselves quite orthodox, toward Theodore Parker, and others of his stamp.
You see I hope, his writings. Our Hicksite Friends are fearful of any approach
to ultraism among us. Few can bear to "have their names cast out as evil" even
for truth's sake. The Vestiges of Creation has been read here by very many.[5] But
the fear of its infidel tendency—not to say Atheistical, has deterred some from
recommending the perusal of it. The sequel to it we have not yet seen.

We have had some valuable productions the past year, on the subject of War
& Capital Punishment. When our E. M. Davis goes over to your land we will
send you copies of these—as well as some of our good AntiSlavery Appeals. The
work of Reform is evidently onward. I wish you were constant readers of the
New York Tribune rather than Bennett's Herald. It has a wide circulation in this
country, as one of the best Whig journals,—and unlike almost every other political Paper takes right ground on the subject of Slavery Capital punishment,
&.c— Moreover it has a Literary department conducted by Margaret Fuller,
which does credit to the *brain* of Woman. It is issued weekly as well as daily.[6]
Cassius M. Clay's 'True American' is doing a good work in Kentucky. The attempts of the mob to suppress it availed little. It is for the present, printed in
Cincinnatti, but mailed & published from Lexington. The Maryland Legislature
has made an unsuccessful attempt to arrest the Editor of one of the Baltimore
Papers because of its Anti-Slavery character. This step has aroused much of the
latent abolitionism of that state—and we hear more from them on that subject
than ever before.[7]

Our own Legislature has received our petitions favorably this winter, for
the removal of the legal facilities given to the slave pursuer;—and a committee from the Anti-Slavery Society has been invited to Harrisburg to be heard
on the question.[8]

These, and many, many more indications of progress in this great cause
satisfy us, that the labors of Abolitionists have not been in vain.

Now, as to matters of family interest, among those with whom you were
acquainted when here, I must leave to our mutual friend A. D. Morrison to inform you. She tells me it is some months since she wrote you—but she intends
to before long. She has been disabled from walking much for some months past
by [*ms. damaged*] slight hurt on her foot or such in stepping into a carriage. She
wished me to say to you, that the book or pamphlet which she mentioned—in

her last letter to you, Sumner's oration—The true grandeur of Nations she would send by Mr.   whom you had introduced to her, was left with the letter at Dr. Morton's. But he, supposing it was sent to him to read, did not hand it to the gentleman with the letter. I have forgotten the name, but presume it is not of sufficient consequence to call again, to learn it. Wm. Morris has had quite a serious attack of varioloid—from which however he has now recovered.[9]

Your and our friend Horace Mann[10] made a short visit to this City, during the winter—in order to deliver a lecture before the Mercantile Library Company— We listened to him with great interest. His subject was Great Britain. He presented her power & greatness in glowing colors—contrasted most touchingly with her oppression and the extreme poverty & suffering of her people—

[ms. damaged] tried to make amends for our want of special attention when he was here with you. He was laborg. under a severe cold wh. prevented his visiting us—further than to make a short call in return. His home attractions are increased by the birth of a little daughter I think.

My husband unites in warmest regards—

yours—    L. Mott

ALS GBNLS Env: "George Combe Esqr, Dr Cox's, Kingston, Surrey"

1. Anna Folger Coffin had died on 26 March 1844. "Drs. Noble & Parrish" were possibly Dr. William Francis Pringle Noble (1827–82), the author of *A Century of Gospel Work* (Philadelphia: H.C. Watts, 1877), and Dr. Isaac Parrish (1811–52), the son of Dr. Joseph Parrish.

2. Thomas would be disowned on 20 May 1846 for marrying his first cousin, Marianna Pelham. Minutes from the Philadelphia Yearly Meeting of 13 May 1840 read: "No marriage between any so near akin as first cousins shall be permitted amongst us" (PSCHi). Queen Victoria of Great Britain (1819–1901) had assumed the throne in 1837; she married Prince Albert of Saxe-Coburg-Gotha in 1840.

3. Thomas Spencer (1796–1853) was the author of *The Rights of the Poor Compared with the Charities of the Rich; or, Thoughts Arising from the Disputes Respecting the Consecration of the Workhouse Burial Ground* (Bath: John and James Keene, 1838).

4. Johannes Ronge (1813–87) had recently published a call to reform the Catholic church in Germany. The article, reprinted from the *Scotsman*, stated that Ronge "simply preached freedom for religious opinions from all lay and clerical domination. He casts the Pope, the Bishops, and the State, equally overboard, and proposes to place religious power in the hands of the people" (*Friends' Intelligencer*, 27 December 1845, 305).

5. The quotation is from Luke 6:22. *Vestiges of the Natural History of Creation*, published anonymously by Robert Chambers in 1844, challenged orthodox interpretations of the creation.

6. James Gordon Bennett (1795–1872) was the editor of the *New York Herald*. Horace Greeley (1811–72), a reformer and a newspaper editor, had founded the *New York Tribune* in 1841. Margaret Fuller (1810–50), an author, a critic, and a transcendentalist, had begun writing for the *New York Tribune* in 1844.

7. Cassius M. Clay edited the *True American* from 1845 to 1846. Initially published in Lexington, Kentucky, it was compelled by proslavery forces to move across the Ohio River to politically friendlier Cincinnati. In Maryland, J. E. Snodgrass, editor of the *Baltimore Saturday Visitor*, struggled to keep his paper alive when a member of the state legisla-

ture accused the paper of being "incendiary" and "calculated to create discontent, and stir up insurrection among the people of color" (*Pennsylvania Freeman,* 5 February 1846, 1–2).

8. On 6 February the Pennsylvania legislature had passed an act instructing the state courts no longer to participate in enforcing the 1793 federal Fugitive Slave Law (*Pennsylvania Freeman,* 11 February 1847, 3).

9. Charles Sumner (1811–74), a Massachusetts politician, had delivered "The True Grandeur of Nations," his antiwar plea, on 4 July 1845 in Boston. "Dr. Morton" was possibly William Thomas Green Morton (1819–68), a Massachusetts dentist and a pioneer in the use of ether. "Wm. Morris" was possibly a medical doctor of Philadelphia and the author of *Ancient Slavery disapproved of God: The Substance of a Lecture* (Philadelphia: Scriptural Knowledge Society, 1862).

10. Horace Mann (1796–1859) was a Massachusetts educator.

## To Elizabeth Pease

Philada. 4 Mo. 28th, 1846.

My dear Elizh. Pease

More than two years have passed, since the reception of thy truly acceptable letter. During that time I have not written to any of our dear English or Irish friends—for after the severe illness which so greatly affected my nervous system I was advised to avoid much reading or writing. Edwd. M. Davis' prospect of again visiting your country & seeing some of our friends revived the desire to communicate with you again. More especially do I wish to convey a line to thee dear Elizh., expressive of the sympathy I feel with thee, in thy late bereavement.[1] Thy long-continued devotion to thy dear Father, doubtless renders this stroke doubly trying to thee. In many ways we feel such a loss! Your feelings & sentiments were congenial upon many points. You could travel together & were each other's helper in the truth. The tear will then naturally flow at the severance of such a tie. And far be it from me to seek to stay it. I know full well the keenness of the separation between Parent & child. My dear Mother was taken from us, when I could illy bear such a shock to my nature. She was companionable in every way. Her Grandchildn. as well as her childn. delighted in her society. She was vigorous in constitution of both body & mind, and promised a longer life than 73— But we had to yield her—and resignation to the event has been a hard lesson. I therefore feel less able to preach it to others. The thought has already occurred to us, now, that thou hast no longer that tender tie to home, whether a visit to this Country may not be effected by thee—gladdening the hearts of many here, and perhaps cheering for the time some lonely hours for thyself. We need not say such a visit would be very pleasant to us, and a hearty welcome would await thee as a guest, under which of our roofs thou might choose to abide.

The contents of thy last letter may not, after so long silence on my part in reply, be familiar to thee now. Thou alluded to our intercourse together, in

England—and thy remarks to H. C. Wright respectg some little restraint that thou afterward thought existed between us.[2] As to thy fear of engrossing too much of our time, & thy regardg us, as among the '*lions* of the Convention' the thought I believe never occurred to us— We felt truly grateful for thy prompt attention to us, while some from Sectarian bigotry were standing aloof. As to the lion part, we felt much more, that we were "counted as *sheep* for the slaughter." That feeling added to the knowledge that many among you were greatly shocked at our supposed heresies, did cause a *little restraint* in our mingling with you. I remember Sarah Pugh reproved me after our first call or visit at your lodgings, because I did not go forward more cordially & offer the hand, in takg. leave of thy Father & Mother. When I was restrained by the feeling, that they would not care to give me the "right hand of fellowship" in any respect. Again, when we met accidentally at Meeting, at the Devonshire house I think, I felt quite a pity for thee, that thou would be brought into a strait after Meeting, whether to speak cordially to us, & thus identify thyself with those, who were "despised & rejected of *Men;*" or to "cut" us, and thus do violence to the promptings of thy kind nature. So, thy after feelings were not without some foundation. But, the more intercourse we had, the more these fears & restraints vanished—and our latter interviews—specially the last, at Liverpool were "free & easy" as any could desire. Since that time, our firm adherance to the great cause, which first bound us together, and the freedom of correspondence have knit us together 'as the heart of one man', and we can greet one another as very friends. As to differences in points of faith sundering us, if that be sufficient cause of division, "oh Lord, who shall stand?"[3] Have not those, who at that time, formed a strong & united phalanx of opposition to "Hicksism", now become divided among themselves, on little hair-splitting points of Theology? Let us rather look, as the truth-loving Jesus recommended, for the fruits which proceed from a good heart—for about these there is no controversy. There is a response in every heart to the exhibition of justice—mercy—love—peace—& Charity, which goes far to ~~convince~~ prove that God has created man upright; and that the counter doctrine of human depravity, has done much to make the heart wicked, and to produce the giant sins that afflict mankind. But I wish not to provoke discussion. A similar feeling to that I have endeavored to express, prevented my calling on thy cousin John Pease, when in this City, & trying to influence him in accordance with thy wish, for the Slave. He did not identify himself with any Anti-Slavery Socy. here. Neither have your pseudo-Abolitionists—the Forsters, Stacey[4] &.c— Have they not shamefully betrayed the cause of the Slave, for their love of sect? Thy letter mentioned a *concern* to write *an out-door* Epistle of sympathy for the Indiana Seceders— Now, that 2 years have passed since the concern arose, has it not ripened into completion? It would doubtless cheer their disappointed hearts, after such a visit from the English bigots—or sectarians— (for I dont want to use hard words—)—and is it not a duty, to do what we can to strengthen one another in this great work. I am ready at any time to sign such an Epistle to our Green Plain Friends—who are set at naught by their rulers. Gennessee Yy. Mg. ^Anti. S. Frds. met in conference last year^ did so—and others will likely follow their example.⁵ We still have much opposition to encounter in our several Meetings, as the accompanyg. documents will shew. But of this, as well as of our progress in the great cause, so constant a reader as thyself of our Liberators & Standard, needs not to be informed. You have Douglass & Buffum with you—good men & true—H. C. Wright also—still stirring the muddy waters of sect—and preachg. humanity. How much need is there of his labors of love, while your National cry is, "Blessed are the *War* makers"—rather than the peace-makers! What dreadful battles on the plains of India! a monstrous sacrifice of human life, by a professedly Christian Nation!⁶

And your poor starved people at home too—overworked & underpaid until driven to desperation. What is to be done, in view of all these evils? The remedy looks at times so hopeless, that I am ready to choose death rather than life, if I must feel as I have done for these classes. There was an extensive Strike of the hand-loom weavers, in this City last winter. They were a month or more idle about twelve hundred—until reduced almost to starvation—deprivg themselves of some 25 or $30.000, wh. they might have recd. even at their all-too low wages. I could ~~not~~ but sympathise with them, in their demand for a better recompense to their early & late toil. But it was most unfortunate for them, for they did not gain the added wages claimed—for "with the Oppressor there is power".⁷ I have written thus far, without telling thee, how much we have felt for Elizh. J. (Neall) Gay during the two or three weeks past, in the extreme illness & death of her Father. She came on from New York soon after he was confined to his bed, and ministered constantly to his wants during his ten days suffering He will be much missed as a friend to the poor—as a liberal-minded overseer of our Meeting, and such are needed, and as the Slave's friend. The Obituary in the Freeman & Standard is a just tribute to his worth—⁸ Poor Elizh. feels it deeply. It will be the breaking up of the pleasant home here, for many of our Anti-Slavery lecturers & friends. He had paid Sydney & Elizh. a very pleasant visit, only a short time before he was taken ill.

I must refer thee to our E. M. Davis for any further particulars of our doings. We shall miss him much from the Mgs. of our Ex. Com. as well as from our family circle. They are settled next door to us, & it has added much to our enjoyment to have them so near us. An added son to their family, prevented Maria's accompanyg. him to England, as was their first plan—when it would not have taken much persuasion to induce J. Mott & self to cross the Atlantic again. Our childn. are all married save one—and all settled in this City. We are lookg. for S. S. Foster & his Abby (Kelly)⁹ next week accompd. by 2 of their frds. from Ohio. Abby Kimber is now in the City. Her company is ever pleasant to us. She & Sarah Pugh—Isaac Winslow & Emily visited us last week. We talked over our visit abroad as we ever do when we meet. We go to Sarah's this eveg. to the Ex. Com. where we always find something interesting to engage us. I dont know whether

Sarah & Abby are writing to thee by Edward— Mary Grew will meet with us this evening. She is putting her talents to good use as editor of the Freeman—

Let me hear from thee soon & please write on thicker paper—so that my old eyes may more easily decipher it. My J. Mott desires most affectionate remembrances—

Thine— L. Mott—

Thy contributn. to our Fair was gratefully recd. as S. Pugh says she wrote thee.

ALS PSCHi-Mott Env: "Elizabeth Pease, Darlington, England"

1. Joseph Pease had died on 16 March 1846 ("Dictionary of Quaker Biography," Library of the Religious Society of Friends, London).

2. Sponsored by the New England Non-Resistance Society, Henry C. Wright toured Britain from 1842 to 1847. According to Walter Merrill, Wright fell in love with Pease while recovering from an illness at her home (*WLG*, 3:16, 126). In her diary LCM described frequent meetings with the Pease family in 1840, including a farewell breakfast in Liverpool (see *Diary*, 23–25, 32, 35, 41, 44, 47–49, 53, 56–58, 77).

3. "Counted as sheep for the slaughter" is from Ps. 44:22; "despised and rejected of men" is from Isa. 53:3. "Oh Lord, who shall stand?" is possibly a variation of "who then is able to stand before me?" (Job 41:10) or "who shall stand when he appeareth?" (Mal. 3:2).

4. This is probably George Stacey (1786–1857), the clerk of the London Yearly Meeting and an anti-Hicksite (*Diary*, 30).

5. In 1845 a delegation from the London Yearly Meeting had gone to Indiana to try to resolve the ideological differences that had led to the 1842–43 split. The Indiana State Anti-Slavery Society, made up mostly of Orthodox Quakers, later protested that the London delegation had sided with the anti-abolitionist stand of the Indiana Yearly Meeting. Further evidence of discord among the Hicksites occurred with the Ohio Yearly Meeting's rejection of the May 1845 epistle from the Green Plain Friends Quarterly Meeting asking for acceptance. In New York some Friends in the Genesee Yearly Meeting had signed an epistle in June 1845 expressing support for the Green Plain Quarterly Meeting and other meetings that had been disowned by the Indiana Yearly Meeting. The epistle criticized the proscriptive spirit that "impugns the actions of brethren and sisters, in their efforts to relieve suffering humanity" and urged Friends to "hold all your meetings in the Power of God" (*Pennsylvania Freeman*, 6 November 1845, 3; *NASS*, 14 August 1845, 42, 21 August 1845, 46, 9 October 1845, 74; see also Thomas Hamm, *God's Government Begun: The Society for Universal Inquiry and Reform, 1842–46* [Bloomington: Indiana University Press, 1995], 63, 67–68).

6. James N. Buffum (1807–87), an abolitionist and the vice president of the Friends of Social Reform, was touring Britain with Frederick Douglass (c. 1817–95), then an agent of the Massachusetts Anti-Slavery Society (*WLG*, 3:138). The British were continuing their conquest of India with a number of victories over the Sikhs in Kashmir.

7. Most weavers worked at home and, in February 1846, those in Moyamensing had struck unsuccessfully for higher wages. Some continued to work "as the only alternative they have to prevent absolute want" (*Philadelphia Public Ledger*, 27 February 1846, 2; Bruce Laurie, *Working People of Philadelphia, 1800–1850* [Philadelphia: Temple University Press, 1980], 159). Eccles. 4:1.

8. Elizabeth Neall had married Sydney Howard Gay (1814–88), an editor of the *NASS*, on 7 November 1845. Daniel Neall had died on 15 April 1846 (*NASS*, 23 April 1846, 3).

9. Stephen S. Foster (1809–81), an antislavery lecturer, had married Abby Kelley on 21 December 1845.

## To Maria Weston Chapman, Caroline Weston,
## Anne Warren Weston, Deborah Weston, Lucia Weston,
## and Emma Weston[1]

Philada. 7 mo. 23rd 1846

My dear M. W. Chapman & sisters

I know not just where to direct, to Caroline Weston, so have adopted this address, in order also, to ask not only her, but her sisters, if they are making ready to come to our Annual Meeting at Kennett and to say to them that it will give us great pleasure to receive them at our house, on the way—and at as much earlier day, so as to make a visit here, as may suit their convenience to come.

The meeting is to be held on the 5th. of next month, as the Papers have doubtless told you.[2] We have not yet heard who is coming—but hope that several from Boston & its neighborhood will give us their company. If Edmund Quincy will come, please say to him, that we have plenty of room & shall be right glad to have him stop at our house. Edward M. Davis & family are passing a few weeks at Germantown—but their house is next door to us, with a communication from the chambers—so that Adin Ballou or any other whom Edward has invited to his house, can come directly to 138 where a hearty welcome awaits them.

We had hoped for Wm. L. Garrison's company & aid at our meeting—but he may do much more by going to England & Scotland, than by remaining at home or coming here, so we try to resign him cheerfully. We think he will remove some of the Sectarian prejudice, that was arrayed against him in 1840. The disposition to receive & hear Fredk. Douglass at the British & Foreign meeting, seemed a little evidence of repentance at their past mis-doings. And I would rather the Standard had not been *quite so severe* in explaining why we had not exchanged more with them.[3] If their conduct manifests a ~~dis~~ more fraternal feeling toward the old organization, let us as far as consistency & *truth* will admit of it, forget "the things that are behind". So, of the parties that have been so hostile to us in this country. I know that Edwd. Davis will not agree with me, for as he says, "he is for *fight*"— Even for poor C. M. Clay—so lamentably fallen & degraded—my cringing soul is continually saying "deal gently with the young man." If it had been any other war than just what it is, it wd. not have surprised us at all, for him to 'buckle on the armor,' for when here he said it would take a great deal to make him a non-resistant, and he liked to tell of his bravery in repelling his enemies. Consistency requires of us to give up his paper—& I suppose to publish him to the world as "such a fool"—but farther than his own conduct has proclaimed that fact, I cant help whispering "tell it not in Gath"![4] His paper reaches many minds in our South land, who would think nothing of his present course, their views of allegiance to Government & to 'the powers that be,' blinding their vision to the clear perception of truth. With this class I have thought, the Anti-Slavery there is in the True American might do good, as they would see it no where else—therefore I would say, let it still circulate there, if they are disposed to take it. So have I always thought of the New organizn & Liberty Party Papers. I wd. rather have Anti-Slavery *in the mixture,* than no Anti-Slavery at all. While those who descend from the higher position which *we* occupy, & unite with these "world's people," need to be "withstood to the face, because they are to be blamed"[5]—and they have been most abundantly.

Now, I expect, when Edward comes in this morning & reads this, he will give me a "blowing up." Do you know, that he had the assurance to call me "Mrs Rogers" last summer? and in the presence of Wm. L. Garrison too![6] I will leave a little space for him to fill— Why cant Wendell P. come—ask him from us—we wd. greet him most cordially—and his Ann too, if her health will admit of her accompyg. him. Our *best bed* shall be made for them, if on return of mail you say they will come. Please answer as soon as it is ascertained who will favor us.

And oblige yours,
for *moral fight*    L. Mott

Kind remembrances to Father Chapman's family[7]—will not Mary G. come? I have the slippers she sent me yet, with their *drab* work, wh. I suppose she thought would best suit me— I love to look at & wear them for her sake. I requested E. M. D. to return thanks for the Liberty Bell. A gentleman from Washington was quite interested in looking over it here lately—— What a calamity poor Nantucket has experienced! We hear of Boston liberality, & are trying to get up a meeting in this City—marked by the slow "growth of what is excellent."[8]

ALS MB Env, written in another hand:
"Maria W. Chapman 58 Federal St Boston Weymouth Ms"

1. Chapman had five unmarried sisters, all of whom were active in the antislavery movement. Not previously identified are Deborah (b. 1814), Lucia (1822–61), and Emma (b. 1825) (Taylor, 4–11).

2. As chairman of the executive committee of the PASS, JM had published a call for abolitionists to gather at the Kennett Meeting House on 5 August 1846 (*Pennsylvania Freeman,* 30 July 1846, 3).

3. Endorsed by the AASS and the Massachusetts Anti-Slavery Society, Garrison had left on 16 July to publicize the antislavery cause in Britain. A request for financial support of the mission had been issued by the executive committee of the PASS in June 1846, signed by LCM, JM, and others (*Liberator,* 10 July 1846, 111). On 19 May Douglass had attended the anniversary meeting of the British and Foreign Anti-Slavery Society (BFASS), which favored the "new organization," the American and Foreign Anti-Slavery Society (AFASS). In a letter to the *Liberator,* Douglass reported that the BFASS's secretary had received no information about the AASS's activities since 1840 (26 June 1846, 103). The *NASS* editorial rebuked the BFASS for refusing to circulate the AASS's reply to attacks from the AFASS. The *NASS* declared that the BFASS's executive committee "STOOD DUMB, AND HAVE ATTEMPTED NO DEFENCE AND MADE NO REPARATION FROM THAT DAY TO THIS!" (9 July 1846, 2).

4. On 13 May Congress had declared war with Mexico. In a letter to Chapman of 30 June, Clay had written that, although he maintained his strong antislavery views, it was

his patriotic duty to take a company of soldiers to Mexico. In her letter of 25 July Chapman had repeated Clay's words on the subject, which asked, was not the war's sole purpose that of "extending Slavery over the unborn fifty millions of Texas, and perpetuating the slave rule over us and our posterity?" (*Pennsylvania Freeman,* 23 July 1846, 3, 13 August 1846, 1). "Tell it not in Gath," 2 Sam. 1:20.

5. Gal. 2:11.

6. "Mrs Rogers" is possibly a reference to a complicated controversy between Garrison and his former ally, Nathaniel P. Rogers. In 1844 AASS leaders had criticized Rogers's paper, the *Herald of Freedom,* for becoming an anti-Garrison publication, a criticism Rogers vehemently denied (Henry Mayer, *All on Fire: William Lloyd Garrison and the Abolition of Slavery* [New York: St. Martin's Press, 1998], 358; *WLG,* 3:285–88).

7. Henry Chapman (1771–1846) was a Boston merchant and an abolitionist.

8. A fire on 13 July had ravaged much of Nantucket. In a letter to Nathaniel Barney (22 July 1846, MNHi), LCM had said she and JM were trying to raise money from local merchants as well as having "a Mg. called here for your relief" (Alexander Starbuck, *History of Nantucket* [Rutland, Vt.: Chas E. Tuttle, 1969], 338). The quotation is possibly an adaptation of Phil. 1:10: "That ye may approve things that are excellent."

## To George Combe

Philada. 4 Mo. 26th. 1847

My dear George Combe

So rapid is the speed of Time, as years & cares increase upon us, that I am quite surprised to find that nearly 11 months have passed, since the date of thy last peculiarly acceptable letter, and no acknowledgement of it from me until now. The sentiments contained in it on the marriage of near relatives, met our decided approval. Our Thomas has a little daughter a few months old [*Isabella*], who though now apparently bright as common, will yet I hope, receive all the added care & attention, which thy suggestions have impressed as necessary. An increasing interest has been manifested in Phrenology here the last winter, through the Lectures & *Manipulations* of Fowler.[1] Some of our children attended them, and thought he had improved since 1838–9—. I did not go to any of his Lectures, not admiring the man, & not caring to descend to second-best. I may be prejudiced, and ought not therefore to say anything to his injury. He had large classes. The truths of Phrenology are evidently receiving more general admission, and the introduction of the principles into some of our Schools, has so simplified the Philosophy there taught, as to leave the brain or mind clear, from complex puzzles & absurdities, for further investigation in after life. Would that this Science could find entrance into the Church & the Theological schools, as a substitute for the dogmas & hidden mysteries there instilled & given forth, in the name of Christianity!

My husband & self have been greatly interested with the Life of Joseph Blanco White.[2] If you have not already enjoyed it, a rare treat is in store for you. The progress of his mind from the darkness of Catholicism to *more* than Unitarian light, and his honesty in the avowal of his opinions from time to time, are truly admirable. His veneration for the Right & the true through all the changes of his theological opinions, and his firm faith & calm trust in "conscientious Reason," & a Great First Cause—up to the close of a life of much physical & not a little mental suffering, inspire his readers with renewed confidence in all that is *good* in Religion; while his great desire, that the fatal errors & absurdities of "articled" Christianity—pretended oracles—& sacerdotal religion, may be more openly opposed; that "Bibleolatry", & the superstitious belief in miracles may give place to rational Christianity & pure worship;—that not only Catholicism— the most mischievous system of Priesthood, but also the narrow, dogmatic teachings of the English Universities—'their wealthy establishments, founded upon the misty twilight of the dark ages,' may be more faithfully & *aggressively* exposed; his ardent wish that a truly philosophical work on the source of knowledge respecting God, should be written, must meet a response in every liberal mind, impressed with the magnitude of the evils & errors he deplores. This work has made me dislike bigotry & bigots more than ever before. I asked James if he had perceived that it had given a coloring to my preaching. Could not George Combe write such a work as the age calls for on this subject?* J. Blanco White's Life has not been re-published in this Country. We hope it may be,—but Orthodoxy will do all it can to suppress it.

By our son-in-law E. M. Davis, last Spring, we sent you & some other of our British friends, a few liberal pamphlets, which we fear were never received. Edward was so excessively Sea-sick, that the Captain advised him to stop at Halifax & return home. His brother, who was with him united with this advice— So he entrusted the various parcels of heretical works to some Orthodox Friends who were on their return from this country. They were slightly tied up—not sealed I think, & no mention being made, from any quarter, of their reception, I am apprehensive or jealous, that the 'pious fraud' was committed, of keeping them back— They were not of much value, only, as shewing the progress of liberal principles here & in New England, we thought they would be interesting. ^I may have done these Friends injustice—so please brush the slander.^

The invitation contained in thy letter to visit you at your nice home, was indeed gratifying to us, and would be most joyfully accepted if we had so good an excuse for crossing the Atlantic, as when we went in 1840. We hear from or of you occasionally, with great pleasure, through those who have visited you. Our correspondent in Dublin—Richd. D. Webb, had much to tell us of Fredk. Douglass' visit at your house— He has now returned to this country & we hope to see him here during the next summer. He has done great credit to himself in his sojourn abroad: And coming home as a free-man, he may feel more secure of Southern arrest; but we do regret that money for his freedom, should be paid to those, who by that means can, & probably will transfer the bonds to another, equally entitled to liberty. The information thou gave, of the success of the Abolition attacks on your Free Church, was acceptable. While thou fears that

some of us—fanatics, may lose influence by "pressing beyond the line of justice,"³ I was amused to percieve, that, in pursuing the subject farther, thou became quite as ultra as the Abolitionists themselves—that is, in making no compromise with the Slave-holders, "while they do not acknowledge the sin &
inhumanity of Slavery" &c— I had that part of thy letter published in the
Penna. Freeman; but the *confidential* remarks, on your pecuniary losses in this
country, have been kept mostly to ourselves, as thou wished. We regret that such
labor as was bestowed here, should lose any—even the least part of its reward—
The more, as your Poor are so much in need just now. What will be done for
famishing, starving Ireland? The ready remittances of the many sympathizers
in America, added to the bounty of British charities, may bring back some from
the gates of Death, if indeed that is to be desired; but we must look beyond the
present exigency, & seek more permanent relief for that subjected, oppressed
people. Their labors have been for ages exacted for the support of the Hierarchy—the Nobility—The Army & Navy—as well as for other claimants of the
soil—their natural right. And until an entire revolution, take place, they must
continue to toil without hope & without reward. Under such circumstances,
prolonged life must be a curse rather than a blessing. It has made me sad, long
before this potato failure, when the hard-working Irish in this country have sent
over their little savings to their friends at home; knowing full well that it was
but aiding to keep up the whole system of oppression a little longer. It was a great
draw-back on the pleasure of our visit & travels in your countries, to see such
an amount of squalid poverty & wretchedness, in the midst of Princely elegance
& the most luxurious indulgence. But I must stop—for while we have three
Millions of abject slaves, robbed of their every right, we have enough to do to
"look at home," and "take the beam out of our own eye."⁴

What added disgrace to our country—that we are engaged in a War of ag-
gression & conquest with a neighboring weak & comparatively defenceless
Nation! May the labors of an Elihu Burritt & an H. C. Wright hasten the time,
when "Violence—shall be no more be heard in the land, wasting & destruction
within her borders"!⁵

We occasionally see the productions of thy pen. The Article or Letter on
Association or Community, we read with interest, & have offered it for re-print-
ing to the Friends Intelligencer.⁶ The Notes on the New Reformation in Germany—&.c—reached us, by way of N. York, with thy well-known hand directing
it to me. How grateful are such tokens of remembrance from those we love! I
read every thing from that quarter with interest. We hear little of Ronge of late.
That pamphlet gave me valuable information of the divisions of Protestantism
in Germany, &.c— — — — Thank thee, for thy contribution to the "Liberty
Bell." I presume our friend M. W. Chapman sent thee a copy.⁷

The subject of Slavery appeared to be the prominent topic of debate, during
our last session of Congress, notwithstandg. all the efforts of the opponents to
ward it off.— Altho' little appears to have been effected by the Anti-Slavery ag-

itation—the number of victims of oppression & cruelty has greatly increased—
the area of Slavery much enlarged—and threatens to be still more so, in our
successful invasion of Mexico— Slave-holdg. rulers are in the ascendant—
General Taylor in anticipation for our next President; yet, to the close discerner
of the signs of the times, the constant agitation of the Abolitionists, has shaken
all these strong holds, and has made the oppressor tremble. That which was once
too "delicate" a subject to be named, is now openly discussed on the high ways
& in public places. Churches are beginning to see their inconsistencies— Merchants & manufacturers are acknowledging themselves "partakers in other men's
sins," in their not "despising the gain of oppression"—[8] Legislat[ors] hear and
answer the prayers of the advocates for freedom—as, in our own State the last
session—abolishg. the "6 months law", & removing the facilities for the recovery of fugitives, and in Delaware, the Bill for the entire abolition of Slavery, passing
the House unanimously & lost in the Senate, by only one vote—[9] The demand
in Kentucky for an Anti-Slavery Paper to be re-established—suspended as it was
by the unworthy apostacy [of] Cassius M. Clay—the readiness with which $5000
have been raised, to place it on a firmer footing, & to secure the services as Editor, of John C. Vaughan, formerly of South Carolina—the establishment of the
National Era in Washington—not an ultra [Pa]per; but even mixed Abolitionism would not have been suffered a few years ago—the admission of appeals for
the slave, into our Political Papers—and other evidences which might be named,
all go to shew, that, incendiaries & fanatics as we were called, our labor has not
been in vain, in the cause of justice & humanity. To those whose "*Hope* springs
eternal," the day has already [crowned?], when "Liberty {shall be} procl[aimed]
throughout all the land, unto all the inhabitants thereof."[10]

Our friends Washington Brown & Wife[11] who visited you last year from this
City, returned greatly pleased with their travel abroad, [&] with the kindness &
hospitality with which they were greeted. They spoke particularly of their pleasant visit to you—of the attention shewn their little daughter & of the kaleidoscope presented,—&.c— They sent messages of kind regards to me, for you
some months since. I may have forgotten in part, what they wished me to say
to you—they however retain a lively sense of the attention shewn by thyself and
Cecilia. To my dear frd. Cecy let me say, that her little additions to thy letters
are ever most welcome—indeed these evidences of your continued regard &
affection would be incomplete without her sisterly "all hail". And so, her poor
dear cousin Fanny Butler has returned to the Stage. Hers has been a chequered
life thus far! I was full of hope for her a few years since, that her talents would
be devoted to the highest good of herself & her fellow beings. I speak thus rather in pity than in censure— Your friend Anne D. Morris[on] was well when I
last saw her—some 6 or 8 weeks since—she then intended to write to y[ou.] Dr.
Hartshorne's family well as usual I believe— We have no social intercourse.
Our Orthodox Friends are divided again on doctrinal points. They have been
engaged the last week at their Yearly Meeting in this City, in a hair-splitting dis-

cussion relative to the Gurney & the Wilbur faith. We-Hicksites too are not agree[ing] on all points. The scriptures are becoming a bone of contention. J. Blanco White exclaims, "Oh, bitter Superstition![ "] Our friend George Parrish,[12] the bearer of this, is a son of our good, benevolent Dr. Parrish. I don't know that he expects to go to Scotland, as his stay will be short—business calling him to England. I have filled the sheet as usual, & have only room to add James Mott's kindest regards & my heart's affections—

Lucretia Mott

*He will perhaps answer, that he has already written several works of the tendency alluded to.

ALS GBNLS

1. Orson Squire Fowler (1809–87), the principal figure in American phrenology, was the editor of the *American Phrenological Journal*. With his brother, Lorenzo Fowler, he founded Fowler and Wells, a phrenological agency and museum in New York City.

2. *The Life of Joseph Blanco White*, edited by John Hamilton Thom (London: J. Chapman, 1845). White (1775–1841), a Spanish priest, journalist, novelist, theologian, and teacher, left his country in 1810 for England, where he converted from Catholicism to the Church of England, attended Oxford, and in 1826 received an honorary master's degree and joined the faculty. He left Oxford when he abandoned the Church of England for Unitarianism. His *Life* reflects his difficult religious journey and "lifelong struggle against orthodoxy," compounded by his poor health (Martin Murphy, *Blanco White: Self-Banished Spaniard* [New Haven, Conn.: Yale University Press, 1989], 195).

3. The quotation is possibly from William Cowper's "Table Talk" (l. 17): "plants in upon the line that justice draws."

4. Matt. 7:5.

5. Elihu Burritt (1810–79) was a Connecticut peace advocate and linguist (*WLG*, 3:301–2). Isa. 60:18.

6. Combe had written that he regarded François Fourier's communitarian system as "impracticable in the present state of society" (*Liberator*, 5 March 1847, 40).

7. In his letter to Maria Weston Chapman of 22 November 1846, Combe had written of American slavery, "If there is a living being in the United States who does not lament and shudder at this scourge of humanity, he is dead, not only to the voice of conscience and of patriotism but to the sense of shame and the honor of his country" (*Liberty Bell* [Boston National Anti-Slavery Fair, 1847], 83–85). The *Friends' Intelligencer* had reprinted "Notes on Germany—State of Protestantism" from the *Scotsman*. This article reported that "Protestantism in Germany is at present divided into three great sections—the 'Pietists,' the 'Friends of Light,' and a middle section, which has taken up ground between these two" (3 January 1846, 313–14).

8. The Mexican War hero General Zachary Taylor (1784–1850) had recently defeated Santa Anna's forces in the Battle of Buena Vista. 1 Tim. 5:22; Isa. 33:15.

9. In February 1847, the Pennsylvania legislature had abolished the "Six Months Law," part of the Act for the Gradual Abolition of Slavery of 1780, which allowed slaveowners to bring their slaves into Pennsylvania and keep them in the state for six months (*Pennsylvania Freeman*, 11 February 1847, 3). It also had abolished a provision that had allowed masters to reclaim fugitives in the state. In Delaware, the House of Representatives had voted for the gradual abolition of slavery in the state, but this act failed to pass in the Senate (*Pennsylvania Freeman*, 25 February 1847, 2, 4 March 1847, 2).

10. John C. Vaughan was a Cincinnati lawyer and an antislavery activist (*Salmon P. Chase Papers,* ed. John Niven, James McClure, and Leigh Johnsen [Kent, Ohio: Kent State University Press, 1993], 1:127). The *National Era,* the official newspaper of the American and Foreign Anti-Slavery Society, had begun publication in 1846. The quotations are from Alexander Pope's "An Essay on Man" and Lev. 25:10.

11. Washington Brown, a merchant, and Susan Allebone Stevenson Brown (d. 1870) were Philadelphia Hicksites.

12. John Wilbur (1774–1856) was a Quaker minister from Rhode Island. He had been disowned by the New England Yearly Meeting in 1845 after speaking out against Joseph John Gurney, and the resulting debate divided Orthodox Quakers. The conservative Wilburites wanted no compromise between Quakerism and modernity and believed that the evangelical Gurneyites endangered Quakerism by making the way to salvation too easy (Thomas Hamm, *The Transformation of American Quakerism: Orthodox Friends, 1800–1907* [Bloomington: Indiana University Press, 1988], 28–29). George Parrish (1820–71) was from Philadelphia.


## To [Martha Coffin Wright?]

*[Philadelphia c. 22 May 1847]*

[*ms. damaged*] the essay it contained has not been published, yet good use has been made of it in "surprisg the Natives," with such a production. S. Pugh liked that & the last sent, wh. is to go to S. H. Gay, for the Standard. Will it do, to appear there as original after being in the Tocsin—?[1] I had scarcely time to look at it till since Yearly Mg.— It is very good. "Who'd 'a thot. o' seeing" her such a author? What a libel on Abolitionists & other Reformers, the charge of irreligion! When they so distinctly & so repeatedly declare their "trust for victory" to be "in God"—that "*they* may be defeated, but their principles, never— Truth, justice, humanity["] being on their side & "plantg their feet" there "as on the everlastg rock" they "go forth conquerg. & to conquer"—or as some one says, "prosperg & to prosper." The close of our Declaration of Sentiments, was beautiful to me when first read, & the repeated evidence of the same trust, has stamped ours as emphatically *the* religious movet. of the age.[2] It is our turn to cry "Infidel" & the pseudo Church knows it too & is trembling in her shoes, if she wear shoes. There is danger however of reformers each makg. their *hobbies* the *only* right manifestn. of faith in God & allegiance to Him—& exercisg. their Benevolence & Conscientiousness, at the expense of their Veneration. The latter organ has received so terrible a shock, in severing it from its Idols—the church, the Bible, & the Ministry, that it is lying in too many instances in a paralyzed state, & needs judicious *Homeopathic* treatment. [*ms. damaged*] saying that he & his daughr. were to sa [*ms. damaged*] remainder of their days with his childn. in Canada; & previously to going thither [*ms. damaged*] to come & make us a visit. He didn't say whether they wd. come in a Steamer, so we cannot tell just when to look for them—but must remain at home till they come. We stopped with them 2 days & enjoyed our visit, & have often wished to see him

here.[3] He is now 7 yrs. older however (as are we) upwards of 70 & has had a
Paralytic stroke— They will likely be here a week or so, & *then* we shall be at
liberty to carry out our plans. In the mean time J. & self propose a *little* tour.

Philada. 6 Mo. 2nd.
4th day morng.

Now we have accomplished it, and are at home again, after havg. attended
the N. E. Convention, which you may possibly notice in some of the papers, as
it has been spread abroad in this way.[4] Jas. has for several years, felt a wish to go
there at that time. He couldn't however decide till a day or 2 before we started,
owing to a suit comg. on, in the Malthouse failure. So that we could not write
to you to meet us there & make our visit to N[antucke]—t at the same time—
because also, the others of our party couldn't go so soon. Mary Brown is to make
one, and she is not yet able to go out of her room much, tho' doing well now.
Martha wrote about the twins— Well, a month or 6 weeks hence, Anna Hopper wd. feel less like takg. a journey, so we persuaded her to turn her back upon
that sweet little Maria & the rest, and bear us compy. We wd. have taken Martha too, but she didn't choose any "Convention," preferg. to go with a party who
wd. stop at the Tremont. So we left her "alone in her glory" to oversee housecleang. & home at Edwd.'s next door. At night, to pass thro' the closet & lodge
in their back chamber. Anne & Elizh. havg. no family but themselves & George
to provide for, had time to begin at the garret— Betsy doing the whitewashg.—
Mary Fisher helpg. scrub a day or so—Mrs. [DeReaux?] puttg down all the straw
carpets, save the 2 parlors wh. after George & Wm. had brot. it from [*ms. damaged*] Elizh.'s ^not Cavender^ help spread down & tacked—was she not smart?

[*P.S.*] all she saw, Boston [*ms. damaged*] in neat order. Anna turned righ [*ms.
damaged*] ready to receive Garrison & others [*ms. damaged*], there was no way
of spendg money so

AL Frag MNS

1. The *Tocsin of Liberty* had become the *Albany Patriot* in 1844. LCM is apparently
referring to its previous name.

2. LCM is quoting from the Declaration of Sentiments written for the 1833 National
Anti-Slavery Convention in Philadelphia (*Liberator*, 14 December 1833, 198).

3. In a letter to Nathaniel Barney, LCM would write of the expected visit of William
Boultbee, a delegate to the 1840 World's Anti-Slavery Convention in London, who had
shown JM and her frequent hospitality in London. LCM and JM had spent five nights
at Boultbee's Birmingham home (7 June 1847, private collection of William Barney;
*Diary*, 27–28, 46, 58–60; JM, *Three Months in Great Britain* [Philadelphia: J. Miller
McKim, 1841], 48–50).

4. The New England Anti-Slavery Convention had met in Boston on 25–26 May 1847.
LCM had been elected to the Business Committee and had spoken on a free produce
resolution (*NASS*, 3 June 1847, 2).

# To Nathaniel Barney and Elisa Barney

*[Added to JM's letter of 26 October 1847]*

Yes it would be very pleasant to us to meet you at Farmington & at Auburn next year, if we live & are in health. It is long now to look forward to, but bear it in mind.

*[Philadelphia]*
7th. day 30th. & 1st. day 31st.

James left this for me to add to, but I have not had an hour to devote to it till now. Yes, we read Nathaniel's letter to Wm. Wharton with much interest; were glad that he had answered the appeal to you as he did—tho' it will not be just what our friends hereaway are desiring for you. We presumed on the confidence reposed in us, so far, as to shew the letter to Geo. & Cathe. Truman, before sending it to Wm. W. George renewed the expression of his desire, that yr. Mg. might be re-opened. I didn't know that the death of G. F. White would not change the aspect of Westbury Qr., & dispose thee, Nathanl., to continue with them. I feel quite satisfied however with yr. decision—only that when travelg. in the neighd. of any of our Mgs. in any part of the country, I wd. rather that yr. right of membership shd. be unquestioned & that Nathanl. shd. exercise his gift in the ministry.[1] George Truman brings rather an encouraging accot. of that state of things in Gennesee Yr. Mg. Farmingn. House was opened, not long since, after havg. been closed against Abolition lectures for 5 years. A better feeling is manifested toward G. M. Cooper and Thos. McClintock—and on the whole there appears to be progress. Danl. Quimby has just been to Baltime. Yearly, attendg. our Mgs. on his way ^Nathanl. Starbuck his companion^.[2] His preachg. was not marked with any invidious slang. A large at[ten]-dance of Ministers as usual, at Balte. Dorothy Golden—Rachel Hicks, & several from hereaway—Jane Johnson[3] John Jackson &.c— Rachel expects to be at our Qy. Mg. a week hence. Now that G. F. W. is gone, she may feel that a double duty devolves on her. New York Mo. Mg. has laid down Marlboro' Preparative, & are preparg. to disown N. Hallock, &.c—

While we were in Ohio & Indiana, a letter was circulating from John Mott proposg. a general conference to take into view the distracted state of things in our Society. Many Friends thereaway wd. unite in a move of that kind. Free & Reform Mgs. too are favorably viewed by them. When a private opp[ortunit]y occurs, I will send for yr. perusal some letters we recd. from Joseph A. Dugdale & Vale. Nicholson[4]—a good man and true, wh. will exhibit the State of things in that neighbd.— As to Indiana Yearly, as a body, less is to be hoped from it, than from any other. They ought to have gone with the Orthodox, at the Separation in—28— Their doings reminded me of Arch St. Mg. the year before the Separation. The business is done by a few around the Clerk's table & in their own way, without regard to any dissentg. voices. They drew the line tighter this year, by requirg. that Ministers shd. have the sanction of the Qy. Mg. before

attendg. any Yearly or other Mg. or Mgs. without their limits, & for an extensive visit *within* their own Yearly— They also made a rule to disown Green Plain
*rebels* in a body—or without the usual form—callg. on them individy.—&
ascertaing. their determinn. & then strikg. off their names from their records,
wh. was well— Joseph Plummer[5] came into the Wom. Mg. with the information sayg—their "Mg had been brot. into exercise & sympathy with Green Plain
*Mo. Mg.,* on accot. of the *rebellious spirit* of some of their members, who had
their records & refused to give them up &.c—&.c—; & in relation to that *rebellion,* it was concluded," &.c. That seems to be a favorite term with them. In
making out so many Meetgs. as Jas. has mentioned, we counted each sittg. of
both Yearly Mgs. as well as those of the Conventions of Garrison & Dougs. There
was a remark in Nathanl.'s letter last summer, respectg Garrison's neglect to
publish some articles sent him, wh. I feared was calculated rather to estrange
that good feeling, wh. has always subsisted between them. I felt like sayg. a word,
suggestive of the idea, that G's seeming neglect, might be nothing more than
his characteristic carelessness as to articles sent for the Liberator. If oppy. offer
therefore, let me hope that there will be a free conversn. together & all jealousy
removed. We were never more impressed with the weight of character & dignity of demeanor of our dear friend—nor with the ability & discretion of our frd.
Dougs. than during the week that it was our privelege to be in their compy. We
regretted that the more Southern parts of the State could not have been edified
with their labors. We were very anxious during G's illness.[6] We were far away, &
only heard occasionally. He is probably at home now—& we hope thoro'ly restored. We were much gratified to meet J. C. Vaughan in Cincina.—successor
to C. M. Clay—Editor of the Examiner.[7] That Paper is doing a good work in
Kentucky & farther South—is preferable to the National Era, in that it has no
party politics to subserve. J. C. Vaughan succeeded in obtaing. sufft. aid when
North & East last winter, to establish the Press & make a beginning—he also
has a good many subscribers in & around Louisville & some farther South. But
to his disappointment, after sendg. the Paper to all C. M. Clay's subscribers this
way & to New England, he had 1800 returns. He is anxious that exertion should
be made to increase its patronage. I promised to do what I could. We have succeeded with a few—also, in collecting $150, subscribed last winter. I mention this,
hoping that some subscribers to the Paper may be found on Nantucket. It appeared to us one of the most important instrumentalities in our great cause.

I dont know that Elisa will thank us for endeavoring to enlist her husband's
interest in this, and in our Church affairs— But I hope it will not be to the injury
of his health or his equanimity— As to any mental exertion, he can judge how
far he may go with safety—& not do as I have done—continually violate Nature's laws. J. A. Dugdale so often reminded me of Nathaniel, that I feel quite a
wish that they should meet.— It was reported in Ohio that we were employed
& *paid* by the A. S. Society for going out & holding these Meetings—& that

therefore we might as well pay board as stop at a Friends' house. Arriving at Richmond Ia. the report reached there—Sarah O. Plummer asked us as to its truth—altho' she said, she had been told that she wd. receive an evasive answer from me,—I wd. not acknowledge it, if so. She however knew me better than that & wished an answer— I told her many false charges had been made, but never before that I was not truthful. James told her so far from that being a fact— we had never at any time received a cent from any Anti Slavery Society, but had paid or given hundreds of dollars. I told her that we had never even availed ourselves of the fund for the Indian Committee's use, while some who censured us for employing Anti S. lecturers—Benjn. Ferris, &.c—had brot. in large bills of their travelg. expenses even to the paper they used in writing letters—&.c— But of how little consequence is all this.

2nd. day 11 mo 1st.

You will miss dear Sarah [*Barney*] from your little family this winter. Is not your high school equal to any boardg. school that could be found? I wrote a hurried line to cousin Phebe by her Edward [*Gardner*], sendg. her our Martha's letters. Will you please tell her that our Anna Hopper added a little son [*George*] to their family yesterday, & is doing well.— Aunt P. [*Hussey*] & Thos. Earle's family are well. We passed last eveg. there pleasantly. Aunt was out at Mg. in the morning, & probably at their Quarterly today. It is a treat to have her with us this winter. Our visit to you is full of pleasant memories— Much love to all our dear friends—including Wm. Henry Knapp. We were kindly recd. by Saml. J. May in Syracuse & had a good meeting there— I did not say just as the correspondt. of the Liberator reported me—about "no greater miracle within the lids of the Bible".[8] I may have queried, whether the successful labors of a Father Mathew & his coadjutors in the Temp[eranc]e. reformn. might not be regarded as among the "greater works" wh. Jesus declared shd. be done, because he went to the Father, & the people were prepared for little in that day— I have also frequently said that the unparrelled success in the Tempe. Cause was one of greatest moral miracles of our days— But the sheet is full. Did I say in our last, that Nathanl.'s & coz Mary Rotch's gifts to Prisa. Cadwalader were forwarded to her, with $25 more from here—& that Elizh. Peart paid her a visit after Indiana Yr. Mg.—that Priscilla was much better than she had been—[9]

yours   L. Mott

I presume our friend George Truman will write to you shortly if he has not already—giving you an accot. of his & Wm.'s travels & the number of interestg incidents connected with the journey. Jas. hasn't told you of a Mg. that we had on board the boat comg. from Cini. to Pittsburg  Rev. Stockton a Methodist of this City[10] & Rev Burgess a Presbytn. of the West took part, and the passengers expressing a wish that I shd. address them I occupied ½ an hour or more  Lindley Hoag[11] was on board sat with us but said nothing— After the Mg. concluded he came to us, smiling said one of the passengers where he sat proposed that a collection be taken up for the *Lady*. I had considerable conversation with Lindley on Gurneyism & Wilburism—& Hicksism—human depravity &.c—&.c—

Altho' decidedly orthodox, he was more open & free in conversation with us than are many of our own side, who are now rank opposers. He attended Ohio—Indiana & Balte. Yearly Mgs. He is going to open a *Free* goods store in New York Friends aiding him.

ALS MNHi

1. Nathaniel Barney had been disowned in 1820 for marrying Elisa Starbuck, a Unitarian. He had become a Hicksite minister in 1831, but a decline in the Nantucket membership caused it to be subsumed by the Orthodox in 1847, and he resigned (Robert J. Leach and Peter Gow, *Quaker Nantucket: The Religious Community behind the Whaling Empire* [Nantucket, Mass.: Mill Hill Press, 1997], 170–74). George F. White had died on 9 October 1847 (*Friends' Intelligencer,* 16 September 1848, 202).

2. Daniel Osgood Quimby (1821–94) was a New England Quaker lawyer and teacher. "Nathanl. Starbuck" is possibly a Quaker from Troy, New York.

3. Jane Johnson (d. 1884) was a Hicksite Quaker minister (*Friends' Intelligencer,* 20 September 1884, 505).

4. LCM and JM had arrived in Ohio in late August. In his part of the letter, JM wrote Barney that they had been "absent 69 days & 6 hours, travelled about 2800 miles, attended 71 mgs. of all kinds, in most of wh. Lucretia took a part." In Salem she had reiterated her allegiance to the Garrisonians and censured the *Constitution* for its proslavery tendencies (*Liberator,* 1 October 1847, 139). John Mott is possibly the publisher of "Copy of a Letter Written by John Mott, to an Orthodox Friend" (c. 1828) and "An Epistle to Friends within the Compass of Philadelphia Yearly Meeting" (c. 1828). Valentine Nicholson (1809–1904) was an Ohio Hicksite abolitionist and a reformer (Thomas Hamm, *God's Government Begun: The Society for Universal Inquiry and Reform, 1842–46* [Bloomington: Indiana University Press, 1995], 32–40, 226–31).

5. In his part of this letter JM had written that, when he and LCM had attended the Indiana Yearly Meeting held in Richmond, they had dined at the home of Dr. John T. Plummer (1807–65). Plummer's wife, Sarah O. Plummer (1804–77), formerly of Pennsylvania, they regarded as an "intimate friend." LCM had complained to the Plummers that she had been feeling ill, "adding if he could cure her she should be willing to give him a larger fee than she would give an A. S. Lecturer; he asked no questions but sat looking very *sober* till she had told him her distress, when with a loud & very trembling voice he said—'Lucretia however my disposition may lead me to extend kindness & hospitality to my friends, such is my affliction at thy rebellion, that I cannot prescribe for thee.'" LCM had responded: "If that is thy feeling Dr. I am glad of the expression of it, & the friends present may judge the spirit we are both of."

6. Garrison and Douglass had embarked on their western tour in early August, visiting Pittsburgh and numerous towns in Ohio. JM wrote in his part of this letter, "We spent nearly a week with Garrison & Douglass, attending their large A. S. conventions, parting with them at Ravenna, they going to Cleaveland where dear Garrison was taken ill." Garrison spent five weeks recovering from his illness and did not return to Boston until early December (*WLG,* 3:465–66, 505, 510, 535).

7. Clay had renamed the *True American* the *Examiner* when he moved the paper to Louisville, Kentucky (*WLG,* 3:314).

8. William Henry Knapp (b. 1812) was a Congregationalist minister. LCM apparently is referring to her speech "Reforms of the Age," delivered in Worcester, not in Syracuse.

Her audience had seemed surprised that she placed theological reform ahead of all other reforms. She reportedly had commended the former slaves William Wells Brown (c. 1816–84) and Frederick Douglass for presenting other reformers with "a moral miracle stranger than *any found recorded within the lids of the Bible.*" The reporter wrote, "Lucretia is a more 'dangerous' person than I expected. She is as 'heretical' in her Theology as she is 'infidel' in her practice" (*Liberator*, 17 September 1847, 150–51).

9. This is probably a reference to Mary Rotch (1777–1848), a member of the New Bedford and Nantucket, Massachusetts, Quaker business and merchant family. Priscilla Coffin Hunt Cadwallader (1786–1859) was a Quaker minister (Ingle, 50–51). Elizabeth M. Peart, the wife of Thomas Peart, was a Philadelphia Hicksite.

10. William Stockton (1785–1860) was the editor of the *Wesleyan Repository,* published in Philadelphia.

11. Lindley Hoag, a New Hampshire Quaker, was received by the New York Monthly Meeting in 1848.

## To Nathaniel Barney

Philada. 3 Mo. 14th. 1848—

My dear Nathaniel—

I would say "Nathanl. & Elisa",—only that our correspondence seems to be, as touchg. you, on Nathanl.'s part alone— Moreover, now that Elisa is so nicely emancipated from sect, and even from *Meetg.,* to her great joy, any participation in our Society twaddle, must be very burdensome to her. And while we form a part of the sectarian 'Humbug,' our letters will necessarily partake of that which helps to mould our character. Let us not err so greatly in judgment, however, as to regard existing religious Assns. a humbug, because no longer profitable to such minds as Elisa's,—& Garrison's, & a *few* others. Consider the vast numbers, who are still saying: "Let not God speak to us lest we die"— These must follow their 'Moses', until "the fulness of time shall come." Nothwithstdg. all the nonsense that is preached of Trinities & Atonements—Divinities and Satanities—Depravities & Regenerations—there is after all so much of *good* mingled with it, that we must "let both grow until the harvest".[1] With all the unmeaning, & superstitious form of worship, displayed equally in the timbrel & the dance—in tumult & noise,—and in "getting into the quiet", there is still so much beautiful appeal to the Veneration,—so much that meets this want in man that, between an *imposed* Sabbath—*forced* observances, and the free exercise of conscience, we must duly discriminate—seeking always to 'illumine that which is dark'. This brings me to the approachg. Convention in Boston. Hast thou become too much of a Gurneyite to sign that 'Call'? or yet to be present in Boston, when the gathering is there? I have a 'Godly jealousy' of thee, while thou attends that meeting, & consents to be a *silent* participant in its worship. "Can a man touch {Orthodox} pitch, & not be defiled"?[2] I agree with thee that there is more liberality—& less drab-colored mint-tything with *thy chosen*, than with the other portion of Bigots—but then they are both bigots after all. We signed that call with our eyes wide open. We knew it wd subject us to added censure & reproach. But it has been a 'testimony' with me for years—not to measure devotion by Sabbath observances—& as zeal has increased in this direction, to try to counteract it— When travellg. last summer, the Sabbath tracts were scattered the length of the cars appealg. to the credulity & gross superstitn. of the Ignorant. I then thot. something should be done to "assert eternal {Liberty} & justify the ways of God to Man".[3] When this Anti-Sabbath move was made, Jas. & self hailed it, among the evidences of a "good time coming". Well pleased should we be to go to Boston, but Jas. has just returned from N. York—a visit of several days to his Mother—now 80 yrs old—& a satisfactory one it was— and he now says, we cant go. Just now too he is not well, from repeated colds, & improper exposures—

So, our journey West is likely to be arrested, at that point of time, by your Bazaar. Jas. says it is too far off to plan much about it— He asks however, if Elisa's influence cant prevail, to have the Bazaar a week earlier? If we go, it must be abt. the time of Gennessee Yearly—so as to meet other members of the Indian Com.—& make a visit to that remnant of a once formidable People. The Canada colony of Colored *ones* also form an attraction thitherward, but whether we shall accomplish all, is another thg. As to our makg. another visit to our loved Island again so soon, kind as was yr. invitatn. and much obliged as we feel, I should be ashamed to shew my face there looking so "very natural". No, you must look at the subject in all its bearings, & report again to us yr. conclusion. No difficulty would arise, I am persuaded, as to yr. right of attendance at the Yearly— The '*living*' there would greet you, as dearly beloveds, & should an objection be raised, it wd. furnish a fine opp[ortunit]y., to expose Sectarian intolerance. We shall not be likely to make much stop at Auburn until returng.— Our sister Martha will probably be here in a few weeks, to stay till about the time that we should go— I shall send by Edwd. G[ardner]., her late letters, for Phebe's perusal—in one of which she expresses how much pleasure it will give her to see you there next summer—

In our Anti Slavery Ex. Com. we have had the subject—repeatedly discussed, of sending an Agent to England—not, just to lecture, but to hold conversational Mgs.—& try to extend the interest in the great cause of human freedom, which now, there as well as here, is confined to too few. J. Miller M'Kim has been proposed as the most suitable agent. We have sometimes talked, just for talk, go with him & take our Martha. Our frds. on the other side the wide water have been written to, as to the probable results of such a measure. We wait their answer— You are aware perhaps, that M. W. Chapman is going in the course of this year, with her 3 childn., to give them the oppy. of a European educatn.—in Germany probably— What will the Boston Com. do without her? Elisa Barney will have to bestow her energies on *that* Fair—and not give all to Nant.— We shall feel an interest in the success of yours—& shall try to send a little—not equal indeed to thy generosity to us hereaway, but as a mite in your treasury. I have the promise of some patterns of silks & ribbons from our E. M. Davis. He has no assortment just now.

The good intentions of dear Andw. Robeson toward W. L. G[arrison]. will not likely be carried out, now that Fortune's tide has turned with regard to him.[4] How sad it is, that he, who was disposed to be so generous, should be deprived the power! What changes have we already seen, in the various branches of that family! Enough to teach us a lesson on the too eager pursuit of wealth. Your only son [*Joseph*] must take care, that gain become not Godliness with him. What has he done with his intended visit this way & to Washn.? We should be very sorry for him to pass thro' this City, without coming to see us. Indeed, it wd. give us great pleasure to have him stop with us long enough for us to shew him the lions of our City. Thy br. Obed is so far from us & his wife—my cousin, not of the most social turn, that we seldom see them.[5]

Cathe. Truman tells me that George has lately written thee— So thou probably has all the Meeting news—and how J. Comly & other of the Repr[esentativ]e. Com. have endeavd. to pass off a creed—&.c— Great efforts are made to lessen John Jackson's influence because of his Peace & War book;[6] greater still to destroy "yr. humble servant" because of her radical preachg. & the free exercise of her individual rights— It is true that some 7 or 8 of the officers &.c— of the Wom. Mg. objected to furnishg me with a minute to appoint Mgs. within the limits of our Yearly Mg. while some 20 or 30 expressed their entire unity—there the matter rested— They cannot however prevent my going as way may open & havg. Mgs. appointed for me as in N. England last year & out West— Some on both sides are quite ready for another attempt at re-organizn. seeing we are already divided on many subjects where harmony is judged by some essential— When will men learn that there are other & more indissoluble bonds of union than agreement in opinion in Creed or form?—

15th.

We hear that our Edwd. Gardner is going tomorw.—& very little have we seen him since he came. This day I have been engaged with our daughr. Marianna Mott—who has another daughter [*Emily*]—and her Mother not here!— We have Telegraphed the important fact & shall look for her next week—

Yours ever—    L. Mott

ALS MNHi Env: "Nathaniel Barney, Nantucket, per coz. Edwd."

1. LCM is adapting Gen. 3:3: "Ye shall not eat of it, neither shall ye touch it, lest ye die." Gal. 4:4; Matt. 13:30.

2. The "Call" for the Anti-Sabbath Convention of 23–24 March 1848 stated, "The attempt to compel the observance of any day as 'THE SABBATH,' especially by penal enactments, is unauthorized by scripture or reason, and a shameful act of imposture and tyranny. We claim for ourselves, and for all mankind, the right to worship God according to the dictates of OUR OWN CONSCIENCES." Not all Garrisonians agreed to sign. The list of signers was headed by William Lloyd Garrison, Theodore Parker, and Henry C. Wright and included LCM and JM (*Liberator,* 21 January 1848, 11, 31 March 1848, 50;

*WLG*, 3:544–45). In her speech at the convention, Mott would go beyond denying the sanctity of the sabbath: "But might we not go further, and shew that we are not to rely so much upon books, even upon the Bible itself, as upon the higher revelation within us? The time is come, and especially in New England it is come, that man should judge of his own self what is right, and that he should seek authority less from the Scriptures" (*Sermons*, 59). LCM is adapting Ecclus. 13:1: "He that toucheth pitch shall be defiled there with."

3. John Milton, *Paradise Lost*, 1:22.

4. Andrew Robeson (1787–1862) was a New Bedford, Massachusetts, businessman, philanthropist, and officer in the American and Massachusetts Anti-Slavery Societies (*WLG*, 3:272).

5. Obed Barney (1798–1875) married Lavinia Coffin (1802–73).

6. John Jackson, *Reflections on Peace and War* (Philadelphia: T. E. Chapman, 1846).


## To Sydney Gay and Elizabeth Neall Gay

Philada. 5 Mo. 1st. 1848

My dear Sydney & Elizh.

Both your kind notes are before me. Not having as pretty paper in the house, as they are written on, I must answer you on such as we have. The invitation to go to your house, we thank you for, as from loving hearts; and gladly would we accept it, if within any reasonable distance; but if we go, the eveg. Mgs. may be as attractive as the others, & then we shall not only wish to attend them, but to have *you* there also, instead of going "away off" to Staten Island to receive company. I do hope however, to be able *one* of the nights of our stay, to go home with you—perhaps the last night.

Several of our Chester Co. frds. are going to the Mg.—Esther Hayes, Hannah Cox, Sarah Coates, &.c—[1] They know not how they shall dispose of themselves. Part of them may go to I. T. Hopper's—others to the Graham House. It is my intention to board where our Mother Mott does—Orchard St. Jas. Mott has not quite decided whether to go or not. Sydney can do as he please, as to the announcement. It is most humbling to me to consent to be made thus public when there are so many "workmen who need not to be ashamed." I should think Elizh. would feel as she did in London, at Wm. Ball's, when frd. Adams had the floor.[2] My eyes are inflamed wh. adds nothing to a body's looks. I have also had an attack of fever & sore throat—all of which make me, if when in Boston last year 65, now 75— But if you'll take me "for better for worse" I'll do what I can, for the glorious cause demands that of us all— What art thou doing, dear Elizh.?

I have no time to say more

ever yours    L. Mott

ALS NNCB-Gay

1. LCM and JM were going to the AASS meeting in New York City, 9–11 May 1848. Esther Hayes was a member of the East Caln Anti-Slavery Society. Hannah Pearce Cox

(1797–1876) was an abolitionist from Chester County (*JGW*, 1:501). The last woman mentioned is possibly Sarah D. Coates (d. 1897) (*Pennsylvania Freeman*, 25 April 1839, 2; *Friends' Intelligencer*, 3 July 1897, 472).

2. 2 Tim. 2:15. William Ball (1801–78), an English Quaker minister, had held a "fancy tea" at his home on 25 June 1840. At it he had announced that anyone could speak who wished, including women. William Adams spoke on nonresistance (*Diary*, 48).

## To Elizabeth Cady Stanton

Auburn [*New York*] 7 Mo. 16th. 48—

Dear Elizabeth

I ought to have answered thy first kind letter of information & invitation, other than by verbal message sent by our mutual friend Mary Ann McClintock,[1] who hoped to see thee a few minutes, on her return from Deruyter— I requested her to tell thee how poorly my husband was, and that it was not likely I should be able to go to Seneca Falls, before the morning of the Convention. James continues quite unwell— I hope however that he will be able to be present the 2nd. day.

My sister Martha will accompany me on 4th. day Morng—& we will with pleasure accept thy kind invite to your house that night if you should not be too much crowded with company. My daughter Martha thinks she is not quite enough of a reformer to attend such a Convention. The true reason however, I presume is, that she is more interested just now, with her cousins here, & her time being short she dont incline to leave them.

James says thy *great* Speech thou must reserve for the Second day, so that he & others may be able to hear it. I was right glad to hear of thy resolve, & hope thou wilt not give out—[2]

The Convention will not be so large as it otherwise might be, owing to the busy time with the farmers, harvest, &.c— But it will be a beginning & we may hope it will be followed in due time by one of a more general character.

I have just returned from a Meeting with the prisoners & many others[3]— have another appointment this evening @ 6 o[clock] at the Universalist Church—

Are you going to have any reform or other Meeting during the sittings of the Convention?

We shall go from the Cars directly to the Meeting on 4th. day Give thyself no trouble about meeting us. There will be enough to conduct us thither.

Lovingly thine    *Lucretia Mott*

ALS DLC-Stanton Env: "Elizabeth C. Stanton, Seneca Falls, N.Y."

1. Mary Ann Wilson McClintock (1800–1884), the wife of Thomas McClintock, was a resident of Waterloo, New York.

2. The Seneca Falls convention would meet on 19–20 July 1848 and would be attended by over one hundred women and men. No record remains of the speeches given at

the convention, but the *Report of the Woman's Rights Convention* (Rochester: John Dick, 1848) mentions that both Stanton and Mott spoke. Mott's speeches on 19–20 July were very well received: "In the evening, Lucretia Mott spoke with her usual eloquence and power to a large and intelligent audience on the subject of Reforms in general." The reporter wrote that on 20 July, "the meeting was closed by one of Lucretia Mott's most beautiful and spiritual appeals" (Gordon, 1:75–88).

3. Mott had spoken at the Auburn State Prison, established in 1820 (Gordon, 1:74–75).

## To Thomas McClintock and Mary Ann McClintock

Auburn [*New York*] 7 Mo. 29th 1848

My dear Friends

You will think us very changeable, when we tell you, we have at length concluded to go to Rochester— I wrote to Amy Post our decision not to go, & recd from her the foregoing "distressing" reply. I had not thought of its being a disappointment to any one—for we did not entirely agree to be there—but on reconsidering the subject, after getting this we wrote again saying that we wd. leave here on 3rd. day n[ext] morning—thus losing part of the exhibition of that day—which we should not so much regret as a part of the day's exercises were such as we did not care to participate in— I write now hoping that some of you and Elizabeth C. Stanton may conclude to go—to help make the Womens Convention interesting.[1]

We are on the eve of a start for Scipio—2 Mgs. tomorrow— I write in the greatest haste— We received the Paper containing the "Declaration" which we have dispatched to Philada. Do send a copy forthwith to the Liberator[2]

Love to all & grateful remembe. of your many kindnesses—

*Lucretia Mott*

Have you recd. the good news from Staten Island? Elizh. Gay has a Son & is doing well—[3]

Our Thos. S. Cavender has been very ill with Dysentery—some deaths near our house, where he was sick—

Rodman Wharton too sick with the same complaint—[4]

ALS NHP Env: "Thomas M'Clintock, Waterloo, NY—"

1. Both Stanton and LCM would participate at the Rochester Woman's Rights Convention, organized by Amy Post and others, on 2 August 1848. As did the meeting at Seneca Falls, this convention emphasized women's economic and political rights. Unlike Seneca Falls, however, a woman, Abigail Bush, presided. LCM spoke several times and argued that women needed education before they could demand their rights: "We cannot expect to do much by meeting in convention, for those borne down by the oppressor, unless the oppressed *themselves* feel and act, and while so little attention is paid to education, and so little respect to woman" (Nancy Hewitt, *Women's Activism and Social Change: Rochester, New York, 1822–1872* [Ithaca, N.Y.: Cornell University Press, 1984], 131–33; *Liberator,* 15 September 1848, 148).

2. The Declaration of Sentiments of the Seneca Falls convention, reprinted in the *Liberator* (25 August 1848, 136), was modeled on the Declaration of Independence. It concluded by demanding equal citizenship for women: "Now, in view of this entire disfranchisement of one-half the people of this country, their social and religious degradation,—in view of the unjust laws above mentioned, and because women do feel themselves aggrieved, oppressed, and fraudulently deprived of their most sacred rights, we insist that they have immediate admission to all the rights and privileges which belong to them as citizens of these United States" (Gordon, 1:80).

3. Elizabeth's son was Walter Gay (1848–50) (Raimund Goerler, "Family, Self, and Anti-Slavery: Sydney Howard Gay and the Abolitionist Commitment," Ph.D. diss., Case Western Reserve University, 1975, 255–56).

4. Rodman Wharton (d. 1854) was the son of William Wharton and Deborah Wharton and the husband of Susannah Dillwyn Parrish (b. 1827).

# To Edmund Quincy

PHILADELPHIA, 8th mo., 24th, 1848.

MY DEAR FRIEND E. Q;

In the absence of our loved Wm. L. Garrison, I address a few lines to thee, to use or reject at discretion.

During the summer, my husband and self have had an interesting travel among the Cataraugus Indians, of Western New York, and the self-emancipated slaves and other colored settlers of Canada West. J. Mott has given some account of these, their location, &c., in the Pennsylvania Freeman.[1] It is worth a journey of many miles, to see 'the colored man *a man*'—in the full exercise of his energies and ingenuity; fertile in expedient, laboring with all the industry and hopeful prospect of a settler in a new country. Many difficulties to contend with, of course, and these mighty to surmount, in view of those, who, wending their way thither from the enervating South, were ill-prepared to meet the giant-forests of their Canaan-land. None, however, seem disposed to return to their worse than Egyptian bondage. They cheerfully toil on, and submit to their present privations, seeing 'a good land and a large' before them.[2]

The education of their children is claiming their attention, and a few years will shew a great change in the character of this people. Especially so, if their friends, the abolitionists, are unceasing in their efforts for the removal of the execrable system of slavery, and its ever-attendant prejudice, which have so sunk and degraded its victims. We had several interesting meetings and conferences with them, at Buffalo, Detroit, Chatham, Dawn, London, and Toronto. The kindness and hospitality extended to us, as well as to many others oft before, give evidence that they are not wanting in the delicacies and refinements of social life. The fugitive from the house of bondage can also speak of the generous aid, with limited means too, bestowed by those who had previously found a resting place there. These demands are happily so frequent, that assistance should be rendered from their friends in the States; guarded, however, against the unwise distribution, that has sometimes been made of money, articles of clothing, &c., sent them.

Few of the settlers are well-informed of the abolition movements, and the progress of the course of human freedom. The postage is so high, that not many of our papers are taken in Canada. But they will not long be dependent upon Anti-Slavery Periodicals, for their lessons of Liberty. The spirit of Freedom is arousing the world; and the press universal will echo the glad sound.

A word for the poor Indians. The few hundreds left of the Seneca Nation at the Cataraugus reservation, are improving in their mode of living, cultivating their land, and educating their children. They, too, are learning somewhat from the political agitations abroad; and, as man is wont, are imitating the movements of France and all Europe, in seeking larger liberty—more independence.

Their Chieftainship is therefore a subject of discussion in their councils, and important changes are demanded and expected, as to the election of their chiefs, many being prepared for a yearly appointment.[3]

Two missionaries are settled among them,[4] and some religious party strife is apparent. The pagans adhere, of course, to the sacred festivals of their fathers, and are not disposed to exchange them for the 'bread and wine' &c., of the Christian party. We had an interesting conference with them, during which their differences were presented; but we declined to decide between them, as, if attempted, we might be found equally discountenancing each form, and recommending our Quaker non-conformity. But, as that was not our mission, we commended them to the 'Great Spirit,' believing that those who danced religiously, might be as nearly perfect, as were those who communed in some other chosen form—neither of these being the test of acceptance. We witnessed their strawberry dance, and grotesque though the figures were, fantastic their appearance, and rude their measured steps, and unharmonious their music, yet, in observing the profound veneration of the hundreds present, some twenty of whom were performers, and the respectful attention paid to the speeches of their chiefs, women as well as men, it was far from me to say, that our silent, voiceless worship was better adapted to their condition, or that even the Missionary Baptism, and Sabbath, and organ, are so much higher evidence of a civilized, spiritual and Christian state.

While in western New York, we attended two Conventions called to consider the relative position of woman in society—one held at Seneca Falls, the other at Rochester. The 'proceedings' have been published in the North Star and several other papers.[5]

The attendance and interest manifested, were greatly encouraging; and give hope that this long neglected subject will soon begin to receive the attention that its importance demands.

I have received some cheering letters upon the subject since our return home—one from Mass.: while, on the other hand, private and public testimony has been borne against the movement.[6] This must serve to impress the necessity of repeated meetings of a similar character. All these subjects of reform are kindred in their nature; and giving to each its proper consideration, will tend to strengthen and nerve the mind for all—so that the abolitionist will not wax weaker in his advocacy of immediate emancipation. He will not love the slave less, in loving universal humanity more.

L. MOTT.

PL *Liberator,* 6 October 1848, 159

1. LCM and JM had been appointed, along with a Quaker from the Baltimore Yearly Meeting, to look into the farm and school the Hicksites operated on the Cattaraugus Reservation (Indian Committee records, Philadelphia Yearly Meeting minutes, 19 May 1848, PSCHi). JM's letter of 20 July 1848 had described their visits to free black communities, settled by fugitive slaves, in Canada (*Pennsylvania Freeman,* 27 July 1848, 3).

2. Exod. 3:8.

3. In 1837, the Seneca had lived on four reservations: Buffalo Creek, Tonawanda, Cattaraugus, and Allegany. The Ogden Land Company successfully set up false chiefs and used other means to take Seneca land, but through the influence of Quaker activists, the compromise treaty of 1842 retained the Cattaraugus and Allegany Reservations for the Senecas. In December 1848, young Senecas would overthrow the system of hereditary chiefs and establish the Seneca Republic, for which they drafted a constitution that provided for a presidential election every two years (Edmund Wilson, *Apologies to the Iroquois* [New York: Farrar, Straus, and Cudahy, 1959], 169–83). The 1848 revolution in France had overthrown King Louis Phillipe in February and had established the Second Republic.

4. One of these missionaries was probably the Reverend Asher Wright (1803–75), a Congregational minister who lived with the Seneca from 1831 to 1875 (ibid., 173).

5. The *North Star* newspaper (not to be confused with the compilation of poetry with the same title) referred to the Seneca Falls convention as "one of the most interesting events of the past week" and offered its support: "Our doctrine is, that 'Right is of no sex.' We therefore bid the women engaged in this movement our humble Godspeed." Of LCM, the *North Star* wrote she was "like a goddess in sacred councils, delivering advice for the benefit of her sex, whose words fell like the inklings of divine inspiration" (28 July 1848, 3, 11 August 1848, 2).

6. A sampling of the published reactions to the Seneca Falls convention, mostly negative or skeptical, is printed in *HWS* (1:802–5), including this extract from the *New York Herald:* "We are much mistaken, if Lucretia would not make a better President than some of those who have lately tenanted the White House."

## To George Combe and Cecilia Combe

Philada. 9 Mo. 10th. 1848—

My dear George & Cecilia Combe

More than a year has actually sped its way, since my last to you. Our frequent travels over parts of our country, and my many engagements, within that time, at home and abroad, have so occupied me, that our loved friends have been neglected, even while they have oft remembered us. The repeated evidence of your continued regard, have been grateful to us. The affecting intelligence of your dear brother's death, reached us, while travelling in Indiana last Autumn. We wished much to hear the particulars of the sad event. His brief visit to this Country, accompanied by his devoted niece, and the little hour we were permitted to enjoy of their Society, had revived & increased the interest I felt in the dear Invalid, on our first acquaintance. We had not heard whether or not, their intention of visiting Boston, Niagara, &c. was fulfilled; & regretted that I had not asked 'Miss' Cox to write to us.

Your absence from him at the time must indeed have added a pang to such a bereavement. The biographical sketch, in the No. of the Phrenological journal sent me, was read with deep interest; confirming the impression that our short acquaintance, & his brother's oft mention of him had made. His Works will long live to bless Mankind.[1] I could readily imagine the mournful blank in your City on your return; but was assured too, before your letter was received, that you would not unprofitably "indulge in lamentations." I cannot forbear mourning, when the good die too soon. You may have heard, that our friend A. D. Morrison is a widow. Her husband died last Spring, after several weeks severe illness—a kind of paralysis of the lungs. Anne laments her loss, more than those who knew her energy of character, were looking for. She goes out but little, and sees less company than she used to— Her means, though lessened by this event, are still sufficient for her to live much as she has done—curtailing some of her generous gifts. She desired love to you—said she had suffered her correspondence with you to close, having little to write.

The state of the European World furnishes so much to think about, and write about, that I hardly know where to begin. When the Reformatory Pope, and the agitator—Ronge, began to overturn the religious world, it seemed as though a new era was breaking in upon us—to say nothing of the "The Constitution of Man," & other "breaker of Images—"[2] But when all Kingcraft & Priestcraft come to be assailed, when even poor, starved subjugated Ireland, begins to array herself in earnest, for the restoration of her long-robbed rights, however ill-judged & inefficient, the means, we can but *hope* for some mighty overturning. Even the non-resistant indulges the secret wish that, if they *will* fight, the right may prevail, and larger liberty diffuse itself over the world. There seems now, however, a temporary settling down, with far less change than was anticipated—especially in revolutionary France. How did you feel, when Lamartine was so soon displaced, & a retrograde movement taking the lead?[3] Is it true that France was not really prepared to go forward as they began? How glad I should be to have Geo. Combe's views on all that has transpired these few months past!

George Parrish goes again to England & is the bearer of this. It is doubtful his visiting Scotland, as business occupies him closely. This is his 3rd. or 4th. visit abroad, & he has not yet been to Ireland or Scotland. His Grand Father [*John*] Cox died last year, aged 93 I think;—leaving the Parrish family in possession of a handsome estate—

I hope to send with this some pamphlets, shewing our doings hereaway, on the Slavery & Peace question—as well as our recent movement for the enlargement of Woman's Sphere. Cecy dear, could not have helped to be interested, had she been at our notable Conventions at Rochester & Seneca Falls. Reform is 'certainly the order of the day'— New laborers are constantly entering the field of pioneer life, which is 'white unto harvest.'[4] Agitation is in all the Churches—ours seems rocked to its centre. Orthodox & Hicksite dividing & subdividing. Several new 'Yearly Meetings' will be held next month—in Ohio Michigan, and Western New York—all on a broader platform—doing away with all that remains of an Hierarchy—or ecclesiastical establishment among us. The undue veneration for the Bible, is freely discussed[,] extracts from Elias Hicks', & other radicals' letters published & circulated. This of course leads to Church action, to secure adherence to "the letter,"—the cry of Infidelity, heresy, &.c. is raised, & all is tumult. We come in for our share of obloquy & sectarian spite—"complaints" followed us from Indiana last year, which our Meeting refused to entertain. This year Genessee Yearly Mg. denounced me—a party rather, & New York has abundantly proved herself Orthodox.[5] This is *our* little "tempest"—other sects might record greater— What is to be the result? Will a Phoenix arise bearing on its pinions "God and Humanity"? Did you see the "Proceedings" of the Anti-Sabbath Convention in Boston last Spring? It was my privilege to be present, & highly did I enjoy it. Theodore Parker took part with the radicals on that occasion. His sermon on 4th of July last I should like to send you, but have it only as published in the Chronotype[6] I would often forward these nice little things, but for subjecting you to so much postage, & but for the probability, in the mission of every thought, that you will already have seen them.

The Pamphlets so kindly sent to us—"Remarks on National Education", "What should Secular Education Embrace?" &.c—were forwarded directly, & read with interest, as you may rest assured every production from that pen will be.[7] We feel obliged, to be thus remembered. The progress of mind, in the Author's inquiries from his boyhood up to his settled convictions, was excellent. Many *think,* but all dare not *express*—and that makes man a blind believer or *assenter* to dark & mysterious Providences. *That same Author's* "Constitution of Man" broke the charm wonderfully—and it is now perceived that Religion, or the Salvation of Man, consists not so much in believing a miracle, & subscribing to a mystery, as in acting out a principle, and conforming to an eternal & unvarying law.

Cecy says, her husband, as well as herself, is "growing old—looks thin and pale"— That was nearly a year ago. May there be a renovation in you both! Geo. Combe once told me that I must not yield to the idea, that memory failed & would not serve me still so now I tell you, dont talk growing old—be young people in advancing life. I dont mean to give up the idea of our meeting again "But how or when, is hid from human eye."[8]

I was glad to find you had read & were interested in the Life of Blanco White. I never read a work of the kind with so much interest It has not been reprinted here. There are few copies in this country. I am lending ours constantly. Would that the existing or rather expiring Church establishment could be overthrown or fairly die out!

We were gratified with your kind notice of Fredk. Douglass. He continues to acquit himself as an abolitionist with ability and propriety. His Paper, The North Star has good circulation among White & Colored.— If you dont take any of our Anti-Slavery Papers, I wish you would borrow occasionally some numbers of the Liberator & read some of Edmund Quincy's articles. He has edited the Paper for some time, in the temporary absence of Garrison, who is still our great pioneer in every advance step in our good cause, and we have many. The religious & political world is fast coming up [to?] our *high elevation,* & indications are abundant, that ere long, from the top of the Mountain of Universal Liberty, the shout will go forth of Freedom to Man!

We were sorry that Burritt should stand so in his own light as not to avail himself of your offered kindness, as it might have been one means of breaking more of the Sectarian shackles which still bind him.[9] He *is* Evangelical, as you supposed—but does not hesitate to associate with Radicals—or heterodox among us—taking care to preserve a non-committal course. He has written to me asking my aid for a correspondence with the Sunday Schools, &.c— Your attention to our frds. Washington Brown & family were duly appreciated by them & ourselves. Their little girl, they bade me say values the kaleidoscope still— They also desired kind remembrances—But I am scarcely leavg. room to say My husband's blessings on you both—as well as manifold from your *loving* friend

L. M.

I must refer you to a late Liberator for a little mention of our travels among the Indians of Western N. York & the colored colonies in Canada this summer. Last year we travelled some thousands of miles*

*& by too great mental exercise I suffered for weeks with a severe Neuralgia affecting the spine.[x]

[x]but as Geo. Combe says—"I repented of my sins," submitted to remedies

& am now well as ever— My James & self are both growg more fleshy Jas. had an attack of Canada fever after returning to the States. We number nine Grandchildn. I want to have the liberty to name the next so as to call him Andw. Combe This is in answer to Cecy's crowded scrap to me. Write more such in each letter. Our Anna M. Hopper has been lookg over this. She laughs at me for writing about our Meetg. squabbles says "The *idea!* just as if they'll be interested with *that*"! Our childn. are all 'come outers.' They go to hear W. H. Furness sometimes I always run out into a free kind of gossipg when writing to those I love as I do you. excuse me

The persons in Boston—Boardman & Dr. Howe[10] carefully forwarded the Phrenological journal & other pamphlets sent. We are ever obliged

ALS GBNLS

1. Andrew Combe had died on 9 August 1847 while visiting his nephew near Edinburgh. The obituary, written by R. Cox, appeared in the *Phrenological Journal* (20 [1847]: 373).

2. Pius IX (1792–1878), pope from 1846 to 1878, instituted reforms in the church and encouraged Italian nationalism but became reactionary when the Italian state began attacking papal territories. LCM refers to Combe's *The Constitution of Man* (New York: William Pearson, 1835).

3. Alphonse Marie Louis de Lamartine (1790–1869), a French romantic poet, had led the provisional government of the Second Republic beginning in February 1848, but by summer his popular support had declined, and in December he would lose the presidency to Napoleon III.

4. John 4:35.

5. Since 1842, the Genesee Yearly Meeting had been divided over women's roles and participation in the antislavery movement and other non-Quaker associations. At its June 1848 meeting, LCM is reported as having given an "impressive sermon." Two hundred people walked out of the meeting and subsequently formed the Congregational Friends. Joseph Dugdale addressed the Genesee Meeting denouncement of LCM: "Two of our number [*LCM and Thomas McClintock*] attended at Waterloo. Upon this fact is based the charge of 'disowned persons' composing the Yearly Meeting in central New York. The body constituting *that movement* has never received any kind of church excommunication." He added that LCM supported the walkout (*Liberator,* 26 October 1849, 172; Judith Wellman, "The Seneca Falls Women's Rights Convention: A Study of Social Networks," *Journal of Women's History* 3 [Spring 1991]: 24–27).

6. LCM may be referring to a "Discourse on the State of the Nation Delivered at the Melodeon, July 2nd," *Liberator,* 14 July 1848, 109.

7. George Combe, *Remarks on National Education* (Edinburgh: Maclachlan, Stewart, 1847), and *What Should Secular Education Embrace?* (Edinburgh: Maclachlan, Stewart, 1848).

8. The quotation is possibly adapted from Job 28:21: "Seeing it is hid from the eyes of all living."

9. Elihu Burritt had traveled to Europe in 1846 and had formed the League of Universal Brotherhood, an international peace society. He had organized the Brussels Peace Conference in 1848, and similar conferences were held in such cities as Paris, London, and Edinburgh.

10. Dr. Andrew Boardman was Combe's friend in New York City (see George Combe,

*Notes on the United States of North America during a Phrenological Visit in 1838–9–40*
[Edinburgh: Maclachlan, Stewart, 1841], preface). Dr. Samuel Gridley Howe (1801–76)
was a Boston reformer.


## To Elizabeth Cady Stanton

Philada. 10 Mo. 3rd. 1848

My dear Elizh.

The letter or parcel sent to the M'Clintocks, by my daughter 3 weeks ago—
I find was kept at Auburn, until last week. You must have thought me very remiss in acknowledging yours, so acceptable—and so I have been, thy last, which
I have read again & again to my own & others' entertainment.[1] I am now trying to awaken sufficient interest, to hold a Woman's Right's Meeting in this
City. It is far more difficult than we found it out West— Still there are members here, who feel a deep interest in the cause. Few however are accustomed
to public speaking. Thou asks if Sarah Pugh & Mary Grew will not take hold
& work— Mary has been very feeble all summer—and continues so much
so, as to be obliged to withhold her active aid in the publication of the Freeman, and rarely meets with our Ex. Com. We could not therefore depend upon
her for anything more than perhaps a short production of her pen. Abby Kimber is much at home with her aged & feeble Mother, and Sarah with hers. But
they would both give all the aid in their power. We have been looking around
for a suitable place to hold a Meeting or Convention in— There will be
difficulty in obtaining one for that object—or such an one as we should like—
Why can't thou & the M'Clintocks come on here to attend such a meeting?
You are so wedded to this cause, that you must expect to act as pioneers in the
work— The writer of that letter from near Boston, which I sent for your
perusal, & which I should be glad to have again, when you have done with it,
would probably come & aid in a meeting— Paulina Wright expects to leave
here soon for Boston, so that we may not depend upon her— There may
however be some unknown "Mrs. Sandfords" to come upon our platform, so
we will be of good courage—[2] If there is any probability of having your company on such an occasion, we could make the time suit your convenience
Please consult Mary Ann & daughters & let me know.[3] I had thought of the
last week in this month, but some time in next would do as well, if you could
better come then.

The Book that thou & Elizh. McClintock are "concocting" I hope will be
forth-coming. It is just what is needed— But you must not depend upon me
for a single chapter. It is not in my line. You can *borrow*[4] from S. M. Grimke's all
the historical part of hers—Bible & all—and from Mary Woolstonecraft much
that is excellent—[5] As to the generality of the works extant on that subject, it is

more surprising that they saw & wrote as far as they did, than that they did not embrace the whole—

The progress that we see in every work of truth & reform ought to lead us to hail each step in the advance-field of Woman's duties & rights. Look back to the days of our Grandmothers & be cheered—

Oliver Johnson is here. He tells me that an Orthodox Minister in the town in Mass. where he has lived the last year, a stranger to me, took occasion lately, to hold me up to his congregation, as the worst of women— I send a low, vulgar scrap from a Paper, published here, which I never see; this & that article from the Boston Paper sent in the other parcel, give evidence of some of the misrepresentation & ridicule we anticipated.

Richard Hunt speaks very favorably of thy Maiden Speech at Waterloo.[6] He says some of their respectable inhabitants were well pleased— He would have preferred the head-dress a little different— It looked rather Theatrical he thought—"a kind of turban & bows"— When thou comes here we can give thee an example of Quaker simplicity. I rejoiced however, that thou wast willing to deliver that lecture—& hope thy talents in that way will be well "exercised by reason of use"— And that Elizh. and Mary M'Clintock will not let their's rust, but will follow thy example & "speak to my people that they go forward".[7] Do you write to Rochester & stir up those women to their duties?

As to the Grimkes, I have little hope of them, after such a flash & such an effectual extinguishment— We must not depend upon them. Nor upon any who have been Apostles before us—but be ready for "those things which shall hereafter appear unto" us—[8]

We are now in the midst of a Convention of the Colored People of this City— Douglass & Delany—Remond & Garnet[9] are here—all taking an active part—and as they include women & *white* women too, I can do no less, with the interest I feel in the cause of the Slave, as well as of Woman, than be present & take a little part— So yesterday, in a pouring rain, Sarah Pugh & self, walked down there, & expect to do the same today—still raining— So even in a hurry I conclude, with the dearest love to you all—

                                              Lucretia Mott

The letter sent with this, I found on our arrival home from the West— Thou wilt see by the date, that the writer had no knowledge of our doings— I presume she has not a thorough acquaintance with our language, by wh. I account for a blindness of style— — I was interested in it, please return it—

We have been begging "a lot" of second hand winter clothing, with some pieces new goods to send to the Refugees in Canada— My husband had two large boxes packed & forwarded last week— We learn by letter from Hiram Wilson[10] & the Female Teacher, that the Steam saw mill is in operation & doing well—they appear encouraged—

                                              ALS DLC-Stanton

1. In her letter to LCM from Seneca Falls written on 30 September, Stanton had described the press coverage of the woman's rights conventions held at Seneca Falls and at Rochester on 2 August: "Imagine the publicity given to our ideas by thus appearing in a widely-circulated sheet like the [*New York*] *Herald*. . . . I fully agree with Mr. [*James Gordon*] Bennett's closing lines, even if you may not" (*Stanton-Anthony Papers,* reel 6, frs. 777–78; see also LCM to Edmund Quincy, 24 August 1848, above).

2. Paulina Wright Davis (1813–76) of Utica had become involved in woman's rights when she petitioned the New York legislature for a married woman's right to own property. At the Rochester meeting, Rebecca M. M. Sanford of Ann Arbor had endorsed "the just claim of woman to an equality with man" (*Liberator,* 15 September 1848, 148).

3. Both Elizabeth McClintock (1821–96, later Phillips) and Mary Ann McClintock (c. 1823–80, later Truman), daughters of Mary Ann McClintock, had addressed the Seneca Falls convention (Gordon, 1:69, 83).

4. The original document contains many underlinings in blue ink. Since LCM used a different ink to write the letter, presumably these underlinings were made by another person and thus they are not indicated here. *Borrow,* here, and *white,* later in the letter, however, were underlined in the same ink used by LCM.

5. LCM had read *Vindication of the Rights of Woman* (1792) by Mary Wollstonecraft (1759–97) in the 1830s (see LCM to Elizabeth Neall Gay, 7 May 1858, below).

6. In her Waterloo speech delivered in September, Stanton had stated that the "time had fully come for the question of women's wrongs to be laid before the public." Richard Hunt (1797–1856), the husband of Jane Master Hunt, a Congregational Friend, and an abolitionist, attended the Seneca Falls convention (Gordon, 1:94–123, 129, quote on 95).

7. LCM is adapting Heb. 5:14: "Who by reason of use have their senses exercised to discern both good and evil." Exod. 14:15.

8. LCM is adapting Rev. 1:19: "Write the things which thou hast seen, and the things which are, and the things which shall be hereafter."

9. Martin Delany (1812–85) was at the time a coeditor of the *North Star.* Henry Highland Garnet (1815–82) was a Presbyterian minister. According to the *Pennsylvania Freeman,* the convention's main purpose was to widen the *North Star*'s circulation (*Pennsylvania Freeman* article reprinted in *Liberator,* 6 October 1848, 159).

10. Hiram Wilson (1803–64) had founded a manual arts school for escaped slaves near London, Ontario, in 1842 (*WLG,* 3:332).

## To George W. Julian[1]

Philadelphia. 11 mo. 14th 1848—

My dear Friend George W. Julian:

I will not attempt to make excuses or apologies for the seeming neglect of thy acceptable and frank letter recieved—(I can hardly believe it) nearly a year ago. That I have not been unmindful of its interesting contents you may be assured when I tell you that I early after reading it, went to our frd. Wm. H. Furness and consulted him as to the works most likely to meet thy wants. I thought he might have some pamphlets or small publication wh he could furnish me with to send thee. He made no offer of any however, except a large work of Prof. Norton's[2] on the Prophecies &c. I had doubts of the propriety of borrowing a book to be sent so far. There is no Unitarian book store here, where their tracts &c can be procured: and the larger works are more expensive I presume than thou art aware of. Theodore Parker has published an elaborate work on the Old Testament the result of much research in the old languages as well as in German & French.[3] Thomas McClintock, of Waterbury N.Y. a minister in our Society and one of the best Bible students we have, says this work is by far the best he has seen. It exposes many errors and false prophecies and clears some Mysteries wh have greatly taxed the veneration of the believer. Theodore Parker's boldness has driven some of the Unitarians of the older School back to the "weak and beggarly elements". Prof. Norton is ready to disclaim his own productions— or rather to doubt the expediency of circulatg. them now.

Wm. H. Channing[4] was with us last winter. I handed him thy letter requesting his opinion. He answered: There are *no* truly good works in the English on the Prophecies and Inspiration. The best that can be easily found are Palfrey's lectures on the Old Testament and parts of Mr. Norton's work on the Genuineness or authenticity of the Gospels. There are two translations from the German & French, wh may be found in Boston: "Introduction to the Old Testament— from Dr. Welte—by Theodore Parker,[5] and a work from the French by some German, Elleria[?]—I think on the Inspiration of the Scriptures. Has your friend ever seen Mr. Furness's book on the Gospels—Life of Jesus?[6] This might help to answer his difficulties. All these books are unfortunately somewhat expensive. There are I believe some Unitarian tracts on the subject" If I recollect right Furness's work was on thy table, when we were at your house. That visit is oft recurred to with interest and pleasure, and I regret to appear so unmindful of your kind hospitalities as to suffer thy letter to lie so long unanswered.

I herewith send you a few Tracts and small works, some of which may prove altogether to radical for thy inquiring mind. That there have been gross impositions practiced upon the believer—the all-to credulous, must be acknowledged. Now that scepticism of the Theology of the Schools, has become some what a duty, free thinkers may go to the other extreme and fail to award to the Scriptures all the beautiful and blessed instruction they contain. I have for some years accustomed myself to read and examine them, as nearly as I would any other book, as Early education and veneration would permit. I have now no difficulty in deciding upon the human and ignorant origin of such parts as conflict with the known and eternal laws of Deity in the Physical creation: be the claim to the miraculous ever so high, & the assumption of the Prophetic and God-inspired, ever so strong. Still less, if possible, do I waver when any violation of the Divine and Eternal law of right, such as murder in any of its forms, Slavery in any of its degrees, and Priestcraft in its various phases as palmed upon the religious world is declared to be "Thus saith the Lord". It is impossible by any Theological ingenuity to reconcile the moral code of the Old & New Testament, as proceeding from Him who is "without variableness or shadow of turning"[7] Far safer, therefore is it, to admit *man* to be fallible than judge God to be changeable. The popular system of faith is fast yielding to a more enlightened philosophy. Of latter time many of the Advocates of that system are beginning to recieve Dr. Channings views and really to regard him quite orthodox. As light advances no difficulty will be found to mould the Bible, that convenient Creed-book, to the present pattern shewn in the mount.

The life of Dr. Channing,[8] just published by his nephew Wm. H Channing, is most interesting. I presume it may be found in Cincinnati. I dont remember whether I spoke of the life of Joseph Blanco White, when with you. I have read it with deep interest. He was a Spanish Priest, who became too enlightened to retain his holy orders. He made his escape from Seville leaving his parents, also two lovely sisters who ended their days in a Convent— arriving in London he became a political editor and translator—recieving an Annuity from the Government during the reign of the Bonaparts in Spain and a pension continued to him. He afterwards joined the Church studied for the Ministry at Oxford in company with Newman & Pusey and others who have since made such a stir in the Church.[9] He once entered the English pulpit; but his views became too enlightened to remain long there. On examination he saw so little difference between the Romish Breviary and the English Liturgy, that he had to renounce the latter also, and became a Unitarian. Archbishop Whately was his most intimate friend. He lived several years in his Palace in Dublin, and corresponded with the learned of the age—Lord Holland—Southey—Coleridge—Newman—Pusey & others—[10] His Unitarian views were the result of his own examination and reflection, with little aid from those of that faith. He was learned in the dead as well as *living* languages. The result of his Bible examinations would suit thee, I doubt not. The work has not been reprinted yet in this Country. The English is $7. a copy, three vol. We have a copy which is now lent out— If thou would like the *loan* of it at some future time, I would gladly send it to thee by some safe conveyance, to be soon returned—as it is in demand, the few copies sent over being all bought up.— Blanco White was 60 years old when he first entered a dissenting meeting-house. The simplicity of the Unitarian preaching delighted him. James Martineau of Liverpool, and his Biographer, J. H. Thom were the preachers who edified him. The latter years of his life he corresponded with Dr. Channing, Dr. Norton, and G. Ripley,[11] on the miracles, Unitarian faith—Bible Authority &c. He went beyond the two former in his scepticism. But he retained to the close of a life of much bodily suffering, all the devotional feeling of a true Christian— — He died in 1842. Dr. Channing said there was not a man in England he so much wished to see as J. Blanco White.— His faith remained unshaken in "The Divine Light within us"—he reviews Geo. Fox—Barclay[12] & John Woolman as clear expounders of their faith, while he could not agree with their mysticisms and superstitions. But I will not fill the sheet with my *pet* author.

The agitations and commotions of religious sects are among the interest-

ing signs of the times. Our Quaker quietude is again disturbed: and both Orthodox and Hicksite are on the eve of another Separation. Several conventions
and new Yearly meetings are being held. Michigan, Western N. York and Green
Plain, Ohio, are all comeing out with a broader platform. We have only recieved
the "Proceedings" of Farmington, N. York. wh I will send as a sample of a broad
"Basis". Thos. McClintock, before spoken of is the writer of that document.[13]
About 200 persons adopted it. The high-handed measures of those in power,
must eventually open the eyes of the people to the impropriety and danger of
conferring such power on our fellow mortals.— The congregational form of
religious association will ultimately prevail as man comes to understand Christian liberty.

In the political world too, there seems to be a tendency strong toward the
breaking up of old parties. In our view, and a discouraging one it is, military
despotism seems to threaten the Country—but the discerner of the signs of the
times, with larger hope, sees republican & true democratic principles on the
advance— The rights of man being recognized to a greater extent and the spirit
of Peace & universal Freedom rising toward the ascendant.— Let us all do our
duty to accelerate the speed of these principles.

I have not written as to a stranger, but have run on in the familiar style of
an old acquaintance. There was something congenial when we met at your
house. Thy letter expressive of an assimilation in mind was gratifying. I know
not that thy enquiring mind can be easily satisfied, but such as I can offer at any
time shall be at thy service.

My husband unites in kind regards to thee & thine—

Sincerely thy friend—
Lucretia Mott

Didst thou recieve a copy of "The Transient & Permanent["] wh I sent thee
some months ago?

C PSCHi-Mott

1. George W. Julian (1817–99), an antislavery politician, would become a Free-Soil
Representative from Indiana to Congress in 1849–51 and 1861–71.

2. Andrews Norton (1786–1853) was a Unitarian minister and a professor at Harvard
Divinity School.

3. LCM possibly means Parker's "An Examination of the Old Testament to Be Divine
Miraculous or Infallible Composition," in *A Discourse of Matters Pertaining to Religion*
(Boston: Charles C. Little and James Brown, 1842), 327–50.

4. William H. Channing (1810–84) was a Unitarian clergyman, the nephew of William
Ellery Channing, and an advocate of temperance, abolition, and woman's rights.

5. *Academic Lectures on the Jewish Scriptures and Antiquities* (Boston: J. Munroe, 1838–
52) by John Gorham Palfrey (1796–1881); Andrews Norton, *The Evidences of the Genuineness of the Gospels* (Boston: J. B. Russell, 1837–44). Parker translated the work of Wil-
helm M. L. De Wette (1780–1849), *A Critical and Historical Introduction to the Canonical
Scriptures of the Old Testament* (Boston: Little and Brown, 1843).

6. Possibly William H. Furness, *Jesus and His Biographers; or, The Remarks on the Four Gospels* (Philadelphia: Carey, Lea, and Blanchard, 1838).

7. "Thus saith the Lord" is from Isa. 7:7; LCM is adapting James 1:17: "With whom is no variableness."

8. *Memoir of William Ellery Channing, with Extracts from His Correspondence and Manuscripts* (Boston: W. Crosby and H. P. Nichols, 1848).

9. On Blanco White, see letter to George Combe, 26 April 1847, above. John Henry Newman (1801–90) and Edward B. Pusey (1800–1882) were both Oxford professors and leaders of the Oxford movement, which sought to protect the Church of England against liberals and disestablishment. Newman had converted to Catholicism in 1845.

10. Richard Whately (1787–1863) was the archbishop of Dublin. Henry Richard Vassall Fox (1773–1840), the third Baron Holland, had met Blanco White in Spain and later became his patron (Martin Murphy, *Blanco White: Self-Banished Spaniard* [New Haven: Yale University Press, 1989], 50–55, 63, 99). Samuel Taylor Coleridge (1772–1834) was a British poet and philosopher.

11. James Martineau (1805–1900) was an English political economist, a Unitarian clergyman, and the brother of Harriet Martineau. John Hamilton Thom (1808–94) was the Unitarian clergyman who edited *The Life of Joseph Blanco White*. George Ripley (1802–80) was a Unitarian minister, a transcendentalist, an editor, and a literary critic.

12. Robert Barclay (1648–90) was an early Quaker leader.

13. After its split from the Genesee Yearly Meeting, the Congregational Friends met in October 1848 in Farmington, New York (see letter to George Combe and Cecilia Combe, 10 September 1848, above). McClintock's "Basis of Religious Association," which the Farmington meeting adopted, called for "liberty of conscience" and "equality in the human family," reflecting the Congregational Friends' belief that a church should impose no constraints on its members, that men and women should meet together, and that there should be no hierarchy in the meeting (Judith Wellman, "The Seneca Falls Women's Rights Convention: A Study of Social Networks," *Journal of Women's History* 3 [Spring 1991]: 24–27; Nancy Hewitt, *Women's Activism and Social Change: Rochester, New York, 1822–1872* [Ithaca, N.Y.: Cornell University Press, 1984], 135; a copy of the "Basis" appeared in the *Friends' Intelligencer,* 20 March 1852, 413–15).

## To Joseph Dugdale and Ruth Dugdale

Philada. 3 Mo. 28th. 1849—

My dear Joseph & Ruth

Having so lately written, both to yourselves & to dear Thos. Borton,[1] I cannot now expect to muster much of interest to you; and should not attempt it, but to notice yours so acceptable, recd. a few days since—handed Jas. by J. M. White, whom I have hoped to see here before this time— Jas. not recollectg. his stoppg. place, has intended to call where his goods are being packed—but these mercantile men sometimes forget their good intentions. I should be sorry he should go away without our seeing him—& wish he would come here without ceremony. We are glad to hear of his becoming a free inquirer; and cannot doubt that your great movement will induce examination & inquiry, among many who will not be so honest as to acknowledge a change of views.

This Congregational form of Church government must obtain eventually—

as the people in their growing intelligence, understand their rights. I have often wondered that so rational a change—made some 30 or 40 years ago ^ay—50 or more^ in Mass., has not spread more generally here away. There is only one Congregational Church of the Orthodox Order—and one Unitarian—Again has it appeared strange, that in Pennsylvania, where one might suppose Unitarianism almost hereditary in its sons—the Father—Penn, being such a radical in his day; that one comparatively small congregation embraces all, who avow themselves Unitarians—unless indeed *our* Quakers may be so called. But really the mass of them scarcely know what they do believe. Still the rational & pure faith of a Priestly—a Worcester[2] & a Channing—to say nothing of a Fox—Penn—Hicks &.c.—has not been preached in vain. All orthodoxy is modifying its creed—or rather, being modified by these heretical writers, it is conforming itself to the more liberal & rational Christianity, demanded by the age.

We have a friend now staying with us—a Unitarian—one of Heaven's own. Saml. J. May of Syracuse N.Y.— You probably know him, as conspicuous in the early A. S. movements—as well as in the Non-Resistant Conventions. He is an advocate for Woman too—it is fitting therefore that this should be his stopping-place. We are trying to get up an Anti S. Mg. for him—but difficulty still attends the procurg. of a suitable room. We had a good Mg. last week—when C. C. B[urleigh]. reviewed Henry Clay's Letter.[3] It was ably done, for Charles you know "doeth all things well", save in the small matter of shaving himself & cutting his hair. Nor is that a *small* matter—if it renders him, with all his powerful mind & happy gift of speech, less effective as the slave's appellant, and the advocate for universal right. He is all packed up now, ready for their removal to N. England, where they will probably reside during his Father's life. His br. Cyrus is our right-hand man—ready to aid in writing, talking, or other Anti-Slavery work— —[4] And here I must tell you what an exciting fugitive case we have had the last week. A citizen of Richmond Va—called at the Office & told Miller & Cyrus that a Slave in that City was meditating his escape, by being placed in a box, as goods, & comg. in the Cars—Adams' Express line. He was told of the great danger of suffocation, as well as the risk of detection—but was not deterred  After some efforts & disapts. or delays—writg to Miller to meet him & callg. him up in vain—one or 2 morngs @ 3 o clk—^until he became quite nervous—& wrote desiring them not to attempt it^ a telegraph at length, apprized them of his approach. The box was recd. at the Depot—more carefully handled, than it had been before—safely deposited at the A. S. Office, where a trembling tap & "all right?" from Miller, was responded to—"all right Sir", from the pent-up man. The lid was removed as quickly as the hoops cd. be loosened, when he as quickly rose, with a "good morng, gent.!" Miller says we can hardly conceive, the relief & excitet. to find the man alive—& the poor fellow's happiness & gratitude—singing a hymn of praise &.c— He is a large man—weighg. nearly 200—& was encased in a box, 2 ft. 10. long—23 in. wide & 3 ft high in a sittg. posture—tho not upright—provided with a few crackers & a bladder filled with water, wh. wd. make no noise, in being turned over, nor yet liable to be broken—he however ate none as it wd. have made him thirsty, & he needed all the water to bathe his head, after the rough turn overs—sometimes restg. for miles on his head & shoulders—when it wd. seem as if the veins would burst. He fanned himself almost constantly with his hat—& bored holes for fresh breathing air, with a gimlet or small auger furnished him.— The cracks of the box had canvass over, to prevent any inspection—& to appear like goods. Dr. Noble says, if he had been consulted—he shd. have sd., it wd. be impossible for the man to be shut up & live 24 hours—the time it took to reach here, & it was his fanning so much wh. kept the exhausted air in motion, & gave place to fresh— Miller took him home—gave him his breakfast & a bath—& then he was conducted here—where he gave us his history. His Master is a rich man— employs an overseer—heartless as such generally are— He was never whipped however He was employed twistg. tobacco, & yielded his Master $200 or more pr year— He had a wife & 3 childn. sold from him a yr. ago—after their own-er—(not his Master) had promised to let him purchase them—a higher offer inducing him to do so— This almost broke his heart—but from that time he resolved on obtaining his own freedom—& havg. no family to provide for, he laid by enough to hire a white man to undertake his removal in the box. One colored man was in the secret & assisted, wh. were all who knew it in Richmond. He had a sore finger—& applied oil of vitriol to make it worse, so as to have leave of absence for a few days—so that he wd. not be missed until 2nd. day—& he was safely here on 7th day last. After restg. over 1st. day, he was sent on East— but we hope the case will not be published for awhile at least. His wife & childn. are now held by a Methodist Minister in North Carolina He has heard from them 2 or 3 times. This & the Crafts case—as well as Isaac Brown's & others not a few,[5] will tell well in history, some time hence, "in the days of freedom oh"!

We shall be right glad to welcome our good Thomas Borton to our home & hearts. Those mental flights hither-ward, as described in his letter to us are to be realized it seems, by the actual, corporeal presence— A union of the spiritual & physical; which I am free to confess is preferable, while in mutability, to either separately. What God has joined, let us not sunder, by any transcendental flights, until the full time for "the dust to return to the earth, & the spirit to God who gave it".[6] We will try also to observe Joseph's cautions about, "eating, drinking, & preaching", so as not to give these bodies any untoward push in the down-hill of life; for I fully unite with Joseph in deploring the fact, that "many leave this beautiful world too soon."

We fear that Thos. Borton will find far too few, among his Jersey kinsfolk, who will be interested in *his* line of progress. Success in money-making is the highest aim of very many in Jersey, as well as in other handy localities to our Philada. Markets.

I dont know whether Rush Plumly has received your letter—as he has been in Baltimore during the last week.[7] You know perhaps that he is our Edward M.

Davis' right hand man in his store— He is rather inclined to throw off his Quaker peculiarities, and seldom attends our Mgs. in the City—but goes to Temp[eranc]e. & other Mgs. in the Country on 1st. days— They live far up-town, and as is too much the case in these large cities, even congenial minds do not often meet. As to George Truman, he seems to be "settling down in the quiet," quite too much; says he is too poor to preach. This new medical profession does not yet yield him much of this world's goods. Cherry St. Mg. does not abound at this present with gifted "workmen who need not be ashamed".[8] Wm. Dorsey seldom says anything and is more conservative than once.— When our Friends begin to feel it wrong to attend A. S. Mgs, "in the mixture", there is little to hope for them. Dr. Griscom is not seen at any of our reform Mgs—though both he & Wm. Dorsey mean to be liberal. They manifested much interest in my Mg. for the students—that was held to good satisfaction—as I think I mentioned in a letter to Thos. Borton—some 20 or 30 rose to go out, while the subject of slavery was pressed upon their attention—[9] Part of this number halted at the door & remained to the close— Many went away for want of room— and a quieter, more attentive audience I have not often had— I sent a few of the "Sermons", by another of yr. merchts. in a parcel of the meanest things! for your acceptance. Some of our coarse free calico was being sold off— I took some for a dress—& thot. Rebecca was at least as humble as I, & perhaps she wd. be willing to wear it. Did you ever receive that parcel we sent from Geo. Thomas?[10]— I know not its content— It was directed to your Mother—perhaps she has acknowledged it to George If so, it is sufficient. We now send another mean parcel—a vest & pants wh. may for a time take the place of some with wh. you have clothed the poor fugitive— Joseph sd. when here, that he was willing to accept 2nd-hand clothg. I have wished to forward another box of clothg. for fugitives—but having so lately acted in the capacity of beggar for those already in Canada, I rather shrunk from the task just now— When Thos. Borton comes, Esther Moore & I will try what we can do.— I will send you some of the Farmington Addresses— Tell us what you think of their "Basis." It will accord with Joseph's expressed views in this letter, as to *toleration* (L. M. Child says she "hates that proud self sufficient word) that is receivg all of every creed and profession—

Ruth asks after our aunt L. P. Mott. She insisted on purchasg. an expensive place near Burlington—against Arthur's[11] & Jas.' judgt.— He ^A.^ went off for a time & indulged in drinkg. to excess— She fell over a trunk the next day after removg. to her house & broke her collar bone—wh. has confined her mostly to the house this winter—she cannot yet dress her hair. Arthur is now at his Mother's & is steady I believe. He only remained away from her a few weeks—

I have filled the sheet without leavg any room for James— He must take another and reply to such parts of your as I have omitted.

I am now going to write a joint letter to our Oakland friends, wh. if I finish may be sent in this parcel for you to forward.

Lydia White has been rather poorly most of the winter. She desires her love—says she wrote you some weeks ago—she gets out to Mg. now

The Clothiers—Evanses, Jacksons &.c &.c are all well[12]

With love unfeigned to you & yours— I must close—say to your dear Mother that our tenderest sympathy flows toward her in her approachg. & added trial. But that she & you all will be sustained—we have strong confidence

AL PSCHi-Mott

1. Thomas Borton, an Ohio Quaker, and his wife, Elizabeth L. Borton (d. 1848), aided fugitive slaves and had participated in the Green Plain Friends' split with the Indiana Yearly Meeting (*Pennsylvania Freeman,* 14 September 1848, 3; LCM to Thomas Borton, Elizabeth Borton, Joseph Dugdale, and Ruth Dugdale, 19 March 1848, copy, Lilly Library, Earlham College, Richmond, Ind.).

2. Joseph Priestley (1733–1804) was a British scientist and Presbyterian minister who embraced Unitarianism. Noah Worcester (1758–1837) was a Congregational minister and the editor of the Unitarian *Christian Examiner.*

3. Clay's letter had appeared in the *Pennsylvania Freeman* (15 March 1849, 1). After outlining a plan of gradual emancipation for Kentucky, Clay added that until the period of emancipation ended, "all the legal rights of the proprietors of slaves, in their fullest extent, ought to remain unimpaired and unrestricted." Burleigh's reply in the same issue found Clay's plan unsatisfactory: "It speaks of the hundred and ninety thousand colored people of Kentucky as though they were all subordinates to the pleasure and the prejudices of the whites. It proposes a scheme under the name of *Emancipation,* which is in fact but a modified system of Slavery, and the cold heartlessness with which it urges that measure makes one shudder to read it" (2–3).

4. Cyrus Burleigh (1810–55) was a temperance and antislavery lecturer.

5. Henry "Box" Brown's escape had been aided by Samuel A. Smith, a white Virginian who helped construct the box. From Philadelphia, Brown went on to Boston, where he became a conductor on the Underground Railroad. Smith served an eight-year prison term for trying to aid two other slaves in a similar manner (Charles Blockson, *The Underground Railroad in Pennsylvania* [Jacksonville, N.C.: Flame International, 1981], 43). Ellen Craft (c. 1826–97) and William Craft (d. 1900) had escaped from slavery in Georgia in December 1848 and passed through Philadelphia. Isaac Brown had been arrested in Philadelphia on 1 May 1847 and was charged with being a fugitive from an assault and battery charge in Maryland, but was released by order of Pennsylvania's attorney general and supreme court. Pennsylvania officials agreed that the charges were contrived to bring him back to Maryland a slave (*Case of the Slave Isaac Brown: An Outrage Exposed* [Philadelphia: n.p., 1847]).

6. Eccles. 12:7.

7. Benjamin Rush Plumly (1816–87).

8. 2 Tim. 2:15.

9. William Dorsey (1811–74) was a Philadelphia Hicksite Quaker and a merchant. Dr. John Hoskins Griscom (1809–74), a New York City Quaker, had received his medical degree from the University of Pennsylvania in 1832. LCM's sermon to the medical students had taken place at the Cherry Street Meeting House on 11 February 1849 and was published by Merrihew and Thompson later in the year. When her audience reacted negatively to her mention of slavery, LCM responded: "It is not strange that the allusion to this subject should create some little agitation among you; and while I can but regret it, I stand here on behalf of the suffering and the dumb, and must express the desire, that there may be a disposition to hear and reflect, and then judge" (*Sermons,* 81–93).

10. George Thomas (1791–1869) was a British reformer and philanthropist.

11. Arthur Mott (1799–1869) was the son of Lydia P. Mott.

12. The Clothiers were Caleb (c. 1807–81), a Hicksite Quaker elder, his wife, Hannah Fletcher Hallowell (1807–55), and their nine children (one of whom was named Lucretia Mott Clothier). The Jacksons were John and Rachel and their son Warner.

## To Richard D. Webb and Hannah Webb

Phila. 5 Mo. 14th. 1849.

My dear Richard & Hannah Webb

It is long since I have had this pleasure—the devotion of a few hours to this kind of intercourse with you. We have several tiny letters from Richard, most acceptable, what there was of them, still unacknowledged. One delivered at the door, when we were not at home, by Henry Chapman, whom I sought at Ellwood Shannon's,[1] and who soon after came and passed part of an evening with us. We were pleased with the young man, and if we had done our part, we might probably have had more of his company— But such is the entire separation between Orthodox & Hicksite Friends, that we scarcely ever come in contact with them, either in a religious or social way. My sister has often spoken of Ellwood Shannon's wife as a fine woman, and I too was much pleased with her, the short interview I had with her.

In the letter alluded to, Richard recommended H. Martineau's Eastern Travel.[2] We had not then read it. Sarah Pugh had, for she always is before us, in reading the nice books that are published. We lost no time in procuring it, and it is passing from one to another in the family, who all agree with the just review in the letter. Neither her writings however, nor those of any other Unitarian, will be fully appreciated in our day. The Reviewers are under Orthodox influence & must cater to their taste— Even the judgment of the more liberal receives its coloring from these sources. "Unhappy Blanco White!" is reiterated by the Unitarians themselves, in that "he found no resting place"; when the man stood firm on every advance tread, finding a happiness with which the stranger could not intermeddle. The demand for its reprint is limited in this Country as yet— but it will appear some day, see if it dont— Our copy is being worn out in the lending. The late application or discovery of electrical affinity—or something else, in the Psychological lectures & experiments, by which the paralytic "rise up & walk", & sundry other seeming miracles are wrought—as also all the animal magnetism wonders, by which so many are "wondering for their bread", all tend to do away the long-cherished belief that the recorded miracles of the New Testament are as essential a part of true faith, as Christian righteousness itself.[3] Since Theodore Parker comes out with such great heresies, the older Unitarians are having credit for being quite orthodox. Many of our Conservatives are reading Channings writings with interest, and indeed are claiming him, as their own. So true is Theodore Parker's remark, that the heresy of one age is the sound faith & orthodoxy of the next. We are anxious to see the Autobiography of Joseph Barker. Every word that Richard wrote of him & his works interested us greatly. Many thanks for keeping us informed of the progress of radicalism among you. The emigrant, to whom was entrusted the tracts, has not yet made his appearance. I hope he will not lose our address, nor neglect to deliver them. All that we have yet seen of Joseph Barker's Writings, was contained in 2 numbers of the Liberator, on the clerical objections to the Abolitionists.[4] There is an originality of style that pleased me. The subject of Anti-Slavery has been so abundantly treated both in public speaking & writing, that it needs to be presented in a unique form, in order to take with the people. It is well for us, that we have the Giddingses[5] & Horace Manns with their great intellects, to pour into the awakening Nation's ear such soul stirring appeals. The Garrisons & Phillips'es & Abby Kellys are still needed, as an advance guard, if that is the right figure. I always hesitate in military symbols— Our Annual Meeting in New York was not less interesting than usual. You will see by the reports that Parker Pillsbury & Wendell Phillips handled the Church & clergy not less severely than in former years. Lucy Stone is an acquisition to our ranks. She is such a thorough woman's-rights woman too. We had a nice Meeting on that subject while she was in this City.[6] Of this too the Standard will inform you, from our precious Sarah Pugh's pen, over her new signature H. H., a la Edmund Quincy. You know I presume that his are the last letters of his name. I tell Sarah she might often contribute a good letter to the Standard—for she is necessarily much confined at home, in the sick chamber of her aged aunt, and infirm Mother.[7] We have had a treat this winter, in the company of Abby Kimber. They have suspended their school for awhile; and Abby came here to devote herself to the study of Mathematics & some other branches, with which she felt herself not sufficiently familiar. So she gave us her company occasionally at our Ex. Com. Mgs., in Sarah Pugh's parlors, and nice times we have had. These meetings are often intellectual & moral feasts—& at other times we have such a "free and easy" time together, that we all hail that evening as a gala day.

I meant to say while on the Church question, that I read with interest the "come-out" of Newanham Travers, at Finsbury Square Chapel, as reported in the Inquirer, was it?—sent we presume, by our ever attentive friend James Haughton. His "S. P. & A. K." Papers come to us occasionally, and we share in the perusal thereof, and bless him for his kindly remembrance of us, from year to year. That large package containing a variety of books & pamphlets, we made the most of—sending some to Ohio, and others to Canada, among our Anti S. colored people there—where indeed few of our Papers find their way—the postage has been so high— Baptist Noel[8] too has left the Church, it seems; while the Newmans & Puseys are going clean-back to Catholicism or Romanism. I watch with interest all these fluctuations in the Sectarian world. As to your & our Politics, precious little interest have I in their various shiftings of opinion, for while their base is physical force, the structure must be evil—so the

O'Connell party—& the young Irelanders—and our Native Americans & Loco focos—& whigs may fight their own battles—as they must while in that dispensation. Richards political leanings have given some coloring to his opinion of O'Connell &.c— We abated somewhat from his strong language. Joseph Barker's Republicanism is going to do much toward overturning wrong governments. And O'Connell's radicalism was not without its effect. I glory in radicalism or ultraism. But I'm talking of that of which I know nothing—so let's pass on.

Tell our good friend Richard Allen to beware how he suffers the "deceitfulness of riches—to choke the divine word, that it become unfruitful".[9] Nothing that we met with in our travels abroad—not even that *World's* Convention (?) impressed us so favorably, as did your united band of Reformers—in your weekly gatherings at the Royal Exchange, exerting such a healthful influence on thousands. It is true that the demand for bread, has for the time almost suspended intellectual & moral improvement—but when you cheer us, as having so wide a field of labor in this extended country, as did Richard in one of those dear little letters lamentg. at the same time over your circumscribed field—bounded by feedg & clothg—the hungry & naked think of the immense power of Barkers' Steam Press & *yours*—think too of the racy letters transmitted to & thro' the Standard, to admiring readers—and if that dont satisfy you, why try again to cross the "narrow frith" that intersects this land & yours; & here we will open the way & help you on to any amount of good— Abby Kelly (Foster) that assumed name has no business there— She is our model for self sacrifice & indomitable energy— She left her little girl of 20 months & came here, when we were already drained in purse, as we plead—& by her perseverance, she gathered $600 to enable the American Society to send Oliver Johnson to Ohio to keep the Bugle notes clear & to stir up afresh the pure mind in that region—[10] The Editor of that Paper B. S. J[ones]. is going to leave it & go to Cleaveland. Abby has since this late effort, labored a few weeks in Eastern N.Y.— Long Island &.c—and the result is over $100 to establish a local interest for the Standard. She & her Stephen are going to devote the coming summer to that work in that neighbd.— She cherishes all a Mother's feelings at the same time by an active corresponde. with her *babe*—a sister of Stephens, acting as amanuensis for *it*. She is almost equal to Harriet Martineau in her knowledge of politics—

We wonder why Maria W. Chapman's pen is so silent— We were expecting rich treats from her contributions to the Liberator & Standard. How we enjoyed Richard's interview with her & hers— But why dont Hannah too partake of more of these blessed interviews? Your childn. are out of arms now— the elder can care for the younger, & you may, as we do, enjoy travel together. We hope the *ass*-back rides have restored your daughter & that no sorrow in any of your families will again sadden your or our hearts. The mention occasionally of the various branches, is grateful to us, & we hope you will continue to keep us informed of yours all—Jas. Haughton's welfare—

We have had more sickness than usual, the past winter among our children
& their families—and an addition of a grandchild too—makg. 10 in all and now
a body cant ascend the platform—without Bennett's Herald reporting her "an
aged woman"[11]—to say nothg. of the Boston reporter, years ago, affixing "65" as
the probable age—  James Mott's Mother—really aged—82, has just made us a
pleasant visit of a few weeks. She is active & bright—& just as if, I mean to admit 56, to be old. She is a thoro' Gurneyite—& how they and the Wilburs dont
like each other & such a tweedledum dispute too! The Wilburs are in the ascendant hereaway—but I don't mean to waste time & paper with the decayings of
the *dead* As a sect Quakerism is doomed! Our Yearly Mg. is now in session—  I
hurried home from the New York Anniversary—received some ½ doz. lodgers—
and began battle with Select Mg. & dead formalisms—plead for the Green Plain
Ohio & Michigan New Yearly Mgs to be recognized by us—but in vain probably—in the Epistle committee "felt drawn particularly to these outcasts"—created an excitement—came home—waited on tables full of company & now tis
                                                            3rd. day Morng. 15th.—

and I have arisen before 5 o clock to finish this & send it by my nephew Ellis
Yarnall—a highly respectable Merchant of this City & an orthodox believer, of
the Oxford School a young widower—his brother [*Thomas*] a clergyman—or
Rector I believe they call it, of a church in West Philada—alias, over Schuylkill.
These are grandchildn. of one of the plainest of the plain elders—who entertained
English & other travelg. Friends—[12] He was as worthy a man as the Select Mg.
wd. let him be—he was one of the ten elders who condemned Ellias Hicks—and
now tell Richard Allen to see what his descendants have come to! I gave Ellis a
letter to him fearing to inflict one upon you or Jas. Haughton lest he should so
soon betray his want of *active* interest in the Anti-Slavery cause, & his dislike of
Radicalism, that you would scarcely give him any hand of fellowship—  To compensate for commending him to Richd. Allen, I herewith send certain Sermons—
wh. I hope may not be put into the Post as that Indian bead work was—subjecting you to expense more than our little mementos are worth—

I might go on if time allowed & tell you a heap of our several friends' doings—how H. C. Wright is radicalizing in Ohio—how lovely Garrison was in
New York—chastened by the recent sore bereavement—how C. C. Burleigh has
retired to his Father's farm for the time being to take care of his Parents in their
old age—Gertrude & 2 childn. sayg. in the expressive language of conduct,
"whither thou goest I will go."[13] how Cyrus his brother is ever faithful & true to
the Penna. Freeman & the cause hereaway—&.c &.c—  But the hour arrives—
I stopped to give breakfast to our household—an now I go to Meeting to help
"take up the State of Society"—& make all sorts of woman's rights speeches.—
Away then with this trifling—how unbecoming an "aged woman"!

Write us a longer letter soon—  Hannah to her part—  Oh—I forgot to say
we Female Socy. are in treaty with Anna Richardson for aid for our Fair—[14] She
will do something if we will devote the proceeds to the free produce question

I meant to tell you of the wonderful escape of the boxed up Slave—& of the attempt of 2 more in the same way being defeated & the man who aided all 3 being lodged in Prison at Richmond—a sad affair—how wonderful the Crafts escape—

ever yours    L. Mott

The correspondence with our Edwd. we have read relative to Hugh [Brady?] His family we hope will reach here before long— June is it? I cant read this over & correct mistakes  Love unfeigned to brothers & all— —

ALS MB

1. Henry Chapman was possibly a relative of Robert Chapman, Webb's business partner. Ellwood Shannon (c. 1804–86) was a Hicksite Quaker and a Philadelphia tea dealer (*Friends' Intelligencer*, 25 September 1886, 617; Philadelphia City Directory, 1850).

2. Harriet Martineau, *Eastern Life, Present and Past* (London: Edward Moxon, 1848).

3. "He found no resting place" is possibly adapted from Matt. 12:43: "He walketh through dry places, seeking rest and findeth none." Mesmerism, an early form of hypnotism popular in the 1830s and 1840s, relied on the existence of a universal magnetic fluid—an "electrical affinity"—conducted by a medium. "Rise up & walk" is probably a reference to "arise and walk" from Matt. 9:5. "Wondering for their bread" is possibly an adaptation of Job 15:23: "He wandereth abroad for bread."

4. Joseph Barker (1806–75) was an English printer, a chartist, a republican, and a former Methodist minister with leanings toward Quakerism and Unitarianism. He was the author of *History and Confessions of a Man as Put Forth by Himself* (n.p.: J. Wortley Barker, 1846). He had toured the United States in 1847 and, after moving to the States permanently in 1851, joined the antislavery movement. Barker had written Garrison: "I am glad you are free from the bondage of sectarianism. I am glad you have thrown off the yoke of human authority, and placed yourself under the authority of Christ alone. There is not a lovelier sight under heaven to me, than the sight of an emancipated soul" (*Liberator*, 10 March 1843, 40).

5. Joshua Reed Giddings (1795–1864) was a Free-Soil Congressman from Ohio.

6. LCM had spoken at the AASS annual meeting, held in New York City on 8 May 1849, stating: "The Constitution is strong, and the Church is strong, but the Truth is stronger than both, it is omnipotent, and it will triumph yet." Wendell Phillips had supported her statement, saying, "There is nothing . . . higher than the *individual conscience;* that is the corner stone of the Reformer" (*Pennsylvania Freeman*, 17 May 1849, 1). Parker Pillsbury (1809–98), living in New Hampshire around this time, had trained as a Congregational minister but had left the ministry to devote himself to the antislavery movement in 1840. Lucy Stone (1818–93), an Oberlin graduate and a woman's rights and antislavery lecturer, had held a series of meetings in Pennsylvania in April. At one talk the *NASS* described her as "graphically depicting the condition of woman, in her social, civil, and religious relations, and the sufferings incident to individuals and to society in consequence of her degradation" (*NASS*, 10 May 1849, 199; *Pennsylvania Freeman*, 26 April 1849, 2).

7. Sarah Pugh, her mother, Catharine Jackson Pugh, and her aunt, Phebe Jackson (c. 1777–1854), had moved to Philadelphia when Sarah was three years old and the women opened a dressmaking business. Sarah had given up teaching in 1841 to care for her elderly mother. She occasionally reported on Philadelphia antislavery news (*NASS*, 10 May 1849, 199; *Friend*, 27 May 1854, 296).

8. Wriothesley Noel (1798–1873) was a minister who had left the Church of England in 1848 to become a Baptist.

9. Matt. 13:22.

10. Foster had convinced Oliver Johnson to edit the *Anti-Slavery Bugle,* which was in financial trouble, if she could raise the money for his salary and additional funds to pay off the Western Anti-Slavery Society's debts. LCM and JM had contributed $100. Paulina Wright "Alla" Foster had been born on 9 May 1847 (Sterling, 249–50).

11. LCM is possibly referring to the *New York Herald*'s reporting of an incident at the AASS anniversary meeting in which "an aged lady" interrupted the speech of a Mr. West, whom she pronounced "deranged" (10 May 1849, 1).

12. In December 1822 Ellis Yarnall (1756–1847) and another elder had challenged Hicks about his questioning of Christ's divinity (Ingle, 109).

13. Garrison's son Charles Follen Garrison had died on 8 April at age six (*Liberator,* 13 April 1849, 59). Matt. 8:19.

14. Anna Richardson and her husband, Henry Richardson, of Newcastle, England, had hosted Frederick Douglass on his visit to England in 1846 and became his benefactors (William McFeely, *Frederick Douglass* [New York: Simon and Schuster, 1991], 137, 150).

## To James Mott and Children

[*Auburn, New York, c. 19 June 1849*]

[*ms. damaged*] the sect. Phil & James went & several more such. Dr. Smith's widow is teachg. their childn., she came & spoke to me, & invited me to visit the school. Perhaps I shall, when it is somethg. cooler. The next Mg. we have, will be the Wom. Rights. I must take time to look over my papers. That Lib. with the letter from M. C. W.[1] on the Wom. of France, has not yet come to hand.[2] On 1st. day I had all our old letters brot. out, wh. if you'll believe it, Martha has kept since 42 or 3—looked over them eno' to find [*ms. damaged*]

4th. day 20th

My dear husband's 61st. birth-day. Would that we cd. pass it together! Will the childn. all gather, & celebrate it, by presenting *their* childn. to be "led about & kept as the apple of the eye"?[3] Forty years that we have loved each other with perfect love, tho' not formally married quite so long. How much longer the felicity is to be ours, who can tell? What the higher joys to be revealed in the spiritual world, no man can utter. Our brother T. M. C's 51st. just passed too, (if he'll allow me to say it) We wish he had allotted the day to us here. We are growg. quite romantic, "as the years draw nigh, in wh. we shall say, 'there is pleasure in them'"[4] David [*Wright*] came up without a letter last eveg., but Frank's early call [*ms. damaged*]

AL Frag MNS

1. Over the initials "C." and "W." LCM wrote "2" and "1," indicating that they should be reversed.

2. In addition to attending sessions of the Congregational Friends in Waterloo on 4–6 June, LCM had spoken in Seneca Falls on woman's rights on 6 June (*New York Tribune,* 18 June 1849, 1). Other unrecorded meetings may have followed this one. Maria Weston Chapman had written from Paris on 15 April 1849 that while French women suffered even more than U.S. women under its legal system, they occupied more posi-

tions in the arts, business, and medicine than their American counterparts (*Liberator,*
18 May 1849, 77).

3. Deut. 32:10.

4. Thomas M. Coffin would die suddenly on 12 July in a Philadelphia cholera epidemic.
LCM is adapting Eccles. 12:1: "Remember now thy Creator, in the days of thy youth, while
the evil days come not, nor the years draw nigh, when thou shalt say, I have no pleasure
in them."

## To Elizabeth Cady Stanton

Philada 10 Mo. 25th. 1849—

My dear Elizabeth

Very neglectful thou are regarding me. But I have not been so unmindful
of the contents of thy letter, as appearances indicate. It was immediately handed to our Edwd. M. Davis, who laid the subject before his partner and the house
here; and after obtaining their opinions, he consulted the New-York house.[1]
Nearly all that passed between them was committed to writing—our Maria
dramatizing a part of it. It made so large a parcel to forward by post, and hearing that our friend Thomas McClintock was very soon to be here, that I have
suffered you to remain thus long in suspense. In truth however, the time necessary for all the consultations, both here and in New York, and the applications
to other houses, occupied many days.

I will now enclose the most important replies, leaving the caricatures, &.c—
to be sent by private conveyance. You will not be at all discouraged I hope, by
the result. There must be a beginning to every thing. The reasons urged for
declinging your, or the suit of Elizh. & Anna, have some weight. The subject has
been discussed among numbers of Merchants, in Market St.—  The fact of a
serious application, flew like wildfire. Morris L. Hallowell,[2] who is in the same
business as Edward, said he thought he should be willing to receive them—
With some conditions however, which would not be so easy of compliance.

All agree that for a beginning, a retail store would be preferable, and no
difficulty in finding a situation in such an one. This City certainly furnishes
facilities over any of our Eastern ones,—because Women have always been
employed in our stores; and some have done quite a large wholesale & retail
business. Sarah Tyndale has lately retired from the China business, with a handsome fortune.[3] Hers was said to be the largest & most handsome Porcelain store
in this country. She is now devoting her time to works of benevolence. She attended our late Anti S. Annual Mg. at Norristown, heard Garrison again & again,
and became quite enthusiastic in the cause.

Other women I could name hereaway, who have retired from business with
a competence. I hope that Elizabeth & Anna will pursue their prospect—come
on here, and they can better judge by personal observation, and inquiry, than
others here can decide for them. As far as we can aid them, our services are at

their command. Cannot thou accompany them and make us the visit so long talked of, and half-promised? It would delight our hearts to have thee as our guest for awhile. Thy Henry too, whom I have always loved, we should be much pleased to entertain at our house— He must not become too much of a *wicked* politician.

We have just had a most interesting Educational Convention in this City. A National gathering to promote Common Schools. Delegates from many States. Horace Mann presiding. Much was said for Woman. The inequality of Salaries where there is equality of capacity, was spoken of by numbers of the more enlightened. The usual eulogistic strain was poured forth also, by those who would deny to woman her just rights. Duncan of Louisiana—where the people are receivg. the benefit of a more enlightened code, & where the salaries of male & female are equal, offered a resolution that no difference should be made on account of sex. Bishop Potter, who in general took the liberal side, opposed this resolution, urging that it would be unwise in that Convention, to introduce such an innovation—that women were inferior by nature, & the object of the convention shd. go no farther than to seek to qualify her for her true position— domestic life— This is as reported to me. I was not present until after that resolution was disposed of. Some few women were delegates to the Convention & their names enrolled, but no voice of Woman was raised there. It opened during our Meeting at Norristown—[4] The Slave having the first claim, of course I could not be present. I was in & out afterward as my 1001 engagements permitted. Never did I long so much to say a word for Woman as in that Convention— and I resolved to do so, following Horace Mann's last speech—but Bishop Potter was so quick with the concluding prayer that I could not. The Convention will assemble here next year, & then if life & health are spared, the latter rather failing now, see what we women will do!

Yes, Elizh., that visit to our dear frd. Gerrit Smith was indeed very pleasant. I shall bear the sweet remembrance of it. How bold *we* were for Woman! I do consider thy cousin remarkably liberal, considering his remarkable adhesion to Jewish rites & Sectarian, or rather denominational observances. His sentiments on the Woman question are really praiseworthy. How far he is indebted to his lovely Ann for the progress he has made,[5] as Wendell Phillips acknowledges *he* is to *his,* we may not decide. But we are all more or less indebted to the good influences around us, for all that we are.

I must close— Say to Thos. M'Clintock please that I have a letter from Nathanl. Barney of Nant., enclosg $10 for him—or rather for congregational Quakerism in Waterloo & other neighbds.— Tell him also that, about the middle of next month, I hope to join him & Mary Ann in helping to Congregationalize Dutchess & Ulster & Westchester Counties & hope that Long Island may unite in the movement. I just received a letter from A. Kelly Foster on the subject, and information also of an Anti Slavery Convention, in the neighbord.

of Nine Partners Boarding School—wh. I hope to attend.— Now I must go to darning old carpets

in dearest love— Lucretia Mott

I almost forgot to tell thee that a Dr. Wilson and wife are here from Ohio, superintending the publication of a work of 3 or 400 pages the labor of 10 years of the wife, growing out of the new-organizatn. on the woman question, in Anti. S. in 1840—[6] They are orthodox in religious faith—of course the arguments are mainly drawn from Scripture authority. I have seen but a few pages of the proofs, which are good. How many can you sell @ $1 a volume—on Rochester & yr. neighbd?

Please say further to Thos. M'Clintock that we have disposed of all "The Reports", and there is demand for more. He will please bring some on— The 1st. Address & Basis we should like a further supply of—[7]

ALS DLC-Stanton Env: "Elizabeth C. Stanton, Seneca Falls, Seneca Co.—, N. York"

1. Stanton had written LCM on 26 September 1849 seeking positions for Elizabeth McClintock and Anna Southwick (1823–1911) in Edward M. Davis's silk importing business: "The spirit of enterprise has seized Elizabeth McClintock & Anna Southwick, & they have decided to be famous silk merchants, in Philadelphia making their annual visits to Paris & other great cities of the world. Preparatory to the realization of these bright hopes they would fain get a clerkship in the establishment of thy noble son Edward Davis" (Gordon, 1:147–48).

2. Morris L. Hallowell (1809–80), a Philadelphia Hicksite Quaker, was a partner in Hallowell, Walton, and Co., importers and wholesalers of dress goods.

3. Sarah Tyndale was a partner in Tyndale and Mitchell, Chinaware (Philadelphia City Directory, 1849).

4. The twelfth annual meeting of the PASS at Norristown had taken place on 15–17 October 1849. LCM stated that although many associations opened their meetings with prayer, it had become "mere cant and form." The PASS "endeavored to avoid this mere formality, at the same time we feel the necessity of asking Divine aid, and depending upon strength superior to our own" (*Pennsylvania Freeman,* 18 October 1849, 2, 25 October 1849, 1–2). At the National School Convention, held on 17–18 October, G. B. Duncan had put forward a resolution on the equalization of pay for male and female teachers. Bishop Alonzo Potter (1800–1865), a Protestant Episcopal bishop of Pennsylvania since 1845, had been a professor of mathematics and natural philosophy at Union College, in Schenectady, New York (Otelia Cromwell, *Lucretia Mott* [Cambridge, Mass.: Harvard University Press, 1958], 147; *Public Ledger,* 18 October 1849, 2, 19 October 1849, 1, 20 October 1849, 1; *Friends' Intelligencer,* 3 November 1849, 250).

5. Gerrit Smith, a Presbyterian, was a first cousin of Stanton on her mother's side. His wife was Ann Carroll Fitzhugh Smith (1805–c. 1875) (Octavius Brooks Frothingham, *Gerrit Smith: A Biography* [New York: G. P. Putnam, 1879], 348). In May 1849 Smith had resolved to give five hundred men and five hundred women parcels of his land, but he later decided that it was "not best" for the women to receive land from him, so he planned to give them $50 each instead (circular, *Liberator,* 18 May 1849, 80; Gerrit Smith, *Circular to John Cochran, Isaac T. Hopper, Daniel C. Eaton, et al.* [Peterboro, N.Y.: n.p., 1850]).

6. Elizabeth Wilson, *A Scriptural View of Woman's Rights and Duties, in All the Important Relations of Life* (Philadelphia: William S. Young, 1849).

7. LCM is referring to Stanton's Waterloo speech given in September 1848 (Gordon, 1:94–123). On the Congregational Friends, see LCM to George W. Julian, 14 November 1848, above.

## To Elizabeth McClintock and Elizabeth Cady Stanton

Philada. 11 Mo. 27th. 1849

My two dear Elizabeths

I would not 'for the world' have thus "slain a {wo} man to my wounding, and a young {wo} man to my hurt.",[1] Why, I had not the slightest idea, that you would receive the answer to your application, and the childish & playful documents accompanying it, as you did.[2] It was very far from Edward M. Davis' feelings, or those of his "*House*", whom he consulted, to treat the matter with the contempt or ridicule, which those caricatures would seem to indicate. Rush Plumly said, if you only knew how given to sketching & caricaturing their boys & young men are; you would not have regarded this, as anything personal to yourselves. When he was travelling West last summer, his letters were made equally the subject of this indulgence, with yours—

He however answered your proposition, or rather entertained it more seriously, and wrote to Elizh. McClintock at large upon the subject, but being called suddenly to Baltimore, he left the rough sketch of his Letter open in his Portfolio, and had not sent it, when yours was received. I urged his copying it off and letting you have it still, as it contained some of those "*weighty* reasons," which I hinted at, but did not feel qualified to pen—thinking too, that Edward would go more fully into the subject. He says that 5 years ago, when he made that proposition to Elizh. McClintock, he was then out of business, and was seriously considering, in what manner he shd. enter again into mercantile life. Something of the Association principle suggested itself to him, giving all in his employm. a proportion of the profits. The idea also then was entertained & seriously too, of engaging the services of women or girls, & he named the thing to Elizh.— for herself, in conjunction with 3 others—Emily Winslow—Elizh. J. Neall & some one else, to enter with him—  At the same time, he saw that his suggestion would not be accepted, because of the difficulties to surmount—  Afterward, he became bound with others, in a different way and now, when told a *part* of the number are ready to comply with his terms as then made, he is not a situation to decide independently of the judgment of those he consulted. He might not think of so *general* a consultation, either in matters of greater, or less moment, than the proposal in question, but in this case, he regarded the subject one in which all were interested, and the opinion of all should be heard. He means to write you again himself, & I hope will state, more clearly than is in my power to do, with my 1001 engagements, even could I embrace all, the objections that have been urged. Rush's letter will give you some idea—

In the drama, so completely returned like for like, *only more so,* you make Janney a dealer with women in his business.[3] You are not aware, I presume, that in Edward's line, there are no dealings with the retailers—men or women. They are importers, and sell to the wholesale dealers, or Jobbers as they are called, who again sell to women retailers—as well as men  Some of these women deal largely—& to some extent in a wholesale line. I still think if Elizh. & Anna could come here & make effort for a situation in one of the largest of *these* stores, it might prepare the way for them to carry out their plans, far more satisfactorily to themselves, than by beginning at the *top*—thus subjecting themselves to *real* ridicule—which if so wounding to a sensitive mind, when nothing at all was meant, would ill be borne, when *personally* applied, because of failure in an enterprise, the difficulties of wh. their *present* circumstances would not enable them to cope with.

I told Rush that Elizh. McClintock was not without experience—that she had been a successful saleswoman & I presumed book keeper also, in her Father's—or rather *their own* store. He admitted all that, still he insisted upon it that "ye know not what ye ask."; and "are ye able"—continues to be the Sceptical interrogatory. I must leave the subject however, with Edwd. & Rush—added to what I have impressed upon Sarah's memory to say to you—  Morris Hallowell, it is true, said, that *he* should be willing to receive you; so did his br. Joshua say,[4] that he should be willing to forego a part of his share of profits, for the sake of carrying out the principle, but Morris Hallowell *& Co.* did not say so—  There are 4 or 5 partners in that *large "House"* and some 15 or 20 clerks— all of whom, would have to be listened to in the matter with greater or less regard—  No, my dear girls, without years of training, so high an aim, however praiseworthy cannot be attained. We poor women shall have to ascend this "mount of transfiguration," by patient and difficult tread. "Discouraged?"— Why no, the farthest from it possible. Come on here, "& try, try again"![5] It would delight us to receive Elizh. & Anna, at our house, while making the effort, & Elizh. Stanton to bear them up, and we would aid all in our power, so grand an undertaking. This proposition is made in all seriousness—  We really should be exceedingly gratified for you to come forthwith to 138 North 9th. St. and I would devote day after day *with you* to such applications, as best wisdom should suggest—  And we would have Woman's rights' Mgs. too, if E. Stanton would bring her lecture along. While Henry is *luxuriating in* your State Senate, let her board out those dear little "Hyenas", and come here & see what can be done—and come before our Fair & 'December Mg.'—  We hope Theodore Parker will be here at that time. We have sent for him. Wm. H. Furness has agreed to take part in that Mg. also—  So, here is a bribe offered, in addition to the claims of the cause of Woman. Mind you let me know what you think of that new work on the subject, by E. Wilson. To those who depend upon Scripture authority, it may be of use. It is well too to see how easily the Bible may be made to prove the *right,* when men begin to be ashamed of flying to it, for authority for the wrong— That is a work of ten years research & hard labor, tho' by one unaccustomed to writg. for the press—a daughr of a Scotch Presbyterian Minister—now, quite an old lady— Her husband—Dr. Wilson is heart & soul with her in the cause—

I need not say, how much amusement the *returns* you made afforded. Sarah can tell you much. I took them to our A. S. Ex. Com. Mg. Edwd. & Rush were present at the readg. there, & at first, with rather an ill grace, bore the "flagellation" regarding it undeserved, if you "could only have known how very respectfully your proposal was received—no ridicule—nothg. to wound unless indeed, their view of the impossibility of carrying out the intent by beginning *so high.*" The fact of its eliciting discussion up & down Market St. was certainly encouraging. I was delighted with *that* & thought when mentiong. it, you would be pleased too— In short, so far from being hurt, or at all daunted, by what has occurred, growing out of this application, I think you or *we* have great reason to be encouraged. I was delighted at the evidence of a determination to *act,* as well as to call Conventions to talk, "*Come* and "let us reason together."[6] We are not expectg any particular company just now, and I will give the subject all the attention in my power, if you 3 will agree to meet here & do what you can— Sarah's visit has been short— We should have been glad to see her much oftener than we have done.

The Temperance papers I fear I shall not be able to do much with hereaway. I was glad to receive the copies & will try what I can do. I am glad for you to have access to the public mind through that medium.

The drama &.c—are going the rounds and doing good too, while, they amuse—and are considered very smart—you know that tho'— I kept no copy of that little pencilling wh. Maria did just for her own amusement, not dreaming that I should make any use of it or send it to you—and I would have been the last to do so, or the caricatures either, if I had an idea of doing more than causing a laugh for the moment. Far be it from me, to wound a bruised spirit. I have become somewhat callous to or by the repeated stripes that have been inflicted upon me, as representative of a larger demand for Woman, and I suppose I judged the younger, more by myself than I ought to do— We have to learn to "endure hardness as good Soldiers,"[7] in all these great reformatory movements.

We had a fine Convention in Duchess Co. tell your Parents, that is Elizh M'C's—notwithstdg. the opposition of worn out Quaker sectarianism. Jas. & self attended some 8 or 10 Mgs— — the Mo. Mgs. occurring at that time—& Danl. Quimby in attendance, with notice given—notice also for me—so that we had large audiences— Some Free Meetings—& closing on 1st. day—eveg— by a large public Mg. in Poughk[eepsi]e. in the Town Hall wh. overflowed by hundreds we were told—a Satisfactory Mg—5 wagon loads of Milton Friends  They spoke of Thomas' late visit among them with Satisfaction, & disaptt. was expressed that he was not at Nine Partners—

With any amount of love,
yours    L. Mott

I doubt much whether any City in this country affords such facilities for Women engaging in business, even in the *retail* line, as this City. In New York & Boston Men have supplanted women. When you have read this—I should be gratified if My sister Martha cd. have the perusal of the whole if you have a copy of the Caricatures sent here—

Stephen & Abby K. Foster are doing a good work in that neighbd. arousing an apathetic people. Our attending the Syracuse Convention is put out of the question, by the Season of the year in wh. it is to be held— I presume you do not ask seriously our opinion of sending all that nonsense to Jane Swisshelm.[8] I will send the 1st letter on the Subject, but please return it to me, when Elizh. or Mary Ann rather, has seen it

ALS MNS

Env: "The two Elizabeths, Waterloo and Seneca Falls, N.Y. kindness of Sarah"

1. Gen. 4:23.

2. The rejection of Elizabeth McClintock and Anna Southwick's application for work at Edward Davis's company can be found in Davis's letter to LCM of 10 October 1849 and its enclosures, including Rush Plumly's undated letter to Lizzie McClintock and an abstract of the meeting, with each employee's comments on the proposed hiring of women. In his letter to McClintock, Plumly stated: "The request was recd. & entertained most respectfully, both from personal regard for you, and from a full recognition of the principle involved, and altho' the debate upon the proposition (a meagre abstract of which will be sent you) resulted unfavorably to your application it was by no means from want of sympathy with your purpose, nor from indifference to that important principle." Cartoons of women working in a warehouse also accompanied Davis's letter (MNS; Gordon, 1:151).

3. The "drama" had been written c. 12 November 1849 by Stanton and Elizabeth McClintock. In the "drama," Jacob Janney stated, "How my eyes would feast themselves on those graceful beings, lightly gliding round midst piles of goods and boxes & these stalwart men" (Gordon, 1:152–61). In Davis's abstract, Janney was recorded as stating: "The social influence of the applicants might be too strong upon the young men of the store, and lessen their attention to business" (Davis to LCM, 10 October 1849, enclosure).

4. Sarah McClintock, the daughter of Thomas McClintock and Mary Ann McClintock, was visiting in Philadelphia (Gordon, 1:151). Joshua Hallowell (b. 1819).

5. William Edward Hickson, "Try and Try Again."

6. Isa. 1:18.

7. LCM is adapting 2 Tim. 2:3: "Endure hardness, as a good soldier of Jesus Christ."

8. The New York State Anti-Slavery Convention had been scheduled for 8 January 1850 (*Liberator,* 30 November 1849, 191). A teacher, a journalist, and an antislavery and woman's rights activist, Jane Swisshelm (1815–84) began her own newspaper, the *Pittsburg Saturday Visiter,* in 1848.

## To Sydney H. Gay

Philada. 12 Mo. 3rd. 1849

My dear Sydney

We notice the time advertized for holding the State Convention at Syracuse, and regret that the season of the year will prevent our attending it. My special object in writing now, however is, to ask if there has been sufficient consultation with the friends of Western N. York, before fixing the time. Fredk. Douglass' English frds. Julia & Eliza Griffetts are in the City.[1] They called here on 7th. day last, and learning that the 15. Proxs.——, was decided upon, they expressed great fears that it might interfere with the Rochester Meeting or Fair in aid of the North Star—as that time had been previously decided upon, and could not well be altered.

I promised them I would write to thee, in reference to it, for I felt sure that there was no intention of doing anything that would at all conflict with the interests of the Western part of the State, or of Frederic's Paper. I hope that no jealousy will be suffered to arise in any quarter of the Old-Organization field. We have had enough of Severance among us. The North Star is struggling doubtless for its life, and the fears of many are, that it will be in vain. But let us be careful how we do anything which jealousy may construe into an indifference as to its life. I did not admit for a moment, to the girls that there was any cause of complaint, nor do I think there is. Still it may be best for us to avoid the appearance of evil. Frederic will probably be with us in a week or two. We shall be glad to have him hold some meetings in this neighborhood. His particular object in coming, we are told, is to be in the City during the Fair that his colored friends are going to hold, in aid of the North Star.[2] We shall much regret it, if there should be any seeming antagonism in our movements. We have ever felt most friendly to Frederic, and desired his success, in whatever field of labor he might be engaged. Some movements among our colored people last winter, led to a hostile spirit on the part of some among them, who have prejudiced others, and the jealousy which has thus been engendered, has weakened their confidence in the Abolitionists. We must do what we consistently can to allay this feeling.

My husband & self were greatly disappointed, that we had not thy company up the North River & at Duchess Co.—— The meetings there were quite encouraging, considering the new ground it was to many of them—— Stephen & Abby Foster have done a good work there and at Milton. But their labors must be followed up by others, lest the interest awakened should prove but temporary. Is it not possible to make a great stir nearer New York City? Or indeed *in* that multitudinous place? You ought to have an efficient Exec. Com. there, constantly divising ways & means to keep up a healthful agitation. It is quite time for that dear, fat baby of your to be cast off a little, and for Elizh.—our energetic Elizh to bestir herself & awaken some dozen men & women who shall enlist in this cause, and then see what we would do! Preparatory to this, she had better come to our approaching Fair, to revive her Anti Slavery spirit. I was hoping you would go to Hingham this Thanksgiving-time, So as not to have the excuse any longer, that the babe had not been presented there, & therefore that your friends elsewhere could not have your company.

How shocking are the developements connected with poor Dr. Parkman's disappearance. We knew the family so well, the Father's I mean, some 40 years ago, when we lived neighbors to them in Boston, that I have partaken more of the excitement of these awful details, than in common cases. Following as it did, the dreadful death of Anna Jenkins & daughter, we had hardly ceased dwelling upon that sad event, when this came upon us.[3]

I am writing more than a mere business letter, as was my only design, in taking the pen, but thou must know, since the very pleasant visit from thee at our Annual Meeting, I feel better acquainted with thee, than before, and love thee better too, not that my affection was in any small measure, previous to that time, for both thee & thy d[ear] Elizabeth, to whom now greeting—

yours    *Lucretia Mott*

James left a letter with thee from our unfortunate frds.—the Vineses. If thou hast done with it, please return it as some of their friends wish to see it.

Our Martha says, "Give my love to him".

ALS NNCB-Gay

1. Julia Griffiths, later Crofts (d. 1894), and her sister, Eliza Griffiths (later Dick), English abolitionists, had come to the United States in 1849. Julia helped Douglass edit the *North Star* and their close relationship caused gossip among abolitionists about a possible extramarital affair (William S. McFeely, *Frederick Douglass* [New York: W. W. Norton, 1991], 163–66).

2. The fair to raise money for the *North Star* would be held on 24–26 December 1849. The *Pennsylvania Freeman* complimented Frederick Douglass and Charles. L. Remond for "their characteristic eloquence. . . . The absence of exclusiveness, or any desire to render this a 'Colored Fair,' and the amicable feeling which seemed to pervade the large assemblage of persons of different complexions, was extremely gratifying to the Philanthropist" (18 December 1849, 3, 3 January 1850, 2).

3. George Parkman (1791–1849), a Boston physician, had been missing for a week before it was discovered that he had been murdered by John White Webster, a professor of chemistry at Harvard. The motive for the murder was $487 that Webster owed Parkman. Parkman's dismembered body was found in a vault under Webster's laboratory (*Liberator*, 7 December 1849, 195). Anna Almy Jenkins and her daughter, Sarah B. Jenkins, had died in a fire in Providence, Rhode Island, where Jenkins had founded the Providence Shelter for Colored Children (Elizabeth Persons, "Lines Composed on the Death of Mrs. Anne A. Jenkins, and Her Daughter Sarah, Who Were Burned to Death in the City of Providence, Nov. 20th, 1849" [Providence: n.p., 1849]).

## To [Martha Coffin Wright]

*[Philadelphia c. 6 February 1850]*

[*ms. damaged*] after doing them awhile, thou made jelly of the juice, & sugared the currants more & dried them, but Eliza W. sd., "no, thou made no jelly with any part." So now, tell us how they are done. Anna H. has lately been makg. a lot of holders, of pieces she has had lying by for years. Maria [*Davis*] had an errand in 8th St. today to get Charlie some buttons, &.c.  So she pursued her walk to Anna's, tho' yestery. she thot. she shd. go out no more very soon. Anna was busy in her kitchen makg. a carpet—rag-list 45c pr yd.—& cuttg her old one into pieces to save the other. I wish she had invited me to go & help her. Thou had not mentioned thy mould candles before. In that & soap-makg. thou hast succeeded, if not in head-cheese. Thy little box of sperms are in our storeroom.[1] I wonder if Eliza's trunk will hold it. She is just made happy with a letter from Ellen Adams. We have not seen that new work of N. P. Willis'. We are now readg. Euthanasy—by a Unitn. Minister near Birmingm. Eng. or—Happy Thoughts near the close of Life.[2] It is a fanciful—beautiful work containg many good, philosophical views; Mary Grew presented it to Edwd [*Davis*]. Thy mourning for the living, & not for the dead, may arise from rather a morbid view of life. We ought not to indulge the habit of looking at life & circumstances around us, through a gloomy medium. When Grace Greenwood was here, Rush Plumly learned from her the particulars of Godey employg. her to write for his Book, & his trying to continue her in an under-hand way.[3] It was mean enough. She & Rush are very good friends. Anna says she can sympathize with thee, havg. lately undertaken a similar task—teachg. Lu. to write. She had her to begin with strokes. Frank [*Wright*]'s teacher is not the only one, who does not find it "profitable". So many send their circulars here, & ask our aid to fill their schools. Thos. Baldwin is doing better this winter than common. I have been visiting 3 or 4 colored schools this morng & distributg 50 garments among them, from our house of Industry.[4] Dr. Atlee is employed as apothecary at the Mullen House down town, where soup is given out for 1200 daily—a school in the house for 100—lodg. rooms for a tempy. home for 50 or more—  Groceries & coal sold out very cheap to the Poor & yet after all, thousands are in want—in rags—in vice & filth. Where is the radical reform?!!!!

[*ms. damaged*] In answer to thy inquiry, "how are we to reconcile the wholesale destructn. of life, occasioned by storms at sea, volcanoes?" &.c. B. Hallowell in his scientific lectures,[5] spoke of these occurrences as strikg. evidences of the impartial operatn. of the natural laws—so does Geo. Combe. We have warng. enough to lead us to build our vessels so strong & secure, that they may withstand storms—increasg. intelligence leads the mariner to avoid icebergs The warnings around volcanoes are sufficient, if obeyed, to lead the inhabitants to remove beyond their danger. So with disease. Fevers—Cholera, &.c. used to be

regarded as special judgments—& so in one sense they are, as the result of neglect of the laws of health. Man has reason & intelligence to avoid these epidem-
ics. I dont know, as to earthquakes. But when whole Cities are destroyed, there
is nothing *partial* in the visitation. B. Hallowell spoke of land-slides, warng.
people not to build too near the edge—Siasconset ought to take warning. Yes,
we have, after all, to confess our knowledge limited. And our very ignorance
should lead us to beware how we judge awful occurrences, to ~~be from~~ "God's
decree." The tendency of this conclusion is to neglect the obvious cause of calamities— New York is investigatg that boiler concern,[6] wh. produced so much
misery, and this care will lead manufacturers, as well as Steam boat & rail road
proprietors to take greater care of such mighty engines of mischief. Your
knockgs. appear likely to be divulged as a great humbug. The supplement to the
Tribune contains Myer's testimony. We have lately recd. letters from Rochester
on the subject—but I cant be interested. Edwd. is—very. Maria not a bit. She
wants thee to hear J. R. Lowells' letter on the subject.[7] He has so little faith in
such grossness as the knockings, being the medium of disembodied spirits, to
communicate with the living. I have thot., among the wonders of mesmerism,
what is passing in the mind of one is conveyed to the clairvoyant, & he gives it
forth to the astonished believer, all in accordance with the "natural laws," if you
only knew what these are, or how they operate—

AL Frag PSCHi-Mott

1. Spermaceti from the head of the sperm whale was used to make candle stock.

2. The prolific writer Nathaniel Parker Willis (1806–67) published several books in
1849–50, among them *Rural Letters* (1849) and *The Gem of the Season for 1850* (1850).
William Mountford (1816–85) wrote *Euthanasy* (1848).

3. Using the pen name Grace Greenwood, Sara Jane Clarke (1823–1904; later Lippincott) had published a card in the *Pittsburg Dispatch* on 22 January 1850 in which she
objected to reinstatement soon after being removed as the editor of *Godey's Lady's Book*
by its publisher, Louis Antoine Godey (1804–78). As Greenwood, Clarke stated that
Godey's attempt to reinstate her "was made without my concurrence or knowledge"
(letter reprinted in *NASS*, 14 February 1850, 150).

4. In October 1847, LCM, Mary Grew, Sarah Pugh, and others had opened the House
of Industry to rehabilitate women "who had led immoral lives" (Lori Ginzburg, "Moral Suasion Is Moral Balderdash: Women, Politics, and Social Activism in the 1850s," *Journal of American History* 73 [December 1986]: 612).

5. Benjamin Hallowell (1799–1877), a Quaker minister, a clerk of the Baltimore Yearly
Meeting, and a lecturer on astronomy, chemistry, and geology, ran a school in Alexan-
dria, Virginia. MCW had posed the question to LCM in her letter of 21 January 1850
(MNS).

6. On 4 February a boiler at a printing press factory had exploded in New York City,
killing an estimated fifty employees (*New York Tribune*, 5 February 1850, 2).

7. The Fox sisters Margaret and Kate, in Hydesville, New York, along with their older
sister Leah Fox Fisher, in Rochester, claimed that they could be in touch with the dead
through mysterious knockings. Edward M. Davis had sent the poet and humorist James
Russell Lowell (1819–91) a letter from Oliver Johnson describing a recent Fox sisters se-
ance. Lowell replied that "these 'spirits' tell us, it seems, what we already know, nothing

else." A letter from Auburn appearing in the *New York Tribune* described how a daughter in the Michael Myers family, by imitating the sounds of the mysterious knockings, exposed them as a hoax (Howard Kerr, *Mediums, and Spirit-Rappers, and Roaring Radicals: Spiritualism in American Literature, 1850–1900* [Urbana: University of Illinois Press, 1972], 4–5, 23; Lowell to Davis, 24 January 1850, *Letters of James Russell Lowell*, ed. Charles Eliot Norton [New York: Harper and Brothers, 1893], 174–75; *New York Tribune*, supp., 4 February 1850, 1).


## To Sydney H. Gay

Philada. 4 Mo 13th. 50

My dear Sydney H. Gay

Bless Richard D. Webb & thy dear Self also, that letter from Liverpool, was answered long ago. It probably reached its destination, about the time that Richard sent his to thee. It is true, we delayed too long, for it is not the easiest thing in the world, to give advice on such an important matter. My husband willingly accepted the transfer of the task to himself, as being better acquainted with farming & the choice of land. But "come to the pinch", he too shrunk from saying, "I would come," or, "I wouldn't." When people are making a comfortable living in their own native land, it is a serious thing to "pull up stakes", and go to a strange country—especially for an Englishman, surrounded with the comforts & elegancies of life, as described by Emerson, Colman, and others, to come here & settle down in our Western Wilds, where such a contrast must be constantly presented.[1] Let the starving millions, & the oppressed operatives come, and every thing here will compare favorably. We did however say all we could to encourage their making the experiment, with the more courage, or hope of their success too, because they contemplated joining Joseph Barker & other emigrants, & forming a neighborhood for themselves, on the Conn. Reserve in Ohio, which indeed is beginning to seem an old country, when compared with the Wisconsins & Iowas & Minesotas.[2] Our correspondent—Suliot by name, ventured the hope that R. D. Webb & family might be induced to come with them. We recd. a short letter from Richd. lately, wh. we intend to answer very soon. Sarah Pugh wrote him one of her prettiest, a short time since. Our subjects are so much in common, that it wont do to follow in too quick succession. I may however accept thy kind offer, & send a few lines to be enclosed in thine.

I am glad to be remembered by thy "Lizzie" in any way and the rebuke contained in the article sent, was so well deserved, I ought to feel it "a kindness", for never had a raft of "curious Qukeresses["] less excuse for thrusting themselves into his clownish presence, "just to get a good look at" him. He shewed himself at that time wanting in sympathy for the Slave, & since he now comes out a negro hater, I feel less ashamed of our rudeness, in "boring" him thus.[3]

Thy words of sympathy, dear Sydney, were grateful to us. Edward & Maria appreciated them, as coming from a heart, touched also with sorrow. Altho' human consolation cannot recal the dead, & therefore seems unavailing, yet it is so natural to crave sympathy, in distress "Have pity upon me, Oh ye my friends, for the hand of God hath touched me"[4] "Ye, who e'er lost an Angel, pity me!" and so natural too, to seek to alleviate grief & human suffering by kindly words, as well as deeds, that none need shrink from the heart's yearning in these directions. I confess however, to the feeling, to such a degree—that what I can offer, can be no alleviation, that I seldom attend a funeral, where expression seems to be called for. At such an hour, the inadequacy of words is paramount— & the inspiration to speak receives a check—

For thy great loss, in the removal of so loved a brother,[5] I did indeed *feel* keenly—& more than once essayed to express it to thee—but failed. I cannot offer the kind of consolation, which many do, & which thou alludes to—"the ways of Providence", &.c—because so firm a believer in the natural laws, that when such useful & beautiful lives, as thy dear br's. & our precious Charlie's are cut off—I can ascribe it to no other cause, than our ignorance of these laws, or our failure to observe them—

This may appear cold unbelief—but commending itself as it does, to my reason it lessens in no wise all veneration for "Him who doeth all things well." equally in the universal operation of his alwise laws as could be by any special act or Providence. Yes, you will probably see the old Quakeress again at the Annual Mg.[6] but if she shd. tell thee she felt "moved to speak at the Tabernacle—the very utterance of it, would withdraw the "motion"— Thanks for the invitatn. to repeat a visit so pleasant to me— If possible it will give me great pleasure— Elizh. must not let [*ms. damaged*] dear boy keep her at home that week—

in fulness of love yrs.    L Mott

I took but a scrap of paper, not expecting to say so much— After filling that, it occurs to me, that I have never acknowledged thine kindly sent in reply to my inquiries relative to the Syracuse Convention & the *notable* English ladies—the Griffeths. Thy explanatn. was altogether satisfactory & in my heart I thanked thee for it. We have our fears for Fredk. [*Douglass*] through the influence of these women—but hope that his strong good sense will preserve him from estrangement.

Thy suggestion relative to employg. S. May Jr. as gen. Agt.[7]—inducg. him to settle in New York, &.c—havg. Quary. Mgs.—& all that reads well, if we could only bring it about. What Penna. would do toward it, we are not able to say; but judgg. from the past, we cannot hope the abolitionists hereaway wd. "shell out" any more liberally. I did not feel qualified to give an opinion, & that is one reason of my not answering thy letter sooner— We must talk the Cause well over when the Society comes together in New York— James Mott expects to be there next week or the week after. If he could see thee at that time, & talk over affairs of the Slave's interest, he could then report to our Ex. Com. before the Annual

Mg. & at least strengthen the interest we all *ought to* feel, in the American Society's arrangements.

It was fully my intention to go to Syracuse—& Miller M'Kim wd. have gone if I had, but our family were so opposed to the winter-journey—that I had to give it up— But that Convenn. was such a Lib. Party affair, that we did not so much regret our absence from it.[8] Moreover Miller wd. not then have gone to Boston, and he did & received good there—

again affecy    L M

ALS NNCB-Gay

1. Apparently a Liverpool resident, Theodore E. Suliot, a teacher and cousin of the Webbs, wished to immigrate to the United States (LCM to Richard D. Webb and Hannah Webb, 28 May 1850, MB; *Anti-Slavery Bugle,* 29 October 1853, 3). Drawing on his tour of Great Britain, the philosopher and essayist Ralph Waldo Emerson (1803–82) lectured in Eastern cities in 1850, including six lectures in Philadelphia in April. After dining with LCM on April 5, Emerson described her as "a blessing & an ornament" (to Lidian Emerson, 6 April 1850, *Letters of Ralph Waldo Emerson,* ed. Ralph L. Rusk [New York: Columbia University Press, 1939], 4:194–95; see also MCW to LCM, 6 February 1852, MNS). Henry Colman published many works on his European travels, including *European Life and Manners: in Familiar Letters to Friends* (Boston: Little and Brown, 1849).

2. After the Revolutionary War, Connecticut had claimed 3.5 million acres in northern Ohio, which later came to be known as the Western Reserve.

3. This is possibly a reference to Father Theobold Mathew. The Irish temperance leader had arrived in the United States in July 1849 and toured the Northeast throughout the fall. His refusal to condemn slavery provoked Garrison and other abolitionists (Rev. Father Augustin, *Footprints of Father Theobald Mathew O. F. M. Cap.* [Dublin: M. H. Gill and Son, 1947], 494–500; *WLG,* 3:640–76).

4. LCM's grandson, Charles Davis, had died on 3 March. Job 19:21.

5. The physician and analytical chemist Dr. Martin Gay (b. 1803) had died on 12 January.

6. The annual meeting of the AASS was to be held on 7–9 May at the Broadway Tabernacle in New York City; LCM would not attend (*New York Tribune,* 10 May 1850, 2; *WLG,* 4:6–15).

7. Samuel May Jr. (1810–99), a Unitarian minister and cousin of Samuel J. May, was then general agent of the Massachusetts Anti-Slavery Society and a strong Garrisonian.

8. Abolitionists meeting in Syracuse on 15 January had discussed the primacy of the AASS and heard a speech by Gerrit Smith supporting the Constitution and the Liberty party (*Liberator,* 1 February 1850, 18).

## To the Salem, Ohio, Woman's Convention

Philadelphia, 4th mo., 13th, '50.

*To the 'Woman's Convention,' to be held in Salem, Ohio, on the 19th inst.:*

The call for this Convention, so numerously signed, is indeed gratifying, and gives hope of a large attendance.[1] The letter of invitation was duly received, and I need scarcely say how gladly I would be present, if in my power. Engagements in another direction, as well as the difficulty of travel, at this season of the year, will prevent my availing myself of so great a privilege.

You will not, however, be at a loss for speakers in your midst; for among the signers of the Call are the names of many whose hearts 'believe unto righteousness;' out of their abundance, therefore, the mouth will make 'confession unto salvation.'[2]

The wrongs of woman have too long slumbered. They now begin to cry for redress. Let them be clearly pointed out in your Convention; and then, not *ask as favor,* but demand *as right,* that every civil and ecclesiastical obstacle be removed out of the way.

Rights are not dependent upon equality of mind; nor do we admit inferiority; leaving that question to be settled by future developments, when a fair opportunity shall be given for the equal cultivation of the intellect, and the stronger powers of the mind shall be called into action.

If, in accordance with your Call, you ascertain 'the bearing which the circumscribed sphere of woman has on the great political and social evils that curse and desolate the land,'[3] you will not have come together in vain.

May you indeed 'gain strength' by your 'contest with difficulty'! May the whole armor of 'Right, Truth and Reason' be yours! Then will the influence of the Convention be felt in the assembled wisdom of *men,* which is to follow; and the good results, as well as your example, will ultimately rouse other States to action in this most important cause.

I herewith forward to you a 'Discourse on Woman,'[4] which, though brought out by local circumstances, may yet contain principles of universal application.

Wishing you every success in your noble effort, I am yours for woman's redemption and consequent elevation,

LUCRETIA MOTT[5]

PL *Liberator,* 17 May 1850, 80

1. The Convention of the Women of Ohio, meeting on 19–20 April 1850, was the first woman's rights conference to be held outside the state of New York (Robert W. Audretsch, ed., *The Salem, Ohio, 1850 Women's Rights Convention Proceedings* [Salem, Ohio: Salem Public Library, 1976]; for the significance of the convention, see Nancy Isenberg, *Sex and Citizenship in Antebellum America* [Chapel Hill: University of North Carolina Press, 1998], ix, 70–71, 212).

2. Rom. 10:10. Other women attending included Josephine S. Griffing, J. Elizabeth Jones, and Mary Ann Johnson.

3. The quotation is from the call "To the Women of Ohio" (*Anti-Slavery Bugle,* 30 March 1850, 114). Another call summoned residents of the Columbiana County area to a mass meeting to urge the upcoming Ohio constitutional convention to grant suffrage "without regard to sex, COLOR or CONDITION" (Audretsch, *Women's Rights Convention Proceedings,* 19–20).

4. LCM had delivered her "Discourse on Woman" on 17 December 1849 in Philadelphia as an answer to a lecture she had heard by the essayist Richard Henry Dana Sr., criticizing the woman's rights movement. In her "Discourse" LCM declared that wom-

en were just as effective as men in solving the world's problems; she set forth the rights to suffrage, property rights, and income that women should be permitted to enjoy as they chose. At the Salem meeting, after reading LCM's letter, Jones read her "Discourse," which "was listened to with marked interest by the whole Convention" (*Liberator,* 17 May 1850, 80; extracts from the "Discourse" were published in the *NASS,* 21 March 1850, 172, and in the *Liberator,* 15 February 1850, 28; see also *Sermons,* 143–62; Bacon, 134–36).

5. After the convention adjourned, a group of male spectators met and adopted a resolution affirming that women should enjoy the same civil and political rights, including suffrage, as men (Audretsch, *Women's Rights Convention Proceedings,* 65). In May the Ohio constitutional convention would defeat, 72-77, a resolution that the word *male* be deleted from Ohio's constitution (Eugene H. Roseboom, *The Civil War Era,* vol. 4 of *A History of the State of Ohio* [Columbus: Ohio State Historical Society, 1944], 235).

## To Joseph Dugdale and Ruth Dugdale

Auburn N.Y. 7 Mo. 12th. 1850

My dear Joseph & Ruth

It was with regret that I left Philada. without replying to Joseph's acceptable letter, received the day before  It had been at our house a day or 2, while I was at Mount. Holly, without your Mother & Sister knowing of it—so that they did not receive the intelligence, they were so longing for, as early as they might have done. I had so much on my mind preparatory to leaving home for 6 weeks absence, that I was not in a fit state to write. The proposal to meet you in Milton [*New York?*] & assist Joseph, in a line for wh he is admirably adapted, & needs no aid, was indeed impracticable for me to comply with, having made an engagement, some weeks before, to be at the Commencement of the Central College, on the 4th., & having promised Harriet Purvis, a *colored* friend of ours, who has sons, students there, to travel thither by the Erie Road, in company.[1] Moreover, an appointment made with a French "Madame" Garnaud, some days before the reception of your letter, to meet her in N. York, on a certain hour, on our way, would again prevent compliance, with an invitation which under other circumstances, would have afforded me great pleasure to accept. Since our visit to our Milton friends & outcasts, we have felt much interest in them, and I felt confident that there would be a Gospel salutation for them thro' you, and in each week that we heard nothg. from you, I presumed you were enjoying a rest somewhere in that beautiful spot. I was glad that Nine Partners meeting was remembered by you likewise. There are some valued friends in that place, who have suffered for the truth's sake.

The accounts from Waterloo Yearly Mg. were rather contradictory. While represented by some in attendance as very interesting, others felt a want of solemnity, and "the good old fashion" of conducting such Meetings.[2] We could readily believe however that you had an interesting time, and were alive to the great interests of truth & humanity. James passed part of a day at Thos. M'Clintock's on his return here from Buffalo, and heard many little particulars, confirming the more favorable side of the picture. Right well pleased were we that you were with them, & that they & you were satisfied.

Joseph's attack of intermittent, was not what we were looking for, but if had thus to suffer, he could hardly have fallen into better hands. We know Elias & Susan Doty right well—& Thos. & Mary Ann are "known & read of all men".[3] The draw-back as regards business, you had to bear, but neighbor's fare you have abundantly in that line; so the hints dropped to Joseph, *not to be too generous,* with his present earnings, must be to his profit. A little competence secured to yourselves is your due. Privations ye have known & felt full long. You have claims & demands near home, from those deservedly beloved & cherished, so, "all these words "to the wise", must be sufficient.

It was what we were least expecting, that you would not return to us, before the time came for us to leave our hot City. To think of your coming so far, and our seeing you so little! We had barely a peep at dear Ruth. Our arrangements could not well be altered, either as respects our Martha's visit at that time, with her Father's escort, or mine as I have told you. It was not pleasant, to leave your dear Mother & Sister, in such an unsettled way, but I hope they succeeded in packing the box, and gathering together such things as were scattered. I felt desirous that the time might be used to the best advantage, and they have oppor[tuni]ty. to see as many of their friends as possible. It was to be sure rather chilling, to find so much conservatism among those, from whom friendly greetings, & close fellowship were expected  This however, has ever been the lot of those who were in advance of their age, and we must strive to be "able to drink the cup, & be baptized with the baptism", which introduces into "newness of life". It is in this sense only that "thro' much tribulation we enter the kingdom".[4] And even this becomes "a small thing," in comparison with the "weight of Glory." But I have not time to sermonize.

My loving & loved husband leaves me this morng to return to Philada., & release our Thomas from close confinement to the counting room, so that he may go to Cape May [*New Jersey*] awhile & recruit his health & strength. I remain here a few weeks for the same purpose, and to be with my dear Sister, as also to receive some Ohio relatives, whom I was obliged to turn my back upon, just as they were about to visit our City. They will probably come out here. James may yet see you again, and who knows but that I may still have that pleasure, on my return some time next month? I shall wish to hear your decision as regards the purchase of the Kennett Place—also the disposal of horses & carriage, how you expect to return, &.c &.c—Johnny will be quite ready, I presume for a start, as he became anxious, as well as his Grand Mother & Aunt, for your return, although he took things easy, and made no complaint. You must give him all the opportunity for school-learning that he ought to have. He was careful not to do anything in your absence, which he thought you would disapprove.

Someone proposed his going to Barnum's Museum[5] he said unless he was sure his Father & Mother wd. like it, he wd. rather not.

I rose early to write, and must now awaken James and make preparation for breakfast, & receive our cousin Yarnalls, 4 in company, who unexpectedly arrived last eveg I have not time nor room to tell you how I shocked the orthodoxy of the Trustees of the Central College, by denying the doctrine of human depravity, & the absurdities thereunto belonging. They are Anti Slavery Baptists—but I had supposed sufficiently liberal to bear opposing views to their own.

The colored professor Charles Reason[6] defended me against the attack of a Methodist Minister, who was sorely grieved. Charles told them that as they had several students who agreed with me in opinion, and who patiently heard *their* views from day to day, it was but fair, that they should hear one in whose opinions they could unite. It caused quite a sensation among them. Whether harm or good was done by their inviting such a heretic, and giving her liberty to choose her subject, time must determine.

I left your letter in Philada. for your Mother & Sister's perusal— So if I have failed to answer any part you will excuse it.

And believe me
yours affectionately    L. Mott—

ALS PSCHi-Mott

1. Harriet Purvis (1810–75), the daughter of James Forten and the wife of Robert Purvis, was active in the PFASS. Her sons Joseph Purvis (b. 1837) and Robert Purvis (c. 1834–62) attended the New York Central College in McGrawville, New York (*WLG*, 5:96).

2. Ruth Dugdale was one of seven members (including Stanton) whom the Congregational Friends Yearly Meeting had appointed to write "a suitable appeal" drawing attention to the rights of women, rights "which belong to her as a human being." The yearly meeting also had adopted a memorial to the U.S. Congress urging the admission of California as a free state, the abolition of slavery in the District of Columbia, and the will to go "to the verge of your constitutional power for the abolition of Slavery in the several slave-holding States of the Union" (*Proceedings of the Yearly Meeting of Congregational Friends Held at Waterloo, N.Y.*, 3–5 June 1850 [Auburn, N.Y.: Henry Oliphant, 1850], 4, 10).

3. Susan R. Doty and Elias J. Doty had signed the Declaration of Sentiments at Seneca Falls in 1848 (Gordon, 1:81–82). 2 Cor. 3:2.

4. "Drink the cup" is from Matt. 20:23. "Newness of life" is from Rom. 6:4. "Thro' much tribulation we enter the kingdom" is from Acts 14:22.

5. The showman Phineas T. Barnum (1810–91) began his career in Philadelphia.

6. Charles Lewis Reason (1818–93) was an abolitionist, a poet, and an educator. At this time he was a professor of belles-lettres, Greek, Latin, and French at Central College.

## To Lucy Stone

Auburn, N.Y. 8 Mo. 6th. 1851—

My dear Lucy Stone

Our frd. M'Kim forwarded to this place, thine of 29th. Ult. It was received 2 days since; but I was too ill at the time, to reply to it—a bilious attack having confined me to my bed. I have not been so unmindful of thy former letter as my silence may have indicated. I consulted early, with the few friends of the Cause, as to the best time & *place* for the next Convention. Opinions were various, as some seemed desirous that Penna. might be decided upon, while Cyrus M. Burleigh & others thought we had not strength for such an undertaking. Should Worcester be decided upon, it is not probable that any of those women who went to that place from Penna. last year, and enjoyed so highly the treat, would go again so soon. I have no expectation of attending one at any place for some time to come. I have been troubled with a constant cough for 6 Mo. past, and now have quite a sore throat, occasioned in part by much speaking. Growing years also admonish me to leave some of the good causes of Reform with younger & fresher hands. These are increasing at the West, and I trust in other parts.

I have corresponded with Amy Post of Rochester, who seemed desirous that we might fix on that place—and that the 10th. of next Month would be a desirable time, as the State Fair will be held there at that time. Some 20 Women met and agreed to propose it to the friends in Mass. and elswhere. They have a fine large Hall, &.c—

They thought at the same time, that many would give Syracuse the preference, where the Convention might be aided by S. J. May. Mrs. Coe of the West was at Buffalo,[1] & would be ready to give her presence and aid, perhaps at either place.

I feel so entirely incompetent to come to any decision, that I must leave the subject in abler hands. I hope Paulina W. Davis' health is improved.

I enclose five dollars, received since the reception of the Proceedings,[2] wh. disappointed many, & met with a slow sale. I have a number of copies still on hand. There may be something to receive from the few sold at the A. S. Office in Philada. If so I will forward the balance on my return home, next week—  I sent some $10 or $22 last Fall. I do not recollect the exact sum.

I have written to the M'Clintocks at Waterloo, relative to the Convention. Our Penna A. S. Mg. will be held about 10th. I think of 10 Mo.

Pray make all allowances for this pitiful scrawl. I rose from bed to write it. May thy youth & health be lengthened out, for every good work—

With much love & all good wishes

Thine    *Lucretia Mott*

I have not seen Elizabeth C. Stanton since being here, but presume the M'Clintocks will confer with her.[3]

I should fear that another Convention held at Worcester so soon would not be so successful, and that our cause would then lose some of [glory?] which was "enough for one day."[4]

ALS MiUc Env: "Lucy Stone, West Brookfield, Mass."

1. Emma Robinson Coe was a woman's rights lecturer in Ohio and Michigan (Gordon, 1:234).

2. *Proceedings of the Woman's Rights Convention, Held at Worcester, October 23d & 24th, 1850* (Boston: Prentiss and Sawyer, 1851).

3. LCM wrote a letter to Stanton similar in content to this one to Stone (Gordon, 1:185–88).

4. Lucy Stone and others issued a call for a convention to "consider the 'Rights, Duties and Relations of Women.'" The convention would be held 15–16 October in Worcester (*Liberator,* 12 September 1851, 147).


## To William Lloyd Garrison and Helen Benson Garrison

Philada. 9 Mo. 11th. 1851—

My dear Wm. L. & Helen Garrison

The prospect of a visit from you both is very pleasant to us; and I write thus early, to assure you that, if a longer time can be allowed us, than merely to attend the Annual Meeting, it will be doubly gratifying to us. Our Kennet friends are desirous of a share of your company. Jas. & self have lately returned from a pleasant excursion through parts of Chester Lancaster & Montgomy. Cos  An earnest wish was expressed by many to have you in their several neighborhoods. If possible to have some Anti S. Mgs. Now is a most important time to sieze on the public mind already aroused, by the enforcement of the atrocious fugitive Slave law, and pour in the truth.[1] There are now willing ears, & that is something, towards reaching the heart & moral sense of this great country.

Our friend Thomas Whitson[2] pointed out a spot in Lancaster Co. commanding an extensive & beautiful view of the extensive Valley & surrounding country, where he said, if notice could be given in time, a very large gathering might be had, to hear Wm. Lloyd Garrison. I promised to write & say so.

The time of the Woman's Convention at Worcester is advertised for the next week after our Meeting. If you contemplate attending that, it will leave little time after ours is over  We would therefore suggest that you come here some time before our Meeting. We shall not have such melting weather much longer probably—the Equinoctial may succeed it—immediately after which will be a good time to ride about & see your friends, and "whatever's to be seen". Need I reassure you that a hearty "All hail" awaits you here, at 338 Arch Street—our new residence.[3]

I have just been reading with great interest a Review of the Woman's Convention of last yr. at Worcester as reported in the Tribune.[4] It is from the Westminster Review, and printed in pamphlet form—a few copies of which were sent to me. I can spare but one to send you which after you have read, you will please direct to Lucy Stone & send it to her. Shall I commission Helen to attend to this, knowing her husband's many cares? I have seen extracts from this Review before—perhaps in the Tribune—maybe in the Liberator. I wish the whole of it could be published in the Liberator. This writer of it was a Mrs. Taylor a widow who has recently married J. S. Mill—one of the conductors of that Review, as you know— Part of it is from his pen. Indeed she says, *he* wrote it—he says, *she* wrote it. Her son is now in this Country—a fine young man.[5] He called here, and furnished me with the few copies I have. You may have read it all, before this. It is very fine.

Hoping soon to hold "communion sweet," face to face, I need not say more now, than kindest remembrances from my Jas. & self to all dear frds.

Lucretia Mott

ALS MB

1. The fourteenth annual meeting of the PASS was to be held in West Chester on 7–9 October 1851 (*Pennsylvania Freeman*, 18 September 1851, 2). The Fugitive Slave Act, requiring Federal officials to return runaway slaves to their owners, would become law on 18 September. At the PASS meeting the following year, LCM would characterize the law as producing "evils" that "are infinite. . . . Is it not better to speak of evil as evil, not deducing from it any consequences which do not strictly belong to it? Does it not tend to weaken our abhorrence of wrong? There is nothing easier than to quote texts of Scriptures in favor of any theory, as every sect supports its faith by such texts. I am not willing to admit that Harriet Beecher Stowe was moved to write Uncle Tom's Cabin by that law; if she says so, I think she mistakes the influences which moved her. I believe, rather that it has been the moral sentiments and truths promulgated by the Liberator, the National Era, and the public discussion of the subject, upon her pure mind, exciting it to feel for the oppressed" (*Pennsylvania Freeman*, 6 November 1852, 2).

2. Thomas Whitson (1796–1864), a founder of the AASS and a Quaker, operated a station on the Underground Railroad in Lancaster County (*WLG*, 4:440).

3. LCM and JM had moved in January 1851 when JM had retired from the wool business (Bacon, 139–40).

4. The Worcester Woman's Rights Convention, held 23–24 October 1850 (reported in the *New York Tribune*, 25 October 1850, 5, 26 October 1850, 5–6), provided the information for an article, "The Enfranchisement of Women," by Harriet Taylor Mill (1807–58) that appeared in the July 1851 issue of the *Westminster Review* and was reprinted in the *New York Tribune* (18 July 1851, 5–6). In her piece Mill praised the work of the convention, at which LCM had spoken. Mill challenged the custom that excluded women from political life and countered objections to women's full participation in it, stating that women were indeed the intellectual equals of men.

5. Harriet Taylor Mill's essay is included in *Dissertations and Discussions* by the English philosopher John Stuart Mill (1806–73) (London: J. W. Parker, 1859, 2:411–49). In his preface to the essay, Mill states that he acted only as "editor and amanuensis" of his wife's work; scholars since then have hotly debated this claim (see, e.g., F. A. Hayek, *John*

*Stuart Mill and Harriet Taylor: Their Correspondence and Subsequent Marriage* [London: Routledge, 1951], 166; Alice S. Rossi, *Essays on Sex Equality: John Stuart Mill and Harriet Taylor Mill* [Chicago: University of Chicago, 1970], 41–45, 93; see also LCM to Elizabeth Cady Stanton, 11 September 1851, and Gordon, 1:185–88). Harriet Taylor Mill's son was Herbert Taylor (b. 1827), a London businessman.

## To Elizabeth Oakes Smith[1]

Philada. 2 Mo. 23rd. 1852—— ——

My dear Friend E. Oakes Smith

Thy candid and friendly letter of 15th. Inst. was duly received, and its contents more particularly noted, than these several days' delay in answering would indicate. We were apprised of thy intention of delivering thy Lectures in this City, by letters from H: K. Hunt,[2] and my cousin Phebe Gardner of Nantucket. Our mutual friend Oliver Johnson too, I found was in correspondence with thee on the subject. Elizabeth Townsend called on me to say she had invited thee to be her guest, altho' she felt at the same time that her interest in the cause of Woman's elevation, was not sufficient to lead to any active effort to promote the object of thy visit. I hope however some zeal may be enkindled in her, by thy coming. She might have influence among a class of our Citizens, who would not be called out, by an appeal from the ultraists, who generally have to take the lead in every reformatory movement. I urged her to notify & consult some of our conservative women—that, judging from the notice of thy lectures in the N Bedford Paper, & other sources, thou would be likely to suit this class. I also called upon a few such as do not usually attend our Meetings, & told them my wish to keep back, & let them go forward, as more likely to secure for thee such hearers as would be most profited by thy appeals.

Thou seems prepared for the difference thou wilt find in Philada., as compared with our Eastern Cities, tho' not so much, as thou supposes, from more conservatism here, as from the lack of intellectual education, combined with moral culture, to prepare the mind to appreciate all that is enjoyed in New England. We are improving however, and thou may find us better, than we have been represented.

The time fixed for thy visit here, 1st. of Next Mo—as far as we can judge, will be favorable for thy Lectures. We may then succeed in getting Subsribers to the proposed Paper—The Egeria.[3] The name, requiring an explanation, will not suit our plain matter-of-fact people, so well as "Woman's Advocate" or some other explicit title, carrying its meaning with it to *common* minds—for, as formerly, it is only these who hear truth gladly.

Some of our Penna. Women, who attended the Worcester Convention, are preparing a Call for a State Convention, to be held at West Chester some time this Spring.[4] We shall hear more of this after thy visit.

It is gratifying as well as encouraging, that the Author of 'Woman and her Needs' feels constrained to lift up her *voice* also in behalf of her Sex.[5] Even tho' not ultra, may that voice wax louder & louder, until every obstacle to Woman's entire enfranchisement shall be removed out of the way.

While we would give no just cause of the charge of "a few embittered, uneasy women," and while we would wish to avoid all angry opposition or ridicule, we must at the same time enter the ranks, prepared to "endure hardness as good soldiers";[6]—and not disclaim the needful antagonism which a faithful presentation of Womans wrongs imposes upon us.

We hail thy coming among us, as among the hopeful signs of the times. The laborers in an unpopular yet common cause cannot feel as strangers.

Very sincerely

thy radical frd.    *Lucretia Mott*

ALS NjP

1. Elizabeth Oakes Smith (1806–93), a woman's rights activist and a writer originally from Maine, had moved to New York City in 1839. She would give a lecture in West Chester on 2 April 1852, accompanied by LCM, and would deliver a series of lectures entitled "Manhood," "Womanhood," and "Humanity" on 6, 8, and 10 April in Philadelphia (*Pennsylvania Freeman,* 1 April 1852, 54, 55).

2. Harriot Kezia Hunt (1805–75), a Boston physician and reformer, had attended her first woman's rights convention in Worcester in 1850.

3. *Egeria* refers to a female advisor or companion. This journal was never published, but Smith would later write for *Una,* a journal begun by Paulina Wright Davis in 1853.

4. LCM (serving as a vice president) and Dr. Hannah E. Longshore of Philadelphia were among the Philadelphians attending the convention in Worcester (*Liberator,* 24 October 1851, 170). The West Chester Woman's Rights Convention would take place on 2–3 June (*Liberator,* 14 May 1852, 79).

5. Smith's *Woman and Her Needs* (New York: Fowler and Wells) had been published in 1851.

6. 2 Tim. 2:3.

## To Nathaniel Barney

Philada. 3 Mo. 19th. 1852

My dear Nathaniel

The sight of thy well-known hand once more in letter directed to me, was welcome—thy continued remembrance of us, truly grateful—especially at such an interesting time and occasion, as that you have just enjoyed. Edwd & Anna M. Hopper as well as our other children appreciate dear Sarah's kindly invitation to them. Of course it was not expected, at this inclement season that they or we would avail ourselves of it, & be present with you. My first impulse was to write a "regret" directly to Alanson & Sarah;[1] but I have to confess, to an instinctive shrinking from penning anything to be read by other than 'own folks', who can make allowance for all defects. Pretty note-paper 'lines' are less in *my line,* than hurried scraps, such as cousin Phebe G—can testify to; and in one of which I sent a message to the bride & groom, as well as to their Parents, which I hope they will entertain.

Thou can hardly conceive the dread I have of answerg. the letters of invitation recd. from Ohio, Western N.Y., Mass., & other places, to attend A. S. & Wom. Conventions; knowing the custom of publishing such answers. When I can prevail on my husband to do it for me, I am happy. So has it ever been, in reference to public speaking. While desirous to "walk worthy the vocation", &.c—it has been a constant 'cross', *without* "despising the shame".[2] And now that nearly threescore years are mine, the prospect of resting, even tho' *not* 'on laurels', is delightful. I was admonished, years ago, in hearg. Ruth Spencer[3] preach after her voice was failing her, that at 60 it would be time for me to give place to the younger. Now that so many able women are in the field, the "gift" may be yielded to them without regret, in full faith that they will "do greater things." Not just in the Quaker field, for, be it acknowledged with humility, few there, whose gifts I would covet; but without the sectarian enclosure, womans mind, as well as powers of speaking *aloud,* will command respect & audience.

We are expecting E. Oakes Smith here next week, to deliver her course of lectures. Mary Ann Johnson too, is instructing classes here & in the country around on Physiology.[4] Paulina Wright, (now Davis) did much for woman in that way. She is now in this City, & I have just engaged a visit from her & her frd. 'Mrs.' Dr. Clark a graduate from Cleveland—also Jas. B. Richards & wife who are here from Boston trying to open an Asylum for "weak-minded" children. Marcus Spring & Reba. & Dr. Earle, just arrived from Cuba are to be of our party, & a cousin Rushmore (orthodox) from L. I.—[5] These, with our several families & cousins, make a party of 30 about; and after preparg. a little for them, I sit down to *thee* awhile. Part of our compy. bidden will be prevented by the sad death of Rebecca (Kite) Brown—Nathanl.'s wife. He is br. to our nephews George & Walter—& cousin to Kate Thornton who is here from N. Bedford, & has enjoyed so much going among her friends, as well as given them pleasure. This death will cast a deep shade, for the present. Rebecca has left 2 little childn. the younger— a yr old— She was taken only a few days since with erysipelas—an epidemic here, & died this afternoon. They had lately bought a handsome house in 9th St & her Mother lived with them—she an only daughr.—[6] These particulars are in part for Aunt Phebe Hussey, to whom please communicate.

If our sympathy could have relieved thy soreness, thou would not have suffered so long. We have hoped from time to time as Coz. Phebe G's letters have been received, that they would report thee better.

Edward interested us with the condition of thy leg, when last here. Jas. was wondering if thou knew the good effects of bandaging—from the foot-up— Some severe flesh wounds & sores have been healed by this means. Our Father Mott suffered for years with a 'breaking out' on his leg. Do try change of air, &

come with Eliza, & yr children & make us a visit. It is quite time you should "know *our* State & see how *we* do." Cold as has been our past winter, and late as our Spring is threatening, the grass is coming up beautifully green, & the willows are putting forth—crocuses too are in bloom. Our children are already preparing to go out to their farms—[7]

Thou asks a question, in reference to the marriage ceremony, which we could answer *for ourselves,* better than we may do for thee. Well then, to me there is great beauty, in the parties asking neither ministerial, nor *magisterial* aid, but in the presence of chosen friends announcing their reciprocal affection, when any present, feeling a word of encouragement, may give utterance to it. Such marriages are legal here performed in private houses. *Our* (Hicksite) Mg. houses are no longer resorted to on such occasions. Your law may require some official aid—if so I should greatly prefer an enlightened "dear frd. Forman" to "Geo Cobb,"[8] provided that part of the *church* marriage, promise, of *obedience on the part of the wife,* were omitted. I could never submit to that. Years ago I remember objecting to a charge against one of our members at 12th St. (Orthodox) Mg of violating our testimony for a free gospel ministry, by employing a clergyman in her marriage. It always has seemed a forced construction of our testimony; & I have often since that time so expressed it, when complaints are brought forward in that way. Our Discipline does not require so strict a construction, altho long custom seems to sanction it. I hope we shall hear that thou yielded to the *reasonable* desire—or choice of the young people—especially [*ms. damaged*] was on her Side. I can hardly imagine it so great a sacrifice as it appeared to thee. Our consciences are so easily moulded by the church, or religious order of our election, that it takes years of liberal thinking to free us from the traditions we receive. What feeble steps have yet been taken from Popery to Protestantism! Our Ecclesiastics, be they Bishops or Quaker Elders, have still far too much sway. Convents we have yet, with high walls, whose inmates having taken the veil, dare not give range to their free-born spirit, now so miserably cramped, & shrouded.

Little is there among us, in the meeting line worth hearing. Our movements are rather retrograde than progressive. Jas. Martin viewing the Society from another stand-point, may have given thee a different account. He is a man of kind, good feelings but sect-bound, therefore knows not what he does. So with very many of our Friends— Priscilla Cadwalader is still poorly at Frankford not having completed her family visits, in Green St. Meeting. She will then perform a similar service at Cherry Street— She has not kept pace with the age— her preaching is of the older school—and has not the "newness of life" of 25 yrs. ago. She avoids parties however, & tries to "follow peace with all men".[9]

At 12th. St. Mo. Mg. last 4th. day, tell aunt P., Hannah Beasley 'opened a concern' to accompany the English Friend Bayes in her travels. Some Wilbur party spirit was shewn & the subject was laid over for consideratn. next Month. "No flesh was glory."[10]

Thou asks after my health. It is pretty good now—only occasional suffering with dyspepsia. I have been out in all weather the past winter, & feel none
the worse for it. Jas. has renewed his youth save in his 'snowy summit'. He is
finely & sends love unmeasured—  Our childn. also to yours—  Now, dear
Nathl., let us hear from thee soon again—  Thine in undiminished affection

                                                                      AL MNHi

1. Nathaniel Barney's daughter, Sarah Barney, had married Alanson Swain (1818–77)
on 17 March 1852 (MNHi records).
2. Eph. 4:1; Heb. 12:2.
3. Ruth Spencer, an associate of Jemima Wilkinson, a former Quaker from Rhode Island, established her own religious colony in western New York.
4. Mary Ann Johnson (1808–72), a reformer, a prison matron, and a lecturer on anatomy and physiology, had married Oliver Johnson in 1832 (*WLG*, 4:251). She gave a series of lectures in the Philadelphia area in March 1852 (*Pennsylvania Freeman*, 4 March
1852, 39, 18 March 1852, 47).
5. James Bardwell Richards (1817–86) devoted his life to the study of mental retarda-
tion. In 1848 he had started the first state school for the mentally retarded in Boston
(*WLG*, 3:554). Marcus Spring (1810–74) and Rebecca Spring (1811–1911), Quaker philan-
thropists and abolitionists, founded the Raritan Bay Union, a communitarian experiment in New Jersey (Gordon, 1:216). The Springs were traveling with Rebecca's cousin
Dr. Pliny Earle (1809–92), a Massachusetts physician and expert on the mentally ill,
through the Carolinas and to Cuba (*Memoirs of Pliny Earle, M.D.,* ed. Franklin B. San-
born [Boston: Damrell and Upham, 1898], 190). "Cousin Rushmore" is Amy Willis Rushmore (1797–1881), who was married to Townsend Rushmore (1792–1870).
6. Rebecca Kite Brown (b. 1814), daughter of the Philadelphia printer Thomas Kite and
Edith Kite (c. 1778–1861), had died on 19 March 1852. She and her husband, Nathaniel
Brown, Orthodox Quakers, had two children, Mary Anna Brown (b. 1849) and Thomas
Brown (b. 1851). Kate Thornton would marry (c. 1854) the Auburn merchant John Hoskin, who had moved to Philadelphia in 1852. A "John Hoskins" is listed as a merchant
in the 1855 Philadelphia City Directory (MCW to LCM, 26 February 1852, 20 February
1854, MNS).
7. In 1851 Thomas Mott and Edward Davis had bought Oak Farm in Chelten Hills,
north of Philadelphia (Bacon, 140).
8. Reverend J. G. Forman was an antislavery minister in Nantucket. George Cobb was
the clerk of the judicial courts in Nantucket (*Liberator,* 23 July 1852, 118, 30 July 1852, 121;
Nantucket Atheneum records).
9. Rom. 6:4; Heb. 12:14.
10. LCM is adapting 1 Cor. 1:29: "That no flesh should glory in his presence."

## To George Combe

                                                      Philada. 5 Mo. 21st 1852—

My dear George Combe
    Again I take the liberty to introduce to thy notice a friend of ours—Clin-
ton Gillingham.[1] He has been the principal Teacher in our 'Friends' Central
School, and has delivered lectures on various scientific subjects. His chief ob-

ject in going abroad is to visit schools & examine into the state of Education in Europe. We know of no one who can give him more or better information than thyself. He is familiar with thy exertions in behalf of secular education in your Country.

We have been much interested lately, in hearing some account of the successful labors of a Mr. Ellis of London, (a friend of thine we are told,) in establishg schools of the right kind.[2] A German, now residing in London—a partner of Herbert Taylor I forget his name, gave us this account. If thou wilt give Clinton G. an introduction to this Mr. Ellis, it may be of some value to him.

We have not yet recd. the last Report of yr Schools—[3] We will gladly pay any expense of transmitg them—   I cannot answer thy enquiry—what is charged on a pamphlet—Jas. can tell—  Those thou hast so kindly sent us, have generally been by private hand—

Thine & Cecilia's last acceptable letter, dated Richmond—Lodge—Ireland— I have never acknowledged. The review of my efforts for Woman's enfranchisement, was read with much interest, as well as some amusement—that you should seem to disclaim, what you *thought* I assumed & urged for my sex—& then conclude with an admission of all I have asked—namely that "the laws & customs of society shd. leave the door open" for such employments & stations as women of intelligence were fitted for—& that their "education should embrace every kind of knowledge calculated to render them intelligent & useful, & every sphere opened to them wh. they are qualified to fill with pleasure & advantage to themselves"—& others—  This would satisfy us entirely. As to the turmoil of political life, *as it is,* or any preparation for the exercise of a government by physical force, I ever distinctly avow a decided & conscientious opposition to it—indeed for men as well as for women—  Still I can but feel the force of the claim of the *right* of suffrage for our sex equally with that of men—and that "taxation without representation" is as unjust to woman as to man.

Thou told me once, not to undervalue myself or my powers—  Now, please to give the same good advice to thy Cecilia. She disparages herself in the comparison she makes. I have been accustomed to *look up* to her, & I cannot have her gratify my Love of Approbation at her own expense—

Did you read that fine article in the Westminster Review of last year?—I dont recollect the number, on our Worcester Convention—written mainly by Mrs. Taylor—now Mrs. Mill—  It is one of the best essays on Woman's Rights that I have seen.

The Conventions & public Mgs. on this Subject have done great good. The public mind is rapidly preparing for Woman's comg. forth in the exercise of her powers, as Physicians—Preachers &.c—  Several graduates of Medicine have entered with promise of Success their appropriate field—  Schools of Design for Women are multiplying in our Country, and in various profitable employments—as artists—takg Daguerres, &.c. women are succeeding admirably.

It is no new thing for the most popular novel-writers to be women—& yet we have hailed, as something extraordinary, the production of "Uncle Tom's Cabin" by Harriet Beecher Stowe—coming as it has, immediately after the passage & execution of the atrocious Fugitive Slave law—and so eagerly seized & read by all classes of Society—many hundred copies finding their way to the South, where our Anti S. Papers are entirely excluded— This unprecedented demand for an American Work—on such a subject—& by a Woman too, is rather gratifying—50.000 copies printed & nearly all sold, yielding her $10.000—[4]

We look upon this as forming an important epoch in Anti-S. history. We have also some new laborers in the field, as public speakers, from whom we hope much. The Presses are more disposed to treat the Abolitionists with fairness & to report our Proceedings, without so much caricature.

We were gratified & greatly obliged by thy letter of introduction to Kossuth's friends & escorts—[5] We saw only Madam Pulszkey & one of the Captains—not her husband, who remained in N York, while they were here. Thy letter was promptly sent to us, & we as promptly went to see them. The call was returned by Madam P., accepting an invitn. for herself & Madam Kossuth to tea with a Select Compy— All were in trim to receive them & eager with expectatn—our son had gone to wait on them, when one of their gent. an intelligt German called with "a regret"— We soon found that there had been some interference of the miserable committee of the City Councils, who had them in charge, to prevent their visiting us—for Anti Slavery reasons.[6] This Captn. remained some time talking in German with our nephew Ellis Yarnall. The next day Madam P. called again, & made all the apology she could— She was obliged also, in the same way to break an engagt.—made at her own request, to visit the Penitentiary— She told my husband that she wished to go in a more private way than with all their attendts.—& *from what Mr. Combe* had told her, she thot. we shd. view subjects somewhat alike.

I regretted much that we were thus deprived of their Society— She invited us to their eveg. party & some of our younger members accepted & went with her afterwd. to one of Kossuth's Mgs & were much gratified with hearg. him.[7] Our children all were delighted with Mrs. Pulszky & it appeared to be mutual—

Such of your friends as time still spares to us, are in usual health— Anne D. Morrison has kept herself in much seclusion since the death of her husband, until lately, she has received into her family a German teacher & his wife & children— wh. seems to give her something worth living for— She lately made us a pleasant visit in co. with Elizh. Oakes Smith, who delivered a course of lectures in our City— We talked of you & affectn. remembrs., were entrusted to me to forward you— The widow of our still lamented Dr. Parrish died about a year since—[8] Our own family remain without further sad breaches by death— Our youngest daughter is expecting to leave us after awhile—or rather to bring to us another—to claim sonship— Our Family Community works admirably—& our childn. are delighted with their summer residences—as farmers—[9]

Would that we could meet you once more in this lower world!

ever most affecy    L. Mott—

My husbands best regards to thee & Cecilia— He mailed the letter to the young man in Virginia—but was afraid the direction was not sufficiently explicit to reach him.

ALS GBNLS

1. Clinton Gillingham (1824–64) was a Hicksite Quaker.

2. William Ellis (1800–1881) had founded several schools emphasizing "political economy" for working-class children (George Combe to LCM, 15 November 1852, GBNLS).

3. Combe had issued a series of pamphlets advocating secular education (see LCM to George Combe and Cecilia Combe, 10 September 1848, above).

4. Originally serialized in the antislavery newspaper the *National Era,* the influential novel by Stowe (1811–96) had been published on 20 March 1852. In remarks later that year, at the PASS meeting of 15 December, LCM warned her colleagues against overemphasizing the novel's influence: "We have much to do yet. . . . The number of slaves is still increasing, and the alarmed slave holders are laboring with unabated zeal to secure new power and fresh markets for their slaves" (*Pennsylvania Freeman,* 23 December 1852, 2).

5. Louis (Lajos) Kossuth (1802–94), a Hungarian political reformer, had led his country's drive for independence from Austria in 1848. After being driven out of Hungary in 1849, he embarked on a tour of Great Britain and the United States. His wife, Terezia Moszlenyi Kossuth (d. 1863), a Hungarian writer, Francis (or Ferencz) Pulszky (1814–97), and Pulszky's wife, Terezia Walder Pulszky (1819–66), were among those accompanying him on his tour (Bonnie Anderson, *Joyous Greetings: The First International Women's Movement, 1830–1860* [New York: Oxford University Press, 2000], 5). In his 15 November letter, Combe replied that he was sorry that Madame Pulszky and Kossuth "disappointed you" (GBNLS).

6. In a December 1863 address to the AASS in Philadelphia, LCM recalled the ostracism she and her family had experienced in 1852: "When Madam PULSKY and her friends came, and we were asked to go with men on a visit to the Penitentiary, and the carriage was at the door, word came that they were discouraged from coming, because we were Abolitionists!" (*Sermons,* 264).

7. Kossuth had delivered a series of lectures in Philadelphia on 23–27 December (*New York Times,* 25 December 1851, 1, 27 December 1851, 1).

8. Susanna Cox Parrish (1788–1851) was the widow of Dr. Joseph Parrish.

9. MML would marry George Lord in 1853. In her letter of 27 March 1851 (GBNLS), LCM informed Combe of her and JM's recent purchase of a farm outside Philadelphia on the York Road.


# To Adeline Roberts[1]

Philada. 7 Mo. 5th. 1852

My dear Friend Adeline Roberts

Again I am under the necessity of answering thy letter of 26th. Ult. in the negative.

While I duly appreciate the kindly regards of the Salem Fem. A. S. Socy. in repeatedly extending the invitation to me, to address their public Meetings, circumstances as yet do not favor my availing myself of their invitations.[2]

My husband & self expect to be absent from home during the latter part of the Summer; & early in the Fall, the Woman's Convention in Syracuse will probably call me thither, which will occupy as much of my time as I shall be able to spare from other duties.[3]

I am pleased to see that your State has the able services of Sally Holly.[4] I have great hope of these new Recruits, who have youth on their side, while some of us—older warriors may begin to retire from the field, and give place to them. We hope to have the stirring labors of Sally Holly in this State before many months.

An interesting Anti Slavery Meeting was held at Norristown yesterday—in which Oliver Johnson Samuel Aaron, B. Rush Plumly & several others took part. We made the 4th. of July the occasion for calling this Meeting, and had *our* Declaration read, as well as those stirring & appropriate lines of J. G. Whittiers "What, Ho! Our Country men in chains?"[5]

We are preparing for an A. S. pic nic for the 1st. of Aug. about 20 miles from the City. Also are we beginning already, as you in Salem are, to create interest for our October Mg— We hope to have Garrison with us at that time.[6] Would it not be well for some of your Society to visit and *address* our Mgs. on that occasion? We shd. in that way become personal friends, as well as mutually interested for the crushed & bleeding Slave.

My husband was out of the City, & I waited his return, to confer with him, before answering thy letter, which accounts for the few days' delay.

I trust you will succeed in finding an able advocate, than would be

Your Sincere friend
*Lucretia Mott*

ALS MSaE

1. Adeline Roberts (d. 1904) was a schoolteacher and the corresponding secretary of the Salem (Mass.) Female Anti-Slavery Society (*WLG*, 3:588).

2. LCM turned down invitations from the Salem Female Anti-Slavery Society, founded in 1834, in letters of 19 September 1850 (MSaE), 8 September 1851 (Haverford College Library, Haverford, Pa.), 12 August 1853 (MSaE), and 15 September 1855 (MSaE). On the society, see Julie Roy Jeffrey, *The Great Silent Army of Abolitionism: Ordinary Women in the Antislavery Movement* (Chapel Hill: University of North Carolina Press, 1998), 102–5.

3. The Syracuse Woman's Rights Convention would meet on 8–10 September (see also LCM to Lucy Stone, 16 August 1852, below).

4. Sallie Holley (1818–93), the daughter of the Rochester, New York, abolitionist Myron Holley, had become an antislavery lecturer and agent of the AASS upon her graduation from Oberlin in 1851. Holley would speak before the Salem Female Anti-Slavery Society on 10 October (*Liberator*, 1 October 1852, 159).

5. LCM had spoken at the antislavery meeting held on 4 July 1852 in Norristown. Sam-

uel Aaron (1800–1865) was a Pennsylvania educator and Baptist minister (*WLG*, 4:374). The *Pennsylvania Freeman* reported that the speakers "took a most encouraging view of the present condition and prospects of the cause, predicting for it a rapid progress and sure triumph in spite of all the machinations of its foes, whether in Church or in State" (10 July 1852, 111). LCM is quoting from "Expostulation," which Whittier wrote after hearing Charles Follen speak in 1834 (*Complete Poetical Works of John Greenleaf Whittier*, ed. Horace E. Scudder [New York: Houghton Mifflin, 1894], 267).

6. When the PASS held its anniversary celebration of West Indian emancipation on 31 July at Spring Hill, in Montgomery County, JM acted as president and "Lucretia Mott made a brief but interesting address" (*Pennsylvania Freeman*, 7 August 1852, 124). Garrison would attend when the PASS held its annual meeting on 25–27 October in West Chester (*NASS*, 7 October 1852, 79; see also LCM to William Lloyd Garrison and Helen Benson Garrison, 31 August 1852, below; Garrison to J. Miller McKim, 18 July 1852, *WLG*, 4:202).


## To Lucy Stone

Philada 8 Mo. 16th. 1852

My dear Lucy Stone

Thine of 12th. Inst. is before me— I agree with thee that the subject of forming a National Society should be duly considered, before coming to any conclusion. The object to be attained may be as fully answered by Conventions in different parts of the Country, as by a more settled organization. Congregational independence will thus be preserved, and the seeds of dissolution be less likely to be sown.

Although the Call does not state the object agreeably to the decision of the Committee, yet the subject will be open for discussion, and we can go with minds prepared to receive the aguments on both sides, and by giving them due weight we may come to a wise conclusion.[1]

We have great reason to take courage, in the successful efforts made thus far. It has been my privilege to attend four Conventions on the subject of Woman's enfranchisement— The 1st at Seneca Falls, one soon after at Rochester, the first held at Worcester, and the late one at West Chester. These have all been conducted with dignity & propriety; and considering the ignorance of Woman, as to conducting public meetings, few mistakes have been made, & very little occured of which we need be ashamed. Beside these gatherings how many laborers have entered the field—lecturing on the subject, in some of our Eastern States, as well as in Ohio, Indiana and Michigan— And the Conventions in Salem, Ohio too were altogether creditable to those engaged in them.

May the approaching gathering at Syracuse be not less interesting, & full of promise, than the others! Use thy influence to induce many of our good New England men, as well as women to attend. Try to have some *short* addresses sent by some who cannot attend in person. Paulina W. Davis will go, will she not? Where is Antoinette Brown now? May we depend upon her presence? Will Wm. H. Channing be there? And Wendell Philips? Indeed we shall want "chief men, a great multitude, and, honorable Women not a few."[2] William L. Garrison has promised to come on here to our State Anti-S. Mg—in the 10 Mo—but let us hope that he & Helen also will be able to go to Syracuse first. We are anticipating the long-talked-of visit from Helen to us this Fall, and I shall come home from my sister's at Auburn, early enough after the Syracuse Mg—to receive them both at our house, and thee too, with much pleasure, if thou wilt come. I have have said thus much, so that if thou should be in Boston & see our friends there, before I write to them more directly, thou may do us the favor to tell them of our wish & hope.

But to the Convention—Saml. J. May will of course be active there—and perhaps E. Oakes Smith. I have heard nothing of her movements lately. It wd. be well to write to her  P. W. Davis is in correspondence with her, I think. The M'Clintocks & Elizh. Stanton, if she can be present, will be a host. Yes, I expect to be there, with my husband; & I mean to do & say all that I can, & that I am qualified for, to help forward the cause of Woman—but as to presiding, that is something I *cannot do,* with any sort of ability. And while there are so many in younger life, every way qualified for the position & who have in addition more of the graces & manner of polished Society, than falls to the lot of the born & bred Quaker, it would be a sad "blunder at the outset," to place me *out of my sphere.* We shall not yet form a National Socy—I presume—   Among all our Presidents, none has given greater satisfaction than Mary Anne Johnson at West Chester.[3] I know not yet that she expects to go to Syracuse—   If she does we shd. do well to place her in that position. P. W. Davis filled the Office well, I [*ms. damaged*] at [Wor]cester. I should be satisfied to have her [again?]. Her opening speech need not be so long as then—   We have less need now of long addresses—   Short & to the point are better. Some forcible Resolutions, we shall depend upon our New Eng. frds. taking with them. Our West Chester Proceedings are out, & I hope before this, a parcel has been sent to New York & Boston. I saw a package, directed to H. K. Hunt, at the Anti S. Office. Oliver Johnson is now in Ohio, & J. M. M'Kim in Chester Co—   So there may have been some delay. My husband & self too have been out of town a good deal and we expect to leave home the last of this week for a Month—   Our E. M. Davis & Maria, & our Martha go to Europe for a few months, & we go to Western N. York— Letters to us can be directed to Auburn, N. Y—care of David Wright Esq.—

I early forwarded to Fowler & Wells—or rather some time in the Spring $16—since which, $3—   they sent receipts for these sums, & credited the Accot.—   They have sent another parcel of the Reports lately—none of which have been sold—   I sent 3 Copies to England lately by a young man who wanted an excuse for calling on Mary Howitt[4] Harriet Martineau &.c—

This is a long scrawl

affecy.—   *L. Mott*

ALS DLC-Blackwell Env: "Lucy Stone, West Brookfield, Mass."

1. The call for the convention in Syracuse on 8–10 September 1852 read: "The time has come not only for the examination and discussion of Woman's social, civil and religious rights, but also for a thorough and efficient organization—a well-digested plan of operation, whereby these social rights, for which our fathers fought, bled and died, may be secured, and enjoyed by us" (*Liberator,* 6 August 1852, 127).

2. Antoinette L. Brown (1825–1921) was a Congregational and Unitarian minister, author, and lecturer. LCM is adapting Acts 17:4: "Of the chief women, not a few."

3. Despite her reluctance to serve, LCM was elected president of the Syracuse convention (*Liberator,* 17 September 1852, 151). In West Chester, President Mary Ann Johnson laid out the demands of that convention in a speech on 2 June: "What then, is the substance of our demand? I answer: We demand for women equal freedom with her brother to raise her voice and exert her influence directly for the removal of all evils that afflict the race; and that she be permitted to do this in the manner dictated by her own sense of propriety and justice." Johnson also asked for educational equality, professional opportunity, and economic independence for women (*Pennsylvania Freeman,* 12 June 1852, 94).

4. Mary Howitt (1799–1888), a Quaker poet and translator of Scandinavian literature, was married to William Howitt.


## To John Ketcham and Rebecca Ketcham

Auburn N. Y. 8 Mo. 30th. 1852

My dear John & Rebecca Ketcham

We are, I know, very neglectful, not to have written to you before leaving home— —the more so, as the last letter contained some money, which should have been acknowledged. Until it came, I did not know that James had sent a Circular to you. Those who have to bear so large a part in the support of the Standard, & the American Society's Mgs. ought not to be *dunned* for a local Paper. It all goes to the same cause however, and the success of our Appeals has been a great help, drained as we were by Christiana trials, & other demands.[1]

The Article sent from W. L. G's pen—Kossuth & Jesus had been already published, not only in the Freeman, but in a separate sheet, & widely circulated—so that it was not thot. best to re-print it. How faithful has W. L. G. ever been to the short-comers! Wendell Phillips too & Edmund Quincy were not behind in marking the inconsistency of the great Hungarian's course. We have been looking for him to speak out more plainly after leaving our Country. His last speech in New York—on behalf of his Mother & Sisters, abounded in useful hints. It was a beautiful production on the Future of this Country—calculated to check its vainglory, & admonishing the boastful, by presenting to view the downfall of other Republics.[2]

The sorrow we felt on account of his timid course of expediency was turned into joy, by the unparralled success of Uncle Tom's Cabin, followed too by the White Slave,[3] which we hope will also be extensively read. The dramatizing of Uncle Tom's Cabin is another good sign of the times. While the enemies of the

Abolitionists are continually charging them with havg. put back the Slave's redemption some 50 years, scarce 20 yrs. of their labor have aroused this slum-
bering Nation to a consideration of its accumulated wrongs—and now the bal-
ads of the North are in favor of the despised Ethiopian—at least they are
changing in their tone & tune, and a tenderness & pathos marks them now, far
different from the old "jump Jim Crow"—    So that whether Freedom be
preached in Novel or Song, therein we do rejoice, yea & will rejoice.

The woven threads of Priestcraft, & of Political demagogueism, by which
they essay to hold back the Express train of Reform are as the green withs to
Sampson's strength. A short time ago we were comforted, as we passed over this
Jordan, with our staff, that *one* "old man eloquent" [*John Quincy Adams*], lifted up his voice among the people—    Now, they are many, who, "before all Israel & the Sun,"[4] proclaim the name of Liberty, "without concealment & without compromise—"

Not alone the *black* Slaves enfranchisement do we seek, but that of Woman
is demanded, at the East & at the West. So successful have the Conventions been
thus far, that we hail the approaching Gathering at Syracuse, and hope very many
of our liberal friends will be there to take part. How is it with you? And cousin
Henry & Catharine Willis and that nice Orthodox cousin of hers, who was in
Philada.? And our valiants Joseph & Mary Post, they can so well attend all the
nice Meetings, that they ought to be there. As to our kind cousins John & Mary
W. they are *Elders* now, of a behind-the-age Organization  We must leave
them—for "behold I say unto you, they have their reward"![5]

What a divided State this said Organization is in! No corner of our Heritage that is not suffering under a blighting, Sectarian Conservatism. You are
aware that our Yearly Mg. confirmed the Intolerance of the Western Qr.—& that
in consequence a real separation is in progress. Jas. & self attended the late Qy.
Mg. of the Liberals, which was held to satisfaction—the small house at Kennett
Square filled. They have not yet decided what distinctive title to bear.[6] They will
doubtless be in sympathy & correspondence with the Congregational Frds. of
Waterloo—the coming Yearly at Salem Ohio—the Green Plain & other Con-
vocations of a similar character. It does not yet appear that the separatn. will be
more than local, in our Yearly Mg—    Time however may reveal a wide-spread
division—for how can we walk much longer together unless we be agreed, more
than for 10 years past? "When ye shall see Jerusalem is compassed about with
armies, then know that the time of desolation draweth thereof is nigh."[7]

John asked months ago for some information, as to spiritual manifestations.
He ought to have been answered before now. As James has paid much more
attention to the subject, than I have, he can better satisfy you. I agree with John,
that the subject ought not to be treated with ridicule, or as wilful deception—
but it requires more faith than I can command, to receive it as direct communion with the departed. There is a grossness about it, not suited to the imagined
aerial State of the "just made perfect." Still the developements are wonderful,

& some of them of an enlightened character. Jas attended a circle for 10 weeks last winter, & was much interested. I have never witnessed anythg. of the kind. Is there not reason to fear the effects of such frequent *reveries,* on Isaac Post's mind? A *Mrs.* Taft of Mass. has lately become quite insane, from that cause.

The information you give from time to time of those dear to us, in your neighbd. is very acceptable. Since the ever-to-be-lamented separation from our well beloved Phebe P. we less frequently hear of the several members of the family circle I meant to have written a note to dear Cathe. Willis by the return of her cousin Rachel Rushmore,[8] with whom we were pleased but she went home without our knowing it. Perhaps it will now do to refer her to this letter, as I have some 5 or 6 unanswered ones that I have resolved to acknowledge while here.

We should be very glad to see coz Henry & Cathe. [*Willis*] in Philada. this Fall—at our Annual Mg at West Chester  Why will not you too plan to be there—& Jos. & Mary—

Rebecca's addition was acceptable. We were glad to hear from your children, as well as from our aged cousin Rachel Willis—[9] The pincushions often remind us of her and of Rebecca's kindness in sending us so many—  She asks if there were enough for all—  Yes, & several of their work-baskets are furnished with them—& the larger ones on the bureaus. The little M'Kims were pleased to be remembered in that way. Their little Charlie has had small pox very thickly covered—  Sarah cured him, without a physician—by the use of water—& watchg him closely—followg his instincts.

Cathe. Willis may not have heard that Priscilla Townsend fell & broke her arm, in comg. out of the bath room. Elizh. was on a visit to Lynn & to Chs. Burleighs, & was sent for home—her Mother was doing well when we left P.

We are just going to Waterloo to stay till tomorw.—  This is 3rd day—31st  I am in great haste—  I was glad of the little mention of poor dear Sarah Hallock[10] I saw a letter of hers to Miller McKim & my heart bled for her—  I wanted to write her my sympathy—but in such a bereavement, words of condolence are of so little avail!

affecy    L Mott

ALS PSCHi-Mott

1. On 11 September 1851 the Maryland slaveholder Edward Gorsuch, his son, and five others had gone to Christiana, Pennsylvania, in search of four fugitive slaves living with William Parker, a former slave. Parker and other free blacks attempted to prevent Gorsuch from capturing the fugitives. Caster Hanway, a Quaker neighbor, tried to keep the group from resorting to violence, but Gorsuch was killed and Parker, the fugitives, and others involved escaped to Canada. Hanway and forty others (thirty-eight of whom were black) were charged with treason for resisting the Fugitive Slave Law. LCM attended the trial in Philadelphia. On 11 December they were acquitted (Thomas Slaughter, *Bloody Dawn: The Christiana Riot and Racial Violence in the Antebellum North* [New York: Oxford University Press, 1991], 43–75, 79–80, 225; *The Selected Papers of Thaddeus Stevens,*

ed. Beverly Wilson Palmer and Holly Byers Ochoa [Pittsburgh: University of Pittsburgh Press, 1997], 1:137–38).

2. In "A Letter to Louis Kossuth, Concerning Freedom and Slavery in the United States: In Behalf of the American Anti-Slavery Society," Garrison had criticized Kossuth for being friendly to slaveholders and proslavery politicians in his efforts to find aid for Hungary (*Liberator,* 20 February 1852, 29, 32). During his time in America, Kossuth had lectured to raise money for his mother and sisters, who had been driven from their home and recently released from prison, so that they might immigrate to the United States. In his final speech delivered on 21 June, Kossuth had argued that no nation could be confident of its future: "As long as the fragile wisdom of political exigencies overrules the doctrines of Christ, there is no freedom on earth firm, and the future of no nation sure. But let a powerful nation like yours raise Christian morality into its public conduct, that nation will have a future against which the very gates of hell itself will never prevail" (*The Future of Nations* [New York: Fowlers and Wells, 1854], 5–8, 39).

3. Richard Hildreth, *The White Slave; or, Memoirs of a Fugitive: A Story of Slave Life in Virginia* (Boston: Tappan and Whittemore, 1852).

4. 2 Sam. 12:12.

5. Matt. 6:2.

6. In 1851 the Kennett Monthly Meeting in Chester County had split and in 1853 formed the Pennsylvania Yearly Meeting of Progressive Friends, which met at Longwood Meeting House (Thomas Drake, *Quakers and Slavery in America* [New Haven, Conn.: Yale University Press, 1950], 174–75).

7. Luke 21:20.

8. Phebe Post Willis had died in 1842. Rachel Rushmore (b. 1830) was the daughter of Townsend Rushmore and Amy Willis Rushmore.

9. This is possibly Rachel Pearsall Willis.

10. Sarah Hull Hallock (1813–86) was a member of the New York Friends of Human Progress and an antislavery activist.


## To William Lloyd Garrison and Helen Benson Garrison

Auburn N. Y. 8 Mo. 31st. 1852

My dear Wm. L. & Helen Garrison

I intended before leaving home for this place, to write a line to you, expressive of the pleasure we feel, that a favorable answer was received, relative to attending our Annual Mg. at West-Chester, and to say further how desirous we are that the long talked-of-visit from Helen shall be made at the same time.

We shall probably remain here until the latter part of next Month—& shall be much pleased to see you and other of our Mass. friends at the approaching Convention at Syracuse— If you are planning to be there & go thence to Philada—we will return with you then—. We shall need all the help we can have, to give interest to the Woman's Convention, & hope that you are planning to be here[1]—& that Wendell Phillips & others will come— If you are not here, I will write again when we fix on a time to leave Auburn, so that your visit to Philada. may not be delayed by supposing us absent from the City. Many there will welcome you—& we may have a real nice time— An increasing interest is felt in attending Anti Slavery Conventions. The disappointment was great last year, that you were not there—

I write in haste, as my Jas., Sister Martha, & self are about starting to pay a visit to our M'Clintock frds. at Waterloo, and to Elizh. C. Stanton—

very affecy—    L. Mott

Jas. sends love without [*ms. damaged*]

XC PSCHi-Mott (Published by permission of the document owner)

1. At the women's rights convention in Syracuse, LCM would celebrate coeducational colleges such as Oberlin, which had conferred degrees on Lucy Stone and Antoinette Brown. LCM would advocate "agitation—in the wisdom of not keeping still." She would declare that "women are degraded by the law, by the monopoly of the Church, and all the circumstances with which she is surrounded. She must therefore boldly affirm her rights" (*Proceedings of the Woman's Rights Convention, Held at Syracuse, September 8th, 9th and 10th, 1852, Stanton-Anthony Papers*, reel 7, frs. 356, 385).

## To Hannah Monaghan Darlington[1]

Philada. 1 mo. 11th 1853

My Dear Hannah

I have received thy letter, with the list of names, which I have forwarded to Saml. J. May. I herewith send a late letter received from him, which thou may like to read. I have not yet returned to him any of the Reports, having distributed so large a number that I have not more than one dozen left— and I have not yet sent copies to all whom he named—not knowing the Post Office address of some of them— Just the directing and mailing take time—an article that I have very little of at command. I began this yestery, ^no-the day before^ it is now the 13th—and with the interruption of more than 20 callers, it is almost impossible to get a letter written. As to those blank petitions, I see no way that I can do anything with them. Scarcely 6 women can be found in this City, who would give the time & attention required to procure signers— Another year we may do something.

The Female Medical Society is trying hard to awaken interest in the public mind in that direction. Dr. H. Longshore repeated her Lecture on 3rd. day eveg., at the Spring Garden Com. Hall—to a good audience. I have been applied to, but feel too ignorant in that branch, to speak for them to any good purpose. I presume Lucy Stone has not interest enough in these separate Institutions to accept an invitation to lecture before the Society. There seems no other way for woman at present—any more than for the colored people. By the way, Sojourner Truth is in the City, & wishes some house procured in which she may make herself heard. I have not yet seen her—[2] Miller McKim is making some arrangets. for her.

Sarah Peter—wife of the British Consul, called on me yesterday, to invite cooperation, for the securing of a High School for Girls—similar to that now established for boys—[3] A new house is about to be built which seems a favorable time to move in the thing— A few women are to meet at her house shortly to agree on a public Meeting for the purpose of getting up a petition to the Legislature. Mary Grew will take part in such a meeting. This aftern. our Fem. A. S. Socy. meets—& each week the Ex. Com. of the State Socy— At our last Mg. we resolved that for every new subscriber obtained for the Freeman, we wd. present a copy of Uncle Tom, & for every 3 subscribers—a copy of the White Slave— So we are still trying to keep Freedoms ball in motion—

Then our miserable Cherry St. organization, with its select as well as its more public Mgs. steal away any time—& here is winter half gone, & work laid out for the beging. of the year, yet untouched!

We had a right pleasant visit on 1st. day last, from Gerritt Smith, on his way to Washn., to secure a house for next year.[4] Our dear Joseph & Ruth Dugdale & Oliver & Mary Johnson made part of our compy.— I wish thou and Chandler too could have been with us— You are to be pitied, if that poor German Reformer inflicted himself upon you long. He tried it here, but we were not so polite to him as I presume you were, & his visit was not long. Such are among the annoyances attendant upon the striking out in any new reformatory movement. I know not what we in Philada. wd. do should we attempt a liberal or progressive Meeting— But it is not wise to anticipate trouble. When the time comes for us to take any step, I hope no unworthy considerations will deter us.

I have spun out an epistle.

very affecy.    Lucretia Mott

Please return S. J. May's  How shall I send thee a parcel of the West Co. Reports?

I have been writg to P. W. Davis & sent her the only letter I had—that from F. D. Gage—[5]

ALS MNHi

1. Hannah Monaghan Darlington (1808–83) lived in Kennett Township, where she and her husband, Chandler Darlington (d. 1879), a farmer, were members of the Longwood Progressive Friends Meeting (WLG, 4:325).

2. Hannah Longshore (1819–1901) and her husband, Thomas E. Longshore, established the Female Medical College of Pennsylvania in 1850. Sojourner Truth (c. 1797–1883), the antislavery and woman's rights lecturer, was born a slave in Ulster County, New York, and was freed in 1827 when the state abolished slavery.

3. Sarah Anne Worthington Peter (1800–1877) was active in women's education in Philadelphia (James Mulhern, A History of Secondary Education in Pennsylvania [Philadelphia: n. p., 1993], 429, 493; see also LCM to Caroline Healey Dall, 5 March 1877, below). Central High School for boys had opened in 1838.

4. Smith would begin his first congressional term as an Independent in December 1853.

5. Frances D. Gage (1808–84) was a writer and a woman's rights and antislavery activist from Ohio.

## To Philadelphia Family

Ohio River<br>
betwn. Maysville [*Kentucky*]<br>
& Steubenville [*Ohio*]<br>
10 mo. 17th. 53—

Dear Home

Can I write amid such a perpetual jarring? The river is so low that only small boats can pass & here we are slowly winding our way to the nearest point of Jas. Ladd's where we hope to find Aunt Mary & daughr. Elizh.—& perhaps Wm. & Julian, who talked of meetg. us there.[1] We talked strongly of taking the boat this morng. to Cincini.—& retracg. our rail-road travel almost to Massillon—then another train to Wellsville, rather than boat up the river in this slow way. But the added expense & not much savg. of time after all deterred us— Beside some uncertainty in our being able to hire a conveyance at Wellesville—some 12 miles or more—

We mailed a letter at Cincini.—but we enquired in vain for one from home. It is too bad, that we have not heard a single word, since leavg. Auburn; except that uncle John P.[2] had recd. on 7th day—a letter from Mari[a].—wh. he chose to make her Mother think contained confidential allusions, & he must not let her see it. All we learned from it was, that they had not yet moved into town—& that all were well, for anythg. sd. to the contrary. He seemed to pretend secrecy more to tease Aunt M[artha]. She thought he carried it rather too far—

Our Mg. at Cini. was all we could ask—both in size & attention—to say nothg. of matter & manner—a very large & handsome Hall, 20c admission—filled to overflowg many standg. & hundreds—some sd. 1000 went away unable to get in—[3] I will enclose a notice of the exercises of the eveg— Several called on us next morng. & urgd our longer stay or our return to have more Mgs.

Sarah Peter, who is just settled there, among our callers— She engaged Lucy S. & Mr. Blackwell to take tea with her that eveg— She wanted to give her some facts. Col. Stevenson's wife also called—expressed great regret that her husbd. was obliged to leave for Philada. & could not be at our Mg. at Maysville—[4] His daughr. came to us after the Mg. & invited us home with her. Jas. Walton's daughr. who married John Mott's son now lives in Cincini.— She & her husband called & expressed full unity with our views—altho opposed by most of her family— Our orthodox cousin Levi Coffin attended our Mg. & waited on us— Debh. Coates' daughr. too—her Mother was out of town—[5] We left Cini. at 11 o clk. & did not reach Maysville till 10 at night— The banks of the river afforded constant & varying scene, & we enjoyed the day—tho' no passengers that were attractive— Uncle John met us at the landg.—his carriage at the Goddard House, where we left our trunks— The ride out in full-moon-light was very pleast.—and the warm reception from the 4 aunts was grateful—a blazing fire added much to the cheerfulness  Their sister in law—Isabel's Mother, Marianna, & another daughr. were there—beside 2 or 3 little childn.—  We were made so entirely at home by their Kentucky hospitality, that we soon felt like old acquaintances. Uncle John is quite at his ease in his own house—  We were sorry to miss receivg. a letter he sent to Cincini. in answer to Aunt Martha's— assurg. us a welcome. Our sleepg. room across the Hall had another large open fire—and in the morng—before we were up—a real slave-lookg. girl came in sans ceremony, & made up the fire anew—

We passed next morng. in free conversation—none going to Mg. save Sis-ter-in-law & daughr. Their table was as generous as their reception in other re-spects—  We went early to town after dinner to [array?] for the Mg. in Town Hall—a crowded house  Slavery spoken of without reserve—well born  much persuasion to have another Mg. wh. we consented to in the eveg. on Woman— a great gathering & apparent satisfaction—[6]

We remained at the Hotel to wait for this shaky boat—uncle J. Aunts Patsy & Ann stayg as long as they thot. wd. do to be from home  We retired to our room—altogether—& about 11 o clk—the boat appeared & here we are—

We shall not reach Jas. Ladds before 4th. day eveg—shall leave there 6th day & make the best of our way home—but we fear it will be 1st. day before we can reach that desirable haven—& then only for a night's rest before going to Nor-ristown—  Aunt E[liza]. will certainly go with us as we shall return nights—

LM

Aunt Martha has not written to Auburn for some days. So you may as well send this elegant production to Eliza, via Succasunna [*New Jersey*] if Pattie is not with you

ALS PSCHi-Mott

1. LCM, JM, and MCW had recently attended the fourth National Woman's Rights Convention in Cleveland, held on 5–7 October 1853, at which LCM had delivered "The Laws in Relation to Woman" (see *Sermons*, 211–25). In an earlier letter to the family LCM had described "3 days most interestg. Mgs. . . . The speeches of Ant[oinett]e. B.,—Lucy S., & others were listened to with the most wrapt attention, & will do great good." LCM, JM, and MCW's destination was probably the residence of James D. Ladd, where they had stayed en route from Cleveland to Cincinnati. "Aunt Mary" was Mary Joy Folger (1778–1858), the widow of Anna Coffin's brother Mayhew Coffin; her daughter Eliza-beth Ladd was the wife of James D. Ladd. "Wm. & Julian" were William H. Folger (c. 1803–?) and his wife, Julia Ann Folger. All four were from Kendal, near Massillon, Ohio (letter of 14 October 1853, Mott Manuscripts, PSCHi; unidentified obituary of Mary J. Folger, Folger family scrapbook, MNHi).

2. John Pelham of Maysville was the brother of MCW's first husband, Peter.

3. The *Cincinnati Daily Commercial* described "the largest audience ever yet assem-bled in and about Smith & Nixon's concert hall" to hear LCM and Stone speak on 14 October. LCM, said the *Commercial*, "wore the usual dress of her sex, leaving the Bloomer costume to the younger laborers in the movement" and spoke of her hope that she would soon see women accorded the vote and "the universal recognition of woman's right." The Bible, declared LCM, had been erected "like a giant scarecrow, across the pathway

of human progression; and the bat like wings of 'authority' had flapped in the face of every reform." LCM then addressed scriptural injunctions against woman's rights, continued the *Commercial,* "at considerable length and with a good deal of genuine wit" (15 October 1853, 2).

4. Sarah Peter had recently returned from Philadelphia to her native Ohio. Stone was visiting the reformer Henry B. Blackwell (1825–1909) at his home in Cincinnati. From Maysville, Thomas B. Stevenson had written LCM that he had advertised her speech locally and regretted that urgent business would prevent him from attending (13 October 1853, Mott Manuscripts, PSCHi).

5. Levi Coffin (1789–1877) operated a free-labor goods store in Cincinnati and was active in the Underground Railroad. "Debh. Coates' daughr." is possibly Emeline Jackson Coates, the daughter-in-law of Deborah Coates and Lindley Coates (Thomas Coates, *Genealogy of the Coates Family* [n.p., 1906], 126–27).

6. Both meetings at the Maysville Court House on 16 October were described by a correspondent for the *New York Tribune:* LCM "presented views bold, startling, and at least, to this community, original. No crying evil of the day escaped exposure and condemnation. . . . Her discourse gave strong evidence of the fact, that woman, when she is qualified properly, has a right to be heard in public assemblages." The writer went on to say that advance notice had prepared the crowd for "a sour, disappointed-looking woman, who . . . was unhappy in her domestic relations," but LCM and JM "gave strong presumptive evidence of a quiet, happy life" (reprinted in the *Liberator,* 4 November 1853, 174).

## To Anne Warren Weston

Philada. 11 mo. 18th. 1853—

My dear Ann:

Come to the second Decade, and hear all I can say to thee, in reply to thy Spicy answer to E. M. Davis, J. &. self, relative to the encouragement proper to give to our friend George Thompson's coming to this country, as an agent for our cause.[1] I would rather talk than write about it. Miller M'Kim & Sarah Pugh thou knows I presume are both favorable to his coming in the way proposed. I know not whether they have yet had an opp[ortunit]y. to talk with Edwd. & hear his objections. I could not recollect which of us named his being a foreigner, as forming one objection, not however to his being welcomed on our platform, but only as to the expediency of making choice of him as an agent, for this & other reasons— Thou says "this would shut the mouth of Miller M'Kim in England".[2] No—as a parallel, the English shd. raise the cry of "down with the Aristocracy"—when it might be a question of expediency, whether their money shd. be used in employing an American Republican as an agent, or one of their own countrymen equally well qualified. But more of this hereafter.

My object now is to bid thee welcome under our roof 338 Arch St. at the coming Anniversary. More than this, to express the hope, that thou wilt come. I have written to Garrison, relative to preparation &.c—as also asking him to extend an invitation to Edmund Quincy to be our guest at that time. Lest he should forget it, wilt thou please say to Edmund that we shall be glad to have his company.

In great haste, & with my husbands best regards

thine,    Lucretia Mott

ALS MB Env: "Anne Warren Weston, Weymouth or Boston,
If in Weymouth will Wm. L. G. please enclose & forward"

1. The AASS planned to commemorate the twentieth anniversary of its founding at Sansom Street Hall in Philadelphia on 3–5 December 1853 (*Liberator,* 18 November 1853, 182). George Thompson had recently been defeated in parliamentary elections in Britain. On 1 September Edward M. Davis had written Weston that the plan to bring Thompson to the United States would be too expensive; Thompson should not come to "live off of the Anti-Slavery Cause & people." In her postscript to Davis's letter LCM had agreed and had expressed fears that Thompson would not be *"reliable,* without more *watching* than cd. be *constantly* exercised" (MB).

2. McKim had recently returned from five months in Great Britain, trying to win more support for Garrison and the AASS (William Cohen, "James Miller McKim: Pennsylvania Abolitionist," Ph.D. diss., New York University, 1968, 255, 260).

## To Thomas Wentworth Higginson[1]

Philada. 4 mo. 6th. 54—

T. W. Higginson
My dear Friend

I hardly know how to apologize for my seeming neglect of thy two letters of Feb. 6 & Mar. 30th— And must just 'own up' to having had "too many irons in the fire". I ought not to accept appointments in our Conventions, for they fail of execution at my hands—

The Circular was altogether suitable. The interest of thyself & Lucy Stone, in issuing it, & calling attention to the subject, deserves our thanks. I early employed a person in this City to collect facts & make out statistics, as requested, but as yet we have had no returns—nothing completed.[2] I hope however to be able to send satisfactory answers, before our next Convention. If possible I will forward them to thee, in the course of a month or two.

Penna. is always slow to work in any progressive or new movement.

I might distribute a *few* of the Circulars with some hope of advantage. A parcel sent by Express—directed to me, or to James Mott 338 Arch St. Philada. would reach us. I noticed in the Paper, that a part of the proceeds of Lucy Stone's lectures in Maine were appropriated to the printing of Tracts on this Subject. We have sent some money to S. J. May for the same purpose.[3] Those who give so freely of their time & talents to the cause, as we & thyself do, should not be allowed to be "out of pocket" too.

The success of Lucy Stone & Antoinette Brown, in their lectures here, give promise of a good attendance at our Convention in the Autumn. We hope you will all come then—not expecting "to be ministered unto, but to minister";[4] for I can assure our Eastern friends, that they will find Philada. 50 years behind them.

It is true that women are employed in retail dry goods stores in this city more than in any other place that I know of—unless it be, in proportion to the number of inhabitants, on Nantucket. There, Women often are the principals in their business—going to Boston, & other places for their supply. Of latter years however they are in danger of being driven out of their legitimate employment, by strangers—Men, going to the Island, & engaging, with perhaps greater advantages in the same business. I was on a visit to this, my native Isle, when thy last letter was recd.—one cause of the delay in answering it.[5]

In the employt. of women in stores, however, as well as teachers in schools, they receive scarcely half the salary of a man for similar duties.

In our Model & Normal Public School in this City—the Male principal's salary was $1200—the Female's $500—the latter performing a greater task—& giving great satisfaction—[6] Some change was lately made in the School-arrangements—and the Salary of the Female Teacher was reduced to $300. The 200 taken from hers was added to his. This has given great dissatisfaction to her friends, where it is known— I have not heard yet all that may be said by the Controllers, for this apparent injustice—there may be reasons, exoneratg. them. I would prefer therefore that no published use be made of this, at present. I will endeavor to obtain the true state of the case—as well as other facts of like injustice, & have them ready for public exposure, at a suitable time.

Thine sincerly    *Lucretia Mott*

ALS NPV

1. Thomas Wentworth Higginson (1823–1911) was a Unitarian minister and reformer from Worcester, Massachusetts.

2. The 1853 Cleveland woman's rights convention had appointed LCM, Wendell Phillips, Ernestine L. Rose (1810–92), Lucy Stone, and Higginson to a committee to prepare reports on educational and business opportunities for women. On 15 January 1854, the committee had issued a flyer (published in the *Liberator* and the *NASS*) requesting information on state legislation regarding women's education, schools to which women were admitted, and the types of employment (and salaries paid) for women. Information was to be sent to Higginson (*Pennsylvania Freeman*, 9 March 1854, 39).

3. In a letter to Lucy Stone, JM had written that LCM was never paid for her lectures and that she donated any money received to the printing of antislavery and woman's rights tracts (17 October 1853, Hallowell, 339).

4. Stone had given the lecture "The Rights of Woman" in the Musical Fund Hall on 11 February to a "respectable" and "attentive" audience (*Liberator*, 17 February 1854, 28). Brown's lecture was "The Creative Genius of Man," given in Philadelphia on 6 March (*Pennsylvania Freeman*, 9 March 1854, 39). LCM is quoting Matt. 20:28.

5. LCM had returned from her Nantucket visit around 1 April (MCW to LCM, 5 April 1854, MNS).

6. The Philadelphia Model School had been founded in 1818 to educate teachers; in 1848 it had become a normal school for female teachers, headed by Dr. A. T. W. Wright (James P. Wickersham, *History of Education in Pennsylvania* [Lancaster, Pa.: Inquirer Publishing Company, 1886], 610–12).

## To Elizabeth Neall Gay

Philada. 10 Mo. 9th. 1854

My dear Elizh.

Cant thou take thy baby, & come to our Woman's Convention? We shall need thee and all other *true* women.

Paulina W. Davis writes doubtfully of her coming, owing to the illness of her brother. Antione. Brown also may be prevented by her own poor health—

We have the promise of Frances D. Gage, Wm. L. Garrison, and Lucy Stone, as well as some others.[1]

I have not succeeded in finding any one to answer that article of John Weiss, as it shd. be answered.[2] I took thy *sharp* letter to Nantucket with me in the Spring, and tried to enlist some clever Unitarian women there against him. Lydia Barney[3] took a copy of thy letter, & sent it to Lydia Green—New Bedford— I understood that John Weiss was likely to see thy criticism of his production. I hope he did— I was proud of it, and read it to Wm. H. Furness, who had rather praised the Article in the Examiner.

We hope Sydney will be at our Annual A. S. Mg. at West Chester— We need him too. Come together, & I will help take care of the babies—[4]

They are very busy at Mt. Holly paperg. & paintg—&.c—coz Ruth [*Chase*] has been quite poorly— Do ask Oliver [*Johnson*] or Sydney to call attention in a short Editorial this week to our Wom. Rig. Con[5]—& their & thy petitioners will ever pray,

L Mott

ALS NNCB-Gay

1. The fifth National Woman's Rights Convention was scheduled to meet in Philadelphia on 18–20 October 1854.

2. John Weiss (1818–79), a Unitarian clergyman from New Bedford, Massachusetts, had written an article, "The Woman Question," in the *Christian Examiner* (January 1854, 1–34). In it Weiss had criticized women's public speaking, from both platform and pulpit. It was permissible when LCM expressed "her convictions in the placid gathering of Friends, the tradition and habit of which place finely harmonize with woman's power of pure and tender exhortation." But women generally were coarsened by public exposure and their rhetorical efforts were unconvincing. Weiss argued that women would be better off "in silent alleviation of some of the evils that implore their intervention" and in helping society cultivate a simpler way of living.

3. Lydia Barney is possibly the daughter of Benjamin Barney of Nantucket, who would die in 1855 (MCW to LCM, 7 April 1855 [2], MNS).

4. JM had published a call to attend the seventeenth annual meeting of the PASS in Westminster on 23–25 October (*Liberator*, 13 October 1854, 163). The Gays had two children, born in 1852 and 1854.

5. Those attending the convention included Gage, Garrison, Higginson, Ernestine L. Rose, and Lucy Stone. On 19 October LCM would support a resolution against establishing a women's newspaper: "Do not let us establish a national organ yet; for there still remains a heavy debt for the publication of our reports. We can retire to our homes, and continue as we have done, up to the present time, labor for the glorious cause of woman." The following day she would attack the clergy's use of Scriptures to justify women's subordinate role: "All reforms were anti-Bible. We must look at things independently. We find woman endowed with certain capacities, and it was of no importance if any book denied her such capacities." LCM would argue that the clergy used the Bible selectively for their own purposes: "It was easy enough to quote Scriptures to sustain a monopoly and tyranny, but there was nothing to quote for equality" (*Philadelphia Evening Bulletin*, 19 and 20 October 1854, *Stanton-Anthony Papers*, reel 8, frs. 69, 72).

## To Elizabeth Cady Stanton

Philada. 3 mo. 16th. 1855—

My dear Elizabeth

Three weeks ago I received thy letter announcing thy plan of a Book,—and 3 weeks ago it ought to have been answered. Repeated absence from home, and the care of a family of 20 when at home, are not sufficient reasons—nor have I any to offer. It is just a dread of entering upon so important a subject.

This is the right work for thee, dear Elizh., and success will no doubt attend the undertaking. All the help I can render shall be most gladly given. Let me suggest then, that the opening Chapter go farther back than the "A. S. split in 1840"—Sarah & Angelina Grimke's labors in Mass. in 1835 & 6 aroused the Clergy; and the 'Clerical Appeal' and 'Pastoral Letter' were issued, which J. G. Whittier and M. W. Chapman satirized in their Poems.[1] The division in the A. S. Socy. began in N. Eng. in 37 & 8—not only against Garrison as a no-governt. man, but against womens public labors also— Some prominent abolitionists who had before given countenance to the Grimkes, now, either secretly or more openly acted against woman's co-operative action with men. C. T. Torrey, A. A. Phelps, A. St. Clair, Drs. Farnsworth, Harris, Woodbury, Scott Codding, Allen, Trask, J. LeBosquet, are names familiar among the opponents—the Tappans—Birney—E. Wright—J. Leavitt & others in New York in 39 & 40 uniting with the New-Eng opposition.[2]

From the time of the 1st. Convention of Women—in New Y 1837—the battle began. A resolution was there warmly discussed & at length adopted by a majority—many members dissenting, "that it was time that woman should move in the sphere Providence assigned her, & no longer rest satisfied in the limits which corrupt custom & a perverted application of the Scriptures had placed her," &. c— During that year Sarah Grimke's Letters were written On the Equal-

ity of the Sexes—the best Work after Mary Woolstonecraft's Rights of Woman—
It would be well in thy Book to give "honor where honor is due—credit where
credit,"[3] by according to M. Woolstonect. great moral courage, in coming out in
that day 60 or 70 years ago with her radical claim of the Rig. of Wom. The early
Quakers still earlier 1660 & 70 asserted & carried out Womans equal claim to the
Ministry—& reciprocal vows in the Marriage covenant—also in acting a part in
the Executive duties of the society—while their women too were & they still are
governed by laws, in the making of which they have no voice—rules of Discipline always issuing from men's Mg— Some advance in this respect in R.I. Yearly—& Genessee; as well as entire equality in the Progressive Frds. Mgs—

But it may not be thy intention to go as far back as I would desire—and to
write a general history of the Woman movement. No one I am persuaded could
do it better than thyself. I could furnish thee a variety of documents & books
bearing on the subject. Cant thou come here and examine them with me? If not,
I might take them, early next summer and either meet thee at Auburn, or at thy
own home— — For thou may make this a very valuable Work, and it must
not be hurried— Thou ought to have access to much that is already History—
and it will take time— Send on thy Chapters, and their headings, and I will
gladly do all I can—

As to Nantucket Women, there are no great things to tell In the early settlement of that Island Mary Starbuck bore a prominent place, as a wise coun-
sellor, & a remarkably strong mind— Divers Quaker women since that time,
have been eminent as preachers. Hannah Barnard of Hudson, a native of Nantucket, of the last century, was regarded one of the greatest ministers in the
Society. She travelled in England, & was there *deposed* by the ruling powers ^in
the Society of course,^ for daring to express doubts of the Divine authority of
the Jewish Wars—as well as ~~far~~ more openly than Friends were wont, to deny
the atonement & scheme of Salvation. She returned home to Hudson & was
much respected thro' a long life for her good works—[4] Priscilla Hunt [*Cadwallader*] another great minister—out west descended from Nant. parents—on the
Fathers side— In the Mo. Mg. of Friends on that Island, the Women have long
been regarded as the stronger part— This is owing in some measure to so many
of the men being away at sea— During the absence of their husbands, Nantucket women have been compelled to transact business, often going to Boston
to procure supplies of goods—exchanging for oil, candles, whalebone—&.c—
This has made them adept in trade— They have kept their own accounts, &
indeed acted the part of men— Then education & intellectual culture have been
for years equal for girls & boys—so that their women are prepared to be companions of man in every sense—and their social circles are never divided. Successive generations of this kind of mental exercise have ~~changed~~ improved the
form of the head, and the intellectual portion predominates— Set down as
much of this to partiality & self-praise as thou please. But to thy questions:
Garrison *did* refuse to take his seat in the London Convention, because the

Women delegates were rejected. He & N. P. Rogers arrived in London after the decision by vote, & they with one or two others, whose names I forget, took their seats in the Gallery. I went up & sat with them awhile, during one sitting. O'Connell went up there to speak to them, and I think Lady Byron did. The Letters of O'Connell & Wm. Howitt on the subject of our exclusion, published in Jas. Mott's 3 Mo. in Great Britain—ought to have a place in thy Book. I will enclose Dr. Bowring's letter to the Liberator.[5] I have for years preserved scraps from the Papers, shewing woman's progress— Most of these may be old to thee—if not, they are at thy service.

Elizh. Fry attended 2 or 3 sittings of the Conventn., and *willingly* accompanied the Duchess of Sutherland to the Exeter Hall Mg.—accepting a seat on the platform from which the American Women delegates were excluded—they being *courteously* shewn to the side seats, and told as a palliative, that it was the Queen's chosen seat, when she visited Exeter Hall. E. Fry did not interest herself in the woman question—nor did any of the Quakers present save J. C. Fuller & Anne Knight, except to vote against us—supposed in part owing to their desire to give no countenance to Hicksites— Harriet Martineau was sick at that time, near Newcastle-upon-Tyne. She wrote us a letter expressive of her sympathy, & invitg. us to visit her.[6] S. Pugh, Abby Kimber, Jas. & self accepted her invitatn.— She did not publish anythg. on the subject to my knowledge.

M. W. Chapman we are informed is coming home this year.[7] She could tell whether the desire of forming a political A. S. party was a cause of dissension, earlier than the opposition to Woman's public labors— Some of the afore-named men may not have actually opposed, while they gave their influence to that side. Amos A. Phelps was one of the first to slip into Angelina G's Mgs. appointed only for women— Others followed his example, and they became mixed audiences, almost before they knew it.

Thou wilt have hard work to prove the intellectual equality of Woman with man—facts are so against such an assumption, in the present stage of woman's developement. We need not however *admit* inferiority, even tho' we may not be able to *prove* equality. The rapid progress of this movement, in so few years of its advocacy, the number of women already in the field, whose talents are appreciated & well rewarded, the willing ear given to the ultra demands made, except indeed by such Priests as "having ears hear not, neither do they understand,"[8] the entrance into the Professions, hitherto monopolised by men, the success as Physicians & lecturers—these all shew womans capability with man, by severe mental labor to attain to honor— Antionette L. B. has done well here— So has Emma R. Coe, who is in Wm. Pierce's office pursuing the study of Law—being regularly entered at our Court—with no opposition—[9] I accompd. her to Harrisbg. this winter & had a hearg. before many members of the Legr. & others. Of Lucy Stone it is not needful that I should speak. Her praise if not "in all the churches," is in the hearts & mouths of all who hear her. Susan B. Anthony too not the least efficient, practical woman— How nobly you all have done at Albany— Ernestine L. Rose is one of our best. Thy Address to the Leg. we circulate unsparingly.[10] It gives great satisfaction.[11] In thy coming Work thou must do thyself justice. Remember the first Convention originated with thee. When we were walking the streets of Boston together in 1841, to find Elizh. Moore's daughter, 'thou' asked if we could not have a Convention for Woman's Rights. Then when Jas. & self were attendg. the Yearly Mg. at Waterloo in 47 or 8 was it? thou again proposed the Convention, which was afterward held at Seneca Falls. I have never liked the undeserved praise in the Report of that Meeting's Proceedings, of being "the moving spirit of that occasion," when to thyself belongs the honor, aided so efficiently by the M'Clintock's—[12]

I was glad to hear of the welfare of that family, for they have long held a high place in my regard & affection.

How glad we should have been of a visit from thee during thy 6 weeks' Stay in New York. We knew not of thy being there, until after thy return home—

I must close this long letter.

Affecy.    Lucretia Mott

ALS DLC-Stanton

1. In July 1837 the Congregational Association of Massachusetts had issued a "Pastoral Letter" protesting women speakers. Responding to the letter, Whittier had written a poem defending the Grimkés (*Liberator,* 20 October 1837, 171; *JGW,* 1:251).

2. Those not previously identified are Amos Farnsworth (1788–1861), a Groton, Massachusetts, physician; the New England clergymen Edwin N. Harris (1805–80); James T. Woodbury (1803–61); "Scott," possibly Orange Scott (1800–1847), a Massachusetts Methodist minister; Ichabod Codding (1811–66), an abolitionist agent; "Allen," possibly George Allen (1792–1883), a Massachusetts abolitionist and Congregational minister; and George Trask (1798–1875) (*JGW,* 1:157, 209, 168, 495, 303; *WLG,* 2:43). The Tappan brothers, Arthur (1786–1865) and Lewis, James G. Birney, and Joshua Leavitt had left the AASS in May 1840 and had formed the American and Foreign Anti-Slavery Society. Elizur Wright Jr. had resigned from the AASS in 1839.

3. At the Anti-Slavery Convention of American Women, held in New York City on 9–12 May 1837, Angelina Grimké had introduced the resolution that LCM is quoting almost verbatim. Grimké's resolution continued: "Therefore that it is the duty of woman, and the province of woman, to plead the cause of the oppressed in our land, and do all that she can by her voice, and her pen, and her purse, and the influence of her example, to overthrow the horrible system of American slavery" (*Liberator,* 16 June 1837, 98). "Honor where honor is due—credit where credit" is a variation of "Render therefore to all their dues: tribute to whom tribute is due; custom to whom custom; fear to whom fear; honour to whom honour" (Rom. 13:7).

4. Mary Coffin Starbuck (1644–45 O.S.–1717 O.S.) was influential in establishing Quaker dominance on Nantucket. Hannah Jenkins Barnard (1754?-1825) had traveled in the British Isles in 1798–1801. She had been censured for preaching that a God of love could have approved of neither the Old Testament wars nor of the Napoleonic wars.

5. The letters of O'Connell and the British writer William Howitt (1792–1879) had protested the convention's rejection of the women delegates. Howitt had declared that the convention's exclusion of women because they were considered "heretics" contradicted Quaker doctrine, which stipulated that "there is no sex in Souls." Dr. John Bowring (1792–1872), a reformer and literary critic, had spoken against the exclusion of

women and had entertained LCM and JM several times in London. His letter of 9 November 1840 to Garrison had appeared in the *Liberator* (25 December 1840, 207; see also *Diary,* 29–30, 41, 53, 57; Hallowell, 474–77).

6. LCM had described as "inconsistent" the seating of Elizabeth Fry (1780–1845), a Quaker minister, and the philanthropist Harriet Elizabeth Georgiana Leveson-Gower, Duchess of Sutherland (1806–68), on the platform at the Exeter Hall meeting on 24 June. According to LCM, the Irish Quaker James C. Fuller had told the women delegates that the convention authorities had been "put on their guard" because "so many of us were not of their faith." LCM and JM had visited Harriet Martineau on 16 August at her home in Tynemouth, where they had spent two or three hours in "pleasant conversation" (Harriet Martineau to LCM, 19 August 1840, *Diary,* 79, see also 30, 45, 73).

7. Maria Weston Chapman would return in November 1855 from seven years' travel in Europe.

8. LCM is adapting Jer. 5:21: "Hear now this, O foolish people, and without understanding; which have eyes and see not; which have ears, and hear not."

9. Antoinette L. Brown had spoken in Philadelphia in January and LCM had described her as giving "great satisfaction" to a full house (LCM to MCW, 24 January 1855, Mott Manuscripts, PSCHi). Emma R. Coe, formerly a lecturer on woman's rights, had registered as a law student in January 1855 in the office of the Philadelphia antislavery leader and judge William Peirce (1815–87).

10. Anthony, Ernestine L. Rose, and Antoinette Brown had recently attended the Albany County Woman's Rights Convention on 13–14 February 1855. In her address of 14 February 1854 to the New York legislature Stanton had reviewed the legal disabilities of women, including the right to vote and a trial by jury, under the current constitution. Stanton also had pointed out that the marriage contract should be treated like other civil contracts, with the two parties retaining their independence and rights (Gordon, 1:234, 302–3, 240–55).

11. Beginning with the following sentence, someone else has underlined all the words to the end of the paragraph in pencil and blue ink, not the brown ink of LCM's letter.

12. The report of the convention stated, "LUCRETIA MOTT, of Philadelphia, was the moving spirit of the occasion" (*Proceedings of the Woman's Rights Conventions held at Seneca Falls and Rochester, N. Y.* [New York: Robert J. Johnston, 1870], 3).

## To George Combe and Cecelia Combe

Philada. 5 Mo. 25th. 1855

My dear Friends George & Cecelia Combe

Our Son & his wife Thomas & Marianna Mott are leaving us for a year's travel & residence in Europe—and as we ever feel a wish that those dearest to us, may share with us the pleasure of your acquaintance, I take the liberty of thus introducing them—

We receive repeatedly, evidences of kindness, in sending not only the published, but the unpublished Works of George Combe— That, on Natural Religion I read[1]—parts of it again & again, with much interest, and regretted that it should be thought best to keep it back, for the benefit of the next generation, rather than to spread all the light before the present—

The Principles of Criminal Legislation—the last production we have received from the same Author, is an enlightened Work—coming up so nearly to my Non-Resistant ideas, that I hail it, as among the evidences that Wars shall eventually "cease to the ends of the earth"[2]—for when once Nations shall be convinced, that retaliatory punishments should not be inflicted for great crimes, how much less disposed will they be, to resort to the sword in settlement of disputes, or for points of honor— The thousands now being slain on the battlefield in Europe—with the sanction & aid too of the most enlightened, & *self-styled* most Christian portion of its people, should arouse the Advocates of Peace on Earth, to greater exertion, in order that they may convince these pious professors, that "they do err, not knowing the Scriptures, nor the power of God".[3]

Our Son Edward M. Davis is in correspondence with your nephew Robert Cox, and receives from him his elaborate writings on the Sabbath question—[4] They are doing great good— Please present to him our many thanks for the Book he sent to us—

His short visit to us is remembered with pleasure— I have entrusted to our Children two small pamphlets I promised to procure for him—not as containg anything new—or any added argument, but because he wished to see all that had been published here on the subject—

Also for dear Cecilia's benefit I send another of our Wom. Rig. Appeals, hoping she by this time is convinced that there is need of Women themselves asserting their rights— Great good has already been effected by the Conventions held, and the demands made for redress of *existing* grievances. The laws of this State & of N. York have been changed[5]—avenues are opened for more lucrative employment—and large numbers of young women are entering and doing credit to themselves as well as increasing their usefulness in society—

You are no doubt posted, as to the progress of the Anti-Slavery movement— Our largest Halls may now be had for lectures on the Subject, and Sumner Giddings—Theodore Parker—Wendell Phillips—Lucy Stone and even Garrison himself, can & do draw large audiences, who listen with applause to the most radical sentiments—

Our family & friends are in usual health— We have 2 grandchildn. [*Isaac Hopper and Charles Cavender*] added to our number—12 in all—

If Anne D. Morrison knew I was writing, she would send love— — I was pleased that your nephew, so quickly discerned, through a rather blunt & rough exterior, her superior mind & character, evincing that so large a brain had not been bestowed in vain—

My husband unites in affectionate remembrances—

Most Sincerely yours—
*Lucretia Mott*
ALS GBNLS

1. George Combe, *An Inquiry into Natural Religion: Its Foundation, Nature, and Applications* (Edinburgh: Neill and Co., 1853).

2. George Combe, *Remarks on the Principles of Criminal Legislation, and the Practice of Prison Discipline* (London: Simpkin, Marshall, and Co., 1854). The quotation is from Ps. 46:9.

3. The Crimean War had begun in September 1853 when the Turks refused the Russian request to protect Christians in their empire and Russia occupied Moldavia and Walachia. The British and French, suspicious of Russian motives, then joined the conflict, which lasted until 1 February 1856. The quotation is from Matt. 22:29.

4. Robert Cox (1810–72), son of Combe's sister Anne Combe Cox, edited the *Phrenological Journal* and wrote *Sabbath Laws and Sabbath Duties; Considered in Relation to Their Natural and Scriptural Grounds, and to the Principles of Religious Liberty* (Edinburgh: Maclachlan and Stewart, 1853).

5. On 8 April 1848 Pennsylvania had revised its laws on the "rights of married women" to state that any property belonging to a single woman "shall continue to be the property of such woman as fully after her marriage as before" (*Pennsylvania House Journal*, 58th sess., 1:907–9, 992). New York had passed a similar law in 1848 (Gordon, 1:68, 76–86). In April 1855, the Pennsylvania legislature had passed a law allowing women who were sole supporters of their families authority over their separate earnings (Marylynn Salmon, "Republican Sentiment, Economic Change, and the Property Rights of Women in American Law," in *Women in the Age of the American Revolution,* ed. Ronald Hoffman and Peter J. Albert [Charlottesville: University Press of Virginia, 1989], 470–71).


## To Elizabeth Pease Nichol

Philada. 5 Mo. 28th. 1855

My dear Elizth. Nichol

I ought before now to have acknowledged, & thanked thee for thy kind remembrance of me, in sending me the Poems of your Son— —[1] I have kept the Volume on the table in our room, and I love to take it up occasionally, and while reading have thee also brought to my mind, in affectionate interest. Of the translations of course, I am not able to judge— The sonnets are discriminating— Ailsa Crag is beautifully descriptive & evinces poetic talent—as do many of the other pieces— Dost thou remember N. P. Rogers' description of Ailsa Crag, in the Herald of Freedom?[2] Some lines of this Poem reminded me of that— I have also a page of Errata, sent by Wendell Phillips at yr. request— I feel obliged by this renewal of thy kind regard, since thy change of situation— J. Miller M'Kim brought us some of the Wedding Cake— When Dr. Nichol was in this City, we saw him only in the Lecture-room, and then sitting at quite a distance from him.

We were promised an introduction, hearing that it would be agreeable also to himself—and Dillwyn Parrish[3] had fixed the time with us, when we were told that the Dr. was called unexpectedly from the City. After learning that he was about to form so interesting an alliance with one we had loved so well, we regretted more than ever the disappointment. Will you not come to this Country together some day? Sarah Pugh gave us a pleasing accot. of her interviews with you—

Our Son & his wife Thomas and Marianna Mott are about to visit your land, and to pass a year or more in Europe. We feel a wish for them to meet with some of our dear Anti-Slavery friends— I thought thou might be in London, during the Anniversaries the coming month, and have asked our children to make inquiry for thee—

We are pleased to hear that thy husband is interested with thee in the movement which first united us— The sympathy & aid of our Abolition friends abroad have been very encouraging & strengthening to us— The Annual Mg— in New York this Spring was considered the best ever held in that City— C. Sumner spoke admirably well— Crowds gathered to hear him & others notwithstandg. the rain, which fell profusely—[4]

My husband unites in warm regards—

Very affectionately
*Lucretia Mott*

ALS MH-H (shelf mark bMS Am 1906 [603])

1. Elizabeth Pease had married Dr. John Pringle Nichol (1804–59), a professor of astronomy at Glasgow University, on 6 July 1853. He had two children by a previous marriage, including a son, John Nichol (1833–94), a literature professor at Glasgow University and the author of *Leaves* (Edinburgh: Ballantyne and Co., 1854).

2. Nathaniel Rogers's article "Ailsa Craig" had appeared in the *Herald of Freedom* on 30 April 1841 (*A Collection from the Newspaper Writings of Nathaniel P. Rogers* [Concord, N.H.: John R. French, 1847], 128–35).

3. Dillwyn Parrish (1809–86) was the son of Dr. Joseph Parrish and Susanna Cox Parrish.

4. The anniversary meeting of the AASS had taken place on 9–11 May 1855 in New York City. Senator Charles Sumner's speech, "The Necessity, Practicability, and Dignity of the Anti-Slavery Enterprise, with Glimpses at the Special Duties of the North," initially given 10 May, was so popular that he delivered it several more times over the course of the following week. Sumner's speech concluded: "Face to face against the SLAVE OLIGARCHY must be rallied the UNITED MASSES of the North, in compact political association—planted on the everlasting base of justice—knit together by the instincts of a common danger, and by the holy sympathies of humanity—enkindled by a love of Freedom not only for themselves but for others—determined to enfranchise the National Government from degrading thraldom" (*Liberator*, 18 May 1855, 78–79; *New York Tribune*, 16 May 1855, 6–7).

## To Maria Mott Davis and Edward M. Davis[1]

Philada. 8 mo. 7th. 55—

I am not going to inflict a long letter upon you, my dear Childn., but thot. you wd. like to hear that all is going on well at the Farm, as far as we know— yr. Father ne'er went out till this aftern.—for Anna [*Hopper*] had to stay at home, to receive Abby Gibbons & childn., who came yester-eveg.—& Edwd's heart wd. have broken, if large Isaac T. [*Hopper*] had not been here, to be shewn to his aunt

& cousins, who thot. him a very fine lovely boy— They all went to Wilmingn. this aftern.—& your carriage & pair just bore of "my sister & my sisters child" beside 2 others of hers & your 2 who have been very happy here, & have given little trouble— Their clothes were rather soiled—havg. a scant supply, & choosg. some of squirtg water from the hydrant—& filling their Grandpa's old shoes & drawg. them up the yard—& then by means of a cane flirting them high up in the air—almost baptizg. Ellen W.[2] who sat under our room window hemmg. the 12th sheet.

They & Ria & Georgie [*Hopper*] have exchanged visits oft— We were glad that 5 days of yr. absence wd. be nearly passed before their home wd. begin to be irksome to them without you— Anna & famy. will now remain during your absence— Ellen Woolley & self are going out there on a spree tomorw.— I have a skirt to cover, & havg. lent my frame, we are going in the 6 o clk. cars, & have already sent our work out in the carriage—& shall quilt it in no time—& then we purpose a drive over to Temple Bar then to Miller's—perhaps take tea there & home in the 8 o clk. cars from there— If yr. Father & Anna had gone yestery. as they intended, we shd. have been more of strangers—but now yr. Father has to come in @ 12 o clk. to attend a preliminary indignatn. Mg.—Morris H. & Miller signg. a kind of private call—[3] Thos. Williamson says he is only afraid Passmore will come out of Prison too soon— Yr. Father went down to Moyamensg. to see him to-day— Yr. Mother proposed last 1st. day that our Frds. shd. call a Mg. & enter a protest— Howard Wilson after Mg. expressed great unity with all that was said, & wished much that somethg. shd. be done, he had never had his feelgs so outraged as at Kanes doings—[4] Jas. Martin thot. the testimony conflictg—tho' he was watchg. with interest, &.c—didn't know whether we were prepared to act officially— We had quite a talk in the yard with some 6 or 8— Saml. Parry standg. in stolid silence— We went out to see Rachel Jackson in the aftern.— She is very sad—but hopes to arouse herself to the duties of the school wh. she presumes will be small[5]—but they intend to try & have issued the prospectus— Her Father & sisters were there— She has John's picture Phototype or some other large type—like that of mine— To-day is our Quary Mg. at Radnor, but we didn't go

The accompg. letters we send 1st. to you—after readg. the 'Furren' please Mail it instanter to Auburn they will think it long-comg— Ask Aunt Martha to forward it to the Flume—& you will please send Aunt Martha's to Thos. & Marianna, care of Baring, Brothers & Co. London—payg. postage—[6] I mention the directn. so that if by any possibility you shall have left Nant. our cousins Edwd. & Phebe [*Gardner*] will forward them— You will of course let them read all if they wish, & tell coz. Phebe how the Auburn letters have to be sent to Europe—& we cannot comply with her request to have them

How glad I am that you are on that dear Island—& can look upon our precious Aunt Phebe [*Hussey*] & all our loved cousins & dear friends to whom affection unmeasured goes forth— We want a letter from you—not havg. yet heard of yr. arrival at the Flume—a nice letter from Elizh. [*Cavender*] was recd. the day you left—  Pattie [*Lord*] & all are well—

AL PSCHi-Mott

1. Maria Mott Davis and Edward Davis had gone to visit relatives in Nantucket, leaving two of their children, probably Henry and Willie, with their grandparents.

2. Ellen Woolley was a seamstress employed by LCM and JM.

3. Morris Hallowell and James Miller McKim were protesting the arrest of the Philadelphia abolitionist and Hicksite Quaker Passmore Williamson (c. 1822–95). He had been charged with carrying off a black female servant, Jane Johnson, and her two children, the alleged property of John Wheeler, minister to Central America. Williamson contended that since Wheeler had brought the slaves into a free state, they were legally free. Edward Hopper was one of several attorneys hired by Thomas Williamson (c. 1796–1871) to represent his son. Hopper appeared in court on July 19 and Passmore Williamson testified on 20 July (*Case of Passmore Williamson* [Philadelphia: Uriah Hunt and Son, 1856], 4, 9–10; *New York Times,* 21 July 1855, 1, 6; *Liberator,* 27 July 1855, 119; *Diary of Sidney George Fisher,* ed. Nicholas B. Wainwright [Philadelphia: Historical Society of Pennsylvania, 1967], 250; *Friends' Intelligencer,* 9 March 1895, 157, 14 October 1871, 122).

4. On 27 July Judge John K. Kane (1795–1858) had ruled that Williamson had interfered with Wheeler's rights and then declared the former in contempt of court (*Liberator,* 3 August 1855, 122; *Case of Passmore Williamson,* 27–28).

5. After her husband's death, Rachel Jackson continued to operate the Sharon Female Boarding School until 1858 (Henry G. Ashmead, *History of Delaware County* [n.p., 1884], 521).

6. Thomas Mott and Marianna Mott had sailed for Europe on 30 May (JM to LCM, 30 May 1855, Mott Manuscripts, PSCHi).

## To Martha Coffin Wright

[*Philadelphia*]
[*September*] 4th day 5th—[*1855*]

[*Continuation of a letter begun 4 September*]

A gathered toe since last 1st. day has bound me fast to home & still prevents my going to Mg. today—so that I can finish & send the parcel wh. was my full intention yestery—but the Ex. Com. met here & some dozen callers & that crazy Elijah Fish who stayed tea & till after 9 oclk— Edwd. & Anna [*Hopper*] came up to tea a rare thing for Edwd.— He has been engaged day & night with this Slave case—[1] All I have said of Ellen [*Wright*]'s coming to Darby, may apply to Hetty [*Wood*] too if Charles should think of sendg. her there—[2] Our Father & Mother used to think there was an advantage in changg. schools & so sent us from Public to Private and from Boston to Nine Partners—& to Westown— Edwd. Hopper was afraid last eveg. that I had praised up Darby too much— He didn't see however what I had written— He went with Joseph Hanson last 7th. day to The Hills, if thats its name, and had a delightful visit over 1st. day—went to Birmingn. Mg. saw Clement Biddle, who kindly invited him to his son's—

didn't accept— Townsd. Sharpless took him over his Place & shewed him all his nice fixtures.[3] Edward thinks the frds. of T. D. Weld couldn't do better than to buy Benjn. Price's Place, wh. was once a boardg. school—[4] Caroe. [*Wood*] will know it I guess—a mile from West Chester—high, healthy situatn. fine productive country—cheaper livg. than any where near Chelton Hills where Ed. Davis & City-limits have raised the price of land, &.c so much— This fine farm might be bought for $10.000— So now, if Charles [*Wood*] & David [*Wright*] & *their wives* are disposed to head a subscription list & send it on, then Edwds. Hopper & Davis & M'Kim & the Wrights & their wives will see what they can do hereaway—& if successful here will be a good school at yr hand, when Chs. & Carole. pull up stakes & bring Hetty & Linn [*Wood*] Laura [*Stratton*] & Mary—Julia & Lou. [*Wood*] *&.c &.c—*

4th. day aftern. 5th—

Last scrap— As the parcel is overweight here goes another heavy ½ sheet. How I wish "our Tommy" wd. write with blacker ink, & in a legible hand. I have to depend altogether upon younger eyes— I tried to look over both his & Mari[a]. [*Mott*]'s—but had to give them up in despair. Eliza [*Yarnall*] says they are quite as difficult to read as Ellis'. Added to *his* hard hand, the paper is so thin that it tempts wicked people to swear—Sarah Pugh's & Miller's used to be just so— Why is it, that 'furrin' travellers are thus licenced? And Caro E. White, simple, green horn to cross-line, 'at that'! Her Mother assured her with a quick step, that she wd. at any time rather pay double postage. Mary [*Earle*] is not mean in *spendg.* her money, albeit she may be somewhat so in supplyg. her table for those who furnish her with the wherewithal. I have mentioned I think, that Richd. & Caro have been to the Giants Causeway—[5] Mary wrote recommendg. to them to go to London before comg. home— She has some transient boarders to help along— Speakg. of letters—have you Thos.' 1st.—and wilt thou send home that & all the others as soon as you have done with them? I have them all collected accordg. to dates, for Charlie Wharton[6]—Josh. Cottringer—Yeamans Gillingm. & others to see, at *their* request—& after all have had them, the pale, illegible things shall be restored to their respective envelopes, wh. also I have preserved, and sent or handed to thee, as the case may be, 'to have & to hold', as all thy own.

As to the Boston trip,[7] I begin to 'shake in my shoes'

now the 5th—latter part of the day

& 'no Barclay yet' & no sign of his comg— James moreover has "clawed off" from going—because Sarah Pugh is talkg. of bearing me compy—& he thinks he will be more in his place at The Oaks—Salem & Plymouth are in our programme & a visit to Gertrude B. & Lizzy Gay is in Sarah's— I have no plan, nor can I have at present but of course I shall write again, as soon as there is anything to write, when there will also be another Furren letter to send, for we are listeng. for the Newsboys to announce the Steamer—so if thou and Chs. &

Caroe. do think at all of Boston, have your trunks ready & start at short notice—
Maybe you will conclude to go without regard to me or mine. If so, give my love
to Lucy S. B—to Antionette [*Brown*] & the rest.

Why didn't thou tell us more of Lucy's private talk with thee at Saratoga?—
Joseph Barker had much to say of Mrs. Rose's lovely character. He scarcely knew
her superior. I was glad to hear him say so—and pleased also that her speaking
was so gratifying to thee, & that Frances Wright's womanhood was vindicated
by her—[8] I have ever or long wished for, & believed the time would come, when
the character of Mary Woolstonecraft & Frances Wright & Robert Owen, would
have justice done them—and the denunciations of bigoted Sectarianism fall into
merited contempt. It was more than I could patiently bear, to see those Scotch
Ecclesiastics at Norristown frown upon Thos. Curtis, when he so well & so carefully, so as not to offend the Orthodoxy of any, presented a beautifully bound
& gilt Bible, with ~~that picture in~~ the frontispiece—Jesus the Consolator, tellg the
Audience how the chained Slave had been stolen out of it & how it now was
presented with the text—"Come unto me all ye," &.c. virtually saying all ye *white*
men, women & childn., who are weary & ["]heavy laden, and I will give you
rest"—[9] That these men should feel that it was a compromise of their cherished
faith, thus to have fellowship with Infidels—& they had been deterred from
acting with us on that account & hoped the speakers wd. beware of calling in
question any part of the Written word, either the old or new Testament— Foss
had sd. what tho' the Levitical law allowed servitude—the higher law sd. "whatsoever ye wd." &.c[10]—& that he used to look *up* when speakg. of Jesus—but now
he saw him in the multitude among the Poor & despised, & oppressed, &.c.—
& I very innocently endorsed sd. sentiments, never dreamg. any body's piety wd.
be shocked, or any reply or disclaimer be called forth— And when we afterwd.
defended our position—they were compelled to say, "we didn't mean yr. Father"

That last letter of thine, came on 2nd. day last— I got James to go up for
Eliza, & she came in—Anna also, & we read it undisturbed The visit to Clifton
wd. have seemed far pleasanter if Hamlet had been there,[11] instead of "left out",
at home— You will have to go again some day— We hope Eliza [*Osborne*]
will experience the benefit after going home if not while there— Isn't she planning to come here this Fall to see our Pattie & hers?— It is no satisfaction tho'
to ask, nor to send pressg. invitatns., till we know more than we now do— Mary
Mott writes more discouraging of her Mother, that she is increasingy feeble &
her symptoms more alarmg—Aunt Mary Hicks still with them at Macinac—
They hope to return home in a week or two, if her Mother shd. be at all able to
bear the journey—(wh. is not likely) A letter from Aunt Lydia acknowledges
the shawl & things sent her for L. Fuller & thanks for the proceeds—& says
Arthur is dull at times—or suffers anxiety because his funds do not allow him
to pay Carpenter, &c as fast as they crave— Next spring they wd. have money
comg. from the West—& other people have to wait for pay— Elizh. Leedom[12]

a poor old worn-out Quaker preacher was then making part of her family & sharing their simple fare—I guess New Y. Frds. are boardg. her there—*low*. She "writes in her kitchen & near noon must go & see to her potatoes"— She wondered that they took Sister Elizh. from home—

A letter has just come from Lucy S. B. to James. He will be glad to have a reply to his so soon— When he came in unexpectedly yestery—he said it was because I was a cripple—but I soon found there was to be a raft there—S. H. Gay Jas & Mary Wright Danl. & Cec Neall[13]—& Kate Hoskin who is stopg. there She & Maria [*Davis*] were over at Brownie's spendg. the day— Edwd. had got up this party—& they had sent over for Maria, as indeed was the plan when she & Kate went—as they expected Sydney to lodge Lue H had an elegant visit there & at Anna B's last week, as I presume she wrote Ellen— Phebe Gardner writes that every body has been to Nant.—& they have had to lend the ocean & Atlantic houses their neat spare chambers to accommodate Ex govrs. & Mayors &.c—

Eliza has been home to dinner & back—no Telegraph from Ellis [*Yarnall*] yet—how we begin to watch Geo. & Pattie [*Lord*] have ventured on a short drive. I have been very careful always to let the choice of a Physician be my *childns*. not mine— Pattie did talk of Hannah Ellis who has large practice—& a Mother, on that accot. preferred to Ann Preston[14] but she is old school & lived far up town—so finally Dr. Griscom is to be the accoucher— Anna H. rather hoped she wd. have Hannah Ellis

AL PSCHi-Mott

1. In an earlier portion of this letter dated 4 September 1855, LCM had written MCW that former slave Jane Wheeler (or Johnson) had been to dinner at LCM and JM's house after testifying in the Passmore Williamson case, but first had to elude possible pursuit: "Her testimony was very clear & satisfacty— We didn't drive slow comg. home  Miller, an Officer—Jane & self—another carriage followg. with 4 Officers for protection and all with the knowledge of the States Attorney— Miller & the Slave passed quickly thro' our house, up Cuthbert St. to the same carriage—wh. drove around to elude pursuit— I ran to the storeroom & fillg. my arms with crackers & peaches, ran after them & had only time to throw them into the carriage" (Mott Manuscripts, PSCHi).

2. Charles Wood had married Caroline Stratton in April 1855 in Philadelphia.

3. Joseph Berry Hanson (1806–68) was a Philadelphia Hicksite Quaker. Clement Biddle (1778–1856) was a Philadelphia Hicksite Quaker. "Townsd. Sharpless" is possibly the Townsend Sharpless who wrote and published *Phonography* (Washington, D.C., 1857).

4. Theodore Weld had opened a coeducational school, Eagleswood, in 1853 as part of a radical Quaker settlement, the Raritan Bay Union, near Perth Amboy, New Jersey. Many radicals, including MCW, sent their children there (William Leach, *True Love and Perfect Union* [New York: Basic Books, 1980], 70–72).

5. Richard White and Caroline White were also traveling in Europe.

6. Charles Wharton (1823–1902), son of William Wharton and Deborah Wharton, was a partner in Edward Davis's firm (Gordon, 1:160). Joseph Cottringer and Yeamans M. Gillingham were listed as merchants in the Philadelphia City Directory, 1849.

7. LCM is referring to the Boston Woman's Rights Convention held on 19–20 September 1855, which she would not attend (*Liberator*, 31 August 1855, 138).

8. The Saratoga Springs Woman's Rights Convention had met on 15–16 August. MCW had been elected president of the convention and Ernestine L. Rose and Lucy Stone had given the principal addresses. Rose had spoken on the "disabilities of woman": "Mrs. R. contended that woman should be thoroughly educated—that all the avocations of life should be open to her, and she said such a state of things would operate vastly to raise both man and woman in the scale of existence, and contribute largely to the happiness, virtue and progress of whatever is right to be done" (*Lily,* 15 September 1855, from *Stanton-Anthony Papers,* reel 8, frs. 279–80). Antoinette L. Brown had described the convention as "the particular outgrowth of a State movement" (*Liberator,* 24 August 1855, 135, 14 September 1855, 148).

9. Thomas Curtis was a Philadelphia bookstore owner (*Philadelphia City Directory,* 1855). LCM is quoting Matt. 11:28.

10. Rev. Andrew Twombley Foss (1803–75) was a New Hampshire Baptist minister who had become an agent of the AASS (*WLG,* 4:317). Foss is quoting Matt. 7:12.

11. "Hamlet" is probably Charles Wood. In a letter to LCM, MCW had written of visiting Wood's home and finding "Hamlet" gone (29 March 1855, MNS).

12. Elizabeth Collins Leedom (d. 1866), a New York City Quaker, was listed as a minister in 1831.

13. Daniel Neall Jr. married Cecilia Anderson (1806–97).

14. Ann Preston (1813–72), a Hicksite Quaker physician, an advocate of woman's rights, and a member of the Clarkson Anti-Slavery Society, would establish the Woman's Hospital of Pennsylvania in 1861. MML would give birth to a daughter, Ellen Lord, on 13 September.

## To Martha Coffin Wright

[*Philadelphia*] 3rd. day—26th.
Last date [*February 1856*]

[*Continuation of a letter begun 25 February*]

I took this up to Eliza's at night yestery—as she sent me word she was too poorly to come here, & that Mary [*Brown*] was there—so I stayed to tea, & we passed a social eveg— Ellis [*Yarnall*] was engaged the latter part, at his frd. Hunter's— He dined at Thos. Cavr's. on 7th. day with Gen. Pomeroy & Henry Carey—came home in the aftern. to shew some of their Balt[imor]e. frds. his pictures—[1] He was disaptd. yestery—as well as the rest of us, that the 2 steamers brot. no letters from Thos. & Mariᵃ.— We presume the Pacific has one on board— There is every thg. to fear for that missg. ship—how awful these winter trips are! And yet Fairman Rogers & bride have just gone out in the Persia— They had engaged a passage in the Pacific— Anne W. Weston & br. gone too—[2] How like M. W. Chapman was that report of their Bazaar— The resolutns. too respectg Harriet Martineau—at the Annual Mg. were hers—& very just they were—[3] Phebe Gardner writes of shipwrecks on their coast—& that they were ice bound 10 days—& went out on the Ocean in sleighs— Edwd. had to go to Boston & New Y. on busins. & was kept away by the ice more than a week—& came home with $15 less in his pocket— Aunt

P. very well & had swallowed 2 vols. of Joseph J Gurney whole—that the Wilburs had been hateful to one of their preachers, because he suffered his son to
learn music at school—& he himself sat at the Examinatn. during the music
exercises—whereupon they at Mg. invited the frd. to a lower seat wh. he resented
& took his departure from them altogether— The death of Joseph Mitchell's
wife had caused quite a sensatn. among them— I cant remember anythg. else
in her letter—unless it is, that they made up a party—each takg. what they had,
& went out to Sconset to Matthew Crosby's house & had a royal, pleast. day—
Wm. Gardner's wife is quite a favorite with them.[4]

Now for thy letter— Tho' lines rather far apart, it was welcome—& good—
We took it up to Eliza's to read— Mary B. was there— It was kind of thee to
praise the trash of letter-scraps sent by Caroe. [*Wood*]— It was the best I could
do—"that's a fact"— This hasn't a foreign letter with it to redeem it— I'm
willing these sheets shd. be a foil to Mari[a]. [*Mott*]'s & her Mother's— I was glad
to have the Peace comments in thine on H. W. Beecher's inconsistency, to read
to Miller & Sarah & Mary Grew, S. Pugh & Rachel Lamborn when they all dined
here with C. Lenox Remond & Robt. Purvis & Adin Ballou last 3rd. day—[5] Miller is not quite a Peace-man—or non-resistant rather—& yet when the speech
of Lucy Stone was read, givg. countenance to suicide, rather than submit to be
a Slave, he thot. it such a horrible doctrine—& that we were in great danger of
becomg. familiar with such views thro' Geo Sands' & other writings—that one
thing led to another—[6] Our advocacy of freedom for the slave, had led to "free
soil"—"free Love" & now "free life"—depend upon it, there was need to pause—
at the same time not prepar'd to admit the inviolability of life—that it might
be taken, for the public good—but never in the shape of suicide to escape personal endurance or sufferg—*that* was purely selfish—& Lucy's "going to God"
was begging the questn.—or somethg. like that He was excited for awhile &
evidently shewed his sectari[a]n educatn.— We had much talk—sat long at
the dinner table—Remond & Purvis blamg. Greeley for his prejudice agnt. col-
or—Miller defendg. him, as havg. done more than any other political Editor for
the colored people &c—[7] Spiritualism came in for a share of the talk, Adin
Ballou havg. lectured the eveg before, on that subject—[8] We went to hear him—
(& "Lord willing"!) At 4½ we repaired to the Ex. Com. Mg—where Miller,
forgettg. part of our talk here, wanted we shd. all read an Article in the Independt.
from H. W. Beecher's pen, on self defence—or fightg— I've not seen the Article— He thot. it so beautifully written & so able, that he wanted we shd. read
it, without reference to the sentiment—we would—"& now," sd. I—"if, followg.
that, if you find another equally well-written defence of suicide in extreme cases,
do read it, laying aside for the time yr. own views"— Miller perceived the
"shot"—& tried to evade it or escape it—but his inconsistency was too glaring—
I wish you cd. have heard the discussn.—then & 1st. day eveg. here, with Gen
Pomeroy—Ths. Cavr.—Mary Grew—Ed Davis, Miller & self—on the Peace
questn.— Pomeroy was a Garrison Man— Peace was dear to him but then—

these Missouri border ruffians—what shd. you do?— David ought to have been here to help the Gen. advocate Sharp's Rifles in this emergency— His accot. of their "hair breadth scapes" was very interestg— Another party met him & Kersey Coates at Thos. Cavr's. to tea last eveg.—Prof Cleveld.[9]—Passmore W. Edwd. Davis & 6 or 8 more—

[P.S.] I was glad that Caroe. was improved in her looks by her visit hereaway  She seemed quite ready to go home & if any homesick feelings have been indulged by her previous to this visit, we here think she will now be better satisfied than ever with her new home— Maria Davis says it has always seemed pleasant to her for Caroe. to have such a settled place of abode—rather than her unsettled life for years past. Coz. Ruth [Chase] sd. if she had not come to see her this winter she shd. certainly have gone to her— She also sd. it was very pleast. to her to have the childn. & it is so natural for them to love to be with their Grandma & Aunt & all their old frds. & acquaintances—hereaway that their Mother & Father too, may well be satisfied for them to stay till warm weather  Augusta [Stratton] has improved with the added year or two of maturer life tho' still a child in some things. She looked well pleased to go back to Holly yestery. & I hope no needless concern on her accot. will be suffered to fill the mind

AL MNS

1. Samuel C. Pomeroy (1816–91) had served as the financial agent of the New England Emigrant Aid Co. and had spent a year and a half in Kansas working to establish it as a free state. In late November 1855 he had been captured by Missouri border ruffians and threatened with execution. Pomeroy had returned to the East in early January (NASS, 5 January 1856, 2). Henry Carey (1793–1879), a Philadelphia economist, was named treasurer of the Republican party in Pennsylvania for the 1856 presidential campaign.

2. Fairman Rogers (1833–1900) was a civil engineer from Philadelphia. Richard Warren Weston (1819–73), a shipping merchant, accompanied his sister to Europe (Taylor, 3; NASS, 23 February 1856, 3).

3. The annual meeting of the Massachusetts Anti-Slavery Society, held in Boston on 25 January, had passed a resolution honoring Martineau for a life "so unreservedly and strenuously devoted to the welfare of mankind" (NASS, 2 February 1856, 3).

4. Matthew Crosby (1791–1878). William Gardner (b. 1829) was a son of Edward Gardner.

5. The Brooklyn preacher and orator Henry Ward Beecher (1813–87) had recently proposed dealing with the admission issue in Kansas by furnishing free state settlers with Sharp's rifles. In an article in the Independent (7 February 1856, 1) Beecher had addressed criticism from the New York Observer for his statement that "there was more moral power in one of those [Sharp's rifles] . . . than in a hundred Bibles." Beecher had maintained that the Kansas settlers' possession of the rifles "would produce a more salutary impression upon vagabond politicians and work more efficiently for peace, than all the moral suasion in the world." Rachel Anna Lamborn (d. 1860) was a member of the Progressive Friends meeting (see LCM to MCW, 17 August 1860, Mott Manuscripts, PSCHi). Robert Purvis (1810–98), born in slavery to a white father and a mulatto mother, was a Philadelphia business leader and a founder of the AASS.

6. In Cincinnati on 13 February, Stone had spoken immediately after the court had adjourned for the day in the trial of Margaret Garner, a slave accused of murdering her

child. After visiting Garner in prison, Stone reported that she believed that Garner was right in proclaiming "'Let us go to God rather than go back to Slavery.' . . . Who that knows the depths of a mother's love, does not estimate the sacrifice she had made? If she had a right to deliver her child, she had a right to deliver herself. So help me Heaven! I would tear open my veins, and let the earth drink my blood, rather than wear the chains of Slavery" (*New York Tribune,* 18 February 1856, 6). The early novels of the French writer George Sand, pen name of Amandine Aurore Lucie Dupin, Baronne Dudevant (1804–76), emphasized characters who defied societal conventions.

7. In recent *New York Tribune* editorials Greeley had strenuously attacked the Fugitive Slave Law and had supported the admission of Kansas as a free state. Remond and Purvis may have been offended, however, by editorials such as one in which Greeley had implied that blacks lacked intelligence. Regarding slaveholders' rejecting democratic principles, Greeley had written, "What if smouldering for so many years the other doctrine [*democracy*] should have penetrated the thick wool of the negroes?" (9 January 1856, 4).

8. Ballou had lectured in Sansom Hall to an audience of spiritualists (*NASS*, 16 February 1856, 2).

9. Kersey Coates (1823–87), a Lancaster attorney and the son of Lindley Coates, had spent 1854–55 in Kansas where, while engaged in real estate, he had allied with the free state faction. Charles D. Cleveland (1802–69) of Philadelphia was a classics professor and editor.


## To Elizabeth Neall Gay

Philada 5 Mo. 27th. 1856

My dear Elizh.

Our dear Mary Shackleton leaves us with her niece this morng., after passing a few days with us—to us very pleasantly— She is anticipating a visit to you this week—& to her I refer thee for all of us & ours that may interest thee— how busy we are settling our Geo. & Pattie [*Lord*] in a little cottage near E. M. Davis's assistg. Thos. & Elizh. Cavr. in movg. out to a similar summer spot nearby preparg. myself for a sudden start to Auburn, with Edwd. & Maria—& little Bel Mott—the latter to see her little sister, who was separated from her a year ago, when their Parents left us for a year in Europe; how pleased we have all been with the opp[ortunit]y. of mingling with those nice young Unitarians at the Progressive Friends Mg. at *Kennett*—and how we laugh'd at thee for not knowg. where Long Wood was—& supposg. that sd. Mg. wd. be held in this City—as inferred from thy few lines introducg D. E Wasson to our notice—[1] Where dost thou keep thyself—not to have heard of *Chester Co.* Yearly Mg.? When Sydney's co-laborer—Oliver J. is so well posted in all their movements! Come out of thy privacy let the babies take care of themselves, just watched by their nurse to keep them out of mischief— I sought thee in vain at the Anniversy. in New Y— Didn't thy *aged* frd. leave babies too, to go there?

I can show thee 3 young Grandchildn. & a niece—[*Anna*] Brown—beside— as well worth being tied down to, as any babies ever born— Didn't thy sd. frd. trot about in all that storm—not only attendg. the Mgs. but going to East Broadway—to look after our br. Richard Mott, who was ill of Typhoid fever & who still is lying there only now considered out of danger J. Mott returng. from him last eveg— And more than all didn't that unwise frd. of thine make a fool of herself by agreeg. to stop longer in N. Y. & try to say somethg. at the City An. Mg.? her powers enfeebled by age at best—then completely exhausted by the previous 2 days' excitement—so pleast. while it lasted. Do read Frothingham's speech—& *repent* that thou wast not there to hear it—[2] I pitied Sydney that eveg—to be so mortified as I knew [he?] must be— But let that pass into oblivion—if it ever will— The young are doing so nobly—Conway—& Wasson & a host comg. up—such brave, outspoken Radicals—leavg. our good Saml. J. May quite in the conservative ranks.[3] The three were here together & Wm. H. Furness with them—& their conversatn. did my heart good— I read them thy letter of 2 or 3 yrs. ago, touchg. Weiss on the Woman questn.— Did any one ever ans. him? I cd.n't find a Champion as thou wished—but he saw thy spirited comments on his weak production, that was somethg.—& hundreds beside have heard it read— — I now have one equally spicy from Lizzy Stanton denying the report of her havg. joined the Church—[4] I must stop— Cant thou meet Ed., Maria [*Davis*], & self—on board the North River boat on 6th. day aftern. next? I shall go on in the 10 oclk line & join them who go on 5th. day eveg.— Edwd. havg. busins. in New Y— It wd. be a little excursion for thy children to take them there & let us see them & *thee* Now rouse thy latent energies—and pass an hour with us on board sd. boat—

Our Holly frds. are well—Coz. Ruth [*Chase*] attended our Yearly—as Mary S. can tell thee—they being roommates—& could talk Ireland together. that is she was with us that week not much at Mg—for her day is nearly over—as well as that of

thy ever loving    *L. Mott*

ALS NNCB-Gay

1. The Progressive Friends had held their yearly meeting at the Longwood Meeting House in Kennett on 18 May 1856. The organization aimed to "unite persons of every shade of theological opinion, in ONE SPIRIT OF LOVE" and to "testify against those systems of popular wickedness which derive their support from a false Church and a corrupt Government" (*NASS*, 3 May 1856, 3). David E. Wasson (1823–87), then a minister with the Free Church of Worcester, Massachusetts, had recently preached in favor of armed resistance to the proslavery forces in Kansas (*NASS*, 16 February 1856, 3).

2. At the AASS annual meeting, held on 7–8 May in the New York City Assembly Rooms, LCM had advocated that speakers "limit themselves as much as they conveniently could" in order that the numerous topics and business issues could be addressed. In his speech on 8 May, Octavius B. Frothingham (1822–95), a Unitarian clergyman from Jersey City, New Jersey, had called for "anti-slavery action" to support the spreading rhetoric against slavery. He had stated that more dangerous than the outright proponents of slavery were the weak Northern men, like President Millard Fillmore, who deceived antislavery adherents into thinking they supported their cause (*Liberator,* 16 May 1856, 79, 6 June 1856, 92).

3. The sermons of the Virginia-born minister-turned-abolitionist Moncure D. Conway (1832–1907) were occasionally printed in the *Liberator* (see e.g., 22 February 1856, 30–31). At the AASS meeting, May had urged the society to take "*gradual steps*" toward the abolition of slavery in Kansas (ibid., 16 May 1856, 79).

4. Apparently MCW had written LCM about the rumors that Stanton had joined the Episcopal church. In a recent letter to MCW, LCM had remarked that Stanton was "too sensible to be caught by sudden conversion—& what will she do with her Woman interest—" (17 April 1856, MNS).

## To Philadelphia Family

Flume House [*New Hampshire*] 8 mo. 20th. 56—

I will not wait till the last minute, before beging. a letter, & then have to hurry it off so, but will give you the best hours of this day—especially as tis too wet, after the night's rain, to go to the Pool— — Anna [*Hopper*]'s acceptable little sheet, was recd. last eveg. also one from Ellis [*Yarnall*],—both givg. a better accot. of you & yours, & ours, than Pattie [*Lord*]'s doleful one wh. came the eveg. before, with Maria [*Davis*]'s ½ sheet—also rather doleful— Elizh. Cavr.'s childn. all sick— Thos. stayg. so much in the hot city— Kitty not being of much assistance—&.c. &.c— Then that forlorn out-pourg. from the tank, when it might have been avoided, by a further outlay—lining it, so much trouble as it is to put down carpets, & make preserves, one dont want the labor lost by a needless freshet— You didn't say whether or not the mattg. was all stained & spoiled. I *feared* the upper part of that tank would do so, & asked if it had not better be secured by leading it— It is poor satisfaction however to say, "I told you so."— — —
— Pattie's experience of country life so far, has been rather of the vexatious order. I reckon she will not incline to remain at RoadSide so long as they talked of in anticipation—even tho' George may be disposed to make as light, of their annoyances, as did their cousin Walter B—of theirs— I was glad to hear of Joseph Lord's intentn. of visiting them.[1] Glad too that Ellis Y. is makg. The Oaks rejoice in his presence. He writes that it is very pleast. to him, insomuch that he readily accepted an invite to prolong his stay. Tell him I am daily growing familiar with his admired frds.—the miss Morrises, & find them *quite* smart, fine girls—not however up to my highest idea of his chosen associates—the elder sister has not intellectual organs so well developed, as ought to suit him—the younger, amiable—lovely, but too delicate, & rather drawls her words. I'll talk more with them however— Now, *that* Miss Mayer, not any handsomer than Miss Morris, the elder, is a finer girl, is she not, Ellis? I have been talkg. with John Weiss this morng., & shewed him Elizh. Gay's letter, on his Woman Article in the Christn. Examr. 2 or 3 years ago— I admire his countenance & agree with him, in many of his views. He is a great pet among his New B. parishioners He joins in the innocent sports of this place—where indeed there is so much free & easy enjoyt. This wet morng., the Kennicotts, & others, includg. the young

Artist Hodgson, have been singg. & playg. all the modern ballads, &.c—to Quaker & other admirg. listeners. Elizh. Cavr. is held in warm rememb[ranc]e here, & Thos. too very kindly spoken of— The Kennicotts are so sorry they are not here— Young Hodgson also expressed himself so— He shewed us last eveg., his essay at Elizh.'s picture ^Aunt E. says it is like Mary Mott^—the hair, & form very good—features not so happy—the dear baby in her lap. I trembled last eveg. when the letter was handed us, with Ellis' directn., lest it shd. contain bad news of little Charlie [*Cavender*], who was on his Mother's lap with fever when the other was sent— These & the late Eng. we sent yestery. to Auburn—so I cant notice all the contents. The fancy party fixins we liked to know of— Ellis wrote that it was successful— — Wm. [*Yarnall*] & Lizzy [*Yarnall*] ought to have gone. Their Father [*Benjamin*] wd. have been none the worse. I wish his spirits cd. be raised. He must try to be bright when Thos. & Mari<sup>a</sup>. [*Mott* ] come home, & enjoy their return, & not dampen their spirits with unavailg. depression. But, alas! how impossible to reason oneself into good spirits & cheerfulness, when disease is shatterg the framework. Nathl. [*Brown*] tries to enjoy what is passing, but when seized with giddiness, it depresses him. He has fallen sometimes when suddenly attacked. Eliza [*Brown*] is alive to every thing, & ready for any spree or scramble. A party of them went yestery. to Mount Lafayette—on horseback— Josh. Ricketson[2] & Fanny [*Cavender*] & Sarah Y. of the number— Eliza B. had rode so much in Madeira, over mountns., that she feared nothg— But the day being windy & rainy, they had rather a perilous ride, & did not quite reach the top—came back wet & muddy—safe however— Thos. Earle & wife were along—& a merry time they had—takg. their dinner with them—^pretendg to us that they went to the tip top—^ We older folk, are satisfied with *part* mountn., & tother part intellectual elevatn. on this plain—the large parlor, where one after another meets you & talks—& where we read together anythg. interestg— The Tribune's Review of Emersons late work for instance, wh. Carry Rowld. read to us this morng., till the singg. & playg. interrupted her, & formed a pleasg. variety.[3]

The beautiful water-falls, & broad streams we enjoy—broader than usual, by late rains.—the deep fissures & wild ravines—& basins & pools cut out by Nature, never tire. It is not strange that this place has Yearly attractns. We told Elizh.'s frds. of her mountn. sickness- The house & table, Nathl. says "are beautiful"— The too-good living, at these fashionable places, is rather the most objectionable part of them—for we are hungry eno' for plain fare— Aunt E. is growg. quite fat, & Mother has gained also— As to yr. Father's health, he was so much better after takg. those nice remedies—Lydia's bl[ac]kb[err]y. syrup, & Maria's camphor, that we forgot to say how well he was, as I felt sure he wd. be, on comg. to his native salt air— And he has ailed nothg. since reachg. Nantucket—

5th. day morng. early—

My time for writg—21st—rainy Dismal weather for climbg. mountns., & seeing distances. Still we have had some fine drives & walks— Did our last mention our Chariot ride to the Profile House? We walked from there to Echo Lake, heard the cannon fired—but *didn't* go out in the boat. Josh. Ricketson called for the echo, "Freedom every where, Slavery no where" some young men were there, & walked away before we did. As we were near the house returng., a spoiled egg was thrown, & broke about a foot from us— What it meant we were left to conjecture— We sd. nothg. about it. The profile is so high on the pointed rock, that it looked smaller than I expected to see, but an exact likeness to a man's face—the dashing waters as we rode along—the basin, wh. we left our Chariott to see, & indeed the whole ride was very interestg.—& part of the way grand— Some 8 or ten horseback riders were in our rear—some on little ponies—and as they rode up to the Profile House—the high mountains all around they looked like pigmies— — The House there is still larger than this—but not so well filled. I have not been sorry that Aunt M. resisted the strong inclin[atio]n. to come here with us, & our equally strong wish to have her compy. for it wd. have been an expensive pleasure, for the very few hours we have had to sit together—Aunt E. & the girls havg. their chosen compy. in Mary's room— nice Barkers from Tiverton, [R.I.] & the Morris's &.c— Only one aftern. & part of one morng. has she sat in our room— Nathl & Eliza have kept much in their room—except evegs. when we all meet in the large parlor, where singing, dancg., & Charades fill the time— We have not yet had the Elephant—the man is sick— As to climbg. wet mountns. and threadg. the way thro' thick forests to the Flume, Pool, &.c—the latter we did yestery in a little rain too, it wd. not be at all to Aunt M's taste—& it wd. fatigue her too much—beside spoilg. clothes so awfully— but if she can "raise the wind" to meet us in Boston, go to see Mr. Mellen[4]—& to Worcester & Prov[idenc]e., & so to New Y. to meet Thos. & Mari[a]. it wd. be prime— Cant [*Anna*] Brownie add to this a small sheet & send it to Aubn.— for it is not likely her aunt can do any such thing, & the least we can do, is to keep her informed of our doings— If another letter come send it on immedy—directed to Anti S. Office Cornhill, Boston & we will read & forwd. it to Auburn—a letter will reach us there mailed as late as the 27th or 28th.

AL MNS

1. The brother of George, Joseph Lord was listed as a New York City broker in 1859; he later became a partner with George in the wool business in New York City and New Jersey (New York City directories, 1859, 1867, 1876).

2. Joseph Ricketson was a New Bedford antislavery activist (*NASS*, 30 January 1845, 139).

3. Emerson's *English Traits* (Boston: Phillips, Sampson, 1856) had been reviewed in the *New York Tribune* (16 August 1856, 6). The reviewer had concluded: "It is rarely that a nation is made to sit for its likeness to so severe, so cold blooded, and so impartial an artist. We believe that every line has been drawn, every color blended, with a high sense

of fidelity to the original." "Carry Rowld." is probably Caroline Rowland (b. 1832), the daughter of James Rowland and Phebe Ann Low Rowland, Philadelphia Hicksites.

4. Charles Mellen, the pastor of the First Universalist Society of Weymouth, Massachusetts, 1855–60, had previously been pastor of the Universalist Church in Auburn, New York (*WLG*, 4:606).

## To Lucy Stone

Philada. 10 Mo. 31st. 1856

My dear Lucy

I know I am remiss, very, in having taken no notice of thy several letters, requiring answers too as they did— All is, I have been full of work, since our return from our summer wanderings, both in our own house, and helping to settle our Thos. & Marianna [*Mott*] on their arrival to us from their long travel abroad— These domestic cares, added to Anti-Slavery Mgs, Fair Circles, a host of company, and some little visiting, have left no time for writing.

When thy first letter was received, announcing the Conventn. for October, I immedy. began to enlist interest in its behalf, & intended sending word to S. Grimke & A Weld— My Sister Martha came prepared to attend it—but thy 2nd. letter informed the time was postponed— It was a relief to me as far as personal considerations went, for it would have been almost impossible to leave home then—

Afterward, in view of the absorbing interest in the Presidential question,[1] as well as the surfeit of Conventions, I rather hoped the year would be suffered to pass, before another Call was issued. I did not like however to say so to thee, lest it might appear a waning of interest in the great Cause. And so, the time passed & I said nothing— Now that another day is fixed upon, of course my sister Martha & self have resolved to be there, and to do all we can to give the Mg. interest, and try to gain all the added strength we can, in the up-hill labor of Reform—

Let there be as much publicity given to it as possible, and as early as may be— Who is there in New York to aid thee in the necessary steps? Ernestine L. Rose out of the country, our dear Antionette otherwise engaged we hear[2]—and we are ready to wish that thou wast too—

T. W. Higginson full of Kansas.[3] He has returned from the West however, and his services must be secured.

Will that nice hard-named German lady, who is aiding Dr. E. Blackwell in the College & Hospital, unite with us in this movement? We were much pleased with her.[4]

Mary Grew's time is so much occupied with preparations for the coming A. S. Fair, that I fear we can not have her services in New York.

We are glad to hear that you are likely to settle permanently, at the East, rather than the West— Wherever you shall be located, my husbands & my best wishes go with you—

Why not add the name of Blackwell—Lucy Blackwell Stone as the French wives do? Its yr. business not mine however—[5]

Lovingly    L. Mott[6]

ALS DLC-Blackwell

1. James Buchanan (Democrat), Millard Fillmore (American/Know-Nothing), and John C. Frémont (Republican) were running for U.S. president. The Republican platform called for congressional control over the extension of slavery in the territories and the admission of Kansas as a free state.

2. Antoinette Brown had married Samuel Charles Blackwell (d. 1901), the brother of Henry Blackwell, on 24 January 1856.

3. After the Kansas-Nebraska Act of 1854, which provided that residents in those territories could determine whether their region was to be slave or free, antislavery forces under the New England Emigrant Aid Company began promoting the free-soil settlement of Kansas. Higginson had been in Kansas on behalf of the Kansas Aid Committee investigating an attack on immigrants there (Gordon, 1:329).

4. Elizabeth Blackwell (1821–1910), the sister of Henry and Samuel, was the first woman to receive a medical degree in the United States. Dr. Marie Elizabeth Zakrzewska (1829–1902) was born in Germany and had immigrated to the United States in 1852. She and Blackwell worked together at a clinic in New York City until 1859, when Zakrzewska moved to Boston to help found the New England Hospital for Women and Children.

5. Although Stone had adopted "Blackwell" as her last name when she and Henry Blackwell were married on 1 May 1855, in July 1856 she had decided that she wished to retain her maiden name and insisted on that nomenclature thereafter (*Loving Warriors: Selected Letters of Lucy Stone and Henry B. Blackwell,* ed. Leslie Wheeler [New York: Dial Press, 1981], 163).

6. At the New York Woman's Rights Convention, held 25–26 November 1856, LCM would be named vice president and MCW would become secretary. LCM would speak on a marriage in which husband and wife were essentially equal and proposed the following resolution, which was adopted: "That as the poor slave's alleged contentment with his servile and cruel bondage only proves the depths of his degradation, so the assertion with regard to woman, that she has all the rights she wants, only proves how far the restraints and disabilities to which she has been subjected have rendered her insensible to the blessings of true liberty" (*Liberator,* 5 December 1856, 196).

## To Lucy Stone

[*Philadelphia 9 December 1856*]

[*Added to JM's letter of the same date*]

Dear Lucy—

As the notice has been so widely extended of thy lecture in that Hall, & as it is now too late to procure another buildg. & give notice, I hope thou wilt consider thy present pledge to the public as binding as thy expressed resolve not again to use that Hall—[1] Were it hired expressly for thee, the case wd. be difft.—

Richardson says thou may enter any protest—that he wd. be as willing as we wd. for certain respectable colored people to come to the lecture— We offered to send tickets to such, & he went directly to the Superintendent to obtain permission but without success Thy Border Ruffian subject[2] can include the wrongs done to our colored people in various ways & perhaps do more good than now to break thy contract wh. would seem too *womanish* & rather capricious. I hope thou wilt not be too firm The colored men who came here that morng to scold thee, did not behave well about it—nor have some others—

AL DLC-Blackwell

1. Stone had been scheduled to deliver her lecture, "Border Ruffians at Home," at the segregated Musical Fund Hall on 11 December 1856. JM encouraged her to keep her engagement and had written in his part of this letter: "While I consider the exclusion of col[ore]d. people to be very wrong & wicked, yet I doubt the propriety of making it so much of an objection, as for thee now to decline lecturing" (see also *Philadelphia Public Ledger,* 9 December 1856, 2).

2. In July 1856 Stone had begun speaking on the struggle between proslavery Missourians, also known as border ruffians, and the Free-Soilers in Kansas (Andrea Moore Kerr, *Lucy Stone: Speaking Out for Equality* [New Brunswick, N.J.: Rutgers University Press, 1992], 97; James M. McPherson, *Battle Cry of Freedom: The Civil War Era* [New York: Oxford University Press, 1988], 146–53).

# PART 3

# *July 1857–January 1868*

⎯⎯⎯⎯⎯⎯⎯⎯

In March 1857 JM and LCM retired to Roadside, the farm they had purchased in 1851 when JM quit his wool business. *Retired,* however, is hardly the word to describe their lives. Logistically the eight-mile distance
from the city center required more concern with transportation and the harsh
weather that might disrupt their obligations in Philadelphia. For example, shortly after the move, LCM wrote Lucy Stone, "Country people can't perform City
duties easily" (1 July 1857). Still, the move did not substantially diminish the
Motts' activism. LCM enjoyed harvesting the vegetables, and JM planted corn
and hauled lumber, but "Ex. Com." meetings of the PASS, attendance at lectures
by Ralph Waldo Emerson or William Lloyd Garrison, and visits to family in the
city continued.

Since many letters to other reformers have disappeared, the record of LCM's
thoughts during a time of great national crisis depends, with a few exceptions,
on letters to her sister MCW or her daughter MML. From these letters we learn
about the hardships caused by the Panic of 1857; John Brown's capture and execution; LCM's constant reading (she preferred factual accounts to "made up
stories"; letter to MCW, Anna Temple Brown, and MML, 21 January 1864) of the
*New York Tribune,* the *NASS,* the *Independent,* and, of course, the paper edited
by her old friend and fellow abolitionist, Garrison's *Liberator.* Portions of LCM's
letters up to and throughout the Civil War provide a running commentary from
a skeptic's point of view. She characterized Lincoln as a "miserable compromiser" and criticized those politicians who decreed that the war was not waged to
end slavery. She admired Senator Charles Sumner because he was *not* a typical
politician, and she praised John C. Frémont's emancipation policy in St. Louis.
As the war neared its close, LCM lamented the split between Wendell Phillips

and Garrison, siding with the former's argument that the antislavery movement must not lapse.

The Civil War should not slow down reform movements, LCM insisted in December 1862. Through her speeches, she remained determined to keep woman's rights before the public: "And when our Meetings are forbidden, & doors closed against us, it is no time to stay away, & thus yield to the enemy," she wrote fellow activist Lydia Mott (22 January 1861). She protested the new periodical *Nation*'s ignoring of women's interests ("it wd. be rather 'a come down' for our Anti Slavery women & Quaker women to consent to be thus overlooked," she wrote MCW and Anna Temple Brown on 10 April 1865). After the war LCM tried to get Wendell Phillips to lend his considerable oratorical powers to the cause of woman suffrage. Although dissension over priorities threatened the cooperation between the representatives of woman's rights and African American rights that had existed since the late 1830s, LCM wrote Susan B. Anthony that she still hoped that the reformers could continue to work in harmony (10 February 1867).

Most of LCM's letters contain a recital of recent deaths of friends and relatives, not unusual in an age of typhoid, pneumonia, risky childbirth, and unreliable medical practices. By 1861, five of her grandchildren had died of sudden illnesses. But in this section we witness two deaths that affected her intensely, even before the one that was to transform her domestic life. Twenty-three-year-old Lue Hopper died in December 1861 of tuberculosis, and in September 1865 Elizabeth Mott Cavender died of cancer at age forty. Then the death of JM in 1868, coming so unexpectedly at the home of daughter MML and George Lord in Brooklyn, left LCM without her companion of over fifty-six years. An earlier expression conveys her anguish over such losses: "how impossible to reason oneself into good spirits & cheerfulness, when disease is shatterg the framework" (letter to Philadelphia family, 20 August 1856).

## To Lucy Stone

Road-Side Montgy Co—
7 mo. 1st. 1857

My Dear Lucy

I could not ans. thy inquiries "at once," for it required time to think about it, & try to come to some satisfactory decision.

I was rather hoping that we should let Conventions "slide" this year. We have had so many, & such a repetition of the same speakers, that I fear they are costing more than they come to— No *National* Convention however has been held in Boston; and if we could ensure a creditable one, it would I think be best to hold it there— —

I should of course try hard to be present, let it be held in either place— Our buildg, and arrangg. &.c. will occupy me all summer & most of the Autumn— Still whenever you should or shall judge best to issue the Call, I shall make the effort to be present.

Yes, herewith is my mite toward the Almanac. I am sure that our devoted T. W. Higginson ought to receive all the aid he requires, in the pursuit of his object— —[1]

My sister Martha sent me a little scrap, which she wrote some weeks since for their Paper 'Auburn Daily Advertiser.' I have intended to offer it to the Wom. Advocate, but I have not yet seen the Editor.[2] Country people can't perform City duties easily, I find.

I will enclose it for thy perusal— When writg. again to let us know yr. decision as to time & place of Conventn., please return the scrap, & I will send it to the Advocate. You should decide soon, so as to circulate information at the West, through the Lily & Bugle, & other Papers— —

We were glad to hear of your location at Orange & will gladly avail ourselves of the kind invitatn. to visit you, when in our power—

Will not Antoinette be able to leave baby & home cares this Fall, & attend the Convention again?[3]

Love to her & to both your husbands & excuse the haste.

Ever thine    L. Mott

My husband's love also to you all & to thee in special.

ALS DLC-Blackwell

1. Higginson was at that time working to bring in Kansas as a free state and organizing a disunion convention (Gordon, 1:346–49).

2. The *Woman's Advocate,* a Philadelphia paper founded in 1855 and operated entirely by women, had been established by Anne E. McDowell (1826–1901).

3. Stone and Henry Blackwell had recently moved to Orange, New Jersey, where they were expecting a baby. Antoinette Brown Blackwell's first child, Florence Brown Blackwell, had been born in November 1856 (Andrea Moore Kerr, *Lucy Stone: Speaking Out*

*for Equality* [Rutgers, N.J.: Rutgers University Press, 1992], 101; Elizabeth Cazden, *Antoinette Brown Blackwell* [Old Westbury, N.Y.: Feminist Press, 1983], 115). No woman's rights convention was held until 13–14 May 1858 in New York City.

## To Martha Coffin Wright

[*Roadside*]
3rd. day 8th [*September 1857*]—

[*Continuation of a letter begun 7 September*]

This was begun yestery— S. Pugh & Abby K. came early in the aftern. to tea—& Anna B. concluded to stay too, as Walter had gone to New Y— Mari[a]. [*Mott*] came to call but we made her stay— Ed. & Maria [*Davis*] stopped for a wonder, from a walk over their extensive domains, & sat while we ate—partakg. of some bl[ac]kb[errie]s. just brot. in— We had quite a pleast. time with them all— Mari[a]. has been here agn. this morng— She waited on Thos. to the cars, & then walked around the road & here for exercise— Just as I had penned the above about Ellis [*Yarnall*], we heard he had come out & was at the Farm— They are all going to Thos. Cavr's to tea—a hut-full—the [*George and Susan*] Barkers, Perots—M'Kims—&.c—[1] Ellis knew not of the party—but they are makg. him go with them— Pattie [*Lord*] has just gone to the Cars for George & then to the party— Jas. & self declined on accot. of room— I preferred too this quiet home to go on with this letter, so as to take it into town tomorw.—
— Phebe Gardner begged for Auburn letters—so I sent to Mary [*Earle*] thy last long one, with stamps for her to forwd. it— It contained several mentions of Caroe. [*Wood*], her *chicken fondness*—her preservg—& yr jelly-makg—& corn pudg. makg—Joe Lord's visit—the rides & drives—& thy comments on our letters— I read it all over before sendg. it, to see if there was anythg not suited to Nant.— 4th. day I asked Mary if twas sent— "Why no! Where was it?["] So much to do it was forgotten  The stamps were not seen—& finally I felt provoked at the want of a little care— Jas. had a busins. letter from Nathl. [*Barney?*] to ans. so I enclosed the two smaller ones from thee, via Flume—Aunt M's visit—& sundry other items will interest them— That lost letter, with one from Eliza [*Osborne*] with it, we now give up in despair  We may find it some day betwn. some Papers— That "Nothing to do" has but just reached our backward region. We have not yet seen it. Pattie is deep now in Aurora Leigh— We are not among the earliest readers— — The Papers take far too much time even tho' we skip so much— Curtis' Lecture I liked to read[2] And yet how little faith you have in all these fancy writers. Curtis is said to be a selfish fellow— Putnam it seems is stopped— The Tribune is complaind of, as deterioratg— — Some of the 1st. Aug. speeches are good eno', if we hadn't already "line upon line"— I liked Garrison's bold reply to Sigma—but Pillsbury's baptism of dogs is worn threadbare— —[3] This week our Anti S. Mgs. begin agn. and the Fair

Circles must meet—and in the midst of this dreadful money-panic, it seems "a forlorn hope"— We have fugitives by the doz. comg. almost every week. Miller & Sarah [McKim] were here to tea on 1st. day, & tho' we wd. "sink the shop" when he comes for a social visit, he has so much of it every day, yet it was necessy. to talk a little of future plans—for we have had few Ex. Com. Mgs. this summer— We are to meet 5th. day— The Disunion Con. is not yet fully decided as to time & place— Syracuse is talked of, & the last of next Mo. proposed—& we must appoint our Annual Mg—so as not to interfere— We hope to have T. W. Higginson to be with us—the Mg. is to be at West Chester  Then the Wom. Rig. Con— When? & where?— Now that Lucy Stone is otherwise occupied— Antionette too, not able to attend, S. B. Anthony lecturg. on Slavery[4] Mrs. Rose very poorly we hear (as usual) inflam[mator]y. rheumm. &.c—who is there to take the lead? Wilt thou?— I have rather hoped this year wd. "slide"—but I'm ready to do the little that remains for me—only I dont want to spend any money in travelg—while we are payg. so many dollars a day to workmen of all kinds— to say nothg. of the cost of furnces & ranges & $100 mantels—no, not quite that neither, but considerably more than 100 for all we have had— The great failures occurg. here, in New Y—& Boston—oh, every where are eno' to alarm us all for our foundatn.—— Thos. says he's sorry eno he didn't keep out of business when he was out, for they "will lose like the mischief now"—not a cent has he made since he re-entered the firm  He may not have meant for me to put this on paper—or even to repeat it so please be careful, & destroy this— Our good neighbr. Stephen Colwell 11th & Arch—author of "New Themes for the Protestt. Clergy—" that grand book, has failed—Robt. Haydk.'s br. George too— Carole. [Wood] knows him, Coffin & Haydock— Charley Wharton went on to New Y—today to see them, & to meet & talk with [V]ibert, who has arrived in the Arago, with his famy., to settle in New Y. [T]his startling panic will frighten him————[5] It is well that Edwd. Hopper hasn't notes to pay— He & Anna did start at last a week ago—were at Elmira the 1st night— Niagara next day & the day after & were to be at Toronto—thence to Quebec—Montreal &.c—& home about the middle of next week— I wish they cd. have been one day at least with you— It is just as "queer" to me, as to thee, that they didn't take the time—even tho they had to pass Dr. Ed. Moore by— Anna sd. it wd. give her great pleasure to see him—so it wd. to be with you all— Edwd. likes to travel in his own way, & "wants none of yr. dictates." Lue & Isaac T. [Hopper] & Cathe. are at the Hut  The other Cathe. at home—the house & Office open every day— Ria [Hopper] not yet returned from New Y— Her parents will probably stop for her— Abby Gibbons has been quite sick—not able to come on here & see Sarah P. in her convalescence———— I have not mentioned that Thos. & Mari[a]., Maria & Anna D went into town last 7th. day aftern., to pay Ellis, as well as Benjn's. famy. all a home comg. visit— I took the word to them in the morng. & found it wd. suit—but I cd.n't stay & enjoy it with them, & come out by moonlight—this splendid harvest moon, wh. we have enjoyed so much— They had 4 a carriage load without me—tho' with 2 horses they begged me to stay, & we cd. ride 3 on the back seat— Eliza also pressed me & the girls too—but I had dined there with Ellis—& heard much that interested me— James had to drive over to Dewey's Lane @ 5 oclk., to take Mary Ann [*Chase?*], & I had agreed to come out in those cars & meet him & ride back with him— Pattie cd.n't leave George who was almost sick with Influenza & Nelly with no nurse— We found Ed. Davis here to tea with all 3 little childn.—so we had a nice time here too— — — I called on Kate [*Hoskin?*] while in town who is right poorly— She was threatened with misca[rriage]. while at Norristn.—was kept there 2 wks longer than she intended to stay, was brot. to the cars on a bed—or pillows— reclined all the way down, & was taken home with great care & confined to her bed—seemed to be doing well for 2 days, when she was much worse—had a Dr. & nurse—& all hope was at an end—till within the last day or 2 the Dr. gives her some encouraget. that she may not lose the precious promise, & she was quite cheerful yestery— — Is yr. Mrs. Sherwood really going to have a fam[il]y.? Was not this about the time? Reba. (Price) Hunt[6] has a son, after a dreadful sufferg. time—her life in great danger for 2 hours—4 doctors with her—the child taken with instruments—its hip broken & the other injured— She was doing better than anybody expected— — We, like you, have been changg. help not in the female departmt., nor yet our faithful Michael, who is a treasure, but poor Citizen who was a liberated slave & allowance therefore to be made. We hurried the house, for his wife & her child to come out (she was a widow) He went in with Edwds. large hay wagon, & brot. out their goods— I fitted an old carpet Anna H. gave them, & all was going on well— The "cats" went away to a Mg. 10 miles distant, & such a play as the mice had! Citizen had gone off to the City—came back at night in liquor—was angry with his wife because the cows were not milked, & fell to beating her— She had been to see a sick sister— — She screamed— Margt. & Mary Ann ran & brot. her & her daughr. here— Jas. & self stopped at Thos. Cavr's. to tea—Geo. & Pattie meetg. us there— We came home about 10—& found all in a great state of excitemt.— Rosanna & child, 9 ys old still here— Jas. went & talked with Citizen who was sob[ered?] down— he sd. his wife *sassed* him— — Jas. came back & sent them home— Citizen slept in the barn, & at early morn put his clothes into a valise & was off & has not since been heard of— — He has been to Sea & talked go again—but we know nothg—only that he has been lately with a low set in Philada. Rosanna has a respectable br. at Abington, who will take her in—& we have another br. & famy—2 childn engaged to take their place— Now if this is a long story, we are even— Mari[a]. said she had no patience with Citizen's coming to our house last winter to beg—Armisted, his br., Edwds. farmer has always done well— The 1st. day a week since when we went to Upper Dublin Mg—by appointmt. we were also summoned to the funeral of Robt. Purvis' son Wm.—[7] Edwd. & Maria went—a large concourse of people—all color distinctn seemed for the time laid aside. Elizh. Paxson preached— Ed. & Maria stayed to tea— Jas. & self went up last 5th. day to tea  They feel the loss much— Harriet [*Purvis*] sd. her daughr. fretted— She spoke of Ellen [*Wright*]'s letters—sd. she had not heard from her lately— I thot. perhaps Ellen now wd. write to her [*ms. damaged*] she cd. sympathise with he[r?]

[*Letter continues dated 9 and 10 September 1857*]

AL MNS

1. In the first portion of this letter, LCM had written: "Ellis means to go to Eng. agn. some day—he is more & more an Englishn." The Perots were probably the family of Elliston Perot (1824–65) and his wife, Caroline Corbit, Philadelphia Hicksites.

2. Elizabeth Barrett Browning, *Aurora Leigh* (New York: C. S. Francis, 1857). The lecture "Patriotism" by George William Curtis (1824–92), an editor and author, supported resistance to unjust laws. For example, if "you must murder your child under two years of age, or prostitute your daughter, or deny a cup of water to the thirsty, or return to savage Indians an innocent captive flying for his life, whom they had stolen from his country, and enslaved for their own gain, under the name of civilizing him, you have no right to obey, because such laws nullify themselves, being repulsive to the holiest human instincts" (*New York Tribune,* 4 September 1857, 3).

3. Curtis had helped start *Putnam's Monthly* in 1852. It had been discontinued in early September 1857 and would merge with *Emerson's United States Magazine* the following month. Sigma, or Lucius Manlius Sargent, had recently published an article in the *Boston Transcript* criticizing the operation of public transportation on Sunday. In this article, he also had brought back an old rumor that Parker Pillsbury had baptized three dogs. Garrison had refuted Sigma's story, calling it "false and malicious," and had defended Pillsbury's speech, which illustrated the bestiality of slavery by comparing the baptism of slaves with the baptism of dogs (*Liberator,* 14 August 1857, 130, 21 August 1857, 134).

4. At the Disunion Convention, held 28–29 October in Cleveland, participants resolved, "That Slavery and Liberty are eternal antagonisms, and can never be peacefully united in the same government" (*Liberator,* 9 October 1857, 164, 6 November 1857, 180). The PASS would hold its annual meeting on 22–23 October; Higginson would not attend (*Liberator,* 6 November 1857, 180). Anthony was on an antislavery lecture tour with Aaron Powell and William Wells Brown (Gordon, 1:353, 365).

5. Stephen Colwell (1800–1871) was a Pennsylvania iron manufacturer and the author of *New Themes for the Protestant Clergy: Creeds without Charity, Theology without Humanity, and Protestantism without Christianity* (Philadelphia: Lippincott, Grambo, 1851). Robert Haydock (1807–94) was a Hicksite Quaker and the husband of Hannah Wharton Haydock. His brother was probably George G. Haydock (c. 1814–98). On 6 January 1858 LCM would write MCW: "Vibert was with us one night—poor fellow! We pity him so much in their sad reverses" (MNS).

6. Rebecca Price (1834–1927), a Philadelphia Hicksite, had married William Hunt, an Orthodox Quaker, in 1852.

7. William Purvis (b. 1832) had died of consumption on 28 August (*NASS,* 5 September 1857, 3).

## To Martha Coffin Wright

Road Side—Montg. Co.
11 Mo. 8th. 57—

Warm, Indn. Sum. Sunday—3 weeks to-day since our dear son left us. A letter from Halifax frm. C. Wharton cheerful—only Thos. too sick & forlorn to write.[1] Mariª., who is here to-day with the childn., says she wrote everythg. durg. my absence of 2 weeks— A real old-fashd., droll, witty sheet was recd. from thee, in that time, wh. was in reserve for me the eveg. of my arrival—the last instalment of wh. came a few days since, with a line or 2 frm. Eliza, in a letter frm. Joh. Lord. Didn't I enjoy the readg. of it all, in my quiet chamber at Thos. Cavr.'s? We wont complain any more of past neglect, if future producn. equal this— The accot. of Willy & Frank's departe. & happiness—Frank's letter— his tryg. to fly—& a' that—Hetty's just estimate of Mr. Weld—Willie's journal, of his needle-work "to pass away time"—Caro [Wood]'s remarks on Auga. [Stratton]'s purchases—her slave-wom. help—her taciturn habit—Mrs. Worden's[2] immoral help—Eliza Gib[bon]s. thief compared to Caleb Some-body— All these items kept me laughg—so well told— Then the more seri-ous part had its weight too—my sister's inability to 'open her mouth for the dumb',[3] wh. we had not before heard of—hope tis open now— Davids remarks on the gamblg. spirit of the age, wh. so exactly spoke my mind. Then these pi-ous gamblers dont pay their 'debts of honor'—but abscond, as you'll see, by the Papers, Allibone has done—& that Sunday School Porter.— — Emmor Haines told me these cases furnished me Capital.—[4] They are certainly the legitimate result of the depravity doctrine— — We felt glad that Munson [Osborne] cd. be cheerful in such awful times—glad too that he sold his house—if it wd.n't have been better to sell yrs. & take that for y'rselves—it looked so pleast., when we went over it, that I wanted Munson & Eliza to have it— Too bad, to lose anythg. on it—& yet the money probably was worth more to him now. We have eagerly read Jos. Lord's letters, hopg. all wd. end well with Munson as well as himself— Our men say, busins. begins to revive a little, & availg themselves of any improvet. they say there may be an unhealthy re-action. What the thousd. exasperated people will do, who are thrown out of employt. is a fearful questn.— You will see the accots. of assembled thousds.— — Can we wonder, when the Banks & other monied Institutns. exhibit such frauds? But can David, or any other say, where *rightful* interest ends, & Usury begins?— Where legitimate trade ends, & gambling begins? Where self-protectn. ends, & injustice & op-pressn. begin?— Wouldn't you like at times to see all swept off, and the world begin anew?— It was a natural conception—*that* flood of ancient time, when "Capt. Noah weighed anchor," when the wickedness of man had become so great— But more modern science teaches, that our "own back-slidgs. reprove us,"[5] & the penalty is, "the fruit of our doings." So we may expect a heap of fruits.

Much will yet have to be traced to American Slavery—even tho the panic is felt north & east first.— — The "counterbalance of good" thou anticipates, must be in our "learng. obedience by the things we suffer"— — — "When the judgts. of the Lord are in the earth, the inhabts. thereof learn righteouss."—[6] This, *just* as true, as if by special Provid[enc]es., & far more reasonable & philosophical— — It was a good time for David to have his old debts paid.— Edwd. D. has had some unexpected incomes—just missed severe losses by failures, where they were accustoned to trust to any amot.—and by his unparalleld facility in busins. matters, he is, for the present, quite easy. Thos.' partners talk encouragingly to Mari[a].— They are makg. some small sales of wool— Mari[a]. keeps up her spirits admirably—quite philosophical in her deserted home—does not want any man at night for protectn.— — She has scarcely been a day or eveg. alone. Henry D. wd. have stayed there nights, had she been timid—but she sd., there was not a livg. man in the Universe whom she wished to have in the house, save Thos.— As coz. Ruth [*Chase*] wrote to Reba. [*Neall*], when she talked of going to Ohio on a visit with Uncle Mayhew [*Folger*] & fam[il]y.— She was at our house in Union St.—our Mother offered Eliza [*Yarnall*] for company for coz. Ruth in her absence— She wrote in reply, "Dearly as I *love* Eliza Coffin, & fond as I am of her compy., *with thine*, it wd. not be the least compensation to have her in thy stead"— Then dwelt on the danger of going to those Western Wilds to be "scalped & tomahawked by the savages of the wilderness"—that it wd. bring their "Mother's grey hairs (if they have turned) with sorrow to the grave".

It has been a questn. with Mari[a]., the keepg. of Eliza—but considg. the advantage to the childn. in Music—& the partners speakg. encouragly. of their bus[ines]s.—moreover *this* wd. be the last winter, for she is to be married to a br. of Mr. Weder, or somebody else—all things considered, she keeps her for the present.— The Leas[7] are dismissg. most of their help, are advertisg. houses & other property for sale— Will Eliza [*Osborne*] have to move agn. in the Spring? I thot. so from some remark in her letter. ^no, that was in a former letter^ We read her letters with as much interest as if we made more comments— I am struck with the grateful spirit that pervades them, for yr. many kindnesses ^sewing machines &.c—her Father doing so much for her^ in the peach, pear, & grape line, as well as for thy care of little Milly— It is a great relief for the time, for Munson to take her in the cars with him— Jas. often takes little darling Nelly [*Lord*], when he has an errand to the neighbg. stores 2 or 3 miles drive— Willy [*Davis*] sometimes likes to go too— It went very hard with Jane, to part from him—poor soul! her sisters' work—makg. vests has been greatly diminished— They are very dull— Jane was glad to go to Sarah M'Kim & sew for a week— While *there*, Willy rode over to see her— She wept over him—& refused to be comforted— It is a questn.—the justice of dismissg. our faithful helps— Edwd. told Jas., he ought to keep his men, as he had done, settg. them to quarryg. stone, at a lower price, rather than turn them away, as winter was settg. in, these terrible times— I told him we must "be just, before we were generous."[8]— We

have too long hired 20 men @ $1.25 pr. day  When our wall & gate are finished—
leavg. the long extent of front wall—gradg., &.c. &.c till next spring—we shall
have expended, to the end of the year $10.000, of the 16.500 our house sold for.
This includes buildg house & barn & out buildgs—new garden & fence—horses,
carts &.c—&.c—farmg. implements in general—years livg., clothg.—(only we
hav bot. none of the latter) ^tho not the price of the place—that is $6.500 more
wh. takes all the house proceeds^—travellg—not to Auburn tho—wh. I feel a
blank in the summer's enjoyt., & yet not a moment's hesitatn. that it was best
under the circumstances—  And thou art not here yet—& David has not been—
wh. may be best too under the pres[en]t. tryg., pinchg. circumsts. Martha
laughed at me, after the letter was gone, & too late to alter it, for writg. as if Eliza had decided not to come this winter, when she gave some encouraget., that
she might come after awhile    The 1st. impressg. was that she wd. *not*, & I suppose that remained—  But be assured, whenever she can break away from her
cares, & have a season of rest here, we shall all hail her comg., for our own sakes
also—  Munson's last call was peculiarly pleast. to us—   Ellen [*Wright*] will
hereafter be the 'young lady' visitor, as the M'Kims now are,—& Lue H. & her
young cozs. from New Y. Gib[bon]s & Brown who have made her happy these
few weeks—  They had Bucks & carriage & drove themselves 2 or 3 days—round
the Wisahickon—Chestnut & Laurel Hill—the Woodlands—& lastly out to visit
us—  We thot. it courageous in Lue—but It was some risk, as Bucks becomes
excited at times, and a man's strength is required to hold him in—gentle as he
is—  The girls will stay some weeks longer—  The Wharton girls are attentive
to them—they have pleast. visits there—   Hetty called in their carriage—a la
Lue, & drove them out to their place, & around the country—  So we see already one advantage in these times—bringg. girls' skill into use, & not dependg.
on coachmen.

Mary & Cannie Mott have decided not to come south this winter—"a pock-
et-cramp" Richd. [*Mott*] says preventg. them—  They hesitate betwn. remaing.
at home or going to Rochester, & write that if Lue H. will go & pass the winter
with them, it will decide them to stay at Toledo—  Lue longs to go—beside the
pleasure, it wd. be such a grand opp[ortunit]y. to take music-lessons—   You
know she has an elegt. piano, that Edwd. bot. low—& is now takg. lessons of
Lucy M'Kim,[9] who has several pupils in the City—  But the 'pocket cramp' will
have to keep Lue at home too, I presume.

But above, I meant to say, when the right time comes, Ellen will be a welcome
visitor here—  That will be, doubtless when Anna D. is at home—  Just think of
that unlooked for home-comg.! I was absent as you know—1st to Westchester—
Jas. & Edwd.—Miller & Lucy—Mattie Griffith & a lot more—a larger Mg. than
was feared—  Garrison disaptg. us—as the letter in the Standd. tells you. Furness' speech was great—a good heart prevailed several hundd. $ subcribed—
Collier did well—[10] He is to be an agent for a month or so—the hammer
fac[tor]y—of wh. he is foreman is stopped, & he has been compelled to work

on the road @ $1 a day— He is happy to go forth for our Socy. He is to be at
Kennett Prog. Mg. next 1st. day, & to lecture in that neighbd.— I had agreed to
join a Com. of the Progressives, in holdg. Anti S. Mgs. this year— So after the
West C. Mg—Jas. returned home, & I went with Thos. Whitson to Christiana—
[Bart.?] Mg—thence to Enterprise with Jos[ep]h. Gibb[on]s.— Phebe had had
a severe fall down stairs in the night, by going in the dark into the childn.'s
room—to see that little Fanny was covered— She mistook the door, ½ asleep,
& walked off the top stairs—they wind down— She struck her hand, head &
face causg. black eyes—pain in her head & a sprained wrist—also an awfully
bruised hand, inside & out—useless since—a week when I was there—her Mother has been with her a few days since—I was there— — She was cheerful & active
doing all she cd. for my comfort, as did Joseph— They invited uncle Joel Wier-
man & Lydia (Lundy) & their Mother to spend the day makg. quite a dinner-
party— Josh. took me 11 miles to Millersville School, wh. is to be the Normal
School— A literary Socy. there, havg. elected Jas. & slf. honorary Mem. & invitg us to speak to them—200 pupils both sexes together—a fine buildg. We had
a gratifyg. time with them— I hoped the 'young ladies' wd.n't be discouraged
even tho' they shd.n't be able at once to solve problems on the black board as
readily as the 'young gent', as I supposed I must call them—to consider how much
longer the latter had had these educational advantages— The Principal saw a
group together, after the Mg.—joined them— They desired him to tell me that
they were quite equal to the boys now— Another compy. came & thanked me
for givg. the wom. questn. 'a lift'— We rode home that night—Phebe sittg up
for us, & takg. that time to give herself a bath by the parlor fire—for they have
no furnace— She is convinced that cold-bathg. has been used to excess. They
have unadvisedly put up a frame kitchen & rooms over it for Josh.'s office garden seeds—medcl. bottles &.c *detached* from the house & such a runng. back &
forth—openg. & shuttg doors—not very gently, with the 4 childn. & the Mother & Father & hired girl—one cellar entrance from our sittg. room, & the only
stairs thro' that room, into the best parlor, windg. up from there—no front or
back entry—door openg. into parlor—back door and a little porch into a shed—
across a cart way near the barn yard—into sd. kitchen—wherein the chickens
can occas[ionall]y— We ate there—except sd. dinner party—when a cold day
the food had to be brot. across—meat-dish covers wantg.— A Mumford cookg
apparatus in sd. kitchen—table up to the wall—bench behind—altogether rather
dismal when for the same outlay they might have been so comfortable—no carpet on sd. kitchen A col[ore]d. wom. washg., in one part of it— — It is a shame
to write this, when they were so kind. Phebe has made a very nice carpet for the
sittg. room—the former kitchen—died the rags red & green—her neighbs. told
her it wd. sell for 87 ½ cts. pr yd—cut so fine & so well woven— She has her
sewg. machine— Mary Anna [*Gibbons*] has learned a little—hemmed her che-
mise—badly eno' to be sure— little Caroe. [*Gibbons*] pared all the apples for
pies & stewg.—made beds, swept &.c— Phebe told Mary Anna she must not

take coz L. out to see her colt, till she had been out & *curry'd* him— She has the care of the fowls—brings in wood, &.c— She told her Father, she "was driven to 3 alternatives—either to tread in the mud with her new shoes—take the wet chips in her clean frock—or apron—or open the gate with her mouth"— I was amused all the time with their talk—but eno' of that visit— The Brussels carpet of her Mothers, really dressed up their parlor— I took cars from there to Columbia where a large Mg. in Odd Fellows Hall was held to satisfactn.—& a request from a Com. to stay & have another—kind hospitality from John & Mary Ann Cooper[11]—Thos. Peart's sister—didn't stay—to York a night with Hannah Dingey & childn. her son married Martha Parker, Theodore's niece, who taught in Margt. Robns. school—a fine girl— they had talked of me that day at dinner—not knowg. of my comg or that I expected to leave home— Martha sd., I had promised her a visit, if ever in neighbd. of York— Isn't there somethg. in Animal magnetism? They each exclaimed as they came in—2 sons— Richd. boarded with Mary Earle & was attached to Caro— Josh. G. thot. he wd. have been so far pref[erab]le. to a Catholic He mourns over Caro—[12] Richd. D. is still single— To Harrisburg next—had several Mg. with the Barnards— Stayed over 1st. day— Agnes Sanders very hospitable & polite—a lady like wom—now a widow— Dost thou remember her? But eno' of this long travel— Jas. wrote me so faithfully— I went to the P.O. before apprisg. the others of my arrival, & had such a nice readg. of his & Pattie's letters, & 2 or 3 hours in my quiet chamber at the hotel, where I took 2 meals, & paid $1— not greadgingly for such a lone, lovely time— Jas. letter mentioned the fire—Anna's return—& the rest— How I did pity little Frank to be left behind, even for one day—and so glad for him to have so much enjoyt. in the short week here— — He made good use of the time— I met him on my return on 2nd. day, at Benjn. [*Yarnall*]'s— He walked with me part way up to Mary Earles, & easily found his way back— I asked him how Philada. compared with New Y., he sd. "no comparison"— "Why, New Y. so far superior? "No—Philada. is superlative"— — He took a fancy to John & Kate [*Hoskin*] called in several times— Kate thinks him a fine little fellow—so does Anna B—so do all indeed— Mari[a]. says she wrote of his doings.

Sarah M'Kim's accot. of their childns. sudden return amused us— She had worked hard to fit them well off. Then turned on to Fall-cleang. before dismissg. their help—wh. they must do, to afford Charlie's going— Lucy was in town givg. music lessons—Sarah in their parlor on the step ladder cleang. paint &.c— Their light dinner eaten—nothg. left—when Lucy arrived & rushed in— "Oh, Mother, I've the best news"! Anythg. of good news, in these times, was of course pleast.— "Anne & Charlie have come—& best of all, Fred. Dennis with them!"— —[13] Anna B. also had a similar pleast. shock— She had been passg. the last day of Mari[a].'s stay at the Farm, with them. On her way home, she met Wilt. the painter, who had been doing jobs at Temple Hill—he called out, "Well the boys are there!" "What?" "Why, your boys have come home". "What boys?" Why, Harry & Wallie— The cause of all these home-comgs. were lost sight of, for the time, in the exceedg. happiness of the young fry— The repairs were so soon accomplished, that no one was burdened with them— Miller & Sarah were very willg. to have such a nice, agreeable, smart, 6 ft. young man— Anna D. was in the 7th Heaven all the time. I was glad our new part was so nearly furnished, as to admit of all movg. in—tho' I wd. have preferred being at home at the time— Piano & valuable camphor trunks of nice beddg. &.c—were brot. here, lest the mob shd. "break thro' & steal"— It was real pleast. to find them here— We manage nicely without added help, except hirg a washer & iron- er— Our colored Isaac's wife has been sick—so we have called in another— — — I was happy eno', to take the load of "sheaves" & travel rapidly to the City on 2nd. day—met S. Pugh by appt. & went to the Assembly Buildgs. to get a deductn. on the price, for the Fair—succeeded—$10 pr day for the 4 days— $40—then to the funeral of Rachel Child—who resembled our Mother—died of paralysis—78 yrs old— A faithful worker at our Fairs, & in other ways— Dost thou remember her?—rather a caricature of Mother, bore my testimony to her Anti S. character, left them to bear her to Fair Hill tomb—called in at the A. S. Office with Sarah, arranged with Miller for an Ex. Com. Mg.—then to Edwd. H's, dined—saw Lue's guests—heard the news of the City—failures, &.c—then to select Qy. Mg—helped Rachel B. M. defend her position agt. John J. White[14]—then to Benjns.—met Frank, aforesd. cd.n't stay tea havg. engaged to meet Anna H. at Thos. Cavrs.—hoped Eliza wd. go with me, but found her with a swelled face & quite poorly— They scolded me for not stoppg. to tea there—as I had agreed to 2 wks. before— But I felt as if I must call immedy. at Mary E's to tell them of my visit & how Phebe was, & to take some apples she sent Caro—but Mary it seems was gone to Enterprise— Richd. [*White*] at home out of buss., tho' his salary going on as yet— Fanny pretty well[15]—a house full of childn. ran thro' the entry—found Anna at Elizhs.—passed a real pleast. eveg Mariᵃ. & Frank came walkg. in the last of the evening— Now dont you think it was a good day's work— I counted the squares, & had walked miles— I stayed the night at Elizhs.— Next day Jas. came in to Qy. Mg—dined at Mariᵃ.'s with Frank—wh. was all I saw of him—for wh. I was sorry— He walked with us part way back— We reached our happy home after dark—a blazg. fire in the *Library*, & the furnace doing its part to the other parts of the house— Car- pets were the order of the day then—till the Attics were covered & furnished— ready for Henry [*Davis*], who had been stayg. nights at his aunt Lydia's— Ellis [*Yarnall*] came out on 6th. day eveg. & over here with Anna B— Walter had been suddenly called agn. to Pittsburg, & Ellis was going to lodge at Temple Hill in his absence— What made their visit the more delectable just then, was, the confidence he had reposed in us, in relatn. to a *marriage engaget. in England*— of a few months' standg. When Thos. had decided to go to Eng., Ellis was so desirous to introd[uc]e. him to his lady-love, that he cd. do no less than divulge his secret— Such a surprise & so many questns. She is the daughr. of his par- ticular frd. Harrison—in the country near London a niece of Mary Howitt's—

Friends by educatn.—Crewdsonites in modern splits—& *Margaret* & her ~~Father &~~ Mother now Church people— She keeps house for an uncle—a Bach-
elor— She is not the eldest of her Father's famy. several younger sisters & a br.
or 2—she is 28 yrs old— Writes a handsome hand—& Anna B says the parts
Ellis read to her were very good— We are pleased that she is of Quaker descent— Ellis knows we shall all like her— He is going to Eng. in the Spring,
to return with her in the Fall—& now the questn. is whether a City or country
resid[enc]e. will be best— Josh. Cottringer's Place we think wd. be 1st. rate—
but there are objectns. to it—so far from RailRoad—

[*P.S.*] Does Caroe. know that there is some talk of Emma Parker's acceptg
that old lover of hers—at the South or West— Mari[a]. knows more about it I
*think,* than she is at liberty to tell— I judged so from her evasive answers—

AL MNS

1. As a result of the depression, beginning in August 1857, Thomas Mott had left for
Europe to find other markets for his wool products (LCM to MCW, 12 October 1857,
MNS).

2. MCW's sons William ("Willy") Wright and Frank Wright attended Theodore Weld's
school, Eagleswood, in New Jersey. Lazette Maria Miller Worden (d. 1875), a friend of
Stanton and MCW, was one of Emma Willard's first students at the Troy Female Seminary (Gordon, 1:433).

3. Prov. 31:8.

4. Thomas Allibone (1809–76) was the president of the Bank of Pennsylvania, which
had failed in September 1857 (*Letter from Thomas Allibone, Esq., Late President of the Bank
of Pennsylvania: To the Public* [Philadelphia: n.p., 1858]). Emmor Haines (b. 1818), a Pennsylvania saw mill operator and an Orthodox Quaker, had married JM's niece Ann Mott
Moore on 27 September 1843.

5. In early October the *New York Tribune* had editorialized that the panic had been
caused by "stock gamblers" who had persuaded bankers to deny loans based on stock
pledges. More recently, a Pittsburgh bank had charged stockbrokers with "obtaining
fraudulently" $185,000; the latter were soon absolved of the charges (*New York Tri-
bune,* 1 October 1857, 4, 23 October 1857, 5, 6 November 1857, 5). LCM is quoting Jer.
2:19.

6. Heb. 5:8. LCM is adapting Isa. 26:9: "When the judgments are in the earth, the inhabitants of the world will learn righteousness."

7. "The Leas" were probably the prominent Philadelphia publishing family. Isaac Lea
(1792–1886) joined Matthew Carey's publishing firm in 1821, when he married Carey's
daughter, Frances Anne Carey. Isaac retired in 1851 and his son, Henry Charles Lea (1825–
1909), took over (*One Hundred and Fifty Years of Publishing, 1785–1935* [Philadelphia: Lea
and Febriger, 1935], 20, 31).

8. LCM may be quoting a proverb that Christopher Smart published in his *Jubilate
Agno* (Rejoice in the Lamb: A Song from Bedlam; n.p., 1758–63).

9. J. Miller McKim's daughter, Lucy McKim, attended Eagleswood, where she studied music. She began teaching piano when she was fifteen (Dena J. Epstein, "Lucy McKim
Garrison, American Musician," *Bulletin of the New York Public Library* 63 [October 1963]:
529–46).

10. Martha ("Mattie") Griffith (c. 1833–1906), a white Southerner, wrote the fictional
*Autobiography of a Female Slave*, published in 1856, and subsequently freed her slaves and
moved North (Gordon, 1:559). Garrison's letter to the PASS saying he would not be able

to attend its meeting had appeared in the *NASS* (31 October 1857, 2). William Furness's speech at the PASS convention of 17 December would be summarized in the *Liberator* (25 December 1857, 207). Benjamin Collier, a British mechanic and a Methodist preacher, was active in U.S. antislavery circles in the late 1850s (*WLG*, 4:571–72).

11. John Cooper and Mary Ann Peart Cooper were Philadelphia Hicksites.

12. Caroline Earle White had recently converted to Catholicism.

13. Frederick Dennis (d. 1886) was the son of Cyrus Dennis and Eunice Dennis of Auburn, New York (Fort Hill Cemetery records, Auburn, N.Y.).

14. Rachel Barker Moore was a Quaker minister from Poughkeepsie, New York. John J. White (1808–79) was a Hicksite Quaker minister of Philadelphia and a supporter of George F. White (*Friends' Intelligencer*, 6 November 1847, 251, 22 March 1851, 409; White Family Genealogy, PSCHi).

15. "Fanny" is possibly Ellen Frances Van Leer Earle, the wife of George H. Earle, Mary Hussey Earle's son.

## To Elizabeth Neall Gay

Road Side, Mont[gomer]y. Co.
5 Mo. 7th. 1858—

My dear Elizabeth

I was so ashamed of the hurried scrap sent thee, in reply to thine, and the confused gathering of pamphlets, at a few minutes notice, that I resolved to write thee more at length in a few days— Now it is a few weeks, since thine was received, and which was not handed me till some days after its date, so that the documents were sent so near the time of the delivery of that *good lecture,* that they could not have been of much use to our brave advocate.

I knew he was not quite satisfied with himself, when in a former lecture some 2 years ago, he cast some riducule, & rather derogatory reflections on Woman, without sufficient allowance for the disabilities under she labored. I told him so, at the time, and he "owned up" so prettily, that it made me love him— I felt quite sure now that he would do fuller justice to the subject.[1]

We read with much interest all that the Tribune furnished, and we gladly would invite him to deliver the lecture in Philada.— — I have consulted some 20 persons on the subject— They united in the desire to hear it—but thought the lecturing season so nearly past, that we had better wait till Fall—

The intelligence of the Age is ripe for the Woman question, and it only needs the *asking* on the part of woman, to *receive*— Will George Curtis, and Sydney H. Gay, & thyself attend the Convention next week in New York, & give your aid to the movement, "before all Israel and the Sun?"[2]

Thou hast had a long furlough in that beautiful Island-home— Come out now into public life, & shew thyself, and help all the good causes along— Sorry enough are we to lose Sydney's able services in the Standard. He will not I know let us lose him altogether—indeed he may be working effectually in his present position. But how he will be missed at this coming Anniversary! I am thankful that Oliver Johnson was good enough to remain, after all the unwise doings of the Boston board—[3]

Jas. & self cant be at the Meeting this year— I long to go, both for the Slave, & for Woman,—that other Slave's Sake— — — You will have with you Barbara Leigh Smith Bodichon—an ardent worker for woman—a clever writer for the new London Magazine—aiding Bessie Parkes the Editor— — She has been in this country with her husband Dr. Bodichon since last Fall—travelling south & west— — She is a niece of Julia Smith, whom we loved so well in 1840— Elizh. Reid's friend— She is also the most intimate friend of Mary Howitt's daughter—& a cousin of Florence Nightingale— Now wont all this commend her to thy kindly notice?[4]

If not let me add, she is like thyself in look & manner, & I loved her all the more for the constant reminder of thee— So do seek her at the Anniversaries— She does not intend to speak publicly— I hope she will be compelled to— — — She is an artist & means to follow painting as a profession, even tho' her income gives her independence.

Dr. Bodichon is a scientific man of some note—much interested in the *Race* question[5]—has passed years in Algiers & can say much of Northern Africa's brain if you could only understand him. They brought letters to us from Mary Howitt & Wm. H. Channing, who officiated at their marriage— — —

We have been somewhat interested in attending a course of lectures, by Eliza Farnham—limited in their scope, but useful nevertheless.— She circulates a Prospectus of a new Paper—Lafga—[6] I hate odd names, needing explanatn.— It contains a disclaimer of Wom. Rig. intent, wh. robs the whole thing of much promise— Of course, I cant promote its circulation— The Paper may be more than it promises—

I will enclose our dear Sarah Pugh's note, speaking of Mrs. Farnham— I dont remember anything about her at the Wom. Rig. Convention. What was the slight? Why didst thou not attend that meetg., & help to keep all things straight, & as they should be?

It is very difficult, when persons come forward, not identified with the movement, and wish to use the valuable time in advocating some fragmentary part of it, ^difficult ought to be down here^ to decide impartially, as to the propriety of granting such claims. But come & see! How we have wanted Lizzie Stanton other than by letter, and the Grimkes, yes, and all of you to "come up to the help," &.c—[7] When art thou coming to see us in our new country home? It is not right to stay away so long— Thy last letter, with the return of the Pamphlets, came in due time—all right, save that Mary Woolstonecraft, my pet book ^or one of them^ was not among them—and as thou says George Curtis has that, he will not wish to retain mine longer— When Sarah Grimke found that book on our Centre table some 20 years ago, she said "Lucretia, I admire thy independence". It is out of print I cannot therefore replace it, or you need not return it— — Miller M'Kim will be in New Y—& can bring it—

Thy account of Curtis' lecture pleased us vastly— Do write again soon— Thy racy, characteristic scraps are valued by me— I have almost worn out that John Weiss letter, reading it over & over— I shewed it to him at the White Mountains 2 years ago—& was pleased that it did not offend him— I dont know that he has improved since he wrote that bad Article— — Such lectures as George Curtis' will tend to enlarge his mind— How I am going on— Love to Sydney— Kiss the childn.— Jas Mott loves you too—

L. Mott

I will enclose also a Note from Mrs. Bodichon

ALS NNCB-Gay

1. On his 1858 lecture tour, George William Curtis delivered "Fair Play for Women," a modified version of the speech he would give at the eighth National Woman's Rights Convention held in New York City, 14–15 May 1858, "An Address Vindicating the Right of Woman to the Elective Franchise." According to the *Liberator,* Curtis also gave a "most radical and eloquent lecture on Woman's Rights" on 7 May at the Lowell Institute in New York City. These speeches were Curtis's first public expression of support for woman's rights (*Liberator,* 14 May 1858, 79, 4 June 1858, 92, 29 October 1858, 173; *HWS,* 1:672; Gordon Milne, *George William Curtis and the Genteel Tradition* [Bloomington: Indiana University Press, 1956], 99–102).

2. The twenty-fifth annual meeting of the AASS would take place on 11–12 May (*Liberator,* 30 April 1858, 70). LCM is adapting 2 Sam. 12:12: "Before all Israel, and before the sun."

3. In November 1857 the AASS had dismissed Oliver Johnson from his position as coeditor of the *NASS.* But when the *New York Tribune* offered Sydney Gay a position in January 1858, Gay resigned from the *NASS* and Johnson was rehired as its editor (Raimund E. Goerler, "Family, Self, and Anti-Slavery: Sydney Howard Gay and the Abolitionist Commitment," Ph.D. diss., Case Western Reserve University, 1975, 264–65).

4. Barbara Leigh Smith Bodichon (1827–91), a British feminist, helped found the *English Woman's Journal,* first published in 1858, with Bessie Rayner Parkes (1829–1925). Bodichon had married Dr. Eugene Bodichon (1810–85), a French medical doctor and resident of Algiers, in July 1857, and the two then left for a trip to the United States. Bodichon had met LCM on 20 April 1858 and wrote, "I never saw such a beautiful old lady. . . . She looks 'full of grace' in every sense of the word. I do not wonder her preaching has stirred so many souls, her aspect is eloquent, her smile full of good things" (Barbara Leigh Smith Bodichon, *An American Diary,* ed. Joseph W. Reed Jr. [London: Routledge and Kegan Paul, 1972], 139–41; Hester Burton, *Barbara Bodichon, 1827–1891* [London: John Murray, 1949], 87–89, 115–19; Candida Ann Lacey, ed. *Barbara Leigh Smith Bodichon and the Langham Place Group* [New York: Routledge, 1986], 4–5, 11). LCM had met Julia Smith, a friend of Harriet Martineau, and Mary Howitt, the mother of Margaret Howitt (b. 1839), in England (*Diary,* 33, 41). LCM reportedly had influenced the career of Florence Nightingale (1820–1910): "When Lucretia Mott was in England in 1840, Florence was a young girl and heard Mrs. Mott talk about the importance of young ladies having some other ambition than that of being married, and how much happier they would be in some career of useful benevolence; and Florence said she would like to live to do good" (John White Chadwick, *A Life for Liberty: Anti-Slavery and Other Letters of Sallie Holley* [New York: Negro Universities Press, 1969], 200).

5. Bodichon believed that "the mixed or colored races are, in point of physiological development, on the whole, in advance of the original constituents from which they

sprung." He drew his conclusions from his research in Algiers and in Louisiana, where he found that the "handsomest" women were "colored" ("Dr. Bodichon on the Mixture of Races," *NASS*, 26 June 1858, 2).

6. Eliza Burhans Farnham (1815–64), a prison reformer and a lecturer, was the author of *Woman and Her Era* (1864). There is no record her proposed newspaper was ever published. At the National Woman's Rights Convention on 14–15 May, she would deliver "Superiority of Woman" (*HWS*, 1:669).

7. LCM is adapting Josh. 10:4: "Come up unto me, and help me."

## To Martha Coffin Wright

Road Side,
7 Mo. 6th. 58—3rd day aftern.—
Cool & pleast.

A sheet, hurried off at last, was sent in to Eliza [*Yarnall*] yestery., to read & forward, via EaglesWd.— I was so dissatisfied with it, that this is forthwith to be finished & sent direct, with the several little notes from Anna B.—— I want to take more notice of thy letters, wh. were so acceptable  Thou had *not* said those smart things before— They were appreciated—especially the "crowg. of the shanghais at Rachel Barkers thrice denial"—[1] She is better however, than S. B. Anthony's letter represented her— She does not "steal the thunder" of others, & appropriate it, but gives forth her own [views], both on Slavery & on Woman, wh. are correct, but from not attendg. any of our Mgs—nor readg. our own Reports, she is ignorant, & thinks the advocates of these causes, are as fanatical as the Papers & popular opinion represent them— S. B. Anthony did right to go to her & complain— I did so once years ago after she had disclaimed Abolitionism in Richmond, after preachg. Anti-Slavery, & raisg a dust—"hush, I'm no Abolitionist." She replied to me, "Oh, my dear, I was not reported right, I sd. 'I'm no *modern* abolitionist"— Now, she knew no better, than to suppose *that* wd. be a satisfacty. explann. to me— The misrepresentns. of our opposers do us & the cause great harm—and havg. suffered for years by false witnesses havg. been suborned, makes me cautious how I receive the testimony of Goodell, or any other, against Pearl Andws. the Free love advocates, Mrs. Farnham, the Spiritualists, & indeed any of the reformer-mono-maniacs—[2]^Rev. Mays came in for a share of Goodells sneers^ Let each & all expound their own creed, & then let us judge righteous judgt.— Miller [*McKim*] is quite troubled that Anti-Slavery shd. be so mixed up with other & objectional isms, as at the Rutland Con., where, he sd. Th. Curtis went to defend Atheism—H. C. W. & Mrs. Cranch to shock the instinct of Modesty in the love & marriage & maternal questn., caterg. to a prurient curiosity  He thot. Conservatism was needed—& I ought to read & understand the views of these ultra free love people, so as to give my influence against them—[3] I didn't feel called to such an ungracious task; & as to readg. what is distasteful, when there is so much of the deepest interest, wh. time fails me to peruse  catch me doing it— I thot. Thos. Curtis sincere in his views—& the others quite as modest as those were, who clung to law & order, as regards woman, makg. her a slave to Man—robbing her of her childn., as by the late decision of Judge—in Pittsburg—sustaing. the will of the Father—& makg. such hateful promises as in the marriage covenant, in Church—[4] I want to write to Lizzie Gay, & send her thy remarks of Pearl Andws. & the other Pearls— I copied them before sendg. thy letter to Nant. Lizzie thinks we shall bring disgrace to our cause, by sufferg. our platform to be free to such people— How excellt. Garrison's speech was, in reply to Foster, on virtue havg. gone out of Abolitionists—if so, it was that they had not stood firm on their Peace & Moral suasion principles, &.c— He is truly a wonderful man. Miller thot. Wendell P. erred, in givg. H. C. Wright such a lift—classg. him with Garrison—[5]— — We were interested in thy comments on Saml. J. May's sermon & visit— I agree with thee that it is a waste of such a man's powers, to appeal to veneratn. in the ordinary way, by shewg. that the "rain *has* a Father."—[6] All thy ink turns black now, & the letters are lovely easy to read—"not so *this*," thou wilt say— I began it 3rd. day— Mattie Griffith, Thos. & Mari^a. [*Mott*] came—also Morris & Elizh. Davis[7]—so that I couldn't go on, in the eveg.— Cool as it was, we had a light in the parlor, & drew in from the piazza— Mari^a. had to lie on the sofa while here with pain—& anticipated a sufferg. night—but the childn. came runng. down next morng. to say Ma was well—the abscess broke in the night— Morris D. magnetized her head & face before she left here, & guessed she wd.n't have more pain. How much that had to do with it, we cant say, any more than we can of Homeop[ath]y. but this we know, that it is sooner gathered than that terrible one in her chamber— I was glad, by thy last letter, to learn that Hetty [*Wood*] was recovg. from her excessive bleeding— Thou seems to have as much care of little Milly & Floy [*Osborne*], as M. Earle always has had of their Florence,[8] as she always chooses to call her, not liking nick names. She dont allow me to say *Ria* H— She poor child is sufferg. with a bad boil, almost a carbuncle, on her neck, or shoulder— It has brot. on fever— It is dischargg. today— They have all been here this week, while paintg. & paperg. are being done at their house. Anna & Lue [*Hopper*] brot. out lots of dress-makg. & other work, wh. with Maria D's & Pattie [*Lord*]'s, keeps the machines going constantly. Edwd. [*Davis*] has only been out one night— He is preparg. to go to Lynchburg, Va., on business— He was at Reading this ^no, last^ week—found it excessive warm travelg Have I ever written that Peter & Fanny Wright have gone to Europe, for Peter's health— for 3 mo— S. Palmer is keepg. house—[9] She made a long visit in New Y. Henry's wife no longer makes one of the fam[il]y— She has gone home to her Parents— Henry is foolishly insolvent, as was his Father's estate—

[*Letter continues dated 8 July*]

AL PSCHi-Mott

Letter from LCM to MCW, 6 July 1858. (Courtesy of the Friends Historical Library of Swarthmore College)

1. In a letter of 20 June 1858 MCW had asked LCM to arrange for Rachel Barker Moore to speak in Auburn (MNS). Moore had earlier preached against Quakers participating in reform movements but later became an active supporter of the antislavery movement (LCM to Nathaniel Barney, c. May 1843, Hallowell, 247–50; *NASS,* 9 March 1843, 2).

2. William Goodell (1792–1878) was a founder of the AASS and of the Liberty party. Stephen Pearl Andrews (1812–86), an abolitionist and a proponent of free love, had spoken at the eighth National Woman's Rights Convention in New York City, 14–15 May 1858. Andrews believed that the woman's rights movement should address "the vital question of marriage" and he had advised women "to change the conditions of that maternity, to experiment . . . and to decide as to the best method of airing and generating the forthcoming population." According to the *New York Herald,* this statement had caused a "sensation" (14 May 1858, 3; Gordon, 1:372–74; *HWS,* 1:668–72). MCW had served as secretary of that convention and had reported to LCM: "I didn't know who that dismal Pearl Andrews was, but as he did not press his views, I suppose there was no great harm done" (17 May 1858, MNS).

3. Goodell had recently attended an antislavery convention in Bradford, Vermont, and had written a letter stating that the convention did not support disunion (*NASS,* 6 March 1858, 2). "Mrs. Cranch" is probably Julia Branch of New York City, who had proposed a controversial resolution at the Free Thought Convention in Rutland, Vermont, on 25–27 June: "That the slavery and degradation of women proceeds from the institution of marriage; that by the marriage contract she loses the control of her name, her person, her property, her labor, her affection, her children, and her freedom." Henry C. Wright, vice president of the Rutland convention and the author of *Marriage and Parentage* (1854), linked sexual control to economic advancement and gave explicit lectures on how married couples could control their sexuality (*Liberator,* 2 July 1858, 106, 107; Lewis Perry, *Childhood, Marriage, and Reform: Henry Clarke Wright, 1797–1870* [Chicago: University of Chicago Press, 1980], 230–55).

4. In 1853 Pennsylvania had passed a law that supported granting child custody to mothers whose husbands abused them or could not support the family. But many women felt that the courts were still biased toward the father in custody cases (Michael Grossberg, *Governing the Hearth: Law and the Family in Nineteenth-Century America* [Chapel Hill: University of North Carolina Press, 1985], 248–50).

5. Garrison's response to Stephen Foster had occurred at the twenty-fifth anniversary meeting of the New England Anti-Slavery Society on 26–27 May in Boston. He had opposed Foster's support for the trend among abolitionists to resort to political, and sometimes violent, means to end slavery. Garrison had replied: "Do not attempt any new political organization; do not make yourself familiar with the idea that blood must flow. . . . I have no other weapon to wield against [*the slaveholder*] but the simple truth of God" (*Liberator,* 4 June 1858, 90). Phillips had praised Wright for standing "outside of the Constitution" in arguing that Massachusetts should refuse to try fugitive slaves (*NASS,* 19 June 1858, 1).

6. On 20 June 1858 (MNS) MCW had written, "The morning sermon disappointed me—it was well enough for anybody else, but not what I wanted people to hear from *him* the text 'Has the rain a father?'" (MNS; the quotation is from Job 38:28). Her impressions of May's afternoon sermon were more favorable.

7. William Morris Davis (1815–91), the brother of Edward M. Davis, was a Republican congressman, 1861–63, and a Philadelphia Hicksite, as was his wife, Elizabeth Jacobs Davis.

8. "All but the care—M—C. W." is interlineated here in another hand.

9. Peter Wright (d. 1870) and Frances Palmer Wright (1828–91) were Philadelphia

Hicksites. Sarah Hopper Palmer (1796–1885) was the daughter of Isaac T. Hopper and Frances's mother.

## To Roadside Family

Baltimore 10 Mo. 27th. 58—

Dear All at Home

I have just finished the 2nd. reading of my beloved's letter, and feel obliged that he should gather so much, to interest us— Ever, when from home, has the reception of family letters, been my most relishing pleasure. We stopped at J. Needles'[1] store, on our way to Mg. yestermorng., & found as we expected said letter, & stood in the sun on their steps, to read it— All the items were acceptable—poor little Willie's night-mare we were sorry for, it will make Ed. & Maria [*Davis*] so fearful to leave him evegs.— — Wm. Bergen is just the one, for a present successor to Geo. B.— — —

If thou Jas. goes to City Mg. to-day, Edwd. will give thee Anna [*Hopper*]'s letter, with my scrap, wh. please keep, Edwd. willing, as a nest-egg for Auburn— Thou might also write a line to coz. Ruth [*Chase*] & Reba. [*Neall*], & send it to them—they desired to hear from us— And we are so pleasantly entertained here, by John & Augusta, that it is due them to read all we can write from their dear childn.'s peaceful home— They will be writg to Auburn & can enclose it with theirs— No, not so, I prefer its going via EaglesWd., so that Anna B. & Laura [*Stratton*] may read it— Let Eliza Y. know of our doings here— Will she be ready to go to Holly with us, after awhile? Eliza Osborne is to choose *her* compy., when she goes. I hope she is enjoyg. herself— I am sorry to lose this week of her visit—

We shall leave here in the 8 ½ Cars, on 6th. day morng— The Mg. will doubtless close tomorw.— We are going on "swimmingly"— Radical preachg. seems to suit the people, and good feeling prevails— Anna & self go to Old-Town Mg. this morng— She is quite a faithful companion—holds out wonderfully— She went with John Needles & self to a large Mg. with the colored people— Chalkley & Kezia Gillingham also accompanied us, & he took part in the exercises, all of wh. appeared satisfacy. to all concerned— Our visits have been pleasant Martha Tyson & daughters did much for our entertainment— — Saml. Townsend & wife have met with us at their br.-in-law Townsend Scott's[2]—a liberal set— We met Saml. Janney last evening at tea at Reba. Turner's son & daughr.'s, where she makes her home— Saml. manifests good feeling— But all are afraid of too much abolition— —

dinner at John Needles— We had Edwd. Needles' escort to Mg. in John's carriage, where we heard long sermons from Miriam Gover— Josh. Foulke, Ann Weaver,[3] & a prayer from Louisa Steer—& all told. After wh. we rode up to the Monument, & called on Elizh. Stanton who will go to Philada. with us &

out to Roadside for the night  So, if convenient to come in with the larger carriage, it will be nice for her to have plenty of room—  She has taken great pains
to find me—has called here, & at John Amos'—  Augusta saw her & invited her
to stop to tea—but she couldn't leave her niece—[4]  She has been here 4 weeks—
She looks lovely—  I hope all will be there to see her—

    Auga. went to Mg. yestery.—the 1st. *sittg.* she was ever at—  They are lib-
eral here to those not members—  Edith Scott[5]—a cousin is a lodger at John's—
Augusta manages nicely—& [*ms. damaged*] to be with her—  She is forward
with her sewing—  Her house hold concerns go on well—  Not much company *here* to-day ^Father Needles^—  Mary Ann is almost sick with a cold—

    Anna may have a word to add—  What a pity that Collyer[6] was not in time
for the cars—such an important Mg!

AL PSCHi-Mott

1. John Needles (1786–1878) was a Hicksite Quaker minister, a cabinetmaker, an abolitionist, and the father of Augusta Stratton Needles's husband, John Amos Needles (b.
1828) (*WLG*, 4:473; Samuel H. Needles, *Record of the Man, Needles, (Nedels) and Ham-
bleton Families* [Philadelphia: Edmund Deacon, 1876], 116, 119).

2. Kezia Warrington Gillingham (1807–72) was a Virginia Quaker and the wife of
Chalkley Gillingham (*Friends' Intelligencer,* 6 April 1872, 89). "Martha Tyson" is probably Martha Ellicott Tyson (1795–1873), a Maryland Quaker. "Saml. Townsend & wife"
are possibly the Philadelphia Hicksite Samuel Townsend (1800–1887) and his second wife,
Mira Sharpless Townsend (d. 1859). Townsend Scott was a Baltimore Hicksite.

3. "Edwd. Needles" is probably Edward Man Needles (1823–1901), a Philadelphia
Hicksite and the brother of John Amos Needles (Needles, *Record,* 116). Miriam G. Gover
was a Virginia Quaker minister (*Friends' Intelligencer,* 22 August 1857, 361). Ann Weaver
was a Philadelphia Hicksite minister.

4. Stanton's niece Harriet Eaton Brown had just given birth to her first child (Gordon, 1:382).

5. Edith Scott (d. 1868), a Hicksite Quaker, was the widow of Israel Scott and the
mother of Townsend Scott (*Friend,* 1 August 1868, 392).

6. Robert Collyer (1823–1912), a British immigrant active in the antislavery movement,
would become a Unitarian minister in 1859. He had met LCM and JM in 1855 when he
was the director of a lyceum in Philadelphia (*Life and Letters of Robert Collyer,* ed. John
H. Holmes [New York: Dodd, Mead, 1917], 1:156–74).

## To Elizabeth Neall Gay

RoadSide, near Philada.<br>12 Mo. 9th. 1858

My dear Elizabeth Gay
    Thine of _____ relative to the paper-weights was recd.—  Edwd. [*Davis*]
had forgotten part of thy message, as he told thee he would be likely to. It is
surprising that he remembers so much, with all his business-cares. We shall
advertise the sea-pebbles, & bring them into notice, in some way, so that they

may sell for their value. Thou knows the utilitarian character of Pennsylvanians, especially of such as patronise our Fairs.—— Why cant thou "make an effort," and come next week, and see how we do, on these great occasions? Sydney being otherwise engaged now, I fear we may look in vain for him. His cheerful presence always added interest to the Fairs, when he *did* favor us, especially to the lovers of fun; and I claim to belong to that class, and,

"Confess,
Fearless, a Soul that does not always think."

We shall have meetings too, during the week, for such as have "the burden of the word of the Lord",[1] and I claim a share in that also— Thou must come. Thy spirit shall "have free course," in either department.

We have had a rich treat, in your noble G. W. Curtis' lectures.— His first, on Democracy & Education was just to my mind, Republican in Principle, and intensely interesting. Then, 'Fair Play for Woman' was fine, unexceptionable in its tone, and so beautiful![2] The satire well deserved, the illustratrations happy— Anti Slavery so throughly sifted in, and borne so well, by the throng in attendance.—— The allusion to Mary Woolstonecraft, bold and so just—("May her tribe increase".) Great good must come from such daring.

"Now mark a spot or two,
That so much beauty would do well to purge."

Edward D. wrote thee, that while we were all delighted with the performance, I had some criticism to make.— I merely wanted to whisper in the dear fellow's ear, that some of the 'breeches' and 'pantaloons' might be omitted.[3] But fearing it would appear needlessly fastidious, I was hesitating, for I hate prudery; when Edwd. mentioned what he had written— So some explanation was called for. G. W. Curtis is so polished—so refined, that anything bordering on the common-place or vulgar, ill-befits him.

We listened to the lecture again last eveg—a large audience—many who were not there the first eveg—& greatly pleased they appeared to be.—— What a *lift* to the Woman's Rights' cause, to have such talents employed in its advocacy! It cannot ultimately be any disadvantage to him. Truth is all powerful & must prevail.

Have you heard Jessie Maritor White Mario on Italy, &.c—?[4] We anticipate her coming here, and hope we may succeed in procuring a good hearing for her. She comes with excellent recommendations to us.

I have never acknowledged thy last characteristic letter—so full of wrath over Pearl Andrews, and our free platform— I was amused— It was not half so bad as thy imagination painted it. Never fear for our cause. We can 'live down' all the harm that 'free-love' or the 'Maternity-question' can do us, only let not our faith fail us—

James Mott joins with me, in the warmest assurances that we are

ever thine most affecy—   L. Mott

Art thou familiar with Shelly's beautiful, poetic dedication of his Work to his wife?—or rather the beautiful allusion & just tribute to her Mother?[5]

REVOLT OF ISLAM

"They say that thou wert lovely from thy birth,
Of glorious parents, thou aspiring Child.
I wonder not—for One then left this earth,
Whose life was like a setting planet mild,
Which clothed thee in the radiance undefiled
Of its departing glory: Still her fame
Shines on thee thro' the tempests dark and wild
Which shake these latter days; and thou canst claim
The shelter from thy Sire, of an immortal name."

ALS NNCB-Gay

1. Zech. 9:1, 12:1; Mal. 1:1.

2. Curtis had given his address, "Fair Play for Women," on 6 December 1858 (*NASS,* 27 November 1858, 3).

3. LCM is quoting William Cowper, *The Task,* book 1, "The Sofa," l. 726. LCM may be referring to a passage in which Curtis criticized British works treating women as "the toy of [*man's*] passionate moments. . . . Precisely the principle inculcated on her daughter by every scheming mamma who means by 'a good match for my darling Jane,' any thing in trousers with twenty thousand dollars a year!" (*Liberator,* 29 October 1858, 173).

4. The Englishwoman Jessie Maritor White Mario (1832–1906) had first gone to Italy in 1854 as a traveling companion to another woman and then became involved in the movement for a unified Italy. She had returned as a correspondent of the *London Daily News* and was imprisoned in Genoa for her "exertions in the cause of Italian liberty." She had met her future husband, Alberto Mario, through this movement, and they had married on 19 December 1857 (*NASS,* 4 December 1858, 2; Elizabeth Adams Daniels, *Jessie White Mario: Risorgimento Revolutionary* [Athens: Ohio University Press, 1972], 5, 14, 71).

5. LCM is quoting from stanza 12 of the dedication to *The Revolt of Islam* by Percy Bysshe Shelley (1792–1822), published in 1818. Mary Godwin Shelley (1797–1851) was Shelley's wife and the daughter of Mary Wollstonecraft and William Godwin. Wollstonecraft had died in 1797 after giving birth to her daughter.

## To Martha Coffin Wright

[*Roadside*] 27th. [*December 1858*]
2nd. day morng.

*[Continuation of a letter begun 26 December]*

We are havg. a quiet day—all the childn. gone to town— Bel & Emmy [*Mott*] described their parlor adorngs.—Christs. green festoons, presents, &.c— in such glowg. colors, & begged so hard for Willie [*Davis*] to go in with them, that his Mother consented, & a happy trio they were— Elizh. Cavr. came down

yesteraftern., & insisted on Willie & Frank [*Wright*] going up there to tea &
lodge—the other childn. to go in the eveg. & see the Christs. tree—    Collyer
also, & his— He was here most of the aftern., readg. with Edwd. aloud parts of
Buckle's Hist. of Civilizn.—[1] Thou may have seen the Reviews of it—only 1 vol.
out, & that but the Introductn.—600 pages— Furness was full of it, at the
Fair—praisg. it up to me—    Josh. Barker says it will do more to break down
superstition & false Theology, than any book that has been published these 150
years.— I have read but 100 pages yet—& laid it aside to do this writg to thee—
Thy last is by me—3rd. Inst.—also 2 to Ellen [*Wright*], wh. we were glad to
read   Anna B. returned the fam. sheet last week—with suitable comments—  I
will give Ellen her letter to enclose to you, as this must go, via EaglesWd.—
Mari[a]. [*Mott*] was sorry that you all had recd. the impressn., that the boys comg.
wd. be a care to her, or dread— I forget now— I only wrote what she did say—
about her Mama being here with them— As Anna B. says, "they are such manly,
nice boys," they will not give trouble to any of us. I wd. have kept them here today & had them taken over to M'Kim's this eveg., where all are to gather, but
Ellen sd. they must go in, to make the needful change in clothg.—   She came
out rather unexpectedly, yesteraftern.—havg. declined the girls invitn. to ride
out with them after Church—as Chs. & Caro [*Wood*] were to dine at
Thos. Clem. afterwd. invited her to drive out with him in the aftern.[2]—& go
back in the eveg. When the time came, she & Miss Shepard & Anna [*Davis?*] were
havg. a good time together, so Henry D. rode in with Clem., & Ellen is still here—
They have just been up to the Farm & brot. arms full of books & are now preparg.
to go over to Miller's to dine—then Ellen will go into town & prepare to come
out to the eveg. party there. Christs. aftern. Anna & Ned Hall[l]. came down &
persuaded our girls to go up there & pass the eveg. Soon after, they, nothg. loth
were gone, the M'Kims & Miss Tallman & Miller drove in—so they followed—
Miller comg. back here to tea, & a pleast. sociable eveg. we had—    Henry D.
came out & followed Suite—    When Miller went up for them @ 9 oclk—they
were far from ready to separate—    Ned promised to see them safe home—so
he took Charley & went home—    Towd. midnight the Hall[l]s. got out their carriage & pair, & the whole 6 drove over to Millers— —  Anna D. & Miss Shepard were in high glee—    Morris & Hanh. H. & Emily are in Boston—so the mice
had a fine play—   Clem. Griscom drove out with Bessie Walton—[3]  Neither Lue
[*Hopper*] nor Ellen were of the impromptu party—    Their enjoyts. were in
town—   Ellen writes I presume.

     Thy accot. of Starr King's Lecture interested us—[4] Yes, it is a pity, you cd.n't
have met at Mrs. Worden's  It is always pleast., to hear of Caroe. visitg thee—  I
want very much to see her, but she will probably go to Holly, before comg. out
here.— —  We have been as greatly pleased, with listening to R. W. Emerson.
His lecture on The Law of Success is full of gems—  Collyer heard him for the
1st. time, & was carried away with delight. He remembd. so much yestery., that

we quite enjoyed hearg. it over. I spoke to him (Emerson) after the Lecture—thanked him for it—he replied, "I got some leaves out of yr. book"—addg. "from yr New Bedford Frds."— I remembd. that his mind was enlightened beyond his Pulpit & Ordinances, about the time of the enlightened Mary Newall's (newlight) comg. out, & I doubt not she had some influence on him—[5] The only objectn. to his philosophy the other eveg. was his makg. Nature *utilize* every thing—the bad as well as the good— That may be in the Animal economy—but in morals, I told him wickedness works only evil & that continually & the only way was to destroy it is with unquenchable fire— EaglesWd. essays, last winter, made good & evil—right & wrong, no longer antagonistic, but runng. in parallel lines— I dont understand it, & want no such quietus to the Conscience— Buckle calls free Will a Metaphysical, while predestn. is a Theological hypothesis or dogma— It was revoltg. to my moral sense years ago, when I heard Dr. Tyng[6] at a Colonizn. Mg. say, that with all the cruelties of the Slave trade, the horrors of the middle passage, & the evils of Slavery in this country, he was prepared to say that Slavery & the Slave trade wd. yet be a blessg. to Africa— At that time Liberia was held up as a great civilizer & evengelizer to that Nation—

If Starr King lecture in the City next Mo., we will try to hear him. Horace Mann had a very rainy eveg. & a poor audience—[7] His lecture was admirable—so said Rachel Jackson— We are expectg. Jessie Mario soon, & I have great fears, lest we shall not be able to secure audiences for her— The season will be so nearly over— Thou may be here in time to hear her. Thou dont say whether Antoine. B's. postponemt. of her visit to Auburn, will keep thee at home all this comg. mo.— The expected accounchmt. too, what effect will that have on thy movements?— Thy nice preparatns. for Betsy was a great lift to her— Eliza Y. has had equal satisfactn., in makg. up for their Biddy divers useful & ornamental articles—a basket from the lumber room, Mary B. varnished, like London, & when lined & filled, it had a temptg appeare.— Sarah & Reba. [*Yarnall*] have been equally busy preparg. Christs dolls, &.c—for all the descendts., who were to assemble as usual there— Reba. has also been knittg. a crib spread for sister Margt. [*Yarnall*]— The girls often go down to Ellis'—but we seldom see him now—& it is a loss to our household— — He gave to the Fair—& Margt. went & bot. some things— Eliza & I met there each day but one— There are however so many calls on me, & the Conventn. too, that sister didn't choose to give her presence to, that we were little together— Maria [*Davis*] was only in one day, & then Jas. Truman (dentist) drew her[8]— Anna D. served tables in her Mother's place, & Lue H. in hers—only Anna [*Hopper*] was down every eveg., to receive the money—$1800 in all—better than we expected—for the Eng. goods did not arrive— Miller sd. we had grown grey in the Cause (alludg. at the time to Isaac Winslows grey Paris wig) & our childn. & childn.'s childn. were takg. the lead— It was even so—how many vacant places there were—no Coateses—Whitsons—Garrets—Dugdales—Coxes—Pierces—(save

Jacob, large as life & old as the [Popes?].) We did have frd. Grew as earnest as ever. Wm. W. B's Drama took very well— We had several Slaveholders prest.— Senator Hammond's son who took part in the debates— He is studyg. Law in the City—⁹ Reba. Potts worked very diligently & sent lots of quilted skirts, drawers, &.c— Elizh. bot. several prs.— Reba. could not feel in spirits to come— No sound of Willie— Sarah M'K. & Margt. Griscom sold a great deal at their table.— So did Lue & Anna Mercy Fraley, Sally Hallᶦ.¹⁰ &.c at theirs— Mary Grew was able to attend at the Book table & that did well— But such a lot of new, little dismals—colored & white promenadg. & childn. without number, makg. such a noise, we concluded, our price of admissn. must be raised next year— — Does all this interest thee more than Dr. Eddy's new philosophy did? I must write what we have— Mariᵃ. begged me to scratch out every one of those "items" from my last—so now I hesitate to make of too much importance, Mrs. Dennis' wrath at her lord's inexcusable neglect¹¹—while I agreed with thee & Anna B. entirely, as to his duty in the matter. I suppose he had no idea of consummatg. the partnership so soon— As to Emma Parker—her ideas are so confused on the Wom. questn., that her opinion has not so much weight with me— She told me she always agreed with me on the subject.— — I was glad yr. shepherdess did so well—& can readily believe the prisoners wd. prefer her appeals, to those of their chaplain No, thou did not write Seward's¹² complimentary speech to thee, twice—only once & we liked to hear it—but we didn't like to see part of the page of thy letter cut off. What was it? I meant above, when on the Prison, to say, what a crying shame it is that the poor inmates must not only be thus incarcerated, but that power is given to put them to torture, even unto death. Why didn't you Auburn people make as much fuss, as the Boston folk did when Dr. Parkman was murdered?— — "Fish o' one & flesh o' the other", is no good Democratic motto. It was quick in Mrs. Dennis to name "br. Gould's" sons.¹³ But then he & his wife left the Quakers— I agree with thee as to Lizzie Gay's judgt. of the Conventn., while sitting at home— It was not wise or knowg I wrote to her, praisg. up Curtis— — He lately lectured in Easton & made quite a good stir there Elizh. Phillips sd.

[P.S.] Thou wast mistaken in thinking Eliza [*Osborne?*] wd dread to go from us. Her visit was so entirely out, that we cd. not have prevailed on her to stay to the Fair if she hadn't wished to have Charles' compy. home. I now must write to our poor Aunt Lydia [*Mott*]. She is in need & the year must not go out till we minister to her wants Mary & Cannie Mott are in New York They with their Father and our niece Mary Hicks are to be here the last of this week¹⁴— And such a party as Lue & Anna are drumg. up for New Year's eve!— It is their turn now, & how soon it will pass away! It suited best for them to unite & bid their frds. out here. Edwd. Hopper has lately been out to Pittsburg & beyond on business— Lucy Gibbons¹⁵ has had several alarmg attacks of falling in a kind of fit— They fear it is the beginning of Epilepsy I called to see Sarah P. & Fanny Wright the other day—the 1st time since Peter & Fanny's return from Europe  So, thou hast been making a new carpet—  Thou accomplishes a great de[al?]

AL PSCHi-Mott

1. Henry Thomas Buckle (1821–62) published his multivolume *History of Civilization in England* between 1857 and 1861 (London: J. W. Parker).

2. Clement Griscom (b. 1841) was a Philadelphia Hicksite.

3. Edward Needles Hallowell (1836–71) was the son of Morris Hallowell and Hannah Smith Penrose Hallowell (1812–99); their daughter was Emily Hallowell (b. 1842). Bessie Walton (d. 1866) (LCM to MCW, 19 March 1866, MNS).

4. Thomas Starr King (1824–64), a Unitarian Universalist minister and a popular lecturer, had delivered his speech "Sight and Insight" in Auburn (MCW to LCM, 3 December 1858, MNS).

5. Emerson had given "The Law of Success" on 16 December at the People's Institute (William Charvat, "Emerson's Lecture Engagements: A Chronological List" [New York: New York Public Library, 1861], 34). Mary Newhall of New Bedford, Massachusetts, was a New-Light Quaker preacher (Frederick B. Tolles, "The New-Light Quakers of Lynn and New Bedford," *New England Quarterly* 32 [September 1959]: 291–319).

6. "Dr. Tyng" is probably Stephen H. Tyng (1800–1885), an Episcopal minister.

7. The Philadelphia correspondent of the *NASS* had expected Mann to speak in Philadelphia early in December (4 December 1858, 3).

8. James Truman (1822–80) was a Philadelphia Hicksite and the husband of Mary Ann McClintock.

9. The twenty-third Anti-Slavery Fair of Pennsylvania had begun on 14 December. William Wells Brown had written two dramas, *The Dough Face* and *The Escape*, and was scheduled to speak at the Pennsylvania Anti-Slavery Convention held in Philadelphia on 15–17 December (*WLG*, 4:441–43; *NASS*, 4 December 1858, 2). A man identifying himself as the son of South Carolina Senator James Hammond had presented a resolution at the convention stating that "Congress had no right, under the Constitution, to declare the slave trade piracy," but no one had seconded his resolution (*Liberator*, 31 December 1858, 211).

10. Margaret Acton Griscom (1819–96) was the mother of Clement Griscom. "Sally Hall[l.]" was possibly Sarah Fraley Hallowell, the second wife of Joshua Hallowell, Morris Hallowell's brother.

11. On 28 November 1858, LCM had written MCW of Dr. Eddy, an English visitor, "He has been explaing. to us, Ericsson's new theory of attractn.—differg. from the Newtonian instd. of gravitatn. & cohesion, his theory simplifies—makes all the result of the same great law of force—" (Mott Manuscripts, PSCHi). Eunice Dennis (d. 1861), the mother of Frederick Dennis, was upset because her husband, Cyrus Dennis (1806–66), a business partner of Charles Wood and Munson Osborne, planned to return to Auburn without consulting her (Cayuga Museum Archives, Auburn, N.Y.; Fort Hill Cemetery records, Auburn, N.Y.; MCW to LCM, 3 December 1858, MNS). The Dennises had moved from Auburn to Buffalo in 1852 (MCW to LCM, 26 February 1852, MNS).

12. William H. Seward (1801–72), an Auburn lawyer and the former governor of New York, was a Whig U.S. senator from New York, 1849–61.

13. In a remark made to MCW, Dennis had referred to the sons of Benjamin Gould of Aurora, New York, as "Quakers gone bad" because they drank and smoked (MCW to LCM, 9 December 1850, 20 March 1854, 3 December 1858, MNS).

14. Mary Hicks (b. 1839) was the daughter of Mary Underhill Mott Hicks and Robert Hicks.

15. Lucy Gibbons (1839–1936) was the daughter of Abby Hopper Gibbons and James Gibbons.

## To [Martha Coffin Wright?]

3rd mo. 8th, 1859.

James and I have had a very satisfactory visit in Baltimore and Washington. Our meetings were large, and people kind and attentive. There was a pleasant reception at Dr. Bailey's on Seventh-day evening; we saw—oh, so many! We visited Miss Miner's school and the colored meeting;[1] also wasted time at the Capitol, looking at those lazy loungers, and listening to "Buncombe." We met there Jessie White Mario, who had brought letters of introduction to us from Professor Nichol of Glasgow University, and traveled with her as far as Baltimore, where she is to lecture Fifth-day evening. I no sooner reached Philadelphia than I went from Dan to Beersheba to make interest for her; have since corresponded with her, and now think we shall get up a lecture or two for her in our city. She is an earnest, pleasing woman—a little too much "*fight* for Italy"—but how smart for her to undertake so much! We are to have a visit from her and her husband, to whom she introduced us. Since our return we have been twenty miles up the country, holding anti-slavery meetings. The first ever held at Gwynned! Mary Grew did admirably. Edward Davis joined us at Horseham and brought me home. It did look so pleasant to see our long tea table.

PL Extr Hallowell, 386–87

1. "Dr. Bailey" is probably Gamaliel Bailey (1807–59), the editor of the *National Era*, an antislavery paper based in Washington, D.C. Myrtilla Miner (1815–64) had founded the Colored Girls School in 1851. Supported by Philadelphia Quakers, the school trained teachers and later was known as the Miner Normal School. Miner had left the school in 1855 due to ill health, but remained involved in promoting the school in the North.

## To Martha Coffin Wright and Anna Temple Brown

[*Roadside and Germantown*]
3'd. day morng—31st. [*May 1859*]

[*Continuation of a letter begun 22, 29, and 30 May*]

Another day gone, with so little writg.— I cant help it. We sat up too late last eveg., tired as I was—& now before 5 oclk. I am up agn., pen in hand—so as to take the sheet with all its familiar narratns., over to Geo [*Brown*]'s, to read to Sister & Mary B— It must go tomorrow— Now I have thy letters by me, & find them so entertaing. to read over, that this sinks into a "poor concern"— I felt nearly as bad as thou did, at the drenchg. of Mrs. Dennis' new carpet—

Indeed all the labor attendt. on such a descent of lime, to say nothg. of the wa-
ter-fall, was eno' to dishearten, after the toil of movg— Do give them my love
& sympathy— I am glad they are safely back in Auburn, & sincerely hope the
busins. will repay them & Chs. Wood too—of course Munson [*Osborne*] has my
*bestest* of wishes in that regard— We noticed, in that bit of a call from Charles,
how characteristically, he had entered into the interests of the firm— We had
no time to ask him ½ the questns. we wished to about you all— We were very
glad that he essayed to see Auga. [*Needles*] in Balt[imor]e., & sorry eno' that she
was from home. We have heard nothg. from her since her return—nor from
Holly in a long time. Thy several mentions of Caroe. [*Wood*] were acceptable.
Dont those sick-headache spells increase? I want to hear of her enjoyg. better
health— After Eliza [*Yarnall*] is settled out at Geo's, she has agreed to go up
with me to Holly—i.e. after Maggie [*Yarnall*]'s confinet.— If thoul't believe
it, here I am sittg. on the floor in Geo's Attic—all alone Mary's travg. trunk to
write on—Eliza & Mary with poor Margt. who is sick— Miller [*McKim*] was
over at Roadside, early this morng. to take Anna Davis home, who stayed there
last night— I rode back with him, to save Jas. *one* drive over, intendg. to walk
from his house, but he wd. bring me quite here— They breakfast late at Ellis'
[*Yarnall*], so I thot. nothg. of findg. only the girl here, & hurried up to this old
carpet to cut out some "geometry work," where the pattern didnt match wh.
Eliza wd.n't let me do yestery., & quite enjoyed being "monarch of all I
survey"ed—[1] About 10 oclk Elly [*Brown*] came from his uncle's bearg. the tidings that aunt Margt. was sick, & his Mother & Grandmr. wd.n't be here— Eliza
might have sent a note, tho.' I didn't agree positively to come today, so she may
think I am not here. How clever that her nurse is with her— She thot. Margt.
had miscalculated & wd.n't need her for a week—& not being well she did not
come for a few days after being asked to lodge out here— She is the same nurse
that Lizzie Hall[l].[2] had, & 1st. rate— I have hoped every hour a bulletin wd. arrive— It is now after 1 oclk—so I'll go down, & dine on ham, potats, bread &
butter— I told the girl to prepare nothg. for me, more than for herself—

                                                      Eveg. 31st. At home agn.—

 didnt accompish much carpet-sewg. Eliza & Mary came toward 4 oclk—
bearg. the news of a daughr's birth @ 12—several hours sooner than Dr. Griscom
expected— It was called a favorable time, but oh, how bad is the best—the last
hour was so severe, that if the Dr. had brot. ether he wd. have given it—such
long-continued forcing pains— She was very sick & vomited freely—& dis-
tressingly at times— The sufferg. far greater than she anticipated— It left her
with headache, but before we left Ellis called in the carriage, for his Mother, &
sd. she was better—quite revived—— Now that event is over. Margt. liked Dr.
Griscom very much— Eliza has gone into town— Sarah [*Yarnall*] says the
Place Geo. has chosen is rightly named—*Idiots' Retreat*. They feel better now
however, as they will move out next week— The strawby. storm has just be-

gun—wind N.E.— Miller & Sarah [*McKim*] came over to tea, bringg. a basket of strawbs. the 1st. we have had— Ours are turng.— Walter B. also walked in., bringg. some trout of his own catchg.—wh. with a shad our man brot. made a good supper for all— We heard of Walter in Ohio, by Richd H's letter, & were quite surprised to see him— He spoke of his visits to you as very pleast.— All the strawby plants he brot. from Aubn. are doing well—at his garden and ours— every one lived—& some in bloom— What a pity that yr grape vines shd. die. Walter says his cuttings are beging. to leaf out— David wanted to know— Our Michael made Geo. Lord wroth by trimg. off all the new wood from our thrifty vine, that he trained with so much care last year— Jas. too had some branches cut from the Poplar in the backyard—quite to Pattie [*Lord*]'s regret— So it goes— We have much to learn.

Late in the eveg.—
last day of May— —

I sent thy letters to Anna B. this eveg., or rather, gave them to Sarah M'Kim for Anne to take tomorw. morng.—& Walter will take this lot [in?] the aftern., so that Anna can rest between the readings.— I am sorry to say, that I have not written to Josh. Dugdale—for the same reason that thou & Anna B. have been neglected, not a moment's time. We go in to Mg. tomorw., & to Ex. Com. Mg., and I will then ask S. Pugh to write to H. M. Darlington, & if successful will forwd. the Reports without delay— — Nothg. could be more ill-judged than Mrs. Dall's readg. that eveg—& nothg. more forced than thy sister's re-marks followg— — I was amused with the comment in the Paper—that "there was nothg. fresh", wh. was a fact.[3] To be stuck up, to speak ½ an hour, with nothg. special to inspire you at the time, is an inflictn. and a bore on the Audi-ence— I have great faith in the Quaker creed, 'to speak, as the Spirit giveth utterance'[4]—so little interest have I, in such Annivs., that you'll not catch me there agn.— Our Anti S. Anniversary Mgs. are becomg. somewhat forced & formal too— Fixed speeches on such occasions are not to be compared to spontaneous discussion. Wendell Phillips of course always is an exceptn.— — Antionette's was good that eveg., & very well delivered— Mrs. Rose's well eno'—[5] She was rather out of humor with me, for callg. 1st. for Wendell P.— I am glad S. B. Anthony has the courage to persevere, glad too that thy interest does not flag— What a nice time you must have had at Mrs. Stanton's—thy accot. of the visit made me wish to see her agn.— What cd. be the cause of such "terrific" sufferg.? the weight of the babe?[6] Nurse thinks Margt's. not more than 7 lbs—a pretty little thing Mary says, & begun immedy. to "live by suc-tion"— You are very good to keep yr. Betsy so long— I can sympathize with thee, in havg. to swallow *affirmations*. That stove pipe is nothg. compared to our stairs— — — — Jas. says 'tis bed time, so good night— —

4th. day—6 mo. 1st.

Rainy morng.—

We go into town—takg. all this stale trash to read to thy daughr. & to Eliza
not being time yestery. for Maria [*Davis*], Elizh. Cavr., Pattie & Nelly [*Lord*] drove
over for me, & we surveyed the house [agn?] Every part is in nice order— Mary
had a wom. to help her girl wash, & then wash all the windows clean stairs, &.c—
Little Ellie does enjoy being out there, & has already made acquaine. with
neighbr. Breakfast bell—good bye—

4th. day aftern. at Thos. Mott's—

& here comes Munson—quite fortunate for Eliz[a?] and I to meet him here.
He might take this, as he expects to leave tomow. & go directly home, but then
Anna B. wd.n't see it, so I must just let it be old news to you, rather than write
these items over to Anna— Maybe Munson will not remember to tell you, that
Margt. talks of namg. her baby, Ethel—what a novel-name!— Pattie desires
all thanks, but she cant bring her mind to leavg. home this summer, by reason
of increasg. size— She says Eliza must do the visitg. till she is prevented by similar circumstances— I have not done answg. thy letters—but will go on—&
fill a small sheet & send to Anna B., by Sarah M'Kim on 7th. day Anna must
add to this & tell you of Walter's rentg. his house to his br. Nathl.—& every thing
else— I have delivd. thy message to Mary Earle— She hopes to accept if her
funds hold out after returng. from Enterprise—

Munson is waitg to take this to Walter—

Hurry it on Anna after fillg this page

lovingly   L. Mott

ALS PSCHi-Mott

1. William Cowper, "Verses Supposed to Be Written by Alexander Selkirk," l. 1 (1782).
2. Elizabeth Corbit Davis Hallowell (b. 1835) was the wife of William Penrose Hallowell.
3. Susan B. Anthony had presided over the National Woman's Rights meeting held in
New York City on 12 May 1859. Caroline Healey Dall (1822–1912), a transcendentalist and
a woman's rights activist from Boston, had read an address "which she said was mostly
extracted from one of a series of lectures delivered last year in Boston" on Mary Wollstonecraft. However, according to the news report, the audience had great difficulty in
hearing Dall, and she finally stopped speaking after repeated interruptions of "'louder,' 'sit down,' 'go on.'" LCM then addressed the group briefly, stating that "the indications of the times were that woman had only to ask for her enfranchisement to have the
request granted. . . . Spheres of usefulness have been opened to her, which she was filling
with honor to herself, and the prediction of Catharine Beecher, thirty years ago, that
woman would enlarge her usefulness, was being realized in medicine, science, art and
industry." LCM's speech was followed by "cheers, hisses, calls for 'Lucy Stone,' 'Rose,'
'Miss Rose,' 'Greeley,' 'Phillips'" (*New York Tribune*, 13 May 1859, 5; *NASS*, 21 May 1859,
4). In its report on LCM's speech at the meeting, the *New York Herald* commented, "Mrs.
MOTT continued to advance several arguments, neither very fresh nor very forcible . . .
and was listened to with a moderate degree of respect to her age, impressive presence
and manifest sincerity" (13 May 1859, 4).
4. Acts 2:4.

5. Phillips had spoken at the AASS meeting on 11 May as had LCM, who had urged the society not to forget its aims of moral suasion "as the most effectual means" to end slavery (*NASS,* 21 May 1859, 3). At the National Woman's Rights meeting, Antoinette Brown Blackwell had asked that women receive equal rights with men. She had urged women to follow Christ's example and eschew modesty in arguing for their cause. Ernestine L. Rose had argued for women to be educated as thoroughly as men: "Educate women, and you needn't 'protect' them any more" (*NASS,* 21 May 1859, 4).

6. After the birth of her son Robert Stanton on 13 March, Stanton had written Anthony that she "had no vitality of body or soul" (10 April 1859, Gordon, 1:387).

## To Caroline Bonsall Kelley[1]

[*Roadside*] 16/7/59—

My dear Carrie

I regret to be obliged to decline this—thy second invitation to visit you— Jas. Mott will go to New York tomorrow, & will not return till early next week— We are expecting John P. Hale[2] to visit us on 6th-day next— He may stay the night— I have invited our frd. Robt. Dale Owen to come out & join him there— And we should be pleased if Judge Kelly & thyself would accompany him to dine or take tea, or both—

In great haste

affecy.    *L. Mott*

ALS NNCB-Kelley

1. In 1854 Caroline Bonsall Kelley (1829–1906), the adopted niece of Sarah Pugh, had married Judge William Darrah Kelley (1814–90), who was later a U.S. congressman from Pennsylvania.

2. John P. Hale (1806–73), a former Free-Soil party presidential candidate, was serving as a Republican U.S. senator from New Hampshire.

## To Anna Temple Brown

RoadSide 1 Mo. 2nd. 60—
2nd. day eveg.
My 1st. date of this year—

Dear precious Anna—

Thou wast "among the missing," at our Fam[il]y. party to-day—and now that Coates & Brown have dissolved partnersp., we are sadly anticipatg. that thou may be more permanently among the missing, at our feasts, by Walter's concludg. that more & better busins. may be done in New York, & therefore that you will go there, "bag & baggage["]— Now be assured we "miss thee at home" as we shall Walter too, if he cease to have business calls to our City— — Aunt Eliza too we no longer have at our gathergs. She fears to go from home this despa'te cold weather— How do you find it? We are nearly frozen up. Our milk in the vault came up ice this morng— The bath tub is ice— And our wood &

coal melt away "like wildfire"— Still we have had great enjoyt. in 2 or 3 parties of late—the EaglesWd. compy., among the number— They can tell you of that, & of all their fun & doings— Henry [*Davis*] has had a large share with them—
— Miller [*McKim*] was over here last eveg. with Dr. Solger,[1] who is going to deliver Lectures in New Y. & Philada.— We had Carole. S. Wood here too for a day or so— Anna Hopper came out last eveg. for the sake of a little of her compy— She is now at Holly with Laura—who can tell thee how they are there, & how much better Eunice Dennis & Eliza Osborne are— We recd. a letter from Aunt Martha today,—a treat after so long silence—except 2 short notes to Maria. [*Mott*] sent with Ellen [*Wright*]'s—both wh. I hope she will enclose to thee tomorw.— We read hers, today at our gatherg—all the daughrs. here includg. Maria.— After Aunt Eliza has had it, I will hurry it on to thee— Walter said we sent thee only parts of Auburn letters by him— I was not aware of it—nor which parts were left behind, so at the risk of disappointg. thee, I have collected all the old ones & put into the box, with Anna D's also & one or 2 of her Mother's wh. she very reluctantly allowed me to send thee—sayg. hereafter Anna's letters shd. not be sent hither & thither I hope however she will let me send them to Auburn—for they complain that they hear very little from Anna— Such a funny time as they have had this below-zero weather, with all their spare rooms occupied— Ned Hall!. went on with Susy & Hanh. Sweeney, & at the last moment, Mother Hall!. concluded not to let Susy go without her watchful care over her, so she went too—& such a surprise to Anna! & such cold nights as they found there! & yet all so pleased with the cottage & its inmates— Norwd.[2] there too—& Andw. Howld., part of the time— Their girl frightened lest she shd.n't cook to suit so particular a lady as Mrs. Hallowell— Ned returned a day or 2 ago, & tells Maria this—& "never wanted to be married, & at housekeepg—so much before, it was so splendid there"—&.c &.c— Morris Hall!. went on, last 6th. day—to reach Medford 7th. day eveg., & all leave tomorw. for home— Anna wrote of her quiet house & lonely feelgs. after her Mother left her—but she has eno' now— Wm. Hall!. thou knows has been to Europe & returned Their little Isaac[3] has been very ill, he is still far from well— They doubt his recovy— This however is in the Aubn. letter, wh. Aunt M. sd. wd. be forwarded to thee in a few days— After thou hast read it, please put it with those I now send thee & return all to me by 1st. *private* opp[ortunit]y— I want to refer to mine, when I write to Nant. if I ever find time— Coz. M. Earle says her Mother is bright— Oh, that too is in your letter— The twin boy is buried— Mary Ann is quite pleased that the daughr. lives— She is doing well— So am I— The swellg. in my face continued 2 or 3 days—nearly closg. one eye & much inflamg. both—but after the boil broke it gradually subsided—no erysipelas or pain followg. to speak of— I have not been out these 10 days—longer that I have been housed than for 10 yrs. It seems an age since I saw Aunt Eliza— Very little have we had of her compy. of late— The death of Edwd. Y—will keep them to themselves awhile, I suppose—[4] Reba. cant bear much exposure—

neither can her Mother— Mary [*Brown*] goes in now & then— I reckon she finds it cold too— We see nothg. of them—or of Ellis & Margt. [*Yarnall*] I have wanted to go & take them a taste of our scrapple & sausage—& Elly a Christs. trifle, but with my lame face, it had to be put off— We killed one 300 lbs pig last week—& such a busy household as we had! Another is to be slain & put up the last of this Mo— Our turkeys are all killed & eaten—ditto ducks—& about 100 fowls—those that remain lay no eggs just now— 3 roastg. pigs we have devoured too— Why are we not as bad as Cannibals?—

Thy letters have been truly acceptable— I have intended to write direct to Reba. Spring—& I will still as soon as I can tell her of any money raised—[5] She deserves credit for remembg. *all* the poor prisoners, with such generous exertions— Lawyer Sennott did not impress us very favorably— Still he may do as well for Stephens as any other—for *he* too will doubtless share the fate of his companions— Morris D[avis]. recd. that sent to him— He came here, & we talked it over—but talkg. thou knows "wont make the pot boil"—tell Reba., wilt thou, that my will is good—but how to do, as yet, I find not—

The Papers are so full of every thg. about all these stirrg events, that there is little left to write—this late corresponde. betwn. Randall & Dana is rich—& how good L. Maria Child's ans. to Mrs. Mason![6] Indeed, good things abound— The leaders in the Eveg. Post are 1st rate— Even our slow, dull North American came out a day or 2 ago—commentg. on Gov. Wise's folly,[7] & the student-stampede— as did the Ledger too—

The Sunday Paper had a broad satire this wk no—last week, in wh. thy Aunt's name figured largely—[8] If uncle Jas. can find it, I'll enclose it—& thou can send it with this to Auburn—& I will enclose a few stamps for the purpose—for I shall not write to aunt M. till several letters are ansd. to my neglected correspondts. I must write & send a New Yrs. gift to poor afflicted Aunt L. P. Mott, who aunt M. writes is decling— Arthur does badly eno'— Our br. Richd. pd. them a visit lately—& heard that Arthur was taken up from the gutter & carried home lately—

AL PSCHi-Mott

1. Reinhold Solger (1817–66) was a German immigrant who lectured on German history and culture.

2. Anna Davis had married Richard P. Hallowell on 25 October 1859 and was living in Medford, Massachusetts. Hallowell relatives not previously identified are Richard's siblings Susan Morris (b. 1845) and Norwood Hallowell (1839–1914), then a student at Harvard University.

3. Isaac Davis Hallowell (b. 1859).

4. Benjamin Yarnall's brother Edward had died on 18 December 1859 (*Friends' Review*, 21 January 1860, 13: 313).

5. Anna Temple Brown had written LCM from Eagleswood on 17 December 1859 about raising money for the prisoners awaiting trial for treason against the state of Virginia in connection with the 16 October raid on the Harpers Ferry arsenal (MNS). John Brown's second wife, Mary Ann Brown, had stayed with LCM and JM en route to her husband

in Virginia, where he awaited execution. On 26 November LCM and Mary Ann had attended a Hicksite meeting near School House Lane, where LCM had preached (*Norristown Times Herald,* 5 December 1959; see also Stephen B. Oates, *To Purge This Land with Blood: A Biography of John Brown* [Amherst: University of Massachusetts Press, 1984], 328, 340, 347, 357). After Brown was hanged on 2 December, James Miller McKim had accompanied Mary Ann Brown with her husband's body to his burial in North Elba, New York. In Eagleswood Rebecca Spring had been trying to obtain funds to pay the expenses of George Sennott, a lawyer for Aaron D. Stevens, one of Brown's followers since the Kansas raids. On 16 March 1860 Stevens, like the rest of Brown's associates, would be executed (*NASS,* 10 December 1859, 2; *Liberator,* 23 March 1860, 48). Of Morris Davis's efforts, Anna Temple Brown had written to LCM that he "is so much interested that I dont believe but that he can stir up the people to prove that all these Union Saving meetings, & mobs, are not going to scare us off" (17 December [1859], MNS). According to the *NASS,* LCM and others were scheduled to speak on the day of Brown's execution; she did speak at antislavery meetings that were held on 21–23 December (*NASS,* 3 December 1859, 3, 24 December 1859, 2; for LCM's comments on Brown, see *Sermons,* 261–62).

6. In a letter of 26 December 1859, Robert E. Randall of Philadelphia had complained to Charles A. Dana (1819–97), managing editor of the *New York Tribune,* that the *Tribune* had insulted him in an editorial by stating that he had, through "senseless noise and interruption," tried to prevent George William Curtis from lecturing. Dana had replied that Randall had no grounds for his charge because he had been arrested for breaking up Curtis's lecture (*NASS,* 31 December 1859, 3). In connection with the Harpers Ferry raid, Margaretta Mason, the wife of James M. Mason, the Virginia senator who was heading the Harpers Ferry investigation, had written Child on 11 November castigating her as one who "would soothe with sisterly and motherly care that hoary headed murderer of Harper's Ferry!" Child had responded on 17 December that the "Abolitionists are not such an ignorant set of fanatics as you suppose. They *know* whereof they affirm. They are familiar with the laws of the slave States, which are alone sufficient to inspire abhorrence in any humane heart or reflecting mind not perverted by the prejudices of education and custom" (*Liberator,* 31 December 1859, 209).

7. The *New York Evening Post* had called Brown's aims "just and generous" even if his means were "misguided and foolish" (1 December 1859, 2). On 27 December the *Post* had called Virginia governor Henry A. Wise (1806–76) to task for describing his state as a "'nursing mother'" when so many of its inhabitants were slaves (2). In an editorial attacking Wise for his accusations against Northern states for interfering with Virginia's laws, an editorialist in the *Philadelphia Public Ledger* had argued, "If the Governor of Virginia wishes to do mischief, and to promote danger to all the national relations of the States, how could he conceive of a more likely way to accomplish such an object than to proclaim his State in arms, to *demand* of Pennsylvania whether she means *bona fide* to adhere to the Constitution?" (12 December 1859, 2).

8. A further exacerbation of North-South tensions was the "student stampede," the decision by medical students from Southern states to leave Philadelphia's medical schools because they considered the climate there unfriendly to Southern interests (*Philadelphia North American,* 22 December 1859, 2). In a satire of the event, a writer for the *Philadelphia Sunday Dispatch* (25 December 1859, 1), reported that the students' "secession" had prompted a meeting, chaired by LCM, "of the notorious club of rowdies and incendiaries known as 'The Quakers,' well-known, unfortunately, as the fruitful authors of the wild outrages and disturbances which have, for years, disgraced our otherwise peaceable city." The medical students tried to depart, but "with a savage howl, the 'Quakers'

were upon them" at Tenth and Locust. The *Dispatch* continued, "The attack was headed by L____ M____, armed with a carboy of vitriol." The medical students retreated
down Tenth Street, where one student from Alabama "was leveled to the dust by a well-
armed blow from a bundle of anti-slavery tracts, wielded by Mrs. Mott." The police chief
finally called out twelve marines, who "bravely charged the insurgents." All the Quakers submitted except "their Amazonian leader, who fought desperately to the last" but
was finally arraigned before "Alderman Slow . . . and was of course immediately discharged without bail."

## To [Martha Coffin Wright]

Roadside 3 mo. 12th. 60—

Rainy washg. day & yet all our clothes dried between the showers— Caroe.
[*Wood*] & Laura [*Stratton*] came out yestery. morng.— Jas. was sick in bed with
a cold a creep & fever the night before—but when he heard they were here, he
sd. he shd. be well now— We of course were not at Mg., for wh. I was glad—
Laura found, if not Anna D—, a trio of young ladies—newly-fledged—'Ria
Hopper Susy Hall[l]. & Han. Sweeney—also Fanny & Harry Cavr. who joined
them at dinner—& then they returned the visit to tea at Chelton corner while
Thos. & Elizh. [*Cavender*] came here, with Thos. Mott & Edwd. H., who made
their weekly visit—walkg. over to Germantn. in the eveg— Mari[a]. [*Mott*] cant
so well come 1st. days— They had Jas. Freeman Clarke at their Ch. in the
morng— Thos. sd not so interestg. as Furness—more manner—not so natural. Furness & wife gone to Boston, Salem, Medford, &.c[1] Wont Anna [*Hallowell*] be glad to see them?— Moreover Thos. sd., they had guests at home, Anna
[*Brown*] & Minnie B— We have enjoyed our share of their visit, & hoped to
have them out here agn. yestery.,— Miller & Sarah [*McKim*] came over in the
eveg— They have had David Potts sick there, with gout preventg. Sarah's comg.
to Elizh. Cavr.'s party— Our talk was (partly) Greely & R. D. Owen, on marriage & divorce— It seemed mean, to cast that fling at Owen, now that he
waived by-gones & was publishg. his Spirit-book— Some of us thot. he defended himself well—others sd. Greely used him up—[2] what did you say of it?
Thou didst not say, if my argument on the good results of evil doing, was con-
vincg.— The next spirit[ed?] discussn. was on Seward's speech—[3] Miller thot.
we ought to judge of it from Seward's stand-point— So much was sd. in its
praise that I anticipated a treat, being generally the last to read these spicy articles. It was a damper, for him, at the outset, to desire "to *allay,* rather than *fo-
ment* the National excitement"—that, "the public welfare & happiness depend
chiefly on institutions, & very little on men"— Mary Grew thot. that very un-
sound— We talked it over, at our Fem. A. S. Mg. on 5th. day I had taken some
note of the objectionable part, & commented on it, while unitg. with the praise
bestowed on other parts of the well-prepared speech— It is prejudicial to sound
morals, to attribute good motives to wicked actions "all unrighteousness is

sin"— Thus: a "virtuous excuse, better than the world can imagine—we have not loved freedom so much less, but the union of our country so much more"— admittg. it to be a questn., whether or not Slavery is a good—"that the States divide on it not perversely"—"with equal tranquility the southern States" chose slavery. Jefferson, whom he quotes, did not hesitate to confess that they had not the courage to divest their families of a property, which however, kept their consciences unquiet—* How could he say that Clay & Webster had gone to honored graves—& that the Whig rep. in an hour of strange bewilderment concurred in removg. the Missouri Comp[romis]e. Such tame rebuke of atrocious wrongs! Then all he says about negro equality & offendg. the white man's pride— If Washn. & Jeff. only desired to exalt *white men* to a political level— not negroes & *Women*, why then they are no models for us. He calls it a *wise* arranget that the South shd. be sovereigns over slavery in their States & we wd. aid them to maintn. what system they pleased, & defend their sover/nty. if assailed. That the South is equally at liberty to reject our system of ethics— How can he say so, with such a Declaratn. of Indap[en]d[enc]e. as they boast? Then that composite structure—a mere matter of choice—askg. who wd. lay violent hands on it— We should de[stroy?] it at once if imperfect, lest great be the fall thereof— It is sickeng. his profound respect for the Vice Pres. & never loved Southern Rep. more than now—[4]

I took the above notes, with others, about the wisdom & justice of the Framers of this Republic—acting in harmony with the condition of Society, & the Spirit of the age—in all its provisions—& made quite a speech, warng. against unqualified praise—especially as the negro was so disparaged. It seemed unexpected—but little reply was made— I then waited for the Standard's comments, & was far from satisfied, that "want of room excluded" them—hopg. *that* Paper wd.n't wait for the Liberator— When that severe, because in the *main just* criticism was read, how glad was I, that Garrison reviewed it, as my instincts had led me to do, & with all the faithful rebuke that ever flows from his pen—[5] I need not therefore say more.

So, to thy letter agn.— With Anna's to Lue [*Hopper*], you will find some notice of thy entertaing. pages. Caroe. read them—she was not frightened at the threatened Circular for the South— — We talked of thy spring visit—So, thou art going or comg. rather to help along the Wom. Rig. Annivy. agn.— I had not intended to go this year—havg. the New-Eng. Conventn. more in my mind, & being rather disheartened with the forlorn Mg. last year.[6] It will be real pleast. to see thee tho', for thou wilt certainly plan to come here, either before or after the Annivy.— I presume Mari[a]. [*Mott*] has written before this time, tho' she has not thy letter returned to her yet—for it has been the rounds—School Lane—Benjn [*Yarnall'*]s.—Edwds. Thos. Cavr. & Roadside, since thy daughr. had the 1st. readg. I will try to hunt up the Standard thou asks for, & send by Caroe., also Anna B's letters— We have distributed ours of that date, but Anna H. may have it— I was very glad thou had such a pleast. time with Elizh. Stanton. Will she be able to come to New Y—? Has Wendell P. been in Auburn yet? & did he stop with you? We are rather hopg., that Lue will stay quietly at Toledo, till this blusterg. weather is over— Yes, I well remember yon promise, & faithfully it was performed until we had a country seat of our own, & until a shade fell over that, before unmixed pleasure—the sad countenance of our dear Caroe.—wh. remaineth unto this day—[7] Still I am ready to accompy. Eliza whenever she can be prevailed upon to go to Auburn— Maria [*Davis*] & self were going to drive Caro & Laura over to Germantn.—call on Mary Earle, & Eliza Needles, & then take them to the 1 oclk. cars but a hard rain set in, so they concluded to go in these cars @ 10 o clk— I shall meet Caroe. at Mari[a].'s on 4th. day—wh. will also be the last Mg. with Anna B. who goes home on 5th. day— We dread her takg. Minnie back to EaglesWd.— She has gained so much hereaway Walter has offered his Place for sale— Thos. has advertised Chelton Corner— So we go— Pattie [*Lord*] took her 2 childn. & rode up to York Road with Caroe. this morng. & spent the remainder of the day at Elizh's—for we mean to have as frequent intercourse as possible, while they are within reach— Part of Elizh.'s carpets are up, & sundry boxs & trunks packed.[8] Thou needn't fear my doing too much on carpets—labor with thy sister Eliza rather, for she still tacks down theirs—stoopg. over, as I cannot do—havg. given up that part, long since—the little sewg. I do, is mere play. I should like to be at it now, up there— Thos. hopes to move the last of this week— We tell him they wd. stall, if thats it, in the crossroad & ought not to attempt it these 10 days— Lue will not be here to lend her aid— She has had a delightful winter at Toledo— Her letters have been very entertaing.— Maria will send her & you some of Anna's, by Caroe. wh. Lue will please bring back— We were amused with Eunice D[ennis]'s plain talk with the Dr.— The tent-Russell we cant explain— Mary E. says it is spelled so—but the origin, we must go to Nant. for— Poor Wm. Folger! It is out of our power to make it easy for him to travel hitherward— how hard, that so many years labor of himself, wife & daughrs. should have yielded so little— He dont say how much the Insure. Compy. paid— I enclosed a trifle a week ago & only wished it a sum worth his acceptance— If by free passes he could reach here, he might, "by hook or by crook", collect a little toward furnishg that to *me*, burdensome Hotel— It is in a nice wide new street—not the filthy narrow one, that thou wast so unhappy in— Our childn. didn't "groan" a bit over the extract from S. B. Anthony's Letter they thot. it interestg— Now if Eliza Osb. and Ellen will not groan over my long comments on Seward's speech—& if they did not over that homily on good & evil, then I will fill another of Edwd.'s French ½ sheets for Anna's next to Lue— The wind is blowg.— Jas has gone to bed with another creep & I must go & attend to him so lovingly farewell—

*Jef. speaks of justice in conflict with Avarice & oppression— The sacred side is gaining new recruits.

3rd day aftern—13th—

I am lookg. over for the last time, thy letters, before sendg. them to Nant., and makg. such comments as they suggest—have covered the blank page in one of Anna B's—& now—take this circular—[9] That foolish, vulgar Valentine came to me thro' the post— Destroy it— I want to say further of Pillsbury— He is so able & effective a speaker, that I long to save him from such estrangement as S. S. Foster now manifests— His rebuke of Oliver J. is undeserved—[10] It is such a pity, for the few Abolitionists to "fall out by the way"— We have great hope of Tilton—he is so friendly—& of such promise—a very pleasg. fellow.— Aaron M Powell too is a good laborer in the field— As to Cheever glad as I am that he is so out-spoken, I cant quite bear the arrogancy of a *Christian* or church A. S. Society—[11] I fear England will be led astray further by that Julia Griffiths & Fredk. Douglass— We have some arrogant colored people among us who are damaging our cause as far as they have influence— What a pity that the Canada settlers are misrepresented too in the Papers—[12] We have need of great faith, to press our labors against such odds— Seward's speech will do harm, in quieting uneasy consciences— I always liked Garrison's remark in his Thoughts on Colonizatn. in the early day "as far as you alleviate the pressure of guilt upon the conscience of evil-doers, you weaken the power of motive to repent & encourage them to sin with impunity"—also Myron Holly[13] in a speech at Rochester 1837 "All experience teaches, that a supine contemplation of atrocious wrongs, impairs the moral sense, weakens the spirit, & degrades the character— It is replete with dangers, & where we have the right & power of active interference eminently criminal. Neither the social sympathies, nor the moral convictions can be disregarded with impunity. They are the ministers of Heaven for good, & they should always be reverently welcomed & obeyed"— I cherish such noble utterances, & want them to be written in letters of gold— So applicable are they to temporizing aspirants, either in Church or State— Have I written how well our out-spoken heterodoxy & our Anti Slavery were received at Reading—

I meant to read what thou wrote of Miller M'K's pastor—Mr. Duffield—to him & Sarah— They were here 1st. day eveg. but there was no time then— It is funny how soon people's speeches reach yr. ears, when least intended—

Maria sd. thy amount of work was wonderful—so much knitting added to all that sewing— "No end" to the quantity Elizh. has rattled off, preparatory to movg. & all summer's work on their large farm— She is in excellent spirits, & says Thos. is as happy as he can be with his prospects— Geo. Lord wd like to buy a small place near them but how shd. we feel to be left in our old age?—

Is Eddy Kniffen[14] still in Scipio? And does his Father yet live? What further do you hear from Aunt Lydia [*Mott*]? I sent $10 lately or 2 mo. since, & have had no acknowledgment of it—

AL PSCHi-Mott

1. James Freeman Clarke (1810–88) was a Unitarian minister at the Church of the Disciples in Boston. Amelia Jenks Furness (d. 1884) accompanied her husband on his speaking engagements, one of which was at Boston's Music Hall on 11 March 1860 (*Liberator,* 9 March 1860, 39).

2. David Potts (1794–1863) was a former Anti-Masonic congressman (1831–39) from Chester County. The correspondence between Greeley and Robert Dale Owen had begun when Greeley published an editorial in the *New York Tribune* criticizing the New York state legislature's attempt to change the divorce laws. Greeley had ridiculed the divorce laws in Indiana, "where the lax principles of Robert Dale Owen" produced a law "which enables men or women to get unmarried nearly at pleasure." In response, Owen had defended the Indiana law and his small role in bringing it about: "You speak of Indiana as 'the Paradise of free lovers.' It is in New York and New-England, refusing reasonable divorce, that free-love prevails." In his published reply to Owen, Greeley, appealing to the Scriptures, had declared that only adultery should be a cause of divorce. "No couple can innocently take upon themselves the obligations of Marriage until they KNOW that they are one in spirit, and so must remain forever" (*New York Tribune,* 1 March 1860, 4, 5 March 1860, 7, 6 March 1860, 4). The exchange, which would continue further into March, was later published as Owen's *Footfalls on the Boundary of Another World* (Philadelphia: J. B. Lippincott, 1860).

3. Seward had delivered his speech in the Senate on 29 February (*Congressional Globe,* 36th Cong., 1st sess., 910–14). In it he had argued for the admission of Kansas as a free state, dwelling on the moral and political evils produced by slavery. He had declared that the Republican party, representing the best interests of the entire nation, favored continued union of the states.

4. LCM took issue with Seward's statement that the Republicans would not "carry" equality for African Americans into the South. He had asked, "Is it then in any, and in which, of the States I have named that negro equality offends the white man's pride?" Seward had declared that the North could not accept the South's "system of capital or its ethics," but the South was "equally at liberty to reject our system and its ethics." He also had stated that because of his "profound respect and friendly regard" for Vice President John C. Breckinridge, he would "weigh carefully" Breckinridge's accusations that the Republican party was hostile to the South (ibid., 912–13).

5. Of Seward's speech Garrison had written that it "evinces, throughout, the adroit, calculating, heartless politician, rather than the wise, courageous, far-seeing statesman." Garrison went on to attack Seward for surrendering the principles of liberty to that of union: "With his recognition of the slaveholding compromises of the Constitution, what does Mr. Seward mean when he says that 'both of these institutions . . . can be saved together'?" (*Liberator,* 9 March 1860, 38).

6. The National Woman's Rights Convention was to be held in New York City on 10 and 11 May, while the New England Anti-Slavery Convention was to meet in Boston on 30 May (*Liberator,* 13 April 1860, 59, 8 June 1860, 90).

7. "The sad countenance of our dear Caroe." is apparently a reference to Caroline Wood's marital difficulties. She had left Auburn to visit her sister in Baltimore, but her husband Charles had refused to join her, conduct LCM labeled "shameful." Charles's affair with another woman was, said LCM, an "outrage. . . . How cruelly he has broken his marriage promise" (to MCW, 8 March 1860, 18 March 1860, Mott Manuscripts, PSCHi; Bacon, 175–76).

8. The Cavender family was moving to Eddington, a farm outside Philadelphia.

9. The letter was written on an invitation to the twenty-sixth National Anti-Slavery Subscription Anniversary meeting held in Boston on 25 January.

10. A letter in the *Liberator* had criticized a recent speech of Parker Pillsbury as hos-

tile to Christianity and the U.S. Constitution (9 March 1860, 38). In his letters to the *NASS*'s editor, Oliver Johnson, Stephen S. Foster had accused the paper of misrepresenting his views and devoting too much space to the Republican party's moderate goals. In a letter published in the *Liberator*, Foster had attacked the "Radical Abolitionists" (e.g., Gerrit Smith in Congress) for adhering too closely to the Republican party's antislavery views (*NASS*, 18 February 1860, 2, 3 March 1860, 2; *Liberator*, 9 March 1860, 39).

11. Theodore Tilton (1835–1907) was the managing editor of the *Independent*, 1855–63, and its editor-in-chief, 1863–70. Aaron M. Powell (1832–99) was then a New York agent of the AASS. George B. Cheever (1807–90), the pastor of the Church of the Puritans in New York City, 1846–67, had recently been reproached by many in his church for his strong antislavery pronouncements and support of John Brown, among other activities (*Liberator*, 17 February 1860, 25; *NASS*, 17 March 1860, 2).

12. An article in the *Liberator*, "Colored Refugees in Canada," addressing recent criticism of former fugitive slaves for behaving irresponsibly, had stated that many were working productively in Canada (2 March 1860, 33).

13. Myron Holley (1779–1841) was a New York state assemblyman, a newspaper editor, and a founder of the Liberty Party.

14. Eddy Kniffen was the son of MCW's neighbor in Auburn (MCW to LCM, 26 October 1858, MNS).


## To [Martha Coffin Wright?]

*[Roadside? c. 5 July 1860]*

I was glad to have such a defence of the resolutions as the letter with the scraps of Parker Pillsbury's & S. B. Anthony's.[1] I have great faith in Elizabeth Stanton's quick instincts & clear insight in all appertaining to woman's rights & [*ms. damaged*] gs, and the fullest confidence in the united judgment of herself & S. B. Anthony, with our sister Martha & P. Pillsbury to back them—    I am glad they are all so vigorous for the work. Every word sent on the subject is most acceptable.* I mean to read all to Miller McKim when I have a chance, he is so dreadfully afraid of Free Love. How little patience he had, with Robt. Dale Owen's views, in that discussion with Greeley. As to Sydney Gay's article, I tho't it was Greeley's, & so it was unfair, & no answer to E. C. S.—[2]—    I shd. have liked to hear her answer the farmer at Junius[3]—& sorry was I, that thou could not go to that Mg. We happen to know a good many fat wives of farmers in this region, so thy illustration wd. not be convincing, but then these are Quaker farmers—and they recipricate, dont they?

*I dont think Garrison wd exclude the marriage & divorce quest[ion] [*ms. damaged*] from the platform—    He took sides in favor of all these subjects being discussed, when we met him at Miller's (McKim's) 2 yrs ago.[4]

C Extr MNS: This extract, entitled "Extract from Lucretia Mott's letter," and written in the hand of MCW, was enclosed with MCW's letter to Elizabeth Cady Stanton dated 5 July 1860 (see Gordon, 1:435).

1. At the tenth National Woman's Rights Convention in New York City, 10–11 May 1860,

at which MCW had presided, Stanton had offered a series of resolutions on marriage that included support for easy access to divorce. Parker Pillsbury had offered his support to Stanton in a May 1860 letter. At the convention, Anthony had stated: "Marriage has ever been a one-sided matter, resting most unequally upon the sexes. By it, man gains all— —woman loses all; tyrant law and lust reign supreme with him— —meek submission and ready obedience alone befit her" (Gordon, 1:433; *HWS*, 1:688–740; *New York Evening Post*, 11 May 1860, 3; *New York Tribune*, 11 May 1860, 7–8).

2. Stanton had written a public letter entitled "Marriage and Divorce" defending her argument that marriage and divorce laws placed all the power in men's hands: "In the case of Divorce, if the husband be the guilty party, he still retains the greater part of the property. If the wife be the guilty party, she goes out of the partnership pennyless" (*Liberator*, 1 June 1860, 88). In an editorial in the *New York Tribune*, Sydney Gay had criticized Stanton's views on divorce: "The Indissoluble Marriage of one man to one woman has always been found, as a general rule, conducive to public morality and personal well-being" (30 May 1860, 4).

3. LCM uses the old term for the monthly meeting that had been part of the Genesee Yearly Meeting before the formation of the Congregational Friends (later Friends of Human Progress) in 1848 (Thomas Hamm, *God's Government Begun: The Society for Universal Inquiry and Reform, 1842–46* [Bloomington: Indiana University Press, 1995], 230). Stanton and Anthony had attended the yearly meeting of Progressive Friends in Waterloo, New York, where similar resolutions on marriage and divorce had been proposed and adopted (Gordon, 1:436).

4. This postscript was written vertically in the margin of the page and may therefore indicate MCW's comment.

# To Martha Coffin Wright

[*Roadside*]
6th. day 27th. Aftern.
[*July 1860*]—

[*Continuation of a letter begun 24 July*]

Waitg. the arrival of the Cars, for Robt. Collyer, Anna H—& we hope Wm. Furness— Jas. is going over to Town's to ask him to join the others— Miller & Sarah [*McKim*], & Reba. Potts are comg. also— Wont it be a pleast. party— I mean to read parts of thy letters—for they are not yet sent to Anna B—and now we have thy new acceptable package with all its enclosures— — We carried out the Holly & Eddingn. visits—found our cousins rather poorly they havg. been all turned up, puttg. in gas pipes—too much for coz. Reba. [*Neall*]—an attack of Cholera morbus followed—then Coz. Ruth [*Chase*] & Auga. [*Needles*], affected in the same way— All better however— John Needles had been there a week & Reba. knew not what she wd. have done without him, so helpful as he was replacing carpets & furniture— They have a new colored girl They welcomed us, as they ever do, & we passed a pleast. day— We took thy letters to read to them Coz. Ruth was on the bed much of the time—tho' down at the dinner table, & carved James means to go up soon & see them all— Auga. &

baby [*Emma Needles*] not the least attractn. I shd. think Caroe. [*Wood*] wd. come
before Auga. returns home in Septemr.— The baby is quite worth a visit— She
is a dear little thing—very fair—& as good as she can be— Auga. is very
handy—[&] has eno' food, she says, for 2 babies— She has no nurse, & does
not seem to need one—so fond as all are of the baby— She is thin, but looks
well, and in fine spirits— — Sarah & Reba. [*Yarnall*] enjoyed the visit— We
had to leave earlier than we need, as the last train went before 5— At Bristol,
we found the Easton train came along @ 6 oclk—& wd. stop at Skink's Statn.
1¼ above Eddingn. So we took *that*, rather than wait there an hour for the eveg.
train—as per agreet. Jas to meet us with the carriage— We walked—& hired a
boy to carry the travg. bag—reached there ½ an hour sooner than to have gone
to Cornwell's— Jas. & Michael both there waitg. for us—but they could drive
faster back with empty carriages—& all ended well— Reba. asked me not to
"put them thro" that night— — They had much to say of the beauty of the
Place— We entered the back way thro' the wood, & by the barn— Elizh. had
been in town all day—only out ½ an hour before we arrived She had little to
do yestery., but sit at sewg. havg. bot. sundry dresses for Fanny [*Cavender*] &
herself— Harry had returned from the shore, rather disaptd., that his Grandfr. didn't let him remain in the water longer at a time— — We left after early
tea—& a shower havg. laid the dust, we had a beautiful moonlight drive home—
reachg. here 9 ½ — I felt as if we had been long from home— The girls will
stay till 2nd. day— Our dear little Bessie [*Lord*] was quite sick when I left here—
& no better when Jas. went up in the aftern.—so that we felt anxious— I was
a relief to find her rather better— I pocketed the new letter till this morng., &
then havg. promised the girls that we wd. let them know of their welfare in
School-Lane, we took an early drive over, & enjoyed the letter & enclosures, with
Eliza [*Yarnall*], & Mary B— — We thot. thine to the Eve. Post very good—
How well I cd. understd. Parker Pillsby's feelings— It was rather a surprise to
find Theode. Parker had to feel in the same way— Parker P's letter to Ellen
[*Wright*] was good too— As to Lizzie Gay, we have always had to take her as
she is— She wd. be as kind to Elizh. Stanton—the dear Queen, as if she hadn't
scolded so—[1] I agree with thee entirely that such phillipics, ^is that spelled
right?^ & editorial hits make no permanent impressn.—& after enduring such
wilful, gross misrepresentn. of our Anti S. motives & actions, we can certainly
bear these little barkings, especially when we find statesmen & legislatures doing our bidding. I was not aware of the determined respectability of the Boston
Conventions—but they attract all the less notice, & do all the less good— —
Now that P. W. Davis his returned from Europe with improved health, she can
join them, & add some feminine graces to their band— Does H. K. Hunt figure
with them? Or is her matrimonial union all-absorbg.?[2] We were amused with
thy supposed cases *in* regard to her— Was it not flat to fill the page of the Libr.
with that minute detail?— It is very pleast. to hear of Caroe. [*Wood*]'s improved
spirits and that you are often together, & that you go frequently to see Eunice

D[ennis]— Eliza O. does perfectly right to put out her sewg.— She must take the best care of her eyes—give them *drink* & fresh air often— A change of air is what she needs—and RoadSide is very pure air— Dearly we should love to have a visit from her out here— So, Ellen [*Wright*] feels as if more school-learng. wd. do her good— Havg. such grown-up correspondents, we were prepared for her to come out an advocate at once— She must be glad to have Parker Pillsby's esteem in such large measure—& S. B. Anthony's too— What a *veteran* it makes thee seem in the cause— We often have discussns. at our table— as also, with regard to smokg.—Lager beer—currant wine—& Geo L. always adds, *Coffee*— I felt rather sorry that Ellen didn't want to go to Willie Seward's weddg.³—because it is so natural for the young to enjoy such excitemts., & our Mother had a horror of anythg. *odd*. Auga. liked to read thy accot. of that weddg.—and all other parts of thy letter she wanted to see— She was very glad that her Grandma had given up all thought of going to Aubn. Caroe. will certainly have to come soon instead— Little Emma looks sweet in her short clothes Auga. dresses her simply, but in good taste— Sister Helen Trump is expectg. her 2nd—a pity—

7th. day 28th—
Cool, beautiful weather—

Did you see that meteor?⁴ We did— Perhaps I have spoken of it before. Maria [*Davis*] saw it on the Sound—Richd. & Anna [*Hallowell*], at their home— Maria is enjoying the quiet there, & the neatness of every part of the house— no flies or midges—cool eno' to sleep under 2 blankets & spread— "Mother Bunch" in good spirits—all ready, willg. & waitg. I saw Willie Furness' wife yestery. in Germantn.— She is in expectatn. some mo. hence—so is Fanny Kemble's daughr.—Mrs. Wistar—& so is Hetty Wharn. Smith— —⁵ Thos. Kimber's daughr. Regina Potts has just made a false alarm— She has had her nurse with her, week after week— It is a singular case— Anna B. will be interested, if this ever reach her— Thou must send it to Newport 1st. for I have not written to Mariᵃ. since Thos. [*Mott*] went there— I will enclose her letter—& thou can send that to Anna, with a nice one from thyself, for her to send to us— Mind & tell me to whose care to direct to her at Pittsfield— I sent one this morng. to New Y—to Walter [*Brown*]—but presume he is not there now— It was very stupid of me, to omit takg. her directn.— Our company came yestery., except Wm. Furness— His wife had just come out to take tea at H. Town's with him & they thot. it wd. not do, to leave & come here— Collyer had called on them in town— He was also up there with them, when Geo. L. called to bring Furness—so he drove back with him ^rode, I like better^ Miller happened to speak of being careful, not to disturb yr neighbs., on Sunday, with Piano, playg. ball, or other amusemt.—even tho' he felt excused from going to Church, & often did little chores about his house & place—but he didn't like noisy plays—&.c— Now, it often happens that, Edwd, Henry [*Davis*] & his young frds. do have exercise of that kind on 1st. day & Edwd. thinks it his duty, to war agt. the pious Sabbath— We had an earnest debate awhile  Collyer did not take much part in it— Miller didn't like I shd. think he ministered to any superstitious observ[anc]e. of the day— I read what thou wrote about going to Church— I had before copied parts, in a letter to Collyer—but I wanted Sarah & Reba. Potts & Miller to hear it—as also, all thou wrote of P. Pillsby. & his, & the letter to the Eve. Post— Was it ever sent to the Post? They thot. it good—& were interested in all—tho' Miller insisted that those Resolutns. were not right— Edwd. D. was surprised to find I had sent Lizzy Gay's letter, to Aubn., & hoped it wd. do no harm, with E. Stanton— Collyer sd. he did not baptise his own childn., but he had, in a few instances the childn. of those who wished it—while he did not deem it necessary— I questioned the advantage, or propriety of it—and of the Commun[io]n. too; in the way, he explained, his administg of that Jewish ceremony— Miller too, held up R. W. Emersn's course as praiseworthy, in withdrawg. from his pulpit, rather than "go to the table unworthily".[6] From that, askg. a blessg. at table was discussed—& *silence* too— Collyer sd., sometimes he did, sometimes he didn't—just as he felt— Then prayers in general came in for discussn. The eveg. was too short— Collyer looks well, & quite dressed up— He went however 1st. to his old workmen at the factory—made a hammer—right well, he sd.—& kind o' apologised to them for comg. here to lodge, rather than accept their invitatns., in their confined close quarters— He is offered $2000 a year, if he will undertake a kind of Circuit revival preachg., among the Unitns. out West— He has brot. his sermon on Theo. Parker, to read to us, after he returns from Long Wood— He & Edwd. went this morng— Anna Hopper ne'er came yestery. Jas. has just driven over for her, hopg. she will come out this aftern.— We devoted this morng. to calls— I have long wanted to go & see Thos. Fisher, who is very poorly—so we had a satisfacy. time there  Wm. & Sarah Wistar & famy. are at Father Fisher's, while their house is being rebuilt. Their son Frank—the 3rd. was taken ill with Typhoid fever there, & has lain 3 weeks much of the time delirious—[7] 2 days ago, they were much alarmed with his sinkg. spells but now they think there is a favorable turn— We didn't go there—as Jas. had promised Martha Earle, as soon as she was able, to take her out to ride— So I got out at School Lane leavg. little Nelly in with him, & walked ¼ mile to Geo. B's—& sat an hour with Eliza & Mary—read Ellis' late letter— They have taken passage in Persia 15 Septr. sister Agnes with them—[8]

AL PSCHi-Mott

1. Theodore Parker had died on 10 May 1860 in Italy. Elizabeth Gay had published a letter in the *New York Tribune* that opposed Stanton's divorce resolutions from the May National Women's Rights Convention: "I was indignant at the introduction of a foreign topic (that of Divorce) upon its platform" (14 May 1860, 5).

2. At the Boston Woman's Rights Convention, held on 1 June 1860, Wendell Phillips, who had opposed Stanton's resolution on divorce at the May convention in New York City, had congratulated the movement on its success: "Right by right had been granted

women, and the ballot would come soon, and this would be in the day of many of the audience" (*Liberator*, 6 July 1860, 106). An announcement of Paulina Wright Davis's return from Europe had been published in the *NASS* (30 June 1860, 3). Harriot K. Hunt had celebrated her "silver anniversary" as a doctor on 27 June. A letter from LCM on the occasion had been published in the *Liberator:* "Then let me cheer thee on thy way; and press upon the young, the duty of entering into similar labors; for the work is only just begun—'the harvest truly is great.' So that when the golden wedding shall be attained [*Hunt's fiftieth year of practicing medicine*], the interdependence of the husband and wife will be equal, their dependence mutual, and their obligations reciprocal" (13 July 1860, 112).

3. William H. Seward Jr. (1839–1920), an Auburn banker, had married Janet McNeil Watson on 27 June (Gordon, 1:435).

4. A meteor had been visible on 20 July (*New York Evening Post*, 21 July 1860, 3).

5. The artist William H. Furness (1828–67), the son of the Unitarian minister, had painted a portrait of LCM in 1858 (Bacon, 170). Fanny Kemble and Pierce Butler had gone through a long, very public divorce in 1848–49. Kemble's daughter Sarah Butler (b. 1835) had married Dr. Owen J. Wister in 1859 (J. C. Furnas, *Fanny Kemble: Leading Lady of the Nineteenth Century Stage* [New York: Dial Press, 1982], 340–46). Their son, Owen (Dan) Wister, (1860–1938) became a novelist. Esther Fisher Wharton (1836–1915), the daughter of William Wharton, had married Benjamin R. Smith in 1859.

6. In 1832 Emerson had resigned as minister of Boston's Second Unitarian Church. The quotation is probably a variation on 1 Cor. 11:27: "Wherefore whosoever shall eat this bread and *this* cup of the Lord, unworthily, shall be guilty of the body and blood of the Lord."

7. Thomas R. Fisher (d. 1861) was a Philadelphia businessman. William Wister (1803–81) had married Sarah Fisher in 1826. Their son was Francis Wister (1841–1905) (*A Philadelphia Perspective: The Diary of Sidney George Fisher, Covering the Years 1834–1871,* ed. Nicholas B. Wainwright [Philadelphia: Historical Society of Pennsylvania, 1967], 438).

8. Martha Earle was the wife of Henry Earle, Mary Hussey Earle's son. Agnes Harrison (1839–1925) was the sister of Margaret Harrison Yarnall (Amice Macdonell Lee, *In Their Several Generations* [Plainfield, N.J.: Interstate Printing Corp., n.d.], 233).

# To Anna Temple Brown

14th. of 12 Mo—60—
Elizh. Cavr.'s 35th. birthday—

That dear daughr. feels lonely up there— She was down a few hours at the Fair—wh. is going on swimmingly, in spite of Union Mgs.—[1] Some 5 or 6 police men sittg. about the room—just as if they were needed, when there has not been the slightest disturbe.—the only insult—the tearg. out the word Slavery from the large sign placarded at the door— It was immedy. replaced— Mari[a]. [*Mott*] tells me that Nathan Southwick is to call this morng., for letters to take to thee—dear Anna—so I will send 2 or 3 from coz. Mary Earle—wh. please send to Aubn. by Munson [*Osborne*], shd. he call next week. We were very glad of the little we had of his compy.; & hope for more on his return— Ellie [*Wright*]'s letters were vastly entertaing— Her original style & mother-wit amused me much— Her appreciatn. of New Eng. heads & countenances, pleased me, for I have often held up their women as examples of Phrenological developet.— How pleast. she makes Medford Cottage & surroundings appear—the Milkman's accommodatg. wagon—& the ride in the 'shay' that bounded like a Kangaroo, over the least appear[anc]e. of a stone—all she says of Anna [*Hallowell*] & the baby—the mite—and the nurse—'the best policy', we liked to hear—her descriptns. are remarkably graphic— She does not impress you with ardent love for Madam, with all her devotional piety, & "scriptur" The contrast with Mr. Weld, is strikg.[2]—the "hour's worth of allegory", & her runng. & joing Madam— & talkg. about the flood, relign. &c"—& their "beging. thanks in a questionable way"—all these witticisms, we laughed over— That ever she shd. be placed with one who is no Abolitionist or Wom. Rig. advocate! She is one after my own heart, in not liking people who dont sympathise with you—kind-hearted in the general, as are our neighbs., how little intimate you can be with suchy— Thos. Mellor tho' did give us $20 worth of trimmings for the Fair—[3]

Mari[a]. says I cant write more for the gentleman has come— I will write more by Munson I made a few notes on this paper

AL MNS

1. The twenty-fifth annual Pennsylvania Anti-Slavery Fair had begun on 11 December 1860. At the same time, Philadelphia business leaders and politicians had held a "great Union meeting" to protest the secession of South Carolina. As the Philadelphia correspondent reported to the *NASS:* "Their language was, in effect, 'Kick us, spit on us, walk over us, and forever despise us; but, for Trade's sake, don't dissolve the Union. We'll catch your slaves, we'll lick your boots, we'll eat our words; we'll do almost anything you ask, if you will only not dissolve the union'" (22 December 1860, 3). Police had guarded the fair after abolitionists were warned not to hold it (*NASS*, 10 November 1860, 3, 22 December 1860, 2).

2. Ellen Wright had attended the Lenox, Massachusetts, school of Elizabeth Buckminister Dwight Sedgwick (1791–1864). In her diary, Ellen had contrasted her experience at Theodore Weld's school with her current experience: "Girls who have been here, love Mrs. Sedgwick & refer with delight to the time spent here—but after Eagleswood, it is just nothing, & very expensive besides! Mrs. Sedgwick doesn't inspire particular *love* in me" (diary entry dated Lenox, November 1860, Smith College Collection, History of Women Microfilm Series, reel 973).

3. Thomas Mellor (1808–82) was a Philadelphia Hicksite and a hosiery importer (Philadelphia City Directory, 1864).

## To Lydia Mott[1]

RoadSide, near Philada.
1 Mo. 22nd—61

My dear Cousin Lydia Mott

Thine of 24th. Ult. was duly received. It was not unexpected that no way opened, for the present, to promote our young friend Anna Dickinson's lecturing tour— We know well the difficulties attendant on one's going forth without means. Anna has been lecturing around Kennet, & in the neighborhood of this City, which may be as well, until she shall be more matured—[2]

Lucy Stone however, was brightest in her early life, when her youthful powers were given to humanity—especially to Woman—  Where is She now? I hoped to see her name among the expected Speakers at the coming Conventions in Albany—[3]

It will be necessary for me to hear from thee once more, before I go to Albany—whether any appointment will be made for me or notice given at Frds. Meeting in the morng. of the 3rd. of the Mo—and at the Unitarian house in the afternoon or evening of that day—  If so, I must go up in the aftern. line on 7th. day—2nd. of the Mo—

My sister Martha is pleased that we can be accommodated as boarders at our friend P. H. Jones's—[4]

My husband will not bear me company this time—he has doubts of my ability to bear the excitement & fatigue of the Meeting—I have suffered so much with dyspepsia for a month or two past—  I am better now however—  And when our Meetings are forbidden, & doors closed against us, it is no time to stay away, & thus yield to the enemy—  We received a Paper from Utica a few days ago giving an account of Beriah Green  S. B. Anthony, & Aaron Powell being denied the Call they had engaged—  We may hope that these demonstrations are only the outbreak of the present desperate effort of the Slave Power[5]—& that by untiring perseverance, the advocates of freedom will eventually find place among all ranks—& "Liberty be Proclaimed throughout all the land"—

Affectionately
thy Cousin   L. Mott

ALS MNS

1. Lydia Mott (1807–75), from Albany, New York, was a Quaker abolitionist, a woman's rights advocate, a teacher, and a distant relative of JM.

2. LCM had attended the twenty-fourth annual PASS meeting held 25–26 October 1860 at Kennett Square, at which Anna Dickinson (1842–1932) of Philadelphia had given her first speech. LCM had remarked that "it was pleasant to greet old friends and see the faces of associates with whom we have so long labored in this most holy cause" and had urged those at the convention to rejoice over the movement's progress (*NASS*, 20 October 1860, 2, 3 November 1860, 2).

3. The fourth annual New York State Anti-Slavery Convention would be held on 4–6 February 1861 and the second annual New York State Woman's Rights Convention would be held on 7–8 February (*Liberator*, 28 December 1860, 217).

4. Phebe Hoag Jones (1812–81) had run a linen manufactory in Troy, New York, until she moved to Albany in 1856 (Gordon, 1:467).

5. Beriah Green (1795–1874), a pioneer abolitionist and a Congregationalist minister, had attended an abolition meeting with Stanton and Anthony held at St. James Hall in Buffalo, New York, in early January that was repeatedly disrupted by vocal antagonists in the audience. At an antislavery convention in Rochester later that month attended by Powell, Stanton, and Anthony, a similar disruption took place (*Liberator*, 18 January 1861, 12; *NASS*, 19 January 1861, 1, 3).

## To William H. Seward

RoadSide, near Philada
3 mo. 3rd. 61—

Wm. H. Seward
My dear Friend
The accompanying letter from our friend Dr. Henry Gibbons was received some time ago— It ought to have been attended to earlier, so that his application should be duly considered— The numerous demands on thy time and attention, have led me to hesitate, as to increasing the number—[1]

We have full confidence in the character, and moral worth of Dr. Gibbons— as also in his medical skill, as far as we are able to judge— His Father [*William*] was for many years, among the first physicians of Wilmington, Del.—and his son had a fair share of practice, both there & in Philada., for a young man, before he removed, with his family, to California—

I am ignorant as to the proper mode of interesting those in power, in cases of this kind, & indeed of all appeals for Governmental appointments— If any deficiency, or if apology be necessary, please supply it, in pity for my—woman's ignorance—

In the hope of our friend—the Doctor's success[2]

I am thy frd.   *Lucretia Mott*

ALS NRU

1. Henry Gibbons (1808–84) was a California physician and the brother of James S. Gibbons. Lincoln had recently appointed Seward secretary of state.
2. This Henry Gibbons may have become acting assistant surgeon for the U.S. Army (George A. Otis, *The Medical and Surgical History of the War of the Rebellion: Part II, Surgical History* [Washington, D.C.: GPO, 1876], 2:64, 818).

## To Martha Coffin Wright and Eliza Wright Osborne

RoadSide 3 mo. 19th. 61—
3rd. day—snowstorm—

Well that our clothes are dried—& ironed neatly  Pattie & Nelly [*Lord*] are just off to town, to make Edwd. & Anna [*Hopper*] a visit of a few days— Little color'd Lizzy is here, while her Father & housekeeper have gone to take in a load of their things—the child is to be with Mrs. Cannon, & go to school in the City— They are to have an auction out here, 5th. day—"who but they"— Poor Isaac is in debt to butcher, store, &.c—so there will be not much clear for him— His cigars & drams have drawn on his purse— — Michael is quite elated with his new position, even tho' more work will be required— he is a very new broom now— he has his house free, instead of havg. to pay $5 per Mo.— Margt. is makg. ready to move on 7th. day, in fine spirits,—her baby is not yet 3 mo—so her sister will come to help her— — Jas. & self are going to drive thro' snow this aftern., to Ellis Y's— We have not called there since Margt. [*Yarnall*]'s confinet.—5 wks. I think— They fear the babe will die— An abscess formed around the navel, wh. has discharged the last week, so much that he now seems sinkg. Dr. Griscom thinks the chances agt. his living— Margt. can't speak of it without tears— Agnes [*Harrison*] has been all-attentn.— She was in the City on 5th. day night & 6th. day, when the girls had invited their coz. Yarnalls to meet her, but before night the carriage was sent in for her little *Oswald* (after a br. who died) was worse— Edwd. H. & Thos. M. took tea there on 1st. day, instd. of here— They were much discouraged then— Geo. Lord saw Ellis yestery. & there was some improvet.— We were away on 1st. day, to an apptd. Mg. at Havreford— Several of our City Frds. were there— Geo. Truman, &.c— We were at the morng. Mg. also—oblgg. us to have early breakft.— the kindest of Frds.—Leedom[1]—gave us dinner & we hurried home to tea, makg. no stop after Mg—, & found a table-full just done—Miller, Sarah, & Charley M'K— Morris & Elizh. Davis—Richd. & Anna D. Hall[1].—Bel & Emmy [*Mott*]— You may know what the subjects were— Morris had lately returned from Washn., & like others of his party, had much praise for Lincoln, who he says is in danger of being driven to death— he longs for rest— Richd. sd., his Inaugural, view'd from an A.S. standpoint, was infernal & diabolical— I thot. so too— and was surprised that it met with so much favor in thy sight— Miller agreed with thee, and Jas. too—yes nearly all who speak of it—& they think it reflects on our judgt. to speak so harshly of it— The Standd. has not pleased such— The Libr. being milder, they think excellt.— Jas. just read from the Bugle, some severe strictures, wh. were certainly just. Shall I use a little of this page in copyg.? It shall be in finer type— Our A.S. Papers shd. not criticise, as party-politicians. "The Southern traitors have rebelled agt. the Union for the sake of Slavery—the Northn. have rebelled agt. Liberty, for the sake of the Union. The Southn. agt. the Fedl. Govt.—the Northn. agt. the Sovereigny & the liberties of the people. The Southn. havg. lost the electn. & the Capitol, trample the Constitutn under foot—the Northn. havg. won the electn. & the Capl., are attemptg. to subvert the Constitutn., by the action of Congs. & the State Legistrs., without even askg. leave of the people,—beyond their power to recover it into their hands agn— The Southn. stole the public funds—&.c— the Northern attempt to steal the People's right to amend their own Constitn.—to take away from them 'in perpetuity,' the constitl. fortress of freedom" Principia "The 1st. great object of the outgoing Pres., "was to protect slave 'property'— the 1st. distinct annuciatn. by the *incomg*. Prest. is, that the same species of 'property' shall be protected as heretofore—of no other property, does he utter a syllable, unless it be to inquire timidly, whether it might not be well to provide" & then quotes that clause— This is also taken from the Principia— Do you know anythg of that Paper?[2]

I dont want to fill much of the sheet with extracts, for I have thy last to acknowle., wh. came a week ago—& was read in town before we had it. Caroe. [*Stratton*]'s too we had about the same time—so the particulars of that intervw., with the "laird of the Valley,"[3] we read, & thot. thou wast fav[ore]d. to "give as good as was sent"— Eliza Y. wd. have liked it better, if thou had not used the words "supreme indiffe.," in ref. to the reports abt. "JoAnna"—we supposed— How strange, that he shd. pretend that the requested intervw., might arrest the wideng. of the breach, when it was an opporty he sought, to arraign Caroe. & thee with railg. accusatns.— You are lucky that such an intimacy shd. be at an end— Caroe. made no allusn. to it in her note— Auga. [*Needles*] & baby are there now— Coz. Reba. in town with Danl. Neall— We hope to have her out here, before she returns home— — You hear from Holly, thro' Caro's letters, more than we can write— The anticipn. of her, and Laura [*Stratton*]'s visit, as well as Anna B's, & yours—includg. Ellen [*Wright*]'s, is exceedy. pleast. We cant bear a word of doubt of Eliza's comg.— David's letter to Edwd. said her little Tommy [*Osborne*] continued so poorly, her comg. was uncertain— We fear she is hurting him with Doctor's visits— I never knew a fam[il]y. so constant- ly givg. little pills— Nature is an excellt. cure-all— That terrible cold, windy weather in Alby. must have touched my head with frost— Some 8 or 10 boils or chillblains or somethg. brokeout & for a week or 2 I had a sore time—but Nature, my only Dr. has cured them— Now do quit tamperg. with that child, & let him get well— Eliza mustn't think of not comg.— Even if he is not quite well, Miss Soule[4] may do better with him than an over-anxs. Mother. I left my only boy when not 2 yrs. old, & after a month's ailg. with summer complt., & went to Ohio—& Betsy Cole cured him. Margt. Yarnls. baby is very sick, as I sd. before—

evening— Jas. & self drove over this aftern.— Mary B. was there— They have more hope of the babe than on 1st. day, when they thot. he wd.n't live the night out— he takes more nourisht., & breathes better— Benjn. & Eliza [*Yar-nall*] came out in the Cars, while we were there— I was hoping to meet sister there— I passed nearly a day with her in town last week— but it is rare for us to be together so long— She seldom comes here this cold weather— The snowstorm cleared at noon today, & we quite enjoyed the winter drive—stopped at Millers—met Wm. Speakman there—heard that Wm. Fisher was ill agn.— these frequent attacks must close his long life— Comg. home we found Thos. M. & Houston had been here, on their way to the 'Corner', & left thy letter of 15th. to Mari[a]., with a nice long one from Anna B— —more encouraging about yr. really comg. The *idea* of thy expressg. any doubts, as in a former letter, be- cause of leavg. thy boys—those grown-up sons! It may be Tommy's teeth that cause the water to flow from his mouth—or is it some poison in homeo[path]y. pills?—quit them— I wish Mari[a]. could have paid both Ellen & you a visit while away— Pattie wd. willingly have stayed longer, for her to have done so, but as she said, the pleasg. expectatn. of seeing all here so soon, made it seem not best to increase the expense now— I hope, with thee, that before this year is out she & the childn. will go to Aubn.—they must long to—& Lenox too, if best— but I always remember, how we, at Nine Partners were 18 months, without seeing a single *kin*—& 2 yrs. & 2 mo. without going home—& just as happy I suppose—knowg. it must be so— I am glad that thou & Caroe. are feeling satisfied with this year's schooling.

As to the best way of comg. & meetg. the learned daughrs., I shd. think the cheapest way decidedly the best— They are old eno', to understd. how to travel to meet you in Albany or New Y— I shall plan to be in Philada the day you arrive, & when ready to come out here, we shall be most happy, &.c— Anna B. writes that they will come the followg. 4th. day, 3rd. of the Mo—and come out here immedy. wh. suits us exactly— We shall go in that morng. to Mg.—prepared to bring her & hers out— It will be quite safe, as she suggests to give her checks to the baggage man impressg. it upon him to have them taken to the North Penn cars—Front & Willow St. in time for the 5 o clk train—when Geo. Lord, or Henry D. will receive & take charge of them— their names might be given the man, or put on the card on the trunks—little bags & things we cd. bring out— The 11 o clk. line, will suit best I shd. think—she will write agn. tho'— And thou too must let us know just how you decide to come— We have arranged nicely to have you here in compy. as often as you can come, *before* the 10th. as well as *after*— Caroe. will want to come & meet you, as early as she can— — There is not a thing about it, that is not 1st. rate pleast. to us to plan— Anna D. H. will come, with baby & nurse, & Maria [*Davis*] has arranged beautifully for them— They were here last 3rd. day, with all our daughrs. & some of the grandchn. Lue, Ria [*Hopper*], 3 Cavrs.—darling little May Mott—the 2nd. time her Mother has brot. her— Richd. came & his sister Anna—[5] It was a pleast. day— I liked to make Anna Hall[l]. listen to some readg. more radical than she is prepared for—on Wom. Rig. & Anti S. "& bugs & things"—parts of thy letter, about Seward, & thy talk with Mr. Fowler—[6] We liked thy plain speakg. and so glad that Mrs. Worden is so strong—yet I cant quite agree with you, that the withdrawal from Fort Sumpter is a compromise— The time may not have come to begin a war—wise judgment may recal Anderson, without sacrifice of principle—indeed, all the Slave States might go—without fightg. about it—as that article in the Standd. "Opportunity" advocated I think—[7] But when Lincoln & Seward & very many of the Republicans promise, or express a willings., to strengthen the pro-Slavery parts of the Constitutn & to yield the claim to rob & murder by thousds.—an infinitely greater number, than in any probable war, might be slain, then "the sacrifice of a few lives", in resisting such iniquitous provisions, may be a questn.

[*Letter continues dated 20 and 21 March*]

AL PSCHi-Mott

1. This is probably the Hicksite Quaker John Leedom, the husband of Elizabeth Leedom.

2. In his inaugural speech, delivered on 4 March 1861, Lincoln had stated: "I have no purpose, directly or indirectly, to interfere with the institution of slavery in the States where it exists. I believe I have no lawful right to do so, and I have no inclination to do so." The *Liberator* had scorned the president's attempts to appease the Confederate states: "The breach is natural, inevitable, and not to be repaired—it is the result of the 'irrepressible conflict' between Justice and Oppression, Right and Wrong, which admits of no conciliation or compromise! LET THERE BE NO CIVIL WAR, but A SEPARATION BETWEEN THE FREE AND SLAVE STATES" (8 March 1861, 38). The *NASS* also had criticized Lincoln's speech: "The speech was made with the face turned toward the South and with both knees bowed down before the idol it worships, as have been all those delivered from the same place for the last quarter of a century" (9 March 1861, 2). An editorial in the *Anti-Slavery Bugle* had stated: "Lincoln is not a great man, and certificates to the contrary do not change the fact" (9 March 1861, 3). The *Principia* was a newspaper published in New York City, 1859–66.

3. Caroline Stratton Wood's divorce from Charles was final in November 1860 (Bacon, 174–76; LCM to MCW, 16, 17, and 18 November 1860, Mott Manuscripts, PSCHi).

4. Lavinia Soule was MCW's dressmaker and a Wright family friend (MCW to LCM, 17 October 1850, MNS).

5. LCM's first great-grandchild was Maria Mott "May" Hallowell (1860–1916); Anna Hallowell (b. 1831).

6. Henry Fowler (1824–72), formerly a newspaper editor and a professor of political economy at the University of Rochester, was the pastor of the Second Presbyterian Church in Auburn, 1858–71.

7. After Lincoln had assumed office, Major Robert Anderson (1805–71) reported that Fort Sumter, one of the last Union forts in the South, was running low on supplies. Lincoln faced a dilemma because sending provisions to Fort Sumter could provoke war (James M. McPherson, *Battle Cry of Freedom: The Civil War Era* [New York: Oxford University Press, 1988], 264–68). The editorial "Opportunity" in the *NASS* stated: "In objecting to the secession of slave States, the Republicans make a blunder fully equal to that by which South Carolina took her slavery from under the protection of the United States Constitution" (2 March 1861, 2).


# To Ellen Wright

[c. March 1861]

James & Lucretia Mott
At Home
4th. Mo 10th. 1861
from 3 to 7 oclock PM.
Golden Wedding

C MNS Env: "Ellen Wright"

# To *NASS* Editor

PHILADELPHIA, 7 mo. 6th, 1861

*To the Editor of The National Anti Slavery Standard.*

RETURNING from our late journey, I observe in THE STANDARD of last week a notice, from the *Boston Bee,* of my discourse at the Music Hall. I am made there to endorse the war, and to 'hope that it will be prosecuted with energy and faith," etc.[1]

This does such injustice to the few remarks made on the subject as to require some correction. I spoke of our country, and of Christendom generally, not having attained to the highest mode of warfare, the weapons of which are "not carnal, but mighty through God,"[2] etc., and expressed the fullest confidence in their efficiency, inasmuch as a labor, begun single-handed and alone, on behalf "of the suffering and the dumb," by earnest appeal and faithful protest, had aroused the country from its alarming lethargy on the slavery question. Advocates not a few had come forth, in the pulpit, and in the literary world, "to plead the cause of the poor and needy."[3]

Now that we are beginning to feel that we are verily guilty concerning our brother, that we must "amend our ways and our doings," and no longer "frame iniquity by law," a hostile spirit is manifested, and instead of the whole armor of God, we have the battle of the warrior, which is ever with confused noise and garments rolled in blood. In its prosecution, now as ever, "all they that take the sword are liable to perish with the sword."[4]

Still, we can understand why Jesus, the Prince of Peace, should say to his disciples, "Ye shall hear of wars and rumors of wars; see that ye be not troubled; for all these things must come to pass."[5] So now, regarding the present calamity as the natural result of our wrong doings, and our atrocious cruelties, terrible as war ever must be, let us hope that it may not be *stayed* by any compromise which shall continue the unequal, cruel war on the rights and liberties of millions of our unoffending fellow-beings, a war waged from generation to generation, with all the physical force of our government, the President himself Commander-in-Chief.

If there should be room in THE STANDARD for this explanation, please insert it, and oblige

L. MOTT.

PL *NASS,* 13 July 1861, 2

1. The *NASS* had quoted from the *Boston Atlas and Bee* on LCM's speech to the Congregational Society in Boston on 16 June 1861: "The closing portion of her address related to the war, which she hoped would be prosecuted with energy and faith, since it was founded upon so good a cause. She thought the greatest danger would be in listening to compromises, which would only result in again fighting the old battle" (29 June 1861, 3).

2. 2 Cor. 10:4.

3. Prov. 31:9.

4. LCM is paraphrasing Jer. 7:3, 7:5, and 26:13 and also Ps. 94:20: "Amend your ways and your doings." LCM is adapting Matt. 26:52: "Shall the throne of iniquity have fellowship with thee, which frameth mischief by a law?"

5. Matt. 24:6, Mark 13:7.

## To Martha Coffin Wright

Roadside 11 mo. 6th. 61—<br>4th. day—

No Mg., by reason of Qy. Mg. yestery.— Fine weather then—rain now— We had arranged to go to Miller [*McKim*]'s, from town, to tea, with Ed. & Maria [*Davis*]—but, as is often our lot, we had to come home, piloting our frds. Jas. & Abigl. Jackson, he a minister from Caln Qr., with a minute to be at several Qy. Mgs— So, our loss was Geo. & Pattie [*Lord*]'s gain—they drivg. over for Ed. & Maria, who went out in the Cars—and havg. rare enjoyt. with the piano & singing while we were left to entertn. our frds. with all the Mg. gossip & such like, that we could muster— They left just now in the rain for Horsham— Abingn. Qr.— Thos. Mellor came over with Sammy Levick, to offer them escort— New times, for Saml. to be callg. on us— Henry [*Davis*] had such a pleast. visit, with Pattie [*Mellor*], at Quakertown, at his house, that I had told Maria she ought to call over at Sister Mellor's, & be agreeable to him & Cathe. Foulke[1]—another old fogy guest of theirs— It is due *our* frds. to say, that, being abolitionists, they have been much interested in all that Edwd. & Jas. have had to say of Fremont, & have as little faith in Seward & *his* Cabinet— As to "old Abe"—he seems now a miserable compromiser— Just as our frds. were departg., the Morng. Press was brot. announcg. the fact, wh. before we cd. hardly believe possible, at this juncture, of Fremont's removal— We all feel it deeply— Pattie's voice faltered as she read his noble parting address—[2] Edwd. looked paler than before— Maria thot. of poor Ned Hall[l]., how he wd. feel— for it is astoundg.—after all the preparatn. by the insertn. of those hateful articles in the Papers, in order to prepare the public mind for the wicked machinatn. of the Administn.— Think of the woful blunders around them—sacrificg. some of the best & brightest of our countrymen—& then, for personal & partisan effect, drumg. up such unmeang., false charges—some so puerile, agt. Fremont— Pattie is indulgg. in a great many naughty hopes— Maria went into town agn. with Edwd., for the day,—and I cd. not settle down to any domestic duty— You must be feelg. just as we do, & trials in common, bring sufferers together—these fam[il]y. sheets—bless them! are the nearest we can approach in communn., so leavg. every thing, let's reason together— — Jas. has sd. from the 1st. that he wd. be removed, he saw the determinatn., & knew the power, but this morng., talkg. with Edwd., he doubted their being so wantg. in wisdom & sound policy, as to act just on the eve of a great battle—he was mistaken— Now we are wonderg. what will be Edwd.'s course— He must go back to St. Louis to attend to his present duties—[3] He has missed his chill these 2 days past—and has intended to go to Washn. tomorw.— It may not be necessy. now— He & Maria go to Boston next week— How sorry they are, that any letters were sent to Aubn., leadg. to so much preparatn. for them— We had sent no word—as their plans were various—and I hoped you wd. not have any intimatn. of their wish, until nearer a decision— A few lines Mari[a]. [Mott] recd. yes[terda]y. made no mention of my ½ sheet sent with hers, with a line added by Anna, after our Westchester Mg—& askg. you for further informn. of Aunt L. P. Mott who A. Lapham wrote,[4] was lying very ill— Jas sent a letter yestery. enclosg. $20— We have looked for her death, but the good news has not yet reached us— Arthur wrote br. Richd. that Scipio frds. wd. take care of her, if he "wd. go either to Califa. or to the Devil"— He is no fool, poor fellow, however depraved— Mari[a]. must have been slow in gettg. that letter off—& another scrap I left with her yestery., as she was going to write immedy. to acknowle. the apples, wh. dear little [Nea.?] was enjoyg. when I was there, & gave me a bite— Some were spoiled on top—they were 2 wks. on the road—wh. is very wrong— I took this sheet in, to begin there, for going in to Select Mg. 2nd. day, I stayed the night—but I found no time to write—the visit to Ann Mather's[5]— & a little darng. on Mari[a].'s heavy Kentucky Counterpane occupied me—except a note to Caroe. [Stratton], sendg. thy letters, & Anna B's—after Mari[a]. had looked over & ansd. them—also another note home to Pattie to apprise her of our comg. with compy., instd. of her havg. the pleasure of their famy. to themselves— Nelly [Lord] however, went to town that morng., with her aunt Maria, aunt Anna H. ^Jas. was with me^ & Lue, who bore the ride better than we feared she wd.— I noticed how weak her cough was—her mouth & throat sore, & just as wasted as she can be—still she was able to go down to dinner, after restg.—& seemed bright— She has to take Morphia in Wild Cherry tincture, her cough is so racking— — We thot. Annie Walton's death[6] wd. affect her sensibly—but she bore it— Anna & Maria D. were at the funeral yesteraftern., not out to the ground— So was I— Our Mg. was not till after 2—but I stepped into the Car—a great convenience, & was there in time  After wh. I went to Thos. & shared a good dinner—found Mari[a]. hadn't written a word, & cd.n't let me have thy letters—so I promised to go there to tea this eveg. & she wd. go with me to the Fair Circle a Dr. Griscom's—as she did last week—away up to Warner Justice's— Isn't she comg. on? Has she written of her beautiful present to Mary Quincy[7]—a time piece for the Mantel— She must describe it—if she have not. She has this Persian floor-cloth down over the worn part of the parlor carpet, & it looks very pretty— A Man came in & put up the curtains there, relievg. her of much climbg. ladders—for her pres[en]t. help does not understd. as Bridget did—who has a baby Bel [Mott] tells me— Now they are deep in

Chamber curtains— I am so glad that May's detested nurse is gone & hope the next will be more pleasg—it was pitiful to see the dear Child shrink so from Sarah— It wd. have been as well, to let the Aubn. help quietly repose in that valley—seeing the Article is so plenty hereaway— How very characteristic & childish that *go* to Syracuse, for that only purpose— Far better to have no further intercourse in any way— Emma Parker has not yet been at our Fair Mgs.— She is in Balt[imor]e. I think— Rush P. is in the City— Reba. was with him at the Continental, wh. certainly is evidence that they have not fairly separated— His game at St. Louis, will in all probability be played out—he never havg. his commission sanctioned at Washn. as Edwd. had— John Hoskin too—what will he do?[8] a most valuable man for the place he fills—& Kate so well satisfied with being there— The Barnum landlady liked her so much, that, when they felt obliged to seek a cheaper boardg. house, she told them that she & her husbd. had been consultg. together, & they wd. reduce their board & make it easy to them to remain— But how dismal St. Louis will seem, with the Stars eclipsed— I am sorry for Ellis Y. just as some explanatns. had brot. him ½ right agn., now to conclude "after all there is a cause"—as we presume he will— He stands alone in the famy. Wm. [*Yarnall*] is an earnest supporter of Fremont—so are his Parents & sisters—& Agnes [*Harrison*]—Margt. too as far as she gives expressn. to her opinions— Aunt Mary Horner was very ill on 2nd. day— We didn't hear yestery. All Benjn.'s famy.—Ellis' & Mary Brown were bidden to the country, to Chs.' to dine— We were sorry it happened the day we were in town— — Tomorw. Thos. R. Fisher is to be buried— Jas. & self are going to drive down there this aftern. awhile—& then I go in the Fisher's Lane Cars— After the funeral tomorw., we go in to the weddg. of Ed. Ferris & Elizh. Jenkins— somethg. every day— Josh. Lord was out here 2nd. day night—he is doing busins. in flour & grain—wh. brings him occas[ionall]y.— Louisa[9] is comg. next week, to visit her Norristn. Frds., & divide her time with us of course— Nelly stayed with Isaac in town last night— We are to have br. Richard & Cannie [*Mott*] in a few weeks— — Richd. Hall[l]. is expected to-day—he may not have time to come out here— Anna is much pleased with havg. the Cummerfords there—Mother & daughr.— I presume she has written Ellen [*Wright*]— — It is a pity that Ellen did not make her visit at Medford— When is Eliza [*Osborne*] comg.? Did C. Wood's going to Washn. make it unnecessy. for Munson to go— Pattie wants her to see her darling, lovely, pretty, good baby [*Mary "Molly" Lord*]—not so large as she might be—or as some of her age—but perfect in her form—& a thicker head of dark hair you never saw on so young a child— Sally Barker[10] is very happy with her little Anna Ferris— Have I written that Elizh. Gay expects to be made happy some day, before very long? But oh, how trifling all these items, when a body's heart & thoughts are full of the great events of the day— I feel almost to despair of any good result from the present commotion— We know full well that the battle field is a precarious resort, to obtain the right—that sorrows multiply there—and as to the moral

sense of corrupt statesmen—alas! "it is seared as with hot iron"— Such spirited protests as attended yr. Mr. Fowler's dismissal, may reach some consciences—and such, as I hope will follow Fremonts removal, may arouse the Nation—& after a long, long while liberty may be proclaimed— There has seemed
rather a stolid determinatn. of late among a class of politicians, that this War
shall have nothg. to do with Slavery—"the Union & nothg. but the Union," is
their cry—as if that were ever agn. possible with the deplorable weight of that
incubus upon it— Time only will reveal to us  Nothg. cd. be more "a tempest
in a teapot," than our petty Select Mg. bickerings on 2nd. day, about answg. the
queries & soundness, &.c— Rachel W. Moore still furnishg. *wind* eno' to create that 'tempest'—& I cant help thinkg. that yr. Church squabbles are of not
much greater importe.— All are the legitimate fruit of Ecclesiastical power—

at Thos. Mott's
5th. day Morng. 7th. & last date—

I came in yestery. to be at the Fair Circle last eveg.—as also to do some
shoppg. with Eliza— We only went to Ann B. Troth's—for the rain stopped
us—we went to Edwd. Hopper's & sat awhile with Lue— I didn't tell Eliza the
black cloud I saw slowly gatherg. in the West— It began to rain on her way
home— I stayed at Edwd.s & such a pour, when the hour arrived to go to Dr.
Griscom's that, short as the distance was I didn't venture out—neither did Mariᵃ.
& her compy— Lue sat up till 8 oclk— She had a hard coughg. spell @ 5 this
Morng  Her throat & mouth are sore—her voice failing—very gradual however every symptom  She asked us last eveg., speakg. of Walton's closed shutters,
not to keep bowed up when *she* died.[11] Comg. here this Morng., found Walter
B—pleast. to see him— Now I go to T. Fisher's funeral

AL PSCHi-Mott

1. Samuel Levick (1819–85) was a Philadelphia Hicksite Quaker minister (*Life of Samuel
J. Levick: Late of the City of Philadelphia,* ed. Hugh Foulke [Philadelphia: W. H. Pile's Sons,
1896]). Catherine P. Foulke (1809–90) was a Quaker minister from the Richland Monthly
Meeting (*Friends' Intelligencer,* 22 August 1857, 361).

2. When John C. Frémont (1813–90), the general in charge of the Department of the
West, had declared the slaves of Missouri rebels free, Lincoln overruled him. Frémont
was removed on 2 November 1861 under allegations that he had given business contracts
to his own staff. In his parting address to his soldiers, Frémont had stated: "I deeply regret
that I shall not have the honor to lead you to the victory which you are just about to
win; but I shall claim the right to share with you in the joy of every triumph, and trust
always to be personally remembered to my companions in arms" (*NASS,* 9 November
1861, 3).

3. Edward M. Davis, a captain under Frémont's command in Missouri, was one of the
staff members with whom Frémont contracted for army blankets, alleged to be of inferior quality (*NASS,* 9 November 1861, 3). In an earlier letter to MCW, LCM had gone into
greater detail about her feelings regarding Edward's military career: "But who wd. have
thot., when Edwd. was exertg. himself—spreadg. Adin Ballou's works, to make converts
to *peace* principles, that he wd. now be among the active officers in this war? He flatter[s?]
himself that the abolitn. of slavery—end, justifies the means— There is a good

understandg. with him & Fremont touchg. measures for emancipatn., wh. of course must not come abroad" (20 August 1861, Mott Manuscripts, PSCHi).

4. Anson Lapham (1804–76), a New York City businessman, a Hicksite Quaker, and a philanthropist, had moved to Skaneateles, where Lydia P. Mott resided, in 1861 (Gordon, 1:47).

5. Ann W. Mather, later Longstreth, was a Philadephia Hicksite Quaker (*Friends' Intelligencer*, 9 January 1864, 697).

6. Annie Hallowell Walton (b. 1841), the daughter of Susannah Hallowell Walton and William Walton, had died on 3 November 1861.

7. This is possibly Mary Jane Miller Quincy (1806–74), the wife of Josiah Quincy, a Boston abolitionist (*WLG*, 5:553).

8. Rush Plumly, a major on Frémont's staff, would later serve under Gen. Nathaniel Banks in the Department of the Gulf. John Hoskin was a captain and aide-de-camp to Frémont (*The War of the Rebellion: A Compilation of the Official Records of the Union and Confederate Armies* [Washington, D.C.: 1880–1901], series 1, 26:704; series 1, 8:398).

9. "Louisa" is probably the wife of Joseph Lord.

10. Sarah Wharton Barker (1821–66) was the daughter of William Wharton and the wife of Abraham Barker (1821–1906).

11. Lue Hopper would die on 31 December 1861.

## To Martha Coffin Wright

Philada. 127 S. 12th. St.
12 Mo. 5th. 61—
Fifth day morng. before breakfast—

It has become a regular course now, to bring in writg. 'fixins,' & employ this early hour thus—a pleast. occupatn. as it ever is— I hoped to say that we had Willie with us here last eveg.— Thos. & Maria. & Emily [*Mott*] went down to the boat & thence to Washn. St. to meet him—in ans. to despatch recd.—but no regiment—no Willie—[1] I waited patiently their return, makg. us very late at the Fair Circle—up Green St. & 17th—Eliza Sproat Randolph's— A large compy. & an interestg. Mg. The Townsends were there but I didn't happen to see them— — The announcement that we cd. have the large room, at the Assembly Buildgs. gave great satisfactn. & now all will turn on & work to make up for lost time— — We had some interestg. subjects—the Prest.'s Message— *rather tame*—Cameron's Report—foolishly modified, as the Tribune had just informed us—that good article in the Eveg. Post—"progress of Opinion"—& matters & things in general— —[2] The same spirit that did such injustice to Fremont, is now at work in other quarters, I guess I was going to say—

It is now another week
12th [*December*]—

at Thos. Motts agn. & not a word written mean-while, even to tell you, that after all, Willie passed thro' in the night & nobody here cd. welcome him— Anna D. H—Anne & Lucy [*McKim*]—Ned H. & some others tried to go, in a

body, at that late hour, & meet the compy. but they failed to bring it about—
And now we have thy fam[ily]. sheet & the little one to Mariᵃ., givg. an accot. of
yr. absorbg. interest in preparg. Willie & yr parting with him—all which was very
interestg.— I knew there wd. be much to feel at last  A strange thing it is that
the glories of War can in any wise reconcile one to the perils, &.c— It is in vain
to say much on the subject now, but my convictns. are strong as ever, that a better
& more effectual way will be found, as civilizn. advances— Even now, the moral
protest & demand of the people, as shewn by the immediate spirited acts of their
representats. in Congress,—seems likely to do more, than any of the armies have
yet accomplished— Petitns. shd. now be poured in from all quarters—so that
poor Abe, M'Clellan & the others, may see how unavailg. all their proslavery
conservatism is—³ The proceedgs. are full of interest now— Can you read
anythg. but the Papers? Oh yes, yr. new church occupies you— We are interested in that too— How natural for a conservative class to shrink from strikg.
off *some* of the heads of the Ecclesiastical Beast— At the time of our Separatn.,
when Wm. Jackson saw how great a part of the Hicksites wished no alteratn. in
the Discipline, and that Select Mgs. were to be retained—that Ecclesiastical rel-
ic—he said he could not go with them the advance was so—⁴ I forget his
speech— I will ask Edwd.— Breakfast is ready—

    It only lays the foundatn. for future trouble & fighting, when, for reputatn.—
'to please men', reformers seek to 'build agn. the things they are called to destroy.' Blanco White, my loved ultra author, says, "Reformers ought to be
satisfied to be destructives— They are too apt to wish to be *Con*structives"—
If they are to be "sharp threshg. instruments havg. teeth" they shd. have some
other name than *re*-formers. I was impressed in our early day, when Lydia Cooke
found that she had only exchanged one set of elders over her, for another, & the
latter, with less sense too, she rose in our Mg., & had "been instructed with the
vision wh. John saw—'the beast had recd. a wound, but was not dead"— She
sat down with 'he that hath ears to hear, let him hear" ∧not that she said so, in
words—∧—⁵ It is well sometimes to leave the applicatn., as the Tribune did its
good hit at the Administn.—quoting Louis Napoleon

> "March at the head of the ideas of yr. age, & then these ideas will follow & sup-
> port you.
> If you march behind them, they will drag you on. (I like such aphorisms.)
> "And if you march against them, they will certainly prove your downfall."

You noticed the good little scrap I doubt not, but I thot. it "vell vorth" copy-
ing.⁶ Now to go to another interestg. subject— Munson & Eliza [*Osborne*] were
to leave home on 2nd. day— Where are they then? Stoppg. in New Y. to see
Anna & Wallie B—? We sat up the longer last eveg., thinkg. they might arrive,
& then Jas. & self meant to "whip over" to Edwd. Hoppers, to sleep for Walter
B. too might come from Washn., & with Minnie B. & Nelly Lord here, the

childn.'s rooms were well filled— — After we retired, a Carriage stopped at the door, & the sound of trunks made us feel sure— Jas. was up in a minute & at the window, but it proved to be an arrival next door— Now I want them to come today, while I am in town— Jas. has just gone home with oysts. for a party this eveg—Laura Stratton Misses Levick & Lester & Pattie Mel[lor] Lucy & Anne M'K. & Fred. Dennis, Willie Potts Anna D. Hall¹. Alfred Mellor—Emily Davis— I shall go out @ 5 oclk— Maria H declines; as also Fanny Cavr. who just came to town—

[*Letter continues dated 13 and 14 December*]

AL PSCHi-Mott

1. Willie Wright had left Auburn in early November to join the Army of the Potomac, prompting LCM to write her sister, "May he survive all battles & return to you deeply impressed with the horrors or barbarous resort to War" (5 November 1861, Mott Manuscripts, PSCHi; Gordon, 1:477).

2. In his 3 December 1861 message, Lincoln had endorsed Congress's act authorizing confiscation of Confederate property (including captured slaves), proposed colonization of these freedpeople, and declared that he sought "to keep the integrity of the Union prominent as the primary object of the contest" (*Congressional Globe,* 37th Cong., 2d sess., appendix, 3). The original report of Secretary of War Simon Cameron (1799–1889), published in both the *New York Times* and the *New York Tribune,* asserted that if captured slaves were found able, "it is the right, and may become the duty, of the Government to arm and equip them, and employ their services against the rebels, under proper military regulation, discipline, and command." The report submitted to the president and published in the *Congressional Globe,* however, did not contain these paragraphs. The *Tribune* commented that Cameron's report had been "modified . . . until it would seem to be more strictly a document emanating *from* the President than one addressed *to* him" (*New York Tribune,* 4 December 1861, 5, 7; 5 December 1861, 4; *Congressional Globe,* 37th Cong., 2d sess., appendix, 18). In an editorial, the *New York Evening Post* criticized those who blamed secession on abolitionists' activities. It noted a "prodigious change" in the public's attitude toward slavery, citing several moderates, such as Edward Everett and George Bancroft, who now saw "that the disposal of slavery is thrust upon us by the inevitable events of the war" (3 December 1861, 2).

3. For example, Thaddeus Stevens had introduced in Congress a resolution declaring that "slavery has caused the present rebellion in the United States; and . . . there can be no solid and permanent peace and union in this Republic so long as that institution exists within it" (*Congressional Globe,* 37th Cong., 2nd sess., 6). Maj. Gen. George B. McClellan (1826–85) commanded the Army of the Potomac and had become general-in-chief of the army in November.

4. William Jackson (b. 1747?) was a Quaker minister from Chester County (Ingle, 185).

5. "Lydia Cooke" is probably Lydia Barton Cooke (d. 1831), who had become a Hicksite in 1827 (Women's Philadelphia Monthly Meeting minutes, 24 October 1827, PSCHi). Rev. 13:14; Matt. 11:15.

6. Louis Napoleon Bonaparte, Napoleon III (1808–73), was then emperor of France. The quotation is from remarks on the English Revolution in his "Historical Fragments." The *New York Tribune* opined that while the war should not necessarily be fought solely to end slavery, neither should the administration's efforts *"be rendered ineffective or fruitless by anxiety to uphold and perpetuate Slavery"* (6 December 1861, 9 December 1861, 4).

## To Philadelphia Family

Auburn [*New York*]
7 Mo. 17th. 62—

My dear Family

I thought after sendg. *that* yestery., there wd. be nothg. more to write, till just before we started on our homeward journey—but this morng. at breakfast, Frank made his appeare.,—2 days earlier than expected—his examinn. successful at Cambridge—he lookg. rather thin, but very well[1]—Willie so happy to have him—Ellen too in high glee—Miss Soule not here today, as good luck wd. have it. The 2 Carries soon here to welcome Frank, & to hear a letter from London— full of sight-seeing—[2] Moreover, a letter from Anna B., with Mari[a]. [*Mott*]'s all so acceptable— I came immedy. to this quiet chamber, & put up all the nice sheets, recd. since we came, & mailed to Anna B. with one from Aunt Martha & self—besides the Ship letters wh. are to be forwarded to you— — Before all this, however I resolved to begin this today, to acknowledge dear Maria's, wh. was so grateful last eveg—

Ar'nt we rich in letters? Not a word too much— Geo. [*Lord*] needn't feel that his were supernumy.—for Mari[a].'s comg. via Milton, his was first-tell of some things— I feel quite obliged by his care of us— Father will attend to the *manure* part, when he returns to-night. Glad shall I be, when the Rochester visit is paid— It is as lonesome to have him gone, as if he did all the talkg.— I can hardly believe that we took so little notice of Edwd.'s letter in the Standard,[3] Look at mine again— It is true, that Aunt Martha hasn't *yet* seen it—for the Papers are all laid aside, till she shall have time to look them over— She is out of the room frequently when anythg. is read—for Willie, tho' so nearly recovd. requires much attentn.[4] You know what the woman sd., abt. waitg on man "with a comg. appetite"— Then Miss Soule comg. as "luck wd. have it", she had lings. & things to hunt up for her, & the machine part to do—so she has little time.

Uncle D. brot. the Standd. to me, sayg. "there's a letter from Edd. M. D."— Maria [*Davis*] may be sure I was not slow to read it—and thot., as she did, that it was good—only Anna H. & self questioned, whether it was needful agn., to advert to those old blankets—great as was the injustice done him— So much however is done to Fremont & numbers more, that he has plenty of compy— When we were at Scipio at Mary Alsop's they spoke of Edwd.'s letter, sayg. they were glad to see it— So did Emily Howland, who is so bright and alive to all that is passing— How well she likes Mary Grew & Margt. Burleigh—[5] Another omission of mine, in yestery.'s letter, to say to Anna, that Lawrence cd.n't tell what the silver was she gave him— He had put it with the rest he had & sold it—so it is likely he has his money's worth— Another—to say, as Aunt Martha desired, how *left* we felt, without Anna [*Hopper*], Maria, & Emmy [*Mott*]— She wd. so have liked for all 3 to stay longer—& how poor little Milly [*Osborne*] hardly knew what to do with herself—believed she'd go & stay with Floy [*Osborne*] that night— Went was soon back—didn't want to stay there— She is quite helpful to her Grandma, uncle & aunt—always ready to run if anythg. is wanted, as Aunt Martha sd. Emily was while here— — I cd. readily believe there was "chatterg.," when she met her sister at Edwd. H's— Aunt Martha has sd more than once, how pleast. that gatherg. of sisters must have been & what a pity that Elizh. cd.n't have stayed! I have thot. much of her & Thos. [*Cavender*] too, with all the harvestg to be done

It was bright for Thos. & Mari[a]. to take their guests a-visiting to Eddingn.— — I am sorry to have miss'd the Peirce visit at Miller's The N. American with his speech we gave Mrs. Worden—[6] She met us at Sewards to tea— We had an affec[tionat]e. welcome there— I was sorry that yr. Father didn't return from Rochester in time to join us— David did at tea, & wd. have taken Willie, had it not looked like rain—it didn't however Ellen went in the eveg. W. Sewd. & wife were there & a wounded officer—able to sit at table with us— Of course war & the times were the only theme— Mrs. Worden severe eno' on McClellan[7]

[*Letter continues dated 20 July from Skaneateles, New York*]

AL PSCHi-Mott

1. LCM and JM had been visiting the Wright family since the end of June (LCM to MCW, 19 June 1862, Mott Manuscripts, PSCHi). Frank Wright would receive his M.A. from Harvard in 1866 (*Quinquennial Catalogue of Harvard University* [Cambridge, Mass.: Harvard University, 1900], 217).

2. Eliza Osborne and Munson Osborne had left in June for several months in Great Britain (Eliza Osborne to Auburn family, 22 August 1862, NSyU).

3. In his letter of 26 June 1862 to the editor of the *NASS* from Ft. Monroe, Virginia, Davis for the first time had publicly addressed charges made against him and others serving with Frémont by the House committee investigating government contracts, in particular the sale of military supplies to the United States for profit. He had testified before the committee and expected vindication soon. When the charges were first brought up in Congress on 7 February, Morris Davis had stated that his brother had been ignorant of the charges against him until they were made public, and he had asked that Edward be given a hearing to prove his innocence. Edward Davis had testified in Washington, D.C., on 12 April that the committee's earlier report wrongly concluded that blankets sold to the U.S. Army were "rotten or condemned." Davis also had declared in the letter that, serving in St. Louis as a brigade quartermaster, his witnessing "the horrors of war and its *necessary* associations" had "driven" him from his position and he was that day resigning from the army (*NASS*, 5 July 1862, 2; *Congressional Globe*, 37th Cong., 2nd sess., 715; "Government Contracts," House Report no. 2, 1862, serial set 1143). Ironically, Davis had recently been disowned by the Cherry Street Monthly Meeting for his military service; after attending the meeting at which Maria Mott Davis's resignation was accepted, LCM wrote: "as Edwd. was disowned, she chose to share with him the release from *Sect*" (Bacon, 182; LCM to MCW, 19 June 1861, Mott Manuscripts, PSCHi). When the investigating committee submitted its report to the next session of Congress, no mention was made of Edward M. Davis.

4. Willie Wright was home on sick leave from the Army of the Potomac.

5. Emily Howland (1827–1929), a New York City Quaker antislavery activist, had taught

at Miner's school for African American girls in Washington, D.C. Margaret Jones Burleigh (1818?–91) was the widow of Cyrus Burleigh (*JGW*, 3:129).

6. "Peirce" is probably Edward L. Pierce (1829–97), who had spent several months at
Port Royal as a special U.S. Treasury agent supervising cotton production. Pierce would
visit Roadside in June 1864 (Willie Lee Rose, *Rehearsal for Reconstruction: The Port Royal Experiment* [Indianapolis: Bobbs-Merrill, 1964], 21; LCM to MML, 4 June 1864, Mott
Manuscripts, PSCHi). McKim, who had resigned from the PASS in January and had
formed the Philadelphia Port Royal Relief Committee, had delivered "The Freedmen of
South Carolina" at Sansom Hall in Philadelphia on 9 July. In it he had reported on his
recent Port Royal visit and the condition of the slaves left behind when plantation owners
abandoned the region. The former slaves' production of fourteen thousand acres of
cotton was, he had declared, "entirely successful." He had called for additional teachers
and administrators to go to South Carolina to assist with the "experiment" (*Philadelphia North American*, 14 July 1862, 1; James M. McPherson, *The Struggle for Equality:
Abolitionists and the Negro in the Civil War and Reconstruction* [Princeton, N.J.: Princeton University Press, 1964], 160–61).

7. Frances Adeline Miller Seward (1805–65) was a graduate of Troy Female Seminary.
After an elaborate campaign on the Virginia peninsula, Maj. Gen. George McClellan had
failed to capture Richmond and, under Lincoln's order, brought his army north toward
Alexandria. To the anger of Radical Republicans, McClellan had opposed any military
action for the purposes of emancipating slaves (James M. McPherson, *Battle Cry of Freedom: The Civil War Era* [New York: Oxford University Press, 1988], 502).

## To Martha Coffin Wright

RoadSide 12 mo. 27th. 62— —

I have longed to have a sheet on hand, but it has seemed impossible  Mari[a].
[*Mott*] sent hers, without my seeing it, wh. I dont allow, but I was in town—
Many engaget. there & here, have occupied us all—  Partg. with our new cook,
after 2 Mo. trial, & seekg. another—puttg. our house in order for Maria [*Davis*]'s
return, last 4th. day, to our rejoicg.—  Then a few Mgs. & funerals—Wm. Dorsey's aunt Rachel Field—good old age—makg. 3 in whom we were interested,
in & around Germantn.—  The last Mg. was near Phoenexve.—saw Uncle
Mayhew [*Folger*]'s house—  The cold intense—water froze in our room, even
tho' a fire when we went to bed ^teeth fast to the basin, like H. Hall[l].'s at Medford—only not hard—^—much as we cd. do to dress—found a warm receptn.
however in the parlor—& in the hearts of Elijah Pennepacker & wife, with 7
childn.—^9 in all—2 died^—a babe 7 mo.—next not yet 2 yrs.—& so up to
18—  Gertrude Burleigh was in the neighbd. visitg. Grace Anna Lewis—  They
came & dined with us—  We had quite a party-visit at S. Pugh's, in honor of
Gertrude & daughr.—  The old Abolitionists—& Dr. & Margt. Griscom—Robt.
& Anna Massey & their sister Rachel—thy frd. Saml. Kimber's widow—so very
homely—but sensible & agreeable—[1]  Miller M'K. always makes himself agreeable, at such times—subjects of such common interest, absorbg. his thoughts—
He has lately been to Washn., on Contraband busins., in wh. we hope he may

be successful—[2] We are preparg. for a public Mg., early after the 1st—shd. 'Abe'
not be driven from his purpose— Haven't we all felt sick at heart of late? We
watched anxiously for dear Willie's safety, & now we wait for his letter— Those
sent have all "been acceptably read," as we say of our Epistles— It is surprising that he & others can write as cheerfully, as they do—when nothg. but de-
feats & retreats await us— Even Seward's removal "flashed in the pan"—[3] It
is some comfort, that I dont mean to become deeply interested in their foolish
doings. Such 'child's play' from the beging.— Yet we must acknowle. an increase of hope for the Slave— Thy letters & comments we have all welcomed—
It is quite time some were sent to Nant., Mary E. will like to read thy comments
on hers—another of hers goes with this— Two of thine Anna B. has not had—
I enclosed Wm. Folgers to her, forgettg. to say it was to be forwarded to thee—
Poor fellow! he must entertain us with such as he has— Those reminiscences
are indeed threadbare— A little more of their own fam[il]y. would have been
acceptable— Levi & Mary we heard were about movg. to New Y— I have not
yet ansd. his letter— I'll let thee—[4] It happened that one from thee the day
his came, asked what of him— After all have read thine, I give one more look
over, to see how neglectful we have been, & then pack them off— The full sheet
of Nov. 17th—& 19th & 20th last date—shall go, before the year goes— That
mentioned thy success in makg. grape wine— Our currant only answers for
mince pies—we had our 1st. last week— Cider has been so plenty this year, that
we are tempted to drink more than temp[eranc]e. advocates ought to— Dr.
Truman recommended my trying it—rather pleast. medicine—2 or 3 swallows
at a time— Thos. often comes in with a pitcher evegs.— On Christs. day all
our help being set at liberty, we were bidden to dine at the farm, on as fine a
turkey as one wd. wish—so 6 or 7 of us, nothg. loth went forth— Maria was
the lion—Mari[a]., the lamb—her cook rather cross at 1st. but all passed off well,
& we had a pleast. day— Ed. & Maria at Morris D's to tea— He just from
Washn., but not very hilarious— — Maria H. & Isaac T. [*Hopper*] came out in
the aftern., & such a time shewg. presents— Bel. [*Mott*] was made happy with
a watch from her father—of course *tiny,* to suit such geese— I offered her mine
to wear a yr or 2, till old eno' to have a new one—but she didn't smile on such
a proposal— They must tell the rest, for I forget— Isaac T. was equally elated, with a beauty, presented by Edwd. Wetherill— He feels as if Edwd. has done
much for him— Our Nelly & Mary [*Lord*] had a box of toys, magic lantern,
&.c. from New Y. so all gathered here in the eveg., & such a time puttg. out fire
& light, pinng. up sheet &.c— We hoped Elizh. Cavr. wd. drive over with her
famy., but only Harry came— She has not been since Thanksgivg., nor have
we been there—so many other engagets.— They too have had trouble with
help, by reason of drink— Robt. the gardener gone— Michael on the point
of being turned away—their cook gone—& so forth— Mother Cavr. about the
same— We have met at Edwd. H's & exchanged *troubles*— Anna's trouble
has been, tearg. down, and buildg. dirt, just after house cleang., paintg. &

paperg.— The Office however will be greatly improved for Edwd.—such a nice little room added—& suffict. light above it for the other Office— If my hurried little pages to Anna B. & to Medford are forwarded to you, this is but repetitn.— Edwd. [*Davis*] left his confusion, havg. busins. at the East, & pleased himself with a visit to Medford— He cd. not wait on Maria from there, but met her in New Y. & they came home together— Our Ex. Com. callg. us, just then, we missed the 1st. homecomg. till evening Henry & Pattie [*Davis*] came out with them—& Thos & Mari[a]. & daughrs. came over—makg. a Circle— Anna H. set out next day, reached 7th. St., when she "let in discouragets." & went home— She may come this aftern. with Edwd., hearg. her father is sick— He awoke me this morng. @ 4 with much pain in his side—extendg. down— I applied hot cloths to no purpose— At 5 called Ed. D. who drove to Jenkintn. 2½ miles, for Dr. Shoem[ake]r.—who came with him in time for breakfast— He pronounced it gravel—prescribed a sitz bath hot—& an applicatn. of hops stewed in vinegar— I had put mustard & Cayenne before he came. The sufferg. was great causg. sick stomach— Now he is sleepg.— Maria went in, to dine at Henry's, by invitatn.—so she agreed to call at Dr. Truman's, & ask him to meet Dr. Shoemr. here @ 4— It is 3 now— We have had our hominy dinner—only Pattie & self to enjoy it, with our new pork—for Nelly must needs be taken sick too, with a chill, and pain under her chin, which may prove mumps—we trust not Dyptheria— She has considerable fever——— Thy accot. of dear little Louis' illness & death was just what we wanted to hear—[5] We thot. Caroe. [*Stratton*] wd. feel it, havg. loved the little fellow, & had such care of him— Chs. sent her a Paper containg. the notice—so Laura [*Stratton*] tells us, who is visitg. Lucy M'Kim in Anne's absence, at Brooklyn, with Sarah Manning, who has been very ill—& still far from well— Laura called at Ed. H's 4th. day on her way to Germantn.— We had heard nothg. from Holly for a long time— Coz. Reba. [*Neall*] has gone to Balt[imor]e. at Auga. [*Needles*]'s urgent call—so that *she* may be released a little from Emma during the holidays— She will stay till the middle of next Mo— She begins to feel too old, to go from home—especially to travel alone—more, Laura says, "than Grandma ever did"— Mary Ann [*Chase*] is passg. a week or so with Caroe., while Laura is away, so that we needn't look for a visit from her yet awhile— I asked Laura how she recd. the news of Louy's death— She said—"quietly—she didn't say much"— While we sat at Edwd.'s on 4th. day, ^no 3rd. day I think^ Anna was called down to the Office to see a gent.— She returned, saying nothg. for some hours, & then informed me, it was Ch. W. who wanted her, to ask where he cd. find Edwd. in New Y.— He didnt find him— Jas. & Mary Truman are expectg. the Townsends before long— Dr. & Mrs. Hall[6] seem to fill the vacancy, yr former associates made— I was very glad to hear of the success of yr. new Church— & hope Mr. Fowler will be as radical a preacher as his highest & best convictions will prompt— What does he think of Bishop Colenso's daring, with the Pentateuch. I wonder who T. L. is—in the Tribune— Are you interested? I am *in the fact* that the Church is thus agitated—after all the Oxford stir with Tracts, &.c—& that it is no longer a solitary Blanco White—followed by a Newman &— a Foxton— —but that *seven* Essayists came upon them in a body—& now, to them still worse, a Bishop & a Missionary[7] How easy it is to raise the cry, of another Voltaire or Paine "come to judgmt.["] but not so easy, blessed be our age of free inquiry, scepticism being a religs. duty to frown down investigatn. into the dogmatic theology of the schools— Edwd. D. brot. out Colenso's book— The Introductn. interested us much—but not the examinatn.—havg. passed thro' that period years ago—when as Ripley (we presume) the reviewer in the Tribune says, Profr. Norton gave similar results to the world—conservative as he was—& intimates that the Bishop may have recd. some ideas from him—[8] I am greatly interested in the onward movement of the various sects— A Scotchman of their Church (Presbytn) sent us a Work on the Trinity, ^disprovg^ wh. I shd. like to pass over to Mr. Fowler—havg. long since been at rest, on that irrational creed— — Thy accot. of your *sparse* meetings of the new Freedman's Assocn. amused us—but if *one can* chase a thousd., when the *Lord* is on the side, you need not be discouraged— The bbls. of clothg. is somethg. I'm sure Edwd. D. & self went last week to our *Frds'* Assocn. Mg. found some 30 or 40 sewg. away 2 or 3 machines going— Several boxes have been sent— the last they fear is lost— The Washn. & Alexria. freedmen are now claimg. attentn.— The Heacock girls start for Port Royal next week—takg. with them, some generous gifts— They are regularly appointed teachers—[9]

Did Mari[a]. write thee of our call on J. Freeman Clarke's Mother, who is boardg. in the City with her daughr.? She is at the head of an Asylum for aged colored wom. in Boston—the only one, she says, in this country—[10] She sent me the Report, wh. Mari[a]. forgot to give me, but I 'mustn't let her know that'— so when we called, wishg. to be agreeable, & being *old* withal, I spoke of her pet Institutn., as an *Orphan* Asylum— She, & *Mari[a]. too,* quickly corrected the mistake, & the old lady was so much interested to tell me about it, that I guess my ignorance passed unperceived— I invited her to go out to our colored Childn.'s Home on the Darby road 2 or 3 miles, but she is too delicate to go from her rooms much in winter— J. F. Clarke is comg. agn. after awhile, & then *we are* to have a visit from them— He preached well for Furness, & for the uptown Church— We asked his opinion of Collyer's takg. Theodore Parker's place at Music Hall— You know they have given him a *call,* don't you? Mr. Clark sd. he had recd. a letter from Collyer givg. him the pros & cons & askg. his advice— wh. was *con*—for various reasons well stated—his usefulness so much more extensive where he was, commanding 4 or 5 States—the diff. in Boston betwn. being a visitor, & being stationed there, where in the social circle he wd. be overlooked—&.c. &.c.— We united with all he said— E. M. Davis had written pretty much so to him, & yestery. recd. an ans. sayg. he had already declined the offer—wh. is another feather in his cap— He little knew when lecturg. here on Geo. Stephn.'s (the engineer) rapid rise from obscure poverty, how "nigh, even at the door" his own elevation was—from a poor Methodist class leader, and a blacksmith fore-man thrown out of work in the panic of 57—& breakg. stone on the high-way @ $1 a day, to the command of the best pulpit in our country & a choice almost equally good of thousands a year at the West—[11] He expected to be at br. Richd.'s—Toledo to-day—

You seem to be havg. yr. share of the magnates, if that's the word— Saml. J. May's visit, & talk interested me— I agree with him that this terrible war will furnish illustratn. plenty, for the advocates of *moral* warfare, as agt. carnal weapons— Strange that any argumt. is needed Of course the nation or governmt. has not attained—& the fact that the cause is glorious does not sanctify the *means*—the resort to bloodshed is barbarous—makg. the innocent suffer for the guilty too— What I most fear, as I ansd. Freeman Clark, when he sd. "The Lord reigns," is, that the Superstitious idea, that, "it is in the hands of the Almighty", will cause indolence—& the *effective instrument*—the moral laborer will cease the exertions wh. have already abolished Slavery in the District of Columbia—the forth-comg. Territs, & on the high seas[12] I was sorry you were disaptd. of F. Douglass' visit—sorry too for S. B. Anthony—a good obituary of her father[13] [*Moncure*] Conway, you will like— Edwd. H. heard him in Boston the other day, & was much pleased— How is it, that he has not a settled pulpit— I asked F. Clark— He sd. the people didn't want to go to Mg. in Concord, where he now lives— Thy ladyship has company there— Was David with thee when thou wast so drowsy, under yr. favorite S. J. May's ministry? & was he as mortified as at Barnes' Church? Mr. Fowler might do much worse than to have Parker Pillsbury—or S. B. Anthony either— I did tell S. Pugh & others, at our Fem. A. S. Mg. that our Standd. was appreciated by Mr. *Pompey.*— It was kind of thee to call & invite Mr. & Mrs. Lee—*or Mrs.*

Thy mention of the Divine compy. at the Freedmen's Mg., reminds me of ours last 1st. day at French Creek—or Charlestown—where 3 or 4 constitute the Assembly— I told them I was aware that the common quotatn. was, for their encouraget., "where two or three are met," &.c—but that my mission was to *dis*courage the continuance of such Mgs. & if their religious wants required it, agree to meet alternately at their homes—Jas. adding—"& *read* perhaps somethg. interestg." It took with them—the expense & trouble of warmg. the house, &.c—was spoken of—& we expect a proposal next Qy. Mg. to "drop" that Mg— The aftern. Mg. our appt., was very large—house full We travelled by Car—the weather too cold to drive— Please say to Mrs. Worden that we shall welcome her heartily at Roadside—& her sister & niece too, if they will come—so also Mrs. Cheesbn.— We thot. when Seward was going to be ousted, that we shd. miss that visit.[14]

[*Letter continues dated 28 December*]

AL PSCHi-Mott

1. Elijah Pennypacker (1804–88) was a former Pennsylvania legislator and a Quaker antislavery activist and was married to Hannah Pennypacker. Grace Anna Lewis (1821–?) was an artist, a nature writer, and an antislavery activist. Susan Konigmacher Kimber was the widow of Samuel Kimber, a son of Emmor Kimber (Gertrude B. Biddle and Sarah Dickinson Lowrie, eds., *Notable Women of Pennsylvania* [Philadelphia: University of Pennsylvania Press, 1942], 161–62, Kimber Genealogy, PSCHi).

2. At this time, McKim was concerned with government appointments to the American Freedmen's Inquiry Commission (see McKim to Charles Sumner, 24 December 1862, *Papers of Charles Sumner,* ed. Beverly Wilson Palmer [Alexandria, Va.: Chadwyck-Healy, 1988], reel 27, fr. 152).

3. Willie Wright had fought in the Battle of Fredericksburg (LCM to Anna Temple Brown, 17 December 1862, Mott Manuscripts, PSCHi). Secretary of State Seward had frequently been criticized by Radical Republicans, and on 18 December a committee of nine Republican senators had urged President Lincoln to make cabinet changes, including removing Seward. Seward promptly submitted a letter of resignation, but Lincoln later rallied cabinet support for Seward and most of the Republican senators withdrew their request (*New York Times,* 21 December 1862, 1, 23 December 1862, 1; *The Diary of Edward Bates,* ed. Howard K. Beale [Washington, D.C.: GPO, 1933], 269–71).

4. Living in Massillon, Ohio, were Levi Rawson, a flour miller, and his wife, Mary Folger Rawson, who was the sister of William Folger and the daughter of LCM's uncle, Mayhew Folger (Folger family scrapbook, MNHi).

5. Charles Wood's son had died on 11 December of diptheria (LCM to Anna Temple Brown, 16 December 1861, Mott Manuscripts, PSCHi; Fort Hill Cemetery records, Auburn, N.Y.).

6. Dr. Edward Hall (d. 1870), then a surgeon at the Pension Office, and his wife (d. 1872) were from Auburn, New York (LCM to MCW, 20 June 1870, 11 October 1872, Mott Manuscripts, PSCHi; *Auburn Daily Advertiser,* 26 August 1869, 3).

7. The British scholar John William Colenso (1814–83), bishop of Natal, had recently published *The Pentateuch and Book of Joshua Critically Examined* (New York: D. Appleton, 1862). According to the reviewer in the *New York Tribune,* Colenso questioned the authenticity of the Scriptures. In response "T. L." wrote a lengthy criticism of the bishop's findings, saying, "In this awful crisis of our national destiny I can see no possible good in any attempt to undermine the most trusting faith in revelation" (13 December 1862, 2, 25 December 1862, 2). Frederick Joseph Foxton (b. 1807) wrote *Popular Christianity, Its Transitional State and Probable Development* (London: J. Chapman, 1849).

8. LCM is referring to the American political theorist and radical Thomas Paine (1737–1809) and the French philosopher François Marie Arouet de Voltaire (1694–1778). The literary editor of the *New York Tribune,* George Ripley, whom LCM is citing, stated that a number of German thinkers had "anticipated" Colenso's ideas; Ripley did not specifically name Professor Norton as one of the bishop's sources, but referred to a "Boston Unitarian divine" (*New York Tribune,* 13 December 1862, 2).

9. The Heacocks were a Quaker family from Bucks and Montgomery Counties. Two of the four unmarried Heacock sisters from Shoemakertown, probably Anne (1838–1932) and Jane ("Jennie"), taught in the Port Royal schools at least until April 1869 (*American Freedman,* December 1866, 141, January 1868, 377, April 1869, 15).

10. James Freeman Clarke's mother, Rebecca Hull Clarke (c. 1790–1865), had established the home in the 1850s. Her daughter was the artist Sarah Freeman Clarke (1808–96) (Arthur S. Bolster Jr., *James Freeman Clarke* [Boston: Beacon Press, 1954], 214).

11. While serving as the minister of Unity Church in Chicago, Collyer also traveled for the U.S. Sanitary Commission. Collyer's final rejection of the Twenty-eighth Congregational Society's offer is printed in John Haynes Holmes, *The Life and Letters of*

*Robert Collyer* [New York: Dodd Mead and Co., 1917], 2:32–34). George Stephenson (1781–1848), a British engineer, is credited with inventing the railroad locomotive. "Nigh, even at the door" is from Mark 13:29.

12. Congress had abolished slavery in the District of Columbia in April 1862 and in the territories in June. On 11 July a treaty with Great Britain to suppress the slave trade more stringently had gone into effect.

13. Daniel Anthony (b. 1794), a champion of progressive causes, had died on 25 November in Rochester, New York. His obituary had appeared in several leading newspapers, including the *NASS* (6 December 1862, 3).

14. In the middle of the following paragraph, LCM notes that the date is now 28 December. It is likely that she ended her 27 December entry with this paragraph.

## To Anne Heacock and Jane Heacock[1]

RoadSide 1 Mo. 2nd. 1863

The year of Jubilee I trust—

I feel very sorry, my dear girls, that the illness of my husband prevented our carrying out our intention of calling on you, on 1st. day last— I called at yr. br. Wms. store to-day, but he was not in— I inquired at the Anti S. Office, if any time was fixed for yr. departure, but could gain no information.[2]

You will go with light hearts I presume, now that the edict of Emancipation has really gone forth— We are all feeling buoyant— I wish you could be at our Mg. to be held on the 10th. Inst.[3]

Our best wishes go with you— Please say to Reuben Tomlinson that I have fully intended to answer his acceptable letter before this time— Kindest remembrances to him and to John Hunn[4]—& your brother We shall be very glad to hear from you—and shall often think of you in your new occupation—

If any of the articles sent are not worth taking, you can leave them with your Mother for passing beggars— The samples Edwd. thinks will amuse the children—

Please accept the copy of the Rejected Stone from yr. sincere & affec[tionat]e. frd.[5]

Lucretia Mott

I have 2 yrs. numbers of the Atlantic Monthly, wh. I intended takg. to you, and will now send them finding yr. br. is in his wagon— You can do as you think best about takg. them— You may find intelligence at Port Royal to appreciate them, if not among the poor, neglected contrabands. Do as you please with them, and all—

ALS PSCHi-Heacock

1. LCM's letter has no salutation but someone has written "To Gayner & Annie Heacock" on a copy in the Mott Manuscripts, PSCHi.

2. "Br. Wm." may be William Heacock (d. 1871), a Hicksite Quaker and a Philadelphia undertaker (*Friends' Intelligencer,* 20 May 1871, 193).

3. JM would preside at the meeting called to celebrate Lincoln's issuance of the Emancipation Proclamation, freeing slaves in all states in the Confederacy. Speakers included LCM, Robert Purvis, Mary Grew, and James Miller McKim (*NASS*, 17 January 1863, 2).

4. Reuben Tomlinson, a former bank clerk, had been sent as a superintendent by the Port Royal Relief Association of Philadelphia in the summer of 1862. John A. Hunn, a Delaware Quaker who had helped fugitive slaves escape, ran a store on St. Helena Island (*The Journal of Charlotte L. Forten,* ed. Ray Allen Billington [New York: Macmillan, 1953], 263, 270; Willie Lee Rose, *Rehearsal for Reconstruction: The Port Royal Experiment* [Indianapolis: Bobbs-Merrill, 1964], 78).

5. Moncure D. Conway, *Rejected Stone; or, Insurrection vs. Resurrection in America* (Boston: Walker, Wise and Co., 1862).

## To Mary Hussey Earle

RoadSide 2 mo. 20th. 1863—
6th. day.

My dear cousin Mary

I am without thy letters—all wh. were very acceptable—two I have sent to Auburn, & the last, recd. this week, sent immedy. to Henry [*Earle*], as directed— They come back regularly from Phebe [*Gardner*], so I have no complaint to make— Thy sister's was rather hard to read, owing to havg. been wet, I suppose, still, she writes such "small print", that I told her, when here, she was hard on old eyes— Her accot. of herself is quite encouraging— They thought they had a very nice chambermaid— I was sorry she proved such a hateful— — Phebe's success in the tobacco line was quite encouragg.— Ten days seemed long to wait for that vessel— I was glad that Edwd. was in good spirits— — It will be a relief to Phebe, that Wm. is in their house, & will see to every thing— —[1] But what is to become of poor Nant., if so many are preparg. to desert their native Isle the comg. Spring?— Thou too hast a visit in prospect, we are glad to learn, among thy childn. & the rest of us hereaway— It may be thy take-leave of Nant. for the present— Thy accot. of thy dear Mother leads us to look for her release before long— Thou hast been a devoted daughter, with many privations— Still on the whole, considerg. Caro [*White*]'s absence, we have thot. thee as pleasantly situated socially, as thou could have been any where— The frds. of our youth are very desirable companions as we grow in years— You have had many interestg. gathergs. this winter— Nathl. [*Barney*] gave me a little accot. of thy good memory adding entertainmt., at your parties—

It saddens me for coz. Philip not to be very well— I cling to the few remaing. of our old relatives, even while rejoicg. in the translatn. of the large no. of strangers mostly in the long list sent in thy letter, from Thos. Macy to whom my thanks for his care— Every day's Paper records the death of one or more very aged people— This mo. & next is favorable for their "crossing over"! Gertrude K. Burleigh was called home last week, before her visit was quite out, by the death of their aged father—blind, deaf, & childish— His married daughr. with him— Anna H. called it "joyful intellige."— Gertrude only called here once— She & her sisters were waitg. for me to be able to receive them for a day, as I assured them I was—& now I am so sorry they didn't come— Moreover, they preferd. not to visit any more, until Willie Kimber's remains were brot. home & buried, wh. was accomplished last wk—frds. invited to meet at Laurel Hill—[2] His new wife walked from the carriage with Susan— — The 1st. call I make, is to be on her—and last week, Jas. being in town, I proposed to Pattie [*Lord*] to drive up there— She discouraged— Had we gone then we shd. Have met Gertrude there— I was sorry, as the next day she was sent for— — — I was sure I was well enough  Again we have been called to resign Joseph Foulke in his 77th. yr.— He died of dry gangrene, beging. in his foot— He wished to have it amputated, & surgeons went from the City for the purpose—but his whole system was affected & of course they did nothing, he lived but a few days after— A large funeral last 3rd. day—met at Gwinned Mg. house— Jas. was there. His son Thos. ministered—also Saml. Levick—Mary S. Lippincott[3]—Joel Lair—Ann Weaver, &.c— You have probably seen Isaac Collins' death in Frds. Review—in his 76th. I think—[4] Does thy Mother still take that Paper?— I can't now go into particulars as to Bishop Colenso & his comg. out so alarmingly to the Church— He is out with a new book on Paul's Epistles— He never was much spoken of before this late heterodoxy—so thou needn't fear to own ignorance— Natal was his field of missionary labor—

I thot. thou wd. understd. my remarks on Liberals judgg. those who went beyond them— It was in reply to thy mention of yr. young Minister brandg. Buckle as almost an Atheist—[5] Just so Martha Wright's frd. Rev. Fowler, so far in advance of many of his brethren, and yet wasn't sure that Parker Pillsbury wasn't an Atheist. How I hate that mad-dog cry! My frd. Erneste. L. Rose has suffered, from the bigotry of very frds.— One or two late letters from Aubn. thou shalt have, after a while— Sister Martha has been quite ill with gastric fever & neuralgia in the head— Wm. M. Folger's visit was not quite so pleast., as if he had found us all well. He was happy to take Westtown School on his way here—and to go to Phoenix V.—(French Creek) & *remenis* to his heart's content— Benjn. & Eliza [*Yarnall*] had their share of his compy.— Also Edwd. & Anna H— He made one or 2 resolves, to call on thy sons, but he is rather lackg. in energy to fulfil all his wishes— Had I been well, & the roads not so exerable—mud thro' & thro'—we shd. have taken him to Eddington— Elizh. [*Cavender*] dined one day at Edwd.'s, when he was expected there, but he failed to reach there— He has gained much flesh—170 or 80 I think— Time has not dealt partially with him— Still he is the same William. His visit to Walter & Anna B. was full of pleast. excitemt.— He hesitated as to stoppg. there— We were glad he did, as Anna wrote how pleased they were to have him— Instd. of a night there, he stayed 3 days— He found sister Martha, like myself in wrapper & night-cap— He planned a day or so with Mary Rawson, on his way home— All their families appeared to be doing well— He spoke of thy br. Edward, but had not seen him very lately—[6]

This is all the news I have to write— The old letters sent thee contain every thg.— Now a word about busins. agn.— Maria [*Davis*] says that Milliken has Men's h[and]k[erchie]fs. the same price as those sent—but rather coarser— Not so now however, they have raised Anna [*Hopper*] hadn't been over to ask them to take back the others— She thot. it so *un*-business like— So now it is all right— Edwd. went yestery. to Sharp's for the 3 doz. thou sent for, & found they had raised the price to $5 per dozen! Of course he didn't buy them— So I took the responsibility to send to Anna to buy the remaing. few of Milliken like those sent, & see what the Men's looked like & let me know— So now please

I write on such paper as my economical port folio furnishes— It is more easily read than thy very thin paper is—tho' I am very glad to get *that,* or any sort thou may have, whereon to commune with me— I sent the parti-colored one to Anna B—in which thou expressed interest in her & hers— She now desires me to say she holds thee in affec[tionat]e. remembrance, and always wants to see thy letters—& enters into thy privations with sympathy—knowg. so well the demands on thy energies & affections— All thou tells of thy precious Mother interests us all—so remember her speeches & let us have them— How wonderful that she retains her power of a choice selectn. of words—for which she was remarkable in earlier life— Her movable cot-bedstead seems very pleast.—so that she can be gratified in lookg. at her "guardian Angel"— one she loves almost as well as she does Mary Earle—that talk was very droll.

Thou dost well in havg. Sophy often, to relieve thee of such constant care— while I can readily believe that partg. with her is also pleast. after a reasonable rest— Thy little companies to tea & good veal pie made me feel as if I must have one made instanter—as did our coz. Rebecca [*Neall*]'s boiled Indian puddg. with milk & eggs, while we were there—"a bit abroad"— Elizh. Pugh sent me some split & twice baked sugar biscuit, wh. I have relished— Our Indian dumplings wont taste as those did in our visits on Nant.

Thou thinks because Nant. revived after the wars of yore, it may again—but the whale fishery *then* cd. be resumed to advantage—now *that* can not be depended on—and so many have gone to California, & other places, that it looks more discouraging then ever before—[7] Agriculture too is so laborious there & its yield so far less than in other parts of our great country, that wisdom & prudence seem to point to other locations— Time however as thou says will reveal— Such social ties & happy realizations our Islanders will look in vain to find 'other where'—but then a new generatn. never knowg. these, will not miss them—

Friends—or Quakers certainly are waning there as never before— What small favors to be thankful for, were the repeated visits of the Wilbur preacher Nathan— Our 12th. St. worshippers have been delighted with a gifted wom-

an-preacher—Comstock from Michigan I think—English by birth—well educated—eloquent, &.c— She stopped long at Charles Yarnall's & visited Rebecca
in her sick room—quoting "They also serve who only stand and wait"—if I have
the line right—perhaps in the singular—*he*.[8] She visited hospitals & prisons, but
had no mission to the Yearly Mg. wh. has just passed without excitemt. A singular act in our Mg. here yestery. at 15th. St—Richd. Cromwell[9] broke up Mg.
at the usual time by reachg. across the aisle & shakg. hands with *me*!— It was
accepted as a kind of public repentance—&.c—

Thou speaks of Nathl. as increasingly nervous & impatient of contradictn.—
We had thot. his health improving— I doubt if whist or euchre wd. add a cubit to the length, either of his or our lives— Jas. *does* take part sometimes in
the new game of Authors, wh. our young people delight in—large circles around
our tables—the Beamens who visit Bel & Emmy [*Mott*]—join in— Eliza Osborne & Ellen W—& Anna D. Hall[l]. with our daughrs. make a lively company—
We are enjoyg. this visit from Anna D. H. & babies— She had thot. she couldn't
come this year—but they bot. the house at Medford & had a furnace to be put
in—& a new range—a pantry made & paintg & paperg. done, so we pressed her
leavg. all—after the much compy. they had had— Edwd. & Norwd. Hall[l]. gettg.
up their colored regiment—[10] Richd. too havg. somethg. to do with it—then
Ellen W. & Lucy M'K. with the compy. they drew—their little cottage was almost overflowg. part of the time—and it was much best for them to spread out
at Roadside, where we have had 18 & 20 in fam[il]y. much of the time this
spring— Our daughrs. takg. every care from me— Mari[a]. [*Mott*] too, often
invited part of ours over there to dine, &.c Martha & Ellen stay there—also
Willie W. who had 2 wks. leave of absence—& David who was with us a few
days— Last 1st. day we had Robt. Purvis & daughr.[11]—Miller M'K & 2
daughrs.—some of ours from town—& Fanny Milton Earle, who walked over—
& Morris & Hanh. Hallowl. who drove out unexpectedly—then some of the
Mellors—with Henry Davis, in the aftern.—countg. all 40, includg. our own
famy. of course— We are now thinning out— Elizh. Cavender has seldom
been able to be with us—her many cares—and the illness of Thos.' Mother
confing. her—& the bad roads & my poor health have prevented our drivg. up
there— It is now 4 or 5 months since Jas. & self were there— Our childn. &
visitors have been once or twice— Anna H. & Maria have had much of the
compy. of all—as well as Benjn. & Eliza, by their often makg. a convenience of
their houses in their shopping—as well as in Concerts & Lectures— Fredk.
Douglass was the last attracn.

Anna E. Dickinson has "found herself famous," as thou may have seen by the
Papers— In New Eng. she has made a great sensatn.— Last week in this City,
she drew a throng, who were carried away almost with her eloquence—[12] Judge
Kelly said her pathos was surpassg— He is delighted with her & her services are
secured for Penna.— She has more *fight* than I can go with— Still her genius
& rare gifts are admirable— Jas. took her under his wing in the beging. of her

youthful career—& he is now much gratified with her success—as I am also—
for some of our Critics saw her defects & were disposed to blame us for encouragg.
her while so young—only 18—

Agnes Harrison is another of our shing. stars— She is very bright— Mariᵃ.
is a great admirer of her—not of course as a public speaker—but comg. out in
the social circle—as at Seward's dinner party in Washn. Thou asks what their
talk was—I cant remember to write it—only that Seward was complaing. of the
English & their want of appreciatn. of our cause when she called his attentn. to
the duchess this & that & Lady such a one, who had come out right—and he
replied as if "oh yes, but they are only Women ^are Duchesses I was speakg. of
Dukes^"—not just so but conveyed that idea— Buckle Discourse on Woman—thou asks how I liked it— I only hurried over it once—& thot. it good as
far as he went as far as an Englishman cd. be expected to go—tho' not by any
means equal to Mrs. Taylor's (Mills) Enfranchisement of Woman, published
after our 1st. Convention at Worcester— Buckle was so full of *inductive* and
*de*ductive in that discourse that I *tired* of it— His remarks on Mill's admirable
Work on Liberty interested me more— That Work is re-printed lately—probably from Buckle directg. attentn. to it—¹³ We have it, but I have not yet read
it— I have lent Buckle to Sarah Pugh, who likes to keep up with the readg. age—
[*George*] Curtis' stories thou speaks of, we are not familiar with— I shd. like
to read Sir Samuel Romilly¹⁴—but there is so much to be read, I cant retain the
little I once could— As to Mrs. Rose's—Pillsbury's & Buckle's atheism—people will cry 'Mad dog' when doctrines or sentiments conflict with their cherished ideas—and I'm glad to say, with the Apostle, "It is a small thing to be
judged by man's judgment"— The Atlantic Article on Buckle I rather liked—
or didn't *dis*like it as ^so—isnt as right there^ much as Edwd. Davis did—for
Wasson is clever at criticism—and we ought not to exempt any favorite author
or preacher from free criticism or review— I shd. like to send thee Robt. Collyer's fault found with some of my sayings, & my defence—¹⁵

[*P.S.*] We are all very sorry for Caro's loss of clothing— A pity they were
not insured— Thank thee for her replies in the Paper They do her credit—
Mariᵃ. borrow'd them & has not yet returned them— I will send better Auburn letters next time— Ellen Wright accompd. her br. Frank to Boston &
Medford last 6th. & 7th. day— This is 1st. day last date—

Joseph Lord just arrived in all the storm—

AL PSCHi-Mott

1. Phebe Gardner and Edward Gardner had been on a voyage to the Navigator Islands,
where he was to be consul. En route from the Fiji Islands their ship sank and all on board
drowned (*Philadelphia Times*, 19 January 1879).

2. Sgt. William Henry Kimber (b. c. 1836) of the Anderson cavalry had been killed near
Nashville on 29 December 1862 (*NASS*, 21 February 1863, 3).

3. Thomas Foulke (1817–90) was a New York City Hicksite Quaker. Mary S. Lippincott (1801–88) was a Quaker minister from Camden, New Jersey.

4. Isaac Collins (c. 1787–1863) was a member of the Orthodox Western District Monthly Meeting of Philadelphia (*Friends' Review,* 14 February 1863, 378).

5. In "Mill on Liberty" Henry T. Buckle had criticized at length a case in which a man accused of writing anti-Christian graffiti was convicted of sacrilege (*Fraser's Magazine* 59 [May 1859]: 509–42).

6. Edward Hussey, Mary Hussey Earle's brother, was a sea merchant (*Philadelphia Times,* 19 January 1879).

7. After the discovery of gold in 1848, many Nantucket residents had left to seek their fortune in California. Because the Nantucket Bar prevented especially large ships from entering its harbor, the port lost its primacy to New Bedford and its population of nearly ten thousand in 1840 had dwindled to only five thousand by 1860 (Emil Guba, *Nantucket Odyssey,* [Waltham, Mass.: n.p., 1951], 136–37).

8. Elizabeth L. Comstock (1815–91). LCM is quoting John Milton's "When I Consider How My Light Is Spent," l. 4.

9. Richard Cromwell (c. 1799–1865) of Garrison, New York, was a Hicksite Quaker minister (*Friends' Intelligencer,* 18 March 1865, 41).

10. In March 1863, Edward Hallowell would become the colonel of the Fifty-fourth Massachusetts Volunteers. Norwood Hallowell was the colonel of the Fifty-fifth Massachusetts, also an African American regiment (*War of the Rebellion: A Compilation of the Official Records of the Union and Confederate Armies* [Washington, D.C.: 1880–1901], series 1, 28:75, 27:819, 47:1036–37, series 2, 6:775–76).

11. Hattie Purvis (b. 1839), the daughter of Robert Purvis and Harriet Purvis, was active in the PFASS and woman's rights movement.

12. Douglass had recently given a speech in New York City on blacks' desire to fight in the Civil War: "Give us fair play, and open here your recruiting offices, and their doors shall be crowded with black recruits to fight the battles of the country" (*NASS,* 14 February 1863, 1). In 1862–63, Dickinson had been delivering lectures around the state supporting the Republican party and arguing that the war was being fought to end slavery (James Parton, Horace Greeley, and Elizabeth C. Stanton, et al., "Anna Elizabeth Dickinson," in *Eminent Women of the Age,* ed. James Parton [Hartford, Conn.: S. M. Betts, 1871], 496–504).

13. Henry Buckle's *The Influence of Women on the Progress of Knowledge* (London: A. C. Fifield, 1875) was first delivered in 1858. John Stuart Mill, *On Liberty* (Boston: Ticknor and Fields, 1863).

14. Samuel Romilly (1757–1818) was an English legal reformer whose *Memoirs* had appeared in 1840.

15. 1 Cor. 4:3. David E. Wasson had written of Buckle: "And as a thinker, I can say nothing less than that Buckle signally failed. His fundamental conceptions, upon which reposes the whole edifice of his labor, are sciolistic assumptions caught up in his youth from Auguste Comte and other one-eyed seers of modern France" ("Mr. Buckle as a Thinker," *Atlantic Monthly,* January 1863, 27–42). Collyer had criticized LCM for becoming too logical and less visionary: "It was the habit in her later life to reason—from premise to conclusion, and let this suffice" (*The Life and Letters of Robert Collyer 1823–1912,* ed. John Hayne Holmes [New York: Dodd, Mead, 1917], 1:159–60).

# To Anne Heacock and Jane Heacock

Roadside 7 mo. 23rd. 63—

My dear Friends

I feel that I have been too neglectful of Anne's kind & interesting letter, recd. so long ago—so, to make some amends, I have put up a small lot of little books, & trimmings for you to dispose of among your interesting children—the account of whom, was so encouraging— Maria has put in some scraps of ribbon, which please little folk—

The visit from John [*Heacock*] has been very pleasant to his friends—we enjoyed our little share with your sister— I hope we did not weary him with our many inquiries— That he & you too should feel so well satisfied—so in your right places must go far to reconcile your parents, & sisters to the separation—and very gratifying to your friends— The privations must be felt by you at times, but the feeling that you are in the path of duty, & doing good to a class whose claims on us all, are so great, will sustain you, & "verily ye shall have your reward"—[1]—

I need not try to tell you any news, as your brother will be the bearer, & will take more than I could tell—

The neighboring Camp seems the absorbing interest just now—[2] Is not the change in feeling, & conduct toward this oppressed class, beyond all that we could have anticipated—& marvellous in our eyes? The recent disgraceful outbreak in New York is but a manifestation of "copperhead" wickedness for political ends—and which must ere long give place to a better feeling.[3]— — There are already generous contributions to the sufferers, especially the blacks.— Our several families are in usual health— 3 of our grandchildn are at a boardg. school in Mass. among the Ber[kshire] [*ms. damaged*] Hills— Dr. Dewey's daug[hter the] [*ms. damaged*] principal[4]—Maria Hopper & Bel & Emily Mott—

Henry & Pattie Mellor Davis are made happy with a little Lucy 3 weeks old—

I am hurrying to take up this to your brother, lest he should go without it— so will close with love—

Lucretia Mott

ALS PSCHi-Heacock

1. LCM is possibly adapting Jer. 31:16: "For thy work shall be rewarded."
2. In January 1863, the Union Army had leased part of Oak Farm from Edward Davis for Camp William Penn, a facility to train African American soldiers (Bacon, 182–83).
3. During the New York City Draft Riots, 12–17 July 1863, whites (primarily the Irish) had rioted to demonstrate their opposition to a draft that allowed men to buy their way out of service for $300. The rioters had targeted blacks, draft offices, men who appeared rich, and Protestant churches. New York and Pennsylvania regiments had been used to suppress the riot (James M. McPherson, *Battle Cry of Freedom: The Civil War Era* [New York: Oxford University Press, 1988], 600–601, 609–10).

4. The Unitarian theologian Orville Dewey (1794–1882) had a daughter named Mary E. Dewey (1821–1910) of Sheffield, Massachusetts.

## To Martha Coffin Wright, Anna Temple Brown, and Marth Mott Lord[1]

Roadside 1 mo. 21st. 64—
Cloudy 5th. day aftern.—

Now this shall be a real family sheet—see if I wont ans. all on hand, from thee, my dear Sister, & from thee, my dear niece—Anna B., & from thee, my dear daughr. Pattie—all wh. letters are at this pres[en]t. scattered abt.—at Eddingn. School Lane, & Philada.—also one from Mariᵃ. to Thos. [*Mott*], givg. us the informn. we wanted, of their arrival, blazg. fire, grouse & other goodies, and of the eveg's employt., lookg. at plans, &.c— It was, as I hoped, that Agnes [*Harrison*] shd. go 1st. with Mariᵃ. to 41st. St— Sorry shall I be if Margt. [*Yarnall*]'s sickness shortens her visit, & hastens her home rather than to Boston— That seemed so pleast., so much as they wd. enjoy together— Margt. is relieved somewhat, tho' not yet sittg. up— Dr. Griscom thinks her liver the trouble— Sarah Y. is with her— Mary B. was one or 2 days— — We were quite alarmed yestery. for Pattie Mellor D.— She had so much fever, the Dr. feared Typhoid, her pulse so irregular— Henry was frightened eno', beside the disapt., after his great interest in the surprise party at their father's new house, for neither to be there— It was a great success, as Thos. will tell the 'Yorkers— The 3 hay-wagons recd. 70 odd at the York Road statn. except those who chose to walk— Our Dearbn. & waiter Clay's 2 wagon loads refreshments dishes &.c, joined them, & all 'processed' to their great gate—alightg. there to avoid noise— Alfred & Geo. saw their parents safely in the parlor after tea, with aunt Margt. Bancroft[2]—& then ran up & lighted the chambers—

Eveg.— Twilight stopped my writg—and I have since filled a ½ sheet or so to Pattie requirg. an ans.— — — What in the world do all those Allen advertisemts. mean sent in a late letter? Now I've noticed one thing— Wasn't Fowler's sermon ra[ther?]— fulsome in its laudatn. of Lincoln? I sent it to Reba. Y. after she expressed dislike of Wendl. P's. criticism, in the lecture she heard in New Y—[3] Reba. has a mind of her own, whether you agree with her or not— She had to give up M'Clellan however after preferg. him to Fremont— As to Ellis, he is nearly lost to us— We rarely see him— I feel it quite a loss, for despite his high Church, he was infinitely agreeable.

At thy instance, I made myself read "A Man without a Country"—The point or moral is good, & it is wonderfully well told—natural to the life, but made up stories cannot interest me, as plain matters of fact do— — I always like to be told what *is* worth readg. in these trashy Periodicals—as Geo. Thompson used to tell me what to admire in our travels in Scotland, & in the galleries of paintings— What do you think of his comg. agn.? I have just read Peirce Butler's story of his married life—[4] What an illustratn. it furnishes of the evil of the church law—requirg. obedience of the wife— the man really cd.n't conceive how any woman cd. demur at such a demand— He was not a fool either, as I inclined to think he was, before readg. his letters—some of wh. are very good— & he was sorely tried at times, with his excitable Fanny— Another illustratn.— of the evils of Slavery—that he so feared the conscientious expression of her abhorrence of it.

1st. day eveg. 24th.—

The letters to be noticed are not yet returned to us—so I will go on with home matters—havg. been very much engaged, fittg. the rat-eaten carpet on our room—& now Mariᵃ. wd.n't know there had been 'a brack' in it— All this week's leisure has been given to it—& to-day I made Mg. give way to it—as part of the aftern. was to be given to the Camp. The Episcopal Minister Parvin had not been told I was going, & had taken a young assistt. expectg. to have the service to themselves— He behaved pretty well however— Edwd. D. lettg. him know, that he was not the appointed Chaplain—only made so by Col. Wagner. Arrangets. were made for me by Col. Kiddoo, who took tea with us on 6th. day eveg—[5] I desired Parvin & his frd. to begin the service, & say what they had to, & I wd. follow—& it was so—& all ended well— It was muddy eno', but our Dearbn. took us to the door— The schoolhouse was filled—many hundred, & all well behaved— That over, we drove up to our neighbr. Brock's, hearg. he was very ill—neumonia—found that he died @ 2 oclk— He was out a week ago yestery—73 yrs. old— It is quite a loss— he was a nice man—not priest-ridden, as too many are— We went in awhile— His son thankd us for callg— On our way we met a messenger invitg. us to the funeral of Wm. Barnard—who lately left the Progresse. Frds.—& returned to old Marlbo. Mg—a minister[6] We cannot go, as Jas. is hardly well eno'—and we are preparg. to leave home on 4th. day not before, havg. many things to attend to, here & in the City— I must go in tomorw. This was to have gone with Anne M'Dennis—but I cd.n't fill it in time— We had quite a party on 6th. day— I plodded on, darng. carpet, till I saw a raft comg. across the orchard— A. D. H & Richd. who came from Boston 2 days before. Norwood & sister Anna [*Hallowell*], Miller M'K. & Jas. Mott, who had been in to the Barclay, aver[rin]g. he was well eno' to go anywhere now—[7] He has barely escaped neumonia, like Brock's— We sent over for Sarah M'K. & daughrs., who drove in nearly the same time— We sent for Anna H. but the contraband sewg. party at Sarah Barker's prevented her comg. Elizh. Cavr. too we longed for, but she says she can never leave home— Willie D. is passg. 2 days there now— Isaac T. [*Hopper*] is here, & was one of our party—and, Pattie, be it known, he sat at the side table & behaved manfully— Col. Kiddoo added interest to the young folk— Singg. & piano interested him—"the new Volunteer"—& "Babylon is fallen", especially—but Anne M'D. can tell you all this— I'm sorry not to send this by her— I wrote the above by twilight—

Philada. 25th. at Edwd. H's

I came in this morng. to do lots of errands, & to call on lots of aged & middle aged—before going to New Y. on 4th. day, for a week's absence—and now Anna proposes that we go up to Eddingn. this aftern.,—I told her, yes, anywhere with her— Jas. & self have been tryg. to plan a visit to Elizh., before leavg. home, but we have not succeeded— It will disapt. him, for us to go without him— The roads have been too muddy to drive so far, this "Jany. thaw"— Willie D. came from Eddington this morng—no change there— Fanny [*Cavender*] sits up part of every day—she may go to some water cure place, after awhile— Thos. wants her to have it applied at home— Miller M'K. had a good deal to say the other eveg. about Ellen [*Wright*] & her headaches. He has been enquirg. her symptoms of Anne, & thinks it is not her spine wh. is affected—& that medical treatment—even water-cure is not so much her needs as strength'ng. her system by a rich, generous diet— Not cakes & candies but substantial food— The many forms of hysteria incline him to the opinion that her nervous system is out of order— He doubts Dr. Herring[8] understandg. her case—

He wd. bring me a Work, wh. he wd. like for me to read— He thinks her headaches may be arrested by proper treatment— *His* health has been poor for several weeks—so that he had not much comfort in his late travel—he is better now— He found it impossible to proceed down the Mississippi—the ice, &.c, &.c Other travellers too givg. such minute accots. of the freedmen thereaway, it did not seem to him necessary— The change in public sentiment he thinks truly wonderful— the prospect for the Slaves is Splendid—'hopeful' doesn't begin to express their condition— He & Saml. Shipley promise to come to our next Freedman's Mg—10 days hence & tell us their observatns. & experience— We are really beging. to *do something.*— The Race St. Sewg. Socy. have made up & forwarded 7000 garments—as many thousd. dollars have been placed at their disposal— Our new Assocn.[9] handed them $1200 last wk— They employ men Tailors to cut out by wholesale— It is amusg. to see the Biddles—Parrishes—Whartons, & such like, all alive to the subject—& preparg. an Address to send thro'out our Yearly Mg——& not a *Meetg.* concern either— any more than the Educational Conferences—and all the better that it is not— Abm. Barker is exceedy. interested, & speaks in our Mgs. Sixty & more meet at private houses to sew & have a simple supper—as they have done at School Lane the year or 2 past—& Fairs at private houses are resorted to, wh. interest the childn.— So our Old Female may well lay down some of our armor—but not quit *watching* & workg— "What I say unto you, I say unto all, *Watch*"—[10] I have always liked thy watchful jealousy & thy criticisms on the Adminstratn.— Tho' now we must admit that Lincoln has done well, *for him*— Doubtful if one *could* have been elected, who wd. have done more— Congress seems as usual to be fritterg. away their time—

What a shame to call our faithful, nice Julian such names— to-be-sure we didn't all rush in to the Continental to see him & his bride, as we might had it been—who shall I say?— We sent a written invite to them to visit us, but they ne'er came, & we were "like Ann Yarnall"! We enjoyed all thou wrote of Fitz & Laura,[11] & I have wanted to shew the letters to Caroline [*Stratton*]—but we have only now got them back agn. not a word from Caroe. since Laura returned home—& now she's gone to Culpepper, as Anne will tell you— Indeed, what can I write that she will not tell— We were glad for Willie to have such enjoyt. in EaglesWd. compy—& only sorry that the Aurora visitor hadn't happened another time—tho' A. D. Hall. had a real lovely visit and was so glad she persevered & went— All say Eliza Osborne is the most wonderful woman they ever saw— Anne M'Kim seems perfectly happy— Lucy [*McKim*] enjoyed her visit too—& they thot. you all did a great deal for them— It was well that Jas. did not attempt to go any further—to be sick on your hands—and to be detained on the road as Anna D. H. was— I meant while on the subject of Laura, to say how my sister mistakes me, when she presumes that war's trappings made the scene a whit more imposing, than a rational citizen's dress— No—it seems childish for men grown to rig out in that Style— We did, tis true, select a *Colonel* to bid to our young people's party the other eveg. rather than the uninterestg. schoolmaster, who had been over several times in the eveg— I *did* quote to Maria, "When thou makest a feast, call in the poor," &c Of course we become accustomed to all these uniforms, wh. meet us at every turn— The AntiS. sentiment is spreadg—not by battles with carnal weapons but the mighty "armor of righteousness on the right hand & on the left"—[12] It is no evidence of inconsistency, to be glad when the right is uppermost in the army—even if yr. depende. is *not* on the arm of flesh— — Yes, the similar service for Caroline only so short time before her daughr's, was impressively before me, durg. the marriage— Mrs. Furness sd. to Caroe.—"I wont speak to you now, I know yr. heart is full"— No allusion probably "to 17 South"— You have Frank with you by this time— What a constant successn. in our several families— When Anna D. H. & bairns & nurse took their departure last 2nd. day—I wondered who wd. come next, beside Thos. Mott—then the Mellor party then ours—& now Anna & I go—& then agn. James & self— Why is it that Thanksgivg. & Christs. are not the chosen time for Harvard vacation— Yes, tell Ellen, I well remember the call from Willie's comrade Lt. Johnson, & thot. him not so animated as the girls were—wh. was natural enough under the circumstances— Our folks say Willie has done right to resign—& William & Norwood Hall. too— We mean to read Parton's history of Butler's Administratn.[13] & every thing else that thou recommends—but Jas' readg. days are nearly over— It is really affectg. to see him choose the strongest light, & after awhile, even then, lay down his book or Paper & say I cant see to read— Maria reads the Tribune aloud every eveg. to him—& we have to read his letters to him, if they are long— Isn't it hard to submit to all these warnings—not that it is sad to die, when our powers & faculties fail us— I wished too that Harry B. cd. have been at Auburn with the others—he has enjoyed young Yale's visit— Walter & Anna

[*Brown*] have had as constant compy. as the rest of us— I'm glad the Chamberlain's is over— I wonder if John & Kate [*Hoskin*] have decided wh. offer to accept— Massillon [*Ohio*] promises most, but they fear chills & fever there— Agnes we think will not go to Boston— Margt. has had a severe attack— Ellis has written I beleive discouragg. her going farther—altho' Margt. is rather better— I sincerely hope Mrs. Worden's health is not going to break down— Thou did just right to encourage Mrs. Gage to postpone her return to Auburn— indeed I have doubts of her success in that line now— Anna E. Dickinson carries the day— What laudatn. of her Washn. Speech[14]— She repeats it here at Music Hall on 4th. day eveg— Church begging is awful— I must send this now, so that George [*Lord*] may open it in New Y. & find we are not going till 4th. day—& after Pattie & Anna have read it send it on to Auburn with any addition of theirs—or of Mari^a.'s if she have returned from Sheffield We hoped to have a letter to-day of their plans I have written this last page in the greatest haste for we must be off—

LM—

Richd. & Anna, & childn. & nurse went to Boston on 7th. Day arrivg yester morn made no stops in New Y— Geo. & Pattie's letters just brot. in very glad to get them and to hear that Ellen is in New York—no time to say more

ALS PSCHi-Mott

1. MML and George Lord had moved in October 1863 to Brooklyn, where George went into the wool business with Walter Brown (LCM to MCW, 18 September 1863, Mott Manuscripts, PSCHi).

2. Margaret Bancroft (1807–84) was the sister of Martha Bancroft Mellor (c. 1813–80), Thomas Mellor's wife. George Mellor is listed as a veterinary surgeon, Alfred Mellor as a manufacturing chemist (Philadelphia City Directory, 1865, 1866).

3. Speaking at the Cooper Institute in New York City on 22 December 1863, Phillips had criticized the president's recent offer of conditions by which the South could return to the Union. Phillips had attacked Lincoln's plan of Reconstruction for giving too much power to Southerners and had suggested that he would not support the president in the election of 1864 (*Liberator*, 1 January 1864, 2–3).

4. Edward Everett Hale (1822–1909), a Unitarian minister, had published the short story "A Man without a Country" in 1863. In *Mr. Butler's Statement* (Philadelphia: J. C. Clark, 1850), Pierce Butler blamed the failure of his marriage to Fanny Kemble on her belief that marriage should be an equal partnership (J. C. Furnas, *Fanny Kemble: Leading Lady of the Nineteenth-Century Stage* [New York: Dial Press, 1982], 346–47).

5. Robert J. Parvin (1823–68). Louis Wagner (b. 1838) of the Eighth U.S. Colored Regiment at Camp William Penn had spoken at the Third Decade Meeting of the AASS, held in Philadelphia on 4–5 December 1863 (*Liberator*, 25 December 1863, 205, 15 January 1864, 11; for LCM's speech at the AASS meeting, see *Sermons,* 263–66). Joseph B. Kiddoo (1840–80), born in Pennsylvania, would become the colonel of the Twenty-second U.S. Colored Troops in June 1864.

6. William Barnard (c. 1800–1864) was a Marlborough (Chester County) Hicksite Quaker and an abolitionist (*NASS*, 30 January 1864, 3).

7. JM served on the board of directors of the Barclay Coal Company (LCM to George Lord, 8 August 1864, Mott Manuscripts, PSCHi).

8. The German physician Constantin Hering (1800–1880) founded a school for homeopathic medicine in Philadelphia.

9. Samuel R. Shipley (1828–1908) was a Philadelphia financier. The Friends' Association for the Aid and Elevation of the Freedman had been founded on 8 January (*Friends' Intelligencer,* 16 January 1864, 712).

10. Abraham Barker was a Philadelphia Hicksite. Mark 13:37.

11. George W. Julian had married Laura Giddings, the daughter of Joshua Giddings, on 31 December 1863 (*NASS,* 23 January 1864, 3). Laura Stratton had married Col. Fitzhugh Birney (d. 1864), the son of James G. Birney, on 25 December 1863. LCM had written MCW about the wedding, the first she had attended in a church: "They made an imposing appear[anc]e. with all the awful regimentals— Furness acted well his part—the whole beautiful—his prayer touchg—especially the close, for Fitz" (25 December 1863, Mott Manuscripts, PSCHi).

12. Luke 14:13; 2 Cor. 6:7.

13. Willie Wright and Lt. W. H. Johnson, members of the First New York Battery, had both been wounded at Gettysburg (*War of the Rebellion: A Compilation of the Official Records of the Union and Confederate Armies* [Washington, D.C.: 1880–1901], series 1, 27:240; LCM to MCW, 26 July 1863, and LCM to Mary Hussey Earle, 1 August 1863, both in Mott Manuscripts, PSCHi). James Parton (1822–91) had published *General Butler in New Orleans* (New York: Mason Brothers) earlier in the year. Maj. Gen. Benjamin Butler (1818–93) was popular early in the war among abolitionists for having declared fugitive slaves "contraband of war" at Fortress Monroe, Virginia, thereby effectively freeing them.

14. Frances Dana Gage was lecturing throughout the northern states on the condition of the freedpeople of the Sea Islands, which she had experienced first hand as a missionary (*NASS,* 2 January 1864, 2, 30 January 1864, 2). Anna E. Dickinson had lectured on behalf of freedpeople in the House of Representatives on 16 January to an audience that included the president and Mary Todd Lincoln; newspapers called it a "splendid personal triumph" (*Liberator,* 29 January 1864, 20).

## To Martha Mott Lord

RoadSide 2 Mo. 5th. 64—

My precious Ones—

I will hurry off a few lines, by Edwd., or you will not hear of our home-comg. before next week— Nothing special on the road—I slept from Newark to Brunswk. The lunch was just eno' & tasted good—sorry we didn't take an Aubn. apple.

We reached Edwd. H's ¼ after 2—no rather earlier than that—found Maria [*Davis*] in—a pleast. surprise—she sd., on purpose to meet us—but also to go to Eddington that aftern.—& stay the night— Edwd. D. dined at Edwd. H's also—

We had no Ex. Com. Mg—so that we cd. sit an hour together after dinner— talked you over— nothg. special from Roadside—Nor any City news—save that Rachel Jackson's father—Isaac Tyson died in Balt[imor]e. & was buried that day— We made no calls— Anna [*Hopper*] took tea with us, at uncle Benjn.

[*Yarnall*]'s, all well there—& glad to hear all we cd. say of you— Reba. sd. she only meant if you *were* going to leave that Cobbett house, she cd. be resigned, because of neighbors—but if *not,* it was very nice there— So we all thought— They seemed in haste for Agnes' [*Harrison*] return— Margt. [*Yarnall*] has had another poor turn—she is better agn.— We tried to induce the girls to go with us to our Freedmans Mg.—but it was "*nogo*"— Debby Kimber was going in there—

Our Mg. was wonderfully interestg. Saml. Shipley gave us an exciting accot. of the suffergs in the Missippi Valley & at the same time, of the contentmt. of the poor Slaves in their escape from *worse* bondage— Hanna Haydock begged him to go to New York to their next Mg. on 4th. day next I think father says 2nd. day— *Do go.* He half agreed to—I think he will— A Methodist Bishop Simpson[1] who had been there Vicksburg then addressed the Mg—and a missioneary school-teacher from there— The house was full down stairs & many in the gallery—among whom Edwd. H. & Abby Gibbons who arrived from Washn. at night after we left Edwds.— They both spoke from up there Abby gave some interestg details— Edwd. praised the Bishop & the Mg— Dr. Joseph Parrish[2] admired the Catholicity & made a neat speech on the breakg. thro' sectarian barriers— So did Abm. Barker—very well too on the import[anc]e. of working Debh. Wharton addressed the Mg. very feelingly—& altogether the audience seemed to think the windows of Heaven opened— Such a shower of blessings Poor things! the first time that many of them had come out of their Sectarian enclosure Some Orthodox Frds. there—

Our Report shewed Zeal—over $2000 raised— I had a letter from Nathl. Barney to read, enclosg. a check for $50 wh. he hoped would reach us by that eveg— He had seen the advertisemt in the Frds. Intelligencer—[3] Yr. father did his part in givg. interest to the Mg—

Nathl. expected to leave Nant., with Elisa [*Barney*] tomorw.— They will be in Brooklyn probably on 1st. day— I will enclose a letter in this—not remember their number or box— Geo. [*Lord*] will oblige me by sending it *tomorrow* to Alanson Swains store.

AL PSCHi-Mott

1. Matthew Simpson (1811–84) was active in the Christian Commission, an organization that distributed Bibles and other aid to soldiers, and later became president of the American Freedmen's and Union Commission (*American Freedman,* April 1866).

2. Dr. Joseph Parrish (1818–91) is probably the son of Dr. Joseph Parrish and Susanna Cox Parrish (*The Parrish Family,* comp. Susanna Parrish Wharton [Philadelphia: George H. Buchanan, 1925], 227).

3. The monthly meeting of the Friends' Association for the Aid and Elevation of the Freedman had been held on 3 February. The announcement had called for "the attendance and co-operation of those interested in the cause of the Freedmen" (*Friends' Intelligencer,* 30 January 1864, 744).

# To William Lloyd Garrison Jr.

RoadSide 3 mo. 4th. 1864—

My dear Wm. L. Garrison Jr.

Thy letter of 24th. Ult. reached us, on our return home, after a few days' absence— Engagements in the City since have delayed the acknowledgment— It is said however that, "silence gives consent"—so thou wilt not construe ours as adverse to thine and Ellen [*Wright*]'s union of hearts— Nor were we altogether unprepared for the announcement, even tho' not looked for from thy pen—

The jokes & predictions of your young friends might not have aroused our suspicions— Neither your correspondence—so common is it in this day, for such interchange to take place, and "Nothing to come of it"—but Sarah McKim's prescience in the heart's affections, led us to watch coming events— We feel gratified by the importance attached to *our* "benediction"—

Rest assured of our heart-felt God-speed,—which I have already sent forth indirectly to our dear Ellen— She is beloved in our family as a daughter and a sister— Her good sense and sprightly wit have interested and amused us—nor has she been wanting in adherence to principle.

Her co-operation with her Mother in reformatory measures has given weight to her character—preserving her from the follies of fashionable life— — And now we can rejoice that, in this most important step she finds a congenial spirit—for we cannot regard her cherished friend as a stranger— — Your family has long seemed almost interwoven with ours, so closely allied in the Slave's cause, as well as in liberal Christianity.

As to "a home adorned with wealth", let me say—*our* early married life was marked with poverty, and many anxieties, still we had our share of enjoyment— and never a cloud overshadowed us in the conjugal relation—

Shall we then send forth our blessing, in the language of the Patriarch:?— "The God, which fed me all my life long, unto this day,—bless the lads"—[1]

very affectionately
Lucretia Mott—

The quotation above is *mis*-printed in the Papers, in the report of my little speech at our late Decade Mg—'bless the *land*'— Should it be issued in pamphlet form, please have it corrected[2]—and oblige &c

L. M—

ALS MNS

1. LCM is adapting Gen. 48:15–16: "The God which fed me all my life long unto this day, The Angel which redeemed me from all evil, bless the lads."

2. The AASS had celebrated its third decade at a meeting held on 3–4 December 1863 in Philadelphia. On that occasion, LCM had stated: "I feel that we older ones may need retire, and thank God that he who has blessed us all our lives long is now blessing the

lads; for there is surely no greater joy than to see these children walking in the anti-slavery path." The *Liberator* had quoted her as stating "blessing the land" (*Sermons*, 263; *Liberator*, 15 January 1864, 10).

## To Marianna Pelham Mott and Martha Coffin Wright

[*Roadside*]
4th. day morng. 7th—[*September 1864*]

[*Continuation of a letter begun 6 September*]

I have risen early to add a word— The Extensn. table is so crowded in behind bureaus, that Thos. [*Mott*] cant well get it out till you begin to move the bulky things into the new house when his aunt-Mother will be welcome to it— but when this rain dries off as it will now soon such a glorious morng., he will send a bbl. sweet potats.— Would that peaches wd. bear transportg— Great beauties $1.—& the last 80c a basket— I saw fine ones for 90 60c not $ I entirely forget what I arose early to write—being in my dotage— I have Eliza [*Osborne*]'s comb & Fanny C's weddg. dress to take and a pr. Candlesticks from Agnes [*Harrison*] to Ellen—[1] she thinks she cant go—but who knows but that at the last min. like Pattie [*Lord*] & me she may "sprunt up" & go— Thos. has hunted up those filagree furbelos—white trash for me to take— Ill enquire for wool to-day—tis very dear— I go in @ 8 oclk in the Cars—stay all day & night by reason of Freedman's Mgs. & Fem. A. S. Society— Mary Grew has come home & we shall now decide I reckon to give up our Anti S. Office—for tis only an expense since Miller [*McKim*] left us—& the work is done now by his Associates I dont wonder that Martha feels as she does about politics & the times. It wd. have done her good to hear Robt. Purvis talk of the injustice to the colored soldier, & other short-comings— He regrets the Lib. & Standard's silence where they ought to blame—but I dont like Conway's impudence nor he either I believe—[2]

Anna [*Hopper*] & self talk of drivg. up to Eddingn. 6th. day— Poor Elizh. wrote such a sad note the Annivy of dear Harry's death[3] I hope Fanny is well— Will she come on with the others or stay till I return I dont know Pattie's stay— The bride & groom must time their visit here, for us to enjoy it I shall not stay more than a week or 10 days at Aubn.— Pattie will not like to be from home longer— Jas. will be alone here too—for Mari[a]. [*Mott*] will want to be going into town to see about their boardg. place—

I know I shall think of somethg. I ought to have written— I am going to call on Richd. White today & hear from Mary Earle

affecy.   L.M

ALS PSCHi-Mott

Roadside, LCM and JM's house outside Philadelphia. *In the foreground, left to right:* A granddaughter, LCM, and JM. (Courtesy of the Friends Historical Library of Swarthmore College)

1. Ellen Wright was to marry Wiliam Lloyd Garrison Jr. on 14 September 1864 in Auburn, in a ceremony performed by Rev. Samuel J. May (*Liberator,* 23 September 1864, 155).

2. On 1 August 1864, the War Department had issued an order that only black soldiers who were freed on or before 19 April 1861 were to receive back pay. The *Liberator* saw this order as an example of the "combined injustice and impolicy" toward African American soldiers (*Liberator,* 12 August 1864, 131, 19 August 1864, 135). But some African Americans clearly felt that abolitionists were not adequately addressing the ill treatment of blacks. In a letter from England, Moncure D. Conway had described what he saw as an insult by the Rev. John Sella Martin, who accused abolitionists of not treating his fellow blacks as equals. LCM may have thought Conway's response impudent when he wrote: "It is my duty to say, that the last time I saw Mr. Martin, until I met him here to-night, he was seated at an Anti-Slavery meeting comfortably between Garrison and Phillips, and did not seem to have any shoe pinching him at all" (*Liberator,* 26 August 1864, 139).

3. Henry Cavender had died in September 1863 at age fourteen.

## To Martha Coffin Wright

Brooklyn [*New York*] 9 mo. 25th. 64—

My dear Sister

Before writg. home, I will begin this scrap to thee, thankg. thee & thine for all your kindly & generous care of us— Up to the last, Munson [*Osborne*] came rushg. into the cars, with his handsful of peaches, & heart-full of good tidings of Eliza— We were so glad to know, before we left, that she was doing well— May this fine, bracg. air soon restore her to her added matronly duties! David & son united found us good seats, & Mr. Hastings,[1] had a pleast. word for us now & then on the journey— Our fellow travellers in the Car next to us, were conspicuous at St. Johnsville,— While "the father" was takg. his dinner after buyg. some pears for them, they promenading outside—before our window, as it might happen  Our lunch was more than suffct. for us— We fared sumptuously on that & the abundt. fruit—sharg. the latter with Mr. Hastgs.— Mr. Sedgwick came to the cars with him at Syrac[us]e. & spoke to us— Arrivg. at Albany, we called at Phebe Jones' who had gone that morng. to Troy— Her daughr. welcomed us—invited us to the parlor—her Mother wd. soon be home—but we preferd. to walk 3 blocks further up street, to Lydia Mott's  A fine house, & some boarders in the parlor— Jane soon appeared—feeble, but agreeable, Lydia out shoppg.— — Garrison stopped there the night he left Aburn & gave up his visit to Ghent—the cars not connectg.— Rev. Mr. Ames & others there in the eveg. & much talk—[2] We left our cousin invalid some of our luscious fruit, & departed— She begged us to stay to tea—but we had shopping to do— Pattie [*Lord*] bot. an India rubber drinkg. cup for Nellie's birthday present—& a baby for baby Lord. She then took me to sd. Restaurant, for a cup of Coffee  I took chocolate, & both, our own bread & butter—thanks to you— Went to the boat—Stateroom all right—aft near the outer deck thanks to Munson—where we sat & soon espied Phebe Jones & Lydia Mott, who followed us "quick-step"—sat an hour with us—talkg. most of the time on the all-too political bearg. of the Standd. & Libr. & the injustice to Wendell P. in Garrison's talk with Ames, who agreed with all he sd.— They fear personal estrangemt. will follow—[3] I hope not—for the Election will soon be over— They felt as I did that F. Douglass letter shd. not receive more favor in our Papers— They were glad to hear from S. B. Anthony, & hoped she wdn't go to Texas— Aaron Powell Lydia thot. about right on the political questn.[4]— — They seemed to know all abt. the weddg.—& enquired with much interest after Ellen—as also after thee— Lydia regrets the givg. up of the Anti S. Office in Albany when they did—for it was never more needed than then—

We sat outside till the train arrived 8½— It was nearer 10 before we were fairly off  Danl. Neall & son & Edwd. Wright agn. on board—[5] They had had too much rain at the Adirondcks. for their enjoyt.— We heard thro' Mr. Hastgs.

that Henry Davis & his compy. had returned— Agn. we shared our goodies—
& still had eno' & more than eno' for breakfast for we didn't arrive till after 9—
Danl. sd. he went down to supper, hopg. to have a good hot meal, but it was
cold—not even *tepid*—so he wd.n't venture in the morng— So the tongue &.c
relished—& if not 7 baskts. full—there were sandwiches to bring home, ye generous bestowers!— A workwoman here with childn. at home, I guess took them
away— We gave our checks to the baggageman & took car to South ferry, in a
drizzle—reached home not wet— Baby Lord & Ellen watchg. for us— Geo
had waited till near 9—& after being at the store awhile, he came over & brot.
letters from home— We found also letters here from Walter & Anna B—wh.
you shall have soon—Walter better—& one from Maria M. D.—written in Geo's
room at the store on 6th. day—& never comg. over here at all—when she might
as well have let Edwd. go on with out her—& stayed the night here, & met us
yesterdy. Wd.n't it have been pleast.? I'll send you her letter, as you'll like to read
her impressns. of the arrival of bride & groom—so entertaing. to us, but old
news of course to you— Mind you send us Ellen's letters— We will be careful of them— This may go to Anna D. H. if worth sendg.— — I wd.n't "stir
up strife" by sendg. it into yon "boardg. school"— Do as you like— Geo. came
home agn. to early tea, & was happy as other husbds. to have his wife agn., who
soon found busins. eno'— Anne not strong yet—every where clean & nice
here— The Lord fam[il]y. in as usual—ever kind— Chs. has just called for
Geo. & Baby to drive to the Park— I have played sick & not been to Meetg—

AL PSCHi-Mott

1. Eliza Osborne's daughter Helen Osborne had been born on 22 September. "Mr.
Hastings" is possibly Hugh J. Hastings (1820–83), an Albany, New York, journalist.

2. "Mr. Sedgwick" is possibly Charles Baldwin Sedgwick (1815–83), a Syracuse, New
York, lawyer elected to Congress (Rep.) in 1859. Phebe Jones's daughter was Margaret
Jones (c. 1835–70). "Jane" was Lydia Mott's sister, Jane Mott (1796–?) (Gordon, 1:517, 557).
Charles Gordon Ames (1828–1912) of Illinois was a wartime lecturer supporting the
Union and abolition (*WLG*, 5:105–6).

3. The *NASS* and the *Liberator* were strong supporters of Lincoln in the 1864 election.
For example, the *Liberator* had rebuked Lincoln's critics: "We regret to see, on the part
of some of whom better things were to be expected, in their opposition to President
Lincoln, manifestly a foregone conclusion of mind to award him no credit for the good
he has done, or the progress he has made in the right direction." Other abolitionists,
such as Wendell Phillips and Edward M. Davis, had criticized Lincoln for not going far
enough in abolishing slavery. Davis and others had given their support to Frémont in
the 1864 election and complained that the *NASS* and the *Liberator* were too partisan
(*Liberator*, 12 August 1864, 130; *NASS*, 6 August 1864, 2).

4. In a letter dated 17 September, Douglass had stated that although he had criticized
Lincoln and hoped that a candidate with stronger antislavery views would be nominated, he now fully supported him: "Every man who wishes well to the slave and to the
country should at once rally with all the warmth and earnestness of his nature to the
support of Abraham Lincoln and Andrew Johnson" (*Liberator*, 16 September 1864, 151,
23 September 1864, 155). Anthony, who had attended Ellen Wright's wedding, planned
to visit her brother in Kansas in early 1865 (LCM to Philadelphia Family, 14 September

1864, Mott Manuscripts, PSCHi; Gordon, 1:534). Aaron Powell's recent statements revealed that he sympathized with Lincoln's critics: "Mr. Lincoln would not have the negro a slave, but he does not want him for a neighbor or a citizen, and does not believe the two races can dwell harmoniously and prosperously together" (*NASS*, 3 September 1864, 2).

5. Daniel Neall's son was Frank Lesley Neall (b. 1844). Edward Needles Wright was a Philadelphia Hicksite.

## To Martha Coffin Wright and Eliza Wright Osborne

Roadside 10 Mo. 31st. 64—
Cloudy washg. day—
the clothes out—

My dear sister—

You ought to have had these letters no. 7, & 8—last week— When read please send them back to Pattie [*Lord*] for safe keepg., with some comments—always Anna [*Hopper*]'s due, for her care in writg., & noticg. ours— Let us know also if all Ellen's & Frank [*Wright*]'s have been returned to you, save the last, with some from Wm. [*Garrison Jr.*]—so good—we are greatly obliged for all—David need have no fears that we shall make a bad use of any of these favors—nor are they made public— Richd. H. wrote how he handled Geo. Thompn. & Garrison without gloves for their severe talk agt. Phillips, at Mrs. Dall's party—and *that*, thro' Lucy M'K. probably, got back to Boston, & Garrison didn't like it—but Anna D. H. sd. he ought not to complain, for their talk was loud—or outspoken—not confidantl. Pardon me, dear, unoffendg. Eliza, for callg. thee names, and attributg. to thee, the veto on our havg. sd. letters to read— On lookg. over thy Mother's agn., I see it is plain eno'—as it was to the others at 1st. but somehow I mistook it— The last from Aubn. is to Mari[a]. [*Mott*], & she will doubtless ans. it, havg., as her, Mother says, leisure— I sent it to Pattie today by Wendl. G. who with Lucy, took tea here last eveg.—[1] Thos., Mari[a]. & Emily [*Mott*] were out but went in before tea, as did Edwd. & Anna H. who dined here on roast pig—Edwd.'s Annual present—& an excelt. one it was, & well cooked—We are expectg. our br. Lindley M. M[oore]. this eveg.—for how long a visit we know not— He has attended their Yearly in Balt[imor]e.—was at Edwd. H's on 7th. day, & out at Havrefd. School yestery.— Maria H. has compy. too—a Miss Briggs from Sheffd. School, another is comg. next week—Abby Gibs. is there now too— She is not going to continue at Beverly long— They have made no arranget. yet with Rosalie, for the future—or for Susan H.— Edwd. has the care of Elizh., & that's his share— That little Craig Ritchie is soon to be married! Carrie Gibbons' cards have just come in—[2] Eliza G's talk of a *farm* has resulted in her buyg. a strip of land of Miller [*McKim*], adj[oinin]g. her cottage, where she & her little son have commenced husbandry, & she's consultg. agricul[tur]e. books— She was inconsolable for awhile after Carrie left her—

Johnsons Dic[tionar]y. has neither Agric-*ist* nor Horlet *ist* or *al*ist either—
Many words in common use now are not found there— Walker has not either— Webster has it, without *al* and Worcester decidedly in pref[erenc]e., &
strange that he admits the *al* at all—see Farmer— he ^Worcester^ uses the
word right there— — I agree with thee that there is only a shade of diff. in the
Cathc & Episl. promises, & in other things too— Isaac T. [*Hopper*] goes to an
Episcopal School, where Thos. Y's sons go— They have church service (as I'm
here) & when *Jesus* is named, they have to bow their heads—& the boys try to
strike the railg. of the form before them—& afterwd. boast how many times they
struck— This was told here last eveg— Wendl. [*Garrison*] added—"thus turng.
reverence into railg." Anna D. H. wd.n't laugh, as she is tryg. to break him of
imitatg. his father in punning— *We* thot. it good, & *did* laugh— Wendl. made
himself very agreeable last eveg— We enjoy their visits— Miller is in Washn.
Jas. M. is in Balte. attendg. the Yearly Mg. after wh. he & Helen Longsth. are going
to Washn. to inspect the Camps, & Hospitals & schools for Freedmen— Our
Iowa Frd. Bennet Walters & Jos. & Ruth Dugde. are also at that Yearly—new
times for Jose— We are to have a visit on their return— Anna Hall¹. is comg.
to tea this aftern. with Sam. Haydk.—³ They are comg. out to Sarah Fisher's 1st.
to call on Fredk. Eustis & daughrs.— A. D. Hall¹. is to drive down for them, &
I with her, to call on them, as they were here last week when we were in Town—
There is somethg. all the time— Mother Jones visited us on 6th. day— We
were at the funeral of Alfred Love's sister, but back in time for dinner—⁴

Thy several visits to Eliza always seem pleast.—and so glad are we, that she
is comg. out of her room in such good ease—with a pleast. fire too in their parlor— I have held her up, as a wonder, in the "hour of her sorrow" to have a
dinner party, & send forth her nice cake for our dessert—how good that coffee
was, & yours too, to us—accustomed to a mixture—tho' we had it pure too,
when the Hall¹. party & Reuben Tomlinson were here,⁵ & Henry & Pattie
[*Davis*]—&.c no, we didn't see Eliza's preserve closet— Our fam[il]y. were all
bidden to Mellors last week, & a great supper they had— Morris D's famy.
too— Jas. & self didn't go—havg. so lately visited them with Bennet Walters—
While writg., 2 Colored men have come in from the camp, for dinner, & to complain that the wife of one is allowed to come out & sell articles, & misbehave,
&.c, wantg. advice, wh. I cd.n't give them— They are now eatg—another came
this morng—for money to help buy the flag for the processn. tomorw.—in
honor of the Maryld. Emancipatn.— We want to hear yr. opinion of Wendl.
P's speech & Garrison's review—severe of course like himself— Phillips too
is like *him*self—severe on Lincoln— I thot. he needn't have made so much of
that Argulla's Case, as he was a base slave trader⁶ only Edwd. says that was not
proved— I shall be glad when the Electn. is over— Chase's speech was good—
but it is tiresome to see so much that amots. to so little—⁷ Maryld. emancipatn.
is indeed glorious— I am sorry thy Contraband shd. be sick— sorry too that
you cd.n't call on Anna E. Dickn.— Why was an *Ante* room chosen?— He

looked anythg. but happy, when we met—*butt*! in the baggage room at Aubn.—
& didn't even nod. Benjn. [*Yarnall*]'s famy. are all nicely moved in, & Eliza is
busy on her carpets— Ellis & Margt. talk go in there this winter while the front
of their house is taken down for the additn.— They will have the 3rd. story—
Sarah & Reba. come down to the 2nd. & have another bed there for Mary when
she visits them— Margt. has had dizzy spells of late, & last week they set out
for a little journey— At Bethlehem Ellis wrote that she was no better & they
wd. come home 7th. day—so Sarah Y. drove over here with their man & up to
York Road for them— they ne'er came, & today their man came agn. with a
note from Mary—that Ellis had written agn. that Margt. had had an attack like
that last winter when Agnes [*Harrison*] was in New Y—& agn. ordered the carriage to York Road for them— Still later he teleghd. for Agnes to go up to Bethlehem next train Margt. had fever—so she went—& agn. the man has come
back without them— he is to go agn. tomorw. or today I might say—for it is
now 3rd. day morng.

1st of 11 Mo—

I wrote as long as I cd. yestery— We made our calls, but our compy. didn't
come out only Henry & Pattie to tea— Have I written that Fanny Cavr. is not
so well, & that she is comg. this week to the Water Cure where Mariᵃ. goes—

[*P.S.*] Wm. Yarnall has to move his store— He was robbed the other day—
over $100 taken from his drawer by a man who asked to look at his Counterft.
detector & he also had his pocket picked of 14 dollars

AL PSCHi-Mott

1. Wendell Phillips Garrison (1840–1907), the son of William Lloyd Garrison, was a
New York City correspondent for the *Liberator*. His engagement to Lucy McKim had been
announced in June 1864 (*WLG*, 5:197, 216).

2. Abby Gibbons was in charge of nursing Civil War soldiers at an army hospital in
Beverly, New Jersey. Edward Hopper's brother John Hopper had recently died, and LCM
is probably referring to the necessity of taking care of his wife, Rosa, and their family.
Elizabeth Hopper (1803–72) was John's sister, and "Susan H." was probably Susanna
Hopper (1817–1908), another sister. "Carrie Gibbons" was probably Caroline Hull Gib-
bons (b. 1840), who had recently married George Q. White (Margaret Hope Bacon, *Abby
Hopper Gibbons: Prison Reformer and Social Activist* [Albany, N.Y.: SUNY Press, 2000],
64, 124; *NASS*, 30 July 1864, 2; *Liberator*, 16 September 1864, 152; LCM to Anna Temple
Brown, 7 August 1864, Mott Manuscripts, PSCHi; LCM to MCW, 26 August 1872, MNS;
Gibbons Papers, PSCHi).

3. Helen Longstreth was a Philadelphia Hicksite Quaker and the secretary of the Female Association of Philadelphia for the Relief of the Sick and Infirm Poor with Clothing (Bacon, 189; *Friends' Intelligencer*, 16 January 1864, 713). Bennet Walters was a Quaker minister (LCM to MCW, 14 October 1964, Mott Manuscripts, PSCHi). Samuel
Haydock (1844–70), a New York City Hicksite, was the son of Hannah W. Haydock.

4. Alfred Love (1830–1913) was a Philadelphia conscientious objector and a wool merchant.

5. In a 14 October letter to MCW, LCM had written of her visit from Tomlinson: "Reuben Tomlinson is here from Port Royal, & is to give an accot. of their progress— What
a shame for the Govt. to let those plantatns. go into speculators' hands—thousands of

acres wh. shd. have been divided into 20 acre lots, wh. the freedmen longed to buy, and were able to pay for, with a little help— Rebn. called here yestery. & interested us an hour or 2 & prevented my writg. He thinks the ardent frds. of the Slave have erred in their estimate of the freedmen, & in holdg. them up to the public as free from the vices inseparable from their abject condition. Miller M'K. among the rest" (Mott Manuscripts, PSCHi).

6. In the summer of 1864, Maryland had held a constitutional convention, and the state's new constitution, ratified on 1 November, ended slavery (Barbara Jeanne Fields, *Slavery and Freedom on the Middle Ground: Maryland during the Nineteenth Century* [New Haven, Conn.: Yale University Press, 1985], 129–30). Phillips's speech, delivered in Boston on 20 October, had criticized Lincoln's position on slavery and the abolitionists who supported him: "I know and regret that some even of those who have stood with me on a disunion platform for twenty years submit, and support Mr. Lincoln as 'the less of two evils.' When, till now, did the anti-slavery cause have such scales to weigh moral evils?" Phillips also had accused Lincoln of acting as a despot in his arrest and deportation of José Arguelles, a Cuban slave trader. Garrison had condemned Phillips's speech: "We cannot allow it to pass with out expressing our regret to perceive what seems to us a set purpose—*prima facie*—to represent Mr. Lincoln in the worst possible light, to attribute to him the worst possible motives, to hold him up as an imbecile and a despot, and to damage his chance of re-election to the utmost extent" (*Liberator,* 28 October 1864, 174–75).

7. Salmon P. Chase (1808–73) was a former Republican governor of Ohio, a U.S. senator, and the secretary of the treasury under Lincoln. In his speech delivered in Covington, Kentucky, on 14 October he supported Lincoln and his policies (*NASS*, 29 October 1864, 1).

## To Martha Coffin Wright, Maria Mott Davis, and Anna Temple Brown

Roadside 1 mo. 17th. 65—

My dear Sister, daughr. Maria, niece Anna B., & others in general—

This is the 6th. day of Maria's absence, and I have not had energy to take the pen— Several letters too, to acknowledge all wh. were thankfully recd.— We hope Edwd. [*Davis*] will bring out one from Maria this aftn., sayg. she's safe— It is an awful miss to have her gone, even tho' Pattie [*Lord*] is still with us, & Anna H. has passed a day & night twice here— Elizh. [*Cavender*] may come tomorw. for a day or so—when Anna H. ½ promises to come agn. & bring Maria.— — Thos. [*Mott*] & Edwd. were out on 1st. day to tea—findg. Miller & Sarah M'K. who had dined here— We sent over for them & Wm. L. Garrison, supposg, as he was advertised to lecture for the colored Socy. on 2nd. day eveg. yestery., that he wd. come with Wendell & Lucy on 7th. day—but ill health prevented— So we hadn't his compy—nor yet Geo. Thompsons, who lectured last eveg. in Garrison's place—[1] Dr. & Rachel W. Moore called in the aftern., & amused our compy., with her talk— She does so much for the Freedmen that we ought to bear with her peculiarities— She has knit over 200 prs. stockgs

for them, & has large circles meetg at their house, makg. socks & clothg. generally, to send where most needed— Anna H. is fairly enlisted too with Margt.
Griscom, & devotes days to the cutting out & packing, &.c— They hire cutters
by wholesale— Maria H. goes twice a week to the Summit Hospital Darby Road,
to help teach the soldiers Colored who learn with avidity—

With all the aforesd. compy., I might have subjects to interest you withal, but
there doesn't seem to be much. Miller & I compared Wendl. P. & Garrison a little— Jas thinkg. it no use, & takg. no part—slippg. off & takg. a nap— Edwd.
D. too purposely not enterg. into the discussn.— — Thos. Cavr. & Elizh. had a
share of our feeling & talk— — A note from Elizh. sd. the seizure of their stock,
&.c. was Village talk, & dear Fanny was feelg. very bad—so as to affect her back
agn— Jas. & Pattie drove up there yestery., found Elizh. as usual— Charlie [*Cavender*] in Town with his father who hadn't been at home for 2 or 3 nights—
Charlie went to Edwd. H's— Their water back was repaired, but they were out
of wood—not even kindling, tho' plenty on the place— One man had strained
himself & was confined to the kitchen with a dreadful swellg. & abscess—attended
by the Dr., who also found proud flesh in Father Cavr.'s knee— Aunt Nelly still
with them— The hearg. before the Judge is today—we wait the result—[2] The
drive home yestery. was very cold—and Jas. stood outside awhile on his return,
with the colored men who had come from Frankfd. to perform that interestg.
operation in our back *well*—the odor of wh. today is diff. from Anna Brown's
Paris perfume— The wind is East however, & a snow storm to boot, so I guess
we can bear it—but when Jas. came in he trembled & shook so, that we soon
perceived he had a severe chill, wh. hot ex[tract]. of ginger wd.n't drive away  He
retired early with fever comg. on—wh. lasted till morng—& now he sits here with
wrapper on—tho better, and missing him just now, there he was, on the piazza,
sweepg. off the snow— — He has had a bad cold for a week past— Pattie found
Martha Mellor's bottle of Elderby Wine—presented some time ago, & made him
a nice tumbler full of hot drink— She is invaluable in Maria's place, to say nothg.
of her good company—but we must part on 5th. day— She is needed at home
her Anne's br. is dying or dead, & she must of course be at the wake, wh. leaves
poor Ellen alone— Geo. [*Lord*] took Nellie home on 1st. day eveg.— The dear
child felt bad to leave her Mother & Sister here, tho she knew it was time she was
in school agn.— These visits from Geo. have been very pleast. He brot. Anna's
No. 13 letter, wh. Edwd. begged to send 1st. to Maria, who is to return it speedily— Nos. 10, 11, & 12 are out on the scout somewhere— It is time they were
collected in— Remember it is not my care now, to send them hither & yon—
and they move slowly— What uninterrupted enjoyt. those travellers are havg.![3]
We were sorry their young companion had to be sent home, on accot. of his
eyes— — We have a little diff. of opinion at times—Mari[a]. not agreeing with
me, that the replies to ours, form so large a part of the value of the letters— I
hope Anna will continue her good practice— It reminds you so nicely of the
contents of our letters—& past events— Not that I wd. lessen the Frenchy part

wh is Maria's & Mari[a].'s delight, & wh. indeed we all like to have—also Walter's artistic creations—& Harry's & Minnie's doings— All interest us— And such neat plain pages too Walter signified that they might return home, in the Spring— That will be delightful if their visit shall be out then—wh. we doubt— ^Pattie says I mistake—only Walter talks so—^ Mari[a]. says there is not the least chance of their joing. them—nor do we see how they cd. leave their new house in its prest. & prospective stage—[4] The plasterers not yet alighted from the parlor ceilg.— So many things to attend to— Thos. Dale's successor Jas. & wife do very well— She keeps us in excellt. butter— It is growg. dark—

[*Letter continues dated 20 January*]

ALS PSCHi-Mott

1. William Lloyd Garrison was to have delivered "The Guilt, Punishment, and Redemption of Our Country," sponsored by the Social, Civil, and Statistical Association of the Colored People of Pennsylvania, at Concert Hall. Instead, George Thompson delivered a "searching examination into the difficulties that surround our country" (*NASS*, 14 January 1865, 3; *Liberator,* 27 January 1865, 16).

2. John Cavender (d. 1869; LCM to MML, 23 November 1869, MNS) had been a conveyancer (Philadelphia City Directory, 1840). LCM was concerned about the Cavenders' recent difficulties with hired help and the management of their farm at Eddington (LCM to MCW, 23 August 1864, Mott Manuscripts, PSCHi). In January the farm had been assumed by creditors, and later in this letter LCM reports that "Roadside seems the best move for Elizh.—not, as final separatn.—that must depend upon circumstances hereafter—we wait events. Some homes are broken up in one way, & some in another" (see also Bacon, 190).

3. Anna Temple Brown, Walter Brown, and their children Harry and Marion had been traveling in Europe since July 1864 (LCM to George Lord, 8 August 1864, Mott Manuscripts, PSCHi).

4. Marianna Mott and Thomas Mott were building a house (which LCM later referred to as the "Palace") on a portion of Oak Farm, part of the property bought earlier with Edward Davis (Bacon, 140, 194).

## To Mary Robbins Post

Roadside 3 mo. 14th. 65—

My dear Mary

It was kind & thoughtful to give us the intelligence of our dear cousin Henry's departure— We had not seen the notice in the Tribune, altho' we had the Paper in the house, as I found after the reception of thy letter— I generally look at the list of the deaths—but that Paper was laid aside, & had escaped my attention— — Jas. & self were speakg. of his & Kate Mott's visits to so many of his dear aged Relatives & friends, only a few days before—and of coz. Henry especially—[1] Recalling our conversation, we found it was about the time of the funeral—

How many sad, as well as some pleasant memories, such events bring to mind!— It has ever made my heart ache to meet any of my dear Phebe P's. loved family, since her death. Often have I felt her spirit near me, as a guardian Angel as she was indeed during life— Coz. Henry's gentle tender spirit may now be re-united to hers, if indeed they have ever really known a separation— — Poor dear Catharine [*Willis*], not to be able to reach her precious father in such an hour! She has been wonderfully sustained in her former bereavement, and I doubt not she will be in this added trial. Samuel [*Willis*] will feel the loss deeply—so closely united as they have been— My sympathy goes forth to them all, with the love I have ever borne them— How soon he has followed his dear brother!—² We received an acceptable letter from his Mary a short time ago— Please say so to her with our love ∧Jas. also endorses all I have said of coz. Henry's fam[il]y.∧— We have not been able to write much since your pleasant visit to us— That indeed at times has seemed almost a dream— I was so unwell soon after— Jas. too just escaped pneumonia—his lungs & breast so much affected by a severe cold— We are both pretty well again—my recovery as once before, attributable to Dr. Truman's Galvanism—

We were two months without our Maria M. D—her daughr. A. D. Hall¹. needing her at Medford—

A little *Jas. Mott* was added to her family—and her Mother left her last 6th. day & returned to us—stoppg. at Brooklyn & inducing Martha L. to come with her for a short visit—leavg. Fanny Cavr. there as housekeeper— All the sisters met here on 7th. & 1st. day— One or other had been with us most of the time of Maria's absence—

We had hoped to keep Elizh. [*Cavender*] & childn. with us, but home cares & duties called her away twice—and now she has returned to us, so very sick that we are not without great anxiety on her accot.— Dr. Ann Preston has been out to see her & will come agn. this aftern. with Dr. Wilson, who has great experience, & whom she wished in consultatn.— Elizh., for months past, has been far from well, but sufferg. no pain, & keepg. about, we were not aware of her dangerous state—until her extreme paleness alarmed us— She is losing her strength—and yesterday was in bed all day with fever— Today she is down stairs again, lying on the sofa— Knowing your sympathising hearts, I have written thus minutely— We can only hope some remedy may be speedily found—

Martha desires me to say how sorry she was, not to be at home when you called, and hopes you will remember her again, when in Brooklyn— Little Nellie [*Lord*] gave her a particular accot. of the call— — If easy to them as to us, to go up to Westbury they would be glad to accept thy invitation, with thanks for the kindness— We may meet in New Y. again this Spring, but *not* at Yearly Meeting. Calculating by the Almanac, we think the Anti Slavery Annual Mg. will come the week before *our* Yearly— If so Jas. has a wish to attend it, and I should incline to accompy. him, if *we are better at home*. Martha will want me with her in the *6th. Mo*—

I wish we had some pleasant City news for you— Several of our aged frds. of Race St. Mg. have passed away—& among the younger or middle aged Rachel Evans—who is much missed—so useful as she was in the Hospitals— Elliston Perot too was buried last week—you dont know him— Sally R. Parrish's son Isaac—& Joshua Hall[l].'s son Edwd.—both about 20 yrs. old—[3] Richard Cromwell's sad & sufferg. death we heard of—

Joseph & Ruth Dugdale made us a pleasant visit of a day or two last week— Joseph is now in the City visitg. Penitentiaries—Alms houses &.c.—[4] He spoke very well to the 500 pupils at our Mg. last 4th. day— They will probably be at our & *your* Yearly Mg. & have recd. an indirect invitatn. to stop at Saml. Willets'

Thy mention of Wendell P. G. & his lecture we cd. understand—as he not long before lectured in our City—about as thou described him— We could wish for more animation— How good the late Inaugural was—And how determined the colored people are to have their right to vote—so we hope the Lib. & Standd. will see more plainly the shortcomings of Banks— Do you see our Freedman's Reports in the Intelligencer?[5] We have had a visit from Catharine E. Beecher lately— She is boardg. for a few weeks with Dr. Ann Preston & Abigl. Woolman—in order to acquaint herself with Friends religious & domestic educatn. of their childn. She is interested in forming an Institution for the Education of girls & young women in housekeepg. & the proper care of children. She has her plans of house &c. and some 5 or 6 Hartford women are joining her in this enterprise  Dillwyn & Susan Parrish,[6] Rachel Jackson, Debh. Wharton & Sally B. & others have had her at their houses with a party of congenial minds  We quite enjoyed her visit here & I have met her at some other places— I have only left room for love—

L. Mott—

Richard Price is lying ill with another attack of paralysis.

ALS Falconi

1. Henry Willis had died on 5 March. "Kate Mott" is either Catherine A. Mott (1841–1916) or Catherine Emily Mott (1841–78), both cousins of JM.

2. Henry Willis's brother, John Willis, had died on 5 October 1864.

3. The *Friends' Intelligencer* reported the deaths of Philadelphia Monthly Meeting members Rachel S. Evans, Elliston Perot (age forty), Isaac Parrish (age nineteen), and Edward Hallowell (age 20) (4 February 1865, 762, 4 March 1865, 825, 18 March 1865, 25).

4. Joseph Dugdale had recently held meetings of African Americans in Maryland and Washington, D.C., and had an interview with President Lincoln (*NASS*, 14 January 1865, 2).

5. LCM is probably referring to the final conciliatory paragraph of Lincoln's Inaugural Address delivered on 4 March. The *NASS* had simply reported the efforts of Nathaniel P. Banks (1816–94), commander of the Department of the Gulf, to establish a government in Louisiana. The *Liberator* had published a lengthy letter from Banks in which he had explained why, under Lincoln's Reconstruction plan, he could not grant suffrage to freed black men in Louisiana, a letter the newspaper had termed "very lucid and satisfactory" (*NASS*, 21 January 1865, 1; *Liberator*, 24 February 1865, 30, 3 March 1865, 34). A

notice of the activities of the Friends' Association for the Aid and Elevation of the Freedman had appeared in the *Friends' Intelligencer* (11 March 1865, 9).

6. An authority on women's domestic responsibilities, Catharine Beecher (1800–1878)
planned with her sister Harriet Beecher Stowe to reopen the Hartford Female Seminary,
which she had previously established in 1823 (Kathryn Kish Sklar, *Catharine Beecher: A
Study in American Domesticity* [New Haven, Conn.: Yale University Press, 1973], 257, 266).
Susannah M. Parrish (1803–84) was the second wife of Dillwyn Parrish (Parrish Genealogy, PSCHi).


## To Martha Coffin Wright and Anna Temple Brown

*[Roadside]*
2nd. day—10th. *[April 1865]*

*[Continuation of a letter begun 9 April]*

Our Annivy.—No party—Our hearts too full of dear Elizh. *[Cavender]*.
Mari[a]. *[Mott]* has come out in this N.E. storm & I have been over to help plan,
but did nothg. but help *look*— Only 2 or 3 of the chambers are finished so that
we cd. stay in them  They are hangg. the windows, & paintg.— Danl. is to put
up a wood stove in one room for the women to work in tomorw. The fire in the
furnace does not warm the house sufficienty while so many doors & windows
are open— What *taste* to prefer such old lookg. wood work, to nice white paint
wh. only adorns the attics—and such heavy ceilg. ornament, rather than neat
mouldgs. like ours—still havg. sd. so much, I own 'twill be a most convent. &
handsome house, & not so burdensome in size as some I've seen ^I hope she
will not give her hired girls each a room—so large as they are^— Give me wide
windows like our Parlor & a wide sill, rather than the obstructn. of a deep column to admit shutters—none outside you know— Mari[a]. means to have sills
put on yet— She has had a number of convent. alterations made—drawers put
under the permanent wash stands for towels— While we were over there, Robt.
Collyer came out here, & stayed 2 hours—keepg. Maria *[Davis]* from Elizh.'s
room—Pattie *[Lord]* & Fanny *[Cavender]* were with her however, & she slept
part of the time, being obliged to take the 2nd. dose of morphia—the ringg. of
the church bell for the surrender keepg. her awake till 3 o clk.— The news
reached the City @ 10 oclk & word sent out here abt. midnight—Wonderful
excitet.—[1] We knew not the cause till breakfast time, & thot. there must be fire
somewhere—tho' no light to be seen— Thy confession, as to the last Inaugural was highly satisfactory to thy *political* sister, who has felt great interest in all
the daily Reports since the war began— She has the first readg. of the Papers
every morng. while I take them as they come often dependg. on the others readg.
to the old folk— Jas' eyes have almost given out for anythg. but the Editorial
type. He hears well however, and is not lame, or bald, or toothless— Richd.
Price is gradually decling.—his speech very imperfect— His son-in-law—Thos.

Richardson is to be buried this aftern., from Richard's— He died in the West Inds., on board a steamer—leavg. a large property— Jas. had to go in, to the Barclay Mg., & stayed to attend the funeral— Geo. L. & Pattie [*Lord*] leave us today— Little Mary Mott L. is happy to go back to her sister as she was to come— Pattie leaves Elizh. rather brighter than for 2 days past—repeated hemor[rha]g[e]s. leavg. her very weak— She is now talkg. with Mari[a].— She has only sat up to have her bed made since 6th. day last, when attemptg. to walk in frm. the bath-room she fainted quite away—& Maria had to call Anna up, to help her & Fanny lift her in, to her bed— Fanny nearly fainted, poor child! We feel that she cannot survive many more such draughts on her system— She too says she is steadily failing— Pattie felt best satisfied to go, independt. of Eliza O's comg.—& wouldn't miss her neither but from necessity— If we are obliged to call her back while Eliza is there, I hope *she* will come with her— The baby wd.n't trouble Elizh. at all— They cd. have the farthest off room— Elizh. liked to have little M'Kim Dennis taken up into her chamber yestery.— Fred. & Anne [*Dennis*] drove over for the 1st. time yestery., with Miller—a hired carriage— We have but one horse, wh. is kept constantly going to the cars & the store— The runaway one is sold & gone—thanks! This one too is sold—only $275 for both— Thos. says we may have one of his greys— Fred. & Anne seem pleased with their house, wh. they will have possessn. of the 17th. I think— She doubtless has written all about it—& havg. Mary Ann Chase to board with them to boot— Fred. was amused with Edwd. H's talk, abt. a witness in court— He & Thos. M. came out as usual—also Thos. Parrish[2] & Susy Hal. to dine—& Maria H— In the aftern. Willie Wright—Emily Davis & Emmy Mott—to tea— Little May Mott was here 7th. & 1st., to Mary Cavr.'s great delight— We have our new girl, and dont mind the number, with 3 to wait on them—such a clearg. out now— Pattie & baby L. just kissed & gone alas—Mari[a]. our only visitor— Anna H. will come tomorrow. Bel couldn't leave Church & hearg. Mr. Collyer to come out— He came to the late Unitarian Conventn.—wh. you saw an accot. of in the Tribune[3]—a hum bug I guess— Wm. Furness wd. have nothg. to do with it, & preached agt. it, after it closed—or before I forget wh— Miller M'Kim is very full of this new Union Associatn., & the Paper to be called "the Nation"— He & Wendl. P. G. to be Editors—[4] They are collectg. money on a large scale—Wm. B. Mann who never before was called on, gives $1000—[5] Miller wd. like all A. S. & Freedman's Societies to be merged in this—a Reconstructive Union— He sent an appeal to our Frds. Associatn.— I told him it was objected, that Woman was ignored in their organizn., & if really a reconstructn. for the Nation she ought not so to be—and it wd. be rather 'a come down' for our Anti Slavery women & Quaker women to consent to be thus overlooked after sufferg. the A. S. Socy. to "split" in 1840 rather than yield—& after claimg. our right so earnestly in London to a seat in the Conventn.— He was rather taken aback sd. "if there seemed a necessity for women he thot. they wd. be admitted["]—to wh. the impetuous reply was "seemed a necessity!! for one half the Nation to act with you!" & the *larger* ½ too we might say—so many men slain! You ought to have been here— He couldnt ask Jas. with quite so good a grace for $1000— He *did* ask tho' but I guess he will not get anything like so much from him—

Thou dont like marginal writings—but I cant take another sheet as this is to go to Europe mind—& via Medford if worth it. Anna D. Hall[1]. begs us to continue to send them to her—and it is the least I can do in return for hers and Ellen W. G[arrison]'s very racy entertaing sheets— Little Charlie Cavr. came from Eddingn. 7th. day, bringg. a shad just caught at their landing and a variety of good things for his Mother—tellg. her privately that the farm was sold  Thos. has been very poorly since 3rd. day last with carbuncles—confined at home— Anna H. had said before thy letter came that she found herself constantly repeatg. that part of Altamont. "Thos. a Monk wd. be" was very good only the "Devil a Monk was he"[6] wd. apply before any change in the [patient?]— Now I must stop now— All thy accot. of the flood interested us—& the *Oil* Company formed— Willy & Mari[a]. answer thy letters I hope— Here is No 16 from Rome—very interestg  You shall have 17—also from Rome soon— Send it to Medford too—

Lovg. you ever I am sadly thy Sister—dear Anna B's Aunt L—

It is so sad that we can anticipate our noble daughrs. death with any reconciling circumstances or alleviation!—

ALS PSCHi-Mott

1. On 9 April 1865, Confederate Gen. Robert E. Lee had surrendered to Union Gen. Ulysses S. Grant at Appomattox Courthouse in Virginia.

2. Thomas Parrish (1847–99) was a son of Edward Parrish.

3. The National Unitarian Convention had met in New York City on 5–6 April. Collyer had spoken briefly on the "needs of the West" for a "liberal gospel." On the convention's second day, Collyer had stated that he had voted against the National Conference of Unitarian Churches' constitution because he considered it a "creed" (*New York Tribune*, 6 April 1865, 8, 7 April 1865, 5).

4. McKim would become the corresponding secretary of the American Freedmen's Union Commission, which combined the secular freedpeople's aid societies (James M. McPherson, *The Struggle for Equality: Abolitionists and the Negro in the Civil War and Reconstruction* [Princeton, N.J.: Princeton University Press, 1964], 387). The *Nation*, originally intended to serve as a successor to the *Liberator*, would first appear on 6 July with Wendell P. Garrison as its literary editor.

5. William B. Mann (1816–?) was a Republican district attorney in Philadelphia.

6. LCM is adapting Rabelais's *Gargantua and Pantagruel* (book 4, chap. 24): "The devil was sick, the devil a monk wou'd be / The devil was well, and the devil a monk he'd be" (trans. Peter Motteux).

# To Martha Mott Lord

Roadside 5 mo. 2nd. 65—

I told Edwd. [*Davis*] he need not write you today, as I shd. send a letter,—
& here it is 3 oclk. & none begun—so many little things to take our attentn.—
Anna H. came out this morng. & of course you want to sit awhile, & hear &
tell some new thing— Then the last Regiment went off from Camp W. P., &
marched thro' our grounds—with the band, & such hurrahg., & takg. off caps,
& biddg. goodbye! All lookg. so nice, & so happy—as I felt for the poor fellows—in the hope that the war is over—& over in the right way—by the Slaveholders' surrender—

There are few left now, & we hear the camp is to be broken up, or at least
changed to some other purpose— There were never more orderly, unoffending men, than the thousands gathered under Col. Wagner from the first— And
he has always thought so much of them, & treated them well— — Mary Fisher's sons write home often— Geo. was among the 1st. to enter Richmond—
He left his bounty money with his Mother, who placed it under Anna H's. care
but the poor soul has drawn it nearly all out— Her son lately wrote, sayg. she
wd. find $60. enclosed—but the envelope was minus the money— They are
cheated in every way— What a *haul* that Jef Davis was allowed to make off
with—but as "murder will out"—*has* out, so we may hope the thief may be
caught— How well it is for wretched Booth to be so speedily put out of the
way—carcase & all—[1]

A whole page, & not a word of our two dear invalids— Yr father is about
agn.—no fever these 2 days—but very feeble, as his voice shews— He drove
up to the store this morng—but he will not go to Town tomorw., altho' 2 Mgs.
he wd. like to attend— He missed the Barclay Annual Mg. yestery., wh. is not
as he wd. wish. Dr. Truman was at Germantn. Mg. on 1st. day, & drove over to
see him—makg. his 3rd. visit—his prescriptns. have done him good— I have
given him boneset tea lately & have some for George [*Lord*]—wish he was here
to take it— If yr. father takes good care of himself, he may be able to go on to
the Annual Mg. & make you a little visit— Maria [*Davis*] tells him it will depend on *that*. Mari³. [*Mott*] will write of her plans, wh. seem rather obscure or
did so when last she was here—7th. day—after being laid up a few days—and
now she is under the weather agn.—so we dont know how she will manage. Her
Mother does not appear any more decided abt. comg. on— We were glad of
her letter, & liked to hear just how Miss Soule & the carpet man made out without Eliza [*Osborne*] & thought she might be easy as regards home— Our colored upholsterer always *overseamed*, instd. of stitchg. back & forth— Maria has
often sd. it was a mistake to take in so much of the edge as many do—a loop or
so of the wool or pattern— Our carpets seem to be everlasting. We dont want
to clean house till it is cleared of Thos. & Mari³.'s things, wh. will not be in a

hurry— Fanny Cavr. is going to Eddingn. this aftern., to help clear their house of every thg. they dont wish the tenants to make use of— It is rented for the season— Thos. [*Cavender*] to board with them keepg. his Library & a lodgg. room—& for Charley at times— The Place is bonafide sold at last we believe to Wm. B. Mann—put up by the Sheriff 1st. last week— The terms we have to guess—& many other things too I presume—

So much more written, and nothg. of our precious Elizh. [*Cavender*]— She was not quite so well the latter part of last week, by reason of a hemorrhage—altho' that was checked before it became excessive—but great weakness follows each attack— Since then she has suffered more pain at times—& had fever for a day or two— Now she is better agn.— She sat up 2 hours this morng.—knittg. part of the time—& sat by the window while all those hundreds of Soldiers passed—& enjoyed the music— They cd. be heard quite up to Shoem[ake]r. town. We have fresh clams brot. to the door twice a wk—as good as yours, & I am learng. to cook them to her liking. Shad too in abund[anc]e.—Plenty of asparagus & salad from our garden— So if you had come on, instead of keepg. Eliza there all the time, you might have fared nearly as well as at Brooklyn in the fish-line— You may come yet if you will— How long is Eliza going to stay?— Art thou so engaged with thy dress-maker as not to be able to write—We want to hear about the wedding, &.c &.c—²

We have little to write of news or anything—No compy.—save Susy Hall¹. & Bel Mott 7th. & 1st. day—Maria Hopper only part of the time—Beverly Soldier school occupyg. her so much— One of the poor fellows wrote her a very good letter—entirely taught by herself in a few weeks— She sent it to Dillwyn P[arrish]. to read— He returned it much pleased—with a note enclosg. $20. for the School— Bel goes often with Maria & both are much interested— I wish Fanny wd. write of her young fry—Tom P[arrish]. seems to like to come—Sam. Haydk. was here on 1st. day—also Darcy Wright & Emily Davis—

Willie W. has just returned from a *trip* to Gettysbg. much pleased with all he saw—his next is to be to Boston I hear— I hope his money will hold out—Anna met him & 2 Parrishes at Thos. Mott's last eveg— Now if you want to know any more Fanny must write it— Helen Yarnall is engaged to be married some time in the future— Her father says they are entirely too young to announce it—

I have written of Wm. Yarnall's robbery—$600 worth fine cutlery—

Now tis time for this to go— Send it off to Aubn. & Boston & Europe & this one from Aunt M.— Edwd. D. is going to Boston last of the week— Anna B's last is not yet sent to Auburn I think—tho' I'm not sure No. 18— Caroline W[hite]. was here on 6th. day last She saw that & aunt Martha's last, in town—

You will have Walter [*Brown*] before long— Will you have room for father if he goes?

Love to everybody—

Joe in particular

Mother

ALS PSCHi-Mott

1. Jefferson Davis (1808–93) and other Confederate officials were still eluding capture by Union forces and hoping to reestablish their government in Texas. Davis would be captured on 10 May in Georgia. "Vanity, like murder, will out," Hannah Cowley, *Who's the Dupe* (1779). John Wilkes Booth (1838–65), Lincoln's assassin, had been caught on 26 April and probably committed suicide.

2. LCM is probably referring to the marriage of Cyrus Dennis to Charlotte Coffin, a woman the same age as Eliza Osborne with two children (MCW to LCM, 30 December 1864, MNS; LCM to MML, 14 April 1865, NSyU).


## To Roadside Family

[*Brooklyn, New York*]
4th. July [*1865*]—

[*Continuation of a letter begun 3 July*]

Cannon firg.—squibs—torpedoes—crackers in every directn.—   Geo. [*Lord*] up @ 4 oclk. at the corner for breakfast with Joe, &.c—& off at 5 for their celebratn.—   Before 6 I am seated at the cool north window in the parlor to finish this, & take it over to the P. O. wh. closes early today—then call at the A. S. Office—   I wish the Standd. wd. change the name of the "ProSlavery" column—call it the *Oppressors* department or corner or somethg for the articles consigned there are not just proslavery—   I send with this Aunt Martha's letter & Parker Pillsbury's  He can't help his morbid tendencies—would that he were more hopeful—so that the Paper might contain some of the more cheerg. signs of the times.[1] I read it with interest  George thinks this last no. very good— Will Aunt Eliza like the long sermons of Cheever's any better than she did Frothingham's[2]  Abby Gibbons sd. *his* 2 wks. ago ought to be printed & circulated—so excellt. & practical—alludg. to the poor in this grt. City being crowded into those wretched Tenement houses—   Are Edward & Isaac [*Hopper*] comg. to New Y. to accept Abby's invitation? Anna [*Hopper*] says they will leave on 5th. day, but does not name their destinatn.—I hope to see them here—say on 6th. day—& then if you dont call me home sooner, I intend to leave on 7th day & try to reach home in the 2.30 train—   It is real nice that Anna intends to "settle down" at Roadside—  Will her father drive over & invite Aunt Eliza & Mary B. to meet me & stay the night? We can take them to their Mg. 1st day on our way to ours—   It will be very pleast. to have them—   Anna says "Maria & father will ans. all inquiries"—they didn't tho'—but never mind—  Yr. father was very good to remember & write so *much*—& I can wait for the rest—   We were glad to know that Care. Gib. White was improvg.—we feared she wd. die—   Maria

Hopper's letters we were glad to have—she seems to be havg. a nice visit—but we can't get over Emmy [*Mott*]'s disapt.— Wendell G. told me how useless it wd. have been to take her out to Cambridge at that late hour— He made himself very agreeable here on 6th. day eveg.—was it? or have I written of his call once? He talked freely of Wm.'s new prospects of busins.—of *father* M'Kim's probable removal to New Y—& of matters & things in general— I wonder if Fanny Garrison & the Baron wont call here today—[3] If I knew they wd. be at Mrs. Anthony's I wd. call on them—

The several items in my beloved's letter interested us—Jay Cooke's *Folly*—[4] All his ^father's^ & Anna D. H.'s calls—The Mellors the harvest so well in— Our raspbs. were not good from the 1st— We have far better here and brot. fresh too—& the vegetables are very good— The butcher keeps their 7th. day's meat in ice for them till 1st. day morng—& we have good fresh churned butter brot.— I just read this to Pattie who is bright this morng. She has gained strength these 2 days—[5] On 6th. day she went into Geo's room while nurse swept hers—& stood at the window admirg. the green & the flowers till she was faint & had to lie on Geo's bed for hours & felt forlorn after it all day— She now hopes to go down stairs on 6th. day—she says it is awful for me to go but she can't say a word— I am always glad to hear of John Cavr.'s calls but it has so happened each time that I have not seen him— Now fare ye well I may go to Mo. Mg. tomorw. & will write once more & hope you will twice— Send this to Aunt Martha I will try to ans. her letter before I leave here— She can send it to Boston & so to Europe for it does not contain a single direction  Maybe Jas. will not say it isn't worth it as he did of one I sent you and I don't wonder he *thot. so.*

affectionately farewell    L. M.

I am sorry Fred. Barley couldn't see Fanny after going out so far for a call—

ALS PSCHi-Mott

1. After the last anniversary meeting of the AASS, on 9 May, William Lloyd Garrison, stating that the work of the antislavery movement had been completed, had retired from the AASS. Other abolitionists, including Parker Pillsbury and Wendell Phillips, disagreed with Garrison and continued the society (*NASS*, 20 May 1865, 1; *WLG*, 5:247–48). Pillsbury had begun editing the *NASS* on 27 May 1865. LCM may be referring to an editorial in which Pillsbury had declared, "The sentiment of gratitude which pervaded the nation has proved too weak to contend with the old prejudice of race, and to-day the political atheism which sees in the Declaration of Independence nothing but a glittering generality is the controlling opinion of the nation" (*NASS*, 3 June 1865, 2).

2. In his sermon entitled "Continued Oppression, and Not God's Judgement, the Reason for Fasting," delivered 1 June, George B. Cheever had expressed the fear that "the South will again rule, and fill society with curses, until again the Almighty rise in vengeance. Such is the prospective result of our committing the great and impious injustice and cruelty of refusing to the colored race the right of voting" (*NASS*, 17 June 1865, 4). Octavius B. Frothingham's sermon "The Saints Coming from the Graves" had praised the recently assassinated Lincoln (*NASS*, 29 April 1865, 2–3).

3. Helen Frances Garrison (1844–1928) was William Lloyd Garrison's daughter; her fiancé was Henry Villard (1835–1900), a journalist from a prominent Bavarian family (*WLG*, 5:276–77).

4. Jay Cooke (1821–1905), a Philadelphia banker, had recently built a mansion near Roadside (Bacon, 194).

5. MML had given birth on 23 June to her fourth daughter, Anna Lord.

## To Martha Coffin Wright

Roadside 10 mo. 2nd. 65—

Bright 3rd. day—making good the lines enclosed in thy letter, my dear Sister, for *us*—& wh. corresponded with my creed, thou knows. Mariana [*Mott*] took home thine recd. last eveg., as she wished to write this morng—but Maria [*Davis*] & Fanny [*Cavender*] have gone over there, & will probably prevent her  There is so much to talk about, when they are together, while I have so much to *think* about, sittg. here alone, as is pleasanter to me than to go anywhere— Some of them will drive over to School Lane this aftern., to take the letters— Anna B's included—& to enquire after the sick— All were better at Ellis' [*Yarnall*] last accot.— We are pained to hear of dear Eliza [*Osborne*]'s hazardous jump, & such a hurt too—near the knee, wh. always seems worse than a broken bone— She must be very careful not to try to walk too soon. It is well *that elaborate* weddg. "came off" first— What a labor for one eveg., aye & *night* too, for that matter— It is wise in the Garrisons, to have less fuss, & array for travelg.— We have scarcely seen Anne McDennis, & not heard ½ we want to, about you. Edwd. [*Davis*]'s 2nd. visit was entirely unexpected to us, as well as to you & to him too— —he has much to say of his nice room, & the cordial receptn.—includg. fruits & flowers—but his absorbg. talk being coalmines & railroads, we dont gather as much from him, as we want— He says he told you all he cd., of our dear victim's last days[1]—wh. was in part repetitn.—and now he starts off agn. this eveg., for Elmira, & I feel strongly tempted to go with him, & have a week or two in quiet sadness with thee, for my sisters & childn. are all I want around me just now— Elizh. Fisher kindly called yestery. & Washn. Brown & Susan, with their daughr.—& last 7th. day Debh. Whartn. & Sarah Palmer passed an hour with us— Debh. said she felt more & more inclined to sit with the sorrowg— She feels anxious for Sally Barker who is very poorly— Our neighbrs. too—the Richardsons & Davises—Lizzie Hall[l]., &.c—have shewn their sympathy—not only in sendg. flowers &.c.—to Elizh., but in calling since— I shrink however from all these visits—as well as from going to Mg. & having to be spoken to by our kind frds.— Still it will not do to indulge in morbid grief— especially when we have so much to be thankful for—that the dear wounded— broken spirit is at rest—free from all future annoyances— Another call we had yestery. wh. I was very glad of—Hariet Tubman.[2] You may see her before this reaches you— I very freely gave her the little I could, to aid her on her way to

Auburn—& Thos. Mott comg. in just then, handed her $5— She will tell you her experience, & shew you her documents— If thou talk with her about the Freedmen & their right to vote—she may reply & enlarge as sensibly as she did here— She is a wonderful woman—

We hoped Anna H. wd. come out this A.M. but no sign of her yet— The sale of a house in Clinton St—wh. Anna & daughr. wd. like, may have kept her in town— Edwd. & Maria meant to attend the sale—near where Ellis Y. lived a year—

It is very pleast. to have Maria at home agn. The 2 wks. seemed 2 mos. I preserved Quinces in her absence— What a pity that yours were stolen! So were our largest pears—2 trees—½ a bush.—& some of the grapes from Benjn. [*Yarnall*]'s yard— They have gathered the remainder & put them up for winter pies— Eliza & daughrs. go in often, to alter carpets & prepare for the new— An Upholsterer engaged to make them—

AL MNS

1. LCM's daughter Elizabeth Mott Cavender had died on 4 September.

2. During the war Harriet Tubman (1820?–1913), a former slave and a conductor on the Underground Railroad, had acted as a spy and a nurse for the Union Army. After the war, she helped build schools for freedpeople in the South and established a home for aged African Americans in Auburn, New York, where she resided. MCW would describe one of Tubman's visits in a letter to LCM dated 16 April 1866: "Harriet Tubman called to acknowledge $10. that I took to her last week & left with her father— Wm. [*Garrison Jr.*] sent it for her, saying his father had a fund of 2 or 300. given him to meet such cases as hers— She said it cd. not have come in a better time, for she wanted to get some potatoes to plant, but she was afraid Mr. Garrison misunderstood her, & tho't they were suffering for food, wh. she sd. wd. not be, while they had so many kind friends here— She has a good deal of that honest pride wh. makes her unwilling to beg— She seems happy & exultant, except for 'the misery' in her shoulder & chest where that Camden & Amboy wretch hurt her—" (MNS).


## To Martha Coffin Wright and Martha Mott Lord

Philada. 11 mo. 2nd. 65—

At Edwd. H's—with a hoarse cold & cough, I can do little else than write. A week to-day since we left home for the West C. Mg—& we have been on the go' almost ever since— Now unfinished carpet-piecg. awaits my return—to say nothg. of other Fall fixins. Our several families are equally busy—& who is not, at this season?— They begin to 'look like London' at Benjn [*Yarnall*]s.—the upholsterer's fittg. & makg. their new carpets, & putting down the 2nd. story, with much planng. & piecg.—[1] The daughrs. with much pleadg., prevailg. with their mother to submit & now she acknowls. that their skill exceeded hers—as I have long since found, when givg. up, even to our 'help'— Mariana [*Mott*]'s rooms are nearly all covered & furnished now— The variety of colors in Eli-

za's carpets please my eye, more than the sameness at 'the Palace'—even tho'
rich red & green abound. The ding. room wd. suit Hannah Fisher—it looks like
Manilla Mattg.—& the antique chair & sofa legs are like unto Hannah Fisher's
too—but how Fashion reconciles every thg.! "Take the house for all in all,"[2] tho'
it is elegant—not preventg. an air of comfort thro' out & the occupants take great
pleasure in each part—very little to wish differt.—

Now is thy time, my dear Sister, to come & enjoy it with them—i.e. as soon
as David [*Wright*]'s strength returns—so as for thee to feel easy to leave him—
& Eliza [*Osborne*]'s lameness is restored, or rather her soundness— We were
daily expectg. to hear of her at Brooklyn crutch & all—& that thou too had
pressed thro' difficulties to meet our dear niece & fam[il]y.— Still when we
heard how quickly they found a house, & how little Mari[a]. & Pattie [*Lord*] had
of Anna [*Brown*]'s compy., we were reconciled—as now we have the visit in
anticipatn., & hope Anna & perhaps Pattie may come before the winter is over—
& make a longer visit than planned now— Returng. from West Chester on 2nd
day last, S. B. Anthony with us, we found thy letter—no it came the next day
when Mary Grew too was with us, & they liked to hear all that was read to
them—about Banks honorg. Mass. &.c— How I wish you cd. have heard Wendell P. on the state of the country— Parker P. too spoke very well but not to his
own satisfactn. He sd. he was not in harness— He cd.n't come home with us—
havg. to hurry back to his post as they were makg. new arrangets. for the Standard— Susan was full of the matter, as well as of the Woman movemt. & brot.
an address by E. C. Stanton for us to endorse—[3] It is well for yr. state to revive
the questn. as the time for revisg. the Constitutn is near—but as a general move,
it wd. be in vain, while the all-absorbg. negro questn. is up— Mary Grew &
Susan had much talk— Anna H. was out too & we had a pleast. time— Susan
came in & went to Mg. with us yestery., & had a little to say to our School
childn.—500 present— Henry Ridgwy also there & sd. much[4]—he was pleased
with Susan & sent his love & approval to her—many spoke to her—but being
Preparative Mg—the men withdrew— We came here & had a lunch & then I
waited on her to the cars—Edwd. D. sendg. up money to pay her expenses—
We remained after the Mg. at West C. to attend the monthly & 1st. day mg—&
a young peoples' gatherg. to discuss our "testimonies"— One dark rainy eveg.
we walked from the mg—Parker—no Wendl. P. & Mary Grew leadg. the way—
We got in to the mud & wet—half fallg. down, & that was the way I got this
cold—wh. I mean now to go home & nurse— Fanny C. was in yestery. with
Bel [*Mott*], to join Maria H. in their 1st. German lesson— Fanny has recovg.
from her tumble down cellar—and wd. be very cheerful, but for her anxiety on
Charlie's accot. His father took him home more than a week ago—& that's the
last of him— The Auction Sale probably absorbg. them—one day rainy—
John Cavr. has moved in— Thos. called in due form the last day of the Mo—
or before—1st at our house, with Mann's son as witness—Jas. not at home—
so he came here—and paid the $5000 to Edwd. with interest—not a word betwn.

them. So much for our 2 Edwds. & their wives urging their father to enter judgmt. if that's the way to express it. Dear Charlie came home from a visit to his father afterwd., with his mind greatly stirred agt. his Grandfr., for "trying to get money out of his father—he didn't *want* to stay here anyhow"— Fanny explained as well as she could—but it shewed the means that wd. be resorted to, to get the dear boy away from us— What a blessing that our precious sufferer is removed from it all!— Edwd. recd. a sympathetic letter from Robt. Collyer since his return from Eng.— His trip & visit were successful. As no doubt Phillips Brooks' will be, but how much he is needed here, to protest agt. that wicked Episcopal Conventn.[5] We were wonderg. if their proceedgs. wd. meet thy eye— We had quite a "fight" here one eveg. with Eliza, who attempted to echo some of Ellis' [*Yarnall*] allowances for their hateful doings. You ought to a' been here—at Roadside I mean, where we are agn. installed, findg. Maria [*Davis*] quite alone—Fanny gone with Bel. to Emily Davis'— We sent over for Eliza a wk. ago—no on 1st. day it was, to make her last visit before they moved in— She stayed the night— On 2nd. we drove to Ellersley with her & made her last call there—the house looks like being finished at last— All the wood is black walnut They will have plenty of room now— The childn. & Agnes are all on the mend now—& things look brighter with them tho' still great confusion— Mari[a]. has had their furniture &.c brot. so gradually, that there has never seemed confusion there only slow work— If you'll believe it, I have not seen that woman 5 min. since she came from Brooklyn, & only had 2nd. hand from Maria, anythg. she had to tell, on her observatns. on her Frenchified cousins— 3rd. day when Susan B. Anthony & Mary Grew were here, it was a steady rain— & tho' it cleared at night & was moonlight, yet Mari[a]. havg. been very busy arrangg. books in the new cases, was too tired to come over— I told Thos. it wd. never do for S. B. Anthony not to see her—so as Mary G. wished to see the house, we drove over early after breakfast yestery. morng., & had 20 min to race from room to room—quite to the 5 attics—& back buildgs— They expressed much—Mary G. wished it understd. that she had not finished & was comg. agn. to see closets &.c &.c—and thats the only time Ive set eyes on thy daughter— So Pattie, my precious, may know we were glad of her letter with the little mention of the weddg—the childn.'s happiness the abrupt departure of Walter & Anna [*Brown*]—bag & baggage— The house must have seemed empty after such a clearing out— It will be pleast. to have a New Y. place to visit if a body ever go agn.— We want 1st. a visit here— If Eliza Osborne come to New Y. as her father seemed to think she wd., why cant you come "over" in a body & make us a visit?— Think of it— Anna & Pattie ought to have fixed days to visit, so as not to cross each other's paths— The *moderate* rent of their house was not named till Mari[a]. came home— Maria says as they are only bound from month to month, it is not so much more than Richard's— That letter, sent the Monday before, was not mean at all—it was we who were mean not to acknowle. it better—but housecleang. & carpets were engrossg. for a time— I have eno' of

that green of Mari[a].'s—for the entry leadg. to our room—so that both chambers & entry will be alike—but then there's a world of piecing, wh. is no dread
on ingrain— You shd. see what Maria did to the old ding. room Brussels, makg.
it look quite bright— Still I shd. like to dump that & the front & back chamber down at Henrietta Dixon's door, & move up our parlor carpet— How Eliza, or even Anna H. wd.n't have done as I did—tack the pieces together, & turn
my back on it all for a week and with my cold I didn't mean to turn on today—
but be a lady & write—& begin anew tomorw— I must go tho', and welcome
Thos. & Martha Mellor home— They came on the 7th. day last after 2 mo.
travel— Edwd. & Maria were there 1st. day— Little Eddy went back to
Prov[idenc]e. last week—& Willie Griscom[6]

I reckon Mari[a]. must have written how Fanny fell— The cellar door of the
Engine or Hose house in 9th. below Arch was open & coal ashes was being taken
out— Edwd. Hallowell complained of the dust & asked her if she cd. get along
at the same time—throwg. the cape of his coat over *his* face & walkg. on—looking back—no Fanny—so he quickly stepped to the trap door—not one of those
*round* holes—& there she lay in a heap stunned—or makg. no ans. as he spoke—
He ran in & down cellar, & with a man or two there lifted her up & carried her
out—there were no cellar steps where she fell— She came to herself by

*still 5th. day 2nd of the mo—*
*east wind & cloudy*

that time. & was able to walk with assistance to Edwd. H.'s where I went in & found
her—pale as death—on the sofa Maria bathg. her head & face—her lip & chin
bleeding—and her knees cut in 2 or 3 places—they supposed by her hoops—her
head much jarred—so that she became sick & cd. eat no dinner—went soon to
bed—lay till night—up *well* except headache—her back not hurt—passed the
eveg. in the parlor—& remained the next day in town quiet since wh. she has made
no complaint—is well & bright with her cousins—especially when the 'boys' come
out as they do—not unfrequently— — Abm. Barker's famy. have moved in

Such a time as the Citizens are havg. to find houses!— Edwd. has had some
offers for his—but not such as he will accept— They won't put the old office
carpet down agn. The Sansom St. occupant wont move—& he cant be forced
till next Spring— Chs. Massey's house is sold—he died some months since—
one of the sisters lives with Wm. & Elizh. the furniture divided among them—
& the sisters divided too— Israel Cope's & Dr. Wistar's houses also sold—[7] All
Arch St. will be stores up to 10th— — I feel sorry for the 'Corner' to be given
up—& hoped one of the brothers & wife wd. occupy part—or some other nice
people—but it may be all right— Wish Charlie much happiness for me—

This letter of course is to ans. the double purpose of ansg. Aunt Martha's &
thine, Pattie— We will send the Auburn one to you soon, with one from Ellen
W. G. wh. we were glad to have— The town house seemed to strike her just as
it did us— We think too that one winter will be eno' for them— How pleast.
for Ellen & Anna [*Hallowell*] to see each other so often—& the headaches so

much less frequent— The weddings are drawg. near—[8] What a change in the Garrison famy—a year or so has made— The father will go to Eng. before long— We wouldn't have believed we cd. hold our Annual Mg. without Miller M'K—& of course we missed him greatly—but we never had a more satisfacty. gathg. The hall well filled—all attentn. from the beging.—and continued—3 sessions till after 10 that eveg—many standing  Some who had never heard Wendell P before were delighted notwithstandg. he came down on the Administratn. so fiercely. C. K. W's leader last week was worthy a Garrison— Theo. Tilton in the Independt. in 3 articles lately has done nobly—he handles his Gamaliel—Beecher, "without gloves"—his last as to appear in the Standard this week—[9] S. B. Anthony hopes much from him— She was glad to hear from Ellen W. G. who is quite a favorite with her— This going out to find suitable bridal presents has become rather a tax— I find a great comfort in keepg. in the simplicity—& to useful articles—& with this cold, pocketh[and]k[erchie]fs. are eminently so— It is not fixed unless lately that Lucy & Wendl. are to be married in Church—the last we heard an eveg. entertainment was talked of— Mari[a]. has driven over there & to Ellis' in the rain—so we shall hear when she returns— Maria & Edwd. drove over to the Cricket ground yestery. where was an exciting game—too exciting I think—these crickets and base balls— Poor Frank! to lose his new coat— We are as sorry as we can be for him— Every body had need earn a mint to live nowadays— Maria H. shewed me this morng. a handsome Photogh. of Willie & Nannie—just recd. I think she said— I hope Willie will make money eno', not to have a long courtship— Yr. house is large eno' for them to be with you, if he continue in business there— I think his Mother wd. be a kind mother-in-law. Maria has just looked over this & says it *is* fixed at last for Lucy to be married in Church—but Wm. & Ellen [*Garrison*] ought to come nevertheless, for we never have had that Bridal visit—& we want to see them here— We enjoyed the eveg. visit we had from his Father—with Miller & Sarah & S. Pugh & Abby K—wh. I have certainly written once—

I am waitg. for Mari[a]. to come over & read this & add if she will— — She has a cook at last— $3 is demanded hereaway too—for *professed* help— Eliza [*Yarnall*] & Mary B. have lately raised their girls' wages— Mary has a new one— Has Harriet Tubman ever called to see thee?— S. B. Anthony told us how badly used she was in the cars— No, I didn't ask her to call & see thee for I presumed of course she wd. That other letter from thee was sent to Brooklyn for Anna B— Have we omitted answerg. it—if so excuse us & we will do better—

Love to All    L Mott

Thank David for so kindly sendg. for me to meet him in Brooklyn & go home with him  I couldn't do it then but some day when Eliza will go too— It was too bad for him to be so near us & not come here for a day or so

L Mott

ALS MNS

1. The twenty-eighth annual meeting of the PASS had been held on 27 October 1865 in West Chester. The Yarnalls were moving from their country residence on School Lane near Germantown into Arch Street for the winter (Eliza Yarnall to LCM, 15 October 1865, Mott Manuscripts, PSCHi; Amice Macdonell Lee, *In Their Several Generations* [Plainfield, N.J.: Interstate Printing Corp, n.d.], 234).

2. LCM is possibly adapting Shakespeare's *Merchant of Venice* (4.1.374–76): "Nay, take my life and all; pardon not that: / You take my house when you do take the prop / That doth sustain my house."

3. Nathaniel Banks had recently been elected to Congress from Massachusetts. At the meeting of the PASS, Wendell Phillips had posited that slavery had not yet been abolished and had questioned whether the Thirteenth Amendment abolishing slavery would be ratified by the requisite number of states. He thus believed that the work of antislavery societies was still needed. Parker Pillsbury had "asked whether it was not evident that the spirit of slavery was still active among ourselves—not to speak of the South." Anthony had spoken in favor of political protection for African Americans and in support of the *NASS*. Stanton's appeal calling for a constitutional amendment to give women the right to vote apparently had met with little favor at the meeting; there is no discussion of woman's rights in the proceedings (*NASS*, 11 November 1865, 2–3; Gordon, 1:558).

4. Henry Ridgway was a Philadelphia Hicksite.

5. Phillips Brooks (1835–93), the Episcopal bishop of the Holy Trinity Church in Philadelphia, had left in July for a fourteen-month trip to Europe and the Middle East. While in England, he had attended some meetings of freedpeople's aid associations (Raymond W. Albright, *Focus on Infinity: A Life of Phillips Brooks* [New York: Macmillan, 1961], 112–21). The Triennial Episcopal Convention, beginning on 4 October in Philadelphia and lasting almost the entire month, had proposed to reunite northern and southern branches of the Episcopal church, which had been divided over slavery. According to the *Independent* reporter, the leaders of the convention had voiced pro-Southern views and largely ignored freed slaves (*Independent*, 12 October 1865, 1, 26 October 1865, 8).

6. Henrietta Troth Austin Dixon (d. 1897) was a Philadelphia Hicksite. William Griscom (1851–97) was the brother of Clement Griscom.

7. Charles Massey, an Orthodox Quaker from Philadelphia, had died on 14 August at age eighty-seven. Possibly this was the house of Israel Cope (1770–1855), a Philadelphia Quaker.

8. Wendell P. Garrison would marry Lucy McKim on 6 December 1865 and Fanny Garrison and Henry Villard would marry on 3 January 1866 (*WLG*, 5:335, 5:278).

9. Charles King Whipple (1808–1900), a journalist and an abolitionist, helped edit the *Liberator*. In his editorial of the previous week he had criticized President Johnson's recent speech to the First Colored Regiment of the District of Columbia as unjust to the African American soldiers: "They have *merited* citizenship, the franchise, an equal standing with others before the law, admission to the witness-box and the jury-box, public respect and honor . . . and yet the public servant in question has the impudence to tell these men that the liberty now accorded to them is simply a liberty to work!" (*Liberator*, 27 October 1865, 170). Theodore Tilton had criticized Henry Ward Beecher's support for President Johnson's policies and had stated his own position on Reconstruction: "We plant ourselves upon the rock of EQUAL SUFFRAGE. Believing this position to be right, to be manly, to be Christian, God forbid our feet to be moved therefrom a single inch—nay, a single hair!" (*Independent*, 26 October 1865, 4, 2 November 1865, 4, 9 November 1865, 4). Gamaliel was a celebrated Jewish teacher (Acts 5:34, 22:3).

# To James Miller McKim

[*Roadside c. 15 April 1866*]

My dear Miller M'Kim

Jas. & self called yesterday to take leave of our friend R.J. Parvin—[1] I spoke of some of our co-laborers in England, whom I hoped he would meet— He suggested my giving him letters— I thought an introduction from thee & other sources would avail him more than from us—but I have ventured on the accompanying, which if thou think worth anything to him, please hand them to him—

He called here with his wife a few days ago— I was not at home— He mentioned to our childn. his hope that thou would accompany him— Sarah [*McKim*] since tells me of thy decision, which I trust will rest easy on thy anxious mind— I shall not be surprised however if on re-consideration thou should feel obliged to follow him—as he so greatly needs thee in such a mission— Only if thou should go, it would seem sufficient without him—

Thou hast not returned me that letter of thine, which I have ever intended to respond & reply to— Thy mention of the many years that we have taken "sweet counsel together" was touching, and grateful to me— Thy varied experiences and Theological shiftings—all resulting so satisfactorily in settled conviction on the liberal side of course gratified thy heterodox friend— And if at any time there threatened a little more leaning to the Conservative side, as our E. M. Davis sometimes thought, why that was most natural, with thy early education— And if thou felt that I was growing more heretical & losing somewhat of the Religious faith which bound us so together, as my *jealousy*, perhaps, whispered, why I comforted myself that thou had heard me less in religious exercise than in years gone by— A few words in the latter part of thy letter were not quite clear— I cannot recollect them now—And the bare mention ^or inference I draw^ that some alienation might have come over our warm friendship gave me pain— Not however very serious—and I cherish the hope that we are too firmly bound in friendships ties, to be easily severed; however we may be pursuing just now—not antagonistic courses—but not exactly working in the same channel together as for years— The Freedmen's interests are very near & dear to me—and I rather dread mixing them with the offspring of Rebels unrepentant—[2]

More when we meet— Let that be soon—

As *ever* thine in warm affection—
Lucretia Mott

Give R. J. Parvin a letter to R. D. Webb—

ALS NN

1. Sailing on 18 April, Robert J. Parvin would travel to Great Britain under the auspices of the American Freedmen's Union Commission to inform the British of the freed slaves' plight (*American Freedman,* April 1866, 4, May 1866, 22, October 1866, 102–3).

2. The American Freedmen's Union Commission sought to promote integrated schools in the South (James M. McPherson, *The Struggle for Equality: Abolitionists and the Negro in the Civil War and Reconstruction* [Princeton: Princeton University Press, 1964], 399–400).

## To Wendell Phillips

Philada. 4 Mo. 17th. 66—

Wendell Phillips
My dear Friend

Yes, I expect to be at the Annual Meeting—and as usual may have a word to say—but it will not be worth heralding— People dread the infliction of the *Old* when younger speakers are present— Moreover I dont know how to prepare a speech, and never tried— Something at the time—from thee or another, may call forth a response or dissent—so take me for what I am and do with me as ye will—[1]

An old colored woman met me in the street, and said, "do you know of anybody who wants a good-for-nothing old cook?" I feel like that old woman— Only as thou says, there is so much to be considered, and done at the coming Mg. that we must all share the responsibility— How *right* it was, to hold on to the Organization! Some who felt & voted for disbanding are coming around to our Side— But we are sadly in need of funds and know not where to apply—

The Woman's Rights Meeting has its claims on us too—[2] It seemed unwise to urge these, just now—as this is emphatically the negro's hour—and we wrote Elizh. Cady Stanton to that effect—and did not use her Petitions—but she mourned over us so—and reasoned with us—that the coming year—(or perhaps this) was the time for the New Y. Legislature to revise the Constitution[3]—& that the attempt made in Congress this session to renew the exclusion of Woman should arouse her advocates[4]—moreover, that the negro's hour was decidedly the fitting time for woman to slip in—these and other reasons so persistently urged— what could we do, but sign & forward the Petitions?— And what can we now do, but go to the meeting, & help her & Susan B. Anthony in their untiring labors? I hope thou too will give thy presence and encouragement—[5]

We need thee *here* also, to lift up the voice of warning in this perilous hour for Liberty—

affecy    *L. Mott*

Dear love to Ann—

ALS MH-H (shelf mark bMS Am 1953 [917])
Env: "Wendell Phillips, Boston, Mass—"

1. Phillips would preside at the AASS meeting held in New York City on 8–9 May. LCM is mentioned as participating "in the discussions of the session" (*NASS*, 19 May 1866, 3).

2. The eleventh National Woman's Rights Convention, which LCM would attend, was to be held in New York City on 10 May.

3. New York had scheduled a convention for 1867 to revise its constitution. Woman's rights leaders were engaged in a campaign to gain suffrage in that state (Gordon, 1:585; see also LCM to the Equal Rights Convention at Albany, 18 November 1866, below).

4. During congressional debates on the Fourteenth Amendment guaranteeing civil rights to all U.S. citizens, the question of equal suffrage arose. Woman's rights leaders protested the introduction, for the first time, of the word *male* into the U.S. Constitution.

5. Speaking informally at the National Woman's Rights Convention on 10 May, Phillips would admit that he did not "feel the keen interest in this question that I have felt in the Anti-Slavery or the Temperance cause." He would acknowledge the potential power women held and would fault them in general for not demanding equal opportunities in the professions and at the voting booth. He would cite LCM's statement at an early convention that women "were launching a cause which had its greatest enemy among its own victims" (*New York Tribune*, 11 May 1869, 8).

## To Elizabeth Cady Stanton

Roadside, near Philadelphia,
4 mo., 22, 1866.

My dear Elizabeth:

I expect to be in New York at the annual meeting of the American Anti-Slavery Society, and I intend to remain and be at the Woman's Rights meeting. I hope Wendell Phillips will stay also, and give woman a lift at that time. I have written to him and said so. Even admitting that this is decidedly the freedman's hour, we may do what we can among ourselves and make what stir we can, especially in your state preparatory to revising the constitution; as also make our appeal to the Congress of the nation, where the attempt in this late day is made to keep woman out.[1]

Affectionately,    Lucretia Mott.

TTR NjRD

1. At the National Woman's Rights Convention held on 10 May 1866, Anthony would offer a resolution: "That the time has come for an organization that shall demand *Universal Suffrage*, and that hereafter we shall be known as the '*American Equal Rights Association*.'" LCM urged that a preamble to the new organization's constitution reflect that the AERA was "an outgrowth of the Woman's Rights movement." Stanton would move that LCM be chosen as president in order that the "office might ever be held sacred in the memory that it had first been filled by one so loved and honored by all" (*Proceedings of the Eleventh National Woman's Rights Convention*, Gordon, 1:584, 586). A 31 May announcement of the AERA meeting signed by LCM as president stated, "This Association is an outgrowth, or wider development, of the National Woman's Rights

Society, into which that body resolved itself at its recent Annual Meeting in New York"
(*NASS*, 19 May 1866, 3).

## To Martha Coffin Wright

Philada. 919 Clinton St.
6th Mo. 10th. ^no it is 2nd. day 11th^ 66
Edwd. Hopper's—In at the dentists—renewing

My dear Sister

Thine—so welcome, with its acceptable enclosures, came on 7th. day, & was
read with great interest by us all— David's accot. of Cyrus D's sudden departure, the funeral, & the feeling of the family, was just what we wanted to hear—
Fred., as I wrote had been communicative, & I was glad I called there, & learned
*so* much—now let us know how they settle the estate, & if all work well together, as Fred seemed confident they would— We cant help feelg. that if this event
had occurred Before the marriage, how much better for them it would have
been— Fred. told me they had "consulted Mr. Wright"— How much David
*felt* with them— Poor Carrie—and yet Maria D. says her future may be brighter,
than her home seemed, after the added family— We wonder if there is any
prospect of increase! Let us have all you hear—for now that Anne has gone to
Auburn, for the summer, & perhaps "for good & all"—and Miller & Sarah
moved clean away from these parts, We have no way of hearg. directly from
them,[1] at least till thou gets back & writes—

It seems very comfortable & pleasant there at Roxbury—Wm.'s prospects so
good, wh. we rejoice with you all in, & Ellen so happy in her anticipations—[2] The
only drawback is the continued sufferg. of their dear father in wh. we heartily
sympathise, & wish we could recommend some cure— If all the rubbing wont
avail, ask him to come & try our air & quiet rest awhile— The LongWood Yearly
is just past,[3] & it had to do without him or Geo. Thompson—as I presumed wd.
be the case— This was the time they were going to Eng. together— That too,
of course, is suspended. Yes, it is a favor that Ellen's afflictn. is not accompd. with
much pain—& then she has so much to sustain & comfort her in the loving devotion of her whole family— — Susan B. Anty was with us yestery. on her return from LongWd. accompd. by Anna E. Dickinson— They drove out & arrived while we were at dinner, entertaining Aaron Powell & John Wildman, with
their wives. They also from Longwd. came out in the morng. cars  J. Wildman is
a correspondt. of the Standard "O." married Cyrus Peirce's youngest daughr.—
Hannah— He is Jay Cooke's book keeper & general clerk—[4]

We had a great deal of talk— Aron Powell confronted Oliver Johnson at
LongWood, who thot. Congress ought not to be found fault with so much—
on the Reconstructn. questn.— Theode. Tilton seconded Aaron & was still
more severe— He "didn't wonder that Oliver J. cd.nt. see that Congress had

surrendered for he had surrendered himself"— Hattie Purvis was there & put up at Isaac Mendenhall's, where Oliver was, & she cd. hardly stay in the room, & hear him denounce Wendell P. as he did, before so large a compy— Had her father been there, as was expected, he cd.n't have stood it, but she felt too young to contradict or oppose him— Susan B. Anty. said Anna E. Dickn. spoke grandly in Boston & very well at Longwood too—[5] I wish Susan cd. have had more talk with thee— She was much disapptd. not to visit you at Roxbury, as she intended to do—but several of her plans were cut short— She and Elizh. C Stantn., & Parker I believe favor a separate periodical rather than take the Standd.'s offer of a page  A little feelg. is up toward Aaron,—they think he ought not to employ Smalley—& that Parker ought to have been kept as Editor—[6] If so, they ought to have sd. so in our preliminary Mg., & Parker ought to have been at the public Mg., when his name was announced— I wish he was not so sensitive, & such a "cross-patch" Edwd. D. says he has had several letters from him, during the past year wishg. he cd. be released from his post— Yes, Susan sd. but of late he had become accustomed to the labor, & liked it better— Then they shd. have sd. so at the time— I weary of such everlastg. complaints— Then Wendl. P. does not satisfy them on the Woman questn—& so we have it— I dont think we cd. begin to raise money eno,' to conduct a Paper— I'm glad sometimes that I shall not have much more to do in any of these movements— A letter of inquiry came from Minnesota, wh. I was glad to hand over to S. B. Anthy— Another from Wm. H. Johnson with 4 or 5 pages of a discussn. he had had on the Wom. questn which he wanted I shd. see— He had read E C. Stanton's excellt. address—[7]

When I took this paper I only intended a short letter, to let thee know that thou alludes to a letter before this last, givg. some accot. of the New-Eng. Con. wh. letter we have not recd.— We dont like to lose one— Thou calls the newly-formed Socy "the Equal Suffrage"— Wasn't it Equal *Rights* Society?— S. B. Anthy. sd. thou presided beautifully & they were pleased with thy speech & with all the part thou took in the Mgs.[8]— So be encouraged & not let it in future be the "skeleton in thy house"

What a nice way this is to use such a lot of letters like this[9]—& if you dont like it, why, you must "*lump* it"—

Ellen & Anna D. Hall[l]. must not let other engagets. prevent their often visitg. & when that cant be done sendg. notes and exchangg. letters sent them—it will keep up the interest in the family circle, wh. otherwise wd. wane.

Love to Wm. & to Richd. Hall[l].—& Ned too & Frank & all—

L. Mott—

ALS PSCHi-Mott

1. Cyrus Dennis had died suddenly on 31 May in Auburn. "Carrie" is probably his daughter, Caroline E. Dennis (d. 1893). James Miller McKim and Sarah McKim had recently moved to Llewellyn Park, New Jersey (Fort Hill Cemetery records, Auburn, N.Y.; LCM to MML and MCW, 19 March 1866, MNS).

2. MCW had gone to Ellen Wright Garrison's home in Massachusetts in anticipation of Ellen's first child. Agnes would be born on 14 June.

3. The yearly meeting of the Progressive Friends at Longwood had met on 7–10 June. At the meeting, both Theodore Tilton and Aaron Powell had advocated universal suffrage without regard to race or sex. Powell had criticized President Andrew Johnson's Reconstruction policies as well as the U.S. Congress's Reconstruction Committee's report, which "had surrendered the vital point at issue with the President." Oliver Johnson, however, had defended Congress as achieving all it possibly could: "The people were not ready to enforce the suffrage question" (*NASS*, 23 June 1866, 3).

4. John Wildman was a Philadelphia banker and a Hicksite Quaker. Cyrus N. Peirce (1829–1909) was a Philadelphia dentist.

5. Isaac Mendenhall (1806–82), active in the Progressive Friends, lived in Hamarton. At the Longwood meeting, Dickinson had urged suffrage for blacks and had criticized Congress for its reluctance to legislate it. Anthony had reminded the members about the new organization, the AERA, and its goal of suffrage for both women and African Americans (*WLG*, 5:44).

6. The *NASS* had announced that Aaron Powell would become its editor and Pillsbury its general agent (16 June 1866, 2). Pillsbury had resigned from the *NASS* in protest of its bias against the equal rights movement (Ellen Carol DuBois, *Feminism and Suffrage: The Emergence of an Independent Women's Movement in America, 1848–1869* [Ithaca, N.Y.: Cornell University Press, 1978], 73–74). George W. Smalley (1833–1916) had previously served as war correspondent for the *New York Tribune*.

7. LCM is probably referring to Stanton's address urging woman suffrage at the National Woman's Rights Convention in New York City on 10 May: "I say stop all this talk about woman's sphere, and place in her hand the ballot, which is the key to all the profitable employments, to education, to civil and political rights, to virtue and independence" (*Proceedings of the Eleventh National Woman's Rights Convention*, in *Stanton-Anthony Papers*, reel 11, fr. 478).

8. As president, LCM had signed the call to the AERA meeting in Boston, which had met on 31 May. At the meeting MCW (whom the *NASS* had described as "a lady better known in New England as sister of Mrs. Lucretia Mott, than for her own long and faithful efforts in reform") had been nominated to preside over the convention (*NASS*, 19 May 1866, 3, 16 June 1866, 2).

9. LCM had written on top of a letter from Esther Smedley asking her to publicize the journal the *Children's Friend*.


## To Philadelphia Family

[Ne]w Y. 11 mo. 15th. 66—
At Walter B's—
No. 28 West 26th St—

My dear Ones All—

Such nice, welcome letters, as we recd., last [7th?] day, from Roadside & Philada— Maria [*Davis*]'s "mice" doings, the party with Mr. Newall added & who I thot. of course was one of the girls beaus—never dreamg. of his being 'the Rev.', till after the letter was sent off to Boston, & then I wanted to look over it agn., to see what the subjects were— It was just the right thing to have him

with you— I have always wanted Mari^a. & Thos. [*Mott*] to shew him marked
attentn., as they are of that faith— When the new Church is done I guess they'll
go oftener I wish he didn't shew his upper gums so— — It was a suitable
compy. to have together. I wondered if you had any cake, & was sorry I hadn't
told Mary Pen to make some— Her head is so full of runng. into town, &
preparg. for marriage, that we shall not have much good of her—[1] — — — —
Carpet work was going on with us at Brooklyn, while you were thus engaged—
both at Roadside & Clinton St.—and indeed *here* also,—Anna [*Brown*] has a
man now, alterg. the stair rod "buttons"— A few closet floors are yet to be
covered with oil cloth— The cellar brick floor is being cleaned—& a man there
sawg. a bin full of kindling from the store Geo. L. has a similar load— Yestery.
4 pots of butter came from Orange—excellt. Anna invited Uncle Richd. &
Cannie [*Mott*] to meet us here yesteraftn.—they came— Such a handsome table
we dont often see—& every thg. so good— They eat at prest. in the basemt.—
a real handsome room— It wd. be a pity to use this back parlor, as they did in
33rd. St—for a ding. room—the delicate Brussels' bot. by Anna in Eng. is far too
handsome to be thus desecrated. The Upholsterer is puttg. up the cornice for
curtains too, so that Anna can't accept an invite to go with us this A. M. & lunch
at Sarah Hicks'— Pattie [*Lord*] too is bidden—she & Geo. were here yestery.—
She doubts being able to go to-day—expectg. a dressmaker & seamstress—not
much escape for me from that craft— One came 2 days after our arrival—on
7th. day she went into the country, & Pattie let her take work eno' to keep her
till to-day—so that we might be free— Sarah Hicks will go tomorw. with Cannie, to meet the bride & groom[2] at Springfield, & go with them to Lebanon,
&.c Yr. father & self are urged by Miller M'K. to go with him tomorw. aftern.
& stay the night— We shd. prefer their comg. to Brooklyn, but Lucy [*Garrison*] away, Sarah cant leave— I have not seen him—yr. father called at his
Office— He was also at the Standd. Office yestery. but Aaron P[owell] was so
busy with the Paper, that he didn't stay long— A letter was recd. from E. M. D.
sayg. a Circular was sent—none had come—so it cd.n't be in this wks Paper I
sent a prompt answ back—"Yes, I'd sign it"—[3] Why didn't Edwd. write a little
home-news with his letter? Nothg. recd. this week— We may get one this
morng. Edwd. H's was like himself—& acceptable—& sent it on with Maria's
to Boston, & I wrote a little—also to Auburn & sent Anna's there— Lucy Stone
^S. B. Anthony I mean^ thinks Aunt Martha must preside at the Albany
Conventn. & as the weddg. is not till the 28th., she can do both—[4] The invitatns.
all arrived in good order—handsomely written, for 3 score & 10—but no cards
with them— Sufficient tho' without them, & lessens labor *so* much Today the
carpets are to be taken to the house—if the paintg. & paperg. & cleang. are done,
they've been smart I dont wonder much that the Martin table wasn't
satisfacty.— I hastened to tell them how *long* it looked when closed— I shd. think
Sarah wd. let her Mother *keep* theirs, & find a more modern one for Race St.

Pattie went with me yestery. to Elizh. Stanton's to lunch— Lucy Stone &

S. B. Anthony meetg. us there— The time all taken up discussg. the comg. Conventn., & readg. an Address in an Eng. Paper from Mrs. Boudichon—very good indeed— She has no childn., & devotes herself to the cause of Woman They live ½ the year in Algeria—the other ½ in England have plenty of means, & do good— H. B. Stanton & 2 or 3 of their sons are engaged in business—the younger as clks. Henry a lawyer— They live near 10th. Av.— North River an Eng. basemt. house—not more than 17 or 18 ft—good depth— Lizzie was like herself—full of spirits—& so pleast.—she has just engaged a housekeeper, & means to go forth & deliver 4 lectures at diff. places the comg. winter— This Equal Rights movet. is no play—but I cant enter into it— Just hearg. their talk & the readg—made me ache all over, & glad to come away, & lie on the sofa here till uncle Richd. & Cannie came—sleepg. in the Car, as we drove along— Hannah Haydk. meant to call here in the aftern., but she ne'er came— I dined there on 1st. day after 15th. St. Mg—Harry B[rown]. going with me, as I stayed here the night before—yr. father being at Cowneck— The Danas were there & a lot of young folk—& when Geo. L. called for me @ 4 oclk., I was quite ready—& findg. S. B. Anthy. waitg. for me I hadn't much rest— She had an urgent message for me from Theo. Tilton to go there they wd. send a carriage & meet Horace Greeley & a Hon. Mr. Griffing— I *couldn't* do it—moreover Susan & Studman[5] & others were to meet me in Joralemon St. to discuss enlarging "The Friend" to admit Equal Rig. seeing the Standd. didn't When Studman came, he wanted us to go & hear Beecher, & have him afterwd. come into our pew, & talk with him preparatory to his speech in Albany I *couldn't do that any more*— So after Susan had taken tea with us, & Geo. L. slipped out—up to his Mother's no—he politely excused himself—the others came & the eveg. passed! You see how little rest, this side Jordan there is for the aged— We are to go home after lunch at S. Hicks' to meet Rev. Mr. & Mrs. Chadwick at Geo's. to tea— Somethg. all the time— The threatened storm kept me from going to 27th. St. Mg.—a block from here— I see in the Tribune the death of a grandchild of Caleb Clothier's whose funeral I shall *not* attend—[6] I wonder if Dr. Swift is living— Mary Earle told me after Qy. Mg. that they were lookg. for his death daily—wh. event wd. be met with great resignatn., as his mind was failg., from bodily disease———— What a disapt. the star-gazers have had—2 or 3 such unsettled nights! Pattie wishes Willie's letters were sent to her— I tried in vain to remember, what the poetic lines were, that May H. wondered she "had never read before"— You dont know how kind & *near* Tom Parrish felt when I met him at Han. Haydks.— I'll try to make Ben. Lyman[7] feel near too, when his visits culminate. We cd. but congratulate Anna [*Hopper*] on the successful result of her anticipated guests, and we do hope Mr. May will be *speedily* successful— Did he call on Mr. Wetherell? Anna's accot. of the "old Female Mg" was acceptable and amusing—

Maria's judicious selection of dry goods as a bonus to that dissatisfied Mrs. Kelly, I was glad of if it wont make her feel more that she was taken in in the sale— Your rush at Edwd.'s that time proved how admirably they receive these influxes— Yes, Anna I did "shed" that "toe pad" at yr. house—& I have wanted it here—but not "awful"— Wont she plan to be at Roadside on 3rd. day next the 20th. We design to leave here in the 10 o'clk line that day  Pattie thinks she cant go with us— Anna B. is expectg Aunt Phebe Horton—wh. will hold her here till near weddg time— She & Pattie may go on together—& Anna asked me if it wd. not be best for her to go out to Thos. first, rather than take her trunk to aunt Eliza's before the wedding— Yes—

Richd. Hall[1]. ought to come on to the Penna. A. S. Mg.— I hope the notice is widely circulated— Yr father will encourage a winding up of the Penna. Organizatn. He says he shall not serve as Prest. any longer— He says No, he shall not withdraw from the Society, if they decide to go on longer— Let's merge in Equal Rights Socy.[8]

Aunt Eliza's hearty & full invitatn. was appreciated by her—glad the day is delayed—

[*Letter continues dated 17 November*]

AL MNS

1. Newall or Newell was the pastor of the Unitarian Church of Germantown (*NASS,* 5 January 1867, 2). A servant in LCM's household, Mary Pen, would be married c. 15 December (LCM to MML, 18 December 1866, MNS).

2. The "bride & groom" are probably Mary Hicks, daughter of JM's niece Sarah Hicks (1818–84) and Elias Hicks, and Peter B. Franklin (b. 1838), who had been married on 8 November (LCM to Philadelphia Family, 9 November 1866, Mott Manuscripts, PSCHi).

3. The circular, signed by Davis, LCM, Robert Purvis, and Mary Grew, invited attendance at the PASS meeting on 22–23 November: "The subject of most vital importance to this nation in its present crisis 'The right of the colored race to full citizenship in order to the security of their full freedom' will be discussed" (*NASS,* 17 November 1866, 2).

4. The AERA was to hold a meeting in Albany on 20–21 November to discuss the proposed convention to revise the New York state constitution. MCW would not attend (*NASS,* 3 November 1866, 3). Sarah Yarnall, LCM's niece, was to marry William H. Abbott.

5. "Studman" is possibly Edwin A. Studwell (b. 1837) of Brooklyn, a member of the AERA, the publisher of the Quaker journal *Friend,* and later the publisher of the *Revolution* (Gordon, 1:591).

6. John White Chadwick (1840–1904), a Unitarian minister in Brooklyn, New York, was married to Annie Horton Hathaway Chadwick (*WLG,* 5:462). Caleb Clothier, the son of William Clothier and Jane Clothier, had died on 14 November (*New York Tribune,* 15 November 1866, 5).

7. This is possibly Benjamin Smith Lyman (1835–1920), a mining engineer then based in Philadelphia.

8. The PASS did not end its work or join the AERA, a decision LCM would support at the November meeting: "These facts show the necessity of our cause, and the continued existence of the Anti-Slavery Society, notwithstanding the legal abolition of the accursed system." The PASS would resolve that "the work of the Abolitionists will not be done until the spirit of slavery is so far exorcised from the nation that the colored man of the South can assert and maintain his actual freedom in the presence of that

dominant class who, defeated on the battlefield, are now striving to win their cause by diplomacy, and to put the negro under their feet" (*NASS*, 1 December 1866, 1).

## To the Equal Rights Convention in Albany

[*Roadside*] 11 Mo. 18th. 66—

My husband and myself would gladly be with you, on this important occasion, were it practicable—

We cordially hail the move-ment at this time for your State, in view of the approaching revision of your Constitution. The negro's hour came with his Emancipation by law, from cruel bondage. He now has Advocates not a few for his right to the ballot— Intelligent as these advocates are, they must see that this right cannot be consistently withheld from woman.[1]

The several conventions of late years, for her equal rights in other respects have led to the removal of many disabilities and legal restraints, in some of the States, and opened the way to her advancement in science and art—securing to herself profitable employment in some of the professions, and in business of various kinds.

We have therefore every encouragement to persevere in this good Work, until the end shall be accomplished.

We pledge fifty dollars toward the necessary funds—

Yours cordially for Equal Rights
*Lucretia Mott.*

ALS CsmH (call number HM 10538)

1. At the meeting held on 20 November, Stanton would report LCM's absence due to "ill health." The convention would appoint a committee consisting of Stanton, Anthony, and Frederick Douglass to protest New York State's ratification of the Fourteenth Amendment (*New York Tribune*, 22 November 1866, 1).

## To Susan B. Anthony

RoadSide, near Philada.
2nd mo. 10th, 66 [*1867*]—

My dear Susan—

I hope the delay in acknowledgg. thine of 3rd will not prevent this reaching thee at Rochester—

I have been troubled lately with dizziness—approaching vertigo wh. has made me shrink from the pen—better now however—

E. C. Stanton's letter was like herself— I cannot cease to regret that some satisfactory arrangement was not made, immediately after our Annual Mg. last Spring, for the co-operation of Anti Slavery as the Standard must advocate it, and Equal Rights, as the new Organization resolved— But we cannot afford to quarrel with seeming unfairness, and I would *swallow* a good deal that is distasteful, rather than stand in an antagonistic relation with our friend & Editor, A. M. Powell— I presume he was ignorant of the important omissions in Elizh's. speech. I was glad to see it in the Standard, and never dreamed of any unfairness.[1]

Your large Meetings are very encouraging. It cheers my heart that young & new advocates are in the field, and that thy energies, dear Susan, are so untiring, and that Elizh's. zeal does not slacken in the least— I was sorry that our dear Lucy Stone did not say more, while in our City— Her husband did himself credit whenever he spoke— — A late No. of the Radical has a grand article from his pen, on Unitarian Theology— I want to thank him for it, and ask him to write more such— The Liberals among Unitarians must "stand fast"— lest the conservatives should "build again the things they have destroyed".[2]

Bartol did well in a former No. and Saml. Johnson always pleases me— Hast thou any time for interest in these discussions?[3]

Theological errors stand so in the way of human progress, that every able assailant should be hailed & encouraged— H. B. Blackwell may have gone too far in attributing so much coldness & indifference to the Unitarians as a body— I hope better things of them—

My Sister Martha is not yet with us—we hope she will soon come. I had no need however, of her aid, to decipher thy letter—and no hesitancy in forwarding with this the $25—thou names, as the balance of our pledge—for surely the least we can do, when at rest in our comfortable homes, is to furnish our mite of pecuniary aid, for the furtherance of the great cause, wh. some of you are making such sacrifice to promote— James paid over $25 last Fall, after our Annual Mg. here—in Philada— I have forgotten what our pledge was—I kept no copy of the letter—

We have had an urgent appeal within a few days, from Louisa De Mortie,[4] on behalf of an Orphan Asylum—in New Orleans— She has been quite successful in raising *thousands*— Our Freedman's Assocn. and that of our Orthodox Frds. contributed—beside a number of private gifts of 25—50—and $100 each— Saml. Willets of New Y. gives 500 toward the $1000 to be raised by the Frds. Assocn. there—

The Peace organization too calls for funds—so we have no lack of demands on our limited resources—[5]

Our nephew Frank Wright and Fanny Pell have decided on an early marriage the coming spring—so that our sister Martha will probably come on before long—[6] The Board of Managers of Eq. Rig. has held one Mg— I was not able to attend, & know not what they did—

Please acknowle. the money, if received—

affecy—    Lucretia Mott

ALS MCR

1. The "main portions" of Stanton's speech before the Judiciary Committee of the New York State Assembly on 23 January 1867 had been reprinted in the *NASS* (2 February 1867, 3). Stanton had argued for woman suffrage and urged members of the committee to allow women and blacks to vote for delegates to the upcoming state constitutional convention (see also Gordon, 2:14–15).

2. Stone had spoken at the Equal Rights Convention held in Philadelphia on 17 January, as did LCM, Stanton, Frances D. Gage, and Susan B. Anthony. The Philadelphia correspondent of the *NASS* had written: "All were imbued with the same exalted purpose, the same beneficent spirit, intent upon increasing the recognized individual rights of women" (*NASS*, 26 January 1867, 2). Blackwell's article "The Theological Dead-Lock" had appeared in the *Radical* (February 1867, 340–45). The quotation is possibly an adaptation of 2 Kings 21:3: "For he built up again the high places which Hezekiah his father had destroyed."

3. Cyrus A. Bartol (1813–1901), a Unitarian clergyman and a transcendentalist of Boston, wrote "The Theological Transition." Samuel Johnson (1822–82), a Unitarian minister from Massachusetts, wrote "American Religion." Both articles appeared in the *Radical* (January 1867, 257–73, 287–96).

4. Louisa De Mortie (c. 1833–67) (*WLG*, 5:452). LCM had frequent requests of a similar sort. On 20 July 1866 she had written MML: "We had another guest last night— Mrs. L. E. Ricks from Washington, the Freedman's friend— She has taken 2 or 300 out West—some to Michigan—& used all her means, of course—" (Mott Manuscripts, PSCHi).

5. LCM, JM, and Alfred Love had founded the Pennsylvania Peace Society in January 1866. According to the call issued in December, the society planned to hold a convention in Philadelphia on 18 January 1867 (*NASS*, 22 December 1866, 3; Bacon, 193).

6. Frank Wright would marry Frances B. Pell on 23 April 1867.

# To the Friends of the AERA

*New York, 12th March, 1867.*

FIRST ANNIVERSARY OF THE American Equal Rights Association.

The first annual meeting of the American Equal Rights Association will be held in the City of New York, at the Church of the Puritans, on Thursday and Friday, the ninth and tenth of May next, commencing on Thursday morning at 10 o'clock.

The object of this Association is to secure Equal Rights to all American Citizens, especially the Right of Suffrage, irrespective of race, color or sex.

American Democracy has interpreted the Declaration of Independence in the interest of slavery, restricting suffrage and citizenship to a *white, male minority.*

The black man is still denied the crowning right of citizenship, even in the nominally free states, though the fires of civil war have melted the chains of chattelism, and a hundred battlefields attest his courage and patriotism.

Half our population are disfranchised on the ground of sex; and though compelled to obey the law and taxed to support the government, they have no voice in the legislation of the country.

This Association then has a mission to perform, the magnitude and importance of which cannot be over-estimated.

The recent war has unsettled all our governmental foundations. Let us see that in their restoration, all these unjust proscriptions are avoided. Let Democracy be defined anew, as *the Government of the people,* AND THE WHOLE PEOPLE.

Let the gathering then at this anniversary, be in numbers and character, worthy in some degree the demands of the hour. The black man, even the black soldier, is yet but half emancipated, nor will he be, until his full suffrage and citizenship *are secured to him in the Federal Constitution.* Still more deplorable is the condition of the black woman; and legally, that of the white woman is no better!

Shall the sun of the nineteenth century go down on wrongs like these, in this nation, consecrated in its infancy to justice and freedom? Rather let our meeting be pledge as well as prophecy to the world of mankind, that the redemption of at least one great nation is near at hand.

In behalf of the American Equal Rights Association.

> LUCRETIA MOTT, Pres.
> SUSAN B. ANTHONY, *Cor. Sec'y.*
> HENRY B. BLACKWELL, *Rec. Sec'y.*

{Communications relating to this Anniversary, and donations in aid of its objects, to be addressed to SUSAN B. ANTHONY, 464 West Thirty-fourth street, New York.}

PL DLC-NAWSA, reel 46

# Memorial of the American Equal Rights Association to the Congress of the United States

*[New York City, 10 May 1867]*[1]

The undersigned, Officers and Representatives of the American Equal Rights Association, respectfully but earnestly protest against any change in the Constitution of the United States, or legislation by Congress, which shall longer violate the principle of Republican Government, by proscriptive distinctions in rights of suffrage or citizenship, on account of color or sex. Your Memorialists would respectfully represent, that neither the colored man's loyalty, bravery on the battle field and general good conduct, nor woman's heroic devotion to liberty and her country, in peace and war, have yet availed to admit them to equal citizenship, even in this enlightened and republican nation.

We believe that humanity is one in all those intellectual, moral and spiritual attributes, out of which grow human responsibilities. The Scripture declaration is, "so God created man in his own image: male and female created he them."[2] And all divine legislation throughout the realm of nature recognizes the perfect equality of the two conditions. For male and female are but different conditions. Neither color nor sex is ever discharged from obedience to law, natural or moral; written or unwritten. The commands, thou shalt not steal, nor kill, nor commit adultery, know nothing of sex in their demands; nothing in their penalty. And hence we believe that all *human* legislation which is at variance with the divine code, is essentially unrighteous and unjust. Woman and the colored man are taxed to support many literary and humane institutions, into which they never come, except in the poorly paid capacity of menial servants. Woman has been fined, whipped, branded with red-hot irons, imprisoned and hung; but when was woman ever tried by a jury of her peers?

Though the nation declared from the beginning that "all just governments derive their power from the consent of the governed," the consent of woman was never asked to a single statute, however nearly it affected her dearest womanly interests or happiness. In the despotisms of the old world, of ancient and modern times, woman profligate, prostitute, weak, cruel, tyrannical, or otherwise, from Semiramis and Messalina, to Catherine of Russia and Margaret of Anjou,[3] have swayed, unchallenged, imperial scepters; while in this republican and Christian land in the nineteenth century, woman, intelligent, refined in every ennobling gift and grace, may not even vote on the appropriation of her own property, or the disposal and destiny of her own children. Literally she has no *rights* which man is bound to respect;[4] and her civil privileges she holds only by sufferance. For the power that gave, can take away, and of that power she is no part. In most of the States, these unjust distinctions apply to woman, and to the colored man alike. Your Memorialists fully believe that the time has come when such injustice should cease.

Woman and the colored man are loyal, patriotic, property-holding, tax-paying, liberty-loving citizens; and we can not believe that sex or complexion should be any ground for civil or political degradation. In our government, one-half the citizens are disfranchised by their sex, and about one-eighth by the color of their skin; and thus a large majority have no voice in enacting or executing the laws they are taxed to support and compelled to obey, with the same fidelity as the more favored class, whose usurped prerogative it is to rule. Against such outrages on the very name of republican freedom, your memorialists do and must ever protest. And is not our protest pre-eminently as just against the tyranny of "*taxation without representation*," as was that thundered from Bunker Hill, when our revolutionary fathers fired the shot that shook the world?

And your Memorialists especially remember, at this time, that our country is still reeling under the shock of a terrible civil war, the legitimate result and righteous retribution of the vilest slave system ever suffered among men. And in restoring the foundations of our nationality, your memorialists most respect-fully and earnestly pray that all discriminations on account of sex or race be removed; and that our Government may be republican in *fact* as well as *form;* A GOVERNMENT BY THE PEOPLE, AND THE WHOLE PEOPLE; FOR THE PEOPLE, AND THE WHOLE PEOPLE.

In behalf of the
American Equal Rights Association,

Theodore Tilton,                              Lucretia Mott, President.
Frederick Douglass,                      Susan B. Anthony, Secretary.
Elizabeth Cady Stanton,
Vice-Presidents

PL *HWS,* 2:226–27

1. The AERA sent this memorial to Congress after its meeting in New York City, 9–10 May 1867 (*HWS,* 2:226).

2. Gen. 5:1–2.

3. Semiramis, a mythical Assyrian queen, was supposedly based on Sammuramat, a ninth century B.C. Assyrian regent. Messalina (22–48 A.D.) was the third wife of the Roman emperor Claudius. Catherine the Great (1729–96) was a German-born empress of Russia. Margaret of Anjou (1430–82) was the wife of Henry VI of England and the leader of the Lancastrians in the War of the Roses.

4. This phrase could be a deliberate reference to one used in Chief Justice Roger B. Taney's decision in the Dred Scott case, that the black race "had no rights which the white man was bound to respect" (Benjamin C. Howard, *Report of the Decision of the Supreme Court of the United States and the Opinions of the Judges Thereof in the Case of Dred Scott* [Washington, D.C.: Cornelius Wendell, 1857], 13).

# To Martha Coffin Wright

Phila. 11th.—[*May 1867*]
7th. day morng.

[*Continuation of a letter begun 8 May from New York City*]

Here we are "bock agn." at Edw. H's our mission satisfactorily accomplished, save not havg. thy presence—[1]  The report in the Papers gives eno' of the speech-es—  There was less than usual of a boring character, large audiences, except at the Peace Mgs. where we were in twice, without losing any of the others— — It was a pity that Wendell P. didn't shew himself at the Equal Rg. Mg., & allay the jealousy existing with Susan & E. C. Stanton— —some erroneous statements of F. D. Gage that he cd. have corrected as I tried to do—that "he was only for *manhood* suffrage, & only limitatn. of labor *for man*", &.c.—  This brot. out a foolish defence from H. C. Wright—[2]  I wished he had stayed at the Peace Mg.— Ernestine L. Rose made a good speech—  She was glad to hear from thee—had hoped thou wd. be there—as had others—  She gave me hers & husbds. Photoghs. & asked for mine, wh. I shall send her—[3]

My health & strength held out pretty well—so that Robt. P[urvis]. leavg. on 4th. day eveg., I took the chair— Anna B. so kindly sittg. near, to wait on me out, if strength failed, as it did 5th. day eveg. Jas. had gone to Brooklyn before dark—not seeg. well. I went home with Anna to lodge—as we both did—on 3rd. day night— Walter & Harry [*Brown*] left home 6th. day for a little excursion North & East— Marion has something. of Intermitt[en]t.—chills every other day—2 wks. ago—& returng. now— Her Mother will take her to Philada. soon—& be with *us* at Roadside a few days—as she wants to see Benjn. [*Yarnall*] agn. before going to Newburgh— He continues abt. the same—the difficulty of walkg. increasg. so that he does not go down stairs at all—sits in the front chamber—Eliza & Reba. or Sarah both assistg. him into the back room adjoining. They say here he will be obliged to have a man I am going there now—before Mg.—Yearly you know

Roadside—1st-day 12th.

At home resting—the Annivy. week gone "with the years beyond the flood"[4]—as go all things! Writg. while attendg. these Mgs. is next to impossible—the long rides back & forth—& if at Walters, late breakfasts—a temptatn. to be lazy in bed—such a lot of letters & Papers as I took to look over & ans., & all brot. back minus a look! to say nothg. of little bundles of sewing, not touched—not even Pattie [*Lord*]'s stockgs. darned—full as *her* hands were, preparg. to send such a load to their country home— This is unlike thy doings while here—but then thou hadn't Mgs. to attend, & 1000 people to speak to— As to visits & calls I declined all— Jas. went to E. Broadway once & to Han. Haydk's. to enquire after Sam who was & still is quite ill—fever & a large abscess on his side, wh. was opened the day we left— Mary (Hicks) Franklin & husband came to one of our Mg. & saw us there. So did Abby Gibbons— Anna B. was with us every day— We hope she will be here the last of this wk. when we get home from Yearly Mg— We returned to the City 6th. day aftern.— E. M. D[avis]. with us— I dreaded to leave before the Mg. was over— Edwd. waited on us down to Edwd. H's & then came out via Germantn.—Jas. Corr driving over for him— Anna [*Hopper*] had a treat of ice cream for us—& a good resting night we had—went to Select Mg. yestery., few strangers & *they* not distingu[ishe]d so we willingly came out last eveg—Jas Corr drivg. in for us— Maria. [*Mott*] & Maria H. & Bel also drove in—Emily [*Mott*] there the night before—so we had a table full at dinner—makg. me glad that I had slipped away from Sam L. Keese, lest he shd. hang on, to be guest with us all the week at Edwd's.— Anna H. came out with us—& such a lot of bundles & luggage! I bot. some 40 in. pillow or bolster case muslin at Steward's as we c'dnt. find it in our City—wh. increased our baggage— We left Pattie full of busins.[5]—all the carpets up—2 bureaus—washstand &.c. brot. down to the back parlor & dozens of other things, ready for the load wh. the farmer they hire the Place of is comg. with his large wagon to take up for them— They all go on 5th. day— It is no doubt the best thing they cd. do—but it seems a great way off.

MAY 1867

I called at Benjns. before the morng. Mg.—found him not much changed—more pain—less ability to walk—the Dr. was glad he no longer attempted to go down stairs. Aunt Sally's chair with wheels has been taken there wh. aids his locomotn. a little—but not so pleast. to sit in— His nights are painful— He now admits that it wd. be impossible to go out of Town at present—

Maria D. met us there after Mg. & thy letter with Ellen [*Garrison*]'s was read—& glad we all were to have it & such pleast. accots. of Frank & Fanny [*Wright*]—while we mourned dear Eliza Osborne's continued inability to go about, & be with you— How often her kindness was before me, as I dressed in her new flannel pet[ticoat]. each morng. at Anna's & Pattie's—quite opportune too, for the golden wed. one was too nearly worn out—& a thick winter one too soiled. What can I do for her? I wish she cd. change the scene by comg. to us awhile— I didn't know till yestery. that Carrie Dennis was going to Eng— Who isnt? How she will be missed at home! Still I think it an advantage to young wives to be house keepers— — Maria has recd. nice letters from S. M'Kim & Wendell—the latter to A. D. Hall[l]. with particulars of *Lloyd's* advent & their happiness—[6] Miller came twice to our Mgs. & had some talk with Edwd. D—& very few min. with us— I had to leave Anna B. with him & go to my *chair*— Many who had never been at a Wom. Rig. Mg. before came & expressed their great joy at being there, & hearg. some they had heard of I might say much of our Mgs., but for time & room & power to give you an idea of the interest of them—full attend[anc]e. thro'out— Anna E. Dickn. attracted many to the AntSlavy. & H. W. Beecher to the Equal Rights— Elizh. Stanton's openg. address was excellt.—[7] Parker Pillsby. read a very able one he had prepared, he sd., on a sick bed shewg. how other governmts. had failed & how ours was on the eve of a similar fate—parts were so discouraging our enormous debt—taxtn. &.c—that I told the audience he had out-Parkered Parker, & I was glad to remember that he had written it on a *sick* bed—he joined heartily in the laugh produced— He sd. if all were true as our Resolutns. & speeches indicated, he might think the millenium near at hand—[8] I do like Parker tho'.

[*P.S.*] I forgot that Aunt Eliza hadn't seen Wm. Folger's letter—please send it back— I hope the Reno postmaster has sent our joint letter to him before this—do write again— I will send Pattie's letters little as they contain except about the country home  Destroy them— Eliza may like to look over them— Wilt thou tell me agn. how thou makes mint sauce— Our garden has much in it, & I mean to have it—should the water be warm—and do you put butter in it? or anything? Tom Parrish stayed out here every night during our absence for pretended protectn.— We are very glad to have him back to the City & his coal business is successful so far—

AL MNS

1. LCM and JM were staying with Anna Temple Brown and Walter Brown while in New York City. They had attended a series of annual meetings: of the AASS on 7 May, of the American Peace Society on 8–9 May, and of the AERA on 9–10 May.

2. In his address to the AASS, Phillips had emphasized the need to "take forever and entirely out of American politics the question of race." He also had named temperance, the improvement of the laborer's status, and woman's rights—"the injustice of one-half of the human race"—as other important causes (*NASS*, 25 May 1867, 1). In remarks at the AERA meeting, Frances D. Gage had declared, "We are told by Mr. Phillips to flood the South with spelling-books. Who is to carry them there? Who, to-day, is teaching the Southern people . . . ? The women of the North, gathering up their strength, have been sent down by all these great societies to teach. The colored men of the South are to vote, while they deny the ballot to their teacher!" Later in the meeting, Henry C. Wright had stated that "no antagonism" should exist between the antislavery and woman's rights organizations. Although both wished "the enfranchisement of both classes, it was no more than right that each should devote his energies to his own movement" (*HWS*, 2:198, 220).

3. Rose and her husband, William E. Rose, a jeweler and silversmith, then lived in New York City. She had concluded her remarks at the AERA by saying, "No 'social evil' was ever yet stopped by force of law. The corrective of our social evil must be commenced in the nursery. . . . Let woman have the franchise, and there will be no further talk about a social evil" (*NASS*, 1 June 1867, 3).

4. LCM is possibly alluding to Gen. 11:10: "Two years after the flood."

5. MML and her family were moving from their Brooklyn home to Suffern, New York, for the summer.

6. Lucy McKim Garrison and her husband, Wendell Phillips Garrison, had recently had a son, Lloyd McKim Garrison (1867–1900).

7. Dickinson had argued at the AASS meeting that the work of the Republican party was far from accomplished; the party must endorse impartial suffrage for freedmen. At the AERA meeting, at which LCM had stated the need for the organization to establish its own newspaper, Henry Ward Beecher is reported to have said that the "black man would be more likely to obtain suffrage if it was demanded at the same time for women." According to the *NASS*, Stanton had declared that suffrage was "a natural right. . . . To woman it was given to save the republic, and to allow her to perform this work she would neither place her at the feet nor the head of man, but on the same level platform of equality with him" (*Proceedings of the First Anniversary of the American Equal Rights Association* [New York: Robert F. Johnston, 1867], 7; *NASS*, 25 May 1867, 1, 1 June 1867, 3).

8. In his AERA speech, "The Mortality of Nations," Parker Pillsbury had expressed his concern about the "physicians" of "doubtful reputation" who were in charge of the young republic. He considered it remarkable that a white male citizen had in his control not one but three ballots: his own, the other two to be *given* to women and to colored men at his pleasure or convenience! Such an idea should never have outraged our common humanity." The AERA's resolutions included one congratulating the woman's rights cause for its success in calling attention to the importance of woman suffrage in both the U.S. Congress and several Northern states (*NASS*, 13 July 1867, 3, 1 June 1867, 3).

# To Octavius B. Frothingham

RoadSide, near Philada—
5 Mo. 20th. 1867—

My dear O. B. Frothingham

Thy letter of invitation to a radical Religious Mg. in Boston on the 30th., deserves an answer.[1] What shall I say? If my friends knew how old, and feeble, and nearly worn out I am, they certainly would not desire my presence, when there are so many young and vigorous women, who do credit to our sex.— Had I replied immediately it would have been to decline the gratifying invitation. But when our Mariana P. Mott read thy letter, she felt a desire to be present, and therefore encouraged my going, and she would take care of me. So it may be that I shall be foolish enough to accept the 'Call'—but please make no announcement—I should be ashamed.

You doubtless have a care that an invitation so extended to all classes of Radicals, may not inflict upon you, or upon the meeting, some who are ever ready to give their presence, and occupy the time, not the most profitably— Should I go you may find me too strong on the side of organization—[x]

> Sincerely thy frd.
> Lucretia Mott—

[x]or rather too favorably inclined—

ALS CULA

1. The Free Religious Association would hold its first meeting on 30 May 1867. A number of prominent woman's rights activists would join the association, an outgrowth of the Unitarian movement, composed of both Christians and Jews, that supported religious reform (William Leach, *True Love and Perfect Union: The Feminist Reform of Sex and Society* [New York: Basic Books, 1980], 7, 86; Bacon, 197). In her speech at the meeting, LCM would state that she represented herself and not the Society of Friends and would call for a recognition of "independence of the mind": "I would desire that the convention may result in so enlarged a charity and so enlarged an idea of religion, and of proper cultivation of the religious nature and element in man, as to be able to bear all things, and to be able to have that extended charity that is not offended, and does not deprecate going on before, and to have charity for those who are behind, and also for those who go on before" (*Sermons*, 296).

## To Anna Mott Hopper and Roadside and Suffern Families

> Medford [*Massachusetts*]
> 5 mo. 30th. 66 [*1867*]—5th day

My dear Anna—& Roadside & Suffern—

I was sorry after Maria [*Davis*]'s letter was gone that I had not thot. to ask you to send it to Pattie [*Lord*], as we have not written to her— If on hand when this is recd., do send it with this— The word from Geo. that dear baby [*Anna Lord*] was no worse, &.c was a great comfort—

Thy letter, Anna, was such a welcome sight, as Richard [*Hallowell*] met us at the Convention & handed out several to Maria— Knowg. thy father was from home, of course I did not expect any direct word from Roadside—

We hoped & looked for Mari[a]. [*Mott*]—in vain I shall watch agn. this morng. for her comg. to the Radical Mg.—but not with much expectatn.—

All the mention of uncle Benjn. [*Yarnall*] was read with great interest & so much sympathy for his continued sufferg.— It is a relief to know that he has a nurse—& that aunt Eliza is better— The daughrs. being able to stay nights will be a great help & comfort to them—

We have been talkg. this morng—of the best way of returng.—to afford a little time to stop in the City on 7th. day & go up there— Maria says the Norwich Line will enable us to reach Philada., so that we can have two or three hours there, before going out home— Possibly Maria may conclude to stay here over 1st. day—so as to see Willie [*Davis*] on his return from his walkg. excursion— She says *not* unless some one shall be going on for company for me— I tell her *any stranger* wd. render all the aid necessy.—just from the car at Norwich to the Boat close by—& then arrivg. at Jersey City to wait on me to the car near by for Philada— We will talk it over at the breakfast table, wh. is later than usual, we were so late reachg. here last eveg—near 12 o'clk—came out in the cars—Richd. & Anna [*Hallowell*] with us— She had to part with her good cook yestermorng—she quarrelled with the other girls—a new one is to come on 7th. day  Anna didn't go into Town till aftern.— — Our Mgs. thro' the day & eveg. were vastly interestg.—even Maria thot. so— Wendell P. great, as usual,—S. Foster combative on the Wom. Res.—ansd. by Wendell, and H. C. Wright who was *very as usual*—Wm. Wells B—and one or two more—Towne—on the Stearns Resolutn.—a few words from yr. aged Mother—also from Abby K. Foster—she in oppositn. to her husbd. on the introductn. of the Wom. questn.— Parker P. opposed to her—a very good speech—not confined to that.[1] We dined in co. with him at that new friend Ellen Johnson's—Parker's daughr. with him— an only child—[2] — The eveg. was too much occupied with antagonistic speeches on the wom. question.

The Papers may contain further notice of the Mg— Christr. C. Hussey was there & talked freely with me.[3] He is pleased with the change he has made— He is now near yr. Falkner frds. who are his best frds.—

Very few familiar faces at the Mg— How I missed the Southwicks—Quincys—Westons &c.— No Maria W. Chapman[4]—"not a Garri."—even Ellen [*Garrison*] didn't find us till the close of the morng. Mg. & had to return immedy. M. A. Johnson still very sick with neumonia— Oliver has come on to assist in nursg— We hope Ellen will come out here tomorw. & have a quiet morng. with us—

L Mott

ALS PSCHi-Mott

1. At the meeting of the New England Anti-Slavery Society, held 29 and 30 May 1867 in Boston, Phillips had stated that the society should be concerned only with black suffrage. Stephen Foster had disagreed with Phillips's stance that the society should not bring up "the woman question." Foster had said, "It was a matter of policy to press both questions now. It would give them two strings to their bow." Agreeing with Phillips, Henry C. Wright had argued that the convention's charge was restricted "to the rights

of the colored man." Addressing the convention on 30 May, William Wells Brown stated that he perceived a tendency to "claim the right of woman to vote, and in so doing to disparage the negro. . . . A dozen Mrs. Mott's or Mrs. Stanton's could not do so much good as the mere presence of Frederick Douglass in Congress." Following Brown, Rev. Edward C. Towne had given a tribute to the changes wrought by the late George L. Stearns (1809–67), a wealthy Boston abolitionist.

LCM had addressed the meeting at its first session on 29 May. She had stated that the "great woman question" was undeniably connected with the issue of black suffrage: the woman question "was no more bringing in an extraneous topic, than the claim of right for the slave to vote would have been considered an extraneous topic a few years ago." She had urged the group to "harmonize together, and feel that we are one. I should greatly lament anything like a feeling of division or opposition among us, because we differ in our views as to some of the questions now agitating the country. We cannot separate these great reformatory movements—and let us feel that we are still united together." In disagreement, Abby Kelley Foster had maintained that the organization's purpose was not to secure suffrage for either freedmen or all women but to "secure freedom from chattel slavery." She believed that, while former slaves were legally free, they were still in economic and political bondage. Rebutting Foster, Parker Pillsbury had stated that women's, as well as freedmen's, suffrage was an appropriate concern of the organization and "it would be a doubtful experiment to give it to black men and not to black women" (*WLG*, 4:693; *NASS*, 8 June 1867, 2, 15 June 1867, 1–3).

2. Ellen Cheney Johnson (1829–99) was a Boston reformer especially concerned with female prisoners' welfare. Parker Pillsbury's daughter was Helen Buffum Pillsbury (b. 1843) (*WLG*, 5:538).

3. Christopher C. Hussey (c. 1820–97), a Nantucket native, was a former Quaker and at this time a Unitarian minister from Billerica, Massachusetts (*Friends' Intelligencer*, 20 November 1867).

4. Thankful Southwick (1792–1867), her daughter, Sarah Southwick (1821–96), and the others named here were all members of the Boston Female Anti-Slavery Society (*WLG*, 5:106, 272).

## To the Public

OFFICE OF THE AMERICAN
EQUAL RIGHTS ASSOCIATION
37 Park Row, (Room 17,) New York,
[*c. July*] 1867[1]

Mr. Editor—

Will you please publish the enclosed Appeal in your paper, and very much oblige

THE EQUAL RIGHTS ASSOCIATION
THE AMERICAN EQUAL RIGHTS ASSOCIATION,
TO THE PEOPLE OF THE UNITED STATES

The Legislature of Kansas has submitted separately, the questions of "Suffrage for Colored Men," and "Suffrage for Women," to a vote of the electors of that State, the coming autumn.

Our Association wishes to send Tracts and Speakers into the State, to make a thorough canvass of every School District, during the months of September and October, feeling sure that with such an agitation, both questions may be easily carried at the November Election.

To do this work, MONEY is needed. Willing hands and hearts are ready, and only wait the means.

FRIENDS OF EQUAL RIGHTS, we ask you to send us your contributions— each according to your ability—the rich, of your abundance, and the poor, the "widow's mite." Help us now, every man and every woman who wishes to see the experiment of UNIVERSAL SUFFRAGE tried; and the morning after the Kansas election, the Telegraph will announce to the world that in Kansas *all women* as well as *all men* are equal before the law.

In behalf of the
American Equal Rights Association,
LUCRETIA MOTT, *President*
ELIZABETH CADY STANTON,
FREDERICK DOUGLAS,               } *Vice Pres.*
HENRY WARD BEECHER
SUSAN B. ANTHONY, *Cor. Sec'y.*
HENRY B. BLACKWELL, *Rec. Sec'y*

Contributions should be sent in Drafts on New York, or Post Office Orders, payable to the Order of the American Equal Rights Association.[2]

Communications should be addressed—SUSAN B. ANTHONY, 37 Park Row, (Room 17,) New York.

PL NSyU

1. In July 1867, Anthony had begun to raise money for her trip to Kansas and, with the support of "eastern friends," had fifty thousand woman's rights tracts printed to distribute there. Stanton and Anthony would leave for Kansas on 28 August; Lucy Stone and others had preceded them in the spring and summer to begin the AERA's campaign for woman and black male suffrage in that state (Ida Husted Harper, *The Life and Work of Susan B. Anthony* [Indianapolis: Hollenbeck Press, 1898], 1:282–83; *HWS*, 2:239; on Stanton and Anthony's efforts in Kansas, see Gordon, 2:88–104).

2. During the campaign, the Republican party withdrew active support for the woman suffrage bill, and in the election on 7 November it would fail to pass, as would the bill for universal male suffrage (Ellen Carol DuBois, *Feminism and Suffrage: The Emergence of an Independent Women's Movement in America, 1848–1869* [Ithaca, N.Y.: Cornell University Press, 1978], 79–80, 86–87, 96).

## To Caroline Healey Dall

Suffern—Erie Road—
30 miles from New York
8 mo. 9th. 67—

My Dear Caroline H. Dall—

Thy two letters ought to have been acknowledged before now; and would have been, had I been at home at the time of their reception—and had thy beautiful present—the Book been received as early as thou intended—[1] It did however come to hand in good order, when I waited to read it, before saying all I wanted to, of thy great kindness, and how much I valued it. But again absence from home, & many engagements prevented my finishing it, until I was called to this Place, to be with our youngest daughter, in her confinement—[2]—

Thy letters are now before me, and deserve more than a passing notice. When thou wrote, early in the Spring, during my illness, I felt much for thee, that so little sympathy and aid were likely to reach thee from our region, where we have ever found progress so slow in every reformatory movement—but that any discouraging words should go forth to thee, from the source thou mentioned to me in Boston, was surprising—   I too was sorry that the brief interview that morning, during the meeting, was all that opportunity offered.

Thy unwearied devotion to the cause of Woman's best developement, has always been most grateful to my feelings. When thou reviewed Bayard Taylor's Work[3] so faithfully, my heart blessed thee—as well as when reading some of thy lectures—   These, as now embodied in this Volume will reach many who never could have heard thee, and will do great good. Not the least valuable too are the biographical sketches of so many women who have lived & labored in advance of their age. I am much interested in these, and especially so in thy rescuing from the intended oblivion of her enemies—Mary Woolstonecraft, whose Rights of Woman I read 40 years ago, and was greatly astonished that such a Work should be thus condemned, and out of print. From that time it has been a centre table book, and I have circulated it, wherever I could find readers. I have at home a few lines written to a friend concerning her, which he had printed in a country Paper, and which I will send thee on my return.

Sarah Grimke in her Work on Woman noticed Mary W. I think in 1835 or 6—   She was impressed much as I was, on first reading her book—   The Reviews of thine, in several of the Papers & Periodicals, we have read with interest—   Harpers Weekly, very good we thought—the Nation—Tribune, &. c. did pretty well.[4] I made effort before leaving home, to have it noticed in our Press, but not much has appeared. Of course an Author has to bear rough treatment— Thou doubtless hast learned to "endure hardness as a good Soldier". I am sorry thou art reaping no pecuniary profit from the Sale—   The mite now enclosed is only in grateful remembrance of thy unceasing effort to elevate Woman

Unworthy as I feel of such a tribute as thou bestows in the Dedication, the less said about that may be best—

Sincerely thy frd.—
Lucretia Mott.

ALS MHi

1. Caroline Healey Dall's book, *The College, the Market, and the Court; or, Woman's Relation to Education, Labor, and Law* (Boston: Lee and Shepard, 1867), focused on notable women such as Harriet Martineau, Mary Wollstonecraft, and Margaret Fuller, and traced the history of women's oppression. It bore a dedication to LCM, who had been "for more than fifty years a preacher and reformer; spotless alike in all public and private relations . . . she is the best example that I know of what all women may and should become."

2. MML's daughter Lucretia ("Lulu") Lord had been born on 5 August.

3. The most recent work of Bayard Taylor (1825–78), the poet, travel writer, and translator of Goethe, was *Colorado: A Summer Trip* (New York: G. P. Putnam, 1867).

4. The *Nation*'s reviewer hoped the book, which advocated woman suffrage, would have "a profitable circulation, in all senses of the word," but also stated that Dall was "perhaps a little too anxious to verify her own credentials" and thus would invite "the charge of pedantry or egotism" (18 July 1867, 46).

## To Martha Coffin Wright

[*Roadside*]
9 Mo. 3rd—2nd. day—[*1867*]

Clear, fine washg. day—large collection—sheets, towels tablecloths, napkins to say nothg. of other things— Your experience must be somewhat similar of late— Mary Q. H. is bravely again and comes regularly to help wash & iron— and when we have a large compy. to dine or tea she is ready when sent for— It is really wonderful how rapidly a settlement has grown where the Camp Wm. Penn was— Edwd. [*Davis*] sold it off in lots— Our Jas. Corr and Henry D's man joined & bot. several acres on speculation, & have made more than $100 by the purchase— Now we can count some 18 small neat houses going up—a doz. finished & inhabited, & instead of the music of the Camp we hear the cries of the sellers of peaches, melons, sweet potatoes, &.c. &.c— Our butcher goes there as regularly as he comes here, & Anna D. H. guesses they buy more meat than we do—she thinks we are "the beater" for eating little meat— Richard [*Hallowell*] wd. frighten us, & she has learned to eat more than she used to— tho' they never have it on tea-table as we do— We always accustomed our childn. not to expect great things in the way of food— — Thou remembers Thos. [*Mott*] askg. his grandmr. if she thot. he was a *horse*, when she offered him so large a piece of cake—

We have run upon egg plants lately—all like them so much—tho' I dont eat them—or anythg. else much— I am indulged now with not going to the table, but have my coffee & tea brot. into the library where I can hear the subjects before them— The sight & smell of food often makes me sick— My stomach seems to be giving out in that direction— Thos. Mott has inherited somewhat of my dyspepsia only I never was thus afflicted till long after his birth— He has had some painful attacks this week or 2 past— Perhaps the care of disposing of his possessions is the exciting cause— There was so large a nibble for the beautiful Place, that we began to feel it as good as sold— Bel [*Mott*] sd. she wd. rather not go to Europe than sell it— Now 'tis all off agn., & they are easy to leave it in Danl.'s & the gardener's charge—Ann to live in the cottage at the gate, & have an oversight of the Palace &.c, &.c.— Jas. Kyle the farmer has gone away— Now if Mariᵃ. [*Mott*] & Bel. have written all this, & you get beside a hurried lot of Oak Lane Buildg. papers scribbled over to Pattie—& a sheet on its way, via Newburgh,[1] this will be dreadful *twoses*!

George L. wastes so much paper running over it in this style, that the least I can do, is to gather up the fragments, & make the most of them— I wrote two or three last week, to one & another—Nathl. Barney, &.c on decent note paper— & now one must certainly go to Parker Pillsbury, who is acting for S. B. Anthony & E. C. Stanton in their absence—raising all the money they can in the dreadful up-hill work of the Equal Rights Society—[2] I never had full faith in its formatn. while there is so much to be done for the Freedmen—neither had thou—for we saw eye to eye at that time—and the work has fallen on such a very few, to labor in yr. State for the Revised Constitution that it could have been done quite as well without an Organizatn. Thou & Eliza [*Osborne*] & Ellen [*Garrison*] have set us such a good example, that I musn't let Susan's urgent appeal to us lie any longer unnoticed  I had hoped to collect a little, *over* as my day is, for anythg,—but namg. it to Sarah Pugh & others  They see no way to make a collectn.—indeed the attempted Mgs. of this State branch, is a failure— I cant for my life remember when they occur—the Committee & Officers I mean, & I have not attended one since we organized last Fall— I sent $25 to Albany then & $25 since to S. B. Anty. for my share, & I now shall send 50 more, & that's all— Thos. & Mariᵃ. have calls constantly— They are drawn upon to the full extent— They heard Susan's letter— They also hear appeals for the Freedmen  We are just meetg. agn. to see if our Frds. Associatn. can possibly raise eno' to keep our 16 teachers at the South, & dare not engage them for more than 6 mo.—& have appointed a large begging com. for *that*.

The Swarthmore College is another constant draft (or [ouch?])—a gatherg. on the ground tomorw. on the completion of another part of the large building—[3] We talk of going, tho' Jas. thinks I'm not well eno'— The Peace Organizatn. draws on us every now & then— They print too much— We were at a Mg. at Germantn. yesteraftern., instd. of going to any in the morng.— The house was filled & a number of good speeches made— Dr. Child always does well— Mr. Newell took part altho' not sound on the subject—& a Mr. Storer from Boston, if I have his name right. I was introduced to him— Rachel Moore

Townsend said much & *well.* She & her husband, & Jas. & self were delegated, with Alfred Love, to attend a Mg. in Boston, of the *Universal* Peace Socy. on the 9th. of next mo.— Rachel told us Saml. couldn't go, but if we wd., she wd. go, *under our wing*!!⁴ I think I see myself takg. her to Medford— We have a prior engaget.—overseers at Joseph Lovering Jr's. marriage on the 10th. of sd. Mo.— Alfred Love's wife⁵ was so ill he c'dn't be at the Mg. yestery.

You may not "make head or tail" of this sheet—and tis of no consequence that you should— I have just written on as if I had been talkg. to my dear Sister here in this Library, with a fire this clear, cool morng. As I hope to do before many weeks— Come before 'tis time for Eliza & Reba. [*Yarnall*] to go back to their "deserted Hall," & then they may be persuaded to come here first, as they have not done yet, much to our regret—for if our sister can meet all those Germantn. Mg. worshippers every week, reason says she might come & sit in our quiet chamber, "with none to molest or make afraid."⁶

My carpet rags have occupied me of late, to add to the 8 or 10 yds. on hand, to cover our kitchen this Fall—still once or twice a week, I have left all & a fam[il]y. of 15 & gone there—the drive alone takg. 2 hours each time— Once we met at Mary Brown's to dine—Maria D. too— Twice, on our way to a Mg. over Schuylkill—& this aftern. Mariana is going to call for Maria & self to go with her & call on Emily Taylor whose father died at Aug[ust]a.-Maine this summer Isaac Winslow—we have written about his last illness I think— We shall stop at Ellerslie as Mariᵃ. often has done to see Agnes [*Harrison*]; & now we have such a nice letter from thee to gladden Eliza's heart with.

Mariana recd. it on 7th. day, just as she was going out—so she kept it till eveg., when we went over & enjoyed it, leavg. Tom [*Parrish*] & Fanny [*Cavender*] to their pleasure—Maria & Edwd., with Anna D. H. & Willie havg. gone to Henry [*Davis*]'s to tea— The graphic accot. of the "narrow escape" of Emily & party amused us so much, that Bel & Maria Hopper who was there, waited on us back to read it to Tom & Fanny— I told them now to read thy Review of Maria Child's *Romance*— I don't like such high-strung fictions— Mariana was in last eveg. & picked up a book from the table, that Steve Parrish brot. from Eng.:⁷—our Grandfr. Mott's "Hints to Young People on the duties of Civil Life". Eng. Friends had it printed & neatly bound— It was only a pamphlet here— wh. I have had in our pile these "100 yrs." I told Mariᵃ. it was thot. excellent when he published it— After lookg. over it a little, she asked to have another book handed her "*not quite so excellent*". She does however read her share of very good works, includg. the Bible— If they dont go till the latter part of November, wh. is not yet decided, thou may be here in time to enjoy the Place & *them* awhile, even if thou waits for Frank & Fanny [*Wright*]'s return

Anna B. will be at home by the middle of the Mo unless they are off to the Adirondacks—geese for wantg. to go away there so late in the season— Henry Davis & his uncle Morris have just returned, & say there was *ice* there before they left— He had great enjoyt. in his trip— Thy "Roland for an Oliver" if that's it, was just what I expected, after my little hint that more of thy own thots. & comments on letters recd. wd. be more interestg. than about people we knew not of— I told Mari[a]. I was lookg. for just that, & had been running over some of the new names in mine It was "a happy hit" we thot., & the whole letter was bright— Have I ever said we all read David's *very long* "*brief*"—& Woods vindictive reply—and the articles in yr. Papers that were sent—& thought there was more personality than was best— It called forth such spiteful return, even tho' disclaimed in the beging— Now we only want to know when the contest is ended, which beat, & if the road is really to be made either route— —[8] We are sorry eno' to hear of Eliza's continued inability to go up & downstairs, &.c.— If she can practice a little every day—not to tire herself, she may be able to travel as far as here & rest awhile— A journey to Ohio cured our Sister when her back was so weak, that she had to ride with a pillow at first— All hereaway wd. welcome her comg. most heartily— In the mean time look out for some sweet potats.—Thos. will send some before long— — Tis new times for Ministers, with such good salaries, to be asking for assistants— Wm. Furness has been doing as S. J. May did— I dont like it much. Indeed the whole system is deplorable  Elisa Barney mourned over the number of young Unitarian ministers, waitg. for a call somewhere—

AL MNS

1. Anna Temple Brown and Walter Brown were then living in Newburgh, New York.
2. In a letter of July 1867 to MCW, Anthony had described the difficulties she and Stanton were experiencing raising money to cover their expenses for their Kansas campaign (Ida H. Harper, *Life and Work of Susan B. Anthony* [Indianapolis: Hollenbeck Press, 1898], 1:282–83).
3. Benjamin Hallowell, Martha Tyson, and Nathan Tyson of the Hicksite Baltimore Yearly Meeting of Friends had provided the main impetus leading to the organization of Swarthmore College in 1860. LCM and JM had been involved in the formation of "a Havreford College of our own" as early as October 1862, and LCM had served on a committee on education. Although the college had been incorporated in May 1864, construction on the first building was slow, for $200,000 was needed to complete it. The *Friends' Intelligencer* would describe admission standards as "exceedingly liberal. Those belonging to other religious denominations can send their children to this institution, while at the same time their religious convictions . . . will be strictly respected" (Richard J. Walton, *Swarthmore College: An Informal History* [Swarthmore, Pa.: Swarthmore College, 1986], 2–3; LCM to MCW, 19 June 1862, Mott Manuscripts, PSCHi; LCM to MML, 15 October 1865, MNS; *Friends' Intelligencer,* 7 September 1867, 427).
4. Henry T. Child (c. 1814–90), a Philadelphia Hicksite Quaker, was the clerk of the Pennsylvania Peace Society. At a meeting on 25 August in Abington LCM had spoken on the "fallacy of war" and Rachel Moore Townsend had expressed her "sympathy with the movement." Love as president and LCM as vice president had issued a call for a general meeting of the Universal Peace Society on 9–10 October (*Friends' Intelligencer,* 21 June 1890, 392; *NASS,* 7 September 1867, 3, 5 October 1867, 3).
5. Susan Henry Brown Love (c. 1830–1913) was a Quaker (*WLG,* 5:177).
6. Benjamin Yarnall had died on 23 June (*Philadelphia North American,* 25 June 1867). The quotation is a variation on several biblical passages: Micah 4:4, Job 11:19, and Jer. 30:10.

7. Lydia Maria Child, *A Romance of the Republic* (Boston: Ticknor and Fields, 1867). Stephen Parrish (1846–1938) was the son of Dillwyn Parrish.

8. Charles Wood advocated a different railroad line than did David Wright, and the two had published their differences in the Auburn newspaper (MCW to William P. Wright, 7 August 1867, MNS).

## To Martha Coffin Wright

Brooklyn [*New York*]
1 mo. 21st. 68—
snowing E [wind?]

My Dear Sister

Would that I could answ. thy letter, recd. shortly before we left home—read by Aunt Eliza &.c—& sent out to us at night, when my eyes & head were in such a watery state from continued severe cold, that I pocketed said letter till morng— Maria [*Davis*] was up at Henry's or she wd. have read them aloud—tho' I always prefer to have the first readg— Early next morng. we were off in the cars to Town— Caroe. White had sent me two numbers of the "Catholic World", containg. a long essay on Woman's culture—so excellt. she knew I wd. be glad to read it.[1] Such a multitude of readg. delayed *that,* till she sent for it to return to the Library. So I had to finish it as we rode into Town & it is indeed very liberal & the most enlarged advocacy of woman's engagg. in Science, inventions, &.c—citing numerous cases of remarkable progress every way. The author, a French distinguished Catholic Bishop—whose name begins with D— If thou can borrow the October & Nov. number of the World, do read it— I stopped at J. Cavrs. & left a nice sack & sontag for Rosa from Fanny toward her fitting out. Rosa has gone to her new place @ $2 pr. week— An auction sale to come off soon— Then I went & delivered the pamphlets to Caro W. found Phebe Gibbons there on a visit— She is more reconciled to her home life— Joseph has some little busins.— — Mary Earle comg. back in March—Anna Folger with her—[2] Fredk. Mitchell lately died—from their circle—a great loss— His wife very hard of hearing— Timy. very childish—all the news I got—

To come to the point,—when about a square from there in Spruce St. my *bag* was among the missing—turng. back, asked a girl cleang. the pave[men]t., if she had seen it—"Yes a woman picked it up & went into that court"—so I went back & forth, & of course found it *not*— Edwd. Hopper advertised it, but no return when we left home— I was glad the articles were delivered before the loss— but such a lot of papers & letters as were to be answd. that day & night & next morng. that we should be in Town— It was that large worked bag—red, green, yellow—by Harriet Purvis for the Fair 10 or 15 yrs. ago—with a brown top sewed on—& used no end in the ten yeas we have lived at Roadside— The 3rd. bag lost since we lived there. Nothg. of much value in this, save *thy* letter—one or

two pocketh[and]k[erchie]fs. & all told—Nathl. Barney's letter with an interestg
accot. of Thos. A. Green's death & Mr. Potter's[3] sermon—a letter to him from
Saml. Rodman—  One from Wm. H. Johnson givg. an interestg. accot. of the
public schools in Bucks & Chester Co. & Lancaster wh. I intended to hand over
to Ed. Parrish & Helen Longstreth for Swarthmore's benefit—beside thine before this last sent to Anna Brown I think—or perhaps "dear Sisters," & wh. had
not been sent to Europe[4]—or maybe it had, for I forget every thing—  So now
all I can do is to mourn said losses, ask you to write over agn. as you may—
Several of Pattie [Lord]'s late letters were among them, some of which I intended to send to you even if Pattie did scold—  Eliza Y. could tell many little items
in Wm. Folger's, as well as in thine—  What a sad loss is Mary F. Ladd![5]

Now for other matters—Fanny Pell [Wright] will tell you we are here, & Jas.
Mott sick in bed every hour since we arrived on 6th. day eveg. 5 oclk. Mary Mott
Lord with us—  He seemed perfectly well when we left home—  We had Jas.
Corr to drive us into Town—& away down "on the Neck" to Edwd. Hopper's—
doing sundry errands, attendg. a Swarthmore Com. Mg. for ½ an hour—then
to Eliza's where tea & bisct. bread & butter &.c. refreshed us, preparatory to drivg.
over to West Philada cars @ 1½ oclk—Mary Cavender with us—to call afterward for Lizzie Parrish to go out with her for a few days at Roadside—  Susy
Hallowell we left there for a week—out of pure sympathy for Fanny—  She is
better gaining every day—  Maria H. & Joe Parrish also meant to go out on 1st.
day—so we trust "the Mice will play"—Henry & Pattie D. with their guests—
coz. Naomi, & Mary J. Lester were to be bidden to add to their mirth in our
absence—[6] It was least expected to have this sickness, to add to Pattie's 1000 &
1 steps—for I am so forlorn with some fever every day, & night sweats, that it is
little help I am——  Nellie is old eno' now to be very useful & when home from
school, she is disposed to be but of course her lessons take much of her time.

2nd sheet  It is no matter how much thick paper I use as this goes by Fanny—no stamps, & as 'twill not be worth sending elsewhere—for one to Philada.
givg. particulars of Jas.' illness will be sent to Boston—& Thou must write another for Europe—  I will enclose Anna D. H.'s & Ellie's when opp[ortunit]y.
occurs return Anna's—  Thou cant call these thick sheets "scraps", or yet "inch
pieces", & I'll fill eno' to make up for all the Circular inside—  Thou may perhaps be able to do more with Julia Holmes' appeal than I have ever done, wh. is
just nothing—& now I mean to do less than ever—[7] I have not even replied to
Lucy Stone's letter—wh. is also in the lost bag—so she has written thee too—
I didn't want to put on paper anything of complaint of our loved co-adjutors,
till they had had more time for defence and explanatn.——  The Revolution
is not satisfactory & I have not the littlest notion of being a subscriber—tho' I
think James said he intended to—  I only wait for the May Mg., to withdraw
from every office. My age & infirmities are reason enough—but I should not
think it wd. do for thee at thy age to cut loose—[8] Lucy Stone feels bad to hear
of such intention from me or any body, when the cause needs all the aid it can

have— It was a great mistake to unite the two—or even to organize a Socy. for Wom. Rig.— The several Conventions held were far more effective, & all that we ought to have attempted— Elizh. Stanton's sympathy for "Sambo" is very questionable—[9] Our feeble attempt to organize a State Aux. Society—S. B. Anthony here to help—S. Pugh—Pres. Several intelligt colored young men & women drawn in—who after all seldom met the Ex. Com. even tho' Sarah Pugh made great effort, & ever at her post—determined to shew our persistent Old Fem. A. S. Socy. that there was a new field opened wh. wd. furnish more needed work, than the continuance of our Socy. cd. do— I found it was all a sham & only met once or twice. They got Frances Harper[10] to deliver one lecture for us— At the last Mg. I moved disbandg. & adjourng. Sine die only 4 or 5 beside myself present— They postponed it a month—only 2 or 3 prest. then, & S. Pugh tells me they agreed to close up— So my more than a hundred dollars contributed, is thus sunk! Im glad I never meant to beg much of others— Our "Fem." holds its own— Mary Grew is preparing her Annual Report— Have I written that she preached twice in the new Unitarian House 2 or 3 wks. ago, & gave great satisfaction—

Now I ought to go up to my husband. He sleeps most of his time, has not yet been clear of fever on 1st. day his pulse 128—no pain—much prostrated— tho' no Typhoid symptoms. As all here employed Homoeopy. & our br. Richd. too preferred it, & had administered the pills, we sent for their Dr. who studied Allopathy & graduated at the New Y. University—but never practised always preferg. homoeopy— He left the 2 tumblers to be given alternately—to produce perspiratn.— Religiously followed up—but not a drop of perspiratn. as yet— Richd. wanted the additn. of bottles of hot water—soakg. feet, &.c. but Dr. Moffett thot. it not necessy. "as there was an equal circulatn."— He thot. him better yestery. but his fever came on after he left—& he has not yet been this morng— On 7th. day after the 1st. chill & fever passed off, Jas. came down & sat here till 10 at night not seemg. sick—but as he was undressg—he coughed, & said he felt like another chill—wh. continued till past midnight— I too have cold hands & feet followd by fever & night sweats—so that we are rather a forlorn old pair— Maria has just sent a nice long letter for Europe wh. we have read & I want you shd. have it, but she says do send it by this next Steamer, so I will look over & see what I can cull from it—

3rd. & last sheet— Maria writes—on her return from Medford: [*Here LCM copies at length directly from Maria's letter in which she discusses home news and the last freedpeople's aid meeting.*]

I might go on & copy her review of Mrs. Davis' new serial in Lippincotts Magazine & other of her writings[11]—but Geo. has just come over to lunch & for the letters for Anna B. to see before tomorw's. Steamer—so I leave much of her Book notices, & scoldg. the Nation—as also her further accot. of the Barclay business drawg. to a close satisfactorily— I wish I cd. say as much of Wm. Abbotts & Geo. Brown's—wh. is any thing but satisfacty.! Now if thou art offended with these mean sheets, just burn them without readg.—& you'll not be the losers for my part— I have asked Fanny [*Cavender*] & *Emily* [*Mott*] all about you I cd. think of, in their short lunch call here— Hope Eliza [*Osborne*] is really gaining but oh, how slowly— I won't close this now—

4th. day morng. 22nd. Last date—

Fine morng. after the snow & rain— Boys will "coast" down Joralemon Hill today "like all-possessed." Jas. had rather less fever last night, and I hope may not be so weak to-day— Dr. say there's no tendency to Typhoid, wh. I feared Today our Quarty. Mg. begins over at 15th. St. How resigned I am to being kept at home! It continues over tomorw. & next day. Deb Wharton will probably be in attendance— I am satisfied to have no call for my bonnet while here, except to go once to Walter B's We hope Anna will find her way here today. She couldn't come to lunch when Walter & the others did—but dined with us the next day—1st. day, as did uncle Richard He is very attentive to his sick br.— A baby was born unto them in Pierpont St. where he stops—br.-in-law Thos. Smith's—where 7 yrs. ago they buried a dear little girl 3 or 4 yrs old, leavg. 2 boys—& none since till now—a *daughr.* & a *joy* Another baby, in East Broadway where our br. also stops—Sarah Hicks— He went over on 2nd. day aftern. found them in commotn. gathered up his night shirt & came back— Yestery. went agn. found a 10½ llb Anne Mott Franklin arrived @ 11 the eveg. before— & all doing well— Bertine & Mary very happy—as indeed all were—tho' Jas Hicks[12] pretended to laugh at them, but evidently as much pleased as the rest— This is all the news—So

L. Mott[13]

ALS PSCHi-Mott

1. LCM and JM had come to New York City for the wedding of Sarah Haydock to Norwood Hallowell on 27 January (LCM to Mary Hussey Earle, 25 January 1868, Mott Manuscripts, PSCHi). "Learned Women and Studious Women" by Monseigneur Felix Antoine Philibert Dupanloup (1802–78) had appeared in the *Catholic World* (October 1867, 24–43, November 1867, 209–26). LCM probably appreciated Dupanloup's support for women's education: "The rights of women to intellectual culture are not merely rights, they are also duties. This is what makes them inalienable" (October 1867, 31).

2. Anna Folger (d. 1870) was LCM's cousin (LCM to MML, 15 October 1870, Mott Manuscripts, PSCHi).

3. This is possibly a son of Alonzo Potter: Henry, Eliphalet, or Horatio Potter (1802–87), all Episcopalian clergymen in New York City.

4. Edward Parrish (1822–72), the son of Dr. Joseph Parrish and Susanna Cox Parrish and the brother of Dillwyn Parrish, helped found Swarthmore College and served as its first president. Thomas Mott and Marianna Mott were traveling in Rome (see LCM to Mary Hussey Earle, 25 January 1868, Mott Manuscripts, PSCHi).

5. Mary Folger Ladd was the daughter of James D. Ladd and Elizabeth Ladd and the granddaughter of Mayhew Folger (Folger Scrapbook, MNHi).

6. Elizabeth Parrish (b. 1856) was the daughter of Edward Parrish and Margaret Parrish. Joseph Parrish (1843–93) was the son of Dillwyn Parrish and his second wife, Sus-

annah M. Parrish. Naomi Lawton (b. 1842), the daughter of Abraham Lawton and Sarah Lawton of New York City, was related to the Mellors.

7. LCM used a letter from Julia Holmes, dated 6 October 1867, as stationery to continue this letter. As a representative of the "Universal Franchise Association" in Washington, D.C., Holmes had written to inform LCM that she had been elected to its advisory committee.

8. LCM is referring to recent divisions in the woman's rights movement and the AERA in particular. After the Republican party in Kansas had turned its back on woman suffrage, Stanton and Anthony had aligned themselves with George Train (1829–1904), an outspoken racist and a Democratic politician, to garner support for woman suffrage in Kansas. Garrison, Stone, and others had strongly objected to this alliance. After the failed campaign, Train helped Stanton and Anthony found a newspaper, the *Revolution,* which published its first issue in January 1868 (Ellen Carol DuBois, *Feminism and Suffrage: The Emergence of an Independent Women's Movement in America, 1848–1869* [Ithaca, N.Y.: Cornell University Press, 1978], 99–103). The AERA was to meet on 14 May in New York City.

9. Stanton had alluded to "Sambo" in a 26 December 1865 letter to the *NASS:* "It becomes a serious question whether we had better stand aside and see 'Sambo' walk into the kingdom first" (Gordon, 1:564). Recently, in a speech in Buffalo, she had protested the enfranchisement of "uneducated men," while "We the educated women" were excluded: "I am opposed to having another man allowed to vote until educated women are allowed too" (*Buffalo Daily Courier,* 3 December 1867; *Stanton-Anthony Papers,* reel 12, fr. 666).

10. LCM is apparently referring to an attempt to start a Pennsylvania branch of the AERA. Frances Ellen Watkins Harper (1825–1911), born in Baltimore to free blacks, had begun her career as an antislavery lecturer in 1854. After the war she had lectured on Reconstruction and woman's rights. Harper had recently spoken at a meeting of the Friends' Association for the Aid and Elevation of the Freedman (*NASS,* 30 November 1867, 2).

11. "Dallas Galbraith" by Rebecca Blaine Harding Davis (1831–1910) first appeared in *Lippincott's* (January 1868, 9–27).

12. Thomas Smith is probably the brother of Elizabeth Mitchell Smith Mott, JM's sister-in-law. Anne Mott Franklin had been born on 20 January to Mary Hicks Franklin and Peter Bertine Franklin. James Hicks (1815–80), the son of Robert Hicks and Mary Hicks, was Mary Hicks Franklin's uncle.

13. On 24 January, the family would telegram Anna Hopper to come to Brooklyn to help nurse JM, who had been growing steadily worse. LCM wrote: "We felt anxious toward night for the Dr. to come—tho' I sd. I was apt to think the patient worse, when the Dr. wd. pronounce him better— But not so now. Yr. father took so little notice of his comg & scarcely ansd. when spoken to—". JM would die on 26 January (LCM to children, 24 January 1868, and LCM to Mary Hussey Earle, 25 January 1868, both in Mott Manuscripts, PSCHi).

# PART 4

*April 1868–December 1879*

Despite the close, loving family surrounding her in the wake of her husband's death, LCM knew she must for the first time since her marriage face life alone. No letters immediately after she became a widow survive (perhaps she wrote few in those first months after 26 January 1868), but one to MML in April devoted only a few lines to missing JM before moving briskly on to other topics. In the same manner did she deal with the passing of other close friends and family: Nathaniel Barney in 1869, her sister Eliza in 1870, and her daughter-in-law Marianna Mott in 1872. Finally, in only a few short months between July 1874 and January 1875, her daughter Anna Hopper, Anna's son Isaac, and her beloved sister MCW all died. Her letter to MCW's daughter Eliza Osborne expressed her concern for the living, especially MCW's husband: "Poor, dear, stricken brother David occupies my thots." The only hint of her own grief was her brief statement that she would miss MCW's "lovely & loving letters" (12 January 1875).

LCM consistently stated her disinclination to become caught up in the woman's rights conflict brewing between the Stone/Blackwell and the Stanton/ Anthony factions, following her earlier efforts at conciliation. Nevertheless, she received frequent appeals for her support and presence at the regional and national meetings of their respective organizations. While refusing most of those requests, she still entertained numerous NWSA visitors. Anthony, Stanton, and Paulina Wright Davis, as well as the peace activist Alfred Love, enjoyed the Roadside hospitality. Decidedly not a recluse, LCM enjoyed sharing acerbic observations about the various women's meetings, formal and informal, with MCW.

In her final years, LCM continued to express a Quaker disdain for extravagant dress and homes, even as her children and grandchildren obviously enjoyed a more material way of life. For example, when her grandson Henry Davis brought fashionable attire back from Europe, she scolded her daughters for their enthusiastic reception of these goods and commented on the exploitation that produced them: "Going to Europe to live cheaper than here, is as if we went South during Slavery days—for tis only by overworkg. the laborer at low wages & oppressg. the Poor that it can be done" (letter to MCW, 7 March 1872).

LCM's varied interests did not abate as she aged. She kept up a keen interest in the establishment of Swarthmore College, attended its inauguration, and followed the school's progress via several of her grandchildren who attended. Since 1867 she had been active in the Free Religious Association, an organization stressing the importance of the individual's own search for the divinity, and regularly read and enjoyed its publication, the *Index*. Although feeble, she still summoned the strength to denounce sectarian beliefs (see her letter to Octavius B. Frothingham, 22 May 1874) and attend meetings of the Boston Radical Club, where she conversed with scholars and writers such as Frederic Henry Hedge and Henry Wadsworth Longfellow. And until the end of her life LCM was following current issues, such as the Comstock censorship law and the freedpeople's settlement in Kansas. That her mind remained active, even as her body declined physically, is evident in these final letters.

LCM died at Roadside on 11 November 1880, surrounded by her children and grandchildren. Tributes poured in from all over the country. Among them was a notice in the *Nation,* the weekly she so frequently criticized for its conservative views, and this accolade would no doubt have amused her. After a survey of her life, the writer concluded, "The fugitive slave knew [*her home*] . . . as a safe harbor, and the poor and needy never left it empty-handed." LCM was known for her "vitality" equally with "the endurance of her mental faculties, and her eager interest to the last in current thought and in all good work for the improvement of mankind" (18 November 1880, 359).

After a private funeral in her home, LCM was buried in Fair Hill Cemetery, north of Philadelphia, in a ceremony attended by over one thousand people. The *New York Times* observed in its obituary that her name "was probably as widely known as that of any other public woman in this or the preceding generation" (12 November 1880, 5, 14 November 1880, 7).

# To Martha Mott Lord

Roadside
4 Mo. 3rd. 68—6th day aftern

My Dear Pattie

It has been as hard for me to get time to write today, as ever it was for thee—Maria [*Davis*] has moved nearly all their treasure from the barn—fillg. the old attics—& we have been trying to bring order out of the heaps of "chaos" up there—i.e. *she* has with a little of Ellen's help— I mean while clearg. up, after takg. my rags to the weaver assorting lots of bags & boxes—lookg. over some of Fanny's things, & giving away others till now there seems a little space for thee & thine— Wm. Wiley—our boy left us on the 1st. to go to his trade, & a real green Erin in his place @ $40 pr. Mo—boards at Jas. Corr's. So Wm.'s room is even full of traps of all sorts, leavg. only room to go around the single bed, if necessity compel any one to lodge there— We are joying in the anticipatn. of your comg. on 2nd. day—& have made several plans for thee & the crib—not yet quite decided— We incline to keep the front spare chamber with only Thos. [*Mott*] in it—as he can be so easily moved up higher on wedding day if best—[1] Aunt Martha has *our!* room—she proposes giving it up to thee & thine and go up to the N.W. attic herself—we say—let Fanny go up there & thou have the crib in thy[+]

We hold ourselves ready however for any change—thou may suggest— So lets leave that till thou come— Fanny is in Town most of her time— She has not been out since last 2nd. day— So many things to attend to—& she evidently prefers Maria Hopper's aid in her purchases to either her obsolete Grandmr.—or little less in *her* judgment, her Aunts— So we let her alone—

Mary has gone in today to choose her present to her sister— Many have been sent— Elegant clock—&.c. &.c—from New York— I've seen nothing yet nor shall I before thou comes— Thos. Mott went in yestery. to make a selection after seeing the other things— He also is in treaty for that Clinton St. house & went to make his last offer yesterday. & dine at Richardson's—then call for aunt Martha at aunt Eliza's, where she went yestery., to go & hear Anna Dickinson last eveg—[2] They will be out soon now & that hurries me so now for this, with one from Mariana [*Mott*] must go to the office at Shoemaker Town or you will not receive it before thou leaves home 2nd. day.

Thy letter & George's—both so welcome I want to answer if the wagon does not come to the piazza & prevent me—

3rd. page— Well I'll try— It is the wisest thing thou can do—to "turn thy back on" every thing & come here for a week—so come along— Ellie Wright [*Garrison*]'s letter came in all good time—so never mind the delay. I've really not found time to read it yet—for we had a large party to dine & tea the day it came 4th. day— Mary Earle, Anna Folger Martha Earle & Laura, Aunt Eliza &

Anna Hopper—Caroe White—& with Aunt Martha & ourselves made 12 to sit down at dinner *all* women kind—not a single man, & the blank was sad indeed! I sat at table as they were all such own folk—but I cant realize it that your precious father is never more to grace our table as he always has done!—& such a miss not to have him go out on the piazza & welcome our friends when they come. Alas where is he not missed?—

You seem to be making progress with your mechanics—no doubt all will be ready in time— I fear the successor will not give your price for the sideboard &.c, &.c—

Glad you are not buying much of the Orange things— Grass will be nicer for the childn. to play over but garden is so nice too that I want you to have part of both— I thot. of you there together yestery—but fear you will not have much of Miller [*McKim*]'s interest in yr. doings, for Sarah writes that he is quite sick with fever—pain in his side &.c—his Spring ailments she says—

Yr. carpets I've no doubt are all right—hope you haven't much shopping to do— Does Geo. want the $2000 sent before he comes? As the payt. was to be the 1st. I thot. he might be dependg. on it  A line to Thos. or Edwd. Hopper & he can have it any time—

Thy visit to Walter [*Brown*]'s seemed pleasant— Glad thou saw & liked Bessie—[3] Wish I could too— Will Harry come to wedding? I believe an inviten. is to be sent tho' I know nothing—haven't even seen the list— Every thing is done in Town. Maria D. is to meet Clay there tomorw.— Glad if my *old* face pleases you—

Yes any kitchen things will do for thy present— I have done nothg. yet but rag carpet & one table cloth— Aunt Martha got one—for her Barnsley very nice & towels &.c  She is markg. every thing beautifully— Dont say to anybody that I am going back with thee— Here's the carriage—

Ive not ½ done—the rest when you come—

+old room & the childn. up in the trundle bed with Fanny. Mary C. sleeps with Aunt Martha

AL PSCHi-Mott

1. Fanny Cavender was to marry Tom Parrish on 10 April.

2. Anna Dickinson's speech given in Philadelphia on 2 April was entitled "The Duty of the Hour" (*NASS,* 4 April 1868, 2).

3. Bessie was Harry Brown's fiancée.

## To the AERA

*[Roadside before 14 May 1868]*

To the annual meeting of the Equal Rights Association to be held on the 14th Inst.

Circumstances prevent my being with you at this time.

While my interest in the great cause for which we are associated remains unchanged, it has occurred to me to suggest for your consideration,—that the claims of the Freedman having many advocates, the *united* efforts of the Society, as an Organization, be discontinued; and that hereafter, as occasion demands, Woman's Rights Conventions, so successfully held in years past, should be resumed.[1]

I herewith resign my office in the Association, tho' a continued subscriber to its funds

Lucretia Mott

ALS DLC-NAWSA, box 65

1. The resolutions adopted by the AERA convention, held on 14 May in New York City, reflected concern over the Republican abandonment of woman suffrage: "Any reconstruction which does not establish woman's right to vote will fail to secure permanent peace and prosperity" (*NASS*, 13 June 1868, 3).

## To Martha Coffin Wright

Orange [*New Jersey*]
12 mo. 3rd. 68—5th. day—[1]

Thou'lt see, my dear Sister how respectfully I am bidden, or *was* rather, to the late convention.[2] But, as going where Susan B. A. & E. C. Stanton were denied wd. be partisan-like, *that* wd. have prevented if age wd.n't— Yes, they had their full share of *bores*. Are we sorry *eno'* for them? E. M. Davis, who has just returned from Boston says "such a Con. has never before been held there, & 'twill do great good"—of course it will—but give me Parker P. before Wasson, & E. C. S. before J. Freeman C—& S. B. Anthony before S. May Jr.— Those worn-out advocates were well eno' for these new beginners— Senator Wilson did his part as a politician— Fredk. Dougs. we can excuse, in his reasonable preference at this hour— Garrison I was rejoiced came out— I wish he wd. at our weak efforts for Peace— Anna H. says if I send her any more notes on Peace Circulars, she will enlist.— — What an exercise of patience that minister-at-large Barnard must have been—& Sewall, it seems lacked freshness— I was amused with Devotion being Olympia B's. fort, rather than argument—[3] These comments grow out of Edwd. D. havg. brot. the accompg. Report, last eveg— the 1st. full notice I've seen—from the Springfield Repub.— If old to thee, hand it to somebody-else— Of course Lucy Stone did well, she always does, *when she does not quarrel*—& her husband I like too—& Mrs. Harper if she wont be egotistical— Thou must want to go to Washn.— Josephe. Griffing is a good speaker—[4] We've not heard who is going— The ball is well in motion, & numbers of new names appear, entering in to the toilsome service of rolling sd. ball— glad my day is over—the grasshopper a burden—these 10 days past, cold, chills, fever sweats, & now cough & sore mouth, & forlorn altogether, as thou wast last spring

Have I sent thee one parcel of letters since coming here nearly 2 wks. ago? I forget—Europe, Boston, Philada. have been all absorbg. besides answerg. a call to Vineland[5] & 2 or 3 other letters—one with a motto—"Take Truth for Authority, not Authority for truth.["] & sent to the modest young man in Boston— Yes, & one to Lady Amberley, with a tiny Indian basket & pr. little moccasins— both very prettily worked, for the little Rachel Lucretia— I'll send you the letter after awhile introducg. Thackeray's daughr. Mrs. Steven, who only made a short call—a pleasg. person—[6] All these letters have kept me busy—for all thine & Ellie [*Garrison*]'s & Eliza O's. I collected, & read nearly all over, before sendg. them to Maria H— Sorry not to see her but not able to go to Jersey City so early in the morng— Pattie went into New Y. the aftern. before & passed an hour or so with Maria at Abby Gibbons'— She was very bright & well, & suitably clad for the voyage Henry & Pattie stayed over in Jersey City all night—to save her strength[7] She coughs a great deal & the night before leavg. home, she had a hemorrhage from the throat they say, but Henry is very anxious Edwd. [*Hopper*] sd. his eyes were red—partg. with those darling childn. & so much to feel every way— Edwd. D. came from Boston yestery. & met them—no 3rd. day—& stayed at Walter B's that night, as did Pattie—& they begged Anna to let them go—early in the morng. & get breakfast down town after the Steamer was off—but they found a good breakfast ready for them— Edwd. came out here last evg. & lodged, & to-day is off to Philada—with a letter from Maria D. who is going to stay another week with Anna— Edwd. sd. their visit at Wm. & Ellen's was very pleast.—& they recd. a cordial welcome when they called at father Garrison's— Some unsettlement as to house just now. at Medford. I guess Ellie will write about that—my head is dizzy.

Last week before I was sick, one visit was made to Anna B. after Pattie & I had shopped a few, to find sd. Indian basket— I stayed a night then—& agreed to go in agn. on 7th. day, & stay 2 nights—& go on to *our* Mg. only a block or so from them— Anna is lookg. much better than I had an idea she wd. for months—and I hope she will have no furthr gashing—let well eno' alone—[8] She was very lovely—& so were the childn.— Walter overpowered me with his kindness & attentn.—hirg. carriage &.c. &.c— Going there on 7th. day I found Anna thinkg. abt. their silver wedding to come off the next eveg. She had told the childn. months ago—that if they wd.n't. be heard to name silver wedding, maybe she'd invite a few— Afterwd. the upset & hurt put it out of the questn.,

& no more was sd. till that day, she consented to ask the Frothms., Bigelows, Haydks., Trimbles, &.c &.c. without form— So that eveg. & early next morng. Walter & Harry went forth & bade them @ 8 oclk— Only Mrs. Frothm. & Bessie to tea—⁹ Mr. was in Provid[enc]e. preachg. in Exch. nearly all came— Lucy Gib. also and Rosalie Hopper—abt. a doz. includg. self—& when all had done their duty to the old lady, & the ice-cream handed I slipped off & retired—happy eno'— Several of them were at Mg. & of course must be pleased—but I grew so hoarse afterwd. that I cd. hardly speak— Anna took me in her carriage to the ferry next morng—cross'd over to Hoboken & sat till the Car was ready to start. I told them I shouldn't go agn. if they felt that they must pay me so much attention. They sd. they always when they had a frd. meant to have the Carriage They keep a single horse and carriage for their own use but ours was a regular hack of no mean order— Saml. Willets called on me the eveg. of the party before any but Mrs. Frothm. & the Haydks. were there— He was going on to Philada. with Han. Haydk. the next day to the Annual Mg. of Swarthmore Col. He told me Wm. Macy¹⁰ had just given $1000—havg. given 500 before— Nelly Lord went on to Thanksgivg at Edwd. H. & went out to Swarthmore & was delighted.*

Im sure these scraps are not so bad to write on— Well, as I was sayg. this corresponde. all around fills a body's time— So, if I haven't made more than 30 aprons for Tubman's Fair, I've written 30 letters, & darned & looked over & rolled up 30 pr. stockings & made *going on* 30 cloths out of old ragged long & short towels, & ravelled & turned new to correspond, & turned a sheet—all but the *hemming on the machine*—wh. also I turned—& hemmed h[and]k[erchie]fs for self & a few & precious few other things—for every day lying on the sofa wrapped well has been more desirable than anything else— One day Sarah M'Kim & Lucy, with Lloyd [*Garrison*] passed here very satisfactorily— Another, they sent their carriage for us Pattie, Mary & Anna, with self went, and had another pleast. day—only such a lot of little drawers to cut out absorbed Lucy & Pattie more than I like in compy— Sarah read parts of Miller [*McKim*]'s letters, by wh. I infer that he is not strong—still very sensitive to drafts—& fears takg. cold—is on his way home now— Sarah & Lucy are comg. here agn. to-morw., hopg. to meet Maria Davis, & how disaptd. they'll be— Edwd. D. wd. have liked to stay to see them— I leave on 7th. day—not to reach Philada. till 2nd. day morng—where I shall stay with Anna till after the Mgs. & Festival—¹¹ How I wish Eliza [*Yarnall*] felt like going to any of these with me— Anna wd. give boot not to go I presume— I enclose her note—her longer ones are hundreds of miles on the ocean— Every thing passes away—& all this will in due time— Thy letters are all gone too, but not before I acknowledged them—& commented a little, save on the one to Dear Sisters recd. since we came here, & wh. has been to Philada. & back with a note from Aunt Eliza to Anna B—sayg. Reba. [*Yarnall*] was better the Dr. sd. so & they thot. so— Eliza has had a bad cold for 2 weeks—better when she wrote— She did not lose her appetite but was confined to the house— Poor Geo. [*Brown*] is very destitute  Edwd. Brown[12] has just been there—says George must have some winter clothing— He was arrested a few days ago, by some creditor, to whom he had broken his promise so many times, that he wd. bear it no longer— What the trouble was we didn't learn— but he was not held in durance very long— We might feel more for him if we hadn't such a vagabond of our own to be tried with— John Cavr. has been very poorly but Nellie says he was at Thos. Cavr.'s when she was there & talked about Thos. takg. Charly from School weeks ago—pretendg. they were going right off to N. Carolina & then he had been out of school, & they'd not gone yet.

[*P.S.*] We have not yet gone on with that *excitg.* novel of Anna E. D's so cant review.[13]

*Lizzie Parrish & Mary Cavr. anticipate enterg. next year—& Nellie hopes to too.

AL MNS

1. MML and George Lord had recently moved from Brooklyn to Orange.

2. The New England Woman's Rights Convention, held 18–19 November in Boston and organized by Lucy Stone, led to the creation of the New England Woman Suffrage Association (*NASS*, 14 November 1868, 3, 28 November 1868, 2). LCM had written to MCW of the split between Stone and Stanton and Anthony in a 5 November letter: "I have written Lucy that I love them all too well to be a partizan with either" (MNS).

3. The *Springfield Republican* (21 November 1868, 4) had reported that Sen. Henry Wilson (1812–75), a Massachusetts Republican, said he voted against woman suffrage in Congress only because "it came in the form of an amendment intended to defeat negro suffrage." At the New England Woman's Rights Convention Charles T. Barnard, a Boston "minister-at-large," had "abused his audience with a weak and rambling speech." Samuel Sewell (1799–1888), a Massachusetts abolitionist, had spoken "on the fact that women are taxed without the right to protect themselves or to direct their contributions to a proper use." Olympia Brown (1835–1926), a Universalist minister and a suffrage activist, had become involved in the woman's rights movement at the first meeting of the AERA in April 1866. She had opened the convention with a prayer and the *Republican*'s reporter opined that "she prays better than she preaches." Frederick Douglass had spoken at the closing session of the convention and had opposed a univeral suffrage resolution, which he claimed "looked to deserting the negro in the hour of need."

4. The *Springfield Republican* had reported that Stone "attended in her usual prompt style to the argument that women do not wish to vote. Her allusions to the old plea that the slaves at the South were happy and didn't wish to be free, were pungent and refreshing" (ibid.). Blackwell had proposed that all citizens should refuse to vote for candidates who did not support woman suffrage. Frances Harper was reported as saying that "she had suffered so much in this republic as a negro that she could not fully realize her wrong as a woman, and proceeded to tell her story right pleasantly and pathetically." Josephine S. Griffing (1814–72), an Ohio abolitionist and a suffrage activist, had moved to Washington, D.C., during the Civil War to devote herself to freedpeople's aid. The National Woman Suffrage Convention was to meet on 19–20 January 1869 in Washington, sponsored by the Universal Franchise Association, of which Griffing was a member (*NASS*, 9 January 1869, 2).

5. On 3 November, 192 women in Vineland, New Jersey, had attempted to vote but had

succeeded in doing so only symbolically by using their own ballots and box. The *NASS*'s reporter noted approvingly the salutary influence of women's presence at the polls: "On this occasion the smokers, who are in the habit of making the atmosphere of the polling places well nigh suffocating with the poisonous fumes of tobacco, were also constrained by the presence and protests of women, to desist." Several weeks later a woman's rights convention would be held in Vineland and Lucy Stone would serve as president (*NASS*, 14 November 1868, 2, 19 December 1868, 2).

6. LCM had befriended Lady Katharine Louisa Stanley Russell Amberley (1842–74) and her husband, Lord John Russell Amberley, a religious and political liberal, the previous year in Boston. The Amberleys named their daughter, Rachel Lucretia Amberley, after LCM (Hallowell, 430–32). Harriet Marian (Minny) Thackeray Stephen (1840–75) was the first wife of Leslie Stephen, a British intellectual.

7. Maria Hopper, Henry Davis, and Pattie Davis were departing for Europe (LCM to MML, 16 November 1868, Mott Manuscripts, PSCHi).

8. MML, Anna Temple Brown, Sarah McKim, and others had been involved in a carriage accident in which Anna's teeth were broken (LCM to children, 28 August 1868, Mott Manuscripts, PSCHi).

9. "Mrs. Frothm." was Caroline Elizabeth Curtis Frothingham (b. 1825), the wife of Octavius B. Frothingham. The "Trimbles" were probably Mary Trimble (1793–1879), a New York City Hicksite, and her family.

10. William Macy (1805–87) was a Pennsylvania Quaker.

11. The PASS would hold its annual meeting on 10 December, the same day of the Pennsylvania Festival of the Friends of Freedom (*NASS*, 12 December 1868, 3).

12. "Edwd. Brown" is possibly Edward Brown (1817–89), a Quaker from Brooklyn (*Friends' Intelligencer*, 23 March 1889, 185).

13. Anna E. Dickinson's *What Answer?* (Boston: Ticknor and Fields, 1868) was, like Lydia Maria Child's *Romance of the Republic,* about racial intermarriage (Lyde Cullen Sizer, *The Political Work of Northern Women Writers* [Chapel Hill, N.C.: University of North Carolina Press, 2000], 234–38).

## To Philadelphia Family

Orange N.J. 2 mo. 1st. 69

My Dear Ones—all—
Here safely arrived— Pattie [*Lord*] the 1st. person seen on reachg. Newark— Isabel[1] had a kiss from her—& then on to New York  The air a few degrees colder than with us—but the ride here in the horse-car pleasant  much to talk about  Dear little Lulu very sick since Geo. came back—better now—running about—tho' her eyes affected as Mary & Anna's have been with a kind of epidemic—the whites becomg. very red—all better—  Geo. & Pattie gone to a concert this eveg.—where Louisa takes part—her br. Charles & Mr. Wiley out, to be there— — —  I find that the proposed reception at Mrs. Winchester's[2] is to be made a great affair—so I have written to Susan B. & Elizh. C. entirely decling.—as I dont feel able to do more than the wedding—perhaps Mo. Mg—& a call or two—  I shall *stick* to that. My strength now is not mighty—& I *will not* be lionized when I can avoid it—  Isabel will write how she passed

my name over to a gentlemanly travelg. companion, when I had so carefully avoided the name of Mott— He made himself very agreeable—kindly giving us his seat—paring & openg. an orange & handg. over to us—an old-school Presbytn. Minister—better than his creed— He left us at Elizabeth after pointing out his Church & grounds to us—

I regret losing these hours of Caroline [*Stratton*]'s visit, & the days of Aunt Martha's—shall be glad to meet Willie in New Y—& I told Jas. Corr to be sure & kill a biddy for his dinner tomorw. & take it in before the butcher called.

Now I'll go on with last week's stockings— It looks pleast. here as ever— Nelly is readg. to Mary—& all are happy— Bel. told her Aunt Pattie she looked lovely {as I'm sure Bel. did also—I was so proud of my travelg. caretaker} wh. is a fact— Geo. came home in good spirits—some stir in wool— Such a welcome as he gives, is worth coming for— More tomorw.—

4th. day morng. 3rd. of the mo.—
snow, rain, sleet—

no go to Mo. Mg.—so resigned! Nothg. pleasanter than to be here "in the quiet." Such a time as we've had about the proposed gathg. at Mrs. Winchester's! S. B. Anthony wrote me that returng. from Florence-Mass. she found that "just mentiong. to 1 or 2 frds. her plan, &.c—has set so many wheels in motion—resultg in $50 being raised & rooms secured for a *reception*— H. Ward Beecher hearg. of this, had offered his Sunday School room & given notice at the close of the morng. Mg. 1st. day" Then she begs me not to withdraw, (as I *had* done) in a note to her, after recg. Anna B's note wh. I enclose—or perhaps will keep it to shew S. Hicks as she was involved somewhat in the plans—to go over to Brooklyn & bear me thence to her house in her carriage for the night— I had not intended callg. on her this time—but I must now after all this muddle— I have sent another *positive decline* of any part in sd. gatherg— This storm keeps Patty & self from Mg. in New Y—wh. we like— Oh, this is said once— We called yestery. at Lucy Stone's—she had just gone to the City— Henry's aged mother recd. us—so lady like—English— Their house pleast. & neat—piano in the parlor the little daughr.[3] fond of music—drawg., paintg. & poetry writes little pieces, wh. they find—as May Hall[1].'s are—is a great reader—absorbed in her book—all wh. may be a set off to her homeliness— In the eveg. Henry B. & Lucy appeared—& stayed late—talked much—*she* did against Train & Anthony—a wide separatn.—no chance of reunion It is astonishg. how perverted the understandg. becomes, when personal dissension exists—as Garrison versus Phillips. Henry was much interested in George's pet bracket lamps

Another grand visit we had yestery. from Miller M'K. He came for a call only, but stayed to dinner—& such a nice talk as we had—on Freedman's Societies— Free produce article— Godkin as an entertaing. gent. dined with them—& his wife last week[4]—"St" Paul's Epistles—Quakers as they *are*—buildg. in Orange—sellg. the Park place—visitg Penna.—no time fixed for that— He looked & seemed very well— Pattie tried to engage them to tea here this eveg. for had

we gone to Mo. Mg. we intended to return this aftern. lunchg. at Anna B's— —
— They may come—

I have not been idle these 2 days—all last & this week's stockgs. are darned
& cuffs hemmed, beside this dreaded corresponde. about the foolish receptn.
doings. The Eveg. Post & other Papers read—

My Bible present was admired— Geo put it up right, havg. been in the
book-busins.— Aunt Martha's Whittier too—wh. was thot. beautiful— I read
many of the pieces—familiar as they were, while Geo. & Pattie were at the Concert— Geo. took the parcels *in* yestery.—

Maria [*Davis*]'s stockings for little Anna were acceptable & thanks— I came
down to breakfast & found Geo. admirg. them—he sd. only one thing he didn't
like—that "*they* were the last she shd. knit"— Anna took them around the
house— The doughnuts we didn't eat were on the tea table— Our Presbytn.
fellow pas. declined our offer—also our candy— Bel had some excelt. cake—
her cook's make.

Now we want to hear from you all—how poor Edwd. H. is—whether Willie will come today in this storm—what Aunt Martha is doing—when Caroe.
left Roadside—what late letters from abroad— Pattie was so glad to have Maria's—sent by Anna to Orange P.O.—wh. was indeed just what we wanted—so
is Mariana [*Mott*]'s sent from Auburn wh. goes with this— How has dear Mary
B. decided as to sellg. their furniture? I wanted her to keep *both* those carpets—
& that nice large Wardrobe & bedstead in yon room—beside the things in theirs.

One of Patties eyes is very red & sore with this epidemic since yestery— She
thinks she will be a sorry spectacle at the Wedding, if indeed she can go— I
want her to cover them with green or blue glasses & go— She may be worse
now for going out with me yestery. & for readg. some letters. Geo. came out in
good spirits yestery. reportg. a sale of wool—remindg me of Edwd D's first *broker*
experience—

My determination at present is, to go with Josh. & Isabel on 1st. day eveg.,
stop at Edwd. H's that night go home 2nd. day in the 2 oclk. line with Edwd D.
if he go then

Has Anna H. engaged a Hall for our Ann. Mg & Mary Grew's Report?[5] Is
my port monaie found? If not, Maria, Ive saved $2 more by not going to New
Y— today. I've only just thot. to tell Pattie of the *tin* gifts & poetry to Ned H. &
Willy S—

AL PSCHi-Mott

1. Isabel Mott had married Joseph Parrish on 3 September 1868.
2. Margaret E. Winchester, the wife of New York City drug company owner Jonas
Winchester, was an AERA executive committee member (Gordon, 1:592).
3. "Henry's aged mother" was Hannah Lane Blackwell (c. 1793–1870); Alice Stone
Blackwell (1857–1950) was Henry Blackwell and Lucy Stone's daughter (Andrea Moore
Kerr, *Lucy Stone: Speaking Out for Equality* [New Brunswick, N.J.: Rutgers University
Press, 1992], 154).

4. Edward L. Godkin (1831–1902), the editor of the *Nation,* was married to Frances Elizabeth Foote Godkin (c. 1835–75) of New Haven, a relative of the Beechers (William M. Armstrong, *E. L. Godkin: A Biography* [Albany: State University of New York Press, 1978], 50, 137).

5. At its annual meeting on 11 February in the Assembly Building, the PFASS would celebrate its thirty-fifth anniversary: "Mary Grew, who read the first report of the Society, presented and read the thirty-fifth on this occasion, giving another shining example of rare devotion, faithfulness, and industry through these many years of struggle with oppression." Describing LCM's speech on this occasion, the reporter would write: "She would have us be brave in well-doing, and courageous in our advocacy of the right. Her words were fraught with beautiful incentive to action, tending to enkindle in our hearts a fervid determination to give our aid wherever humanity calls" (*NASS,* 20 February 1869, 2).

# To the U.S. Senate

*[Philadelphia c. 3 February 1869]*[1]

To The Senate of The United States:

The Philadelphia Female Anti-Slavery Society respectfully petition your Honorable Body to adopt such an Amendment to the Constitution of the United States, as shall secure the right of suffrage to the colored people of this Nation. We earnestly ask for this, in order that their personal freedom, recently declared by the Constitution,[2] shall be completed and secured.

Signed, on behalf of the Society, by
Lucretia Mott Pres.
Mary Grew, ⎫
Gulielma M. Jones ⎬ Secretaries[3]

LS DNA

1. A note accompanying this petition reveals that it was referred to the Committee on the Judiciary on this date.

2. Ratification of the Fourteenth Amendment had been announced on 28 July 1868. Congress would pass the Fifteenth Amendment, establishing universal male suffrage, on 26 February.

3. Gulielma M. Jones (1824–1910) was an Orthodox Quaker. Like other abolitionists, LCM was very concerned with the fate of the Fifteenth Amendment. On 5 March 1869 LCM would write MML, "What a good Address—or Message Grant's is—15th. Amendt. & all— Edwd. D. came over delighted yestery" (Mott Manuscripts, PSCHi). In his inaugural speech of 4 March, Grant would state: "It seems to me very desirable that the question [*of male suffrage*] should be settled now, and I entertain the hope and express the desire that it may be by the ratification of the fifteenth article of amendment to the Constitution" (*The Papers of Ulysses S. Grant,* ed. John Y. Simon, William M. Ferraro, and J. Thomas Murphy [Carbondale: Southern Illinois University Press, 1995], 19:142).

# To Josephine Butler[1]

Roadside, near Philadelphia,
4 mo. 20th, 1869.

MY DEAR FRIEND,

Thy letter of Feb. 1st I would have answered immediately, as thou requested, if only to say that, unaccustomed to write for the press, I must decline, as I
have done when urged to furnish articles for the Anti-Slavery or Woman's
Rights' papers, to prepare an Essay on either of the subjects proposed, worthy
such a work as your publisher, Macmillan, designs.[2]

Still, on further reflection, my age and experience enabling me to state facts
connected with the Society of Friends, and the Woman's Rights' movements,
and desiring to give all the aid in my power, I venture to make some statements
from which some one of your writers may produce an Essay.

The stand taken by George Fox, the founder of our Society, against authority as opposed to the immediate teachings of the "light within," gave independence of character to women as well as men. Their ministry recognised, as a free
gospel message, they went forth among the nations "preaching the Word," and
spreading their principles. Adopting no theological creed, their faith was shown
by their works in the everyday duties of life, "minding the Light" in little things
as well as in the greater; thus keeping a conscience void of offence toward God
and toward men.

In the executive department of the Society, the right conceded to woman
to act conjointly with man has had its influence, not only in making her familiar with the routine of business relating to our "Discipline," but in giving her
self-reliance in mingling with the various reformatory societies in the great
movements of the age.

In the Marriage union, no ministerial or other official aid is required to
consecrate or legalise the bond. After due care in making known their intentions, the parties, in presence of their friends, announce their covenant, with
pledge of fidelity and affection, invoking Divine aid for its faithful fulfilment.
There is no assumed authority or admitted inferiority; no *promise* of *obedience.* Their independence is equal, their dependence mutual, and their obligations reciprocal. This of course has had its influence on married life and the
welfare of families. The permanence and happiness of the conjugal relation
among us have ever borne a favourable comparison with those of other denominations.

The "Testimonies" of the Society against war, slavery, the forced mainte-
nance of the ministry, and the extravagant and luxurious indulgences of the age,
intoxicating drinks, &c., which are revived yearly and quarterly in our meetings
of discipline, have prepared our members to unite in many reformatory movements of the day, demanding a "righteousness exceeding that of the Scribes and

Pharisees."[3] The restraint placed on the young from light and unprofitable read-ing has had a good effect also on the character in after-life.

Do not understand, however, that the Society is free from surrounding in-jurious influences. By birthright membership, without judicious training, and from other causes, many have "gone halting," as regards these testimonies, and our women themselves have much to learn from the more enlightened, as to their equal place in the community. {See Clarkson's Portraiture of Quakerism.}[4] But not to dwell too long on our own Society,—The co-operation of women of all classes with men in anti-slavery, temperance, and other moral reform societies, has prepared woman to act more decidely in her own behalf. In 1840, when the World's Anti-Slavery Convention was called in London, the Ameri-can Society sent delegates of women with men (the greater number Friends). Our English abolitionists, afraid of the "ridicule of the morning papers," ruled us out, extending at the same time courtesy and flattery in lieu of right. Daniel O'Connell, William Howitt, Dr. Bowring, and others, pleaded our cause ably— in vain. Their appeals were published.[5] If not easily obtained, I can furnish a copy. I might go on with a history of woman's advancement, from Mary Wool-stonecraft, Frances Wright, and your own *Westminster Review,* down to our more recent efforts,—woman's journals, parliamentary action, and in this country woman's conventions, petitions, and appeals to our legislatures, reform in our state laws, public lectures, women entering the professions, schools of design, telegraph operations, &c. &c. Our woman's conventions originated with Eliza-beth Cady Stanton, twenty years ago. They attracted much notice and no little opposition and misrepresentation; nevertheless, women were greatly encour-aged to persevere in their work. Numbers travelled over our country, holding meetings, delivering lectures, inviting discussion on the Bible arguments, the laws, &c., maintaining that the time had come for woman to move in her prop-er sphere, no longer resting satisfied in the circumscribed limits with which corrupt custom and a perverted application of the Scriptures had encircled her. Thus has she been prepared intelligently to make application for her rights, until at last the ballot is demanded as a legitimate claim. We have several periodicals specially advocating woman's rights, some of them edited by women.

In the Social relations, the sacred duties of wife and mother are fulfilled with no less assiduity than where woman is kept in a subordinate position. The most refined of our sex are among its most able advocates. I hope to enlist one of these to write for you, Dr. Ann Preston, who, with many other women practitioners, is gaining recognition and respect every year. Thirty-five students were kindly welcomed this winter to the clinical lectures, delivered in Philadelphia by lead-ing medical teachers.

In the Educational department also, woman holds her place. In *some* of our public schools her salary is equal to those of our best male teachers.

These mere facts are about all I feel able to write in compliance with thy request. It is with great reluctance I take the pen for more than family letters.

Make such use of the foregoing as may be of any avail. If I can further aid in any way, save in a clever essay, my poor services shall be freely rendered.

Thine, for woman's elevation,
LUCRETIA MOTT.

PL *Woman's Work,* xlv–xlvii:
A fragment of LCM's original letter is in the Butler Papers, Fawcett Library, London.

1. Josephine Butler (1828–1906), a British woman's rights leader, was especially active in the campaign on behalf of prostitutes to repeal the Contagious Diseases Acts (see LCM to Richard D. Webb, 22 January 1871, note 4, below).

2. Butler's *Woman's Work and Woman's Culture: A Series of Essays* (London: Macmillan, 1869) contained essays by both British men and women on education, medicine, and suffrage.

3. Matt. 5:20.

4. Thomas Clarkson, *A Portraiture of Quakerism* (New York: Samuel Stansbury, 1806).

5. See LCM to Daniel O'Connell, 17 June 1840, to Maria Weston Chapman, 29 July 1840, and to Elizabeth Cady Stanton, 16 March 1855, all above.

## To Susan B. Anthony

Roadside—Philada.
6 Mo. 6th. 69—

My Dear Susan B. Anthony

Sitting up in bed I hasten to reply to thy letter, recd. last eveg.

I had not heard of our dear frd.—Ernestine L. Rose's intention of going to Europe— May her health be restored by again breathing her native air![1]

I have long esteemed her for her honest, out-spoken radicalism, her discerning & discriminating mind, and her enlarged charity & forbearance toward the ignorant criminal and wrong doer—as well as wrong *thinker*—

All this before she was associated with us in the Wom. Rig. movement. Her lectures always attracted me—so rare is candor in unpopular heterodoxy— A warm attachment is the result— She has the best wishes of

her lovg. frd.    Lucretia Mott.

ALS PSCHi-Mott

1. Ernestine L. Rose would soon leave for a European vacation with her husband. Years of activity in reform movements had left her suffering from neuralgia and rheumatism. She settled permanently in London.

# To Martha Coffin Wright

[*Roadside*] 1st. day morng—
bright & beautiful—
6th. of the Mo—[*June 1869*]

[*Continuation of a letter begun 5 June*]

Still in bed—tho' sitting up most of yestery. I hoped to fill & send this by last eveg's mail—so that you might early have Mariana [*Mott*]'s last & Thos.'— but found I cd. do no more than the foregoing—& sew some carpet rags— We have been troubled by receivg a Telegram from Henry D. askg. for Mother Mellor or Naomi [*Lawton*] to go with the childn.— Pattie's last was so decided that she shd. come home with Henry next mo. or Aug., that we fear she is growg. worse—as indeed she was then—temporarily, they thot.—owing to the fatigue of the journey to Paris, & poor lodggs. there for a few days— Edwd. [*Davis*] has written to Naomi askg. if she will go the 16th— Martha Mellor wd. go too if her husband were not so opposed to it— The plan is to take Lucy & leave Charley here—[1] We have been quite in a state of excitement—

Willie Davis arrived yestery. for 2 wks. before startg. on his expeditn.— — Mary Cavr. was delighted to come out & see him— He is lookg. well & lovely as ever— Your Willie has passed us by we suppose— Geo. L. wrote that he was with them a day or so, "as pleast. & obliging as ever"— Pattie sd. he was brown as a native— I hope Ellen [*Garrison*] will be able to take her childn. & go to Auburn while he is there— That continued pain in her side shd. have early care— I am not yet able to take a long breath without a catch or stitch— & wear a Belladonna plaster if thats it— I was so glad thou cd. stay & help Ellen till they were settled—but I wd.n't have had that forlorn cook one day— It was just the thing to have that shed or outer kitchen put up— Richd. [*Hallowell*] thinks the wool busins. will revive in the Fall— It was indeed news that Fanny Pell [*Wright*] had *prospects.* She did nobly in encouragg. thy long stay— Eliza O—gave us the impressn. that she was only makg. the best of her hard lot. She thot. the mice were havg. rare play in yr parlor &.c &.c—but it must have been a comfort to find all cleang. done. Thou soon had to invite parties— Miller & Sarah [*McKim*]'s visit was unexpected— Poor Anne to suffer so much! David's being at home seemed very pleast.—& cool weather lucky for thee  Mrs. Worden's bed in her parlor a good plan—love to her

I agree with thee that the Hutchn's. singg. is an interruption I thot. so at the Brooklyn Mgs. the 3 or 4 times they took the time— That Olive play actor was horrid—immodest, &.c— she needed rebuke— Anna C. Field sd. I went there for that rebuke to her & for that speech, wh. seemed anythg. but good to me sick as I was—[2] no doubt this illness wd. have come, go or not go— Ill send S. B. Anthony's letter with my reply— I was very sorry for thee & S. Pug. to lose the Club Mg. & hearg. J. Weiss[3]—sorry too for Sarah to be alone at the Parker

House. Glad tho' that I wasn't thar, how reconciled I am to the prevention—all thgs. considered.

How little I thot. that the renowned Mrs. Livermore was that Universalist Minister's wife at Auburn— She dined at Anna C. Field's that day, & told me she was introduced to me at yr. house— I thot. it was in our walks tho' I didn't say so to her— She spoke admirably well that aftern. in Brooklyn—& Lucy Stone they sd. made a magnificent closg. speech— Her husband is a very genial man not at all as thou fancied him—& very liberal—[4] They seem very happy together— I didn't like Susan B. A. & E. C. S. sittg. there on the back ground like—a side box on the platform— Altho' they may make some mistakes—and perhaps mis statements—as Richd. H. thinks Elizh. C. S. did as regards her invitatn to Boston & then being withdrawn[5]—yet I cant bear to have them ignored in any way & I took pains to ascribe to them the present progress of our Cause in my speech— These 11th. hour J. W. Howes are not to be compared with them— Lucy Stone too I honored in my eveg. speech—I forgot to name her in the aftern.—[6] I agree with thee as to whisperg. & unsettlemt. on the platform, & stand corrected as far as I am implicated— As to liberal views on Sunday travel &.c—be encouraged It is a shame tho' for the P. M. general to stop the Mails.

Now haven't I ansd. thy letter? Bel. Mott P. is sewg. for good life makg. many things herself— Maria D. is hemg. diapers & sewg. double some— Anna H. interestg. herself for her too— She & Joe [Parrish] are happy with their prospects— Tom & Fanny [Parrish] drove out one aftern. this week—he was sick a day with fever afterwd.— They all took tea at father Edwd's on 6th. day with Steve & Bessie— I'm spun out now— This goes 1st. to Pattie & Anna B—her notes are ever welcome—

[P.S.] Have you heard of aunt Louisa Wait's illness & just as she began to recover seized with parallysis & now lying speechless—right side affected—cant take solid food—still is *better*. Aunt Mary Flagg[7] affected somewhat on the other side—from over exertion & sympathy but very slight—

Pattie's hands full Their company next door taken in *there* as well as their own— I fear she parted with her childs nurse too soon. She is far from well herself such giddy spells I must send you one or 2 of her letters only she does not allow me to do so—

AL MNS

1. LCM is referring to Henry Davis and Pattie Mellor Davis's children, Lucy (1863–1951) and Charles (1865–1951).

2. The Hutchinsons had performed at the anniversary meeting of the AERA on 12–13 May and at the Friends of Woman's Suffrage meeting in Brooklyn on 14 May. Members of the AERA convention had defeated a resolution to oppose the Fifteenth Amendment granting universal male suffrage. Anna Cromwell Field (1823–1912) was a member of the AERA executive committee and the president of the suffrage meeting in Brooklyn. The *New York Tribune* had reported that at the Brooklyn meeting, Olive Logan (1839–1909), an Elmira, New York, actress, "dealt numerous severe blows at the other sex. Her many

sarcastic and humorous hits elicited great applause." LCM had responded to this speech by calling for women to speak with a "dignity of demeanor" to further the cause: "We must understand the great needs of the human race, we must have such clear insight as to be prepared to speak more from the inspiration of the time—with dignity rather than with levity." After these meetings Stanton and Anthony formed the NWSA because they thought the AERA did not take a strong enough stand on woman suffrage (*New York Tribune*, 13–14 May 1869, 5, 15 May 1869, 3; *HWS*, 2:381, 398–401; Gordon, 2:241–43; Ellen Carol DuBois, *Feminism and Suffrage: The Emergence of an Independent Women's Movement in America, 1848–1869* [Ithaca, N.Y.: Cornell University Press, 1978], 187–90; *Loving Warriors: Selected Letters of Lucy Stone and Henry B. Blackwell*, ed. Leslie Wheeler [New York: Dial Press, 1981], 380).

3. John Weiss had delivered a speech entitled "Fatality" at the meeting of the Radical Club in Boston on 26 May (*NASS*, 5 June 1869, 2).

4. Mary A. Livermore (1820–1905) was a woman suffrage advocate and the wife of Daniel Parker Livermore, who had replaced Charles Mellen as the pastor of the Universalist church in Auburn, New York, in 1855. She spoke on the right of women to serve as jurors. Lucy Stone had ended the Brooklyn meeting with a speech advocating woman suffrage (*New York Tribune*, 15 May 1869, 3).

5. LCM is probably referring to the New England Woman's Suffrage Convention, held 25–26 May in Boston, to which LCM had sent a letter of regret (*NASS*, 12 June 1869, 3, 19 June 1869, 2). Stanton's invitation was inadvertent; the committee had made clear that they did not want her to attend (Elisabeth Griffith, *In Her Own Right: The Life of Elizabeth Cady Stanton* [New York: Oxford University Press, 1984], 135).

6. Julia Ward Howe (1819–1910), the author of "Battle Hymn of the Republic," a reformer, a suffrage advocate, and the wife of Samuel Gridley Howe, was the president of the New England Woman Suffrage Association. LCM had spoken thus of Stone at the Brooklyn meeting's evening session: "When I consider what Lucy Stone did when she was at Oberlin College, and the Faculty discouraged her reading the Thesis which she had prepared, and endeavored to persuade her to allow a man to read it, when she felt that it would not be consistent with her ideas of right, and read it herself, then, indeed, I felt that there was room for hope and congratulation." LCM had also been called upon to speak in the afternoon, but declined until the audience begged her to deliver a few remarks. "This venerable pioneer of Woman's Rights expressed her congratulations for the great progress of the cause to which she had devoted so much of her life. But she would not detain the audience, as she was expected to speak at night" (*New York Tribune*, 15 May 1869, 3).

7. Louisa Wait and Mary Flagg (d. 1873) were sisters of George Lord's mother (LCM to MCW, 20 April 1873, Mott Manuscripts, PSCHi).

## To Martha Coffin Wright

Nantucket 9 mo. 9th. 69—

Precious Sister

Unexpectedly I date from this place— Receivg. the within last 7th. day, while in the City to see our new grandbaby, I seemed impressed to come here—knowg. full well too, that the funeral wd. be over—[1] Mentiong it to Edwd. & Anna [*Hopper*]—with a suggestn. to Edwd. to wait on me—they encouraged—Edwd. havg. said he shd. like to come here this summer— After Mg. & dinner 1st. day went home—hadn't quite so much encouraget. there—tho' a willingness—wrote to Pattie [*Lord*] to join us—she never havg. been here—& put off her visit to Roadside till 7th. day—but she cdn't leave her 4 easy—so only met us, with Geo. on board the Fall River boat—& sat till we started— Lucy Stone & Henry Blkl. were on board—going to Boston—thence to Chicago—workg. hard for the proposed National Socy. Her talk was mainly on the subject—less asperity than in former talks— Just after partg. with her at the Junction—Lucy & Sarah Chase came into our car—so we were *blest* all the way—[2] They were comg. here for the 1st. time— Edwd. was glad of their compy. None sick on the Boat—very smooth sea—a doz. takg. their dinner or lunch in our Saloon— Not a familiar face there or on our arrival, tho' many on the wharf— We are boardg. at Joseph Swain's—a clean nice place—his wife a Gardner from Griffeth M. Cooper's neighbd. Farmington—her father havg. gone on a farm there from this Island— The Chases also here— Edwd.'s frd. Josh. Mitchell Unitaran has paid us every attentn.— We took tea there last eveg— Then went to the Church where Robt. Collyer was expected but didn't come, so I had the service—short notice—not very large audience—but satisfactory bore testimony to Nathl's. worth wh. was great indeed— Several of his famy. present includg. Elisa [*Barney*]— I had dined with her, as well as called the eveg. before—with Edwd. the 1st. place—was recd. so lovingly! Elisa shewed me letters—from Garrison & L. M. Child— Called twice also on Anna Folger & Eliza Mitchell— Mary Earle came down from Sconset in the aftern. & was like herself— Caroe. going this morng. in the boat with us— She has had a cottage at Sconset with Tommy, while Richd. [*White*] went to Ireland—now on his return  Timy. H. quieter than he has been but very silly— Now I must stop— Edwd. will leave me at ½ way house & go to Boston for a day— Caro' White all the way to New Y—when I go to Orange & home with Pattie & 2 childn. 7th. day— I wish David & thee cd. have met us here—but no time to send word— I hope to find a letter from thee at home—

AL PSCHi-Mott

1. Ethel Parrish, daughter of Bel Parrish and Joseph Parrish, had been born on 3 September. Nathaniel Barney had died on 2 September.

2. "The proposed National Socy." is probably a reference to Stone's plans to form a national woman's suffrage society. Stone and others favored enfranchisement of freedmen prior to a campaign for woman suffrage. Soon after the final AERA meeting, members of the New England Woman Suffrage Association began to organize what would become the AWSA (Ellen Carol DuBois, *Feminism and Suffrage: The Emergence of an Independent Women's Movement in America, 1848–1869* [Ithaca, N.Y.: Cornell University Press, 1978], 189–96). The Chase sisters Lucy (1828–1909) and Sarah (1836–1915), Worcester, Massachusetts, Quakers, had been working among freedpeople in Virginia and Washington, D.C.

## To Martha Mott Lord and George Lord

Phila. 11 mo. 13th. 69—
bright, clear day

My dear One & All—

Not an hour since dear Pattie left us, have I had, to "hold sweet communion" with you— Our house-confusion—puttg. in Latrobe & registers, the paper-hangers at the same time, in back entry & Library, Edwd. & Maria [*Davis*] hurryg. off to the Oil Region, I promising not to stay a night there alone, durg. their absence—gatherg. up duds for a week's stay here in Clinton St—of course planng. a world of sewg. & writg & readg and loadg. my bags accordingly ^all in vain^—comg. in via Germantn. to call on Mary Earle—shopping there to send things home—arrivg. here late—callg. at Photograph's in Chestnut St. to ans. an appointt. agreed to go agn. on 5th day—called for mended gold pen— (now so good) reached here—no, aunt Eliza's in time for a little chat—learned of Ellis [*Yarnall*] & co's safe arrival abroad—went to Select Mg. to hear a tirade from J. J. White—then out to Roadside agn. for the last eveg. with Ed. & Maria & Henry—hurryg. in agn. to Quarty. Mg. 3rd day examined alteratns. in the Discipline for Wom. Mgs. heard much preachg—Debh Wharton & others—held till near 3 oclk—dined at Aunt Eliza's—good rich soup—expected Mary Earle but she not at Mg— Rachel W. Townsd. made a strong appeal for the poor old Freedmen in Washn. where she had just been—another from Mary Jeans for the Indians—money & clothes wanted for all—Sarah Gillingh for Aged Col[ore]d. Home, & for Cold. Orphan Asylum—eno' to craze one— —came here at last— found Thos. M. Joe & Bel [*Parrish*] here to tea—no, that was 4th day eveg—so I forget 3rd day eveg— Anna [*Hopper*] out at Swarthmore all that day—preparg. for the inauguratn. 4th. day—[1] Now I remember— Thos. Mott went out with me 3rd day eveg. to help Jas Corr about our Oak trees ^such a comfort to have my dear son^—& we all came in together 4th. day morng.—& out in the 11 oclk. train—trees & Jas Corr by privilege—as all such things must go in freight trains—very many went out there—& 7 car loads in the special train @ 2 oclk— 3 or 400—a thousd. & more there altogether—many drivg. over from the country around—a large number came on from New Y—Several from Balt[imor]e. & quite [out?] to Indiana— Before enterg. the house, they joined our large gatherg. at the tree-plantg., wh. was a success. G. Truman made an appropriate speech—a photograph taken of the assemblage there & of the College &c.— Then all called to the large ding. room of 40 or 50 tables—a good collatn.—*free* then up to the fine collectg. room—all the pupils there—the Programme embracg. hours' work—good & satisfacy. no women called out—so poor I had to thrust in an improviso[2] Nelly Lord may have written all you'll want to hear— so you can hurry this on to Aubn.—I cant write direct— Our childn. indeed all the scholars seemed perfectly happy—& well they may be—for 'tis a perfect Establishmt.

Wm. Dorsey introduced a little of his orthodox Theology but the Pres[iden]ts. & J. Hicks' addresses were very liberal—[3] I hope aunt Martha will visit Swarthmore some day. As to Aunt Eliza I have lost all hope of her ever going with me anywhere—not from inability—tho' that may be at present, but from growg. indispositn. to leave her home—makg. more of her slight deafness than it deserves—for that is really better than a year or 2 ago— Dr. Turnbull[4] still sees her & Reba. occasy. & prescribes for both— Well to go on—we all rushed in @ 5 & 6 oclk—& twas then we so pleasantly found Thos., Joe & Bel here— Poor Marianna [Mott] in bed with toothache & general cold & hoarseness— Thos. was just here—had been to Mahlon Kirk & who wd. attend to her at once—so he has gone for a Cab to take her there— I met Mary Brown there on 5th. day, & had a pleast. call for an hour. Mari^a. in bed then— That morng. I had to sit an hour at Hurn's Photo[grap]h. at his request—then to aunt Eliza's agn.—hopg. she cd. go with me to the Fem. A. S. Mg. in the aftern.—but no— Reba. had just been out & thot it too cold—& in truth I thot. so too— We had a lively mg.— Mary Grew always gives interest to these occasions— Next week will be the last Annual Mg. of the State Society—[5] Wendll. P. cant come then, but he will be here next Mo— Chs. Burleigh is comg.—&c. &c.— That aftern. I had to call at Dr. Truman's to beg Cathr. to come out to Roadside—on 2nd day, to help entertain Reba. Turner who wished to make us a visit & that her only day— It will be a [poult?] to Maria to arrive home that morng & find a party— This eveg. was their time for returng. but a Telegram says 2nd. day morng—via North Penn-York Road Now I've got to yestery—omittg calls here from Sarah Pugh—plang. Wom. Rig. Mg—Lillie Parrish talkg. free trade, & all the other incidentals that filled every min. of time—

Yestermorn Anna & Maria H. looked over their wardrobe & made a large pile for Washn. & Iowa—for be it known we have a box nearly filled to send there— I arranged for Jas. Corr to come in this morng.—bring in what fowls & produce he can collect—then drive around with me & gather up the gifts & take to House of Ind[ustr]y. & to Race St. School-room where Mary Jeans & Lydia Gillingm. are attending to packg. a box for Washn.—then @ 2 oclk I am to meet Lucy Stone & Henry B[lackwell]. at Dr. Childs, with as many as can go on so short notice, to consult as to a Mg. here this Winter,[6] &c— Anna H. will not be able to go being summoned to Swarthmore today— So you see I am still tied here— After sundry calls yestery. I whipped into the cars & out to Roadside—saw how nicely all had been done there as ordered—took a cup of tea & toast & in agn. 4½—givg. Jas. Corr the above directns.—for I found to hire a cab here for 2 hours wd. cost 4 or $5—& I'm bent on savg. every dollar these begging times—so I hadn't my shawl & bonnet off after breakft. till arrivg. at John Wildman's to tea with Cyrus P. & his blind good Ruth—& daughrs.— all of whom I hadn't seen since the sad death of John's lovely Hannah— A call too I made yestery. on Saml. Townsd., whose son Geo. died suddenly of disease of the heart—at last it is whisper'd by suicide—his suffergs. have been great of late—[7] Rachel not at home—now here's this nice paper filled all about our-selves, when I always love to dwell at length on the pleasure your letters give us—& not ans. them so imperfectly as I have done of late. no word from any of you this week— Pattie must not let her letters to Nellie, rob us of our weekly mis-sives— I have a little *tax* on dear Anna B's time, viz: When in New Y. at that nice store 21st. St., if twas that where I got that toilet set— I saw a toast rack—English plate they sd., @ $5—I think—maybe 5.50— I told them I might send for it from here—they promised to remember—, & told me how to ask for it—wh. of course I entirely forgot— Anna directed us to the Shop—but Maria was not with me when I looked at *that*— She had gone to Stewarts— It was at the right hand side as you enter the shop—now I shall be much obliged if Anna will try to find it—& pay the $5 I herewith enclose—& more if I was mistaken— I cant get one here I like so well under $12— This is plated on *hard* metal— It can be sent to Geo. L's store—he will be comg. here soon, I hope— I now goes with Jas. Corr everywhere—

                                                        AL MNS

1. Sarah Gillingham (d. 1874), a Philadelphia Hicksite, was the widow of Charles Gil-lingham. Swarthmore College had opened on 8 November with 180 students of both sexes. Its inaugural was held on 10 November. In June, Anna Hopper had been elected to Swarthmore's board of managers (LCM to MML, 20 June 1869, MNS; *Friends' Intel-ligencer,* 20 November 1869, 602; *NASS,* 20 November 1869, 3).

2. At the inauguration, LCM had planted two oak trees (which had been raised from acorns by JM) "as fitting memorials of his interest in the cause of education and in the erection of this College." LCM had advised students to pay "heed to the 'inner light' as an inestimable source of instruction, at the same time directing their attention to the value of the teachings of such good men as Elias Hicks, and the beautiful and simple truth taught by Jesus of Nazareth" (*NASS,* 20 November 1869, 3).

3. Swarthmore president Edward Parrish then spoke, positing that "intellectual cul-ture is only valuable as it is joined with influences calculated to mould the character into forms of purity and truth." John D. Hicks (c. 1828–1907), a Hicksite Quaker of West-bury, Long Island, and a member of the Swarthmore Board of Managers, had remarked: "We have superadded a system for the joint education of the sexes, carrying out the principle we have long recognized in our Society of equal rights, not for all men, but for all men and *women*" (*Proceedings of the Inauguration of Swarthmore College* [Phila-delphia: Merrihew and Son, 1869], 12, 14; *Friends' Intelligencer,* 11 January 1908, 29).

4. Laurence Turnbull (b. 1821) was a Philadelphia physician.

5. The thirty-second annual meeting of the PASS was to be held on 17 November. The announcement read that the executive committee was "joyful in the hope that this may be the last Anniversary Meeting of this organization, and that a few more months will consummate its work and usher in the grand jubilee of American freedom" (*NASS,* 30 October 1869, 2).

6. The "Mg. here this Winter" is probably the jubilee celebration of the passage of the Fifteenth Amendment to be held in March 1870 (Bacon, 205).

7. Hannah Peirce Wildman had died on 12 June 1869 at the home of her parents, Cyrus Peirce and Ruth Peirce, all Philadelphia Hicksites. The Peirces had at least one other daughter, Sarah Harriet Peirce (1822–98) (*NASS,* 19 June 1869, 3). George Craft Townsend, the son of Samuel Townsend and his first wife, Rebecca, had died on 6 November.

## To Martha Coffin Wright

Roadside 12 mo. 5th 69—
Rain instd. of Snow
as threatened yestery.—

My Dear Sister

Thy lovely letter was enjoyed by us all last eveg—i.e. by all out here—only Ed & Maria [*Davis*] & self— Josh. Gibbons & daughr. Caroe. were coming but failed—so we had to be resigned— Edwd. & Thos. Mott went to Towanda & Barclay Mines on 5th. & 6th. days, & only returned last eveg—Thos. not stoppg. here— Mari[a]. [*Mott*] recd. thine with Eliza [*Osborne*]'s & Ellen [*Garrison*]'s entertaing. enclosures, while I was in Town 3 days ago— We were quite excited with the romantic story—and amused with Ellen's wit, & her Agnes' understandg. of Mabel's name— What a sick time they had there! So sorry were we that Anna D. H. missed findg. them at home, & that Eliza didn't get to Medford. She must go again before long—& Ellen must come here with Anna D. H. before the winter is over— Anna B. we hope will come after awhile What a blessg. that the operatn. was a success—[1] Her courage was great— I thot. I put Walter's accot. of it in my last to Aubn. but the other day it lay in an envelope—so if found, here goes—with one or 2 of Pattie [*Lord*]'s— We find one of thy letters must have miscarried— It certainly never reached us—*that* "to every body"— We wondered that thou let a whole month pass after such a harrowg. accot. of dear Fanny [*Wright*]'s sufferg. without letting us know how she & baby fared—& its name &.c. &.c— Do try to think what was in that letter—whether any more extracts from J. W. Howe's learned effusions—[2] We were much amused with all in Mari[a].s & in that recd. yestery. We agreed with thee in regard to the late & our former Conventions—i.e. Maria & I did— Edwd. means to hold his prejudices—tho' he agreed with us that John Wildman's Report of the Cleveld. Con. in the Standard was very unfair—entirely to leave out so important an item as a special invitatn. from the platform to Susan B. A. and her noble speech—[3] I was much gratified— So havg. a letter of invitatn. from Henry B. B. & Lucy S. to the Annual Mg. of the N. Jersey State Socy. to be held in Newark Opera house 8th & 9th—[4] I have ansd. affirmatively for one day—the 9th—so as not to be out in the eveg— I shall go to Orange on 4th. day aftern.— wilt thou meet me there?—& return home on 7th. day— Geo. Lord is comg then to go out to Swarthmore 1st. day with me— Canst thou do that too? If so, call & see Susan B. A. & learn her accot. of the Mg— I was sorry eno' that our dear Wm. L. G. cd. find it in his heart to write such a paragraph in his otherwise good letter to the Conventn.—[5] But we see from such diff. Standpoints. Give me also the "ring of the early Conventions"— Did the lost letter mention a visit from Caroe. [*Stratton*]? She was in Town last week & we dined together @ 5½ oclk at Edwd. H's— She mentioned going with Bettie[6] to Aubn.

What a long visit she made at Geneva [*New York*]— Mary Earle is going to [*Mt.*] Holly [*New Jersey*] soon, to tell them of her pleast. visit at Brattlebr. Our cousins so lovely— Anna H. still has her hands full— Painters & paperers the last nuisance—now all done—& the carpets beging. to be put down—Swarthmore twice a week—thro' it all— They have their troubles out there— The house allowed to get too cold at night the drain clogged filling that part of the buildg. with bad odor— The housekeeper too much to do, given out—broken down & sent in her resignatn. Helen Longstreth a bad cold—very hoarse— Anna Hall[l]. almost sick—has to lie down after givg. her lessons— Money wanted *dreadful*, to finish Laundry, Piazzas, grading & 1000 other things— Managers meet 3rd. day & in the aftern. the Annual Stockholders' Mg.— So we'll see!

I dont mean this as a regular letter—only to let thee know that one of thine has failed to reach us— I can't find Walter Brown's after all I'll look again— I have had about as many letters to write as thou hast—2 today before this to Blackwells—& John Wildman He wants me to help form an Auxiliary State Suffrage Socy—[7] I say yes if it shall include all our Pioneers—not else— S. Pugh has been trying for some time to arouse Philadelphians to call a Convention—

Mari[a]. was bright on 6th. day, after her more than usual ordeal,—had to resort to morphia 2 nights— She & the others I forget who, are invited to Mrs. John Field's party this week— Maria D. & self went to Robt. Collyer's Lecture on 4th. day eveg—no 6th. day—eveg—very good—clear grit—large audience—[8] We couldn't speak to him He left the City that night— Maria H. Joe & Bel [*Parrish*], Tom & Fanny [*Parrish*], the Hunts, & Dawes Furness had their Shakespeare Readg. that night & couldn't go with us—Anna H. too tired—

That baby of Bel's [*Ethel*] grows lovely—holds up her head, & "he got sense"— Our Cathe. Corr not yet confined—tho' our little cow is today—

We dont know yet how father Cavr's. estate is going to turn out some few thousands are safe & some good Oil Stock— Not a word from his wretched son [*Thomas*] of course— All thou copied from Willie [*Wright*]'s was very acceptable It takes a *Woman* to make pioneer settlers & lives cheerful Flora did just the right thing to go at once to her home & help clear up— It may be best for Willie & his partner to divide possessions— May it all be done without a quarrel— Even in our little Peace Society "I hear there are divisions & I partly believe it" alas![9]

It was in character for Willie to find an Oleander flower for Flora— Glad there was a "wonderful sunset" for them. *Was* the marriage published?[10] We were sorry eno, that sickness prevented their partakg. of that real wedding collation at Anna B's.— We were glad for Harry & Bessie [*Brown*] to visit you— Thou hast thy full share— They have not been here yet— Thou says nothg. of thy health—but if able to do so much & read so much & write so much, & have a Dennis & Osb[orn]e. party beside I trust thou art better— *We* havent yet read S. J. Mays book quite thro'— Garrison presented it to me when we met at Llewellyn Park that pleast. eveg—so that didn't grudge the $5 hire of the Carriage to go there—(much) Higginson's book we haven't read either. What busins. had he to hesitate when S. B. Anthony was called for?— We had the *World's* Report & Maria was savg. it for thee—but you've had it—[11] Maria thot. it the best of all— Isn't the Livermore Paper that is to be moved to Boston, to be considered the "Organ"?— I dont know & dont care—so that as Susan sd., they will work hard for the Suffrage Let Mrs. Howe have her hifoluton "generalities"—[12] Was there ever such nonsense? The Cleveld. Papers were sent to us too—& so to S. Pugh— She is true to Susan & Elizh. She heard Elizh. at Kennet 2 or 3 wks. ago & was much pleased— It was nice for thee to be countenanced in Syracuse— The Nation always finds fault with somethg— Miller M'Kim furnished that accot.* He has taken rooms in Walnut St—or a room—& Sarah comg. to *visit him* soon— Yes that Richardson affair is a pity—a pity too we thot. for Beecher & Frothingham to officiate in the marriage & *prayer*—[13] Oliver Johnson too— Why, of course, at Grandfr. Cavr's. *age* we admit that death was a blessg.— Thou wrote as if we didn't want people to die "not never"— It is for the young & useful we mourn— Richardson was too young to die, & as thou says, *bright*—

As to married people's quarrels I dont mean to enter into them—unless as near home as Caroline's We say just so of the Commonwealth—& the Radical

Mr. Fowler seems to have "kittened less & less." I was wonderg. the other day what use the increasg. number of Churches wd. be put to, as Civilizatn. outgrew them Thou wilt see quite a change around Eliza [*Yarnall*]'s house That large Masonic Hall up to the 2nd. Story, & the Church in front finished outside— Yr. professor Hopkins' address was somethg. like Dr. Bellows'[14] at the Dedicatn. of the new Unitarian— I am always glad for thee to go often to see Mrs. Worden. Now I've ansd. nearly every part of thy nice letter— Thy daughr. & Eliza shall have it tomorw. & Anna B's note too

It is gettg too dark to write & Ive done little else today—save mending my old shoes & darning old napkins Our Library is comfortable, but we fear thou wilt not find the room above as warm as the little stove made it— If so thou can go into Fanny Cavr's. room where the stove is & where David slept and asked next morng. if he might take that bed home—come again

so good bye    L Mott

*not the article

ALS MNS

1. Frank Wright and Fanny Wright's daughter Mabel Wright had been born on 30 October 1869. In a letter to MML, LCM had mentioned Anna Temple Brown's fifty-five-minute operation (21 November 1869, MNS).

2. MCW may have quoted from Howe's *From the Oak to the Olive: A Plain Record of a Pleasant Journey* (Boston: Lee and Shepard, 1868).

3. John K. Wildman's report of the AWSA's founding meeting in Cleveland, Ohio, on 24–25 November had appeared in the *NASS* (4 December 1869, 3). In a letter written 6 December, Wildman would respond to LCM's criticism of his article: "The fault and

omission referred to rest not with me. I mean to be fair and just towards all people. I entertain no unkind feelings towards Susan B. Anthony, and would do her no intentional wrong" (Harriet Beecher Stowe Center, Hartford, Conn.). He would go on to explain that the editor of the *NASS* had omitted the portion of his article that discussed Anthony's speech. At the Cleveland convention, Anthony had urged the AWSA to work for a sixteenth amendment to the Constitution for "the question would then be decided by the most intelligent portion of the people. If the question is left to the vote of the rank and file, it will be put off for years." Although Anthony thought the convention would "nullify" the NWSA, she had told the audience: "If you will do this work in Washington so that this amendment shall be proposed, and go with me to the several Legislatures and *compel* them to adopt it, I will thank God for this Convention as long as I have the breath of life" (*Revolution,* 2 December 1869, 343; see also Gordon, 2:284–85).

4. Stone, Blackwell, and LCM would attend the New Jersey Women's Suffrage Association meeting on 8–9 December in Newark (*NASS,* 18 December 1869, 3).

5. In his letter, read at the convention, Garrison had advised those who did not "sanction" the AWSA to "evince a just sense of the fitness of things by not enrolling themselves as members of the convention, nor taking any part in its proceedings." He also had suggested that the society and its "organ" should not "mistake rashness for courage, folly for smartness, cunning for sagacity, badinage for wit, unscrupulousness for fidelity" (*Revolution,* 2 December 1869, 342).

6. Bettie Birney (b. 1864) was the daughter of Laura Stratton Birney and Fitzhugh Birney.

7. A meeting to form an auxiliary to the AWSA was to be held at the Mercantile Library in Philadelphia on 22 December (*NASS,* 18 December 1869, 3).

8. "Mrs. John Field" is probably the wife of the Philadelphia merchant John Field. Collyer had given his lecture "Clear Grit" on 4 December in Philadelphia (*NASS,* 11 December 1869, 3).

9. The Pennsylvania Peace Society had recently celebrated its third anniversary at a meeting held on 22–24 November in Philadelphia. LCM had delivered the final address of the meeting: "She saw much to encourage the friends of peace. The United States, she said, is advancing in civilization and enlightenment, and as they press on, the moral sentiments come more actively into play. One thing alone was gratifying to her—the doing away of corporeal punishment at home and in the public schools. It was a specie of barbarism that our intellects had outgrown" (*NASS,* 11 December 1869, 3).

10. Willie Wright had married Flora McMartin (1843–98), the niece of Elizabeth Cady Stanton, on 28 October.

11. S. J. May, *Some Recollections of Our Anti-Slavery Conflict* (Boston: Fields, Osgood, 1869); Thomas Wentworth Higginson, *Army Life in a Black Regiment* (Boston: Lee and Shepard, 1869). At the Cleveland convention, the chairman, Judge James Bradwell, had moved that Anthony be invited to take a seat on the platform. "Mr. Higginson thought it unnecessary, as a general invitation had been extended to all desiring to thus identify themselves with the movement. Mr. Bradwell insisting, the resolution was put and carried. Miss Anthony walked to the stage and her appearance was greeted with much applause" (*Revolution,* 2 December 1869, 342). The *New York World* had described Anthony's presence at the convention as "persistent and conspicuous . . . what some people would call earnestness and other people 'cheek'" (*New York World,* 26 November 1869, 4).

12. When Mary Livermore's Chicago paper, the *Agitator,* merged with the *Woman's Journal,* Livermore moved to Boston and became its editor. At the Cleveland convention, Julia Ward Howe had stated: "Hold service in your right hand, and you will always hold empire in your left. But grasp empire in your right hand, and service will be lame

and hampered in your left. The ballot is empire where it means service; where it does not it is anarchy and treason" (*NASS*, 4 December 1869, 3). In an earlier letter to MCW, LCM had written: "We always had to labor with every variety of mind in the Anti S. struggle—& while rejoicg. in such accession as Julia W. H.—Mrs. Livermore & others, still we must not turn from such pioneers as E. C. S. & Susan B. A." (23 September 1869, Mott Manuscripts, PSCHi).

13. In its 2 December issue, the *Nation* had ridiculed the fashionable attire of many woman's rights leaders. It also had opined that sympathy for Albert Deane Richardson (1833–69), a journalist and an abolitionist who had been shot on 25 November by Daniel McFarland, the former husband of Richardson's fiancée, was excessive (479–80, 474–75). Henry Ward Beecher, assisted by Octavius B. Frothingham, had married Richardson and his fiancée, Abby Sage, a few days before Richardson's death from the wound on 2 December (*New York Tribune,* 1 December 1869, 5).

14. Henry W. Bellows (1814–82), a Unitarian clergyman, had been president of the U.S. Sanitary Commission during the war.

## To Josephine S. Griffing

RoadSide, near Philada.
12 mo. 25th. 69

My Dear Josephine

Thy kind "call" to your Wom. Rig. Mg. in Washingn., I cannot respond to favorably— My children object to my going far from home this winter— So many young & vigorous have entered the field, there is less need now for the aged & worn-out to "cumber the ground"— A new State organization was formed in Philada. this week auxiliary to the late Cleveland formation—[1] I felt excused from that also—desirous to avoid all party movements— Still I would attend any of the meetings if in my way— Susan B. Anthony did right to go to Cleveland—

Our dear Rachel W. Townsend has indeed exerted herself to the utmost to gather the temporary relief for thy poor sufferg. charge—[2] Another box she tells me is on the way— The claims of the Indians—so long injured & cheated & wronged in so many ways, seem now, with many of our Friends, to take the place of the Freedmen—so that we can hardly collect money eno' to pay our 8 or 10 teachers—South, for the end of this year—i.e. till next Summer—

We have also our Aged Col[ore]d. Wom. Home here & the Orphan Cold. Childn.'s Home besides the many individual demands—so that we must not be judged too sparing toward your greater necessities— If you could have a Soup-house it wd. aid you much in supplyg. the daily hunger—

I presume thou recd. my letter enclosg—a little sum—$20 I think from S. Pugh & others— It was sent with Rachel W T's first or second— Our neighbr. Martha Mellor sent me a large package of clothg. (cast offs) & boots & shoes &.c—&.c—some very good—old cloth table covers for shawls, &.c—wh. were packed in the box with the rest— If noticed among the things of more value,

I shd. like to tell her you recd. them— Thy letters I know have acknowledged fully—but all dont see them out here in the country—

I herewith send $10—better than nothg. I am a poor beggar—

Affecy.   L. Mott

Thy labors I know are blessed to the poor creatures—and thou art "not weary in well doing"— "Enter thou!"[3] LM

ALS NNCB-Griffing

1. The NWSA would meet on 18–20 January 1870 in Washington, D.C. Although LCM would not attend, MCW would, bearing "a message from Lucretia Mott, to the Convention, that she sent her 'God Speed' to the movement, and regretted that sickness prevented her being present" (*Revolution,* 27 January 1870, 52). The Pennsylvania Woman Suffrage Association would meet on 22 January as an auxiliary to the AWSA. Officers included Mary Grew, Edward M. Davis, Annie Heacock, and John K. Wildman (*NASS,* 18 December 1869, 3, 1 January 1870, 3).

2. The minutes of the PFASS meeting on 13 January 1870 record: "A very interesting letter from Josephine Griffing was read, which gave a graphic account of the suffering which had existed in Washington and thanking those who had so generously contributed to their aid" (Pennsylvania Abolition Society Papers, reel 30, PHi).

3. Gal. 6:9 and 2 Thess. 3:13; Matt. 25:21.

# To Fellow Abolitionists

[*December 1869*]

*Dear Friend and Fellow Laborer:*

This Circular is addressed to you, personally, in the belief that you have been long laboring for the emancipation of the slave, and his elevation to the full liberty and rights of an American citizen; or that, at least, you are at this time interested in the efforts made to secure all this for him. We ask your attention to a few facts. The doctrine of the American Anti-Slavery Society, as set forth in its DECLARATION OF SENTIMENTS, is "*That all persons of color, who possess the qualifications which are demanded of others, ought to be admitted forthwith to the enjoyment of the same privileges, and the exercise of the same prerogatives, as others.*" Its purpose, as declared in the 3d Article of its Constitution, is "*to elevate the character and condition of the people of color,*" and to remove "*public prejudice, that thus they may, according to their intellectual and moral worth, share an equality with the whites, of civil and religious privileges.*" The personal freedom of the colored men in the South cannot be complete and secure without the right of suffrage. The ratification of the Fifteenth Amendment will so secure to them and to colored men of the North this right, that they can never be deprived of it, except by the consent of three-fourths of the States of the Union. To promote this ratification is the end to which the American Anti-Slavery Society and its coadjutors are now working. Our main instrumentality is the National Anti-Slavery Standard, which is doing most effective service in this cause. That its influence cannot be safely spared in the present crisis, we have the testimony of such men as Charles Sumner, Henry Wilson and Wm. D. Kelley, who, from time to time, exhort the Abolitionists not to disband their organizations, and not to permit the Standard to be discontinued until this work shall be accomplished.[1]

Six months ago we confidently hoped that this Amendment would be ratified within this year, and that at its close we should be able to announce that the colored man was legally and constitutionally invested with the rights of an American citizen, and the special work of the Anti-Slavery Societies accomplished. These hopes will not be realized; and we have no alternative but to continue our organizations and publish our paper a few months longer. We trust that it will be but a few months; and that within that time the ratification will be accomplished. Then we shall ask you to join us in a jubilee over the consummation of the grandest Moral Revolution of the nineteenth century. *Now* we appeal to you for a generous donation towards the support of the Standard until the work to which we are pledged shall be finished. And we appeal with confidence, knowing that our cause is yours and the Nation's, and that the race for whom we plead and work have claims upon all of us which this nation will never cancel.

As a Moral Reform nears its accomplishment, though increasing numbers applaud it, its closing tasks are often left to the hands of a few of its friends who, in the flush of victory, do not forget that all may be lost by neglecting to secure what has been won. On comparatively few the burden of our work now falls. It is useless for us to ask aid of those who care little whether the colored man is protected in his rights, or left to struggle for them unaided. We ask it of you, because we know that you sympathize with him. And we ask you to respond to our appeal with liberality proportioned to your ability.

| | |
|---|---|
| Lucretia Mott | Robt. Purvis |
| Benjamin C. Bacon | E M *Davis* |
| Alfred H Love | W Still[2] |
| Margaret J. Burleigh | S H Peirce |
| J. K. Wildman. | Mary Grew |

PLS PSCHi-Mott

1. In December, the *NASS* had regarded the ratification of the Fifteenth Amendment as "well nigh certain" and had planned to change its mission accordingly. The newspaper had eliminated "Anti-Slavery" from its title after the amendment was officially proclaimed in late March 1870 and had proposed to continue its work as an "independent journal of Reform and Literature" (*NASS*, 18 December 1869, 2; 26 February 1869, 2, 5 March 1870, 2).

2. William Still (1821–1902), a Pennsylvania abolitionist who was the son of fugitive slaves, was best known for his work on the Underground Railroad.

# To Edward N. Hallowell

Roadside 2 mo. 1st 1870—

My Dear Edward—

I should have acknowledged thy letter of 18th. Ult. sooner had I known just how to answer thy inquiries— It is true that Friends, in their collective capacity gave no countenance to "modern Abolitionism", as they called it—that they often in their meetings misjudged & misrepresented the action of those engaged in the cause—many of their ministers trying to preach them down, & succeeding so far as to disown I. T. Hopper, Chs. Marriott & a few others—the only "persecution" they could practice. The Meetg. of Green Plain Ohio was laid down by Indiana Yearly Mg—& numbers were disowned— They sent complaints agt. me for appointg & attendg. lectures—on Anti S. & Temp[eranc]e., in Richmond, Ind. also—Nine Partners' Qy. Mg.—but not being done according to order, they were never acted upon— An effort was made to remove me from the Mg. of Min. & Elders, but that too failed for the same reason—after being on their records some 9 or 10 Mos. No charge of Abolition was made— but that "she had lost her gift in the ministry."[1] The body of the Mg however, especially the younger part of the society, wherever I went always sustained me— as was generally the case with such of our ministers as travelled, bearing their testimony against Slavery. When any of our AntiSlavery lecturers held Mgs. in the neighborhds. of Friends, there were always eno.' found, ready to entertain them, & to aid in forming A. S. Societies—but the use of our Mg. houses was seldom granted— — When our Yearly Mg. was pressed for a testimony against Slavery, they could only, "encourage Friends to avail themselves of every right opening," &c.—implying that our measures were not of that character— At length a large com. was appointed—Dr. Parrish, Dr. Gibbons Debh. Wharton & others— Dr. Gibbons hoped that Com. wd. not be identified with the popular movements, which had put the cause back 50 years, &.c &.c— I replied to him—he thot. "the phillipic underservd" & comg to me afterwd., I told him such charges we were familiar with, from the ignorant, but we had a right to think better of him— He received it kindly, saying with a smile, "Well I'll tell thee what it is, I'll try to think better of you"—which he did—for in 1840 or 41, after Dr. Parrish's earnest, but too tame an appeal—in pamphlet form, Dr. Gibbons produced a Report, full of strong arguments, & striking facts, gathered from T. D. Weld's "Slavery as it is—or the Testimony of a thousand witnesses".[2] saying he pitied the person who could read that Work & remain neutral—or not be impressed; I forget his exact words in the Com.— The Yearly Mg. could not go so far & dissolved the committee. Dr. Parrish had died a short time before— and our Anna Hopper bore her testimony agt. such a backward step, when the righteous labors of such a man were so fresh before us—her exact words too I forget— We were in England at that time— Friends there had always assisted

Clarkson & his co-workers agt. the Slave trade—& were ready to join in calling a World's Conventn. for the entire Abolitn. of Slavery—some abstained from slave-labor product

I cannot say as to the Orthodox Frds. of other Yearly Mgs. than Philada.— Here *they* gave no more countenance to the movement than did ours— When some English Friends—Joseph Sturge & John Candler & wife[3] in 1841 were here, after the latter had visited the West Indies, & wished to report the success of Emancipatn. there, Arch St. Mg. house was denied them, even the little middle room— So that it may safely be said that no encouraget. was given in a collective capacity—* When Joseph John Gurney was in this country—some of their Frds. were asked why his mouth was closed on the Anti Slavery subject—open as it was at home— The reason given was that, "his mission here was to preach the Gospel"—!! In Indiana Orthodox Yearly Mg. an antiSlavery separatn. took place & a smaller Yearly Mg. was held at Newport I think—some 10 or 12 miles from Richmond, Ind.

In the limits of our own Yearly Mg. too,—Western Quarter—Kennet Mg. divided—& Longwood was established—owing to the treatment of Joseph Dugdale & others in Ohio—& many Frds. in Chester Co.—Penna— This however is familiar to you—as much of the foregoing long accot. must be to Richard— I hope to see his Discourse—[4]

11th [February]—

This was begun as dated—when I was called to the City to my dear Sister Yarnall's sick bed—since which, I have felt unable to finish it—[5] And now thou wilt have to make allowance for this unsuccessful effort—wh. however is freely made—

by thy Sincere frd.<br>Lucretia Mott—

*but rather that obstacles were placed in their path— The Periodicals of Friends came out in opposition—contrasting the labors of Anthony Benezet & John Woolman with such as were crying aloud and sparing not in our day. Our Intelligencer is now printing Benjn. Lay's, Ralph Sandiford—Anthony Benezets labors agt. Slavery—[6] I sd. to one of the Editors, "how much more good they wd. have done had they been in that Paper years ago—when we needed such testimony["]—but they were carefully excluded then—except some accot. of Warner Mifflin's[7] travels & testimony—at the South where he was so careful not to offend the Slave holders—something like this— Now you can decide in the "difference of opinions between you, which is nearest right—

ALS Davis Env: "Edward [S.?] Hallowell, care Hallowell & Coburn, Boston, Mass"

1. See LCM to Elizabeth Pease, 28 April 1846, and LCM's portion of JM's letter to Nathaniel Barney and Elisa Barney, 26 October 1847, both above. From 1843 to 1858 LCM did not receive a traveling minute. According to Margaret Hope Bacon, she would have been told informally not to apply for one, since her application would most likely have

been denied (research by Margaret Hope Bacon, Monthly Meeting of Friends of Philadelphia [Hicksite] records, PSCHi).

2. The minutes of the Hicksite Philadelphia Yearly Meeting of 17 May 1839 record the
formation of a committee "to take charge of the Concern of this Meeting, as connected
with the welfare of the People of Colour." Members included Joseph Parrish and William Gibbons. The committee's report, read in the yearly meeting on 14 May 1840, stated that "the painful state of public sentiment . . . calls loudly upon us to guard equally
against a state of indifference on the one hand & on the other, from taking any step in
the advancement of this righteous cause, which is not dictated by that Spirit which
breathes peace on earth & good will to men." It ordered that ten thousand copies of an
"address, calling the attention of Friends to this interesting concern" be published and
circulated among Friends. The following year (on 12 May 1841) a subcommittee, which
included Gibbons, revised the 1840 report and had ten thousand copies printed and
distributed. The committee reported that "Education of the Coloured population" was
a significant concern of the meeting and called attention to the "five fold" increase in
the number of slaves in the United States along with continued "cruelty injustice &
oppression." The committee concluded "that it is only as we withdraw from the confusion that is in the world & submit our own wills, that we can know our own feet shod
with the preparation of the Gospel of peace & thus be qualified to advance the cause of
justice, mercy & truth" (Philadelphia Yearly Meeting minutes, PSCHi). Theodore D.
Weld's work was published in 1839 (New York: American Anti-Slavery Society).

3. John Candler (1787–1869) was married to Maria Candler (1792–1870).

4. On the Longwood meeting, see LCM to John Ketcham and Rebecca Ketcham, 30
August 1852, above. Richard Hallowell's *The Quakers in New England* was published in
Philadelphia (Merrihew and Son, 1870).

5. Elizabeth Yarnall had died on 4 February 1870.

6. The Philadelphia Quakers and reformers were Anthony Benezet (1713–84), a school-
teacher; Benjamin Lay (1677–1759), a British immigrant; and Ralph Sandiford (1693–
1733), a merchant and a former slaveholder. Called "Sketches of Friends," articles on
Sandiford, Woolman, Benezet, and Lay appeared in the *Friends' Intelligencer* (8 January
1870, 705–8, 15 January 1870, 721–25, 29 January 1870, 753–55, and 5 February 1870, 769–
72).

7. Warner Mifflin (1745–98), a Delaware Quaker, was an antislavery activist and the
grandfather of Elizabeth Neall Gay.


## To Richard D. Webb

Roadside, near Philada.
2 mo. 24th. 1870.

My Dear Richard D. Webb—

Thy kind & thoughtful attention in sending me the pamphlet containg.
Archbishop Whately's miserable objections to furnishg. Thom with such letters
& testimony as would have added value to the biography of Blanco White,[1]
deserved earlier notice and thanks than I have given it, but please even now
accept the assurance that thy attentions were appreciated, in that & in the Papers sent since, all which have been read by us with interest— —   The great
questions of the time—Woman's Rights &.c—seem to be claiming simultaneous

interest in Europe & America— Poor man has only to meet coming results with the best grace he can— The lectures of Horace Greely and others, stating how far they are disposed to *let* woman exercise her rights, are simply amusing because so childish—so behind the demands of *now*. As also J. Stahl Pattersons Phrenological measurement of the brain, in the last Radical.[2] Dost thou see that Periodical? Let Woman's intellect be cultivated for a few generations, as man's has been, & then judge— Geo. Combe told me the sculls of the native Anglo Saxon, in the earliest day were far inferior to our later developements— Nantucket women's frontal organs are more prominent than those of women whose intellectual powers & business talents have not been called into action— But this scrap is not for a Wom. Rig. letter— I am so glad that Edwd. Davis & thyself keep up correspondence— We were far from ready for thee to go home & leave us—such a little heap of our Hicksite Frds. writgs., & some others still more heterodox, as I had gathered to shew thee & talk over, but not worth sending, *without the talk,* are now scattered again— It gave me a kind of pain when thy dear Deborah[3] told us thou wast more settled at home, & said less of coming back— We want thee back, & want thee to feel that thou would be happier to come & settle among us— I had just begun to feel acquainted with Debh., when she left us— I called at the door of her cousin too late to see her again— I was surprised to find her leang. to Spiritualism— Does her interest increase? I must call again & enquire more about her— Sarah Pugh is very kind in keepg. me informed— But of late my time & feelings have been absorbed with the illness & death of my dear Sister Elizh. C. Yarnall with whom we visited together when thou wast in Philada.— She was in poor health then, but kept up till 3 or 4 weeks since an attack of Pneumonia proved too much for her reduced strength— She was 75 yrs. old We were like twin sisters 10 months the longest time we were ever separated— The loss is very great to me— My Sister Martha C. Wright was with her during her illness— She is still here—& a great comfort to us to dwell on our bereavet. together— I expected to go first & now so soon to follow, it may seem that at our age I might rejoice rather than mourn but all our speculations as to "what we shall be" are unavailing,

> "when the heart is torn—
> "The human drops of bitterness will steal,
> Nor can we lose the privilege to mourn
> While we have left the faculty to feel."

Indeed all guess work as to the future is so vain, that we may as well content ourselves with the certainty that both here & hereafter "we are secure to be as blest as we can bear"— Amen—

affecy.   L. Mott

ALS MB

1. Archbishop Richard Whately had criticized the autobiography of Blanco White, edited by John Hamilton Thom, for being too morbid and personal (Martin Murphy, *Blanco White: Self-Banished Spaniard* [New Haven, Conn.: Yale University Press, 1989], 195–96; see also LCM to George W. Julian, 14 November 1848, above).

2. In a speech given in Pennsylvania entitled "The Woman Question," Greeley had argued that women should not participate in politics or government because these arenas were not in their sphere. The *Revolution* frequently accused Greeley's *New York Tribune* of biased reporting on the woman's rights movement (*NASS*, 26 February 1870, 1; see, e.g., *Revolution*, 27 January 1870, 58). In "Woman and Science: A Chapter on the Enfranchisement and Education of Woman" (*Radical*, March 1870, 169–85), Patterson would examine the differences between men and women. He would conclude that women were emotionally superior, but men were intellectually superior: "Woman takes the affectional sphere of activity; man, the sphere of thought and execution; and, whatever exceptions might be named, this general truth would remain unaffected."

3. Webb's daughter Deborah Webb (1837–1921) was visiting the United States (Richard S. Harrison, *Richard Davis Webb: Dublin Quaker Printer* [Skeagh, Ireland: Red Barn Publishing, 1993], 19, 84).

## To William Lloyd Garrison

Roadside 3 mo. 8th. 70—

My Dear Long-loved William Lloyd Garrison

Our E. M. Davis is now in Boston— He will confer with our friends there, as to the time of holding the Commemorative Mg. of the 15th. Amendmt. and of the great events of the few years past—[1] Since he left us I have regretted that I did not urge him to call on thee and ask if thou cannot, in view of so great a movement, leave the things that are behind and unite with all who may be disposed to come together to celebrate these marvelous events— I called on Mary Grew yestery.— She agreed with me in this desire, & said the Ex. Com. would doubtless send a special invitation— May we not hope that it will be accepted,—and that Edmund Quincy, Samuel May Jr. & other of our long tried friends may again co-operate with us in a measure that involves no compromise? Let us not hope in vain— We have not met I think since the pleasant eveg. we passed at J. M. M'Kim's—& thy Wendell's—in Llewellyn Park— Then thou presented me Saml. J. May's Book on the Anti Slavery Conflict— On lookg. over it with so much interest, I have wanted to thank thee again for it— His notes & memory do not furnish a thorough history, but his beautiful spirit marks the book throughout— I wish Miller M'K. & thyself would unite in presenting to the public just what is needed as none other it seems to me can do it so well— Clarkson's Slave Trade tho' necessarily egotistical not offensively so, could not have been written by his *helpers,* as by himself— Senator Wilson will doubtless give the Political history as well—*as we cd. expect*— He has applied to some of our Philada. Abolitionists, for facts in the life & labors of Thos. Shipley, Evan Lewis & Lindley Coates—[2] If I succeed in begging thee to take part in our coming jubille, I shall be encouraged to ask thee, & Wendell Phillips too to sink past differences in Wom. Rig. struggle & let the May meetg. be *one & undivided*—[3] Amen—

Love in full measure to thy dear Helen & to your household—

L. Mott

ALS MB

1. The commemorative meeting to celebrate the Fifteenth Amendment would be held on 9 April in New York City.

2. Thomas Clarkson published a number of works on the slave trade, including *A Summary View of the Slave Trade* (London: J. Phillips, 1787); *An Essay on the Impolicy of the African Slave Trade* (London: J. Phillips, 1788); *An Essay on the Slavery and Commerce of the Human Species Particularly the African* (London: J. Phillips, 1788); *Letters on the Slave Trade* (London: J. Phillips, 1791); and *The History of the Rise, Progress, and Accomplishment of the Abolition of the African Slave Trade* (London: R. Taylor, 1808). Henry Wilson's multivolume *History of the Rise and Fall of the Slave Power in America* (Boston: James R. Osgood, 1872–74) included several mentions of Pennsylvania's role in the abolition of slavery and named a number of the state's important abolitionists, including LCM, Coates, and Thomas Shipley (c. 1787–1836), an Orthodox Quaker (see, e.g., 1:421, 2:51). Evan Lewis (d. 1834) was a Hicksite Quaker.

3. Garrison would not attend the jubilee; Wendell Phillips would preside. LCM's name was on the call, and she also would speak: "But with all their faith and confidence in the overruling power of justice and love, they had never anticipated a victory like the present. After so many years, there was no thought of ceasing their work. Their motto was still onward. With this in view, there was nothing sad in being called together for a final meeting" (*NASS*, 5 March 1870, 3, 2 April 1870, 2, 16 April 1870, 1).

## To Theodore Tilton

Roadside 3 mo. 18th. 70—

Theodore Tilton
My Dear Friend

I have just received thy letter with the proposed appeal to our divided ranks in the labor for Womans Suffrage— I most willingly have my signature attached,—only please not place the name first, but rather far below those who have prepared this Circular—[1]

I had interviews last Fall with the active workers on both sides in Boston & New York, and plead with them, that at the then coming Convention in Cleveland they should merge their interests in one common cause, and have one universal society— This however was not done— Still I hope it is not too late for this proposed union to take place—

I had observed with regret that the Anniversary Meetings in New York, are appointed for the same time— —

I shall not be present at either—our Yearly Meeting of Friends in Philada. occurs at the same time, which will keep me here—[2]

I love the pioneer & earnest labores on both sides too well to become a partizan—and shall be glad to attend any meetings when in my power—

very cordially    Lucretia Mott

In great haste[3]

ALS NBu

1. Theodore Tilton's call quoted from both AWSA and NWSA constitutions, arguing that "no sufficient reason exists to justify the future permanence of the disunion which we at present deplore." Other signers included John White Chadwick and Frances Dana Gage (*Revolution*, 27 March 1870, 189; *Independent*, 31 March 1870, 4).

2. The NWSA anniversary meeting was to be held on 10–11 May and the AWSA meeting on 11–12 May in New York City (*New York Times*, 11 May 1870, 1, 12 May 1870, 8, 13 May 1870, 5). Although LCM was not present at these, she would attend the last meeting of the PFASS on 24 March and the last meeting of the PASS on 5 May 1870 (*NASS*, 2 April 1870, 3, 16 April 1870, 2).

3. Tilton would print LCM's letter, with only minor changes, in the *Independent* along with a number of others endorsing the union of the two societies (31 March 1870, 4).


## To Martha Coffin Wright

Orange [*New Jersey*]
4 mo. 7th. 70—
5th. day morng. bright & clear,
after a wk of N.E. weather

My Dear Sister—

With thy 3 letters open, I begin an ans. direct not remembg. the contents of the 2 or 3 sent you via Orange & N.Y. Another of thine to Anna B. she sent to Mari[a]. [*Mott*]—we here have not seen it— From Anna B's accot., we fear poor little Tom [*Osborne*] is still alarmgly. ill, & only wish his Mother were with him—[1] Geo. L. says she ought to be here now—unless the N.E. storm has delayed the arrival— Pattie [*Lord*] & self lunched at Walter [*Brown*]'s yestery. & *so* hoped she wd. appear while we were there— We left early to go to the reconciliatn. Mg. called by Theo. Tilton, wh. you will see reported in the Tribune—[2] Pattie was admitted by courtesy, as my escort— About a dozen present— Quite a free talk, & several proposals made—none of wh. acceded to, by the 3 from Boston— Pattie inclined to their side, as did Anna B. from our report to her— She thinks the Revolution has so many foolish things in it—all those pres[en]ts., & flattering saygs. to S. B. Anthony— Tilton they thot., or Pattie did, too much a partizan on their side to be an impartial outsider—ditto her mother— I shd. have been glad if P. Pillsbury had been willing as one, to drop the National Socy., & join in a body the American, as Lucy S. & Higginson said the Olive Branch was extended to all—& E. C. Stanton wrote as if willg. for anythg.[3] I went "not expectg. great things, & I didn't get 'em"— Glad to be out of it all, & never mean to join another Organizatn. Parker was quite affected when speakg. of the misrepresentatns.—after his Southern letter,—the Republican Papers, with one exceptn. (Curtis' Harpers Weekly) chargg. him with favorg. the Democts.[4] Some dispute arose betwn. Higginson & Tilton as to H. Ward Beechers position—each denyg. the other's statemt.— Also Higginson tried to disprove Tilton's accot. of the Provid[enc]e. Mg—before the Cleveld Con., insistg that he was opposed to that— Tilton sd. "no, only to the proposed form & Constitutn.—only delegates to vote["] &.c—but he cd. shew 3 articles in the Independt. approvg. the Cleveld. Mg. &.c—[5] I didn't like Higginson's spirit & his & Lucy's flushed face & Curtis' determined spirit & manner—so little idea of yieldg. 1 iota— Pattie didn't admire Tilton's indiff[erenc]e., when they were speakg. & his all-attentn. when Pillsby. began—who I did not observe—whereupon she thot. *my* leangs. were as decidedly to the Stanton-Anthony side— I did express regret at the occasional flings in the Wom. Journal—& not less at Pillsbury's severe comments on their treatment, as in the late Revolutn.[6] But all is of little avail—& we were quite ready to leave— Mrs. Wilbour urged our stayg. to the dinner they had ordered—but we had dined eno'—Anna B. havg. hurried up their lunch—& havg. another hour, we went back there & had a good time. Walter met us at the corner & went back, with us—nourishd. my exhausted powers with his good wine, & then went on his way— Anna is settling all their home affairs, & has made numerous calls— She looked well & was very lovely—comg. home found Geo. with a stiff neck, wh. indeed had kept him awake hours the night before—better this morng—gone to his busins., as he did yestery. also— Miller M'K. called this morng., on his way to Philada. on busins.—returng. early in the week, to meet Charlie who is well on his way home—Sarah busy preparg. for Debh. Webb, who is comg. from Ohio, on *her way home* to Dublin— I hope to see her, as well as Charlie— I may stay long eno' to go to Yonkers next week—hearg. that our sister Sarah [*Cornell*] is very poorly—the cancer extendg. above her eyebrows—!! Sarah Hicks & daughrs. also confined to the house—all sick— Mary [*Franklin*] recovg. tho'—so I goes there too— Am I to meet thee on 7th. day in New Y—? We fear not, as Tom continues ill— Pattie is real sorry to lose thy visit here— Miller spoke of thy ans. to his letter, of course not satisfacy.[7] We have not yet seen it— He "alluded to both thee & Maria, in that letter to me, not meang. offensively, but you were too easily taken with a kind of reasong." Oh, I forget what he did say—*nothg*. Only I was glad he included Maria, & "didn't mean yr. father." He talked incessantly the short ½ hour before runng. to the Cars & didn't want to hear, determined, as Pattie sd. *I* was, to talk too— He is very well now, & wants to decide what to do—

Now, for thy letters & Ellen [*Garrison*]'s & Eliza [*Osborne*]'s, & copy of Willie's & Flora [*Wright*]'s— All wh. have been read to satisfactn. save the 1st parcel of Eliza's wh. Mari[a]. promised to let me have, & then being sick, she never sent me— I called to see her 3rd. day before comg. here—found her still in bed, tho' she did sit up a little on 1st. day— Emily [*Mott*] too was quite poorly—sittg. in the parlor— Thos. waited on us over to the Depot—carryg. the childn's bags & things & seeing us seated in the cars—then waited & checked Pattie's trunk— She wd.n't *stay* & finish her visit as I wanted her to— Tom & Fanny [*Parrish*] were out at Roadside 2nd. day eveg. We hoped Joe & Bel [*Parrish*] wd. join them but they cd.n't. leave baby who was quite sick—teething— Nelly Lord was with us from 7th. day aftern., only leavg. us at the Depot—Mary Cavr. & May Mott also out—so that there was fun eno', with plays—Theatricals & recitatns.—all of their own gettg. up—for our small audience. Anna H. was out 2 days & one night while Pattie was with us, & on 2nd. day they had quite a *holder* bee—17 stitched together & most of them finished— I had to leave Pattie 1st day morng. & go in to a colored Mg. when lo! Dillwyn P. was not well & the Mg. didn't come off—so to compensate Anna went out with me— I called 1st. day on the Yarnall sisters & left thy letters with them— Thos. Y's son Tom 4 yrs old had been very ill with dyptheria & croup—they were all over there, & much alarmed a consultg Physicn. was called, who seemed to regard it so hopeless that he proposed no change in the treatmt.—but it proved the turn of the disease & he grew better from that time, but since then a relapse has kept them anxious—he was no worse however on 3rd. day, when Pattie & I were there— Mary B. was lookg. better than since her sickness, & all are more cheerful— So they may hail *Easter's* approach—

Anna H. on 7th. day had another large tea party—that wh. was talked of when thou wast with us—Drs. Smith & Morton & wives—neighrs. Huttons & Hopkins—& several more—I forget—so that she had a morng's clearg. up before she cd. go with me— I wd.n't. go so into detail if thou had not been with us of late— How little thou hast had of David's compy. since thy return— So essential as thy presence was to dear Tom made us all feel that it was well that thy going was thus hastened— I'm sure the Mg. yestery. needn't cause any regret that thou had not delayed on that accot.— It must be a great satisfaction to Eliza that thou went immedy. on hearg. that he was real sick— Thy 1st. letter misdirected Walnut St., Thos. soon traced as Mariᵃ. had doubtless written thee— How in character it was for Eliza to give her br. & sister the treat of a trip with them & taking the provision to them was also so like her—such a generous soul— Yes, not being so generous as to expense as thy daughr., I presume I shd. have sd.—"needn't telegh. if all's right & safe going home for we can infer so"— & I think thou agreed with me—so far but if necessity for speed, as of course when Tom's symptoms were so alarmg. why of course telegrh.— So as regards $3 for one night's sleep, when there was a probability that thou would be needed in a sound good state of health immedy. on reachg home, why, grudge *not* the $3— I only speak as to common travelg., when plenty of time to rest afterwd., & speak of it too as *my* preference—not judgg. for others, *if they have the means,* that I wd. rather take my chance for a comfortable lodgg. at the common price— I never objected to a stateroom on the boat with my husband, save once when our precious, careful sister was with us & protested agt. the additl. 50c— She would have opened her eyes very wide if $3 had been named to her—for she never felt that she *had* the means—good, economical dear that she was— A recurrence to any litle savings of that kind, & in the way of hotel & steamboat tables, ever brings peace to my mind— Now I can give the same amt. to each of the Wom. Rig. movets.—, & to Garrison & Powell abolitnists. without feelg. that I have spent the money needlessly, & now cant afford it— I did mean to buy a pr new gloves for this great occasion, but time passed & I forgot it— So Pattie's keen eye spying my old beavers, worn all winter, brot. forth from her treasure a nice partly worn pr. brown kid, with a pretty white rim around them, & thou dont know how dressed I felt, with aunt Phebe's nice merino dress & cloth shawl, surmounted with that stunng. Angola—for we were havg. snow & quite cold weather—& my black cloak & fur cape were left at home— I hope the fellow-passenger, who *didn't* get the upper-berth found a lodgment without such *offensive* *"proximity"*— In a gen'ral way I rather like Fredk. Dougls' "I can stand it if you can." Flora's letters we are pleased with— They are so cheerful & smart— It *is* rather confusg. for thee to use so many scraps—economy out of the question—makg. it difficult to find wh. date they belong to— If Miller had stayed long eno' I shd. have liked to read to him thy comments on his letter in the Nation, tho' it wd. have done no good in his present dispensation—& he always shrinks from my readg. anythg. to him— the undisputed floor is his choice—needn't shew Anne this— There are few whom I prefer to listen to for all— We liked thy remarks— Miller sd. he had often noticed that failure of argument in Maria Davis much as he liked her Miller thot. women erred so much in laying all the blame of fallen women on men— It wd. be found that Women themselves were as bad—not just so either was his talk—but in that strain, & it had been and still was a great exercise to his mind— Educatn. & not voting was most needed— He met with oppostn. at home— Sarah & Lucy didn't agree with him—&.c &.c— I hope Mariᵃ. has ansd. thy letters better than I have  All was interestg

so goodbye    L. M.[8]

ALS PSCHi-Mott

1. MCW had cut short her visit to LCM in March because of her grandson's illness (LCM to MML, 29 March 1870, Mott Manuscripts, PSCHi).

2. Tilton and LCM had met with Laura Curtis Bullard (b. c. 1834), an officer in the Brooklyn Equal Rights Association and a friend of Tilton, at the Fifth Avenue Hotel in New York City on 6 April. Representing the NWSA were Parker Pillsbury, Josephine S. Griffing, and Charlotte Beebe Wilbour (1833–1914, president of the New York Sororis and a member of NWSA's executive committee); representing the AWSA unofficially (the "3 from Boston") were George W. Curtis, Thomas W. Higginson, and Lucy Stone. At the meeting, both Curtis and Stone had stated that the "olive branch [*to join the AWSA*] was extended at Cleveland." Pillsbury and Wilbour had declared themselves in favor of uniting the two organizations, as did Tilton and Bullard. LCM had said, "I believe that the two Societies should unite by all means—by such concessions each should make to the other." Shortly after these statements, the AWSA representatives and LCM left the

conference, with Brooklyn businessman and suffrage activist Francis D. Moulton taking LCM's place. The remaining members decided to form the American Woman's Franchise Society with Tilton as president. Tilton stated that he had hoped LCM would serve, "but she had already, before leaving the convention, expressed her emphatic unwillingness to accept the position" (*New York Tribune,* 7 April 1870, 5; *Independent,* 14 April 1870, 4; Gordon, 2:357, 259). The *Woman's Journal*'s account of the meeting was similar to that of the other two periodicals, but concluded that the constitution for the new society "follows mainly in name and form that of the 'National Woman Suffrage Association' and abandons the plan of a *delegated* society, which is the essential principle of that formed at Cleveland" (9 April 1870, 104).

3. Stanton, then president of the NWSA, had written from Minnesota that she declined any office in the new organization (*Independent,* 14 April 1870, 4).

4. In an article, "The South As It Is," Pillsbury had declared Reconstruction a failure in terms of economic and political progress for freedpeople. He had recounted numerous instances of poverty and degradation in the Southern states and had concluded, "Neither political party understood the situation during the war of rebellion. Neither party understands it to-day." From Beaufort, South Carolina, John Hunn had criticized Pillsbury's discounting the progress freedpeople had made (*Independent,* 4 November 1869, 1, 2 December 1869, 4). Assessing Pillsbury's article and the reaction to it, an editorial in *Harper's Weekly* had stated that Pillsbury did not devalue work of the antislavery movement, as some newspapers had claimed; Pillsbury had concluded "that the sad condition of the colored population at the South is directly due to Slavery" (4 December 1869, 771).

5. Beecher was then president of the AWSA. In October the *Independent* had termed the formation of yet another woman's rights organization, moreover one based on "mere existing state organizations," as "unwise, illiberal and unjust." In the same article, the *Independent* had criticized the upcoming Cleveland convention's voting procedures, mentioning in passing the Rhode Island Woman's Suffrage Association meeting held in Providence on 20–21 October. The paper subsequently described the Cleveland convention as a gathering of "intelligent and thoughtful men and women," and the convention's goals as making "the delegated body of representatives from states and societies the controlling power, being so framed as to prevent a central power in any locality from managing or controlling without consent of members at a distance" (*Independent,* 28 October 1869, 4, 2 December 1869, 3; *Revolution,* 28 October 1869, 257–58, 4 November 1869, 281).

6. In the 2 April issue of the *Woman's Journal,* Stone had responded to the call for a conference to unite the two organizations by saying, "We are satisfied with the organization [*AWSA*]. . . . Its friendly door is wide open for any who wish to join it. Do we need any other?" (100). In his editorial, Pillsbury had called the AWSA "a rival and hostile movement" casting "every false, slanderous, and abusive epithet" against the NWSA (*Revolution,* 31 March 1870, 201).

7. In two letters from Orange signed "M.," published in the *Nation,* McKim had written that if women were granted suffrage, the United States could certify even more voters of "ignorance and unfitness." Granting that women were deserving of equal treatment, McKim had argued that men were suited for war and politics, and women for peace and the domestic sphere. Although he had quoted from LCM's 1849 "Discourse on Woman" without naming the speaker, he had concluded by referring explicitly to LCM; he did not see how the right to vote could possibly "increase the influence which she now exerts for the benefit of her sex and other good purposes." In a letter signed "M. C. W." appearing in the next issue of the *Nation,* MCW had countered McKim's assertion that women had been granted all the equal rights they sought. She had declared,

"It is paying a poor compliment to the schools and press and pulpits of our land to imagine that our ship of state must inevitably sink under its load of ignorance and crime, if the principles of republican government are fairly carried out" (*Nation,* 24 March 1870, 189–90, 31 March 1870, 205–6, 7 April 1870, 222–23).

8. Stone would write LCM expressing hope that she would attend the AWSA meeting on 10 May: "If I could hear that you would do so, I should be very glad to announce your name next week in the Journal" (24 April 1870, Mott Manuscripts, PSCHi).

## To Josephine S. Griffing

Roadside, near Philada.
5 mo. 17th. 70—

Josephine S. Griffing
My dear Friend

I was sorry not to have a longer time with thee last week—to hear more of the New Y. Wom. Suff. Mg— The Papers give but a meagre accot.—[1]

Before seeing thee I had made an appeal to our Meeting on behalf of the aged suffering Poor of Washington— After our interview I thought one more attempt might not be in vain so I ventured—informing our friends that I would remain after the Mg—to receive any sums which might be contributed— Quite a number came forward—some with the "widows mite"— Counting up on returning home, I found nearly $50, so I herwith send the check or draft for that amount, which I know thou wilt distribute wisely— We shall not be likely to collect more this season—if indeed hereafter; for the opinion has spread abroad that if this individual effort were discontinued, the Governmt. or Authorities of Washington would take charge of these poor, sufferg. people—

I have no doubt thy unwearied labor & sympathy have been most timely & effective— I greatly hope the appropriation thou spoke of will be made— Our Freedman's Assocn. had sent out to our Monthly Meetgs. this Spring an appeal for the Schools south, as we feared they wd. have to be closed before the usual vacation[2] A return however of a few hundred dollars enables us to go on— This made it harder to ask again—but I rejoiced that it was not all in vain—

Please acknowledge—

And believe me earnest in the desire for all the help we can contribute to your good work—

thy Sincere frd.   L. Mott—

ALS NNCB-Griffing

1. Griffing had attended the meeting of the Union Woman's Suffrage Society, an attempt at reconciliation initiated by members of the NWSA, on 10–11 May. The *New York Times* reported that she had spoken briefly and added: "Every female employe in Washington was praying for the success of the Convention." The Union Society had resolved to meet with the AWSA "with a view to the harmonization of all the friends of woman suffrage into a national organization." At its 12 May meeting, the AWSA had passed a

resolution, however, stating that the members believed such a national organization already existed (12 May 1870, 8, 13 May 1870, 5).

2. The *Revolution* had quoted a *New York World* correspondent that Congress had appropriated $30,000 for poor relief and that "this fund last year was entrusted mainly to one good woman, Mrs. Josephine Griffing" (3 March 1870, 137). The Friends' Association for the Aid and Elevation of the Freedman had begun its appeal in January: "The payment of moneys due the teachers of our thirteen schools, finds us with an exhausted treasury. Will Friends allow these teachers to be recalled, or will they, by a small contribution, enable us to continue them until the end of the season?" (*Friends' Intelligencer*, 1 January 1870, 699).

## To Roadside Family

[*Orange, New Jersey*]
Continuatn. 23rd—Noon—[*May 1870*][1]

We go @ 2.30— Pattie [*Lord*] is doing 500 last things— One large Valise is to hold all our clothes—my carpet bag reposes— Notice was in the Paper that Sojr. Truth & self wd. be at Mg.—Young Men's Christn. Union Hall—a nicer place than ever before here—& well filled[2] Geo. [*Lord*] waited on me—& Chs. Steele who called here  People very attentive & many expressed satisfactn. & thanked me— Sojourner did very well  The Audience seemed interested in her— She is going to "labor with the colored people of Jersey." She homes with Rowld Johnson[3] who had about a doz. beside to dine there—his wife invited me but this quiet retreat was preferred— I called in next door, comg. home— Mother Lord poorly with rheumatm.— I had quite a nap after dinner—then looked over a *bushel* of carpetrags & seamstress' leavgs—came down at 6—to find Dr. Green & wife here to tea— Geo. rode up to Miller [*McKim*]'s—none of them out— Lucy prepared to be at Mg—but her cold was so bad she had to give it up— Sarah, many regrets that she c'dnt come to see me. Mr. Rouse called in the eveg— They are living 2 or 3 miles off— Chs. Steele also here to tea— So tis well that Pattie & I had that *social* ride from Newark here, or I shd. feel as if I hadn't yet arrived— She had a good quiet time to do every thing while we were at Church— Mary Mott & Anna [*Lord*] with us—the latter "very tired— didn't like it"!! And I guess the former too if the truth was known— Dear little soul— She had 4 little bouquets—very fragrant—filling the parlor with their perfume gathered from the front lawn—little Anna sd. "she got them all for me on 7th day["]— They are beautiful still—& so sweet in her to welcome Grandma. thus

Now I must go & collect my duds & be off—no time to call at the Revolutn. Office, even if I knew where to find it— Do send us a letter by Mari[a]. [*Mott*] if she delays till 4th. day & then write for us to rec[eiv]e. it 6th. day in Boston— Our plan is to leave there 6th. day aftern.—Stay quietly here till 2nd. day when

I shall hasten home to help Fanny [*Parrish*] if all is settled as to the House—
Maybe Pattie will add—

AL Frag PSCHi-Mott

1. This fragment is dated by references to LCM's travels and the season of the year.

2. Repeated searches of New York City and New Jersey newspapers have not uncovered a record of the meeting at which Truth and LCM spoke. Truth had attended the AWSA meeting in New York City in May 1870 but LCM had not (Nell Irvin Painter, *Sojourner Truth* [New York: W. W. Norton, 1996], 232, 258).

3. Rowland Johnson (1816–86) was a broker and a New Jersey Quaker. Truth frequently stayed with Johnson when in Orange (Carleton Mabee, *Sojourner Truth: Slave, Prophet, Legend* [New York: New York University Press, 1993], 120–21; *Narrative of Sojourner Truth: A Bondswoman of Olden Time* [Chicago: Johnson Publishing, 1970], 190, 198, 212–13).

## To Martha Coffin Wright

Roadside 7 mo. 16th. 70—<br>"Hot as heaters" this 7th. day morng—!!

With a pile of letters to ans. seemingly mountn. high,—thine, my dear Sister, of June 20th. & July 10th. I think—shall be 1st. honored, while I am fresh—tho' to tell the truth, neither on hand just now— S. Abbott keepg. them for Mary B[rown]. to see who is out at Ellersley, keepg. house, while Margt. [*Yarnall*] is visitg. cousin at Burlingn.— I took some notes however—so "here goes"— Yes, thy 1st. date lay at Edwd. D's office awhile & then taken into Edwd. H's. while he & Joe [*Parrish*] were both away, we ne'er recd. it till after my return from Orange—July 9th.— It was acceptable even then, containg. many items of news—& thy wonderful works in preparatn. for such lots of dear ones—How admonishg. such after-wearin[es]s., that thy age demands rest—& thou ought not to do ½ as much as before thy health failed & strength diminished now do be careful— We shall be afraid to go to Aubn., lest thou exert thyself too much for our reception— Thou sd. nothg. of a sprain or strain in steppg. down 2 or 3 stairs, when shewg. Eliza [*Osborne*] all yr neat rooms Mari[a]. [*Mott*] must have mentioned it— I do hope thou'lt go to Saratoga— It will be too bad, to call a Conventn. there, & for none who can give it interest to attend it—E. C. Stant[on] will need thee, & thou ought to be willing to preside— I agree with thee in a willingness for the Revoln. to *close*.[1]

Paulina W. D. has sent me a long letter about a comg. Con. in Philada.—*called* the 2nd. Decade[2]—another to S. Pugh— Now, we wornout-individls. are the only depende. for getting up sd. Con., & I cant pos[sibly]. take a step toward it—all the interest in our City is auxiliary to the Cleveld. organizatn. [*AWSA*]—I have answd. Paulina (one of my skeletons) to that effect— She & her Com. are preparg. an extensive call—& "wd. I have my name appended"— Yes, I sd., "if sent to Boston & all interested without regard to party"— Little notion wd.

*they* have of attendg., however independt. the Conventn. might be—for Garrison, Lucy Stone, & Henry too, Wendll. P. & a few others are very *sot* agt. workg. with S. B. Anthy., E. C. Stanton, & even Paulina D— — Mary Grew sd. when here, she didn't like her principles on the marriage & divorce questn.[3]—too [easy?]—&.c— If she & many others wd. simply say, "I dont agree with her"—instd. of makg it a *principle,* it wd. be less arrogant— The marriage & divorce law is certainly undergoing severe review now— Truth will stand I wanted more of E. C. Stanton's visit[4]—what you talked abt. &.c., She & Susan will do well to confine themselves to lecturg., & holg. independt. Conventns. where they can be got up well—and let Boston do all the good it can with the able speakers & excellt. Journal—only not antagonise the pioneers— Paulina writes that *she* originated our 1st. Con. with Sarah Tynall such a strife for supremacy![5] Aunt Phebe was always laughed at for her claim—"I thought of't first"—afterwd. a by word— Not strange that all were pleased with Flora [*Wright*]— She made a similar favorable impression in Roxbury & New York—among Willie's frds.— It will be *long* for him to be away from his Florida busins. & house-buildg. too, if Flora's confinet. is not till December— Wont it affect his name for a driving busins. man?— What wd. Nant. say, for husband not to sail when the ship was ready—but wait 4 or 5 mos. *for a baby?* excuse free criticism— — All the brs. & sisters meetg. must be delightful—& Ellen [*Garrison*] ought to lay in a stock of strength for future use— We want her very much to come here next Fall— If we carry out our Nant. plan, & she & Wm. can be there at the same time, it will add much to our pleasure—specially Pattie [*Lord*]'s I presume— We can only *hope* for *thee*— Mariana wd.n't want to be in thy way—she cd. whip off to Newport, wh. wd. just suit her— I must send you her letter. What a flittg. generatn. this is! Maria Hopper, in part, agrees to join Thos. Mott & Emily—not to stay at Sharon Springs—but to visit her Hopper relatives in New Y. 1st. not havg. seen them since her return from Europe, & then join her uncle & Emily somewhere on their journey— Anna H. is plannng. no trip— She was out here a few days last week & this while I was alone, & yestery. after Edwd. & Maria's return—wh. was pleast.—heart-broken as they were, after partg. with dear Willie for a long 3 years—[6] He too broke down at the leave-takg. at Portland A letter last eveg. however was cheerful—not a doubt as to his decision to engage in the undertakg., & a very satisfacty. letter from Mr. Rock—his compann., promisg. all attentn. to him, from his wife & self— They were on board ship—waitg. for wind— 3 yrs. have passed at Cambridge, & he the same good boy—but oh, how diff., say his parents, when they cd. hear from him so often, & see him 3 or 4 times a year— Now, unless they speak a vessel & send a letter, no news for 100 days!— Is it strange, they—I may say *We* feel the pang of separatn.— Florida seemed far off for *yr.* Willie but oh how near now in comparison

Aftern. still 16th. & a very hot day—thermr. above 90 all day— It is a comfort to be in undress & have no callers— Anna Hopper says she shd. like to lock up her front door—take the bell out & then live quietly from all formal visitors thro' the summer. ~~I suppose she means this special summer~~— I mistook thinkg of Anna D. Hall[1]. Maria [*Davis*] never was in a house so entirely to her mind & taste—no grandeur, but every convenience—plenty of room—good furniture—many antique pieces Anna D. H. has picked up, & bot. at auction— No part too good to enjoy— — — — Glad as Tom & Fanny [*Parrish*] were to have that nice house (not large) near their uncle & aunt [*William and Rebecca*] Hunts, they were not at all dissatisfied with their "nut shell" while it was best for them to have no more than 450 rent to pay— Now the interest on the purchase—taxes, & repairs—to say nothg. of little improvets. will double their rent—wh. Thos. thot. his busins. *promised to pay*— Their relatives helped furnish the additional rooms— Mother Parrish[7] straw mattg. for lower floor & up to 2nd. story chamber doors— Thos. Mott $100 for a lounge & some other things— That, bot. at auction for their boardg. house proved such a mean one, that after offerg. it to Fanny, Thos. Mott sd. it was not worth acceptg. so sent it to auction, & gave her sd. money to buy another— Anna H. sent her what she cd.—& I the carpets from our parlor, wh. just covered their 2 chambers—not an inch over & our partly worn kichen carpet— It doesn't begin to need turng.— I was surprised that yours did. At Orange too, the same pattern has not worn near so well as ours— It must be shoddy as much of modern carpenterg. is

It was an exciting time while the purchase of sd. house was under consideratn.— Tom & Fanny so anxious to get it—just what they wanted— single back buildg.—ding. room above the kitchen, & a good little lumber or trunk room above— I shall let them have $1000 toward payg. for it when the mortgage is to be paid— Thou needn't reply to this item—plenty of yard room grass plot—a little outer shed with a stove pipehole— Now come & see how happy they are with it— Tom lately went to Steubenville by free ticket sent by Charley Hall[1].[8] with an earnest invitatn. to him & Fanny—but she had too much on hand to leave home, so Clem. Hunt went with her ticket, & a nice excursn. it was—for they meant to deny themselves all "sprees & larks & things"—returng. after a wks. absence, Tom sd. their house looked pleasanter than any one he had ever seen, br. Edwd. Parrish—younger than Tom—home from College stayd. with Fanny The older br. Clem. is to make one of their fam[il]y. & lessen their rent so much—[9] He is engaged to Dr. Wilson's daughr.— While interested in every part of their movg., I cd. appreciate thy labor on Wm. & Ellen [*Garrison*]'s Roxbury house—yes, & yr. own too—going from room to room—after thy hard work—how much you had to do! I rather enjoyed Marias comg. & findg. our "Aunt Eliza" one all spread even—lookg. as if down for good—& so we mean it shall be while this terrible burng. weather lasts—for no Upholsterer can come now— — Mary Cavr. was comg. out at noon today—the childn. May & Pen. went over to City Line to meet her—[10] she didn't come—so they slowly walked back in the heat— She just came was prevented earlier by havg. cut off the end of her finger—next the little one, in the grocery store—trying to catch flies, struck it agt. the sharp butcher knife— She ran home with it hangg. down— almost makg. Fanny sick— She sent her to uncle Dr. Hunt near—Spruce St.— he not at home—his wife—Reba. (Price) gave her stickg. plaster—told her it must be replaced & grow on agn.— So the perseverg. child had it thus dressed & here she is— Her Pa. was in town last wk—called to see them—sd. little— but wd. come agn. & that's the last of him— Fanny & Mary urged Charly comg. to Swarthmore—he asked when the Fall term wd. open & thats all— Now for thy letter agn.— Anna Dennis wd. be a dull scholar, not to have learned from Miller [*McKim*] that "educated Suffrage" is all that shd. be claimed for Black or woman"— He is a strange talker now a days—"no interest in '*Reform*'"— "Social Science & the Nation will do every thing" He is a good talker tho' still— & often called & sat an hour at Orange.

And that old lady Wood is gathered at last— Emma [*Parker Wood*] must have had her hands full— Only *owny dony* ought to have such a charge— It is oft the fate of *wives* tho— I had forgotten that her sister Townsend still lived— Emma's uncle Joseph Sharpless died 10 days since—opposite Benjn. Y's— The bill was off our dear sister's house as I passed there yestery— Still all shut up, & lookg. sad, & dismal eno'! Reba. [*Yarnall*] says there's the greatest diff in Arch & Race—the childn. the narrow st.,—the smells—a grocery so near—indeed every thg. contrasts—a more wo-be-gone face you rarely see— Sarah wishes she wd. go to Nant. with us—or somewhere— She is quite uneasy about her— I wonder she didn't go out with Mary B. to Ellersley— Sarah didn't like to come out here with her sisters

[*P.S.*] Where's Watch Hill pray? The diamond ring needs a glossary too— Yes—big A. little A's mention of the other Meetg. was very mean He lessens himself by all such doings more than he can those he aims *at*.[11]

Very glad for Mrs. Hall— It was a generous act— Benjn. Gould's marriage just as you might expect

What Ann was it who gained $25000— Smart to make a wrapper so soon I have begun*

*to make doubles from Anna's old sheets—bibs from napkins—&.c for Sarah— Pattie sent her baby clothes—

AL PSCHi-Mott

1. The New York State Suffrage Society had announced a meeting to be held in Saratoga on 28–29 July and chaired by Matilda Joslyn Gage. Anthony would attend; neither Stanton nor MCW would (*Revolution*, 14 July 1870, 26). Financial pressures had forced Stanton and Anthony to give up the *Revolution* and form a joint stock company to continue it. There were no issues in June 1870, and beginning with the July issues, Laura Curtis Bullard edited the paper (Gordon, 2:357).

2. The Second Decade Convention celebrating twenty years of woman's rights activism would be held on 19–22 October in New York City (*HWS*, 2:428).

3. At the Second Decade Convention, which both LCM and MCW would attend, Paulina Wright Davis would deliver a history of the national woman's rights movement

in which she praised Stanton's drive to reform marriage and divorce laws. About marriage she stated, "It is slowly beginning to be felt that in that relation there is a vast amount of legalized prostitution, bearing the semblance of virtue, which is rotten below the fair exterior" (*A History of the National Woman's Rights Movement, for Twenty Years* [New York: Journeymen Printers' Co-operative Association, 1871], 22). In an article on LCM in the *Revolution,* Davis would refer to LCM's marriage: "As a wife, I often noted her affectionate freedom, mingled with a rarely delicate deference toward her husband, James Mott, a man who impressed me as one without guile—pure, noble, upright, peace-loving and peace-making." In the same article Davis would respond to LCM's hope that the Second Decade Convention would not be "partizan": "We know it will not be, as it has been more than a year in preparation, and looked forward to for years as a great and solemn event" (4 August 1870, 68).

4. In a letter of 9 July to Paulina Wright Davis from Johnstown, New York, Stanton had described how she and Gerrit Smith spoke at a "grand temperance lecture in Syracuse . . . to two thousand people" (*Stanton-Anthony Papers,* reel 14, fr. 871).

5. In *A History of the National Woman's Rights Movement, for Twenty Years,* Davis described Sarah Tyndale of Philadelphia as "one of the first to sign the call. Indeed, the idea of such a convention had often been discussed in her home, more than two years before, a home where every progressive thought found cordial welcome" (14).

6. After graduating with honors from Harvard University, Willie Davis had left for Buenos Aires to help establish an observatory there (*NASS,* 30 July 1870, 1).

7. Margaret Shreve Hunt Parrish (1824–72) was the mother of Tom Parrish.

8. Charles Hallowell (1842–75) was the son of Joshua Hallowell and the cousin of Richard Hallowell.

9. Edward Parrish Jr. (b. 1850) and Clemmons Parrish (b. 1848) were children of Susannah Parrish and Edward Parrish, the son of Dr. Joseph Parrish and Susannah Cox Parrish.

10. Maria Mott Hallowell and Penrose Hallowell (1862–72) were the children of Anna Hallowell and Richard Hallowell.

11. LCM refers to an unidentified article in the *NASS* (LCM to MCW, 22 July 1870, Mott Manuscripts, PSCHi).

## To Martha Mott Lord

Roadside 1 mo. 22nd. 71—
Windy—clear—pretty cold—

My dear Pattie—

So lately a letter gone to you, that this broken sheet will ans. for all I have to say now— Maria [*Davis*] says she will add the Line she thinks you had better come in on 5th. day next— Be sure you write to Nellie to meet you here— Geo. had better not try to go to the City for busins. till he has rested here a few days— I know all about recovg. from neumonia— Catarrh too has been slow— But well now as are all our invalids, unless Sarah Abbott's baby be an exceptn.— We hope to hear from them & Thos. Yarnall's son when Edwd. H. & Thos. M. come out by & by—[1] It is one of our pleasantest *expects* every 1st. day— We were so glad that Paulina D. & S. Pugh's visits were 6th. day night & yestermorng. rather than today— They were very agreeable—gave a glowg. accot. of the Washn. Mg.—i.e. as much as Paulina ever does *glow*— She is rather monotonous & lack-a day's a cal—but very decided in the part she takes— Sarah seemed to enjoy it to the full— She slept next me in the far room— Paulina goes back to Washn. to the Room they have there, where she & Mrs. Hooker mean to keep the Judiciary Com. in motion— They want to get many signers to the 14th. Amendt. demand[2]—& Paulina wondered if my sister Martha wdn't go to Albany & try to get signers there  Do send her this immedy. so that no time may be lost, *if she will*— It was really distressg. to hear their determined plans—& how we cd. set the ball in motion in Philada.— "Cd. *I* see Ann Preston & have the Medical School to sign—& Lydia Gillingm., & wd. Mrs. Hopper see Susan Leslie," &c. &.c— Sarah wd. go to Adeline Thompson[3]—Gulaelma Jones— Huldah Justice—& Germantn  It brot. on water brash— I excused my self & retired—had a great "frowg. up" time—then slept well & next morng. enjoyed their talk till 11 oclk—when they went to Town to meet Paulina's daughr. from Swarthme.

Maria wrote a headg. wh. she & Edwd. signed as did their Mother & that's about all I mean to undertake, for I cant do it— I'm past all but going to Orange now & then— Thine & Geo's letters were sent out last eveg. I read them over—not much callg. for reply— What about that carriage you went to New Y. to look at? All this tho' when we meet— Look around once more for my glasses—so mysteriously they disappeared. Bring my carpet rags— Fanny C. P. was pleased with her Xmas gift for her kitchen stairs late as it came— It is really nice. A heap of presents you'll have to see—some very pretty—A chair Mother Parrish had made for them—her work— I am sorry Maria H. and Bel [*Parrish*] will be away— I was glad of all Geo. wrote of Eliza O's visit & her loveliness to say nothg. of her dress maker's charges—but you *are* to have neé Basset's aid after all— It was so nice for thee to be able to go in to New Y. with Eliza & have "an enjoyable time"— Nice too that Eliza's old frd. Joe [*Lord?*] was with you while she was there & that Louisa's music charmed them— The good Report of all our fam[il]y. Wool-merchts. was not the least part welcome in George's pages— He says truly that much of our comfort in life depends on success—& helps to make the grateful hearts he acknowledges— Dear little Anna [*Lord*]'s wish for so near a *kin* to her Aunt Maria & that she lived at Deckers, was very touchg. Even little Lulu echoes the love for Aunt Maria— Our dears Lucy & Charlie [*Davis*] are out visitg. their little cousin Evans'— I was amused yestery. when the 4 came here yestery., & findg. only me in here, askg. so earnestly, "Where's Grandma. Davis?" She was soon found & plenty of toys & apples for them— Lizzie Evans made quite a long, pleast. call with them— she is *lovely*.

Thieves are a very provokg. set— So sorry are we for that plated teakettle to be borne off— 'Twill teach their girls a lesson— It is surprisg. that our basket of silver has escaped when access to our ding. room is so easy— Here comes

dinner—no Edwd. & Thos. yet— Both our girls went to Church this morng.—
I stays at home— Edwd. walked up in all this high wind to Geo. Evans'[4] to see
his grandchildn.

When in Town 4th. day Mari[a]. [*Mott*] shewed me a letter from her Mother—I cant remember much now—only that her rheumatism continued & she
didn't mean to go out much while the bad walkg. continued— Thou can read
her letters when thou comes I'll not send them now, for coz. Caroe. [*Stratton*]
called at Edwd.'s office on her way to Balt[imor]e. & asked to have letters sent
to her— Aunt M's last date was 16th. & 17th. She seemed pretty well then—&
apologized for undervalug. mine from Orange—& insists my cold was in mixg.
mince for Maria's pies—a great mistake— As to keepg. up good fires— We
have no lack—only that day leavg. the Library long eve forgot to add coal— She
seems to think it was Miller M'K. who caviled—he sd. not a word— — It was
Godkin— I seem to have hard work to make her understd. me— Elizh. Fisher told S. Pugh The Nation made her so mad, she resolved agn. & agn. she wd.
give it up—[5] I too was very sorry that E. Stanton was not at the Washn. Conventn— Sorry was I too not to have a visit from Susan either before or after
the Con.— Mrs. Hooker had it her own way—not in Parliamenty. order— No
Pres. or Sec or busins. com. apptd.—& introduced each Speaker in a queer way—
by a speech herself— Still it seemed to call forth no remark—& on the whole
was a very gratifying Mg—large & attentive—& did good  The Press make less
fun for their readers—that Mrs. Woodhull made a good impressn. & if her
$10.000 be forthcomg. it will equal the Boston Bazer—[6]

AL PSCHi-Mott

1. Sarah Abbott's son, Charles Abbott, had been born in October 1870. Thomas Yarnall had been visiting his son William Yarnall in the South (LCM to MML, 15 October
1870, and LCM to MCW, 20 December 1870, both in Mott Manuscripts, PSCHi).

2. The NWSA meeting had been held on 11 January 1871 at the First Congregational
Church. The association wished to persuade the Judiciary Committee of the House of
Representatives that, under the Fourteenth and Fifteenth Amendments to the Constitution, women were citizens and thus already possessed the right to vote. The spiritualist and reformer Victoria Claflin Woodhull (1838–1927) and Isabella Beecher Hooker
(1822–1907), an officer in the NWSA, had met with the Judiciary Committee on 11 January to present Woodhull's petition urging Congress to enact laws "for carrying into
execution the right vested by the Constitution in the citizens of the United States to vote
without regard to sex" (*New York Times*, 14 January 1871, 1, 12 January 1871, 1). In a document entitled "Declaration and Pledge of the Women of the United States concerning
the Right to, and Their Use of the Elective Franchise," Elizabeth Cady Stanton, LCM,
Maria Mott Davis, Julia Ward Howe, Isabella Beecher Hooker, Susan B. Anthony, and
eight others stated that the rights of citizenship most recently "confirmed" by the Fourteenth and Fifteenth Amendments allowed women to "accept the duties of franchise in
our several States, so soon as all legal restrictions are removed" ([January 1871], *Stanton-Anthony Papers*, reel 15, frs. 371–74).

3. Mary Adeline Thomson (1811–95), a Hicksite Quaker, and her sister, Anna Thomson (1806–85), of Philadelphia were civil engineers (Gordon, 2:498).

4. George O. Evans had married Elizabeth Mellor, the daughter of Thomas Mellor and

Martha Mellor, on 12 June 1860 and was in the hosiery business with Thomas Mellor (Philadelphia City Directory, 1864).

5. An editorial in the *Nation* on 24 November 1870 had ridiculed the feud between the Boston and New York City woman's rights organizations, singling out the New York organization's mission of "Emilie J. Merriam" as a peacemaker in the Franco-Prussian War: "We think it was a little premature for the New York branch to send a female 'peace advocate and commissioner' to Bismarck and Jules Favre and for Mrs. Howe, of the Boston branch, to 'declare war' against the former because he would not make peace with the French on her terms" (346). The 22 December issue had carried an item stating that "M. C. W." had written to say that the mission of Emilie J. Meriman (later Loyson) of New York City had not been an act of the convention, but was taken on her own initiative. The *Nation* had conceded that point but insisted that the work of the women was "gross folly" and not worthy of "respectful mention" (414; *New York Times,* 5 December 1909, 13).

6. LCM had earlier expressed the fear that Isabella Hooker was "too green" to preside at the NWSA meeting, a concern also expressed by MCW in a letter to Elizabeth C. Stanton (LCM to MCW, 10 January 1871, Mott Manuscripts, PSCHi; MCW to Stanton, 6 January 1871, *Stanton-Anthony Papers,* reel 15, fr. 324). Hooker had spoken on 11 and 13 January, emphasizing the importance of woman suffrage toward achieving temperance and educational reform and restraining men's sexual behavior. Woodhull had pledged $10,000 to cover the expenses of gathering petitions and lobbying the Judiciary Committee (*Washington Daily Chronicle,* 12 January 1871, 14 January 1871, *Stanton-Anthony Papers,* reel 15, frs. 327, 331; *New York Times,* 14 January 1871, 1).


## To Richard D. Webb

Roadside, near Philada.
1 mo. 22nd—1870 [*1871*]—

My dear Richard Webb—

I fear thou must think me very heartless, after such a letter as thou sent me more than 2 mos. since, with the heart-rending inclosure of details of the awful ravages and sufferg. from the war in France, that no response has yet been made. What shall I say? Apologies & excuses for omissions ever seem worthless. Could I have returned such a list of contributors as thy envelope contained, surely an ans. would have been forth-*going*— But about that time *two* Bazars' were begun, on behalf of non-combatant sufferers both in France & Germany or Prussia, in which a few Friends of both sides took part—so that any attempt to raise money as proposed seemed a useless effort.

The Hicksites have few rich—& the Orthodox prefer a distinct fund. They may have been appealed to from England—and not in vain.—Will not this terribly devastating war tend to open the eyes & consciences to the unchristian— the wicked—the barbarous resort to murderous weapons? There is certainly more life and interest in Peace meetings now than ever before. The conventions are well attended & higher ground. is taken— Julia Ward Howe—your Josephine Butler & some *men* too are calling attention to the subject, with a determined purpose— A Peace Congress is resolved upon—when & where, here-after to be decided— It only needs the *will of the people,* to substitute other settlements of claims & redress of grievances & thus, to make "War a game that Kings shall not play at." Charles Sumner lately delivered a grand lecture on the subject, in which he called attention to the fact of the Working Men's Union in England having come out with a protest against war—[1] Is that so? Even the woman question, as far as voting goes, does not take hold of my every feeling as does War— Cant we meet in London yet—old as I am, in another Worlds Convention? Wouldn't I try to?

But this little space for communing with thee must not all be devoted to my hobbies—so we'll let woman go, after sayg. a large & good meetg. has lately been held in Washn. by the Stanton-Anthony side—and a very successful Bazar in Boston by the Stone-Blackwell party[2]—each advocating the self-same measures—

Thy correspondts. in New Y. & Germantn. doubtless informed thee of the sad bereavemt. in Robt. & Hanh. Haydocks family of their eldest son[3]—a fine good young man— They try hard to bear it even cheerfully—but in a call on Hannah, I was really glad to see the mother's heart betray itself— "Nor can we lose the privilege to mourn /While we have left the faculty to feel!" Death has made other sad inroads this winter— I believe E. M. D. will fill the last page—so with dear love to Deborah—whose pretty poetic lines were read to me the other day, & a full lot to thyself, with a wish not yet abandoned that you will come back someday & settle among us I will close— Sarah Pugh was here yestery. She hears from you all thro' her faithful correspt. Mary Estlin— The women in Eng. are doing nobly—agt. the Contagious disease Acts. We enjoy Margt. Lucas' society—[4]

Lucretia Mott.

ALS MB

1. In November 1870, Howe and other women had held a meeting in Boston on the subject of war and peace. In her address at this meeting, Howe had proclaimed, "It is now time to count the votes of the bleeding hearts. You say that women should not vote because they cannot fight; and I say that women should vote because they cannot fight." Howe had sent an appeal to women in the United States and Europe and hoped to call a women's peace congress in London (*Independent,* 1 December 1870, 6; Julia Ward Howe, *Reminiscences* [Boston: Houghton Mifflin, 1899; reprint, New York: Negro Universities Press, 1969], 327–30). Sumner had begun a tour in October, delivering his lecture on the Franco-Prussian War, "The Duel between France and Germany, with Its Lesson to Civilization" (*Charles Sumner: His Complete Works* [Boston: Lee and Shepard, 1900], 18:177–253).

2. The AWSA had held a bazaar in December 1870 that raised $8,000 (Andrea Moore Kerr, *Lucy Stone: Speaking Out for Equality* [New Brunswick, N.J.: Rutgers University Press, 1992], 158–60; *Woman's Journal,* 5 November 1870, 348).

3. Samuel Haydock had died on 6 December.

4. Mary Estlin was a British abolitionist, a suffrage advocate, and a member of the Ladies' National Association for the Repeal of the Contagious Diseases Acts, which allowed the police to incarcerate, and sometimes abuse, prostitutes. The association stat-

ed its objections to the laws, passed in 1866 and 1869, as singling out only women: "Any woman can be dragged into court, and required to prove that she is not a common prostitute." Other members included Margaret Lucas (1818–90), a British temperance reformer and the sister of John Bright, Josephine Butler, and Elizabeth Pease Nichol (*Revolution*, 3 February 1870, 70–71).

## To Martha Coffin Wright

Roadside 2 mo. 4th 70 [*1871*]—
Beautiful day—thawg.

I wonder if this handsome paper will redeem the page in my dear Sister's estimate— I'll try 'any how' if tis any easier to write on, than such as I buy cheap.

Thou cant bring *thy* mind to letter-writg. when you have compy.— Perhaps I shd. be disinclined too, if our compy. had not gone to Town for the day— Pattie & childn. Mary Mott to Swarthmore— Geo. [*Lord*] hardly strong eno' to go far. He goes in @ 11 o'clk. & does what busins. he can, & comes out tired— He has bot. several 1000 lbs. wool tho'—& receives encouragg. letters from Joe [*Lord*]— Maria [*Davis*] often says "success is every thing"—so we are hopg. Munson [*Osborne*]'s lawsuit decision involvg. so much will not despoil him of success on the whole— We shd. like to hear more about that— We are sorry as we can be that the Dennis brs. have had to give up their Paper—[1] Thou speaks of it as a *failure*— Is it more than want of success in that undertakg.? We may remember tho', H. B. Stanton's talk when we were there of the great expense of a Periodical—& how many subscribers were needed to make it 'pay'—also Abolitionists have cause to remember the repeated drafts to sustain the Liberator, Standd., Freeman—A Kentucky Paper—Lundy's 'Genius'—&.c— The Boston compy. took the Liberator's financial part into their own hands & released Garrison from all care— We are sorry to see that Theode. Tilton is about to begin agn. with another.[2] He is in danger of running himself into the ground—

What a pity as thou says that Care. Dennis let her share go beyond her control— Women will be slow to learn to assume responsibility, even of their own— Ever taught to confide & trust in men in pecuniary matters, they risk more than they ought to where they have no exercise of judgt.— Our Mother had no faith in French Creek Works, & in our father's endorsg. thousands for John James, & used to beg him to quit before he was involved so deeply—but he went on, till they were sadly in debt—the $9000 to be paid in 60 days—the Works sold *well*, tis true, but our father's advances & accots. in conductg. the sales &.c. were disputed by the Odiornes, because of their inability to pay—& before the referees decided our dear sufferer was removed from it all—leavg. his fam[il]y. poor, includg. Jas. Mott whom he had taken in as a partner in the kindness of his heart— In the windg. up there being a deficiency & Jas. part ⅓ being $3000—he gave his note—& one of our noble Mother's first acts, as a widow, was to destroy that note—[3] Think of lettg. my pen run thro' all this old familiar story! As thou says Fred. & Roland are young & with their energy they may do well in some business— Their printg. paid, didn't it? before they had a Paper? No wonder Roland was so sick last summer— That was the way it affected Jas., dear soul, when our little new shop in 4th. St. was going behind— It was only the last time Miller [*McKim*] called at Orange, he was speakg. of his niece Ellen Mulvany who has married so well, and of Anne Dennis—how they both were really better off than his own daughr.—remindg. me of Anna Brown & others then named— How often we see such revolutns. of the Wheel of Fortune— Speakg. of Revols., think those green-horns will be able to hold out much longer? What a curious fact, that proper Mrs. Hooker shd. be so linked in with Mrs. Woodhull—& what an added handle for the Boston compy. agt. S. B. Anthony—who was so innocent of it all— Paulina D. was confined some time at Rachl. Jackson's, after leavg. us, with a bad cold—so that she cd. not go to Swarthme. for awhile to see her daughr.— I cant summon much interest for signers to our Petitn. to the Judiciary Com.[4] S. Pugh does her part— She has just sent us a letter to read speakg. in the highest terms of praise of Josephe. Butler & her public labors agt. the Cont[agious] Disease Acts. Margt. Lucas often lends me her Papers to read— She was very sorry not to be in Washn. at the Conventn.— S. Pugh wd. have gone with her, had she known of her wish to be there— She is going with Thos. & Martha Mellor before Congress closes— She & Esther Bancroft[5] & 2 other Women cousins from Athens have just been to Niagara for a Winter view—& were delighted Margt. sd. it exceeded in grandeur any thing she had seen here the massive blocks of ice going over the Falls, &.c &.c—

Pattie took thy letter, recd. on 5th. day—to Town this A.M. also one Mari[a]. [*Mott*] recd. 3rd. or 4th. day—so that I may fail to notice some parts—but not thy terrible vertigo & fall— Eliza [*Osborne*] did right to have the Dr.— Thou must learn to move about more slowly & carefully— I am not willg. to believe it a "warning" of apoplexy—but whatever it is, it ought not so to be— Better hurry off to Florida— Those extracts were entertaing. & we are very glad for all Willie [*Wright*]'s good luck— Thos. Yarnall was full of praise of all he cd. see in 20 min The River was magnificent— — His poor son [*William*] was brot. home with difficulty—immedy. taken to the Asylum & is so violent that 2 of the keepers are afraid to go near him he has taken such a dislike to them— Have I written that Annie Harrison is engaged to be married to a Scotch gent[6] Maria & Pattie had a fine sleighride as far as Ellis' the other day—with all the childn.—but meetg. them also givg. theirs a drive—or a sleigh-ride I shd. say, they didn't stop—only to exchange a few words— Yestery. the snow much melted they ventured agn. to Thos. Mellor's, met them comg. here—they insisted on turng. back—so the call was that I was resigned— Findg. Pattie was going to Swarthme. that kindest of women sent down 2 boxes cakes this A.M.— 1 for Nellie & Charlie Cavr. & the other for Susan P. Wharton's son & daughr.[7]

also to us a plate of little fancy pads of butter of her make— Our Kitty makes 6 or 7 llbs. a week very good butter—even now with the additn. to our famy. some 4 or 5 llbs. were made yestery. & we have plenty of cream on table too— Thos. Mott was out on 1st. day— Edwd. had busins. in Town— I too was in at a Mg. with the Old Col[ore]d. Wom. Home—& told them of the funeral of Thos. Garrett the day before wh. Edwd. D. & self attended[8] Aaron Powell was there & spoke admirably well—also a Methodist Minister of repute & a fine intelligt. cold. man Such a concourse of all sects & colors we never before saw thousands—the street lined for ½ a mile to the Mg. house where he was taken—& nearly as many outside as in— 6 colored men bore him that distance & then into the grave yard adjoing—the coffin opened at the Mg. house altho hundreds & hundreds cold. & white had passed thro' his house to take the last look & lay their hands on his face— The table of simple refreshts. had a set of beautiful silver (plated likely) waiter with coffee & teapots &.c &.c—presented after the 15th Amendt. passed as a memorial by the colored people of Wilmington We expected Garrison & Oliver Johnson but neither were there Several went from the City—many from Kennett & the Country around— We returned the same eveg— Edwd. quite home— I stayed in havg. the apptmts. with sd. colored people. Thos. came out with me in time for a late dinner— On 4th. day Pattie & self were in agn. a rainy day She went directly to Pine St. & was the whole morng with Mari[a].—Anna H. and I joing. them at noon—& had a real nice call only I was sick with water brash & "frowg. up["]— Mariana seemed better than common—tho' keepg. in her chamber— Anna H was out here on 3rd. day last Maria & Isabel [Parrish] went to Medford the 5th. day before I guess Ellen [Garrison] will write you of Bel & Maria's visit—so I will not annoy my dear Sister further with these interlinings Maria H. has come home leavg Bel there to finish her visit— Mari[a]. & Emily love to have that bright Ethel with them— The music lesson hurried Maria home so soon— Pattie hopes to have Bel to stop with them a day or 2 on her return— Geo. will go on 3rd. day leavg. Pattie & childn. here till next 5th. day— Now paper full & items spun out—I close—

[P.S.] Edwd. just sent out Riddle's Speech—[9] Have you one?

Geo. will dine at Thos. Mott's & come out in the 5 oclk Line Edwd. D. will stay in too to some Mg.

[Letter continues dated 5 February]

ALS MNS

1. Frederick Dennis and his brother Roland Dennis (1845–1917) had been publishing the Auburn Morning News, a Republican paper, since July 1868 (Elliot G. Starke, "History of the Press of Cayuga County, from 1798 to 1877," Collections of Cayuga County Historical Society [Auburn, N.Y.: Cayuga County Historical Society, 1889], 74, History Room, Seymour Library, Auburn, N.Y.).

2. In January 1839, Francis Jackson, Edmund Quincy, and William Bassett had assumed responsibility for the Liberator's finances (WLG, 2:415, 417). Tilton had assumed editorship of the Brooklyn Union in 1870.

3. Thomas Coffin had invested in a cut nail factory outside Philadelphia in 1809 and JM had become a partner shortly thereafter (Bacon, 27; Otelia Cromwell, *Lucretia Mott* [Cambridge, Mass.: Harvard University Press, 1958], 22; see also LCM to Adam Mott and Anne Mott, 8 November 1813, above).

4. On 30 January 1871, the Judiciary Committee of the House of Representatives had issued a report rejecting the claims of Woodhull's memorial for woman suffrage. The majority report stated that the claim "does not, in the opinion of the Committee, refer to privileges and immunities of citizens of the United States other than those privileges and immunities embraced in the original text of the Constitution, article 4, section 2" (*New York Times*, 31 January 1871, 1).

5. Esther Bancroft (1813–87) was a Hicksite Quaker from Philadelphia.

6. Anne Harrison (1841–1930), who had visited her sister Margaret Yarnall in 1869, would marry James Macdonnell in 1871 (Amice Macdonnell Lee, *In Their Several Generations* [Plainfield, N.J.: Interstate Printing, n.d.], 296).

7. The Hicksite Quaker Susan Dillwyn Parrish Wharton (b. 1827), the wife of Rodman Wharton, had two children at the time, Susannah Parrish Wharton (b. 1852) and William R. Wharton (b. 1854).

8. Thomas Garrett (1789–1871), a Wilmington, Delaware, Quaker, had been an active abolitionist.

9. Albert Gallatin Riddle (1816–1902), a lawyer and a former U.S. congressman (Rep., Ohio), was representing the women petitioners to the Judiciary Committee. His speech, delivered at the NWSA convention in Washington on 11 January, "On the Right of Women to Exercise the Elective Franchise under the Fourteenth Article of the Constitution," was issued in a sixteen-page pamphlet and excerpted in the *Woman's Journal* (18 February 1871, 50).

## To Mary Grew

Roadside 2 mo. 24—71—

My Dear Mary Grew

I ought to begin by thanking for the honor conferred in the suggestion that I might occupy our frd. Farrington's place on 1st. day next—but I will only hasten to say that I have two appointments on that day among our *Presbyterian* colored people[1]—if a hoarse cold I have had all this week do not prevent my fulfilling these engagements—

Thou wilt not certainly permit the Germantown Congregation to suffer for the bread of life— I should like to partake of that communion with thee— This little service among our colored people has been on my mind for a year or two past, as a parting legacy—havg. long mourned with those who mourned, now to rejoice with them who do rejoice— So far, in the six Mgs. held there has been a reciprocal All hail!

affecy.   L. Mott—

It is time to have another visit from thee & Margaret [*Burleigh*]—.

ALS NPV

1. In a letter to MCW, LCM had referred to a conversation with "Mr. Farrington" on Unitarian meetings (4 June 1870, Mott Manuscripts, PSCHi). The first African Presbyterian church had been founded in Philadelphia in 1807 (Gary Nash, *Forging Freedom: The Formation of Philadelphia's Black Community, 1720–1840* [Cambridge, Mass.: Harvard University Press, 1988], 199–201).

## To Paulina Wright Davis

Roadside 4 mo. 7th. 71—

My dear Paulina

Ten days since the date of thine, & had memory served me a more prompt answer would have been returned—

I listened with great interest to thy opening speech at the 2nd. Decade Mg., & thought it a faithful account of the 1st. Mg[1]—or Convention at Worcester, as well as a correct history of the striking events of the succeeding 20 years— As I expressed at the time—immediately following thee—and added one or two interesting items not noticed in thy speech—but memory entirely fails me as to just what I said, as also the facts or incidents I referred to—[2]  So thou'lt have to accept the privilege of Old age *to forget*—  I doubt not thy book will be sufficiently interesting without any word of mine—

Affectionately    Lucretia Mott.

ALS NPV

1. The proceedings of the Second Decade Convention held on 19–21 October 1870 in New York City were included in Davis's *A History of the National Woman's Rights Movement, for Twenty Years* (New York: Journeymen Printers' Co-operative Association, 1871). In her speech Davis had traced the history of the woman's rights movement, beginning with Frances Wright's lectures in 1828, and described the first National Woman's Rights Convention held in Worcester, Massachusetts, in 1850 (6–31).

2. LCM had spoken on the significance of the history of the woman's rights movement to future efforts and regretted that many records had been lost. She had emphasized the gender equality women Quakers enjoyed in Nantucket, her childhood home: "Among Quakers there had never been any talk of woman's rights—it was simply human rights" (ibid., 31).

## To Martha Coffin Wright

Orange 5 mo. 4th.[3] 71—
cloudy & cool—

My dear Sister—

Now for a clean ½ sheet. Thy fun poked for my poor letter, came near being lost on me—  I tried to make sense & then passed it over, for the more interestg parts of that acceptable sheet, even tho' rendered almost illegible to thy

Sisters old eyes, by reason of its *thinness*! I had to lay white under it, when readg. it to Geo. & Pattie [*Lord*] in the eveg—& only then did I perceive what thou wast driving at, in thy wit—in thus travestying my very plain marginal penmanship on only an ⅛ of one page— Still Pattie thot. it droll—who cares? Geo. agreed with me that such awful thin paper was worse & harder to read—so now! He rather liked my economy & had no difficulty in readg—beside I thus get rid of so many dear Reformers letters—givg others the benefit of them, rather than make lamplighters of them— I have just filled 1 to Edwd. D. on a sheet he had sent me from a California Wom. Rig. secy. begg[in]g. a letter to be read at their comg. mg.—¹ A letter before askg. for Photos. & autos. I had *honored*—sendg. ½ doz with my name & had read this letter before leavg. home, & hadn't the least notion of ans. it—for many letters read at Annivs. are always a bore—beside I never write *sichy*— So I *blessed* Edwd. when eagerly openg. the envelope to hear from home—to find sd. old letter & one from "great A. little a)." askg. me to go to the Standd. Festival wh. I rise to say I shant²—not meang. to attend any *eveg*. mgs. by reason of no strength— Edwd. only addg. "All well" Wasn't I mad?

I didn't mean to fill the whole page so— Thy thin sheet shall be preserved for Europe— It contains many comments on time-worn sermons, translatns. to Heaven & the like, that I think will amuse Anna B. as much as they did us— I was sorry too that Susan B. A. didn't stop on her way down— I was glad to see the notice of the National *CosmoPolitical* Mg. in the Tribune for I feared there wd. be *no* Annivy.—³ Elizh. C. S. & Susan B. A. being rather disposed to draw off & leave the Boston Socy. to have all the glory— I go this aftern. to the Essex Co. Mg. a mile or so from here—in a private parlor— — Mrs Hussey's glad of a Jersey movemt. of any kind—⁴ Indeed there seems to be rather a dispositn. to quit fightg. & try to unite agn.—if, indeed, this late junctn. with V. Woodhull & cosmo-politico—wont make another bone of contention. Miller M'K. was here yestery., & thot. the foolishness of *her* own name as Pres. was eno' to stamp her with Geo. Francis Train—& as to her capability in argument & writg. books—so were the Tammany Hall Democrats The prejudice he manifested was painful— I agreed with him that thus advertisg. herself was an injury to her—but didn't men aspirants do so too— "No" he sd. Geo. L. ansd. "Yes, they did in a round a bout way & *she* was deservg. credit for her honesty"—tis of no use to talk with him at pres[en]t.— Let the Nation die & then see—⁵

All are pleased with the time suitg. so well for David & thyself to come together— We shall be happy to have you both here—& hope thou'lt be *well* Thy trunk of course can only be checked to New Y—then the baggage man will take it to the Morris & Essex Depot foot of Barclay St—where you will rec[eiv]e. it & then check it agn. to Brick Church, where a man is stationed to rece. it—& brings it here if directed to for a trifle— I will enclose letters from home so that thou may read them on the way, & not have to take time after gettg. here— 'pears as if we shall have much to say—even tho' partg. so lately— Will Bel

[*Parrish*]'s prospects be as new to thee as to us? Those 2 "awful Conigmachers["]
are in the Asylum—   They were too much for Susan K. to bear—

What an amot. you had to do—equal to *here* for Pattie with all the building
Dont make thyself sick with hard work

AL PSCHi-Mott

1. LCM is perhaps referring to the San Francisco County Woman's Suffrage Society,
which had written LCM on 10 February 1871 (MNS) asking for autographed photographs
to be sold at a forthcoming bazaar.

2. LCM would speak at the first anniversary meeting of the Reform League on 9 May
in New York City. She may have called it a "Standard Festival" in this letter because the
evening session, a fund-raiser chaired by *NASS* editor Aaron Powell, offered entertainment. In her remarks during the daytime meeting, LCM would object to one of the resolutions, which "advocates the killing of human beings. . . . If we had fixed opinion right
when the Rebellion broke out, all need not have met it with the sword; we might have
met it with intelligent argument" (*New York Tribune*, 10 May 1871, 8).

3. Included in the New York City anniversary meetings for May were those of the
AWSA to be held on 10 May at Steinway Hall, and the NWSA convention (or what the
*New York Tribune* called the "Cosmo-Politico Party" after Victoria Woodhull's party by
that name) on 11–12 May at Apollo Hall (1 May 1871, 5; Mary Gabriel, *Notorious Victoria*
[Chapel Hill, N.C.: Algonquin Press, 1998], 95–96). At the latter meeting, LCM would
say that although the woman's rights movement was "somewhat divided or separated
in some of our measures, yet I believe that on the great principles on which we get out,
we are one." She went on to say that she had come to the meeting, "although in feeble
health, to identify myself so far with this branch" because of "certain resolutions" passed
at the AWSA on 10 May that "I greatly regret." She probably meant the AWSA resolution that deplored "recent attempts in this city and elsewhere to associate the Woman
Suffrage cause with the doctrine of Free Love, and to hold it responsible for the crimes
and follies of individuals" (*New York Tribune*, 12 May 1871, 2, 11 May 1871, 8).

4. At a meeting of the Essex County Woman Suffrage Society on 3 May, LCM had
spoken on her role in the woman's rights movement. Cornelia Collins Hussey (1827–
1902) was the society's corresponding secretary (*Woman's Journal*, 10 June 1871, 178;
*Loving Warriors: Selected Letters of Lucy Stone and Henry B. Blackwell*, ed. Leslie Wheeler [New York: Dial Press, 1981], 384).

5. An editorial in the *Nation* (25 May 1871, 350) would characterize the woman's rights
movement as a "scene of frightful commotions." Regarding recent evidence on the background of Woodhull (who had divorced both her first and her second husband, but had
remarried the second, a doctor practicing "under divers aliases"), the *Nation* would
conclude that "if anybody says, on reading the above, that this is very disgusting stuff
to introduce into the *Nation,* we can assure him we entirely agree with him. . . . We have
been pointing out for two years what this Woman's Rights movement as it has been
conducted, was tending to; and now that we almost have our hand on the proofs of the
soundness of our previsions, we are not going to be driven off by foul sights or foul
smells."

# To Richard D. Webb

Orange, N. Jersey
5 mo. 4th. 1871—

My dear friend
Richard D. Webb

A longer time than I meant should pass, since receiving thy letter, with the *radical* pamphlets for my perusal & opinion of them— Well, I have read them more than once & parts of them to others—& have sent them to professor Magill[1] & the other teachers at our Swarthmore College—so thou may see I am not much afraid of spreading such heresy— Indeed it is cause of rejoicing that Religious-minded persons dare to speak & write so plainly, who cannot be charged, as were Voltaire, Paine & others, with ribaldry—Atheism &.c— The criticisms are so just & the reasons so good, why they ^the Scriptures of the Jews^ should not be read indiscriminately in schools or in any elementary training I expressed very similar opinions in a 1st. day School Conference of Friends in Baltimore during their Yearly Mg. week—much to the wounding of the Bible advocates This was more than 3 years ago—& as thou says, I have read all that has come in my way on this subject & other radical points as well—and I am much pleased with the tone of these Essays, & agree entirely with the reasons given for judging rightly of this Idol of Christendom— At the same time I love the Scriptures & can say with Theodore Parker: "You cannot open this book any where, but from between its oldest & newest leaves there issues forth truth—words that burn even now tho' they are 2 or 3000 yrs. old"— I may not have quoted it quite right from memory, & I am not at home to get the book & correct it—[2]

Thy late letter to S. Pugh gave us a pleasant view of your home—& of Deborah thy dear left one—who made herself dear to many—or numbers of us here too— I always feel rather a wish for you not to be quite so satisfied with settling down in Dublin or near there—in the fond hope that you might yet come to Pennsylva. for a permanency.

Now my ½ sheet is full & I cant often exceed that— Thou hast had from S. Pugh & S. Bowman I presume a full account of the all-too sudden passing from us of our loved Abby Kimber[3]—maybe wrong to say too sudden for it is better so than long years paralysis but we miss her cheerful loving company so sadly— A severe blow to our dear Sarah Pugh They were as Sisters— Edwd. Davis writes thee of all of us— So I need not try to say more than that I am ever thy very warmly attached frd.

Lucretia Mott

ALS MB

1. Edward Hicks Magill (1825–1907) was a professor of languages and the future president of Swarthmore.

2. LCM might be attempting to quote a portion of Parker's "A Discourse of the Bible," book 4 (1842): "Then we see the true relation the Bible sustains to the soul; the cause of the real esteem in which it is held is seen to be in its moral and religious truths; their power and loveliness appear. These have had the greatest influence on the loftiest minds and the lowliest hearts for eighteen hundred years. How they have written themselves all over the world, deepest in the best of men! What greatness of soul has been found amid the fragrant leaves of the Bible, sufficient to lead men to embrace its truths, though at the expense of accepting tales which make the blood curdle!" (*A Discourse of Matters Pertaining to Religion* [Boston: American Unitarian Association, 1907], 2:336).

3. Abby Kimber had died on 22 March at age sixty-seven (*Friends' Intelligencer,* 1 April 1871, 73).

## To Martha Coffin Wright

Orange 6 mo. 6th. 71—Cloudy—dry—

Precious Sister, whom we haven't set eyes on—much as we wished to— Better *so,* we thot., too during those very hot days in Boston— Maria [*Davis*] cd. hardly bear it—while I was "as cool as a cucumber," (almost) We attended 2 Mgs. each day—& went out to lovely Medford at night— Anna D. H. longed to go in with us, but a new girl comg. & a sewg. wom. there & her 4 childn. kept her at home, save the 1st. day—the Club Mg. at J. T. Sargeants extra when Dr. Hedge read his Essay & Weiss, Wendell P., Froth[ingha]m. Wasson Longfellow &.c—commented—hifluton as parts were, scientific & metaphysical as other parts, I listened to all with great interest & much unity & then they listened to thy sister indulgently—[1] There Ellen W. G. appeared, bright as a morng. star— as I guess she has written— We were going to see her that aftern., but instd. of it, Anna engaged her & Wm. to join Margt. Lucas & Esther Banc[rof]t. at their house—so we had that pleasure— And she has "gone & been" as private as Bel [*Parrish*] was! Thou *may* have stayed at home *now* as October will call thee thither—but that wont do *us* any good— All the Mgs. were good & very interestg.— The Papers dont begin to do justice to them— Maria was much pleased with Mrs. Hooker & her speech— The Mg. & the platform set heard all with patience & apparent interest—tho' determined to pass an endorsemt. to the New Y. Resolution— Who cares? Every body seemed kindly disposed I never had a more lovg. welcome even tho' almost the only opponent to that Resolutn.—till the vote was taken & then a hearty minority of No—followed the loud majority—[2] J. W. Howe bade us then to lunch with a nice set— Margt. Lucas, Lucy Stone Mrs. Hazlett—Mrs. Wilbour—Mrs. Glyn Dallas that Scotch actress—Stephen Foster, Henry Blackwell &.c.— Such a grand lunch! That was the only place we visited—oh, yes we were specially urged to stay to lunch with Dr. Hedge Mr. Weiss, Wendell P.—[*George W.*] Smalley—just arrived from Eng. Caroe. Severance[3] & 2 or 3 others, at J. T. Sargeants—& a good talkg., as well as eatg. time we had—icecream at both places—plenty of cake—tea &

coffee—lobster salad boiled salmon &.c— Theo. Parker's frd. Miss Stevenson invited us there to dine with Mr. & Mrs. Potter but we were engaged[4]—i.e. we had planned to slip away from all the dear, kind frds. & walk down away from the multitude, to Café below the Mall & have a quiet hour to ourselves—& didn't we enjoy it 2 of the 4 days?— We were stopped in the Street agn. & agn.—"Isn't this Mrs. Mott"— Even when ploddg. thro' the dirty Washn. Market in New Y. yestery. a nice-lookg. butcher sd. "is this Lucre. Mott? Well thee's been at our house in Waterloo— I'm Saml. Lundy's son" &.c— In Boston a Miss Shannon stopped me in that way & presented me Mr Weiss' new Book—American Religion[5] wh. I am very glad to have & tryg. hard to read understand.gly—

Roadside 6 mo. 13th—

Only think— All these days & not a word written— Well I can only say— wait till you are nearly 4 score & then see if you can do more than I have been doing of late—not an hour that I cd. take the pen without interruptn.—& brain too full for ability to write any how— Maria being with me in Boston & Orange was elegant & we enjoyed all we met with, but memory now fails me to narrate—so as to interest thee This must be finished & hurried off—only barely acknowlg. thine with Eliza [*Osborne*]'s wh. Ellen sent us & wh. were read with great interest—glad thou felt easy with thy decision not to attempt the journey in the heat—much as we longed for thee, we feared thou cd. hardly endure it— for Maria suffered—I didn't—at all And David has been in Philada. agn. & we have not seen him—& Mari[a]. [*Mott*] & fam[il]y. gone to Newport as she doubtless has written you— We have not yet had a scrap from her— Bel is comg. out here tomorw. & may bring letters— Anna D. H. writes that her baby too has taken the whoopg. cough & tis pullg. him down— Ethel is mending— Ned Hall[l.]'s wife was confined the day after we left there—another daughr.—Emily— doing well—poor Ned seems decling.—more poorly or so late letters say— Bright letters from his sister— They had a fine passage— Robt. Collyer a lovely companion &.c—&c[6] I haven't time now to make a single comment on Woodhull or Mrs. Hooker or anybody—for we are expectg. Wm. L. Garrison to tea with the Miss Browns—Thos. & Martha Mellor—Geo. & Lizzie Evans & others Sarah Pugh is not at home yet. We were together at the Progrs. Mg. at Longwood—but 1st—after gettg. home we had quite a party here Robt. Purvis & son[7]—Dr. with his bride & the Heacocks & Shoem[ake]rs. Penrose & Lydia Mather & a young lady Eleanor Rockwd. from Boston Anna Hopper—&.c— about 18 or 20—selves included—this was the next day after our return home— the followg. we were off for Kennett—3 days absent—every thg. to do on comg. home, to be ready to receive Garrison &.c—but he stays with the young Browns in Dobbins' enclosure—[8] We were there last eveg. with 20 or 30— Dr. Ann Preston—Edith Atlee[9]—the Davises & Hallowells & a host of young talkers— beautiful music—plenty of ice cream & cake—today I have called with him & Mary B. in her carriage on Martha Mellor & bade them here & now tis time they came

I promise thee I will take a clean sheet & write better as soon as I hasten off a little letter to Pattie not havin sent a line since we left Orange—for I went to Bristol on 7th. day without comg. home—was at Mg. there 1st day—

L. Mott

ALS PSCHi-Mott

1. John Turner Sargent (1807–77), a Unitarian minister, was a founder of the Boston Radical Club. Others not previously identified are Frederick Henry Hedge (1805–90), a professor of ecclesiastical history at Harvard Divinity School, and the poet Henry Wadsworth Longfellow (1807–82). At the Boston Radical Club meeting, in response to Hedge's essay defending pantheism, LCM recalled a statement Hedge had made not long after the split between the Hicksite and the Orthodox that had helped her to "disregard the condemnation of others. . . . She learned then how fiercely people could do battle for words and formulas" (Mary Fiske Sargent, ed., *Sketches and Reminiscences of the Radical Club* [Boston: James Osgood and Co., 1880], 158–59).

2. At the New England Woman Suffrage Association meeting held 29–30 May 1871, Isabella Hooker had declared that women were equally fit for political activity and that woman suffrage could eradicate evils such as drunkenness and prostitution. LCM had opposed as being "out of place" a resolution passed at the New York City AWSA convention and presented by Henry Blackwell in New England denying that the woman suffrage cause had any connection with "the doctrines of free love" (*New York Tribune*, 31 May 1871, 5; see also LCM to MCW, 3 May 1871, above).

3. Mary Adelle Hazlett (1837–1911), president of the Northwestern Suffrage Association, had spoken at the meeting, as had Charlotte B. Wilbour (*Woman's Journal*, 3 June 1871, 172–73; Gordon, 2:333). Caroline M. Severance (1820–1914) had organized the New England Woman's Club in 1868.

4. Hannah Stevenson (c. 1807–87) was Parker's secretary and the assistant secretary of the Free Religious Association (*WLG*, 4:533). William J. Potter (1829–93), secretary of the Free Religious Association, had spoken at its meeting on 2 June, and LCM had remarked on the "great advance in liberality even among the strictest sects." Potter's wife was Elizabeth Babcock Potter (*New York Tribune*, 3 June 1871, 1; *Sermons*, 360).

5. "Miss Shannon" is probably Mary C. Shannon of Newton, Massachusetts, mentioned as a donor to the *Woman's Journal* (7 June 1873, 180). John Weiss, *American Religion* (Boston: Roberts Brothers, 1871).

6. Charlotte Wilhelmina Sweet Hallowell (d. 1919) was the wife of Edward N. Hallowell (*Friends' Intelligencer*, 24 January 1920, 59). Collyer had sailed for England on 19 May (*New York Tribune*, 1 May 1871, 5).

7. Charles Burleigh Purvis (1842–1929) was on the medical faculty at Howard University.

8. Later in 1871 Eleanor D. Rockwood was asked to edit the *Lawrence [Massachusetts] American* (*NASS*, 9 December 1871). While attending the Progressive Friends meeting in Longwood on 8–10 June, Garrison had stayed with Mary de Benneville Brown (1785–1874), a philanthropist living on Arch Street. He had written to Helen Garrison on 9 June that at the Longwood meeting LCM "made a tolerably long but somewhat disconnected speech . . . chiefly occupied with her reminiscences of the rise and progress of the Woman's Rights' movement, but was listened [to] with much interest as well as great reverance" (*WLG*, 6:201).

9. Edith Willets Atlee (1823–92) was a Hicksite Quaker.

# To Martha Mott Lord

Clinton St. [*Philadelphia*]
12 mo. 29th. 71—cloudy

My dear Pattie

Thy sweet letter was a welcome sight last eveg. when we came here from V. Woodhull's able lecture on political economy—Bankg. & Land monopolies—Rail Road ditto, & the workingman's & people's Rights—a full house at Broad & Spring Garden—Spiritualists Hall—  Edwd. D. & self had taken tea at Dr. Child's with her only I didn't go to the table, havg. dined late at Henry Earles[1] & came in with Maria [*Davis*] who preferred to come here to tea, even tho' Edwd H. and Anna were engaged to tea at Mr. Hopkins'—  She went to the lecture too & was pleased—

We were glad to hear of thy safe comg. out of your large party—save the Idiocy! Fanny Palmer Wright had a similar gatherg. of her br[ethre]n. & families—30 in all—for her Mother [*Sarah Palmer*]—and without lettg her know—Chs & fam[il]y arrived the eve before—  Every preparatn. was made by Fanny only 1 girl, without the old lady perceivg a thing about it—  Now we say thou ought to let the others do the next xmas g[athering].—  That the next day found thee in usual health was a relief—  Do be careful. Sorry for dear Aunt Mary's head to trouble her glad for your childn. to be made so happy with their little guest—  I had hoped your presents for them wd.n't be so profuse as last year—All the exchanges hereaway gave satisfaction—  Thou shalt hear of them when thine & Eliza Osborne's visit comes off wh. is to us a very pleast. anticipatn.—so send this to her & hurry her along—  We have no engagt. for that time—& no Mgs. that week or 2—

Havg. so lately filled a sheet to Aubn. via Orange, I haven't any thing new now only that Theo. Tilton & wife & Dinah Mendenhl. dropped in unexpectedly with Edward the other eveg—*they* to tea & eveg. only, *she* to stay the night—Woodhull talk—& Theo's lectures at WestChester & Kennett—plain talk with him about his Woodhul book—[2]

The next is Jacob Barker's death[3]—& his funeral this morng—  Mary Earle is just here to with us—Anna & Maria too—none to the ground—  We go home to dinner—& want Anna to go, but she wont—havg. clearg. up to do after Eliza  She wrote a hurried letter to Maria yestery—amid many interruptns., wh she thot. Maria wd. be displeased with—  Mary Earle sends love & I must close  send back aunt Martha's letter—  Anna & the rest haven't seen it—

Mother

ALS PSCHi-Mott

1. Woodhull had delivered "The Material Relations of Humanity" on 28 December (*Philadelphia Public Ledger,* 28 December 1871). In a 24 December 1871 letter to MCW, LCM had written of Woodhull: "We think Victoria's advocates are increasg.

notwithstandg. her unwise utterances—as to the '*right* of doing wrong'—so misunder-
stood—givg. such a handle to her enemies" (Mott Manuscripts, PSCHi). Henry Earle
(1829–74), married to Martha Earle, was the son of Mary Hussey Earle.

2. Elizabeth Richards Tilton (1834–97) was married to Theodore Tilton. Dinah Han-
num Mendenhall (1807–89) was a member of the Progressive Friends of Longwood,
Pennsylvania, and the wife of Isaac Mendenhall (*WLG*, 5:44). Theodore Tilton had published the *Biography of Victoria Woodhull Claflin* (New York: Golden Age, 1871) and was
one of her biggest supporters. As LCM had noted in a letter to MCW on 8 November
1871, "Tilton is going so far in praise of Victoria, that there is a danger of hurtg. her future labors" (Mott Manuscripts, PSCHi).

3. Jacob Barker (1779–1871) was a well-known Hicksite Quaker merchant, a financier
whose businesses repeatedly failed, and possibly a distant relative of LCM. He had died
at the home of his son, Abraham Barker, on 26 December.

# To Martha Coffin Wright

[*Roadside*] 7th. [*March 1872*]

[*Continuation of a letter begun 6 March*]

Eliza [*Osborne*] & Pattie [*Lord*] came out so tired after all their errands in the
wind, that they retired before Henry came from his tea visit at Wm. Hall[l].s'—such
heaps of candies as they brot. & handed 'round— Eliza's the beater for buying,
tho Pattie did her part this time— See what a suitable light Delaine or Mohair
dress—cheap too, she bot. for Nellie. Tis quite a relief to see anythg. of moderate price—so sad is it to hear Henry tellg. them they cant get such & such shawls
under from 400 to $900—[1] Even our simple Maria [*Davis*] listeng. to his gettg.
her an India heavy one for $100!!! I tell them going to Europe to live cheaper than
here, is as if we went South during Slavery days—for tis only by overworkg. the
laborer at low wages & oppressg. the Poor that it can be done— Eliza wishes
Wm. & Ellen G. could go to Germany with their famy. for a few years—now that
Wm. will be out of busins. awhile—[2] How right the InterNational workmen are
to protest *aloud* agt. the great sum expended in the parade for the Prince's recovy. And John Bright too, to despair of economy in the Govermt while £7000000
sterling are taken from the Nation's industry  What a pity that his brain is so
overworked!—[3] What foolish balls & dressing in Washn. & in this City too! Why
cant a Republic set a better example of public receptions & such like?— It does
seem of late as if ours ^Republic^ is in danger of decay as Kossuth prophesied
in his last Lecture in this Country—The Future of Nations.

Edwd. [*Davis*] brot. out last eveg. thy letter with its enclosures wh. were all
read aloud, except Paulina [*Davis*]'s  What a pity for E. C. Stanton to be thus
disappointed & to have to disappt. so many—dear, earnest enthusiastic Mrs.
Beecher Hooker among the number— Wast thou not surprised at the mis-
spellg. &.c. &.c. of Paulina?— Her estimate of earnest, faithful Josephe. Griffing
I liked to see— Hast thou recd. those newspaper obituaries I sent?[4] I want them
agn.

When I see "Pug." thy love shall be given— A letter from Margt. Lucas sends similar affection to thee, & to S. Pugh too— She has entered into busy life, since reachg. home, Martha Mellor says, helpg. her children with their sewg. &c— Poor Lizzie Evans is still *unhelped*—a new girl came who proved to be simple & they had to despatch her in the next Car— George & Lizzie came sociably to tea the other eveg., at Henry's invite to go up to his room—*a cold place* & see the pretty things he had brot.—among them 2 made dresses for Lizzie full of furbelows!

Our compy. has been well timed—always a long table full & yet no overflow as we feared wd. be, if Edwd. carried out his desire to ask Morris & Elizh. [*Davis*] the night Henry arrives— I sd. it wd.n't do—but when we found Alfred [*Love?*] & Isabella [*Parrish*] & br. Edwd. were not comg. we sent the Dearborn for them just at tea time & Elizh. said they were rejoiced to come— Her sickness lasted abt. a week—not dangerous but leavg. her very weak— They will not be without help again— Eliza & Pattie have been in Town agn. today, if thou'lt believe it, & have just come out laden— So as I've seen very little of them, I stops, for they go with Maria to Martha Mellors to tea— Tomorw. they go with Ellen [*Lord*] to Swarthmore—Anna H. with them Edwd. D. stays in tonight to go to Wendl. Phillips' lecture & to have some of his compy—

Pity he c'dn't be with me when "Dogtails" success was read in the suit brot. agt. him by Bennet Walters—a long quarrel.

AL PSCHi-Mott

1. Henry C. Davis had recently returned from Europe for a brief visit (LCM to MCW, 29 February 1872, Mott Manuscripts, PSCHi).

2. William Lloyd Garrison Jr., seriously injured in a railroad accident in August 1871, had successfully sued the railroad company for $25,000 in damages (ibid.; *WLG*, 6:210, 227).

3. The *New York Tribune* had carried an account of the expensive ceremonies held in London on 26 February 1872 to celebrate the recovery of Edward, Prince of Wales (1841–1910), from typhoid fever. In March, the British Liberal leader John Bright (1811–89) had sent a letter to the Anti-Income Tax Association seeking a reduction in Britain's income tax. He had criticized the Liberal government that taxed "the nation's industry" in the amount of £70,000,000 a year (28 February 1872, 1, 6 March 1872, 1). LCM's figure was low by a factor of ten.

4. Stanton had written MCW that the illness of her daughter Harriet Stanton (1856–1940, later Blatch) prevented her from a planned lecture tour in the Midwest (c. 1 March 1872, *Stanton-Anthony Papers*, reel 16, fr. 52). An obituary of Josephine S. Griffing, who had died on 18 February, had praised her as an "untiring, unselfish" friend of the poor and the freed slaves and a woman of strong principles (*Woodhull and Claflin's Weekly*, 9 March 1872, 8).

# To Elizabeth Cady Stanton

Roadside—Philada. 3 mo. 25th. 72—

My dear Elizabeth

Had I not supposed that my good amanuensis—E. M. D. had written, acknowledgg. the reception of thy generous gift of many colors, with the letter—so like thee, & the sweet, sentimental verses—almost poetry, I shd. have tried my best, to thank thee before this late date—[1] The pen is ever a dread, & the 10 days past I have felt so near 4 score, as to give up almost every thing—so a dozen letters are on hand unanswered—

After our amusement over said bright effusion—& wondering if I could not rhyme too in return—in vain tho', I opened the bag, & enjoyed looking over each piece, opening every pinned up bundle, amazed that thou had collected so much—& that thou bore my carpet rag mania in mind— Part of the glowg. colors already in one ball, & a little leisure of each day cuttg. others in strips. I hope thou hast reserved enough to mend thy daughrs.' torn dresses at boarding school— Thy kind remembrance in this way has my hearty thanks, & I am trying to think of something when the good bag is returned to fill it withal.

Sarah Pugh has thy letter & poetry, so that I cant comment as they deserve. That thy daughr. should have to leave her school, & to suffer so long with fever, & that thou should have to disappoint so many, have called forth our sympathy & regret— It may not be too late yet for the appointments to be again made—if so it will be only such a rest of thy voice & abundant travel as is essential—

As to all the plans of perseverg. Isaba. B. Hooker & thyself for Spring work, and our E. M. Davis' untiring energy to form a new Organizatn. in Philada., it is really distressg., & I must be allowed to be a cypher— I did tho' go in with Maria D[avis]. & listened to Laura De Force's good argumentative lecture last week—& to the proposed plan for sd. Organization—[2] Such a new set as are now interested in, the Suffrage question, able, young minds ought to inspire new life, & would if my day were not so nearly over— Edwd. M. D—cant seem to understand it, that we are not all on the alert—as he is—— His club mgs. are increasing in numbers & interest—

My sister Martha sends us her letters from Susan & thyself, wh. we are glad to have. Martha now is wholly absorbed—nearly alone with David thickly covered with varioloid, they wd. fain call it—really small pox— He was engaged some days in New York in Court—& came here to rest over 7th. & 1st. day went back & finished his case—travelled all night, reachg. home—quite sick— The Dr. thot. it a bilious attack—from over-work—& not till the eruption appeared did they dream of small pox— Last date he was on the mend—no one allowed to go to the house— Eliza Osborne goes to the yard and talks with her Mother from the piazza— Their hired girls & man havg. had the disease have no fears—

but even they are not allowed to go near his room— The Board of Health keepg. close watch— Martha writes cheerfully—finds such nursg. quite easy—& while Help is at hand in the kitchen & outside she will not complain. How much worse had David been taken sick in New Y— —

Kindest regards to Henry—

Thine affecy.   Lucretia Mott.

ALS MNS

1. Stanton had sent LCM a package of clothing remnants along with several stanzas of rhyme: "Not Grant himself, 'the present taker', / Boasts such as these, my charming Quaker, / In fact, though nearing now threescore, / Ne're heard I of such gifts before. . . . Oftimes I have wished myself / Some horrid man, or bird, or elf / But now I'd gladly be a scarlet rag / To live forever in *thy* carpet bag" (Tenafly, N.J., 13 March [1872], Mott Manuscripts, PSCHi).

2. Davis was organizing the Citizen's Suffrage Association, based on the principle that women were citizens and deserved the franchise (*NASS,* December 1872, 2). Laura De Force Gordon (1838–1907), a journalist and a lawyer, had founded the California Woman Suffrage Society in 1870.

## To Martha Coffin Wright

New York—at Robt Haydock's
5 Mo. 27th. 72—

My dear Sister

I have succeeded in a short letter to Anna Brown with a tremblg. hand, & now let's see what can be done for thee— Also an autograph for a Hanover N. H. applicant—& tired eno' of such requests!

Medford [*Mass.*]—6 mo. 1st.

Only so far with my letter, great as was the desire to fill this sheet. So many callers in New Y—not ½ hour to write, no visits paid either save tea once at Saml. Willets' & dined at Mary Trimble's where Pattie [*Lord*] agreed to meet me on 3rd. day & wait on me to Orange—& a sweet Orange it was—so satisfied to let the dear Frds. enjoy the remaing. days of the Mg— Did you see the Herald's accot. of 1st. day preachg.?[1] It was not true that my "bonnet was handed to a Sister"—a thing I never do—nor was "a h[and]k[erchie]f. unfolded & laid over the railing"—as is the way some do— A great change has come over *that* & other yearly Mgs.— They do more than eno' now of hearty welcome & fellowship. But how few cotempories in age remain! These few I loved to meet— & so glad to see some of the young comg. out—"wiser than their teachers"— Han. Haydk. tries hard to keep their 1st. day school clear of old Orthodoxy— They make judicious selections from the Scriptures—& read poetry & nice little stories, &.c— Not singing yet but 'twill come by & by— Wm. Dorsey's daughr. has it in her Germantn. School—

I only had one day at Orange before Edwd. D. met me on the Boat for Boston—Pattie going or comg to New Y. with me, & we enjoyed watchg. the passengers comg. till Edwd. appeared— I was pretty sick—water-brash &.c—so at dusk the berth was most grateful—& such sound sleep was refreshg. while Edwd. had scarcely any— The passage was so rough—not a single acquainte. on board—tho' one who knew me last yr. happened to get into our Carriage, & was very cordial— She is a Universalists minister's daughr., & came with a large box of flowers to strew over her br.'s grave—Decoratn. day—& such a playg. soldier as there was!—'tis awful— It was my intentn. to go right out to Roxby. hoping to catch Ellen [*Garrison*] & childn. before they were off for Auburn— but a Club Mg. extra at Sargeants prevented— An excellt. scientific discourse we had on the Darwin theory, from Willie D's teacher at Cambridge—Shaler—² Dr. Hedge's comments on it—more favorable than one wd. expect from him—also Longfellows—Chadwk.'s Mrs. Cheny's³ & others—a very interestg Mg—no hard words—only anthropomoroporism (if thats it) once—now breakft. time— up to write before 6—

Orange [New Jersey]<br>6 mo. 2nd—1st. day noon—

"As true as I live" not a min. has there been to go on with this—for sickness on the way to Medford obliged lying down when Norwd. & Sally [*Hallowell*] were not there—then the Mgs & travel back & forth occupied every wakg. hour— These 7, 8 hours sleep are my livg.— I cant eat—as Ive said a time or two!

We meant to stay a little longer at Medford & "rest the Sabbath day accordg. to the commandt." but Edwd. found Sunday bigotry run no boats on Sunday *night* even, & he had to be in Philada. Monday, so there's the cause of our hasteng. back here— The same hateful proscriptn forbade our reachg. here by any car today, so we had to pay 12 dollars & toll to be driven here—arrivg. before 10 o'clk—telegrh. our comg., Geo. [*Lord*] had a fine Barouche to meet us at the boat—& Pattie had breakft. in waitg. for us—altho' we had had a cup of coffee on the boat, with biscuit that Anna D. H. spread for us— Just as if that wd. satisfy hungry Edwd.—the restless man walkg. miles from end to end of the boat—back & forth—beside carryg. his & my Valise—&.c—at every turn—to be sure mine wasn't heavy—not even a change of dress—agt. the grain as it was to travel in this good 2nd. hand rich silk—made from the great width of Maria [*Davis*]'s—really none the worse tho' for the wear—as to night clothes, they were pinned at my back to make a Grecian bend—or that other stickout—what is it called? oh, Paniers— Well we had a real pleast. visit & the best speakg. of any Free Relig. Mg. I have been at of wh. you'll see accots.— I had to go to dear Alfred [*Love*]'s Peace Mg., but not to the exclusn. of a single session of the Free Relig.— Several fine wom. welcomed me Ednah Cheeney—Miss Shannon who presented me John Weiss' American Relign. last year, & now gave me Dr. Bar-

tol's new Book—I forget the title—[4] Mrs. Frothingm. took pains to find me—
She had just returned from Newburg— Harry & Bessie [*Brown*] are there—&
happy &.c Walter & Anna [*Brown*] we hear are not comg. till Fall— I or we
were invited to the Wom's Club Festival—but the break in our stay prevented
our acceptg— Giles Stebbins was there with his new Book—the Bible of the
Ages—Extracts of the best words from Pagan & Heathen Philosophy—from our
Bible—a little & from the best writers—quite a good collectn.[5] He *presented* me
a copy, so I bot. ½ a doz. $2 a copy—left 2 or 3 at Medford—sent one to H. Haydk.
to use in her 1st. day school—shall do the same for Philada. & Wilmingn ditto— So come & see if thou wants a copy— Edwd. D. has them for sale— I
c.dn't hear in Boston or New Y. whether the Coffin Gatherg. was to come off
on Nantuckt.

Wm. Garrison came, & spoke to me at the close of the aftern. Mg—lookg
lovely as ever I cd.n't see any mark, in that passage way, of his terrible hurt—
for I didn't recognise *him* immedy.—not that he had altered a bit—but that I
was 4 score— His father was not able to be at the Mg—for wh. we were very
sorry, apart from his suffg. complaints— He is so tho'ro'ly liberal that he belongs to that platform so truly religious too—without Sectarian bigotry—
Gladly wd. I have called on him & wife had it been possible in the limited time—
Love to dear Ellen [*Garrison*]— As soon as her visit is out she & Wm. must go
agn. & look at that Medford House They can easily modernize it—& then the
Hall[l]. brothers & Wm. can buy the pretty green 5 or 6 acre lot wh. will be such a
beautiful play-ground for the childn., & their Parents will be in reasonable reach
if indeed they do not sell & follow them to another Place wh. will probably be
for sale sometime Anna [*Hallowell*] & I talked it over & quite raised my hopes.
How lovely it is for Ellen & co to be at Auburn & how I enjoy being here with
my dear ones!

AL PSCHi-Mott

1. LCM had read an article on a Quaker yearly meeting in Rutherford, New Jersey,
describing the discrepancy in attire between the young and the more elderly Friends.
LCM was depicted "in drab, with a face that shows the signs of patient struggles, soft-
ened by an expression of steadfast inspiration and of hope." The writer praised LCM's
demeanor as she had addressed the subject of the U.S. ratification of the recent Treaty
of Washington, in which Great Britain had agreed to pay the United States for damages
wrought by a British-built ship, the CSS *Alabama,* in the Civil War. "Beginning in a low,
tremulous tone, her thoughts seem to gather strength and pour upon her like a summer flood, so that her voice grows at length more distinct, clear and loud." The writer
stated that LCM had made "a strong appeal for the perpetual continuance of harmony
between England and America. She deprecated THE SHEDDING OF BLOOD in an age
like this, when civilization and culture are so advanced. . . . Since the beginning of the
trouble between the two countries in relation to the Alabama claims she had ever hoped
and prayed for the settlement by peaceful means. . . . If the Society of Friends kept firmly
to that defence and advocacy of peace which had so distinguished it, it could not be long
ere the principle would triumph in the world." LCM had closed by advising "young ladies

on the subject of dress, the extravagance and showiness of which were evils of the time" (*New York Herald,* 27 May 1872, 5).

2. Endorsing Charles Darwin's theory of biological evolution at a Radical Club meeting, Nathaniel Southgate Shaler (1841–1906), a professor of paleontology at Harvard University, had declared, "When man took the beast for his kinsman, empty heads laughed; but there can be no doubt that when he chose to come up from the worm, rather than down from the god, there was the basis laid for a moral revolution which exceeded any that our world has seen." (Mary Fiske Sargent, ed., *Sketches and Reminiscences of the Radical Club* [Boston: James Osgood and Co., 1880], 261).

3. Ednah Dow Cheney (1824–1904) was a Boston reformer and a member of the Free Religious Association. At the meeting, LCM had said she had come to recognize science "as a friend, not to fear it as a foe. She considered the conjunction of theology with religion lamentable, and would fain depose the usurper, theology" (ibid., 265).

4. Octavius B. Frothingham, Cyrus A. Bartol, Bronson Alcott, and LCM were among the speakers at the Free Religious Association meeting in Boston on 31 May (*New York Herald,* 3 June 1872, 8; see *Sermons,* 360–62). Cyrus A. Bartol's *Radical Problems* was published in 1872 (Boston: Roberts Brothers).

5. Giles Stebbins (1817–1900) of Rochester, New York, a Congregational Friend and an antislavery activist, published *Chapters from the Bible of the Ages* (Detroit: the author, 1872).


## To Martha Coffin Wright

[*Roadside*]
1st day 29th—[*September 1872*]

[*Continuation of a letter begun 26 and 27 September*]

Bel [*Parrish*] says thou'st had the letter[1]

Now that we have had a nice little visit from S. B. Anthony, there is eno' to fill this page—so thou shalt have it forthwith.

She came out with Edwd. [*Davis*] on 6th. day eveg., after happeng. just in time to be at Edwds. Suffrage Mg. at his Office—rather a common kind of gatherg.—Reporters, getting word, were there—& this appeared in the Press—[2] Maria was rather sorry to see it—

Susan made herself very agreeable— I felt the better for her visit—& was so glad to see & hear her agn.— She shews such good judgmt.—as to Blackwell's political managemt., & opposed to E. C. S. receivg. his suggestns. & being drawn into a corresponde. with him—[3] She is delighted with the success of the Rochester Mg—[4] Her appointmts. are made far ahead—to be in Hartford tomorw. so that she cd. only stay with us one night— We drove over to ^Bel drove the pair—Maria [*Davis*] with us^ S. Pughs early yestermorng. for Sarah had to go to her cousin's funeral to meet @ 11 oclk—Yardley Warner's wife—Reba. Allen's daughr. Hannah a minister—[5] Susan had much talk with Sarah while Mrs. Pugh was with me— I cared less havg. heard it all from Susan—Bel was quite interestd. to hear her— Joe didn't come out that night havg. to

meet his cos. Parrishes to decide who shd. Administer[6]—they fixed on Tom—
I am going in now to go to the Aged Col[ore]d. Mg. this aftern.—shall pass the
morng. with Fanny [*Parrish*] & write agn. soon—  Isaac T. [*Hopper*] returned
yes[terda]y. & came out—no 6th. day he came—his mother & Maria to follow
yesteraftern. I shall lodge there tonight—  Enclosed see Anna's letter

in great haste    L. Mott—

S. B Anthony went in from S. Pugh's—then we went to Earle's asked her to
come home with us—but she had to attend to the Cruelty busins. & cdnt come
till next 5th. day—no more now

S. B. Anthony spoke with delight of thy letter to her was it? comments on
HB letter—[7] She longs to have a day to pass with thee—  We got thy few lines
with Europe letter

ALS MNS

1. In an earlier part of this letter dated 27 September, LCM had asked if MCW had
seen a letter from Anna Temple Brown.

2. At the Citizen Suffrage Association meeting held on 27 September, Anthony had
spoken for woman suffrage and had defended her support of the Republican party,
noting that it "has shown us more consideration than the other party, and have recognized us in their platform, which is something gained" (*Philadelphia Press,* 28 September 1872, 2).

3. LCM is probably referring to differing strategies on the part of the AWSA and the
NWSA to gain Republican support for woman suffrage in the approaching national
election. Over the summer and into September, Henry Blackwell, Stanton, and Anthony had exchanged numerous letters regarding the speakers at various functions. In a letter
to Blackwell of 15 September 1872, Stanton had complained about the lack of cooperation from Stone and others in organizing campaign rallies. Shortly thereafter Blackwell
had written Stanton apologizing for neglecting to cover her recent "grand meeting" in
the *Woman's Journal,* but promised its inclusion in the next issue. He had suggested that
Stanton should organize twenty more rallies in New York and Pennsylvania (*Stanton-
Anthony Papers,* reel 15, frs. 289–91, 398, 469–70; see also Gordon, 2:518–21).

4. Stanton and Matilda J. Gage were principal speakers at the meeting of "Ladies all
Republican" in Rochester on 19 September, which, according to the *Rochester Evening
Express,* attracted an overflow crowd, turning away from one thousand to fifteen hun-
dred people (21 September 1872, *Stanton-Anthony Papers,* reel 16, fr. 410).

5. Rebecca Leeds Allen (1815–90), an Orthodox Quaker, had five daughters. Hannah
W. Smith was an Orthodox Quaker minister (LCM to MCW, 17 March 1872, Mott Manuscripts, PSCHi).

6. Joe Parrish and Thomas Parrish's father, Edward, had died on 9 September.

7. In a letter to Anthony of 17 September, MCW had thanked her for the copy of Blackwell's letter "with so much gratuitous advice" (*Stanton-Anthony Papers,* reel 16, fr. 401).

# To Martha Mott Lord

Roadside 2 mo. 27th. 73—snowing

My dear Pattie

This isn't my day for thee, but Maria [*Davis*] consents to my sendg. May H[allowell]'s letter, so 'here goes'— We have had a week's constant company & visitg, & attendg. Mgs.— Today left to ourselves & the reaction has been hard on me—so good-for-nothing & unable to do anythg but 'mope' & sleep—

You must come soon without others, for we had only ½ of you with such divided interest, Edwd. *may* bring out a letter sayg. how they fared in yr. absence— One from Fanny P. W. to Isabel [*Parrish*] says she is comg. next week— for, among the unlooked for events with us, Frank [*Wright*] is going next mo. to Europe on busins.— They had given up their house & were over at Pa Wright's and Fanny might follow Frank after awhile.* I have not seen the letter & may not have it right So much for them— We fear A. D. Hall. will not be well eno' to leave her home as early as tomorw.— Maria has written her to stay with you to a later train than 9 o'clk 7th. day—& that we will send to the junction for the 12 oclk.— It is very pleast. to be expectg. them—but she has much to do to make ready & tis doubtful her being able so soon—

Now for our own affairs—1st.ly send back the Auburn letters I want to ans. them—next ask dear Anna B. to take the time to come with thee very soon & finish out that too short visit— We are not expectg. any Emily Faithfuls now—[1] We saw she was at the Continental on 3rd. day & lost no time to call—early 4th. day morng with E. C. Stanton, but she had gone to New Y—& I was sweetly resigned— Elizh. Stanton asked me if I had written to her invitg. her here— Oh, no—said I "I never write— E. M. D. called & asked her to come when she 1st. came to Philada., & as soon as she returned here from Auburn *I* called—but she had hastened on to Washn."— Well Elizh. sd.—"You'll write & tell her so, wont you?—"*No,* Ill ask Edwd. to"— She didn't incline to be mixed with the Suffragists so there seemed no necessity to "tear her clothes"— It was good of aunt Martha to pay her so much attention, & to speak so kindly of her & her self-sacrifice for the oppressed working women— And I'm sure I should have been glad of *one* day's visit—*not a night*—for it wd.n't have suited to make a blazg. fire in our front chamber & for 8 oclk. to be too early for breakfast—& then her companion[2] was a dread.

Dear Elizh. Cady S. was nothg. but a pleasure & a nice short visit with S. Pugh & Adeline Thomson from 3rd. day morng. till 4th. day morng— Adeline returned the same eveg—her sister too poorly to be left— We were very glad we thot. to invite her— Edwd. went on purpose—good, thoro' soul that he is— S. B. Anthony spoke very highly of Adeline—

Maria had to go in on 2nd. day, to see about that stove, & agreed with the man to change it if she found it must be after tryg. smaller coal in it—& so thot.

she wd. surprize Edwd. & make him happy by stayg. to the eveg. lecture—& it was a great success,— She was so sorry that Anna & Maria H. & Isabel hadn't heard her— The place was crowded chairs in every spot & many standg— The Convention members listened with intense interest—& not a word Maria sd., that she wd. have spared all extemporaneous & delivered with great dignity Many were introduced afterwd. & expressed their pleasure to her— Maria over heard one say to others: "Now which of us cd. make such an extemporaneus speech in that Hall?"— Every body was delighted. Edwd. has sent you the Press' report, wh Maria says hardly gives an idea of the beauty of the speech[3] I was so sorry not to dare go in such an intensely cold eveg—after being sick, & "frowg. up" 2 hours— Maria says she felt as if she wd. never discourage me agn.— She regretted so that I didn't hear her, but she feared I wd. faint by the way— After our unsuccessful call on Emily Faithful Elizh. Cady went with me to Mg. & saw the 700 pupils of the schools come in & be seated with such order— I sat by her on a side seat till 2 or 3 of the schools came in— Our preachg. was not very interestg— John J White was there & had much to say—then Mary S. Lippincott good eno' but too long—Wm. Dorsey a little— Elizh. thot. the children were very patient— In the aftern. we were at Edwd's Club Mg—70 or 80 people present—several new ones— Elizh. delivered a very good address on The Poor and the Rich—wh. will be one of her coming lectures now—[4] Do hear her if you have opporty. Then we went to Thos. M'Clintks.—to tea—S. Pugh havg. been there in the morng. to announce the visit Edwd. D. with us— They "were delighted"—& such a sumptuous table! I went to the 3rd story to see poor Aunt Margt. Pryor in her 89th. year; brighter than she had been—able to read the Papers— She was anxious to see Elizh. so we went up separately— She has a nice Vineland nurse with her[5] a great relief to Mary Ann We had a very lively eveg— Edwd. & self left for the 10 30 Train— & found Thos. & Maria with a good fire & cut oranges waitg for us— I lost my supper before retirg—but none the worse for that—so endeth Stanton Saml. Pennock & wife stayed in the City till the Club Mg. Be it known to aunt Martha that he said he hadn't slept so well for many nights as when in our front chamber with only as much warm air as we send up in the eveg—for the stove pipe was not fitted in—

Send this to Auburn— Maria says write that Mr. Richardson has bot. Pepper's Place for $50.000— no more news—

ever    Mother & sister

Edwd ansd. this letter— Did she find aunt Martha?

*Maria says her plan is to go with Eliza the latter part of April—

ALS MNS

1. Emily Faithfull (1835–95) was a British woman's rights advocate and the founder of the Victoria Press. In chapter 7 of her book, *Three Visits to America* (Edinburgh: David Douglas, 1884), she described her visit to Philadelphia.

2. The word *companion* was written here in another hand over an erased word or words.

3. Elizabeth Cady Stanton had delivered "Woman Suffrage" on 24 February at the Constitutional Convention Hall in Philadelphia. After being introduced by Edward M. Davis, she had connected the struggle for woman suffrage to the American Revolution and the Civil War: "No just government can be formed without the consent of the governed. This we have heard for a century. We have gone over the question of slavery—all the questions of taxation; and having answered them so often, must the arrangement be gone over again to convince the people on this question of woman suffrage? Taxation without representation is tyranny" (*Philadelphia Press*, 25 February 1873, 8).

4. Stanton had given her address, "Rich and Poor," at the Radical Club on 26 February after an introduction by LCM. Stanton had argued that "the gravest of all questions of political economy is that of a nation's money. This question is now for the first time being philosophically considered by the masses themselves. Gold is not and never can be made to meet the requirements for which money is demanded" (from *Philadelphia Inquirer*, 27 February 1873, reprinted in *Woodhull and Claflin's Weekly*, 22 March 1873, *Stanton-Anthony Papers*, reel 17, fr. 1).

5. Margaret Wilson Pryor (b. c. 1785) was a sister of Mary Ann McClintock and the wife of George Pryor. Margaret and George were Hicksite Quakers and woman's rights and antislavery activists. Margaret Pryor had moved to Vineland, New Jersey, in 1868, to an experimental community, where she regularly went to the polls to vote (Gordon, 1:44–45; Thomas Hamm, *God's Government Begun: The Society for Universal Inquiry and Reform, 1842–46* [Bloomington: Indiana University Press, 1995], 156).

## To Martha Coffin Wright

Roadside 3 mo. 18th. 73—<br>
Blowg. up the Equinochl. storm—

My dear Sister—

What a flittg. family we are!!

I can't let Thos. [*Mott*] & Pattie [*Lord*] go in upon you, without 1st acknowledgg. thy late letters—one via Ellen [*Garrison*]  They were read with interest by us, & the Yarnalls—  Caroe. S[tratton]. has not been here for weeks—we have not yet sent them to her—nor has Mary Earle been near us, since Maria [*Davis*] & I called there last mo—  I generally keep thine for her readg., save now & then a page or 2 she had better not have—  Sarah Pugh is thankful for all she can have of thine——  Edwd. D. keeps up an active corresponde. with E. C. Stanton & S. B. Anthony—  He may send some of their letters by Pattie for thy perusal. That to Pres. Grant is excellt.—[1]—  I wish, when lookg. over thine, that Maria wd. take the pen sometimes & comment on thy Reviews of the late Works thou has read—& wh. I never read—"Yesterds with Authors" & such like— Thos. reads to us evegs—sometimes translates as he reads—now he has a young Englishman's Travels in Spain—quite entertaing.—  While I am more than satisfied with Abbott's late productn. in the Index—drawg. such a good distinctn. between Theology & Religion. Even Thos. Mott read it at my recommendan.

& thot. it very good—& so well written— I care not how radical the free-enquirer may become, if a regard for *true* religion is preserved— Garrison always kept that in view, in his speeches, & his Bible selections— Theologies & forms are dying out—even tho' too slowly, I must look up some nice Peace Articles & send thee— Have you read Herbert Spencer's Article in the Popular Science Mo.ly.?—Our 2 Religions—Amity & Enmity— I cut it from the World,—— Also an defence of Suicide & homicide by F. W. Newman, & a Dr. Lionell somethg[2]—both wh. herewith—also a slip on the Beauties of Winter— This is about all of the intellectual & moral, for this time—

If a letter or telegram reach you tomorw saying that Thos. & Pattie will be with you on 7th. day, dont go to work & sweep thy house over agn., lest a little dust be somewhere— Thos. cd.n't decide till he got Eliza [*Osborne*]'s answer this morng— He may have to go New Y. today to see about the Steamer for some change is made since he engaged the berths & they may have to take another— Their visit to you must be short, for Pattie has to be at home on 5th. day of next week— Eliza can therefore have more time to come here & let us enjoy her compy.— Fanny [*Wright*] writes that she has decided *not* to come to a Philada. dentist—a disappointmt. to Bel. [*Parrish*] & the rest of us— She may come yet before she leaves the Country— Anna Massey was so sorry to learn that Anna D. H. went alone—only a day or so before Anna Lea[3] went also alone, when they might have gone in the same steamer— A Telegram yesteraftn. says, the Silesia arrived at Plymouth on 1st. day— You'll see that report tho' before this reaches us

Thy extracts from Willie & Flora [*Wright*]'s letters we read with interest, & so sorry for the frost to agn. nip their buds— We feared it when the Papers reported the cold storms—no way but to hope "better luck next time"— Tom & Fanny [*Parrish*] still write cheerfully—tho' beging. to say "dear East", & to long to hear all that Maria H. & the others will write— Edwd. H. was out at Swarthmore 1st. day, & there found his *br.* Cavr. visitg his childn.— —no recognitn.— Dear May Hall[1]. is perfectly happy there—says she "has not been a speck homesick"— Maria is only waitg. for her little ones to be better, to go & see May & the others— Mott's cold & cough affected his hearg. so, that he had to be taken in to Dr. Turnbull who found his nose & throat involved, & much has to be done for him— Lu has fever daily & coughs much, tho' not confined to house—little Frank is better of his cold—but they all need attentn.,[4] & our Kitty (cook) was in bed 2 days with Epizoodic I guess—& Maria had her hands full—& sent for Dr. Smith—who made light of it— I have my share of the same kind of cold & cough Our Hannah is complaing now—& we have had Alice from the Cottage daily for a week past— I have not written to Pattie as Thos. was in correspe. with her—so if she care to look over this, why let her have it—

Wm. Abbott's father was buried last 5th. day—in his 85th. yr— I was at the house awhile— Mary Brown & Reba. Y. were there but not up stairs with Wm. & Sarah— I called afterwd. on Dr. Cleveld. & pd. my sub to the Med. Col. also

$5 from Thos. who liked to continue Mariᵃ.'s sub— Dr. Cleveld. said she was not expectg. to hear of her death—hopg. that after a few years she wd. be releaved of those sufferg. spells of pain—[5] Dr. Eliza E. Judson delivd. a beautiful address the eveg. before at the Horticultural Hall—a tribute to Dr. Preston's life & works—& to her memory— I was sorry not to hear it— It will be printed tho'— I was at the Commencemt. on 4th. day a short time— You didn't miss so very much when Anna Dickn. lectured— She seems to be rather losing her radical ground of late—[6] Indeed, it *is* a relief to feel that you can stay by yr. fireside—even when Wendell P. & Fredk. D. are the speakers— How little thou understd. my not going to hear Wendl. that time— I had decided not to without regard to takg. Isaac T. [*Hopper*] that stormy eveg—who *did* go out—a little way— I may not have written clearly about it— Dougherty delighted a crowded house last eveg—[7] It was nice for Garrison to be so pleased with Phillips— What a pity for yr nice Dr. Landford to have such a spell of sickness—

I cant remember now what we paid for Hay— Edwd must tell Thos. this eveg—& sundry other things we must try to think of & send word by Thos— The scraps from the Papers &.c—he will take—& now I must stop— We pay $1.25 for potats—& we too are just out of apples Edwd. bot. some this week— & we buy sweet potats. of our oyster man 30c ½ peck— Our one bbl lasted till a week or 2 ago— Turkeys are 25c pr lb in Market— Willie & Flora were favored as we were in havg. venison sent them. Glad *did* see Willie's frd. Col. Cowen[8]

We are only just clear of snow— Now with love to Eliza & Munson [*Osborne*] & hope he is better—& to Frank & Fanny & glad they are with you & a kiss for Mabel [*Wright*] darling

yr. worn out L. *Mott*—

I am keepg. thy piece of the letter with comments on the hateful treatment of Victoria for S. Pugh to see—[9] I only get a peep at her, once in a great while— We can arrange nicely for Eliza & Pattie even tho' some of our rooms are nursery & hospital— Anna H. was out here last night— Maria had a dressmaker 3 or 4 days of last week & was in a whirl for a time while cook & all were so sick— send back Anna B's letter—also May Hallowells her father will want to see it—

ALS PSCHi-Mott

1. Elizabeth Cady Stanton had written President Ulysses S. Grant (1822–85), whom she had supported in the 1872 election, congratulating him on his inauguration and his inaugural speech. She also had chastised him for forgetting "to mention the 20,000,000 disfranchised women" (*Woman's Journal*, 29 March 1873, 99).

2. James T. Fields, *Yesterdays with Authors* (Boston: J. R. Osgood, 1872). The "young Englishman's Travels in Spain" is possibly Augustus J. C. Hare's *Wanderings in Spain* (London: Strahan, 1873). Francis Ellingwood Abbot (1836–1903), a former Unitarian minister, was a member of the Free Religious Association and the editor of its journal, the *Index*. His recent article was "A Study of Religion: The Name and the Thing" (8

March 1873, 109). Herbert Spencer (1820–1903), an English philosopher, published "The Study of Sociology—Subjective Difficulties" (*Popular Science Monthly,* January 1873, 257–80) and "Our Two Religions: The Religion of Amity and the Religion of Enmity" (*New York World,* 6 March 1873, 2). LCM is also referring to another article in the *New York World,* "The Duty of Suicide: Euthanasia versus Lingering and Hopeless Maladies" (10 March 1873, 2), which included letters from both Francis William Newman (1805–97), a British scholar and the brother of John Henry Newman, and Lionel Tollemache.

3. This is possibly Anna Jaudon Lea (1825–1909), the wife of Henry Charles Lea, or their daughter, Anna Lea. Anna Hallowell had sailed for Europe on 6 March, leaving her children with Maria Mott Davis (LCM to MCW, 3 March 1873, MNS).

4. Anna Hallowell's children are James Mott (1865–1928), Lucretia (1867–1958), and Frank (1870–1933).

5. Dr. Emeline Horton Cleveland (1829–78) had been a professor of obstetrics and the diseases of women and children at the Female Medical College of Pennsylvania since 1862. Marianna Mott had died in Switzerland on 3 July 1872 of a stroke.

6. Dr. Ann Preston had died on 18 April 1872. Eliza E. Judson's "Address in Memory of Ann Preston, M.D.: Delivered by Request of the Corporation and Faculty of the Woman's Medical College of Pennsylvania" had been given on 11 March 1873. Dickinson had recently begun to deliver her lecture "What's to Hinder," which offended a number of woman's rights activists because she made light of women's struggles. As one writer in the *Woman's Journal* commented, "A woman fighting, single handed, for a principle, or a mother, earning for her helpless ones, finds much to hinder" (22 February 1873, 58).

7. In a 14 February 1873 letter to MML, LCM had described in further detail the snowstorm that had prevented her from attending Wendell Phillips's lecture on the Irish on 13 February (MNS). Daniel Dougherty (b. 1820), a Philadelphia lawyer, had given a benefit lecture for the Home of the Good Shepherd (*Philadelphia Public Ledger,* 13 March 1873, 2).

8. Captain Andrew Cowan of the First Independent Battery New York Volunteers had served with Willie Wright at the Battle of Gettysburg (*The War of the Rebellion: A Compilation of the Official Records of the Union and Confederate Armies* [Washington, D.C.: 1880–1901], series 1, 27:240, 689–91; MCW to LCM, 25 June 1865, MNS).

9. In the 2 November 1872 issue of *Woodhull and Claflin's Weekly,* Woodhull had published an account of Henry Ward Beecher's affair with Elizabeth Tilton, one of his parishioners and the wife of Theodore Tilton. Shortly thereafter, Woodhull was arrested on obscenity charges. She was in and out of jail for most of the spring until found not guilty in June 1873. Writing LCM in February, Woodhull had asked for LCM's support: "The issue now, is *not* Victoria Woodhull, *but* Free Speech *and* free press to the rescue of which from their present threatened positions everyone ought to hasten." Woodhull signed it "Your affectionate would-be-daughter" (27 February 1873, MNS; Mary Gabriel, *Notorious Victoria: The Life of Victoria Woodhull, Uncensored* [Chapel Hill, N.C.: Algonquin Press, 1998], 183–203, 212).

# To Martha Coffin Wright

Roadside 5 mo. 23rd. [*1873*]—
Growg. warmer—rain ceased—

My dear Sister— —

So many letters & other writg., that it has been almost impossible to fill a sheet to Auburn or Orange—so my dear ones have been neglected—also our Colorado precious children—

Thou may have been in Rochester, & so absorbed with Susan B. A. & her trial,[1] as not to be lookg for letters— I see in this A.M. Paper that her cause is postponed— Thy letter & parcels, by David were very acceptable— I was sorry not to have anythg. to send in return— The candy served a good purpose in Mg— It is as thou says soothing, & Susan Parrish shared some of it, to ease her Bronchial tendency— The soap came in the right time—for we had none but that rosin smell & soft soap, wh. Kitty succeeds well in makg. I had told Maria I shd. get some in Town— We only saw David [*Wright*] a minute (as it were)— He had had tea & wd.n't. go up to the ding. room with us—preferg. he sd. a quiet meetg. Joseph & Mary Post were takg. tea with us, & stayed so long that it left little time to enjoy David—tho' he did his part nicely with our compy., whom he remembered meetg. before. Edwd. & Anna [*Hopper*] had only 2 guests save their mother— Saml. Brown (Rachel's husband) & Henry Powell, who was there last year— Some few to breakft. & quite a party on 7th. day to tea when I came home to stay over the public Mg— Han. Haydk., Margt. Corlies, Phebe Foulke[2] &.c. &.c— They wanted Maria D. to go in—just as if she would have trusted me to care for the childn. with Bridget's help— She makes herself a Recluse if not a slave to them—& will go no where, except as she takes them with her to Germantn., & other calls & errands over the country—

Their Mother [*Anna Hallowell*] has reached Paris agn. & bendg. down to her drawg. lessons—delighted with all she has seen in Rome & other Places— Emily Hall[l]. with her, boardg. where Emily Mott & May are Henry [*Davis*] was greatly pleased to go to Rome with them & stay as long as he was easy to leave Pattie who really seems better last accots.— Willie D. will soon join them now— His letter recd. 2 days ago rejoiced our anxious hearts, that he was safely over the mountns., & at Valpar[ais]o. ready for the Steamer to Lisbon— Emily Hall[l]. letter sent out to us to read, says how pleased all were to meet with Frank W. in Paris— What wonderful flitting! Caroe. White (Earle) & Reba. Watson are off— Reba.'s Mother died 2 wks. since, before her daughr. reached her—on Nantt. Mary Earle has waited their departure before going to Holly— We go on 3rd. day-next— Now for thy letter— I sent it to Caroe. [*Stratton*] a week ago, or I shd. have tried to reply— Takg. a carriage from the Coleman House was just the right thing—& saved anxiety for the trunk's arrival in time—but how I wd.n't. have paid the extra for Pullman— I rather like the *smell* of tobacco—

& I dont see dirt except, on myself, & prefer not to sit opposite to cleaner passengers & have to be polite.— Anna B. was wise to discourage yr. takg. a carriage—such a diff. in price—& only a few short blocks to the cars—a little wettg. from the passg. crowd soon dries—

I dont know how thou wd. have borne a large Yearly Mg. Frd. next to me, havg. been caught in a shower, & pressg. up close to make room for her compann.— The smell of cloth shawl &.c—wet is worse than tobacco smoke— to say nothg. of the wrinkles such a *fatty's* dampness makes in a body's Sunday best— I didn't wear my new Popluin once—not I. We did move along nicely—only almost preached to death—no opposition to changes in Discipline— Temperance &.c—6 visitors from Men's Mg—mostly strangers—& when our Rachel Rogers[3] "had a concern" to visit the brethren, "way didn't open" to receive her—"time was so short["] & they had so much to do, the last day— It was a pity that thou didn't know of the direct Train—as I didn't in going alone to Holly last year & had to sit an hour & ½ at the Depot, waitg. for the Omnibus not being able to tug my bag up— Now Caroe. has written wh. car to take— Thou ought not to have fasted so long.—"the banquet Hall deserted" was a happy quotation. We were real sorry to lose that last few hours—almost a day, of thy stay at Orange, when every own-folk time is so desirable— But wasn't that a pleast. dinner party, and wasn't I proud of E. C. Stanton's able defence, & replies to Miller [*McKim*]?—& to see Sarah so swallowg. it all—& uniting with *her* rather than with her husband— I was glad too of the few words that Susan & thou put in & you ought to have said more. I always mean to take my share— Miller is not so good a listener as he used to be— Lucy & her baby Catharine [*Garrison*] are doing well—born the 10th—good nurse Our Mary Quin Hagen is just about givg birth to *her* 3rd—& hopes that will be a girl too I guess—havg. 2 boys. I am makg. her doubles &c— Widow Coffin Dennis' fixins & house interested me—as did all thou wrote of yr poor sick & dying— As to hired nurses for little childn., blessed were we to be without them— We see the evil of them in these now brot under their dear Grandma Davis' care. The extracts from Eliza [*Osborne*]'s, Flora [*Wright*]'s & all we thanked thee for & yet were afraid thou copied too much for thy health—sittg so long at the table writg—

Now if all that 3rd. page is skipped thou'lt not lose much— Charlie Cavr. writes that he is gettg. along very well in the Office has worked every thing up that was behind hand in his line—fillg up & endorsg. deeds—copyg letters & attendg to some of the corresponde., then payg. bills runng. with Telegrams, &.c & thinks he "will have a raise in June["]— His time from Monday morng. till Saturday night is pretty well taken up—has only Sunday to look around—but has a pretty good time— Nothg. of his health—so we hope he is well— Fanny [*Parrish*] much interested in their new buildg—[4]

Maria has just gone with the childn. & Edwd. has stopped at Oak Lane & sent word that two strangers from the West Indies are comg. out in the 4 o clk train—& they did come to my sorrow—& I had to sit more than an hour with them before Edwd. & Maria came— A Methodist missionary—English liberal—& daughr.—from Jamaica & the Bahamas where he has been these 30 yrs. sendg. his childn. to Eng. to be educated— He was at one of our Annual Anti S. Mgs. 15 years ago. remembd. James' presidg.—& now wished to see me & introduce his daughr. I was amused to see how quickly Edwd. interested them with his Photos. & talk about the people thus pictured. The daughr. was real bright— They had to leave before tea—as no other train till after 9—did I cry?—

[*Letter continues dated 24 May*]

AL PSCHi-Mott

1. Anthony and fourteen other women had been arrested in Rochester, New York, for voting in the 1872 election, but Anthony's was the only case brought to trial. At her trial on 17–19 June 1873, she would be convicted and fined $100, but she would refuse to pay the fine: "Your denial of my citizen's right to vote, is the denial of my right of consent as one of the governed, the denial of my right of representation as one of the taxed, the denial of my right to a trial by a jury of my peers as an offender against law, therefore, the denial of my sacred rights to life, liberty, property" (*An Account of the Proceedings of the Trial of Susan B. Anthony, on the Charge of Illegal Voting, at the Presidential Election in Nov., 1872* [Rochester: *Daily Democrat and Chronicle*, 1874], v–vi, 4–5, 82; Gordon, 2:524–29, 608–17).

2. Samuel Brown (c. 1794–1882) was a New York City Hicksite Quaker and the husband of Rachel Hopper Brown. Henry Powell was a Chatham, New York, Quaker. "Corlies" is possibly Margaret N. Corlies (1814–75), a New York City Hicksite Quaker. Phebe Foulke (b. 1847) was the daughter of Charles Foulke and Ann Foulke.

3. Rachel C. Rogers (d. 1882) was a Philadelphia Hicksite minister.

4. Charlie Cavender had left Philadelphia in April to join his sister Fanny Parrish and her husband, Tom Parrish, in Colorado Springs (LCM to MCW, 20 April 1873, Mott Manuscripts, PSCHi).

# To Martha Coffin Wright

Orange [*New Jersey*]
6 mo. 1st. 73—1st. day aft.—

All gone to drive & to tea at Miller M'K's—so I shd. have a nice time to write if the reaction of all this late excitemt. were not so disqualifyg.—even tho' thy welcome sheet, recd. in Roxbury [*Mass.*] is by me ready for comment— We hoped to meet & enjoy the great pleasure of a visit to Wm. & Ellen [*Garrison*] together & looked out for thee as we drew near instd. of that great gratificatn., Wm. met us as we left the car, with word that Ellen was in bed with head-ache— The poor child made the exertion to receive us, & wait on us at breakft.—& shew us her sweet little Frank—the prettiest flower of the three. The others wanted to pay us every attentn.—chips of the Garrison block— They have grown tall especially Agnes, & give their parents little trouble—behavg. so nicely.

The Stoningn. route suited admirably— It was too hot, as yr. thermomr. sd. to go up to Anna B's room so we went to the boat on our arrival, secured our room cooled ourselves—ate our lunch—read some letters—walked about, & watched the comg. passengers—not a great crowd—went early to rest, to be called up @ 2— I slept of course but @ 11 poor Caroe. [*Stratton*] must needs be up & dressed—no matter now tho'— It didn't prevent our enjoyg the rest of the travel or of her eatg. her thick slices of brown bread & butter, while I preferred her cookies— Ellen had excellt. Indn. cakes & a variety of good relishes— Boston fare always tastes so good— Thy letter was handed in soon after, wh. Ellen was able to read to us—then I lay down & slept while Father Garrison called—& told Caroe. the right car to take us to Medford— He meant to wait on us to the Lowell Depot—but we were off before he got back, wh. was best, for I was at home then—& we had no difficulty—arrivg at Richds. [*Hallowell*] empty house, the hired man came along & told us that the other houses were also deserted—Charlotte & Sallie H. gone to Town— We went over & saw the girl who soon found the key of Richd.'s, wh. was all we cared for as we only had an hour— she went over with us & I took pleasure in shewg Caroe. each room & the number of odd pieces of furniture, & the pictures too but as thou sd., deserted halls are not pleast.—so back we went—Caroe. well paid to have now a good idea of Anna's home— returng., the Conductor thot. the back way to J. T. Sargent's wd. be the shortest & put us out near the Revere House—& *such a tramp* as we had up hills & thro' windg. streets.! makg. the walk twice as long as to go in the cars up Washn. to Winter St—& then walk across the common to Chesnut St—a way I knew "like a book" instead of havg. to enquire ½ doz. times in those new streets We reached it at last—& such a parlor full!— not just a Club Mg. as we supposed, but a receptn. for Miss Carpenter refreshmts. in an adjoing little room—& oh, such a 1000 & 1 to speak to—some very nice people—Dr. Hedge—Abbott, T. W. Higginson, *E Peabody,* Mattie Griffith, Abby Hutchn Patton,[1] some new dignitaries (as our Mother called them) to be introduced to—till glad was I when we cd. leave, & go across that beautiful common to Tremont St—& so let Caroe. see the many new streets & the extent of Boston in the 30 yrs. absence— she did enjoy all—did a little shoppg. in Washn. St—& then went to a Restaurt. & had tea & waited till T. W. Hig[ginson]. called for us to go to the eveg. mg. of the bus[ines]s. Free Relign. wh. was interestg.— tho' nothg. very special—a good letter read—addressed to us from one of the Chunder Sen Theists in British India— J. Weiss made good remarks F. E. Abbott, & others on Organizatn. &.c—[2] Richd. Hall[l]. had the Treasurer's accot—& Wm. Potter the Annual Report Richd. was with us as much as he possibly cd. with all the attentn. to the several Mgs. & to the Festival[3]—Wm. Gar[riso]n. [*Jr.*] was there to wait on us out— Ellen had to take her bed agn. when we left in the morng—& cd.n't leave it till the next morng—when she sd. she was all right—but not able to go in & be at the Mgs. till the eveg. at the festival when she enjoyed meetg with some of her choice frds. & hearg. good sing-

ing—the Hutchinsons & a celebrated Miss Sterling  We didn't close till late—
11 oclk when we reach'd home—  Ellen none the worse & had a good night—
    2nd scrap—Same date Sunday aftn.—near night—  I had not so much time
to go around in Ellen's rooms as I desired—& didn't see her lodg. room at all
where the parlor carpet is—  The new one is pretty—& odd—tho fashionable—
white ground but needs a little green & red—  Every where looked nice—&
pleast. to Caroe.—  She takes great notice of childn. & is now going to Roadside with me tomorw. to see me safe home she says but more I guess to see our
Hall[l]. childn.—  We had early breakfast yestermorng. to take the 8½ Train—  I
thot. the cook smart, to have warm rolls, toast fish balls, &.c—&.c—so early—
Ellen was able to go into Town with us—Wm. of course, & supply generously
apples & bananas—in additn. to a paper bag full of bread & butter, crullers,—
so good & a lemon wh. Caroe. liked to have—  The childn. ran along with us to
the Norfolk cars—  It was Agnes' birth day—  I gave her what few pennies I
had in my pocket, & Carole. havg. Charlie's hand put some in his, when he began to ask his Mother what he shd. "get for Miss Carolina"—  Agnes at the same
time askg. to buy somethg. for herself—  Ellen told her what Charlie was sayg.—
when in a few min. she sd. "Aunt Lucretia, do you like popcorn?"—"yes" not
thinkg why she asked, & away she flew across the street to buy some—  We called
her back & sd.—not so soon after breakft.—  I was much amused—& so glad
to see the dear childn. their parents agn.—  Now if Ellen *has* written all this, it
may be told twice to Grandparents—  It is really wonderful how much hospitality Wm. can bestow, with his great heart & his open hand & *a half!*—dear
Man—  George & Frank we saw too[4]  Caroe. had a beautiful ride with Wm. &
his Mother—  She missed the last sittg of the Mg—Weiss & Abbott—  I was
sorry—  I was to have gone out to tea at father Garrison's but Richd Hall[l]. was
so urgent for me to be at the eveg festival & brot such a pressing invitatn from
Ednah Cheeney & Mary Shannon that I broke the engaget to tea & didn't see
Mother G—at all much to my regret—  We came here all the way by cars in
time for the 6 o clk Orange Train  We found Maria Hopper here & Julia Gibbons[5] had come out that aftern. & they had had tea & were just going to take a
drive—so Pattie & we had a little good time together. Today Geo & Pattie [*Lord*]
went to hear Geo Truman & Caroe. & I went to the Park—

Last scrap—<br>
Roadside 2nd. of the Mo—<br>
safe at home—Last date.

    I hoped to finish & send this off from Orange, but it was impossible  I had
not done telling of our Boston visit—  When we were preparg. to go in on 6th.
day to the Mg. the childn. ran in sayg. there's a great fire in Boston—[6]  Wm. went
to the top of the house & sure eno'!—  We cd. only reach Essex St.—father
Garrison with us when the crowd was so great the cars cd. go no further—so
we walked toward Tremont St & in another car went nearly to Park St.—no ½

way there, when enjines & hose & the crowd—& Decoratn. (as when we hunted Mr. Mellon) obliged us to walk as we cd. to Tremont Hall  The Mg. not so
large, on accot. of the fire, but a goodly no. of very intelligt. nice people, & all
the speakg, save R. D. Owens—20 min. on Spiritualism & his books, very good—
Saml. Longfellows[7] & F. E. Abbott's excellt.—  Then the last 10 min. my only
effort was well recd.—  I cd.n't. resist the pressing invitn. to go direct to the Hall
for tea & eveg. & no poor old lady was ever more heartily welcomed  ever so
many new young people introduced—& all bringg. me bouquets & the best of
the goodies—such excellt, real plum cake—& ice cream in the eveg  Then "if I
wd. only go on the platform & say 5 words" &.c &.c—so the old goose did that
too—& begged the dear young people to simplify their costume, &.c. & such a
huge bouquet as they brot. me—for Ellens parlor—  She was no worse for going in, & we came away next morng—more than satisfied—

Now no room is left to say all that ought to be said of thy nice letter—so
prettily written. We cd.n't—complain that thou didn't start off & join us in
Boston, but oh, how glad we shd. have been! We had "Heaven" to-be-sure, as it
was—for we agree that Ellen's head ache was the only alloy—unless we add,
Caroe.'s missing that last good meetg—  Did I say she *did* go in to the eveg.
festival—  We had no ache or pain from the time we left home till we got here
@ 1 oclk—Maria [*Davis*] meetg. us at the junctn. with such good news from
Thos. [*Mott*] & Bel [*Parrish*] & more still—a Telegm. that Willie Davis—dear
soul, was safe in Paris—further when I've read the letters—& to go from the
sublime, that poor sufferg. Mary Quin Hagen has a daughr. & is well—  We have
had dinner & Caroe. sits here asleep snoring & at 4 we are going to drive over
to see Mary Earle—

We are sorry to learn that thou still feels not very well able to do all thou
wishes to toward yr. house cleang. but it is much best for thee not to try—& best
too I presume, that thou didn't attempt to go to Boston—  Thy extracts from
Florida were very acceptable—to think of sendg. cucumbers all the way to New
York! Willie [*Wright*] has my best wishes—  Do encourage David to put by all
he can so as to go to Florida—  Think of *thy* offerg. to take care of Maria's 3 for
her & Edwd to go to the copper-mines—  poor Mrs. Boucher is near her confinet & is *insane!*[IX]

Thou wast all right not to go that late party—but do go all thou can & not
rust out at home alone—

Caroe. says do tell us abt. the Bank defalcation & Starin.[8]

I shall be so glad when Munson & Eliza & the childn. are settled at home
again—  It is worthy of note that we took the dismal lonesome Palace car from
Boston to New York—  Emily Mott writes that tis so lovely to be able to sit &
look at her father & Bel & the childn.—  Anna D. H.—takes but one lesson a
day havg. so many commissions to attend to—  How blessed for the 3 to be
together—after 3 yrs separatn.—

Now I must close this & take a bit of a nap before we go to Germantn.—&
mail this—with ever so much love—

L. Mott

XMrs. Boucher was better last accot.—

ALS MNS

1. "Miss Carpenter" is probably the British philanthropist Mary Carpenter (1807–
77), active in prison and school reform. Elizabeth Peabody (1804–94) was a Boston transcendentalist and an educational reformer. Abby Hutchinson (1829–92), a member of
the Hutchinson family singers, had married Ludlow Patton in 1849.

2. Keshub Chunder Sen (1838–84) was the leader of a rationalist, monotheistic sect
of Hinduism, similar to Unitarianism. The *Index* would reprint a report from the *Boston Investigator* on the Free Religious Association meeting, which described Weiss's
speech: "John Weiss was holding forth, and we judged from what he said that . . . the
end and aim of Free Religion, as he understands it, is to mystify and befog the whole
subject." The report continued, "Col. Higginson, and Messrs. Frothingham, Abbot,
Morse, and Robert Dale Owen, of that party, are rather more practical and understand-
able" (14 June 1873, 240).

3. In conjunction with its anniversary meeting on 29–30 May, the Free Religious
Association had held a "Social Donation Festival." At that time, Richard Hallowell was
the treasurer (*Index,* 26 April 1873, 184). LCM had spoken at the meeting on 30 May, stating that it was "probably the last opportunity I shall have of meeting with this Association." She had urged members to "give evidence of a deep sense of religion which will
put an end to all the vain and false theologies and useless forms in Christendom and in
Heathendom" (*Sermons,* 362–64).

4. George Thompson Garrison (1836–1904) and Francis Jackson Garrison (1848–
1916) were sons of William Lloyd Garrison.

5. Julia Gibbons (1837–89) was the daughter of James Gibbons and Abby Hopper
Gibbons.

6. On 30 May the Globe Theater in Boston had burned, taking with it numerous
businesses (*New York Times,* 31 May 1873, 3).

7. Samuel Longfellow (1818–92) was a New York City Unitarian minister.

8. This is possibly John Henry Starin (1825–1909), a New York City transportation
entrepreneur elected to Congress in 1877.

## To Ulysses S. Grant

Philadelphia
Eleventh Mo 12. 1873

U. S. Grant
President of the United States
Respected Friend:[1]

The accompanying letter was presented this day by a convention of the Pennsylvania Peace Society and friends of peace from this & other States and was unanimously adopted and ordered to be signed by the Officers of The Society and forwarded

Respectfully    Lucretia Mott.

LS IaDPm

## To Ulysses S. Grant

Philadelphia
Eleventh Mo 12th. 1873

Ulysses S. Grant
President of the United States
Respected Friend:

In deep sympathy with the recent executions in Cuba, growing out of the capture of the ship "Virginius", and gratified that the Government has endeavoured to withhold the murderous hand, we, as friends of peace, uncompromisingly in favor of the emancipation of Slavery in Cuba, as well as throughout the world, are at the same time strongly opposed to the taking of human life, and we earnestly desire that no step may be taken that may involve this nation in war.[2]

In the expedition of the "Virginius" we see a violent war measure, aiding and abetting in the sacrifice of human life, and opposed to the course so strongly deprecated by this Government in the action of the Alabama and other vessels during the late rebellion, and after the long controversy with England, and the satisfactory adjustment of all difficulties by the Geneva award,[3] we appeal for that consistency with our late position, which will prevent the fitting out of vessels of war from this country against a friendly power, and thus maintain that grand peace message, "Let us have peace".

Respectfully    Lucretia Mott. President
Alfred H Love
Rachel W. Townsend, Vice Presidents
John M. Spear[4]

T. Ellwood Chapman Trea[surer]
Henry T. Child 2nd    ⎱
Lydia A. Schofield    ⎰    Secretaries

LS OHi

1. LCM had met Grant in 1873 when he was visiting Jay Cooke. She had urged him to pardon six Modocs who had been condemned to death for resisting forced settlement in California. Her pleas were apparently heard to some extent since only four were hanged (Bacon, 215–16; William S. McFeely, *Grant: A Biography* [New York: W. W. Norton, 1981], 436).

2. Cuba was currently engaged in the Ten Years' War (1868–78) to liberate itself from Spain. On 31 October 1873, Spain had seized the Cuban ship *Virginius,* which was falsely flying U.S. flags, and executed fifty-three passengers and crew, including U.S. and British citizens. To avoid war with the United States, Spain eventually returned the ship and paid $80,000 to the families of the executed Americans. Slavery would not be abolished in Cuba until 1886.

3. In September 1872 Geneva arbitrators had ruled that Britain had to pay over £3 million ($15.5 million) for damages caused by the Confederate cruiser *Alabama* and other British-built ships (*London Times,* 14 September 1872, 5).

4. John Murray Spear (b. 1804) was a spiritualist.


# To Catharine Fish Stebbins[1]

Roadside near Philada.
3 mo. 30th. 74—

My dear Catharine

Thy oft-repeated kindness & remembrance of me deserves more notice & acknowledget.—than four score & upwards is now able to give— The pen is almost laid aside— Memory is deserting me, and feeble health unfits me for almost every thing— Still I enjoy life—read some every day—of late J. S. Mill's & Mrs. Somerville's autobiography with no common interest—also many of the just tributes to our greatly lamented Chs. Sumner—Saml. Johnson's in the Index—& Anthony's of R. Isld.—especially—[2] Thou asks how I am— Here is the ans— I might add, that Wm. J. Potter's article in a late no. of the Index— or rather his Lecture in Boston—reported in the Index, on Religion & the Science of Religion—pleased me greatly—[3] How much there is to read now-a-days Giles [*Stebbins*] will have to bring forth another Bible of the Ages— So far without thanking thee for the choice extracts of thy dear Mother's collecting— I have read them with much interest, & placed them among some I have been wont to collect, when readg. an Author's Works of uncommon interest— Have you had Matthw. Arnold's Literature & Dogma?[4] It is well worth readg. His nice distinctions in the Bible—bringg. so into notice the "not ourselves" "which makes for righteousness"—an honor I have often given to the Israel's Religion in the old Testament—& so fully borne in the *New*—

No—I was not in Washington—and I shall not probably ever go there again, but trust to our E. M. Davis, & my sister Martha Wright to give me the occurrences of interest—[5] My sister was not there this year— She was in Florida at her son Wm's. whose wife had a claim on her in the birth of her 2nd. daughr.— We are now expectg. her return— Should thou or Giles be comg. this way at any time we should be pleased to see you here— Our br. Richard Mott & daughr. Cannie made us a short visit in the Fall—or early winter—

How gratifying that the cause of Woman is making such progress and has so many advocates—

affecy.   Lucretia Mott—

ALS NRU

1. The Quaker Catharine Fish Stebbins (b. 1823), a peace and woman's rights activist, was one of the signers of the Seneca Falls Declaration of Sentiments (Gordon, 1:81, 85).

2. *Personal Recollections, from Early Life to Old Age, of Mary Somerville. With Selections from Her Correspondence by Her Daughter, Martha Somerville,* by the British astronomer Mary Fairfax Somerville (1780–1872), was published in 1874 (Boston: Roberts Bros.). The *Index* had published two tributes to Sumner after his death on 11 March 1874, but none by Samuel Johnson (see "Notes and Comments," and an editorial, 19 March 1874, 133, 138). In his remarks in the Senate on 12 March, Henry B. Anthony (1815–84; Republican, R.I., 1859–84) had described Sumner as "admired for his genius and his accomplishments, reverenced for the fidelity with which he adhered to his convictions, illustrious for his services to the Republic and to the world" (*Congressional Record,* 43d Cong., 2d sess., 2142).

3. William J. Potter had delivered "Religion and the Science of Religion" to the Free Religious Association on 8 March (*Index,* 26 March 1874, 146–49).

4. Catherine Stebbins's mother, Sarah Fish of Rochester, had helped organize the 1848 Rochester Woman's Rights Convention and had been dismissed from the Genesee Yearly Meeting for her antislavery activities (Nancy A. Hewitt, *Women's Activism and Social Change: Rochester, New York, 1822–1872* [Ithaca, N.Y.: Cornell University Press, 1984], 131, 143). *Literature and Dogma: An Essay towards a Better Apprehension of the Bible* (Boston: J. R. Osgood, 1873) was written by the poet and critic Matthew Arnold (1822–88).

5. Edward M. Davis had attended the NWSA meeting held on 15 January (*New York Times,* 16 January 1874, 1; LCM to MML, 17 January, Mott Manuscripts, PSCHi).

## To Octavius B. Frothingham[1]

ROADSIDE, 5th mo. 22nd. [*1874*]

"The objects of the Free Religious Association are to promote the scientific study of *theology,* and to increase fellowship in the spirit," &c.

Doubting the propriety of calling theology a science, I would suggest an amendment in this wise: to encourage the scientific study of the religious nature or element in man—the ever-present Divine inspiration.

W. J. Potter and others have written on this subject, once alluding to my objection; but they have not met the distinction I would make. Saml Longfellow thought my dislike of the term was because of the abounding erroneous, or false theology. No; it is more than this: it is the study to "find out," or define God. Abbot says, "Index," 267, "If we make an image of Him, even in our own thoughts, to bow down before and worship, it will be hard to realize His presence in our own souls, out of which grow our holiest feelings, our noblest living."[2]

John Weiss, in his speech at our first Free Religious meeting,[3] directed us to the ever present inspiration in our own minds or souls, apart from all miracle or super-naturalism. I would add, apart from all verbal creeds and theologies, and from all sectarian or conventional observances as well.

> "These little *systems* have their day,
> They have their day and cease to be;
> They are but broken lights of Thee,
> And Thou, O Lord, art more than they."[4]

Combe, in his Essay on Natural Religion, says, "It is greatly to be regretted that theology has ever been connected with religion; and religion so much injured by the conjunction."[5]

Is not the basis of all science, fact, demonstration, or self-evident truth? Can we create a science on our speculations? Some writer has said: "The heathen make graven images, we make verbal ones, and they do not worship more ardently the work of their hands than we do the work of our pens. Language is inapplicable to such speculations, and can no more explain what eye hath not seen or ear heard, than we can by taking thought add one cubit to our stature."

Will not the above apply to much that has been written on the importance of faith in a personal God?

Let us rather use our time and efforts for the promotion of a higher righteousness than is yet demanded by *our* Scribes and Pharisees.[6]

LUCRETIA MOTT.

PL Hallowell, 425–26

1. Octavius B. Frothingham served as president of the Free Religious Association from 1867 to 1878 (J. Wade Caruthers, *Octavius Brooks Frothingham, Gentle Radical* [University: University of Alabama Press, 1977], chap. 5).

2. LCM is possibly referring to issue 167 of the *Index,* which included Francis Abbot's "A Study of Religion: The Name and the Thing" (see LCM to MCW, 18 March 1873, above).

3. In a speech before the Free Religious Association in Boston on 30 May 1873, LCM had cited Weiss's reference to "the science of the inspiration of the human mind" at the first meeting (*Sermons,* 362–64).

4. Alfred Lord Tennyson, "In Memoriam A. H. H.," prologue, ll. 17–20 (emphasis added by LCM).

5. LCM probably means George Combe's *An Inquiry into Natural Religion: Its Foundation, Nature, and Applications* (Edinburgh: Neill and Co., 1853).

6. At its 1874 meeting, the Free Religious Association had approved LCM's amendment

to its constitution "to encourage the scientific study of man's religious nature and history" (Stow Parsons, *Free Religion* [New Haven, Conn.: Yale University Press, 1947], 53).

## To Martha Coffin Wright

Roadside 7 mo. 14th. 74—
very warm—near 90—

So very kind & thot.ful, my dear sister, to send Ellen [*Garrison*]'s excellt. letter to us—after a hasty readg—& so sick thyself too, that 24 hours ought not to have passed without acknowlg & thanking most heartily for it— Bel [*Parrish*] has it now— Mary B. so anxious to hear often, shall have it tomorw., & 2 of Pattie [*Lord*]'s recd. since she & Mary Earle were here last 5th. day—coz. Caroe. [*Stratton*] too longs for letters—she sent us thine with a note, herein— It takes all my time, to arrange for all interested, to hear the latest news— Fanny C. P. writes for more— She has been sufferg. with her eyes—cd. neither read nor sew— Mary Cavr. has been quite a help to her—and continues very happy there— letters to-day

I was so sorry for thee to be sick—so alone as thou art now— Ellen must hurry along—only added numbers may not be so desirable to u while thou art so weak— Take yr flaxsd. candy— It is as well that little Anne[1] so feeble has not been with you during the sickness— Didst thou take cold going into yr. bath tub so often— It needs great care— I have, only once been in the tub— such a skin & bone frame can soon have all the water necessy. from a basin— twice a day—now that gardening causes profuse perspiratn—so conducive to health— I am entirely free from any usual ailment, since takg. regularly Pepsine powders—no whiskey needed—or the wine of pepsine—pulverised & taken in a little hot water has cured me— I can ride over to Germantn. & back easy— or walk from City Line station, as last week—comg. out in an earlier train than was fixed—& bringg. crackers and cucumbers—our garden failg. of them

Maria [*Davis*] has just come from a drive with Isabel, who has read all the letters sent her, & says, "by all means send Ellen's direct to her father for it is so very interestg—let her have it after Mary B. has seen it & she will send it"—so as we dont know Eliza [*Osborne*]'s address, we will let her have it— To-days date i.e yesterys. says dear Anna had a poor night, & was feeling miserable— tho' her voice was better & she ate a little more—[2] Dr. Morton left that day— sd. her pulse was good & she might last some time— Edwd. may have to come home for a few days this week— Its so difficult to manage her hair, she wants it cut off & I hope they will do so— Pattie had to sit with her arms around her & hold her up while Maria arranged it—& she was so exhausted she cd.n't turn to the other side of the bed—she coughed less but raised a great deal— I will enclose 1 or 2 letters— I have one from Sarah M'Kim to send to Caroe. and she will want to see Pattie's too & as 'twill be but a day's delay for thee it may as well go via Holly—  If any great change I will write agn. direct—

4th. day—

15th Clinton St—[*Philadelphia*]

Here without my glasses & only watered ink—waitg in the hope that Edwd. D. will send up a letter by today's mail—  Caroe. will please send Patties & this to Auburn & come here & read ours from Auburn—  The envelopes will not hold them—

AL MNS

1. Anne McMartin, the daughter of Flora Wright and Willie Wright, had been born on 7 October 1872. Flora had written MCW from Johnstown about Anne's illness (quoted in MCW to Anthony, 25 June 1874, *Stanton-Anthony Papers,* reel 18, fr. 60).

2. Anna Hopper had been diagnosed with throat cancer in March. At the time LCM had written MML, "It is all inexpressibly sad, & I have no life for anythg—" (6 March 1874, MNS). On 5 July MML had written her mother from York, Maine, where the doctor had sent Anna, about the latter's worsening condition (MNS).

## To Lydia Love[1]

Roadside 9 mo. 17th. 74

My dear Lydia

Thy feeling, characteristic lines I recieved last evening, on returning from our dear Edwards Hopper's house of deep mourning—his lovely Isaac T. having "departed this life" with so very short notice—only a few days confined to his bed—leaving his again stricken sister alone with her father—the last of 5 dear children—their precious Mother recently "called higher"![2] I can say no more now, than that thy sympathy meets a grateful heart—beating with you too in your sorrow—[3]

Lucretia Mott—

C PSCHi-Mott

1. Lydia Love was probably a sister-in-law of Alfred Love (Alfred Love Diary, 9 September 1874, Universal Peace Union records, Peace Collection, PSCHi).

2. Anna Hopper had died on 3 August in York, Maine. Her son Isaac Hopper had died on 15 September of typhoid fever (MCW to Elizabeth Cady Stanton, 3 October 1874, *Stanton-Anthony Papers,* reel 18, fr. 99).

3. Alfred Love's father, William H. Love, had died on 1 August.

## To Eliza Wright Osborne

12th. [*January 1875*]

My heart is so constantly with you, that I must add a word to go with Maria [*Davis*]'s, just to say how poor, dear, stricken brother David occupies my thots.—and how I plan one way after another for him—[1]

If he prefer to remain in his house whether some nice woman wd. rent it for a boardg. house—he choosing his rom— Maria thinks that will not suit him—then we hope he will go 1st. to Florida & consult Willie & Flora [*Wright*]— I want much to see him & have comfort in mutual sympathy!

Yes, dear Eliza, I have kept the shawl near to look at it often, and feel grateful for being so soon thot. of—

Now do write either to Pattie [*Lord*] or direct to us here; telling just how thou hast arranged every thing in that full house—now made so desolate! Dont I know every feeling when I go to the deserted 919 Clinton St.?[2]

We are thankful to see Maria Hopper—dear lonely Maria, so cheerful when we go there—& comg. out here with her father repeatedly—

All about yr. moving too we want, & just how the splendid mansion is suiting you all—& how distributed as to lodgg. rooms, &.c &.c— We have no lovely & loving letters any more, so eagerly recd. when Edwd. comes out with the mail— Of course from Auburn I mean— Dear Pattie will still be faithful—

Maria just hands me one from Caroline [*Stratton*], wh. you may like to see— We shall be glad of our share of Sarah M'Kim's & Anne D's visit hereaway—

If thou writes to Florida, do assure Willie & Flora, they have my heart's warmest sympathy & love— Oh yes all the dear bereft ones— Ellen [*Garrison*] so favored to have had her precious mother with her so many weeks— Frank & Fanny [*Wright*] so far away!— It will be a severe blow to them too—

How sad it all is! Is thy fathers lameness any better?

My love to Mrs. Worden I know she is a mourner with us—

AL MNS

1. MCW had died on 4 January 1875, after a brief illness.
2. This was the home of Edward Hopper and the late Anna Hopper.

## To Susan B. Anthony

Roadside 7 mo 21st 76

Dear Susan

I forgot to take the parcel of tea I promised thee—so please accept it now— thankg. thee for so oft remembg. me with the cool ice drinks of it— It is rather superior to the oulon tea generally imported, & we like it better than the breakft. tea.

After leavg. you so hurriedly yestery.,[1] I felt that thou wast still short of an even balance, & now enclose another ten, for thy own *personal*—use. It is too hard for our widely extended National Socy. to suffer thee to labor so unceasingly without a consideratn.

affecy.    L. Mott

Love to dear Elizh. Osborne. What a good time you will have together—a rest I hope to thee—indeed to you both—again with dear love

L. Mott

ALS MNS

1. Anthony had been in Philadelphia to attend the nation's centennial celebration. During the 4 July event at Independence Hall, Anthony had interrupted the ceremony, from which suffrage advocates had been excluded, to present the NWSA's "Declaration of the Rights of the Women of the United States." Suffrage advocates then held a separate convention in the nearby First Unitarian Church, at which LCM presided. LCM apologized for her weak voice but "reviewed the history of the movement, and said there is no law in existence fit to govern the American republic." Another report described her speech as "being of unusual power" (*Philadelphia Evening Bulletin,* 5 July 1876, and *Ballot Box* [Toledo, Ohio], August 1876, in *Stanton-Anthony Papers,* reel 18, frs. 859, 1861).

## To Anna Davis Hallowell

Brier Hall [*East Orange, New Jersey*]
13th. [*September 1876*]

[*Added to Maria Mott Davis's letter to LCM of 12 September from Roadside Annex, to be sent on to Anna Davis Hallowell*]

Thy Mother, dear Anna, leaves a page for me to fill, as if hers wdn't. be more to thee than any thing I can add—    There is however now thy postal to acknowle., containg. what I most wanted, & wh. was impressed, before a word was read,—the good news that you wd. be in Centre St. to close yr. Nant. residence. Thy Mother must see that in a moral as well as physical point of view it promises well—    You are in time for corn-puddgs.[x] & maybe late bl[ac]kb[err]y. ditto—    Nant. fare any how, in wh. I hope, you'll not be disaptd.—    The added mechanics to the Enos fam[il]y. may make her loss of yr. board less felt—I'm sure  I wish her well & glad you didnt leave abruptly—

Yr. change has revived the longing I have had, since our brief visit on the Island, for a longer stay, & if possible I wd. be off at once & have a few days more with you—    Could 'coz. Elizh.'[1] give me a little corner in some room or Hall—no matter how *upper,* in that little cot of thine, if thou bot. it, & wd. she be willg. to take in such a heterodox believer? Tell her the Wilbour Frds. have always seemed to me nearer the faith of Geo. Fox's good "inward Light" believers, than the Gurneys, who now have almost adopted the popular creed—in great sincerity no doubt, but I cant go with them.[2] I asked Geo. & Pattie [*Lord*] last eveg. if they'd go with me— Geo. said he wd. or shd. like to go as far as Newport— This A.M. I hastened on thy scrap or card, askg. thy parents if they didn't long to see *u* in yr. Nant. home & if so wd. they come on to the Fall River boat abt. the 26th—& after a few days with you, *they* cd. stop at Newport in returng. & Geo. & Pattie join me on board the boat & return here— If thy father had to hasten home frm. Newport thy Mother cd. go on to Boston with thee or after thee & thine, & help thee re-arrange your house &.c. &.c All wh. is submitted—

This is Ellen [*Lord*]'s 21st. birth-day— The childn. had each a present for her— Their Mother thot. birthday eve wd. be best to produce them, as School hastens them off in the morng.— And such an Oh ing! as there was— A very pretty work basket from her Mother—various useful contents—needle book, pincushn. cotton railroad—6 spools—sewg. silk, scissors the best I ever saw, button hole ditto—&.c—then lying over, neck ties—ribbon & lace—combs— chain & hook called a *page* isn't it? to fasten up foolish trains or [*symbol or drawing resembling a reverse 9*]—a hat fastener—and all with each sister as the giver— It was a merry time— Father added silver not grn. backs It was new to me that all this was in progress, so I had only time to bring forth my Nant. basket with a new silver, not *gold* thimble, wh. was rather large for me, bot. in Chesnt. St. & a few silver ½s. that thy father had furnished me, assuring us he liked green Paper far better—& I confessed so too—[3]

We are all in fair health here— Mother Lord & Louisa [*Lord?*] passg. the day in honor of Nellie's 21st.— One of the beaus coming out to tea & for the night. Mary Mott may tell of all the foregoing when she ans. that nice letter frm. May. Thy fuller letter I am anticipating  Do write every thing & love to all—

Thy own lovg. grandmother<br>
L. Mott—

[x]We have corn puddg. nearly every eveg. teatime—& the garden still yields all their vegetables— ½ doz. peach trees have furnished a peck a day—their 1st bearing—

ALS MNS

1. This is possibly Elizabeth Easton Macy (b. 1840), the widow of Thomas Macy's son James Macy.

2. By the 1870s the Gurneyites had become increasingly evangelical, fostering the conversion experience, the singing of hymns, and emotional expression in worship (Thomas Hamm, *The Transformation of American Quakerism: Orthodox Friends, 1800–1907* [Bloomington: Indiana University Press, 1988], 75).

3. From 1862 until 1875, paper notes, or "greenbacks," had circulated as legal tender. The Resumption Act, which had gone into effect in January 1875, called for a gradual retirement of greenbacks and provided for their redemption in gold coins (Margaret G. Myers, *A Financial History of the United States* [New York: Columbia University Press, 1970], 192–93).

## To Caroline Healey Dall

Roadside near Philada
3 mo. 5th. 1877—

Dear Caroline Dall—

Thy letter of 2nd. Inst. just recd. I hasten to ans. Sarah Peter, whose death was reported in the Cincini. Paper, was the founder of the School of Design in this City—[1] She was much interested for a higher & better education for girls, than our Schools furnished 30 or 40 yrs. ago— It was not quite at my suggestion that this Institution was started—but hearing me relate an instance of our daughter drawing a plan of an addition to our house, which the builder said would *do*,—he said to her father, he had met with many *men* whom he could not make understand a a draught on paper—he never before met with a *woman* who could draw one—

This drew from Sarah Peter some remarks on teaching girls such branches—and when a year or two after, this School was opened, it occurred to me that she might have had something to do in starting it—but makg. no inquiry, I never heard until 2 years ago—the School's vacation was longer than usual for some repairs, when the public were invited to see the success of the students—in their drawings on the walls—then giving credit to Sarah Peter as the founder I think of the Institution—

Return of mail forbids another word—

Sincerely thy frd.
Lucretia Mott—

ALS InFwL

1. Sarah Peter had founded the Philadelphia School of Design for Women in 1848, the first of many such schools established to train educated women for careers in commercial design. The school is now Moore College of Art and Design (Nina De Angeli Walls, "Art and Industry in Philadelphia: Origins of the Philadelphia School of Design for Women, 1848 to 1876," *Pennsylvania Magazine of History and Biography* 117 [July 1993]: 177–79).

## To Daniel Neall Jr.[1]

Roadside 1 mo 24th. '78.

Dear Danl. Neall—

Thou greatly obliged me by allowing my little contribution to go with thine & the others, to our dear J. G. Whittier—[2] And all thou wrote of him pleased me it was so like thee— If I had thy ready pen I might say something pretty too—

Also was my heart tenderly touched with thy allusion to a certain visit I made thee when fearing an unnecessary Discipline might be allowed to be passed upon thee— I well rember the feeling at the time—wd. now—say somethg., if I knew how—

Thy repeated remembrances of me are very grateful—& the kind invitations too— The neat little box, I keep near me— I want to call when it may not be an intrusion, to ask thee how I can best offer a little parcel of Eng. Autographs of 1840's collection, to thy sister [*Elizabeth Neall Gay*]'s acceptance—

so now affecy   L. Mott.

ALS PHi

1. This letter was written by LCM on a pamphlet announcing the eleventh anniversary of the Pennsylvania Peace Society, 27 November 1877, with LCM listed as president.
2. At a seventieth birthday party sponsored by the *Atlantic Monthly* on 17 December 1877, John Greenleaf Whittier had received many gifts and letters wishing him well (*JGW*, 3:383–84).

## To Elizabeth Smith Miller[1]

Roadside near Philadelphia
1 mo. 23rd. 79—

My dear Elizabeth

What words shall I use to express my warm thanks for thy beautiful gift? So unexpected—with such kind remembrances—all so undeserved—

Well as I have loved to meet thee, ever since, when a little girl, thy parents induced Lydia Shipley[2] to overstep her Quaker prohibitions, & have a piano in her little parlor for thy benefit, and dear as thy father & mother were to me ever after, still I fail to find any claim to such special regard, grateful as it is—

Only a few days' ago, a note from the Express Agent at Germantn. informed of a package, which we soon sent for & received— Company that day, & havg to go into the city yest[erda]y—prevented acknowledgg. till now, further than our E. M. D's postal that it was safely here—so neatly enclosed, I wd. not suffer impatience to cut the string, as my father used to say, "never cut when you can untie"—and when in its inmost enclosure the very pretty little pitcher & thy loving letter were found, with yet another gift to beautify my carpet balls— Most opportune too— I hardly know how to thank thee for all— That pleasant little social meeting in the cars S. Pugh & I talk over & she will be pleased with thy message, wh. I shall hasten to give—

How gladly would we welcome a visit from thee— If dear Betty B. is still in New York, will she not attract thee hitherward?—& then Sarah Pugh & we here might draw thee to us—

We miss my dear sister Martha Wright's visits & letters so sadly—and then death also deprived us of our loved Caroe. Stratton! The loving mention they both made of thee, increased ours— — Count me about as thou stands as to the Comstck. stir—glad Heywood is at liberty— Sorry Abbott is such a partisan in the matter— Comstock's power ought to be limited or taken away—[3]

Most affecy.    Lucretia Mott—

C PSCHi-Mott

1. The papers of Anna Davis Hallowell (PSCHi) indicate that she had identified the recipient as "Elizabeth S. Miller" and our research supports this designation. Elizabeth Smith Miller (1822–1911), a Geneva, New York, reformer and woman's rights activist, the daughter of Gerrit Smith, and a close friend of Elizabeth Cady Stanton, had attended a Quaker school in Philadelphia from 1839 until at least 1841. She had visited LCM and JM while there (see LCM to Stanton, 23 March 1841, Gordon, 1:22).

2. Lydia Shipley (1789–1885) was a Philadelphia Orthodox Quaker.

3. In 1873 Anthony Comstock (1844–1915), a reformer from New York City, had helped pass national legislation, known as the "Comstock laws," to prohibit sending obscene material through the mails. In November 1877 Comstock had arrested Ezra Heywood (1829–93), a Massachusetts pamphleteer and an advocate of free love, for *Cupid's Yokes,* a pamphlet on marriage reform. Heywood had been convicted in June 1878 but was pardoned by President Rutherford B. Hayes after serving only six months because of the outcry over his imprisonment. The National Liberal League, an organization devoted to secularization, protested the Comstock laws. Its president, Francis Abbot, supported a modification of the laws, though most members of the league wanted the laws repealed; he resigned his position in 1878 (Janet Farrell Brodie, *Contraception and Abortion in Nineteenth-Century America* [Ithaca, N.Y.: Cornell University Press, 1994], 263, 272, 278–80).


# To Martha Mott Lord

Roadside 11 mo. 7th. 79

snow melted

Dear Martha

Not quite noon— What can you think there will be to write—alone as we are, & not a week since you 3 lovely Visitors left us? Let's think!— Well Quarly. Mg. 1st. preachg. very good & plenty of it—makg. our 1st. Mg. long— As the men were about to retire to their end, I stopp'd them, to make an appeal for Kansas immigts.[1] was patiently heard— S. Levick stoppg as he went out to say he took my letter to Girard Ave. Mg. on 1st. day eveg. & made an appeal to them— Dr. Child came to ask me to give notice that he would take any parcels in his carriage to Joshua Bailey's Office—being well acquainted with him. Another met me afterwd. & put $3 in my hand to buy a comfortable— And before we began busins Debh. Wharton expressed full unity with my thus bringg. the subject before them  Before next letter I hope to be able to report results— Maria H's sweet smilg face met me, as we closed, to wait on me any where—

she hadn't sat for the Mg! So, callg. awhile at Dillwyn P's. she *would* keep with me quite to the 5th. St. Cars—where some of my frds. came up & quite out beyond city Line.

Maria's only news for me was that Thos. Mott & May wd leave Newport last eveg & be here today—& that she was fillg. an order for Fanny Cavr. Parrish. Thos. P. has not yet shewn hisself here. or frm. New Yk yet  Maria D. had been busy as ever all day—no compy—  We sat in here all the eveg. only Henry [*Davis*] callg—he brot. good accots. from Edwd. successful meetg with his frds.—his health good &.c. &c. that he wdn't be home before 4th. day of next wk.

Maria was "struck up" when told that I was going next P.M. to the Peace Ex. Com. "So much to do she cdnt. go", but reconsidg., *that other* H. of Ind[ustry]. decided her going & up 17th. St. to Norris far north of Girard Ave & for $2 buyg. & *bringg. away* a very pretty *real* patchwork quilt red & mixed—calico not large— wh. I have concluded to send to Will & Nellie's attic spare chamber—² She left another not so pretty wh. will do for Hannah's room—if not sold when she goes in tomorw—another Pinafore or somethg. else—  My pen is givg. out & spoils this nice clean page—all the pens good-for-nothg  Maybe I can put down the few nothgs. to pen—  Comg. home 4th. day eveg. Maria was bidden to go into Henry's at once to tea with Richd. Hallˡ. Nothg. loth she was off,—kindly leavg. with me Lucy D. & Emma M. *junr.* both to stay the night. Wasn't it kind? After I had refused an [in]vit[atio]n.  There was a good fire in the parlor then, for Richard wd. come here after tea & go back to Town @ 9 & to Swarthmore the next day—  Oh yes today  It was a real pleast. hour or so we had with him & Henry & Naomi—³ He cd. tell how nicely the Free Religs. Mg. was planng. & beging a very good practical work  I doubt not at Felix Adler's suggestn. at the last Annual Mg he presided & his openg address was more practical than Frothingham's used to be—⁴

Our young guests are with us still to tea & lodge & bkft., & are real company for Maria—  Emma just came in to say good bye.—  Her mother at the gate with baby & nurse—stopped to take her in—baby 5 wks. old—sun out—fine day for them

AL PSCHi-Mott

1. By the late 1870s thousands of Southern blacks had migrated to Kansas as a result of poverty and the failure of Reconstruction. Aid societies formed around the country to help the refugees (Nell Irvin Painter, *Exodusters: Black Migration to Kansas after Reconstruction* [New York: Knopf, 1977], 230–31).

2. Will Davis would marry Ellen "Nelly" Bliss Warner (1859–1913) on 25 November 1879.

3. Henry Davis had married Naomi Lawton in 1876.

4. As president of the Free Religious Association, 1878–82, Felix Adler (1851–1933) steered the society toward social reform. After breaking with Reform Judaism, he founded the Society for Ethical Culture in 1876 (Horace L. Friess, *Felix Adler and Ethical Culture: Memories and Studies* [New York: Columbia University Press, 1981], 69).

# To Dr. Alexander M. Ross[1]

[*Roadside?*] 12 Mo 13th. 1879.

Dr. Alexander M Ross Montreal
My Dear Friend

Dread of the pen now in my 88th. year has prevented an earlier acknowledgement of thy printed lecture on "Spiritism" which was read with interest and profit. Give my Love to thy dear Little Garibaldi Ross and tell him to frequently read the following Lines which were set for me as copies in Learning to write when about 9 or 10 years old— I have never seen the book since from which they were taken but they were fixed in my memory.

> "Learn to avoid what thou believist is sin.
> Mind what reproves or justifies within.
> No act is good, that doth disturb thy peace.
> Or can be bad, which makes true joy increase".[2]

I hope thy son will grow up to be a comfort and blessing to thee.

Thy sincere friend    Lucretia Mott

C PSCHi-Ross: A note to Maria Mott Davis from Alexander M. Ross enclosed with this copy informed her that the original was pasted in an album.

1. Alexander M. Ross (1832–97) was a Canadian physician and the author of *Recollections and Experiences of an Abolitionist* (Toronto: Rowsell and Hutchinson, 1876); he had been a friend of John Brown and had previously served as a physician for the Union Army.

2. In a scrap dated 1868, LCM had written out the entire poem, noting that it was an "Alphabetical Acrostic, by one of our 'early Friends', committed to memory, 1802 or 3— by writing in her Copy book on Nantucket" (MNS).

# Appendix: Guide to
# Lucretia Coffin Mott Correspondence

Although two repositories, Swarthmore College and Smith College, contain the vast majority of LCM's correspondence, other letters are scattered among other institutions, private collections, and printed sources. The list below is the most comprehensive accounting of the surviving correspondence to date.

Much of the information relating to specific characteristics and sources of the documents in the entries below has been abbreviated. Although the entries contain some abbreviations that have been used elsewhere in the text, a complete listing of the abbreviations that appear in this guide follows. Each entry provides information on the recipient or sender of the document, its date, the location from which it was sent, its format and length, any accompanying documents or identifying characteristics, and its source. Information that does not appear in the document itself is in brackets. For example, here is a representative entry:

Anthony, Susan B.
[c. 8 June 1869] Fr    ?    PL 1p Extr    Harper

Judging from either internal evidence or other letters we can place this document as being written around 8 June 1869. We know that Susan B. Anthony sent it to LCM, but the location from which it was sent is unknown. This printed letter runs for one page but was extracted from a longer piece. It appeared in Ida Husted Harper's *The Life and Work of Susan B. Anthony* (Indianapolis: Hollenbeck Press, 1898).

Women are listed by their married surnames in the entries, even if the woman was unmarried as of the date on the letter. Letters written in installments over more than one day are listed separately under each dated entry; thus, a letter written in four daily installments, for example, will have four entries below. Similarly, letters written to or from more than one person have an individual listing under each correspondent. States or countries have not been indicated for well-known cities, such as Philadelphia, Boston, and London. All other cities or towns with no state designations are located in Pennsylvania.

## Abbreviations of Document Information

AGS         autograph, with inscription
AL          autograph letter
ALS         autograph letter with signature
AMs         autograph manuscript
AN          autograph note
ANS         autograph note with signature
c.          circa
C           contemporary copy
Dam         damaged
Dft         draft
Enc         enclosure
Env         envelope
Extr        extract
Frag        fragment
Inc         incomplete
JL          joint letter
Lbk         letterbook copy
LS          letter signed
PL          printed letter
PLS         printed letter with holograph signature
PS          postscript
pTTR        partial transcription
TR          our transcription
TTR         transcription from another source
XC          photocopy of original
*           recipient/sender is inferred from evidence
**          recipient/sender is guessed
?           information is unknown or guessed
~           included in this volume
#           extract in Hallowell

## Abbreviations of Original Sources

Barney      Private collection of William Barney, Boca Grande, Fla.
*BBox*      *Toledo Ballot Box*
Bru         Private collection of Jack Brubaker, Lancaster, Pa.
BWP         Private collection of Beverly Wilson Palmer, Claremont, Calif.
Comly       John Comly, *Journal of the Life and Religious Labours of John Comly*
            (Philadelphia: T. Ellwood Chapman, 1853)
*CongRec*   *Congressional Record*
CSmH        Huntington Library, San Marino, Calif.
CtHSD       Harriet Beecher Stowe Center, Hartford, Ct.
CtY         Manuscripts and Archives Department, Yale University

CULA        Box 121, Collection 100, Miscellaneous Manuscripts Collection, Depart-
            ment of Special Collections, Charles E. Young Research Library, Univer-
            sity of California, Los Angeles
Davis       Private collection of Hester Davis, Fayetteville, Ark.
*Diary*     *Slavery and "The Woman Question": Lucretia Mott's Diary of Her Visit to
            Great Britain to Attend the World's Anti-Slavery Convention of 1840,* ed.
            Frederick B. Tolles (Haverford, Pa.: Friends Historical Association, 1952)
DLC         Blackwell Family Papers (Blkw), Lucretia Coffin Mott Papers (Mott),
            National American Woman Suffrage Association Papers (NAWSA), Eliz-
            abeth Cady Stanton Papers (Stan), Thaddeus Stevens Papers (Stev), and
            Western Anti-Slavery Society Papers (WASS), Manuscript Division, Li-
            brary of Congress, Washington, D.C.
DNA         Records of the U.S. Senate, 40th Cong., 3d sess., RG 46, National Ar-
            chives, Washington, D.C.
*ECS*       Theodore Stanton and Harriot Stanton Blatch, eds., *Elizabeth Cady Stan-
            ton as Revealed in Her Letters, Diary, and Reminiscences* (New York: Har-
            per and Bros., 1869)
Falconi     Private collection of Elizabeth Post Falconi, Newtown, Pa.
FRA         Free Religious Association, Proceedings
*FrdsInt*   *Friends' Intelligencer,* Philadelphia
Fuller      Private collection of Helen Fuller, Wilbraham, Mass.
GB-Fw       Fawcett Library, London
GBNLS       Combe Papers, National Library of Scotland, Edinburgh
Gordon      *Selected Papers of Elizabeth Cady Stanton and Susan B. Anthony,* ed. Ann
            D. Gordon, vol. 1 (New Brunswick: Rutgers University Press, 1997)
Hallowell   *James and Lucretia Mott: Their Life and Letters,* ed. Anna D. Hallowell
            (Boston: Houghton Mifflin, 1884)
Harper      Ida Husted Harper, *The Life and Work of Susan B. Anthony* (Indianapolis:
            Hollenbeck Press, 1898)
*HWS*       Elizabeth Cady Stanton, Susan B. Anthony, and Matilda Joslyn Gage,
            *History of Woman Suffrage,* vols. 1 and 2 (New York: Fowler and Wells,
            1881)
IaDHi       State Historical Society of Iowa
IADPm       Putnam Museum of History and Natural Science, Davenport, Iowa
ICHi        Chicago Historical Society
InEar       Earlham College, Richmond Indiana
InFwL       Lincoln Museum, Fort Wayne, Indiana
Layton      Private collection of William W. Layton, Washington, D.C.
*Lib*       *Liberator*
*LibBl*     *Liberty Bell*
*LMC*       *Lydia Maria Child: Selected Letters,* ed. Milton Meltzer and Patricia G.
            Holland (Amherst, Mass.: University of Massachusetts Press, 1982)
MB          Rare Books and Manuscripts, Boston Public Library
MCR         Schlesinger Library, Radcliffe Institute, Harvard University, Cambridge,
            Mass.
MH-H        Houghton Library, Harvard University, Cambridge, Mass.

| MHi | Caroline Wells Healey Dall Papers (Dall), Horace Mann Papers (Mann), and Grenville H. Norcross Autograph Collection (Nor), Massachusetts Historical Society, Boston |
| --- | --- |
| MiUc | Diedrich Collection, Manuscripts Division, William L. Clements Library, University of Michigan, Ann Arbor |
| MNHi | Nantucket Historical Association, Nantucket, Mass. |
| MNS | Garrison Family Papers, Sophia Smith Collection, Smith College, Northampton, Mass. |
| *Mo Rep* | *Missouri Republican* |
| MSaE | Salem Female Anti-Slavery Society Papers, Phillips Library, Peabody Essex Museum, Salem, Mass. |
| MWA | American Antiquarian Society, Worcester, Mass. |
| *NASS* | *National Anti-Slavery Standard* |
| *Nat Rep* | *National Republican,* Washington, D.C. |
| NBu | James Fraser Gluck Collection, Grosvenor Rare Book Room, Buffalo and Erie County Public Library, Buffalo, N.Y. |
| *NEnq* | *National Enquirer* |
| NHP | Women's Rights National Historical Park, Seneca Falls, N.Y. |
| NICO | May Anti-Slavery Collection (#4601), Division of Rare and Manuscript Collections, Cornell University Library, Ithaca, N.Y. |
| NjP | General Manuscripts, Bound, CO199, Department of Rare Books and Special Collections, Princeton University Library, Princeton, N.J. |
| NjRD | Elizabeth Cady Stanton Memorial Collection, Mabel Smith Douglass Library, Rutgers, the State University of New Jersey, New Brunswick |
| NN | Maloney Collection of McKim-Garrison Family Papers, Manuscripts and Archives Division, New York Public Library, Astor, Lenox, and Tilden Foundations |
| NNCB | Sydney Howard Gay Papers (Gay), Josephine S. Griffing Papers (Griff), and Caroline Bonsall Kelley Papers (Kell), Rare Book and Manuscript Library, Columbia University, New York |
| NNMor | Pierpont Morgan Library, New York City |
| NPV | Vassar College Library, Poughkeepsie, N.Y. |
| NRU | Department of Rare Books and Special Collections, Rush Rhees Library, University of Rochester, Rochester, N.Y. |
| NSyU | Osborne Family Papers (Osb) and Gerritt Smith Papers (Smith), Syracuse University Library, Syracuse, N.Y. |
| OHi | Charles E. Rice Papers, Archives/Library Division, Ohio Historical Society, Columbus |
| OMC | Dawes Library, Marietta College, Marietta, Ohio |
| *PFrm* | *Pennsylvania Freeman* |
| PHC | Haverford College Library, Haverford, Pa. |
| PHi | Pennsylvania Abolition Society Papers (PAS) and Society Collection (Soc), Historical Society of Pennsylvania, Philadelphia |
| PSCHi | Hallowell Manuscripts (Hal), Heacock Manuscripts (Hea), Janney Manuscripts (Jan), Mott Manuscripts (Mott), Ogden Manuscript Collection (Og), Peace Collection (P), and Ross Manuscripts (Ross), Friends Historical Library, Swarthmore College, Swarthmore, Pa. |
| PStH | Pennsylvania State University, Harrisburg |

| S-A Papers | *Papers of Elizabeth Cady Stanton and Susan B. Anthony,* ed. Patricia G. Holland and Anne D. Gordon, microfilm ed. (Wilmington, Del.: Scholarly Resources, 1992) |
|---|---|
| *3 Mos* | James Mott, *Three Months in Great Britain* (Philadelphia: J. Miller McKim, 1841) |
| Truth | Sojourner Truth, *Narrative of Sojourner Truth; A Bondswoman of Olden Time, with History of Her Labors and Correspondence Drawn from Her "Book of Life"* (New York: Oxford University Press, 1991) |
| TxU | Harry Ransom Humanities Research Center, University of Texas at Austin |
| ViU | Alderman Library, University of Virginia, Charlottesville |
| VtMiM | Middlebury College Library, Middlebury, Vt. |
| WHi | State Historical Society of Wisconsin, Madison |
| *Wm's Wk* | Josephine Butler, ed. *Woman's Work and Woman's Culture: A Series of Essays* (London: Macmillan, 1869) |

| Name and Date | Location | Document Type and Length | Source |
|---|---|---|---|
| _____, Elizabeth | | | |
| 22 Apr. 1859 To | Roadside | ALS 4p+TR | DLC-Mott |
| _____, Martha | | | |
| 2 Nov. 1877 To | Roadside | AL 4p | PSCHi-Mott |
| _____, Rebecca | | | |
| 29 Dec. 1861 To | Roadside | ALS 1p | NPV |
| Allen, Anne | | | |
| 10 Sept. 1848 To | Philadelphia | AL 4p JL# | MB |
| Allen, George R. | | | |
| 18 May 1872 Fr | New York City | AL 2p JL | PSCHi-Mott |
| Allen, Mary P. | | | |
| 5 June 1877 To | Roadside | PL 2p | Hallowell |
| Allen, Richard | | | |
| 25 June 1842 To | Philadelphia | ALS 2p~ | OHi |
| 10 Sept. 1848 To | Philadelphia | AL 4p JL# | MB |
| Amberley, Kate | | | |
| 30 June 1868 Fr | London | PL 1p | Hallowell |
| American Freedmen's Aid Committee | | | |
| 1 Nov. 1863 Fr | Philadelphia | AL 2p JL | MNS |
| Anthony, Susan B. | | | |
| 18 Oct. 1854 To | ? | PL 1p Extr | Harper |
| 11 June 1855 To | Philadelphia | PL 2p | *HWS* |
| [c. Oct. 1865] To** | [Roadside?] | PL 1p Extr | Harper |
| 10 Feb. [1867] To | Roadside | ALS 4p~ | MCR |
| [pre–3 Apr. 1869] Fr | N.Y. City | ALS 2p | PSCHi-Mott |
| 6 June 1869 To | Roadside | ALS 1p~ | PSCHi-Mott |
| [c. 8 June 1869] Fr | ? | PL 1p Extr | Harper |
| 21 July 1876 To | Roadside | ALS 2p~ | MNS |
| 26 Apr. 1879 To | Roadside | PL 1p | *HWS* |
| 28 Apr. 1879 To | Roadside | PL 1p JL | *Mo Rep* |
| Anti-Slavery Societies | | | |
| 10 Nov. 1836 To | Philadelphia | PL 1p JL~ | *NEnq* |
| Ashman, Howard N. | | | |
| 5 Aug. 1875 Fr | Philadelphia | PL 1p JL | NSyU-Osb |

| Name and Date | Location | Document Type and Length | Source |
|---|---|---|---|
| Barney, Elisa | | | |
| 8 Nov. 1839 To | Philadelphia | ALS 4p+Env JL~# | MNHi |
| 23 Nov. 1839 To | Philadelphia | ALS 2p Env JL~ | MNHi |
| 17 Sept. 1844 To | Philadelphia | ALS 4p+Env JL | MNHi |
| 22 Feb. 1846 To | Philadelphia | ALS 3p JL | MNHi |
| 19 June 1846 To | Philadelphia | ALS 4p+Env JL | MNHi |
| 22 July 1846 To | Philadelphia | AL 4p+Env JL | MNHi |
| 30 Oct. [1847] To | Philadelphia | ALS 2p Inc PS JL~ | MNHi |
| 31 Oct [1847] To | Philadelphia | ALS 2p Inc PS JL~ | MNHi |
| 1 Nov. [1847] To | [Philadelphia?] | ALS 1p Inc PS JL~ | MNHi |
| Barney, Nathaniel | | | |
| 8 Nov. 1839 To | Philadelphia | ALS 4p+Env JL~# | MNHi |
| 23 Nov. 1839 To | Philadelphia | ALS 1p+Env JL~ | MNHi |
| [6 Mar. 1841] To | [Philadelphia] | ALS 1p PS~ | MNHi |
| 11 Apr. 1841 To | Philadelphia | PL 2p | Hallowell |
| 21 May 1841 To | Philadelphia | AL 4p+Env# | MNHi |
| 22 Nov. 1841 To | Philadelphia | PL 3p | Hallowell |
| 8 Oct. 1842 To | Philadelphia | PL 3p | Hallowell |
| 14 Feb. 1843 To | Philadelphia | PL 4p~ | Hallowell |
| [post–5 May 1843] To | [Philadelphia] | PL 4p | Hallowell |
| 17 Sept. 1844 To | Philadelphia | ALS 4p+Env JL | MNHi |
| 22 Feb. 1846 To | Philadelphia | ALS 3p JL | MNHi |
| 19 June 1846 To | Philadelphia | ALS 4p+Env JL | MNHi |
| 22 July 1846 To | Philadelphia | AL 4p+Env JL | MNHi |
| 7 June 1847 To | Philadelphia | ALS 5p | Barney |
| 10 June 1847 To | Philadelphia | ALS 4p | Barney |
| 30 Oct. [1847] To | [Philadelphia?] | ALS 2p Inc PS JL~ | MNHi |
| 1 Nov. [1847] To | [Philadelphia?] | ALS 1p Inc PS JL~ | MNHi |
| 14 Mar. 1848 To | Philadelphia | ALS 3p~ | MNHi |
| 22 May 1848 To | Philadelphia | ALS 3p+Env TR | MNHi |
| 29 July 1849 To | Philadelphia | ALS 4p | MNHi |
| 7 Feb. 1850 To | Philadelphia | ALS 1p | MNHi |
| 23 May 1850 To | Philadelphia | AL 2p Inc? | MNHi |
| 19 Mar. 1852 To | Philadelphia | ALS 4p~# | MNHi |
| 7 Apr. 1861 Fr | Nantucket, Mass. | AL 4p JL Dam | PSCHi-Mott |
| 18 June 1865 Fr | Yonkers, N.Y. | AL 1p+Enc | PSCHi-Mott |
| 21 June 1868 Fr | Philadelphia | ALS 4p | PSCHi-Mott |
| Barrett, J. O. | | | |
| 14 Aug. 1867 Fr | Sycamore, Ill. | ALS 2p+Enc | PSCHi-Mott |
| Borton, Elizabeth | | | |
| 19 Mar. 1848 To | Philadelphia | C 3p JL | InEar |
| Borton, Thomas | | | |
| 19 Mar. 1848 To | Philadelphia | C 3p JL | InEar |
| Boston Anti-Slavery Society | | | |
| 25 Jan. [1860] Fr | Boston | PL 1p JL | PSCHi-Mott |
| Bowman, Sarah R. | | | |
| 3 Oct. 1869 Fr | Philadelphia | ALS 1p | MNS |
| Brown, Anna Temple | | | |
| [c. 1855] Fr | [Eagleswood, N.J.?] | ALS 1p | PSCHi-Mott |
| 24 Nov. [1856?] Fr | Eagleswood, N.J. | ALS 4p | MNS |
| [c. Aug. 1857] To | [Roadside] | AL 2p Inc | PSCHi-Mott |
| 5 July 1858 To* | [Roadside] | AL 2p Inc JL | PSCHi-Mott |

| Name and Date | Location | Document Type and Length | Source |
|---|---|---|---|
| 4 Aug. 1858 Fr | Trenton Fallls, N.J. | ALS 4p | MNS |
| 13 Aug. 1858 To | Roadside | ALS 6p | PSCHi-Mott |
| 10 Oct. [1858?] Fr | Eagleswood, N.J. | ALS 4p | MNS |
| 5 Nov. [1858] To | Philadelphia | AL 2p Inc | PSCHi-Mott |
| [11 Nov. 1858] To** | [Roadside] | AL 2p+TTR | MNS |
| 12 Nov. 1858 To** | Roadside | AL 2p | MNS |
| 26 Nov. 1858 To | Roadside | ALS 2p | PSCHi-Mott |
| 27 Nov. 1858 To | Roadside | ALS 7p | PSCHi-Mott |
| 15 Dec. 1858 To | Philadelphia | ALS 2p | PSCHi-Mott |
| 30 Dec. 1858 To | Roadside | AL 3p Inc | PSCHi-Mott |
| 2 Jan. 1859 To | Roadside | ALS 6p+TTR | PSCHi-Mott |
| 3 Jan. 1859 To | Roadside | TTR 1p | MNS |
| 6 Jan. 1859 To | Roadside | ALS 6p | PSCHi-Mott |
| 31 May 1859 To* | Roadside | ALS 2p JL~ | PSCHi-Mott |
| 1 June 1859 To* | Roadside | ALS 2p JL~ | PSCHi-Mott |
| 17 Sept. [1859] Fr | Eagleswood, N.J. | ALS 4p | MNS |
| 30 Sept. 1859 To | Roadside | AL 6p | PSCHi-Mott |
| 16 Nov. [1859] Fr | Eagleswood, N.J. | ALS 4p | MNS |
| 17 Dec. [1859] Fr | Eagleswood, N.J. | ALS 4p | MNS |
| 2 Jan. 1860 To | Roadside | AL 4p~ | PSCHi-Mott |
| 12 May 1860 To* | Roadside | AL 4p JL | PSCHi-Mott |
| 28 May 1860 To | Roadside | AL 8p# | PSCHi-Mott |
| 21 July 1860 To | Roadside | ALS 4p | PSCHi-Mott |
| 27 [July 1860?] To* | [Roadside?] | AL 2p Inc JL Dam | PSCHi-Mott |
| [c. 17 Aug. 1860] To** | [Roadside] | ALS 3p Inc JL | PSCHi-Mott |
| 18 [Aug. 1860] To** | [Roadside] | ALS 1p Inc JL | PSCHi-Mott |
| 14 Dec. 1860 To* | [Roadside?] | AL 2p~# | MNS |
| [8? Jan. 1861] To** | [Roadside?] | AL 8p Inc JL Dam | PSCHi-Mott |
| 16 Dec. 1862 To | Philadelphia | ALS 3p | PSCHi-Mott |
| 17 Dec. 1862 To | Roadside | ALS 2p | PSCHi-Mott |
| 21 Jan. 1864 To | Roadside | ALS 1p JL~ | PSCHi-Mott |
| 24 Jan. 1864 To | Roadside | ALS 1p JL~ | PSCHi-Mott |
| 25 Jan. 1864 To | Philadelphia | ALS 3p JL~ | PSCHi-Mott |
| 12 Apr. 1864 To | Roadside | PL 2p | Hallowell |
| 18 May 1864 To | Brooklyn, N.Y. | ALS 2p | PSCHi-Mott |
| 7 Aug. 1864 To | Roadside | AL 3p | PSCHi-Mott |
| 20 Sept. 1864 To* | Roadside | AL 2p | PSCHi-Mott |
| 22 Sept. 1864 To | Roadside | AL 2p Dam JL | PSCHi-Mott |
| 17 Jan. 1865 To | Roadside | AL 4p JL~ | PSCHi-Mott |
| 10 Apr. 1865 To* | Roadside | ALS 1p JL~ | PSCHi-Mott |
| 10 Jan. 1866 To | Roadside | AL 2p | PSCHi-Mott |
| 20 July [1866?] Fr | Pittsfield, Mass. | ALS 8p | MNS |
| 23 Sept. 1866 To | Philadelphia | AL 4p JL | PSCHi-Mott |
| 24 Sept. 1866 To | Philadelphia | ALS 2p JL | PSCHi-Mott |
| 27 Aug. 1867 To* | Roadside | AL 4p Dam JL | PSCHi-Mott |
| 1 July 1868 To | Mt. Holly, N.J. | AL 7p JL | PSCHi-Mott |
| 30 Jan. 1872 Fr | Dresden, Ger. | ALS 8p | MNS |
| 10 June 1872 To | Orange, N.J. | ALS 2p JL | PSCHi-Mott |
| 12 Apr. 1873 To | Roadside | AL 2p Inc | PSCHi-Mott |
| Brown, Mary Yarnall | | | |
| 3 Dec. [1866] Fr | Ellersleigh | AL 1p | MNS |
| [c. 1879] Fr | [Philadelphia] | ALS 2p | PSCHi-Mott |

| Name and Date | Location | Document Type and Length | Source |
|---|---|---|---|
| Brown, M. L. | | | |
| 21 Jan. 1868 Fr | Washington, D.C. | ALS 6p | PSCHi-Mott |
| Brown, Moses | | | |
| 9 July 1836 Fr | Providence, R.I. | ALS 2p+Env | PSCHi-Og |
| Brown, Samuel | | | |
| 11 Mar. 1821 Fr | Winchester, [Va.?] | C 2p | PHi-Soc |
| Brown, Walter | | | |
| 10 June 1872 To | Orange, N.J. | ALS 2p JL | PSCHi-Mott |
| ? Fr** | [New York City?] | ALS 1p | PSCHi-Mott |
| Burleigh, Charles C. | | | |
| 4 July 1841 Fr | Montrose | ALS 4p+Env | MB |
| Burleigh, Margaret J. | | | |
| 3 Feb. 1868 Fr | Philadelphia | LS 3p JL | PSCHi-Mott |
| Butler, Josephine | | | |
| 20 Apr. 1869 To | Roadside | PL 1p~ | *Wm's Wk* |
| [20 Apr. 1869] To* | [Roadside] | ALS 1p Frag | GB-Fw |
| Byron, Anne Milbanke | | | |
| 4 July [1840] Fr | London | ALS 2p | PSCHi-Mott |
| Carr, Henry S. | | | |
| 12 Jan. 1874 Fr | New York City | ALS 1p | MNS |
| Cavender, Charles | | | |
| 16 June 1872 Fr | Swarthmore | ALS 1p | PSCHi-Mott |
| 10 Sept. 1872 Fr | Swarthmore | ALS 2p | PSCHi-Mott |
| 1 June 1873 Fr | Colorado Springs, Colo. | ALS 1p | PSCHi-Mott |
| Cavender, Elizabeth Mott | | | |
| 5 May 1839 Fr | Kimberton | ALS 1p | MNS |
| 1 Aug. [1855] Fr | Flume House, N.H. | ALS 6p JL | MNS |
| 17 Oct. [1855] Fr | Philadelphia | ALS 2p+Env | MNS |
| Cavender, Mary | | | |
| 30 July 1874 Fr | Colorado Springs, Colo. | ALS 7p JL | MNS |
| Champeix, Leonie Bera | | | |
| 20 Sept. 1870 Fr | Paris | ALS 3p JL | NPV |
| Channing, William Henry | | | |
| 2 July 1847 To | Philadelphia | ALS 1p | PSCHi-Mott |
| Chapman, Maria Weston | | | |
| 29 May 1839 To | Philadelphia | ALS 2p+Env~ | MB |
| 16 Oct. [1839] To | Philadelphia | ALS 3p+Env | MB |
| 16 Dec. 1839 To | Philadelphia | ALS 4p+Env~ | MB |
| [20 Feb. 1840] To | [Philadelphia] | ALS 4p+Env~ | MB |
| 13 May 1840 To | Philadelphia | ALS 4p+Env~ | MB |
| 29 July 1840 To | Dublin, Ire. | ALS 4p+Env~ | MB |
| [post–16 Aug. 1840] To | [London?] | ALS 1p+Env Frag | MB |
| 19 Oct. 1842 Fr | Boston | ALS 2p | PSCHi-Mott |
| 30 Nov. 1842 To | Philadelphia | ALS 4p+enc, Env | MB |
| 23 July 1846 To | Philadelphia | ALS 2p+Env JL~ | MB |
| 28 July 1847 To | Philadelphia | ALS 2p | MB |
| Chase, Lydia H. | | | |
| 19 Sept. 1850 To | Philadelphia | ALS 2p+TR JL | MSaE |
| Chase, Mary Ann | | | |
| 19 Feb. 1867 To | Roadside | ALS 4p | PSCHi-Mott |
| Child, Henry T. | | | |
| 10 Aug. 1868 To | [Roadside] | ALS 1p+Env | PSCHi-Mott |

| Name and Date | Location | Document Type and Length | Source |
|---|---|---|---|
| 30 Jan. 1871 Fr | Philadelphia | ALS 1p | MNS |
| 30 Jan. [1871] To | Roadside | ALS 2p | PSCHi-Mott |
| Child, Lydia Maria | | | |
| 5 Mar. 1839 Fr | Northampton,Mass. | ALS 4p+Env# | PSCHi-Mott |
| 3 Sept. 1843 Fr | New York City | ALS 3+Env | ViU |
| 26 Feb. 1861 Fr | Medford, Mass. | PL 2p | *LMC* |
| Clarke, Clara Catlin | | | |
| 27 Jan. 1873 Fr | Syracuse, N.Y. | ALS 2p | MNS |
| Clute, Oscar | | | |
| 11 Nov. 1871 Fr | Vineland, N.J. | ALS 1p | PSCHi-Mott |
| 15 Nov. 1871 To | Roadside | ALS 1p | IaDHi |
| Coffin, Anna Folger | | | |
| 3 Aug. 1835 To | Philadelphia | ALS 2p+TTR Dam | MNS |
| 4 Aug. 1835 To | Philadelphia | ALS 3p+TTR Dam | MNS |
| 6 Aug. 1835 To | Philadelphia | ALS 1p+TTR Dam | MNS |
| [11 Dec. 1842] Fr | [Auburn, N.Y.] | AL 2p | MNS |
| 18 Dec. 1842 Fr | Auburn, N.Y. | AL 4p+Env, TTR JL | MNS |
| [c. 1842] Fr | [Auburn, N.Y.] | AL 1p Inc | MNS |
| Collin, John? | | | |
| 25 Jan. 1871 Fr | Philadelphia | ALS 1p | MNS |
| Combe, Cecilia | | | |
| [19 Nov. 1840] To | [Philadelphia] | ALS 4p JL | GBNLS |
| 24 Mar. 1843 To | Philadelphia | ALS 4p JL~ | GBNLS |
| 2 Mar. 1846 To | Philadelphia | ALS 4p+Env JL~ | GBNLS |
| 10 Sept. 1848 To | Philadelphia | ALS 4p JL~ | GBNLS |
| 19 Oct. 1848 Fr | [Edinburgh] | ALS 1p+Env JL | NPV |
| 28 May 1850 To | Philadelphia | ALS 2p JL | GBNLS |
| 21 Aug. 1852 To | New York City | ALS 4p JL | GBNLS |
| 25 May 1855 To | Philadelphia | ALS 4p JL~ | GBNLS |
| [5 Nov. 1856] To | [Philadelphia] | ALS 2p JL | GBNLS |
| Combe, George | | | |
| 13 June 1839 To | Philadelphia | ALS 4p+Env~ | GBNLS |
| 15 July 1839 Fr | White Mountains, N.H. | Lbk 4p | GBNLS |
| 8 Sept. 1839 To | Philadelphia | ALS 4p+Env | GBNLS |
| 5 Nov. 1839 Fr | Boston | ALS 3p+Env | PSCHi-Mott |
| 25 Nov. 1839 To | Philadelphia | ALS 3p+Env~ | GBNLS |
| [19 Nov. 1840] To | [Philadelphia] | ALS 4p JL | GBNLS |
| 8 Feb. 1841 Fr | Slateford, Scot. | ALS 4p+Env | PSCHi-Mott |
| 8 Feb. 1841 Fr | Slateford, Scot. | Lbk 7p Dam | GBNLS |
| 10 Apr. [1841] To | Philadelphia | ALS 4p+Env | GBNLS |
| 17 Apr. [1841] To | Philadelphia | ALS 1p+Env | GBNLS |
| 24 Mar. 1843 To | Philadelphia | ALS 4p JL~ | GBNLS |
| 8 Oct. 1844? Fr | ? | Lbk 1p | GBNLS |
| 10 Oct. 1844 Fr | Edinburgh | Lbk 3p | GBNLS |
| 2 Mar. 1846 To | Philadelphia | ALS 4p+Env JL~ | GBNLS |
| 26 Apr. 1847 To | Philadelphia | ALS 4p~ | GBNLS |
| 28 Oct. 1847 Fr | Edinburgh | Lbk 2p Inc, Dam | GBNLS |
| 10 Sept. 1848 To | Philadelphia | ALS 4p JL~ | GBNLS |
| 19 Oct. 1848 Fr | Edinburgh | ALS 3p+Env JL | NPV |
| 28 May 1850 To | Philadelphia | ALS 2p JL | GBNLS |
| [24?] Nov. 1850 Fr | Edinburgh | Lbk 4p | GBNLS |
| 27 Mar. [1851] To | Philadelphia | ALS 8p | GBNLS |

| Name and Date | Location | Document Type and Length | Source |
|---|---|---|---|
| 21 May 1852 To | Philadelphia | ALS 8p~ | GBNLS |
| 21 Aug. 1852 To | New York City | ALS 4p JL | GBNLS |
| 22 Oct. 1852 Fr | Edinburgh | ALS 4p | PSCHi-Mott |
| 15 Nov. 1852 Fr | Edinburgh | Lbk 4p | GBNLS |
| 22 Apr. 1853 To | Philadelphia | ALS 3p Dam | GBNLS |
| 25 May 1855 To | Philadelphia | ALS 4p JL~ | GBNLS |
| [5 Nov. 1856] To | [Philadelphia] | ALS 2p JL | GBNLS |
| Corbit, Sarah | | | |
| 28 Apr. 1851 To | [Philadelphia] | ALS 1p | PSCHi-Mott |
| Daggett, J. G., Jr. | | | |
| 16 Nov. 1868 Fr | Boston | ALS 1p | MNS |
| Dall, Caroline Healey | | | |
| 9 Aug. 1867 To | Suffern, N.Y. | ALS 4p~ | MHi-Dall |
| 5 Mar. 1877 To | Roadside | ALS 2p~ | InFwL |
| Darlington, Hannah M. | | | |
| 7 Feb. 1852 To | Philadelphia | ALS 3p+Env | PSCHi-Mott |
| 11 Jan. 1853 To | Philadelphia | ALS 1p~ | MNHi |
| 13 Jan. 1853 To | Philadelphia | ALS 3p~ | MNHi |
| Davis, Edward M. | | | |
| 18 June 1838 To | Philadelphia | ALS 2p+Env~ | MH-H |
| 10 Oct. 1849 Fr | [Philadelphia] | ALS 2p+Enc | MNS |
| 16 [May 1851] To | Philadelphia | ALS 2p | MNS |
| 7 Aug. 1855 To* | Philadelphia | AL 2p JL~ | PSCHi-Mott |
| 14 [Apr. 1865] To* | Roadside | AL 2p JL | MNS |
| 6 July 1865 To** | Brooklyn, N.Y. | AL 2p JL | PSCHi-Mott |
| 28 Feb. 1866 Fr | Philadelphia | ALS 2p | MNS |
| 24 June 1870 To | Roadside | ALS 2p | PSCHi-Mott |
| 25 June 1870 To | Roadside | ALS 1p | PSCHi-Mott |
| 13 Feb. 1873 Fr | [Philadelphia?] | ALS 1p | MNS |
| Davis, Maria Mott | | | |
| 27 Mar. 1850 To | [Philadelphia] | ALS 1p+Env PS | MH-H |
| 7 Aug. 1855 To* | Philadelphia | AL 2p JL~# | PSCHi-Mott |
| 10 Aug. [1856] Fr | Oak Farm | AL 1p JL | MNS |
| 14 Dec. 1857 To* | Philadelphia | ALS 4p JL | MNS |
| 23 Aug. 1860 To | Roadside | AL 4p | PSCHi-Mott |
| 11 [Sept. 1860] To* | [Roadside] | AL 3p+TTR | MNS |
| 4 Nov. 1862 To | New York City | AL 4p | PSCHi-Mott |
| 5 Nov. 1862 To | Philadelphia | AL 3p | PSCHi-Mott |
| 20 Nov. 1862 To* | Roadside | ALS 4p JL | PSCHi-Mott |
| 27 Aug. 1864 To** | Roadside | ALS 2p JL | PSCHi-Mott |
| 17 Jan. 1865 To | Roadside | AL 4p JL~ | PSCHi-Mott |
| 14 [Apr. 1865] To* | Roadside | AL 2p JL | MNS |
| 8 July 1866 To* | Roadside | AL 4p | MNS |
| 18 July 1866 To* | Philadelphia | ALS 4p JL | MNS |
| 23 July 1866 To | Roadside | AL 4p | PSCHi-Mott |
| 24 July 1866 To | Roadside | AL 3p | PSCHi-Mott |
| 31 July 1866 To** | Roadside | AL 7p Inc? | PSCHi-Mott |
| [c. 1866] Fr | [Philadelphia?] | ALS 2p Inc | MNS |
| [Nov. 1869?] Fr | [Philadelphia] | ALS 1p | PSCHi-Mott |
| 29 June 1870 To | Orange, N.J. | AL 3p | PSCHi-Mott |
| 30 June 1870 To | Orange, N.J. | AL 1p | PSCHi-Mott |

| Name and Date | Location | Document Type and Length | Source |
|---|---|---|---|
| 5 Sept.[1871?] Fr | Roadside | AL 2p | MNS |
| 28 May [1873] Fr | Roadside | ALS 2p | MNS |
| [pre–13 Sept. 1876] Fr | Roadside Annex | ALS 2p | MNS |
| Davis, Paulina Wright | | | |
| 12 Feb. 1871 To | Roadside | AL 1p | NPV |
| 7 Apr. 1871 To | Roadside | ALS 1p~ | NPV |
| Davis, Thomas W. | | | |
| 29 Mar. 1879 Fr | Philadelphia | ALS 1p | PSCHi-Mott |
| Dugdale, Joseph A. | | | |
| 19 Mar. 1848 To | Philadelphia | C 3p JL | InEar |
| 28 Mar. 1849 To | Philadelphia | AL 4p JL~ | PSCHi-Mott |
| 12 July 1850 To | Auburn, N.Y. | ALS 4p JL~ | PSCHi-Mott |
| [pre–29 Mar. 1870] Fr | Mt. Pleasant, Ia. | ALS 1p | PSCHi-Mott |
| Dugdale, Ruth | | | |
| 19 Mar. 1848 To | Philadelphia | C 3p JL | InEar |
| 28 Mar. 1849 To | Philadelphia | AL 4p JL~ | PSCHi-Mott |
| 12 July 1850 To | Auburn, N.Y. | ALS 4p JL~ | PSCHi-Mott |
| Dugdale, Sarah | | | |
| 7 Oct. 1845 To | Philadelphia | ALS 3p+Env~ | PSCHi-Mott |
| Earle, Mary Hussey | | | |
| 9 Oct. 1856 To | Roadside | ALS 6p JL | PSCHi-Mott |
| 16 Sept. 1858 To | [Roadside] | PL 1p | Hallowell |
| 19 Nov. 1860 Fr | Buckdell? | ALS 4p | MNS |
| 28 Dec. 1860 To* | Roadside | AL 4p JL | PSCHi-Mott |
| 30 Dec. 1860 To* | Roadside | AL 1p JL | PSCHi-Mott |
| 14 May 1862 Fr | Nantucket, Mass. | ALS 8p | MNS |
| 11 Jan. 1863 To** | Philadelphia | AL 2p Inc? | PSCHi-Mott |
| 20 Feb. 1863 To* | Roadside | AL 4p~# | PSCHi-Mott |
| 22 Feb. 1863 To* | Roadside | AL 1p~# | PSCHi-Mott |
| 27 Apr. 1863 To | New York City | AL 4p | PSCHi-Mott |
| 1 Aug. 1863 To | Roadside | AL 4p | PSCHi-Mott |
| 19 July 1864 To | Roadside | AL 4p | PSCHi-Mott |
| 26 Apr. 1865 To | Roadside | ALS 4p | PSCHi-Mott |
| [pre–1867] Fr | Germantown | ALS 3p | MNS |
| 25 Jan. 1868 To | Brooklyn, N.Y. | AL 3p | PSCHi-Mott |
| 11 Aug. 1868 To | Roadside | ALS 1p+Env | PSCHi-Mott |
| 23 Jan. 1869 Fr | Germantown | ALS 1p | MNS |
| 13 Feb. [1870?] To | Roadside | ALS 1p | NPV |
| 19 Feb. 1872 Fr | Germantown | ALS 1p | MNS |
| 27 Sept. 1872 Fr | [Germantown?] | ALS 1p | MNS |
| 5 Apr. 1875 Fr | Germantown | ALS 2p | MNS |
| Edwards, George H. | | | |
| 3 Jan. 1879 Fr | Philadelphia | PL 1p JL | Hallowell |
| Emerson, Ralph Waldo | | | |
| 25 Nov. 1852 To | Philadelphia | LS 3p JL | MH-H |
| Equal Rights Advocates | | | |
| [pre–12 May 1869] To | [New York City] | PL 1p JL | *HWS* |
| Equal Rights Association | | | |
| [pre–14 May 1868] To | [Roadside] | ALS 1p JL~ | DLC-NAWSA |
| [pre–12 May 1869] To | New York City | PL 1p JL | PSCHi-Mott |

| Name and Date | Location | Document Type and Length | Source |
|---|---|---|---|
| Equal Rights Convention, Albany | | | |
| 18 Nov. 1866 To | [Roadside?] | ALS 2p JL~ | CSmH |
| Equal Rights Party | | | |
| 11 June 1872 Fr | New York City | LS 1p JL | PSCHi-Mott |
| Equal Rights Party, Central Committee | | | |
| 18 May 1872 Fr | New York City | AL 2p JL | PSCHi-Mott |
| Farrington, C. L. | | | |
| 8 Dec. 1871 Fr | Healyoke? | ALS 1p | PSCHi-Mott |
| Fellow Abolitionists | | | |
| [Dec. 1869] To | [Philadelphia] | PLS 1p JL~ | PSCHi-Mott |
| Fisher, Elizabeth Rodman | | | |
| 24 Jan. 1870 To | Roadside | ALS 1p | PHi-Soc |
| Fisher, William L. | | | |
| 25 Nov. 1858 To | Roadside | ALS 4p | PHi-Soc |
| Fisher, W. L. | | | |
| [Oct. 1857?] Fr | [Philadelphia?] | ANS 1p | MNS |
| Foster, Abigail Kelley | | | |
| 18 Mar. 1839 To | Philadelphia | ALS 3p+Env~ | MWA |
| Fowler, Henry | | | |
| 11 May 1868 Fr | Auburn, N.Y. | ALS 3p | PSCHi-Mott |
| Fracker, A. H. | | | |
| 3 Jan. 1879 Fr | Philadelphia | PL 1p JL | Hallowell |
| Free Produce Association | | | |
| 20 Oct. 1840 To | Philadelphia | PL 1p JL | *PFrm* |
| Free Religious Association Members | | | |
| [pre–22 Aug. 1879] To | [New York City?] | PL 2p JL | PSCHi-Mott |
| A Friend | | | |
| 4 Apr. 1843 To | Philadelphia | PL 1p | Hallowell |
| [1872] To | [Roadside?] | PL 2p | Hallowell |
| Friends and Friendly People | | | |
| [pre–24 Jan. 1873] To | [Philadelphia] | PL 1p JL | PSCHi-Mott |
| Friends of Equal Rights | | | |
| [15 Apr. 1852] To | [Philadelphia] | PL 1p JL | *PFrm* |
| Friends of Freedom | | | |
| [c. 2 Nov. 1867] To | [Philadelphia] | PL 1p JL | *NASS* |
| Friends of Philadelphia | | | |
| 6 Nov. 1863 Fr | Philadelphia | PL 1p JL | PSCHi-Mott |
| Friends of the AERA | | | |
| 12 Mar. 1867 To | New York City | PL 1p JL~ | DLC-NAWSA |
| Frothingham, Octavius B. | | | |
| 20 May 1867 To | Roadside | ALS 2p~ | CULA |
| 22 May [1874] To | Roadside | PL 2p~ | Hallowell |
| Gage, Frances D. | | | |
| 9 July 1852 Fr | Mt. Airy | ALS 4p | PSCHi-Mott |
| Gardner, Eunice | | | |
| 19 June 1833 To | Nantucket, Mass. | ALS 3p+env | MWA |
| Gardner, Phebe Hussey | | | |
| 26 Mar. 1852 To | Philadelphia | ALS 2p+TR | MNS |
| [c. 21 Apr. 1855] To** | [Philadelphia] | AL 2p | MNS |
| 9 Oct. 1856 To | Roadside | ALS 6p JL | PSCHi-Mott |
| 28 Dec. 1860 To* | Roadside | AL 4p JL | PSCHi-Mott |
| 30 Dec. 1860 To* | Roadside | AL 1p JL | PSCHi-Mott |

| Name and Date | Location | Document Type and Length | Source |
|---|---|---|---|
| **Garrison, Ellen Wright** | | | |
| [pre–10 Apr. 1861] To | [Roadside] | C 1p+Env~ | MNS |
| 10 July 1864* Fr | [Auburn, N.Y.] | ALS 1p JL | MNS |
| 1 Jan. 1867* To | Roadside | ALS 4p JL | PSCHi-Mott |
| **Garrison, Francis Jackson** | | | |
| 1 May 1862 To | Roadside | ALS 1p+Env | TxU |
| **Garrison, Helen Benson** | | | |
| 11 Sept. 1851 To | Philadelphia | ALS 2p JL~ | MB |
| 31 Aug. 1852 To | Auburn, N.Y. | ALS 3p JL XC~ | PSCHi-Mott |
| **Garrison, Lucy McKim** | | | |
| [6 July 1874] Fr | [Llewelln Park, N.J.] | ALS 2p JL | MNS |
| **Garrison, William Lloyd** | | | |
| 28 Apr. 1840 Fr | Boston | ALS 4p+Env | PSCHi-Mott |
| 8 May 1845 Fr | ? | C 1p Extr+PL | MH-H |
| 10 Jan. 1848 Fr | Boston | PL 1p | Hallowell |
| 11 Sept. 1851 To | Philadelphia | ALS 2p JL~ | MB |
| 31 Aug. 1852 To | Auburn, N.Y. | ALS 3p JL XC~ | PSCHi-Mott |
| 12 Sept. 1865 Fr | Boston | ALS 3p | PChHi-Mott |
| 8 Apr. 1867 Fr | Roxbury, Mass. | ALS 4p# | PSCHi-Mott |
| [30 Jan. 1868] Fr | [Roxbury, Mass.?] | PL 2p | Hallowell |
| 8 Mar. 1870 To | Roadside | ALS 4p~ | MB |
| 1 Sept. 1871 To | Orange, N.J. | ALS 3p | MNS |
| 25 May 1875 To | Roadside | ALS 2p+Env TTR | PSCHi-Mott |
| **Garrison, William Lloyd, Jr.** | | | |
| 4 Mar. 1864 To | Roadside | ALS 3p~ | MNS |
| 4 Feb. 1867* To | Philadelphia | ALS 1p+TTR | MNS |
| **Gay, Elizabeth Neall** | | | |
| 9 July 1844 To | Auburn, N.Y. | ALS 3p | NNCB-Gay |
| [pre–29 May 1845?] To | [Philadelphia] | ALS 2p+Env | NNCB-Gay |
| 24 Dec. 1847 To | Philadelphia | ALS 3p+Env | NNCB-Gay |
| 18 Apr. 1848 To | Philadelphia | AL 2p | NNCB-Gay |
| 1 May 1848 To | Philadelphia | ALS 1p JL~ | NNCB-Gay |
| 27 Nov. 1850 To* | Philadelphia | ALS 4p JL | NNCB-Gay |
| 9 Oct. 1854 To | Philadelphia | ALS 2p~ | NNCB-Gay |
| 27 May 1856 To | Philadelphia | ALS 4p~ | NNCB-Gay |
| 7 May 1858 To | Roadside | ALS 6p~ | NNCB-Gay |
| 9 Dec. 1858 To | Roadside | ALS 3p~ | NNCB-Gay |
| 15 Mar. 1870 To | Roadside | ALS 3p | NNCB-Gay |
| 1 May 1870 To | Roadside | ALS 2p | NNCB-Gay |
| **Gay, Sydney H.** | | | |
| 1 May 1848 To | Philadelphia | ALS 1p JL~ | NNCB-Gay |
| 3 Dec. 1849 To | Philadelphia | ALS 3p~ | NNCB-Gay |
| 13 Apr. 1850 To | Philadelphia | ALS 4p~ | NNCB-Gay |
| 27 Nov. 1850 To* | Philadelphia | ALS 4p JL | NNCB-Gay |
| **Gibbons, James S.** | | | |
| 17 Feb. 1843 Fr | New York City | ALS 7p | MB |
| **Gibbons, Phebe Earle** | | | |
| [Sept. 1880?] To | [Roadside] | PL 2p | Hallowell |
| **Grant, Ulysses S.** | | | |
| 12 Nov. 1873 To | Philadelphia | LS 2p JL~ | OHi |
| 12 Nov. 1873 To | Philadelphia | LS 1p JL~ | IaDHi |

| Name and Date | Location | Document Type and Length | Source |
|---|---|---|---|
| Greene, L. M. | | | |
| [July 1873] Fr | ? | ALS 1p | PSCHi-Mott |
| Greene, Lydia | | | |
| 22 Nov. 1838 To | Philadelphia | ALS 3p+Env JL~ | MNS |
| Greene, Thomas | | | |
| 22 Nov. 1838 To | Philadelphia | ALS 3p+Env JL~ | MNS |
| Grew, Mary | | | |
| [post–26 Jan. 1868] Fr | [Philadelphia] | PL 1p | Hallowell |
| 3 Feb. 1868 Fr | Philadelphia | LS 3p JL | PSCHi-Mott |
| 24 Feb. 1871 To | Roadside | ALS 2p~ | NPV |
| 8 Sept. 1880 Fr | Whitefield, N.H. | ALS 2p | PSCHi-Mott |
| Griffing, Josephine Emma | | | |
| 26 June [1871] Fr | Washington, D.C. | ALS 1p | PSCHi-Mott |
| Griffing, Josephine S. | | | |
| 25 Dec. 1869 To | Roadside | ALS 2p~ | NNCB-Griff |
| 15 Apr. 1870 Fr | Washington, D.C. | PL 5p | *HWS* |
| 1 May 1870 To | Roadside | PL 1p | *HWS* |
| 17 May 1870 To | Roadside | ALS 2p~ | NNCB-Griff |
| Hale, W.? C.? | | | |
| 11 Mar. [1874] Fr | New York City | ALS 2p | MNS |
| Hallowell, Anna Davis | | | |
| 9 Aug. 1867 To* | Suffern N.Y. | AL 2p | PSCHi-Mott |
| 23 Aug. 1867 To | Roadside | AL 2p | PSCHi-Mott |
| 13 [Sept. 1876] To* | [Orange, N.J.] | ALS 2p~ | MNS |
| Hallowell, Edward N. | | | |
| 1 Feb. 1870 To | Roadside | ALS 4p+Env~ | Davis |
| 11 Feb. 1870 To | Roadside | ALS 1p+Env~ | Davis |
| Hallowell, Mary | | | |
| 9 Feb. 1876 Fr | Swarthmore | ALS 1p XC JL | PSCHi-Mott |
| Hallowell, Morris L. | | | |
| 18 Feb. 1872 Fr | Byberry | ALS 1p | PSCHi-Mott |
| ? To | ? | AGS 1p | PSCHi-Mott |
| Hallowell, S.? W. | | | |
| 6 Dec. 1870 Fr | [Philadelphia] | ALS 2p | PSCHi-Mott |
| Harris, George | | | |
| c. 1 Aug. 1840 Fr | Glasgow, Scot. | PL 1p JL | *3 Mos* |
| Haughton, James | | | |
| 10 Sept. 1848 To | Philadelphia | AL 4p JL# | MB |
| Haughton, Mrs. James | | | |
| 10 Sept. 1848 To | Philadelphia | AL 4p JL# | MB |
| Haydon, Benjamin Robert | | | |
| 20 June 1840 Fr | London | ALS 1p XC | PSCHi-Mott |
| Hayes, Lucy Webb | | | |
| 23 Oct. [c. 1878] To | [Philadelphia] | PL 2p JL | WHi |
| Heacock, Anne | | | |
| 2 Jan. 1863 To | Roadside | ALS 3p JL~ | PSCHi-Hea |
| 23 July 1863 To | Roadside | ALS 4p JL~ | PSCHi-Hea |
| 4 Aug. 1869 Fr | ? | ALS 1p Dam | PSCHi-Mott |
| Heacock, Jane | | | |
| 2 Jan. 1863 To | Roadside | ALS 3p JL~ | PSCHi-Hea |
| 23 July 1863 To | Roadside | ALS 4p JL~ | PSCHi-Hea |

| Name and Date | Location | Document Type and Length | Source |
|---|---|---|---|
| Hick, G. H. | | | |
| 24 June 1871 Fr | New York City | ALS 1p | PSCHi-Mott |
| Higginson, Thomas Wentworth | | | |
| 6 Apr. 1854 To | Philadelphia | ALS 4p~ | NPV |
| 27 May 1855 To | Philadelphia | ALS 2p | NPV |
| Hoffman, Emily Osborne | | | |
| ? Apr. 1878 To | [Roadside] | ALS 1p | Fuller |
| Hoffman, Miss H. N. | | | |
| 29 Aug. 1873 Fr | St. Paul, Minn. | ALS 2p JL | MNS |
| Holland, Frederic W. | | | |
| 18 Feb. 1843 To | Philadelphia | ALS 3p+Env# | DLC-Mott |
| Holmes, Julia Archibald | | | |
| 6 Oct. 1867 Fr | Washington, D.C. | ALS 12p | PSCHi-Mott |
| Hopper, Anna Mott | | | |
| 17 Oct. 1853 Fr* | Philadelphia | ALS 4p | MNS |
| 11 Nov. 1854 To | Succasunna, N.J. | ALS 3p+Env JL | MH-H |
| 12 Nov. 1854 To | Succasunna, N.J. | ALS 3p+Env JL | MH-H |
| 1 May [1855?] Fr | [Philadelphia] | ALS 2p+TTR | MNS |
| 27 June 1855 Fr | Philadelphia | ALS 4p | MNS |
| 9 [July 1856] Fr | Philadelphia | ALS 3p PS | MNS |
| 11 Aug. [1856] Fr | Oak Farm | ALS 1p JL | MNS |
| 16 Aug. [1856] Fr | Roadside | ALS 4p | MNS |
| [c. 1860] Fr | [Philadelphia] | ALS 2p | MNS |
| 9 July 1861 To* | Roadside | ALS 4p+TTR | MNS |
| [c. July 1866] Fr* | [Philadelphia?] | ALS 2p | MNS |
| 30 May [1867] To* | Medford, Mass. | ALS 2p JL~ | PSCHi-Mott |
| 12 July 1869 Fr* | Toledo, Ohio | ALS 4p | MNS |
| [c. Aug. 1869] Fr | [Philadelphia] | ALS 2p | NSyU-Osb |
| 27 June 1870 To | Orange, N.J. | ALS 2p | PSCHi-Mott |
| 5 July 1870 To | Orange, N.J. | ALS 2p | PSCHi-Mott |
| Hopper, Edward | | | |
| 11 Nov. 1854 To | Succasunna, N.J. | ALS 3p+Env JL | MH-H |
| 12 Nov. 1854 To | Succasunna, N.J. | ALS 3p+Env JL | MH-H |
| 11 Aug. 1856 Fr | Philadelphia | ALS 2p | MNS |
| Howitt, Mary | | | |
| post–5 Oct. [1848] Fr | Bangor, Wales | ALS 3p+Env | NPV |
| Howitt, William | | | |
| 27 June 1840 Fr | London | PL 4p | Hallowell |
| Hunt, Harriot | | | |
| 21 June 1860 To | Roadside | PL 1p | Lib |
| J____, M____ K____ | | | |
| 26 Feb. 1875 Fr | ? | C 1p | PSCHi-Mott |
| Jackson, Jane T.? | | | |
| 9 May 1864 Fr | West Grove | ALS 1p | PSCHi-Mott |
| Janney, Samuel M. | | | |
| [c. 1835] Fr* | ? | AL 3p | PSCHi-Jan |
| Johnson, Mary | | | |
| 17 Jan. 1842 To | Philadelphia | ALS 4p+Env JL | PSCHi-Mott |
| Johnson, Oliver | | | |
| 22 Oct. 1880 Fr | New York City | ALS 7p | PSCHi-Mott |
| ? Fr | [Philadelphia?] | ANS 2p Frag | PSCHi-Mott |

| Name and Date | Location | Document Type and Length | Source |
|---|---|---|---|
| Johnson, William | | | |
| 17 Jan. 1842 To | Philadelphia | ALS 4p+Env JL | PSCHi-Mott |
| Jones, Benjamin S.? | | | |
| 17 Nov. 1840 To | ? | AGS 1p | DLC-WASS |
| Julian, George W. | | | |
| 14 Nov. 1848 To | Philadelphia | C 6p~# | PSCHi-Mott |
| Keep, Charles D. | | | |
| 1 Apr. 1873 Fr | Hartford | ALS 1p | MNS |
| Keep, Howard N. | | | |
| 16 Dec. 1872 Fr | Hartford | ALS 1p | MNS |
| Kelley, Caroline Bonsall | | | |
| 16 July 1859 To | [Roadside?] | ALS 1p~ | NNCB-Kell |
| Ketcham, John | | | |
| 16 Mar. 1850 To | Philadelphia | ALS 3p+Env JL | PSCHi-Mott |
| 30 Aug. 1852 To | Auburn, N.Y. | ALS 4p JL~ | PSCHi-Mott |
| 31 Aug. 1852 To | Auburn, N.Y. | ALS 1p JL~ | PSCHi-Mott |
| Ketcham, Rebecca | | | |
| 16 Mar. 1850 To | Philadelphia | ALS 3p+Env JL | PSCHi-Mott |
| 30 Aug. 1852 To | Auburn, N.Y. | ALS 4p JL~ | PSCHi-Mott |
| 31 Aug. 1852 To | Auburn, N.Y. | ALS 1p JL~ | PSCHi-Mott |
| Kilgore, Damon Y. | | | |
| 26 Aug. 1867 Fr | Philadelphia | ALS 1p | MNS |
| Kimber, Abigail | | | |
| 3 Feb. 1868 Fr | Philadelphia | LS 3p JL | PSCHi-Mott |
| L____, C____ | | | |
| 21 May 1871 Fr | ? | C 1p | PSCHi-Mott |
| Labar, Richard E. | | | |
| 29 Aug. 1879 Fr | Philadelphia | ALS 2p | PSCHi-Mott |
| Laing, H. M. | | | |
| 21 Dec. 1871 Fr | Philadelphia | ALS 1p | PSCHi-Mott |
| 23 Dec. 1871 Fr | Philadelphia | ALS 1p | PSCHi-Mott |
| Leo, Andre | | | |
| 7 Sept. 1870 Fr | Paris | PL 2p JL | *HWS* |
| Lewis, Grace Anna | | | |
| 9 Aug. 1852 To | Philadelphia | ALS 2p | PSCHi-Mott |
| 31 July 1860 To | Roadside | ALS 4p | PSCHi-Mott |
| Lippincott, Aaron S. | | | |
| 8 Dec. 1840 To | Philadelphia | ALS 3p+Env~ | PSCHi-Mott |
| Lloyd, Mary L. | | | |
| 9 Sept. 1825 Fr | Wednesbury, Eng. | ALS 3p+Env | PSCHi-Mott |
| London Yearly Meeting | | | |
| [c. 14 Apr. 1830] To | Philadelphia | PL 4p JL~ | Comly |
| Lord, George W. | | | |
| 11 Nov. 1854 To | Succasunna, N.J. | ALS 3p+Env JL | MH-H |
| 12 Nov. 1854 To | Succasunna, N.J. | ALS 3p+Env JL | MH-H |
| 20 Oct. 1863 To* | Philadelphia | ALS 3p JL | PSCHi-Mott |
| 30 Oct. 1863 To* | Roadside | AL 4p JL | PSCHi-Mott |
| 8 Nov. 1863 To | Roadside | AL 3p JL | PSCHi-Mott |
| 10 Nov. 1863 To | Roadside | AL 1p JL | PSCHi-Mott |
| 26 Nov. [1863?] To* | Eddington | ALS 8p JL | PSCHi-Mott |
| 8 Aug. 1864 To | Philadelphia | ALS 4p | PSCHi-Mott |

| Name and Date | Location | Document Type and Length | Source |
|---|---|---|---|
| [13? Apr. 1865] Fr | [New York City?] | ALS 1p | MNS |
| 29 Aug. 1867 Fr* | Suffern, N.Y. | ALS 2p JL | MNS |
| 27 Mar. 1868 To | Roadside | AL 3p# | PSCHi-Mott |
| 21 May 1868 Fr | New York City | ALS 1p | PSCHi-Mott |
| 29 May 1868 Fr | New York City | ALS 2p | PSCHi-Mott |
| 9 June 1868 Fr | New York City | ALS 1p | PSCHi-Mott |
| 12 June 1868 Fr | New York City | ALS 1p | PSCHi-Mott |
| 14 June 1868 To | Roadside | ALS 4p JL | MNS |
| 15 June 1868 To | Roadside | ALS 5p JL | MNS |
| 13 Nov. 1869 To* | Philadelphia | AL 4p JL~ | MNS |
| 24 Nov. 1869 Fr | Orange, N.J. | ALS 1p | MNS |
| 21 Mar. 1871 To* | Roadside | ALS 4p+TTR JL | MNS |
| 23 Mar. 1871 To* | [Roadside] | ALS 2p+TTR JL | MNS |
| 24 Mar. 1871 To* | Roadside | ALS 1p JL | MNS |
| Lord, Martha Mott | | | |
| 27 Oct. 1853 Fr | Brooklyn, N.Y. | ALS 4p | MNS |
| 30 Jan. 1854 To | Philadelphia | AL 2p | PSCHi-Mott |
| 6 Aug. 1854 To | Philadelphia | AL 4p | PSCHi-Mott |
| 17 Sept. 1854 Fr | Succasunna, N.J. | ALS 4p | MNS |
| 21 Sept. 1854 To | Philadelphia | AL 2p | PSCHi-Mott |
| 27 Sept. 1854 To* | Philadelphia | AL 4p# | PSCHi-Mott |
| 29 Sept. 1854 To* | Philadelphia | AL 2p | PSCHi-Mott |
| [Sept. 1854] To* | [Philadelphia?] | ALS 2p Inc | PSCHi-Mott |
| 28 June [1855?] Fr | Philadelphia | AL 4p | MNS |
| 13 [Aug. 1855] To** | Philadelphia | AL 3p | PSCHi-Mott |
| 17 June 1856 Fr | Roadside | ALS 4p | MNS |
| 6 July 1856 Fr | Roadside | ALS 4p | MNS |
| 8 July 1856 Fr | Roadside | AL 2p | MNS |
| [26 Aug. 1856] To** | [Gloucester, Mass.] | AL 1p | MNS |
| 14 Dec. 1857 To* | Philadelphia | ALS 4p JL | MNS |
| [1857] To* | [Roadside?] | ALS 2p Inc | MNS |
| [Jan. 1858] To** | Philadelphia | PL 1p | Hallowell |
| 10 Aug. [1860?] Fr | Roadside | ALS 4p | MNS |
| 20 Oct. 1863 To* | Philadelphia | ALS 3p JL | PSCHi-Mott |
| 22 Oct. 1863 To* | Roadside | ALS 4p | PSCHi-Mott |
| 23 Oct. 1863 To* | Roadside | ALS 4p | PSCHi-Mott |
| 24 Oct. 1863 To* | Philadelphia | ALS 1p | PSCHi-Mott |
| 29 Oct. 1863 To* | Roadside | ALS 4p | PSCHi-Mott |
| 30 Oct. 1863 To* | Roadside | AL 4p JL | PSCHi-Mott |
| 1 Nov. 1863 To* | Roadside | ALS 6p JL | PSCHi-Mott |
| 5 Nov. 1863 To* | Roadside | AL 2p Inc | PSCHi-Mott |
| 8 Nov. 1863 To* | Roadside | AL 3p JL | PSCHi-Mott |
| [pre–8 Nov. 1863] To | [Roadside?] | ALS 2p Inc | PSCHi-Mott |
| 10 Nov. 1863 To* | Roadside | AL 1p JL | PSCHi-Mott |
| 10 Nov. 1863 To* | Roadside | AL 2p Inc | PSCHi-Mott |
| 24 Nov. 1863 To* | Roadside | ALS 4p JL | PSCHi-Mott |
| 26 Nov. [1863] To* | Eddington | ALS 8p JL | PSCHi-Mott |
| 15 Dec. 1863 To* | Roadside | AL 4p | PSCHi-Mott |
| [c. 1863] To | Philadelphia | ALS 2p | NSyU-Osb |
| 14 Jan. 1864 To* | Roadside | AL 4p | PSCHi-Mott |
| 21 Jan. 1864 To | Roadside | ALS 1p JL~ | PSCHi-Mott |

| Name and Date | Location | Document Type and Length | Source |
|---|---|---|---|
| 24 Jan. 1864 To | Roadside | ALS 1p JL~ | PSCHi-Mott |
| 25 Jan. 1864 To | Philadelphia | ALS 3p JL~ | PSCHi-Mott |
| 5 Feb. 1864 To* | Roadside | AL 4p~ | PSCHi-Mott |
| [post–4 Mar. 1864] To* | [Roadside?] | C 1p Extr | MNS |
| 18 Mar. 1864 To | Roadside | ALS 4p | NSyU-Osb |
| 28 Mar. 1864 To | Philadelphia | ALS 4p | NSyU-Osb |
| 22 Apr. 1864 To* | Roadside | AL 7p | PSCHi-Mott |
| 23 Apr. 1864 To* | Roadside | AL 2p | PSCHi-Mott |
| 2 June 1864 To* | Roadside | AL 1p Inc | PSCHi-Mott |
| 3 June 1864 To* | Roadside | AL 6p Inc | PSCHi-Mott |
| 4 June 1864 To* | Roadside | AL 7p Inc | PSCHi-Mott |
| [5 June 1864] To* | [Roadside?] | AL 2p Inc | PSCHi-Mott |
| 21 June 1864 To* | Roadside | AL 2p Inc | PSCHi-Mott |
| 23 June 1864 To* | Roadside | AL 1p Inc | PSCHi-Mott |
| 3 July 1864 To* | Roadside | AL 3p | PSCHi-Mott |
| 4 July 1864 To* | Roadside | AL 7p | PSCHi-Mott |
| 5 July 1864 To* | Roadside | AL 1p | PSCHi-Mott |
| 17 July 1864 To* | Roadside | AL 3p | PSCHi-Mott |
| 18 July 1864 To* | Roadside | AL 2p | PSCHi-Mott |
| 6 Aug. [1864?] Fr | Brooklyn, N.Y. | ALS 4p | MNS |
| [c. 20 Aug. 1864] To* | [Roadside] | ALS 2p Inc | PSCHi-Mott |
| 23 Aug. 1864 To* | Roadside | AL 3p Dam | PSCHi-Mott |
| 24 Aug. 1864 To* | Roadside | AL 1p Dam | PSCHi-Mott |
| 27 Aug. 1864 To | Roadside | ALS 2p JL | PSCHi-Mott |
| 31[Aug.] 1864 To* | Philadelphia | ALS 2p | PSCHi-Mott |
| 21 Oct. 1864 To* | Roadside | ALS 3p | PSCHi-Mott |
| 22 Oct. 1864 To* | Roadside | ALS 4p | PSCHi-Mott |
| [c. Oct. 1864] To* | [Roadside?] | ALS 2p Inc | MNS |
| [28? Nov. 1864] To* | [Roadside?] | AL 1p Inc | PSCHi-Mott |
| 29 [Nov. 1864] To* | [Roadside?] | AL 1p Inc | PSCHi-Mott |
| [c. Nov. 1864] To* | [Roadside?] | AL 2p Inc | MNS |
| 4 Dec. 1864 To* | Roadside | ALS 2p | PSCHi-Mott |
| 5 Dec. 1864 To* | Roadside | ALS 3p | PSCHi-Mott |
| [c. 20 Dec. 1864] To* | [Roadside] | ALS 3p Inc PS | PSCHi-Mott |
| 26 Dec. 1864 To* | Roadside | ALS 4p | PSCHi-Mott |
| [Feb. 1865] To | [Roadside] | AL 2p | MNS |
| 27 [Mar. 1865] To* | [Roadside] | AL 2p | MNS |
| 14 Apr. 1865 To | Philadelphia | ALS 6p | NSyU-Osb |
| 28 Apr. 1865 To* | Roadside | ALS 4p | PSCHi-Mott |
| 2 May 1865 To* | Roadside | ALS 4p~ | PSCHi-Mott |
| 28 May 1865 To* | Roadside | ALS 1p PS | PSCHi-Mott |
| 11 June 1865 To | Roadside | ALS 3p | PSCHi-Mott |
| 17 June 1865 To | Roadside | AL 4p | PSCHi-Mott |
| 9 July 1865 To | Roadside | AL 2p | PSCHi-Mott |
| 10 July 1865 To | Roadside | AL 2p | PSCHi-Mott |
| 12 July 1865 To | Philadelphia | ALS 2p | PSCHi-Mott |
| 18 July 1865 To* | Roadside | AL 2p | PSCHi-Mott |
| 20 July 1865 To | Roadside | ALS 4p | PSCHi-Mott |
| 22 July 1865 To | Roadside | ALS 4p | PSCHi-Mott |
| 24 July 1865 To | Roadside | ALS 4p | PSCHi-Mott |
| 28 Sept. 1865 To* | Roadside | ALS 4p | MNS |

| Name and Date | Location | Document Type and Length | Source |
|---|---|---|---|
| 5 Oct. 1865 To | Roadside | ALS 2p | PSCHi-Mott |
| 15 Oct. 1865 To* | Roadside | AL 4p+TR | MNS |
| 15 [Oct. 1865] To* | [Roadside?] | AL 2p | MNS |
| 2 Nov. 1865 To* | Philadelphia | ALS 6p JL~ | MNS |
| 7 Nov. 1865 To* | Philadelphia | ALS 4p | MNS |
| 16 Nov. 1865 To* | Roadside | AL 4p | MNS |
| 23 Nov. 1865 To* | Roadside | AL 4p | MNS |
| 24 Dec. 1865 To* | [Roadside?] | ALS 2p Inc | MNS |
| [post–24 Dec. 1865] To* | [Roadside?] | AL 2p# | MNS |
| 14 Jan. [1866?] Fr | Brooklyn, N.Y. | AL 4p Inc | MNS |
| 24 Jan. 1866 To | Philadelphia | AL 4p | PSCHi-Mott |
| 31 Jan. 1866 To | Philadelphia | AL 3p | PSCHi-Mott |
| 1 Feb. 1866 To | Philadelphia | AL 1p | PSCHi-Mott |
| 4 Feb. 1866 To* | Roadside | AL 4p+TR JL | MNS |
| 5 Feb. 1866 To* | Roadside | AL 1p JL | MNS |
| 12 Mar. 1866 To | Roadside | AL 6p | PSCHi-Mott |
| 19 Mar. 1866 To* | Roadside | ALS 4p+TR JL | MNS |
| 26 Mar. 1866 To* | Roadside | ALS 2p | PSCHi-Mott |
| 5 Apr. 1866 To** | Roadside | AL 2p | PSCHi-Mott |
| 22 Apr. 1866 To | Roadside | AL 6p | PSCHi-Mott |
| 30 Apr. 1866 To | Roadside | AL 4p | PSCHi-Mott |
| 3 May 1866 To* | Roadside | AL 6p | MNS |
| 28 May 1866 To | Roadside | AL 4p | PSCHi-Mott |
| 3 June 1866 To | Roadside | AL 2p | PSCHi-Mott |
| [8 June 1866] To | [Roadside] | AL 2p Inc | MNS |
| 8 June 1866 To* | Roadside | AL 4p | PSCHi-Mott |
| [c. 10 June 1866] To* | [Roadside?] | ALS 2p Inc | PSCHi-Mott |
| 28 June 1866 To | Roadside | AL 4p | PSCHi-Mott |
| 9 July 1866 To | Roadside | ALS 3p | PSCHi-Mott |
| 11 July 1866 To* | Philadelphia | ALS 2p | MNS |
| 17 July 1866 To | Roadside | AL 3p | PSCHi-Mott |
| 18 July 1866 To* | Philadelphia | ALS 4p JL | MNS |
| 20 July 1866 To | Roadside | AL 2p | PSCHi-Mott |
| 21 July 1866 To | Roadside | AL 1p | PSCHi-Mott |
| 14 Aug. 1866 To | Roadside | AL 4p JL | PSCHi-Mott |
| 24 Aug. 1866 To | [Newburgh, N.Y.] | ALS 4p JL | PSCHi-Mott |
| 23 Sept. 1866 To | Philadelphia | AL 4p JL | PSCHi-Mott |
| 24 Sept. 1866 To | Philadelphia | ALS 2p JL | PSCHi-Mott |
| 28 Oct. 1866 To* | Roadside | ALS 2p JL | MNS |
| 29 Oct. 1866 To* | Roadside | ALS 5p JL | MNS |
| [post–3 Dec. 1866] To* | [Roadside?] | AL 4p | MNS |
| [c. 15 Dec. 1866] To** | [Roadside?] | ALS 2p Inc | MNS |
| 18 Dec. [1866] To* | [Roadside] | ALS 1p | MNS |
| 18 Dec. 1866 To* | Philadelphia | ALS 6p | MNS |
| 19 Dec. [1866] To | [Roadside] | ALS 2p | MNS |
| 10 Jan. 1867 To* | Philadelphia | AL 4p | MNS |
| [pre–23 Jan. 1867] Fr | Brooklyn, N.Y. | ALS 1p Inc | MNS |
| [post–12 Mar. 1867] To* | [Roadside] | ALS 2p Inc | PSCHi-Mott |
| 21 Apr. [1867] To | Roadside | ALS 3p | PSCHi-Mott |
| 22 Apr. [1867] To | Roadside | ALS 1p | PSCHi-Mott |
| 28 Apr. 1867 To* | Roadside | AL 4p+TTR JL | MNS |

| Name and Date | Location | Document Type and Length | Source |
|---|---|---|---|
| 12 May [1867] To** | Roadside | AL 2p | PSCHi-Mott |
| 27 June 1867 To* | Roadside | AL 3p Inc JL | MNS |
| 28 June 1867 To* | Roadside | AL 1p Inc JL | MNS |
| 27 Aug. 1867 To** | Roadside | AL 4p Dam JL | PSCHi-Mott |
| 29 Aug. 1867 Fr | Suffern, N.Y. | ALS 2p JL | MNS |
| 2 Sept. 1867 To* | Roadside | ALS 4p | MNS |
| 3 Sept. 1867 Fr | Suffern, N.Y. | ALS 4p | MNS |
| 13 Sept. 1867 To | Roadside | ALS 4p | PSCHi-Mott |
| 11 Oct. 1867 To* | Roadside | AL 2p | PHC |
| 17 Oct. [1867] Fr | Brooklyn, N.Y. | ALS 7p | MNS |
| [pre–1867] To** | [Roadside] | PL 1p | Hallowell |
| 5 Mar. 1868 To | Roadside | ALS 2p | PSCHi-Mott |
| 26 Mar. 1868 To | Roadside | PL 1p | Hallowell |
| 27 Mar. 1868 To | Roadside | ALS 2p | PSCHi-Mott |
| 29 Mar. 1868 To | Roadside | ALS 2p | PSCHi-Mott |
| 30 Mar. 1868 To | Roadside | ALS 1p | PSCHi-Mott |
| 3 Apr. 1868 To | Roadside | AL 5p~ | PSCHi-Mott |
| 2 [June 1868?] To* | [Roadside] | AL 1p Inc | PSCHi-Mott |
| 11 June 1868 To | Roadside | AL 2p | PSCHi-Mott |
| 14 June 1868 To* | Roadside | ALS 4p JL | MNS |
| 15 June 1868 To* | Roadside | ALS 5p JL | MNS |
| 16 June 1868 To | Roadside | ALS 4p | PSCHi-Mott |
| 26 June 1868 To* | Roadside | AL 2p# | MNS |
| 1 July 1868 To | Mt. Holly, N.J. | AL 7p JL | PSCHi-Mott |
| 6 July 1868 To* | Roadside | AL 1p | PSCHi-Mott |
| 7 July 1868 To* | Roadside | AL 2p# | PSCHi-Mott |
| 4 Nov. 1868 To* | Roadside | ALS 5p JL | MNS |
| 5 Nov. 1868 To* | Roadside | ALS 2p JL | MNS |
| 16 Nov. 1868 To | Roadside | ALS 4p | PSCHi-Mott |
| [? Jan. 1869?] To* | [Roadside?] | ALS 2p Inc | PSCHi-Mott |
| 23 Apr. 1869 To | Philadelphia | AL 4p | PSCHi-Mott |
| 5 May 1869 To* | Roadside | AL 4p | PSCHi-Mott |
| 25 May [1869] Fr | Orange, N.J. | ALS 3p | MNS |
| 28 May 1869 To | Philadelphia | AL 2p | PSCHi-Mott |
| 13 June 1869 To* | Roadside | AL 4p | MNS |
| 14 June 1869 To* | Roadside | AL 1p | MNS |
| 20 June 1869 To* | Roadside | ALS 4p | MNS |
| [21? June 1869] To* | [Roadside] | AL 2p | MNS |
| 23 June 1869 To* | Roadside | ALS 6p JL | PSCHi-Mott |
| 16 July 1869 To | Roadside | ALS 4p | PSCHi-Mott |
| 22 July 1869 To* | Roadside | ALS 3p | MNS |
| 13 Aug. 1869 To | Roadside | AL 2p | PSCHi-Mott |
| 23 Aug. 1869 To | Roadside | ALS 4p | PSCHi-Mott |
| 2 Sept. 1869 To | Roadside | ALS 4p | PSCHi-Mott |
| 12 Sept. 1869 To | Roadside | AL 4p | PSCHi-Mott |
| [c. 5 Oct. 1869] To* | [Roadside?] | ALS 1p Inc | MNS |
| 8 Oct. 1869 To* | Philadelphia | ALS 2p | MNS |
| [c. Oct. 1869] To** | [Roadside?] | ALS 1p | MNS |
| 13 Nov. 1869 To* | Philadelphia | AL 4p JL~ | MNS |
| 21 Nov. 1869 To* | Roadside | ALS 1p | MNS |
| 23 Nov. 1869 To* | Philadelphia | ALS 3p | MNS |

| Name and Date | Location | Document Type and Length | Source |
|---|---|---|---|
| [c. Nov. 1869] To* | [Roadside?] | ALS 2p Inc | PSCHi-Mott |
| 22 Dec. [1869?] Fr* | Orange, N.J. | ALS 4p | MNS |
| 31 Dec. 1869 To | Roadside | AL 4p | PSCHi-Mott |
| [c. Jan. 1870] To** | [Roadside?] | AL 1p Inc | MNS |
| 2 Feb. 1870 To* | Philadelphia | AL 2p | MNS |
| 3 Feb. 1870 To* | Philadelphia | ALS 2p JL | MNS |
| 4 Feb. [1870] To* | Philadelphia | ALS 2p JL | MNS |
| 29 Mar. 1870 To | Roadside | ALS 4p | PSCHi-Mott |
| 12 May 1870 To | Philadelphia | AL 2p | PSCHi-Mott |
| 17 May 1870 To | Roadside | AL 4p JL | PSCHi-Mott |
| 4 June 1870 To* | Philadelphia | ALS 2p JL | PSCHi-Mott |
| 20 June 1870 To* | Roadside | AL 4p JL | PSCHi-Mott |
| 21 June 1870 To* | Roadside | AL 1p JL | PSCHi-Mott |
| 8 Oct. 1870 To | Roadside | ALS 4p | PSCHi-Mott |
| 15 Oct. 1870 To | Roadside | AL 2p | PSCHi-Mott |
| 19 Dec. 1870 To* | Roadside | AL 4p | PSCHi-Mott |
| 20 Dec. 1870 To* | Roadside | AL 1p | PSCHi-Mott |
| [c. 1870] To** | [Roadside?] | AL 2p | MNS |
| 9 Jan. 1871 To | Roadside | AL 2p | PSCHi-Mott |
| 16 Jan. 1871 To | Roadside | AL 4p | PSCHi-Mott |
| 20 Jan. 1871 To | Roadside | AL 4p | PSCHi-Mott |
| 22 Jan. 1871 To | Roadside | AL 4p~ | PSCHi-Mott |
| 21 Mar. 1871 To* | Roadside | ALS 4p+TTR JL | MNS |
| 23 Mar. 1871 To* | [Roadside] | ALS 3p+TTR JL | MNS |
| 24 Mar. 1871 To* | Roadside | ALS 2p+TTR JL | MNS |
| 6 Apr. 1871 To | Roadside | ALS 4p# | PSCHi-Mott |
| 18 May 1871 To | Roadside | ALS 4p | PSCHi-Mott |
| 22 May 1871 To* | Roadside | AL 4p | PSCHi-Mott |
| 14 July 1871 To | Roadside | AL 3p Inc | PSCHi-Mott |
| 1 Aug. 1871 To | Roadside | AL 3p | PSCHi-Mott |
| 4 Aug. 1871 To | Roadside | ALS 4p | PSCHi-Mott |
| 20 Sept. 1871 To* | Roadside | AL 4p | PSCHi-Mott |
| 27 Sept. 1871 To | Philadelphia | AL 2p | PSCHi-Mott |
| [c. Sept. 1871] To* | [Roadside?] | AL 2p Inc | PSCHi-Mott |
| 24 Nov. 1871 To | Philadelphia | ALS 4p | PSCHi-Mott |
| 2 Dec. 1871 To | Roadside | ALS 8p JL | PSCHi-Mott |
| 15 Dec. 1871 To | Roadside | AL 4p | PSCHi-Mott |
| 23 Dec. 1871 To | Roadside | AL 4p | PSCHi-Mott |
| 29 Dec. 1871 To | Philadelphia | ALS 2p~ | PSCHi-Mott |
| 2 Feb. [1872?] To | Roadside | AL 3p | PSCHi-Mott |
| 12 Mar. 1872 To* | Roadside | ALS 1p JL | PSCHi-Mott |
| 13 Mar. 1872 To* | Roadside | ALS 3p JL | PSCHi-Mott |
| 14 June 1872 To | Roadside | ALS 4p | PSCHi-Mott |
| 4 Aug. 1872 To* | Philadelphia | ALS 2p | MNS |
| 12 [Aug. 1872] To | [Roadside?] | AL 4p | PSCHi-Mott |
| [pre–26 Aug. 1872] Fr** | [Orange, N.J.?] | ALS 3p Inc | MNS |
| 6 Sept. 1872 To* | Roadside | AL 2p | MNS |
| 14 [Sept. 1872] To* | [Roadside?] | AL 1p Inc? | MNS |
| 16 [Sept. 1872] To* | [Roadside?] | AL 2p Inc? | MNS |
| [post–16 Sept. 1872] To* | [Roadside?] | ALS 2p Inc TTR | MNS |
| [c. Sept. 1872] To** | [Roadside?] | AL 4p Inc? TTR | MNS |

| Name and Date | Location | Document Type and Length | Source |
|---|---|---|---|
| 11 Oct. 1872 To | Roadside | ALS 4p | PSCHi-Mott |
| 17 Oct. 1872 To* | Roadside | ALS 4p | MNS |
| 10 Nov. 1872 To | Roadside | ALS 2p | PSCHi-Mott |
| 13 Dec. 1872 To | Roadside | ALS 4p | PSCHi-Mott |
| 17 Jan. 1873 To* | Roadside | ALS 6p+TTR | MNS |
| 26 Jan. [1873?] Fr* | Orange, N.J. | AL 4p | MNS |
| 14 Feb. 1873 To* | Roadside | ALS 4p JL | MNS |
| 27 Feb. 1873 To* | Roadside | AL 4p~ | MNS |
| 2 Mar. 1873 To* | Roadside | ALS 4p | MNS |
| [7 Apr. 1873] To* | [Roadside] | ALS 2p Inc | PSCHi-Mott |
| 12 Apr. 1873 To | Roadside | AL 2p Inc JL | PSCHi-Mott |
| [4 July 1873] To* | [Roadside] | ALS 4p | PSCHi-Mott |
| 25 July 1873 To | Roadside | AL 2p | PSCHi-Mott |
| 26 July 1873 To | Roadside | AL 3p | PSCHi-Mott |
| [July 1873?] To* | [Roadside] | AL 2p Inc | PSCHi-Mott |
| 8 Aug. 1873 To* | Roadside | AL 3p | PSCHi-Mott |
| 16 Oct. 1873 To* | Roadside | ALS 4p JL | MNS |
| 17 [Oct. 1873?] To* | [Roadside] | ALS 2p TTR JL | MNS |
| 9 Jan. 1874 To | Roadside | AL 2p | PSCHi-Mott |
| 17 Jan. 1874 To | Roadside | AL 2p | PSCHi-Mott |
| 23 Jan. 1874 To | Roadside | AL 4p | PSCHi-Mott |
| 30 Jan. 1874 To** | Roadside | ALS 4p | PSCHi-Mott |
| 6 Mar. 1874 To* | Roadside | ALS 4p+TTR | MNS |
| 13 Mar. 1874 To* | Roadside | AL 6p+TTR Dam | MNS |
| 20 Mar. 1874 To* | Roadside | AL 6p+TTR | MNS |
| 27 Mar. 1874 To* | Roadside | AL 3p+TTR | MNS |
| 10 Apr. 1874 To* | Roadside | AL 4p+TTR | MNS |
| 13 [Apr.] 1874 To* | Roadside | ALS 4p+TTR# | MNS |
| 24 Apr. 1874 To* | Roadside | AL 4p+TTR | MNS |
| 5 July [1874] Fr* | York, Me. | ALS 4p | MNS |
| 6 July 1874 Fr* | [York, Me.] | AL 4p | MNS |
| [10 July 1874] Fr* | York, Me. | ALS 4p | MNS |
| 20 July [1874] Fr* | Marshall House, Me. | ALS 4p | MNS |
| 4 Dec. 1874 To | Roadside | AL 3p Inc | PSCHi-Mott |
| 25 Dec. 1874 To | Roadside | ALS 4p | PSCHi-Mott |
| [pre–1874] To** | [Roadside] | ALS 2p | MNS |
| 20 Feb. 1875 To | Roadside | AL 2p | PSCHi-Mott |
| 9 Apr. 1875 To* | Roadside | ALS 7p+TTR | MNS |
| 16 Apr. 1875 To* | Roadside | ALS 4p+TTR | MNS |
| 21 May 1875 To* | Roadside | ALS 4p | MNS |
| 22 Oct. 1875 To | Roadside | AL 3p | PSCHi-Mott |
| 12 Nov. 1875 To | Roadside | AL 4p | PSCHi-Mott |
| 15 Nov. 1875 To | Roadside | AL 3p | PSCHi-Mott |
| 19 Nov. 1875 To | Roadside | AL 3p | PSCHi-Mott |
| [c. Nov. 1875] To* | [Roadside] | AL 2p Inc | PSCHi-Mott |
| 7 Jan. 1876 To | Roadside | AL 4p | PSCHi-Mott |
| 14 Jan. 1876 To | Roadside | AL 3p | PSCHi-Mott |
| [c. Oct. 1876?] To* | [Roadside?] | ALS 4p Inc | PSCHi-Mott |
| 18 [Jan. 1878] To** | [Roadside?] | AL 2p | MNS |
| 11 Feb. 1878 To | Roadside | ALS 2p | MCR |
| 5 July 1878 To | Roadside | AL 2p Inc | MNS |
| 24 Apr. 1879 To | Roadside | AL 5p | PSCHi-Mott |

| Name and Date | Location | Document Type and Length | Source |
|---|---|---|---|
| 25 Apr. 1879 To | Roadside | AL 2p | PSCHi-Mott |
| 8 May 1879 To | Roadside | AL 2p Inc | PSCHi-Mott |
| 23 May 1879 To | Roadside | AL 4p | PSCHi-Mott |
| [May 1879] To | [Roadside?] | ALS 2p Inc | PSCHi-Mott |
| 19 June 1879 To | Roadside | AL 4p | PSCHi-Mott |
| 6 July [1879] Fr* | East Orange, N.J. | ALS 4p | MNS |
| 20 July [1879] Fr* | Newport, R.I. | ALS 4p | MNS |
| [pre–7 Aug. 1879] To | [Roadside] | ALS 2p Inc | PSCHi-Mott |
| 7 Aug. 1879 To | Roadside | AL 3p | PSCHi-Mott |
| 22 Aug. 1879 To | Roadside | AL 4p | PSCHi-Mott |
| 18 Sept. 1879 To | Roadside | AL 6p | PSCHi-Mott |
| 7 Nov. 1879 To | Roadside | AL 2p~ | PSCHi-Mott |
| 5 Dec. 1879 To | Roadside | AL 4p | PSCHi-Mott |
| 20 [? 1879] To** | Philadelphia | ALS 1p Inc | PSCHi-Mott |
| Lossing, Benjamin J. | | | |
| 22 Feb. 1879 To | [Roadside] | C 2p | PSCHi-Mott |
| 20 Mar. 1879 Fr | [Plains, N.Y.?] | ALS 2p | PSCHi-Mott |
| Love, Alfred H. | | | |
| 22 Aug. 1867 To | Roadside | ALS 2p | PSCHi-Mott |
| pre–9 Oct. 1867 Fr | Philadelphia | AN 1p+Enc | PSCHi-Mott |
| 27 Dec. 1867 To | Roadside | ALS 2p | PSCHi-Mott |
| 3 Feb. 1868 Fr | Philadelphia | LS 3p JL | PSCHi-Mott |
| 5 Feb. 1872 Fr | [Philadelphia] | ALS 1p | PSCHi-Mott |
| 26 Nov. 1874 To | Roadside | TTR 1p JL | PSCHi-Mott |
| Love, Lydia | | | |
| 1 Sept. 1874 To | Roadside | C 3p | PSCHi-Mott |
| 17 Sept. 1874 To | Roadside | C 1p~ | PSCHi-Mott |
| 26 Nov. 1874 To | Roadside | TTR 1p JL | PSCHi-Mott |
| Lundy, Benjamin | | | |
| 19 Sept. 1835 Fr | Philadelphia Prison | ALS 1p | PSCHi-Mott |
| Magill, Edward H. | | | |
| 14 May 1872 Fr | Swarthmore | ALS 1p | PSCHi-Mott |
| Mann, Horace | | | |
| 31 Dec. 1851 To | Philadelphia | LS 3p JL | MHi-Mann |
| Marriott, Charles | | | |
| 8 June 1835 Fr | Sunnyside | Dft 3p | PSCHi-Mott |
| Martin, Angelique | | | |
| 1 Oct. 1854 To | Philadelphia | ALS 3p | OMC |
| Martin, Rachel Cutler | | | |
| 19 June 1871 To | New York City | ALS 3p | PSCHi-Mott |
| Martineau, Harriet | | | |
| [pre–24 June 1840] Fr | [Tynemouth, Eng.] | PL 1p | *Diary* |
| 9 Aug. 1840 Fr | Tynemouth, Eng. | C 4p JL | PSCHi-Mott |
| May, Samuel J. | | | |
| 25 Aug. 1852 Fr | Syracuse, N.Y. | ALS 1p | PSCHi-Mott |
| Mayo, Amory D. | | | |
| 2 Sept. 1860 To | Auburn, N.Y. | ALS 1p | NNMor |
| McAllister, John A. | | | |
| 28 Feb. 1864 To | Roadside | AL 2p | PHi-Soc |
| McClintock, Elizabeth | | | |
| 13 Nov. 1849 Fr | Waterloo, N.Y. | TTR 2p | NSyU-Osb |
| 27 Nov. 1849 To | Philadelphia | ALS 6p+Env JL~ | MNS |

| Name and Date | Location | Document Type and Length | Source |
|---|---|---|---|
| McClintock, Mary Ann | | | |
| 29 July 1848 To | Auburn, N.Y. | ALS 3p+Env JL~ | NHP |
| McClintock, Thomas | | | |
| 29 July 1848 To | Auburn, N.Y. | ALS 3p+Env JL~ | NHP |
| McKim, James Miller | | | |
| 1 Jan. 1834 To | Philadelphia | PL 2p | Hallowell |
| 8 Apr. 1834 To | Philadelphia | ALS 4p+Env | NICO |
| 8 May 1834 To | Philadelphia | ALS 3p+Env~# | PSCHi-Mott |
| 25 Sept. 1834 To | Philadelphia | ALS 4p+Env | NICO |
| 27 Jan. 1837 To | Philadelphia | ALS 4p+Env | NICO |
| [13 Nov. 1837] To | [Philadelphia] | ALS 2p+Env | MB |
| 15 Mar. 1838 To | Philadelphia | ALS 3p+Env~# | PSCHi-Mott |
| 19 Mar. 1838 To | Philadelphia | ALS 1p+Env~ | PSCHi-Mott |
| [22 July 1838] To | [Philadelphia?] | ALS 2p+Env | PSCHi-Mott |
| 19 July 1839 To | Philadelphia | ALS 1p+Env~ | NICO |
| 23 July 1839 To | Philadelphia | ALS 4p+Env~ | NICO |
| 24 July 1839 To` | Philadelphia | ALS 1p+Env~ | NICO |
| 29 Dec. 1839 To | Philadelphia | ALS 4p+Env~ | PSCHi-Mott |
| 31 May 1861 To | New York City | AL 2p | NICO |
| 3 June [1863?] Fr | Philadelphia | ALS 2p | PSCHi-Mott |
| 1 Mar. 1866 Fr | New York City | ALS 1p | PSCHi-Mott |
| [c. 15 Apr. 1866] To | [Roadside?] | ALS 3p~ | NN |
| McKim, Sarah Speakman | | | |
| 12 Apr. 1838 To | Philadelphia | AL 3p+Env | PSCHi-Mott |
| 6 July [1874] Fr | Llewellyn Park, N.J. | ALS 4p JL | MNS |
| Mellor, Martha Bancroft | | | |
| 9 Dec. [1868?] Fr | Bilbro Oaks | ALS 1p | MNS |
| 15 Nov. [1872?] Fr | Bilbro Oaks | ALS 1p | PSCHi-Mott |
| Mellor, Thomas | | | |
| 29 Mar. 1871 Fr | Bilbro Oaks | ALS 1p | PSCHi-Mott |
| Miller, Elizabeth Smith | | | |
| 23 Jan. 1879 To* | Roadside | C 2p~ | PSCHi-Mott |
| Mitchell, Mary M. | | | |
| 1 Sept. 1871 Fr | Nantucket, Mass. | ALS 4p | MNS |
| Moore, M. and E. | | | |
| 26 June 1842 To | Philadelphia | XC 1p | PSCHi-Mott |
| Morgan, John | | | |
| 11 July 1840 To | London | PL 1p | *Diary* |
| Mott, Adam | | | |
| [8 Nov. 1813] To | [Philadelphia] | ALS 2p+Env PS JL~ | PSCHi-Mott |
| 1 Apr. 1817 To | Philadelphia | PL 1p JL | Hallowell |
| 12 Mar. 1819 To | [Philadelphia] | PL 1p JL | Hallowell |
| 18 June 1820 To | Philadelphia | PL 1p PS JL | Hallowell |
| [29 Dec. 1822] To | [Philadelphia] | ALS 2p JL~# | Davis |
| 30 [Jan. 1825] To | [Philadelphia] | ALS 2p+Env JL | Davis |
| 15 [May 1825] To | [Philadelphia] | ALS 1p PS JL# | Davis |
| 23 Apr. 1826 To | Philadelphia | PL 1p PS JL~ | Hallowell |
| 19 Sept. 1826 To | Philadelphia | PL 1p JL | Hallowell |
| Mott, Anna Caroline ("Cannie") | | | |
| 27 July 1871 Fr | Manhasset, N.Y. | ALS 2p | PSCHi-Mott |
| Mott, Anne | | | |
| 8 May 1811 Fr | New Rochelle, N.Y. | PL 2p JL | Hallowell |

| Name and Date | Location | Document Type and Length | Source |
|---|---|---|---|
| [8 Nov. 1813] To | [Philadelphia] | ALS 2p+Env PS JL~ | PSCHi-Mott |
| [Oct. c. 1814] To | [Philadelphia] | PL 1p | Hallowell |
| 1 Apr. 1817 To | Philadelphia | PL 1p JL | Hallowell |
| 12 Mar. 1819 To | [Philadelphia] | PL 1p JL | Hallowell |
| 2 Feb. 1820 To | Philadelphia | PL 1p | Hallowell |
| 18 June 1820 To | Philadelphia | PL 1p PS JL | Hallowell |
| [29 Dec. 1822] To | [Philadelphia] | ALS 2p JL~# | Davis |
| 30 [Jan. 1825] To | [Philadelphia] | ALS 2p+Env JL | Davis |
| 15 [May 1825] To | [Philadelphia] | ALS 1p PS JL# | Davis |
| 23 Apr. 1826 To | Philadelphia | PL 1p PS JL~ | Hallowell |
| 19 Sept. 1826 To | Philadelphia | PL 1p JL | Hallowell |
| 26 Feb. 1827 To | Philadelphia | PL 1p~ | Hallowell |
| 29 Dec. 1828 To | Philadelphia | PL 1p | Hallowell |
| 16 May 1830 To | Philadelphia | PL 1p | Hallowell |
| Mott, Catharine Emily | | | |
| 1 July 1863 To | Roadside | ALS 3p | PHC |
| Mott, James | | | |
| 9 June 1849 To | Auburn, N.Y. | AL 2p Inc# | MNS |
| [19 June 1849] To* | [Auburn, N.Y.] | AL 1p Frag~# | MNS |
| 20 [June 1849] To* | [Auburn, N.Y.] | AL 1p Frag~# | MNS |
| 11 Nov. 1854 To | Succasunna, N.J. | ALS 3p+Env JL | MH-H |
| 12 Nov. 1854 To | Succasunna, N.J. | ALS 3p+Env JL | MH-H |
| 30 May 1855 Fr | New York City | ALS 3p JL | PSCHi-Mott |
| 24 Nov. 1863 To* | Roadside | ALS 4p JL | PSCHi-Mott |
| 29 Sept. 1864 To | Brooklyn, N.Y. | ALS 2p JL | PSCHi-Mott |
| 30 Sept. 1864 To | Brooklyn, N.Y. | ALS 2p JL | PSCHi-Mott |
| 24 June 1865 To | Brooklyn, N.Y. | ALS 2p | PSCHi-Mott |
| 26 June 1865 To | Brooklyn, N.Y. | ALS 2p | PSCHi-Mott |
| 3 July 1865 Fr | Roadside | AL 4p | PSCHi-Mott |
| 4 July 1865 Fr | Roadside | AL 3p | PSCHi-Mott |
| 5 July 1865 Fr | Philadelphia | AL 2p | PSCHi-Mott |
| 13 Sept. 1866 To | Nantucket, Mass. | AL 4p | PSCHi-Mott |
| [15 Sept. 1866] To | Middleboro, Mass. | AL 4p+TR | PSCHi-Mott |
| 15 Sept. 1866 To | Hyannis, Mass. | AL 6p+TR | PSCHi-Mott |
| 16 [Sept. 1866] To | Brooklyn, N.Y. | AL 1p | PSCHi-Mott |
| Mott, James, Sr. | | | |
| 23 May 1812 Fr | New York City | PL 1p JL | Hallowell |
| 3 Jan. 1818 Fr | ? | PL 1p JL | Hallowell |
| 8 Feb. 1818 Fr | New Hartford | PL 1p JL | Hallowell |
| 24 Jan. 1819 To | Philadelphia | PL 1p~ | Hallowell |
| 6 Feb. 1819 Fr | New York City | PL 1p JL | Hallowell |
| 6 Jan. 1820 Fr | Skaneateles, N.Y. | PL 1p JL | Hallowell |
| 7 May 1820 Fr | New York City | PL 1p JL | Hallowell |
| 15 Mar. 1822 To | Philadelphia | ALS 4p+Env TR~ | Davis |
| [10 May 1822] To | [Philadelphia] | ALS 4p | Davis |
| 29 June 1822 To | Philadelphia | PL 1p~ | Hallowell |
| 26 July 1822 Fr | New York City | PL 1p | Hallowell |
| ? Feb. 1823 Fr | New York City | PL 1p | Hallowell |
| Mott, John | | | |
| 11 Feb. 1846 Fr* | Clermont Co., Ohio | ALS 3p | MNHi |
| Mott, Lydia | | | |
| 22 Jan. 1861 To | Roadside | ALS 3p~ | MNS |

| Name and Date | Location | Document Type and Length | Source |
|---|---|---|---|
| Mott, Lydia P. | | | |
| 4 Mar. 1851 Fr | Cuyahoga Falls, Ohio | ALS 1p+Env | PSCHi-Og |
| 30 Apr. 1861 To | Roadside | PL 2p | *HWS* |
| Mott, Marianna Pelham | | | |
| 14 Sept. 1848 Fr* | Auburn, N.Y. | AL 2p+Env | MNS |
| [30 May 1855] Fr* | Aboard *Baltic* | AL 1p JL | PSCHi-Mott |
| 2 June 1855 To* | Philadelphia | AL 4p JL | PSCHi-Mott |
| [18 Sept. 1855] To* | [Philadelphia] | AL 2p JL | MNS |
| 26 Nov. 1855 To* | [Philadelphia] | AL 3p JL | PSCHi-Mott |
| 7 July 1861 To* | Roadside | AL 4p | PSCHi-Mott |
| 27 Aug. 1864 To | Roadside | ALS 2p JL | PSCHi-Mott |
| 7 Sept. 1864 To* | Roadside | ALS 2p JL~ | PSCHi-Mott |
| 1 Jan. 1867 To* | Roadside | ALS 4p JL | PSCHi-Mott |
| 3 Feb. [1870] To* | Philadelphia | ALS 2p JL | MNS |
| 4 Feb. [1870] To* | Philadelphia | ALS 2p JL | MNS |
| 7 July 1870 To | Orange, N.J. | ALS 2p | PSCHi-Mott |
| 10 June 1872 To | Orange, N.J. | ALS 2p JL | PSCHi-Mott |
| Mott, Thomas | | | |
| 2 June 1855 To* | Philadelphia | AL 4p JL | PSCHi-Mott |
| [18 Sept. 1855] To* | [Philadelphia] | AL 2p JL | MNS |
| 26 Oct. 1855 Fr* | Dresden, Ger. | AL 3p JL | MNS |
| 29 Oct. 1855 Fr* | Berlin | AL 1p JL | MNS |
| 16 Nov. [1855] Fr* | Paris | AL 4p+Env JL | MNS |
| 26 Nov. 1855 To* | [Philadelphia] | AL 3p JL | PSCHi-Mott |
| 11 Dec. [1855] Fr* | Paris | AL 2p JL | MNS |
| 19 Dec. 1855 Fr* | Paris | AL 4p JL | MNS |
| 25 Dec. [1855] Fr* | Paris | AL 5p JL | MNS |
| 3 Jan. 1856 Fr* | Naples | AL 6p JL | MNS |
| 13 Jan. [1856] Fr* | Naples | AL 4p JL | MNS |
| 3 Feb. 1856 Fr* | Rome | AL 4p+Env JL | MNS |
| 5 Feb. [1856] Fr* | Rome | AL 6p JL | MNS |
| 11 Feb. [1856] Fr* | Rome | AL 4p JL | MNS |
| 20 Feb. [1856] Fr* | Rome | AL 4p JL | MNS |
| 16 July [1856] Fr* | St. Poar,? Neth. | AL 4p+Env JL | MNS |
| 6 May 1864 To | Brooklyn, N.Y. | AL 2p | PSCHi-Mott |
| 8 Jan. 1868 Fr* | Naples | AL 8p JL | MNS |
| 10 June 1872 To | Orange, N.J. | ALS 2p JL | PSCHi-Mott |
| Musical Fund Bazaar Patrons | | | |
| [c. 1847] To | [Philadelphia] | PL 2p JL | PHi-PAS |
| "My dear" | | | |
| ? To | [Roadside?] | AN 1p | MNS |
| Myers, Leonard | | | |
| 21 Mar. 1851 To | Philadelphia | LS 2p+enc JL? | DLC-Mott |
| Myers, Myles L. N. | | | |
| 18 Nov. 1869 Fr | Brooklyn, N.Y. | ALS 1p | MNS |
| *National Anti-Slavery Standard* Editor | | | |
| 6 July 1861 To | Philadelphia | PL 1p~ | *NASS* |
| Neall, Daniel, Jr. | | | |
| 24 Jan. 1878 To | Roadside | ALS 1p~ | PHi-Soc |
| Neall, Rebecca Chase | | | |
| [pre–5 Sept. 1855] Fr* | [Mt. Holly, N.J.] | ALS 2p | PSCHi-Mott |

| Name and Date | Location | Document Type and Length | Source |
|---|---|---|---|
| 15 Apr. 1856 Fr* | Mt. Holly, N.J. | AL 1p+enc TTR | MNS |
| 10 Nov. 1858 Fr* | Mt. Holly, N.J. | ALS 1p+Env | MNS |
| Nichol, Elizabeth Pease | | | |
| [pre–25 Aug. 1840] Fr | ? | PL 1p | *Diary* |
| 18 Feb. 1841 To | Philadelphia | AL 4p+Env~# | PSCHi-Mott |
| 28 Apr. 1846 To | Philadelphia | ALS 4p+Env~ | PSCHi-Mott |
| 28 May 1855 To | Philadelphia | ALS 3p~ | MH-H |
| 10 Nov. 1859 To | Philadelphia | ALS 2p | MH-H |
| 15 Apr. 1866 To | Philadelphia | ALS 3p | MHi-Nor |
| No Addressee | | | |
| 15 Dec. 1819 To | [Philadelphia] | PL 1p~ | Hallowell |
| 16 July 1839 To | Philadelphia | AMs 1p | DLC-WASS |
| 3 July 1844 To | [Philadelphia?] | AGS 1p | PStH |
| [c. 1 Dec. 1855] To | [Philadelphia] | AL 2p Inc | PSCHi-Mott |
| [c. 1856] To | ? | ALS 2p Inc | MNS |
| Jan. 1864 To | [Roadside?] | AGS 1p | ICHi |
| Jan. 1864 To | ? | AGS 1p | OHi |
| Jan. 1864 To | ? | AGS 1p | MH-H |
| 26 Mar. 1865 To | ? | AGS 1p | OHi |
| [1869] To | ? | AL 1p Frag | MNS |
| 1870 To | ? | AGS 1p | PSCHi-Mott |
| 1870 To | Philadelphia | AGS 1p | NPV |
| 1873 To | ? | AGS 1p | PSCHi-Mott |
| [1874] To | ? | AGS 1p | MNS |
| 1877 To | [Roadside?] | AGS 1p | BWP |
| 22 Sept. 1878 To | [Roadside] | ALS 1p+Enc | PSCHi-Mott |
| 1879 To | ? | AGS 1p | PSCHi-Mott |
| 1879 To | ? | AGS 1p | PSCHi-Mott |
| 1879 To | ? | AGS 1p | PSCHi-Mott |
| [1880] To | [Roadside?] | AL 2p Inc | OHi |
| ? To | [Roadside?] | PL 1p | Hallowell |
| ? To | ? | AL 2p Inc? | MNS |
| No Signature | | | |
| [c. Oct. 1849] Fr | ? | AL 4p | MB |
| [pre–1861] Fr | [Boston] | AL 3p | PSCHi-Mott |
| 8 Dec. 1872 Fr | New York City | AL 1p Inc | MNS |
| O'Connell, Daniel | | | |
| 17 June 1840 To | London | PL 1p~ | *PFrm* |
| 20 June 1840 Fr | London | PL 1p# | *PFrm* |
| Oliver, John | | | |
| 1 Dec. 1875 Fr | Philadelphia | ALS 1p | PSCHi-Mott |
| Osborne, David Munson | | | |
| 17 Apr. 1877 Fr | Auburn, N.Y. | ALS 4p | PSCHi-Mott |
| Osborne, Eliza Wright | | | |
| [4 Oct. 1845] To | [Philadelphia] | ALS 2p+Env | NSyU-Osb |
| 26 June 1856 To | Auburn, N.Y. | ALS 2p | NSyU-Osb |
| 4 July [1856] To | Auburn, N.Y. | ALS 2p | PSCHi-Mott |
| 14 [July] 1856 To | Auburn, N.Y. | ALS 2p+Env | NSyU-Osb |
| 19 Mar. 1861 To* | Roadside | AL 3p JL~ | PSCHi-Mott |
| 20 Mar. 1861 To* | Roadside | AL 2p JL | PSCHi-Mott |
| 21 Mar. 1861 To* | Roadside | AL 1p JL | PSCHi-Mott |

| Name and Date | Location | Document Type and Length | Source |
|---|---|---|---|
| [22 Aug. 1862] Fr** | London | ALS 8p | NSyU-Osb |
| 29 Apr. 1863 To** | New York City | ALS 4p | NSyU-Osb |
| [June 1864?] To | [Roadside?] | AL 1p PS | NSyU-Osb |
| 31 Oct. 1864 To | Roadside | AL 3p JL~ | PSCHi-Mott |
| 3 Apr. 1865 To** | Roadside | ALS 3p PS | MNS |
| 12 [Jan. 1875] To* | [Roadside] | AL 3p+TTR~ | MNS |
| 4 Apr. 1875 To | Roadside | AL 4p+TTR | MNS |
| 17 Apr. 1876 To | Roadside | ALS 2p | PSCHi-Mott |
| 7 Sept. 1877 To | Roadside | ALS 2p | PSCHi-Mott |
| Parrish, Frances Cavender | | | |
| 24 Aug. 1866 To** | [Newburgh, N.Y.] | ALS 4p JL | PSCHi-Mott |
| 30 July 1874 Fr* | Colorado Springs, Colo. | ALS 2p JL | MNS |
| Parrish, L. G. | | | |
| 1 Nov. 1863 Fr | Philadelphia | ALS 2p | MNS |
| Parrish, Samuel | | | |
| 23 Apr. 1872 To | [Roadside?] | C 2p# | PSCHi-Hal |
| Parrish, Thomas C. | | | |
| 16 [June] 1869 Fr | Philadelphia | ALS 1p | MNS |
| Peace Advocates | | | |
| [pre–19 Feb. 1867] To | Providence | PL 1p JL | PSCHi-Mott |
| [pre–1 Dec. 1872] Fr | Philadelphia | PL 1p JL | PSCHi-Mott |
| [pre–1 Dec. 1874] To | Philadelphia | PL 1p JL | MNS |
| [pre–19 June 1879] To | Philadelphia | PL 2p JL | PSCHi-Mott |
| Peace Advocates, Exeter, Eng. | | | |
| [c. 15 June] 1846 To | Philadelphia | PL 1p JL | PSCHi-P |
| Peace Advocates, Philadelphia | | | |
| 28 Apr. 1846 Fr | Exeter, Eng. | LS 1p JL | PSCHi-P |
| Peirce, Charlotte L. | | | |
| 18 Oct. [1870?] Fr | Bristol | ALS 2p | PSCHi-Mott |
| 13 Apr. ? Fr | ? | ALS 1p | PSCHi-Mott |
| Peirce, Sarah H. | | | |
| 3 Feb. 1868 Fr | Philadelphia | LS 3p JL | PSCHi-Mott |
| Pennock, C. W. | | | |
| 26 Oct. 1843 To | Philadelphia | ALS 2p~ | PSCHi-Mott |
| Pennslvania Abolition Society | | | |
| 29 Sept. 1836 To | [Philadelphia] | LS 1p JL | PHi-PAS |
| Pennsylvania Anti-Slavery Society | | | |
| [pre–26 Dec. 1867] Fr | Philadelphia | PL 1p JL | PSCHi-Mott |
| 3 Feb. 1868 Fr | Philadelphia | LS 3p JL | PSCHi-Mott |
| *Pennsylvania Freeman* | | | |
| 29 Jan. 1844 To | Philadelphia | PL 2p | *PFrm* |
| Pennsylvania Peace Society | | | |
| [pre–10 Dec. 1872] To | Philadelphia | PL 1p JL | PSCHi-Mott |
| [pre–27 Nov. 1877] To | [Philadelphia] | PL 1p JL | PHi-Soc |
| Pennsylvania Peace Society, Executive Committee | | | |
| [pre–4 June 1873] Fr | [Philadelphia] | LS 1p JL | PSCHi-Mott |
| [pre–17 June 1873] Fr | [Philadelphia] | PL 1p JL | PSCHi-Mott |
| Philadelphia Family | | | |
| 15 June 1840 To | London | C 4p | NRU |
| 27 June 1840 To | London | C 6p | NRU |
| 14 Oct. 1853 To | Cincinnati | ALS 4p | PSCHi-Mott |

| Name and Date | Location | Document Type and Length | Source |
|---|---|---|---|
| 17 Oct. 1853 To | Ohio River | ALS 4p~# | PSCHi-Mott |
| [17 ? 1856] To | [Philadelphia] | AL 2p PS | *PFrm* |
| 20 Aug. 1856 To* | Flume House, N.H. | AL 3p~ | MNS |
| 21 Aug. 1856 To* | Flume House, N.H. | AL 2p~ | MNS |
| 9 June 1861 To* | Nantucket, Mass. | AL 4p | PSCHi-Mott |
| 11 June [1861] To* | Nantucket, Mass. | AL 3p | PSCHi-Mott |
| 12 June [1861] To* | Nantucket, Mass. | AL 2p | PSCHi-Mott |
| 16 July 1862 To | Auburn, N.Y. | AL 4p | PSCHi-Mott |
| 17 July 1862 To | Auburn, N.Y. | AL 3p~ | PSCHi-Mott |
| 20 July 1862 To | Skaneateles, N.Y. | ALS 2p | PSCHi-Mott |
| 23 July 1862 To | New Milford | ALS 2p | PSCHi-Mott |
| 23 July 1862 To | Herrick Center | ALS 3p | PSCHi-Mott |
| 12 May 1864 To | Brooklyn, N.Y. | AL 2p | PSCHi-Mott |
| 14 Sept. 1864 To | Auburn, N.Y. | AL 4p | PSCHi-Mott |
| 15 Sept. 1864 To | Auburn, N.Y. | AL 1p | PSCHi-Mott |
| 20 Sept. 1864 To | Auburn, N.Y. | AL 2p | PSCHi-Mott |
| 22 Sept. 1864 To | Auburn, N.Y. | AL 2p Dam | PSCHi-Mott |
| 29 Sept. 1864 To | Brooklyn, N.Y. | ALS 2p JL | PSCHi-Mott |
| 30 Sept. 1864 To | Brooklyn, N.Y. | ALS 2p JL | PSCHi-Mott |
| 9 Nov. 1866 To | Brooklyn, N.Y. | ALS 4p | PSCHi-Mott |
| 15 Nov. 1866 To | New York City | AL 4p~# | MNS |
| 17 Nov. 1866 To | Brooklyn, N.Y. | ALS 2p# | MNS |
| 11 Aug. 1867 To | Suffern, N.Y. | ALS 4p | PSCHi-Mott |
| 24 Jan. 1868 To | Brooklyn, N.Y. | AL 3p Inc | PSCHi-Mott |
| [c. 20 Aug. 1868?] To | [Orange, N.J.] | AL 1p Frag | PSCHi-Mott |
| 22 Aug. 1868 To | Orange, N.J. | AL 4p | PSCHi-Mott |
| 28 Aug. 1868 To | Orange, N.J. | ALS 4p | PSCHi-Mott |
| 1 Feb. 1869 To | Orange, N.J. | AL 3p~ | PSCHi-Mott |
| 3 Feb. 1869 To | Orange, N.J. | AL 2p~ | PSCHi-Mott |
| 27 June 1869 To | Orange, N.J. | ALS 2p | MNS |
| 29 June 1869 To | Orange, N.J. | ALS 3p | MNS |
| 30 June 1869 To | Orange, N.J. | ALS 2p | MNS |
| 31 Mar. 1872 To | Orange, N.J. | AL 2p | PSCHi-Mott |
| 3 Apr. 1872 To | Orange, N.J. | ALS 2p | PSCHi-Mott |
| 29 May 1872 To | Orange, N.J. | ALS 6p | PSCHi-Mott |
| 9 Oct. 1875 To | Orange, N.J. | AL 3p | PSCHi-Mott |
| 1 Nov. [1877] To | [Roadside] | AL 2p | PSCHi-Mott |
| ? To* | ? | AL 1p Inc | PSCHi-Mott |
| Philadelphia Yearly Meeting, Executive Committee | | | |
| 5 Sept. 1863 Fr | Philadelphia | PL 1p JL | PSCHi-Mott |
| Phillips, Wendell | | | |
| 8 June 1839 To | Philadelphia | ALS 1p+Env | MH-H |
| 3 July 1845 Fr | [Boston?] | ALS 2p | VtMiM |
| 17 Apr. 1866 To | Philadelphia | ALS 3p+Env~ | MH-H |
| Pickering, D. C. | | | |
| 15 May 1873 Fr | Providence, R.I. | ALS 1p | PSCHi-Mott |
| Pierce, Cyrus | | | |
| 13 Mar. 1843 To | Philadelphia | PL 3p | Hallowell |
| Pierce, James L. | | | |
| 15 Jan. 1849 To | Philadelphia | PL 9p | Hallowell |

| Name and Date | Location | Document Type and Length | Source |
|---|---|---|---|
| **Plumly, Rush** | | | |
| [post–10 Oct. 1849] Fr | [Philadelphia] | ALS 1p | MNS |
| **Post, Joseph** | | | |
| [12 Feb. 1858] To | [Roadside] | AL 2p+TTR PS JL | Falconi |
| 12 [Sept. 1859] To | [Roadside] | ALS 2p PS JL | Falconi |
| [c. 12 Sept. 1861] To** | [Roadside] | AL 2p+TTR Inc JL | Falconi |
| **Post, Mary Robbins** | | | |
| [12 Feb. 1858] To | [Roadside] | AL 2p+TTR PS JL | Falconi |
| 12 [Sept. 1859] To | [Roadside] | ALS 2p PS JL | Falconi |
| [c. 12 Sept. 1861] To** | [Roadside] | AL 2p+TTR Inc JL | Falconi |
| 18 Aug. 1863 To | Roadside | ALS 4p+TTR | Falconi |
| 20 Aug. 1863 To | Roadside | ALS 5p+TTR | Falconi |
| 14 Mar. 1865 To | Roadside | ALS 4p~ | Falconi |
| 4 Sept. 1871 To | Orange, N.J. | ALS 2p+TTR | Falconi |
| **Potter, William J.** | | | |
| 12 Apr. 1869 To | Roadside | PL 1p | FRA |
| 11 June 1879 Fr | Grantville, Mass. | ALS 4p | PSCHi-Mott |
| **Preston, Ann** | | | |
| 12 Mar. 1849 Fr | West Grove | ALS 4p | PSCHi-Mott |
| 28 May 1866 To | [Roadside] | ANS 1p+Env | PSCHi-Mott |
| **Price, Lydia** | | | |
| 25 Dec. 1869 To | Roadside | ALS 2p+Env | PSCHi-Mott |
| **The Public** | | | |
| Oct. 1844 To | Philadelphia | PL 1p JL | *PFrm* |
| [18 Nov. 1852] To | [Philadelphia] | PL 1p JL | *PFrm* |
| [28 July 1853] To | [Philadelphia] | PL 1p JL | *PFrm* |
| [23 Mar. 1854] To | [Philadelphia] | PL 1p JL | *PFrm* |
| [c. 12 May 1866] To | [New York City] | PL 1p JL | *NASS* |
| [c. Dec. 1866] To | ? | PL 1p JL | *NASS* |
| [c. July] 1867 To | New York City | PL 1p JL~ | NSyU-Smith |
| [c. Sept. 1870] To | [New York City] | PL 2p JL | PSCHi-Mott |
| [Jan. 1871] To | Philadelphia | LS 2p JL | *S-A Papers* |
| 4 July 1876 To | Philadelphia | PL 2p JL | *BBox* |
| **Pugh, E. H.** | | | |
| [? 1869] Fr | [Philadelphia?] | ALS 1p | PSCHi-Mott |
| **Pugh, Sarah** | | | |
| 31 [Mar. 1853] To* | [Philadelphia?] | AL 1p Inc | CtY |
| 3 Feb. 1868 Fr | Philadelphia | LS 3p JL | PSCHi-Mott |
| 3 Jan. 1873 Fr** | [Philadelphia] | ALS 2p | MNS |
| **Pugh, T. B.** | | | |
| 28 Nov. 1870 Fr | Philadelphia | ALS 2p | PSCHi-Mott |
| **Purvis, Robert** | | | |
| 3 Feb. 1868 Fr | Philadelphia | LS 3p JL | PSCHi-Mott |
| **A Quaker** | | | |
| [c. 1876] Fr | [Philadelphia?] | PL 1p | Hallowell |
| ? Fr | ? | PL 1p | Hallowell |
| **Quincy, Edmund** | | | |
| 24 Aug. 1848 To | Philadelphia | PL 1p~ | *Lib* |
| **R., E. H.** | | | |
| [c. 14 Mar. 1844] To | [Philadelphia] | PL 5p~ | *LibBl* |
| **Race Street Meeting, Friends Commmittee** | | | |
| [pre–7 Feb. 1873] Fr | Philadelphia | PL 1p JL | PSCHi-Mott |

| Name and Date | Location | Document Type and Length | Source |
|---|---|---|---|
| Roadside Family | | | |
| 27 Oct. 1858 To | Baltimore | AL 4p~ | PSCHi-Mott |
| 30 Apr. 1864 To | New York City | AL 2p | PSCHi-Mott |
| 1 May 1864 To | New York City | AL 2p | PSCHi-Mott |
| 3 May 1864 To | Brooklyn, N.Y. | ALS 4p | PSCHi-Mott |
| 4 May 1864 To | Brooklyn, N.Y. | ALS 1p | PSCHi-Mott |
| 9 May 1864 To | Brooklyn, N.Y. | AL 2p | PSCHi-Mott |
| 24 June 1865 To | Brooklyn, N.Y. | ALS 4p | PSCHi-Mott |
| 29 June 1865 To | Brooklyn, N.Y. | AL 6p | PSCHi-Mott |
| 3 July 1865 To | Brooklyn, N.Y. | AL 3p | PSCHi-Mott |
| 4 July 1865 To | Brooklyn, N.Y. | AL 2p~ | PSCHi-Mott |
| 28 Aug. 1866 To | Danby, Vt. | AL 5p | PSCHi-Mott |
| 1 Sept. 1866 To | Danby, Vt. | AL 2p | PSCHi-Mott |
| 2 Sept. 1866 To | Rensaleer, N.Y. | AL 1p | PSCHi-Mott |
| 5 Aug. 1867 To | Suffern, N.Y. | AL 3p | PSCHi-Mott |
| 6 Aug. 1867 To | Suffern, N.Y. | AL 3p | PSCHi-Mott |
| 23 [May 1870] To | Orange, N.J. | AL 2p Frag~ | PSCHi-Mott |
| Roberts, Adeline | | | |
| 19 Sept. 1850 To | Philadelphia | ALS 2p+TR JL | MSaE |
| 8 Sept. 1851 To | Philadelphia | ALS 3p+Env | PHC |
| 5 July 1852 To | Philadelphia | ALS 2p~ | MSaE |
| 12 Aug. 1853 To | Philadelphia | ALS 1p | MSae |
| 15 Sept. 1855 To | Philadelphia | ALS 2p | MSae |
| Rodman, Elizabeth Rotch | | | |
| [Apr. 1840] Fr | ? | PL 1p | Hallowell |
| [Apr. 1840] To | [Philadelphia?] | PL 1p | Hallowell |
| Rosine Association | | | |
| 5 Apr. 1866 Fr | ? | PL 1p | PSCHi-Mott |
| Ross, Alexander M. | | | |
| 8 Aug. 1875 To | Roadside | ALS 1p | ICHi |
| 13 Dec. 1879 To | [Roadside?] | C 1p~ | PSCHi-Ross |
| Rotch, William, Jr. | | | |
| June 1846 Fr | Philadelphia | ALS 1p | PSCHi-Og |
| San Francisco County Woman's Suffrage Society | | | |
| 10 Feb. 1871 Fr | San Francisco | LS 1p JL | MNS |
| Sands, J. I.? | | | |
| 18 May 1872 Fr | New York City | AL 2p JL | PSCHi-Mott |
| Schofield, Martha | | | |
| 7 Apr. 1877 Fr | Aiken, S.C. | ALS 4p | PSCHi-Mott |
| Severance, Caroline M. | | | |
| 18 Sept. 1855 To | Philadelphia | ALS 4p | MHi-Dall |
| 10 Nov. 1868 Fr | West Newton, Mass. | ALS 2p | MNS |
| Seward, William H. | | | |
| 3 Mar. 1861 To | Roadside | ALS 2p~ | NRU |
| Shanks, John P. C. | | | |
| 18 Jan. 1869 Fr | [Harrisburg?] | ALS 1p | MNS |
| Shoemaker, F. | | | |
| 21 Apr. 1869 To | Roadside | ALS 1p+enc | PSCHi-Mott |
| Shrigley, James | | | |
| 28 Apr. 1869 Fr | Philadelphia | ALS 1p | PSCHi-Mott |
| Smedley, Esther R. | | | |
| 14 May 1866 Fr | Philadelphia | ALS 1p | PSCHi-Mott |

| Name and Date | Location | Document Type and Length | Source |
|---|---|---|---|
| Smith, Elizabeth Oakes | | | |
| 23 Feb. 1852 To | Philadelphia | ALS 3p~ | NjP |
| 9 [Mar. 1852?] To | [Philadelphia] | AL 1p+Env | ViU |
| Smith, Mrs. A. S. | | | |
| 4 Nov. 1880 Fr | Philadelphia | ALS 2p | PSCHi-Mott |
| Snodgrass, J. E. | | | |
| 26 Nov. 1842 Fr | Baltimore | ALS 1p | NPV |
| Snow, Mary F. | | | |
| 10 Feb. 1871 Fr | San Francisco | LS 1p JL | MNS |
| Society for the Prevention of Cruelty to Animals | | | |
| [pre–9 Jan. 1871] Fr | Philadelphia | PL 1p JL | PSCHi-Mott |
| Society of Friends | | | |
| 27 Feb. 1847 To | Philadelphia | PL 1p JL | *FrdsInt* |
| Somerville Literary Society | | | |
| 9 Feb. 1876 Fr | Swarthmore | ALS 1p XC JL | PSCHi-Mott |
| Speakman, Micajah | | | |
| 12 Feb. 1838 To | Philadelphia | C 1p | PSCHi-Mott |
| Speakman, Priscilla | | | |
| 3 July 1871 To | Roadside | ALS 1p | PSCHi-Mott |
| Speakman, T. H. | | | |
| [pre–19 Feb. 1869] Fr | [Swarthmore?] | PL 1p JL | PSCHi-Mott |
| Spear, Caroline H. | | | |
| 10 Feb. 1871 Fr | San Francisco | LS 1p JL | MNS |
| 11 June 1872 Fr | New York City | ALS 1p JL | PSCHi-Mott |
| Stanton, Elizabeth Cady | | | |
| 23 Mar. 1841 To | Philadelphia | ALS 4p~ | DLC-Stan |
| 16 July 1848 To | Auburn, N.Y. | ALS 3p+Env~ | DLC-Stan |
| 30 Sept. 1848 Fr | Seneca Falls, N.Y. | TTR 2p | NjRD |
| 3 Oct. 1848 To | Philadelphia | ALS 4p~ | DLC-Stan |
| 26 Sept. [1849] Fr | Seneca Falls, N.Y. | TTR 2p | NSyU-Osb |
| 25 Oct. 1849 To | Philadelphia | ALS 4p+Env~ | DLC-Stan |
| [Oct. 1849?] Fr | [Seneca Falls, N.Y.] | C 2p Enc | MB |
| 12 Nov. 1849 Fr | Seneca Falls, N.Y. | PL 2p | Gordon |
| 27 Nov. 1849 To | Philadelphia | ALS 6p+Env JL~ | MNS |
| 11 Sept. 1851 To | Philadelphia | PL 3p | Gordon |
| 27 Nov. 1852 To | Philadelphia | TTR 1p | NjRD |
| 16 Mar. 1855 To | Philadelphia | ALS 5p~ | DLC-Stan |
| 22 Apr. 1866 To | Roadside | TTR 1p~ | NjRD |
| 12 Jan. [1867] Fr | New York City | ALS 1p | PSCHi-Mott |
| 21 Jan. 1869 Fr | Washington, D.C. | PL 1p | *ECS* |
| 1 Apr. [1871] Fr | Newcastle, Del. | ALS 8p | NPV |
| 13 Mar. [1872] Fr | Tenafly, N.J. | ALS 4p | PSCHi-Mott |
| 25 Mar. 1872 To | Roadside | ALS 4p~ | MNS |
| 16 July 1872 Fr | Tenafly, N.J. | TTR 1p | NjRD |
| 19 July 1876 Fr | Tenafly, N.J. | PL 2p | *BBox* |
| Stebbins, Catharine Fish | | | |
| 30 Mar. 1874 To | Roadside | ALS 3p~ | NRU |
| Stevens, Mrs. E. Pitts | | | |
| 10 Feb. 1871 Fr | San Francisco | LS 1p JL | MNS |
| Stevens, Thaddeus | | | |
| 15 Oct. 1866 To | Philadelphia | LS 2p JL | DLC-Stev |

| Name and Date | Location | Document Type and Length | Source |
|---|---|---|---|
| **Stevenson, Thomas B.** | | | |
| 13 Oct. 1853 Fr | Maysville, Ky. | ALS 1p | PSCHi-Mott |
| **Still, William** | | | |
| 3 Feb. 1868 Fr | Philadelphia | LS 3p JL | PSCHi-Mott |
| 29 Mar. 1875 Fr | [Philadelphia] | ALS 1p | MNS |
| **Stone, Lucy** | | | |
| 6 Aug. 1851 To | Auburn, N.Y. | ALS 3p+Env~ | MiUc |
| 16 Aug. 1852 To | Philadelphia | ALS 4p+Env~ | DLC-Blkw |
| 15 Nov. 1852 Fr | [Ambler, Pa.?] | ALS 2p | PSCHi-Mott |
| 14 Jan. [1855?] Fr | Bangor, Me. | ALS 2p | DLC-Blkw |
| 31 Oct. 1856 To | Philadelphia | ALS 3p~ | DLC-Blkw |
| 9 Dec. 1856 To | Philadelphia | AL 2p PS~ | DLC-Blkw |
| 1 July 1857 To | Roadside | ALS 3p~ | DLC-Blkw |
| 24 Apr. 1870 Fr | Boston | ALS 1p | PSCHi-Mott |
| 1 Nov. 1880 Fr | Boston | ALS 2p | PSCHi-Mott |
| **Stratton, Caroline Chase** | | | |
| 18 Dec. [1863] Fr* | Mt. Holly, N.J. | ALS 3p | PSCHi-Mott |
| 2 June 1870 Fr | [Mt. Holly, N.J.?] | ALS 1p | PSCHi-Mott |
| 10 Sept. 1872 Fr | Mt. Holly, N.J. | ALS 1p | MNS |
| 8 Oct. 1872 To* | Roadside | AL 4p | PSCHi-Mott |
| 11 Oct. 1875 To | Orange, N.J. | ALS 6p | PSCHi-Mott |
| **Taylor, Alfred B.** | | | |
| 5 Dec. 1870 Fr | Philadelphia | ALS 1p | MNS |
| **Taylor, O. A.** | | | |
| 17 Nov. [1871?] Fr | [Derry?] | ALS 1p Dam | PSCHi-Mott |
| **Tilton, Theodore** | | | |
| 18 Mar. 1870 To | Roadside | ALS 3p~ | NBu |
| **To Whom It May Concern** | | | |
| 13 Dec. 1866 To | [Roadside?] | TTR 1p | Bru |
| **Townsend, R. B.** | | | |
| 21 Aug. 1879 Fr | [Philadelphia] | ALS 1p | PSCHi-Mott |
| **Trask, George** | | | |
| 4 Jan. 1870 Fr | Fitchburg, [Mass.?] | ALS 1p | PSCHi-Mott |
| **Trout, Jenny K.** | | | |
| 5 Mar. 1874 Fr | Philadelphia | ALS 1p+TTR | MNS |
| **Truth, Sojourner** | | | |
| Nov. 1869 To | Roadside | PL 1p | Truth |
| **Universal Franchise Association** | | | |
| [pre–18 Jan. 1870] To | [Roadside] | PL 1p Extr | *Nat Rep* |
| **Universal Peace Society** | | | |
| 9 Oct. 1867 Fr | Boston | PL 1p JL | PSCHi-Mott |
| **U.S. Congress** | | | |
| 16 Apr. 1836 To | Philadelphia | LS 1p JL | DNA |
| [c. 1846] To | [Philadelphia?] | LS 1p JL | DNA |
| [c. 10 May 1867] To | [New York City] | PL 2p JL~ | *HWS* |
| 16 Jan. 1880 To | Philadelphia | PL 1p JL | *CongRec* |
| **U.S. Senate** | | | |
| [c. 3 Feb. 1869] To | [Philadelphia] | LS 1p JL~ | DNA |
| **Waldmen, J. [R.?]** | | | |
| 3 Feb. 1868 Fr | Philadelphia | LS 3p JL | PSCHi-Mott |

| Name and Date | Location | Document Type and Length | Source |
|---|---|---|---|
| **Webb, Hannah Waring** | | | |
| 16 Aug. 1840 To | Newcastle, Eng. | ALS 2p JL | MB |
| 12 Oct. 1840 To | Philadelphia | ALS 3p+Env JL# | MB |
| Mar. 1841 To | Philadelphia | ALS 1p PS JL | PSCHi-Mott |
| 2 Apr. 1841 To | Philadelphia | ALS 4p+Env JL~# | MB |
| 10 Aug. 1841 To | Philadelphia | ALS 2p+Env JL | MB |
| 25 Feb. 1842 To | Philadelphia | ALS 7p+Env JL~# | MB |
| 7 Mar. 1842 To | Philadelphia | ALS 3p+Env JL~# | MB |
| 12 Mar. 1842 To | Philadelphia | ALS 1p+Env JL~# | MB |
| 17 Mar. 1842 To | Philadelphia | ALS 1p+Env JL~# | MB |
| 17 Mar. 1843 To | Philadelphia | ALS 4p+Env JL~ | MB |
| 23 Mar. 1846 To | Philadelphia | PL 7p JL | Hallowell |
| 29 [Apr. 1846] To | [Philadelphia] | ALS 1p PS JL Inc? | MB |
| 10 Sept. 1848 To | Philadelphia | AL 4p JL# | MB |
| 14 May 1849 To | Philadelphia | ALS 4p JL~# | MB |
| 15 May 1849 To | Philadelphia | ALS 1p JL~# | MB |
| 28 May 1850 To | Philadelphia | ALS 4p+TR# JL | MB |
| 5 Apr. 1852 To | Philadelphia | ALS 4p JL | MB |
| **Webb, Richard D.** | | | |
| 16 Aug. 1840 To | Newcastle, Eng. | ALS 2p JL | MB |
| [pre–25 Aug. 1840] Fr | Dublin, Ire. | PL 1p | *Diary* |
| 12 Oct. 1840 To | Philadelphia | ALS 3p+Env JL# | MB |
| Mar. 1841 To | Philadelphia | ALS 1p PS JL | PSCHi-Mott |
| 2 Apr. 1841 To | Philadelphia | ALS 4p+Env JL~# | MB |
| 10 July 1841 To | Tarrytown, N.Y. | AN 1p+Enc | MB |
| 10 Aug. 1841 To | Philadelphia | ALS 2p+Env JL | MB |
| 25 Feb. 1842 To | Philadelphia | ALS 7p JL~# | MB |
| 7 Mar. 1842 To | Philadelphia | ALS 3p JL~# | MB |
| 12 Mar. 1842 To | Philadelphia | ALS 1p JL~# | MB |
| 17 Mar. 1842 To | Philadelphia | ALS 1p JL~# | MB |
| 17 Mar. 1843 To | Philadelphia | ALS 4p+Env JL~ | MB |
| 23 Apr. 1843 To | Philadelphia | ALS 1p | MB |
| 23 Apr. 1846 To | Philadelphia | PL 7p JL | Hallowell |
| 29 [Apr. 1846] To | [Philadelphia] | ALS 1p JL PS Inc | MB |
| 21 Feb. 1847 To | Philadelphia | TR 2p# | MB |
| [26 Apr. 1847] To | [Philadelphia] | ALS 1p PS +TR# | MB |
| 10 Sept. 1848 To | Philadelphia | AL 4p JL# | MB |
| 8 Feb. 1849 Fr | Dublin, Ire. | ALS 4p+Env JL | PSCHi-Og |
| 14 May 1849 To | Philadelphia | ALS 4p JL~# | MB |
| 15 May 1849 To | Philadelphia | ALS 1p JL~# | MB |
| 14 Apr. 1850 To | Philadelphia | ALS 4p# | MB |
| 28 May 1850 To | Philadelphia | ALS 4p+TR JL# | MB |
| 5 Apr. 1852 To | Philadelphia | ALS 4p JL | MB |
| 21 May 1852 To | Philadelphia | ALS 8p | MB |
| 13 Aug. 1852 Fr | Dublin, Ire. | ALS 4p JL | PSCHi-Mott |
| 22 Apr. 1853 To | Philadelphia | ALS 4p | MB |
| 9 Oct. 1862 To | Philadelphia | ALS 3p | MB |
| 4 Sept. 1868 To | Roadside | ALS 4p | MB |
| 24 Feb. 1870 To | Roadside | ALS 2p~ | MB |
| 22 Jan. [1871] To | Roadside | ALS 2p~ | MB |
| 4 May 1871 To | Orange, N.J. | ALS 2p~ | MB |

| Name and Date | Location | Document Type and Length | Source |
|---|---|---|---|
| Weiss, John | | | |
| 1 Feb. 1868 Fr | Watertown, Mass. | ALS 4p# | PSCHi-Mott |
| Weston, Anne Warren | | | |
| 7 June 1838 To | Philadelphia | ALS 1p+Env PS~ | MB |
| 18 July 1841 To | Philadelphia | ALS 2p+Enc | MB |
| 23 July 1846 To | Philadelphia | ALS 2p+Env JL~ | MB |
| [1 Sept. 1853] To | [Philadelphia] | ALS 1p PS | MB |
| 18 Nov. 1853 To | Philadelphia | ALS 4p+Env~ | MB |
| Weston, Caroline | | | |
| 23 July 1846 To | Philadelphia | ALS 2p+Env JL~ | MB |
| Weston, Deborah | | | |
| 23 July 1846 To | Philadelphia | ALS 2p+Env JL~ | MB |
| Weston, Emma | | | |
| 23 July 1846 To | Philadelphia | ALS 2p+Env JL~ | MB |
| Weston, Lucia | | | |
| 23 July 1846 To | Philadelphia | ALS 2p+Env JL~ | MB |
| Whitney, George H. | | | |
| 26 Feb. 1872 Fr | Haverhill, Mass. | ALS 1p | PSCHi-Mott |
| Wilbur, Julia A. | | | |
| 7 July 1853 To | Auburn, N.Y. | ALS 2p | NPV |
| Wildman, John K. | | | |
| 6 Dec. 1869 Fr | Philadelphia | ALS 3p | CtHSD |
| Willets, Sam | | | |
| 29 May 1872 Fr | New York City | ALS 1p | PSCHi-Mott |
| Willetts, Jane C. | | | |
| 19 Jan. 1878 To | Roadside | ANS 1p+Env | PHC |
| Willis, Phebe Post | | | |
| 16 Mar. 1831 To | Philadelphia | ALS 4p+Env | NRU |
| 26 July 1833 To | Philadelphia | ALS 6p | NRU |
| 22 Oct. 1833 To | Philadelphia | ALS 4p+Env | NRU |
| 1 Mar. 1834 To | Philadelphia | AL 3p+Env~ | NRU |
| 9 Mar. 1834 To | Philadelphia | AL 1p+Env~ | NRU |
| 13 Sept. 1834 To | Philadelphia | ALS 6p+Env~ | NRU |
| 10 Mar. 1835 To | Philadelphia | ALS 4p+Env | NRU |
| 20 Apr. 1835 To | Philadelphia | ALS 4p+Env | NRU |
| 2 Sept. 1835 To | Philadelphia | AL 3p+Env~ | NRU |
| 3 Sept. 1835 To | Philadelphia | AL 1p+Env~ | NRU |
| 26 Mar. 1836 To | Philadelphia | ALS 4p+Env | NRU |
| 19 May 1836 To | Philadelphia | ALS 4p+Env | NRU |
| 28 Aug. 1836 To | Philadelphia | ALS 4p+Env | NRU |
| 12 Feb. 1838 To | Philadelphia | ALS 4p+Env | NRU |
| 6 Sept. 1838 To | Philadelphia | ALS 3p+Env | NRU |
| 1 Nov. 1838 To | Philadelphia | ALS 2p+Enc | NRU |
| 25 Apr. 1840 To | Philadelphia | ALS 4p+Env | NRU |
| 6 Jan. 1842 To | Philadelphia | ALS 4p+Env~ | NRU |
| 28 Apr. 1842 To | Philadelphia | ALS 4p+Env | NRU |
| Woman's Association for the Promotion of Physiological and Hygienic Knowledge | | | |
| [pre–27 Mar. 1875] Fr | Philadelphia | PL 1p | PSCHi-Mott |
| Woman's Christian Association | | | |
| 29 Aug. 1873 Fr | St. Paul, Minn. | AL 2p JL | MNS |
| Woman's Convention, Salem | | | |
| 13 Apr. 1850 To | Philadelphia | PL 1p JL~ | *Lib* |

| Name and Date | Location | Document Type and Length | Source |
|---|---|---|---|
| Woman's Rights Friends | | | |
| [1 Sept. 1853] To | [Philadelphia] | PL 1p JL | *PFrm* |
| 15 Jan. 1854 To | ? | PL 1p JL | *PFrm* |
| 23 Dec. 1871 To | ? | PL 1p JL | *S-A Papers* |
| Woman Suffrage Advocates | | | |
| [pre–10 Jan. 1872] To | ? | PL 2p JL | *HWS* |
| Wood, Emma Parker | | | |
| [c. 1858] To | [Roadside?] | ALS 1p | PSCHi-Mott |
| Woodhull, Victoria C. | | | |
| 13 July 1871 Fr | ? | ALS 1p | MNS |
| 27 Feb. 1873 Fr | New York City | ALS 1p+TTR | MNS |
| Wright, David | | | |
| 4 June 1838 To | [Philadelphia] | AL 1p+Env JL | PSCHi-Mott |
| 5 June 1838 To | [Philadelphia] | AL 2p+Env JL | PSCHi-Mott |
| 6 June 1838 To | [Philadelphia] | AL 1p+Env JL | PSCHi-Mott |
| 28 Aug. [1841] To | Philadelphia | AL 2p JL~# | MNS |
| 3 Sept. 1843 To | Philadelphia | AL 3p+Env JL# | MNS |
| 13 Sept. 1843 To | Philadelphia | AL 1p+Env | MNS |
| 8 Aug. 1875 To | Roadside | ALS 4p | NSyU-Osb |
| Wright, Martha Coffin | | | |
| [1837] To | [Philadelphia] | PL 1p | Hallowell |
| 22 Feb. 1838 To | [Philadelphia?] | C 1p | PSCHi-Mott |
| 23 Feb. 1838 To | [Philadelphia?] | C 1p | PSCHi-Mott |
| 26 Feb. 1838 To | [Philadelphia?] | C 1p | PSCHi-Mott |
| 4 June 1838 To | [Philadelphia] | AL 2p+Env JL | PSCHi-Mott |
| 5 June 1838 To | [Philadelphia] | AL 1p+Env JL | PSCHi-Mott |
| 6 June 1838 To | [Philadelphia] | AL 1p+Env JL | PSCHi-Mott |
| 9 Aug. 1839 Fr | [Auburn, N.Y.] | AL 4p+Env Inc | MNS |
| 11 Mar. 1841 Fr | [Auburn, N.Y.] | TTR 7p | MNS |
| 5 Apr. 1841 Fr | [Auburn, N.Y.?] | ALS 4P+TTR, Env | MNS |
| 28 Aug. [1841] To | Philadelphia | AL 2p JL~# | MNS |
| 7 Nov. 1841 Fr | [Auburn, N.Y.] | AL 4p+Env TTR | MNS |
| 19 Nov. [1841] Fr | [Auburn, N.Y.] | AL 4p+Env TTR | MNS |
| [Dec. 1841?] Fr | [Auburn, N.Y.] | AL 4p+Env TTR | MNS |
| 7 Jan. 1842 Fr | Auburn, N.Y. | AL 4p+Env TTR | MNS |
| [Apr. 1842?] Fr | [Auburn, N.Y.] | C 2p+TTR | MNS |
| 27 Nov. 1842 Fr | Auburn, N.Y. | AL 1p+Env JL | MNS |
| 11 Jan. 1843 Fr | Auburn, N.Y. | AL 4p+Env TTR | MNS |
| 3 Feb. 1843 Fr | Auburn, N.Y. | AL 4p+Env TTR | MNS |
| 3 Sept. 1843 To | Philadelphia | AL 4p+Env JL# | MNS |
| 2 Jan. 1844 To | [Philadelphia] | PL 1p | Hallowell |
| [12 Jan. 1844] To* | [Philadelphia] | AL 1p Inc~ | MNS |
| 22 Feb. [1844?] To | [Philadelphia] | PL 1p | Hallowell |
| 11 Mar. 1844 Fr | Auburn, N.Y. | AL 3p+TTR | MNS |
| 17 Mar. 1844 To* | Philadelphia | AL 1p PS | PSCHi-Mott |
| 12 Sept. 1844 Fr | Auburn, N.Y. | AL 6p+Env TTR | MNS |
| 23 Sept. 1844 Fr | Auburn, N.Y. | AL 4p+Env TTR | MNS |
| 31 Oct. 1844 Fr | Auburn, N.Y. | AL 4p+Env TTR | MNS |
| 21 Dec. 1844 Fr | Auburn, N.Y. | AL 4p+Env TTR | MNS |
| 15 Jan. [1845] Fr* | Auburn, N.Y. | TTR 3p | MNS |
| 7 Feb. [1845] Fr* | Auburn, N.Y. | TTR 10p | MNS |

| Name and Date | Location | Document Type and Length | Source |
|---|---|---|---|
| 8 Mar. 1845 Fr | Auburn, N.Y. | AL 4p+Env TTR | MNS |
| 27 Mar. [1845?] Fr | Auburn, N.Y. | AL 4p Inc | MNS |
| 7 June [1845] Fr | Auburn, N.Y. | AL 4p+Env TTR | MNS |
| 23 June [1845] Fr* | Auburn, N.Y. | TTR 6p | MNS |
| 25 June [1845] Fr | Auburn, N.Y. | AL 4p+TTR | MNS |
| 30 Sept.[1845] Fr | Auburn, N.Y. | AL 3p+Env pTTR | MNS |
| 6 Oct. [1845] Fr | Auburn, N.Y. | AL 2p+Env pTTR | MNS |
| 7 Oct. [1845] Fr | Auburn, N.Y. | AL 3p+Env TTR | MNS |
| 14 Oct. [1845] Fr | Auburn, N.Y. | AL 1p+TTR | MNS |
| 16 Oct. [1845] Fr | Auburn, N.Y. | AL 4p+TTR | MNS |
| 23 Oct. 1845 Fr* | Auburn, N.Y. | TTR 1p | MNS |
| 28 Oct. 1845 Fr | Auburn, N.Y. | AL 4p+TTR | MNS |
| 14 Dec. [1845] Fr | Auburn, N.Y. | AL 6p+Env TTR | MNS |
| 23 [c. 1845] Fr* | [Auburn, N.Y.?] | TTR 3p | MNS |
| [c. 1845] Fr* | [Auburn, N.Y.?] | TTR 5p | MNS |
| 1 Jan. 1846 Fr | Auburn, N.Y. | AL 3p+TTR | MNS |
| 5 Jan. 1846 Fr | Auburn, N.Y. | AL 2p+TTR | MNS |
| 6 Jan. 1846 Fr | Auburn, N.Y. | AL 4p | MNS |
| 27 Jan. 1846 Fr | Auburn, N.Y. | AL 1p+TTR | MNS |
| [Jan. 1846] Fr | Auburn, N.Y. | AL 1p+Env TTR | MNS |
| 3 Feb. 1846 Fr | Auburn, N.Y. | AL 1p+Env TTR | MNS |
| 7 Feb. 1846 Fr | Auburn, N.Y. | AL 1p+Env TTR | MNS |
| 9 Feb. 1846 Fr | Auburn, N.Y. | AL 2p+Env TTR | MNS |
| 11 Feb. 1846 Fr | Auburn, N.Y. | AL 2p+Env TTR | MNS |
| 16 Feb. 1846 Fr | Auburn, N.Y. | AL 2p+Env TTR | MNS |
| 17 Feb. 1846 Fr | Auburn, N.Y. | AL 1p+Env TTR | MNS |
| 18 Feb. 1846 Fr | Auburn, N.Y. | AL 1p+Env TTR | MNS |
| 20 Feb. 1846 Fr | Auburn, N.Y. | AL 2p+Env TTR | MNS |
| 28 Feb. 1846 Fr | Auburn, N.Y. | AL 2p+Env TTR | MNS |
| 2 Mar. 1846 Fr | Auburn, N.Y. | AL 5p+Env TTR | MNS |
| 10 Mar. 1846 Fr | Auburn, N.Y. | AL 1p+TTR | MNS |
| 11 Mar. 1846 Fr | Auburn, N.Y. | AL 2p+TTR | MNS |
| 20 Mar. 1846 Fr | Auburn, N.Y. | AL 3p+TTR | MNS |
| 21 Mar. 1846 Fr | Auburn, N.Y. | AL 1p+TTR | MNS |
| 10 Apr. [1846] Fr | Auburn, N.Y. | AL 2p+pTTR | MNS |
| 10 Apr. 1846 To | Philadelphia | PL 1p | Hallowell |
| 14 Apr. 1846 Fr | Auburn, N.Y. | AL 2p+pTTR | MNS |
| 17 Apr. 1846 Fr | Auburn, N.Y. | AL 2p+pTTR | MNS |
| 22 Apr. 1846 Fr | Auburn, N.Y. | AL 2p+pTTR | MNS |
| 23 Apr. [1846] Fr | Auburn, N.Y. | AL 1p+Env TTR | MNS |
| 25 Apr. [1846] Fr | Auburn, N.Y. | AL 1p+Env TTR | MNS |
| 29 Apr. [1846] Fr | Auburn, N.Y. | AL 2p+Env TTR | MNS |
| 7 May [1846] Fr | Auburn, N.Y. | AL 1p+Env TTR | MNS |
| 8 May [1846] Fr | Auburn, N.Y. | AL 3p+Env TTR | MNS |
| 9 May [1846] Fr | Auburn, N.Y. | AL 1p+Env TTR | MNS |
| 13 May 1846 Fr | Auburn, N.Y. | AL 2p+pTTR | MNS |
| 22 May 1846 Fr | Auburn, N.Y. | AL 3p+pTTR | MNS |
| 2 June 1846 Fr | Auburn, N.Y. | AL 1p+Env pTTR | MNS |
| 15 June 1846 Fr | Auburn, N.Y. | AL 2p+Env pTTR | MNS |
| 18 June 1846 Fr | Auburn, N.Y. | AL 3p+Env pTTR | MNS |
| [8? July 1846] Fr | [Auburn, N.Y.] | AL 4p+Env | MNS |

| Name and Date | Location | Document Type and Length | Source |
|---|---|---|---|
| 9 [July 1846] Fr | [Auburn, N.Y.] | AL 1p+Env | MNS |
| 13 July 1846 Fr | Auburn, N.Y. | AL 1p+pTTR | MNS |
| 18 July 1846 Fr | Auburn, N.Y. | AL 4p+pTTR | MNS |
| 20 July 1846 Fr | Auburn, N.Y. | AL 1p+Env pTTR | MNS |
| 25 July 1846 Fr | Auburn, N.Y. | AL 2p+Env pTTR | MNS |
| 27 July 1846 Fr | Auburn, N.Y. | AL 3p+Env pTTR | MNS |
| 2 Aug. 1846 Fr | Auburn, N.Y. | AL 1p+Env pTTR | MNS |
| 4 Aug. 1846 Fr | Auburn, N.Y. | AL 1p+Env pTTR | MNS |
| 11 Aug. 1846 Fr | Auburn, N.Y. | AL 2p+TTR | MNS |
| 15 Aug. 1846 Fr | Auburn, N.Y. | AL 2p+pTTR | MNS |
| [21] Aug. 1846 Fr | Auburn, N.Y. | AL 3p+pTTR | MNS |
| 23 Aug. 1846 Fr | Auburn, N.Y. | AL 2p+pTTR | MNS |
| 24 Aug. 1846 Fr | Auburn, N.Y. | AL 1p+Env TTR | MNS |
| 27 Aug. 1846 Fr | Auburn, N.Y. | AL 1p+Env TTR | MNS |
| 31 Aug. 1846 Fr | Auburn, N.Y. | AL 1p+Env TTR | MNS |
| 4 Sept. 1846 Fr | Auburn, N.Y. | AL 1p+Env TTR | MNS |
| 5 Sept. 1846 Fr | Auburn, N.Y. | AL 1p+Env TTR | MNS |
| 7 Sept. 1846 Fr | Auburn, N.Y. | AL 1p+Env TTR | MNS |
| 20 Jan. 1847 Fr | Auburn, N.Y. | AL 1p+pTTR | MNS |
| 26 Jan. 1847 Fr | Auburn, N.Y. | AL 1p+pTTR | MNS |
| 29 Jan. 1847 Fr | Auburn, N.Y. | AL 3p+pTTR | MNS |
| 5 Feb. 1847 Fr | Auburn, N.Y. | AL 3p+pTTR | MNS |
| 7 Feb. 1847 Fr | Auburn, N.Y. | AL 2p+TTR | MNS |
| 8 Feb. 1847 Fr | Auburn, N.Y. | AL 2p+TTR | MNS |
| 11 Feb. 1847 Fr | Auburn, N.Y. | AL 2p+TTR | MNS |
| 16 Feb. 1847 Fr | Auburn, N.Y. | AL 1p+TTR | MNS |
| 25 Feb. 1847 Fr | Auburn, N.Y. | AL 4p+pTTR | MNS |
| [28] Feb. 1847 Fr | Auburn, N.Y. | AL 1p+pTTR | MNS |
| 17 Mar. 1847 Fr | Auburn, N.Y. | AL 3p+pTTR | MNS |
| 21 Mar. 1847 Fr | Auburn, N.Y. | AL 1p+pTTR | MNS |
| 22 Mar. 1847 Fr | Auburn, N.Y. | AL 1p+pTTR | MNS |
| [c. 22 May 1847] To** | [Philadelphia] | AL 2p Frag Dam~ | MNS |
| 2 June [1847] To** | [Philadelphia] | AL 1p Frag Dam~ | MNS |
| 28 June 1847 Fr | Auburn, N.Y. | AL 2p+Env TTR | MNS |
| [11?] July 1847 Fr | Auburn, N.Y. | AL 3p+Env TTR | MNS |
| 13 July 1847 Fr | Auburn, N.Y. | AL 2p+Env TTR | MNS |
| 14 July 1847 Fr | Auburn, N.Y. | AL 1p+Env TTR | MNS |
| 14 [1847?] Fr | Auburn, N.Y. | AL 2p+pTTR | MNS |
| 17 Feb. 1848 Fr | Auburn, N.Y. | AL 2p+Env pTTR | MNS |
| 25 Feb. 1848 Fr | Auburn, N.Y. | AL 5p+Env pTTR | MNS |
| 7 Mar. 1848 Fr | Auburn, N.Y. | AL 1p+Env pTTR | MNS |
| 23 May [1848] Fr | Auburn, N.Y. | AL 4p+Env | MNS |
| 5 Aug. 1848 Fr | Auburn, N.Y. | ALS 2p+Env pTTR | MNS |
| 11 Aug. 1848 Fr | Auburn, N.Y. | ALS 2p+Env pTTR | MNS |
| 21 Aug. 1848 Fr | Auburn, N.Y. | AL 4p+pTTR | MNS |
| [2? Sept. 1848] Fr | [Auburn, N.Y.] | AL 2p+Env Inc? | MNS |
| 3 [Sept. 1848] Fr | [Auburn, N.Y.] | AL 1p+Env Inc? | MNS |
| 4 Sept. 1848 Fr | Auburn, N.Y. | AL 2p+Env pTTR | MNS |
| 14 Sept. 1848 Fr | Auburn, N.Y. | AL 2p+Env pTTR | MNS |
| 20 Sept. 1848 Fr | Auburn, N.Y. | ALS 2p+pTTR | MNS |
| 21 Sept. 1848 Fr | Auburn, N.Y. | ALS 2p+pTTR | MNS |

| Name and Date | Location | Document Type and Length | Source |
|---|---|---|---|
| [c. Sept. 1848] Fr | [Auburn, N.Y.] | TTR 3p | MNS |
| 1 Oct. 1848 Fr | Auburn, N.Y. | AL 1p+pTTR | MNS |
| 3 Oct. 1848 Fr | Auburn, N.Y. | AL 2p+pTTR | MNS |
| 4 Oct. 1848 Fr | Auburn, N.Y. | AL 2p+pTTR | MNS |
| 9 Oct. 1848 Fr | Auburn, N.Y. | AL 2p+pTTR | MNS |
| 14 Oct. 1848 Fr | Auburn, N.Y. | AL 1p+pTTR | MNS |
| 16 Oct. 1848 Fr | Auburn, N.Y. | AL 2p+Env pTTR | MNS |
| 28 Oct. 1848 Fr | Auburn, N.Y. | AL 3p+Env pTTR | MNS |
| 29 [Nov.] 1848 Fr | Auburn, N.Y. | AL 2p+Env TTR | MNS |
| 1 Dec. 1848 Fr | Auburn, N.Y. | AL 3p+Env TTR | MNS |
| 6 Dec. 1848 Fr | Auburn, N.Y. | AL 2p+pTTR | MNS |
| 19 Dec. [1848] To | [Philadelphia] | AL 1p PS | PSCHi-Mott |
| 20 Dec. [1848] To | [Philadelphia] | AL 1p PS | PSCHi-Mott |
| 27 Dec. 1848 Fr | Auburn, N.Y. | AL 3p+pTTR | MNS |
| 28 Dec. 1848 Fr | Auburn, N.Y. | AL 1p+pTTR | MNS |
| [Dec. 1848] To | [Philadelphia] | PL 1p | Hallowell |
| [c. 1848] To** | [Philadelphia?] | AL 2p Inc Dam | PSCHi-Mott |
| 9 Jan. [1849] Fr | [Auburn, N.Y.] | AL 2p+Env pTTR | MNS |
| 12 Jan. 1849 Fr | Auburn, N.Y. | AL 4p+Env pTTR | MNS |
| 3 Feb. 1849 Fr | Auburn, N.Y. | AL 4p+Env pTTR | MNS |
| 13 Feb. 1849 Fr | Auburn, N.Y. | AL 2p+Env pTTR | MNS |
| 19 Feb. 1849 Fr | Auburn, N.Y. | AL 3p+Env pTTR | MNS |
| 20 Feb. 1849 Fr | Auburn, N.Y. | AL 3p+Env pTTR | MNS |
| 5 Mar. 1849 Fr | Auburn, N.Y. | AL 6p+Env | MNS |
| 25 Mar. 1849 Fr | Auburn, N.Y. | AL 1p+Env | MNS |
| 2 Apr. 1849 Fr | Auburn, N.Y. | AL 3p+Env pTTR | MNS |
| 9 Apr. 1849 Fr | Auburn, N.Y. | AL 1p+Env pTTR | MNS |
| 6 May [1849] Fr | [Auburn, N.Y.] | TTR 5p | MNS |
| 7 May [1849] Fr | [Auburn, N.Y.] | TTR 2p | MNS |
| 8 May [1849] Fr | [Auburn, N.Y.] | TTR 1p | MNS |
| 6 July 1849 To* | Philadelphia | AL 3p# | PSCHi-Mott |
| 8 July 1849 To* | Philadelphia | AL 1p# | PSCHi-Mott |
| 9 July 1849 To* | [Philadelphia] | AL 2p | PSCHi-Mott |
| 13 July 1849 To* | Philadelphia | AL 1p Dam | PSCHi-Mott |
| 14 July 1849 To* | Philadelphia | AL 6p Dam | PSCHi-Mott |
| 15 July 1849 To* | Philadelphia | AL 1p | PSCHi-Mott |
| 17 July 1849 To* | Philadelphia | AL 2p | PSCHi-Mott |
| 25 July 1849 To* | Philadelphia | AL 5p | PSCHi-Mott |
| 26 July 1849 To* | Philadelphia | AL 1p | PSCHi-Mott |
| 28 July 1849 To* | Philadelphia | AL 4p Dam | PSCHi-Mott |
| 3 Aug. 1849 To* | Philadelphia | AL 2p | PSCHi-Mott |
| 6 Aug. 1849 To* | Philadelphia | AL 1p | PSCHi-Mott |
| 21 [Nov. 1849] To | Philadelphia | AL 4p Inc?# | PSCHi-Mott |
| 26 Dec. [1849?] To* | [Philadelphia] | AL 2p Inc Dam | PSCHi-Mott |
| 3 Jan. 1850 Fr | Auburn, N.Y. | AL 2p+Env pTTR | MNS |
| 8 Jan. 1850 Fr | Auburn, N.Y. | AL 3p+Env pTTR | MNS |
| 15 Jan. 1850 Fr | Auburn, N.Y. | AL 3p+Env pTTR | MNS |
| 21 Jan. 1850 Fr | Auburn, N.Y. | AL 4p+Env TTR | MNS |
| 27 Jan. 1850 Fr | Auburn, N.Y. | AL 4p+Env TTR | MNS |
| 29 Jan. 1850 Fr | Auburn, N.Y. | AL 3p+Env pTTR | MNS |
| [c. Jan. 1850] To* | [Philadelphia] | AL 2p Frag | PSCHi-Mott |

| Name and Date | Location | Document Type and Length | Source |
|---|---|---|---|
| [c. 6 Feb. 1850] To** | [Philadelphia] | AL 2p~ | PSCHi-Mott |
| 13 Feb. 1850 Fr | Auburn, N.Y. | AL 6p+Env pTTR | MNS |
| 16 Feb. 1850 Fr | Auburn, N.Y. | AL 1p+Env TTR | MNS |
| 23 Feb. 1850 Fr | Auburn, N.Y. | AL 4p+Env TTR | MNS |
| 27 Feb. 1850 Fr | Auburn, N.Y. | AL 3p+Env TTR | MNS |
| 4 Oct. 1850 Fr | Auburn, N.Y. | AL 2p+TTR | MNS |
| 6 Oct. 1850 Fr | Auburn, N.Y. | AL 2p+TTR | MNS |
| 8 Oct. 1850 Fr | Auburn, N.Y. | AL 3p+TTR | MNS |
| 17 Oct. 1850 Fr | Auburn, N.Y. | AL 1p+TTR | MNS |
| 2 Nov. 1850 Fr | Auburn, N.Y. | AL 2p+TTR | MNS |
| 3 Nov. 1850 Fr | Auburn, N.Y. | AL 2p+TTR | MNS |
| 20 Nov. 1850 Fr | Auburn, N.Y. | AL 3p+Env TTR | MNS |
| 21 Nov. 1850 Fr | Auburn, N.Y. | AL 1p+Env TTR | MNS |
| 24 Nov. 1850 Fr | Auburn, N.Y. | AL 3p+Env TTR | MNS |
| 30 Nov. 1850 Fr | Auburn, N.Y. | AL 2p+Env TTR | MNS |
| 9 Dec. 1850 Fr | Auburn, N.Y. | AL 5p+Env pTTR | MNS |
| 14 Dec. 1850 Fr | Auburn, N.Y. | AL 2p+Env pTTR | MNS |
| 16 Dec. 1850 Fr | Auburn, N.Y. | AL 1p+Env pTTR | MNS |
| 30 Dec. 1850 Fr | Auburn, N.Y. | AL 3p+Env TTR | MNS |
| 15 [1850?] Fr | [Auburn, N.Y.] | AL 2p+TTR Inc | MNS |
| 16 [1850?] Fr | [Auburn, N.Y.] | AL 1p+TTR Inc | MNS |
| 2 Jan. 1851 Fr | Auburn, N.Y. | AL 2p+Env TTR | MNS |
| 14 Mar. 1851 Fr | Auburn, N.Y. | AL 3p+pTTR | MNS |
| 19 Mar. 1851 To* | Philadelphia | AL 4p+TTR | MNS |
| 20 Mar. 1851 Fr | Auburn, N.Y. | AL 1p+pTTR | MNS |
| 21 Mar. 1851 Fr | Auburn, N.Y. | AL 2p+pTTR | MNS |
| 24 Mar. 1851 Fr | Auburn, N.Y. | AL 1p+pTTR | MNS |
| 13 May 1851 Fr | Auburn, N.Y. | AL 2p | MNS |
| 16 May 1851 Fr | Auburn, N.Y. | AL 3p | MNS |
| 2 June 1851 Fr | Auburn, N.Y. | AL 3p | MNS |
| June 1851 Fr | Auburn, N.Y. | AL 2p | MNS |
| 6 Feb. 1852 Fr | Auburn, N.Y. | AL 2p+Env pTTR | MNS |
| 8 Feb. 1852 Fr | Auburn, N.Y. | AL 2p+Env pTTR | MNS |
| 13 Feb. 1852 Fr | Auburn, N.Y. | AL 4p+Env pTTR | MNS |
| 26 Feb. 1852 Fr | Auburn, N.Y. | ALS 3p+pTTR | MNS |
| 28 Feb. 1852 Fr | Auburn, N.Y. | ALS 2p+pTTR | MNS |
| 1 Mar. 1852 Fr | Auburn, N.Y. | ALS 3p+pTTR | MNS |
| [22 Apr. 1852] Fr | Auburn, N.Y. | AL 3p+Env Inc | MNS |
| 24 [Apr. 1852] Fr | Auburn, N.Y. | AL 4p+Env Inc | MNS |
| 5 Sept. 1852 To** | Philadelphia | AL 3p# | PSCHi-Mott |
| 29 Sept. [1852] Fr | Auburn, N.Y. | AL 1p+pTTR | MNS |
| 5 Oct. [1852] Fr | Auburn, N.Y. | AL 2p+pTTR | MNS |
| 11 Oct. [1852] Fr | Auburn, N.Y. | AL 3p+pTTR | MNS |
| [1852] Fr | ? | TTR 2p | MNS |
| 27 Feb. [1853] To* | Philadelphia | AL 2p Dam | PSCHi-Mott |
| 31 Mar. [1853] To* | [Philadelphia] | AL 2p Inc | PSCHi-Mott |
| 28 Jan. 1854 Fr | Auburn, N.Y. | AL 4p+pTTR Dam | MNS |
| 29 Jan. 1854 Fr | Auburn, N.Y. | AL 2p+pTTR Dam | MNS |
| 30 Jan. 1854 To* | Philadelphia | AL 4p | PSCHi-Mott |
| 5 Feb. 1854 Fr | Auburn, N.Y. | AL 3p+pTTR Dam | MNS |
| 20 Feb. 1854 Fr | Auburn, N.Y. | AL 3p+pTTR | MNS |

| Name and Date | Location | Document Type and Length | Source |
|---|---|---|---|
| 21 Feb. 1854 Fr | Auburn, N.Y. | AL 2p+pTTR | MNS |
| 27 Feb. 1854 Fr | Auburn, N.Y. | AL 4p+pTTR | MNS |
| 8 Mar. 1854 Fr | Auburn, N.Y. | ALS 4p+pTTR Dam | MNS |
| 20 Mar. 1854 Fr | Auburn, N.Y. | AL 4p+pTTR | MNS |
| 5 Apr. 1854 Fr | Auburn, N.Y. | AL 4p | MNS |
| 6 Aug. 1854 Fr | Auburn, N.Y. | ALS 12p+pTTR | MNS |
| 14 Jan. 1855 Fr | Auburn, N.Y. | TTR 6p | MNS |
| 16 Jan. 1855 To | Philadelphia | ALS 4p | PSCHi-Mott |
| 19 Jan. 1855 Fr | Auburn, N.Y. | AL 1p+pTTR | MNS |
| 20 Jan. 1855 Fr | Auburn, N.Y. | TTR 1p | MNS |
| 22 Jan. 1855 Fr | Auburn, N.Y. | AL 1p+pTTR | MNS |
| 22 Jan. 1855 To | Philadelphia | ALS 3p Dam | PSCHi-Mott |
| 23 Jan. 1855 To | Philadelphia | ALS 1p Dam | PSCHi-Mott |
| 24 Jan. 1855 To | Philadelphia | AL 3p Dam | PSCHi-Mott |
| 25 Jan. 1855 To | Philadelphia | ALS 2p | PSCHi-Mott |
| 29 Jan. 1855 Fr | Auburn, N.Y. | TTR 2p | MNS |
| 1 Feb. 1855 To | Philadelphia | ALS 4p | PSCHi-Mott |
| 12 Feb. 1855 Fr | Auburn, N.Y. | ALS 8p+pTTR Dam | MNS |
| 14 Feb. 1855 Fr | Auburn, N.Y. | AL 4p+pTTR | MNS |
| 18 Feb. 1855 To | Philadelphia | ALS 5p Dam | PSCHi-Mott |
| 19 Feb. 1855 To | Philadelphia | ALS 1p | PSCHi-Mott |
| 27 Feb. 1855 Fr | Auburn, N.Y. | AL 3p+pTTR Dam | MNS |
| 27 Feb. 1855 To* | Philadelphia | PL 2p | Hallowell |
| 28 Feb. 1855 Fr | Auburn, N.Y. | AL 4p+pTTR Dam | MNS |
| 5 Mar. 1855 To | Philadelphia | ALS 16p | PSCHi-Mott |
| 6 Mar. 1855 To | Philadelphia | ALS 3p | PSCHi-Mott |
| 12 Mar. 1855 To | Philadelphia | ALS 4p Dam | PSCHi-Mott |
| 15 Mar. [1855?] Fr | Auburn, N.Y. | AL 4p+pTTR | MNS |
| 17 Mar. [1855?] Fr | Auburn, N.Y. | AL 1p+pTTR | MNS |
| 26 Mar. 1855 To | Philadelphia | ALS 4p | PSCHi-Mott |
| 27 Mar. 1855 To | Philadelphia | ALS 2p | PSCHi-Mott |
| 29 Mar. 1855 Fr | Auburn, N.Y. | AL 1p+pTTR | MNS |
| 2 Apr. 1855 To | Philadelphia | ALS 6p Dam | PSCHi-Mott |
| 7 Apr. 1855 Fr | Auburn, N.Y. | ALS 4p+pTTR | MNS |
| 7 Apr. 1855 Fr | Auburn, N.Y. | ALS 4p+pTTR | MNS |
| 11 Apr. 1855 Fr | Auburn, N.Y. | ALS 2p+pTTR | MNS |
| 13 Apr. 1855 Fr | Auburn, N.Y. | ALS 2p+pTTR | MNS |
| 16 Apr. 1855 To | Philadelphia | AL 2p Dam | PSCHi-Mott |
| 17 Apr. 1855 To | Philadelphia | AL 3p Dam | PSCHi-Mott |
| 21 Apr. 1855 To | Philadelphia | ALS 4p | PSCHi-Mott |
| 22 Apr. 1855 To | Philadelphia | ALS 1p | PSCHi-Mott |
| 23 Apr. 1855 Fr | Auburn, N.Y. | ALS 2p+pTTR | MNS |
| 23 Apr. 1855 To | Philadelphia | ALS 1p | PSCHi-Mott |
| 24 Apr. 1855 Fr | Auburn, N.Y. | ALS 2p+pTTR | MNS |
| 25 Apr. 1855 Fr | Auburn, N.Y. | ALS 3p+pTTR Dam | MNS |
| 26 Apr. 1855 Fr | Auburn, N.Y. | ALS 1p+pTTR Dam | MNS |
| 26 Apr. 1855 To* | Philadelphia | ALS 4p | PSCHi-Mott |
| 27 Apr. 1855 To* | Philadelphia | AL 6p# | PSCHi-Mott |
| 27 Apr. 1855 Fr | Auburn, N.Y. | ALS 2p+pTTR Dam | MNS |
| 28 Apr. 1855 Fr | Auburn, N.Y. | ALS 2p+pTTR Dam | MNS |
| 30 Apr. 1855 To* | Philadelphia | AL 3p# | PSCHi-Mott |

| Name and Date | Location | Document Type and Length | Source |
|---|---|---|---|
| 1 May 1855 To* | Philadelphia | AL 1p# | PSCHi-Mott |
| 4 May 1855 Fr | Auburn, N.Y. | ALS 3p+pTTR | MNS |
| [5] May 1855 Fr | Auburn, N.Y. | ALS 1p+pTTR | MNS |
| 10 May 1855 To* | Philadelphia | ALS 4p | PSCHi-Mott |
| 11 May 1855 To* | Philadelphia | ALS 1p | PSCHi-Mott |
| 14 May 1855 To* | Philadelphia | AL 7p# | PSCHi-Mott |
| 19 May 1855 To* | Roadside | AL 4p | PSCHi-Mott |
| 21 May 1855 To* | Roadside | AL 2p | PSCHi-Mott |
| 22 May 1855 To* | Roadside | AL 1p | PSCHi-Mott |
| [post–30 May 1855] To* | [Philadelphia?] | AL 1p | PSCHi-Mott |
| 4 June 1855 To* | Philadelphia | AL 4p | PSCHi-Mott |
| 7 June 1855 To* | Philadelphia | AL 2p | PSCHi-Mott |
| 4 July 1855 To* | Philadelphia | AL 2p | PSCHi-Mott |
| 5 July 1855 To* | Philadelphia | AL 2p | PSCHi-Mott |
| 14 Aug. 1855 To* | Philadelphia | AL 2p | PSCHi-Mott |
| 15 Aug. 1855 To* | Philadelphia | AL 2p | PSCHi-Mott |
| 16 Aug. 1855 To* | Philadelphia | AL 2p | PSCHi-Mott |
| 29 Aug. 1855 Fr | Auburn, N.Y. | ALS 2p | MNS |
| 30 Aug. 1855 Fr | Auburn, N.Y. | ALS 2p | MNS |
| 4 Sept. 1855 To* | Philadelphia | AL 4p+TR | PSCHi-Mott |
| 5 Sept. 1855 To* | Philadelphia | AL 6p~ | PSCHi-Mott |
| 7 Sept. 1855 To* | Philadelphia | AL 2p | PSCHi-Mott |
| 8 Sept. 1855 Fr | Auburn, N.Y. | ALS 3p+pTTR JL | MNS |
| 9 Sept. 1855 Fr | Auburn, N.Y. | ALS 2p+pTTR JL | MNS |
| 10 Sept. 1855 Fr | Auburn, N.Y. | ALS 1p+pTTR JL | MNS |
| 11 Sept. 1855 To* | Philadelphia | AL 4p Inc | PSCHi-Mott |
| 12 Sept. 1855 To* | Philadelphia | AL 1p Inc | PSCHi-Mott |
| 13 Sept. 1855 To* | Philadelphia | AL 1p Inc | PSCHi-Mott |
| [post–13 Sept. 1855] Fr | [Auburn, N.Y.] | AL 2p+pTTR | MNS |
| 17 Sept. 1855 To* | Philadelphia | AL 3p | PSCHi-Mott |
| 18 Sept. 1855 To* | Philadelphia | AL 2p | PSCHi-Mott |
| 19 Sept. 1855 To* | Philadelphia | AL 1p | PSCHi-Mott |
| 4 Oct. 1855 To* | Philadelphia | AL 4p | PSCHi-Mott |
| 10 Nov. 1855 To* | New York City | ALS 4p | PSCHi-Mott |
| 16 Nov. 1855 To* | Philadelphia | AL 5p | PSCHi-Mott |
| 17 Nov. 1855 Fr | Auburn, N.Y. | AL 2p+pTTR | MNS |
| 20 Nov. 1855 To* | Philadelphia | AL 1p | PSCHi-Mott |
| 22 Nov. 1855 Fr | Auburn, N.Y. | AL 3p+pTTR | MNS |
| 24 Nov. 1855 To* | Philadelphia | AL 3p | MNS |
| 24 Nov. 1855 Fr | Auburn, N.Y. | AL 1p+pTTR | MNS |
| 25 Nov. 1855 To* | Philadelphia | AL 2p | MNS |
| 26 Nov. 1855 Fr | Auburn, N.Y. | AL 1p+pTTR | MNS |
| 26 Nov. 1855 To* | Philadelphia | AL 1p | MNS |
| 29 Nov. [1855] Fr | [Auburn, N.Y.] | ALS 2p+pTTR | MNS |
| 30 Nov. [1855] Fr | [Auburn, N.Y.] | ALS 1p+pTTR | MNS |
| 4 Dec. [1855] To* | [Philadelphia] | AL 4p | PSCHi-Mott |
| 5 Dec. [1855] To* | [Philadelphia] | AL 1p | PSCHi-Mott |
| 7 Dec. 1855 Fr | Auburn, N.Y. | AL 3p+pTTR | MNS |
| 9 Dec. 1855 Fr | Auburn, N.Y. | AL 2p+pTTR | MNS |
| 9 Dec. 1855 To* | Philadelphia | AL 3p | PSCHi-Mott |
| 10 Dec. 1855 To* | Philadelphia | AL 2p | PSCHi-Mott |

| Name and Date | Location | Document Type and Length | Source |
|---|---|---|---|
| 10 Dec. 1855 Fr | Auburn, N.Y. | AL 1p+pTTR | MNS |
| 13 Dec. 1855 Fr | Auburn, N.Y. | AL 4p+pTTR | MNS |
| 18 Dec. 1855 To* | Philadelphia | AL 2p | PSCHi-Mott |
| 31 Dec. 1855 To* | Philadelphia | AL 2p+TR | PSCHi-Mott |
| 1855 To** | [Philadelphia] | PL 3p | Hallowell |
| [c. 1855] To** | [Philadelphia?] | AL 2p Inc | PSCHi-Mott |
| 1 Jan. 1856 To* | Philadelphia | AL 3p | PSCHi-Mott |
| 6 Jan. 1856 Fr | Auburn, N.Y. | ALS 2p+pTTR | MNS |
| 7 Jan. 1856 To* | Philadelphia | AL 4p | PSCHi-Mott |
| 8 Jan. 1856 To* | Philadelphia | AL 4p | PSCHi-Mott |
| 8 Jan. 1856 Fr | Auburn, N.Y. | ALS 2p+pTTR | MNS |
| 10 Jan. 1856 Fr | Auburn, N.Y. | ALS 2p+pTTR | MNS |
| 18 Jan. 1856 To* | Philadelphia | AL 4P+TTR | MNS |
| 19 Jan. 1856 To* | Philadelphia | AL 1P+TTR | MNS |
| 26 Jan. 1856 To* | Philadelphia | AL 2p+TTR Inc? | MNS |
| 29 Jan. 1856 Fr | Auburn, N.Y. | TTR 2p | MNS |
| 29 Jan. 1856 Fr | Auburn, N.Y. | TTR 4p | MNS |
| 9 Feb. 1856 To* | Philadelphia | AL 4p+TTR Inc | MNS |
| 10 [Feb. 1856] To* | [Philadelphia] | AL 2p Inc | MNS |
| 14 Feb. 1856 Fr | Auburn, N.Y. | ALS 4p+pTTR | MNS |
| 15 Feb. 1856 Fr | Auburn, N.Y. | ALS 1p+pTTR | MNS |
| 25 Feb. 1856 To* | Philadelphia | AL 3p | MNS |
| 26 Feb. 1856 To* | Philadelphia | AL 1p~ | MNS |
| 1 Mar. 1856 Fr | Auburn, N.Y. | TTR 1p | MNS |
| [4?] Mar. 1856 To* | Philadelphia | AL 2p+pTTR | MNS |
| 11 Mar. 1856 To* | Philadelphia | AL 6p | MNS |
| 13 Mar. 1856 To* | Philadelphia | AL 6p | MNS |
| 14 Mar. 1856 To* | Philadelphia | AL 2p | MNS |
| 3 Apr. 1856 To | Philadelphia | AL 4p+TR | MNS |
| 17 Apr. 1856 To* | Philadelphia | AL 4p+TTR | MNS |
| [post–17 Apr. 1856] To* | [Philadelphia?] | AL 2p+Enc TTR | MNS |
| 18 [Apr. 1856] To* | [Philadelphia] | AL 1p+Enc TTR | MNS |
| 18 Apr. 1856 To* | Philadelphia | AL 6p+TTR | MNS |
| 29 Apr. 1856 To* | Philadelphia | AL 4p+TTR | MNS |
| 1 May 1856 To* | Philadelphia | AL 1p+TTR | MNS |
| 14 May 1856 To* | Philadelphia | AL 3p | MNS |
| 15 May 1856 To* | Philadelphia | AL 2p | MNS |
| 16 May 1856 To* | Philadelphia | AL 1p | MNS |
| 7 [June? 1856] To* | [Roadside] | AL 2p Inc | PSCHi-Mott |
| 9 Aug. 1856 To* | Nantucket, Mass. | AL 4p+TTR | MNS |
| 18 Aug. 1856 To* | Flume House, N.H. | AL 2p+TTR | MNS |
| 19[Aug.? 1856] To | Flume House, N.H. | AL 2p Inc? | MNS |
| [c. 21 Aug. 1856] To** | [Flume House, N.H.] | AL 2p | MNS |
| 22 Aug. 1856 Fr | [Auburn, N.Y.] | AL 1p+TTR Frag | MNS |
| 26 Aug. 1856 To* | Gloucester, Mass. | ALS 1p+TTR | MNS |
| 28 Aug. 1856 To* | Boston | ALS 1p+TTR | MNS |
| 21 Sept. 1856 To* | Roadside | AL 1p | PSCHi-Mott |
| 22 Sept. 1856 To* | Roadside | AL 4p | PSCHi-Mott |
| 19 Feb. 1857 To* | Philadelphia | AL 1p+pTTR | MNS |
| 24 Feb. 1857 To* | Philadelphia | AL 2p+pTTR | MNS |
| 25 Feb. 1857 To* | Philadelphia | AL 2p+pTTR | MNS |

| Name and Date | Location | Document Type and Length | Source |
|---|---|---|---|
| 27 Feb. 1857 To* | Philadelphia | AL 2p+pTTR | MNS |
| 1 Mar. 1857 To* | Philadelphia | AL 2p | MNS |
| [1 Mar.? 1857] To* | [Roadside] | AL 1p+pTTR | MNS |
| 2 [Mar. 1857] To* | [Roadside] | AL 2p | MNS |
| 17 Mar. [1857] To* | Philadelphia | AL 4p+pTTR | MNS |
| [Mar. 1857?] To* | [Philadelphia?] | AL 1p Frag +TTR | MNS |
| [1] Apr. [1857] To* | [Philadelphia] | AL 4p | PSCHi-Mott |
| 2 Apr. [1857] To* | [Philadelphia] | AL 4p | PSCHi-Mott |
| 11 Apr. 1857 To* | Roadside | AL 3p+TR | MNS |
| 13 Apr. 1857 To* | Roadside | AL 1p+pTTR | MNS |
| [17 Apr. 1857] To* | [Roadside] | AL 5p | MNS |
| [c. Apr. 1857] To* | Philadelphia | AL 1p Inc | MNS |
| [c. Apr. 1857] To* | [Roadside] | AL 2p Inc | MNS |
| 6 May 1857 To* | Roadside | AL 2p+pTTR | MNS |
| 7 May 1857 To* | Roadside | AL 4p+pTTR | MNS |
| 25 May 1857 To* | Roadside | AL 1p+pTTR Dam | MNS |
| 29 May 1857 To* | Roadside | AL 2p+pTTR Dam | MNS |
| 1 June 1857 To* | Roadside | AL 1p+pTTR Dam | MNS |
| 2 June 1857 To* | Roadside | AL 1p+pTTR Dam | MNS |
| [c. 4 June 1857] To* | [Lancaster?] | AL 2p Inc | MNS |
| 12 June 1857 To* | Roadside | AL 3p | MNS |
| 20 June 1857 To* | Roadside | AL 2p | MNS |
| 21 [June 1857] To* | [Roadside] | AL 1p | MNS |
| 24 [June 1857] To* | Philadelphia | AL 2p | MNS |
| 9 July 1857 To* | Roadside | AL 2p+pTTR | MNS |
| 10 July 1857 To* | Roadside | AL 1p+pTTR | MNS |
| 11 [July 1857] To* | Roadside | AL 1p+pTTR | MNS |
| 13 July 1857 To* | Philadelphia | AL 1p+pTTR | MNS |
| 7 Sept. 1857 To* | Roadside | ALS 2p+pTTR | MNS |
| 8 Sept. 1857 To* | Roadside | AL 3p~ | MNS |
| 9 Sept. 1857 To* | Philadelphia | ALS 2p | MNS |
| 10 Sept. 1857 To* | Philadelphia | ALS 1p | MNS |
| 13 Sept. 1857 To* | Roadside | ALS 2p+pTTR | MNS |
| 18 Sept. 1857 To* | Philadelphia | ALS 3p+pTTR | MNS |
| 22 Sept. 1857 To* | Roadside | ALS 3p | MNS |
| 23 Sept. 1857 To* | Roadside | ALS 1p | MNS |
| 12 Oct. 1857 To* | Roadside | AL 6p+pTTR | MNS |
| 18 Oct. 1857 To* | Roadside | AL 2p | MNS |
| 8 Nov. 1857 To* | Roadside | AL 4p~ | MNS |
| 12 [Nov. 1857?] To* | Roadside | AL 2p+TTR | MNS |
| 14 [Nov. 1857?] To* | Roadside | AL 3p+TTR | MNS |
| 24 Nov. 1857 To* | Roadside | AL 3p | MNS |
| [26] Nov. 1857 To* | Roadside | AL 1p | MNS |
| 28 Nov. 1857 To* | Roadside | AL 1p | MNS |
| 29 Nov. 1857 To* | Roadside | AL 3p | MNS |
| 9 Dec. 1857 To* | Roadside | AL 3p | MNS |
| 10 Dec. 1857 To** | Roadside | AL 2p | MNS |
| 10 Dec. 1857 To* | Roadside | AL 2p | MNS |
| 20 Dec. 1857 To* | Philadelphia | AL 1p | MNS |
| 21 Dec. 1857 To* | [Philadelphia] | AL 2p | MNS |
| 22 Dec. 1857 To* | [Philadelphia] | AL 2p | MNS |

| Name and Date | Location | Document Type and Length | Source |
|---|---|---|---|
| [post–26 Dec. 1857] To* | Roadside | AL 2p+TTR | MNS |
| [1857?] Fr | [Auburn, N.Y.?] | AL 2p | MNS |
| [1857?] Fr | [Auburn, N.Y.] | AL 2p Frag | MNS |
| 6 Jan. 1858 To* | Philadelphia | AL 2p | MNS |
| 7 Jan. 1858 To* | Philadelphia | AL 2p | MNS |
| 14 Jan. 1858 To* | Philadelphia | AL 8p+TTR | MNS |
| 14 Jan. 1858 Fr | Auburn, N.Y. | AL 4p JL Dam | MNS |
| 16 May 1858 To* | Roadside | AL 3p | MNS |
| 17 May 1858 Fr | Auburn, N.Y. | AL 4p | MNS |
| 19 May 1858 To* | Roadside | AL 2p | MNS |
| 20 May 1858 To* | Philadelphia | AL 1p | MNS |
| 27 May 1858 To* | Roadside | AL 11p | MNS |
| 29 [May 1858] To* | Philadelphia | AL 1p | MNS |
| 13 June 1858 To* | Roadside | ALS 2p | PSCHi-Mott |
| 14 June 1858 To* | Roadside | ALS 2p | PSCHi-Mott |
| 15 June 1858 To* | Roadside | ALS 2p | PSCHi-Mott |
| 20 June 1858 Fr | Auburn, N.Y. | ALS 4p | MNS |
| 21 June 1858 Fr | Auburn, N.Y. | AL 2p | MNS |
| 29 June 1858 To* | Roadside | AL 4p | PSCHi-Mott |
| 5 July [1858] To* | [Roadside] | AL 2p Inc JL | PSCHi-Mott |
| 6 July 1858 To* | Roadside | AL 2p~# | PSCHi-Mott |
| 8 July 1858 To* | Roadside | AL 3p# | PSCHi-Mott |
| 7 Aug. 1858 To* | Roadside | AL 3p | PSCHi-Mott |
| 8 Aug. 1858 To* | Roadside | AL 1p | PSCHi-Mott |
| 9 Aug. 1858 To* | Roadside | AL 1p | PSCHi-Mott |
| 24 Aug. 1858 To* | Roadside | AL 4p | PSCHi-Mott |
| 27 Aug. 1858 To* | Roadside | AL 1p | PSCHi-Mott |
| 29 Aug. 1858 To* | Roadside | ALS 2p | PSCHi-Mott |
| 30 Aug. 1858 To* | Roadside | ALS 3p | PSCHi-Mott |
| 1 Sept. 1858 To* | Philadelphia | AL 2p | PSCHi-Mott |
| 10 Sept. 1858 To* | Roadside | AL 2p | PSCHi-Mott |
| 11 Sept. 1858 To* | Roadside | AL 1p | PSCHi-Mott |
| 12 Sept. 1858 To* | Lawrenceville, N.J. | AL 3p | PSCHi-Mott |
| 13 Sept. 1858 To* | Roadside | AL 3p | PSCHi-Mott |
| [28 Sept. 1858] To* | [Roadside] | AL 2p Inc | PSCHi-Mott |
| [29 Sept. 1858] To* | [Roadside] | AL 1p Inc | PSCHi-Mott |
| 14 Oct. 1858 To* | Roadside | AL 4p | PSCHi-Mott |
| 16 Oct. 1858 To* | Roadside | AL 4p# | PSCHi-Mott |
| 18 Oct. 1858 To* | Roadside | AL 3p Inc | PSCHi-Mott |
| [19 Oct. 1858] To* | [Roadside] | AL 1p Inc | PSCHi-Mott |
| 26 Oct. 1858 Fr | Auburn, N.Y. | ALS 2p JL | MNS |
| 27 Oct. 1858 Fr | Auburn, N.Y. | ALS 2p JL | MNS |
| [28] Oct. 1858 Fr | Auburn, N.Y. | ALS 1p JL | MNS |
| [29] Oct. 1858 Fr | Auburn, N.Y. | ALS 1p JL | MNS |
| 3 Nov. 1858 To* | Philadelphia | AL 4p | PSCHi-Mott |
| 10 Nov. 1858 Fr | Auburn, N.Y. | AL 4p | MNS |
| 28 Nov. 1858 To | Roadside | AL 6p+TR# | PSCHi-Mott |
| 3 Dec. 1858 Fr | Auburn, N.Y. | AL 4p | MNS |
| 13 Dec. 1858 To* | Philadelphia | AL 4p | PSCHi-Mott |
| 26 Dec. 1858 To* | [Roadside] | AL 2p# | PSCHi-Mott |
| 27 Dec. 1858 To* | [Roadside] | AL 2p~# | PSCHi-Mott |

| Name and Date | Location | Document Type and Length | Source |
|---|---|---|---|
| 20 Jan. 1859 To* | Roadside | AL 3p | PSCHi-Mott |
| 24 Jan. 1859 To* | Roadside | AL 3p | PSCHi-Mott |
| 25 Jan. 1859 To* | Roadside | AL 1p | PSCHi-Mott |
| 8 Mar. 1859 To** | [Roadside] | PL 2p~ | Hallowell |
| 22 May 1859 To* | Roadside | ALS 1p JL | PSCHi-Mott |
| 29 May 1859 To* | Roadside | ALS 1p JL | PSCHi-Mott |
| 30 May 1859 To* | Roadside | ALS 2p JL | PSCHi-Mott |
| 31 May 1859 To* | Roadside | ALS 2p JL~ | PSCHi-Mott |
| May 1859 To** | [Roadside] | PL 1p | Hallowell |
| 1 June 1859 To* | Roadside | ALS 2p JL~ | PSCHi-Mott |
| 3 Aug. 1859 To* | Roadside | AL 4p Dam | PSCHi-Mott |
| 19 [Oct. 1859] To* | Roadside | AL 2p | PSCHi-Mott |
| 8 Mar. 1860 To* | Philadelphia | AL 4p | PSCHi-Mott |
| 12 Mar. 1860 To* | Roadside | AL 4p~# | PSCHi-Mott |
| 13 Mar. 1860 To* | Roadside | AL 4p~ | PSCHi-Mott |
| 18 [Mar. 1860?] To* | Roadside | AL 2p | PSCHi-Mott |
| 12 May 1860 To* | Roadside | AL 4p JL | PSCHi-Mott |
| 13 May 1860 To* | Philadelphia | AL 3p+TR | PSCHi-Mott |
| 14 May 1860 To* | Philadelphia | AL 1p | PSCHi-Mott |
| 16 May 1860 To* | Philadelphia | AL 2p | PSCHi-Mott |
| [c. 5 July 1860] To* | [Roadside?] | C 1p Extr~ | MNS |
| 24 July 1860 To* | Roadside | AL 2p | PSCHi-Mott |
| 27 July 1860 To* | Roadside | AL 1p~ | PSCHi-Mott |
| 28 July 1860 To* | Roadside | AL 1p~ | PSCHi-Mott |
| 12 Aug. 1860 To* | Roadside | AL 2p Inc | PSCHi-Mott |
| 13 Aug. 1860 To* | Roadside | AL 2p Inc | PSCHi-Mott |
| 14 Aug. 1860 To* | Roadside | AL 2p Inc | PSCHi-Mott |
| [c. 17 Aug. 1860] To* | [Roadside] | ALS 3p Inc JL | PSCHi-Mott |
| 18 [Aug. 1860] To* | [Roadside] | ALS 1p Inc JL | PSCHi-Mott |
| 24 Aug. 1860 To* | Roadside | AL 1p Inc | PSCHi-Mott |
| 13 Sept. 1860 To* | Roadside | AL 8p | PSCHi-Mott |
| 21 Sept. 1860 To** | Roadside | ALS 4p | PSCHi-Mott |
| 8 Oct. 1860 To | Roadside | AL 4p# | PSCHi-Mott |
| 11 Oct. 1860 To | Philadelphia | AL 1p# | PSCHi-Mott |
| 16 Nov. 1860 To* | Roadside | AL 2p# | PSCHi-Mott |
| 17 Nov. 1860 To* | Roadside | AL 3p# | PSCHi-Mott |
| 18 Nov. 1860 To* | Roadside | AL 1p# | PSCHi-Mott |
| 20 Nov. 1860 To* | Roadside | AL 1p | PSCHi-Mott |
| 23 Nov. 1860 To* | Roadside | AL 1p | PSCHi-Mott |
| 27 Nov. 1860 To* | Roadside | AL 2p | PSCHi-Mott |
| 4 Dec. 1860 To* | Roadside | AL 6p | PSCHi-Mott |
| 20 [Dec. 1860] To* | [Roadside?] | ALS 2p Inc | PSCHi-Mott |
| 20 [Dec. 1860?] To* | [Roadside] | ALS 2p Inc | PSCHi-Mott |
| [c. Dec. 1860] To* | [Roadside?] | AL 4p Inc | PSCHi-Mott |
| [8 Jan. 1861?] To* | [Roadside?] | AL 8p JL Dam | PSCHi-Mott |
| 15 Jan. 1861 To* | Roadside | AL 2p | PSCHi-Mott |
| 17 Jan. 1861 To* | Roadside | AL 2p | PSCHi-Mott |
| 18 Jan. 1861 To* | Eddington | AL 2p | PSCHi-Mott |
| 22 Jan. 1861 To* | Roadside | AL 1p | PSCHi-Mott |
| 19 Mar. 1861 To* | Roadside | AL 3p JL~ | PSCHi-Mott |
| 20 Mar. 1861 To* | Roadside | AL 2p JL | PSCHi-Mott |

| Name and Date | Location | Document Type and Length | Source |
|---|---|---|---|
| 21 Mar. 1861 To* | Roadside | AL 1p JL | PSCHi-Mott |
| 21 Mar. 1861 To** | Roadside | PL 1p | Hallowell |
| 18 Aug. 1861 To* | Roadside | AL 1p | PSCHi-Mott |
| 19 Aug. 1861 To* | Roadside | AL 3p | PSCHi-Mott |
| 20 Aug. [1861] To* | [Roadside] | ALS 3p+TR Inc | PSCHi-Mott |
| 21 Aug. [1861] To* | [Roadside] | ALS 2p Inc | PSCHi-Mott |
| 15 Oct. 1861 To** | Roadside | AL 1p | PSCHi-Mott |
| [4 Nov.?] 1861 To* | Philadelphia | AL 4p | PSCHi-Mott |
| 6 Nov. 1861 To* | Roadside | AL 2p~# | PSCHi-Mott |
| 7 Nov. 1861 To* | Roadside | AL 1p~# | PSCHi-Mott |
| [c. 10 Nov. 1861] To* | [Roadside] | AL 4p Inc | PSCHi-Mott |
| 5 Dec. 1861 To* | Philadelphia | AL 1p~ | PSCHi-Mott |
| 12 Dec. 1861 To* | Philadelphia | AL 1p~ | PSCHi-Mott |
| 13 Dec. 1861 To* | Roadside | AL 3p | PSCHi-Mott |
| 14 Dec. 1861 To* | Roadside | AL 1p | PSCHi-Mott |
| 12 Jan. 1862 To* | Roadside | AL 4p# Inc? | PSCHi-Mott |
| 13 June 1862 To* | Philadelphia | AL 2p | PSCHi-Mott |
| 16 June 1862 To* | [Roadside?] | AL 1p | PSCHi-Mott |
| 19 June 1862 To* | Roadside | AL 3p | PSCHi-Mott |
| 17 Aug. 1862 To* | Roadside | ALS 4p | PSCHi-Mott |
| 18 Aug. 1862 To* | Roadside | ALS 1p | PSCHi-Mott |
| 20 Nov. 1862 To* | Roadside | ALS 4p JL | PSCHi-Mott |
| 27 Dec. 1862 To* | Roadside | AL 4p~# | PSCHi-Mott |
| 28 Dec. 1862 To* | Roadside | ALS 2p | PSCHi-Mott |
| 28 Feb. 1863 To* | Roadside | AL 2p+TR# | MNS |
| 1 Mar. 1863 To* | Roadside | AL 2p# | MNS |
| [Apr. 1863] To* | [Roadside] | PL 1p | Hallowell |
| 23 May 1863 To* | Roadside | ALS 2p | PSCHi-Mott |
| 2 June 1863 To* | Roadside | AL 4p# | PSCHi-Mott |
| 26 July 1863 To* | Roadside | ALS 4p | PSCHi-Mott |
| 27 July 1863 To* | Roadside | ALS 1p | PSCHi-Mott |
| 21 Aug. 1863 To* | Roadside | AL 3p+TTR# | PSCHi-Mott |
| 22 Aug. 1863 To* | Roadside | AL 1p# | PSCHi-Mott |
| 23 Aug. 1863 To* | Roadside | AL 2p# | PSCHi-Mott |
| 25 Aug. 1863 To* | New York City | AL 1p# | PSCHi-Mott |
| 12 Sept. 1863 To* | Roadside | ALS 3p | PSCHi-Mott |
| 18 Sept. 1863 To* | Roadside | ALS 4p | PSCHi-Mott |
| 1 Nov. 1863 To* | Roadside | ALS 6p JL | PSCHi-Mott |
| 20 Dec. 1863 To* | Roadside | AL 1p | PSCHi-Mott |
| 21 Dec. 1863 To* | Roadside | AL 1p | PSCHi-Mott |
| 23 Dec. 1863 To* | Roadside | AL 1p | PSCHi-Mott |
| 24 Dec. 1863 To* | Roadside | AL 4p | PSCHi-Mott |
| 25 Dec. 1863 To* | Eddington | AL 2p | PSCHi-Mott |
| 26 Dec. 1863 To* | Eddington | AL 1p | PSCHi-Mott |
| 27 Dec. 1863 To* | [Roadside] | ALS 4p | PSCHi-Mott |
| 27 Dec. 1863 To* | Roadside | ALS 2p | PSCHi-Mott |
| 28 Dec. 1863 To* | Philadelphia | ALS 1p | PSCHi-Mott |
| 29 Dec. 1863 To* | Philadelphia | AL 2p Inc? | PSCHi-Mott |
| 21 Jan. 1864 To | Roadside | ALS 1p JL~ | PSCHi-Mott |
| 24 Jan. 1864 To | Roadside | ALS 1p JL~ | PSCHi-Mott |
| 25 Jan. 1864 To | Philadelphia | ALS 3p JL~ | PSCHi-Mott |

| Name and Date | Location | Document Type and Length | Source |
|---|---|---|---|
| [post–10 Apr. 1864] To | Roadside | PL 1p | Hallowell |
| 19 Apr. 1864 To* | Roadside | ALS 2p | PSCHi-Mott |
| 22 Apr. 1864 To* | Roadside | ALS 2p | PSCHi-Mott |
| 23 Apr. 1864 To* | Roadside | ALS 1p | PSCHi-Mott |
| 10 July 1864 Fr | Auburn, N.Y. | ALS 8p JL | MNS |
| 27 July 1864 Fr | Auburn, N.Y. | ALS 8p | MNS |
| 16 Aug. 1864 To* | Philadelphia | AL 4p | PSCHi-Mott |
| 23 Aug. 1864 To* | Roadside | ALS 6p | PSCHi-Mott |
| 26 Aug. 1864 Fr | Auburn, N.Y. | ALS 7p JL | MNS |
| 27 Aug. 1864 Fr | Auburn, N.Y. | ALS 1p JL | MNS |
| 6 Sept. 1864 To* | Roadside | ALS 4p JL | PSCHi-Mott |
| 7 Sept. 1864 To* | Roadside | ALS 2p JL~ | PSCHi-Mott |
| 25 Sept. 1864 To* | Brooklyn, N.Y. | AL 4p~ | PSCHi-Mott |
| 3 Oct. 1864 To | Brooklyn, N.Y. | ALS 4p | PSCHi-Mott |
| 13 Oct. 1864 To* | Philadelphia | AL 2p | PSCHi-Mott |
| 14 Oct. 1864 To* | Roadside | AL 3p+TR | PSCHi-Mott |
| 19 Oct. 1864 Fr | Auburn, N.Y. | AL 4p JL | MNS |
| 22 Oct. 1864 To* | Roadside | AL 2p | PSCHi-Mott |
| 29 Oct. 1864 Fr | Auburn, N.Y. | ALS 4p JL | MNS |
| 31 Oct. 1864 To | Roadside | AL 3p JL~ | PSCHi-Mott |
| 1 Nov. 1864 To | Roadside | AL 1p JL~ | PSCHi-Mott |
| 14 Nov. 1864 To* | Roadside | AL 4p# | PSCHi-Mott |
| 30 Dec. 1864 Fr | Auburn, N.Y. | ALS 6p JL | MNS |
| 3 Jan. 1865 To* | Roadside | ALS 4p | PSCHi-Mott |
| 9 Jan. 1865 Fr | Auburn, N.Y. | ALS 6p JL | MNS |
| 17 Jan. 1865 To | Roadside | AL 4p JL~ | PSCHi-Mott |
| 20 Jan. 1865 To | Roadside | AL 5p JL | PSCHi-Mott |
| 24 Jan. 1865 Fr | Auburn, N.Y. | ALS 8p JL | MNS |
| 11 [Feb. 1865] Fr | Auburn, N.Y. | ALS 4p JL | MNS |
| 16 Feb. 1865 To* | Roadside | ALS 4p+TR | PSCHi-Mott |
| 21 Mar. 1865 Fr | Auburn, N.Y. | ALS 6p JL | MNS |
| 26 Mar. 1865 Fr | Auburn, N.Y. | ALS 2p JL | MNS |
| 9 Apr. 1865 To* | Roadside | ALS 3p+TR | PSCHi-Mott |
| 10 Apr. 1865 To* | Roadside | ALS 1p JL~ | PSCHi-Mott |
| 17 Apr. 1865 To* | Roadside | AL 4p+TR# | PSCHi-Mott |
| [post–21 June 1865] To | [Roadside?] | AL 2p | PSCHi-Mott |
| 25 June 1865 Fr | Auburn, N.Y. | ALS 8p JL | MNS |
| 5 July 1865 Fr | Auburn, N.Y. | ALS 4p JL | MNS |
| 10 July 1865 Fr | Auburn, N.Y. | ALS 4p JL | MNS |
| 11 July 1865 To* | Roadside | AL 1p | PSCHi-Mott |
| 27 July 1865 To* | Roadside | ALS 4p | PSCHi-Mott |
| 7 Sept. 1865 Fr | Auburn, N.Y. | ALS 4p JL | MNS |
| 2 Oct. 1865 To* | Roadside | AL 2p~ | MNS |
| 2 Nov. 1865 To* | Philadelphia | ALS 6p JL~ | MNS |
| 4 Feb. 1866 To* | Roadside | AL 4p JL | MNS |
| 5 Feb. 1866 To* | Roadside | AL 1p JL | MNS |
| [post–28 Feb. 1866] To | [New York City] | AN 1p | MNS |
| 19 Mar. 1866 To* | Roadside | ALS 4p+TR JL | MNS |
| 6 [Apr. 1866?] To | [Roadside?] | AL 2p Inc | PSCHi-Mott |
| 16 Apr. 1866 Fr | Auburn, N.Y. | ALS 8p JL | MNS |
| 11 May 1866 To* | Philadelphia | AL 1p+TR | MNS |

| Name and Date | Location | Document Type and Length | Source |
|---|---|---|---|
| 12 May 1866 To* | Roadside | AL 1p+TR | MNS |
| [c. 8 June 1866] To | [Roadside?] | PL 1p Extr | Harper |
| 10 June 1866 To** | [Roadside?] | PL 1p | Hallowell |
| 11 June 1866 To** | Philadelphia | ALS 4p~ | PSCHi-Mott |
| 13 [c. June 1866] To* | [Roadside] | AL 4p Inc | PSCHi-Mott |
| 14 [c. June 1866] To* | [Roadside] | AL 1p Inc | PSCHi-Mott |
| [c. July 1866] To** | [Roadside?] | AL 2p Inc? | MNS |
| 14 Aug. 1866 To | Roadside | AL 4p JL | PSCHi-Mott |
| 28 Oct. 1866 To* | Roadside | ALS 2p JL | MNS |
| 29 Oct. 1866 To* | Roadside | ALS 5p JL | MNS |
| 12 Nov. 1866 To* | Brooklyn, N.Y. | ALS 4p Dam PL | MNS |
| 15 Nov. 1866 To** | Brooklyn, N.Y. | PL 1p | Hallowell |
| 30 Nov. 1866 To* | Roadside | ALS 6p | MNS |
| 1 Dec. 1866 To* | Roadside | ALS 5p+TR | MNS |
| 24 Dec. [1866?] To* | [Roadside?] | ALS 2p Inc | MNS |
| 1 Jan. 1867 To | Roadside | ALS 4p JL | PSCHi-Mott |
| 1 Jan. 1867 To* | Roadside | ALS 8p | MNS |
| 22 Jan. 1867 To* | Roadside | AL 4p +TTR | MNS |
| 30 [c. Jan. 1867] To* | [Roadside?] | ALS 2p | MNS |
| [Jan. 1867] To* | [Roadside] | AL 4p Inc | MNS |
| 6 Feb. 1867 To | Philadelphia | AL 4p# | PSCHi-Mott |
| 28 Apr. 1867 To* | Roadside | AL 4p+TTR JL | MNS |
| 8 May [1867] To* | New York City | AL 2p+TR | MNS |
| 11 May [1867] To* | Philadelphia | AL 2p~ | MNS |
| 12 May [1867] To* | Roadside | AL 2p~ | MNS |
| 26 May [1867] To** | Suffern, N.Y. | AL 4p | PSCHi-Mott |
| 5 June 1867 To** | West Chester | PL 1p | Hallowell |
| 27 June 1867 To* | Roadside | AL 3p Inc JL | MNS |
| 28 June 1867 To* | Roadside | AL 1p Inc JL | MNS |
| 7 July 1867 To* | Roadside | ALS 4p | MNS |
| 28 July 1867 To | Roadside | AL 6p | PSCHi-Mott |
| [c. 1 Aug. 1867] To* | [Roadside] | ALS 1p Inc | MNS |
| 5 Aug. 1867 To* | Suffern, N.Y. | AL 3p JL | PSCHi-Mott |
| 6 Aug. 1867 To** | Suffern, N.Y. | AL 2p JL | PSCHi-Mott |
| [c. 6 Aug. 1867] To* | [Suffern, N.Y.] | AN 2p Inc | MNS |
| 27 Aug. 1867 To* | Roadside | AL 4p Dam JL | PSCHi-Mott |
| 1 Sept. 1867 To* | [Roadside] | AL 4p | MNS |
| 3 Sept. 1867 To* | [Roadside] | AL 4p~ | MNS |
| 1867 To** | [Roadside?] | PL 1p | Hallowell |
| [pre–1867] To** | [Roadside] | PL 1p | Hallowell |
| 21 Jan. 1868 To* | Brooklyn, N.Y. | ALS 12p~ | PSCHi-Mott |
| 22 Jan. 1868 To* | Brooklyn, N.Y. | ALS 1p~ | PSCHi-Mott |
| [pre–10 Apr. 1868] To | [Roadside] | AL 2p Frag | MNS |
| [10 Apr. 1868] To* | [Roadside] | AL 2p Inc | PSCHi-Mott |
| 16 May 1868 Fr | Auburn, N.Y. | ALS 6p JL | MNS |
| 30 May 1868 Fr | Auburn, N.Y. | ALS 8p JL | MNS |
| 13 June 1868 Fr | Roxbury, Mass. | ALS 6p JL | MNS |
| 24 June 1868 Fr | Roxbury, Mass. | ALS 2p JL | MNS |
| 27 June 1868 Fr | Roxbury, Mass. | ALS 6p JL | MNS |
| 1 July 1868 To | Mt. Holly, N.J. | AL 7p JL | PSCHi-Mott |
| 31 July 1868 Fr | Auburn, N.Y. | ALS 4p JL | MNS |

| Name and Date | Location | Document Type and Length | Source |
|---|---|---|---|
| 23 Aug. 1868 Fr | Auburn, N.Y. | ALS 4p JL | MNS |
| 25 [Aug. 1868] Fr | [Auburn, N.Y.] | ALS 4p Inc | MNS |
| 30 Aug. 1868 Fr | Auburn, N.Y. | ALS 4p JL | MNS |
| 6 Sept. 1868 Fr | Auburn, N.Y. | ALS 4p JL | MNS |
| 8 Oct. 1868 Fr | Auburn, N.Y. | ALS 4p JL | MNS |
| 4 Nov. 1868 To* | Roadside | ALS 5p JL | MNS |
| 5 Nov. 1868 To* | Roadside | ALS 2p JL | MNS |
| 3 Dec. 1868 To* | Orange, N.J. | AL 6p~ | MNS |
| [c. Dec. 1868] To* | [Orange, N.J.] | AL 1p+TTR Inc? | MNS |
| 10 Mar. 1869 Fr | Roxbury, Mass. | ALS 6p | MNS |
| 13 Mar. 1869 To** | Roadside | ALS 2p | PSCHi-Mott |
| 16 Mar. 1869 To** | Roadside | ALS 3p | PSCHi-Mott |
| 3 Apr. 1869 To* | Roadside | AL 2p | PSCHi-Mott |
| 5 Apr. 1869 To* | Roadside | AL 3p | PSCHi-Mott |
| 28 May 1869 To* | Philadelphia | ALS 1p | MNS |
| 5 June 1869 To* | Roadside | AL 3p | MNS |
| 6 June 1869 To* | Roadside | AL 1p~ | MNS |
| [c. 10 June 1869] To | [Roadside?] | PL 1p Extr | Harper |
| 23 June 1869 To* | Roadside | ALS 6p JL | PSCHi-Mott |
| 12 July 1869 To* | Roadside | AL 4p | MNS |
| 16 July 1869 Fr | [Auburn, N.Y.] | AL 4p+Env Inc | MNS |
| 18 July 1869 To* | Roadside | AL 2p Inc?# | MNS |
| 26 July 1869 To* | Roadside | AL 4p | MNS |
| 27 July 1869 To* | Roadside | AL 1p PS | MNS |
| 22 [Aug.? 1869] To** | [Roadside] | AL 1p | NSyU-Osb |
| 9 Sept. 1869 To* | Nantucket, Mass. | AL 2p~ | PSCHi-Mott |
| 23 Sept. 1869 To* | Roadside | AL 2p | PSCHi-Mott |
| 18 [Oct. 1869] To** | [Roadside?] | AL 2p Inc | MNS |
| 21 Oct. 1869 To* | Philadelphia | AL 2p | PSCHi-Mott |
| 22 Oct. 1869 To* | [Roadside] | AL 2p | PSCHi-Mott |
| 26 Nov. 1869 To* | Roadside | AL 2p | MNS |
| 27 Nov. 1869 To* | Roadside | ALS 3p | MNS |
| 5 Dec. 1869 To* | Roadside | ALS 6p~ | MNS |
| [c. Dec. 1869] To* | [Roadside?] | AL 6p Inc? | MNS |
| 30 [Jan. 1870] To* | [Roadside] | ALS 2p Inc | PSCHi-Mott |
| 24 Mar. 1870 To* | Roadside | ALS 2p | PSCHi-Mott |
| 25 Mar. 1870 To* | Roadside | ALS 2p | PSCHi-Mott |
| 7 Apr. 1870 To* | Orange, N.J. | ALS 4p~ | PSCHi-Mott |
| 17 May 1870 To* | Roadside | AL 4p JL | PSCHi-Mott |
| 4 June 1870 To* | Philadelphia | ALS 2p JL | PSCHi-Mott |
| 20 June 1870 To* | Roadside | AL 4p JL | PSCHi-Mott |
| 21 June 1870 To* | Roadside | AL 1p JL | PSCHi-Mott |
| 8 July 1870 To | Orange, N.J. | ALS 2p | PSCHi-Mott |
| 16 July 1870 To | Roadside | AL 4p~ | PSCHi-Mott |
| 22 July 1870 To | Roadside | ALS 2p | PSCHi-Mott |
| 28 [July? 1870] To* | [Roadside] | AL 2p Inc | PSCHi-Mott |
| 27 Oct. 1870 To* | Orange, N.J. | ALS 1p | PSCHi-Mott |
| 28 Oct. 1870 To* | Orange, N.J. | ALS 1p | PSCHi-Mott |
| 29 Oct. 1870 To* | Roadside | ALS 2p | PSCHi-Mott |
| 30 Oct. 1870 To* | Roadside | ALS 1p | PSCHi-Mott |
| 31 Oct. 1870 To* | Orange, N.J. | ALS 1p | PSCHi-Mott |

| Name and Date | Location | Document Type and Length | Source |
|---|---|---|---|
| 2 [Dec.? 1870] To | Philadelphia | AL 1p | PSCHi-Mott |
| 3 [Dec. 1870] To | Roadside | AL 4p | PSCHi-Mott |
| 29 Dec. 1870 To* | Orange, N.J. | AL 4p | PSCHi-Mott |
| 10 Jan. 1871 To* | Roadside | AL 4p | PSCHi-Mott |
| 4 Feb. [1871] To* | Roadside | ALS 4p~# | MNS |
| 5 Feb. [1871] To* | Roadside | ALS 2p | MNS |
| 26 Feb. 1871 To | Roadside | ALS 2p | PSCHi-Mott |
| 13 Apr. 1871 To* | Roadside | ALS 7p | MNS |
| 28 Apr. 1871 To | Orange, N.J. | AL 3p Inc | PSCHi-Mott |
| 29 Apr. 1871 To | Orange, N.J. | AL 4p | PSCHi-Mott |
| 3 May 1871 To | Orange, N.J. | AL 2p~ | PSCHi-Mott |
| 28 May [1871] To* | Philadelphia | AL 1p | PSCHi-Mott |
| 2 June [1871] To* | West Medford, Mass. | AL 1p | PSCHi-Mott |
| 6 June 1871 To | Orange, N.J. | ALS 2p~ | PSCHi-Mott |
| 13 June 1871 To | Orange, N.J. | ALS 3p~ | PSCHi-Mott |
| [c. June 1871] To** | [Roadside?] | AL 2p Inc | MNS |
| 17 July 1871 To | Roadside | ALS 2p | PSCHi-Mott |
| 28 Aug. 1871 To | Mt. Holly, N.J. | AL 3p | PSCHi-Mott |
| 29 Aug. 1871 To | Mt. Holly, N.J. | AL 1p | PSCHi-Mott |
| 30 Aug. 1871 To | Orange, N.J. | AL 2p | PSCHi-Mott |
| [c. Sept. 1871] To* | [Roadside?] | AL 2p Inc | PSCHi-Mott |
| 9 Sept. 1871 To | Manhassett, N.Y. | AL 4p Dam | PSCHi-Mott |
| 30 Oct. 1871 To* | Roadside | ALS 2p | PSCHi-Mott |
| 8 Nov. 1871 To* | Roadside | ALS 2p | PSCHi-Mott |
| 2 Dec. 1871 To* | Roadside | ALS 8p JL | PSCHi-Mott |
| 7 [Dec. 1871] To* | Roadside | ALS 6p Inc | PSCHi-Mott |
| 24 Dec. 1871 To* | Roadside | AL 5p | PSCHi-Mott |
| 26 Dec. 1871 To* | Roadside | ALS 1p | PSCHi-Mott |
| 23 Feb. 1872 To* | Roadside | ALS 2p | MNS |
| 24 Feb. 1872 To* | Roadside | ALS 1p | MNS |
| 29 Feb. 1872 To | Roadside | AL 2p | PSCHi-Mott |
| 6 Mar. 1872 To | Roadside | AL 4p | PSCHi-Mott |
| 7 Mar. 1872 To | Roadside | AL 2p~ | PSCHi-Mott |
| 12 Mar. 1872 To* | Roadside | ALS 1p JL | PSCHi-Mott |
| 13 Mar. 1872 To* | Roadside | ALS 3p JL | PSCHi-Mott |
| 16 [Mar. 1872] To* | [Roadside?] | AL 2p Inc | PSCHi-Mott |
| 17 [Mar. 1872] To* | [Roadside?] | AL 4p Inc | PSCHi-Mott |
| 18 [Mar. 1872] To* | [Roadside?] | AL 1p Inc | PSCHi-Mott |
| [c. 20 Mar. 1872] To* | [Roadside] | AL 2p Inc | PSCHi-Mott |
| 21 Mar. 1872 To | Roadside | AL 3p | PSCHi-Mott |
| 23 Apr. 1872 To | Roadside | ALS 4p | PSCHi-Mott |
| 28 [Apr. 1872] To | Roadside | AL 2p Inc | PSCHi-Mott |
| 1 May 1872 Fr | Auburn, N.Y. | AL 8p | MNS |
| 6 May 1872 Fr | Auburn, N.Y. | AL 4p | MNS |
| 13 May 1872 To | Philadelphia | AL 6p | PSCHi-Mott |
| 14 May 1872 To | Philadelphia | AL 3p | PSCHi-Mott |
| 27 May 1872 To | New York City | AL 1p~ | PSCHi-Mott |
| 1 June 1872 To | Medford, Mass. | AL 2p~ | PSCHi-Mott |
| 2 June 1872 To | Orange, N.J. | AL 3p~ | PSCHi-Mott |
| 20 July 1872 To | Orange, N.J. | ALS 2p | PSCHi-Mott |
| 21 July 1872 To* | [Roadside] | AL 7p | PSCHi-Mott |

| Name and Date | Location | Document Type and Length | Source |
|---|---|---|---|
| 11 Aug. 1872 To | Roadside | AL 4p | PSCHi-Mott |
| 26 Aug. 1872 To* | Roadside | ALS 2p# | MNS |
| 26 Aug. 1872 To* | Roadside | ALS 4p | MNS |
| 5 Sept. 1872 To* | Roadside | ALS 4p | MNS |
| 10 Sept. 1872 To | Roadside | AL 2p | PSCHi-Mott |
| 11 Sept. 1872 To | Roadside | AL 1p | PSCHi-Mott |
| 14 Sept. 1872 To | Roadside | AL 1p | PSCHi-Mott |
| 26 Sept. 1872 To* | Roadside | ALS 3p# | MNS |
| 27 Sept. 1872 To* | Roadside | ALS 2p# | MNS |
| 29 Sept. 1872 To* | Roadside | ALS 1p~# | MNS |
| [30 Sept. 1872] To* | [Roadside] | ALS 2p | MNS |
| 10 Oct. 1872 To | Roadside | ALS 6p | PSCHi-Mott |
| 11 Oct. 1872 To | Roadside | ALS 1p | PSCHi-Mott |
| 4 Dec. 1872 To | Philadelphia | AL 2p | PSCHi-Mott |
| 5 Dec. 1872 To | Philadelphia | AL 3p | PSCHi-Mott |
| 25 Dec. 1872 To* | Roadside | AL 7p Dam | MNS |
| 27 [Dec. 1872] To* | Roadside | AL 3p | MNS |
| [post–26 Jan. 1873] To* | [Roadside?] | AN 1p | MNS |
| 29 Jan. 1873 To* | Orange, N.J. | AL 3p Inc Dam | MNS |
| 7 Feb. 1873 To* | Roadside | AL 4p | MNS |
| 14 Feb. 1873 To* | Roadside | ALS 4p JL | MNS |
| 3 Mar. 1873 To* | Roadside | AL 7p | MNS |
| [4 Mar. 1873] To** | [Roadside] | AL 1p | MNS |
| 18 Mar. 1873 To | Roadside | ALS 4p~ | PSCHi-Mott |
| 27 Mar. 1873 To | Roadside | AL 4p | PSCHi-Mott |
| 28 Mar. 1873 To | Roadside | AL 1p | PSCHi-Mott |
| 20 Apr. 1873 To | Roadside | AL 6p | PSCHi-Mott |
| 21 Apr. 1873 To* | [Roadside] | AL 2p | PSCHi-Mott |
| 22 Apr. 1873 To* | [Roadside] | AL 1p | PSCHi-Mott |
| 11 May 1873 Fr | Auburn, N.Y. | ALS 8p | MNS |
| 23 May [1873] To | Roadside | AL 4p~ | PSCHi-Mott |
| 24 May [1873] To | Roadside | AL 1p | PSCHi-Mott |
| 1 June 1873 To* | Orange, N.J. | ALS 4p~ | MNS |
| 2 June 1873 To* | Roadside | ALS 2p~ | MNS |
| [c. June 1873] To** | [Roadside] | AL 2p Inc | PSCHi-Mott |
| 8 July [1873] To* | Roadside | AL 4p | PSCHi-Mott |
| 11 July [1873] To* | Roadside | AL 2p | PSCHi-Mott |
| [c. Aug. 1873] To* | [Roadside] | AL 2p Inc | PSCHi-Mott |
| 5 Oct. 1873 To* | Roadside | C 3p+TTR | MNS |
| 7 Oct. 1873 To* | Roadside | C 1p | MNS |
| 16 Oct. 1873 To* | Roadside | ALS 4p JL | MNS |
| 17 [Oct.? 1873] To* | [Roadside] | ALS 2p+TTR JL | MNS |
| 11 Dec. 1873 Fr | Jacksonville, Fla. | ALS 6p | MNS |
| 14 Dec. 1873 Fr | Mt. Royal, Fla. | ALS 4p | MNS |
| 22 Dec. 1873 Fr | Mt. Royal, Fla. | ALS 4p | MNS |
| 16 Feb. 1874 To | Roadside | ALS 5p | PSCHi-Mott |
| 17 Mar. 1874 To* | Roadside | ALS 3p+TTR | MNS |
| 10 May 1874 To* | Roadside | ALS 2p+TTR | MNS |
| 4 June 1874 Fr | Auburn, N.Y. | ALS 6p | MNS |
| 9 June 1874 Fr | Auburn, N.Y. | AL 4p | MNS |
| 14 July 1874 To* | Roadside | AL 2p~ | MNS |

| Name and Date | Location | Document Type and Length | Source |
|---|---|---|---|
| 15 July 1874 To* | Philadelphia | AL 1p~ | MNS |
| 23 July 1874 To* | Roadside | AL 3p+TTR | MNS |
| 24 July 1874 To* | Roadside | AL 3p+TTR | MNS |
| 2 Oct. 1874 To* | Roadside | AL 5p+TTR | MNS |
| 2 Nov. 1874 Fr | Auburn, N.Y. | ALS 2p | MNS |
| 7 Dec. 1874 Fr | Roxbury, Mass. | AL 4p | MNS |
| 12 Dec. 1874 Fr | Roxbury, Mass. | ALS 4p | MNS |
| [pre–1874] To** | [Roadside] | PL 1p | Hallowell |
| [pre–1874] To** | [Roadside] | PL 1p | Hallowell |
| [pre–1874] To** | [Roadside] | PL 1p | Hallowell |
| [pre–1874] To | [Roadside?] | PL 1p | Hallowell |
| Yarnall, Eliza Coffin | | | |
| 1 Aug. [1855] Fr | Flume House, N.H. | AL 1p PS JL | MNS |
| 7 Aug. 1856 To** | Nantucket, Mass. | AL 4p+TTR | MNS |
| 16 July 1857 To* | Roadside | AL 4p | MNS |
| 17 July 1857 To* | Roadside | AL 2p | MNS |
| 27 July 1857 To* | Roadside | AL 8p | MNS |
| [c. July 1857] Fr** | Flume House, N.H. | AL 2p+Enc | MNS |
| 13 Aug. 1857 To* | Roadside | AL 7p | MNS |
| 28 Aug. 1857 To* | Roadside | AL 1p | MNS |
| 12 May 1864 To* | Brooklyn, N.Y. | AL 2p | PSCHi-Mott |
| 6 July 1865 To | Brooklyn, N.Y. | ALS 2p JL | PSCHi-Mott |
| [pre–1868] Fr** | [Philadelphia?] | AL 2p Frag | MNS |
| Yarnall, Margaret Harrison | | | |
| 3 Dec. [1866] Fr | Ellersleigh | AL 1p JL | MNS |
| Yarnall, Sarah Price Rose | | | |
| [pre–22 Aug. 1872] Fr | Philadelphia | ALS 1p JL | PSCHi-Mott |
| [c. Mar. 1873] Fr | West Philadelphia | ALS 2p | MNS |
| Yarnall, Thomas Coffin | | | |
| 10 Aug. 1872 Fr | Philadelphia | ALS 2p | MNS |
| [pre–22 Aug. 1872] Fr | Philadelphia | ALS 1p JL | PSCHi-Mott |
| Yarrington, J. T. | | | |
| 1 Feb. 1873 Fr | Carbondale | ALS 2p | PSCHi-Mott |
| "Young Frankie" | | | |
| 23 June 1861 To | Boston | ANS 1p | Layton |

# Index

LCM's opinions on various subjects are indexed under the topic (e.g., Antislavery movement, Marriage). Numbers in bold italics indicate pages with identifications.

BEVERLY WILSON PALMER is the editor of *The Selected Letters of Charles Sumner* (1990) and *The Selected Papers of Thaddeus Stevens* (1997–98). She is also the coordinator of the writing program at Pomona College.

HOLLY BYERS OCHOA is the associate editor of *The Selected Papers of Thaddeus Stevens* (1997–98) and volume 5 of *The Salmon P. Chase Papers* (1998).

CAROL FAULKNER is an assistant professor of history at SUNY Geneseo, specializing in women's history, the Civil War, and Reconstruction.

## Women in American History

Composed in 10.5/12.5 Adobe Minion
by Jim Proefrock
at the University of Illinois Press
Manufactured by Cushing-Malloy, Inc.

University of Illinois Press
1325 South Oak Street
Champaign, IL 61820-6903
www.press.uillinois.edu